CLYMER MARINE REPAIR SERIES

OMC COBRA
STERN DRIVE SHOP MANUAL
1986-1989 (Includes King Cobra Models)

RANDY STEPHENS
Editor

CLYMER PUBLICATIONS
The world's finest publisher of mechanical how-to manuals

INTERTEC PUBLISHING CORPORATION
P.O. Box 12901, Overland Park, Kansas 66212

FIRST EDITION
First Printing July, 1988

SECOND EDITION
Updated to include 1989 models
First Printing October, 1989
Second Printing October, 1990

Printed in U.S.A.

ISBN: 0-89287-455-4

Technical illustrations by Mitzi McCarthy, Steve Amos, Diana Kirkland and Carl Rohkar.

Tools shown in Chapter Two courtesy of Thorsen Tool, Dallas, Texas. Test equipment shown in Chapter Two courtesy of Dixson, Inc., Grand Junction, Colorado.

With thanks to Mike Trevett, Newport Pacific, Pomona, California, and Valley Marine, Burbank, California.

COVER: Photographed by Mark Clifford, Los Angeles, California. Boat courtesy of Galaxie Boat Center, Canyon Country, California.

Contents

CHAPTER FIVE
LAY-UP, COOLING SYSTEM SERVICE AND FITTING OUT 101

CHAPTER SIX
INLINE ENGINES 112

CHAPTER SEVEN
GM V6 AND V8 ENGINES 177

CHAPTER EIGHT
FORD V8 ENGINES 220

CHAPTER NINE
FUEL DELIVERY SYSTEM 269

CHAPTER TEN
COOLING SYSTEM 303

CHAPTER ELEVEN
ELECTRICAL SYSTEMS 326

CHAPTER TWELVE
STERN DRIVE AND UPPER GEAR HOUSING 349

CHAPTER THIRTEEN
GEARCASE HOUSING (LOWER UNIT) 371

QUICK REFERENCE DATA

ENGINE OIL VISCOSITY

Anticipated temperature range	Recommended viscosity
Above 32° F (0° C)	SAE30
Zero° F (-18° C) to 32° F (0° C)	SAE20W-20
Below zero° F (-18° C) or adverse operating conditions	SAE 10W

APPROXIMATE ENGINE OIL CAPACITIES

	Capacity (qt.)[1]		Filter type		
Engine	w/filter	w/o filter	OMC	AC	Purolator
2.3L	5.0	4.0	173231	PF-2	PER 1
2.5L/3.0L	4.0	3.5	173232	PF-25	PER 49
4.3L	4.5	4.0	173834	PF-51	PER 173
5.0L/5.7L	6.0	5.0	173233[2]	PF-35	PER 40
5.8L	6.0	5.0	173231	PF-2	PER 1
7.5L	6.8	5.8	173231[3]	PF-2	PER 1

1. All capacities in this table are approximate. To assure correct oil level and prevent overfilling the engine, always use the dipstick as recommended in text.
2. For Ford 302 cu. in., use filter type shown for 5.8L engine.
3. For 1989 models, an OMC 174796 is recommended.

APPROXIMATE STERN DRIVE CAPACITIES

Model	Capacity[1]
2.3L/2.5L/3.0L	60 oz. (1,774 ml)
4.3L/5.0L/5.7L/5.8L	64 oz. (1,892 ml)
7.5L	108 oz. (3,194 ml)

1. Capacity is only approximate. When refilling a stern drive after draining all lubricant, recheck level after a one-minute run-in period to eliminate air pockets which may develop during filling. If necessary, top up after rechecking to bring the lubricant to the correct level.

RECOMMENDED LUBRICANTS, SEALANTS AND ADHESIVES

Lubricant	Application
OMC Cobra® Premium 4-cycle motor oil	Engine crankcase
OMC Hi-Vis gearcase lubricant	Vertical drive
OMC Triple-Guard grease	Steering ram
OMC Marine Wheel Bearing grease	Power steering actuator valve
OMC Needle Bearing Grease	Bearings
OMC 2 + 4 Fuel Conditioner	Fuel tank
OMC Rust Preventative	Engine
OMC Power Trim/Tilt Fluid	Power trim/tilt system
OMC Storage Fogging Oil	Carburetor
OMC Moly Lube	Remote control cables
Sealer/Adhesive	
OMC Black Neoprene Dip	
OMC Pipe Sealant with Teflon	
OMC Gasket Sealing Compound	
RTV adhesive sealant	
OMC Locquic Primer	
OMC Ultra Lock	
OMC Nut Lock	
OMC Spline Lock	
OMC Screw Lock	
OMC Adhesive M sealant	

TUNE-UP SPECIFICATIONS

1986					
Engine displacement	Spark plugs Type	Spark plugs Gap (in.)	Breaker points Dwell (degrees)	Breaker points Gap (in.)	Timing (RON 93 fuel)[1]
2.5L/3.0L	AC-MR43T	0.035	31-34	0.019	4° BTDC
4.3L	AC-MR43T	0.035	39 ±2	0.019	6° BTDC
5.0L[3]	AC-MR44T	0.032	30 ±2	0.018	13° BTDC
5.7L	AC-MR43T	0.032	30 ±2	0.018	10° BTDC
Engine displacement	**Timing (RON 90 fuel)[2]**	**Idle speed (rpm)**	**Full throttle range (rpm)**	**Fuel pump (psi)**	
2.5L/3.0L	1° ATDC	500-600	4,200-4,600	3.5-6.0	
4.3L	1° BTDC	500-600	4,200-4,600[4]	5.75-7.0	
5.0L[3]	9° BTDC	500-600	4,200-4,600	5.75-7.0	
5.7L	5° BTDC	500-600	4,200-4,400	5.75-7.0	

1. Anti-knock index 89.
2. Anti-knock index 86.
3. GM 305 cu. in.
4. 4,400-4,800 rpm with 4-bbl. carburetor.

(continued)

TUNE-UP SPECIFICATIONS (cont.)

1987

Engine displacement	Spark plugs Type	Spark plugs Gap (in.)	Breaker points Dwell (degrees)	Breaker points Gap (in.)	Timing (RON 93 fuel)[1]
2.3L	AWSF-32	0.035	36 ±2	0.018	10° BTDC
3.0L	AC-MR43T	0.035	31-34	0.019	6° BTDC
4.3L	AC-MR43T	0.035	39 ±2	0.019	6° BTDC
5.0L[3]	AC-MR44T	0.032	30 ±2	0.018	10° BTDC[4]
5.7L	AC-MR43T	0.032	30 ±2	0.018	10° BTDC[5]
7.5L	ARF-32	0.035	31 ±2	0.017	15° BTDC

Engine displacement	Timing (RON 90 fuel)[2]	Idle speed (rpm)	Full throttle range (rpm)	Fuel pump (psi)
2.3L	10° BTDC	600-650	5,200-5,600	3.5-6.0
3.0L	1° ATDC	500-600	4,200-4,600	3.5-6.0
4.3L	1° BTDC	500-600	4,200-4,600[8]	5.75-7.0
5.0L[3]	5° BTDC[6]	500-600	4,200-4,600	5.75-7.0
5.7L	5° BTDC[7]	500-600	4,200-4,400	5.75-7.0
7.5L	10° BTDC	600-650	4,400-4,800	5.0-6.0

1. Anti-knock index 89.
2. Anti-knock index 86.
3. GM 305 cu. in.
4. Models 504AMFTC and 504APFTC, 13° BTDC.
5. Models 574AMARY and 574APARY, 8° BTDC.
6. Models 504AMFTC and 504APFTC, 8° BTDC.
7. Models 574AMARY and 574APARY, 3° BTDC.
8. 4,400-4,800 rpm with 4-bbl. carburetor.

1988

Engine displacement	Spark plugs Type	Spark plugs Gap (in.)	Breaker points Dwell (degrees)	Breaker points Gap (in.)	Timing (RON 93 fuel)[1]
2.3L	AWSF-32	0.035	36 ±2	0.018	10° BTDC
3.0L	AC-MR43T	0.035	31-34	0.019	4° BTDC
4.3L	AC-MR43T	0.035	39 ±2	0.019	6° BTDC
5.0L[3]	AC-MR44T	0.032	29 ±2	0.017	10° BTDC
5.7L	AC-MR43T	0.032	29 ±2	0.017	8° BTDC
7.5L	ARF-32	0.035	31 ±2	0.017	15° BTDC

Engine displacement	Timing (RON 90 fuel)[2]	Idle speed (rpm)	Full throttle range (rpm)	Fuel pump (psi)
2.3L	10° BTDC	600-650	5,200-5,600	3.5-6.0
3.0L	1° ATDC	500-600	4,200-4,600	3.5-6.0
4.3L	1° BTDC	500-600	4,200-4,600[4]	5.75-7.0
5.0L[3]	5° BTDC	500-600	4,200-4,600	5.75-7.0
5.7L	3° BTDC	500-600	4,200-4,400	5.75-7.0
7.5L	10° BTDC	600-650	4,400-4,800	5.0-6.0

1. Anti-knock index 89.
2. Anti-knock index 86.
3. GM 305 cu. in.
4. 4,400-4,800 rpm with 4-bbl. carburetor.

(continued)

TUNE-UP SPECIFICATIONS (cont.)

1989					
Engine displace-ment	Spark plugs Type	Gap (in.)	Breaker points Dwell (degrees)	Gap (in.)	Timing (RON 93 fuel)[1]
2.3L	AWSF-32	0.035	36 ±2	0.019	10° BTDC
3.0L	AC-MR43T	0.035	31-34	0.019	4° BTDC
4.3L	AC-MR43T	0.035	39 ±2	0.019	6° BTDC
5.0L[3]	AC-MR44T	0.030	29 ±2	0.018	10° BTDC
5.7L	AC-MR43T	0.035	29 ±2	0.018	8° BTDC
5.8L	AC-MR43T	0.030	29 ±2	0.018	10° BTDC
7.5L	ASF-32M	0.035	29 ±2	0.018	10° BTDC

Engine displace-ment	Timing (RON 90 fuel)[2]	Idle speed (rpm)	Full throttle range (rpm)	Fuel pump (psi)
2.3L	10°BTDC	600-650	5,200-5,600	5.75-7.0
3.0L	1° ATDC	550-600	4,200-4,600	5.75-7.0
4.3L	1° BTDC	550-600	4,200-4,600[4]	5.75-7.0
5.0L[3]	10° BTDC	550-600	4,000-4,400	5.75-7.0
5.7L	3° BTDC	550-600	4,200-4,600	5.75-7.0
5.8L	10° BTDC	550-600	4,000-4,400	5.75-7.0
7.5L	10° BTDC	600-650	4,400-4,800	5.0-6.0

1. Anti-knock index 89.
2. Anti-knock index 86.
3. Ford 302 cu. in.
4. 4,400-4,800 rpm with 4-bbl. carburetor.

TEST WHEEL RECOMMENDATIONS

Model	Test wheel part No. Standard rotation	Counter rotation
2.3L/2.5L	982036	
3.0L	384933	
4.3L/5.0L (305 cu. in.)	387388	398673
5.0L (302 cu. in.)/5.8L	982038	985624
5.7L	982038	985624
King Cobra		
262	387388	398673
350	982038	985624
460	985007	985626

OMC COBRA
STERN DRIVE SHOP MANUAL
1986-1989 (Includes King Cobra Models)

Introduction

This Clymer shop manual covers the service and repair of all OMC Cobra stern drive units used for pleasure boating and equipped with 2.3L through 7.5L engines from 1986-1989, including the King Cobra models. Step-by-step instructions and hundreds of illustrations guide you through jobs ranging from simple maintenance to complete overhaul.

This manual can be used by anyone from a first-time amateur to a professional mechanic. Easy to read type, detailed drawings and clear photographs give you all the information you need to do the work right.

Having a well-maintained engine and stern drive will increase your enjoyment of your boat as well as assure your safety offshore. Keep this manual handy and use it often. It can save you hundreds of dollars in maintenance and repair costs and make yours a reliable, top-performing boat.

Chapter One

General Information

This detailed, comprehensive manual contains complete information on maintenance, tune-up, repair and overhaul. Hundreds of photos and drawings guide you through every step.

Troubleshooting, tune-up, maintenance and repair are not difficult if you know what tools and equipment to use and what to do. Anyone not afraid to get their hands dirty, of average intelligence and with some mechanical ability can perform most of the procedures in this book. See Chapter Two for more information on tools and techniques.

A shop manual is a reference. You want to be able to find information fast. Clymer books are designed with you in mind. All chapters are thumb tabbed. Important items are indexed at the end of the book. All procedures, tables, photos, etc., in this manual assume that the reader may be working on the machine or using this manual for the first time.

Keep this book handy in your tool box. It will help you to better understand how your machine runs, lower repair and maintenance costs and generally increase your enjoyment of your marine equipment.

MANUAL ORGANIZATION

This chapter provides general information useful to marine owners and mechanics.

Chapter Two discusses the tools and techniques for preventive maintenance, troubleshooting and repair.

Chapter Three describes typical equipment problems and provides logical troubleshooting procedures.

Following chapters describe specific systems, providing disassembly, repair, assembly and adjustment procedures in simple step-by-step form. Specifications concerning a specific system are included at the end of the appropriate chapter.

NOTES, CAUTIONS AND WARNINGS

The terms NOTE, CAUTION and WARNING have specific meanings in this manual. A NOTE provides additional information to make a step or procedure easier or clearer. Disregarding a NOTE could cause inconvenience, but would not cause damage or personal injury.

A CAUTION emphasizes areas where equipment damage could result. Disregarding a CAUTION could cause permanent mechanical damage; however, personal injury is unlikely.

A WARNING emphasizes areas where personal injury or even death could result from negligence. Mechanical damage may also occur. WARNINGS *are to be taken seriously*. In some cases, serious injury or death has resulted from disregarding similar warnings.

TORQUE SPECIFICATIONS

Torque specifications throughout this manual are given in foot-pounds (ft.-lb.) and either Newton meters (N•m) or meter-kilograms (mkg). Newton meters are being adopted in place of meter-kilograms in accordance with the International Modernized Metric System. Existing torque wrenches calibrated in meter-kilograms can be used by performing a simple conversion: move the decimal point one place to the right. For example, 4.7 mkg = 47 N•m. This conversion is accurate enough for mechanics' use even though the exact mathematical conversion is 3.5 mkg = 34.3 N•m.

ENGINE OPERATION

All marine engines, whether 2- or 4-stroke, gasoline or diesel, operate on the Otto cycle of intake, compression, power and exhaust phases.

4-stroke Cycle

A 4-stroke engine requires 2 crankshaft revolutions (4 strokes of the piston) to complete the Otto cycle. **Figure 1** shows gasoline 4-stroke engine operation. **Figure 2** shows diesel 4-stroke engine operation.

2-stroke Cycle

A 2-stroke engine requires only 1 crankshaft revolution (2 strokes of the piston) to complete the Otto cycle. **Figure 3** shows gasoline 2-stroke engine operation. While diesel 2-strokes exist, they are not commonly used in light marine applications.

FASTENERS

The material and design of the various fasteners used on marine equipment are not arrived at by chance or accident. Fastener design determines the type of tool required to work with the fastener. Fastener material is carefully selected to decrease the possibility of physical failure or corrosion. See *Galvanic Corrosion* in this chapter for more information on marine materials.

Threads

Nuts, bolts and screws are manufactured in a wide range of thread patterns. To join a nut and bolt, the diameter of the bolt and the diameter of the hole in the nut must be the same. It is just as important that the threads on both be properly matched.

The best way to tell if the threads on 2 fasteners are matched is to turn the nut on the bolt (or the bolt into the threaded hole in a piece of equipment) with fingers only. Be sure both pieces are clean. If much force is required, check the thread condition on each fastener. If the thread condition is good but the fasteners jam, the threads are not compatible.

Four important specifications describe every thread:

a. Diameter.
b. Threads per inch.
c. Thread pattern.
d. Thread direction.

Figure 4 shows the first 2 specifications. Thread pattern is more subtle. Italian and British standards exist, but the most commonly used by marine equipment manufacturers are American standard and

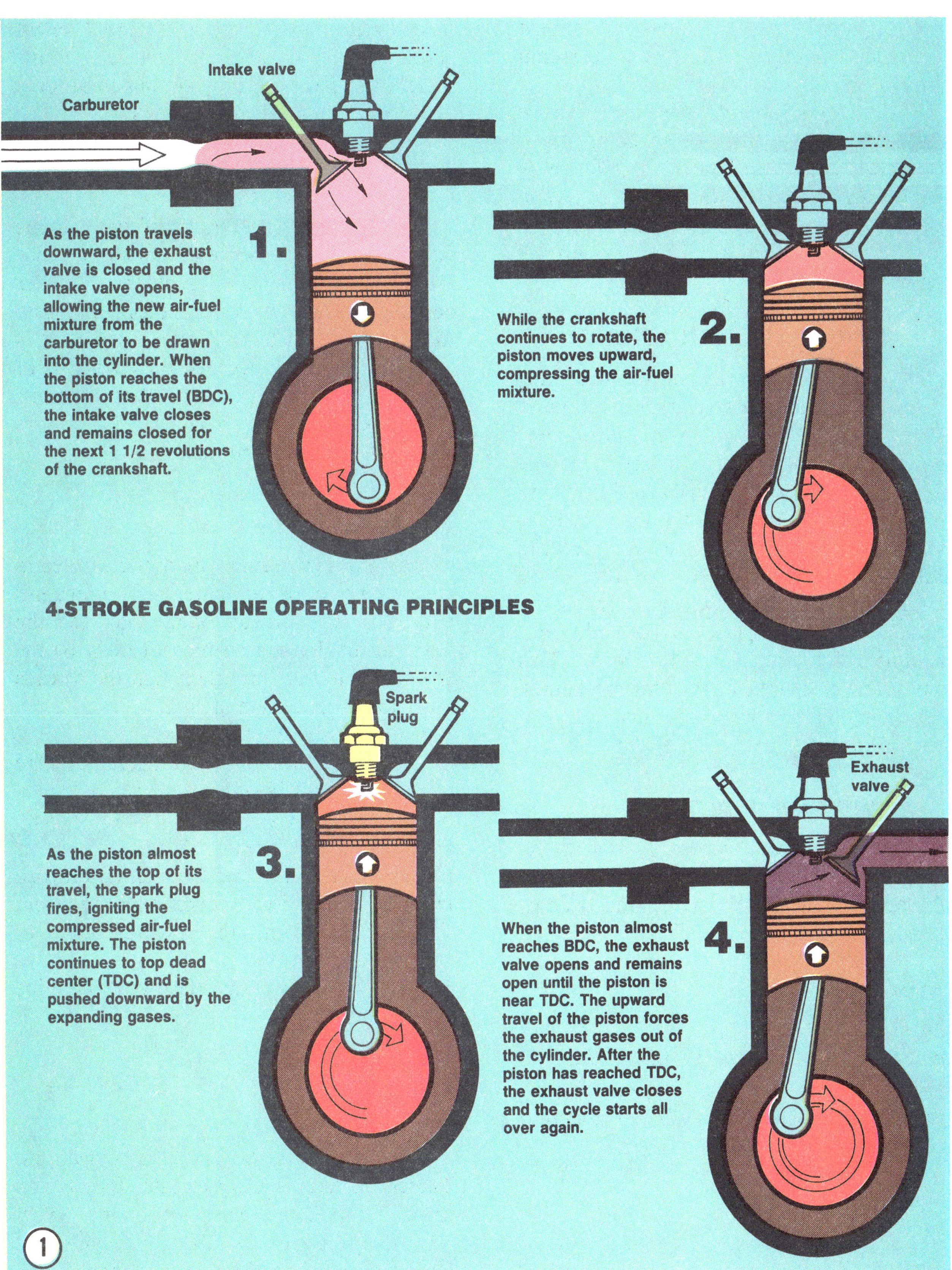
Intake valve
Carburetor
1.
As the piston travels downward, the exhaust valve is closed and the intake valve opens, allowing the new air-fuel mixture from the carburetor to be drawn into the cylinder. When the piston reaches the bottom of its travel (BDC), the intake valve closes and remains closed for the next 1 1/2 revolutions of the crankshaft.
2.
While the crankshaft continues to rotate, the piston moves upward, compressing the air-fuel mixture.
4-STROKE GASOLINE OPERATING PRINCIPLES
Spark plug
3.
As the piston almost reaches the top of its travel, the spark plug fires, igniting the compressed air-fuel mixture. The piston continues to top dead center (TDC) and is pushed downward by the expanding gases.
Exhaust valve
4.
When the piston almost reaches BDC, the exhaust valve opens and remains open until the piston is near TDC. The upward travel of the piston forces the exhaust gases out of the cylinder. After the piston has reached TDC, the exhaust valve closes and the cycle starts all over again.
1

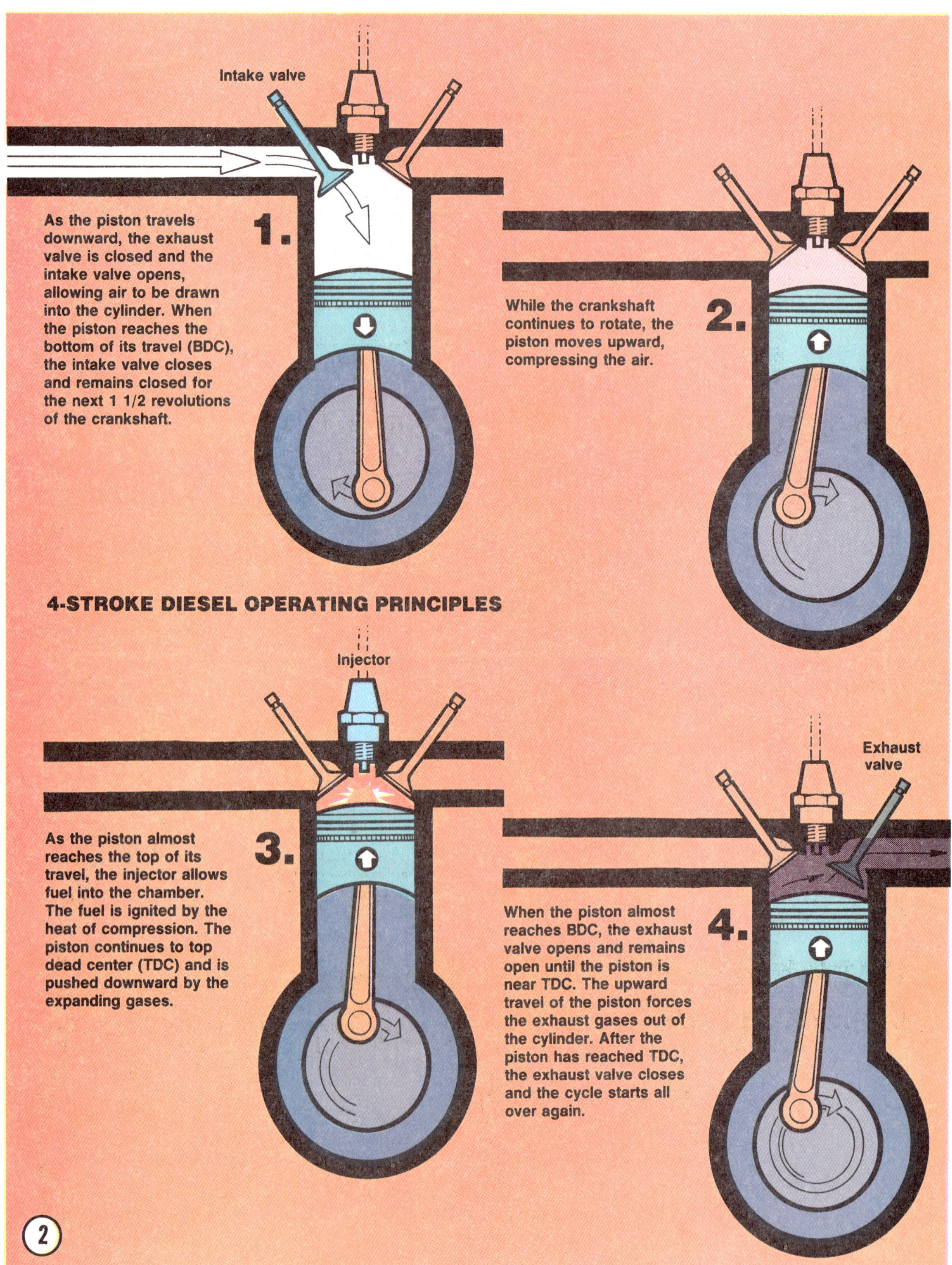
Intake valve
1.
As the piston travels downward, the exhaust valve is closed and the intake valve opens, allowing air to be drawn into the cylinder. When the piston reaches the bottom of its travel (BDC), the intake valve closes and remains closed for the next 1 1/2 revolutions of the crankshaft.
2.
While the crankshaft continues to rotate, the piston moves upward, compressing the air.
4-STROKE DIESEL OPERATING PRINCIPLES
Injector
3.
As the piston almost reaches the top of its travel, the injector allows fuel into the chamber. The fuel is ignited by the heat of compression. The piston continues to top dead center (TDC) and is pushed downward by the expanding gases.
Exhaust valve
4.
When the piston almost reaches BDC, the exhaust valve opens and remains open until the piston is near TDC. The upward travel of the piston forces the exhaust gases out of the cylinder. After the piston has reached TDC, the exhaust valve closes and the cycle starts all over again.
2

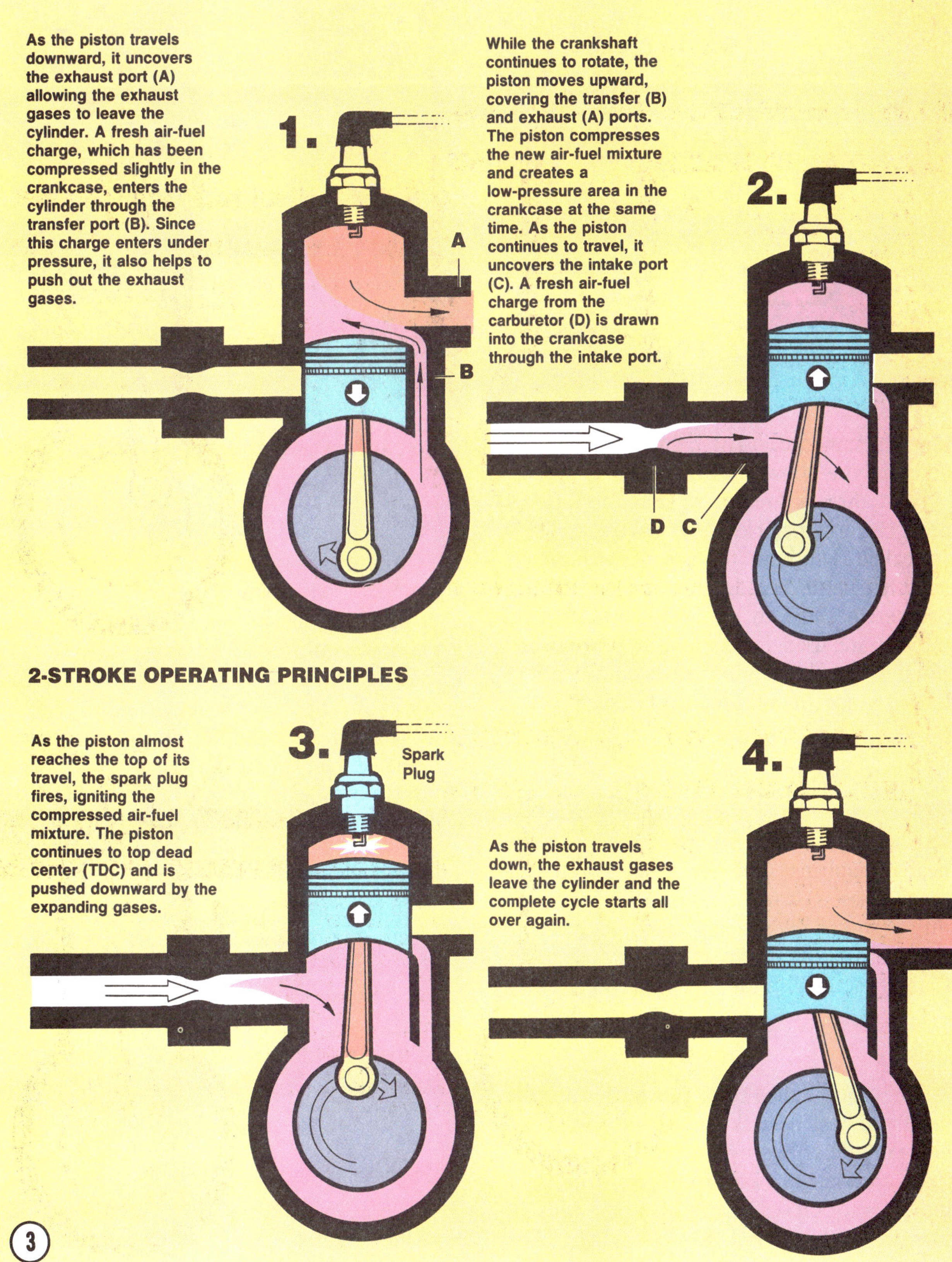
As the piston travels downward, it uncovers the exhaust port (A) allowing the exhaust gases to leave the cylinder. A fresh air-fuel charge, which has been compressed slightly in the crankcase, enters the cylinder through the transfer port (B). Since this charge enters under pressure, it also helps to push out the exhaust gases.
1.
A
B
While the crankshaft continues to rotate, the piston moves upward, covering the transfer (B) and exhaust (A) ports. The piston compresses the new air-fuel mixture and creates a low-pressure area in the crankcase at the same time. As the piston continues to travel, it uncovers the intake port (C). A fresh air-fuel charge from the carburetor (D) is drawn into the crankcase through the intake port.
2.
D
C
2-STROKE OPERATING PRINCIPLES
As the piston almost reaches the top of its travel, the spark plug fires, igniting the compressed air-fuel mixture. The piston continues to top dead center (TDC) and is pushed downward by the expanding gases.
3.
Spark Plug
4.
As the piston travels down, the exhaust gases leave the cylinder and the complete cycle starts all over again.

3

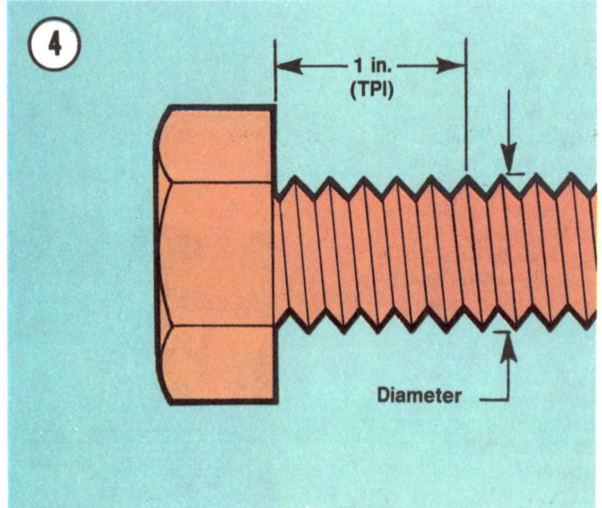

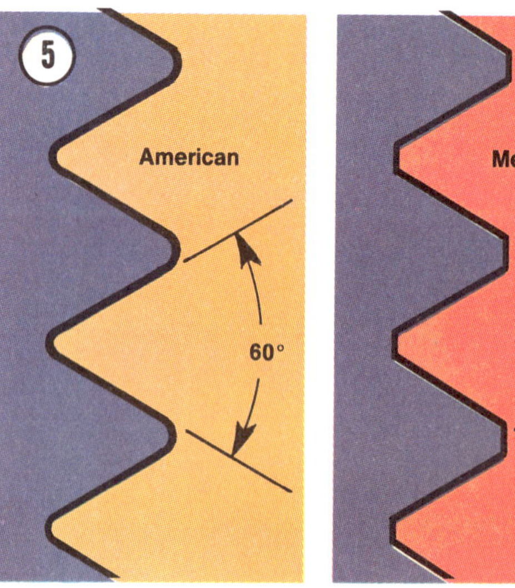

metric standard. The threads are cut differently as shown in **Figure 5**.

Most threads are cut so that the fastener must be turned clockwise to tighten it. These are called right-hand threads. Some fasteners have left-hand threads; they must be turned counterclockwise to be tightened. Left-hand threads are used in locations where normal rotation of the equipment would tend to loosen a right-hand threaded fastener.

Machine Screws

There are many different types of machine screws. **Figure 6** shows a number of screw heads requiring different types of turning tools (see Chapter Two for detailed information). Heads are also designed to protrude above the metal (round) or to be slightly recessed in the metal (flat) (**Figure 7**).

Bolts

Commonly called bolts, the technical name for these fasteners is cap screw. They are normally described by diameter, threads per inch and length. For example, 1/4-20×1 indicates a bolt 1/4 in. in diameter with 20 threads per inch, 1 in. long. The measurement across 2 flats on the head of the bolt indicates the proper wrench size to be used.

Nuts

Nuts are manufactured in a variety of types and sizes. Most are hexagonal (6-sided) and fit on bolts, screws and studs with the same diameter and threads per inch.

Figure 8 shows several types of nuts. The common nut is usually used with a lockwasher. Self-locking nuts have a nylon insert which prevents the nut from loosening; no lockwasher is required. Wing nuts are designed for fast removal by hand. Wing nuts are used for convenience in non-critical locations.

To indicate the size of a nut, manufacturers specify the diameter of the opening and the threads per inch. This is similar to bolt specification, but without the length dimension. The measurement across 2 flats on the nut indicates the proper wrench size to be used.

Washers

There are 2 basic types of washers: flat washers and lockwashers. Flat washers are simple discs with a hole to fit a screw or bolt.

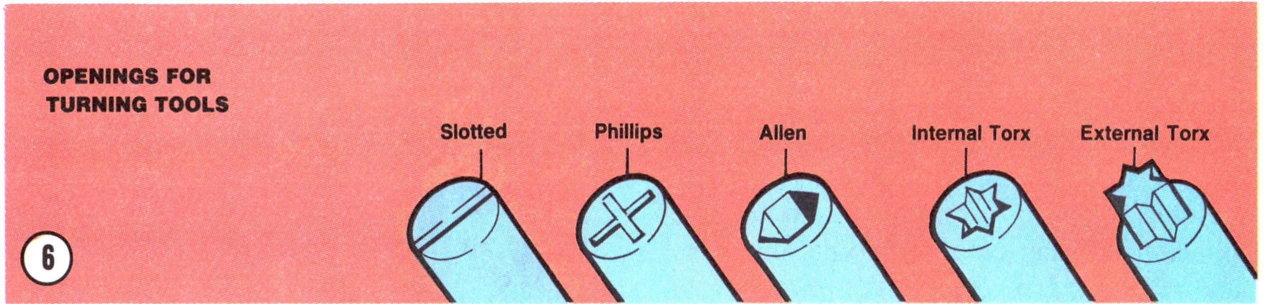

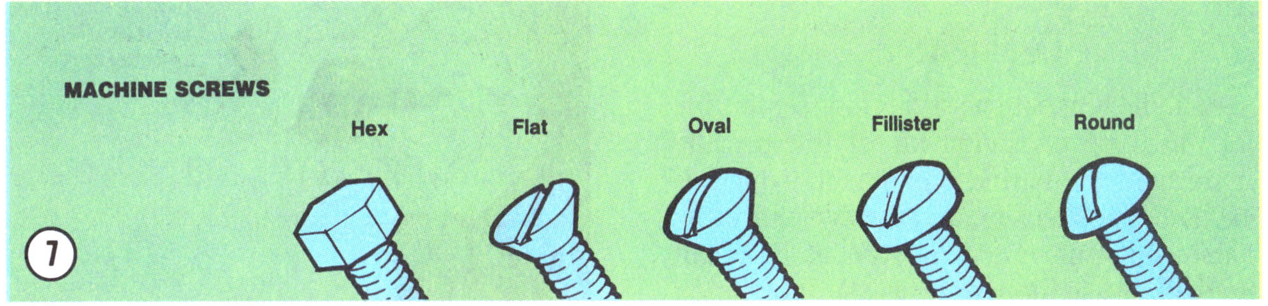

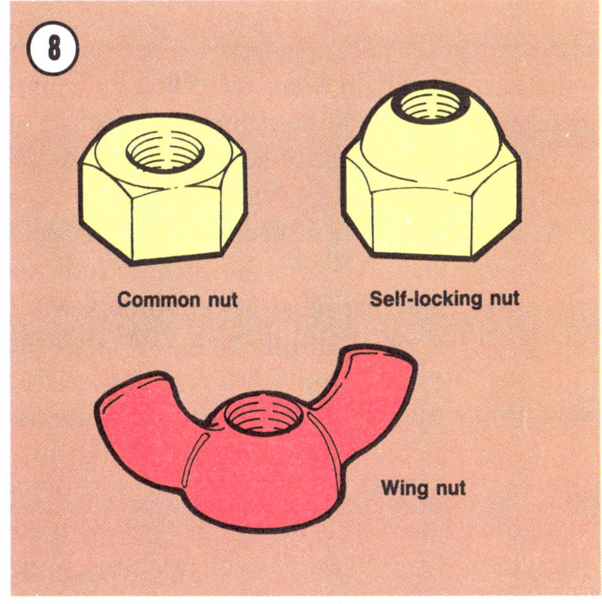

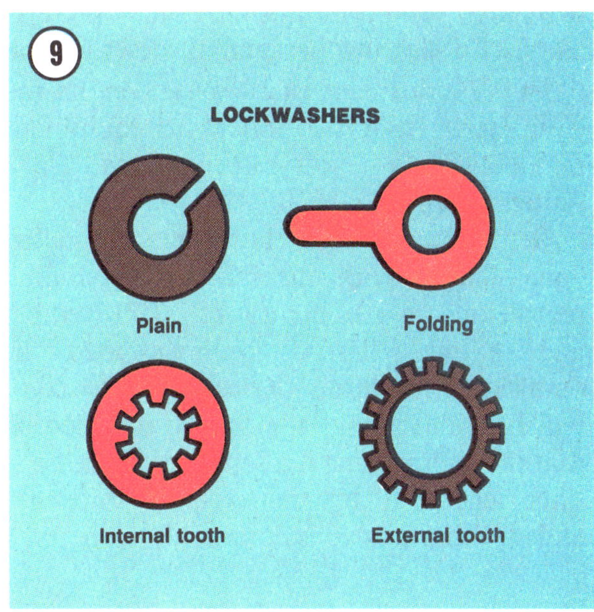

Lockwashers are designed to prevent a fastener from working loose due to vibration, expansion and contraction. **Figure 9** shows several washers. Note that flat washers are often used between a lockwasher and a fastener to provide a smooth bearing surface. This allows the fastener to be turned easily with a tool.

Cotter Pins

Cotter pins (**Figure 10**) are used to secure special kinds of fasteners. The threaded stud must have a hole in it; the nut or nut lock piece has projections which the cotter pin ends wrap around. Cotter pins should not be reused after removal.

Snap Rings

Snap rings can be of an internal or external design. They are used to retain items on shafts (external type) or within tubes (internal type). Snap rings can be reused if they are not distorted during removal. In some applications, snap rings of varying thickness can be selected to control the end play of parts assemblies.

LUBRICANTS

Periodic lubrication assures long service life for any type of equipment. It is especially important to marine equipment, which is exposed to salt or brackish water and other harsh environments. The *type* of lubricant used is just as important as the lubrication service itself, although in an emergency the wrong type of lubricant is better than none at all. The following paragraphs describe the types of lubricants most often used on marine equipment. Be sure to follow the equipment manufacturer's recommendations for lubricant types.

Generally, all liquid lubricants are called "oil." They may be mineral-based (including petroleum bases), natural-based (vegetable and animal bases), synthetic-based or emulsions (mixtures). "Grease" is an oil to which a thickening base has been added so that the end product is a semi-solid. Grease is often classified by the type of thickener added; lithium soap is commonly used.

4-stroke Engine Oil

Oil for 4-stroke engines is graded by the American Petroleum Institute (API) and the Society of Automotive Engineers (SAE) in several categories. Oil containers display these ratings on the top or label (**Figure 11**).

API oil grade is indicated by letters; oils for gasoline engines are identified by an "S" while oils for diesel engines are identified by a "C." Most modern gasoline engines require SE or SF graded oil. Automotive and marine diesel engines use CC or CD graded oil.

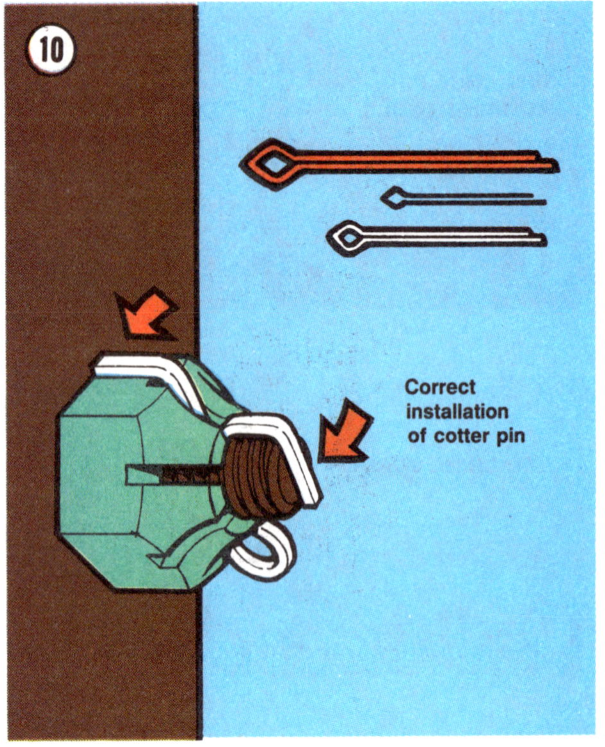

Viscosity is an indication of the oil's thickness. The SAE uses numbers to indicate viscosity; thin oils have low numbers while thick oils have high numbers. A "W" after the number indicates that the viscosity testing was done at low temperature to simulate cold-weather operation. Engine oils fall into the 5W-20W and 20-50 range.

Multi-grade oils (for example, 10W-40) are less viscous (thinner) at low temperatures and more viscous (thicker) at high temperatures. This allows the oil to perform efficiently across a wide range of engine operating temperatures.

2-stroke Engine Oil

Lubrication for a 2-stroke engine is provided by oil mixed with the incoming

fuel-air mixture. Some of the oil mist settles out in the crankcase, lubricating the crankshaft and lower end of the connecting rods. The rest of the oil enters the combustion chamber to lubricate the piston rings and cylinder walls. This oil is burned during the combustion process.

Engine oil must have several special qualities to work well in a 2-stroke engine. It must mix easily and stay in suspension in gasoline. When burned, it can't leave behind excessive deposits. It must be appropriate for the high temperatures associated with 2-stroke engines.

The National Marine Manufacturer's Association (NMMA) and the Boating Industry Association (BIA) have set standards for oil for use in 2-stroke, water-cooled engines. This is the BIA TC-W (two-cycle, water-cooled) grade (**Figure 12**). The oil's performance in the following areas is evaluated:

a. Lubrication (prevention of wear and scuffing).
b. Spark plug fouling.
c. Preignition.
d. Piston ring sticking.
e. Piston varnish.
f. General engine condition (including deposits).
g. Exhaust port blockage.
h. Rust prevention.
i. Mixing ability with gasoline.

In addition to oil grade, manufacturers specify the ratio of gasoline to oil required during break-in and normal engine operation.

Gear Oil

Gear lubricants are assigned SAE viscosity numbers under the same system as 4-stroke engine oil. Gear lubricant falls into the SAE 72-250 range (**Figure 13**). Some gear lubricants are multi-grade; for example, SAE 85W-90.

Various additives are put into gear oils to tailor them for specific uses; these additive packages are graded by the API and identified by the letters "GL" and a number. GL-4 and GL-5 are the most commonly used.

Grease

Greases are graded by the National Lubricating Grease Institute (NLGI). Greases are graded by number according to the consistency of the grease; these ratings range from No. 000 to No. 6, with No. 6 being the most solid. A typical multipurpose grease is NLGI No. 2 (**Figure 14**). For specific applications, equipment manufacturers may require grease with an additive such as molybdenum disulfide (MOS^2).

GASKET SEALANT

Gasket sealant is used instead of pre-formed gaskets between some engine mating surfaces. Two types of gasket sealant are commonly used: room temperature vulcanizing (RTV) and anaerobic. Since these 2 materials have different sealing properties, they cannot be used interchangeably.

RTV Sealant

This is a black silicone gel supplied in tubes (**Figure 15**). Moisture in the air causes RTV to cure. Always place the cap on the tube as soon as possible when using RTV. RTV has a shelf life of one year and will not cure properly when the shelf life has expired. Check the expiration date on RTV tubes before using and keep partially used tubes tightly sealed.

Applying RTV Sealant

Clean all gasket residue from mating surfaces. Surfaces should be clean and free of oil and dirt. Remove all RTV gasket material

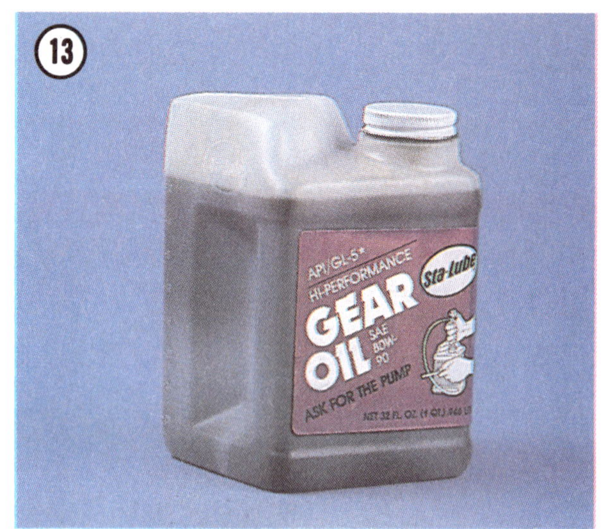

13

14

15

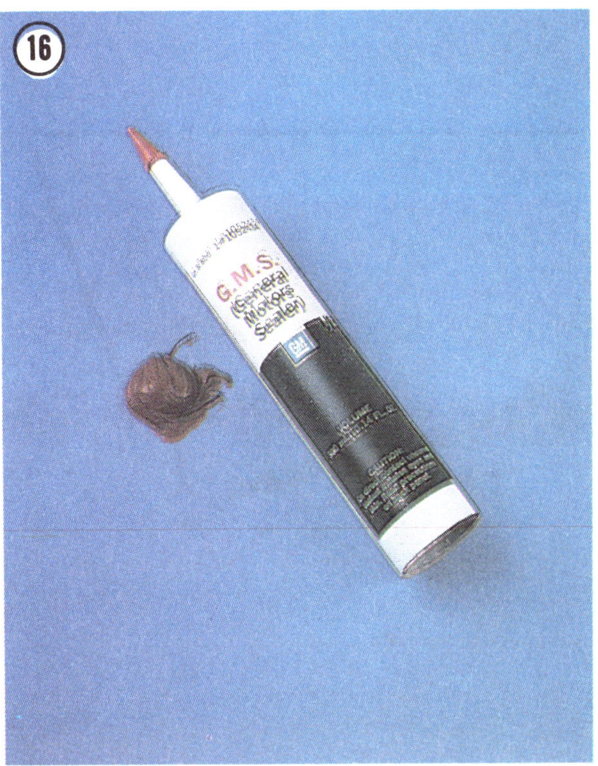

from blind attaching holes, as it can cause a "hydraulic" effect and affect bolt torque.

Apply RTV sealant in a continous bead 2-3 mm (0.08-0.12 in.) thick. Circle all mounting holes unless otherwise specified. Torque mating parts within 10 minutes after application.

Anaerobic Sealant

This is a red gel supplied in tubes (**Figure 16**). It cures only in the absence of air, as when squeezed tightly between 2 machined mating surfaces. For this reason, it will not spoil if the cap is left off the tube. It should not be used if one mating surface is flexible.

Applying Anaerobic Sealant

Clean all gasket residue from mating surfaces. Surfaces must be clean and free of oil and dirt. Remove all gasket material from blind attaching holes, as it can cause a "hydraulic" effect and affect bolt torque.

Apply anaerobic sealant in a 1 mm or less (0.04 in.) bead to one sealing surface. Circle all mounting holes. Torque mating parts within 15 minutes after application.

GALVANIC CORROSION

A chemical reaction occurs whenever 2 different types of metal are joined by an electrical conductor and immersed in an electrolyte. Electrons transfer from one metal to the other through the electrolyte and return through the conductor.

The hardware on a boat is made of many different types of metal. The boat hull acts as a conductor between the metals; even if the hull is wood or fiberglass, the slightest film of water within the hull provides conductivity. Water is an electrolyte. This combination creates a good environment for electron flow (**Figure 17**). Unfortunately, this electron flow results in galvanic corrosion of the metal involved. That is, one of the metals is corroded or eaten away by the process. The amount of electron flow (and therefore the amount of corrosion) depends on several factors:

a. The types of metal involved.
b. The efficiency of the conductor.
c. The strength of the electrolyte.

Metals

The chemical composition of the metals used in marine equipment has a significant effect on the amount and speed of galvanic corrosion. Certain metals are more resistant to corrosion than others. These electrically negative metals are commonly called "noble"; they act as the cathode in any reaction. Metals which are more subject to corrosion are electrically positive; they act as the anode in a reaction. The more noble metals include titanium, 18-8 stainless steel

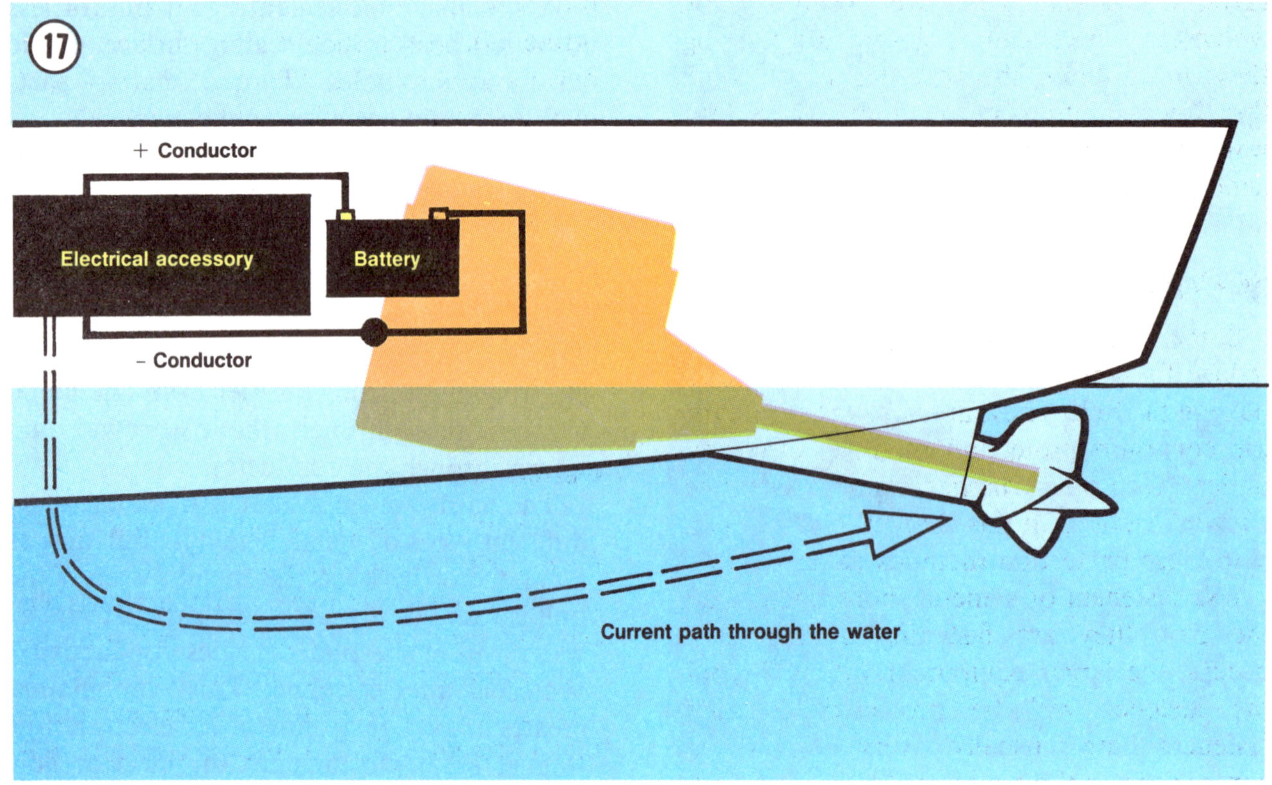

and nickel. Less noble metals include zinc, aluminum and magnesium. Galvanic corrosion becomes more severe as the difference between the two metals increases.

In some cases, galvanic corrosion can occur within a single piece of metal. Common brass is a mixture of zinc and copper; when immersed in an electrolyte, the zinc portion of the mixture will corrode away as reaction occurs between the zinc and the copper particles.

Conductors

The hull of the boat often acts as the conductor between different types of metal. Marine equipment such as an outboard motor or stern drive unit can also act as the conductor. Large masses of metal, firmly connected together, are more efficient conductors than water. Rubber mountings and vinyl-based paint can act as insulators between pieces of metal.

Electrolyte

The water in which a boat operates acts as the electrolyte for the galvanic corrosion process. The better a conductor the electrolyte is, the more severe and rapid the corrosion.

Cold, clean fresh water is the poorest electrolyte. As water temperature increases, its conductivity increases. Pollutants will increase conductivity; brackish or salt water is also an efficient electrolyte. This is one of the reasons that most manufacturers recommend a fresh-water flush for marine equipment after operation in salt water.

PROTECTION FROM GALVANIC CORROSION

Because of the environment in which marine equipment must operate, it is practically impossible to totally prevent galvanic corrosion. There are several ways by which the process can be slowed; after taking these precautions, the next step is to "fool" the process into occuring only where *you* want it to occur. This is the role of galvanic anodes and impressed current systems.

Slowing Corrosion

Some simple precautions can help to reduce the amount of corrosion taking place outside the hull. These are *not* a substitute for the corrosion protection methods discussed under *Galvanic Anodes* and *Impressed Current Systems* in this chapter, but they can help these protection methods do their job.

Use fasteners of a metal more noble than the part they are fastening. If corrosion occurs, the larger equipment will suffer but the fastener will be protected. Because fasteners are usually very small in comparison to the equipment being fastened, the equipment can survive the loss of material. If the fastener were to corrode instead of the equipment, major problems could arise.

Keep all painted surfaces in good condition. If paint is scraped off and bare metal exposed, corrosion will rapidly increase. Use a vinyl- or plastic-based paint which acts as an electrical insulator.

Be careful when using metal-based anti-fouling paints. These should not be applied to metal parts of the boat or they will actually react with the equipment, causing corrosion between the equipment and the layer of paint. Organic-based paints are available for use on metal surfaces.

Where a corrosion protection device is used, remember that it must be immersed in the electrolyte along with the rest of the boat to have any effect. If you raise the power unit out of the water when the boat is docked, any anodes on the power unit will be removed from the corrosion cycle and will not protect the rest of the equipment that is still immersed. Also, such corrosion protection devices must not be painted, as that would insulate them from the corrosion process.

Any change in the boat's equipment (such as the installation of a new stainless steel propeller) will change the corrosion process. Keep in mind that when you add new equipment or change materials, you should review your corrosion protection system to be sure it is up to the job.

Galvanic Anodes

Anodes are usually made of zinc, a far from noble metal. They are specially made lumps of metal designed to do nothing but corrode. Properly fastening such pieces to the boat will cause them to act as the anode in *any* galvanic reaction that occurs; any other metal present will act as the cathode and will not be damaged.

Anodes must be used properly to be effective. Simply fastening lumps of zinc to your boat in random locations won't do the job.

You must determine how much zinc surface area is required to adequately protect the equipment's surface area. A good starting point is provided by Military Specification MIL-A-818001, which states that one square inch of new zinc anode will protect either:

a. 800 square inches of freshly painted steel.
b. 250 square inches of bare steel or bare aluminum alloy.
c. 100 square inches of copper or copper alloy.

This rule is for a boat at rest. When underway, more anode area is required to protect the same equipment surface area.

The zinc must be fastened so that it has good electrical contact with the metal to be protected. If possible, the zinc can be attached directly to the other metal. If that is not possible, the entire network of metal parts in the boat should be electrically tied together so that all pieces are protected.

Good quality anodes have inserts of some other metal around the fastener holes. Otherwise, the zinc could erode away around the fastener. The anode can then become loose or even fall off, removing all protection.

Another Military Specification (MIL-A-18001) defines the type of alloy preferred, which will corrode at a uniform rate without forming a crust which could reduce its efficiency after a time.

Impressed Current Systems

An impressed current system can be installed on any boat that has a battery. The system consists of an anode, a control box and a sensor. The anode in this system is coated with a very noble metal (such as platinum) so that it is almost corrosion-free and will last indefinitely. The sensor, under the boat's waterline, monitors the potential for corrosion. When it senses that corrosion could be occuring, it transmits this information to the control box.

The control box connects the boat's battery to the anode. When the sensor signals the need, the control box applies positive battery voltage to the anode. Current from the battery flows from the anode to all other metal parts of the boat, no matter how noble or non-noble these parts are. This battery current takes the place of any galvanic current flow.

Only a very small amount of battery current is needed to counteract galvanic corrosion. Manufacturers estimate that it would take 2 or 3 months of constant use to drain a typical marine battery, assuming the battery is never recharged.

An impressed current system is more expensive to install than simple zinc anodes but, considering its low maintenance requirements and the excellent protection it provides, the long-term cost may actually be lower.

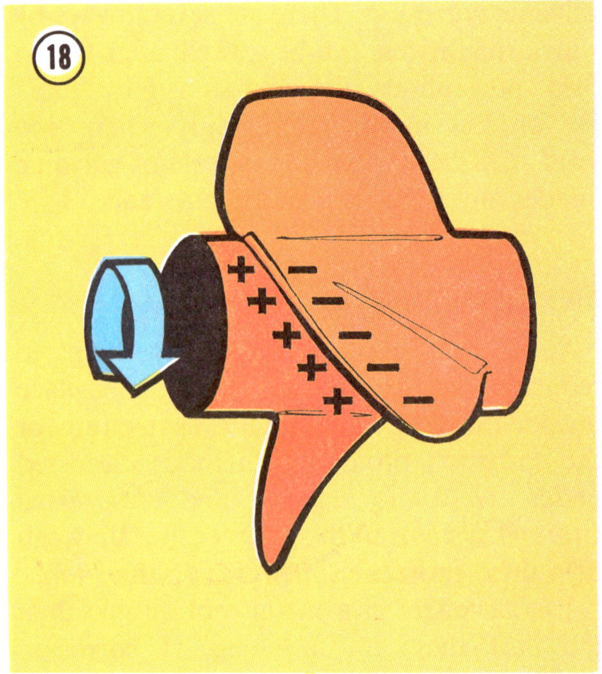

PROPELLERS

The propeller is the final link between the boat's drive system and the water. A perfectly maintained engine and hull are useless if the propeller is the wrong type or has been allowed to deteriorate. Although propeller selection for a specific situation is beyond the scope of this book, the following information on propeller construction and design will allow you to discuss the subject intelligently with your marine dealer.

How a Propeller Works

As the curved blades of a propeller rotate through the water, a high-pressure area is created on one side of the blade and a low-pressure area exists on the other side of the blade (**Figure 18**). The propeller moves toward the low-pressure area, carrying the boat with it.

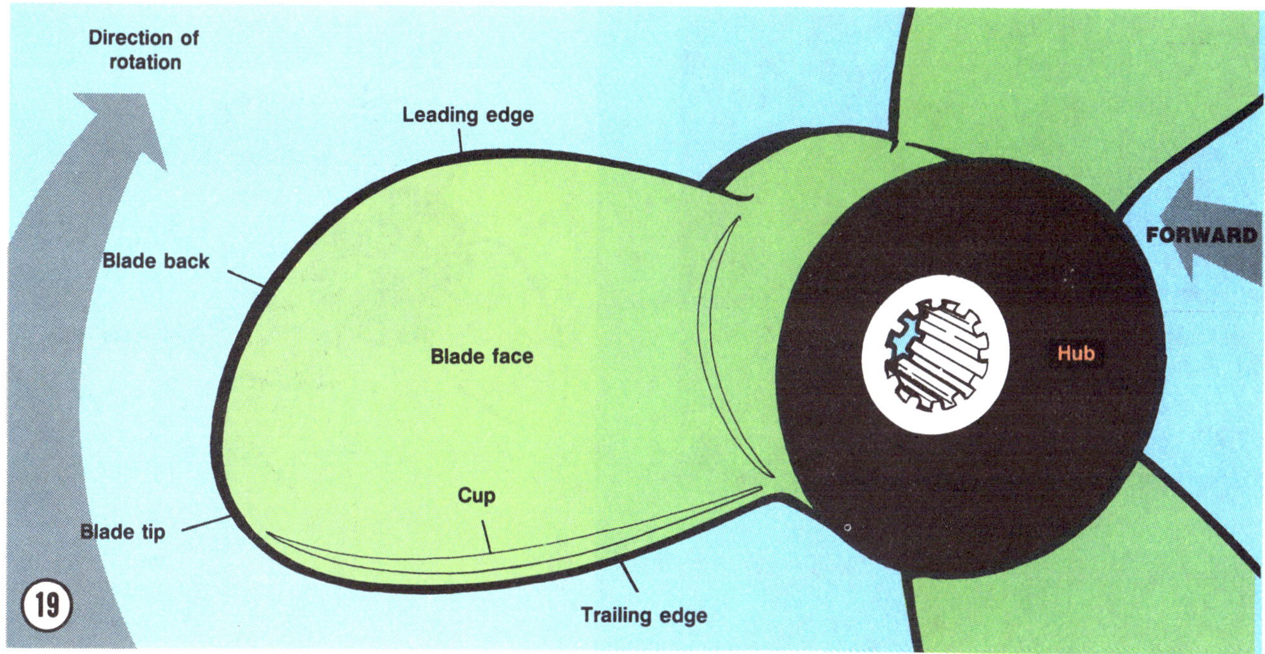

Propeller Parts

Although a propeller may be a 1-piece unit, it is made up of several different parts (**Figure 19**). Variations in the design of these parts make different propellers suitable for different jobs.

The blade tip is the point on the blade farthest from the center of the propeller hub. The blade tip separates the leading edge from the trailing edge.

The leading edge is the edge of the blade nearest to the boat. During normal rotation, this is the blade that first cuts through the water.

The trailing edge is the edge of the blade farthest from the boat.

The blade face is the surface of the blade that faces away from the boat. During normal rotation, high pressure exists on this side of the blade.

The blade back is the surface of the blade that faces toward the boat. During normal rotation, low pressure exists on this side of the blade.

The cup is a small curve or lip on the trailing edge of the blade.

The hub is the central portion of the propeller. It connects the blades to the propeller shaft (part of the boat's drive system). On some drive systems, engine exhaust is routed through the hub; in this case, the hub is made up of an outer and an inner portion, connected by ribs.

The diffuser ring is used on through-hub exhaust models to prevent exhaust gases from entering the blade area.

Propeller Design

Changes in length, angle, thickness and material of propeller parts make different propellers suitable for different situations.

Diameter

Propeller diameter is the distance from the center of the hub to the blade tip, multiplied

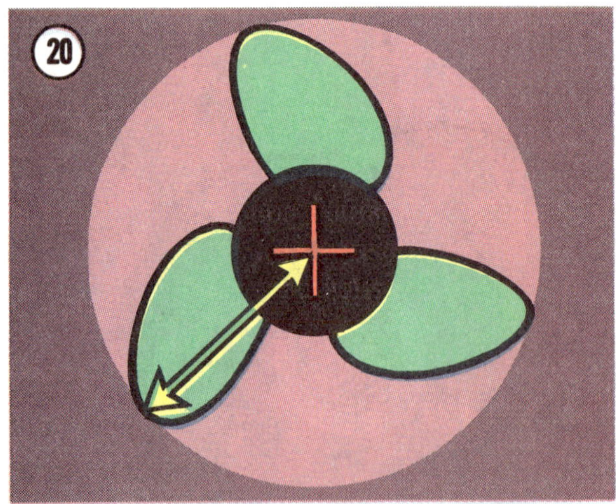

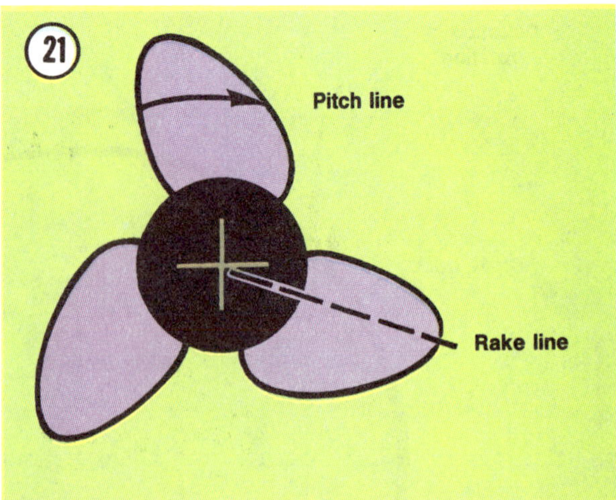

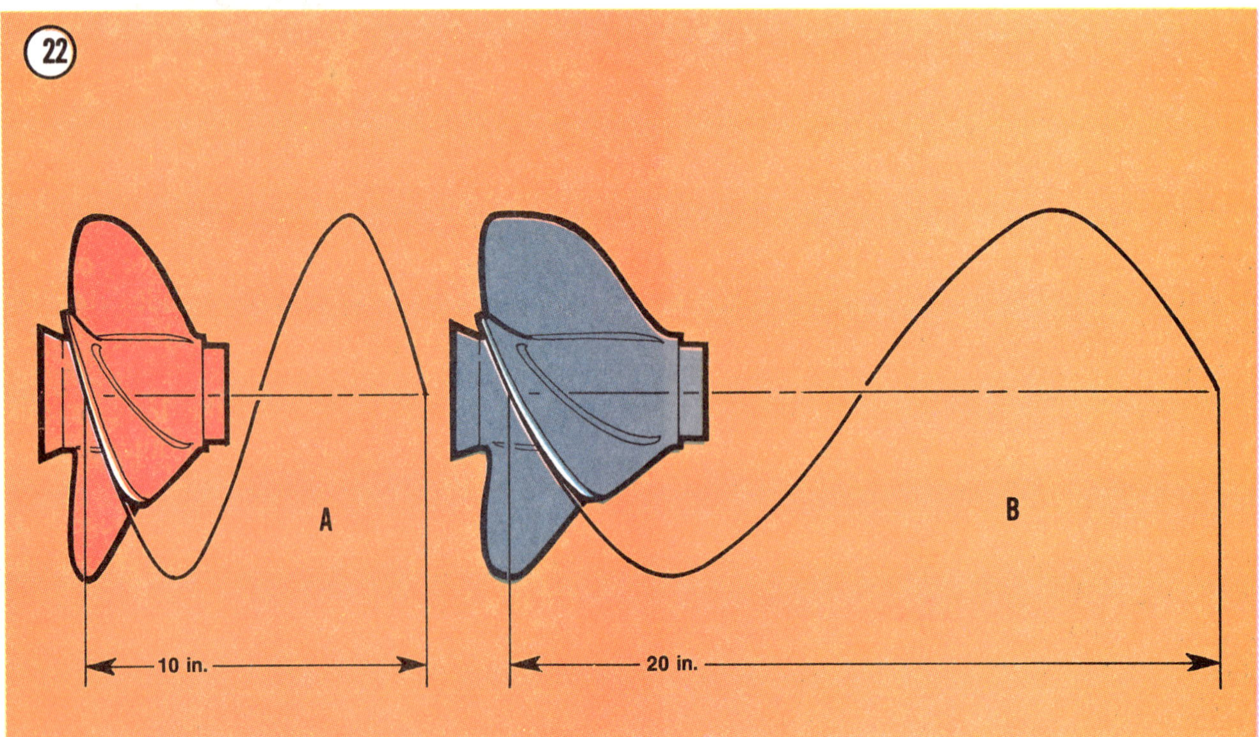

by 2. That is, it is the diameter of the circle formed by the blade tips during propeller rotation (**Figure 20**).

Pitch and rake

Propeller pitch and rake describe the placement of the blade in relation to the hub (**Figure 21**).

Pitch is expressed by the theoretical distance that the propeller would travel in one revolution. In A, **Figure 22**, the propeller would travel 10 inches in one revolution. In B, **Figure 22**, the propeller would travel 20 inches in one revolution. This distance is only theoretical; during actual operation, the propeller achieves about 80% of its rated travel.

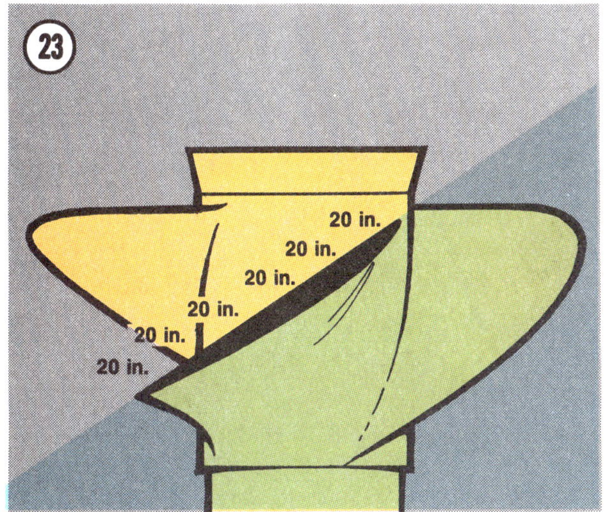

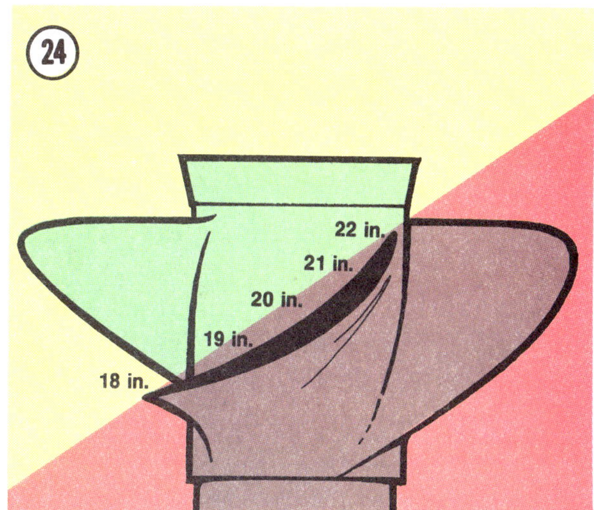

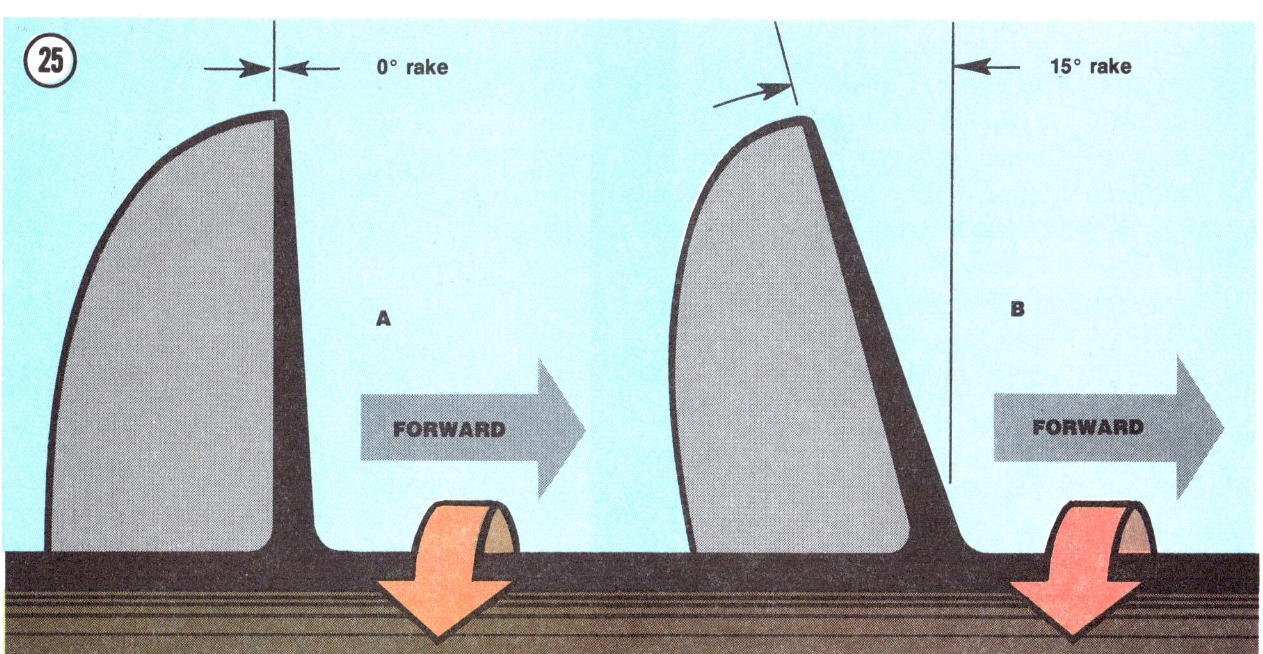

Propeller blades can be constructed with constant pitch (**Figure 23**) or progressive pitch (**Figure 24**). Progressive pitch starts low at the leading edge and increases toward the trailing edge. The propeller pitch specification is the average of the pitch across the entire blade.

Blade rake is specified in° and is measured along a line from the center of the hub to the blade tip. A blade that is perpendicular to the hub (A, **Figure 25**) has 0 degree of rake. A blade that is angled from perpendicular (B, **Figure 25**) has a rake expressed by its difference from perpendicular. Most propellers have rakes ranging from 0-20°.

Blade thickness

Blade thickness is not uniform at all points along the blade. For efficiency, blades should be as thin as possible at all points while retaining enough strength to move the boat. Blades tend to be thicker where they meet the hub and thinner at the blade tip (**Figure 26**). This is to support the heavier loads at the hub section of the blade. This thickness is dependent on the strength of the material used.

When cut along a line from the leading edge to the trailing edge in the central portion of the blade (**Figure 27**), the propeller blade resembles an airplane wing. The blade face, where high pressure exists during normal rotation, is almost flat. The blade back, where low pressure exists during normal rotation, is curved, with the thinnest portions at the edges and the thickest portion at the center.

Propellers that run only partially submerged, as in racing applications, may have a wedge-shaped cross-section (**Figure 28**). The leading edge is very thin; the blade thickness increases toward the trailing edge, where it is the thickest. If a propeller such as this is run totally submerged, it is very inefficient.

Number of blades

The number of blades used on a propeller is a compromise between efficiency and vibration. A one-bladed propeller would be the most efficient, but it would also create high levels of vibration. As blades are added, efficiency decreases, but so do vibration levels. Most propellers have 3 blades, representing the most practical trade-off between efficiency and vibration.

Material

Propeller materials are chosen for strength, corrosion resistance and economy. Stainless steel, aluminum and bronze are the most commonly used materials. Bronze is quite strong but rather expensive. Stainless steel is

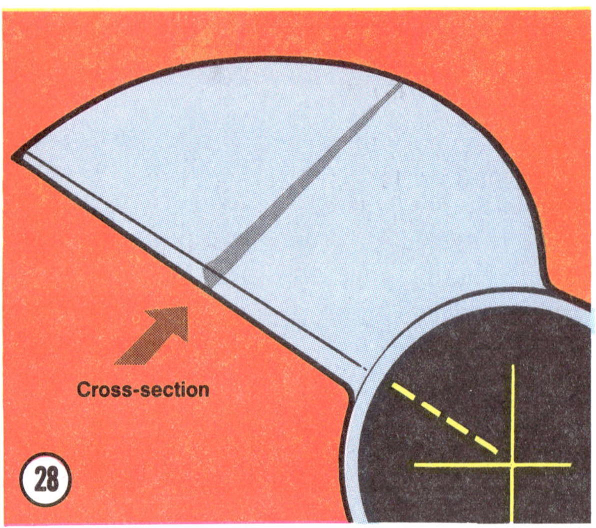

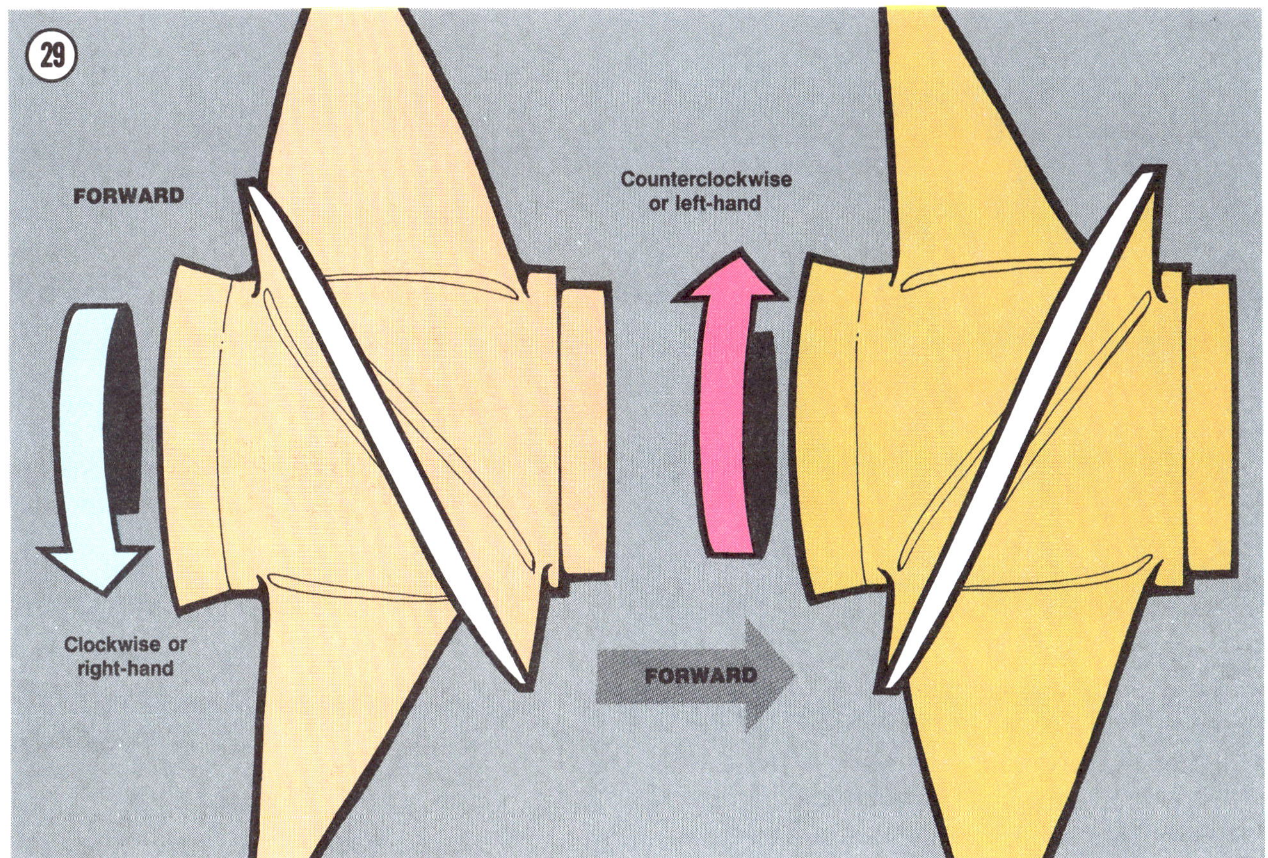

more common than bronze because of its combination of strength and lower cost. Aluminum alloys are the least expensive but usually lack the strength of steel. Plastic propellers may be used in very low horsepower applications.

Direction of rotation

Propellers are made for both right-hand and left-hand rotation, although right-hand is the most commonly used. When seen from behind the boat in forward motion, a right-hand propeller turns clockwise while a left-hand propeller turns counterclockwise. Off the boat, you can tell the difference by observing the angle of the blades (**Figure 29**). A right-hand propeller's blades slant from the lower left to the upper right; a left-hand propeller's blades are the opposite.

Cavitation and Ventilation

Cavitation and ventilation are *not* interchangeable terms; they refer to 2 distinct problems encountered during propeller operation.

To understand cavitation, you must first understand the relationship between pressure and the boiling point of water. At sea level, water will boil at 212° F. As pressure increases, such as within an engine's closed cooling system, the boiling point of water increases—it will boil only at some temperature higher than 212° F. The opposite is also true; as pressure decreases, water will boil at a temperature lower than 212° F. If pressure drops low enough, water will boil at typical ambient temperatures of 50-60° F.

We have said that, during normal propeller operation, low pressure exists on the blade back. Normally, the pressure does not drop

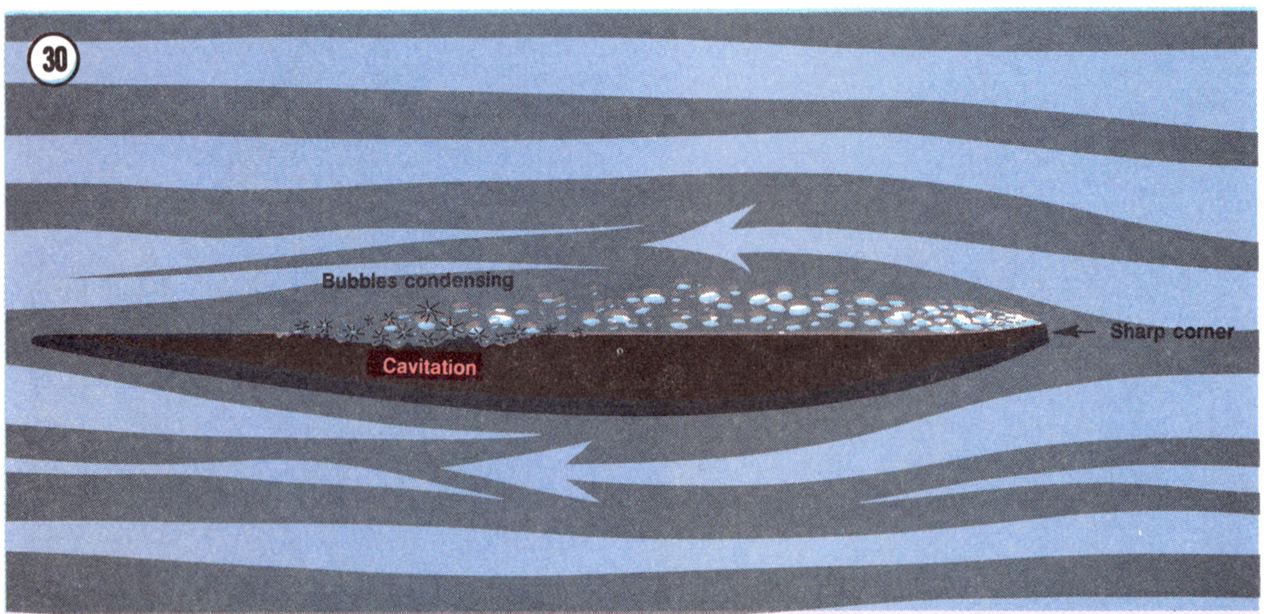

low enough for boiling to occur. However, poor blade design or selection or blade damage can cause an unusual pressure drop on a small area of the blade (**Figure 30**). Boiling can occur in this small area. As the water boils, air bubbles form. As the boiling water passes to a higher-pressure area of the blade, the boiling stops and the bubbles collapse. The collapsing bubbles release enough energy to erode the surface of the blade.

This entire process of pressure drop, boiling and bubble collapse is called "cavitation." The damage caused by the collapsing bubbles is called a "cavitation burn." It is important to remember that cavitation is caused by a decrease in pressure, *not* an increase in temperature.

Ventilation is not as complex a process as cavitation. Ventilation refers to air entering the blade area, either from above the surface of the water or from a through-hub exhaust system. As the blades meet the air, the propeller momentarily over-revs, losing most of its thrust. An added complication is that as the propeller over-revs, pressure on the blade back decreases and massive cavitation occurs.

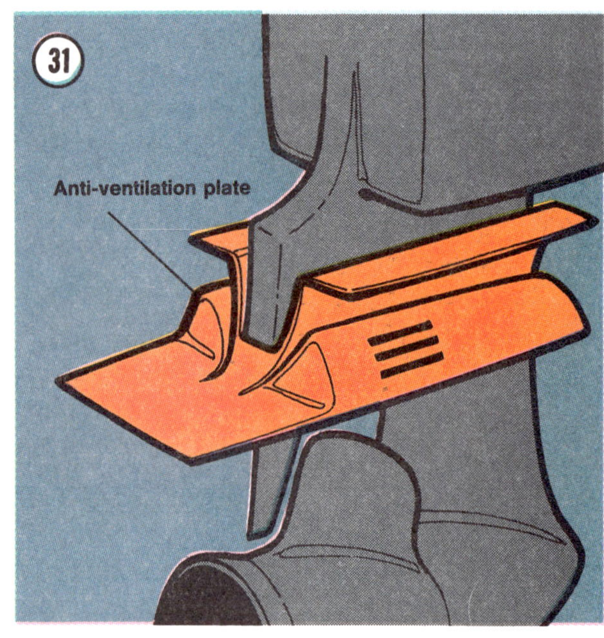

Most pieces of marine equipment have a plate above the propeller area designed to keep surface air from entering the blades (**Figure 31**). This plate is correctly called an "anti-ventilation plate," although you will often *see* it called an "anti-cavitation plate." Through-hub exhaust systems also have specially designed hubs to keep exhaust gases from entering the blade area.

Chapter Two

Tools and Techniques

This chapter describes the common tools required for marine equipment repairs and troubleshooting. Techniques that will make your work easier and more effective are also described. Some of the procedures in this book require special skills or expertise; in some cases, you are better off entrusting the job to a dealer or qualified specialist.

SAFETY FIRST

Professional mechanics can work for years and never suffer a serious injury. If you follow a few rules of common sense and safety, you too can enjoy many safe hours servicing your marine equipment. You can hurt yourself or damage the equipment if you ignore these rules.

1. Never use gasoline as a cleaning solvent.
2. Never smoke or use a torch near flammable liquids such as cleaning solvent. If you are working in your home garage, remember that your home gas appliances have pilot lights.
3. Never smoke or use a torch in an area where batteries are being charged. Highly explosive hydrogen gas is formed during the charging process.
4. Use the proper size wrenches to avoid damage to fasteners and injury to yourself.
5. When loosening a tight or stuck fastener, think of what would happen if the wrench should slip. Protect yourself.
6. Keep your work area clean, uncluttered and well lighted.
7. Wear safety goggles during all operations involving drilling, grinding or the use of a cold chisel.
8. Never use worn tools.
9. Keep a Coast Guard approved fire extinguisher handy. Be sure it is rated for gasoline (Class B) and electrical (Class C) fires.

BASIC HAND TOOLS

A number of tools are required to maintain marine equipment. You may already have some of these tools for home or car repairs. There are also tools made especially for marine equipment repairs; these you will have to purchase. In any case, a wide variety of quality tools will make repairs easier and more effective.

Keep your tools clean and in a tool box. Keep them organized with the sockets and related drives together, the open end and box wrenches together, etc. After using a tool, wipe off dirt and grease with a clean cloth and place the tool in its correct place.

The following tools are required to perform virtually any repair job. Each tool is described and the recommended size given for starting a tool collection. Additional tools and some duplications may be added as you become more familiar with the equipment. You may need all English size tools, all metric size tools or a mixture of both.

Screwdrivers

The screwdriver is a very basic tool, but if used improperly it will do more damage than good. The slot on a screw has a definite dimension and shape. A screwdriver must be selected to conform with that shape. Use a small screwdriver for small screws and a large one for large screws or the screw head will be damaged.

Two types of screwdriver are required: a common (flat-blade) screwdriver (**Figure 1**) and Phillips screwdrivers (**Figure 2**).

Screwdrivers are available in sets which often include an assortment of common and Phillips blades. If you buy them individually, buy at least the following:

a. Common screwdriver—5/16×6 in. blade.
b. Common screwdriver—3/8×12 in. blade.
c. Phillips screwdriver—size 2 tip, 6 in. blade.

Use screwdrivers only for driving screws. Never use a screwdriver for prying or chiseling. Do not try to remove a Phillips or Allen head screw with a common screwdriver; you can damage the head so that the proper tool will be unable to remove it.

Keep screwdrivers in the proper condition and they will last longer and perform better.

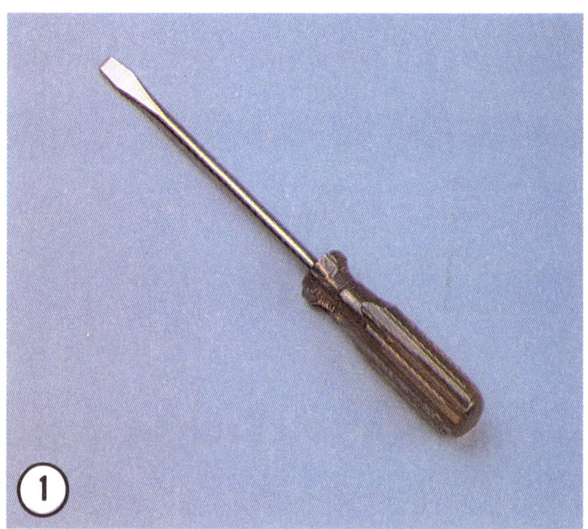
1

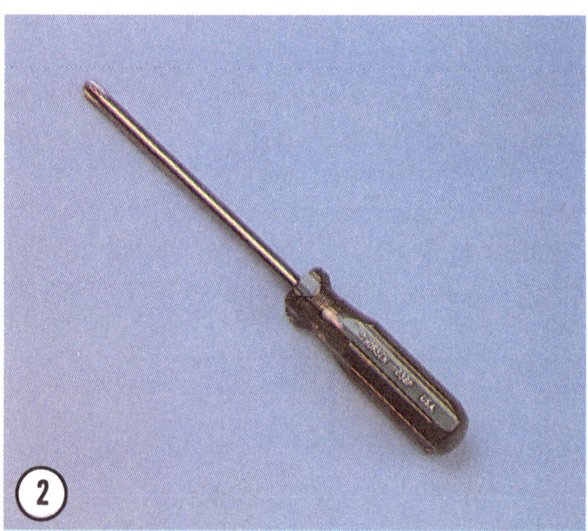
2

Always keep the tip of a common screwdriver in good condition. **Figure 3** shows how to grind the tip to the proper shape if it becomes damaged. Note the parallel sides of the tip.

Pliers

Pliers come in a wide range of types and sizes. Pliers are useful for cutting, bending and crimping. They should never be used to cut hardened objects or to turn bolts or nuts. **Figure 4** shows several types of pliers.

Each type of pliers has a specialized function. Gas pliers are general purpose pliers

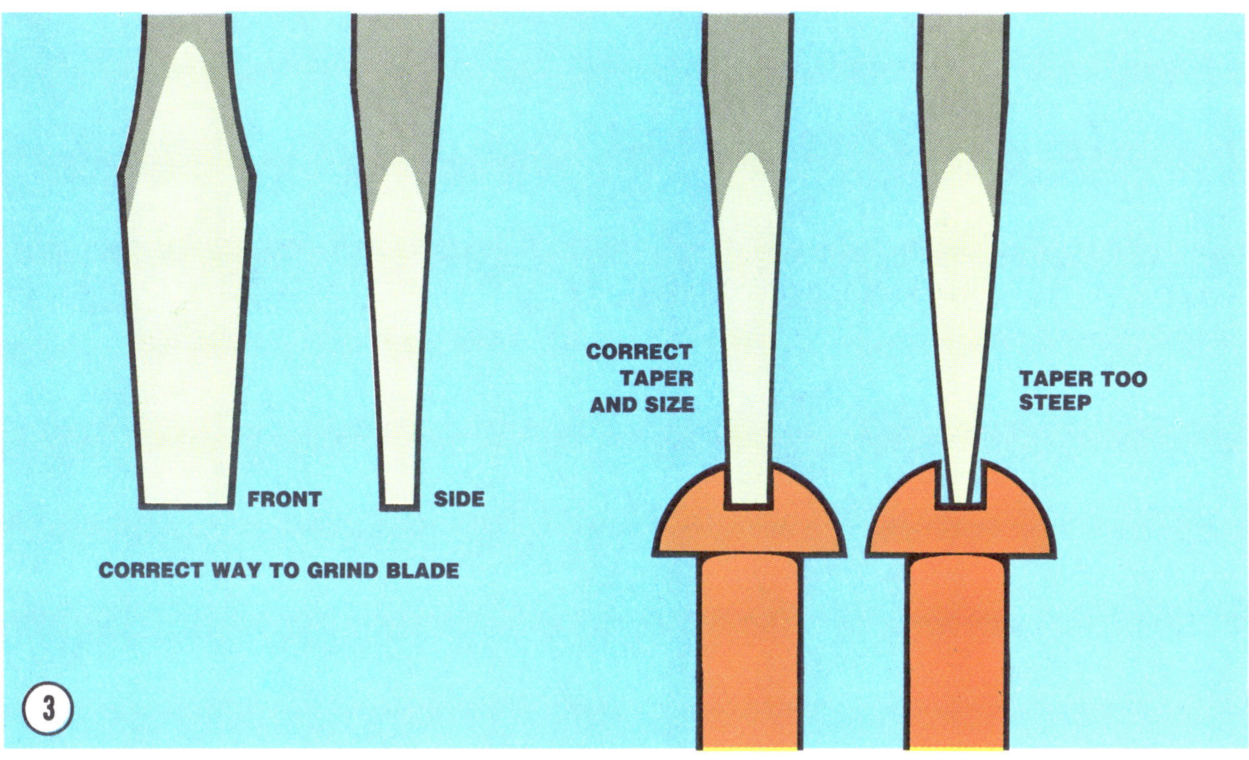

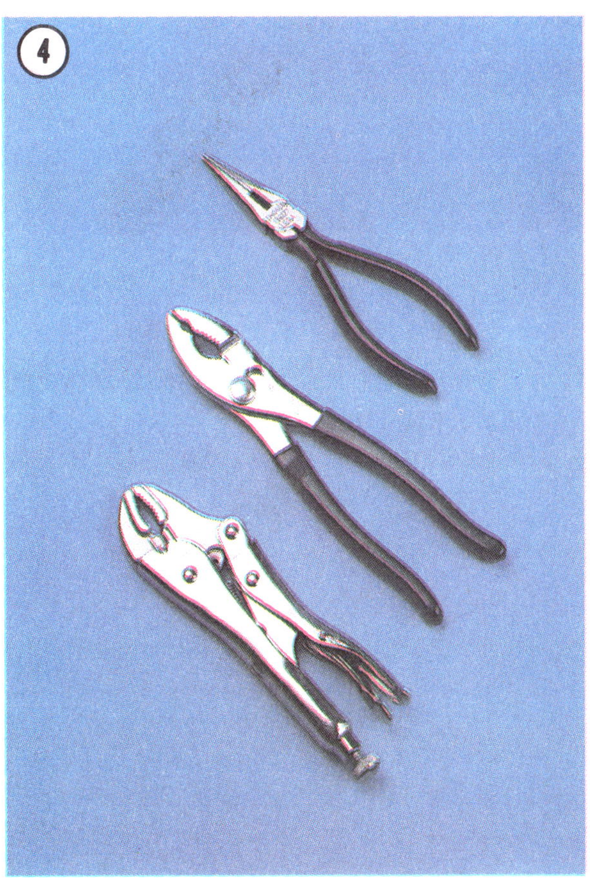

and are used mainly for holding things and for bending. Vise Grips are used as pliers or to hold objects very tight like a vise. Needlenose pliers are used to hold or bend small objects. Channel lock pliers can be adjusted to hold various sizes of objects; the jaws remain parallel to grip around objects such as pipe or tubing. There are many more types of pliers. The ones described here are the most commonly used.

Box and Open-end Wrenches

Box and open-end wrenches are available in sets or separately in a variety of sizes. See **Figure 5** and **Figure 6**. The number stamped near the end refers to the distance between 2 parallel flats on the hex head bolt or nut.

Box wrenches are usually superior to open-end wrenches. An open-end wrench grips the nut on only 2 flats. Unless it fits well, it may slip and round off the points on the nut. The box wrench grips all 6 flats. Both 6-point and 12-point openings on box

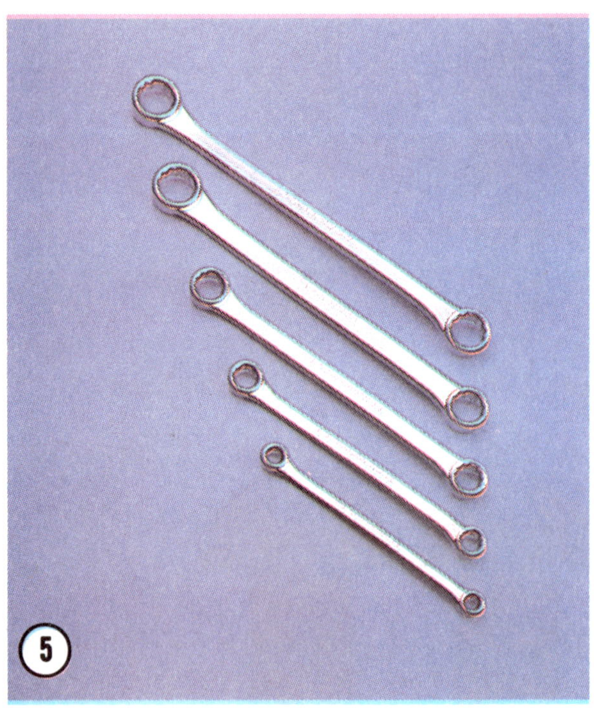

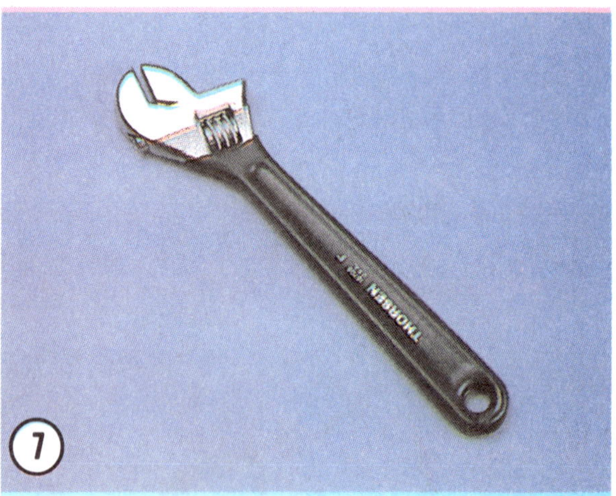

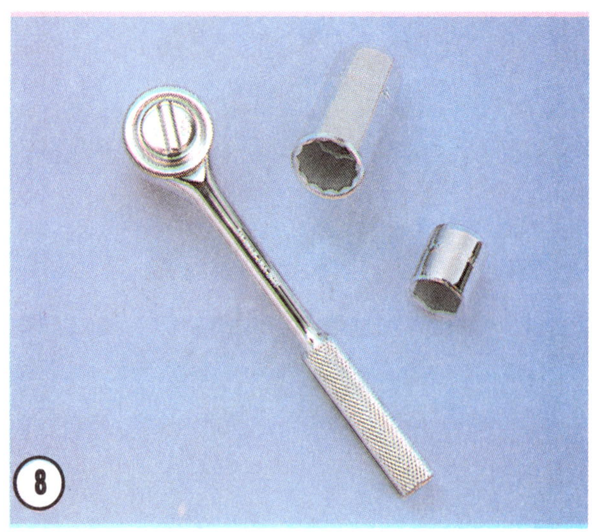

wrenches are available. The 6-point gives superior holding power; the 12-point allows a shorter swing.

Combination wrenches which are open on one side and boxed on the other are also available. Both ends are the same size.

Adjustable (Crescent) Wrenches

An adjustable wrench (also called crescent wrench) can be adjusted to fit nearly any nut or bolt head. See **Figure** 7. However, it can loosen and slip, causing damage to the nut and maybe to your knuckles. Use an adjustable wrench only when other wrenches are not available.

Crescent wrenches come in sizes ranging from 4-18 in. overall. A 6 or 8 in. wrench is recommended as an all-purpose wrench.

Socket Wrenches

This type is undoubtedly the fastest, safest and most convenient to use. See **Figure 8**. Sockets which attach to a ratchet handle are available with 6-point or 12-point openings

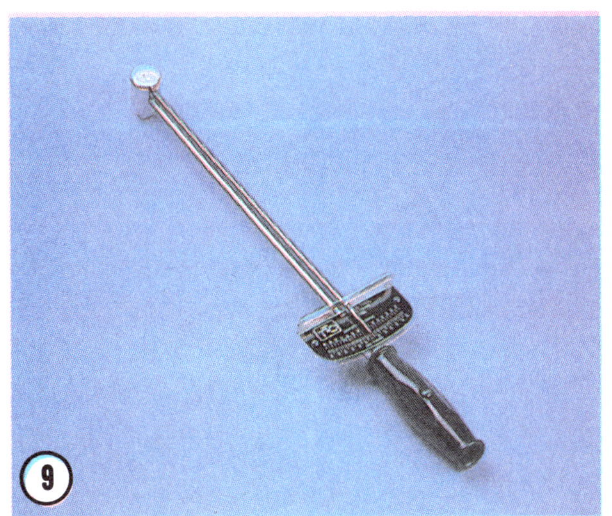

9

12

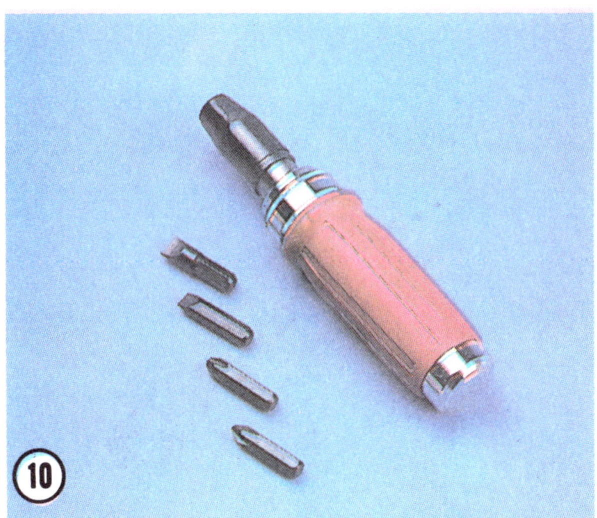

10

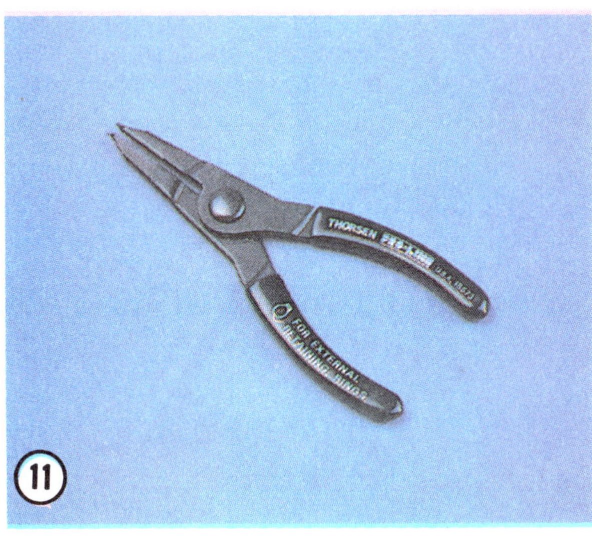

11

and 1/4, 3/8 and 3/4 inch drives. The drive size indicates the size of the square hole which mates with the ratchet handle.

Torque Wrench

A torque wrench (**Figure 9**) is used with a socket to measure how tight a nut or bolt is installed. They come in a wide price range and with either 3/8 or 1/2 in. square drive. The drive size indicates the size of the square drive which mates with the socket. Purchase one that measures 0-140 N•m (1-100 ft.-lb.).

Impact Driver

This tool (**Figure 10**) makes removal of tight fasteners easy and eliminates damage to bolts and screw slots. Impact drivers and interchangeable bits are available at most large hardware and auto parts stores.

Circlip Pliers

Circlip pliers (sometimes referred to as snap-ring pliers) are necessary to remove circlips. See **Figure 11**. Circlip pliers usually come with several different size tips; many designs can be switched from internal type to external type.

Hammers

The correct hammer is necessary for repairs. Use only a hammer with a face (or head) of rubber or plastic or the soft-faced type that is filled with buck shot (**Figure 12**). These are sometimes necessary in engine tear-downs. *Never* use a metal-faced hammer as severe damage will result in most cases. You can always produce the same amount of force with a soft-faced hammer.

Feeler Gauge

This tool has either flat or wire measuring gauges (**Figure 13**). Wire gauges are used to measure spark plug gap; flat gauges are used for all other measurements. A non-magnetic (brass) gauge may be specified when working around magnetized parts.

13

Other Special Tools

Some procedures require special tools; these are identified in the appropriate chapter. Unless otherwise specified, the part number used in this book to identify a special tool is the marine equipment manufacturer's part number.

Special tools can usually be purchased through your marine equipment dealer. Some can be made locally by a machinist, often at a much lower price. You may find certain special tools at tool rental dealers. Don't use makeshift tools if you can't locate the correct special tool; you will probably cause more damage than good.

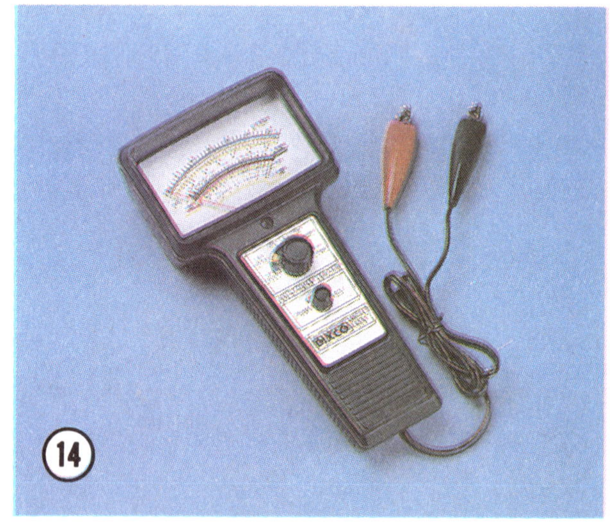

14

TEST EQUIPMENT

Multimeter

This instrument (**Figure 14**) is invaluable for electrical system troubleshooting and service. It combines a voltmeter, an ohmmeter and an ammeter into one unit, so it is often called a VOM.

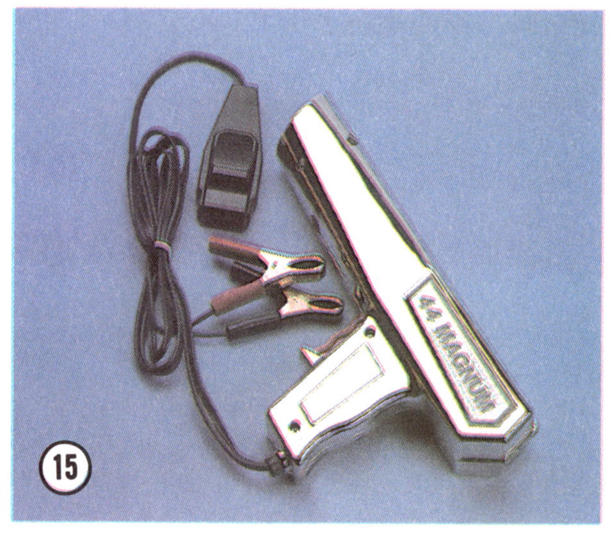

15

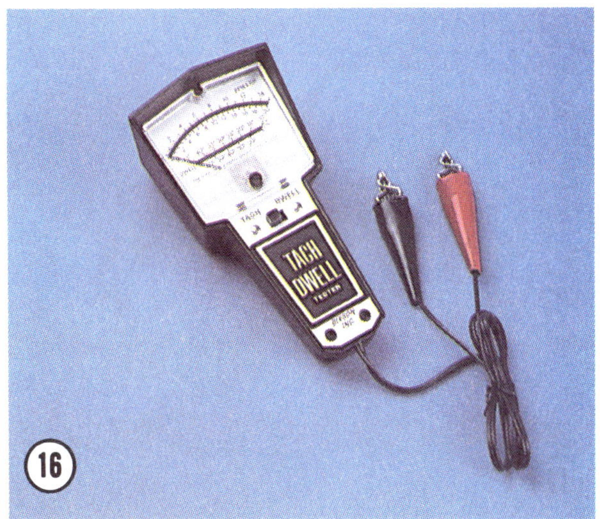

16

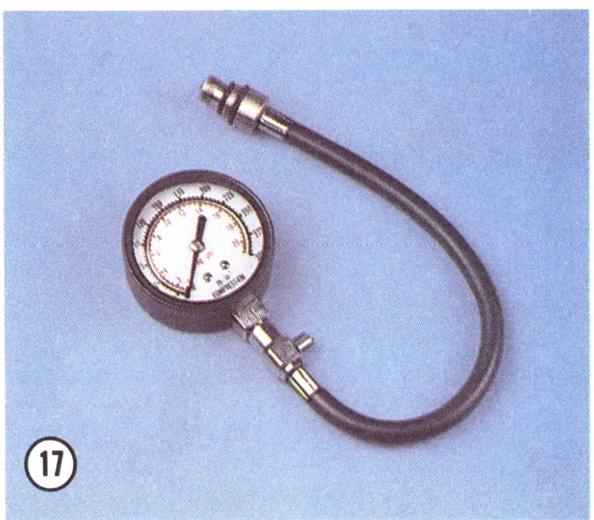

17

Strobe Timing Light

This instrument is necessary for dynamic tuning (setting ignition timing while the engine is running). By flashing a light at the precise instant the spark plug fires, the position of the timing mark can be seen. The flashing light makes a moving mark appear to stand still opposite a stationary mark.

Suitable lights range from inexpensive neon bulb types to powerful xenon strobe lights. See **Figure 15**. A light with an inductive pickup is best, as it eliminates any possible damage to ignition wiring.

Tachometer/Dwell Meter

A portable tachometer is necessary for tuning. See **Figure 16**. Ignition timing and carburetor adjustments must be performed at the specified idle speed. The best instrument for this purpose is one with a low range of 0-1,000 or 0-2,000 rpm and a high range of 0-4,000 rpm. Extended range (0-6,000 or 0-8,000 rpm) instruments lack accuracy at lower speeds. The instrument should be capable of detecting changes of 25 rpm on the low range.

A dwell meter is often combined with a tachometer. Dwell meters are used with breaker point ignition systems to measure the amount of time the points remain closed during engine operation.

Compression Gauge

This tool (**Figure 17**) measures the amount of pressure present in the engine's combustion chamber during the compression stroke. This indicates general engine condition. Compression readings can be interpreted along with vacuum gauge readings to pinpoint specific engine mechanical problems.

The easiest type to use has screw-in adaptors that fit into the spark plug holes. Press-in rubber-tipped types are also available.

Vacuum Gauge

The vacuum gauge (**Figure 18**) measures the intake manifold vacuum created by the engine's intake stroke. Manifold and valve problems can be identified by interpreting the readings; when combined with compression gauge readings, other engine problems can be diagnosed.

Some vacuum gauges can also be used as fuel pressure gauges to trace fuel system problems.

Hydrometer

Battery electrolyte specific gravity is measured with a hydrometer (**Figure 19**); this indicates the battery's state of charge. The best type has automatic temperature compensation; otherwise, you must calculate the compensation yourself.

Precision Measuring Tools

Various tools are needed to make precision measurements. A dial indicator (**Figure 20**), for example, is used to determine run-out of rotating parts and end play of parts assemblies. A dial indicator can also be used to precisely measure piston position in relation to top dead center; some engines require this measurement for ignition timing adjustment.

Vernier calipers (**Figure 21**) and micrometers (**Figure 22**) are other precision measuring tools used to determine the size of parts (such as piston diameter).

Precision measuring equipment must be stored, handled and used carefully or it will not remain accurate.

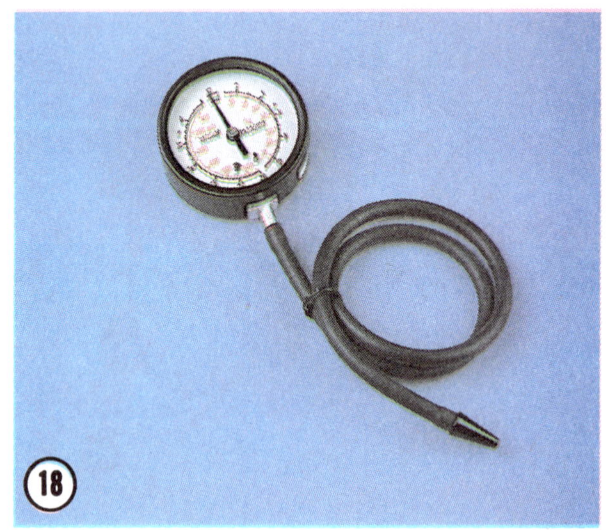

18

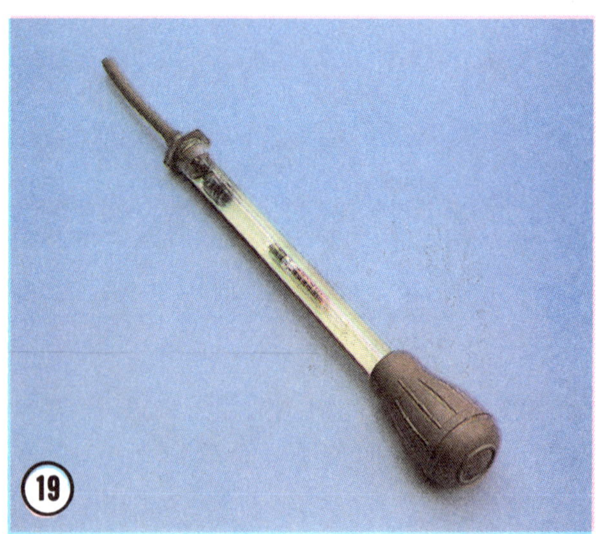

19

20

SERVICE HINTS

Most of the service procedures covered in this manual are straightforward and can be performed by anyone reasonably handy with tools. It is suggested, however, that you consider your own skills and toolbox carefully before attempting any operation involving major disassembly of the engine or gearcase.

Some operations, for example, require the use of a press. It would be wiser to have these performed by a shop equipped for such work,

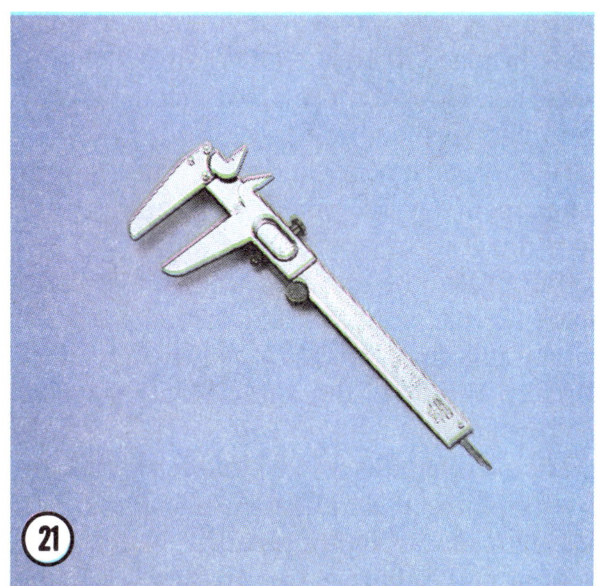

21

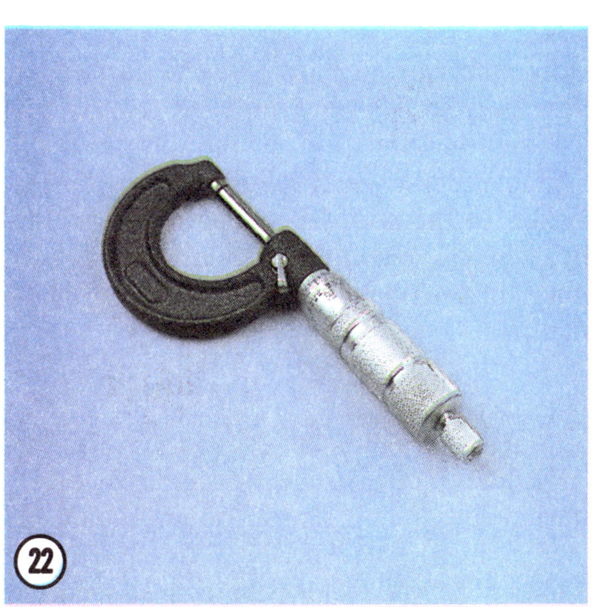

22

rather than trying to do the job yourself with makeshift equipment. Other procedures require precise measurements. Unless you have the skills and equipment required, it would be better to have a qualified repair shop make the measurements for you.

Preparation for Disassembly

Repairs go much faster and easier if the equipment is clean before you begin work. There are special cleaners, such as Gunk or Bel-Ray Degreaser, for washing the engine and related parts. Just spray or brush on the cleaning solution, let it stand, then rinse it away with a garden hose. Clean all oily or greasy parts with cleaning solvent as you remove them.

WARNING

Never use gasoline as a cleaning agent. It presents an extreme fire hazard. Be sure to work in a well-ventilated area when using cleaning solvent. Keep a Coast Guard approved fire extinguisher, rated for gasoline fires, handy in any case.

Much of the labor charged for repairs made by dealers is for the removal and disassembly of other parts to reach the defective unit. It is frequently possible to perform the preliminary operations yourself and then take the defective unit in to the dealer for repair.

Once you have decided to tackle the job yourself, read the entire section in this manual which pertains to it, making sure you have identified the proper one. Study the illustrations and text until you have a good idea of what is involved in completing the job satisfactorily. If special tools or replacement parts are required, make arrangements to get them before you start. It is frustrating and time-consuming to get partly into a job and then be unable to complete it.

Disassembly Precautions

During disassembly of parts keep a few general precautions in mind. Force is rarely needed to get things apart. If parts are a tight fit, such as a bearing in a case, there is usually a tool designed to separate them. Never use a screwdriver to pry apart parts with machined surfaces (such as cylinder heads and crankcases). You will mar the surfaces and end up with leaks.

Make diagrams (or take an instant picture) wherever similar-appearing parts are found. For example, head and crankcase bolts are often not the same length. You may think you can remember where everything came from, but mistakes are costly. There is also the possibility you may be sidetracked and not return to work for days or even weeks, in which interval carefully laid out parts may have become disturbed.

Tag all similar internal parts for location and mark all mating parts for position. Record number and thickness of any shims as they are removed. Small parts such as bolts can be identified by placing them in plastic sandwich bags. Seal and label them with masking tape.

Wiring should be tagged with masking tape and marked as each wire is removed. Again, do not rely on memory alone.

Protect finished surfaces from physical damage or corrosion. Keep gasoline off painted surfaces.

Assembly Precautions

No parts, except those assembled with a press fit, require unusual force during assembly. If a part is hard to remove or install, find out why before proceeding.

Cover all openings after removing parts to keep dirt, small tools, etc., from falling in.

When assembling 2 parts, start all fasteners, then tighten evenly in an alternating or crisscross pattern if no specific tightening sequence is given.

When assembling parts, be sure all shims and washers are installed exactly as they came out.

Whenever a rotating part butts against a stationary part, look for a shim or washer. Use new gaskets if there is any doubt about the condition of the old ones. Unless otherwise specified, a thin coat of oil on gaskets may help them seal effectively.

Heavy grease can be used to hold small parts in place if they tend to fall out during assembly. However, keep grease and oil away from electrical components.

High spots may be sanded off a piston with sandpaper, but fine emery cloth and oil will do a much more professional job.

Carbon can be removed from the cylinder head, the piston crown and the exhaust port with a dull screwdriver. *Do not* scratch either surface. Wipe off the surface with a clean cloth when finished.

The carburetor is best cleaned by disassembling it and soaking the parts in a commercial carburetor cleaner. Never soak gaskets and rubber parts in these cleaners. Never use wire to clean out jets and air passages; they are easily damaged. Use compressed air to blow out the carburetor *after* the float has been removed.

Take your time and do the job right. Do not forget that a newly rebuilt engine must be broken in the same as a new one. Use the break-in oil recommendations and follow other instructions given in your owner's manual.

SPECIAL TIPS

Because of the extreme demands placed on marine equipment, several points should be kept in mind when performing service and repair. The following items are general suggestions that may improve the overall life of the machine and help avoid costly failures.

1. Unless otherwise specified, use a locking compound such as Loctite Lock N' Seal No. 2114 (blue Loctite) on all bolts and nuts, even if they are secured with lockwashers. This type of Loctite does not harden completely and allows easy removal of the bolt or nut. A screw or bolt lost from an engine cover or bearing retainer could easily cause serious and expensive damage before its loss is noticed.

When applying Loctite, use a small amount. If too much is used, it can work its way down the threads and stick parts together not meant to be stuck.

Keep a tube of Loctite in your tool box; when used properly it is cheap insurance.

2. Use a hammer-driven impact tool to remove and install screws and bolts. These tools help prevent the rounding off of bolt heads and screw slots and ensure a tight installation.
3. When straightening out the fold-over type lockwasher, use a wide-blade chisel such as an old and dull wood chisel. Such a tool provides a better purchase on the folded tab, making straightening out easier.
4. When installing the fold-over type lockwasher, always use a new washer if possible. If a new washer is not available, always fold over a part of the washer that has not been previously folded. Reusing the same fold may cause the washer to break, resulting in the loss of its locking ability and a loose piece of metal adrift in the engine.

When folding the washer over, start the fold with a screwdriver and finish it with a pair of pliers. If a punch is used to make the fold, the fold may be too sharp, thereby increasing the chances of the washer breaking under stress.

These washers are relatively inexpensive and it is suggested that you keep several of each size in your tool box for repairs.

5. When replacing missing or broken fasteners (bolts, nuts and screws), always use authorized replacement parts. They are specially hardened for each application. The wrong 50-cent bolt could easily cause serious and expensive damage.
6. When installing gaskets, always use authorized replacement gaskets *without* sealer, unless designated. Many gaskets are designed to swell when they come in contact with oil. Gasket sealer will prevent the gaskets from swelling as intended, which can result in oil leaks. Authorized replacement gaskets are cut from material of the precise thickness needed. Installation of a too thick or too thin gasket in a critical area could cause equipment damage.

MECHANIC'S TECHNIQUES

Removing Frozen Fasteners

When a fastener rusts and cannot be removed, several methods may be used to loosen it. First, apply penetrating oil such as Liquid Wrench or WD-40 (available at any hardware or auto supply store). Apply it liberally and let it penetrate for 10-15 minutes. Rap the fastener several times with a small hammer; do not hit it hard enough to cause damage. Reapply the penetrating oil if necessary.

For frozen screws, apply penetrating oil as described, then insert a screwdriver in the slot and rap the top of the screwdriver with a hammer. This loosens the rust so the screw can be removed in the normal way. If the screw head is too chewed up to use a screwdriver, grip the head with Vise Grip pliers and twist the screw out.

Avoid applying heat unless specifically instructed, as it may melt, warp or remove the temper from parts.

Remedying Stripped Threads

Occasionally, threads are stripped through carelessness or impact damage. Often the threads can be cleaned up by running a tap (for internal threads on nuts) or die (for external threads on bolts) through threads. See **Figure 23**.

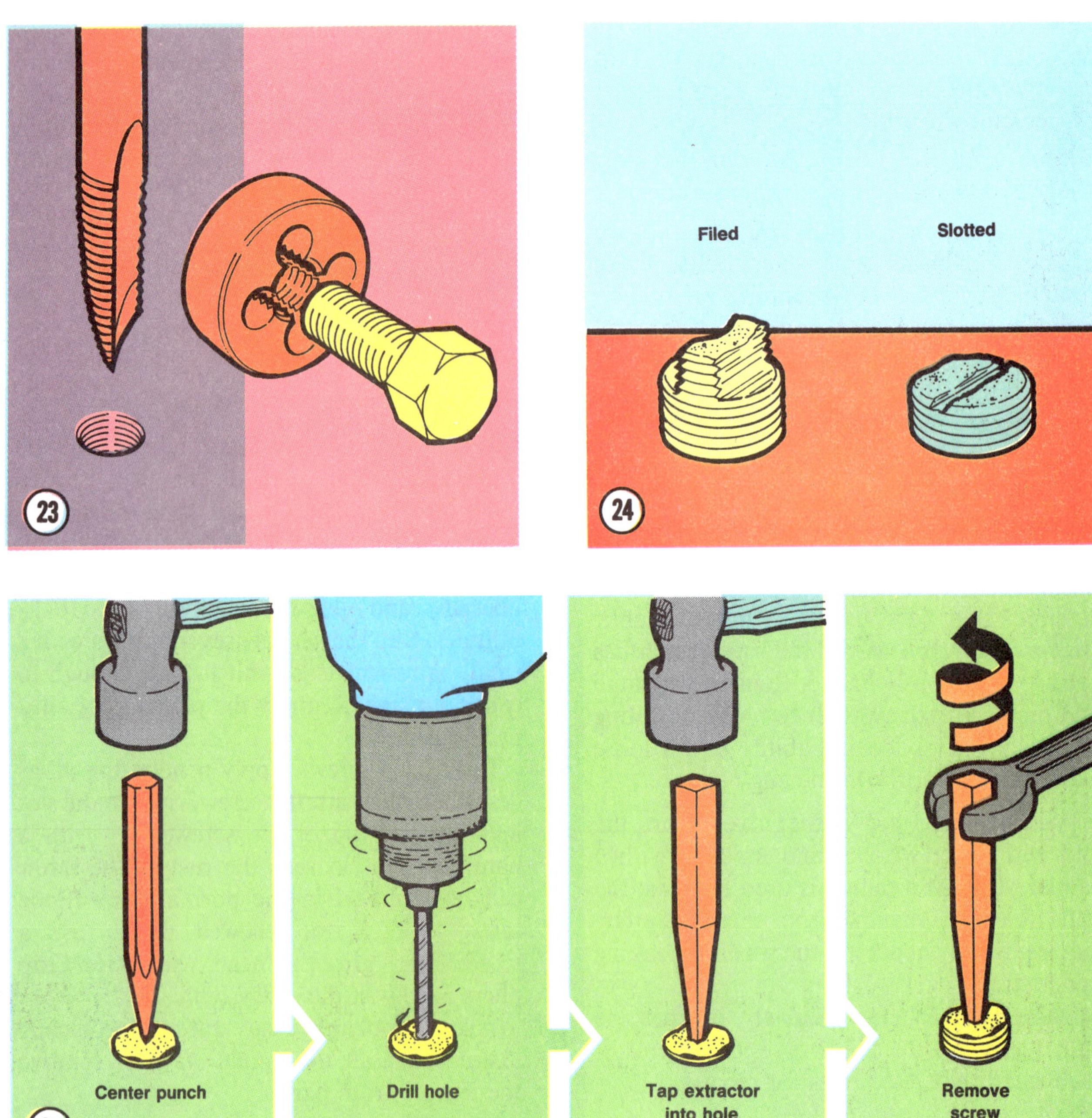

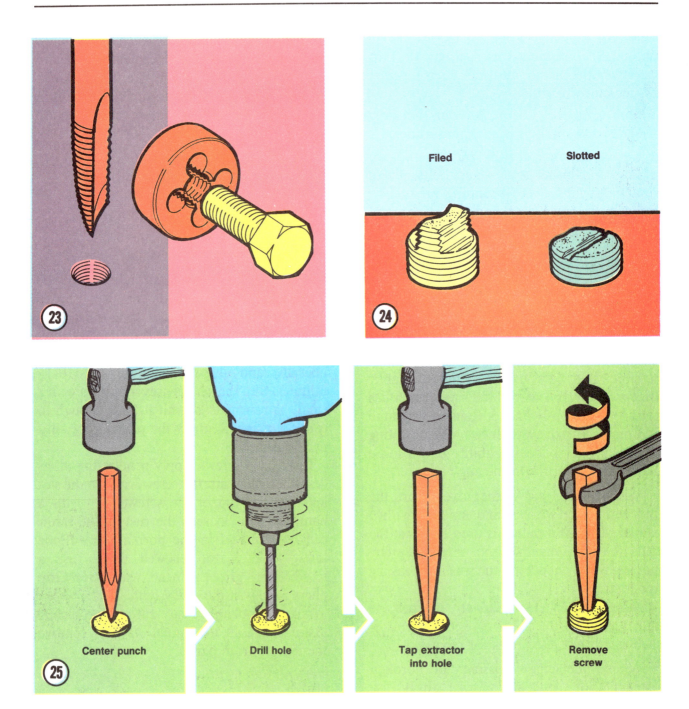

Removing Broken Screws or Bolts

When the head breaks off a screw or bolt, several methods are available for removing the remaining portion.

If a large portion of the remainder projects out, try gripping it with Vise Grips. If the projecting portion is too small, file it to fit a wrench or cut a slot in it to fit a screwdriver. See **Figure 24**.

If the head breaks off flush, use a screw extractor. To do this, centerpunch the remaining portion of the screw or bolt. Drill a small hole in the screw and tap the extractor into the hole. Back the screw out with a wrench on the extractor. See **Figure 25**.

Chapter Three

Troubleshooting

Every internal combustion engine requires an uninterrupted supply of fuel and air, proper ignition and adequate compression. If any of these are lacking, the engine will not run.

Troubleshooting is a relatively simple matter when it is done logically. The first step in any troubleshooting procedure is to define the symptoms as fully as possible and then localize the problem. Subsequent steps involve testing and analyzing those areas which could cause the symptoms. A haphazard approach may eventually solve the problem, but it can be very costly in terms of wasted time and unnecessary parts replacement.

There are two axioms to remember about troubleshooting.

a. The source of the problem is seldom where you think it is.
b. When all else fails, go back to basics—simple solutions often solve complex-appearing problems.

Never assume anything. Don't overlook the obvious. If the engine suddenly quits when running or refuses to start, check the easiest and most accessible spots first. Make sure there is fuel in the tank, and that the spark plugs and all wiring harnesses are properly connected. Something as simple as a loose terminal connection on the ignition coil can allow the primary wire to come off while boating, especially if the vessel has been subjected to turbulent waters. It is costly and embarrassing to call for help in such a case.

You should be familiar enough with the engine compartment to know which wires go where. If a quick visual check of the obvious does not turn up the cause of the problem, look a little further. Learning to recognize and describe symptoms accurately will make repairs easier for you or a technician at the shop. Saying that "it won't run" isn't the same as saying "it quit at high speed and wouldn't start."

Gather as many symptoms together as possible to aid in diagnosis. Note whether the engine lost power gradually or all at once, what color smoke (if any) came from the exhaust and so on. Remember, the more complicated engine systems are, the easier it is to troubleshoot them because symptoms point to specific problems.

After the symptoms are defined, test and analyze those areas which could cause the problem(s). You don't need fancy or complicated test equipment to determine whether repairs can be attempted at home.

The electrical system is the weakest link in the chain. More problems result from electrical malfunctions than from any other source. Keep this in mind before you blame the fuel system and start making unnecessary carburetor adjustments. A few simple checks can keep a small problem from turning into a large one. They can also save a large repair bill and time lost while the boat sits in a shop's service department.

On the other hand, be realistic and don't attempt repairs beyond your abilities or with make shift tools. Stripping the threads on a carburetor fuel inlet while trying to change the fuel filter will cost you several hundred dollars for a new carburetor. Marine service departments also tend to charge heavily for putting together a disassembled engine or other component that may have been abused. Some won't even take on such a job—so use common sense and don't get in over your head or attempt a job without the proper tools.

Proper lubrication, maintenance and periodic tune-ups as described in Chapter Four will reduce the necessity for troubleshooting. Even with the best of care, however, every marine engine is prone to problems which will eventually require troubleshooting.

If replacement components are to be installed, do *not* use automotive parts. While marine components such as carburetors, starters, alternators, etc. may appear to be the same as automotive components, they are not. Marine components have been designed to withstand the unique requirements of marine service, as well as to provide a measure of safety that is not required of automotive service. For example, a marine starter is flashproofed to prevent possible ignition of fuel vapors in the bilge. The use of an automotive starter as a replacement can result in an explosion or fire and possible serious injury or loss of boat and life.

This chapter contains brief descriptions of each major operating system and troubleshooting procedures to be used. The troubleshooting procedures analyze common symptoms and provide logical methods of isolation. These are not the only methods. There may be several approaches to a problem, but all methods used must have one thing in common to be successful—a logical, systematic approach.

Troubleshooting diagrams for individual systems are provided within the chapter. A master troubleshooting chart is provided in **Table 1** at the end of the chapter.

STARTING SYSTEM

The starting system consists of the battery, starter motor, starter solenoid, assist solenoid, ignition switch, shift control (if so equipped) and the necessary connecting wiring and fuses. A Delco-Remy marine starter motor is used on all 2.5, 3.0, 4.3, 5.0 (305 cu. in.) and 5.7 liter engines. A Motorcraft positive engagement marine starter motor is used on all 2.3, 5.0 (302 cu. in.), 5.8 and 7.5 liter engines.

Delco-Remy Starting System Operation

When the ignition switch is turned to START with the shift control in NEUTRAL, the assist solenoid closes and battery current is transmitted to the starter solenoid, which mechanically engages the starter with the engine flywheel. Once the engine has started and the ignition switch is released, the assist solenoid is de-energized. Without current to hold the solenoid in position, the starter

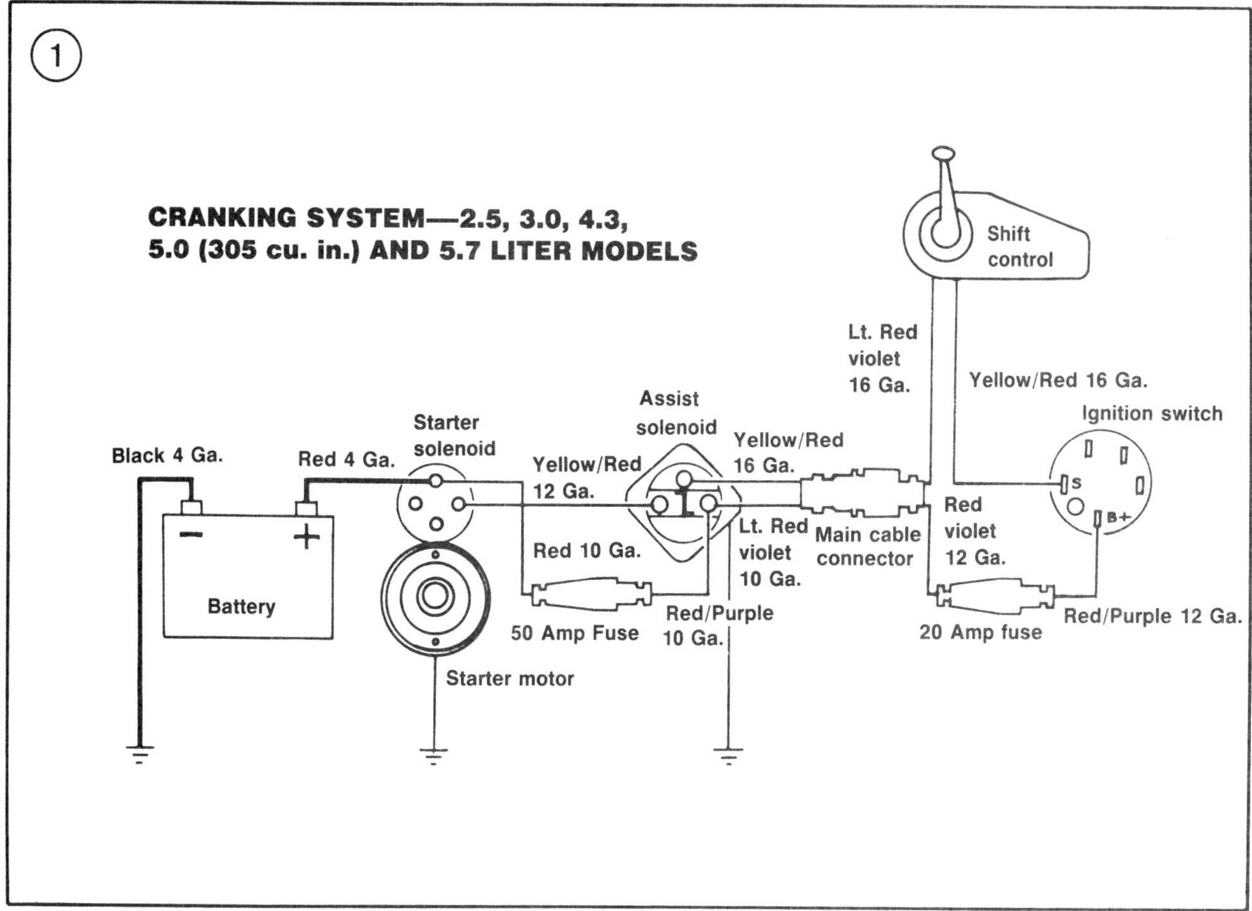

motor overrunning clutch disengages the starter pinion from the flywheel. **Figure 1** is a schematic of the Delco-Remy starter system.

Motorcraft Positive Engagement Starting System Operation

When the ignition switch is turned to START with the shift control in NEUTRAL, the assist solenoid closes and battery current is transmitted to a grounded field coil inside the starter motor. The grounded field coil operates a movable pole shoe attached to the starter drive plunger, forcing the drive to engage with the engine flywheel. As the movable pole shoe reaches the end of its travel, it opens the field coil ground and a holding coil then takes over to maintain the pole shoe in place until the engine has started. Once the engine has started and the ignition switch is released, the assist solenoid is de-energized. Without current to hold the movable pole shoe in position, the starter motor drive plunger disengages from the flywheel. **Figure 2** is a schematic of the Motorcraft starter system.

Troubleshooting

Starting system problems are relatively easy to find. In most cases, the trouble is a loose or dirty electrical connection.

On-boat Testing

Two of these procedures require a fully charged 12-volt battery, to be used as a booster, and a pair of jumper cables. Use the jumper cables as outlined in *Jump Starting*, Chapter Eleven, following all of the

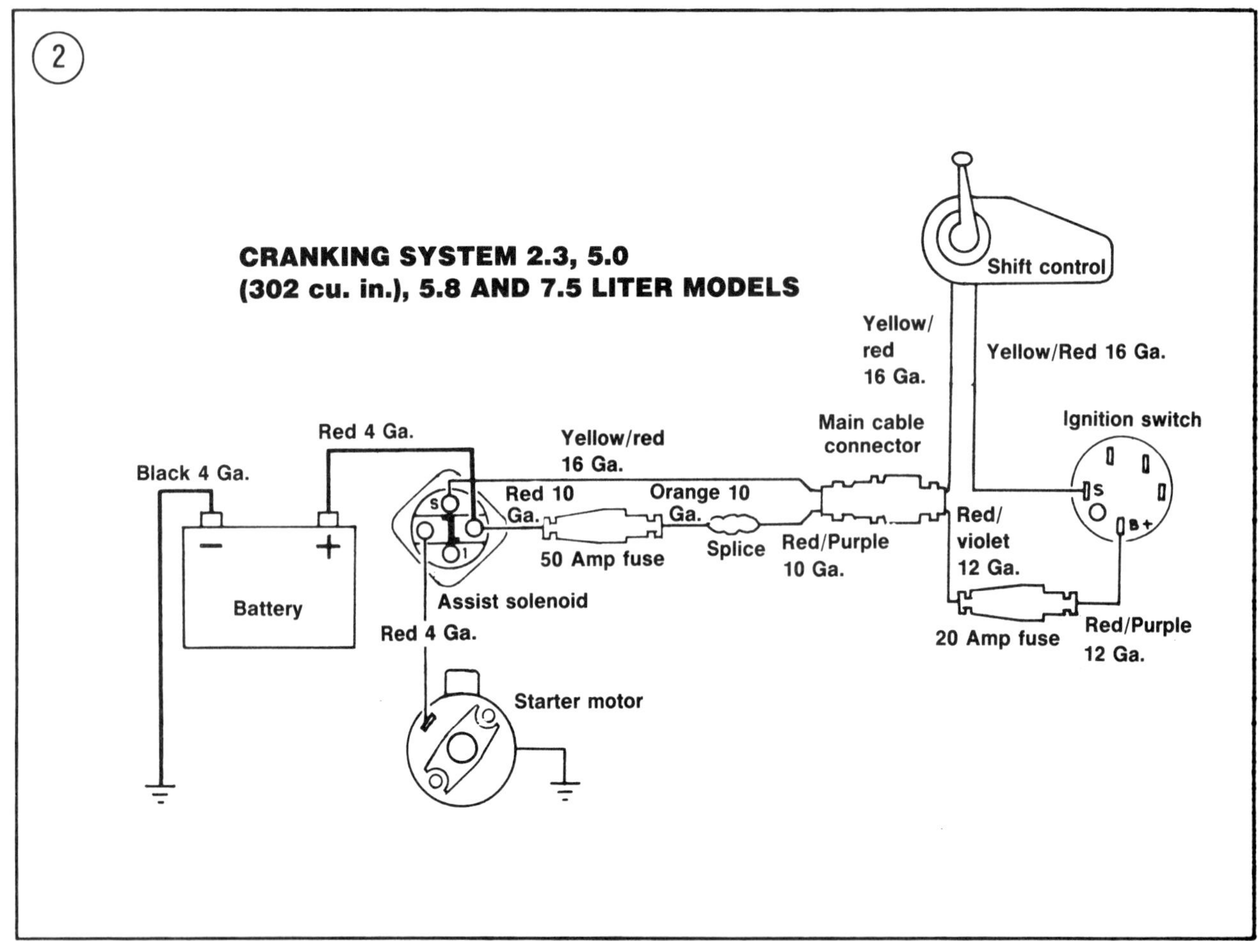

precautions noted. Disconnect the wiring harness and leads at the rear of the alternator before connecting a booster battery for these tests. This will protect the alternator diodes from possible damage.

Slow cranking starter

1. Connect the 12-volt booster battery to the engine's battery with jumper cables. Listen to the starter cranking speed as the engine is started. If the cranking speed sounds normal, check the battery for loose or corroded connections or a low charge. Clean and tighten the connections as required. Recharge the battery if necessary.
2. If cranking speed does not sound normal, clean and tighten all starter solenoid connections and the battery ground on the engine.
3. Repeat Step 1. If the cranking speed is still too slow, replace the starter.

Starter solenoid clicks, starter does not crank

1. Clean and tighten all starter and solenoid connections. Make sure the terminal eyelets are securely fastened to the wire strands and are not corroded.
2. Remove the battery terminal clamps. Clean the clamps and battery posts. Reinstall the clamps and tighten securely.
3. If the starter does not crank, connect the 12-volt booster battery to the engine's battery with the jumper cables. If the starter still does not crank, replace it.

Starter solenoid chatters (no click), starter does not crank

1. Check the S terminal wire connection at the starter solenoid; clean and tighten if necessary.
2. Disconnect the S terminal wire at the starter solenoid. Connect a jumper wire between this terminal and the positive battery post.
3. Try starting the engine. If the engine starts, check the ignition switch, neutral start switch (cut-out) switch and the system wiring for an open circuit or a loose connection. If the engine does not start, replace the starter solenoid.

Starter spins but does not crank

1. Remove the starter. See Chapter Eleven.
2. Check the starter pinion gear. If the teeth are chipped or worn, inspect the flywheel ring gear for the same problem. Replace the starter and/or ring gear as required.
3. If the pinion gear is in good condition, disassemble the starter and check the armature shaft for corrosion. See *Brush Replacement*, Chapter Eleven for disassembly procedure. If no corrosion is found, the starter drive mechanism is slipping. Replace the starter with a new or rebuilt marine unit.

Starter will not disengage when ignition switch is released

This problem is usually caused by a sticking solenoid but the pinion may jam on the flywheel ring gear of high-mileage engines.

Loud grinding noises when starter runs

This can be caused by improper meshing of the starter pinion and flywheel ring gear or by a broken overrunning clutch mechanism.
1. Remove the starter. See Chapter Eleven.
2. Check the starter pinion gear. If the teeth are chipped or worn, inspect the flywheel ring gear for the same problem. Replace the starter and/or ring gear as required.
3. If the pinion gear is in good condition, disassemble the starter and check the overrunning clutch mechanism (Delco-Remy) or starter drive plunger mechanism. See *Brush Replacement*, Chapter Eleven for disassembly procedure.

CLYMER QUICK TIP

The engine starts fine when cold and restarts easily when used for short distance boating. After a trip of longer duration, however, the starter will not crank and restart the hot engine. After the engine cools for 1-3 hours (depending upon ambient temperature), the starter works normally. An open-circuit test and hydrometer check of the battery indicates that it is in satisfactory condition.

Disregard helpful hints about resetting the ignition timing or mechanics who tell you that this is typical of Chevrolet or Ford marine engines. The key here is your battery, especially if it has been replaced recently. Check the cold cranking amperage rating of the battery installed in the vehicle and compare it to specifications. If a replacement battery has been installed, the odds are high that while the battery has sufficient power for a cold start, it is insufficient to cope with the high internal resistance in the starter and reduced engine operating tolerances which result from engine operation, especially in extremely warm weather.

Many owners buy a replacement battery according to the length of the guarantee and their pocketbook. While a 12-month battery seems satisfactory (and the price is right), it does not have the power and stamina to handle the starting requirements of your engine.

Starter Resistance Test

The following test will determine the amount of voltage reaching the starter motor during cranking and will indicate any excessive resistance in the circuit.

Delco-Remy starter

Refer to **Figure 3** for this procedure.

1. Check the battery and cable condition. Clean the battery terminals, replace suspect cables or recharge the battery as required.
2. Start the engine and warm to normal operating temperature.
3. Shut the engine off. Disconnect the distributor primary lead at the coil negative terminal to prevent the engine from starting.
4. Connect the positive lead of a voltmeter to the bottom terminal on the solenoid, then

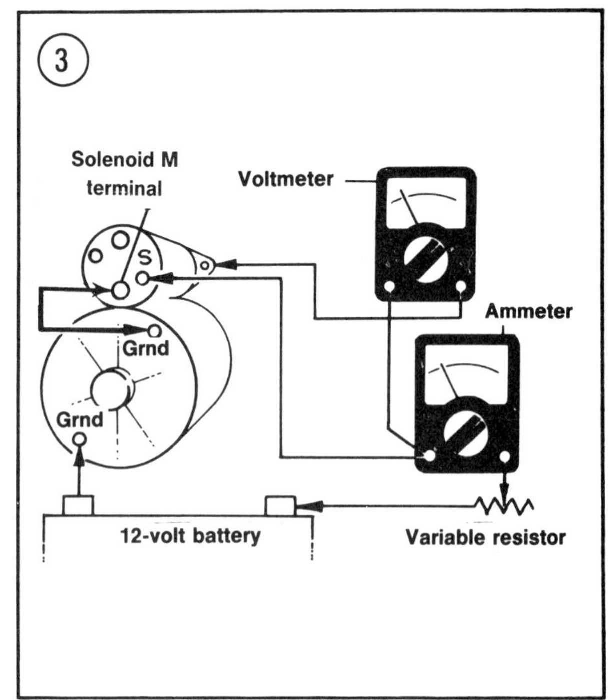

4

Solenoid M terminal

Starter motor

A

Battery terminal

Solenoid M terminal

Starter motor

B

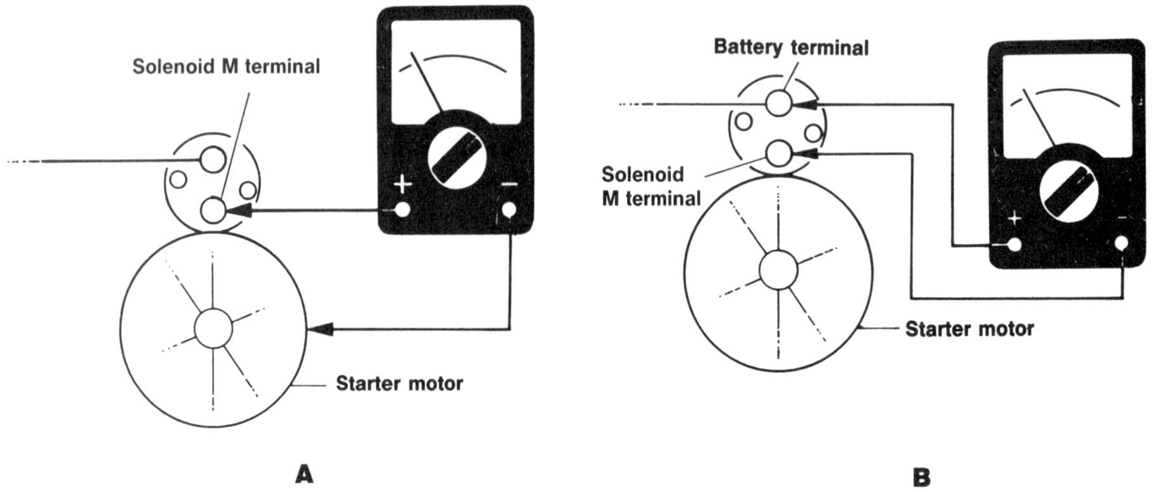

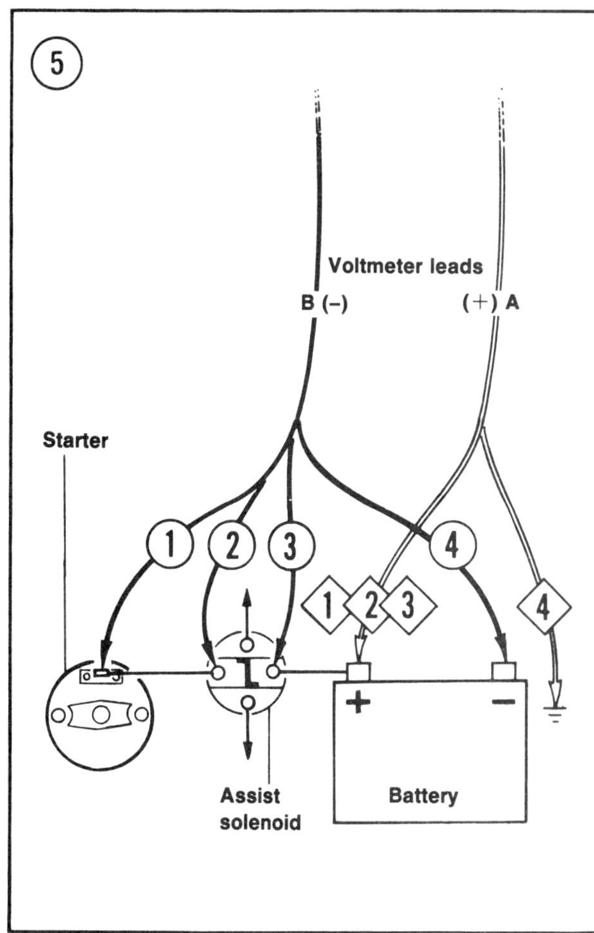

ground the negative lead to the starter frame. See A, **Figure 4**.

CAUTION
Do not crank the engine for more than 10 seconds in Step 5. Wait for at least 2 minutes before recranking the engine or it may overheat and damage the starter motor.

5. Crank the engine for a few seconds while noting the voltmeter reading. If it reads less than 9 volts, connect the voltmeter as shown in B, **Figure 4**.
6. While cranking the engine, switch the voltmeter from its high to low scale, take the reading, then switch the meter back to its high scale and stop cranking the engine. If the voltmeter reading is more than 1/10 volt, replace the solenoid.

7. If the voltmeter reads less than 1/10 volt in Step 6, check the current draw of the solenoid windings as follows:

a. Remove the solenoid terminal screw **(Figure 3)** and bend the field leads enough so they will not touch the terminal. Ground the solenoid M terminal to the starter motor frame with a jumper wire.
b. Connect a battery, a variable resistor and an ammeter with a 0-100 amp scale in series with a solenoid S terminal as shown in **Figure 3**. Ground the starter frame to the negative battery terminal.
c. Connect the voltmeter between the solenoid frame and S terminal.
d. Adjust the variable resistor slowly until the voltmeter shows 10 volts, then note the ammeter scale. The current draw of both windings in parallel should be 47-55 amps at 10 volts (room temperature).
e. Remove the jumper wire installed between the M terminal and starter frame. Readjust the variable resistor until the voltmeter shows 10 volts, then note the ammeter scale. The current draw of the hold-in winding should be 14.5-16.5 amps at 10 volts (room temperature).
f. If the solenoid windings do not perform as specified, replace the solenoid.

Motorcraft starter

Refer to **Figure 5** for this procedure.

1. Check the battery and cable condition. Clean the battery terminals, replace suspect cables or recharge the battery as required.
2. Start the engine and warm to normal operating temperature.

3

3. Shut the engine off. Disconnect the distributor primary lead at the coil negative terminal to prevent the engine from starting.

CAUTION
Connect the voltmeter only while cranking the engine in the following steps to avoid possible damage to the meter. Do not crank the engine for more than 10 seconds in any step. Wait for at least 2 minutes before recranking the engine or it may overheat and damage the starter motor.

4. Connect the negative voltmeter lead (B) to the starter terminal. Crank the engine and connect the positive voltmeter lead (A) to the positive battery terminal. See connections 1, **Figure 5**. The meter should read 0.5 volt.
5. Connect the negative voltmeter lead (B) to the assist solenoid starter terminal. Crank the engine and connect the positive voltmeter lead (A) to the positive battery terminal. See connections 2, **Figure 5**. The meter should read 0.3 volt.
6. Connect the negative voltmeter lead (B) to the assist solenoid starter terminal. Crank the engine and connect the positive voltmeter lead (A) to the positive battery terminal. See connections 3, **Figure 5**. The meter should read 0.1 volt.
7. Connect the negative voltmeter lead (B) to the negative battery terminal. Crank the engine and connect the positive voltmeter lead (A) to a good engine ground. See connections 4, **Figure 5**. The meter should read 0.1 volt.
8. If the voltmeter readings are not as specified, look for loose or dirty connections or damaged/deteriorated wiring in that portion of the circuit which fails the test.

CHARGING SYSTEM

The charging system consists of the alternator, voltage regulator, battery, ignition switch, starter and/or assist solenoid, instrument panel ammeter, the necessary connecting wiring and fuses.

A drive belt driven by the engine crankshaft pulley turns the alternator, which produces electrical energy to charge the battery. As engine speed varies, the voltage output of the alternator varies. The regulator maintains the voltage to the electrical system within safe limits. The ammeter on the instrument panel signals when charging is not taking place.

All 1986 models use a Delco-Remy SI-series marine Delcotron alternator with internal solid-state regulator; all 1987 and later models use a Motorola marine alternator with an attached solid-state regulator. The output rating is stamped on the alternator frame. **Figure 6** shows the SI-series charging circuit. **Figure 7** (GM engines) and **Figure 8** (Ford engines) show the Motorola charging circuit.

Complete troubleshooting of the charging system requires test equipment and skills which the average home mechanic does not possess. However, there are basic tests which can be done to pinpoint most problems.

Charging system troubles are generally caused by a defective alternator, voltage regulator, battery or a blown fuse. They may also be caused by something as simple as incorrect drive belt tension.

The following are symptoms of problems you may encounter.

1. *Battery dies frequently, even though the ammeter indicates no discharge*—This can be caused by a drive belt that is slightly loose. With the engine off, grasp the alternator pulley with both hands and try to turn it. If the pulley can be turned without moving the belt, the drive belt is too loose. As a rule, keep the belt tight enough so that it can be deflected only about 1/2 in. under moderate thumb pressure applied between the pulleys. The battery may also be at fault; test the

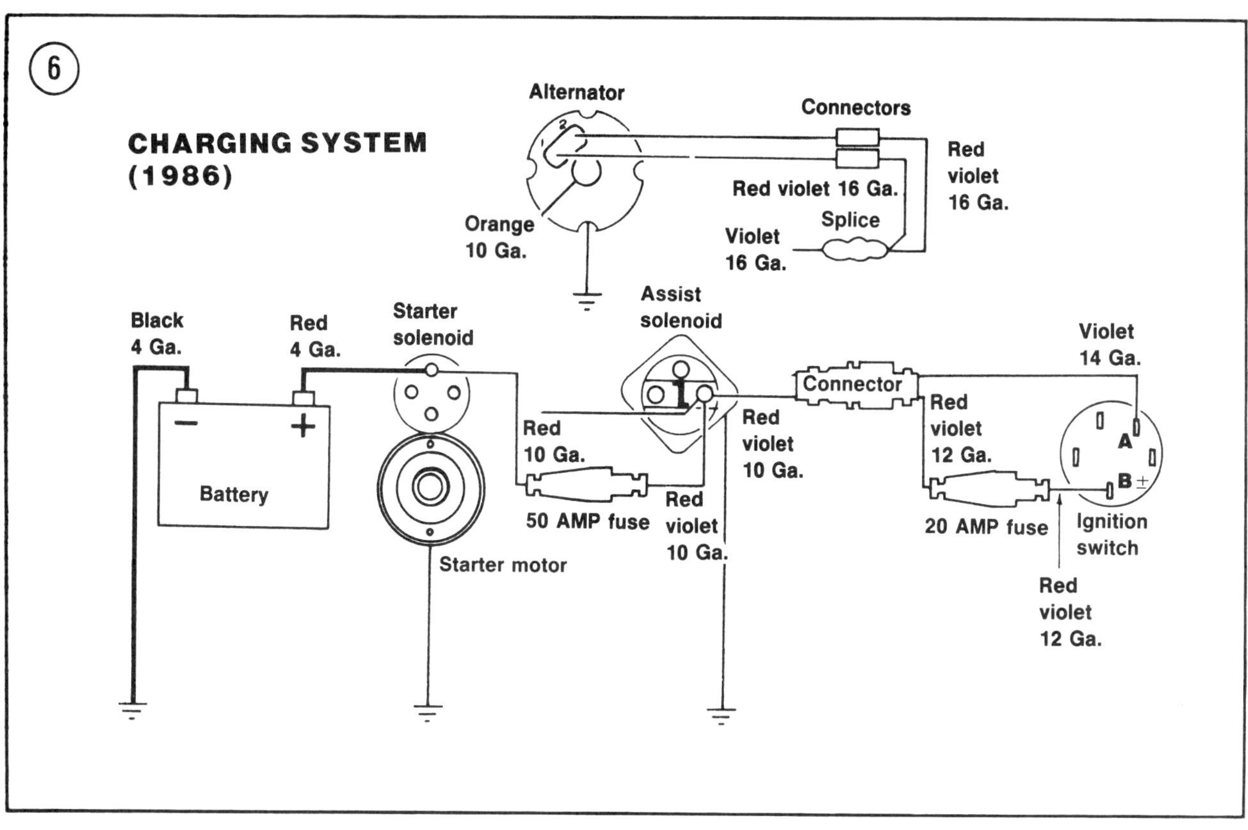
6
CHARGING SYSTEM (1986)
Alternator
Connectors
Red violet 16 Ga.
Red violet 16 Ga.
Splice
Violet 16 Ga.
Orange 10 Ga.
Assist solenoid
Black 4 Ga.
Red 4 Ga.
Starter solenoid
Violet 14 Ga.
Connector
Red violet 12 Ga.
Red violet 10 Ga.
Red 10 Ga.
Battery
50 AMP fuse
Red violet 10 Ga.
20 AMP fuse
Ignition switch
Starter motor
Red violet 12 Ga.
A
B

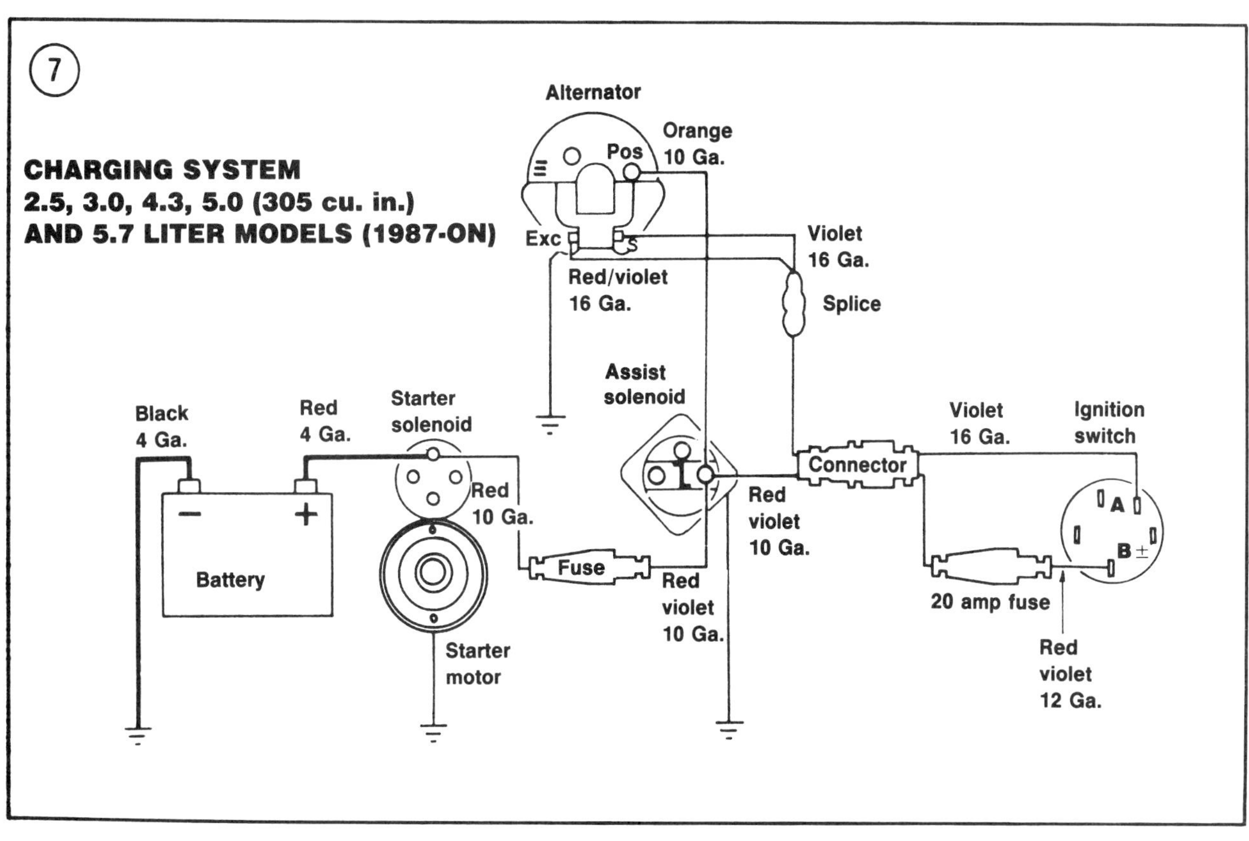
7
CHARGING SYSTEM
2.5, 3.0, 4.3, 5.0 (305 cu. in.) AND 5.7 LITER MODELS (1987-ON)
Alternator
Pos
Orange 10 Ga.
Exc
S
Violet 16 Ga.
Red/violet 16 Ga.
Splice
Assist solenoid
Black 4 Ga.
Red 4 Ga.
Starter solenoid
Violet 16 Ga.
Ignition switch
Connector
Red 10 Ga.
Red violet 10 Ga.
Battery
Fuse
Red violet 10 Ga.
20 amp fuse
Starter motor
Red violet 12 Ga.
A
B

battery condition as described in Chapter Eleven.

2. *Ammeter needle does not move when ignition switch is turned ON*—This may indicate a defective ignition switch, battery, voltage regulator or ammeter. Try to start the engine. If it doesn't start, check the ignition switch and battery. If the engine starts, remove and test the ammeter. If the problem persists, the alternator brushes may not be making contact. Perform the *Charging System Test* in this chapter.

3. *Ammeter needle fluctuates between "Charge" and "Discharge"*—This usually indicates that the charging system is working intermittently. Check drive belt tension first, then check all electrical connections in the charging circuit. As a last resort, check the alternator.

4. *Ammeter needle stays on "Discharge"* — This usually indicates that no charging is taking place. First check drive belt tension, then the battery condition. Check all wiring connections in the charging system. If this does not locate the problem, check the

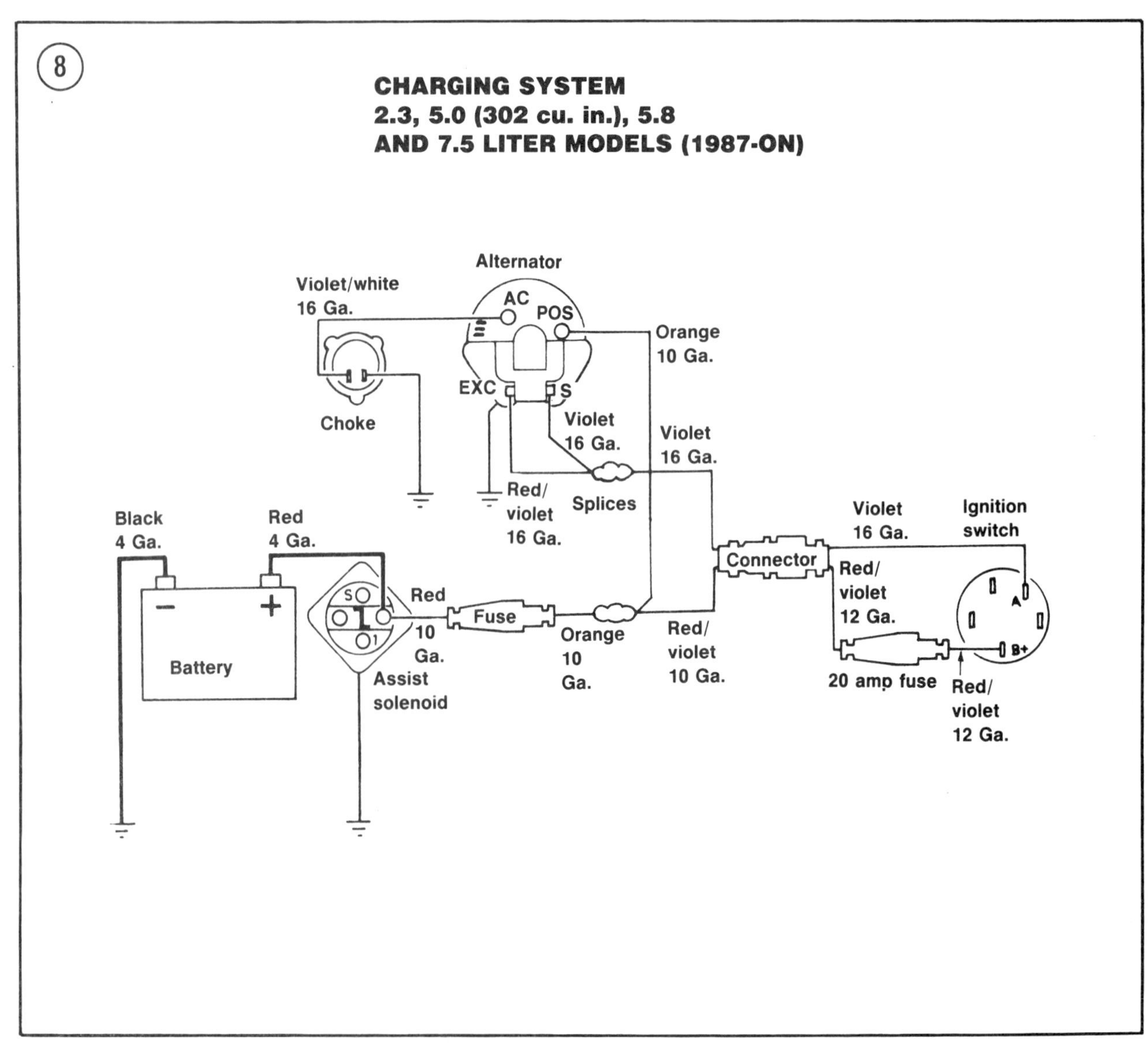

alternator and voltage regulator as described in this chapter.

5. *Battery requires frequent addition of water or lamps require frequent replacement*—The alternator is probably overcharging the battery. The voltage regulator is most likely at fault.

6. *Excessive noise from the alternator* — Check for loose mounting brackets and bolts. The problem may also be worn bearings or (in some cases) lack of lubrication. If an alternator whines, a shorted diode may be the problem.

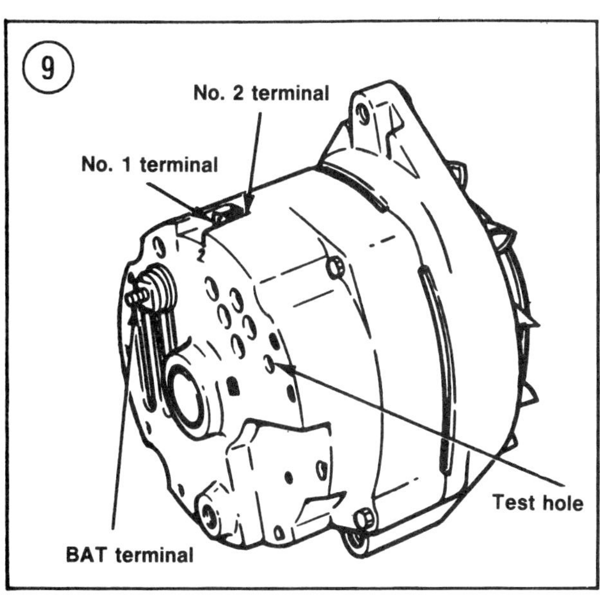

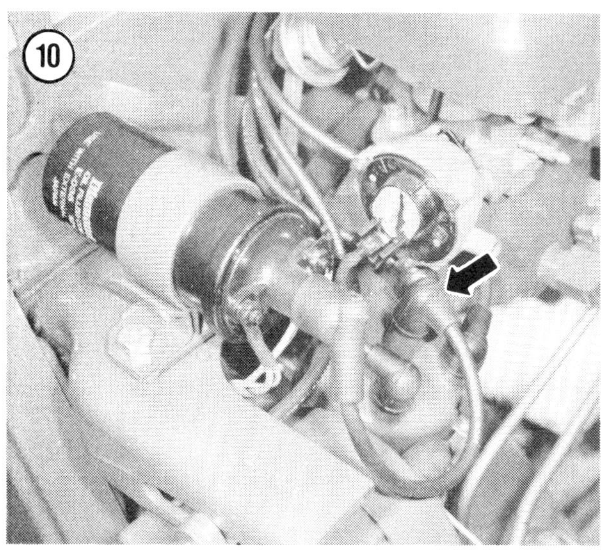

SI-SERIES DELCOTRON CHARGING SYSTEM TROUBLESHOOTING

The Delcotron alternator used on 1986 models contains a non-adjustable voltage regulator inside the alternator. The wiring harness containing the No. 1 and No. 2 alternator leads also has a diode in the No. 1 lead circuit. Use of a harness without the diode can result in damage to the alternator's diode trio. If the harness diode is shorted, the engine may continue to run from power supplied by the alternator after the ignition switch is turned OFF.

Alternator Output Test

A voltmeter with a 0-20 volt scale, an ammeter with a 0-50 amp scale and an engine tachometer are required for an accurate charging system test. Refer to **Figure 6** for this procedure.

1. Check the alternator drive belt tension. See Chapter Eleven.
2. Check the battery terminals and cables for corrosion and/or loose connections. Disconnect the negative battery cable, then the positive battery cable. Clean the cable clamps and battery terminals if necessary.
3. Check all wiring connections between the alternator and engine to make sure they are clean and tight.
4. Disconnect the orange lead at the alternator BAT terminal (**Figure 9**). Connect the negative lead of a DC ammeter to the alternator BAT terminal and the positive lead to the disconnected orange wire.
5. Connect the voltmeter between the alternator output terminal and a good engine ground. Reconnect the positive battery cable, then the negative battery cable.
6. Disconnect the coil secondary (thick) lead from the center tower of the distributor (**Figure 10**, typical) and ground it to the engine block with a jumper lead.

7. Turn all accessories on and crank the engine for 15-20 seconds to remove any surface charge from the battery.
8. Turn all accessories off and reconnect the coil lead to the distributor cap.
9. Connect the tachometer to the engine according to manufacturer's instructions. Connect a carbon pile across the battery.
10. Start the engine and run at 1,500-2,000 rpm. Adjust the carbon pile to obtain maximum alternator output. The ammeter should read a minimum of 37 amps. If a lower or no output reading is obtained, shut the engine off. Remove the alternator and have it bench-tested by a dealer or qualified electrical shop.
11. Disconnect the carbon pile and allow the battery to return to full charge. Check the voltmeter when the charging current tapers to 5 amps or less. It should read 14.7-15.2 volts at room temperature.
12. If the output reading obtained is within specifications in Step 10 and Step 11, remove the spark suppression or flame arrestor screen from the rear of the alternator (**Figure 11**).

CAUTION
Exercise care when inserting a screwdriver in the test hole in Step 13. The ground tab is located about 3/4 in. inside the end frame. If the screwdriver is inserted too far, it can contact the rotor and cause alternator damage.

13. Insert a thin screwdriver blade inside the test hole in the rear end frame. See **Figure 12**. Repeat Step 10 and Step 11 while noting the ammeter scale.
14. If the reading obtained in Step 10 is obtained, have the regulator replaced. A low output requires further bench testing of the alternator by a dealer or qualified electrical shop.
15. Reconnect all disconnected leads, reinstall the spark suppression or flame arrestor screen and remove all test equipment.

MOTOROLA CHARGING SYSTEM TROUBLESHOOTING

Alternator Output Test

A voltmeter with a 0-20 volt scale, an ammeter with a 0-50 amp scale and an engine tachometer are required for an accurate charging system test. Refer to **Figure**

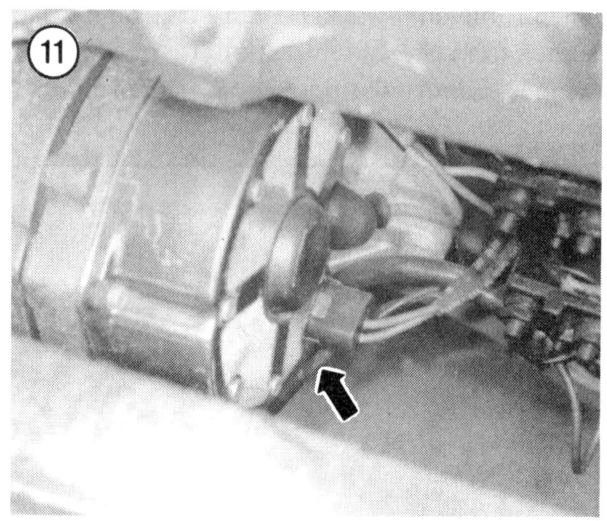

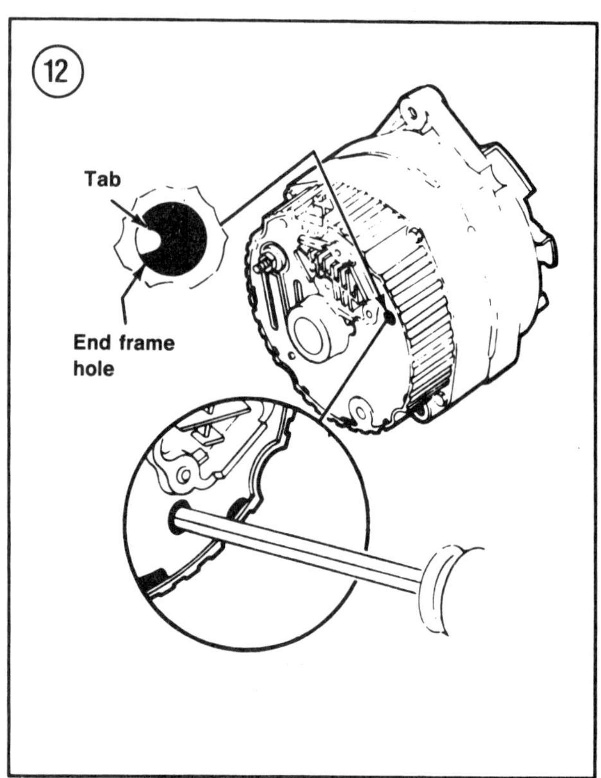

7 (GM engine) or **Figure 8** (Ford engine) for this procedure.

1. Check the alternator drive belt tension. See Chapter Eleven.
2. Check the battery terminals and cables for corrosion and/or loose connections. Disconnect the negative battery cable, then the positive battery cable. Clean the cable clamps and battery terminals if necessary.
3. Check all wiring connections between the alternator and engine to make sure they are clean and tight.
4. Disconnect the orange lead at the alternator POS terminal. Connect the negative lead of a DC ammeter to the alternator POS terminal and the positive lead to the disconnected orange wire. See connections 1 and 2, **Figure 13**.

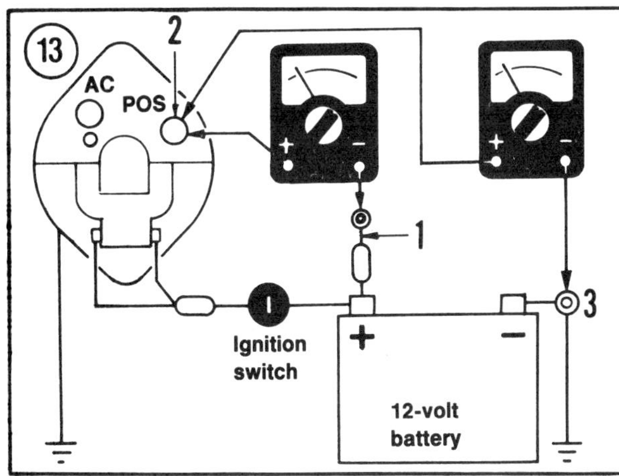

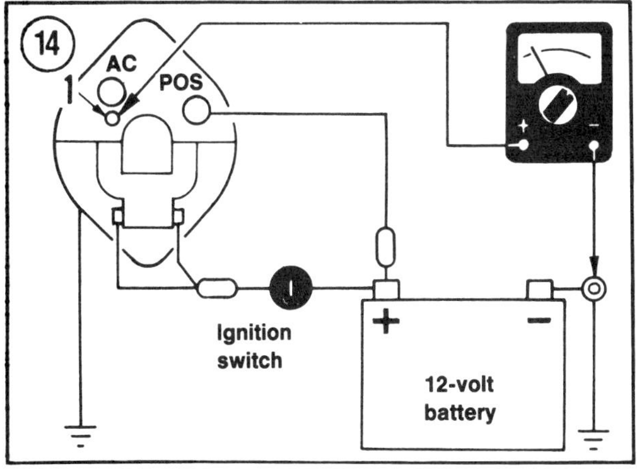

5. Connect the voltmeter between the alternator POS terminal and a good engine ground. See connections 2 and 3, **Figure 13**. Reconnect the positive battery cable, then the negative battery cable.
6. Disconnect the coil secondary (thick) lead from the center tower of the distributor (**Figure 10**, typical) and ground it to the engine block with a jumper lead.
7. Turn all accessories on and crank the engine for 15-20 seconds to remove any surface charge from the battery.
8. Turn all accessories off and reconnect the coil lead to the distributor cap.
9. Connect the tachometer to the engine according to manufacturer's instructions. Connect a carbon pile across the battery.
10. Start the engine and run at 650 rpm. Adjust the carbon pile to obtain maximum alternator output. The ammeter should read a minimum of 20 amps.
11. Increase engine speed to 1,500 rpm. Adjust the carbon pile to obtain maximum alternator output. The voltmeter should read 13.0-14.7 volts.
12. Increase engine speed to 3,000 rpm. Adjust the carbon pile to obtain maximum alternator output. The ammeter should read a minimum of 45 amps.
13. If the readings obtained are not as specified in Steps 10-12, shut the engine off.
14. Unscrew the protective cap from the LIGHT terminal stud on the rear of the alternator. Connect a voltmeter between the stud and the negative battery terminal as shown in **Figure 14**. Turn the ignition switch on, but do not start the engine. If the voltmeter does not read 1.5-3.0 volts, replace the voltage regulator. If the voltage reading is within specifications, continue with Step 15.
15. Install a jumper wire (1) between the POS terminal stud (2) and the LIGHT terminal stud (3) as shown in **Figure 15** to bypass the diode trio inside the alternator. Connect a voltmeter between the POS stud

and a good engine ground. Start the engine and run at idle. If charging voltage is present, the diode trio is defective.

16. If the alternator performs as specified in both Step 14 and Step 15, replace the voltage regulator and repeat the test procedure. If the unit still does not meet the specified amperage/voltage readings with a new regulator, remove the alternator and have it bench-tested by a dealer or qualified marine shop.

17. Reconnect all disconnected leads, reinstall the LIGHT terminal cap and remove all test equipment.

CLYMER QUICK TIP
The charging system seems to be working properly, but 1 or 2 cells of your unsealed battery require water quite frequently. A visual inspection of the battery and charging system turns up nothing and you suspect an overcharge condition. Remove the battery from the engine compartment and check the case carefully for a crack before having the alternator tested. When only 1 or 2 cells are thirsty, the chances are good that the battery has been damaged from moving around in the battery case or from a battery hold-down that was tightened excessively.

IGNITION SYSTEM

The ignition system on all models is a mechanical contact breaker point type. Most problems involving failure to start, poor performance or rough running stem from trouble in the ignition system. Many novice troubleshooters assume that these symptoms point to the fuel system instead of the ignition system (remember our axioms?).

Note the following performance symptoms:

a. Engine misses.
b. Stumbles on acceleration (misfiring).
c. Loss of power at high speed (misfiring).

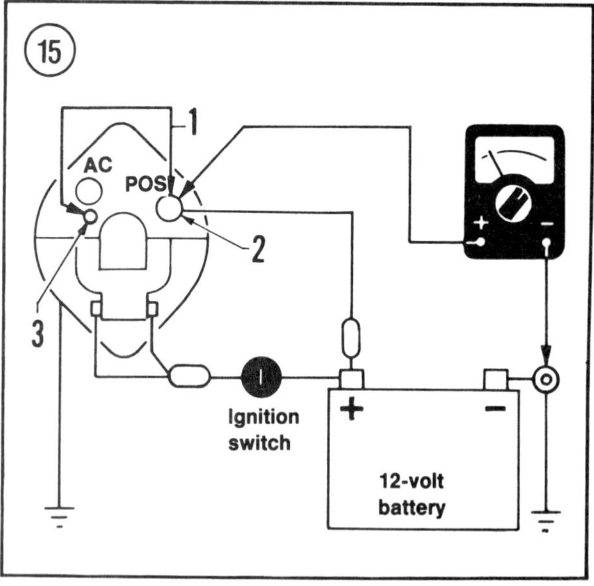

d. Hard starting (if at all).
e. Rough idle.

These symptoms may be caused by one of the following:

a. Spark plugs.
b. Secondary wires.
c. Distributor cap and rotor.
d. Ignition coil.

Most of the symptoms can also be caused by a carburetor that is worn or improperly adjusted, or a fuel pump that is about to fail. But considering the law of averages, the odds are far better that the source of the problem will be found in the ignition rather than the fuel system.

Ignition system troubles may be roughly divided between those affecting only one cylinder and those affecting all cylinders. If the problem affects only one cylinder, it can only be in the spark plug, secondary wiring or that part of the distributor associated with that particular cylinder. If the problem affects all cylinders (weak or no spark), then the trouble is in the ignition coil, rotor, distributor or associated wiring.

Some tests of the ignition system require running the engine with a spark plug or ignition coil wire disconnected. The safest

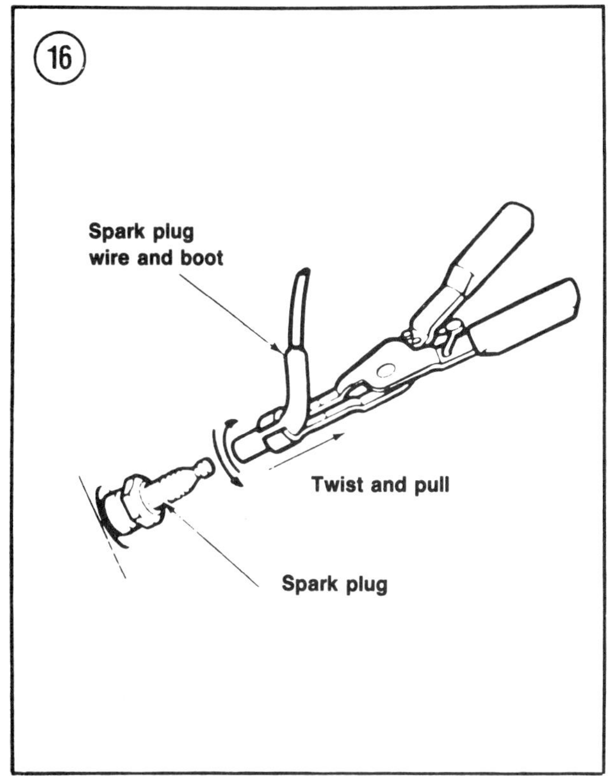

way to do this is to disconnect the wire with the engine stopped, then hold its end next to a metal surface with insulated pliers as shown in **Figure 16**.

WARNING
Never disconnect a spark plug or ignition coil wire when the engine is running. The high voltage in the ignition system could cause serious injury or even death.

Spark plug condition is an important indicator of engine performance. Spark plugs in a properly operating engine will have slightly pitted electrodes and a light tan insulator tip. **Figure 17** shows a normal plug and a number of others which indicate trouble in their respective cylinders.

The troubleshooting procedures outlined in **Figure 18** will help you to isolate ignition problems quickly. These procedures assume that the battery is in good enough condition to crank the engine over at its normal rate.

CLYMER QUICK TIP
If the engine runs roughly after you or someone else has worked on it, check the spark plug wire routing. The wires may have been connected to the plugs correctly, but improperly routed, resulting in a condition known as cross-fire or induction leakage.

Cross-fire is caused by induced magnetism whenever ignition cables are positioned closely together and in parallel for a distance. It is most likely to occur between consecutive firing cylinders when the cylinders are located side-by-side in the engine block.

3

FUEL SYSTEM

Fuel system problems should be isolated to the fuel pump, fuel lines, fuel filter or carburetor. The following procedures assume that the ignition system is working properly and is correctly adjusted.

1. *Engine will not start*—Make sure there is gas in the tank and that it is being delivered to the carburetor. Remove the flame arrestor, look into the carburetor throat and operate the throttle linkage several times. There should be a stream of fuel from the accelerator pump discharge tube each time the linkage is moved. If not, check the fuel pump pressure as described in Chapter Nine. Also check the float condition and adjustment. If the engine will not start, check the automatic choke parts for sticking or damage. If necessary, rebuild or replace the carburetor as described in Chapter Nine.
2. *Engine runs at fast idle*—Check the choke setting, idle speed and mixture adjustments.
3. *Rough idle or engine miss with frequent stalling*—Check choke linkage for proper adjustment. Check throttle stop screw adjustment. Check for sticking throttle plates. Set idle speed to specifications. Check float adjustment.

(17)

SPARK PLUG CONDITION

NORMAL

- Identified by light tan or gray deposits on the firing tip.
- Can be cleaned.

GAP BRIDGED

- Identified by deposit buildup closing gap between electrodes.
- Caused by oil or carbon fouling. If deposits are not excessive, the plug can be cleaned.

OIL FOULED

- Identified by wet black deposits on the insulator shell bore and electrodes.
- Caused by excessive oil entering combustion chamber thorugh worn rings and pistons, excessive clearance between valve guides and stems, or worn or loose bearings. Can be cleaned. If engine is not repaired, use a hotter plug.

CARBON FOULED

- Identified by black, dry, fluffy carbon deposits on insulator tips, exposed shell surfaces and electrodes.
- Caused by too cold a plug, weak ignition, dirty air cleaner, too rich a fuel mixture, or excessive idling. Can be cleaned.

LEAD FOULED

- Identified by dark gray, black, yellow, or tan deposits or a fused glazed coating on the insulator tip.
- Caused by highly leaded gasoline. Can be cleaned.

WORN

- Identified by severely eroded or worn electrodes.
- Caused by normal wear. Should be replaced.

FUSED SPOT DEPOSIT

- Identified by melted or spotty deposits resembling bubbles or blisters.
- Caused by sudden acceleration. Can be cleaned.

OVERHEATING

- Identified by a white or light gray insulator with small black or gray brown spots and with bluish-burnt appearance of electrodes.
- Caused by engine overheating, wrong type of fuel, loose spark plugs, too hot a plug, or incorrect ignition timing. Replace the plug.

PREIGNITION

- Identified by melted electrodes and possibly blistered insulator. Metallic deposits on insulator indicate engine damage.
- Caused by wrong type of fuel, incorrect ignition timing or advance, too hot a plug, burned valves, or engine overheating. Replace the plug.

4. *Engine "diesels" (continues to run) when ignition is switched off*—Check carburetor ignition timing and idle speed (probably too fast). Check linkage to make sure the fast idle cam is not hanging up. Check for engine overheating.

5. *Stumbling when accelerating from idle*—Check accelerator pump action (Step 1). Check for a clogged fuel filter, low fuel pump volume, plugged bowl vents or a power valve that is stuck closed.

6. *Engine misses at high speed or lacks power*—This indicates possible fuel starvation. Check accelerator pump action (Step 1). Check float setting and needle valve operation. Check for a plugged pump discharge nozzle or leaking nozzle gasket. Check for a clogged fuel filter or dirty flame arrestor.

7. *Engine stalls on deceleration or during a quick stop*—Adjust the idle speed to specifications. Check throttle positioner functioning. Check for leaking intake manifold or carburetor gasket(s).

8. *Engine will not reach wide-open throttle; top speed and power are reduced*—Check

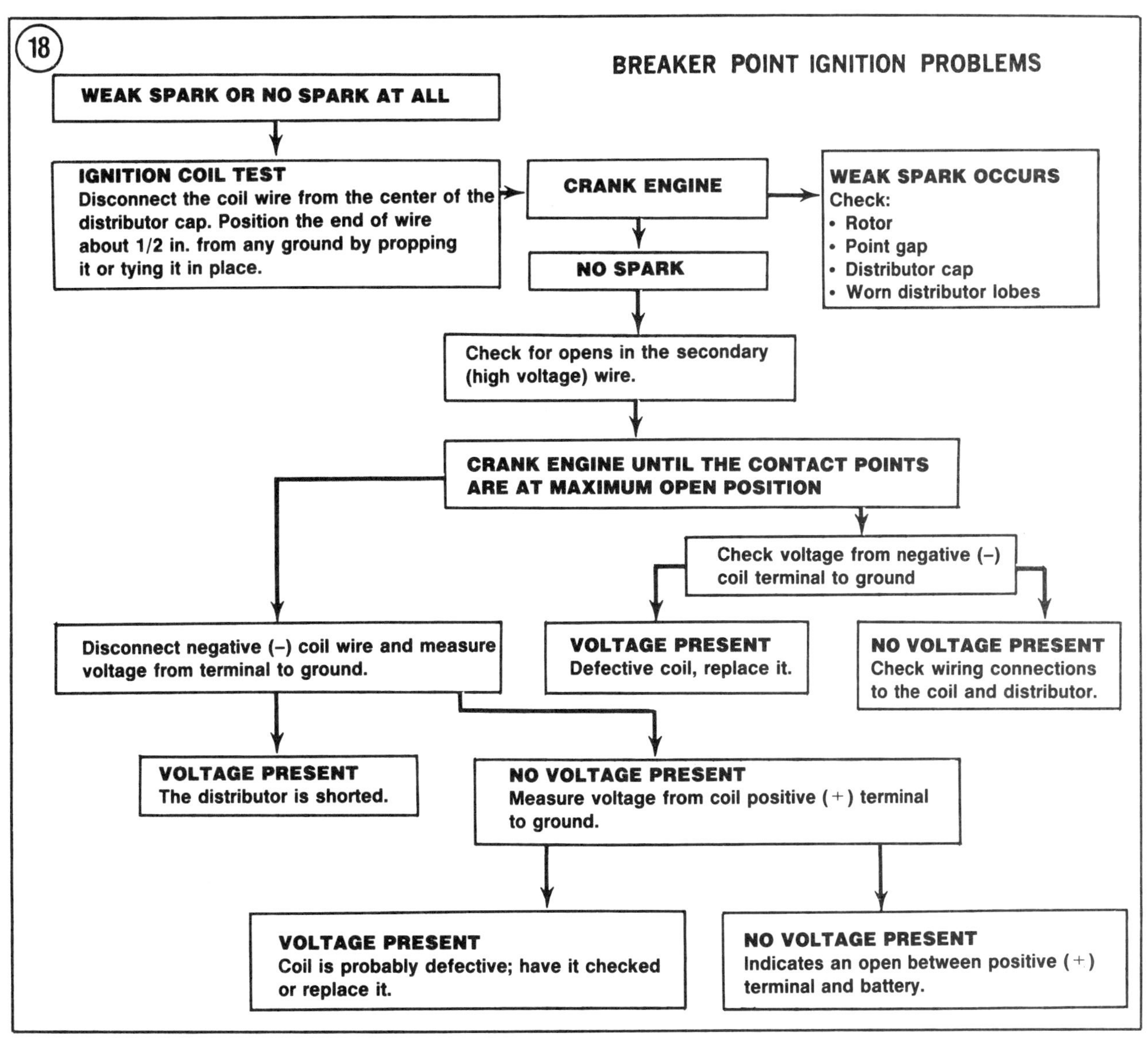
18
BREAKER POINT IGNITION PROBLEMS
WEAK SPARK OR NO SPARK AT ALL
IGNITION COIL TEST
Disconnect the coil wire from the center of the distributor cap. Position the end of wire about 1/2 in. from any ground by propping it or tying it in place.
CRANK ENGINE
WEAK SPARK OCCURS
Check:
• Rotor
• Point gap
• Distributor cap
• Worn distributor lobes
NO SPARK
Check for opens in the secondary (high voltage) wire.
CRANK ENGINE UNTIL THE CONTACT POINTS ARE AT MAXIMUM OPEN POSITION
Check voltage from negative (–) coil terminal to ground
Disconnect negative (–) coil wire and measure voltage from terminal to ground.
VOLTAGE PRESENT
Defective coil, replace it.
NO VOLTAGE PRESENT
Check wiring connections to the coil and distributor.
VOLTAGE PRESENT
The distributor is shorted.
NO VOLTAGE PRESENT
Measure voltage from coil positive (+) terminal to ground.
VOLTAGE PRESENT
Coil is probably defective; have it checked or replace it.
NO VOLTAGE PRESENT
Indicates an open between positive (+) terminal and battery.

throttle linkage for binding. Check for low fuel pump volume, incorrect float drop, a clogged fuel filter, stuck power valve or an inoperative secondary system.

9. *Engine surges at cruising speed*—Check for a plugged fuel filter. Adjust float level and drop. Check for low fuel pump volume or pressure. Check fuel for contamination. Check for blocked air bleeds or leaking plugs/lead seals.

10. *Black exhaust smoke*—Check for an excessively rich mixture. Check idle speed adjustment and choke setting. Check for excessive fuel pump pressure, leaky float or worn needle valve.

11. *Excessive fuel consumption*—Check for an excessively rich mixture or misblended gasohol. Check choke operation. Check idle speed and mixture adjustments. Check for excessive fuel pump pressure, leaky float or worn needle valve.

CLYMER QUICK TIP

Contrary to what manufacturers would have you believe, the composition material used in floats ***does*** *gradually absorb fuel over a period of time. Such fuel absorption increases the weight of the float and prevents it from operating properly when set to correct specifications.*

To check a composition float for fuel absorption, remove it from the carburetor, hold it between a thumb and finger and gently press a fingernail into the surface. If moisture appears where your fingernail pressed, the float has started to absorb fuel.

Since floats are quite expensive, the best way to determine if fuel absorption has affected float performance is to weigh it with an inexpensive float scale available in most auto supply stores. The scale comes with weight specifications for all new floats and can immediately pinpoint a fuel system problem that is often overlooked.

CLYMER QUICK TIP

The engine stumbles during acceleration, misses at high speed and generally lacks power. The diagnosis is a malfunctioning accelerator pump in the carburetor but an overhaul does not cure the problem for long.

You are probably using a blended fuel (alcohol and gasoline). The alcohol in the fuel causes the accelerator pump cup to swell, restricting its travel in the pump bore. When the carburetor is removed and disassembled, the alcohol evaporates and the pump cup returns to normal size, allowing the pump to work properly. Carburetors with a tapered pump bore are especially prone to this problem. Look for tell-tale marks on the cup lip and pump bore which indicate cup scuffing. Installing a new pump cup will only temporarily solve this problem—the only real cure is to change the brand of gasoline used.

CLYMER QUICK TIP

Your fuel economy has dropped off considerably and you can smell gasoline fumes. You suspect a leak in the fuel system, but a quick check turns up no signs of the tell-tale stains such a leak would leave on the carburetor or intake manifold. It's not an uncommon problem with Rochester Quadrajet carburetors.

The Quadrajet contains 2 brass plugs in the secondary fuel well which tend to leak over a period of time. The solution requires carburetor removal and disassembly to reach the plugs. After scraping the area around each plug clean, seal it with epoxy. Let the epoxy cure for 24-48 hours before reassembling the carburetor.

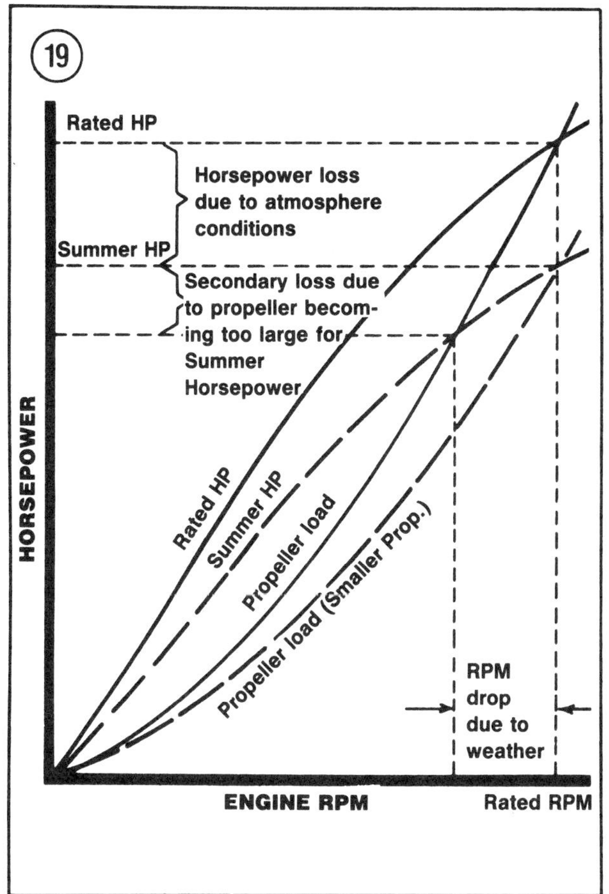

ENGINE PERFORMANCE

Elevation and weather have definite effects on the wide-open throttle power of any internal combustion engine. As elevation increases, the air gets thinner and the engine air/fuel mixture becomes overrich. Installation of a lower pitch propeller will regain some of the lost performance, but the basic problem remains: The diameter of the propeller is too large for the reduced power available. Your OMC dealer can calculate how much diameter must be removed from a lower pitch propeller to provide good performance at high elevations. You may find it helpful to make a gear ratio change to provide more reduction.

Heat and humidity affect the density of the air in a similar manner. This is particularly noticeable when your engine is propped out on a cool, dry spring day or seems to lose its pep during hot, humid summer days. You may lose up to 14 percent of the available horsepower, resulting in a 2-3 mph reduction in speed and an inability to get the boat on plane. **Figure 19** shows the relationship between horsepower and weather conditions.

A number of other factors can make the engine difficult or impossible to start or cause rough running, poor performance and so on. The majority of novice troubleshooters immediately suspect the carburetor as the cause of the problem. In most cases, however, the problem lies in the ignition system.

The troubleshooting procedures outlined in **Figures 20-23** and **Table 1** will help you solve the majority of engine performance problems in a systematic manner.

ENGINE OVERHEATING

There are numerous causes of engine overheating, some of which are often overlooked during troubleshooting:

a. A loose alternator belt. This prevents the water pump from operating at the proper speed.
b. Excessively advanced or retarded ignition timing.
c. A plugged or restricted water passage in the stern drive due to operation while the drive unit was submerged in sand or silt.
d. Water supply hoses that are defective inside. This is most often the result of delamination, in which the hose disintegrates from inside.
e. A plugged or restricted inlet screen on the stern drive lower unit.
f. A worn or damaged engine circulating or stern drive water pump.
g. Leakage of air or exhaust into the suction side of the stern drive water pump.

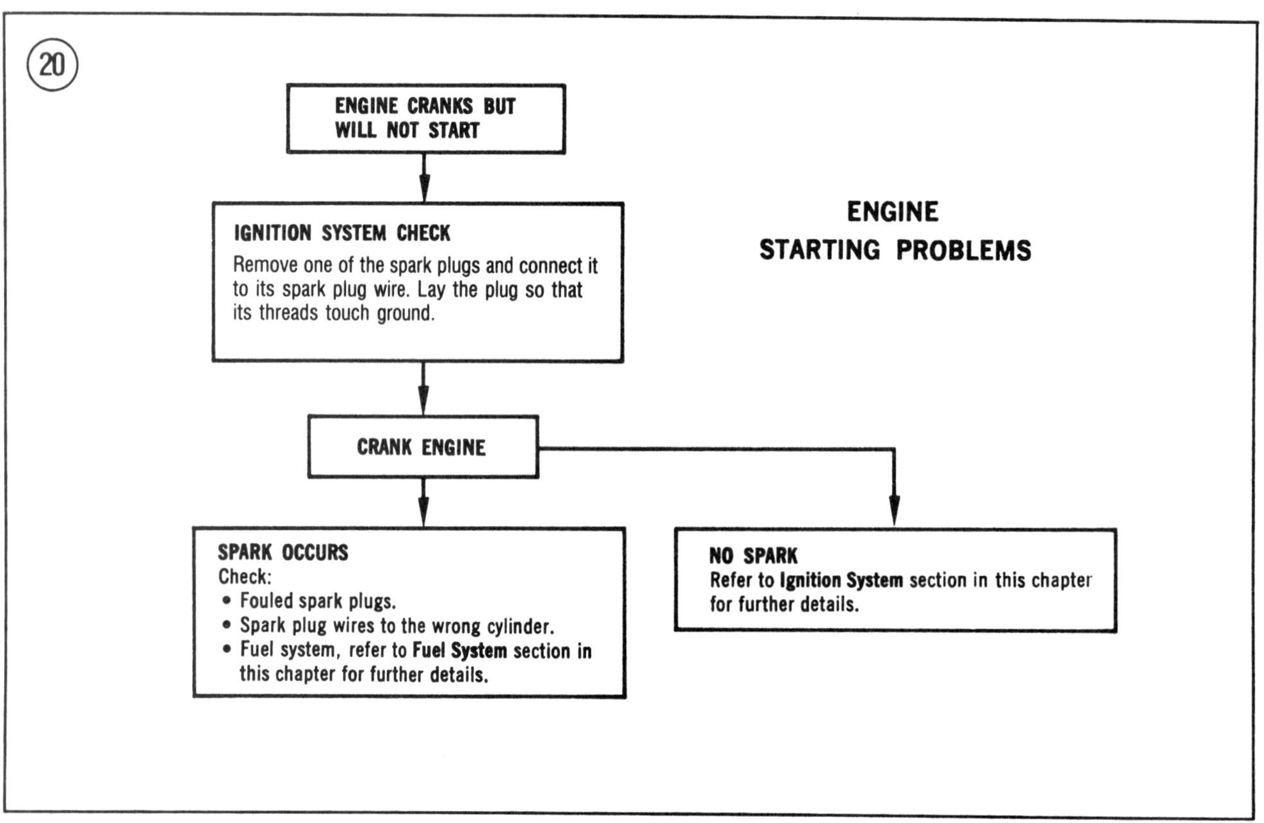
20
ENGINE CRANKS BUT WILL NOT START
IGNITION SYSTEM CHECK
Remove one of the spark plugs and connect it to its spark plug wire. Lay the plug so that its threads touch ground.
ENGINE STARTING PROBLEMS
CRANK ENGINE
SPARK OCCURS
Check:
• Fouled spark plugs.
• Spark plug wires to the wrong cylinder.
• Fuel system, refer to Fuel System section in this chapter for further details.
NO SPARK
Refer to Ignition System section in this chapter for further details.

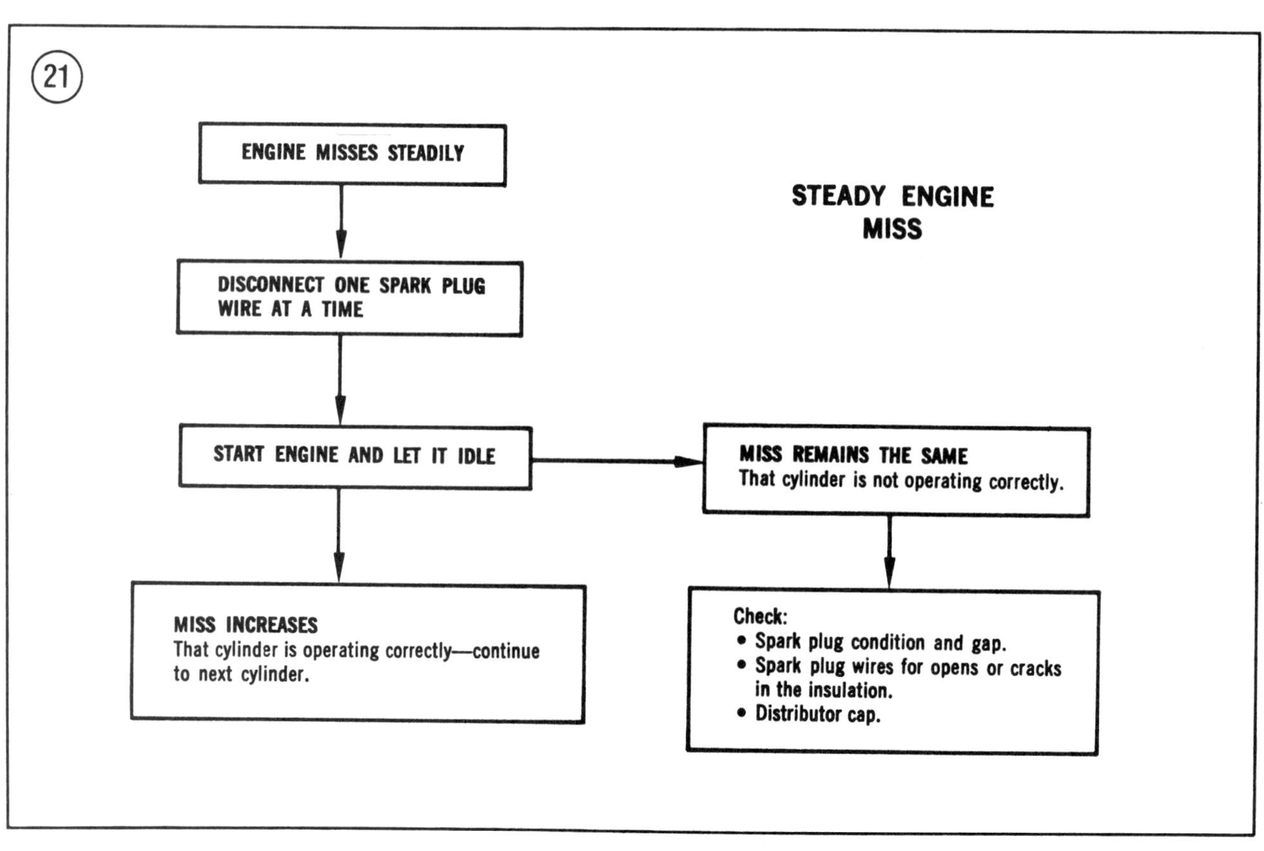
21
ENGINE MISSES STEADILY
STEADY ENGINE MISS
DISCONNECT ONE SPARK PLUG WIRE AT A TIME
START ENGINE AND LET IT IDLE
MISS REMAINS THE SAME
That cylinder is not operating correctly.
MISS INCREASES
That cylinder is operating correctly—continue to next cylinder.
Check:
• Spark plug condition and gap.
• Spark plug wires for opens or cracks in the insulation.
• Distributor cap.

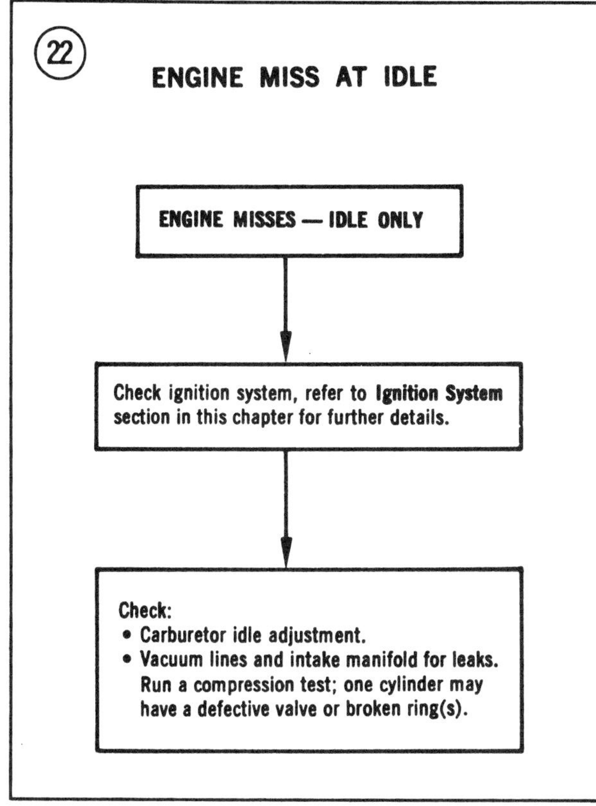

22
ENGINE MISS AT IDLE
ENGINE MISSES — IDLE ONLY
Check ignition system, refer to Ignition System section in this chapter for further details.
Check:
• Carburetor idle adjustment.
• Vacuum lines and intake manifold for leaks. Run a compression test; one cylinder may have a defective valve or broken ring(s).

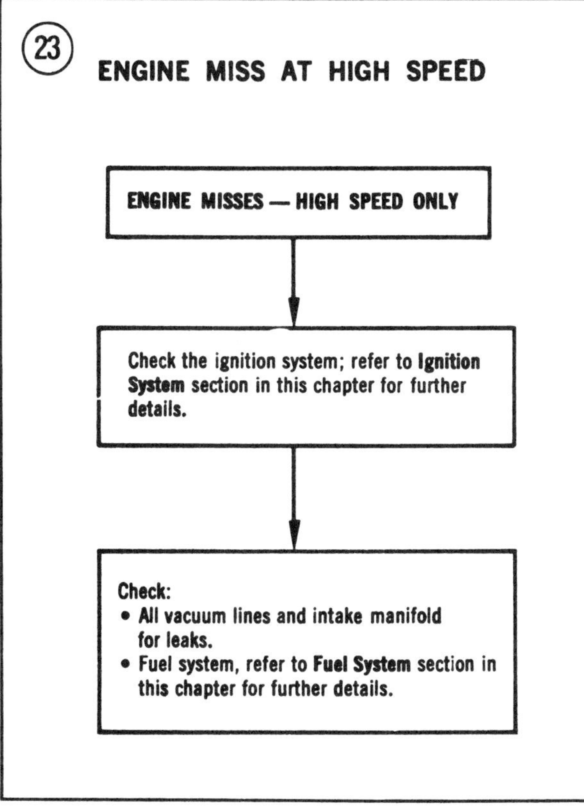

23
ENGINE MISS AT HIGH SPEED
ENGINE MISSES — HIGH SPEED ONLY
Check the ignition system; refer to Ignition System section in this chapter for further details.
Check:
• All vacuum lines and intake manifold for leaks.
• Fuel system, refer to Fuel System section in this chapter for further details.

h. Too much oil in the crankcase. Excessive oil will cause overheating at wide-open throttle.
i. A defective thermostat. See Chapter Ten.

3

ENGINE OIL PRESSURE INDICATOR

Proper oil pressure is vital to the engine. If oil pressure is insufficient, the engine can destroy itself in a comparatively short time.

The oil pressure warning circuit monitors oil pressure constantly. If pressure drops below a predetermined level, the warning light comes on.

Obviously, it is vital that the warning circuit be in working order to signal low oil pressure. Each time you turn on the ignition, but before starting the engine, the warning light should come on. If it doesn't, the trouble is in the warning circuit, not the oil pressure system. See **Figure 24** to troubleshoot the warning circuit.

Once the engine is running, the warning light should remain off. If the warning light comes on or acts erratically while the engine is running, there is trouble with the engine oil pressure system. *Stop the engine immediately.* Refer to **Figure 25** for possible causes of the problem.

ENGINE OIL LEAKS

Like automotive engines, OMC marine engines are subject to oil leaks. Boat installation, however, may make it difficult to determine exactly where the leak is. Many owners of new boats discover oil in the bilge. Generally, this oil leaks into the sealed flywheel housing through the rear main oil seal if the boat is shipped at too high an angle. It is not a serious problem and is self-correcting, as long as the boat is not stored at a high angle. The oil that leaks past

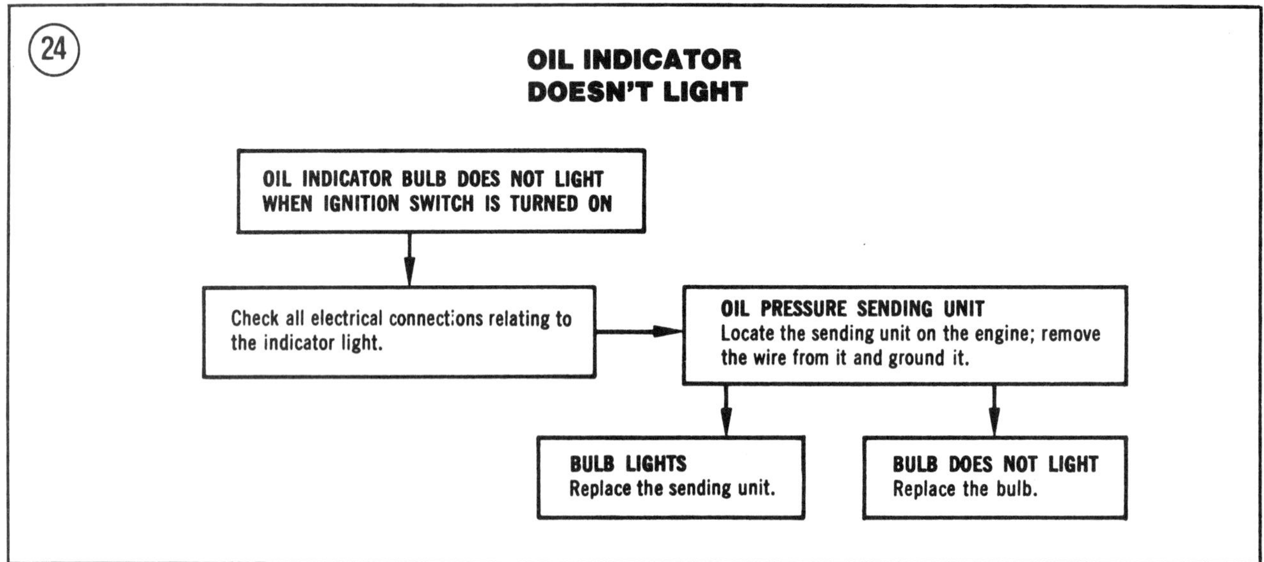

the seal will spray out of the water pump vent on the starter motor side of the engine and can be wiped up.

More common oil leaks are found as hours are put on the engine. A leaking rear main oil seal will allow oil to run down the outside of the flywheel housing when the engine is running. Replacing the seal will stop the leak.

A leaking oil pan gasket will also allow oil to drip down the outside of the flywheel housing when the engine is running. The leaking oil is usually found on the starter motor side of the engine. The most common cause of a leaking pan gasket is overtightening of the pan attaching screws. If a leak is traced to the oil pan, replace the gasket and check the pan gasket surface for possible warpage.

ENGINE NOISES

Often the first evidence of an internal engine problem is a strange noise. That knocking, clicking or tapping sound which you never heard before may be warning you of impending trouble.

While engine noises can indicate problems, they are difficult to interpret correctly; inexperienced mechanics can be seriously misled by them.

Professional mechanics often use a special stethoscope (which looks like a doctor's stethoscope) for isolating engine noises. You can do nearly as well with a "sounding stick" which can be an ordinary piece of doweling, a length of broom handle or a section of small hose. By placing one end in contact with the area to which you want to listen and the other end near your ear, you can hear sounds emanating from that area. The first time you do this, you may be horrified at the strange sounds coming from even a normal engine. If you can, have an experienced friend or mechanic help you sort out the noises.

Clicking or Tapping Noises

Clicking or tapping noises usually come from the valve train and indicate excessive valve clearance. A sticking valve may also sound like a valve with excessive clearance. In addition, excessive wear in valve train components can cause similar engine noises.

Knocking Noises

A heavy, dull knocking is usually caused by a worn main bearing. The noise is loudest when the engine is working hard, such as

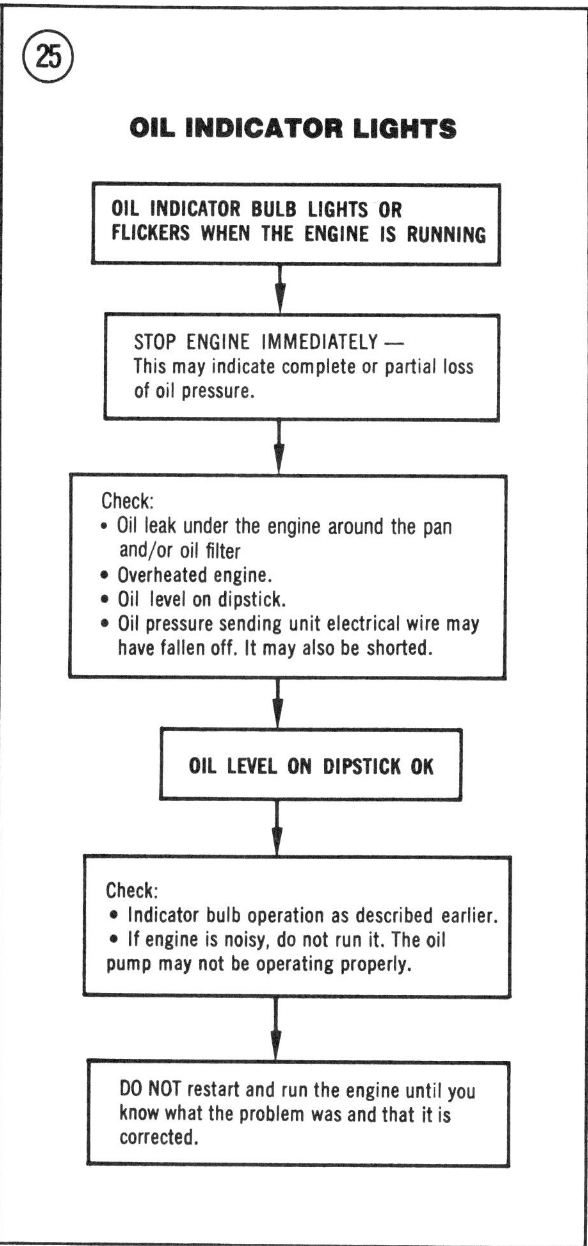

accelerating at low speed. You may be able to isolate the trouble to a single bearing by disconnecting the spark plugs one at a time. When you reach the spark plug nearest the bearing, the knock will be reduced or disappear.

25
OIL INDICATOR LIGHTS
OIL INDICATOR BULB LIGHTS OR FLICKERS WHEN THE ENGINE IS RUNNING
STOP ENGINE IMMEDIATELY — This may indicate complete or partial loss of oil pressure.
Check:
• Oil leak under the engine around the pan and/or oil filter
• Overheated engine.
• Oil level on dipstick.
• Oil pressure sending unit electrical wire may have fallen off. It may also be shorted.
OIL LEVEL ON DIPSTICK OK
Check:
• Indicator bulb operation as described earlier.
• If engine is noisy, do not run it. The oil pump may not be operating properly.
DO NOT restart and run the engine until you know what the problem was and that it is corrected.

Worn connecting rod bearings may also produce a knock, but the sound is usually more metallic. As with a main bearing, the noise is worse during acceleration. It may increase just as you go from acceleration to coasting. Disconnecting the spark plugs will help isolate this knock as well.

A double knock or clicking usually indicates a worn piston pin. Disconnecting spark plugs will isolate this to a particular piston; however, the noise will *increase* when you reach the affected piston.

A loose flywheel and excessive crankshaft end play also produce knocking noises. While similar to main bearing noises, they are usually intermittent, not constant, and they do not change when spark plugs are disconnected. When caused by a loose flywheel or coupling, the noise is generally heard at idle or during rapid deceleration. It is a good idea to recheck flywheel/coupler nut torque whenever the engine is removed from the boat.

Some mechanics confuse piston pin noise with piston slap (excessive piston clearance). The double knock will distinguish piston pin noise. Piston slap will always be louder when the engine is cold.

ENGINE TROUBLESHOOTING

These procedures assume the starter cranks the engine over normally. If not, refer to the *Starter* section of this chapter.

Engine Won't Start

This can be caused by the ignition or fuel system. Refer to *Ignition System* section of this chapter and perform a spark intensity test. If sparks occur, the problem is more likely in the fuel system. If they do not occur, check the ignition system.

Engine Misses Steadily

Remove one spark plug wire at a time and ground the wire. If engine miss increases, that cylinder is working properly. Reconnect the wire and check another. When a wire is disconnected and engine miss remains the same, that cylinder is not firing. Perform a spark intensity test as described in this chapter. If no spark occurs for the suspected cylinder, check the distributor cap, wire and spark plug. See Chapter Four. If a spark occurs properly, check cylinder compression and intake manifold vacuum (Chapter Four).

Engine Misses Erratically at All Speeds

Intermittent problems can be difficult to locate. This could be in the ignition system, exhaust system or fuel system. Start with the secondary ignition wiring and follow the troubleshooting procedures for each system to isolate the cause.

Engine Misses at Idle Only

The problem could be in the ignition system or carburetor idle adjustment. Have the idle mixture adjustment checked and inspect the idle circuit for restrictions.

Engine Misses at High Speed Only

Check the accelerator pump operation and fuel pump delivery. Look for a restricted fuel line. Check the spark plugs and wires.

Low Performance at All Speeds, Poor Acceleration

Usually an ignition or fuel system problem. May also be an intake manifold or carburetor vacuum leak.

CLYMER QUICK TIP

To check for a leaking V6 or V8 intake manifold gasket, use a garden hose to run water along the mating surface on each side with the engine idling. The V-design of the engine will allow enough water to accumulate to temporarily seal any leak. If the engine idle suddenly smooths out, the gasket is leaking.

Although oil or carburetor cleaner is often used to troubleshoot this problem, water is preferred, as it is both cleaner and safer. Water does not leave the messy residue of oil and is not dangerous like carburetor cleaner.

Tighten the bolts on a leaking intake manifold first to see if this eliminates the problem. However, tightening the manifold on engines which use a metal valley cover with laminated gasket sections will not work. The laminated gasket material is causing the leak and the entire valley cover will have to be replaced.

Excessive Fuel Consumption

Check for a plugged or restricted air cleaner filter element. Misblended gasohol will also cause the problem, although there will be performance problems at the same time.

Engine Overheats

Usually caused by a cooling system problem, although late ignition or valve timing can be responsible. Check the coolant level in the cooling system. Check the condition of the drive belt. Check the cooling system hoses for leaks and loose connections.

Engine Stalls As It Warms Up

The choke valve may be stuck closed, the engine idle speed may be set too low, or the PCV valve may be defective.

Engine Stalls After Idling or Slow-speed Cruising

This can be caused by a defective fuel pump, overheated engine, incorrect float level or idle adjustment, or a defective PCV valve.

Engine Stalls After High-speed Cruising

Vapor lock within the fuel lines caused by an overheated engine and/or hot weather is the usual cause of this trouble. Inspect and service the cooling system (Chapter Ten). If the problem persists, change to a different fuel or shield the fuel line from engine heat.

Engine Backfires

Thre are several possible reasons for this problem: incorrect ignition timing, overheating, excessive carbon, spark plugs with an incorrect heat range, hot or sticking valves and/or a cracked distributor cap.

Smoky Exhaust

Blue smoke indicates excessive oil consumption usually caused by worn piston rings. Black smoke indicates an excessively rich fuel mixture.

Excessive Oil Consumption

This can be caused by external leaks through broken seals or gaskets, or by burning oil in the combustion chambers. Check the oil pan and the front/rear of the engine for signs of oil leakage. If the oil is not leaking externally, valve stem clearances may be excessive, valve seals may be defective, piston rings may be worn, or cylinder walls may be scored.

COOLING SYSTEM

The temperature gauge usually signals cooling system problems before there is any damage. As long as you stop the engine at the first indication of trouble, serious damage is unlikely.

With standard cooling systems in which seawater is drawn into the engine, circulated and then expelled, cooling system problems are generally mechanical—a faulty pump, defective thermostat, loose or broken drive belt or passages plugged with contamination or foreign material.

Closed cooling systems are more complex in that they use a heat exchanger which transfers heat from the engine coolant to seawater without the two coming in contact. The "closed" portion of the cooling system is pressurized (like an automotive cooling system) and uses a 50/50 mixture of ethylene glycol antifreeze and pure soft water. This system should be checked periodically to make sure it can withstand 15 psi.

Heat exchangers used in closed cooling systems collect salt, lime and other contaminants in their passages, leading to a gradual decrease in cooling efficiency. For this reason, they should be removed every 2 years and the seawater passages cleaned with a wire brush and compressed air.

POSITIVE CRANKCASE VENTILATION SYSTEM

A closed crankcase ventilation system is used to recycle crankcase vapors into the combustion chambers for burning. A vent hose connects the flame arrestor to the valve cover breather cap. This provides a positive flow of air through the crankcase. Fresh air and crankcase vapors are drawn into the intake manifold through a PCV valve containing a spring-loaded plunger. The position of the plunger in the PCV valve varies depending upon engine vacuum and thus controls or meters the flow of crankcase vapors into the intake manifold. The PCV valve is located in a line between the intake manifold and crankcase on 2.3L engines (**Figure 26**). On all other engines, the PCV valve is installed in the valve cover (**Figure 27**). A typical V8 system is shown in **Figure 28**.

A malfunctioning PCV valve or a clogged ventilation line will cause a rough or loping engine idle. If such an idle condition

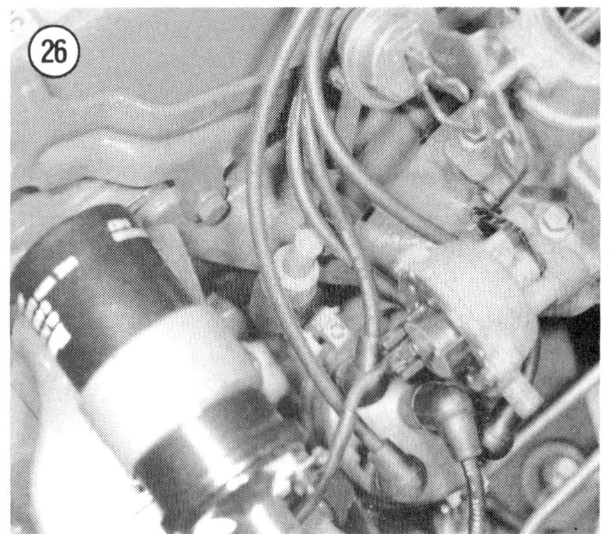
26

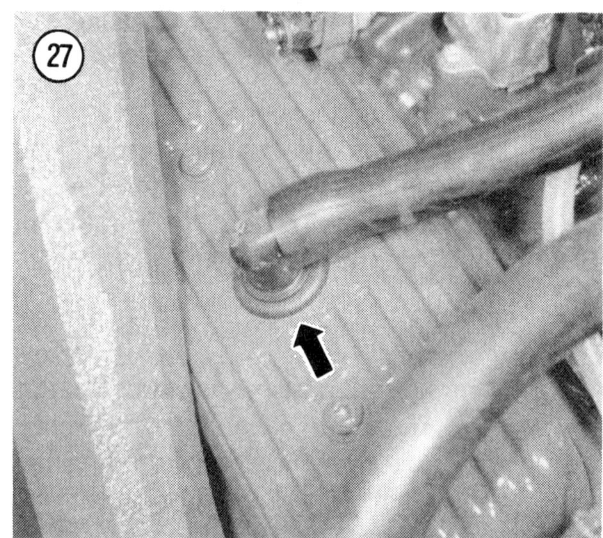
27

28

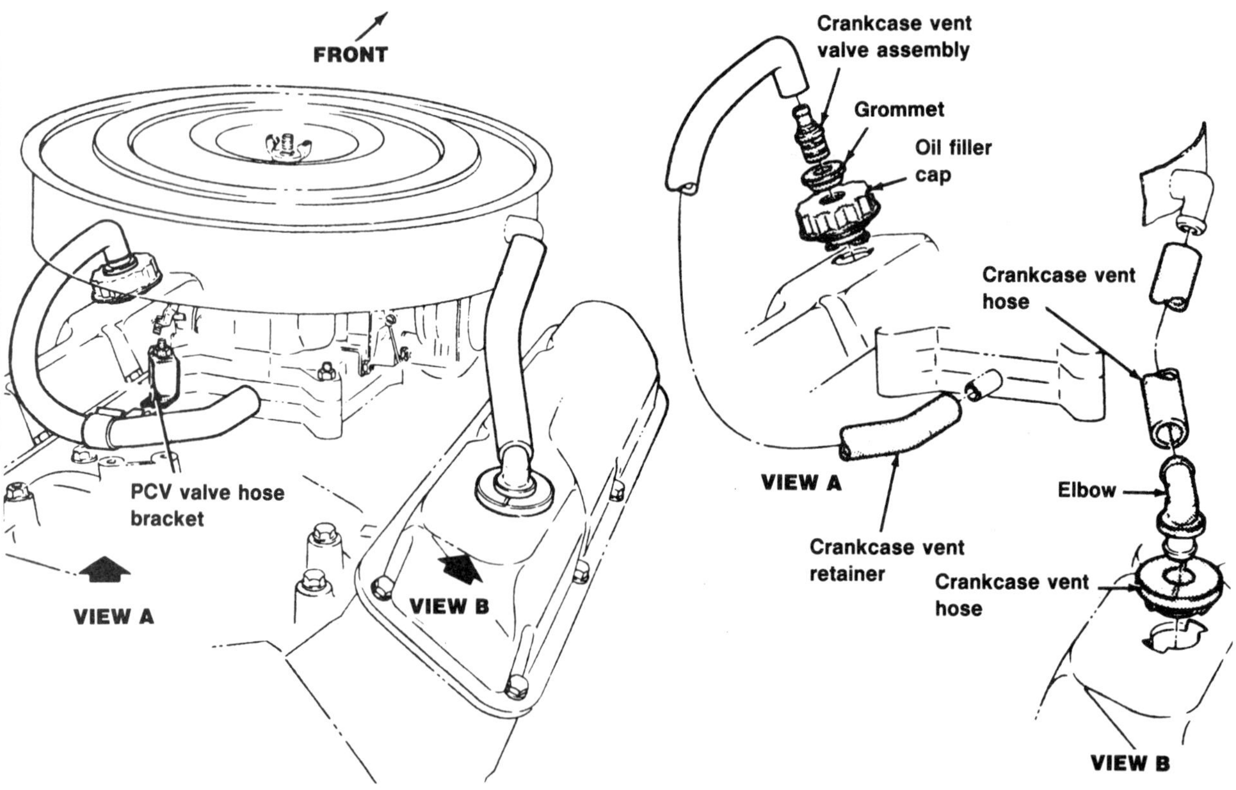

FRONT

PCV valve hose bracket

VIEW A

VIEW B

Crankcase vent valve assembly

Grommet

Oil filler cap

VIEW A

Crankcase vent retainer

Crankcase vent hose

Elbow

Crankcase vent hose

VIEW B

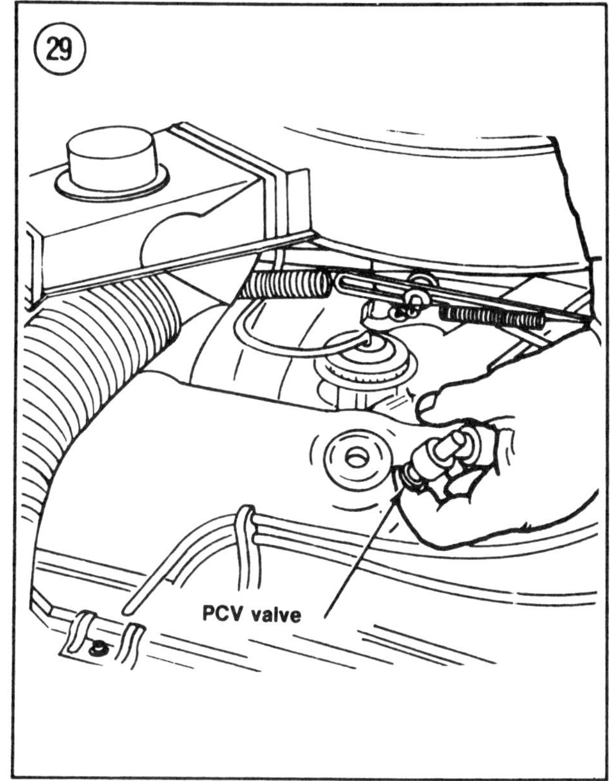

develops, do not attempt to correct it by readjusting the idle speed or by disconnecting the PCV system. Readjusting the idle will not solve the problem for long; disconnecting the PCV system will affect fuel economy in the short run and result in premature engine wear which will shorten the engine's service life in the long run.

PCV System Check

If a rough or loping engine idle develops, test the PCV system as follows:

1. Check the condition of all system hoses. Replace any damaged, deteriorated or plugged hose. Make sure that all connections are tight and that there is no leak in the system.
2. Start the engine and run at idle. Remove the PCV valve from the intake manifold line (2.3L) or valve cover (all others). A hissing noise should be heard as air passes through the valve and a strong vacuum should be felt when a finger is placed over the end of the valve (**Figure 29**). If not, check for a plugged hose. If none is found, install a new PCV valve.
3. Reinstall the PCV valve in the intake manifold line or valve cover. Disconnect the air inlet hose at the flame arrestor. Hold a piece of stiff paper, such as a parts tag or a 3×5 memo card, over the inlet hose opening. Wait about 60 seconds for crankcase pressure to be reduced. Shortly thereafter, the paper should be sucked to the hose with a noticeable force. If it is not, check for a plugged hose.
4. Shut the engine off. Reattach the hose to the flame arrestor and remove the PCV valve a second time. Shake the valve and listen for the rattle of the check needle in the valve. If no rattle is heard, install a new PCV valve.

STERN DRIVE UNIT

In normal straight-ahead operation, a stern drive makes very little noise. Changing direction to port or starboard will increase the noise level from the universal joints, but it should not be objectionable.

If U-joint noise is suspected, attach a flush-test device (*Cooling System Flushing*, Chapter Four) and run the engine at idle. Have an assistant turn the stern drive first to port and then to starboard while you listen for noise at the gimbal housing. Any unusual noise during this test indicates either U-joint wear or a defective gimbal bearing.

Propeller damage may occur without being obvious. If the propeller has hit many underwater objects, it may slip on its hub.

If water leaks into the boat, inspect the gimbal housing seal, U-joint bellows or shift cable bellows.

A shift handle that is difficult to move may be caused by a problem in the stern drive, transom shift cable, shift box or remote control cable. To isolate the trouble, disconnect the remote control cable at the transom plate. If shifting is still difficult, the shift cable or control box is at fault. If shifting is normal, the problem is in the stern drive. Have an assistant turn the propeller by hand while you move the shift cable back and forth between the stern drive and transom plate. If the cable does not move freely, replace it.

Tilt/trim system problems may be mechanical, electrical or hydraulic. Any of these can prevent the stern drive from moving to a full UP or full DOWN position. First check to make sure that the stern drive is in FORWARD gear. If it is in REVERSE, the shift interlock switch will prevent the power trim system from operating.

Mechanical problems result from frozen U-joints, lack of proper lubrication or non-use over a lengthy period. Electrical problems involve the pump motor wiring circuit. Hydraulic problems are most often caused by low or contaminated hydraulic fluid.

Table 1 ENGINE TROUBLESHOOTING

Trouble	Probable cause	Correction
Starter will not crank engine	Discharged battery	Charge or replace battery
	Corroded battery terminals	Clean terminals
	Loose connection in starting circuit	Clean and tighten all connections
	Defective starting switch	Replace switch
	Starting motor brushes dirty	Clean or replace brushes
	Jammed Bendix gear	Loosen starter motor to free gear
	Faulty starter motor	Replace motor
Starter turns but does not crank engine	Partially discharged battery	Charge or replace battery
	Defective wiring or wiring capacity too low	Locate and replace defective wiring
	Broken Bendix drive	Remove starter motor and repair drive
Engine will not start	Empty fuel tank	Fill tank with proper fuel
	Flooded engine	Remove spark plugs and crank engine several times; replace plugs.
	Water in fuel system	Clean fuel tank, lines and carburetor; refill with proper fuel.
	Inoperative or sticking choke valve	Check choke, linkage and choke rod/cable for proper operation.
	Improperly adjusted carburetor	Adjust carburetor
	Clogged fuel lines or defective fuel pump	Disconnect fuel line @ carburetor. If fuel does not flow freely when engine is cranked, clean fuel line and sediment bowl (if so equipped). If fuel still does not flow freely after cleaning, repair or replace fuel pump.

(continued)

Table 1 ENGINE TROUBLESHOOTING (continued)

Trouble	Probable cause	Correction
Engine will not start (poor connections and other causes)	Air leak around intake manifold	Check for leak by squirting oil around intake connections. If leak is found, tighten manifold and replace gaskets, if necessary.
	Loose spark plugs	Check all plugs for proper seating, gasket and tightness. Replace all damaged plugs and gaskets.
	Loosely seating valves	Check for broken or weak valve springs, warped stems, carbon and gum deposits and insufficient tappet clearance.
	Damaged cylinder head gasket	Check for leaks around gasket when engine is cranked. If a leak is found, replace gasket.
	Worn or broken piston rings	Replace worn or broken rings; check cylinders for out-of-round and taper
Engine will not start (ignition system)	Ignition switch OFF or defective	Turn on switch or replace
	Fouled or broken spark plugs	Remove plugs and check for cracked porcelain, dirty electrodes or improper gap
	Improperly set, worn or pitted distributor points.	Adjust or replace as needed
	Defective ignition coil	Remove center wire from distributor cap and hold within 3/8 in. of engine block. Crank engine. A clean, sharp spark should jump between wire and block when points open. Clean and adjust points. If spark is weak or yellow after point adjustment, replace condenser. If spark is still weak or not present, replace ignition coil.
	Wet, cracked or broken distributor cap	Dry inside surfaces of cap with clean cloth. Inspect for cracks or other defects. Replace if necessary.
	Engine timing wrong	Set engine timing
Hard starting when cold	Choke out of adjustment	Check choke adjustment
	Stale or sour fuel	Drain fuel tank and refill with fresh fuel.
	Defective fuel pump	Replace fuel pump.
	Malfunction in ignition system	Check ignition system.
	Improper engine timing	Check and adjust timing.
Hard starting when hot	Choke out of adjustment	Check choke adjustment
	Incorrect spark plugs	Replace with plugs of the proper heat range.
	Defective coil and/or condenser	Test and replace if necessary.
	Water in fuel	Drain and clean fuel tank, lines and carburetor; refill with proper fuel.

(continued)

Table 1 ENGINE TROUBLESHOOTING (continued)

Trouble	Probable cause	Correction
Excessive coolant temperature	No water circulation	Check for clogged water lines and restricted inlets/outlets. Check for broken or stuck thermostat. Look for worn or damaged water pump or water pump drive.
	Defective thermostat	Replace thermostat
No oil pressure	Defective gauge	Replace gauge
	No oil in engine	Refill with proper grade oil
	Dirt in pressure relief valve	Clean oil pump valve
	Defective oil pump, oil line leak or broken oil pump drive	Check oil pump and oil pump drive for worn or broken parts. Tighten all oil line connections.
Low oil pressure	Oil leak in pressure line	Inspect all oil lines; tighten all connections
	Weak or broken pressure relief valve spring	Replace relief valve spring
	Worn oil pump	Replace oil pump
	Worn or loose bearings	Replace bearings
Oil pressure too high	Engine oil viscosity too thick	Drain crankcase and replace with oil of proper viscosity
	Pressure relief valve stuck	Clean or replace valve
	Dirt or obstructions in lines	Drain and clean oil system; check for bent or flattened oil lines and replace where necessary
Rpm loss	Damaged propeller	Repair or replace propeller
	Bent rudder	Repair
	Misalignment	Realign engine to stern drive
	Dirty boat bottom	Clean boat bottom
Vibration	Misfiring or preignition	See "Preignition"
	Loose mounting or mounting bolts	Tighten
	Loose crankshaft balancer or flywheel	Tighten bolts
	Loose alternator	Tighten bolts
	Propeller shaft bent or out-of-line	Repair or replace
	Propeller bent or pitch out-of-true	Repair or replace
Preignition	Defective spark plugs	Check all spark plugs for broken porcelain, burned electrodes or incorrect gap; replace all defective plugs or clean and reset gap
	Improper timing	Set timing to specs
	Engine carbon	Remove cylinder head and clean out carbon
	Engine overheating	See "Excessive Coolant Temperature"

(continued)

Table 1 ENGINE TROUBLESHOOTING (continued)

Trouble	Probable cause	Correction
Backfiring	Insufficient fuel reaching engine due to dirty lines, strainer or blocked fuel tank vent; water in fuel	See "Engine will not start"
	Improper distributor adjustment	See "Engine will not start"
Sludge in oil	Infrequent oil changes	Drain and refill with proper oil
	Water in oil	Drain and refill; if trouble persists, check for cracked block, cracked head or defective head gasket
	Dirty oil filter	Replace oil filter

Table 2 COBRA DRIVE MODELS

Model No.	Engine	Steering	Drive
	1986		
252AMKWB	2.5L 2-bbl.	Mechanical	983841
252APKWB	2.5L 2-bbl.	Power	983841
302AMKWB	3.0L 2-bbl.	Mechanical	983841
302APKWB	3.0L 2-bbl.	Power	983841
432AMKWB	4.3L 2-bbl.	Mechanical	983842
432AMWXS	4.3L 2-bbl.	Mechanical	983842
432APKWB	4.3L 2-bbl.	Power	983842
432APWXS	4.3L 2-bbl.	Power	983842
434AMKWB	4.3L 4-bbl.	Mechanical	983842
434AMWXS	4.3L 4-bbl.	Mechanical	983842
434APKWB	4.3L 4-bbl.	Power	983842
434APWXS	4.3L 4-bbl.	Power	983842
504AMKWB	5.0L 4-bbl.	Mechanical	983843
504AMWXS	5.0L 4-bbl.	Mechanical	983843
504APKWB	5.0L 4-bbl.	Power	983843
504APWXS	5.0L 4-bbl.	Power	983843
574AMKWB	5.7L 4-bbl.	Mechanical	983843
574AMWXS	5.7L 4-bbl.	Mechanical	983843
574APKWB	5.7L 4-bbl.	Power	983843
574APWXS	5.7L 4-bbl.	Power	983843
	1987		
232AMFTC	2.3L 2-bbl.	Mechanical	984540
232APFTC	2.3L 2-bbl.	Power	984540
232APSRC	2.3L 2-bbl.	Power	985193
302AMARJ	3.0L 2-bbl.	Mechanical	984042
302AMFTC	3.0L 2-bbl.	Mechanical	984042
302APFTC	3.0L 2-bbl.	Power	984042

(continued)

Table 2 COBRA DRIVE MODELS (continued)

Model No.	Engine	Steering	Drive
		1987 (cont.)	
302APSRC	3.0L 2-bbl.	Power	985194
302APSRY	3.0L 2-bbl.	Power	985194
432AMFTC	4.3L 2-bbl.	Mechanical	984541
432AMARY	4.3L 2-bbl.	Mechanical	984541
432APKWB	4.3L 2-bbl.	Power	984541
432APARY	4.3L 2-bbl.	Power	984541
432APSRC	4.3L 2-bbl.	Power	985195
432APSRY	4.3L 2-bbl.	Power	985195
434AMFTC	4.3L 4-bbl.	Mechanical	984541
434AMARY	4.3L 4-bbl.	Mechanical	984541
434APFTC	4.3L 4-bbl.	Power	984541
434APARY	4.3L 4-bbl.	Power	984541
434APSRC	4.3L 4-bbl.	Power	985195
434APSRY	4.3L 4-bbl.	Power	985195
504AMFTC	5.0L 4-bbl.	Mechanical	984542
504AMARY	5.0L 4-bbl.	Mechanical	984542
504APFTC	5.0L 4-bbl.	Power	984542
504APARY	5.0L 4-bbl.	Power	984542
574AMFTC	5.7L 4-bbl.	Mechanical	984543
574AMARY	5.7L 4-bbl.	Mechanical	984543
574APFTC	5.7L 4-bbl.	Power	984543
574APARY	5.7L 4-bbl.	Power	984543
574APSRC	5.7L 4-bbl.	Power	985196
754APFTC	7.5L 4-bbl.	Power	984544
754APSRC	7.5L 4-bbl.	Power	985197
754BPFTC	7.5L 4-bbl.	Power *	984544
754BPSRC	7.5L 4-bbl.	Power *	985197
		1988	
232AMRDGP	2.3L 2-bbl.	Mechanical	985267
232AMRDGE	2.3L 2-bbl.	Mechanical	985267
232APRDGP	2.3L 2-bbl.	Power	985267
232APRDGE	2.3L 2-bbl.	Power	985267
302AMRDGP	3.0L 2-bbl.	Mechanical	985268
302APRDGP	3.0L 2-bbl.	Power	985268
432AMLGDP	4.3L 2-bbl.	Mechanical	985270
432APRGDP	4.3L 2-bbl.	Power	985269
432APRGDE	4.3L 2-bbl.	Power	985269
434AMLGDP	4.3L 4-bbl.	Mechanical	985270
434AMRGDP	4.3L 4-bbl.	Power	985269

(continued)

Table 2 COBRA DRIVE MODELS (continued)

Model No.	Engine	Steering	Drive
		1988 (cont.)	
502AMLGDP	5.0L 2-bbl.	Mechanical	985272
502APRGDP	5.0L 2-bbl.	Power	985271
504AMLGDP	5.0L 4-bbl.	Mechanical	985272
504APRGDP	5.0L 4-bbl.	Power	985271
574AMLGDP	5.7L 4-bbl.	Mechanical	985274
574APRGDP	5.7L 4-bbl.	Power	985273
574BMLGDP	5.7L 4-bbl.	Mechanical *	985274
574BPRGDP	5.7L 4-bbl.	Power *	985273
754BMLGDP	7.5L 4-bbl.	Mechanical *	985276
754BMLGDE	7.5L 4-bbl.	Mechanical *	985276
754BPRGDP	7.5L 4-bbl.	Power *	985275
754BPRGDE	7.5L 4-bbl.	Power *	985275
		1989	
232BMRMEF	2.3L 2-bbl.	Mechanical	985683
232BMRMED	2.3L 2-bbl.	Mechanical	985683
232BPRMED	2.3L 2-bbl.	Power	985683
232BPRMEF	2.3L 2-bbl.	Power	985683
302AMRMED	3.0L 2-bbl.	Mechanical	985684
302APRMED	3.0L 2-bbl.	Power	985684
432AMLMED	4.3L 2-bbl.	Mechanical	985686
432APRMED	4.3L 2-bbl.	Power	985685
262AMLMED	4.3L 4-bbl.	Mechanical*	985686
262APRMED	4.3L 4-bbl.	Power*	985685
502BPRMED	5.0L 2-bbl.	Power	985687
502AMLMED	5.0L 2-bbl.	Mechanical	985688
502APRMED	5.0L 2-bbl.	Power	985687
574AMLMED	5.7L 4-bbl.	Mechanical	985690
574APRMED	5.7L 4-bbl.	Power	985689
350AMLMED	5.7L 4-bbl.	Mechanical*	985690
350APRMED	5.7L 4-bbl.	Power*	985689
584AMLMED	5.8L 4-bbl.	Mechanical	985690
584APRMED	5.8L 4-bbl.	Power	985689
460AMLMED	7.5L 4-bbl.	Mechanical*	985692
460APRMED	7.5L 4-bbl.	Power*	985691

* King Cobra model with thru-transom exhaust.

Chapter Four

Lubrication, Maintenance and Tune-up

All gasoline engines used with OMC Cobra drives are based on automotive engines. The average pleasure boat engine, however, is subjected to operating conditions which are far more severe than those encountered by the average automobile engine. This is particularly true if the engine uses raw water cooling and is used in salt or polluted water. Regular preventive maintenance and proper lubrication will pay dividends in longer engine and stern drive life, as well as safer boat operation.

This chapter provides the basis for such a program. The lubrication and maintenance intervals provided in **Table 1** are those recommended by OMC for normal operation. When the boat is used for continuous heavy duty, high-speed operation or under other severe operating conditions, maintenance and lubrication should be performed more frequently. If the boat is not used regularly, moisture and dirt will collect in and on the engine and stern drive. This eventually leads to rust, corrosion and other damage. Active use of the boat will help to prevent such deterioration.

It is also a good idea to keep the engine and accessory units clean and free of dirt, grime and grease buildup. Such a buildup will eventually reduce the engine's capacity for cooling by preventing heat from radiating from the metal. Keeping the engine clean will assure that it can perform at its top efficiency and has the added benefit of allowing you to locate leaks almost immediately, as they will be far more apparent on a clean engine than on one that has been allowed to accumulate a coating or buildup of contamination.

Tables 1-7 are at the end of the chapter.

PRE-OPERATIONAL CHECKS

Before starting the engine for the first time each day, perform the following checks:

1. Remove the engine compartment cover or hatch and check for the presence of raw gasoline fumes. If the boat is equipped with a bilge blower, turn it on for a few minutes. If

strong fumes can be smelled, determine their source and correct the problem before proceeding.

WARNING
Always have a Coast Guard-approved fire extinguisher close at hand when working around the engine.

2. Check the engine oil level with the dipstick as described in this chapter. Add oil if the level is low.
3. Check the electrolyte level in each battery cell as described in this chapter. Add distilled water, if necessary.
4. Check the power steering pump fluid level, if so equipped.
5. Check the condition of all drive belts. If a belt is in doubtful condition, replace it. Spare belts are difficult to obtain offshore.
6. Check all water hoses for leaks, loose connections and general condition; repair or replace as required.
7. Check the oil level in the stern drive unit as described in this chapter. Add lubricant if necessary.
8. Check the fluid level in the trim/tilt reservoir, if so equipped. Add fluid if required.
9. Check the bilge for excessive water. Drain or pump dry if present.
10. Check the propeller for nicks, dents, missing metal, etc. Repair or replace if damaged.
11. Turn on the fuel tank valve(s).
12. Connect the battery cables to the battery (if disconnected).
13. Reinstall the engine compartment cover or hatch.

STARTING CHECKLIST

After performing the pre-operational checks, the following starting check list should be followed:

1. If equipped with a bilge blower, operate it for at least 5 minutes before starting the engine.
2. Make sure the stern drive unit is fully down and in operating position.
3. If the engine is cold, prime it by operating the throttle one or two times.
4. Make sure the gearshift lever is in NEUTRAL.

WARNING
Always have a fully charged fire extinguisher at hand before attempting to start the engine.

5. Start the engine and let it run at idle speed for a few minutes.

CAUTION
Prolonged operation of the engine with the gearshift lever in NEUTRAL can cause damage to gears in the stern drive unit due to improper circulation of the lubricant.

6. Note the gauges and warning lights to make sure that the engine is not overheating, that proper oil pressure is present and that the battery is not discharging. If any of these conditions occur, shut the engine down at once. Determine the cause and correct the problem before proceeding.

POST-OPERATIONAL CHECKS

Perform the following maintenance after each use:

1. If the boat was used in salt or polluted water, flush the cooling system with fresh water as described in this chapter. This will minimize corrosion and buildup of deposits in the cooling system.
2. Disconnect the battery cables from the battery. You may want to remove the battery from the boat to prevent its theft.
3. Shut off the fuel tank valve(s).
4. Top off the fuel tank(s), if possible. This will minimize the possibility of moisture condensation in the tank(s).
5. If water is present in the bilge, either drain or pump dry.

6. Wash the interior and exterior surfaces of the boat with fresh water.

COOLING SYSTEM FLUSHING

Flushing procedures differ depending upon the location of the water pump. Regardless of pump location, cooling water must *always* circulate through the stern drive whenever the engine is running to prevent damage to the pump impeller. On models equipped with a closed cooling system and a seawater pump in addition to the seawater pump in the drive unit, *both* pumps must be supplied with cooling water.

WARNING
When the cooling system is flushed, make sure that there is sufficient space to the side and behind the propeller and that no one is standing in the vicinity. If possible, remove the propeller to prevent the possibility of serious personal injury.

Standard Cooling System

A flush-test device must be used with this procedure to provide cooling water. **Figure 1** shows a typical unit in use.

1. Attach the flush-test device directly over the intake holes in the gear housing. Connect a hose between the device and the water tap.

CAUTION
Do not use full water tap pressure in Step 2.

2. Partially open the water tap to allow a low-pressure flow of water into the device.

CAUTION
Do not run the engine above idle speed while flushing the system in Step 3.

3. Place the gearshift lever in NEUTRAL. Start the engine and run at normal idle until the engine reaches normal operating temperature, as shown on the temperature gauge.

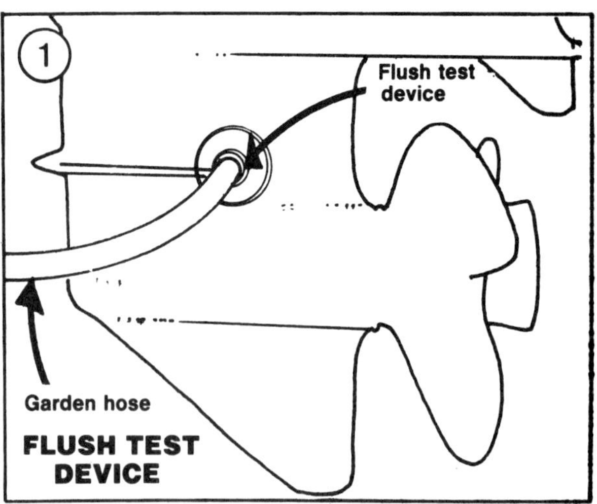

FLUSH TEST DEVICE

4. Watch the water being flushed from the cooling system. When the flow is clear, shut the engine off.
5. Shut the water tap off. Disconnect and remove the flush-test device from the gear housing.

Closed Cooling System

If the engine is to be flushed with the boat still in the water, a seawater petcock must be installed between the water pickup and pump inlet.

1. If the boat is to remain in the water for this procedure, close the seawater petcock.
2. Loosen the water intake hose clamp and remove the hose from the water pump inlet.
3. Connect a length of garden hose between the water pump inlet and a water tap.

CAUTION
Do not use full water tap pressure in Step 4.

4. Partially open the water tap to allow a low-pressure flow of water into the pump inlet.

CAUTION
Make sure that water is being discharged from the exhaust outlets in Step 5. If not, shut the engine off immediately and check the flushing hose connections.

5. Place the remote control handle in NEUTRAL. Start the engine and run at idle until the engine reaches normal operating temperature, as shown by the temperature gauge.

6. Watch the water being flushed from the cooling system. When the flow is clear, shut the engine off.

7. Shut the water tap off and remove the garden hose from the water pump inlet and water tap. Reconnect the water intake hose to the pump inlet and tighten the clamp securely.

8. Open the seawater petcock.

ENGINE MAINTENANCE AND LUBRICATION

The maintenance tasks discussed in this section should be performed at the intervals indicated in **Table 1**. These intervals are only guidelines, however. Consider the frequency and extent of boat use when establishing the actual intervals. You should perform the tasks more frequently if the boat is used under severe service conditions.

Engine Oil Level Check

All engines will consume a certain amount of oil as a lubricating and cooling agent. The rate of consumption is highest during a new engine's break-in period, but should stabilize after approximately 100 hours of operation. It is not unusual for a 4-cylinder engine to consume up to a quart of oil in 5-10 hours of wide-open throttle operation.

For this reason, you should check the oil level at least every 15 days. If the boat is used more frequently, check the level each time the engine is shut down, allowing approximately 5 minutes for the oil in the upper end to drain back into the crankcase oil pan.

1. With the boat at rest in the water and the engine off, pull out the dipstick. See **Figure 2** (inline) or **Figure 3** (V6 and V8) for typical locations. Wipe it with a clean rag or paper towel, reinsert it and pull it out again. Note the oil level on the dipstick.

NOTE
Some dipsticks have ADD and FULL lines. Others read ADD 1 QT. and OPERATING RANGE. In either case, keep the oil level above the upper line.

2. Top up to the FULL or OPERATING RANGE mark on the dipstick, if necessary, using OMC Cobra® Premium 4-cycle SAE

4

30 motor oil. If this is not available, any good quality automotive oil carrying an API designation of SF may be used. See **Table 2** for the proper single viscosity oil to be used (OMC does not recommend the use of multi-viscosity oils). Remove the oil filler cap and add oil through the hole in the valve cover. See **Figure 4** (inline) or **Figure 5** (V6 and V8), typical.

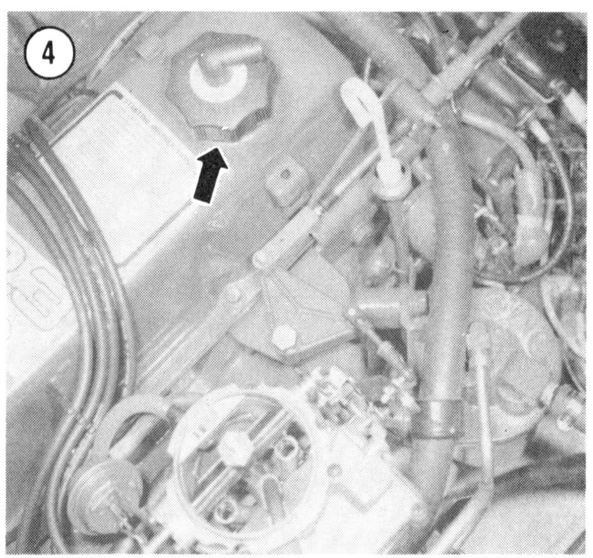

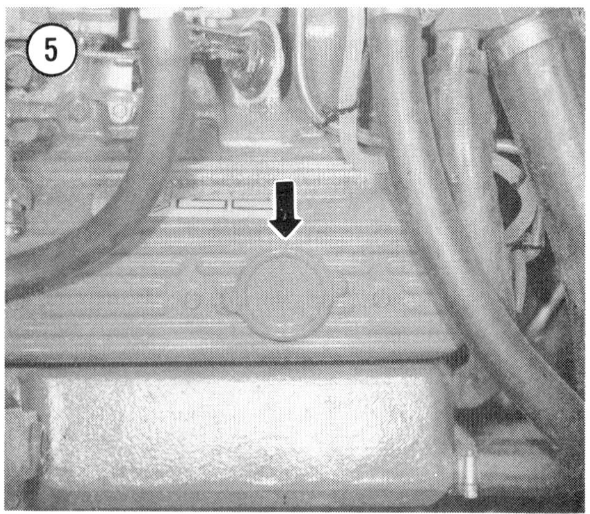

Engine Oil and Filter Change

The engine oil and filter should be changed at the end of the 20 hour break-in period, then every 50 hours of operating time or 6 months, whichever comes first. At a minimum, the oil and filter should be changed at least once per season. OMC recommends the use of its Cobra® Premium 4-cycle SAE 30 motor oil. If this is not available, any good quality automotive oil carrying an API designation of SF may be used. See **Table 2** for the proper viscosity oil (OMC does not recommend the use of 10W-30 and 10W-40 multi-viscosity oils) according to the lowest ambient temperature expected during the period the boat will be used.

Most installations do not leave enough space to permit the use of the oil pan drain plug. For this reason, an oil drain suction pump is the most common device used to drain the crankcase oil. The pump has a long flexible hose which is inserted into the oil withdrawal tube (2.5L and 3.0L) or oil dipstick tube (all others) and fed into the crankcase. OMC offers an oil drain kit (part No. 172473); several makes of pumps are also available from marine supply dealers. Some are hand-operated, some are motorized and others are designed to be operated with an electric drill (**Figure 6**).

The used oil should be discharged into a sealable container and properly disposed of. There are several ways to discard the old oil safely. Many auto supply stores sell an oil disposal kit which contains a quantity of sawdust-like material designed to absorb the oil. After pouring the oil into the bag containing this material, the bag is sealed and the entire box disposed of.

Plastic bleach and milk containers are also excellent for oil disposal. The oil can then be taken to a service station for recycling or, where permitted, thrown in your household trash.

NOTE
Check local regulations before disposing of oil in the trash. Never

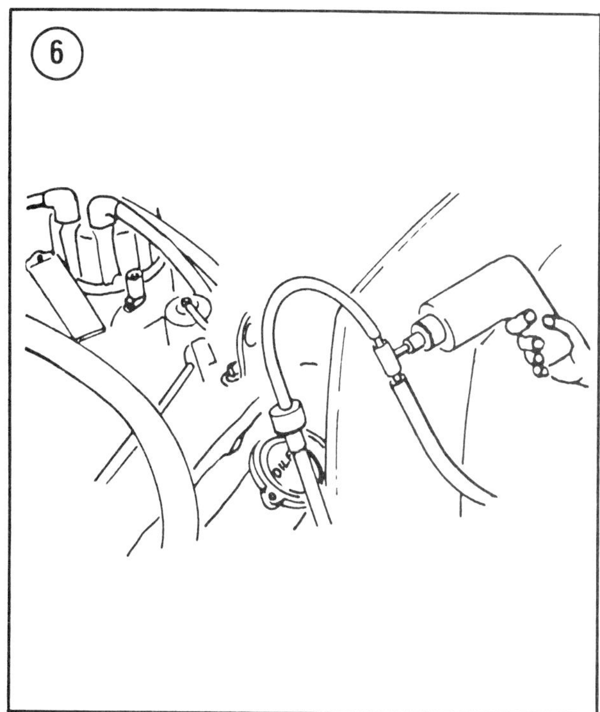

dump used oil overboard or on the ground.

Oil filters are the disposable spin-on type. An inexpensive oil filter wrench can be obtained from any auto parts or marine supply store. This wrench is handy in removing oil filters, but should *not* be used to install the new filter. A firm fit is all that is required; overtightening the filter can damage it and/or cause an oil leak.

The installed angle of the engine affects oil level in the crankcase. To assure that the oil is drained and replaced properly, perform the following procedure with the boat at rest in the water.

1. Start the engine and warm to normal operating temperature under load, then shut it off.
2. Remove the dipstick, wipe it clean with a lint-free cloth or paper towel and place it to one side out of the way. On 3.0L engines, remove the cap from the withdrawal tube.
3. Insert the oil drain pump hose into the oil withdrawal tube (3.0L) or dipstick tube (all others) as far as it will go.
4. Insert the other pump hose into a sealable container large enough to hold the oil from the crankcase. Most engine crankcases hold 4-6 quarts of oil. Refer to **Table 3** to determine the capacity of your engine crankcase.
5. Operate the pump until it has removed all of the oil possible from the crankcase. Remove the pump hose from the withdrawal or dipstick tube.
6. Place a drain pan or other suitable container under the filter to catch any oil spillage when the filter is removed. See **Figure 7** (typical).
7. Unscrew the filter counterclockwise. Use the filter wrench if the filter is too tight or too hot to remove by hand.
8. Wipe the gasket surface on the engine block clean with a paper towel.
9. Coat the neoprene gasket on the new filter with a thin coat of clean engine oil.
10. Screw the new filter onto the engine *by hand* until the gasket just touches the engine block. At this point, there will be a very slight resistance when turning the filter.
11. Tighten the filter another 1/2-3/4 turn *by hand.* If the filter wrench is used, the filter will

probably be overtightened. This can damage the filter or cause an oil leak.

12. Remove the oil filler cap from the valve cover. See **Figure 4** (inline) or **Figure 5** (V6 and V8), typical.

13. Reinstall the dipstick in the dipstick tube or the cap on the withdrawal tube.

14. Refer to **Table 3** to determine the crankcase capacity of your engine. Pour the specified amount of oil into the valve cover opening and install the oil filler cap. Wipe up any spills on the valve cover with a clean cloth as they occur.

NOTE

Check the area under and around the oil filter for leaks while the engine is running in Step 15.

15. Start the engine and let it idle for 5 minutes, then shut the engine off.

16. Wait approximately 5 minutes, then remove the dipstick. Wipe the dipstick clean with a lint-free cloth or paper towel and reinsert it in the dipstick tube. Remove the dipstick a second time and check the oil level. Add oil, if necessary, to bring the level up to the FULL or OPERATING RANGE mark, but do *not* overfill.

Power Steering Service

If equipped with power steering, check the fluid level in the pump reservoir each time the oil is changed as described in this chapter. Top up if necessary with GM Power Steering Fluid. If this is not available, DEXRON II automatic transmission fluid or OMC Power Trim and Tilt Fluid may be used.

Fuel System Service

This service is particularly important, especially if the boat is equipped with fiberglass fuel tanks. Some types of fiberglass tanks contain a residue of particles which will prematurely clog the filter. Others contain a wax used in their manufacture which dissolves in gasoline. This wax is trapped by the filter, but since it cannot be seen, the filter appears to be clean. The resulting lean-out condition can only be cured by installing a new filter.

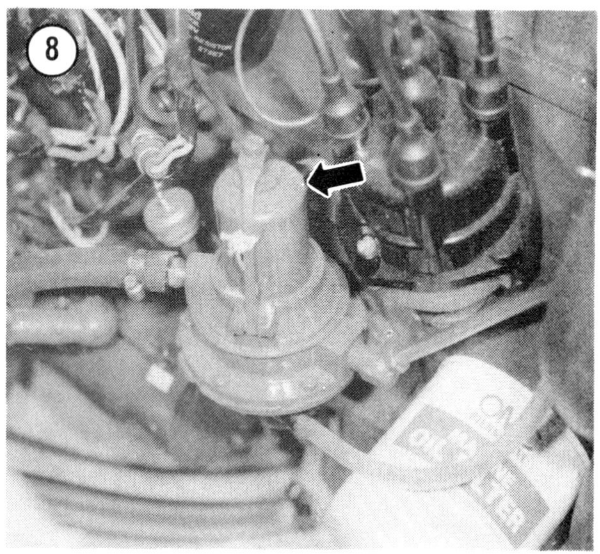

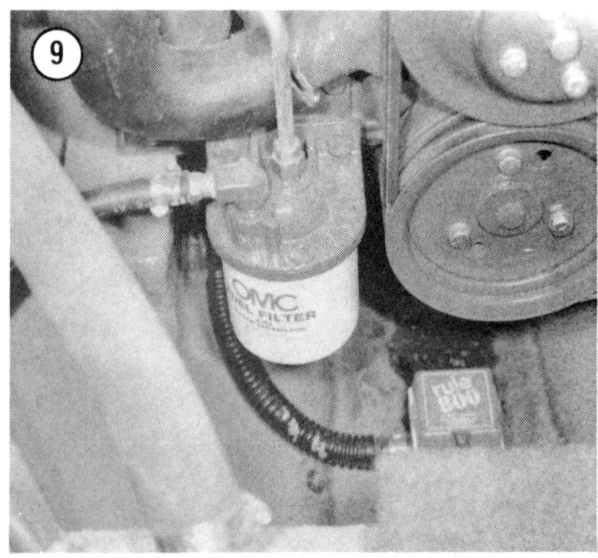

All fuel lines should be checked for deterioration or loose connections at the intervals specified in **Table 1** and replaced or tightened as required.

Replace the 3.0L fuel pump filter (**Figure 8**), canister-type filter (**Figure 9**) and

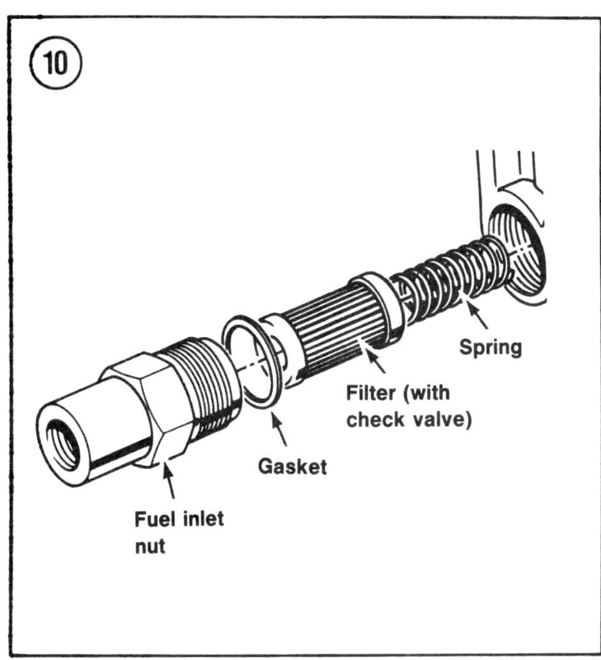

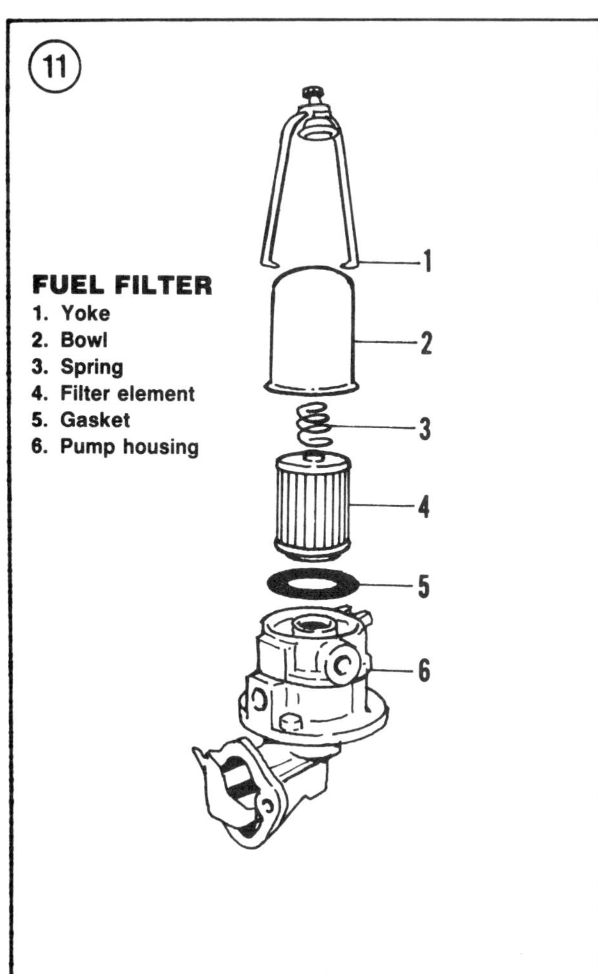

FUEL FILTER
1. Yoke
2. Bowl
3. Spring
4. Filter element
5. Gasket
6. Pump housing

carburetor fuel inlet filter (**Figure 10**) at least once a year and more often if operating conditions are severe. Clean the fuel inlet nut screen used with 7.5L carburetors at the same intervals.

NOTE
In areas where only poor quality fuel is available or where moisture tends to condense in fuel tanks, it is advisable to install an inline fuel filter to remove moisture and other contaminants. These are sold as accessory items by marine supply dealers.

Fuel Pump Sediment Bowl Filter Replacement

Refer to **Figure 11** for this procedure.

1. Loosen the sediment bowl yoke screw. Swing the yoke over the bowl. Remove the bowl and filter spring.
2. Remove and discard the filter and bowl gasket.
3. Wash the bowl thoroughly in clean solvent and blow dry with compressed air.
4. Installation is the reverse of removal. Tighten the yoke screw securely. Start the engine and check for leaks.

Canister-type Filter Replacement

This type of fuel filter looks like an oil filter (**Figure 9**) and is replaced using a procedure similar to that for oil filter replacement. Unscrew the filter canister from the filter adapter (using a filter wrench, if necessary) and discard. Wipe the neoprene gasket on the new filter with a thin film of clean engine oil and screw the filter onto the adapter until it is snug—do not overtighten. Start the engine and check for leaks.

Carburetor Fuel Inlet Filter Replacement

Refer to **Figure 10** for this procedure.

1. Remove the flame arrestor or cover (**Figure 12**) if necessary to provide adequate working clearance.
2. Place one wrench on the carburetor inlet nut (A, **Figure 13**). Place a second wrench on the fuel line connector nut (B, **Figure 13**). Hold the fuel inlet nut from moving and loosen the connector nut.
3. Disconnect the fuel line from the inlet nut fitting.
4. Remove the filter element and spring from the carburetor fuel inlet.
5. Remove and discard the inlet nut gasket.
6. Installation is the reverse of removal. Make sure the end of the filter with the hole faces the inlet nut. Use a new gasket. Tighten the inlet nut and connector nut snugly.
7. Install the flame arrestor, if removed. Start the engine and check for leaks.

Fuel Quality

Gasoline blended with alcohol and sold for marine use is widely available, although this fact may not be advertised and it is not legally required to be labeled as such in many states. Using such fuels is not recommended unless you can determine the nature of the blend. A mixture of 10 perecent ethyl alcohol and 90 percent unleaded gasoline is called gasohol.

Fuels with an alcohol content tend to slowly absorb moisture from the air. When the moisture content of the fuel reaches approximately one percent, it combines with the alcohol and separates from the fuel. This separation does not normally occur when gasohol is used in an automobile, as the tank is generally emptied within a few days after filling it.

The problem does occur in marine use, however, because boats often remain idle for days or even weeks between start-ups. This length of time permits separation to take place. The water-alcohol mixture settles at the bottom of the tank where the fuel pickup

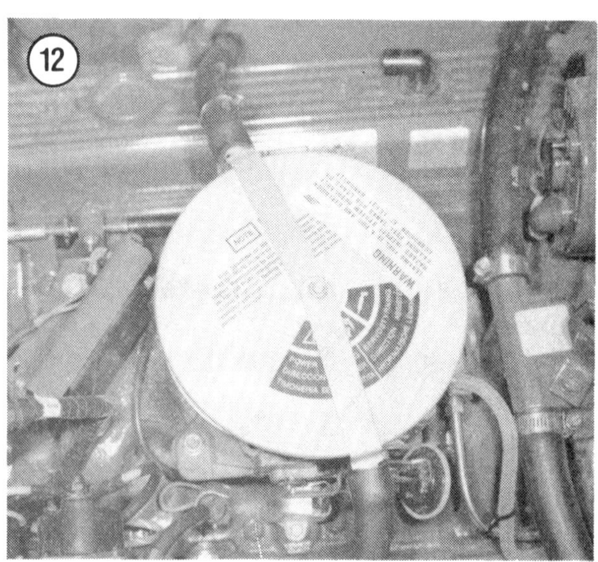

carries it into the fuel line. Since the engine will not run on this mixture, it is necessary to drain the fuel tank, flush out the fuel system with clean gasoline and then remove and clean the spark plugs before the engine can be started. If it is necessary to operate an engine on gasohol, do not store such fuel in the tank(s) for more than a few days, especially in climates with high humidity.

Some methods of blending alcohol with gasoline now make use of cosolvents as suspension agents to prevent the water-alcohol from separating from the gasoline. Regardless of the method used, however, alcohol mixed with gasoline in any manner can cause numerous and serious problems with a marine engine and fuel system. Among them are performance problems (such as vapor lock, hard starting or a low-speed stall), fuel tank corrosion and deterioration of fuel lines and other nonmetallic fuel system components (O-ring seals, inlet needle tips, accelerator pump cups and gaskets).

The problem of gasoline blended with alcohol has become so prevalent around the United States that Miller Tools (32615 Park Lane, Garden City, MI 48135) and Kent-Moore 28635 Mound Road, Warren,

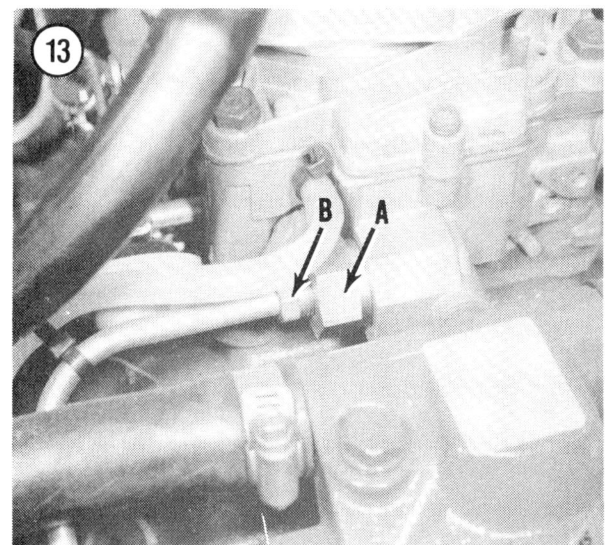
13
B
A

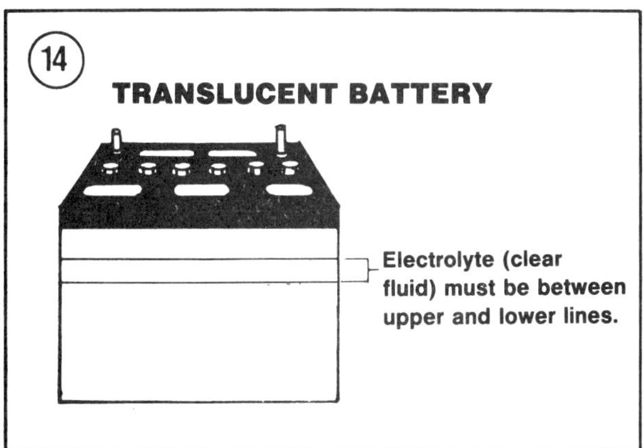
14
TRANSLUCENT BATTERY
Electrolyte (clear fluid) must be between upper and lower lines.

MI 48092) now offer Alcohol Detection Kits so owners can determine the quality of the fuel being used.

The detection procedure is performed with water as a reacting agent. However, if cosolvents have been used as suspension agents in alcohol blending, the test will not show the presence of alcohol unless ethylene glycol (automotive antifreeze) is used instead of water as a reacting agent. It is suggested that a gasoline sample be tested twice using the detection kit: first with water and then with ethylene glycol (automotive antifreeze).

The procedure cannot differentiate between types of alcohol (ethanol, methanol, etc.) nor is it considered to be absolutely accurate from a scientific standpoint, but it is accurate enough to determine whether or not there is sufficient alcohol in the fuel to cause the user to take precautions. Maintaining a close watch on the quality of fuel used can save hundreds of dollars in marine engine and fuel system repairs.

Flame Arrestor

The flame arrestor (**Figure 12**, typical) serves as both an air filter and as a safety precaution against engine backfiring that might cause a dangerous explosion in the engine compartment. Remove and service the flame arrestor every 25 hours of operation or once per season. Wash in solvent and air dry thoroughly. Make sure the air inlet screen is not deformed and reinstall the flame arrestor.

Battery

Remove the battery vent caps and check battery electrolyte level. On translucent batteries, it should be between the marks on the battery case (**Figure 14**). On black batteries, it should be about 3/16 in. above the plates or even with the bottom of the filler wells. See **Figure 15**. Test the battery condition with a hydrometer (**Figure 16**). See Chapter Eleven.

Steering System Lubrication

The steering ram should be lubricated every 60 days with OMC Triple-Guard grease. See **Figure 17** (mechanical steering) or **Figure 18** (power steering).

If equipped with power steering, lubricate the actuator valve fitting (**Figure 19**) every 6 months with approximately 1 ounce of OMC Marine Wheel Bearing Grease or OMC Extreme Pressure Grease. Move the actuator back and forth to purge any air pockets and distribute the grease evenly. This lubrication

15

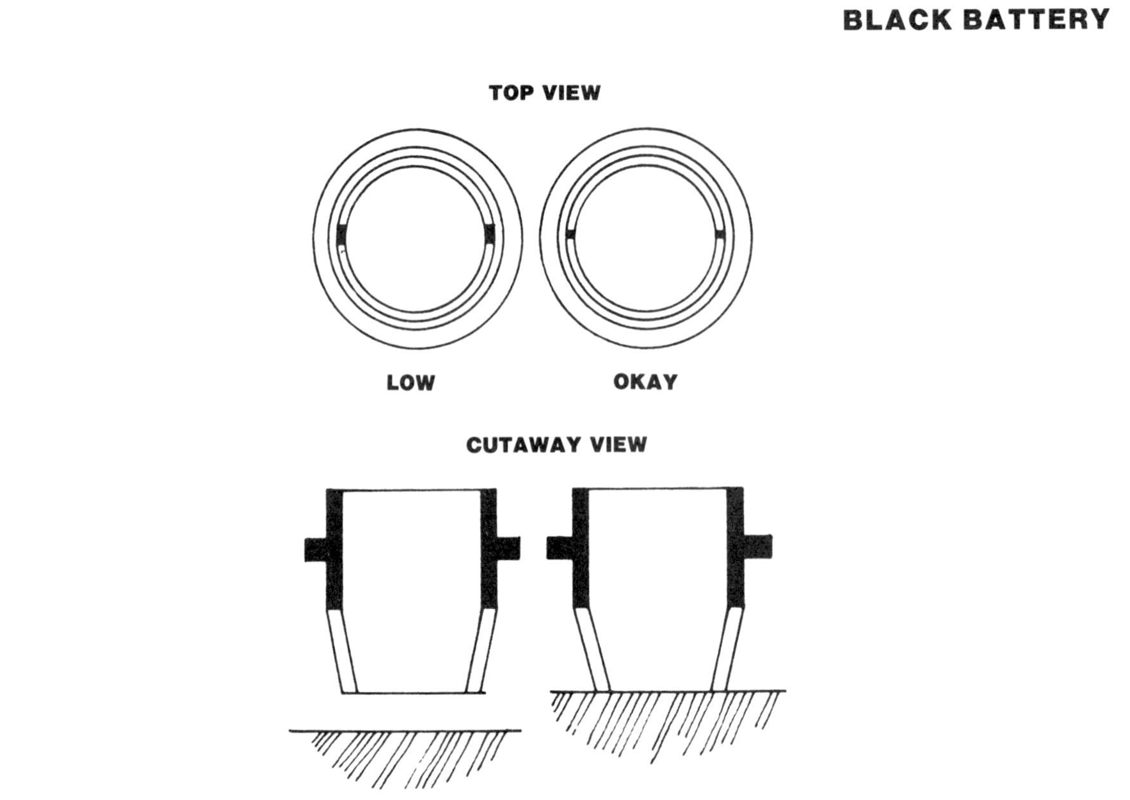

BLACK BATTERY
TOP VIEW
LOW
OKAY
CUTAWAY VIEW

16

Hydrometer
Read with
hydrometer level
Cell

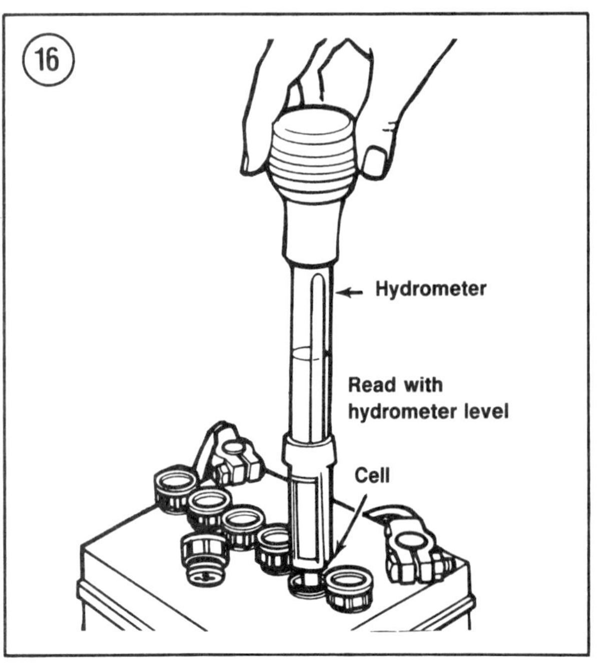

17

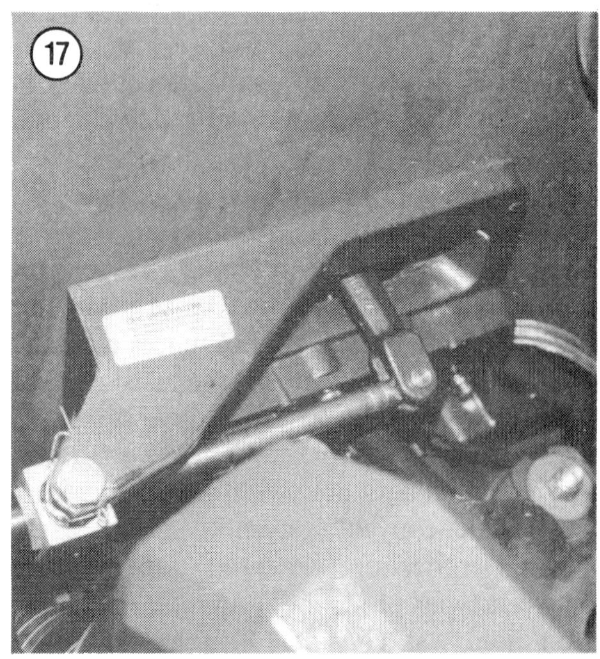

is vital to maintaining proper steering control and should not be overlooked.

STERN DRIVE LUBRICATION

The lubrication tasks described in this section should be performed at the intervals indicated in **Table 1**. These intervals are only guidelines, however. Consider the frequency and extent of boat use when setting actual intervals and perform the tasks more frequently if the boat is used under severe service conditions.

Stern drive capacities are listed in **Table 4**; recommended lubricants are provided in **Table 5**. Lubricate all Cobra drives with OMC Hi-Vis Lubricant. Use of regular automotive grease or other substitute lubricant will result in premature failure. Dispose of old lubricant properly. Disposal methods discussed under *Engine Oil and Filter Change* in this chapter are applicable.

Fluid Check

Check stern drive lubricant level when the unit is cool.

1. With the drive unit in a vertical position, unscrew and remove the dipstick on the top of the drive unit (**Figure 20**).
2. Wipe dipstick clean with a lint-free cloth or paper towel, then thread it back in place.
3. Wait a few seconds, then remove the dipstick a second time and check the oil level.
4. Loosen and momentarily remove, then reinstall the oil drain plug. If more than a teaspoon of water drains from the hole or if the lubricant has a milky-white or milky-brown color, have the stern drive checked by a dealer to determine and correct the problem before running the unit again.
5. If the oil level is low, reinstall the dipstick tightly and remove the oil fill plug from the

side of the gearcase. See A, **Figure 21.** This creates an air lock which holds the lubricant in the gearcase.

6. Add sufficient OMC Hi-Vis lubricant to bring the level to the FULL mark on the dipstick, then install the oil fill plug.

7. Remove the dipstick a second time and recheck the oil level. It may be necessary to repeat this action more than once, but do *not* overfill.

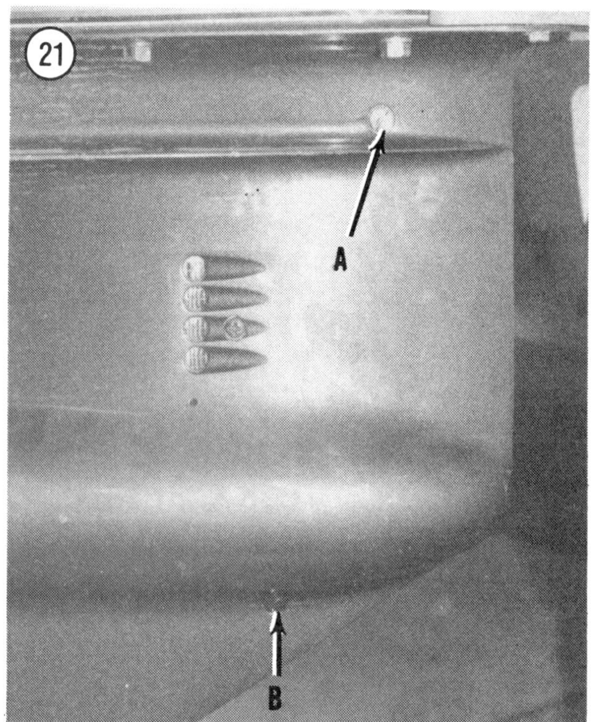

Fluid Change

1. With the drive unit in a vertical position, place a suitable container underneath the oil drain plug.
2. Unscrew and remove the dipstick on the top of the drive unit (**Figure 20**) and the oil drain plug (**Figure 21**).
3. Allow the drive unit lubricant to drain *completely,* then reinstall the oil drain plug.
4. Remove the oil fill plug (A, **Figure 21**) and fill the drive unit with the required amount of OMC Hi-Vis lubricant. Reinstall the oil fill plug.
5. Wipe the dipstick clean with a lint-free cloth or paper towel and insert it in the dipstick hole but do *not* thread it in place—simply let the dipstick cap rest in the hole. This method results in a slight overfill to compensate for the oil level drop that will occur as a result of trapped air being purged from the system when the drive is operated.
6. When lubricant level is correct, reinstall the dipstick and tighten securely.

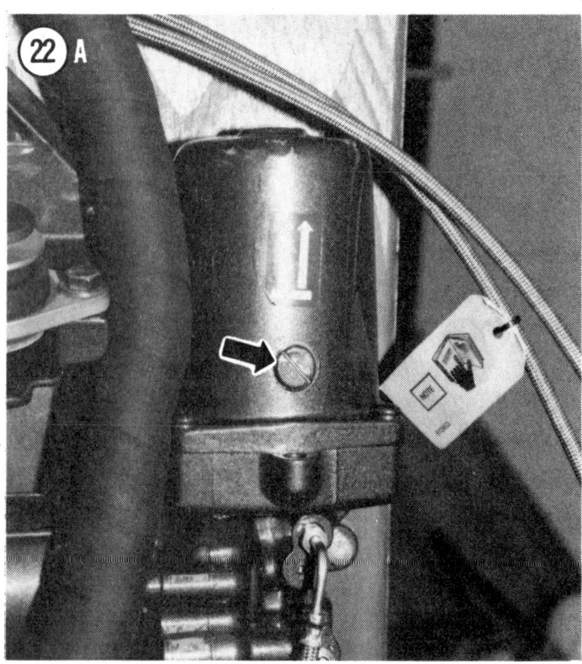

Gimbal Housing and U-joint Lubrication

The gimbal housing bearing and universal joints must be lubricated at least once a year or permanent damage to the stern drive unit will result. Lubrication requires removal of the stern drive unit as described in Chapter Twelve.

The gimbal bearing grease fitting is located on the starboard side of the gimbal housing. The U-joint grease fittings are located on the double cardan U-joint. Each fitting should be lubricated with OMC Marine Wheel Bearing

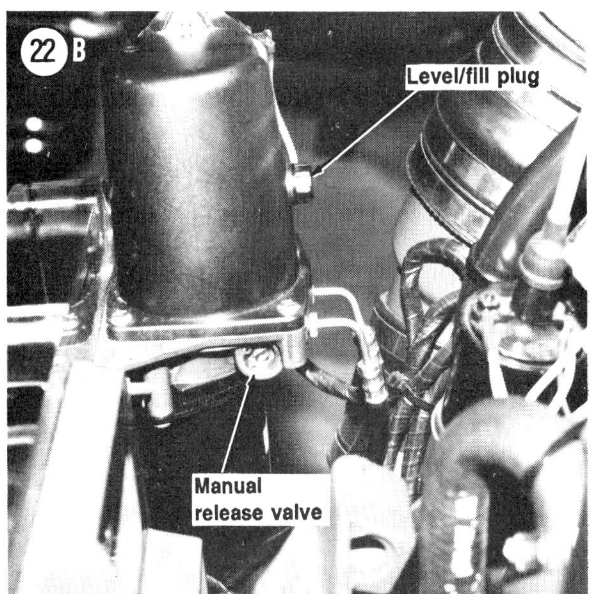

grease until the old grease has been forced out and new grease appears. Wipe the fitting and remove all excess grease.

Before reinstalling the drive, lubricate the U-joint shaft splines with OMC Triple-Guard grease and apply a light coat of engine oil to the O-rings on the shaft. Check the bellows for damage and/or deterioration and replace as required. Once the stern drive unit has been reinstalled, check engine alignment as described in Chapters Six-Eight, according to your engine.

Power Trim/Tilt Reservoir Fluid Check

The trim/tilt unit reservoir, hydraulic pump and motor are a combined self-contained unit. At the start of each season, check the reservoir fluid level as follows.

WARNING

If the level/fill plug is removed with the stern drive unit down, pressure in the reservoir will force an oil spray from the plug hole which could result in serious personal injury if it were to spray in your face or eyes.

1. With the stern drive unit tilted up, remove the level/fill plug from the reservoir housing. See **Figure 22A** for 1986-1988 models and **Figure 22B** for 1989 models.
2. If the fluid level is not at the bottom of the fill hole with the stern drive unit at full tilt, add OMC Power Trim and Tilt fluid to bring the fluid to its correct level.
3. Reinstall the level/fill plug and tighten securely.

Power Trim/Tilt Reservoir Fluid Change

1986 models

1. Raise the stern drive unit to its full UP position and prop it up to prevent its weight from pressurizing the system and resulting in a messy fluid spill.
2. Mark the TOP hydraulic line. Place a suitable container under the reservoir and open the manual release valve one full turn. See **Figure 23**.
3. Slowly remove the level/fill plug (**Figure 22**) in case of residual pressure in the reservoir.
4. Remove the manufacturing plug (**Figure 24**) and drain the fluid from the valve body. While the fluid is draining, manually lower the stern drive unit to force any oil from the base of the trim/tilt cylinders.

4

5. When the fluid has drained, return the stern drive to its full UP position. Reinstall the manufacturing plug and add OMC Power Trim and Tilt fluid through the reservoir fill hole. When fluid level is at the bottom of the hole, bleed the system by cycling the stern drive unit at least 5 times, then add fluid as required to bring the level to the bottom of the hole. Reinstall the level/fill plug and return the drive unit to its full DOWN position.

1987-1988

1. Raise the stern drive unit to its full UP position and prop it up to prevent its weight from pressurizing the system and resulting in a messy fluid spill.
2. Place a suitable container under the reservoir and slowly remove the level/fill plug (**Figure 22**) in case of residual pressure in the reservoir.
3. Remove the manual release valve (**Figure 23**) and drain the fluid from the valve body. While the fluid is draining, manually lower the stern drive unit to force any fluid from the base of the trim/tilt cylinders.
4. When the fluid has drained, return the stern drive to its full UP position. Reinstall the manual release valve and add OMC Power Trim and Tilt fluid through the reservoir fill hole. When fluid level is at the bottom of the hole, bleed the system by cycling the stern drive unit at least 5 times, then add fluid as required to bring the level to the bottom of the hole. Reinstall the level/fill plug and return the drive unit to its full DOWN position.

1989

1. Raise the stern drive unit to its full UP position and prop it up to prevent its weight from pressurizing the system and resulting in a messy fluid spill.

2. Place a suitable container under the reservoir and slowly remove the level/fill plug (**Figure 22B**) in case of residual pressure in the reservoir.
3. Remove the manual release valve (**Figure 22B**) and drain the fluid from the valve body. While the fluid is draining, manually lower the stern drive unit to force any fluid from the base of the trim/tilt cylinders.
4. When the fluid has drained, return the stern drive to its full UP position. Reinstall the manual release valve and add OMC Power Trim and Tilt fluid through the reservoir fill hole. When fluid level is at the bottom of the hole, bleed the system by cycling the stern drive unit at least 5 times, then add fluid as required to bring the level to the bottom of the hole. Reinstall the level/fill plug and return the drive unit to its full DOWN postion.

ENGINE TUNE-UP

A smooth running, dependable marine engine is more than a convenience. At sea, it can mean your life. To keep your engine running right, you must follow a regular program of preventive maintenance.

Part of any preventive maintenance program is a thorough engine tune-up. A tune-up is a series of accurate adjustments necessary to restore maximum power and performance. In addition, some ignition parts

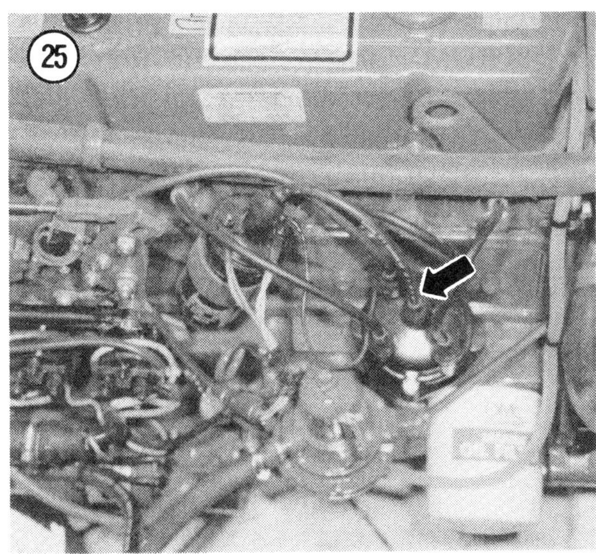

25

which deteriorate with use must be replaced. Engine tune-ups are generally recommended at 50-hour intervals. If the engine is used infrequently, a tune-up should be performed at least once a season. Tune-up specifications are provided in **Table 6** at the end of the chapter.

Whenever a tune-up is performed, the propeller should be replaced by the recommended OMC test wheel (**Table 7**). Use of the propeller or an incorrect test wheel can result in engine damage. Never operate the engine above the maximum recommended rpm.

a. Compression check.

b. Ignition system work.

c. Carburetor inspection and adjustment.

Careful and accurate adjustment is crucial to a successful engine tune-up. Each procedure in this section must be performed exactly as described and in the order presented.

WARNING
Marine components are more expensive than comparable automotive parts (contact breaker points, distributors, carburetors, etc.), but they are designed to operate in different environments. Automotive parts should ***not*** *be substituted for safety reasons, as well as long component life. Major reasons for this are found in Section 183.410 (a) of the Coast Guard Electrical and Fuel Systems Standards.*

COMPRESSION CHECK

An engine with low or uneven compression cannot be properly tuned. A compression test measures the compression pressure that builds up in each cylinder. Its results can be used to assess general cylinder and valve condition. In addition, it can warn or developing problems inside the engine.

1. If the boat is not in the water, install a flush-test device to provide water before operating the engine.
2. Warm the engine to normal operating temperature, then shut it off.
3. Remove the flame arrestor and make sure that the choke and throttle valves are completely open.
4. Disconnect the coil high tension (thick) lead at the distributor cap tower (**Figure 25**, typical) and ground the lead at the engine block.
5. Remove the spark plugs as described in this chapter.
6. Connect a remote start switch to the starter solenoid or assist solenoid according to manufacturer's instructions. Leave the ignition switch in the OFF position.
7. Connect a screw-in compression tester to the No. 1 cylinder according to manufacturer's instructions. Refer to **Figure 26** for the location of the No. 1 cylinder according to engine.
8. Crank the engine at least 5 turns with the remote start switch or until there is no further increase in compression shown on the tester gauge.
9. Remove the compression tester and record the reading. Relieve the tester pressure valve.

10. Repeat Steps 7-9 for each remaining cylinder.

When interpreting the results, actual readings are not as important as the difference between readings. The lowest reading on Ford engines should be 75 percent of the highest. Any variation of less than 20 percent (GM) or 25 percent (Ford) is acceptable. Greater differences indicate that an engine overhaul is required because of worn or broken rings, leaky or sticking valves or a combination of all.

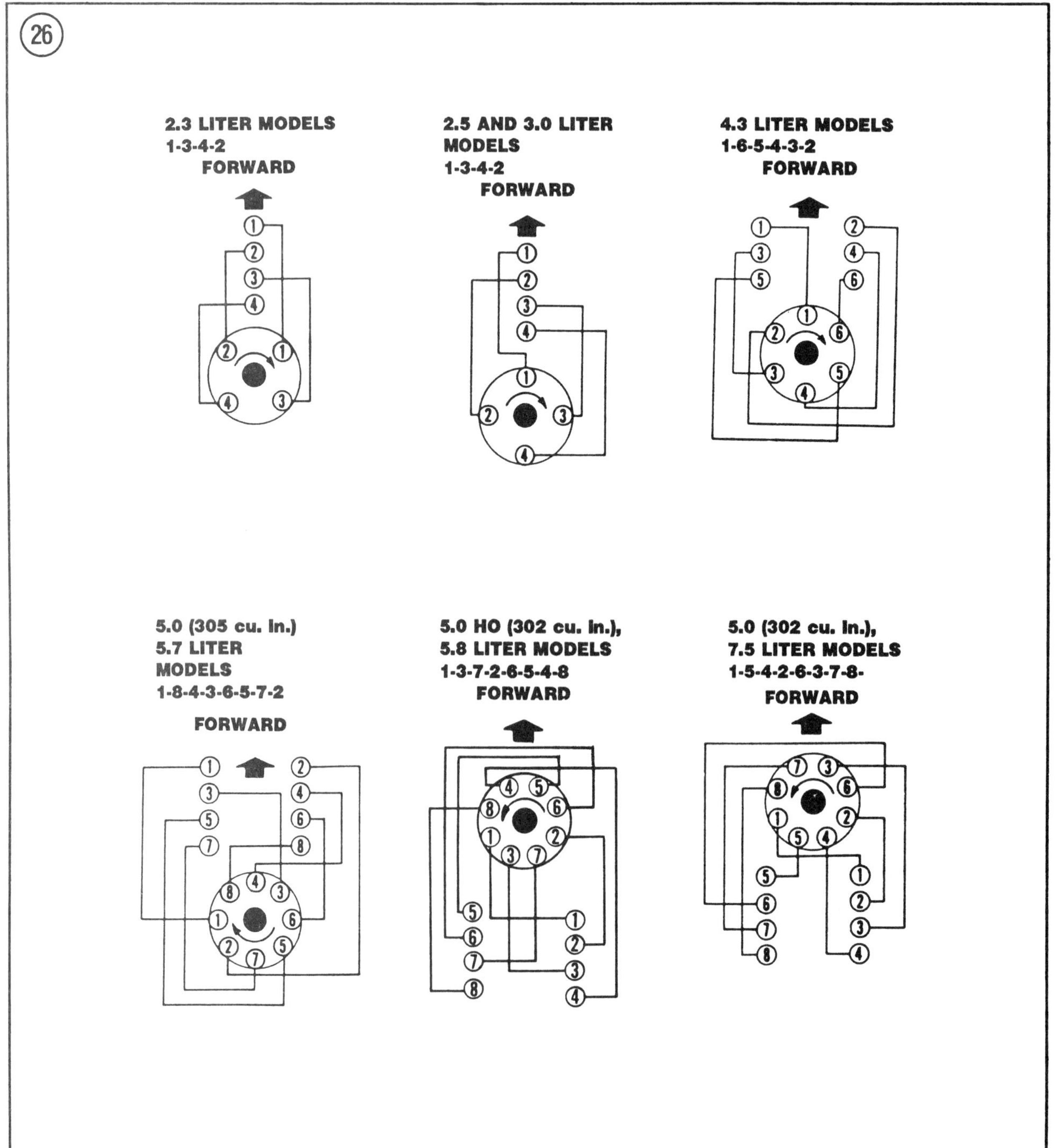

If the compression test indicates a problem (excessive variation in readings), isolate the cause with a wet compression test. This is performed in the same way as the dry test, except that about 1 tablespoon of heavy engine oil (at least SAE 30) is poured down the spark plug hole before performing Steps 7-9. If the wet compression readings are much greater than the dry compression readings, the trouble is probably caused by worn or broken rings. If there is little difference between the wet and dry readings, the problem is probably due to leaky or sticking valves. If 2 adjacent cylinders read low on both tests, the head gasket may be leaking.

Use a vacuum gauge and compare the vacuum gauge and compression tester readings to isolate the problem more closely. **Figure 27** provides interpretation of vacuum gauge readings.

IGNITION SYSTEM

A mechanical contact breaker point ignition system is used on all engines covered in this manual. The ignition system may contain a Delco-Remy, Mallory or Prestolite distributor. **Figure 28** (GM engines) and **Figure 29** (Ford engines) show the major components and wiring of the ignition system.

Spark Plug Removal

Refer to **Figure 26** for spark plug routing according to engine.

CAUTION

Whenever the spark plugs are removed, dirt from around them can fall into the spark plug holes. This can cause expensive engine damage.

1. Blow out any foreign matter that may have accumulated around the spark plugs with compressed air. Use a compressor if you have one or a can of inert gas available at photo stores.
2. Disconnect the spark plug wires by twisting the wire boot back and forth on the plug insulator while pulling upward (**Figure 30**). Pulling on the wire instead of the boot may break it. In some cases, you may find spark plug wire removal pliers (**Figure 31**) useful, especially when working around a warm or hot engine.
3. Remove the plugs with an appropriate size spark plug socket. Keep the plugs in order so you know which cylinder each came from. See **Figure 32**.
4. Examine each spark plug and compare its appearance with the illustrations in Chapter Three. Electrode appearance is a good indication of performance in each cylinder and permits early recognition of trouble.
5. Discard the plugs. Although they could be cleaned, regapped and reused if in good condition, they seldom last very long. New plugs are inexpensive and far more reliable.

Spark Plug Gapping and Installation

New plugs should be carefully gapped to ensure a reliable, consistent spark. Use a special spark plug tool with a wire gauge. See **Figure 33** for two common types.

1. Remove the plugs from their boxes. Tapered plugs do not use gaskets. Some plug brands may have small end pieces that must be screwed on before the plugs can be used.
2. Determine the correct gap setting from **Table 6**. Insert the appropriate size wire gauge between the electrodes. If the gap is correct, there will be a slight drag as the wire is pulled through. If there is no drag or if the wire will not pull through, bend the side electrode with the gapping tool (**Figure 34**) to change the gap, then remeasure with the wire gauge.

CAUTION

Never try to close the electrode gap by tapping the spark plug on a solid surface. This can damage the plug internally. Always use the gapping/adjusting tool to open or close the gap.

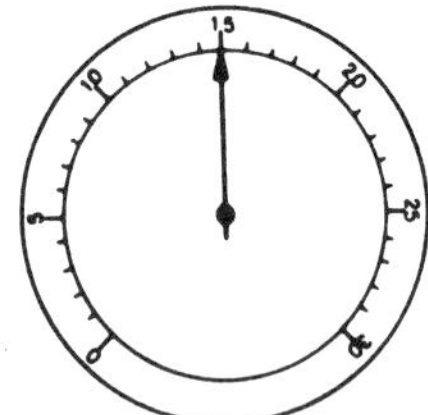

1. NORMAL READING
Reads 15 in. at idle.

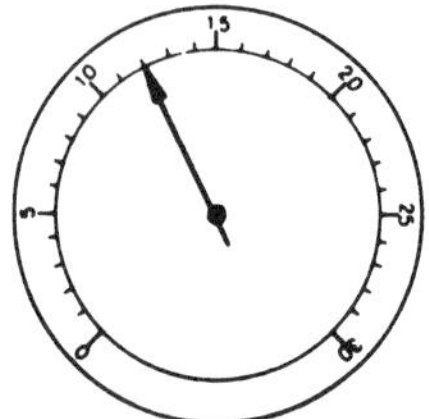

2. LATE IGNITION TIMING
About 2 inches too low at idle.

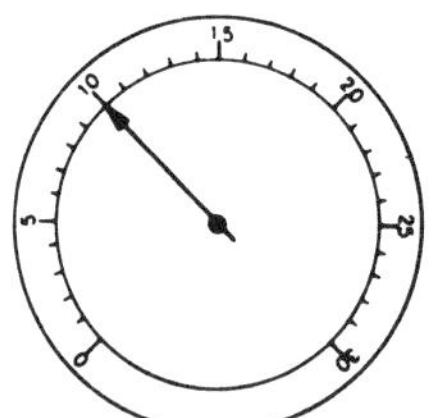

3. LATE VALVE TIMING
About 4 to 8 inches low at idle.

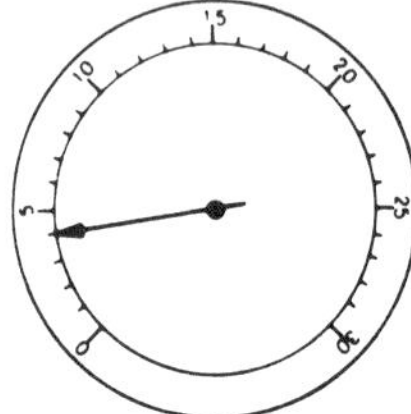

4. INTAKE LEAK
Low steady reading.

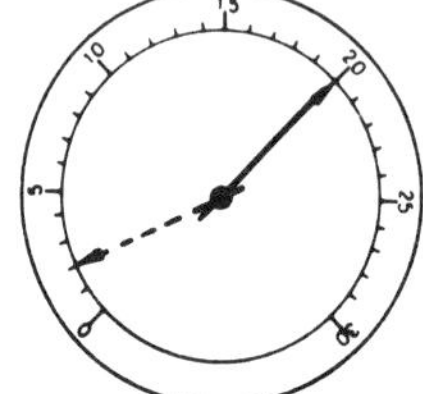

5. NORMAL READING
Drops to 2, then rises to 25 when accelerator is rapidly depressed and released.

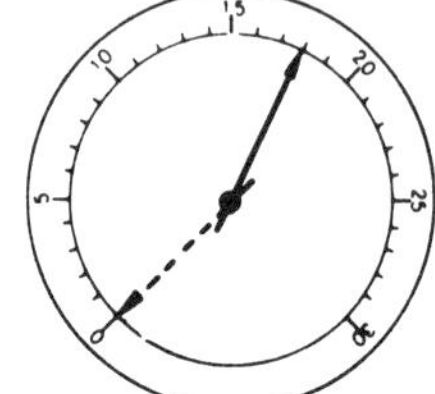

6. WORN RINGS, DILUTED OIL
Drops to 0, then rises to 18 when accelerator is rapidly depressed and released.

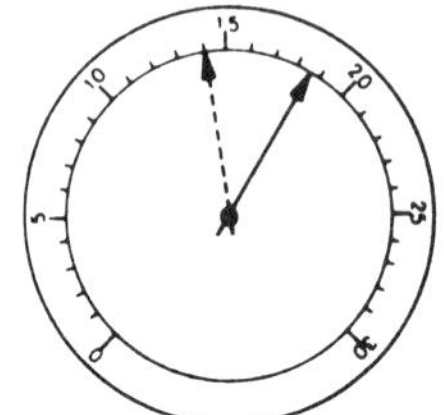

7. STICKING VALVES(S)
Normally steady. Intermittently flicks downward about 4 in.

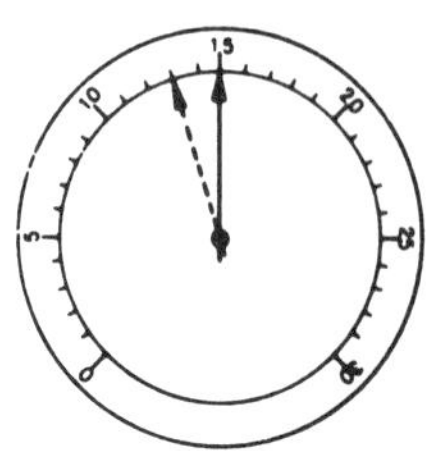

8. LEAKY VALVE
Regular drop about 2 inches.

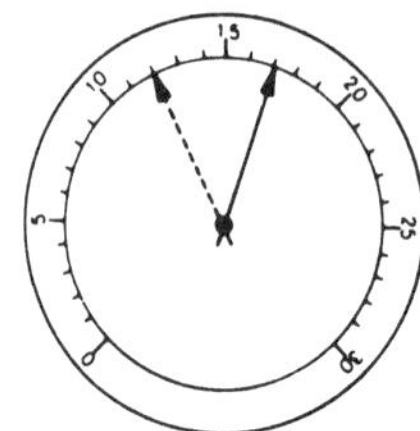

9. BURNED OR WARPED VALVE
Regular, evenly spaced down-scale flick about 4 in.

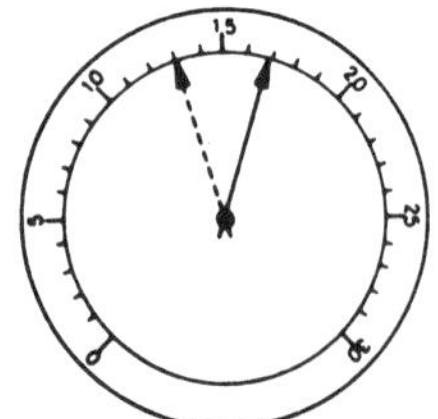

10. WORN VALVE GUIDES
Oscillates about 4 in.

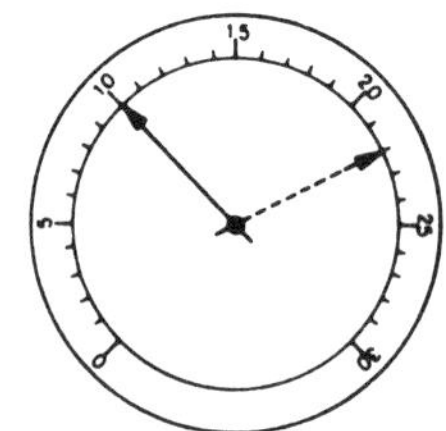

11. WEAK VALVE SPRINGS
Violent oscillation (about 10 in.) as rpm increases. Often steady at idle.

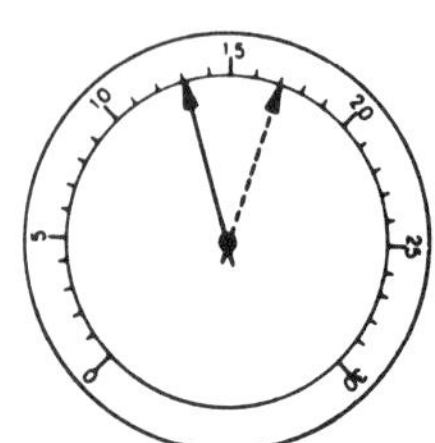

12. IMPROPER IDLE MIXTURE
Floats slowly between 13-17 in.

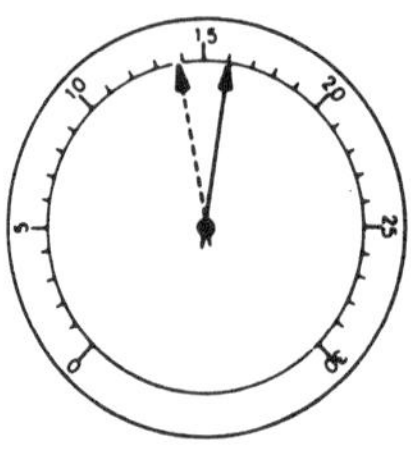

13. SMALL SPARK GAP or DEFECTIVE POINTS
Slight float between 14-16 in.

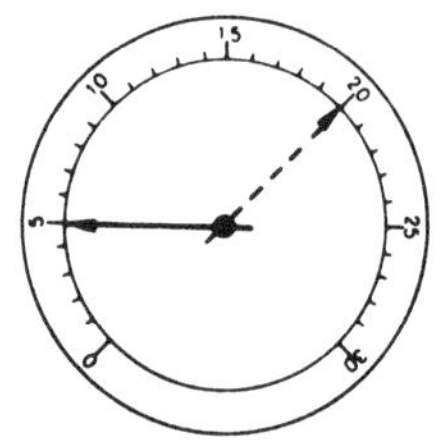

14. HEAD GASKET LEAK
Gauge floats between 5-19 in.

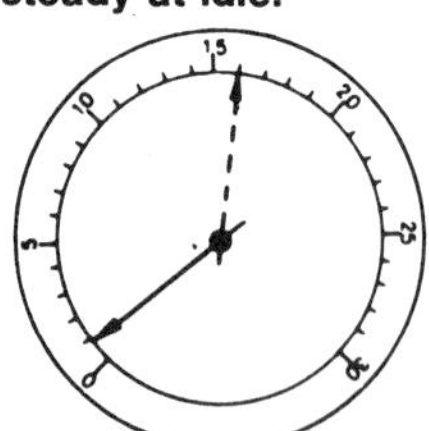

15. RESTRICTED EXHAUST SYSTEM
Normal when first started. Drops to 0 as rpm increases. May eventually rise to about 16.

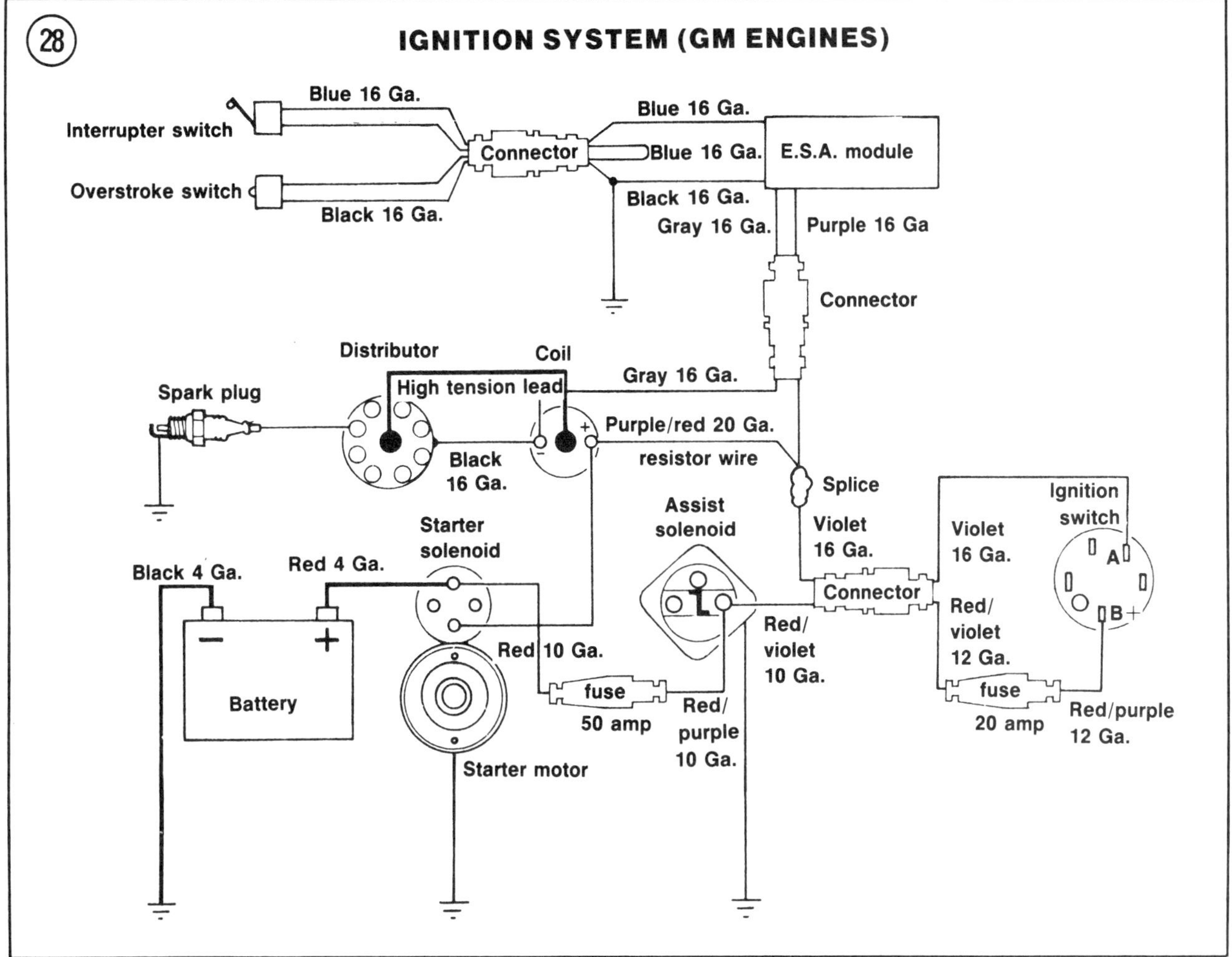

3. Apply a drop of engine oil to the threads of each spark plug. Screw each plug in by hand until it seats. Very little effort is required. If force is necessary, the plug is cross-threaded. Unscrew it and try again.
4. Tighten the spark plugs. If you have a torque wrench, tighten to 15-20 ft.-lb. (20-30 N•m). If not, tighten the plugs with your fingers, then tighten an additional 1/16 turn (tapered seat) or 1/4 turn (gasket-type) with the plug wrench.
5. Reinstall the wires to their correct cylinder location. See **Figure 26**.

Distributor Cap, Wires and Rotor

1. Wipe all ignition wires with a cloth slightly moistened in kerosene. Carefully bend each wire and inspect the insulation, cable nipple and spark plug boot for abrasions, cracks or deterioration. Clean any corroded terminals. Replace wires as required.
2. Unsnap, unscrew or turn the distributor cap attachment devices as required and remove the cap. See **Figure 35**. Pull cap straight up and off the distributor to prevent rotor blade damage.
3. Check the carbon button and electrodes inside the distributor cap for dirt, corrosion or arcing. See **Figure 36**. Check the cap for cracks and make sure the vent screen is clean and fits correctly. Replace the cap and rotor as a set if necessary.
4. Lift the rotor straight up and off the distributor shaft (**Figure 37**). Wipe the rotor

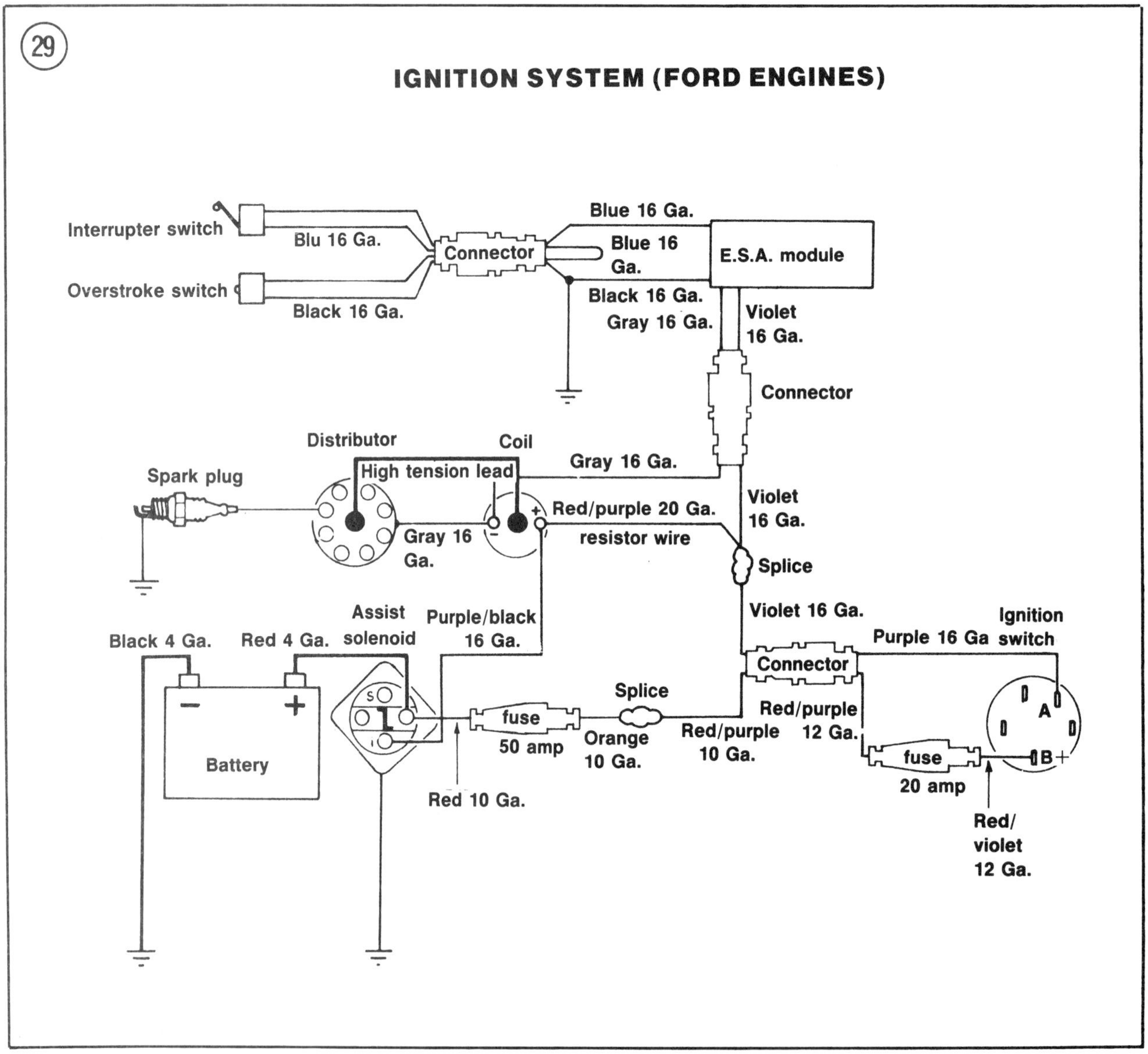

29
IGNITION SYSTEM (FORD ENGINES)
Interrupter switch
Blu 16 Ga.
Overstroke switch
Black 16 Ga.
Connector
Blue 16 Ga.
Blue 16 Ga.
E.S.A. module
Black 16 Ga.
Gray 16 Ga.
Violet 16 Ga.
Connector
Distributor
Coil
Spark plug
High tension lead
Gray 16 Ga.
Red/purple 20 Ga. resistor wire
Gray 16 Ga.
Violet 16 Ga.
Splice
Violet 16 Ga.
Assist solenoid
Purple/black 16 Ga.
Black 4 Ga.
Red 4 Ga.
Ignition switch
Purple 16 Ga
Connector
Battery
Splice
fuse 50 amp
Orange 10 Ga.
Red/purple 10 Ga.
Red/purple 12 Ga.
fuse 20 amp
Red 10 Ga.
Red/violet 12 Ga.

30
Spark plug boot

31
Spark plug wire and boot
Twist and pull
Spark plug

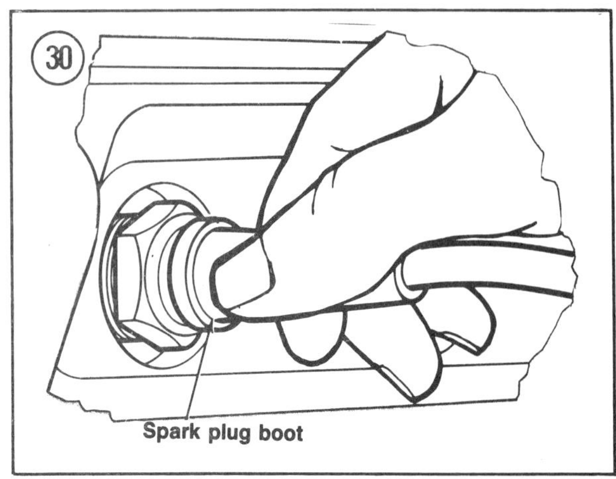

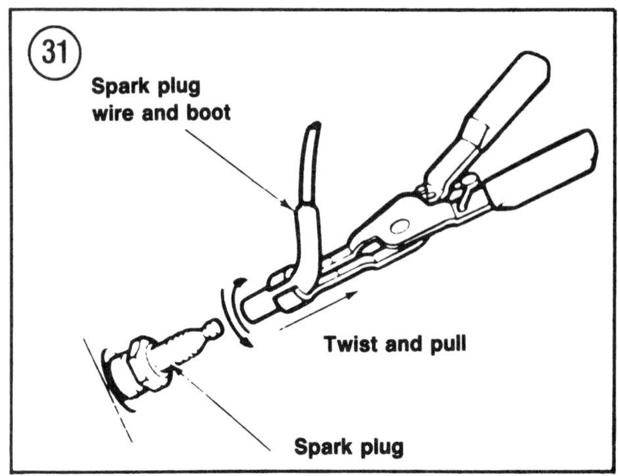

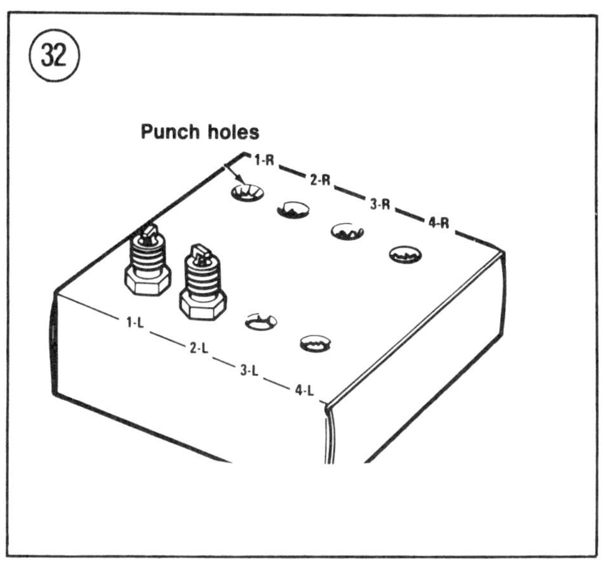

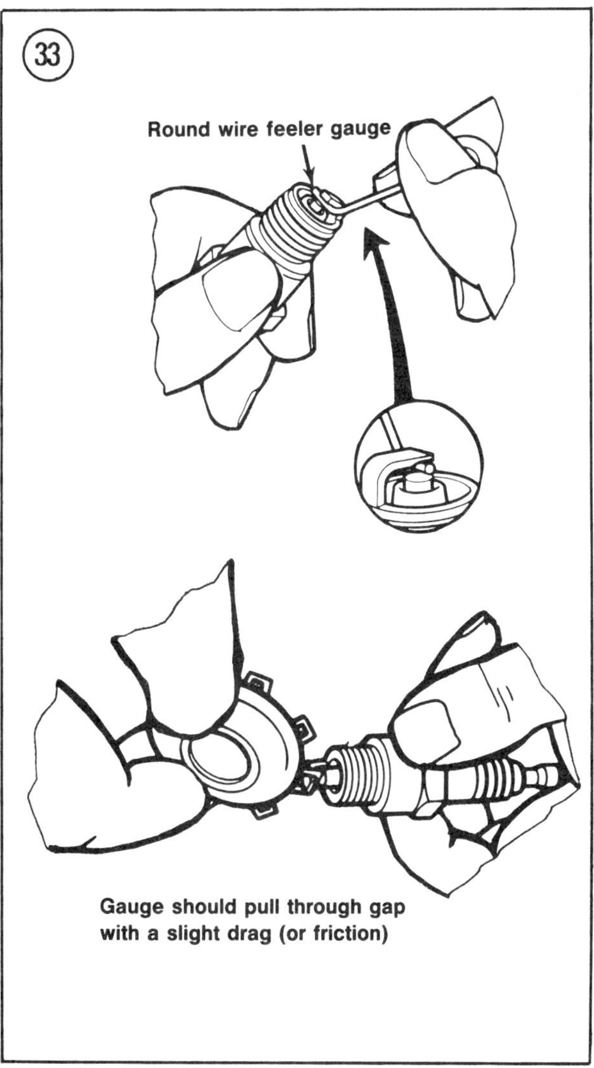

with a clean, damp cloth. Check for burns, arcing, cracks and other defects. Replace the rotor and cap as a set if necessary.

5. To reinstall, align the tang inside the rotor with the slot in the distributor shaft. Press rotor onto shaft until it is fully seated.

6. Grasp the rotor, twist it clockwise (GM engines) or counterclockwise (Ford engines) and then release it. The rotor should return quickly to its original position when released. If not, the distributor advance mechanism requires service. This should be done by a dealer.

7. Install the distributor cap. Snap the clips in place, turn the cap latches or tighten the screws as required. See **Figure 35**.

4

Contact Breaker Point Replacement

The breaker points and condenser should be replaced during a tune-up. Copy the distributor number and use it to obtain the correct replacement parts. Set dwell to specifications (**Table 6**), then check ignition timing.

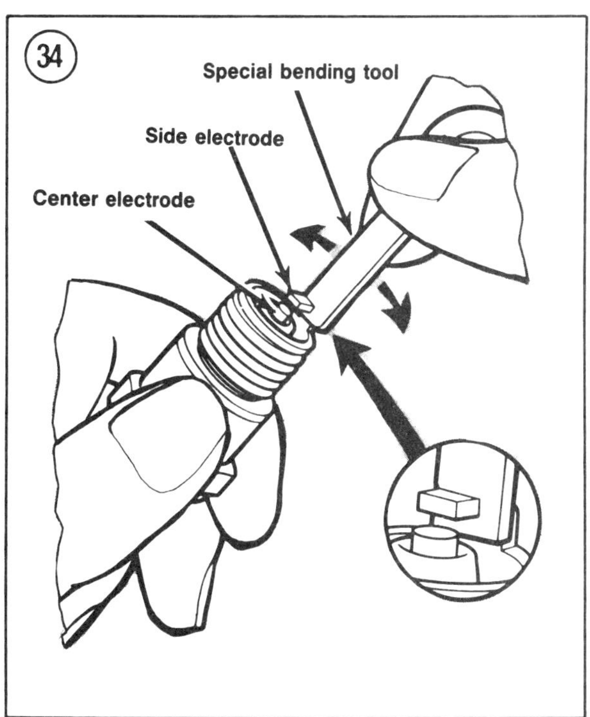

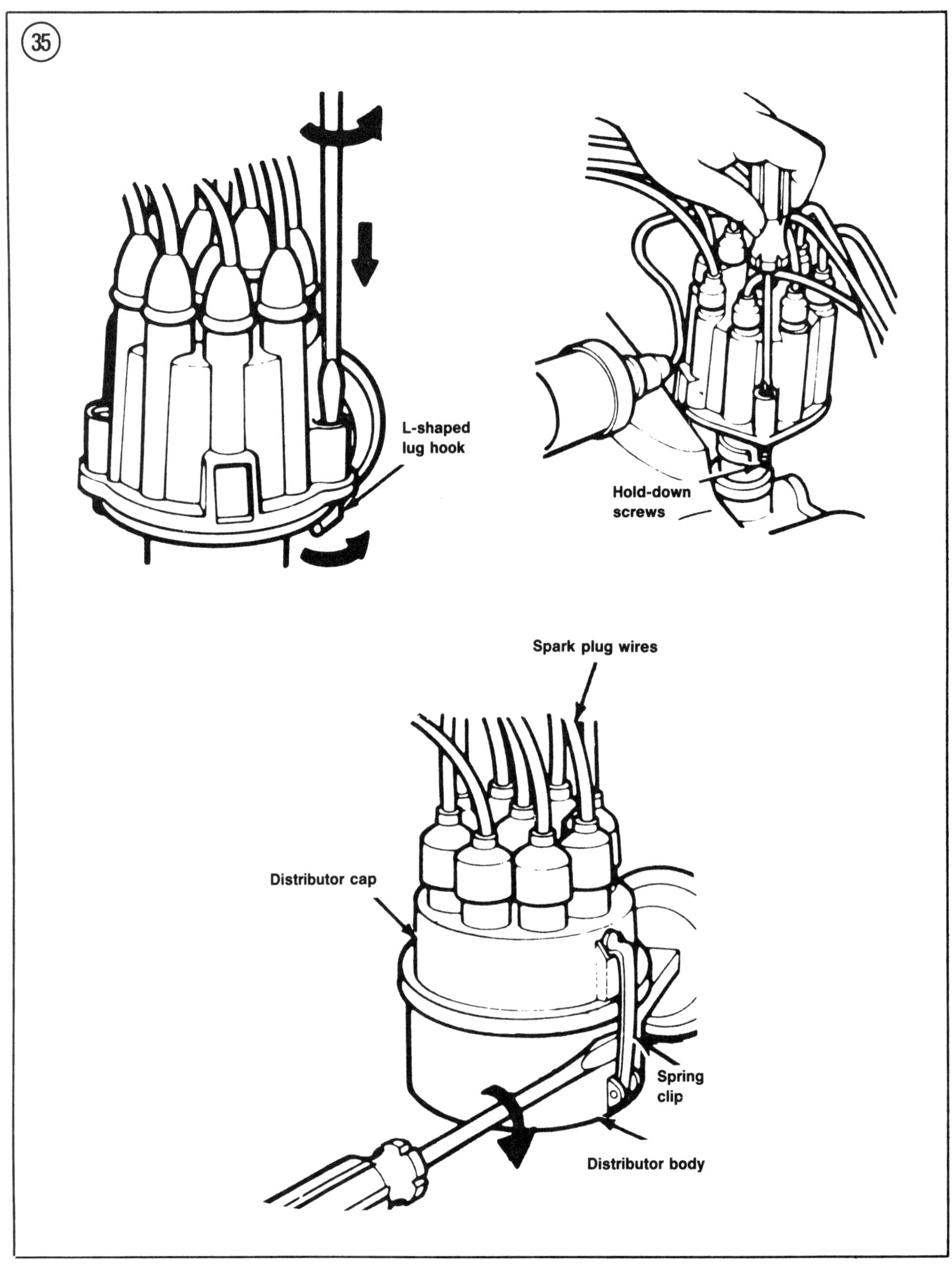
35
L-shaped
lug hook
Hold-down
screws
Spark plug wires
Distributor cap
Spring
clip
Distributor body

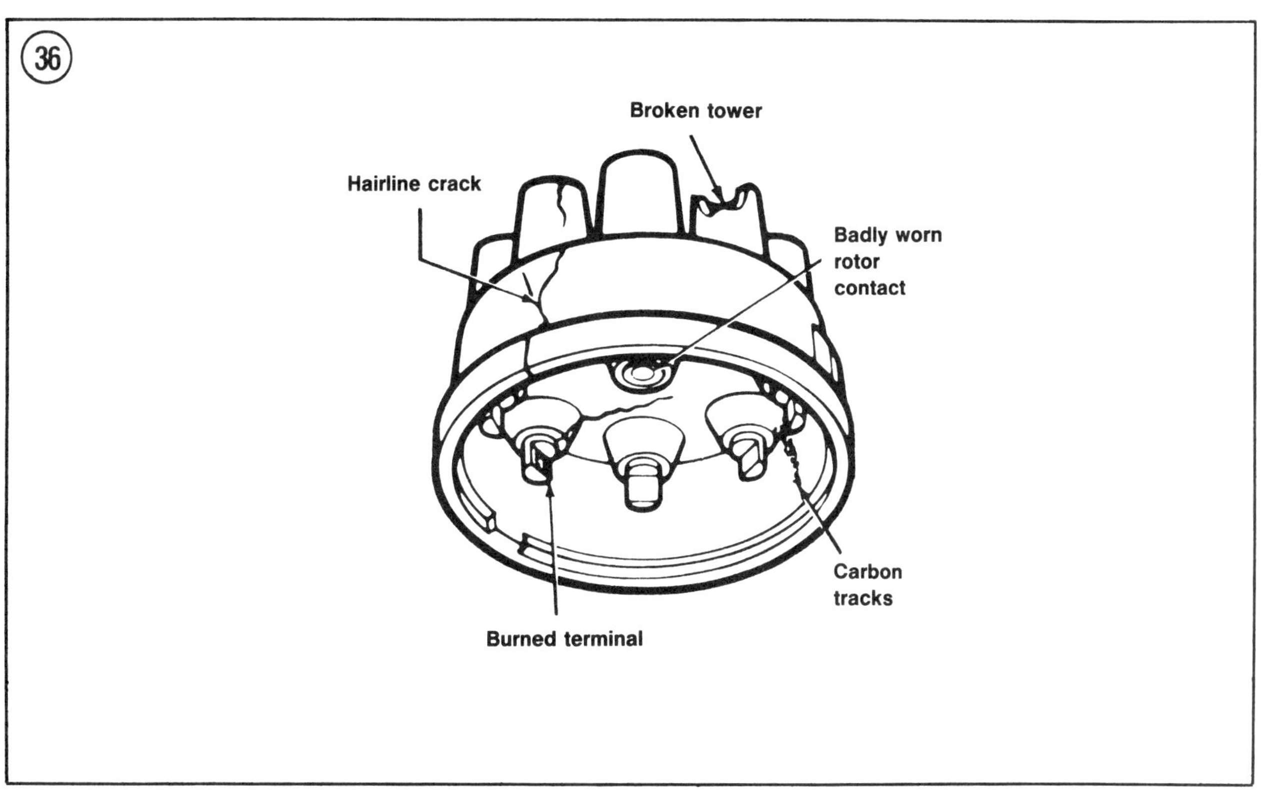
36
Broken tower
Hairline crack
Badly worn
rotor
contact
Carbon
tracks
Burned terminal

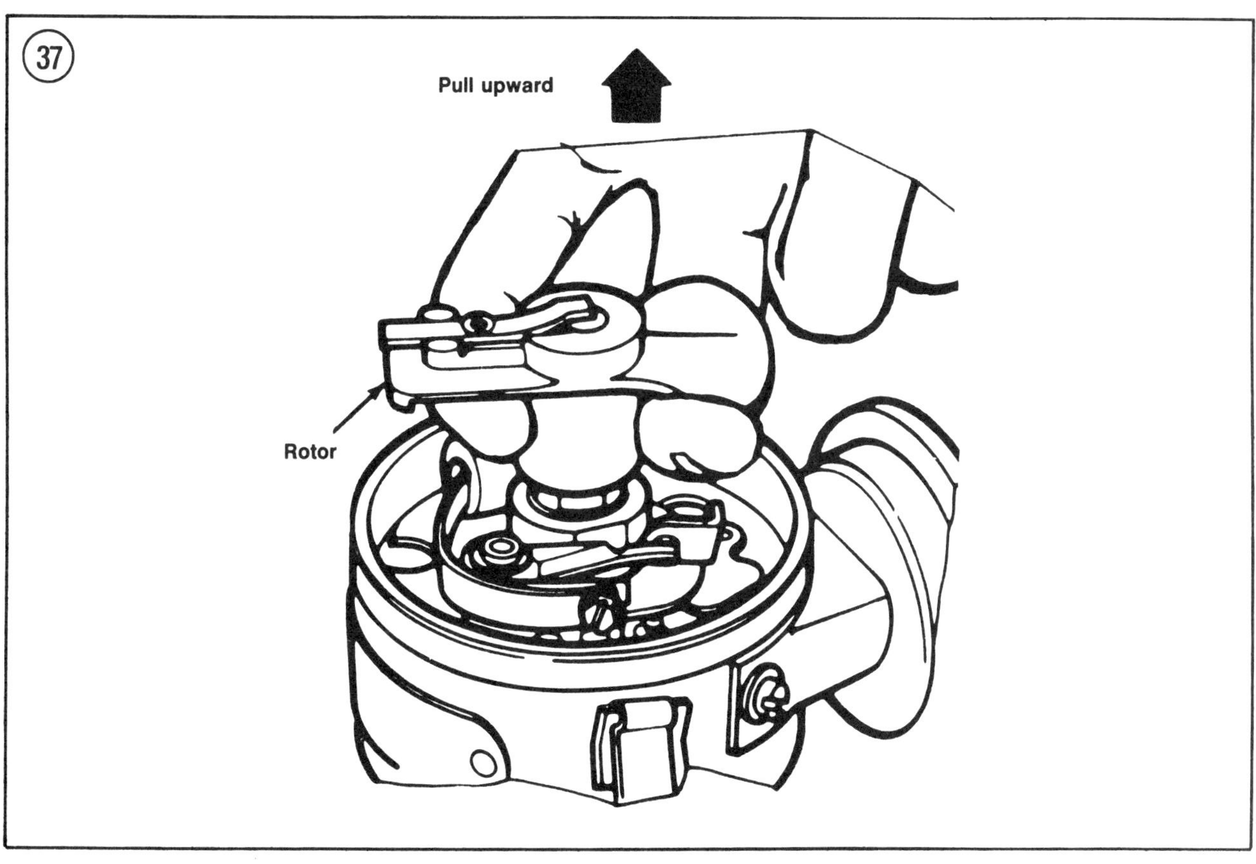
37
Pull upward
Rotor

NOTE
Breaker point sets used in marine distributors have corrosion-resistant springs. Do not use automotive breaker points as a replacement. Use only B.I.A. marine-approved parts.

1. Remove the distributor cap and rotor as described in this chapter.
2. Loosen the primary terminal nut and disconnect the primary lead. See **Figure 38** (typical).
3. Unscrew the retaining screw(s) from the condenser and breaker assembly. Note the location of the ground wire so it may be reinstalled in the same place, then remove the condenser and breaker point assembly from the distributor. See **Figure 39** (typical).

NOTE
*On distributors using a felt lubricating cam wick (**Figure 40**), install a new wick and proceed with Step 5.*

4. Wipe the cam and breaker plate clean. See **Figure 41**. Lightly coat the cam with special distributor grease. Never use oil or common grease; they will break down under the high temperature and frictional load and are likely to find their way onto the contact points.
5. Install the new contact breaker assembly and condenser in the distributor, but do not tighten the locking screw. Make sure the ground wire, condenser lead and primary lead are installed exactly as they were before. Double check the connections and screw to ensure that they are tight.
6. With the points closed, make certain the contact surfaces are properly aligned with each other (**Figure 42**). Make adjustments as required, bending the stationary arm of the point set only. If reusing old points, they should not be realigned.
7. Check inside of the distributor shaft. If a felt wick is installed, lubricate with 1-2 drops of SAE 30 engine oil (**Figure 43**).

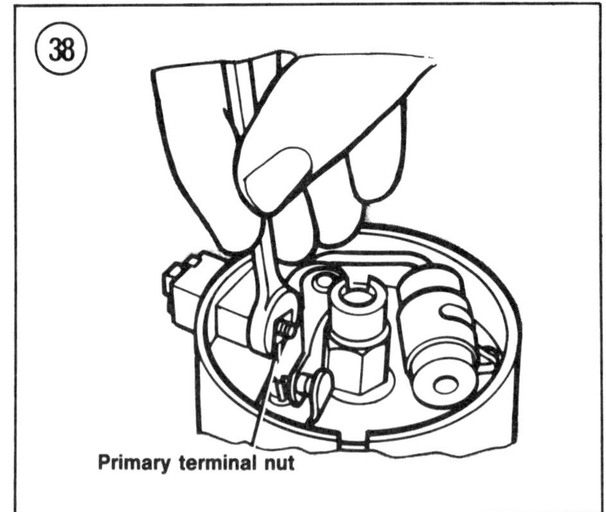

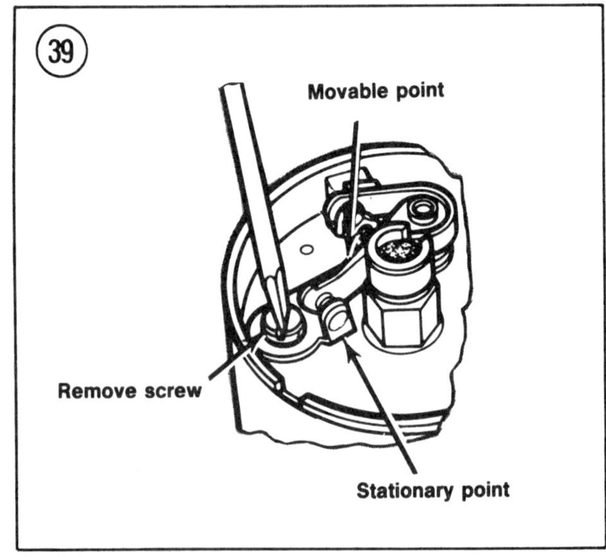

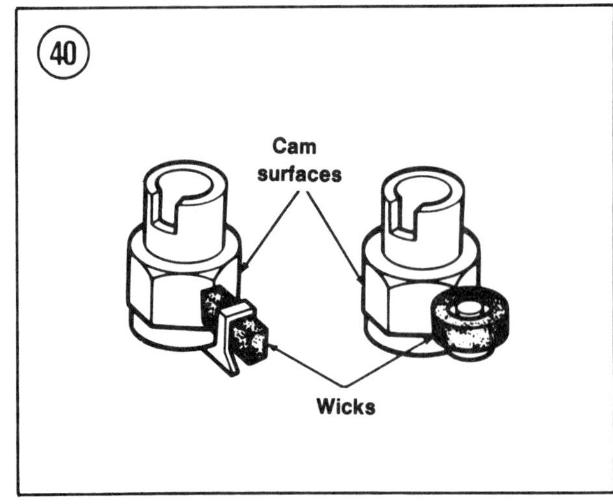

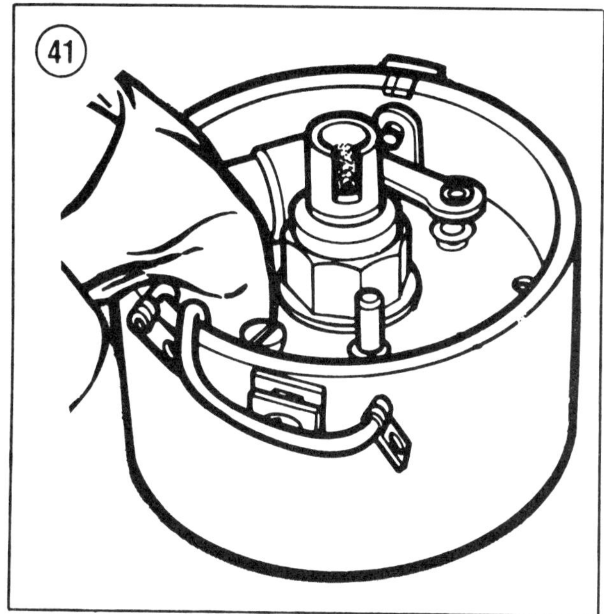

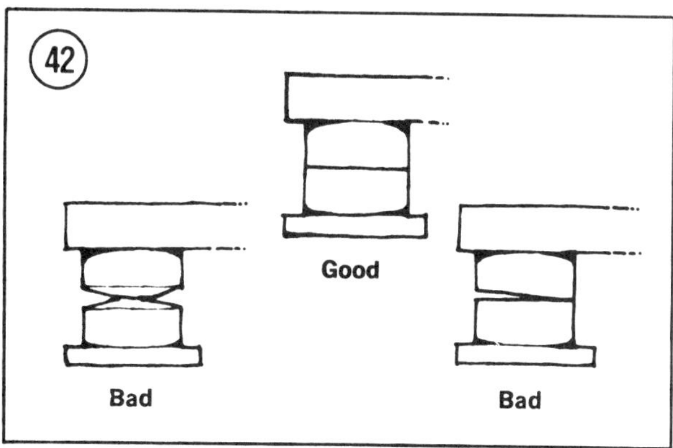

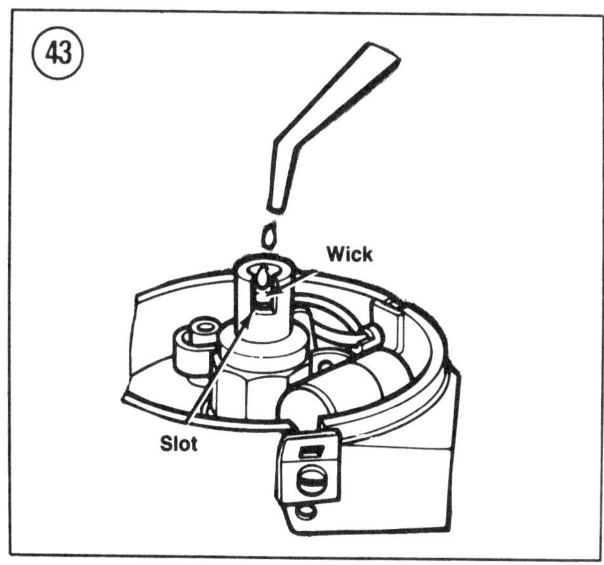

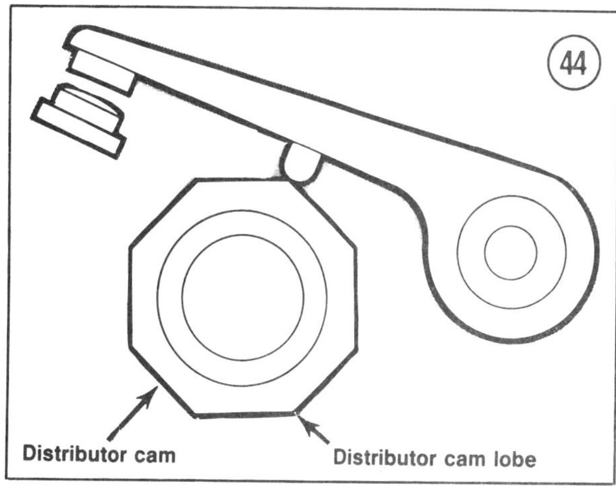

8. Adjust breaker point gap as described in this chapter.

Breaker Point Gap Adjustment

There are two ways to adjust the breaker point gap:

a. Feeler gauge.
b. Dwell meter.

The dwell meter method is the most accurate.

To set the gap with a feeler gauge

1. Disconnect the ignition coil high tension (thick) lead and ground it at the engine block.
2. Connect a remote starter button to the starter solenoid or assist solenoid according to manufacturer's instructions and crank the engine over until the breaker point rubbing block rests precisely on a distributor cam lobe, as shown in **Figure 44**. At this position, the points are open to their fullest.
3. Insert a flat feeler gauge between the open points (**Figure 45**) and compare the gap to specifications (**Table 6**). Gap adjustment is made either with an adjusting screw or with a screwdriver inserted in the slotted hole in the point set/breaker plate. See **Figure 46**. When a slight drag is felt on the gauge blade, tighten the locking screw. Recheck gap to make sure the points did not move during tightening.

To adjust point gap with a dwell meter

1. Remove the distributor cap and rotor as described in this chapter.
2. Connect a dwell meter and remote starter button according to manufacturer's instructions.
3. Crank the engine with the remote starter button and read the dwell angle on the meter.
4. Adjust the dwell by varying the breaker point gap. Decrease the gap to increase dwell; increase the gap to decrease dwell.
5. Tighten the breaker point locking screw.
6. Repeat Step 3 to recheck the dwell.
7. Install the distributor rotor and cap as described in this chapter.

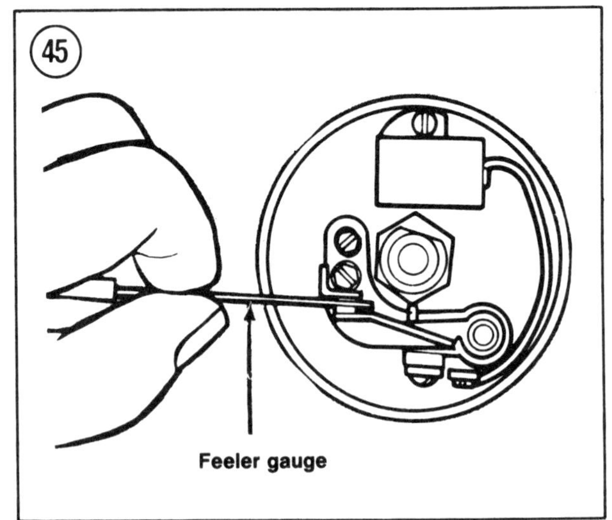

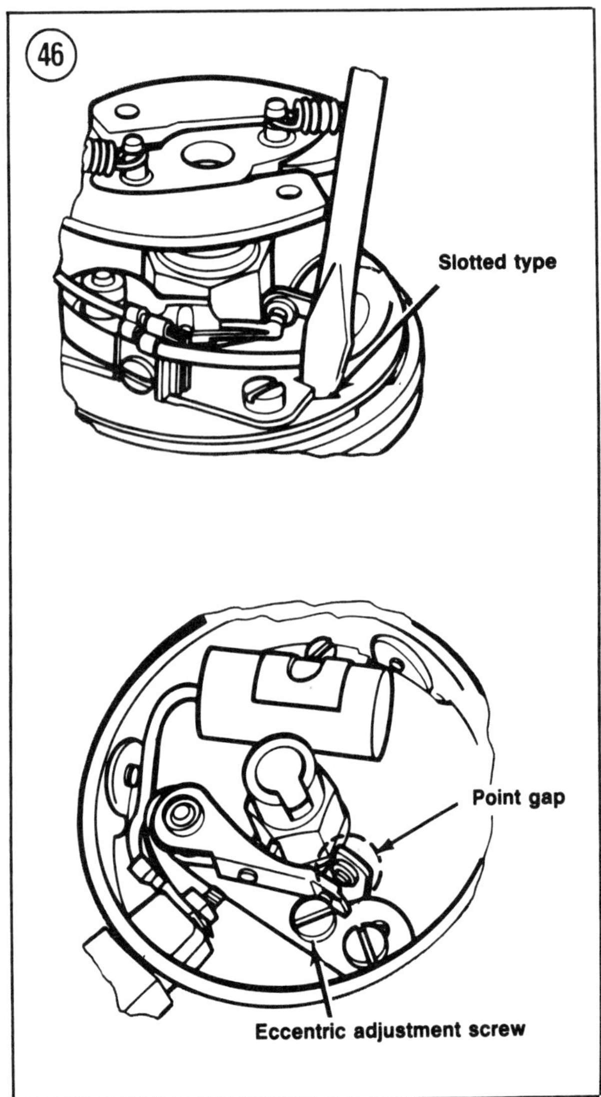

Ignition Timing

The No. 1 cylinder is the front cylinder on all inline engines. It is the front cylinder on the port side of GM V6 and V8 engines and the starboard side of Ford V8 engines.

If the engine is being operated on a blended gasoline/alcohol fuel, be sure to use the correct setting as specified in **Table 6** or engine performance will be adversely affected.

1. Connect a timing light to the No. 1 spark plug wire according to manufacturer's instructions. See **Figure 26**.
2. Connect a tachometer according to manufacturer's instructions.
3. Locate the timing marks on the engine timing cover or block and crankshaft pulley or harmonic balance. See **Figure 47** for typical arrangements.
4. Clean the timing marks. Apply a coat of white paint or chalk so they can be more easily seen.
5. Start the engine and run at slow idle. Refer to **Table 6** for timing specifications and aim the timing light at the timing marks. If the engine timing is correct, the moving mark wil appear to stand still opposite the stationary mark.

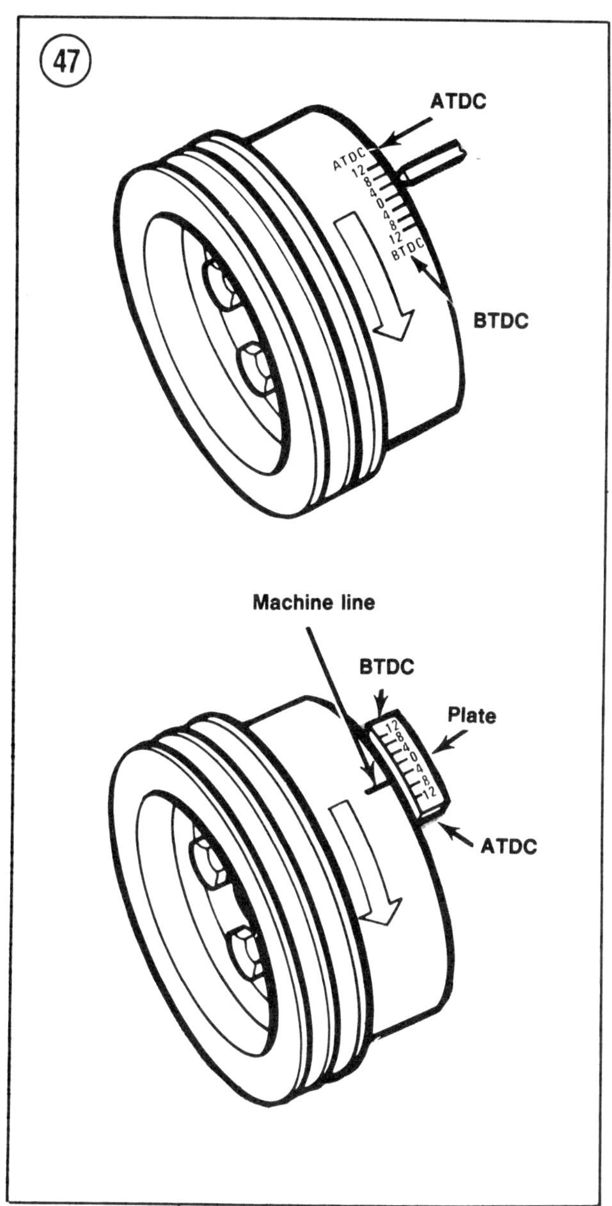

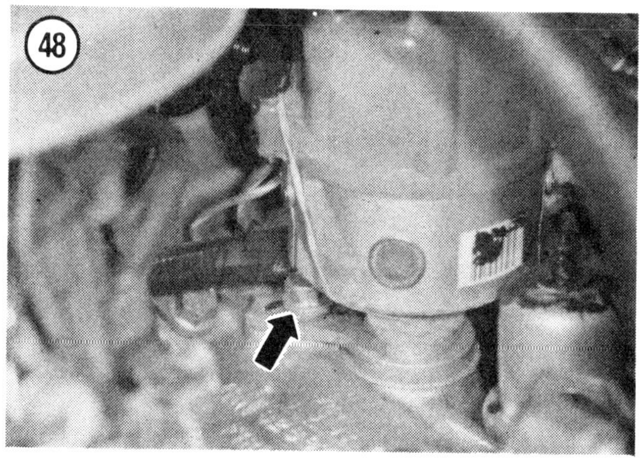

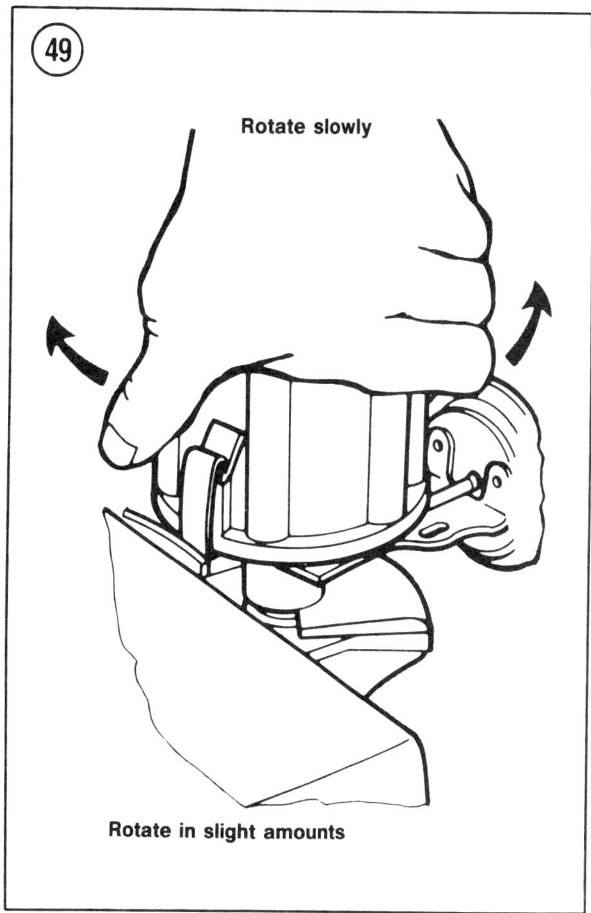

6. If the timing marks are not properly aligned, loosen the hold-down bolt at the base of the distributor (**Figure 48**, typical) just enough so the distributor body can be turned by hand with some resistance.

7. Slowly rotate the distributor body clockwise or counterclockwise as required until the marks come into alignment. See **Figure 49**.

8. Tighten the hold-down bolt without further moving the distributor. Recheck timing with the timing light. Repeat Step 6 and Step 7 if timing was disturbed while tightening the bolt.

9. After setting initial timing, check the operation of the centrifugal advance mechanism. With the engine operating at slow idle, note the position of the timing marks with the timing light.

NOTE
If the timing mark moves with jerky motion or does not start to move within 50-100 rpm of the specified speed in Step 10, the distributor centrifugal advance is not working properly and must be cleaned or repaired.

10. Gradually increase the engine speed to about 1,800 rpm while observing the timing marks. The moving mark should move steadily in a direction opposite to engine rotation.
11. Decrease engine speed to slow idle while observing the timing marks. The moving mark should move back smoothly as speed decreases.

CARBURETOR

Refer to specifications in **Table 6** for the proper idle speed for your engine. Do not remove the flame arrestor for this procedure. **Figures 50-54** show the location of idle mixture needles and idle stop screws for the carburetors used on all engines.

1. Connect a tachometer according to manufacturer's instructions.
2. Locate the idle mixture screw(s) on your carburetor. This is usually a spring-loaded screw near the carburetor base.
3. Locate the idle stop screw on the carburetor throttle linkage.
4. Start the engine and run at fast idle until normal operating temperature is reached.
5. Once the engine is warmed up, bring it back to a normal idle. Shift into FORWARD gear and note the idle speed on the tachometer. If necessary, adjust the idle stop screw to bring the idle speed back within specifications (**Table 6**).
6. Adjust the idle mixture screw to obtain the highest rpm possible. If the carburetor has 2 mixture screws, adjust them alternately until the highest rpm reading is obtained.

7. Readjust idle speed to bring it back within specifications, if necessary.

8. Repeat Step 6 and Step 7 as required until the smoothest engine operation possible is obtained at the specified idle speed.

9. Shut the engine off and remove the tachometer.

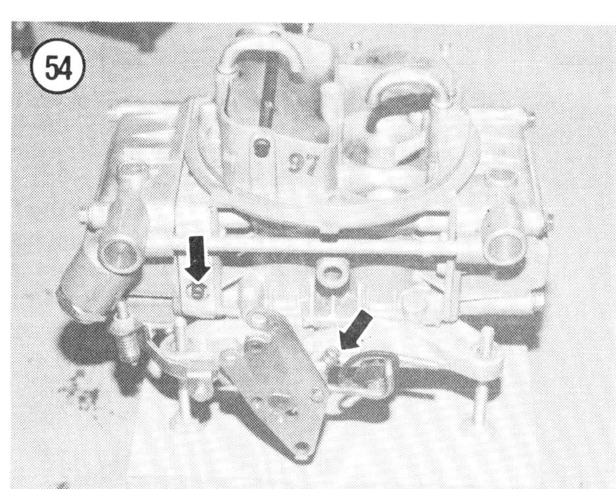

Table 1 OMC COBRA LUBRICATION AND MAINTENANCE SCHEDULE

ENGINE	
Daily	• Check crankcase oil and power steering fluid level • Check fuel pump overflow line for leakage • Check for fuel system leaks • Check fuel supply • Check all electrical connections • Check for cooling system leaks • Check control linkage operation
Every 2 months	• Lubricate steering ram
Every 6 months	• Lubricate power steering actuator valve
At 20 hours of operation	• Have dealer perform service check to maintain warranty
Every 25 hours of operation	• Check battery condition • Check all electrical connections • Clean and check flame arrestor • Check/adjust alternator and power steering drive belt tension

(continued)

Table 1 OMC COBRA LUBRICATION AND MAINTENANCE SCHEDULE (continued)

ENGINE (CONT.)	
Every 50 hours of operation	• Change crankcase oil and filter • Check ignition system connections • Check and clean PCV valve (if so equipped) • Adjust or replace breaker points as required • Check/adjust ignition timing • Check distributor cap, rotor and ignition wires
Every 100 hours of operation	• Replace PCV valve (if so equipped)
Once a season	• Replace spark plugs • Replace fuel filter • Check power trim/tilt system for leakage and proper fluid • Check/adjust carburetor idle speed and mixture • Check cooling system and hose condition[1] • Check for loose, missing or damaged components • Have dealer check engine alignment
STERN DRIVE	
Daily	• Check lower gearcase for smooth shifting in all gears
Every 30 days	• Check condition of sacrificial anodes
Every 25 hours of operation	• Have dealer adjust steering cable tension
Every 50 hours of operation or twice a season	• Drain and refill vertical drive unit
Once a season	• Lubricate gimbal bearing and stern drive U-joint fittings • Check propeller for damage

1. Drain after operating in freezing temperatures or during a seasonal lay-up.

Table 2 ENGINE OIL VISCOSITY

Anticipated temperature range	Recommended viscosity
Above 32° F (0° C)	SAE30
Zero° F (-18° C) to 32° F (0° C)	SAE20W-20
Below zero° F (-18° C) or adverse operating conditions	SAE 10W

Table 3 APPROXIMATE ENGINE OIL CAPACITIES

Engine	Capacity (qt.)[1] w/filter	w/o filter	Filter type OMC	AC	Purolator
2.3L	5.0	4.0	173231	PF-2	PER 1
2.5L/3.0L	4.0	3.5	173232	PF-25	PER 49
4.3L	4.5	4.0	173834	PF-51	PER 173
5.0L/5.7L	6.0	5.0	173233[2]	PF-35	PER 40
5.8L	6.0	5.0	173231	PF-2	PER 1
7.5L	6.8	5.8	173231[3]	PF-2	PER 1

1. All capacities in this table are approximate. To assure correct oil level and prevent overfilling the engine, always use the dipstick as recommended in text.
2. For Ford 302 cu. in., use filter type shown for 5.8L engine.
3. For 1989 models, an OMC 174796 is recommended.

Table 4 APPROXIMATE STERN DRIVE CAPACITIES

Model	Capacity *
2.3L/2.5L/3.0L	60 oz. (1,774 ml)
4.3L/5.0L/5.7L/5.8L	64 oz. (1,892 ml)
7.5L	108 oz. (3,194 ml)

* Capacity is only approximate. When refilling a stern drive after draining all lubricant, recheck level after a one-minute run-in period to eliminate air pockets which may develop during filling. If necessary, top up after rechecking to bring the lubricant to the correct level.

Table 5 RECOMMENDED LUBRICANTS, SEALANTS AND ADHESIVES

Lubricant	Application
OMC Cobra® Premium 4-cycle motor oil	Engine crankcase
OMC Hi-Vis gearcase lubricant	Vertical drive
OMC Triple-Guard grease	Steering ram
OMC Marine Wheel Bearing grease	Power steering actuator valve
OMC Needle Bearing Grease	Bearings
OMC 2 + 4 Fuel Conditioner	Fuel tank
OMC Rust Preventative	Engine
OMC Power Trim/Tilt Fluid	Power trim/tilt system
OMC Storage Fogging Oil	Carburetor
OMC Moly Lube	Remote control cables
Sealer/Adhesive	
OMC Black Neoprene Dip	OMC Ultra Lock
OMC Pipe Sealant with Teflon	OMC Nut Lock
OMC Gasket Sealing Compound	OMC Spline Lock
RTV adhesive sealant	OMC Screw Lock
OMC Locquic Primer	OMC Adhesive M sealant

4

Table 6 TUNE-UP SPECIFICATIONS

1986

Engine displacement	Spark plugs Type	Spark plugs Gap (in.)	Breaker points Dwell (degrees)	Breaker points Gap (in.)	Timing (RON 93 fuel)[1]
2.5L/3.0L	AC-MR43T	0.035	31-34	0.019	4° BTDC
4.3L	AC-MR43T	0.035	39 ±2	0.019	6° BTDC
5.0L[3]	AC-MR44T	0.032	30 ±2	0.018	13° BTDC
5.7L	AC-MR43T	0.032	30 ±2	0.018	10° BTDC

Engine displacement	Timing (RON 90 fuel)[2]	Idle speed (rpm)	Full throttle range (rpm)	Fuel pump (psi)
2.5L/3.0L	1° ATDC	500-600	4,200-4,600	3.5-6.0
4.3L	1° BTDC	500-600	4,200-4,600[4]	5.75-7.0
5.0L[3]	9° BTDC	500-600	4,200-4,600	5.75-7.0
5.7L	5° BTDC	500-600	4,200-4,400	5.75-7.0

1. Anti-knock index 89.
2. Anti-knock index 86.
3. GM 305 cu. in.
4. 4,400-4,800 rpm with 4-bbl. carburetor.

1987

Engine displacement	Spark plugs Type	Spark plugs Gap (in.)	Breaker points Dwell (degrees)	Breaker points Gap (in.)	Timing (RON 93 fuel)[1]
2.3L	AWSF-32	0.035	36 ±2	0.018	10° BTDC
3.0L	AC-MR43T	0.035	31-34	0.019	6° BTDC
4.3L	AC-MR43T	0.035	39 ±2	0.019	6° BTDC
5.0L[3]	AC-MR44T	0.032	30 ±2	0.018	10° BTDC[4]
5.7L	AC-MR43T	0.032	30 ±2	0.018	10° BTDC[5]
7.5L	ARF-32	0.035	31 ±2	0.017	15° BTDC

Engine displacement	Timing (RON 90 fuel)[2]	Idle speed (rpm)	Full throttle range (rpm)	Fuel pump (psi)
2.3L	10° BTDC	600-650	5,200-5,600	3.5-6.0
3.0L	1° ATDC	500-600	4,200-4,600	3.5-6.0
4.3L	1° BTDC	500-600	4,200-4,600[8]	5.75-7.0
5.0L[3]	5° BTDC[6]	500-600	4,200-4,600	5.75-7.0
5.7L	5° BTDC[7]	500-600	4,200-4,400	5.75-7.0
7.5L	10° BTDC	600-650	4,400-4,800	5.0-6.0

1. Anti-knock index 89.
2. Anti-knock index 86.
3. GM 305 cu. in.
4. Models 504AMFTC and 504APFTC, 13° BTDC.
5. Models 574AMARY and 574APARY, 8° BTDC.
6. Models 504AMFTC and 504APFTC, 8° BTDC.
7. Models 574AMARY and 574APARY, 3° BTDC.
8. 4,400-4,800 rpm with 4-bbl. carburetor.

(continued)

Table 6 TUNE-UP SPECIFICATIONS (cont.)

1988

Engine displacement	Spark plugs Type	Spark plugs Gap (in.)	Breaker points Dwell (degrees)	Breaker points Gap (in.)	Timing (RON 93 fuel)[1]
2.3L	AWSF-32	0.035	36 ±2	0.018	10° BTDC
3.0L	AC-MR43T	0.035	31-34	0.019	4° BTDC
4.3L	AC-MR43T	0.035	39 ±2	0.019	6° BTDC
5.0L[3]	AC-MR44T	0.032	29 ±2	0.017	10° BTDC
5.7L	AC-MR43T	0.032	29 ±2	0.017	8° BTDC
7.5L	ARF-32	0.035	31 ±2	0.017	15° BTDC

Engine displacement	Timing (RON 90 fuel)[2]	Idle speed (rpm)	Full throttle range (rpm)	Fuel pump (psi)
2.3L	10° BTDC	600-650	5,200-5,600	3.5-6.0
3.0L	1° ATDC	500-600	4,200-4,600	3.5-6.0
4.3L	1° BTDC	500-600	4,200-4,600[4]	5.75-7.0
5.0L[3]	5° BTDC	500-600	4,200-4,600	5.75-7.0
5.7L	3° BTDC	500-600	4,200-4,400	5.75-7.0
7.5L	10° BTDC	600-650	4,400-4,800	5.0-6.0

1. Anti-knock index 89.
2. Anti-knock index 86.
3. GM 305 cu. in.
4. 4,400-4,800 rpm with 4-bbl. carburetor.

1989

Engine displacement	Spark plugs Type	Spark plugs Gap (in.)	Breaker points Dwell (degrees)	Breaker points Gap (in.)	Timing (RON 93 fuel)[1]
2.3L	AWSF-32	0.035	36 ±2	0.019	10° BTDC
3.0L	AC-MR43T	0.035	31-34	0.019	4° BTDC
4.3L	AC-MR43T	0.035	39 ±2	0.019	6° BTDC
5.0L[3]	AC-MR44T	0.030	29 ±2	0.018	10° BTDC
5.7L	AC-MR43T	0.035	29 ±2	0.018	8° BTDC
5.8L	AC-MR43T	0.030	29 ±2	0.018	10° BTDC
7.5L	ASF-32M	0.035	29 ±2	0.018	10° BTDC

Engine displacement	Timing (RON 90 fuel)[2]	Idle speed (rpm)	Full throttle range (rpm)	Fuel pump (psi)
2.3L	10°BTDC	600-650	5,200-5,600	5.75-7.0
3.0L	1° ATDC	550-600	4,200-4,600	5.75-7.0
4.3L	1° BTDC	550-600	4,200-4,600[4]	5.75-7.0
5.0L[3]	10° BTDC	550-600	4,000-4,400	5.75-7.0
5.7L	3° BTDC	550-600	4,200-4,600	5.75-7.0
5.8L	10° BTDC	550-600	4,000-4,400	5.75-7.0
7.5L	10° BTDC	600-650	4,400-4,800	5.0-6.0

1. Anti-knock index 89.
2. Anti-knock index 86.
3. Ford 302 cu. in.
4. 4,400-4,800 rpm with 4-bbl. carburetor.

Table 7 TEST WHEEL RECOMMENDATIONS

Model	Test wheel part No. Standard rotation	Counter rotation
2.3L/2.5L	982036	
3.0L	384933	
4.3L/5.0L (305 cu. in.)	387388	398673
5.0L (302 cu. in.)/5.8L	982038	985624
5.7L	982038	985624
King Cobra		
262	387388	398673
350	982038	985624
460	985007	985626

Chapter Five

Lay-up, Cooling System Service and Fitting Out

LAY-UP

Boats that are to be stored for more than 4 or 5 weeks should be carefully prepared. This is necessary to prevent damage to the engine and the stern drive unit from freezing, corrosion or fuel system contamination. Preparation for lay-up should begin, if possible, while the boat is still in the water.

If the boat has been removed from the water, a supply of cooling water must be made available to the engine. This is best accomplished by using a flushing adapter kit available from your OMC dealer. If a flushing adapter or flush/test device is used, you should remove the propeller to prevent any possible interference and always start the water flow before starting the engine.

The suggestions for lay-up preparation which follow are based on recommendations made by OMC. See Chapter Four for lubricants recommended by OMC.

In-the-water Preparation

1. If the boat is not in the water, attach a flushing adapter to the stern drive. See *Cooling System Flushing*, Chapter Four.

2. Make sure the fuel contains OMC 2+4 Fuel Conditioner. Refer to the container for the recommended amount to add according to the size of your tank and the amount of fuel inside. This additive prevents gum and varnish from forming in the fuel system.

3. Start the engine and run under load (boat in water) or at idle (boat out of water and a flushing adapter used) until it reaches normal operating temperature, then shut the engine off.

4. Drain the engine oil and install a new oil filter (**Figure 1**, typical). See Chapter Four.

5. Refill the crankcase with the proper amount of fresh SF engine oil. See Chapter Four.

6. Make sure the stern drive is in its full DOWN position. Restart the engine and run at fast idle for several minutes to circulate the fresh oil throughout the engine. Check for leaks around the new filter and oil pan while the engine is running.

7. Shut the engine off and wait approximately 5 minutes, then check the oil

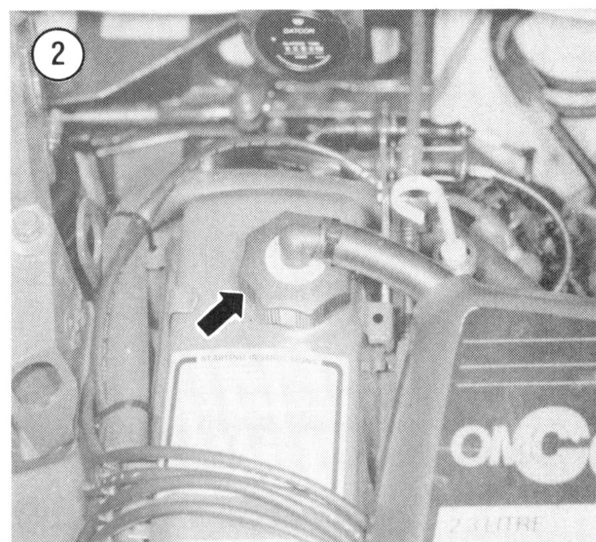

level on the dipstick. See Chapter Four. Add oil, if necessary, through the filler hole (**Figure 2,** typical) to bring the level up to the FULL mark on the dipstick.

8. Drain the lubricant from the unit and refill with OMC Hi-Vis gearcase lubricant. See Chapter Four.

9. Drain the trim/tilt reservoir and refill with OMC Power Trim and Tilt Fluid. See Chapter Four.

10. Shut the fuel supply off at the fuel tank.

NOTE
A thick smoke will develop in Step 11. This is normal.

11. Remove the flame arrestor (**Figure 3**) from the carburetor intake and restart the engine. Increase engine speed to a fast idle (1,200-1,500 rpm) and slowly pour 2/3 of a 1/2 pint can of OMC Storage Fogging oil into the carburetor throat (**Figure 4**, typical) to fog the internal surfaces of the induction system. As the engine runs out of fuel, quickly pour the remaining 1/3 of the can into the carburetor and turn off the ignition.

12. Clean the flame arrestor with solvent, blow dry with compressed air (if available) and reinstall on carburetor air horn.

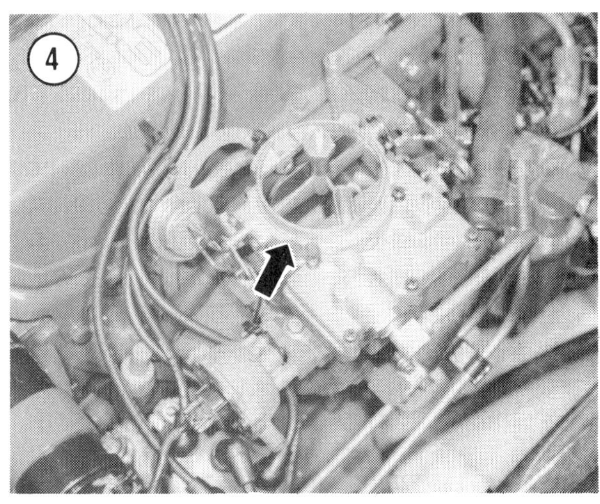

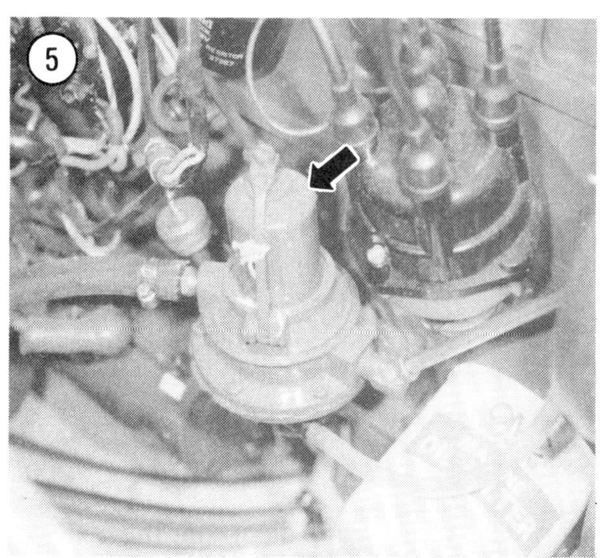

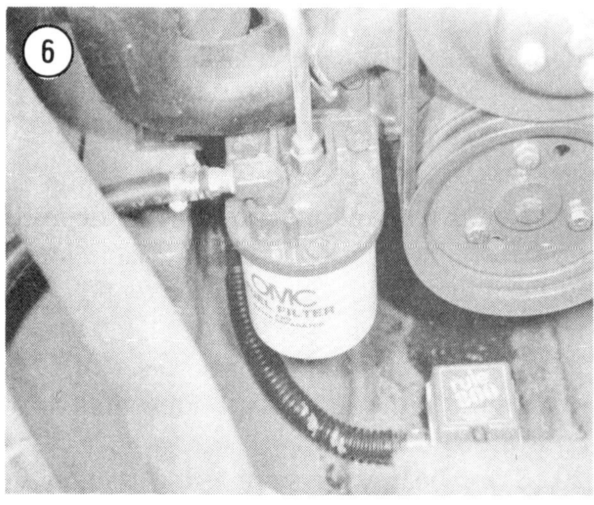

13. Replace the fuel filters as follows:
   a. 2.5/3.0L engine—Install a new filter in the top of the fuel pump. See **Figure 5** (typical).
   b. All others—Install a new fuel filter canister. See **Figure 6** (typical).
   c. All except 5.0L (302 cu. in.), 5.8L and 7.5L—Install a new filter in the carburetor fuel inlet nut. See **Figure 7** (typical).
   d. 5.0L (302 cu. in.), 5.8L and 7.5L—Remove the fuel inlet nut and clean the screen, then reinstall the screen and inlet nut.

14. Remove the boat from the water, keeping the bow higher than the stern if possible to assist in draining the exhaust system.

Out-of-water Preparation

1. Adjust trailer or cradle so that the engine is in a level position. Lower the stern drive unit to its full DOWN position.
2. Loosen drive belt tension and inspect condition of all belts. Replace as required. Tighten accessory unit adjusting bolts without placing tension on drive belts.
3. Drain the cooling system as described in this chapter.
4. Check all hoses for signs of deterioration, cracks or other defects. Replace hoses as required.
5. Remove the spark plugs and pour one ounce of SAE 30 SF engine oil into each cylinder.
6. Disconnect the coil high tension (thick) lead at the coil center terminal. Ground the lead and crank the engine over for 15-20 seconds with the starter to coat the cylinder walls with oil.
7. Wipe up any excess oil from the plug holes. Wipe a thin film of SAE 30 SF engine oil on the spark plug threads. Reinstall the spark plugs and connect the coil lead.
8. Remove the valve cover(s) and check for signs of condensation in the rocker arm area. Carefully wipe away any oil/water mixture found. Coat valve mechanism and inside of rocker arm cover(s) generously with SAE 30 SF engine oil. Reinstall the valve cover(s) using new gasket(s).
9. Refill the closed cooling system, if so equipped, as described in this chapter.
10. Cover the flame arrestor and carburetor with a plastic bag and tape tightly in place. This prevents moisture from entering the carburetor and intake manifold.
11. If equipped with power steering, place a suitable container under the oil cooler and

remove the drain plug. On 7.5L models, drain the engine oil cooler.

12. With the stern drive unit in a vertical position, remove the water drain plug located on the port side of the pivot housing. Crank the engine 1-2 turns to expel any water from the drive pump, then run the drive to its full tilt position and allow the unit to continue draining. When no more water is expelled, run the drive back to a vertical position. Allow any additional water to drain, then reinstall the drain plug.

13. Remove the battery from the boat. Tape vent holes closed and clean battery case with baking soda solution to remove any traces of corrosion and acid, then rinse with cold water. Check electrolyte level in each cell and top up with distilled water as required. Cover terminals with a light coat of petroleum jelly or spray with a can of CRC-6-66 (available from your OMC dealer) or equivalent. Store the battery in a cool, dry place.

NOTE
Remove the battery from storage every 30-45 days. Check electrolyte level and slow-charge for 5-6 hours at 6 amperes.

14. Remove the stern drive unit from the boat. This permits the drainage of any water trapped in the transom bracket cavities. It also provides access to the universal joint fittings that should be lubricated. See Chapter Four.

15. Insert a length of wire in the stern drive water pickup screen to make sure there are no obstructions. Reinstall the stern drive unit to the boat.

16. Tape the exhaust outlets to prevent moisture from entering the exhaust manifolds and valve chambers.

17. Clean engine exterior thoroughly and retouch any blemishes with engine touch-up paint. Apply a film of OMC Rust Preventative or equivalent on the exterior surfaces.

CAUTION
Do not paint sacrificial zinc rings, plugs or bars, if present. These must be left unpainted in order to prevent galvanic corrosion.

18. Remove all marine growths and deposits from the stern drive unit. Clean metal surfaces that have become exposed and cover with touch-up paint.

19. Wipe or spray exterior surfaces of stern drive unit with OMC Rust Preventative or equivalent.

20. Store boat with stern drive unit in its normal operating position.

COOLING SYSTEM DRAINING

The engine cooling system must be properly drained for storage during the winter months in areas where temperatures fall below 32° F (0° C). If it is not, the engine block may be cracked by expansion of frozen water.

Inline engines tend to crack horizontally just below the core plugs or along the upper edge below the cylinder head. A V-block will usually crack near the hydraulic lifters or in the valley of the block below the intake manifold.

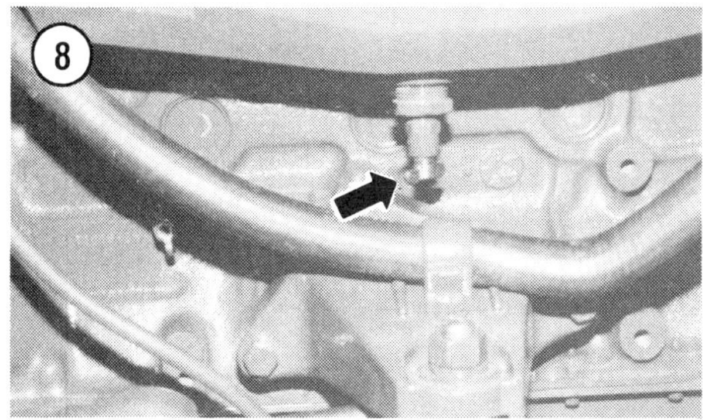

The following procedures are designed to help you prevent unnecessary engine damage during winter storage.

To assure that the cooling system is completely drained, adjust the trailer or cradle so that the forward end of inline engines is higher than the aft end. With V6 and V8 engines, adjust the trailer or cradle so that the engine is level—the bow of the boat will be higher than the stern.

Standard Cooling System (Inline Engines)

1. Place suitable containers under the exhaust manifold and engine block drain pints, if space permits. This will prevent water from draining into the bilge.
2. Cover any exposed components such as the alternator or starter motor with plastic to protect them from water during this procedure.
3. Open one exhaust manifold drain valve and one cylinder block drain valve. **Figure 8** and **Figure 9** show the 2.3L engine; the 2.5L/3.0L is similar.
4. Locate the longest hose that connects to the thermostat housing. This is the transom bracket water (inlet) hose. Unclamp and disconnect the hose from the thermostat housing.
5. Unclamp and disconnect the water supply hose between the thermostat housing and water pump. See **Figure 10** (typical).
6. If equipped with power steering, remove the drain plug from the lower end of the power steering oil cooler. See **Figure 11** (typical).
7. Allow the cooling system to drain *completely*, then disconnect and ground the ignition coil high tension (thick) lead to the engine block. Crank the engine over several times to purge any water remaining in the water pump.
8. Leave the drain valves open. Reconnect the hoses and install the power steering cooler drain plug, if so equipped.

Standard Cooling System (V6 and V8 Engines)

1. Place suitable containers under the exhaust manifold and engine block drain points, if space permits. This will prevent water from draining into the bilge.
2. Cover any exposed components such as the alternator or starter motor with plastic to protect them from water during this procedure.

3A. 4.3L/5.0L (302 cu. in.)/5.8L—Open the exhaust manifold drain valve and cylinder block drain valve on each side of the engine. See **Figures 12A, 12B and 13**.

3B. 5.0L (305 cu. in.)/5.7L—Unclamp and remove the rubber cap(s) on each exhaust manifold. Some installations will use one cap; others have two caps. Open the cylinder block drain valve on each side of the engine. See **Figure 14** (port) and **Figure 15** (starboard).

3C. 7.5L—Unclamp and remove the rubber cap on each exhaust manifold. Open the cylinder block drain valve on each side of the engine. See **Figure 16** (port) and **Figure 17A** and **Figure 17B** (starboard).

4. Insert a wire in the exhaust manifold drains to clear away any corrosion and permit complete drainage.

5. Locate the longest hose that connects to the thermostat housing. This is the transom bracket water (inlet) hose. Unclamp and disconnect the hose from the thermostat housing. See A, **Figure 18** (typical).

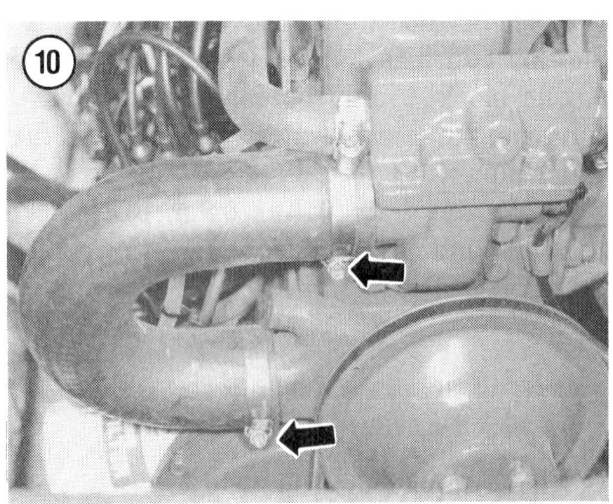

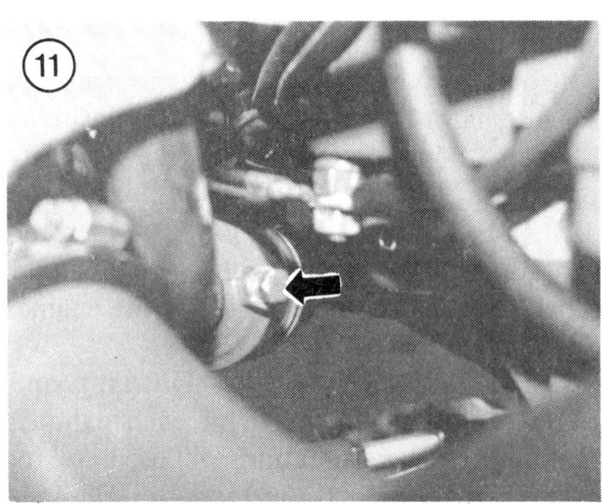

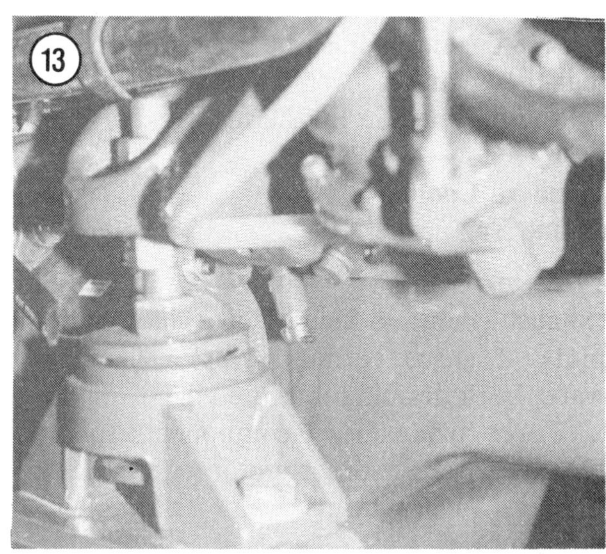

14

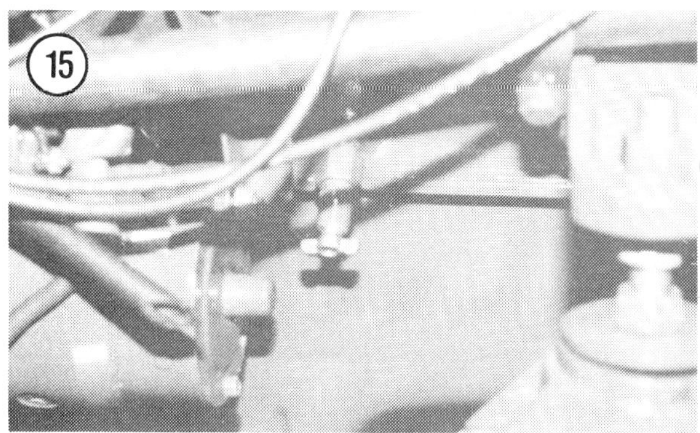
15

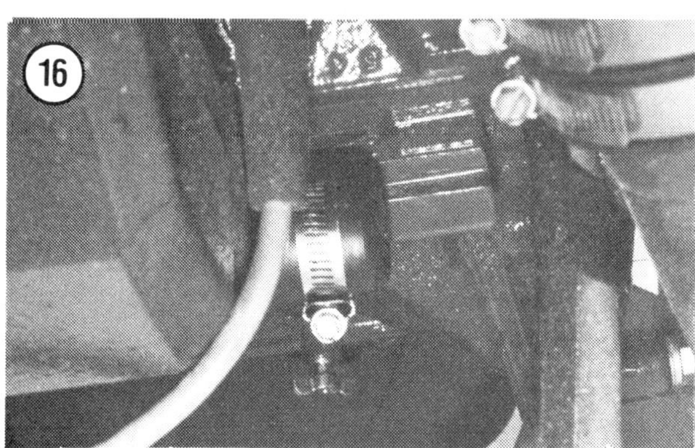
16

17A

17B

6. Unclamp and disconnect the water supply hose between the thermostat housing and water pump. See B, **Figure 18** (typical).
7. If equipped with power steering, remove the drain plug from the lower end of the power steering oil cooler. See **Figure 11** (typical).
8. 7.5L—Remove the oil cooler drain plug located on the starboard rear of the engine (**Figure 19**).
9. Allow cooling system to drain *completely*, then disconnect and ground the ignition coil high tension (thick) lead to the engine block (**Figure 20**, typical). Crank the engine over several times to purge any water remaining in the water pump.

Closed Cooling System (All Engines)

The fresh water section of a closed cooling system need not be drained during winter months, provided it is kept filled with a 50/50 solution of pure soft water and ethylene glycol antifreeze. However, the seawater section must be drained *completely*.

Seawater section

1. Place a container under the seawater pump, if space permits. This will prevent water from draining into the bilge.
2. Remove both hoses at the seawater pump to drain the pump and heat exchanger.
3. Lift and flex the hoses to make sure they are completely drained.

4. Remove the exhaust elbow drain plugs and drain the elbows.
5. Allow seawater section to drain *completely*, then reconnect the hoses to the seawater pump and install the exhaust elbow drain plugs.

Fresh water section

1. Place containers under drain points, if space permits. This will prevent coolant from draining into the bilge.
2. Remove the pressure fill cap from the reservoir. See **Figure 21** (typical).
3. Remove the engine block drain valves. See **Figure 8** and **Figure 9** (inline engine, typical) or **Figures 12-17** (V6 and V8 engines) as required.
4. Disconnect the large hose at the engine water pump. See C, **Figure 18** (typical). Lower the hose and flex it several times to drain any remaining coolant.
5. Disconnect the coolant recovery tank line at the heat exchanger, if so equipped. Drain the recovery tank.

NOTE

If coolant will not be reinstalled, disconnect the ignition coil high tension (thick) lead and ground it at the engine block. Crank the engine over several times to remove all water from the

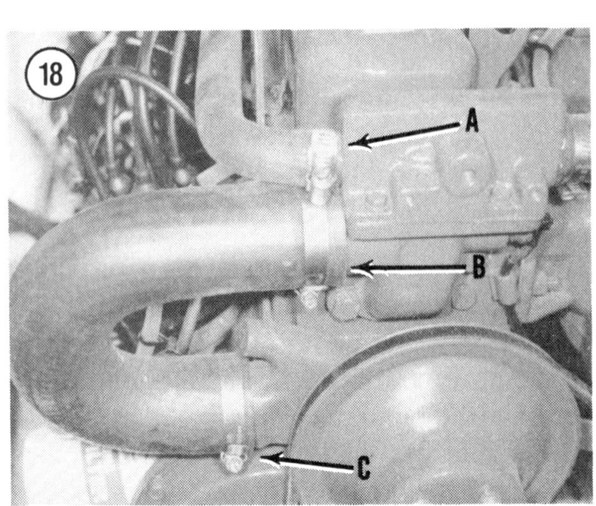

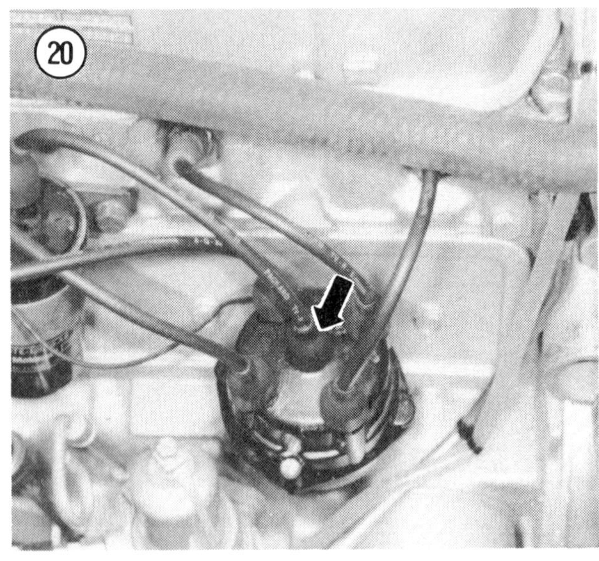

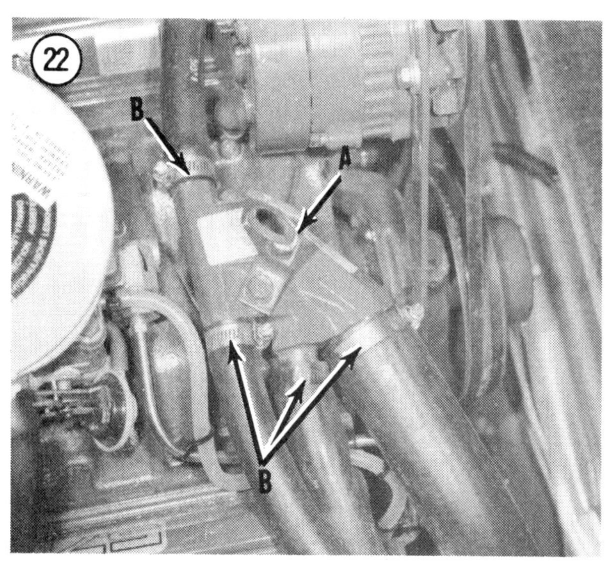

water pump before performing Step 6. Leave the drain valves open after installation.

6. Allow fresh water section to drain *completely*, then install the engine block drain valve. Reconnect the large hose to the water pump and the lower hose to the coolant recovery tank, if so equipped.

COOLING SYSTEM REFILLING

In Preparation for Storage

Under normal circumstances, the fresh water section of a closed cooling system would not be drained until just before the boat is to be returned to service from winter storage. The following procedure pertains to standard cooling systems and is designed to provide additional protection against freeze damage during winter temperatures.

CAUTION
Do not run the engine after performing the storage cooling service procedure that follows. Before returning the boat to service, drain the coolant as described in this chapter and tighten all fasteners and clamps to specifications.

1. Close all drain valves. Replace any rubber hoses, caps, plugs or clamps that exhibit signs of deterioration.
2. Remove the thermostat housing. See A, **Figure 22** (typical).
3. Remove the thermostat and gasket. Discard the gasket.
4. Pour a 50/50 solution of pure soft water and ethylene gylcol antifreeze into the thermostat housing until the cylinder head, block and manifold are full.
5. Reinstall thermostat with a new gasket. Reinstall thermostat housing and tighten fasteners securely.
6. Disconect the hoses at the thermostat housing. See B, **Figure 22** (typical).
7. Pour coolant mixture into each hose until full, then reconnect to the thermostat housing. Under some circumstances, the long hose connected to the thermostat housing may not fill completely. This is normal, but do not pour more than 1 quart of coolant into the hose.

NOTE
The antifreeze may leak through the stern drive water pump housing after Step 8 has been performed. Although this is normal and should not be a cause for alarm, OMC recommends that you place a plastic bag over the drive unit to retain the antifreeze.

8. With the stern drive in a vertical position, crank the engine over 1-2 times to route coolant into the stern drive water pump housing.

Returning the Engine to Service

Most ethylene glycol antifreeze solutions used in closed cooling systems tend to become corrosive after approximately 3 years of use or if a blown head gasket allows exhaust gases to enter the cooling system. While such corrosive tendencies will not cause significant damage to the engine, they

5

do produce loose particles that can plug the coolant side of the heat exchanger.

The increasing usage of aluminum components in engines, water pumps, manifolds and recovery tanks has led to the development of an antifreeze formulation recommended for use with aluminum engines.

This new type antifreeze formula should be used with all OMC marine engine closed cooling systems. Check the antifreeze container and make sure it meets one of the major automakers' specifications, such as Ford specification ESE-M97B44-A or GM specification 1825M.

1. Remove the pressure fill cap from the heat exchanger.
2. Fill the fresh water section with a 50/50 mixture of pure soft water and ethylene glycol antifreeze until the fluid level is approximately one inch below the top of the filler neck.

CAUTION
Water must flow through the stern drive pump in Step 3 or possible damage to the pump and engine may result.

3. If the boat is not in the water, connect a flushing device and adjust water flow. Start the engine and run at about 1,000 rpm, adding coolant to the heat exchanger as necessary to maintain the coolant level at approximately one inch below the top of the filler neck. When the engine reaches normal operating temperature and coolant level remains constant, reinstall the pressure fill cap.
4. If equipped with a coolant recovery system, remove the reservoir cap and fill with coolant to the FULL mark on the reservoir.
5. Check for leaks while the engine is running and note the position of the engine temperature gauge—it should be normal.

WARNING
Do not remove the pressure fill cap when the engine is warm or hot. You may be seriously scalded or burned by coolant escaping under pressure.

6. Shut the engine off and allow it to cool for 30 minutes. Turn the pressure fill cap to the first detent and allow any pressure to escape, then remove the cap.
7. Recheck the coolant level in the heat exchanger and add coolant as required to bring it to the specified level.

FITTING OUT

Preparing the boat for use after storage is relatively easy if the engine and stern drive unit were properly prepared before storage. The following suggestions for fitting out are based on the recommendations made by OMC.

1. Clean the engine and stern drive unit with a solvent such as kerosene to remove any accumulated dirt and preservative oil. Retouch any paint blemishes.

NOTE
If the boat is to be left in the water for an extended period of time, it may be advisable to cover the underwater surfaces (including the stern drive unit) with an antifouling paint. Do ***not*** *use a paint containing copper or mercury, as these elements may increase galvanic corrosion.*

2. Remove any protective covers installed on the flame arrestor, carburetor and exhaust outlets.
3. Drain antifreeze from standard cooling systems, if installed.
4. Make sure all drain valves and plugs are tightly closed and that all cooling system hoses are securely clamped in place.

5. Inspect all hoses for cracks, weak walls and leaks. Replace any that appear questionable.
6. Check all through-hull fittings for leaks and proper valve operation.
7. Remove, clean and reinstall the flame arrestor.
8. Check the fuel system. Refill the tanks if they were drained. Turn the fuel shut-off valve(s) on and check all fuel lines for leaks.
9. Check battery electrolyte level and fill if necessary. Make certain battery has a full charge (recharge if necessary). Clean the battery terminals and install the battery. Connect the positive cable, then the negative cable, making certain the cables are connected with proper polarity. Cover battery terminals with a light coat of petroleum jelly or spray with a can of CRC-6-66 (available from your OMC dealer) or equivalent.
10. Check the crankcase oil level. Add oil, if necessary. If oil was not changed at time of lay-up or if engine has been in storage for an extended period of time, change the oil and oil filter.
11. Check the power steering and power trim hydrauic pump oil levels (if so equipped) and top up as required.
12. Check and adjsut drive belt tension.
13. Remove the distributor cap and examine the distributor contact breaker points. Replace point set if any wear is evident. If old points are to be reused, clean thoroughly with alcohol or acetone to remove any traces of oil. Clean the inside of the distributor cap with a soft cloth and spray with a can of CRC-6-66 (available from your OMC dealer), then reinstall the cap.
14. Make a thorough check of the boat, engine and stern drive unit for loose or missing nuts, bolts and/or screws. Tighten, replace or take such other corrective actions as may be necessary.
15. Examine the sacrificial zinc elements and replace if more than 25 percent eroded.

WARNING
If your boat is not equipped with a bilge blower, make sure the engine cover or hatch is open and properly supported before performing Step 16. This will prevent the buildup of any fumes that might result in an explosion if there is a fuel leak.

16. Provide a source of water for engine cooling. Make certain a Coast Guard-approved fire extinguisher is handy, then start the engine. While the engine is warming up, watch the instrument panel gauges to make certain that all systems are operating as they should. You should also check for any signs of fuel, oil or water leaks.
17. Proceed with engine tune-up. See Chapter Four for instructions and specifications.

ENGINE SUBMERSION

If the engine should become submerged in water for any reason, it should be retrieved as soon as possible and taken to an OMC dealer for immediate disassembly and lubrication of all internal parts. All electrical components should also be dried and then checked for water damage. Delay in retrieval, disassembly and lubrication can result in extensive and costly engine damage.

Chapter Six

Inline Engines

This chapter covers the GM 2.5L and 3.0L 4-cylinder engines and the Ford 2.3L OHC engine used with Cobra stern drives. Although differing in displacement, the GM engines are essentially the same design with many interchangeable parts. All engines are marine versions of popular automotive engines used in many GM and Ford automobiles. The procedures given in this chapter apply to all 3 engines, except where specifically noted.

The GM engines are a pushrod design; the Ford engine is an overhead cam design. The cylinders are numbered 1-2-3-4 from front to rear; the firing order on all engines is 1-3-4-2. The cast iron GM cylinder head contains intake and exhaust valves with integral valve guides. Rocker arms are retained on individual threaded shoulder bolts. A ball pivot valve train is used, with camshaft motion transferred through hydraulic lifters to the rocker arms by pushrods. No lash adjustment is necessary in service or during assembly unless some component in the valve train has been removed or replaced.

The gear-driven camshaft is located above the crankshaft and is supported by 3 bearings. The oil pump mounted at the bottom front of the engine block is driven by the camshaft via the distributor.

The crankshaft is supported by 5 main bearings, with the rear bearing providing the crankshaft thrust surfaces. Crankshaft rotation is counterclockwise when seen from the drive unit end of the engine.

The cylinder block is cast iron with full length water jackets around each cylinder.

The Ford valve train uses pivot-type rocker arms with hydraulic valve lash adjusters at the fulcrum point of the rocker arm.

The belt-driven camshaft is located in the cylinder head and is supported by 4 bearings. The cogged belt which drives the camshaft also operates an auxiliary shaft. The auxiliary shaft drives the oil pump, fuel pump and distributor. Tension is maintained on the camshaft drive belt by a locked idler pulley riding on the outside of the belt.

The crankshaft is supported by 5 main bearings, with the No. 3 bearing providing the

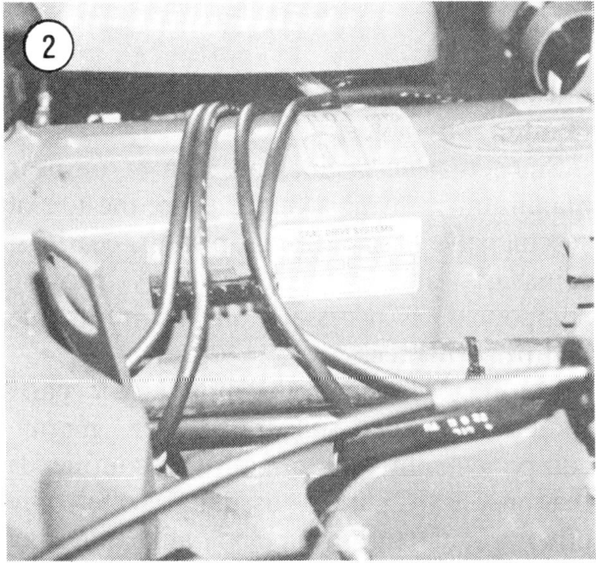

crankshaft thrust surfaces. Crankshaft rotation is counterclockwise when seen from the drive unit end of the engine.

The cylinder block is lightweight cast iron with full length water jackets around each cylinder.

Engine specifications (**Table 1** and **Table 2**) and tightening torques (**Tables 3-5**) are at the end of the chapter.

ENGINE SERIAL NUMBER

An engine identification number is stamped on a plate or decal located on the valve cover. See **Figure 1** (GM) or **Figure 2** (Ford). This information indicates if there are unique parts or if internal changes have been made during the model year. It is important when ordering replacement parts for the engine.

SPECIAL TOOLS

Where special tools are required or recommended for engine overhaul, the tool numbers are provided. GM tool part numbers have a "J" prefix. Ford tool part numbers have a "T" prefix. While these tools can sometimes be rented from rental dealers, they can be purchased. Order tools for GM engines from Kent-Moore, Inc., 28635 Mound Road, Warren, Michigan 48089. Order tools for Ford engines from Owatonna Tools, Inc., 2013 4th Street N.W., Owatonna, Minnesota 55060.

GASKET SEALANT

Gasket sealant is used instead of pre-formed gaskets betwen numerous mating surfaces on the engines covered in this chapter. Two types of gasket sealant are used: room temperature vulcanizing (RTV) and anaerobic. Since these 2 materials have different sealing properties, they cannot be used interchangeably.

Room Temperature Vulcanizing (RTV) Sealant

This black silicone gel is supplied in tubes and is available from your OMC dealer or any automotive dealer. Moisture in the air causes RTV to cure. Always place the cap on the tube as soon as possible when using RTV. RTV has a shelf life of one year and will not cure properly when the shelf life has expired. Check the expiration date on RTV tubes before using and keep partially used tubes tightly sealed.

Applying RTV Sealant

Clean all RTV residue from mating surfaces. They should be clean and free of oil and dirt. Remove all RTV gasket material from blind attaching holes, as it can cause a hydraulic effect and affect bolt torque.

Unless otherwise specified, apply RTV sealant in a continuous bead 3-5 mm (1/8-3/16 in.) thick. Apply the sealant on the inner side of mounting holes. Torque mating parts within 10 minutes after application.

Anaerobic Sealant

This is a colored gel supplied in tubes. It cures only in the absence of air, as when squeezed tightly between 2 machined mating surfaces. For this reason, it will not spoil if the cap is left off the tube. It should not be used if one mating surface is flexible.

Applying Anaerobic Sealant

Clean all gasket residue from mating surfaces. They should be clean and free of oil and dirt. Remove all gasket material from blind attaching holes, as it can cause a hydraulic effect and affect bolt torque.

Unless otherwise specified, apply anaerobic gasket material in a continuous 1 mm (0.04 in.) or narrower bead to one sealing surface. Apply the sealant on the inner side of mounting holes. Torque mating parts within 15 minutes after application.

REPLACEMENT PARTS

Various changes are made to automotive engine blocks used for marine applications. Numerous part changes are required due to operation in fresh and salt water. For example, the cylinder head gasket must be corrosion-resistant. Marine engines use head gaskets of copper or stainless steel instead of the standard steel used in automotive applications. Brass expansion or core plugs

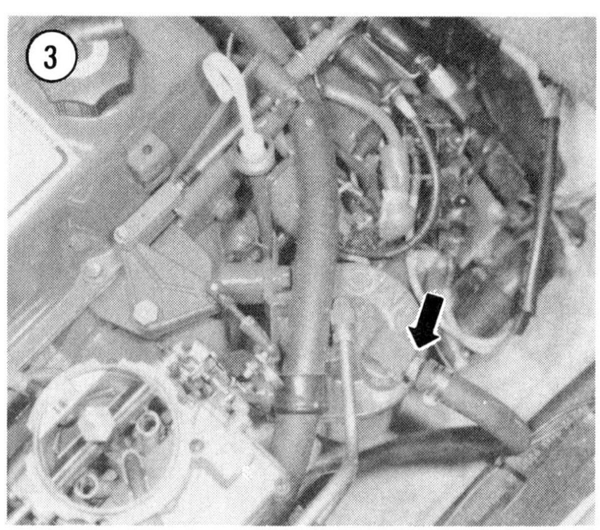

must be used instead of the steel plugs found in automotive blocks.

Since marine engines are run at or near maximum rpm most of the time, the use of special valve lifters, springs, pistons, bearings, camshafts and other heavy-duty moving components is necessary for maximum life and performance.

For these reasons, automotive-type parts should not be substituted for marine components. In addition, OMC recommends that only OMC parts be used. Parts offered by other manufacturers may look alike, but may not be manufactured to OMC specifications. Any damage resulting from the use of other than OMC parts is not covered by the OMC warranty.

ENGINE REMOVAL

Some service procedures can be performed with the engine in the boat; others require removal. The boat design and service procedure to be performed will determine whether the engine must be removed.

If the clearance between the front of the engine and the engine compartment bulkhead is less than 6 in., the stern drive unit must be removed in order to disengage the driveshaft from the engine coupler.

The stern drive must also be removed if engine mount height must be altered during engine removal.

WARNING

The engine is heavy, awkward to handle and has sharp edges. It may shift or drop suddenly during removal. To prevent serious injury, always observe the following precautions.

1. Never place any part of your body where a moving or falling engine may trap, cut or crush you.

2. If you must push the engine during removal, use a board or similar tool to keep your hands out of danger.

3. Be sure the hoist is designed to lift engines and has enough load capacity for your engine.

4. Be sure the hoist is securely attached to safe lifting points on the engine.

5. The engine should not be difficult to lift with a proper hoist. If it is, stop lifting, lower the engine back onto its mounts and make sure the engine has been completely separated from the vessel.

1. Remove the engine hood cover and all panels that interfere with engine removal. Place the cover and panels to one side out of the way.

2. Disconnect the negative battery cable, then the positive battery cable. As a precaution, remove the battery from the boat.

3. Use a flare nut wrench to loosen and disconnect both power steering hydraulic lines at the actuator unit. Cap the lines and plug the actuator fittings to prevent leakage and the entry of contamination. Secure the lines at a point higher than the engine power steering pump during the remainder of this procedure to prevent damage or the loss of fluid.

4A. *Ford*—Disconnect the fuel inlet line from the tank to the fuel filter canister at the filter canister (**Figure 3**). Cap the line and canister fitting to prevent leakage and the entry of contamination.

4B. *GM*—Disconnect the fuel inlet line from the tank to the fuel pump at the pump (**Figure 4**). Cap the line and the pump fitting to prevent leakage and the entry of contamination.

5. Locate and unplug all electrical harness connectors. This step will include the:

a. Rubber 2-wire trim/tilt sender connector.
b. Plastic 3-wire trim/tilt wire connector.
c. Rubber 3-wire trim/tilt instrument cable connector.
d. Rubber instrument cable connector.
e. Battery cable lead at the starter solenoid.
f. Black ground lead at engine stud near starter motor.

6A. *Ford*—Loosen the 8 exhaust hose clamps. See **Figure 5**. Lubricating the exhaust pipe with dishwashing liquid will make it easier to move the lower hose. Pry or twist the lower hose from the exhaust adapter and slide it down the exhaust pipe. Remove the adapter and upper hose from the exhaust manifold.

6B. *GM*—Loosen the 4 exhaust hose clamps. See **Figure 6**. Lubricating the exhaust pipe with dishwashing fluid will make it easier to move the hose. Pry or twist the hose from the elbow and slide it down onto the exhaust pipe.

7. Refer to **Figure 7** and remove the remote control (A) and transom bracket (B) shift cables from the engine shift bracket. Remove the cables from each of the anchor pockets (C) and disconnect from the shift lever (D). Secure the adjustable trunnion to the remote control cable with tape to prevent misadjustment when the cable is reinstalled.

8. Disconnect the throttle cable at the carburetor and manifold anchor block. See **Figure 8** (typical).

9. Loosen the water supply hose clamp and remove the hose from the transom bracket water tube.

10. Attach a suitable hoist to the engine lifting brackets. The hoist must have a minimum lift capacity of 1,500 lb. Raise the hoist enough to remove all slack.

NOTE
At this point, there should be no hoses, wires or linkage connecting the engine to the boat or stern drive unit. Recheck this to make sure nothing will hamper engine removal.

11. Remove and save the self-locking nut and flat washer from each rear engine mount. See **Figure 9**.

12. Remove and save the lag screws at each front engine mount. See **Figure 10**.

13A. If the stern drive was removed, lift the engine up and out of the engine compartment.

13B. If the stern drive was not removed, lift the engine enough to pull it forward and disengage the driveshaft from the engine flywheel coupler. Once the driveshaft is free of the coupler, lift the engine up and out of the engine compartment.

14. If the exhaust pipe requires service, remove the 4 retaining screws and the top

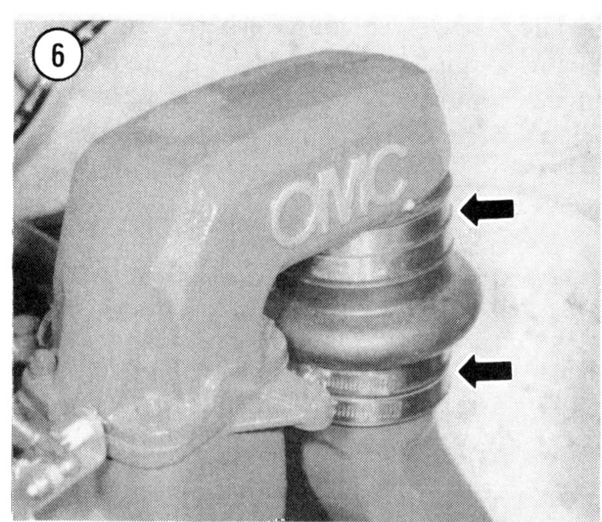

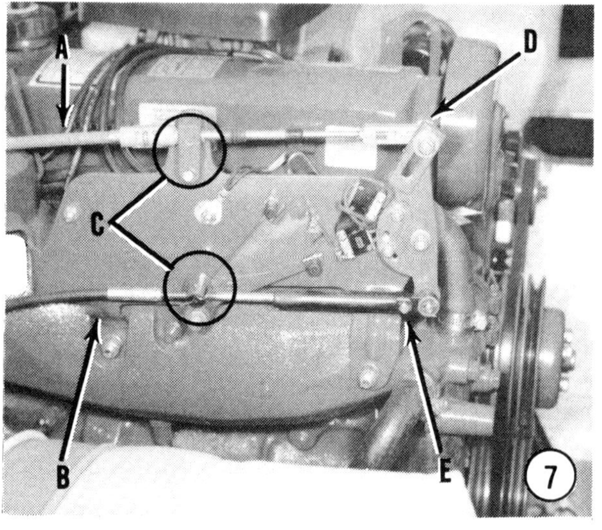

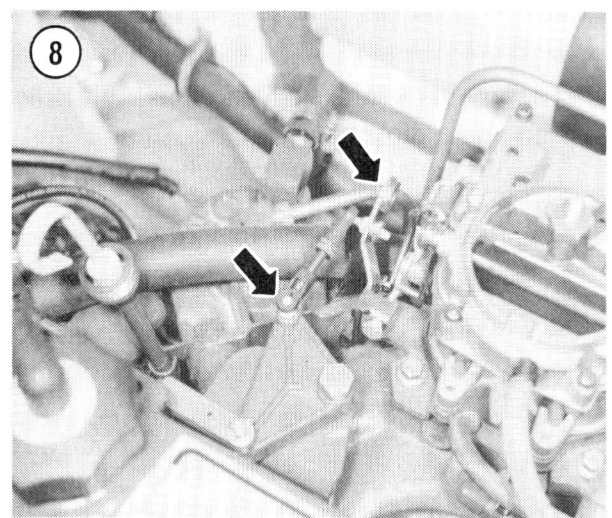

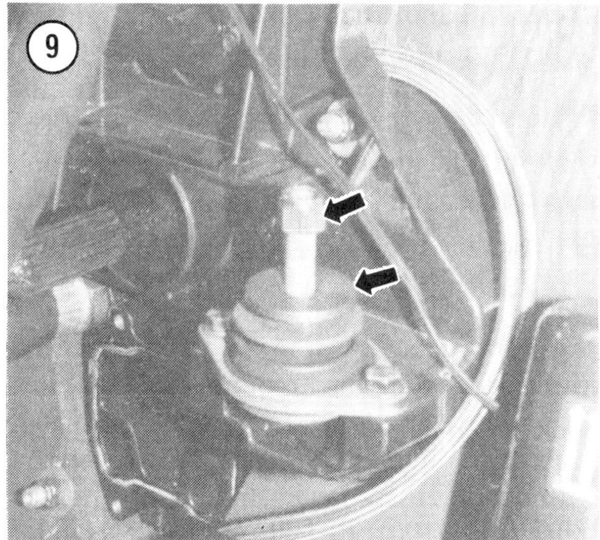

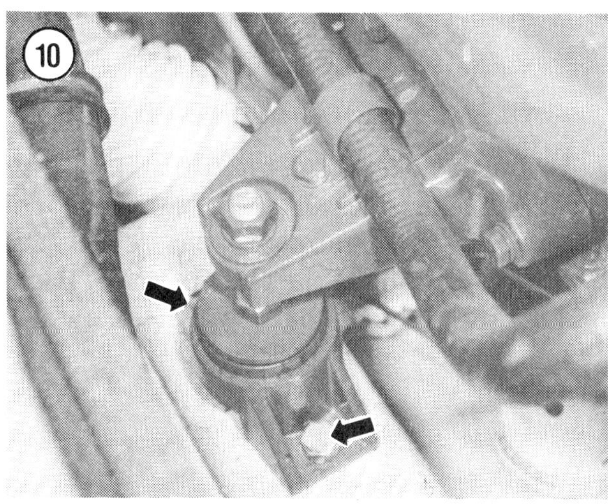

port trim line clamp, if so equipped. Remove the exhaust pipe and discard the seal. Clean all residue from the transom bracket and exhaust pipe surface.

ENGINE INSTALLATION

Engine installation is the reverse of removal, plus the following:

1. If the exhaust pipe was serviced, coat a new seal with OMC Adhesive M and install in transom bracket groove. Wipe exhaust pipe screw threads with OMC Gasket Sealing Compound. Install exhaust pipe to transom bracket and tighten screws to 10-12 ft.-lb. (14-16 N•m).
2. Install any shims or adapters used with the engine mounts.
3. Install forward mount lag screws securely and tighten the rear mount self-locking nuts to 28-30 ft.-lb. (38-40 N•m).
4. If stern drive was removed, perform the *Engine Alignment* procedure as described in this chapter after securing the engine mounts.
5. Lubricate the transom bracket shift cable anchor with OMC Triple-Guard grease.
6. Fill the engine with an oil recommended in Chapter Four.
7. Fill the cooling system, if equipped with a closed system. See Chapter Five.
8. Adjust the drive belts. See Chapter Ten.
9. Adjust the timing as required. See Chapter Four.

REAR ENGINE MOUNTS

WARNING

The engine is heavy and may shift or drop suddenly. Never place your hands or any part of your body where the moving engine may trap or crush you. If you can't remove the mounts without placing your hands where the moving engine may injure them, support the engine with a jackstand as well as a hoist to be certain the engine can't fall on you.

Engine mounts are non-adjustable and rarely require service. Replace any broken or deteriorated mounts immediately to reduce strain on remaining mounts and drive line components.

Removal

1. Attach a suitable hoist to the engine lifting brackets. The hoist must have a minimum lift capacity of 1,500 lb. Raise the hoist enough to remove all slack.
2. Remove and save the self-locking nut and flat washer from each rear engine mount. See **Figure 9**.
3. Lift the engine off the rear mounts with the hoist, then remove the screws and washers holding the mount assembly. Remove the mount assembly from the transom plate.
4. To disassemble the mount, clamp it in a vise. Hold the square nut with a suitable open-end wrench and remove the bolt. Separate the mount and 2 flat washers (early models) or 1 flat and 1 conical washer (late models).
5. To reassemble the mount, place a flat washer (early model) or conical washer (late model) on the bolt (the concave side of the conical washer should face the mount). Install bolt through the flat side (bottom) of the mount. Place the other washer on the bolt and install the nut finger-tight.

NOTE
The 90 degree relationship established between the nut and mounting holes in Step 6 must be maintained or the engine mount pad slot will not engage the rear mount during installation.

6. Clamp the mount assembly in a vise. Align the mount holes 90° to any side of the square nut. Holding the mount in this position, tighten the bolt to 18-20 ft.-lb. (24-27 N•m).
7. Position the mount assembly on the transom plate. Reinstall the screws with washers and tighten to 20-25 ft.-lb. (27-34 N•m).
8. Lower the engine with the hoist until the mount pad slot engages the square nut. Reinstall the flat washer and self-locking nut. Tighten nut to 28-30 ft.-lb. (38-41 N•m).

ENGINE ALIGNMENT

To assure satisfactory engine/drivetrain life, engine alignment must be checked during reinstallation whenever stern drive unit removal is required for engine removal. Correct alignment is provided by adjusting the front mounts up or down as required. OMC alignment tool part No. 912273 with universal handle part No. 311880 is required to perform this procedure.

Slide the alignment tool through the gimbal housing from outside the boat. The tool must fit through the gimbal bearing and into the engine coupler easily. If the tool binds, adjust the front engine mounts in the proper direction to remove the binding.

Engine mount adjustment is made by readjusting the position of the upper and lower nuts on the mount screw. When alignment is correct, retighten the front mounts to maintain alignment. Hold one nut with an open-end wrench and tighten the other nut to 100-120 ft.-lb. (136-163 N•m) for Ford engines or 115-140 ft.-lb. (156-190 N•m) for GM engines.

DISASSEMBLY CHECKLISTS

To use the checklists, remove and inspect each part in the order mentioned. To reassemble, go through the checklists backwards, installing the parts in order. Each major part is covered in its own section in this chapter, unless otherwise noted.

Decarbonizing or Valve Service

1. Remove the valve cover.

2. Remove the intake and exhaust manifolds.
3. Remove the rocker arms.
4. Remove the cylinder head.
5. Remove and inspect the valves. Inspect the valve guides and seats, repairing or replacing as required.
6. Assemble by reversing Steps 1-5.

Valve and Ring Service

1. Perform Steps 1-5 of *Decarbonizing or Valve Service.*
2. Remove the oil pan and oil pump.
3. Remove the pistons with connecting rods.
4. Remove the piston rings. It is not necessary to separate the pistons from the connecting rods unless a piston, connecting rod or piston pin needs repair or replacement.
5. Assemble by reversing Steps 1-4.

General Overhaul

1. Remove the engine from the boat.
2. Remove the flywheel.
3. Remove the mount brackets and oil pressure sending unit from the engine.
4. If available, mount the engine on an engine stand. These can be rented from equipment rental dealers. The stand is not absolutely necessary, but it will make the job much easier.
5. Remove the following accessories or components from the engine, if present:
   a. Alternator and mounting bracket.
   b. Power steering pump and mounting bracket.
   c. Spark plug wires and distributor cap.
   d. Carburetor and fuel lines.
   e. Oil dipstick and tube.
   f. Seawater pump, if so equipped.
6. Check the engine for signs of coolant or oil leaks.
7. Clean the outside of the engine.
8. Remove the distributor. See Chapter Eleven.
9. Remove all hoses and tubes connected to the engine.
10. Remove the fuel pump. See Chapter Nine.
11. Remove the intake and exhaust manifolds.
12. Remove the thermostat. See Chapter Ten.
13. Remove the valve cover and rocker arms.

14A. *Ford*—Remove the crankshaft pulley, timing belt cover and timing belt.

14B. *GM*—Remove the crankshaft pulley, front hub, front cover and camshaft/crankshaft sprockets.

15. Remove the camshaft.
16. Ford—Remove the auxiliary shaft.
17. Remove the cylinder head.
18. Remove the oil pan and oil pump.
19. Remove the pistons and connecting rods.
20. Remove the crankshaft.
21. Inspect the cylinder block.
22. Assemble by reversing Steps 1-20.

VALVE COVER

Removal/Installation

Ford engine

Refer to **Figure 11** (typical) for this procedure.

1. Disconnect the crankcase ventilation hose at the valve cover oil cap (**Figure 12**).
2. Disconnect the spark plug cables at the plugs and remove the plug cable retainers from their brackets on the cover. See **Figure 13**.
3. Remove the cover attaching screws.
4. Rap the valve cover with a soft-faced mallet to break the gasket seal. Remove the valve cover.
5. Clean any gasket residue from the cylinder head and valve cover with degreaser and a putty knife.

6. Coat one side of a new gasket with an il-resistant sealer. Install the gasket sealer-side down on the cylinder head.
7. Position the valve cover on the cylinder head.
8. Install the attaching screws and tighten to specifications (**Table 4**).
9. Install the spark plug cable retainers on the valve cover brackets. Connect the wires to the appropriate spark plugs. See Chapter Four.
10. Reconnect the crankcase ventilation hose to the valve cover oil cap.

GM engine

1. Disconnect the crankcase ventilation hose at the PCV valve on the valve cover.
2. Unclip or detach any wires attached to the valve cover.
3. Remove the cover attaching screws.
4. Rap the valve cover with a soft-faced mallet to break the gasket seal. Remove the valve cover.
5. Clean any gasket residue from the cylinder head and valve cover with degreaser and a putty knife.
6. Install a new gasket in the valve cover. Gasket tabs must engage cover notches.
7. Position the valve cover on the cylinder head.
8. Install the attaching screws and tighten to specifications (**Table 3**).
9. Reconnect the crankcase ventilation hose to the PCV valve.

INTAKE AND EXHAUST MANIFOLDS

The Ford engine uses separate intake and exhaust manifolds. The GM engine intake and exhaust manifolds are combined in a single unit.

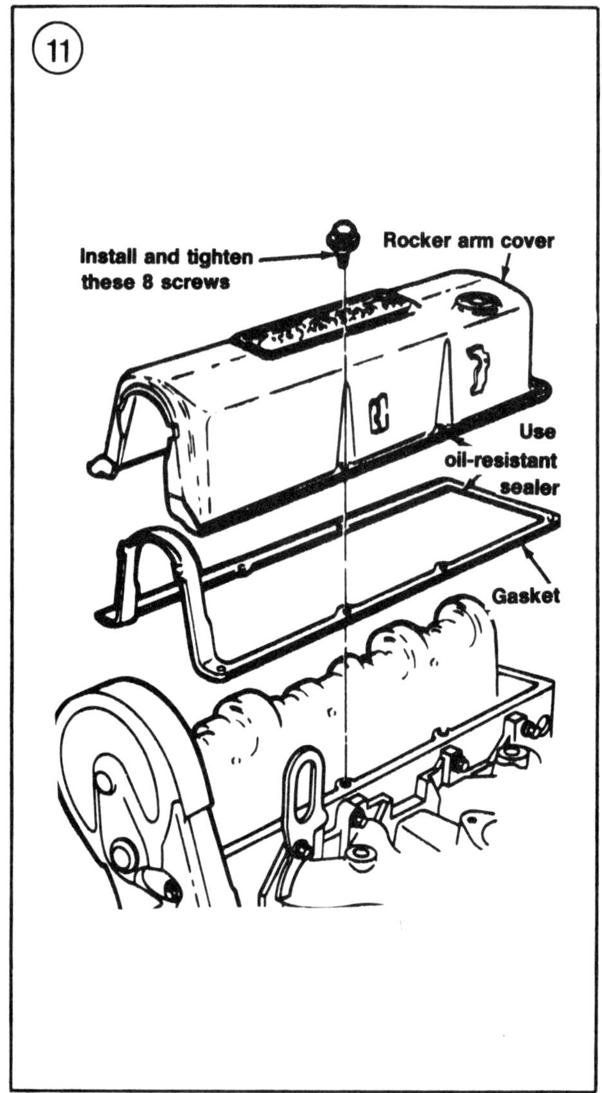

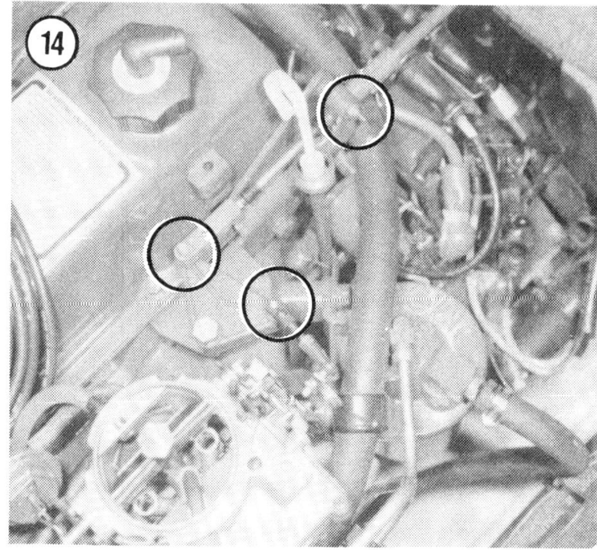

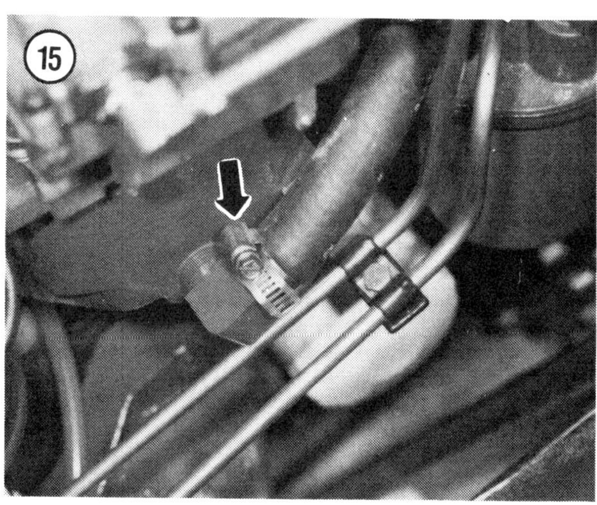

Ford Engine Intake Manifold Removal/Installation

Refer to **Figure 14** for this procedure.

1. Disconnect the negative battery cable.
2. Open the cylinder block water drain and allow all water to drain.
3. Disconnect the throttle cable from the bellcrank and anchor block. Disconnect the carburetor linkage at the bellcrank. See **Figure 14.**
4. Disconnect the fuel lines at the carburetor and fuel filter assembly. Cap the lines and fittings to prevent leakage and the entry of contamination.
5. Remove the fuel lines from the intake manifold clamp and disconnect both lines from the fuel pump. Cap the lines and pump fittings to prevent leakage and entry of contamination.
6. Unbolt and remove the fuel filter assembly from the intake manifold.
7. Unclamp and disconnect the water hose at the manifold elbow. See **Figure 15.**
8. Remove flame arrestor and carburetor. See Chapter Nine.
9. Disconnect all secondary leads at the distributor cap, then remove the distributor cap and rotor. See Chapter Eleven.
10. Disconnect the PCV valve from the crankcase hose. See **Figure 16.**
11. Remove the 2 upper rear manifold bolts. Place throttle cable bracket to one side out of the way.
12. Remove the 2 upper front manifold bolts and lifting bracket.
13. Remove the lower manifold attaching bolts. Note that end bolts have a clamp attached.
14. Remove the manifold and gasket from the cylinder head. Discard the gasket.
15. Clean all gasket residue from the manifold and cylinder head mating surfaces with degreaser and a putty knife.

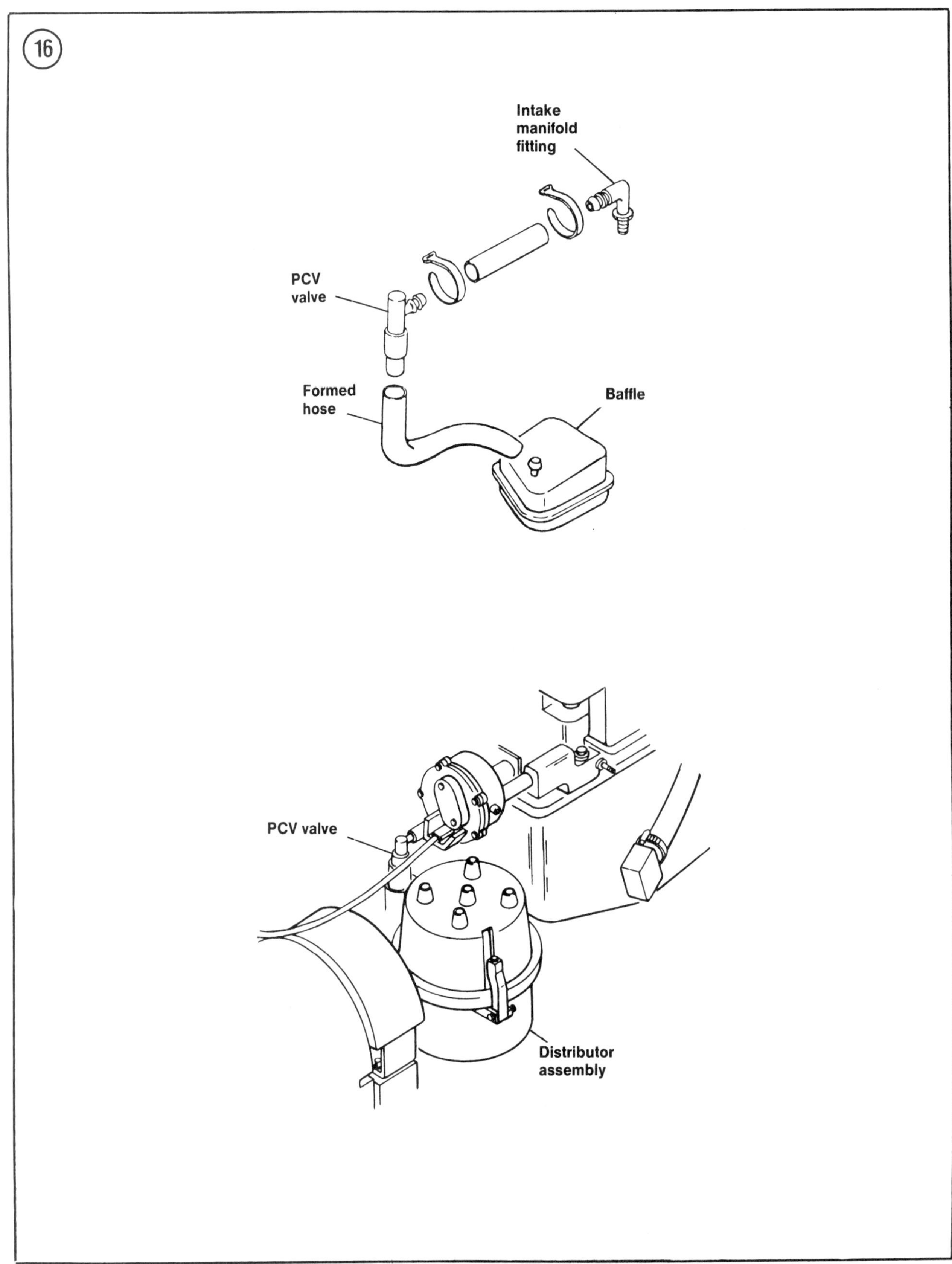
16
Intake
manifold
fitting
PCV
valve
Formed
hose
Baffle
PCV valve
Distributor
assembly

16. Inspect the manifold as described in this chapter.

17. Installation is the reverse of removal, plus the following:

a. Use new manifold and carburetor gaskets.

b. Install all manifold fasteners finger-tight, then tighten to 60-84 in.-lb. (6.8-9.5 N•m) and retighten to 14-18 ft.-lb. (19-24 N•m) following the sequence shown in **Figure 17**.

c. Run the engine and check for fuel and water leaks.

Ford Engine Exhaust Manifold Removal/Installation

1. Open the cylinder block water drains and allow all water to drain. Loosen the clamps holding the exhaust hoses to the exhaust elbow.
2. Use a soapy water solution to lubricate the top of the exhaust pipe and then slide the lower hose down off the elbow.
3. Lubricate the upper end of the elbow and twist it out of the high-rise exhaust hose.
4. Disconnect the shift cables from the shift bracket. Unbolt the shift bracket from the manifold and high-rise elbow. Place shift bracket out of the way on the engine.

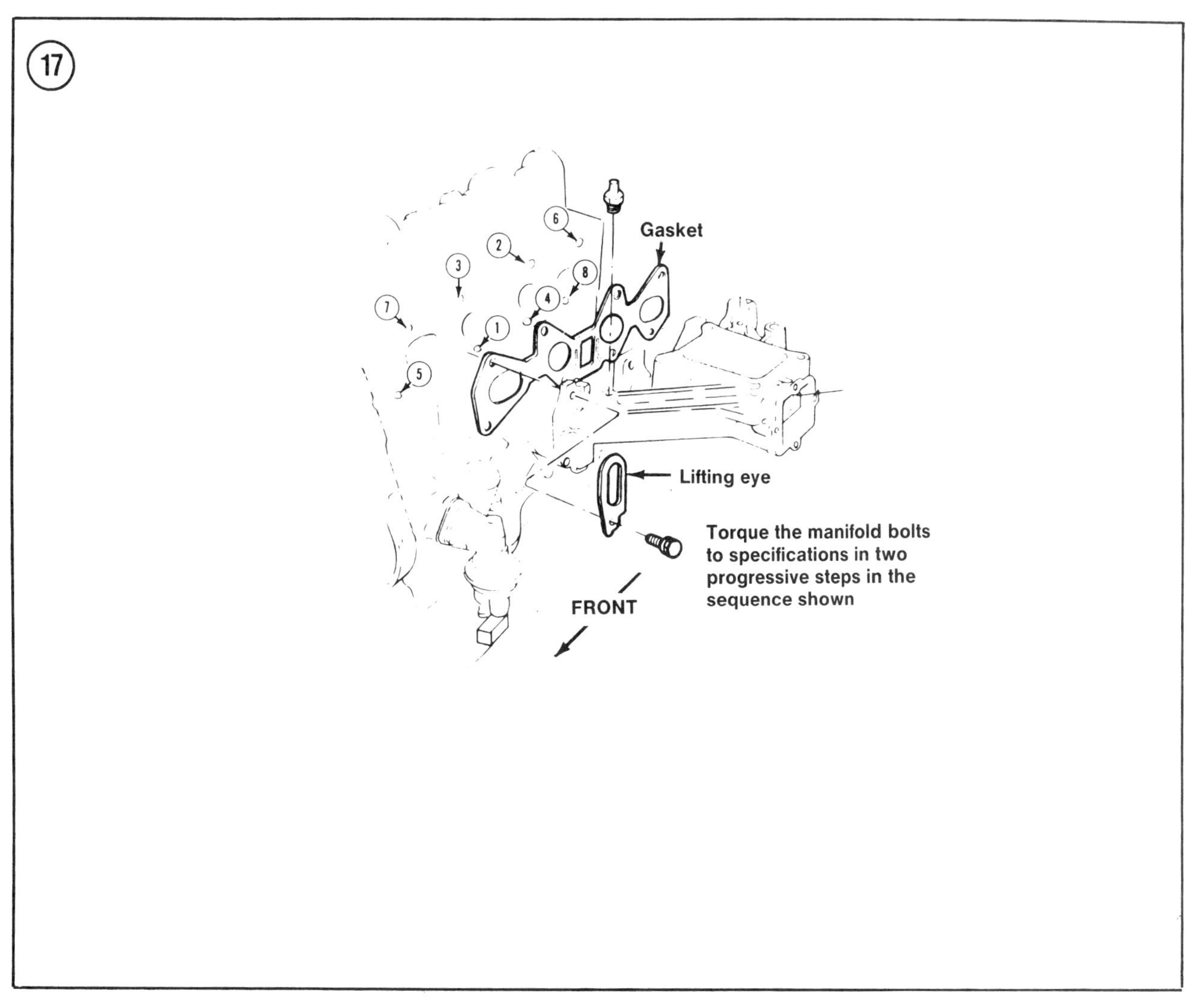

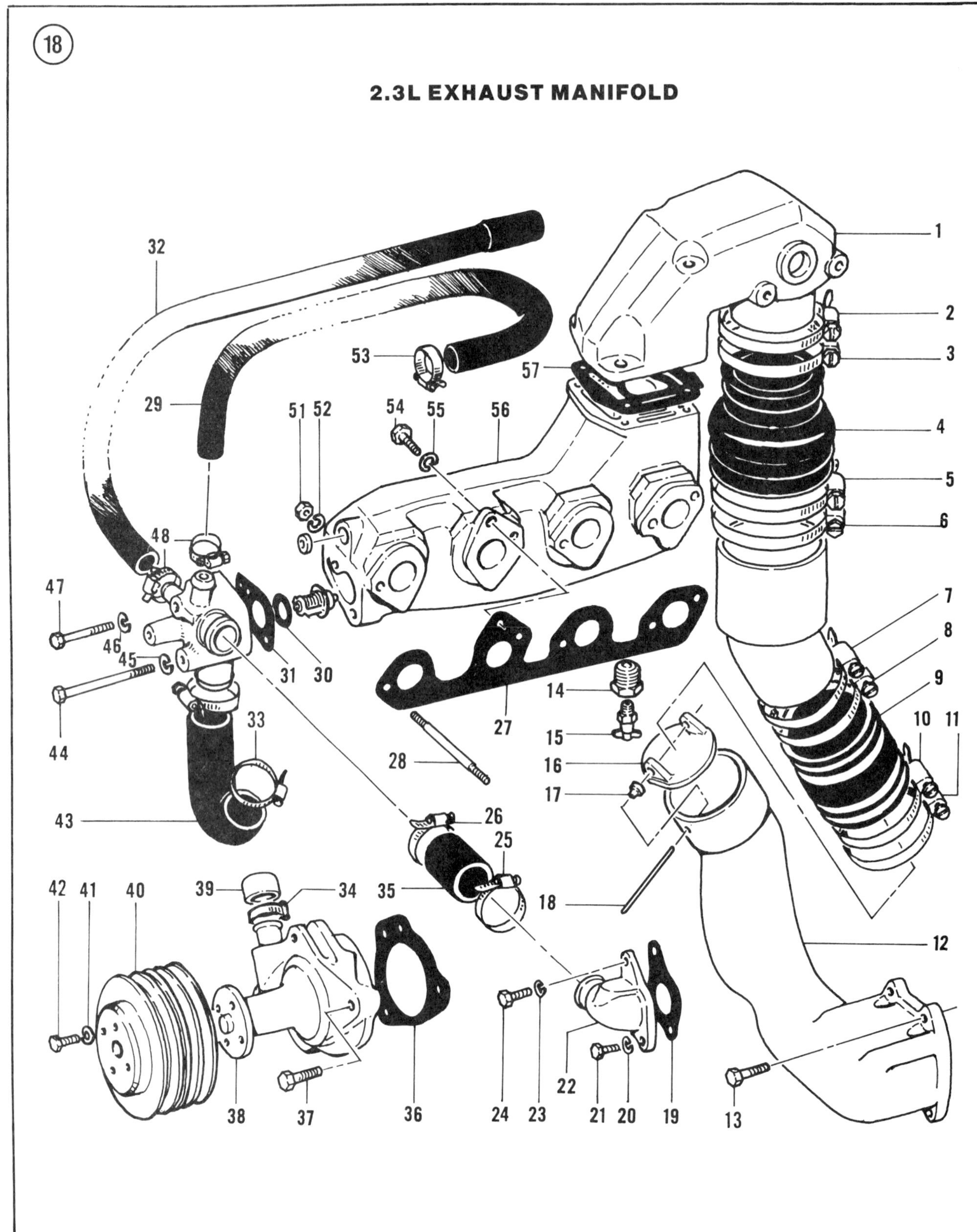
18
2.3L EXHAUST MANIFOLD
1
2
3
4
5
6
7
8
9
10
11
12
13
14
15
16
17
18
19
20
21
22
23
24
25
26
27
28
29
30
31
32
33
34
35
36
37
38
39
40
41
42
43
44
45
46
47
48
51
52
53
54
55
56
57

1. Exhaust elbow
2. Clamp
3. Clamp
4. Hose
5. Clamp
6. Clamp
7. Clamp
8. Clamp
9. Hose
10. Clamp
11. Clamp
12. Exhaust pipe
13. Exhaust pipe screw
14. Fitting
15. Drain valve
16. Exhaust door
17. Bushing
18. Pivot pin
19. Gasket
20. Lockwasher
21. Bolt
22. Water outlet elbow
23. Lockwasher
24. Bolt
25. Clamp
26. Clamp
27. Manifold gasket
28. Manifold stud
29. Hose
30. Gasket
31. Gasket
32. Hose
33. Clamp
34. Clamp
35. Hose
36. Gasket
37. Bolt
38. Water pump (engine circulating)
39. End cap
40. Water pump pulley
41. Lockwasher
42. Pulley bolt
43. Hose
44. Bolt
45. Lockwasher
46. Lockwasher
47. Bolt
48. Clamps

5. Unbolt and remove the high-rise exhaust elbow and hose assembly from the manifold.
6. If equipped with power steering, remove the power steering pump and bracket assembly from the thermostat housing on the exhaust manifold.
7. Disconnect the water hose from the starboard side of the thermostat housing. Remove the thermostat housing fasteners. Rap the housing with a soft-faced mallet to break the gasket seal. Remove the thermostat housing, gasket and thermostat. Discard the gasket.
8. If equipped with power steering, unbolt the oil cooler assembly and reposition it away from the exhaust manifold.
9. Remove the remaining manifold fasteners. Remove the manifold from the cylinder block studs. Remove and discard the gasket.
10. Remove all gasket residue from the cylinder block, thermostat housing, high-rise elbow and manifold mating surfaces with degreaser and a putty knife.
11. Inspect the manifold as described in this chapter.
12. Installation is the reverse of removal, plus the following:
   a. Use a new manifold gasket without sealer.
   b. Use a new thermostat housing gasket coated on both sides with OMC Gasket Sealing Compound.
   c. Use a new carburetor gasket with rounded projections facing toward the engine.
   d. Tighten all fasteners to specifications (**Table 4**).

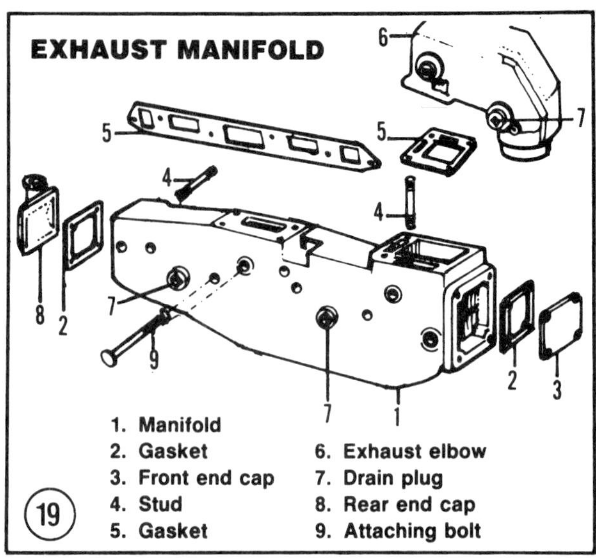

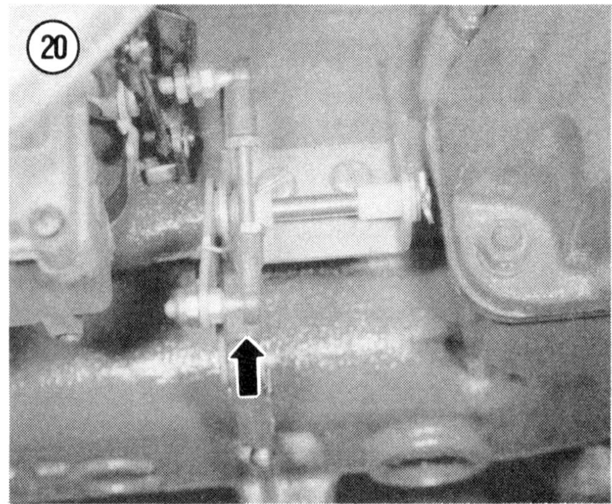

GM Manifold Assembly Removal/Installation

If the combination manifold assembly is not properly torqued, it can gradually pull away from the intake passages. This will result in air entering the intake manifold portion and leaning the air/fuel mixture. When this happens, the engine will run roughly, hesitate on acceleration and may suffer valve problems. To prevent such occurrences, observe the torque specifications and tightening sequence faithfully. Refer to **Figure 19** for this procedure.

1. Disconnect the negative battery cable.
2. Remove the throttle cable from the actuating bracket and anchor block.
3. Open the cylinder block water drain and allow all water to drain.
4. Disconnect the throttle arm-to-manifold link (**Figure 20**).

5. Remove the carburetor. See Chapter Nine.
6. Unclamp and disconnect the water hose at the manifold (**Figure 21**), then disconnect it at the thermostat housing and remove from the engine.
7. If equipped with power steering, remove the alternator (Chapter Eleven). Remove the oil cooler and mounting plate.
8. Loosen the clamps holding the exhaust hose to the high-rise elbow. See **Figure 6**. Unbolt and remove the elbow with the hose attached.
9. Unbolt and remove the manifold from the cylinder head. Discard the gasket.
10. Unbolt and remove the end cap from the manifold. Discard the gasket.
11. Clean all gasket residue from the cylinder head, high-rise elbow and manifold mating surfaces with degreaser and a putty knife.
12. Inspect the manifold assembly as described in this chapter.
13. Installation is the reverse of removal, plus the following:
   a. Use a new manifold gasket without sealer.
   b. Use a new elbow gasket with sealer.
   c. Use a new carburetor gasket.
   d. If end cap is removed, reinstall with a new gasket.
   e. Tighten all fasteners to specifications (**Table 3**). When tightening the manifold fasteners, work from the center outward.
   f. Start and run the engine. Check for fuel leaks.

Intake Manifold Inspection

1. Check the intake manifold for cracks or distortion. Replace if distorted or if cracks are found.
2. Check the mating surfaces for nicks or burrs. Small burrs may be removed with an oilstone.
3. Place a straightedge across the manifold flange/mating surfaces. If there is any gap between the straightedge and surface, measure it with a flat feeler gauge. Measure each manifold from end to end and from corner to corner. If the mating surface is not flat within 0.006 in. (0.15 mm) per foot of manifold length, replace the manifold.

Exhaust Manifold Inspection/Cleaning

1. Inspect the engine exhaust ports for signs of rust or corrosion. Replace manifold if such signs are found.
2. Check water passage in exhaust elbow for clogging.
3. Remove pipe plugs in manifold and exhaust elbow, if so equipped. Check for sand, silt or other foreign matter.
4. Every 300 hours or 3 years, soak the manifold and elbow for 90-120 minutes in muriatic acid (available from swimming pool supply houses) to loosen deposits. Wash thoroughly with fresh water and use a stiff rod to break free any deposits inside. Repeat the washing process a second time, then wash and blow dry with compressed air.

ROCKER ARMS

Removal/Installation

Ford engine

1. Remove the valve cover as described in this chapter.
2. Rotate the camshaft by hand until the low side of the camshaft lobe contacts the rocker arm being removed.
3. Using Ford tool part No. T74P-6565-A or T74P-6565-B, collapse the valve spring and slide the cam follower over the lash adjuster and out of the head. See **Figure 22**. If necessary, lift the lash adjuster out of the head.
4. Repeat Step 2 and Step 3 for each rocker arm to be removed.
5. Installation is the reverse of removal. Each valve spring must be collapsed and released after the camshaft follower is reinstalled before rotating the camshaft to another position.

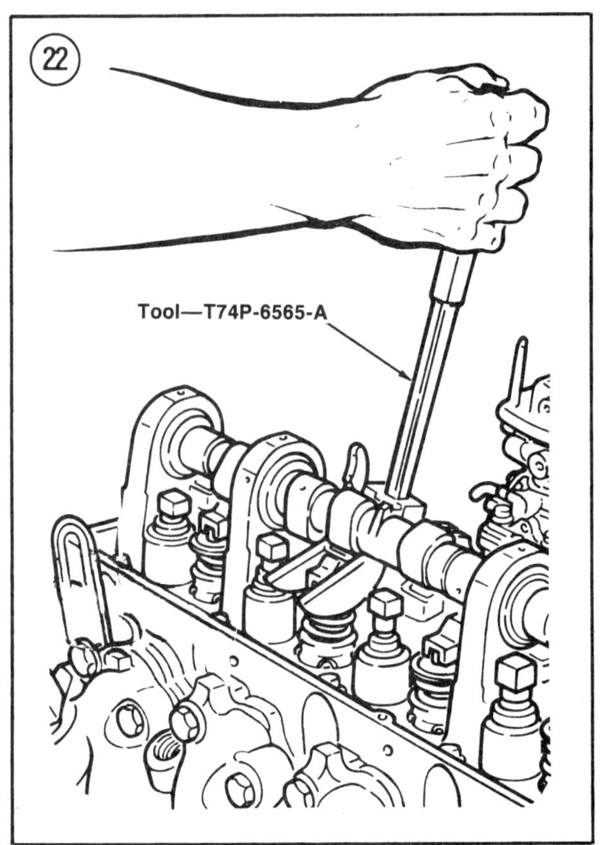

GM engine

Each rocker arm moves on its own pivot ball. The rocker arm and pivot ball are retained by a nut. It is not necessary to remove the rocker arm for pushrod replacement; simply loosen the nut and move the arm away from the pushrod. To remove the entire assembly, refer to **Figure 23** and proceed as follows.

1. Remove the valve cover as described in this chapter.
2. Remove the rocker arm nut and ball.
3. Remove the rocker arm.
4. Remove the valve pushrod from the cylinder block.
5. Repeat Steps 2-4 for each remaining rocker arm. Place each rocker arm and pushrod assembly in a separate container or use a rack to keep them separated for reinstallation in the same position from which they were removed.

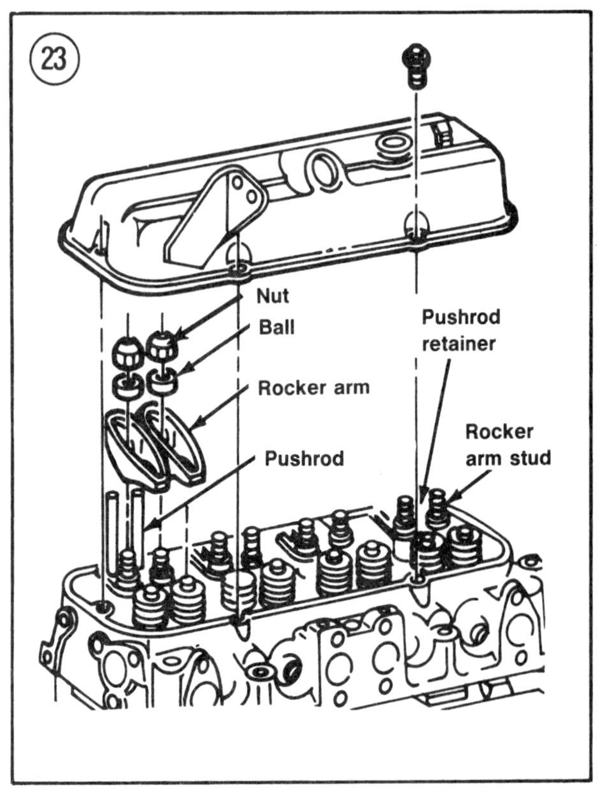

6. Installation is the reverse of removal. If new rocker arms or balls are being installed, coat contact surfaces with engine oil or Molykote. Make sure pushrods fit into lifter sockets. Adjust the valve clearance as described in this chapter.

Inspection (Ford Engine)

1. Clean all parts with solvent and blow dry with compressed air.
2. Check the rocker arms for nicks, scratches, scoring or scuffing.
3. Check the pad at the valve end of the rocker arm for excessive wear or scuffing. Replace the rocker arm if the pad is grooved—do not try to correct by grinding.

Inspection (GM Engine)

1. Clean all parts with solvent and use compressed air to blow out the oil passages in the pushrods.
2. Check each rocker arm, ball, nut and pushrod for scuffing, pitting or excessive wear; replace as required. If one component is worn, replace all components servicing that valve.
3. Check pushrods for straightness by rolling them across a flat, even surface such as a pane of glass. Replace any pushrods that do not roll smoothly.
4. If a pushrod is worn from lack of lubrication, replace the corresponding lifter and rocker arm as well.

Valve Clearance Check/Adjustment

Valve stem-to-rocker arm clearance must be within specifications when the zero-lash adjuster (Ford) or hydraulic lifter (GM) is completely collapsed. If valve clearance is insufficient, the valve opens early and closes late, resulting in a rough engine idle. Excessive clearance lets the valve open too late and close too early, causing valve bounce and damage to the camshaft lobe.

Valve clearance check and/or adjustment is required only when the cylinder head valve train has been disassembled. Check/adjust the valves with the lifter on the base circle of the camshaft lobe.

Ford engine

1. Use Ford tool part No. T74P-6565-A or T74P-6565-B and slowly apply pressure to the cam follower to completely collapse the lash adjuster.
2. Hold the cam follower depressed and measure the clearance between the cam follower and the base circle of the cam with a flat feeler gauge.
3. Compare the measurement obtained in Step 2 with specifications (**Table 2**). If the clearance is not within specifications:
   a. Remove the cam follower and check it for wear or damage.
   b. If the follower is satisfactory, measure the valve spring assembled height (to make sure the valve is not sticking) and compare to specifications (**Table 2**).
   c. If the valve spring height is correct, remove the camshaft as described in this chapter and check the camshaft lobes for excessive wear or damage.
   d. If the camshaft is satisfactory, remove the lash adjusters and have them cleaned and tested by a dealer.
4. Repeat Step 1-3 for each remaining cam follower.

GM engine

1. Rotate the crankshaft until the pulley notch aligns with the zero mark on the timing tab. This positions the No. 1 cylinder at TDC. This position can be verified by placing a finger on the No. 1 rocker arms as the pulley notch nears the zero mark. If the valves are moving, the engine is in the No. 4 firing position; rotate the crankshaft pulley one full turn to reach the No. 1 firing position.

NOTE
The intake valves are those closer to the intake manifold. Exhaust valves are closer to the exhaust manifold.

2. With the engine in the No. 1 firing position, adjust the valves for No. 1 cylinder. To adjust each valve, back off the adjusting nut until lash is felt at the pushrod, then turn the nut to remove all lash. When lash has been removed, the pushrod will not rotate. Turn the nut in another full turn to center the lifter plunger. See **Figure 25.**
3. Rotate the crankshaft ½ turn to place No. 3 cylinder at top dead center. Adjust the valves for No. 3 cylinder as described in Step 2.
4. Rotate the crankshaft ½ turn to place No. 4 cylinder at top dead center. Adjust the valves for No. 4 cylinder as described in Step 2.
5. Rotate the crankshaft ½ turn to place No. 2 piston at top dead center. Adjust the valves for No. 2 cylinder as described in Step 2.
6. Install the valve cover as described in this chapter.

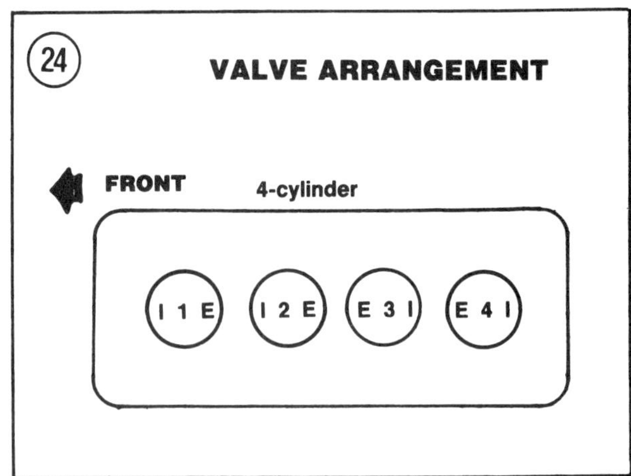

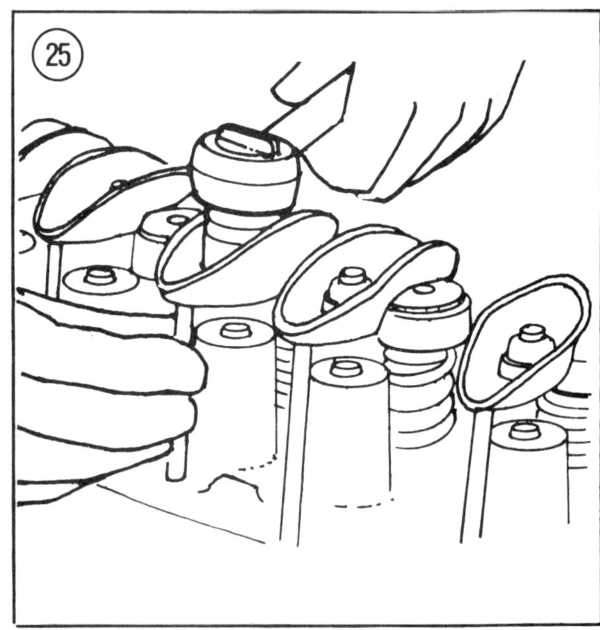

CRANKSHAFT PULLEY AND FRONT HUB (2.5L ENGINE)

Removal/Installation

1. Remove the alternator and power steering (if so equipped) drive belt(s). See Chapter Ten.
2. Remove the pulley attaching bolts. See **Figure 26**. Remove the pulley from the hub.
3. Remove the pulley-to-hub bolt and washer.
4. Install puller part No. J-6978-E or equivalent to the pulley hub with pulley attaching bolts and remove the hub. See **Figure 27**.
5. Lubricate the front cover seal lip with clean engine oil.

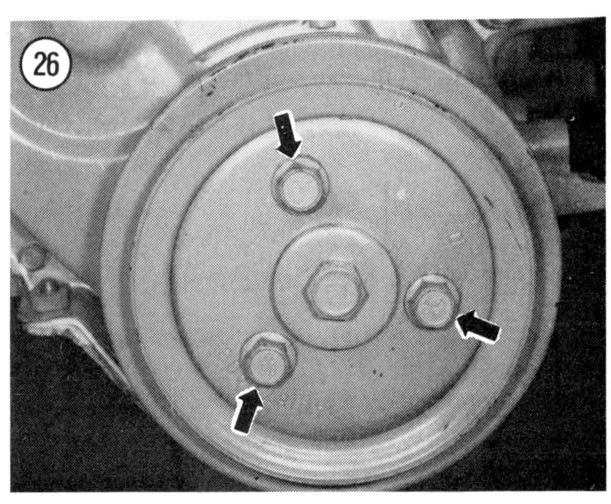

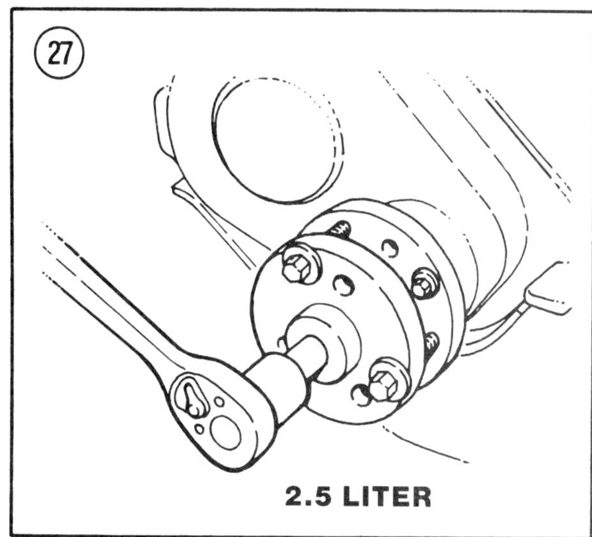

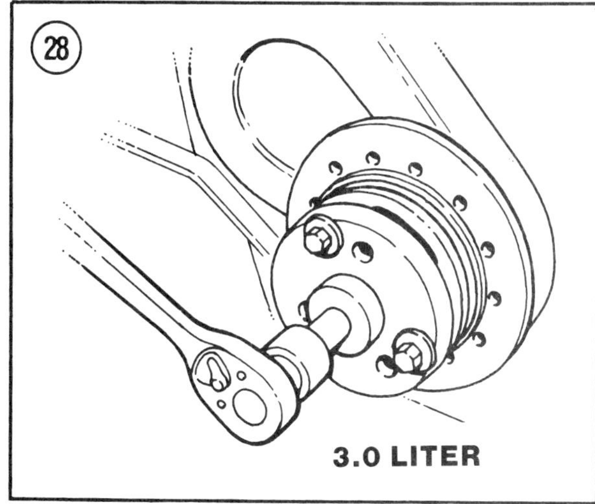

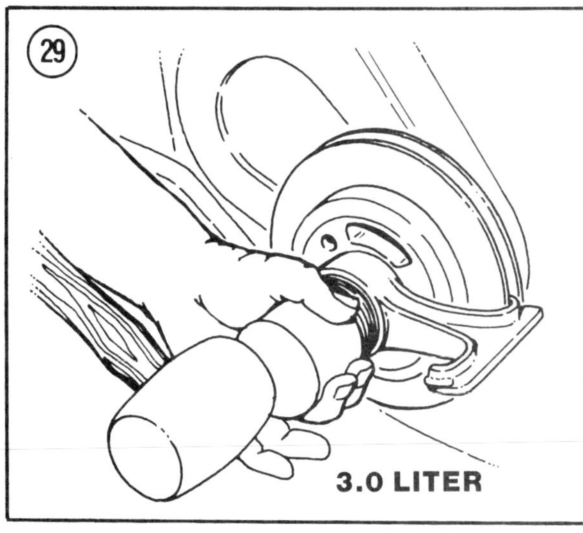

6. Position hub on crankshaft end and start with a mallet, then use tool part No. J-5590 to strike the hub until it is fully seated against the crankshaft sprocket. Crankshaft will extend through the hub slightly when bottomed.
7. Install pulley on hub.
8. Install and adjust the drive belt(s). See Chapter Ten.

CRANKSHAFT PULLEY AND HARMONIC BALANCER (3.0L ENGINE)

Removal/Installation

1. Remove the alternator (and power steering, if so equipped) drive belt(s). See Chapter Ten.
2. Install puller part No. J-6978 or equivalent to the pulley hub with the 3/8-24 bolts and remove the harmonic balancer. See **Figure 28**.
3. Lubricate the front cover seal lip with clean engine oil.
4. Position harmonic balancer on crankshaft end and start with a mallet, then install tool part No. J-5590 and drive the balancer in place until fully seated against the crankshaft sprocket. See **Figure 29**.
5. Install and adjust the drive belt(s). See Chapter Ten.

CRANKSHAFT PULLEY AND DAMPER (FORD ENGINE)

Removal/Installation

Refer to **Figure 30** for this procedure.

1. Remove the alternator and power steering (if so equipped) drive belt(s). See Chapter Ten.
2. Remove the pulley and damper attaching bolt and washer.
3. Remove the crankshaft damper.
4. Installation is the reverse of removal. Tighten pulley bolt to specifications (**Table 4**). Adjust the drive belt(s). See Chapter Ten.

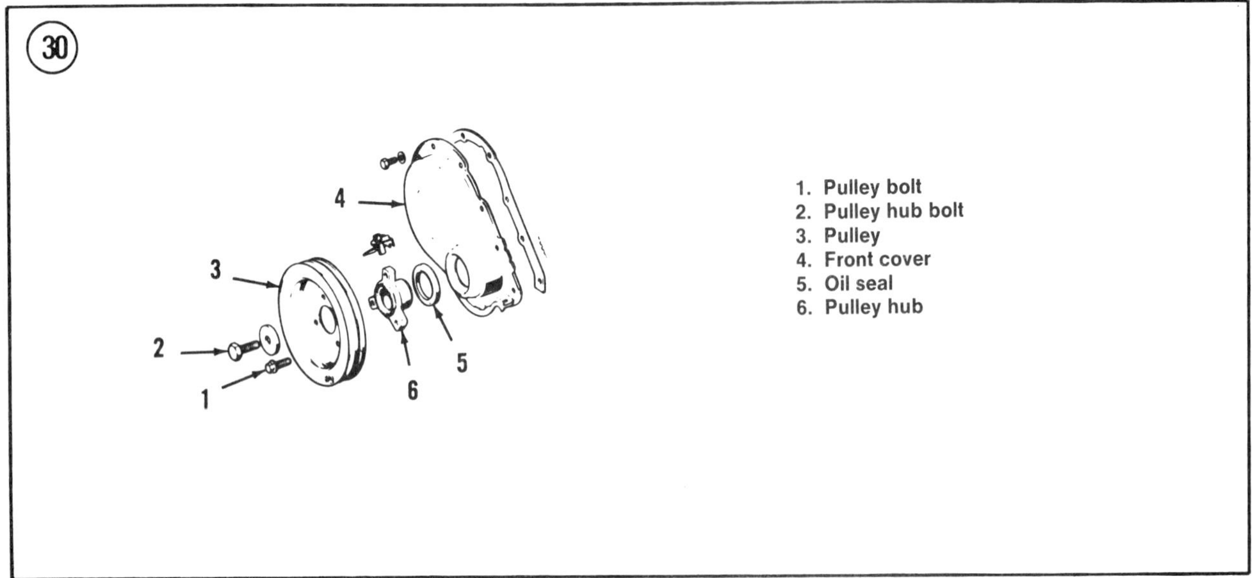

CRANKCASE FRONT COVER AND OIL SEAL (GM ENGINE)

Cover Removal/Installation

This procedure can generally be performed without removing the engine from the boat, providing you are careful in cutting the oil pan seal in Step 4. Refer to **Figure 30**.

1. Open the engine block drain valves and drain all the water from the block.
2. Drain the crankcase oil. See Chapter Four.
3. Remove the crankshaft pulley and front hub/harmonic balancer as described in this chapter.
4. Remove the screws holding the front of the oil pan to the front cover. Pull the front cover slightly away from the block.
5. Use a sharp X-acto knife to cut the oil pan seal flush with the cylinder block face. See **Figure 31**.
6. Remove the front cover attaching bolts. Remove the front cover and gasket. Discard the gasket but retain the cut portion of the pan seal for use as a template in Step 8.
7. Clean the gasket mounting surfaces on the block and cover with degreaser and a putty knife.

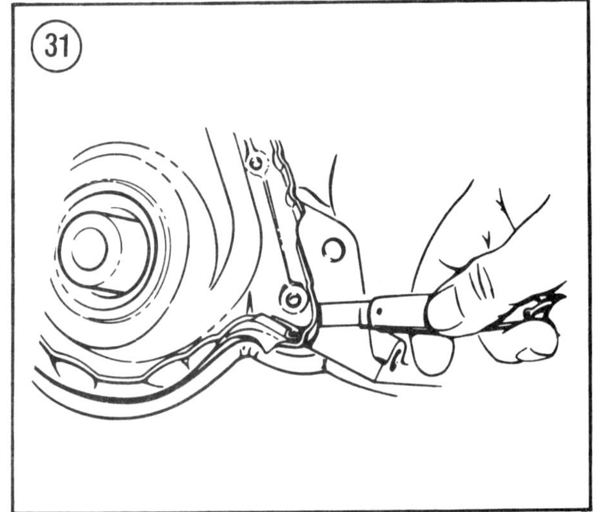

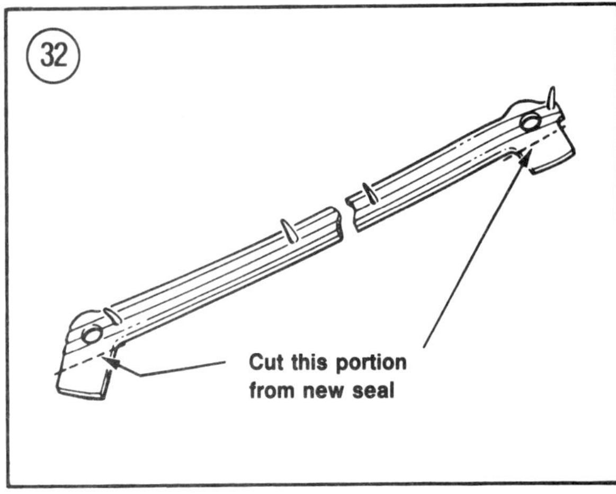

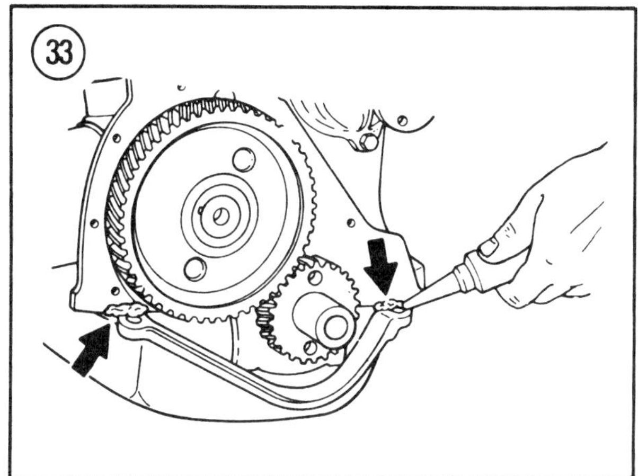

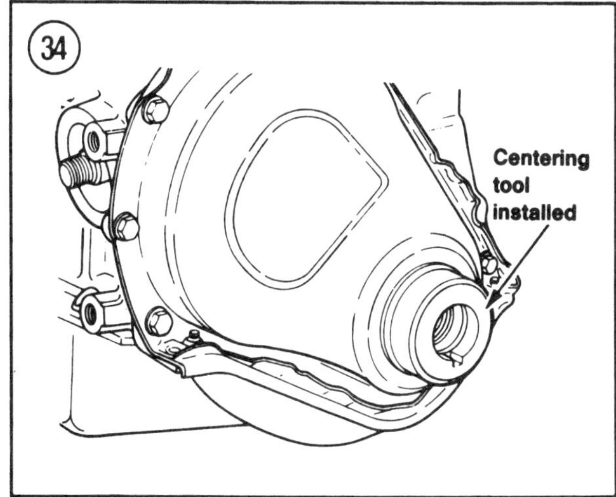

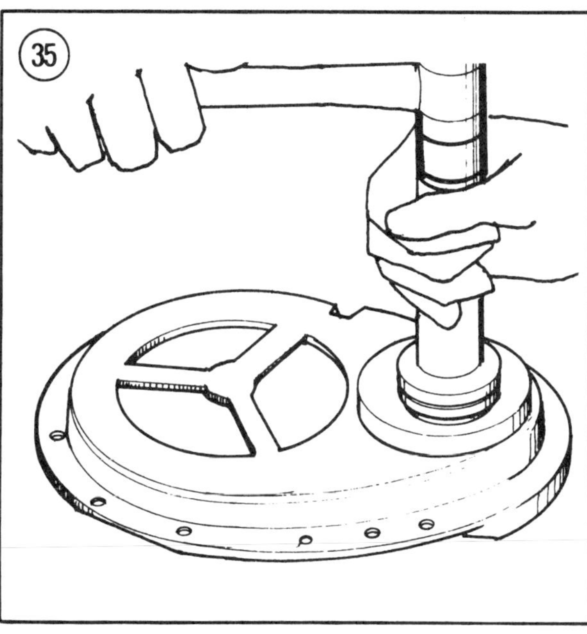

8. Use the cut portion of the oil pan seal as a template and cut a matching section from a new seal for use in Step 9 (**Figure 32**).
9. Install the cut portion of the seal to the bottom of the front cover, inserting the seal tips into the cover holes. Apply a 1/8 in. bead of RTV sealant along the joint on each side where the oil pan meets the block. See **Figure 33**.
10. Install alignment tool part No. J-23042 through the front cover seal. Position the front cover on the engine block with a new gasket. Work carefully to prevent damage to the oil seal or movement of the gasket. See **Figure 34**.
11. Apply upward pressure on the oil pan and install the pan attaching screws.
12. Install the cover attaching bolts. Tighten cover bolts and oil pan screws to specifications (**Table 3**).
13. Remove the alignment tool and install the crankshaft pulley and hub/harmonic balancer as described in this chapter.

Front Cover Seal Replacement

The seal can be replaced without removing the front cover. If the cover has been removed and seal replacement is necessary, support the cover on a clean workbench and perform Steps 2-4.

1. Remove the crankshaft pulley and hub as described in this chapter.
2. Pry the old seal from the cover with a suitable screwdriver. Work carefully to prevent damage to the cover seal surface.
3. Clean the seal recess in the cover with solvent and blow dry with compressed air.
4. Position a new seal in the cover recess with its open end facing the inside of the cover. Drive seal into place with installer part No. J-23042. See **Figure 35**.
5. Install the harmonic balancer/hub and crankshaft pulley as described in this chapter.

CAMSHAFT BELT OUTER COVER (FORD ENGINE)

Removal/Installation

1. Remove the crankshaft pulley as described in this chapter.
2. Remove the camshaft belt outer cover bolts. Remove the outer cover.
3. Installation is the reverse of removal. Tighten the cover bolts to specifications (**Table 4**).

TIMING GEAR REPLACEMENT (GM ENGINE)

1. Remove the camshaft as described in this chapter.

NOTE
Make sure the thrust plate is aligned with the Woodruff key in the camshaft before performing Step 2.

2. Install the camshaft in a press plate and use an arbor press to remove the camshaft from the gear.
3. Installation of the gear is the reverse of removal. Press the gear onto the camshaft until it bottoms against the gear spacer ring.
4. Check the thrust plate end clearance with a flat feeler gauge as shown in **Figure 36**. It should be 0.001-0.005 in. If less than specified, replace the spacer plate. If greater than specified, replace the thrust plate.

CAMSHAFT BELT (FORD ENGINE)

Removal/Installation

Refer to **Figure 37** for this procedure.

1. Remove the camshaft belt outer cover as described in this chapter.
2. Draw an arrow on the camshaft belt with chalk to indicate the normal direction of rotation (clockwise as seen from the front). If the belt is to be reused, it must be installed to move in the same direction.

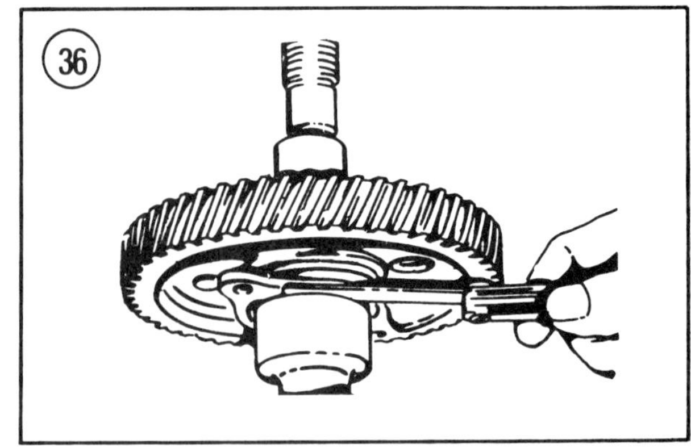

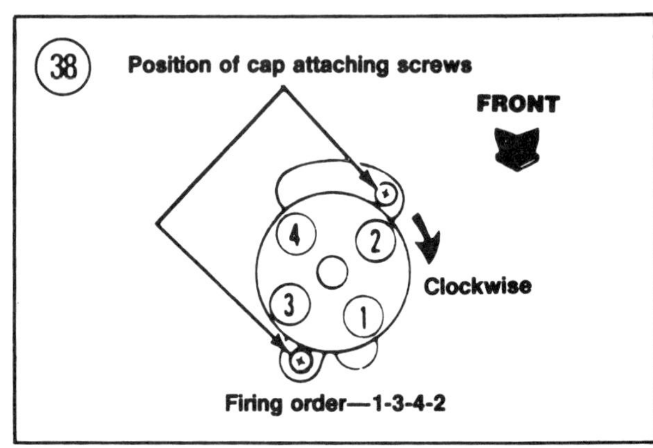

3. Reinstall the crankshaft pulley bolt. Place a wrench on the bolt and rotate the engine in a clockwise direction until the No. 1 piston is at top dead center on the compression stroke.

CAUTION
Rotate the engine only in its normal direction (clockwise as seen from the front of the engine). Rotating the engine backward may cause the camshaft belt to slip off the sprockets, changing the valve timing.

When the crankshaft is positioned correctly, the 0° (TDC) mark on the vibration damper will align with the timing pointer on the front of the engine and the camshaft timing mark will align with the camshaft sprocket timing mark. Remove the distributor cap and make sure the rotor is pointing to the No. 1 terminal in the cap (**Figure 38**).

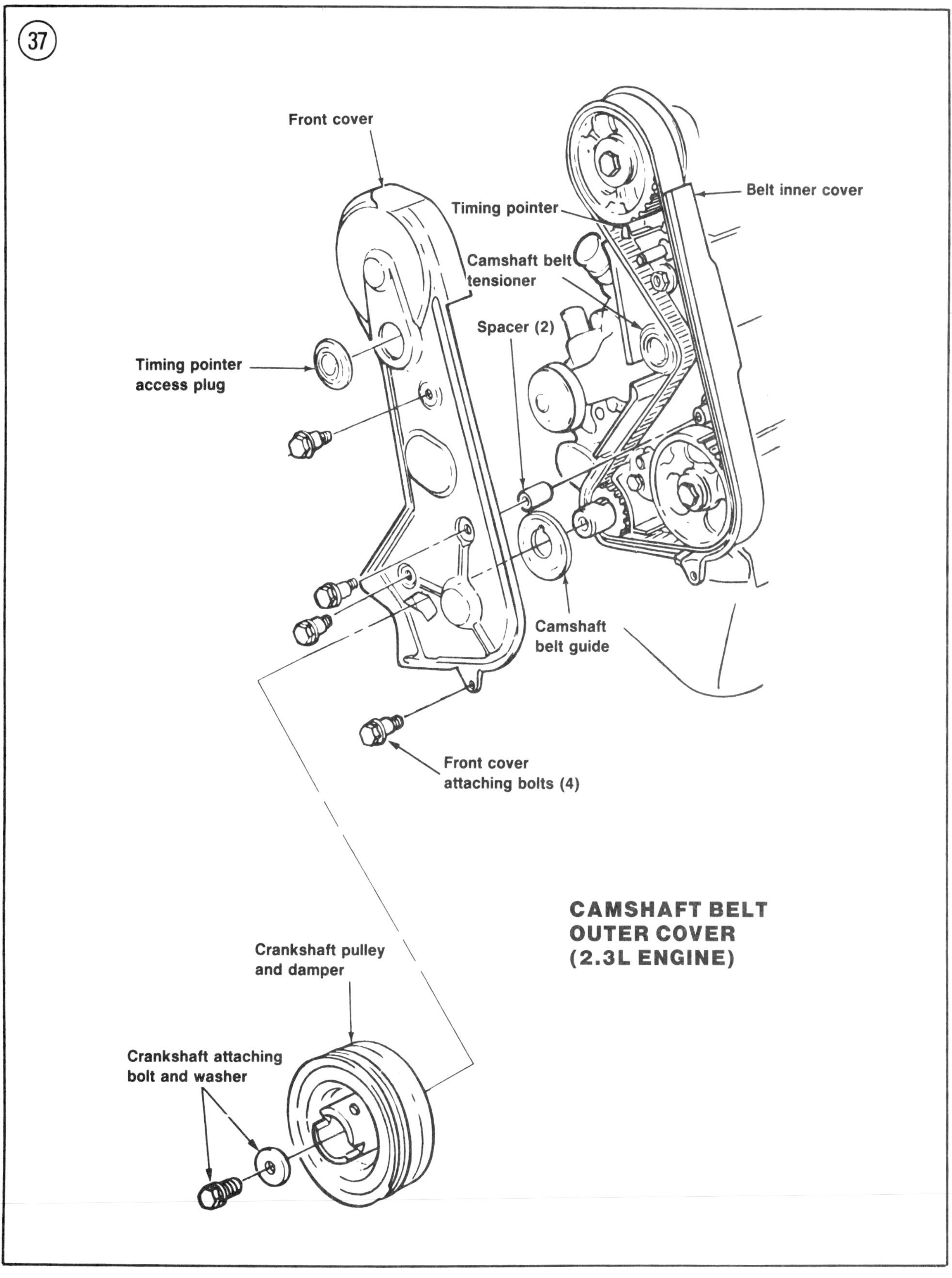
37
Front cover
Timing pointer
Belt inner cover
Camshaft belt tensioner
Spacer (2)
Timing pointer access plug
Camshaft belt guide
Front cover attaching bolts (4)
CAMSHAFT BELT OUTER COVER (2.3L ENGINE)
Crankshaft pulley and damper
Crankshaft attaching bolt and washer

4. Loosen the camshaft belt tensioner adjustment bolt (**Figure 39**) and install tensioner adjusting tool part No. T74P-6254-A on the tension spring rollpin. Use the tool to release the belt tension as far as possible, then tighten the adjustment bolt to hold the tensioner in its fully released position.

5. Remove the crankshaft pulley attaching bolt. Remove the camshaft timing belt guide.

CAUTION

During the next steps, do not bend or twist the camshaft belt. Do not use sharp instruments to pry it off. Handle the belt with clean hands and keep grease and lubricants from touching it as they will cause the belt to deteriorate, resulting in a premature failure. Do not rotate any of the belt sprockets while the belt is removed, as that would change engine timing.

6. Remove and check the camshaft belt for wear, missing teeth or other damage. Replace the belt if any of these conditions are found.

7. Make sure the timing marks on the camshaft sprocket and timing pointer are properly aligned (**Figure 40**) and that the

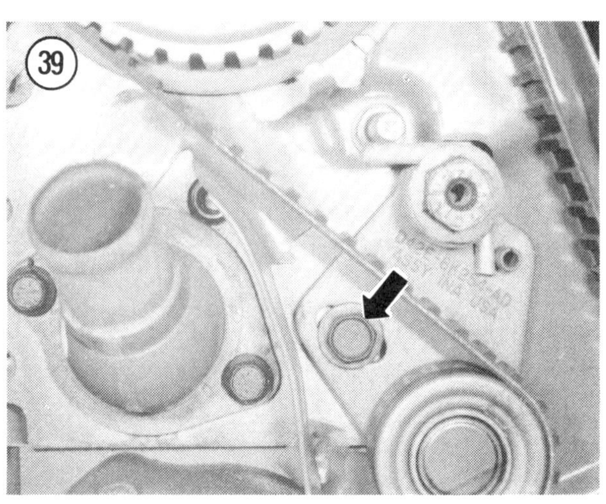

39

40

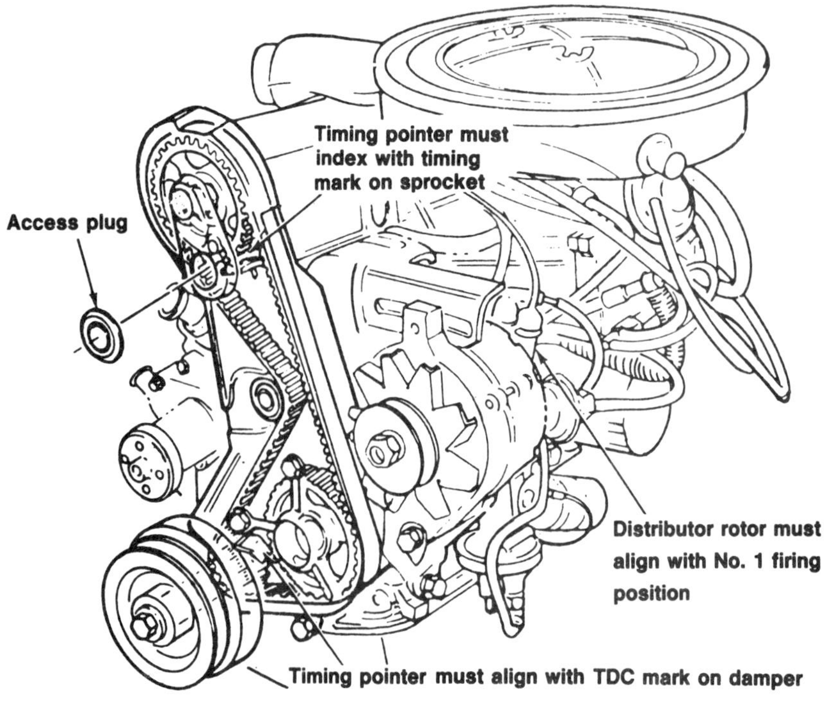

Timing pointer must index with timing mark on sprocket

Access plug

Distributor rotor must align with No. 1 firing position

Timing pointer must align with TDC mark on damper

distributor rotor points toward the No. 1 terminal in the distributor cap (**Figure 38**).

8. Install the camshaft belt around the 3 drive sprockets and camshaft belt tensioner as shown in **Figure 37**. Align the belt properly on the sprockets.

9. Loosen the belt tensioner adjusting bolt (**Figure 39**) and let the tensioner move against the belt.

CAUTION
The spark plugs must be removed in Step 10 before rotating the engine or the camshaft belt may jump the sprocketed teeth during engine rotations.

10. Remove the spark plugs. Rotate the crankshaft clockwise (as seen from the front) 2 complete revolutions to remove any slack from the camshaft belt.

11. Tighten the tensioner adjusting and pivot bolts to specifications (**Table 4**).

12. Recheck timing mark alignment as described in Step 7.

13. Install the camshaft belt guide.

14. Reinstall the camshaft belt outer cover as described in this chapter.

SPROCKET AND FRONT SEAL REPLACEMENT (FORD ENGINE)

Replacement procedures for the camshaft drive sprocket, the auxiliary shaft drive sprocket, the crankshaft sprocket and the camshaft, auxiliary shaft and camshaft belt cover seals are provided in the following steps.

A multi-purpose puller (Ford part No. T74P-6256-A) is required to remove and install the camshaft or auxiliary sprockets. Ford tool part No. T74P-6306-A is required to remove and install the crankshaft drive sprocket. A seal remover (part No. T74P-6700-B) is required to remove each of the 3 seals. Seal installer part No. T74P-6150-A is used to install each of the seals.

1. Remove the camshaft belt cover and camshaft belt as described in this chapter.

2. If the camshaft, auxiliary shaft or crankshaft drive sprockets are to be removed, refer to the tool list above and use the proper tool or equivalent.

3. Installation of the sprocket is the reverse of removal. The threaded insert in the sprocket puller must be removed during camshaft or auxiliary shaft sprocket installation to permit the center attaching bolt to be installed and tightened. Torque values are provided in **Table 4**. No special tool is necessary to install the crankshaft sprocket.

CAUTION
Always use a new camshaft sprocket bolt or wrap the old bolt threads with Teflon tape. If Teflon tape is not available, coat the bolt threads with Teflon paste.

4. To replace the camshaft seal or auxiliary shaft seal, use the proper seal removal tool. When removing the camshaft seal, make sure the jaws of the tool grip the thin edges of the seal very tightly before operating the jaw-screw part of the tool.

5. To replace the camshaft belt cover seal, use the proper seal removal tool described in the list above. Use tool part No. T74P-6150-A to install the new seal.

CAMSHAFT

Removal/Installation

Ford engine

Refer to **Figure 41** for this procedure. It may be necessary to remove the engine from the boat, depending on boat design.

1. Remove the camshaft belt outer cover and belt as described in this chapter.

2. Remove the valve cover as described in this chapter.

6

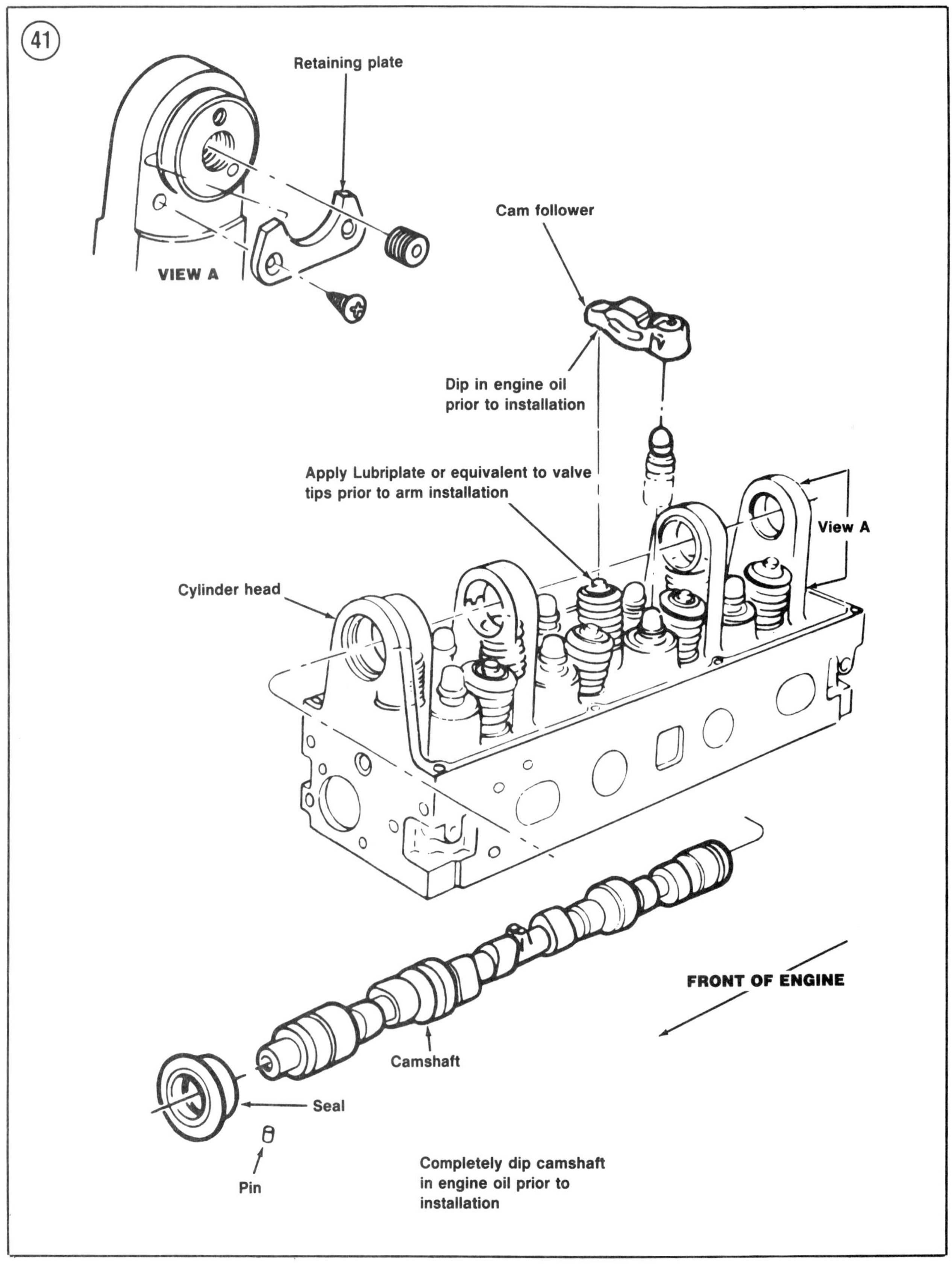
41
Retaining plate
VIEW A
Cam follower
Dip in engine oil
prior to installation
Apply Lubriplate or equivalent to valve
tips prior to arm installation
View A
Cylinder head
FRONT OF ENGINE
Camshaft
Seal
Pin
Completely dip camshaft
in engine oil prior to
installation

3. Check camshaft end play before removal. Push the camshaft as far as it will go toward the rear of the engine. Install a dial indicator on the front of the cylinder head with its plunger touching the front of the camshaft sprocket. Set the indicator gauge to zero, then pry the camshaft forward as far as possible with a large screwdriver. If the dial indicator reading exceeds 0.009 in., replace the camshaft retaining (thrust) plate during installation.

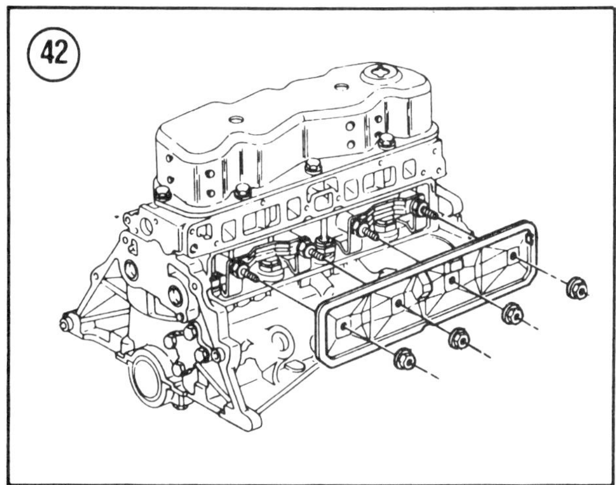

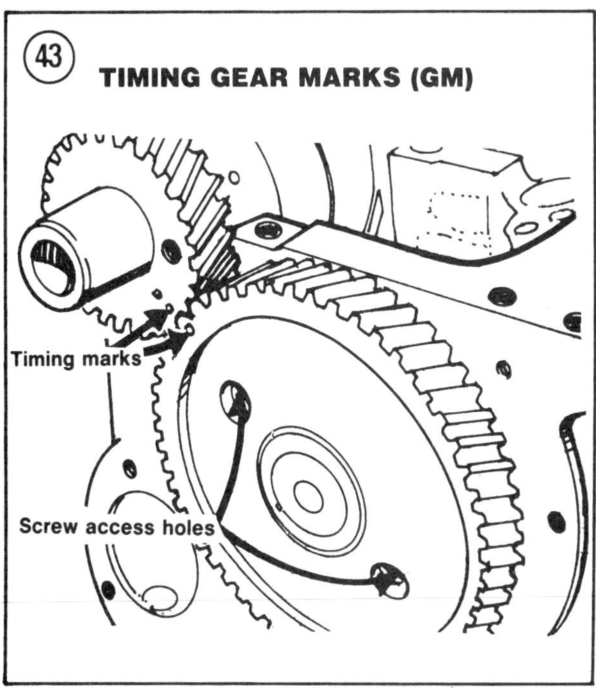

4. Remove the rocker arms as described in this chapter.

5. Remove the camshaft sprocket and seal as described in this chapter.

6. Remove the retaining (thrust) plate from the rear camshaft support stand on the cylinder head.

7. Carefully remove the camshaft from the cylinder head support stands with a rotating motion. Do not let the cam lobes touch or nick the bearings.

8. Installation is the reverse of removal. Dip the camshaft completely in engine oil before installation. Carefully install the camshaft with a rotating motion to prevent bearing damage. Tighten the retaining plate screws to 6-9 ft.-lb. (8-12 N•m). Align all timing marks as described for camshaft belt installation.

GM engine

1. Remove the valve cover as described in this chapter.
2. Remove the front cover as described in this chapter.
3. Remove the fuel pump. See Chapter Nine.
4. Remove the distributor. See Chapter Eleven.
5. Loosen the rocker arm adjusting nuts, swivel the arms off the pushrods and remove the pushrods.
6. Identify each pushrod for reinstallation in its original location.
7. Remove the pushrod cover. See **Figure 42** (typical). Discard the gasket.
8. Remove the valve lifters with a pencil-type magnet. Place them in a rack in order of removal for reinstallation in their original location.
9. Rotate the camshaft to align the timing gear marks (**Figure 43**).

10. Working through the access holes in the camshaft gear, remove the 2 camshaft thrust plate screws. See **Figure 43**.

CAUTION
Do not cock the camshaft during removal. This can damage the camshaft or its bearing thrust surfaces.

11. Carefully withdraw the camshaft from the front of the engine with a rotating motion to avoid damage to the bearings.
12. Installation is the reverse of removal. Coat the camshaft lobes with Lubriplate or equivalent and the journals with heavy engine oil before reinstalling in the block. Check runout and backlash as described in this chapter.

Inspection (All Engines)

1. Check the journals and lobes for signs of wear or scoring. Lobe pitting in the toe area is not sufficient reason for replacement unless the lobe lift loss exceeds specifications.
2. Check all machined surfaces of the camshaft for nicks or grooves. Minor defects may be removed with a smooth oilstone. Severe damage or wear beyond that specified in **Table 1** or **Table 2** requires replacement of the camshaft.

NOTE
If you do not have precision measuring equipment, have Step 3 done by a machine shop.

3. Measure the camshaft journal diameters with a micrometer (**Figure 44**) and compare to specifications (**Table 1**). Replace the camshaft if the journals exceed the wear or out-of-roundness specifications.
4. Suspend the camshaft between V-blocks and check for warpage with a dial indicator. See **Figure 45**. Replace if reading is greater than 0.002 in.

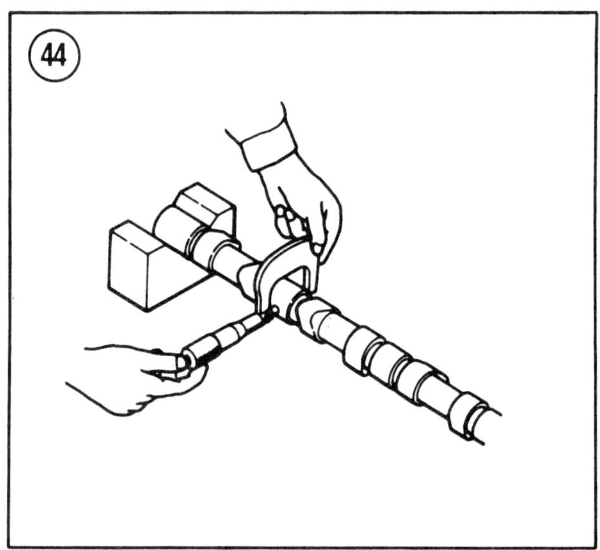

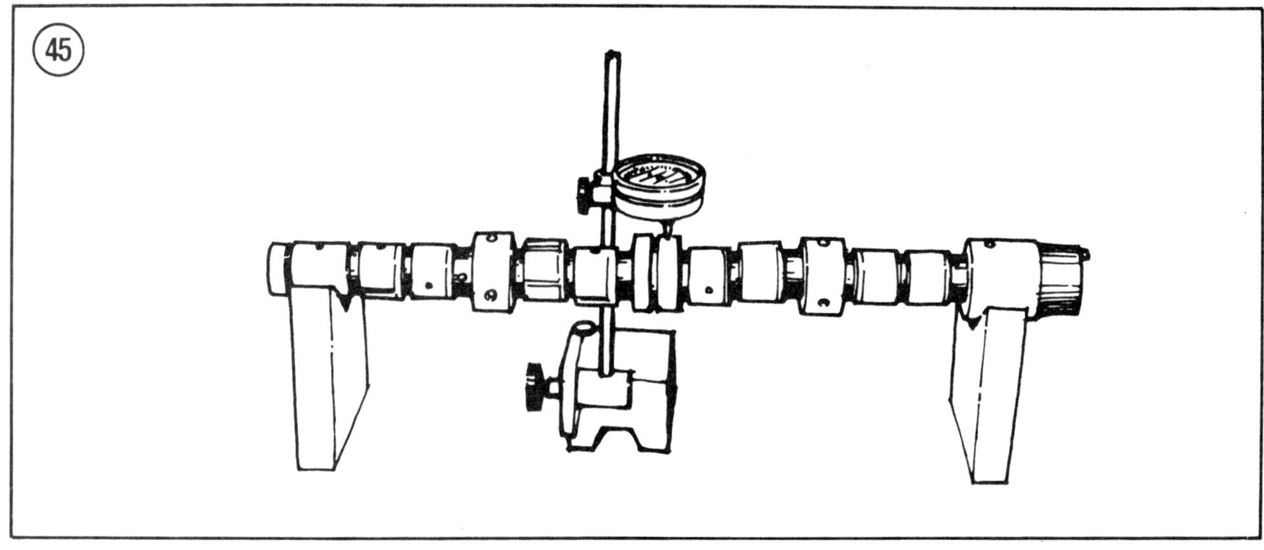

5. Check the inner diameter of the camshaft bearings, being careful not to damage the bearing material. If the bearings are excessively worn, grooved, pitted or scored, have them replaced by a dealer or competent machine shop (Ford) or replace them as described in this chapter (GM).

CAUTION
All camshaft bearings should be replaced, even if only one bearing is damaged or worn. If not, the camshaft may be out of alignment when reinstalled.

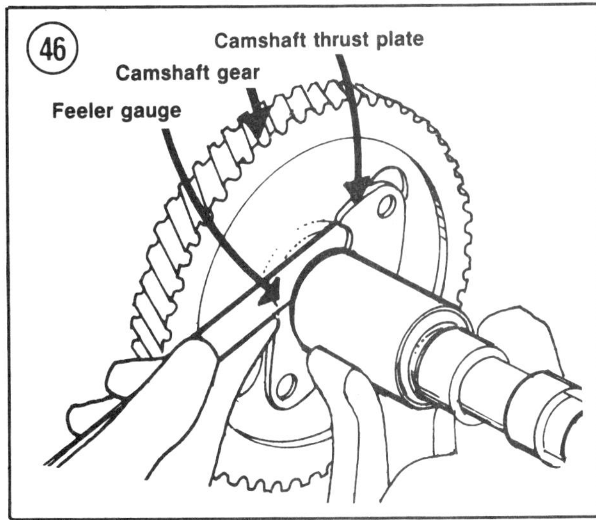

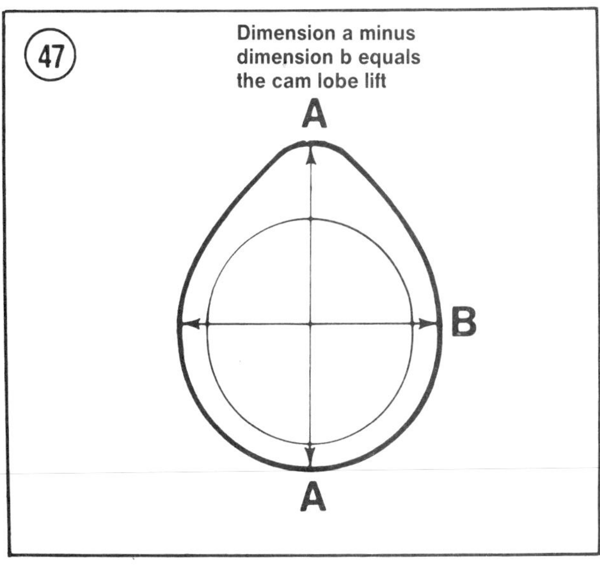

6. Check the oil pump and distributor drive gears for excessive wear or damage.
7. Check camshaft gear and thrust plate for wear or damage.
8. GM engine—Insert a flat feeler gauge between the thrust plate and camshaft to measure end play. See **Figure 46**. If end play exceeds 0.005 in., remove the camshaft gear as described in this chapter and replace the thrust plate.

Lifter Inspection

Keep the lifters in proper sequence for installation in their original position in the head. Clean lifters in solvent and wipe dry with a clean, lint-free cloth. Inspect and test the lifters separately to prevent intermixing of their internal parts. If any part requires replacement, replace the entire lifter.

Inspect all parts. If any lifter shows signs of pitting, scoring, galling, non-rotation or excessive wear, discard it. Check the lifter plunger. It should drop to the bottom of the body by its own weight when dry and assembled.

6

Lobe Lift Measurement

Camshaft lobe lift can be measured with the camshaft in the block and the cylinder head in place.

Ford engine

1. Remove the valve cover as described in this chapter.
2. Use a vernier caliper to measure the distance between the major and minor diameters of each cam lobe (**Figure 47**). Record the readings.
3. Subtract dimension B from dimension A. The difference equals the lobe lift. If lobe lift is less than 0.2381 in. on one or more lobes, replace the camshaft.
4. Reinstall the valve cover as described in this chapter.

GM engine

The lifters must be bled down slowly in Step 6 or the readings will be incorrect.

1. Remove the valve cover as described in this chapter.
2. Remove the rocker arms and pivot assemblies as described in this chapter.
3. Remove the spark plugs. See Chapter Four.
4. Install a dial indicator on the end of a pushrod. A piece of rubber tubing will hold the dial indicator plunger in place on the center of the pushrod. See **Figure 48** (typical).
5. Rotate the crankshaft in the normal direction of rotation until the valve lifter seats on the heel or base of the cam lobe (**Figure 49**). This positions the pushrod at its lowest point.
6. Set the dial indicator at zero, then slowly rotate the crankshaft until the pushrod reaches its maximum travel. Note the indicator reading and compare to specifications (**Table 1**).
7. Repeat Steps 4-6 for each pushrod. If all lobes are within specifications in Step 6, reinstall the rocker arm assemblies and adjust the valves as described in this chapter.
8. If one or more lobes are worn beyond specifications, replace the camshaft as described in this chapter.
9. Remove the dial indicator and reverse Steps 1-3.

Bearing Replacement (Ford engine)

Have camshaft bearings replaced by a dealer.

Bearing Replacement (GM engine)

Camshaft bearings can be replaced without complete engine disassembly. Replace bearings in complete sets. Camshaft bearing and installer tool part No. J-6098 is required for bearing replacement.

1. Remove the camshaft as described in this chapter.
2. Remove the crankshaft as described in this chapter. Leave pistons in cylinder bores.
3. Drive the camshaft welch plug from the rear of the cylinder block.
4. Secure the connecting rods to the side of the engine to keep them out of the way while replacing the cam bearings.
5. Index the bearing pilot in the inner bearing.
6. Install nut on puller screw until screw can be threaded into pilot with nut extending from front of block.
7. Install remover section to puller screw, then insert screw through cam bore and thread into pilot.
8. Hold the puller screw with one wrench. Turn the nut with a second wrench until the bearing has been pulled from its bore. See **Figure 50** (typical).
9. When bearing has been removed from bore, remove tool and bearing from puller screw. Install pilot on drive handle with shoulder facing handle.

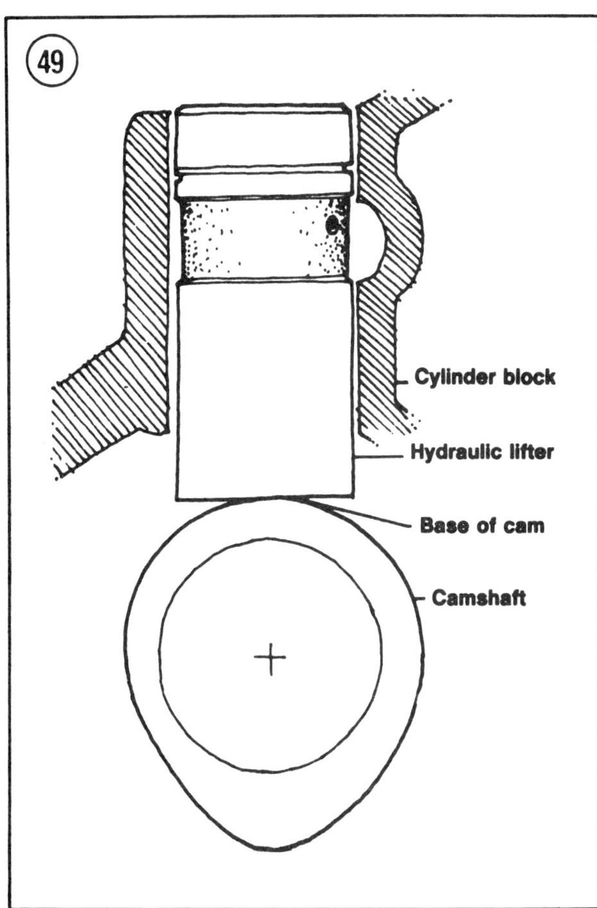

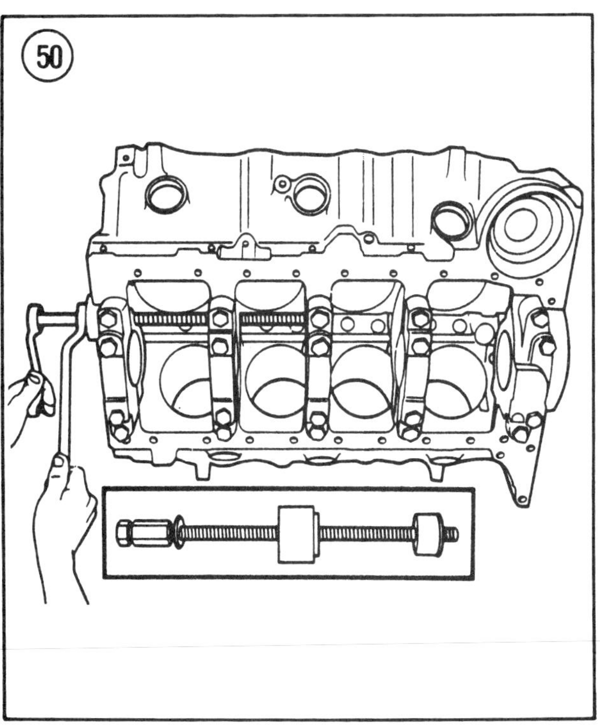

10. Remove the front and rear bearings by driving them toward the center of the block.

CAUTION
Improper alignment of the rear bearing during Step 11 will restrict oil pressure reaching the valve train.

11. Installation is the reverse of removal. Use the same tool to pull the new bearings into their bores. Bearing oil holes must align with those in the block. Since the oil hole is on the top of the bearings and cannot be seen during installation, align bearing oil hole with hole in bore and mark opposite side of bearing and block at bore to assist in positioning the oil hole during installation.
12. Wipe a new camshaft welch plug with an oil-resistant sealer and install it flush to 1/32 in. deep to maintain a level surface on the rear of the block.

CAMSHAFT AND CRANKSHAFT GEAR (GM ENGINE)

Runout and Backlash Check

1. Install a dial indicator as shown in **Figure 51**. Rotate camshaft 360° to check runout. If camshaft gear runout exceeds 0.004 in., replace the gear.
2. Reposition the dial indicator so its contact plunger touches the face of the crankshaft gear. Repeat Step 1. If runout exceeds 0.003 in., replace the gear.
3. Install dial indicator as shown in **Figure 52** to check gear teeth backlash. If backlash is not 0.004-0.006 in., replace both gears.

Camshaft Gear Replacement

If inspection indicates that the camshaft, gear or thrust plate should be replaced, press the gear from the camshaft with an appropriate size support sleeve. Position the thrust plate so that it will not be damaged by the Woodruff key in the shaft when it separates from the gear. If the gear is to be reused, support its hub before applying pressure or it will be ruined. Install the camshaft gear by pressing it onto the shaft, then check end play as described under *Inspection* in this chapter.

AUXILIARY SHAFT (FORD ENGINE)

Removal/Installation

1. Remove the camshaft belt outer cover, camshaft belt and auxiliary shaft sprocket as described in this chapter.
2. Remove the distributor (Chapter Eleven) and fuel pump (Chapter Nine).
3. Remove the auxiliary cover from the block.
4. Remove the 2 screws holding the auxiliary shaft retaining plate to the engine block. Remove the retaining plate.
5. Carefully withdraw the auxiliary shaft from the engine block, making sure that the fuel pump eccentric and distributor drive gear do not touch the auxilairy shaft bearing surfaces.
6. Check the auxilairy shaft bearings for wear or damage. If any bearing is visibly worn or defective, remove all with an internal puller (part No. T58L-101-A) and a slide hammer.
7. Installation is the reverse of removal. If the auxiliary shaft bearings were removed, use a suitable size hollow drift or Ford tool part No. T57T-7003-A to install the new bearings. Tighten all fasteners to specifications (**Table 4**).

CAUTION
Make sure the oil holes in the auxiliary shaft bearings are aligned with those in the engine block during installation.

OIL PAN

Removal

Refer to **Figure 53** (typical) for this procedure.

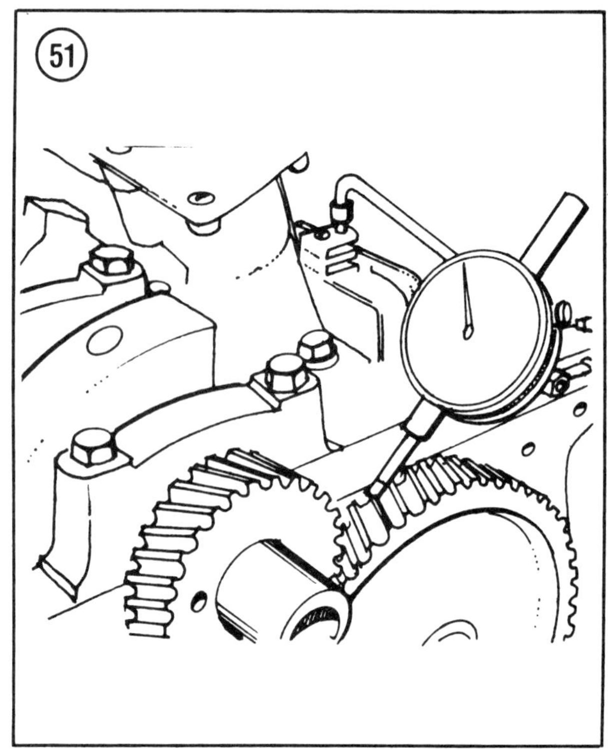

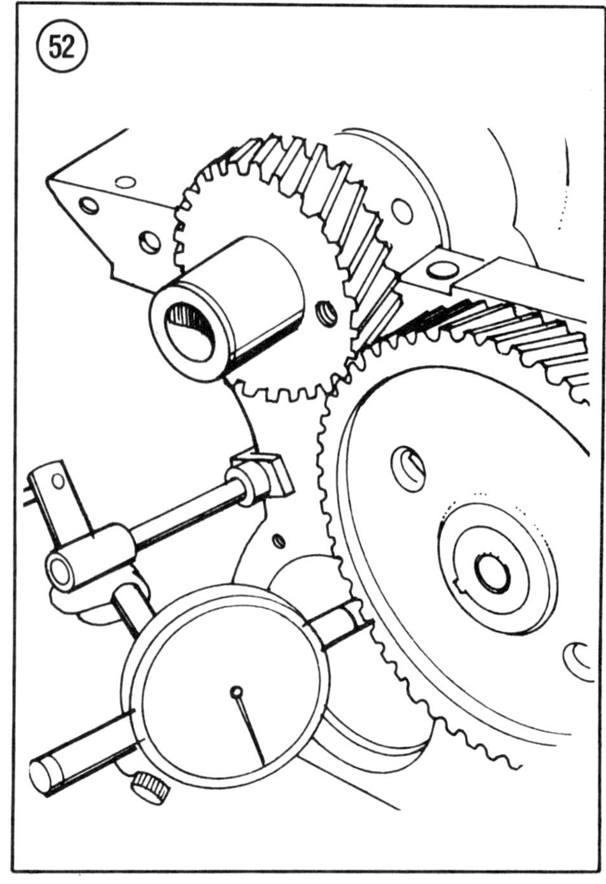

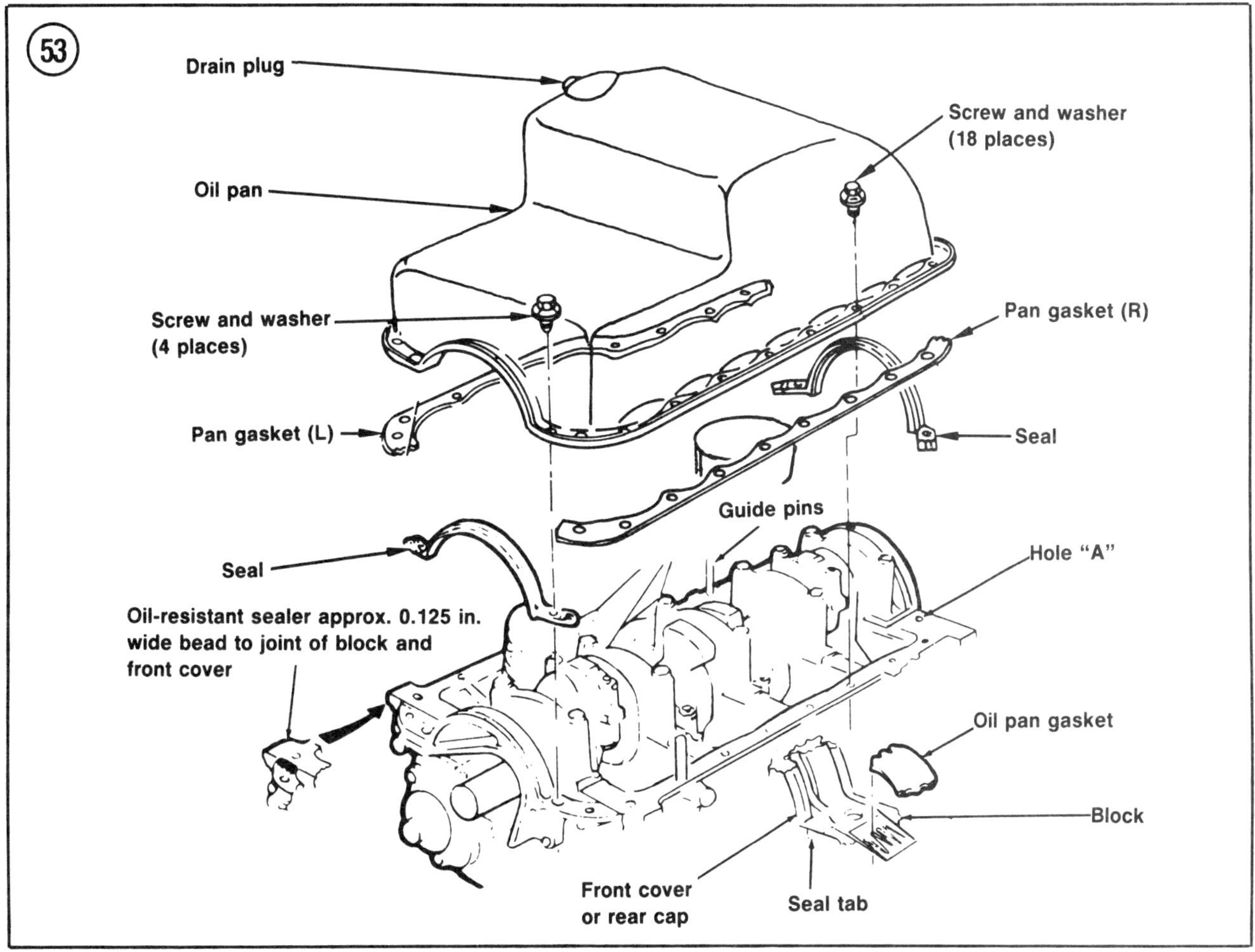

1. Remove the engine as described in this chapter.
2. Place a suitable container under the oil pan drain plug. Remove the plug and let the crankcase drain. Reinstall the drain plug.

NOTE
A modification kit is available from marine dealers to assist in draining the oil when the engine is in the boat. This kit can be installed on any engine oil pan when the engine is removed for service.

3. If mounted in an engine stand, rotate the engine 180° to place the oil pan in an upright position.
4. Remove the oil pan attaching screws. Remove the oil pan.
5. Remove and discard the 2-piece pan gasket and the front/rear seals.

Inspection and Cleaning

1. Clean any gasket residue from the oil pan rail on the engine block and the oil pan sealing flange with degreaser and a putty knife.
2. Clean the pan thoroughly in solvent and check for dents or warped gasket surfaces. Straighten or replace the pan as required.

Installation

Refer to **Figure 53** (typical) for this procedure.

1. Coat the block side rails with grease and position the 2 side gaskets on the side rails.
2. Install the front pan seal on the front cover, pressing the seal into the cover holes. Tuck the side gasket front ends into the gap between the front seal groove and block.
3. Install the rear seal on the rear main bearing cap. Tuck the seal ends into the block groove openings.
4. Carefully place the oil pan in position. Make sure the gaskets and seals are not misaligned and then install a pan attaching screw finger-tight on each side of the block.
5. Install the remaining screws and tighten all to specifications (**Table 3** or **Table 4**). Work from the center outward in each direction.
6. Install the engine in the boat as described in this chapter and fill the crankcase with an oil recommended in Chapter Four.

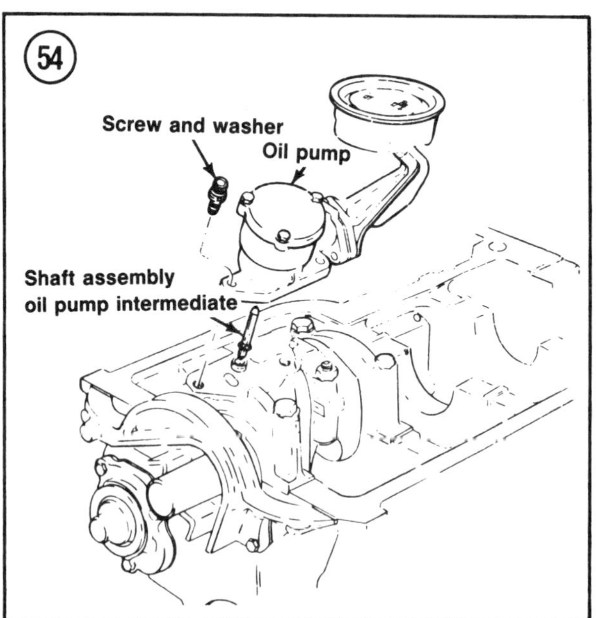

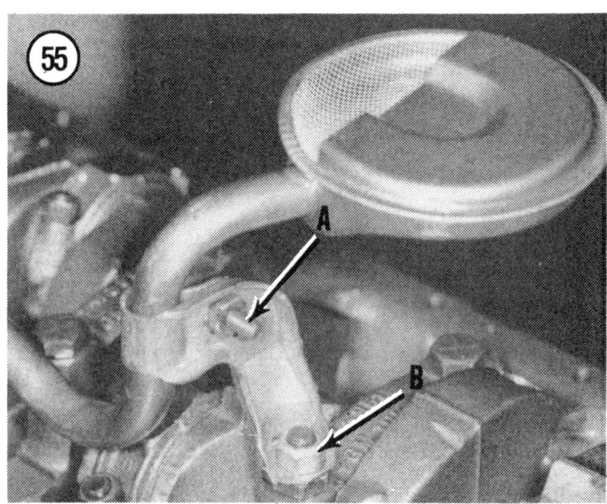

OIL PUMP

Removal/Installation

Ford engine

1. Remove the oil pan as described in this chapter.
2. Remove the 2 pump attaching screws and washers. Remove the oil pump and intermediate shaft assembly. **See Figure 54.**

NOTE
Prime the pump by filling it with engine oil and rotating the pump drive shaft to circulate oil through the pump before installation.

3. Installation is the reverse of removal. Tighten all fasteners to specifications (**Table 4**).

GM engine

1. Remove the oil pan as described in this chapter.

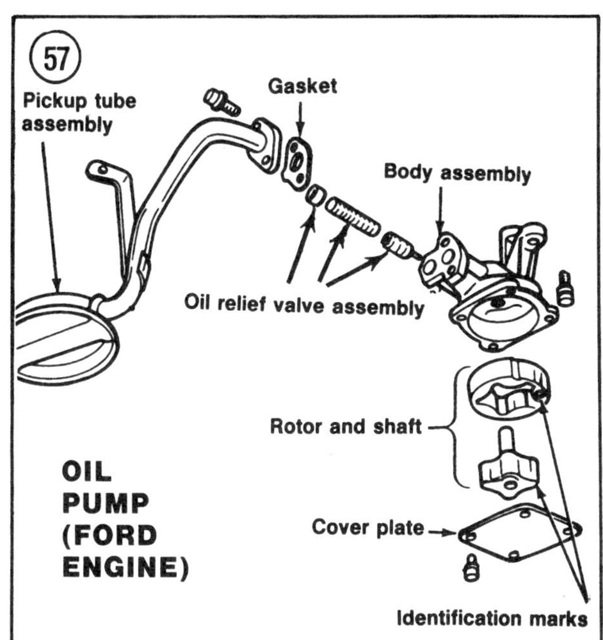

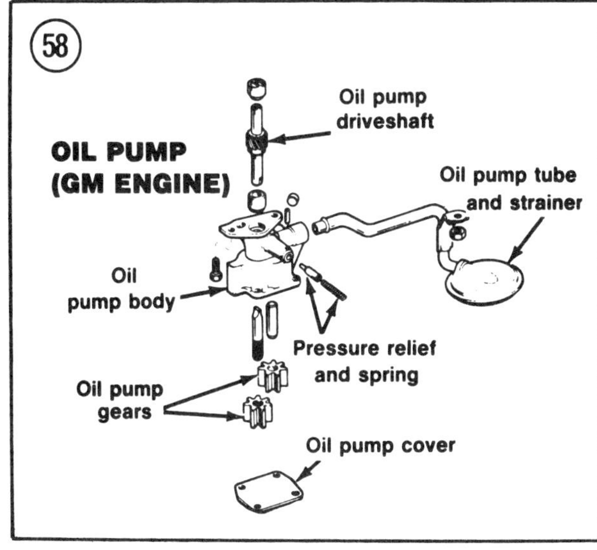

NOTE
The oil pump pickup tube and screen are a press fit in the pump housing and should not be removed unless replacement is required.

2. Loosen the pickup tube bracket bolt (A, **Figure 55**). Remove bracket attaching nut (B, **Figure 55**).
3. Remove the oil pump attaching bolts (**Figure 56**). Remove the oil pump, gasket and pickup tube/screen as an assembly. Discard the gasket.
4. To install, align the pump gear shaft slot with the distributor shaft drive tang.
5. Install pump to block with a new gasket (if used). Tighten fasteners to specifications (**Table 3**).
6. Reinstall the oil pan as described in this chapter.

Disassembly/Assembly

Ford engine

Refer to **Figure 57** for this procedure.
1. Remove the cover screws, cover and gasket. Discard the gasket.
2. Mark the gear teeth for reassembly indexing and then remove the idler and drive gear with shaft from the body.
3. Remove the pressure regulator valve pin, regulator, spring and valve.
4. Lubricate all parts thoroughly with clean engine oil before reassembly.
5. Assembly is the reverse of disassembly. Index the gear marks, install a new cover gasket and rotate the pump drive shaft by hand to check for smooth operation. Tighten cover bolts to specifications (**Table 4**).

GM engine

Refer to **Figure 58** for this procedure.
1. Remove the cover screws, cover and gasket. Discard the gasket.
2. Mark the gear teeth for reassembly indexing and then remove the idler and drive gear with shaft from the body.
3. Remove the pressure regulator valve pin, regulator, spring and valve.
4. Remove the pickup tube/screen assembly *only* if it needs replacement. Secure the pump body in a soft-jawed vise and separate the tube from the cover.

CAUTION
Do not twist, shear or collapse the tube when installing it in Step 5.

5. If the pickup tube/screen assembly was removed, install a new one. Secure the pump body in a soft-jawed vise. Apply sealer to the new tube and gently tap in place with a soft-faced mallet. See **Figure 59**.
6. Lubricate all parts thoroughly with clean engine oil before reassembly.
7. Assembly is the reverse of disassembly. Index the gear marks, install a new cover gasket and rotate the pump drive shaft by hand to check for smooth operation. Tighten cover bolts to specifications (**Table 3**).

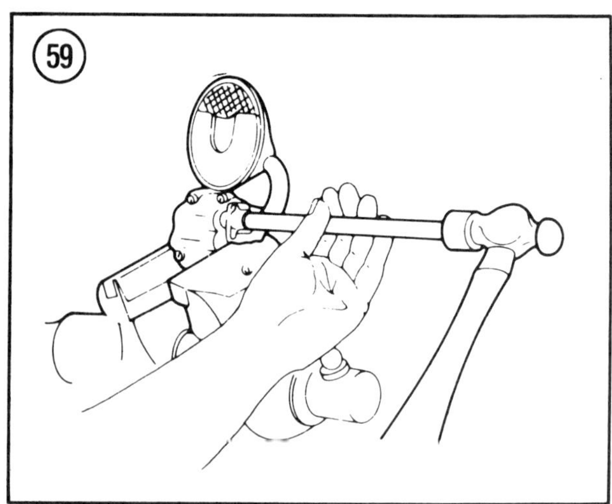

Cleaning and Inspection

Ford engine

NOTE
The inner rotor, shaft and outer race are serviced as an assembly. If one component is defective, replace the pump.

1. Clean all parts thoroughly in solvent. Brush the inside of the body and pressure relief chamber to remove all dirt and metal particles. Dry with compressed air, if available.
2. Check the pump body and cover for cracks or excessive wear.
3. Check the pressure relief valve spring. If worn, damaged or collapsed, replace the spring.
4. Check the relief valve plunger for scoring. Check for free operation in the pump bore.
5. Install outer race in pump body and check the clearance with a flat feeler gauge (**Figure 60**). If clearance exceeds specifications (**Table 2**), replace the pump assembly.
6. Install the rotor/shaft assembly in the pump body. Place a straightedge over the assembly and body. Measure end play between the rotor/outer race and straightedge. See **Figure 61**. If end play exceeds specifications (**Table 2**), replace the pump assembly.

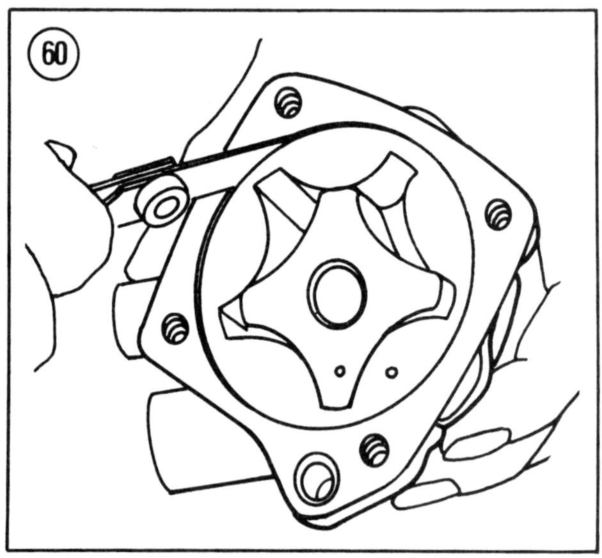

GM engine

NOTE
The pump and gears are serviced as an assembly. If one or the other is worn or damaged, replace the entire pump. No wear specifications are provided by GM.

1. Clean all parts thoroughly in solvent. Brush the inside of the body and the pressure regulator chamber to remove all dirt and metal particles. Dry with compressed air, if available.
2. Check the pump body and cover for cracks or excessive wear.

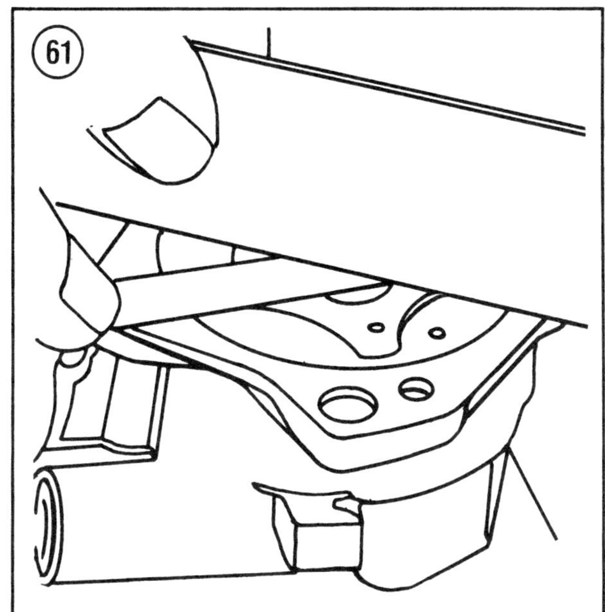

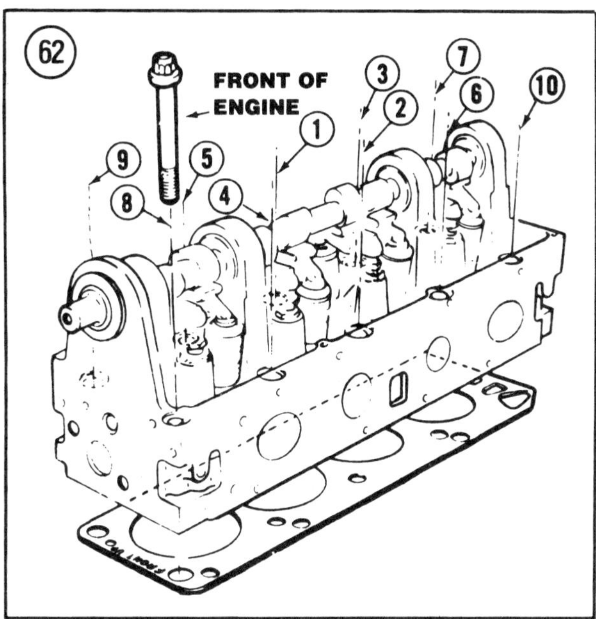

3. Check the pump gears for damage or excessive wear.
4. Check the drive gear shaft-to-body fit for excessive looseness.
5. Check the inside of the pump cover for wear that could allow oil to leak around the ends of the gears.
6. Check the pressure regulator valve for a proper fit.

CYLINDER HEAD

Removal (Ford)

1. Open the engine block drain valves and drain all water from the block.
2. Remove the oil dipstick tube.
3. Remove the alternator and bracket from the cylinder head. If a low-mounted alternator is used, this step may not be necessary.
4. Remove the intake and exhaust manifolds as described in this chapter.
5. Remove the valve cover as described in this chapter.
6. Disconnect the oil pressure sending unit lead.
7. Remove the outer timing belt cover and timing belt tensioner as described in this chapter.
8. Remove the tensioner spring stop stud from the cylinder head.
9. Disconnect the spark plug wires and remove the wire looms from the cylinder head. Remove the spark plugs (Chapter Four).
10. Loosen the cylinder head bolts in the sequence shown in **Figure 62**. The bolts should be loosened in progressive stages to prevent warping of the cylinder head.
11. Remove the head bolts. Rap the end of the head with a soft-faced hammer to break the gasket seal. Remove the head from the engine.

CAUTION
Place the head on its side to prevent damage to the head gasket surface.

12. Remove and discard the head gasket. Clean all gasket residue from the head and block mating surfaces.

Removal (GM)

1. Open the engine block drain valves and drain all water from the block.

2. Remove the intake and exhaust manifolds as described in this chapter.
3. Unclamp and disconnect the coolant hoses at the thermostat housing. Disconnect the fuel line clips at the cylinder head and thermostat housing. Disconnect the temperature sending unit lead. Remove the thermostat housing.
4. Disconnect the spark plug wires and remove the wire looms from the cylinder head. Remove the spark plugs (Chapter Four).
5. Remove the valve cover as described in this chapter.
6. Loosen the rocker arms and rotate them to one side. Remove the pushrods and identify each for reinstallation in their original position.
7. Remove the ignition coil and bracket.
8. Loosen the cylinder head bolts, working from the center of the head to the end in each direction.
9. Remove the head bolts. Rap the end of the head with a soft-faced hammer to break the gasket seal. Remove the head from the engine.

CAUTION
Place the head on its side to prevent damage to the head gasket surface.

10. Remove and discard the head gasket. Clean all gasket residue from the head and block mating surfaces.

Decarbonizing (All Engines)

1. Without removing the valves, remove all deposits from the combustion chambers, intake ports and exhaust ports. Use a fine wire brush dipped in solvent or make a scraper from hardwood. Be careful not to scratch or gouge the combustion chambers.
2. After all carbon is removed from the combustion chambers and ports, clean the entire head in solvent.

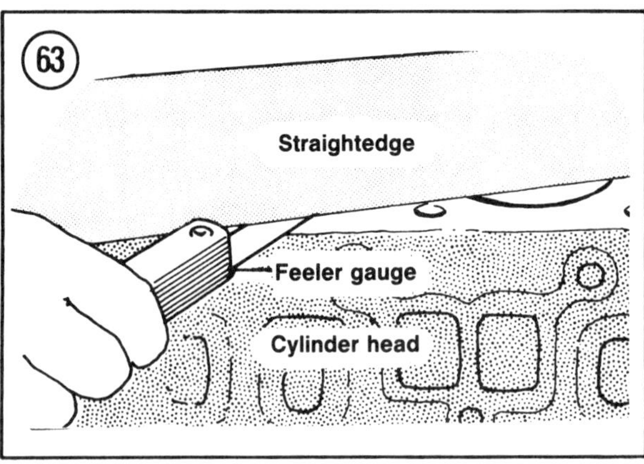

3. Clean away all carbon on the piston tops. Do not remove the carbon ridge at the top of each cylinder bore.
4. Remove the valves as described in this chapter.
5. Clean the pushrod guides, valve guide bores and all bolt holes. Use a cleaning solvent to remove dirt and grease.
6. Clean the valves with a fine wire brush or buffing wheel.

Inspection (All Engines)

1. Check the cylinder head for signs of oil or water leaks before cleaning.
2. Clean the cylinder head thoroughly in solvent. While cleaning, look for cracks or other visible signs of damage. Look for corrosion or foreign material in the oil and water passages. Clean the passages with a stiff spiral brush, then blow them out with compressed air.
3. Check the cylinder head studs for damage and replace if necessary.
4. Check the threaded rocker arm studs or bolt holes for damaged threads; replace if necessary.
5. Check the spark plug holes for damaged threads. Have repairs made by a dealer, if required.
6. Check for warpage of the cylinder head-to-block surface with a straightedge and feeler gauge (**Figure 63**). Measure diagonally,

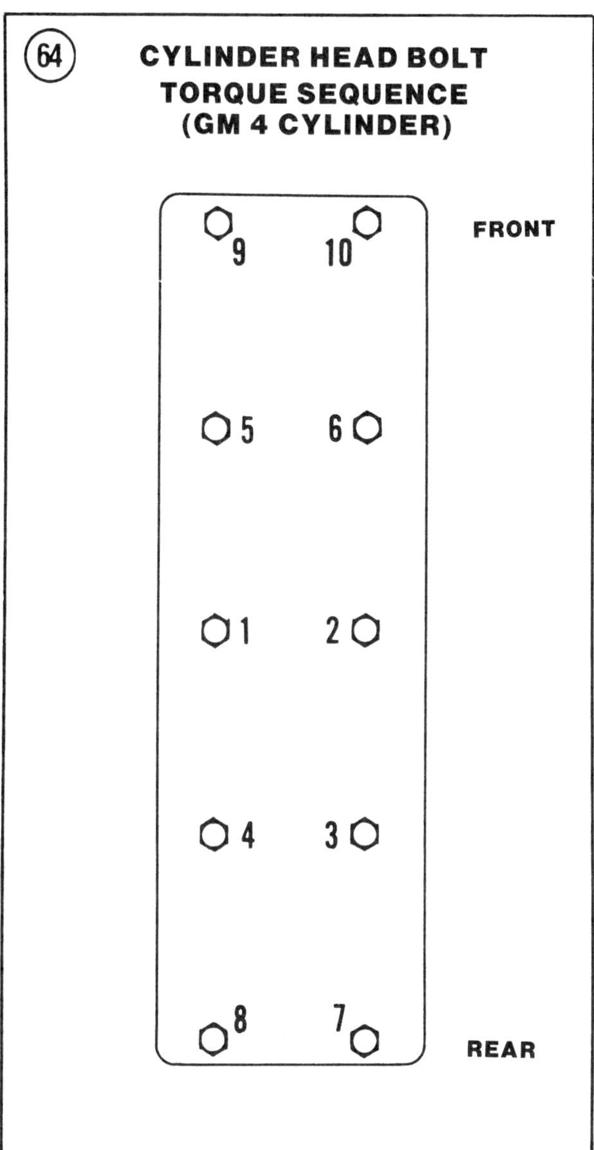

as well as end to end. If the gap exceeds specifications (**Table 1** or **Table 2**), have the head resurfaced by a machine shop. If head resurfacing is necessary, do not remove more than 0.010 in. Replace the head if a greater amount must be removed to correct warpage.

Installation (All Engines)

1. Make sure the cylinder head and block gasket surfaces and bolt holes are clean. Dirt in the block bolt holes or on the head bolt threads will affect bolt torque.
2. Recheck all visible oil and water passages for cleanliness.

CAUTION
Do not use any type of sealer with head gaskets. OMC marine head gaskets are coated with a special lacquer which provides a proper seal once the engine is warmed up.

3. Fit a new head gasket over the cylinder dowels on the block.
4. Carefully lower the head onto the cylinder block, engaging the dowel pins.
5. Wipe all head bolt threads with OMC Gasket Sealing Compound or equivalent. Install and tighten the head bolts finger-tight.
6. Tighten the head bolts 1/2 turn at a time following the sequence shown in **Figure 62** (Ford) or **Figure 64** (GM) until the specified torque is reached. See **Table 3** or **Table 4**.
7. Reverse Steps 1-9 (Ford) or Steps 1-7 (GM) of *Removal* in this chapter. On GM engines, adjust the valves as described in this chapter. Check and adjust ignition timing as required. See Chapter Four.

VALVES AND VALVE SEATS

Servicing the valves, guides and valve seats must be done by a dealer or machine shop, since they require special knowledge and expensive machine tools. Others, while possible for the home mechanic, are difficult or time-consuming. A general practice among those who do their own service is to remove the cylinder head, perform all disassembly except valve removal and take the head to a dealer or machine shop for inspection and service. Since the cost is low relative to the required effort and equipment, this is usually the best approach, even for experienced mechanics. The following procedures are given to acquaint the home mechanic with what the dealer or machine shop will do.

Valve Removal

Refer to **Figure 65** (typical) for this procedure.

1. Remove the cylinder head as described in this chapter.
2. Remove the rocker arm assemblies as described in this chapter.
3. Compress the valve spring with a compressor like the one shown in **Figure 66**. Remove the valve keys or cap locks and release the spring tension.
4. Remove the valve spring cap (or exhaust valve rotator) and valve spring.
5. Remove the valve stem seal with a pair of pliers (**Figure 67**). Discard the seal. Remove the shim and spacer, if used.

CAUTION
Remove any burrs from the valve stem lock grooves before removing the valves or the valve guides will be damaged.

6. Remove the valve and repeat Steps 3-5 on each remaining valve.
7. Arrange the parts in order so they can be returned to their original positions when reassembled.

Inspection

1. Clean the valves with a fine wire brush or buffing wheel. Discard any cracked, warped or burned valves.
2. Measure valve stems at the top, center and bottom for wear. A machine shop can do this when the valves are ground. Also measure the length of each valve and the diameter of each valve head.

NOTE
*Check the thickness of the valve edge or margin after the valves have been ground. See **Figure 68**. Any valve with a margin of less than 1/32 in. should be discarded.*

3. Remove all carbon and varnish from the valve guides with a stiff spiral wire brush.

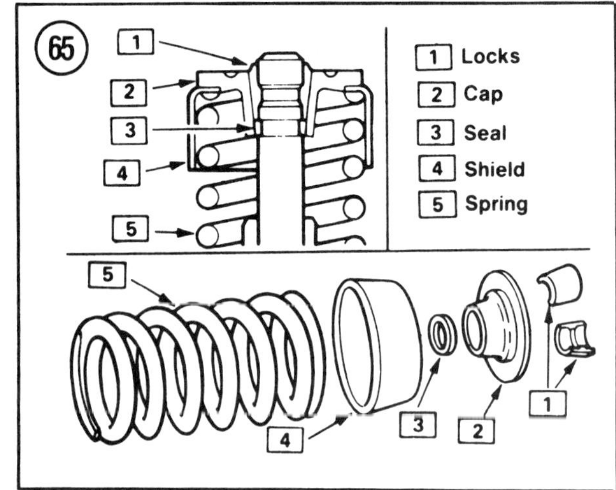

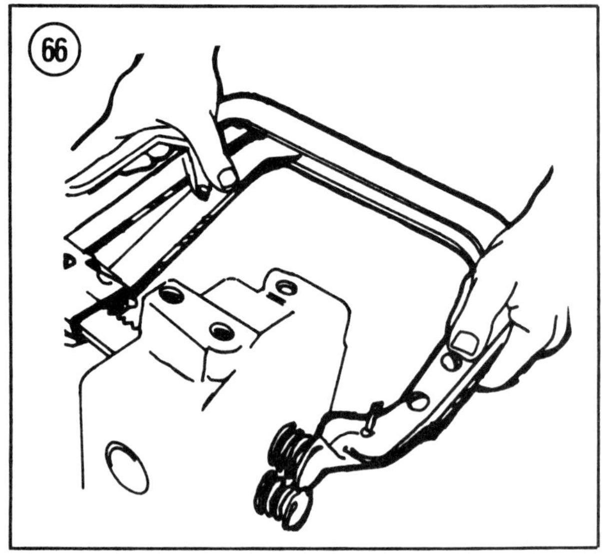

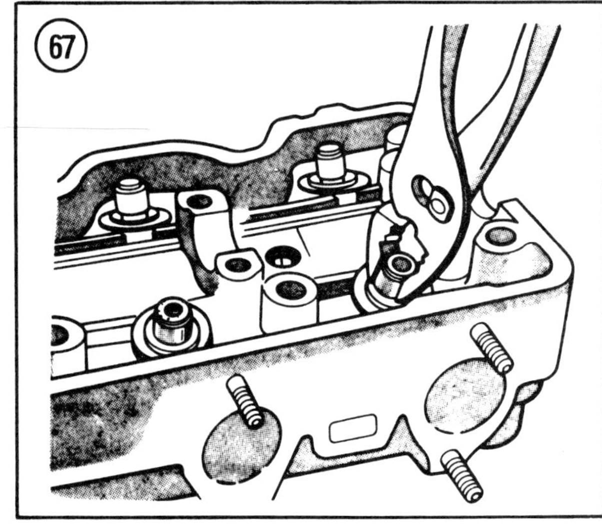

NOTE
The next step assumes that all valve stems have been measured and are within specifications. Replace valves with worn stems before performing this step.

4. Insert each valve into the guide from which it was removed. Holding the valve just slightly off its seat, rock it back and forth in a direction parallel with the rocker arms. This is the direction in which the greatest wear normally occurs. If the valve stems rocks more than slightly, the valve guide is probably worn.
5. If there is any doubt about valve guide condition after performing Step 4, have the valve guide measured with a valve stem clearance checking tool. Compare the results with specifications in **Table 1** or **Table 2**. Worn guides must be reamed for the next oversize valve stem.
6. Test the valve springs under load on a spring tester (**Figure 69**). Replace any weak springs.
7. Check each spring on a flat surface with a steel square. See **Figure 70**. Slowly revolve the spring 360° and note the space between the top of the coil and the square. If it exceeds 5/16 in. at any point, replace the spring.
8. Inspect the valve seat inserts. If worn or burned, they must be reconditioned. This is a job for a dealer or machine shop, although the procedure is described in this chapter.
9. Check each valve lifter or lash adjuster to make sure it fits freely in the block and that the end that contacts the camshaft lobe is smooth and not worn excessively.

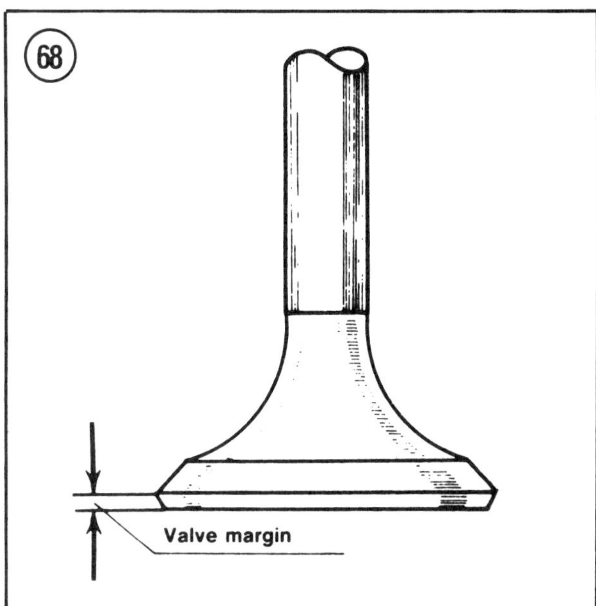

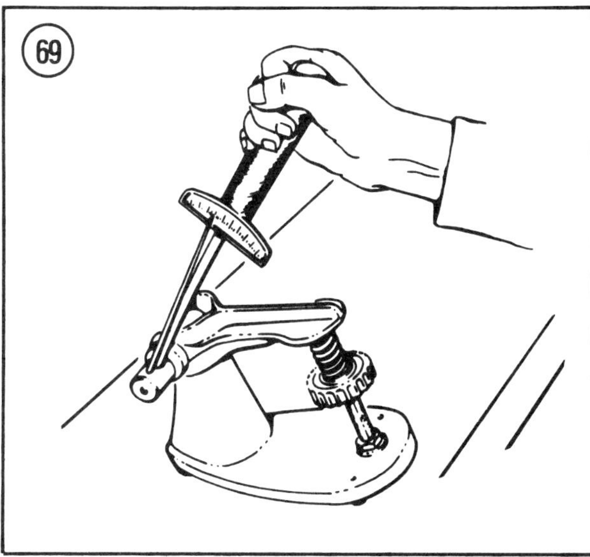

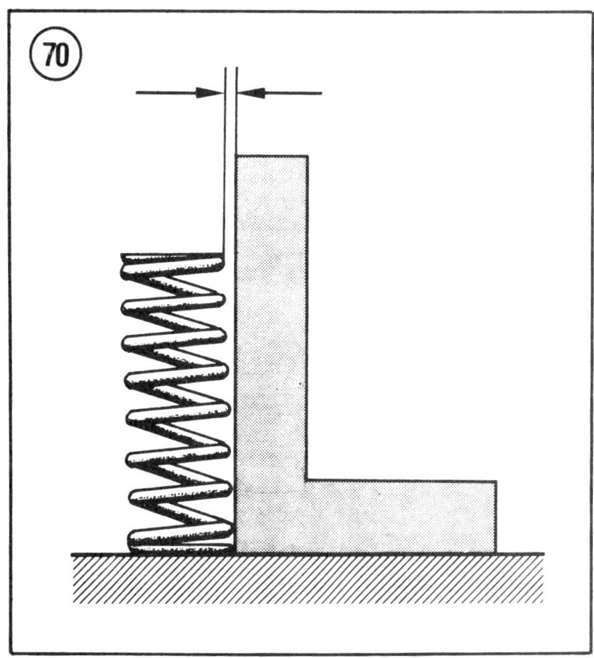

6

Valve Guide Reaming

Worn valve guides must be reamed to accept a valve with an oversize stem. These are available in 3 sizes for both intake and exhaust valves. Reaming must be done by hand (**Figure 71**) and is a job best left to an experienced machine shop. The valve seat must be refaced after the guide has been reamed.

Valve Seat Reconditioning

1. Cut the valve seats to the specified angle (**Table 1** or **Table 2**) with a dressing stone. Remove only enough metal to obtain a good finish.
2. Use tapered stones to obtain the specified seat width when necessary.
3. Coat the corresponding valve face with Prussian blue dye.
4. Insert the valve into the valve guide.
5. Apply light pressure to the valve and rotate it approximately 1/4 turn.
6. Lift the valve out. If it seats properly, the dye will transfer evenly to the valve face.
7. If the dye transfers to the top of the valve face, lower the seat. If it transfers to the bottom of the valve face, raise the seat.

Valve Installation

NOTE
Install all parts in the same positions from which they were removed.

1. Coat the valves with engine oil and install them in the cylinder head.

2A. *Ford engine*—Use installer tool part No. T73P-6571-A (**Figure 72**) and install new oil seals on each valve as follows:

a. Lubricate plastic installation cap and fit over valve stem end (A, **Figure 73**).
b. Carefully start seal over cap. Depress seal until jacket contacts top of guide (B, **Figure 73**).
c. Remove plastic installation cap. Bottom seal on valve guide with installation tool (C, **Figure 73**).

2B. *GM engine*—Install new oil seals on each valve. Seal should be flat and not twisted in the valve stem groove.

3. Drop the valve spring shim/spacer (if used) around the valve guide boss. Install the valve spring over the valve, the install the cap or retainer.
4. Compress the springs and install the keys. Make sure both keys seat properly in the upper groove of the valve stem.
5. GM engine—Measure the installed spring height between the top of the valve seat and the underside of the cap or rotator, as shown in **Figure 74**. If height is greater than specifications, install an extra spring seat shim about 1/16 in. thick and remeasure the height.

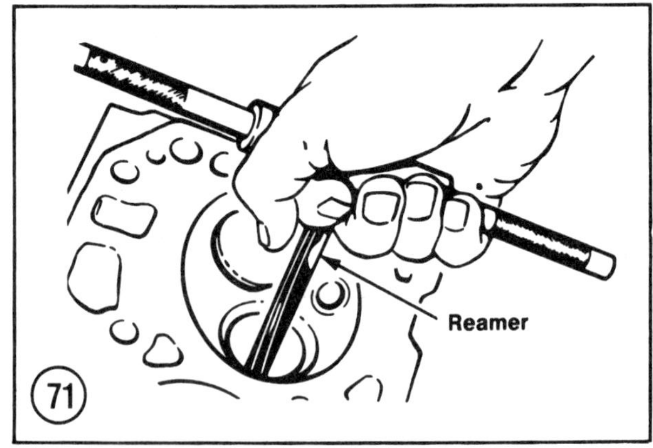

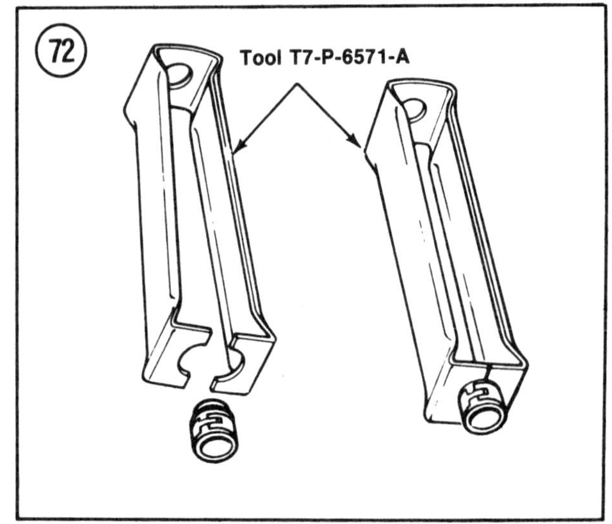

VALVE LIFTERS/LASH ADJUSTERS

Removal/Installation (Ford Engine)

See *Rocker Arm Removal/Installation* in this chapter.

Removal/Installation (GM Engine)

1. Remove the rocker arm assemblies, pushrods and pushrod cover (if so equipped) as described in this chapter.
2. Remove the valve lifters. This can be done without special tools, although tool part No. J-3049 will make the job easier and faster.
3. Installation is the reverse of removal.

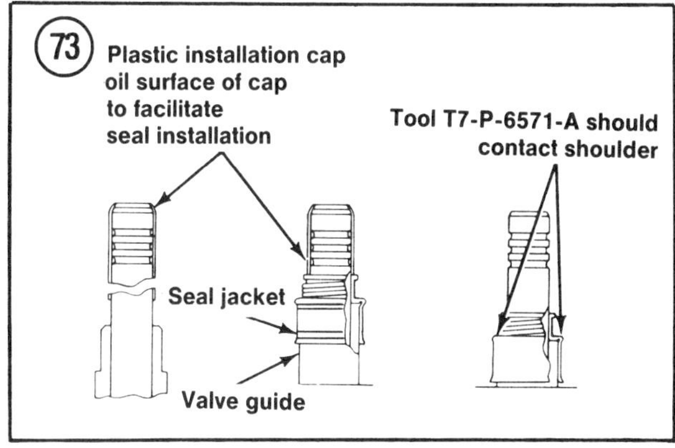

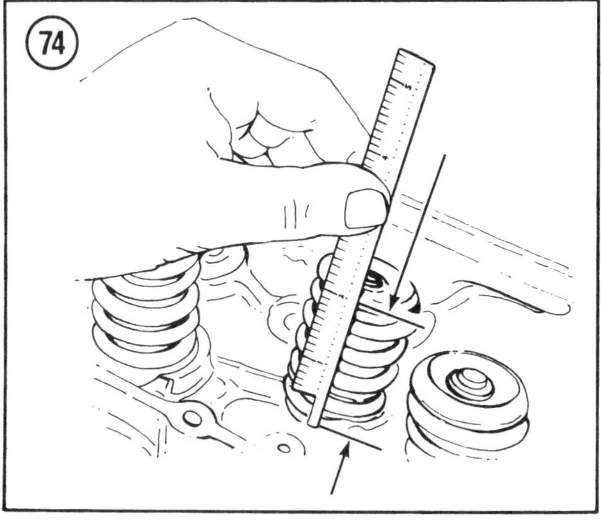

PISTON/CONNECTING ROD ASSEMBLY

Piston/Connecting Rod Removal

1. Remove the engine as described in this chapter.
2. Place a suitable container under the oil pan and remove the drain plug. Let the crankcase oil drain, then reinstall the drain plug.
3. Remove the intake and exhaust manifolds as described in this chapter.
4. Remove the cylinder heads as described in this chapter.
5. Remove the oil pan and oil pump as described in this chapter.
6. Rotate the crankshaft until one piston is at bottom dead center. Pack the cylinder bore with clean shop rags. Remove the carbon ridge at the top of each cylinder bore with a ridge reamer. These can be rented for use. Vacuum out the shavings, then remove the shop rags.
7. Rotate the crankshaft until the connecting rod is centered in the bore. Measure the clearance between the connecting rod and the crankshaft journal flange with a flat feeler gauge (**Figure 75**). If the clearance exceeds specifications (**Table 1** or **Table 2**), replace the connecting rod during reassembly.
8. Remove the nuts holding the connecting rod cap. Lift off the cap, together with the lower bearing insert.

NOTE
If the connecting rod caps are difficult to remove, tap the studs with a wooden hammer handle.

9. Use the wooden hammer handle to push the piston and connecting rod from the bore.

NOTE
Mark the cylinder number on the top of each piston with quick-drying paint. Check the cylinder numbers or

6

*identification marks on the connecting rod and cap. If they are not visible, make your own **(Figure 76).***

10. Remove the piston rings with a ring remover (**Figure** 77).
11. Repeat Steps 6-10 for all remaining connecting rods.

Piston Pin Removal/Installation

The piston pins are press-fitted to the connecting rods and hand-fitted to the pistons. Removal requires the use of a press and support stand. This is a job for a dealer or machine shop equipped to fit the pistons to the pins, ream the pin bushings to the correct diameter and install the pistons and pins on the connecting rods.

Piston Clearance Check

Unless you have precision measuring equipment and know how to use it properly, have this procedure done by a machine shop.

1. Measure the piston diameter with a micrometer (**Figure 78**) just below the rings at right angles to the piston pin bore.
2. Measure the cylinder bore diameter with a bore gauge (**Figure** 79). **Figure 80** shows the points of normal cylinder wear. If dimension A exceeds dimension B by more than 0.003 in., the cylinder must be rebored and a new piston/ring assembly installed.

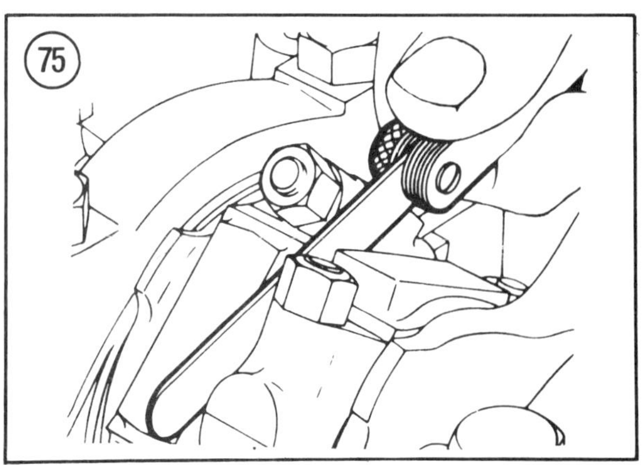
75

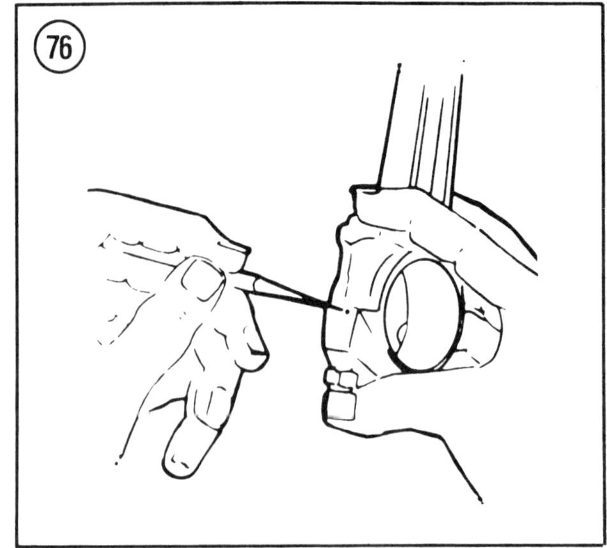
76

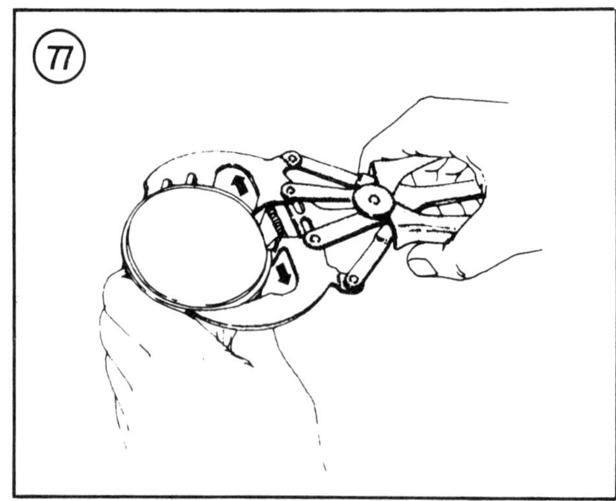
77

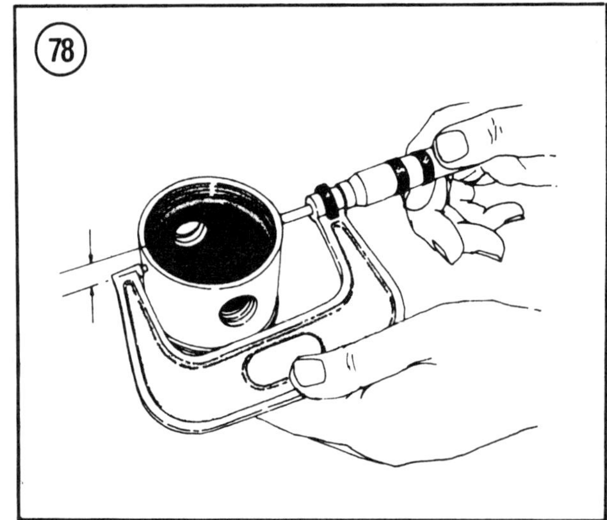
78

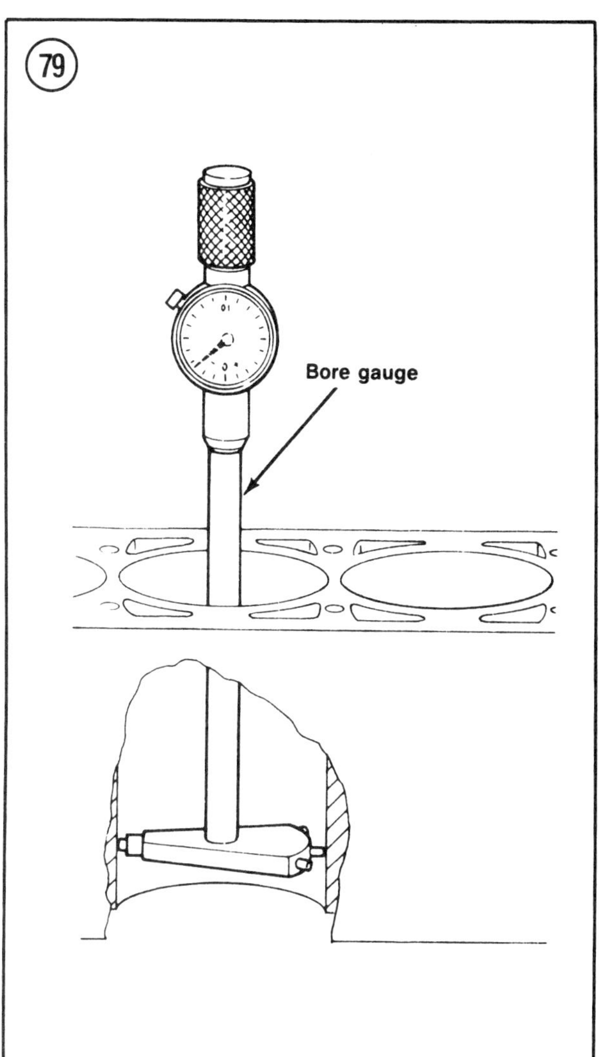

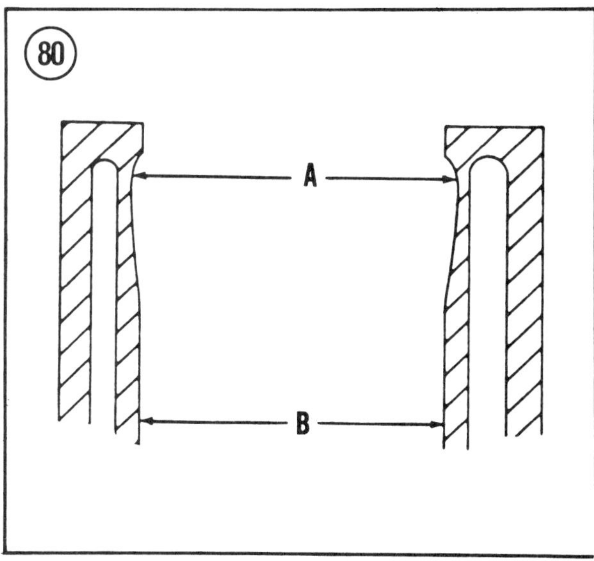

3. Subtract the piston diameter from the largest cylinder bore reading. If it exceeds the specifications in **Table 1** or **Table 2**, the cylinder must be rebored and an oversized piston installed.

NOTE
Obtain the new piston and measure it to determine the correct cylinder bore oversize dimension.

Piston Ring Fit/Installation

1. Check the ring gap of each piston ring. To do this, position the ring at the bottom of the ring travel area and square it by tapping gently with an inverted piston. See **Figure 81.**

NOTE
If the cylinders have not been rebored, check the gap at the bottom of the ring travel, where the cylinder is least worn.

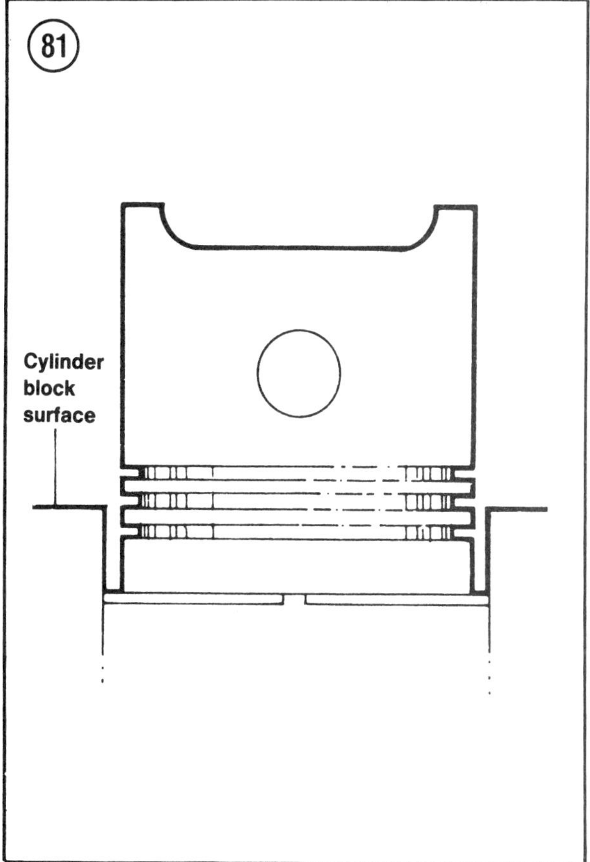

2. Measure the ring gap with a feeler gauge as shown in **Figure 82**. Compare with specifications in **Table 1** or **Table 2**. If the measurement is not within specifications, the rings must be replaced as a set. Check gap of new rings as well. If the gap is too small, file the ends of the ring to correct it (**Figure 83**).
3. Check the side clearance of the rings as shown in **Figure 84**. Place the feeler gauge alongside the ring all the way into the groove. The feeler gauge should slide all the way around the piston without binding. Any wear that occurs will form a step at the inner portion of the ring groove's lower edge. Compare the inserted feeler gauge size with the specifications in **Table 1** or **Table 2**. If the measurement is not within specifications, either the rings or the ring grooves are worn. Inspect and replace as required.
4. Using a ring expander tool (**Figure 85**), carefully install the oil control ring, then the compression rings. Oil rings consist of 3 segments. The wavy segment goes between the flat segments to act as a spacer. Upper and lower flat segments are interchangeable.
5. Position the ring gaps as shown in **Figure 86** (Ford) or **Figure 87** (GM).

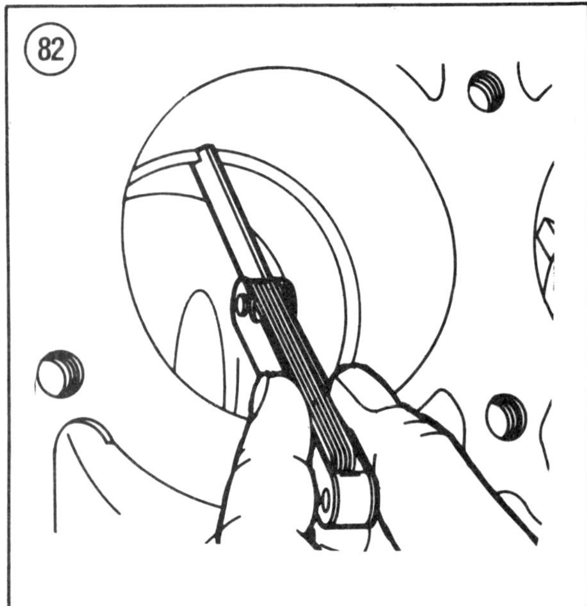

Connecting Rod Inspection

Have the connecting rods checked for straightness by a dealer or machine shop. When installing new connecting rods, have them checked for misalignment before installing the piston and piston pin. Connecting rods can spring out of alignment during shipping or handling.

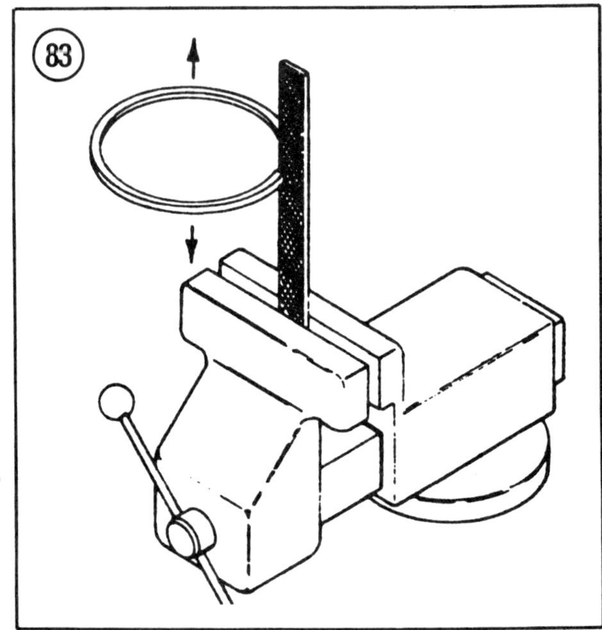

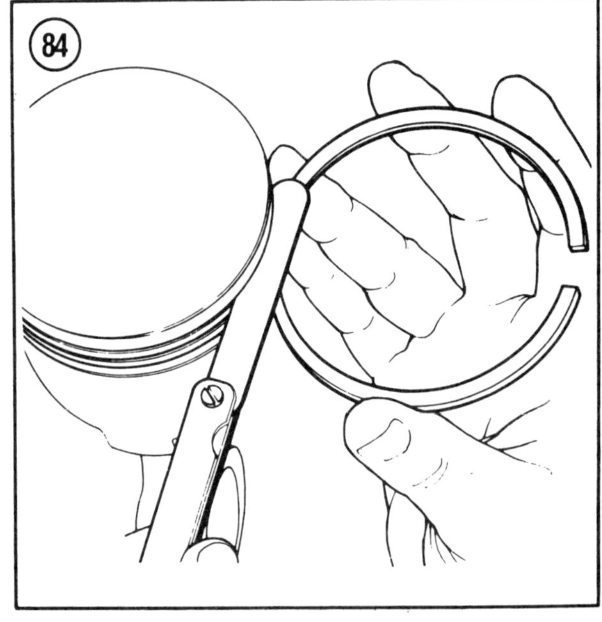

Connecting Rod Bearing Clearance Measurement

1. Place the connecting rods and upper bearing halves on the proper connecting rod journals.
2. Cut a piece of Plastigage the width of the bearing. Place the Plastigage on the journal (**Figure 88**), then install the lower bearing half end cap.

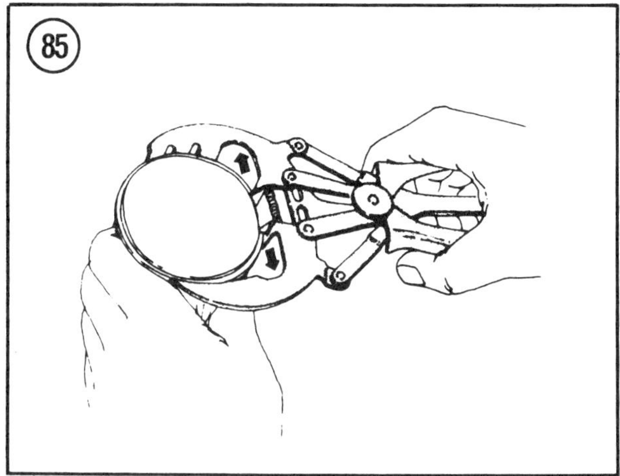
85

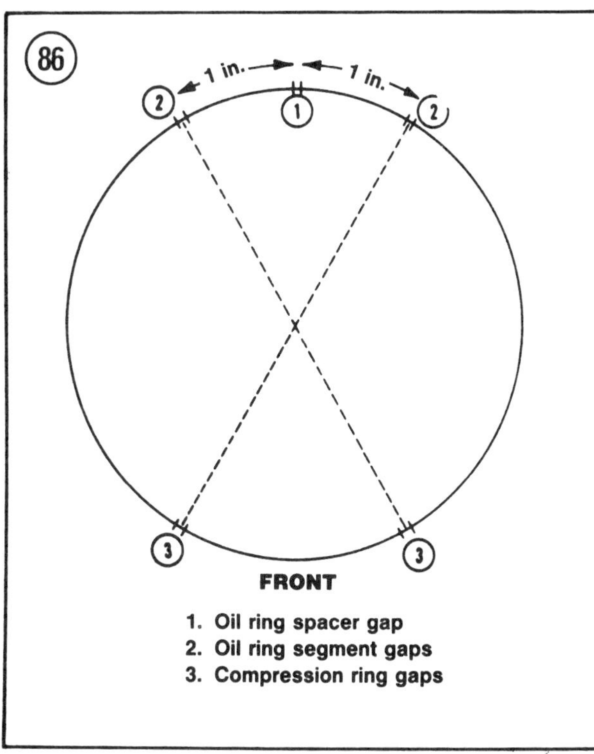

86

1. Oil ring spacer gap
2. Oil ring segment gaps
3. Compression ring gaps

NOTE
Do not place Plastigage over the journal oil hole.

3. Tighten the connecting rod cap to specifications (**Table 3** or **Table 4**). Do not rotate the crankshaft while the Plastigage is in place.
4. Remove the connecting rod caps. Bearing clearance is determined by comparing the width of the flattened Plastigage to the markings on the envelope (**Figure 89**). If the clearance is excessive, the crankshaft must be reground and undersize bearings installed.

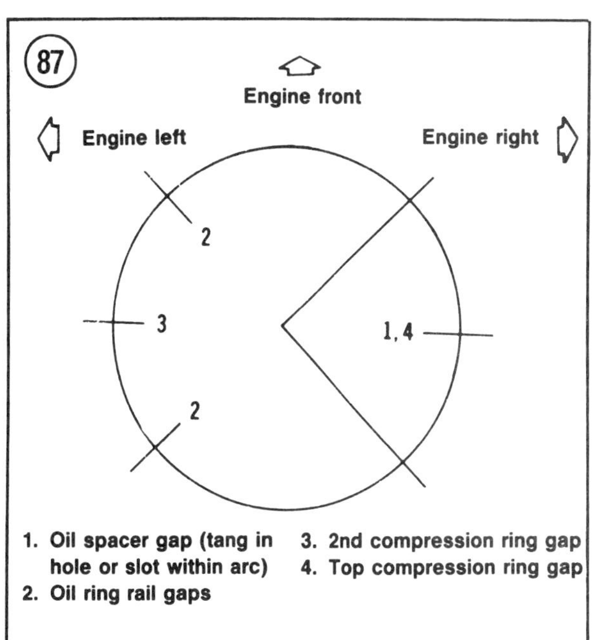

87

1. Oil spacer gap (tang in hole or slot within arc)
2. Oil ring rail gaps
3. 2nd compression ring gap
4. Top compression ring gap

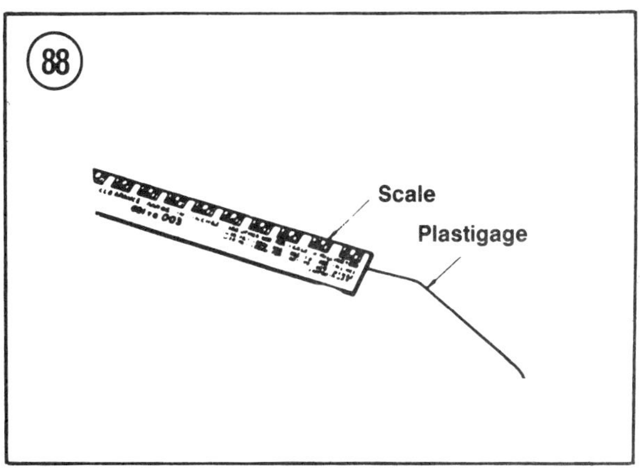

88

Piston/Connecting Rod Installation

1. Make sure the pistons are correctly installed on the connecting rods, if they were separated:
   a. On Ford pistons, the notch on the piston crown must face to the front of the engine with the connecting rod boss on the port side (seen from front of piston).
   b. On GM pistons, the flange or heavy side of the connecting rod must face toward the cast depression in the top of the piston head.
2. Make sure the ring gaps are positioned as shown in **Figure 86** (Ford) or **Figure 87** (GM).
3. Slip short pieces of hose over the connecting rod studs to prevent them from nicking the crankshaft. Tape will work if you do not have the right diameter hose, but it is more difficult to remove.
4. Immerse the entire piston in clean engine oil. Coat the cylinder wall with oil.

CAUTION
Use extreme care in Step 5 to prevent the connecting rod from nicking the crankshaft journal.

5. Install the piston/connecting rod assembly in its cylinder with a piston ring compressor as shown in **Figure 90**. Tap lightly with a wooden hammer handle to insert the piston. Make sure that the cylinder number painted on the piston top before removal corresponds to the cylinder number, counting from the front of the engine.

NOTE
The notch on the piston must face the front of the engine. See ***Figure 91***.

6. Clean the connecting rod bearings carefully, including the back sides. Coat the journals and bearings with clean engine oil. Place the bearings in the connecting rod and cap.

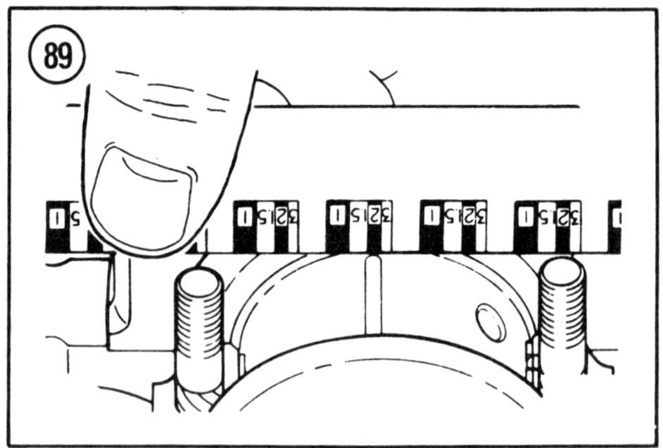

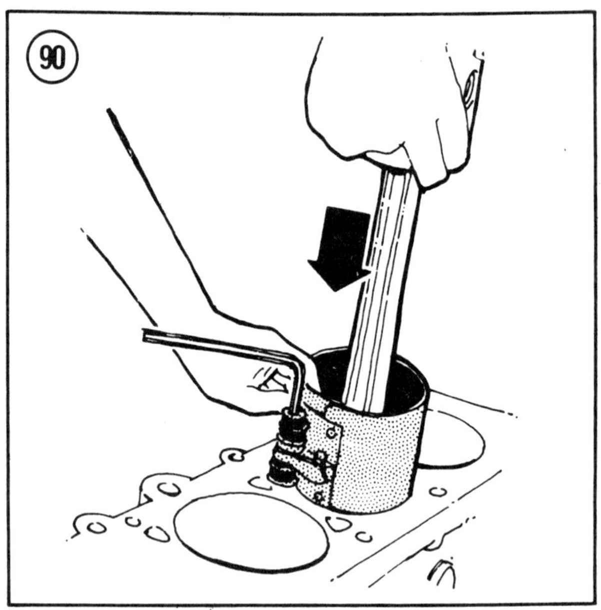

7. Pull the connecting rod and bearing into position against the crankpin. Remove the protective hose or tape and lightly lubricate the connecting rod bolt threads with SAE 30 engine oil.
8. Install the connecting rod cap. Make sure the rod and cap marks align. Install the cap nuts finger-tight.
9. Repeat Steps 4-8 for each remaining piston/connecting rod assembly.
10. Tighten the cap nuts to specifications (**Table 3** or **Table 4**).
11. Check the connecting rod big-end play as described under *Piston/Connecting Rod Removal* in this chapter.

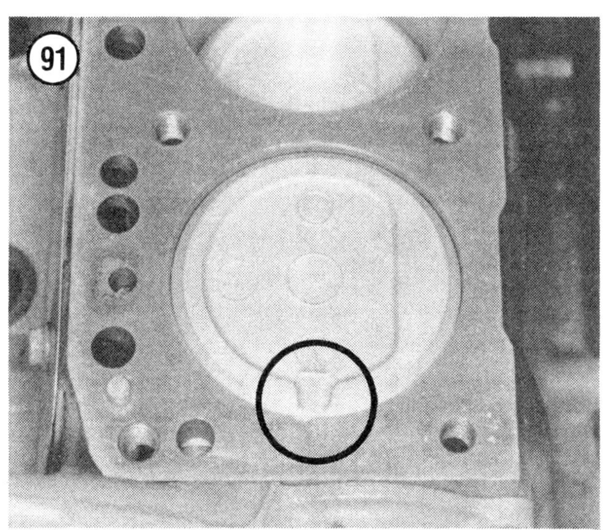
91

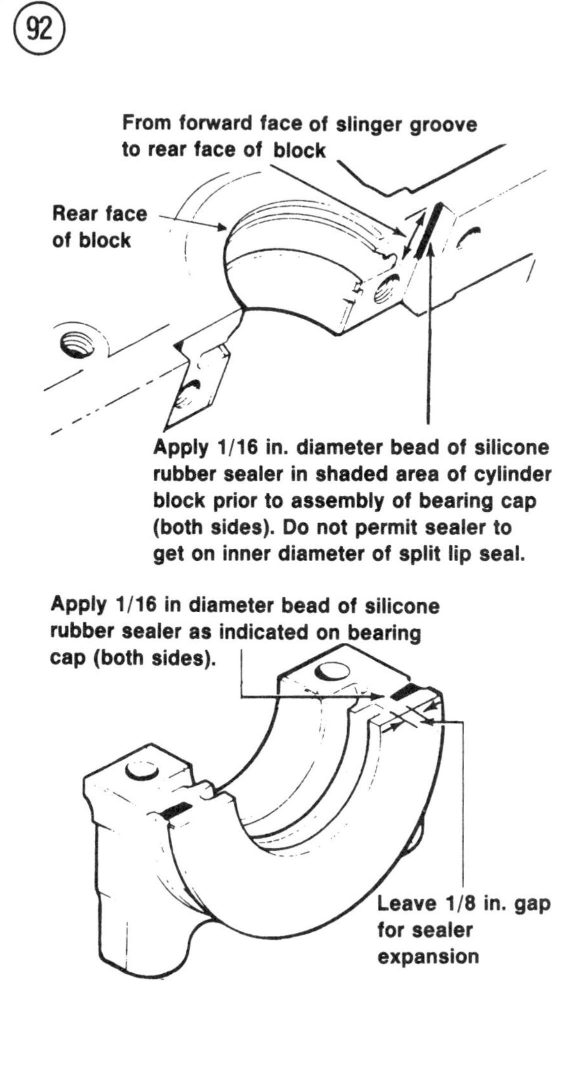
92
From forward face of slinger groove to rear face of block
Rear face of block
Apply 1/16 in. diameter bead of silicone rubber sealer in shaded area of cylinder block prior to assembly of bearing cap (both sides). Do not permit sealer to get on inner diameter of split lip seal.
Apply 1/16 in diameter bead of silicone rubber sealer as indicated on bearing cap (both sides).
Leave 1/8 in. gap for sealer expansion

REAR MAIN BEARING OIL SEAL

Ford engines may use a 2-piece rear crankshaft seal or a circular 1-piece seal. GM engines use a 2-piece neoprene seal. In each case, the seal can be replaced without crankshaft removal.

CAUTION

Make sure no rubber is shaved from the outside of the seals by the groove edges in the cylinder block or rear main bearing cap during installation. Do not allow any engine oil to drip on the area of the cylinder block or rear main bearing cap to which silicone rubber sealer will be applied later.

Ford 2-piece Seal Replacement

1. Remove the engine from the boat as described in this chapter.
2. Remove the oil pan as described in this chapter.
3. Remove the rear main bearing cap. Remove the 2 halves of the crankshaft rear oil seal from the cylinder block and rear main bearing cap, then discard them. It may be necessary to loosen the remaining main bearing bolts to let the crankshaft lower about 1/16 in. at the rear. Use a pin punch to start removal of the cylinder block seal half; once seal extends from the groove, grasp its end with needlenose pliers and remove it from the block.
4. Clean the rear oil seal grooves in the cylinder block and rear main bearing cap with a brush and solvent such as lacquer thinner. Also clean the areas where silicone rubber sealant is to be applied before installing the rear main bearing cap to the cylinder block (**Figure 92**).
5. Dip the halves of the seal in clean engine oil.
6. Carefully install half of the seal in its groove in the cylinder block and the other half of the seal in its groove in the rear main

6

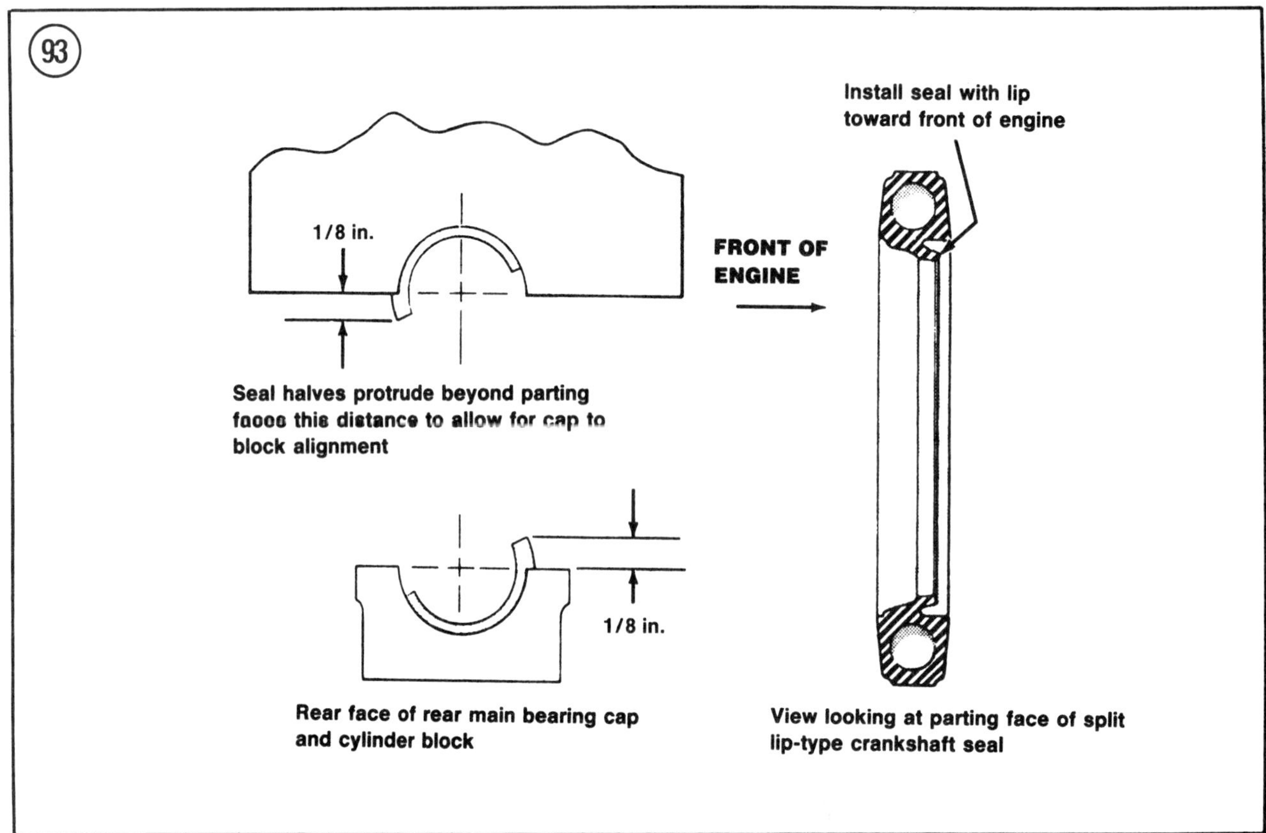

bearing cap as shown in **Figure 93**. The lip of the installed seal must face the front of the engine as shown in **Figure 93**. If main bearing caps were loosened in Step 3, retighten to specifications (**Table 4**) at this time.

7. Apply a 1/16 in. diameter bead of silicone rubber sealant to the areas of the cylinder block and rear main bearing cap shown in **Figure 92**. Install the rear main bearing cap and tighten the cap bolts to specifications (**Table 4**).
8. Reinstall the oil pan as described in this chapter.
9. Reinstall the engine in the boat as described in this chapter.

Ford 1-piece Seal Replacement

1. Remove the engine from the boat as described in this chapter.
2. Remove the oil pan as described in this chapter.
3. Punch 2 holes opposite each other in the seal case with an awl. Install 2 sheet metal screws into the seal holes. Grasp the screws with pliers and work the seal from the block. Work carefully to avoid damage to the crankshaft seal bore.
4. Carefully clean the seal groove in the cylinder block.
5. Lubricate the new seal and seal mating surface with clean engine oil.
6. Fit the new seal on seal installer tool part No. T82L-6701-A with its spring side facing the engine.
7. Attach installer tool with seal to the crankshaft using the 2 bolts supplied with the tool. See **Figure 94**.
8. Alternately tighten the bolts until the seal is seated within 0.005 in. (0.127 mm) of the rear face of the block.
9. Remove the seal installer tool and reinstall the oil pan as described in this chapter.

94

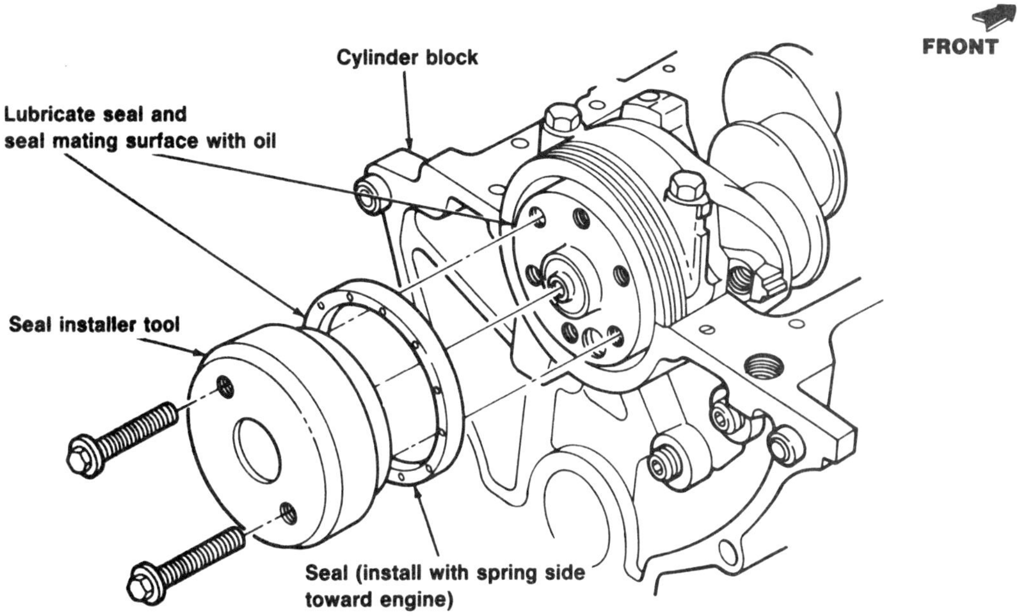

Cylinder block
FRONT
Lubricate seal and seal mating surface with oil
Seal installer tool
Seal (install with spring side toward engine)

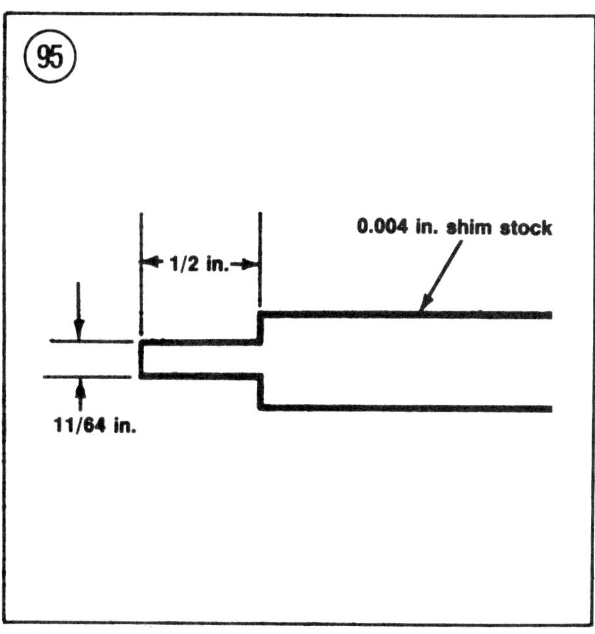

10. Reinstall the engine in the boat as described in this chapter.

GM 2-piece Seal Replacement

Always replace upper and lower seals as an assembly. Make sure to clean the crankshaft surface before installing a new seal. The seal lip must face toward the engine.

1. Fabricate a seal installation tool as shown in **Figure 95** to protect the seal bead when positioning the new seal.
2. Remove the oil pan and oil pump as described in this chapter.
3. Remove the rear main bearing cap. Pry the oil seal from the bottom of the cap with a small screwdriver.

4. Remove the upper half of the seal with a brass pin punch. Tap the punch on one end of the seal until its other end protrudes far enough to be removed with pliers.
5. Clean all sealant from the bearing cap and crankshaft with a non-abrasive cleaner.
6. Coat the lips and bead of a new seal with light engine oil. Do not let oil touch seal mating ends.
7. Position tip of seal installer tool (fabricated in Step 1) between crankcase and seal seat. Position seal between crankshaft and tip of tool so seal bead touches tool tip. Make sure oil seal lip faces toward front of engine. See **Figure 96**.
8. Use seal installer tool as a shoehorn and roll seal around crankshaft, protecting seal bead from sharp corners of seal seat surfaces. Keep tool in position until seal is properly seated, with both ends flush with the block.
9. Remove the tool carefully to prevent pulling seal out with it.
10. Use seal installer tool as a shoehorn again and install seal half in bearing cap. Feed seal into cap with light thumb and finger pressure.
11. Install rear main bearing cap with seal and tighten to 10-12 ft.-lb. (14-16 N•m). Tap end of crankshaft to the rear, then to the front to align the thrust surfaces.
12. Retighten bearing cap to specifications (**Table 3**).

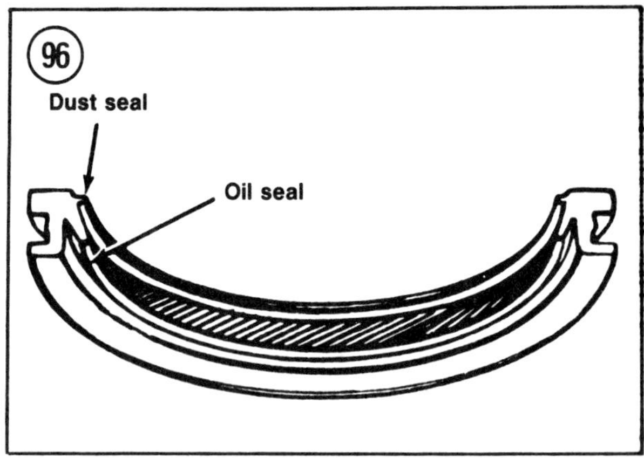

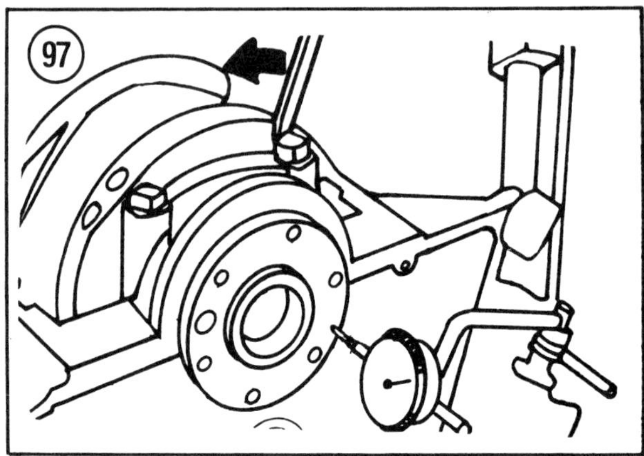

CRANKSHAFT

End Play Measurement

Ford engine

1. Pry the crankshaft to the rear of the engine with a large screwdriver.
2. Install a dial indicator with its contact point resting against the crankshaft flange. The indicator axis should be parallel to the crankshaft axis. See **Figure 97**.
3. Set the dial indicator gauge to zero. Pry the crankshaft forward as far as it will go and compare the reading to specifications (**Table 2**).
4. If the end play is excessive, replace the thrust (No. 3) bearing. If less than specified, remove the crankshaft and recheck the thrust bearing faces for scratches, nicks, burrs or dirt. If none of these are found, improper alignment is probably the cause.

GM engine

1. Pry the crankshaft to the front of the engine with a large screwdriver.
2. Measure the crankshaft end play at the front of the rear main bearing with a flat feeler gauge. See **Figure 98**. Compare to specifications in **Table 1**.
3. If the end play is excessive, replace the rear main bearing. If less than specified, remove the crankshaft and recheck the thrust bearing

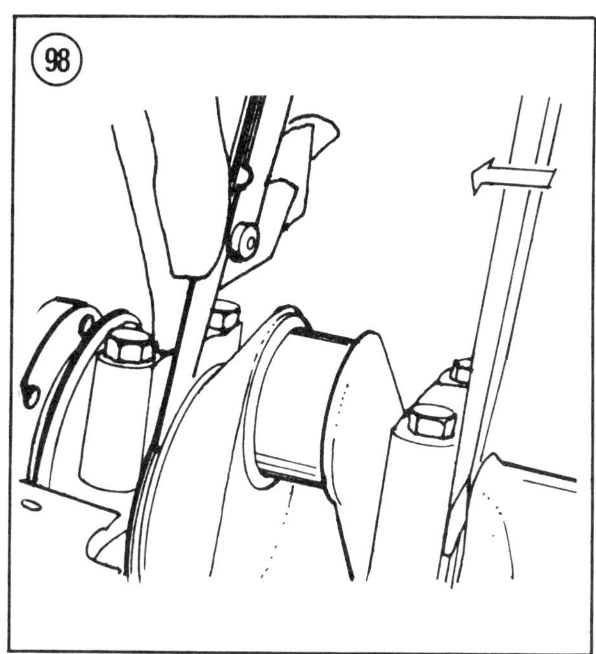

faces for scratches, nicks, burrs or dirt. If none of these are found, improper alignment is probably the cause.

Removal (All Engines)

1. Remove the engine from the boat as described in this chapter.
2. Remove the flywheel as described in this chapter.
3. Mount the engine on an engine stand, if available.
4. Remove the starter motor. See Chapter Eleven.
5. Invert the engine to bring the oil pan to an upright position.
6. Remove the oil pan and oil pump as described in this chapter.

7A. *Ford engine*—Remove the vibration damper, outer belt cover and timing belt as described in this chapter.

7B. *GM engine*—Remove the pulley and front hub or harmonic balancer, front cover and timing gear as described in this chapter.

8. Remove the spark plugs to permit easy rotation of the crankshaft.
9. Measure crankshaft end play as described in this chapter.
10. Rotate the crankshaft to position one connecting rod at the bottom of its stroke.
11. Remove the connecting rod bearing cap and bearing. Move the piston/rod assembly away from the crankshaft.
12. Repeat Step 10 and Step 11 for each remaining piston/rod assembly.
13. Check the caps for identification numbers or marks. If none are visible, clean the caps with a wire brush. If marks still cannot be seen, make your own with quick-drying paint.
14. Unbolt and remove the main bearing caps and bearing inserts.

NOTE
If the caps are difficult to remove, lift the bolts partway out, then pry them from side to side.

15. Carefully lift the crankshaft from the engine block and place it on a clean workbench.
16. Remove the bearing inserts from the block. Place the bearing caps and inserts in order on a clean workbench.
17. Remove the main bearing oil seal from the cylinder block and rear bearing cap.

Inspection

1. Clean the crankshaft thoroughly with solvent. Blow out the oil passages with compressed air.
2. Check the main and connecting rod journals for wear, scratches, grooves, scoring or cracks. Check oil seal surface for burrs, nicks or other sharp edges which might damage a seal during installation.

NOTE
Unless you have precision measuring equipment and know how to use it, have a machine shop perform Step 3.

3. Check all journals against specifications (**Table 1** or **Table 2**) for out-of-roundness and taper. See **Figure 99**. If necessary, have the crankshaft reground and install new undersize bearings.

Main Bearing Clearance Measurement

Main bearing clearance is measured with Plastigage in the same manner as connecting rod bearing clearance as described in this chapter. Excessive clearance requires that the bearings be replaced, the crankshaft be reground or both.

Installation (All Engines)

1. Install a new rear main bearing oil seal as described in this chapter.
2. Install the main bearing inserts in the cylinder block. Bearing oil holes must align with block oil holes and bearing tabs must seat in the block tab slots.

NOTE
Check cap bolts for thread damage before reuse. If damaged, replace the bolts.

3. Lubricate the bolt threads with SAE 30 engine oil.
4. Install the bearing inserts in each cap.
5. Carefully lower the crankshaft into position in the block. On Ford engines, work carefully to avoid damage to the sides of the No. 3 (thrust) bearing.

6A. Ford engine:
   a. Install all main bearing caps except the rear cap and the No. 3 cap. Make sure the arrows on the top of the caps face toward the front of the engine.
   b. Apply a 1/16 in. diameter bead of RTV sealant to the areas of the cylinder block and rear main bearing cap shown in **Figure 92**.
   c. Install the cap bolts and tighten to specifications (**Table 4**).

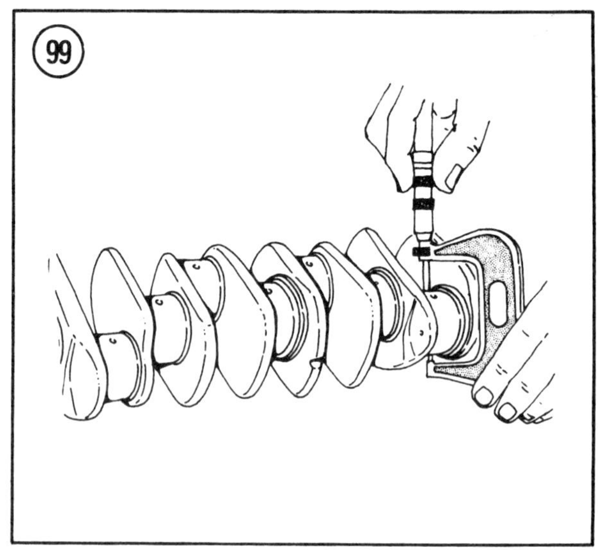

   d. Install the No. 3 bearing cap and tighten the bolts finger-tight.
   e. Use a large screwdriver or pry bar to force the crankshaft as far to the rear of the block as possible and the No. 3 bearing cap as far to the front as possible. This aligns the 2 halves of the thrust bearing. Holding the crankshaft and thrust bearing cap in this position, tighten the cap bolts to specifications (**Table 4**).

6B. GM engine:
   a. Install the bearing caps in their marked positions with the arrows pointing toward the front of the engine and the number mark aligned with the corresponding mark on the journals.
   b. Install and tighten all bolts finger-tight. Recheck end play as described in this chapter, then tighten all bolts to specifications (**Table 3**).

7. Rotate the crankshaft to make sure it turns smoothly at the flywheel rim. If it binds or the crankshaft becomes hard to turn, stop and find out why before continuing. Check for foreign material on the bearings and journals. Make absolutely certain that the bearings are the correct size, especially if the crankshaft has been reground. Never use undersize

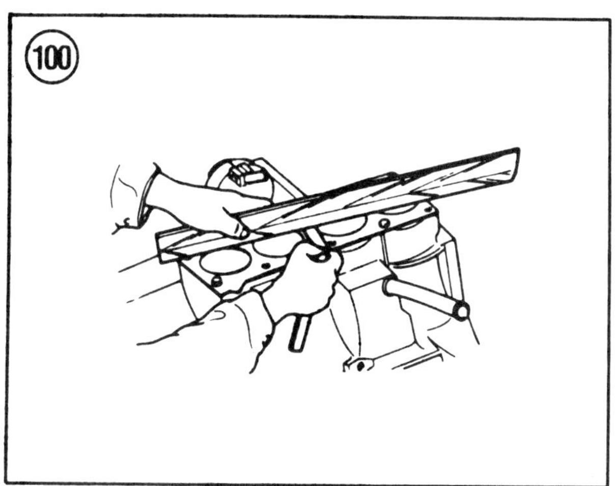

bearings if the crankshaft has not been reground.
8. Reverse Steps 1-11 of *Removal* in this chapter.

FLYWHEEL

Removal/Installation

1. Remove the engine from the boat as described in this chapter.
2. Remove the flywheel housing and drive plate or coupling, if so equipped.
3. Unbolt the flywheel from the crankshaft. Remove the bolts gradually in a diagonal pattern.
4. To install, align the dowel hole in the flywheel with dowel in crankshaft flange and position the flywheel on studs.
5. Fit the drive plate or coupling on the studs. Install the washers and locknuts. Tighten nuts to 40-45 ft.-lb. (54-61 N•m).
6. Install a dial indicator on the machined surface of the flywheel and check runout. If runout exceeds 0.008 in., remove the flywheel and check for burrs. If none are found, replace the flywheel.
7. If flywheel runout is within specifications, install the flywheel housing and tighten screws to 28-36 ft.-lb. (38-49 N•m).
8. Reinstall the engine in the boat as described in this chapter.

Inspection

1. Visually check the flywheel surface for cracks, deep scoring, excessive wear, heat discoloration and checking. If the surface is glazed or slightly scratched, have the flywheel resurfaced by a machine shop.
2. Check the surface flatness with a straightedge and feeler gauge.
3. Inspect the ring gear for cracks, broken teeth or excessive wear. If severely worn, check the starter motor drive teeth for similar wear or damage; replace as required.

CYLINDER BLOCK

Cleaning and Inspection

1. Clean the block thoroughly with solvent. Remove any gasket or RTV sealant residue from the machined surfaces. Check all core plugs for leaks and replace any that are suspect. See *Core Plug Replacement* in this chapter. Remove any plugs that seal oil passages. Check oil and coolant passages for sludge, dirt and corrosion while cleaning. If the passages are very dirty, have the block boiled out by a machine shop. Blow out all passages with compressed air. Check the threads in the head bolt holes to be sure they are clean. If dirty, use a tap to true up the threads and remove any deposits.
2. Examine the block for cracks. To confirm suspicions about possible leak areas, use a mixture of 1 part kerosene and 2 parts engine oil. Coat the suspected area with this solution, then wipe dry and immediately apply a solution of zinc oxide dissolved in wood alcohol. If any discoloration appears in the treated area, the block is cracked and should be replaced.
3. Check flatness of the cylinder block deck or top surface. Place an accurate straightedge on the block. If there is any gap between the block and straightedge, measure it with a flat feeler gauge (**Figure 100**). Measure from end

to end and from corner to corner. Have the block resurfaced if it is warped more than 0.004 in. (0.102 mm).

4. Measure cylinder bores with a bore gauge (**Figure 101**) for out-of-roundness or excessive wear as described in *Piston Clearance Check* in this chapter. If the cylinders exceed maximumum tolerances, they must be rebored. Reboring is also necessary if the cylinder walls are badly scuffed or scored.

NOTE
*Before boring, install all main bearing caps and tighten the cap bolts to specifications in **Table 2**.*

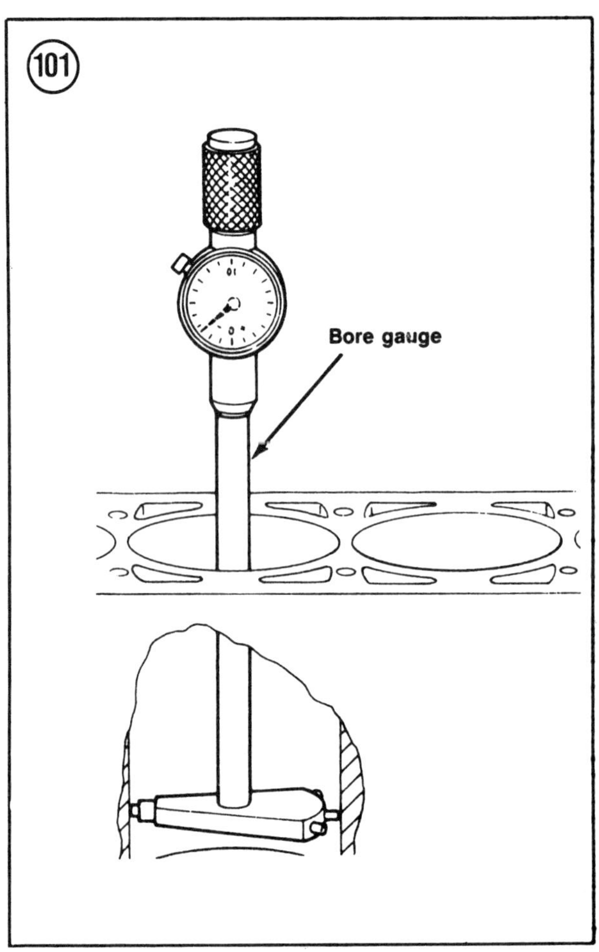

CORE PLUG REPLACEMENT

The condition of all core plugs in the block and cylinder head should be checked whenever the engine is out of the boat for service. If any signs of leakage or corrosion are found around one core plug, replace them all.

Removal/Installation

CAUTION
Do not drive core plugs into the engine casting. It will be impossible to retrieve them and they can restrict coolant circulation, resulting in serious engine damage.

1. Tap the bottom edge of the core plug with a hammer and drift. Use several sharp blows to push the bottom of the plug inward, tilting the top out **(Figure 102).**
2. Grip the top of the plug firmly with pliers. Pull the plug from its bore **(Figure 103)** and discard.

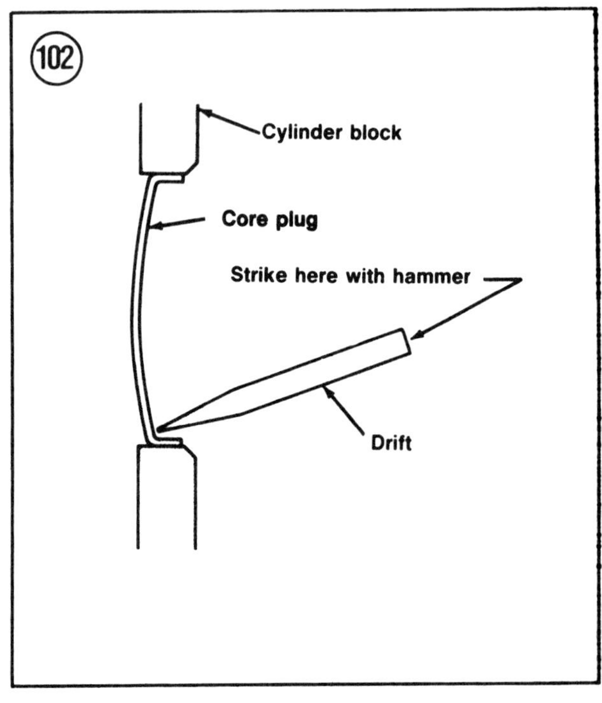

NOTE
Core plugs can also be removed by drilling a hole in the center of the plug and prying them out with an appropriate size drift or pin punch. On large core plugs, the use of a universal impact slide hammer is recommended.

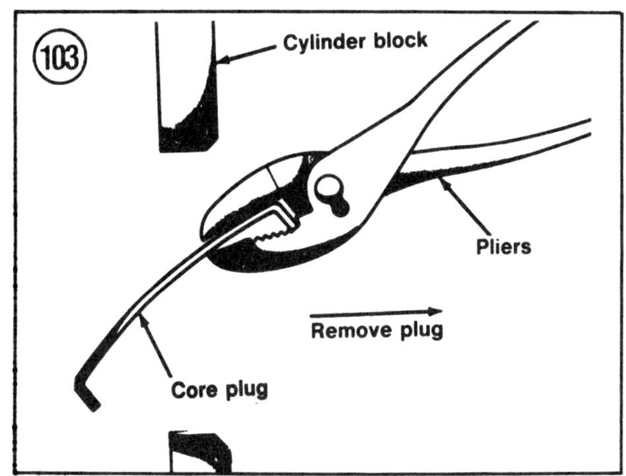

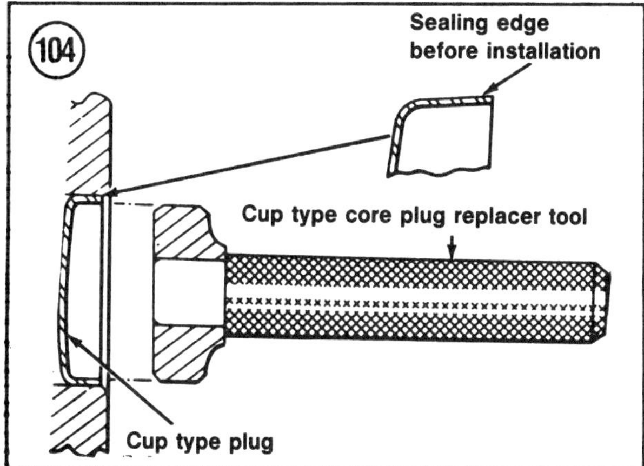

3. Clean the plug bore thoroughly to remove all traces of the old sealer. Inspect the bore for any damage that might interfere with proper sealing of the new plug. If damage is evident, true the surface by boring for the next oversize plug.

NOTE
Oversize plugs can be identified by an "OS" stamped in the flat on the cup side of the plug.

4. Coat the inside diameter of the plug bore and the outer diameter of the new plug with sealer. Use an oil-resistant sealer if the plug is to be installed in an oil gallery or a water-resistant sealer for plugs installed in the water jacket.
5. Install the new core plug with an appropriate size core plug replacer tool (**Figure 104**), driver or socket. The sharp edge of the plug should be at least 0.02 in. (0.5 mm) inside the lead-in chamfer.
6. Repeat Steps 1-5 to replace each remaining core plug.

Tables are on the following pages.

Table 1 GM 4-CYLINDER ENGINE SPECIFICATIONS

Engine type	Inline 4-cylinder
Bore	
3.0L	4.00 in.
2.5L	3.875 in.
Stroke	
3.0L	3.60 in.
2.5L	3.25 in.
Displacement	
3.0L	181 cid
2.5L	153 cid
Firing order	1-3-4-2
Cylinder arrangement	1-2-3-4
Cylinder bore	
Out-of-round	
Production	0.0005 in. max.
Service	0.001 in. max.
Taper	
Production	0.0005 in. max.
Service	0.001 in. max.
Pistons	
Type	
3.0L	Flat—sump head
2.5L	Flat—notched head
Clearance	
At top land	
3.0L	0.0255-0.0345 in.
2.5L	0.0245-0.0335 in.
At skirt	
3.0L	0.0025-0.0035 in.
2.5L	0.0005-0.0015 in.
Ring groove depth	
Compression	
3.0L	0.209-0.211 in.
2.5L	0.200-0.208 in.
Oil	
3.0L	0.190-0.199 in.
2.5L	0.194-0.202 in.
Piston ring	
Width	
Compression	0.0775-0.0780 in.
Oil	0.188-0.189 in.
Ring gap	
3.0L	
Top	0.010-0.020 in.
2nd	0.013-0.025 in.
Oil	0.015-0.055 in.
2.5L	
Compression	0.010-0.020 in.
Oil	0.015-0.055 in.

(continued)

Table 1 GM 4-CYLINDER ENGINE SPECIFICATIONS (continued)

Piston pin	
Length	2.990-3.010 in.
Diameter	0.9270-0.9273 in.
Clearance	
In piston (new)	
3.0L	0.0003-0.0004 in.
2.5L	0.00015-0.00025 in.
Wear limit in piston	0.001 in.
Fit in rod	0.0008-0.0021 (press)
Camshaft	
Lobe lift	
3.0L	0.2525 in.
2.5L	0.2325 in.
Journal diameter	1.8687 in.
Runout	0.0015 in. max.
Crankshaft	
Main journal diameter	2.2983-2.2993 in.
Taper	0.0002 in.
Out-of-round	0.0002 in.
Main bearing clearance	0.0003-0.0029 in.
End play	0.002-0.006 in.
Crankpin	
Journal diameter	
3.0L	2.099-2.100 in.
2.5L	1.999-2.000 in.
Taper	0.0003 in.
Out-of-round	0.0002 in.
Connecting rod	
Bearing clearance	
3.0L	0.00085-0.00135 in.
2.5L	0.0007-0.0027 in.
End play	0.008-0.015 in.
Valve train	
Lifter	Hydraulic
Rocker arm ratio	1.75:1
Valve lash	3/4 to 1 turn down from zero lash
Face angle	45°
Seat angle	46°
Seat width	
Intake	1/32-1/16 in.
Exhaust	1/16-3/32 in.
Stem clearance	
Intake	0.0010-0.0027 in.
Exhaust	
3.0L	0.0010-0.0027 in.
2.5L	0.0015-0.0032 in.
Valve spring	
Free length	2.08 in.
Load	
Closed	78-86 lb. @ 1.66 in.
Open	170-180 lb. @ 1.26 in.

6

Table 2 FORD 4-CYLINDER ENGINE SPECIFICATIONS

Engine type	Inline overhead cam 4-cylinder
Bore	3.78 in.
Stroke	3.126 in.
Displacement	140 cid (2.3 liter)
Firing order	1-3-4-2
Cylinder arrangement	1-2-3-4
Cylinder bore	
Diameter	3.7795-3.7831 in.
Out-of-round	0.0015 in. max.
Taper	0.010 in. max.
Head gasket surface flatness	0.003 in. in 6 in.
Pistons	
Diameter	
Code red	3.7780-3.7786 in.
Code blue	3.7792-3.7798 in.
0.003 oversize	3.7804-3.7810 in.
Clearance	0.0014-0.0022 in.
Ring groove width	
Compression	0.080-0.081 in.
Oil	0.188-0.189 in.
Ring width	
Compression	0.077-0.078 in.
Side clearance	
Compression	0.002-0.004 in.
Oil	Snug
Ring gap	
Compression	0.010-0.020 in.
Oil	0.015-0.055 in.
Piston pin	
Diameter	
Standard	0.9119-0.9124 in.
Length	3.010-3.040 in.
Clearance	0.0002-0.0004 in.
Camshaft	
Lobe lift	0.2437 in.
Journal diameter	1.7713-1.7720 in.
Journal to bearing clearance	0.001-0.003 in.
Runout	0.005 in.
Out-of-round	0.005 in.
End play	0.001-0.007 in.
Crankshaft	
Main journal diameter	2.3990-2.3982 in.
Taper	0.0006 in.
Out-of-round	0.0006 in.
Main bearing clearance	0.0008-0.0015 in.
End play	0.004-0.008 in.
Crankpin	
Diameter	2.0464-2.0472 in.
Taper	0.0006 in.
Out-of-round	0.0006 in.
Connecting rod	
Bearing clearance	0.0008-0.0015 in.
Side clearance	0.0035-0.0105 in.

(continued)

Table 2 FORD 4-CYLINDER ENGINE SPECIFICATIONS (continued)

Valve train	
Lifter	Hydraulic
Rocker arm ratio	1.64:1
Valve arrangement	EIEIEIEI
Face angle	44°
Seat angle	45°
Seat width	
Intake	0.060-0.080 in.
Exhaust	0.070-0.090 in.
Stem clearance	
Intake	0.0010-0.0027 in.
Exhaust	0.0015-0.0032 in.
Stem diameter	
Standard	
Intake	0.3416-0.3423 in.
Exhaust	0.3411-0.3418 in.
0.003 oversize	
Intake	0.3446-0.3453 in.
Exhaust	0.3441-0.3448 in.
0.015 oversize	
Intake	0.3566-0.3573 in.
Exhaust	0.3561-0.3568 in.
0.030 oversize	
Intake	0.3716-0.3723 in.
Exhaust	0.3711-0.3718 in.
Head diameter	
Intake	1.73-1.74 in.
Exhaust	1.49-1.51 in.
Face runout	0.0020 in. max.
Valve spring	
Free length	1.89 in.
Installed height	1 17/32-1 19/32 in.
Out-of-square	0.078 in.
Load	
Closed	71-79 lb. @ 1.56 in.
Open	159-175 lb. @ 1.16 in.
Oil Pump	
Relief valve tension	15.2-17.2 lb. @ 1.20 in.
Drive shaft-to-housing bearing clearance	0.0015-0.0030 in.
Relief valve clearance	0.0015-0.0030 in.
Rotor assembly end clearance	0.0010-0.0040 in.
Outer race-to-housing radial clearance	0.001-0.0013 in.

Table 3 GM 4-CYLINDER TIGHTENING TORQUES

Fastener	in.-lb.	ft.-lb.
Camshaft thrust plate	72-90	
Connecting rod caps		35
Cylinder head bolts		90-100
Distributor clamp		20
Engine mount-to-block		20-24
Exhaust manifold		
V6	18-22	24-30
V8		
Attaching nuts	20-26	27-35
High rise elbow	10-12	14-16
Flywheel housing-to-engine		35-40
Flywheel-to-crankshaft coupling		60-65
Manifold		
Attaching fasteners		20-25
Elbow		12-14
Main bearing caps		60-70
Oil pan		
End	165	
Side	80	
Oil pump		
Attaching bolts	110-120	
Cover screws	65-75	
Pulley-to-balancer hub		15-20
Pushrod cover	50	
Temperature sending unit		20
Timing gear cover	72-90	
Valve cover	45	
Water pump		13-17

Table 4 FORD 4-CYLINDER TIGHTENING TORQUES

	ft.-lb.	N•m
Auxiliary shaft		
Gear bolt	28-40	38-54
Thrust plate	6-9	8-12
Cover bolt	6-9	8-12
Belt tensioner		
Adjusting bolt	14-21	19-28
Pivot bolt	28-40	38-54
Camshaft		
Gear bolt	80-90	108-122
Thrust plate bolt	6-9	8-12
Carburetor fasteners	12-14	16-19
Connecting rod nut	30-36	41-49
Crankshaft damper	100-120	136-162
Cylinder front cover	6-9	8-12
Cylinder head bolts	See note 1	See note 1

(continued)

Table 4 FORD 4-CYLINDER TIGHTENING TORQUES (continued)

	ft.-lb.	N•m
Distributor clamp bolt	14-21	19-28
Exhaust manifold		
Attaching nuts	30-35	41-47
Attaching screw	20-25	27-34
Shift bracket-to-manifold	30-35	41-47
High-rise elbow	10-12	14-16
Shift bracket-to-elbow	12-14	16-19
Thermostat housing	20-25	27-34
Flywheel	54-64	71-87
Fuel pump	14-21	19-28
Intake manifold	See note 2	See note 2
Main bearing cap	80-90	108-122
Oil pump		
Pickup tube-to-pump	14-21	19-28
Pump-to-block	14-21	19-28
Oil pan		
Drain plug	15-25	21-33
M6	6-8	7-11
M8	8-10	11-13
Timing belt cover		
Inner stud	14-21	19-28
Outer bolt	6-9	8-12
Water jacket drain plug	14-21	19-28
Water outlet	14-21	19-28
Water pump	14-21	19-28

1. Stage 1: 50-60 ft.-lb. (68-81 N•m); Stage 2: 80-90 ft.-lb. (108-122 N•m).
2. Stage 1: 5-7 ft.-lb. (7-9 N•m); Stage 2: 14-18 ft.-lb. (19-24 N•m).

Table 5 STANDARD TORQUE VALUES

Fastener	ft.-lb.	N•m
Grade 5		
1/4-20	8	11
1/4-28	8	11
5/16-18	17	23
5/16-24	20	27
3/8-16	30	40
3/8-24	35	47
7/16-14	50	68
7/16-20	55	75
1/2-13	75	100
1/2-20	85	115
9/16-12	105	142
9/16-18	115	156

(continued)

Table 5 STANDARD TORQUE VALVES (continued)

Fastener	ft.-lb.	N•m
Grade 6		
1/4-20	10.5	14
1/4-28	12.5	17
5/16-18	22.5	31
5/16-24	25	54
3/8-16	40	34
3/8-24	45	61
7/16-14	65	88
7/16-20	70	95
1/2-13	100	136
1/2-20	110	149
9/16-12	135	183
9/16-18	150	203

Chapter Seven

GM V6 and V8 Engines

Cobra drive installations may use one of three small block marine V6 and V8 engines manufactured by Chevrolet: a 262 cid (4.3 liter) V6, a 305 cid (5.0 liter) V8 or a 350 cid (5.7 liter) V8. Since the 4.3L and 5.0L engines are both derived from the 5.7L V8, there is little difference in the repair and service procedures for these engines. The procedures given in this chapter apply to all 3 engines, except where specifically noted.

The V6 engine cylinders are numbered from front to rear: 1-3-5 on the port bank and 2-4-6 on the starboard bank. The firing order is 1-6-5-4-3-2. The V8 engine cylinders are numbered from front to rear: 1-3-5-7 on the port bank and 2-4-6-8 on the starboard bank. The firing order is 1-8-4-3-6-5-7-2.

The cast iron cylinder head contains intake and exhaust valves with integral valve guides. Rocker arms are retained on individual threaded shoulder bolts. A ball pivot valve train is used, with camshaft motion transferred through hydraulic lifters to the rocker arms by pushrods. No lash adjustment is necessary in service or during assembly unless some component in the valve train has been removed or replaced.

The chain-driven camshaft is located above the crankshaft between the 2 cylinder banks and supported by 4 (V6) or 5 (V8) bearings. The oil pump mounted at the bottom of the engine block is driven by the camshaft via the distributor.

The crankshaft is supported by 4 (V6) or 5 (V8) main bearings, with the rear bearing providing the crankshaft thrust surfaces. Crankshaft rotation is counterclockwise when seen from the drive unit end of the engine.

The cylinder block is cast iron with full length water jackets around each cylinder.

Engine specifications (**Table 1**) and tightening torques (**Table 2** and **Table 3**) are at the end of the chapter.

ENGINE SERIAL NUMBER

An engine identification number is stamped on a pad located near the thermostat housing (**Figure 1**). This information indicates if there are unique parts or if internal changes have been made during the model year. It is important when ordering replacement parts for the engine.

SPECIAL TOOLS

Where special tools are required or recommended for engine overhaul, the tool numbers are provided. While these tools can sometimes be rented from rental dealers, they can be purchased from Kent-Moore, Inc., 28635 Mound Road, Warren, MI 48089.

GASKET SEALANT

Gasket sealant is used instead of pre-formed gaskets betwen numerous mating surfaces on the engines covered in this chapter. See *Gasket Sealant*, Chapter Six.

REPLACEMENT PARTS

Various changes are made to automotive engine blocks used for marine applications. Numerous part changes are required due to operation in fresh and salt water. For example, the cylinder head gasket must be corrosion-resistant. Marine engines use head gaskets of copper or stainless steel instead of the standard steel used in automotive applications. Brass expansion or core plugs must be used instead of the steel plugs found in automotive blocks.

Since marine engines are run at or near maximum rpm most of the time, the use of special valve lifters, springs, pistons, bearings, camshafts and other heavy-duty moving components is necessary for maximum life and performance.

For these reasons, automotive-type parts should not be substituted for marine components. In addition, OMC recommends that only OMC parts be used. Parts offered by other manufacturers may look alike, but may not be manufactured to OMC specifications. Any damage resulting from the use of other than OMC parts is not covered by the OMC warranty.

ENGINE REMOVAL

Some service procedures can be performed with the engine in the boat; others require removal. The boat design and service procedure to be performed will determine whether the engine must be removed.

If the clearance between the front of the engine and the engine compartment bulkhead is less than 6 in., the stern drive unit must be removed in order to disengage the driveshaft from the engine coupler.

The stern drive must also be removed if engine mount height must be altered during engine removal.

WARNING

The engine is heavy, awkward to handle and has sharp edges. It may shift or drop suddenly during removal. To prevent serious injury, always observe the following precautions.

1. Never place any part of your body where a moving or falling engine may trap, cut or crush you.

2. If you must push the engine during removal, use a board or similar tool to keep your hands out of danger.

3. Be sure the hoist is designed to lift engines and has enough load capacity for your engine.

4. Be sure the hoist is securely attached to safe lifting points on the engine.

5. The engine should not be difficult to lift with a proper hoist. If it is, stop lifting, lower the engine back onto its mounts and make sure the engine has been completely separated from the vessel.

1. Remove the engine hood cover and all panels that interfere with engine removal. Place the cover and panels to one side out of the way.
2. Disconnect the negative battery cable, then the positive battery cable. As a precaution, remove the battery from the boat.

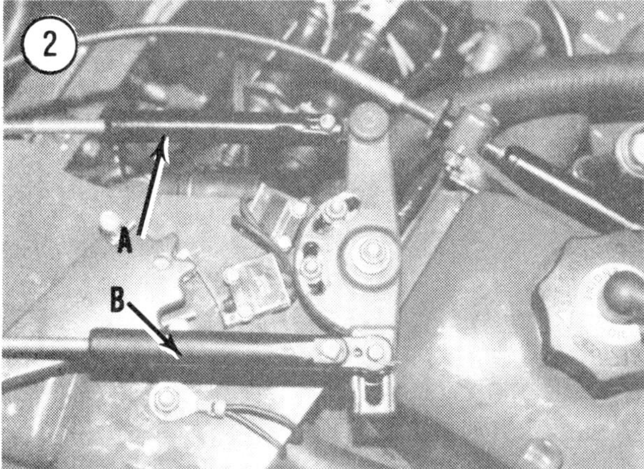

3. Use a flare nut wrench to loosen and disconnect both power steering hydraulic lines at the actuator unit. Cap the lines and plug the actuator fittings to prevent leakage and the entry of contamination. Secure the lines at a point higher than the engine power steering pump during the remainder of this procedure to prevent damage or the loss of fluid.
4. Disconnect the fuel inlet line from the tank to the fuel filter canister at the filter canister. Cap the line and canister fitting to prevent leakage and the entry of contamination.
5. Locate and unplug all electrical harness connectors. This step will include the:
   a. Rubber 2-wire trim/tilt sender connector.
   b. Plastic 3-wire trim/tilt wire connector.
   c. Rubber 3-wire trim/tilt instrument cable connector.
   d. Rubber instrument cable connector.
   e. Battery cable lead at the starter solenoid.
   f. Black ground lead at engine stud near starter motor.

NOTE
Some early 5.0L and 5.7L installations use a short exhaust hose with only 4 clamps and no adapter. Disconnection is essentially the same as described in Step 6.

6. Loosen the 8 exhaust hose clamps. Lubricating the exhaust pipe with dishwashing liquid will make it easier to move the lower hose. Pry or twist the lower hose from the exhaust adapter and slide it down the exhaust pipe. Remove the adapter and upper hose from the exhaust manifold.
7. Refer to **Figure 2** and remove the remote control (A) and transom bracket (B) shift cables from the engine shift bracket. Remove the cables from each of the anchor pockets and disconnect from the shift lever. Secure the adjustable trunnion to the remote control cable with tape to prevent misadjustment when the cable is reinstalled.
8. Disconnect the throttle cable at the carburetor and manifold anchor block. See **Figure 3.**
9. Loosen the water supply hose clamp and remove the hose from the transom bracket water tube.
10. Attach a suitable hoist to the engine lifting brackets. The hoist must have a minimum lift capacity of 1,500 lb. Raise the hoist enough to remove all slack.

NOTE
At this point, there should be no hoses, wires or linkage connecting the engine to the boat or stern drive unit. Recheck this to make sure nothing will hamper engine removal.

11. Remove and save the self-locking nut and flat washer from each rear engine mount. See **Figure 4**.

12. Remove and save the lag screws at each front engine mount. See **Figure 5**.

13A. If the stern drive was removed, lift the engine up and out of the engine compartment.

13B. If the stern drive was not removed, lift the engine enough to pull it forward and disengage the driveshaft from the engine flywheel coupler. Once the driveshaft is free of the coupler, lift the engine up and out of the engine compartment.

14. If the exhaust pipe requires service, remove the 4 retaining screws and the top port trim line clamp, if so equipped. Remove the exhaust pipe and discard the seal. Clean all residue from the transom bracket and exhaust pipe surface.

ENGINE INSTALLATION

Engine installation is the reverse of removal, plus the following:

1. If the exhaust pipe was serviced, coat a new seal with OMC Adhesive M and install in transom bracket groove. Wipe exhaust pipe screw threads with OMC Gasket Sealing Compound. Install exhaust pipe to transom bracket and tighten screws to 10-12 ft.-lb. (14-16 N•m).
2. Install any shims or adapters used with the engine mounts.
3. Install forward mount lag screws securely and tighten the rear mount self-locking nuts to 28-30 ft.-lb. (38-40 N•m).
4. If stern drive was removed, perform the *Engine Alignment* procedure as described in this chapter after securing the engine mounts.
5. Lubricate the transom bracket shift cable anchor with OMC Triple-Guard grease.
6. 5.0L and 5.7L engines—Pry engine lifting bracket toward the valve cover until it is vertical before installing the throttle cable.
7. Fill the engine with an oil recommended in Chapter Four.
8. Fill the cooling system, if equipped with a closed system. See Chapter Five.
9. Adjust the drive belts. See Chapter Ten.
10. Adjust the timing as required. See Chapter Four.

REAR ENGINE MOUNTS

WARNING

The engine is heavy and may shift or drop suddenly. Never place your hands or any part of your body where the moving engine may trap or crush you. If you can't remove the mounts without placing your hands where the moving engine may injure them, support the engine with a jackstand as well as a hoist to be certain the engine can't fall on you.

Engine mounts are non-adjustable and rarely require service. Replace any broken or deteriorated mounts immediately to reduce strain on remaining mounts and drive line components.

Removal

1. Attach a suitable hoist to the engine lifting brackets. The hoist must have a minimum lift capacity of 1,500 lb. Raise the hoist enough to remove all slack.
2. Remove and save the self-locking nut and flat washer from each rear engine mount. See **Figure 4**.
3. Lift the engine off the rear mounts with the hoist, then remove the screws and washers holding the mount assembly. Remove the mount assembly from the transom plate.
4. To disassemble the mount, clamp it in a vise. Hold the square nut with a suitable open-end wrench and remove the bolt. Separate the mount and 2 flat washers (early models) or 1 flat and 1 conical washer (late models).
5. To reassemble the mount, place a flat washer (early model) or conical washer (late model) on the bolt (the concave side of the conical washer should face the mount). Install bolt through the flat side (bottom) of the mount. Place the other washer on the bolt and install the nut finger-tight.

NOTE
The 90 degree relationship established between the nut and mounting holes in Step 6 must be maintained or the engine mount pad slot will not engage the rear mount during installation.

6. Clamp the mount assembly in a vise. Align the mount holes 90° to any side of the square nut. Holding the mount in this position, tighten the bolt to 18-20 ft.-lb. (24-27 N•m).
7. Position the mount assembly on the transom plate. Reinstall the screws with washers and tighten to 20-25 ft.-lb. (27-34 N•m).
8. Lower the engine with the hoist until the mount pad slot engages the square nut. Reinstall the flat washer and self-locking nut. Tighten nut to 28-30 ft.-lb. (38-41 N•m).

ENGINE ALIGNMENT

To assure satisfactory engine/drivetrain life, engine alignment must be checked during reinstallation whenever stern drive unit removal is required for engine removal. Correct alignment is provided by adjusting the front mounts up or down as required. OMC alignment tool part No. 912273 with universal handle part No. 311880 is required to perform this procedure.

Slide the alignment tool through the gimbal housing from outside the boat. The tool must fit through the gimbal bearing and into the engine coupler easily. If the tool binds, adjust the front engine mounts in the proper direction to remove the binding.

Engine mount adjustment is made by readjusting the position of the upper and lower nuts on the mount screw. When alignment is correct, retighten the front mounts to maintain alignment. Hold one nut with an open-end wrench and tighten the other nut to 100-120 ft.-lb. (136-163 N•m).

DISASSEMBLY CHECKLISTS

To use the checklists, remove and inspect each part in the order mentioned. To reassemble, go through the checklists backwards, installing the parts in order. Each major part is covered in its own section in this chapter, unless otherwise noted.

Decarbonizing or Valve Service

1. Remove the valve covers.
2. Remove the intake and exhaust manifolds.
3. Remove the rocker arms.
4. Remove the cylinder heads.
5. Remove and inspect the valves. Inspect the valve guides and seats inspected, repairing or replacing as required.
6. Assemble by reversing Steps 1-5.

Valve and Ring Service

1. Perform Steps 1-5 of *Decarbonizing or Valve Service.*
2. Remove the oil pan and oil pump.
3. Remove the pistons with connecting rods.
4. Remove the piston rings. It is not necessary to separate the pistons from the connecting rods unless a piston, connecting rod or piston pin needs repair or replacement.
5. Assemble by reversing Steps 1-4.

General Overhaul

1. Remove the engine from the boat.
2. Remove the flywheel.
3. Remove the mount brackets and oil pressure sending unit from the engine.
4. If available, mount the engine on an engine stand. These can be rented from equipment rental dealers. The stand is not absolutely necessary, but it will make the job much easier.
5. Remove the following accessories or components from the engine, if present:
   a. Alternator and mounting bracket.
   b. Power steering pump and mounting bracket.
   c. Spark plug wires and distributor cap.
   d. Carburetor and fuel lines.
   e. Oil dipstick and tube.
   f. Seawater pump, if so equipped.
6. Check the engine for signs of coolant or oil leaks.
7. Clean the outside of the engine.
8. Remove the distributor. See Chapter Eleven.
9. Remove all hoses and tubes connected to the engine.
10. Remove the fuel pump. See Chapter Nine.
11. Remove the intake and exhaust manifolds.
12. Remove the thermostat. See Chapter Ten.
13. Remove the valve covers and rocker arms.
14. Remove the crankshaft pulley, harmonic balancer, timing case cover and water pump. Remove the timing chain and sprockets.
15. Remove the camshaft.
16. Remove the cylinder heads.
17. Remove the oil pan and oil pump.
18. Remove the pistons and connecting rods.
19. Remove the crankshaft.
20. Inspect the cylinder block.
21. Assemble by reversing Steps 1-19.

VALVE COVERS

Removal/Installation

Refer to **Figure 6** (typical) for this procedure.

1. Disconnect the crankcase ventilation hose at the valve cover **(Figure 7)**.
2. Disconnect the spark plug cables at the plugs and remove the plug cable retainers from their brackets on the cover.

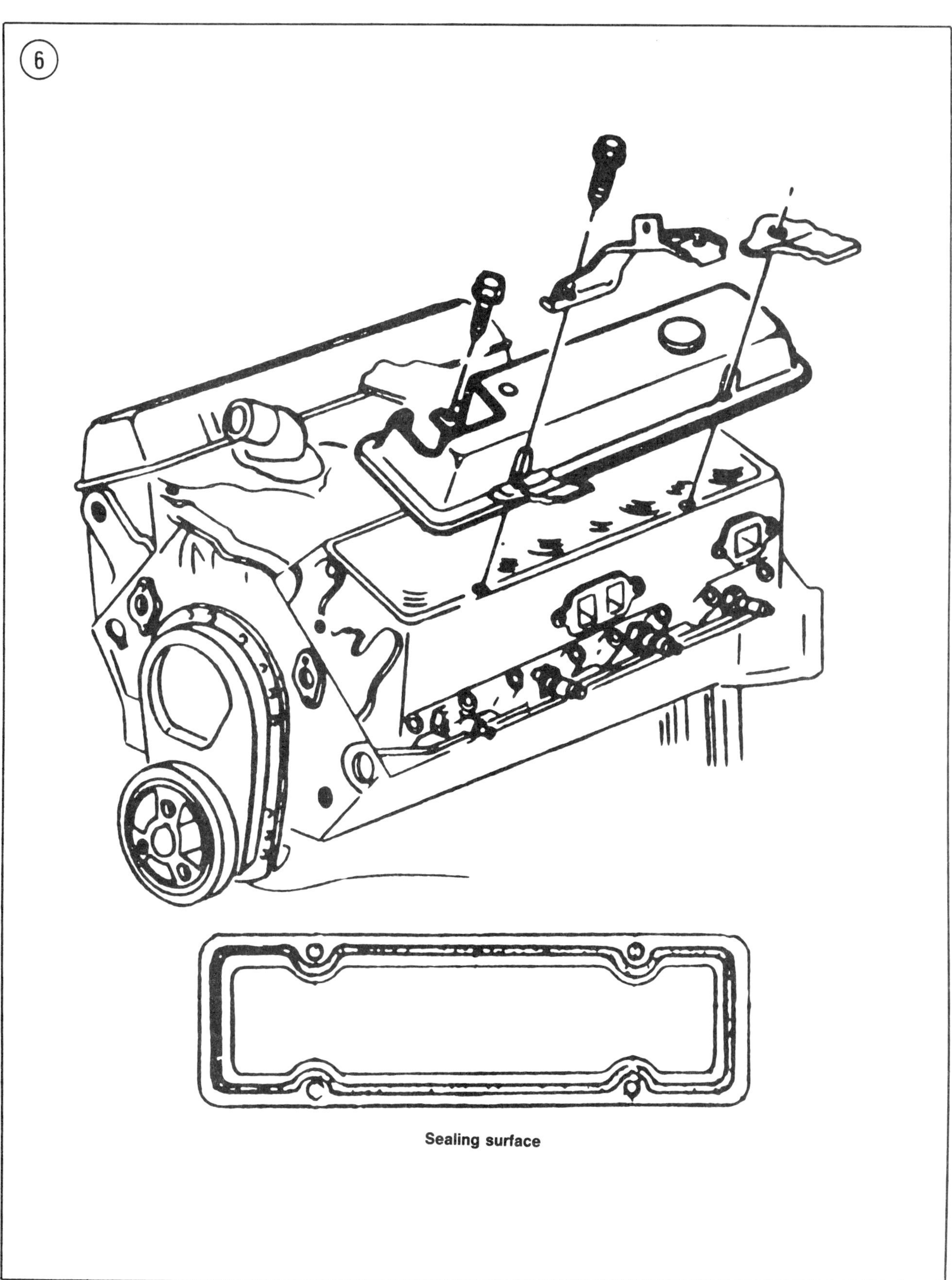

Sealing surface

7

3. Remove the cover attaching screws.
4. Rap the valve cover with a soft-faced mallet to break the gasket seal. Remove the valve cover.
5. Clean any gasket residue from the cylinder head and valve cover with degreaser and a putty knife.
6. Coat one side of a new gasket with an oil-resistant sealer. Install the gasket sealer-side down on the cylinder head.
7. Position the valve cover on the cylinder head.
8. Install the attaching screws and tighten to specifications (**Table 2**).
9. Install the spark plug cable retainers on the valve cover brackets. Connect the wires to the appropriate spark plugs. See Chapter Four.
10. Install the crankcase ventilation hose in the valve cover.

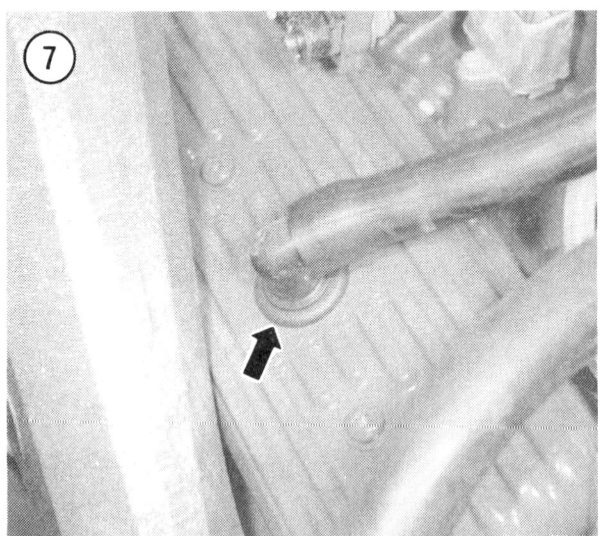

INTAKE MANIFOLD

Removal/Installation

Refer to **Figure 8** for this procedure.

1. Disconnect the negative battery cable.
2. Disconnect the crankcase ventilation hose from each valve cover (**Figure 7**).
3. Remove the flame arrestor.
4. Open the cylinder block water drains and allow all water to drain. Disconnect the water hoses at the manifold, thermostat housing (**Figure 9**, typical) and water pump.
5. Disconnect the throttle cable linkage at the carburetor and anchor block. See **Figure 10** (typical).
6. Disconnect the temperature gauge sender unit.
7. If equipped with power steering, disconnect the engine wiring harness at the alternator. Remove the alternator and mounting bracket. See Chapter Eleven.
8. Disconnect the spark plug cables. Remove the cable retainers from the valve covers.

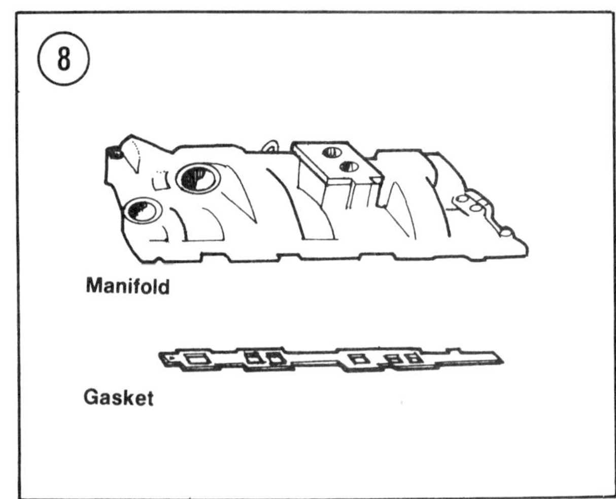

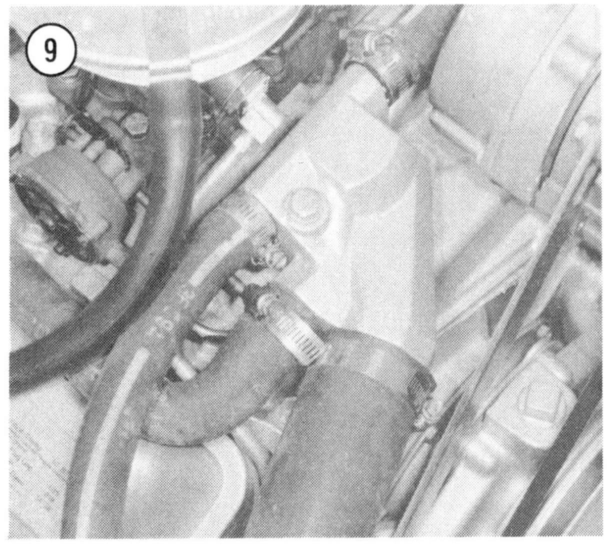

9. Disconnect the ESA module (if so equipped), secondary and primary ignition leads at the ignition coil. Disconnect the oil pressure sender lead.
10. Disconnect the fuel pump vent hose.
11. Remove the distributor cap and place it (with plug cables attached) to one side out of the way.
12. Mark the position of the distributor rotor relative to the intake manifold. Loosen the hold-down clamp and remove the distributor. See Chapter Eleven.
13. Disconnect the fuel inlet line at the carburetor. Cap the line and plug the fitting to prevent leakage and the entry of contamination.
14. Loosen the intake manifold fasteners. Remove the fasteners and solenoid bracket. Pry the manifold loose and remove it from the engine block.
15. Remove and discard the intake manifold gaskets and seals. Discard the attaching bolt sealing washers.
16. Clean all gasket residue from the block, cylinder heads and intake manifold with degreaser and a putty knife.
17. If the intake manifold is being replaced, transfer the carburetor, thermostat and housing, throttle cable anchor block unit, distributor clamp, temperature sending unit and ESA module, if so equipped, as well as any other hardware that might be installed.
18. Coat the areas where the gaskets butt together and all gasket areas around the water passages with a water-resistant sealer.

NOTE
*Front and rear manifold seals are not provided for some engines. Run a 3/16 in. bead of GM silicone sealer on the front/rear of the cylinder block and extend it 1/2 inch up each head to hold and seal the manifold side gaskets. See **Figure 11**.*

19. Install new seals on the cylinder block. Install new manifold side gaskets on the cylinder heads. Make sure that the gaskets interlock with the seal tabs, and that the holes in the gaskets are aligned with the holes in the cylinder heads.
20. Lower the intake manifold into position on the cylinder block. Check the seal area to make sure the seals are in their proper position. If not, remove the manifold, correct the seal position and reinstall the manifold.
21. Install the manifold attaching fasteners. Tighten the manifold fasteners to specifications (**Table 2**) in the sequence shown in **Figure 12**.

22. Reverse Steps 1-13 to complete installation. Coat all electrical connections with OMC black neoprene dip (part No. 909570).

Inspection

1. Check the intake manifold for cracks or distortion; replace if distorted or if cracks are found.
2. Check the mating surfaces for nicks or burrs. Small burrs may be removed with an oilstone.
3. Place a straightedge across the manifold flange/mating surfaces. If there is any gap between the straightedge and surface, measure it with a flat feeler gauge. Measure each manifold from end to end and from corner to corner. If the mating surface is not flat within 0.006 in. (0.15 mm) per foot of manifold length, replace the manifold.

EXHAUST MANIFOLDS

Removal/Installation

Refer to **Figure 13** (typical) for this procedure.

1. Disconnect the negative battery cable.
2. Open the cylinder block water drains and allow all water to drain.
3. Disconnect the water hose(s) from the manifold(s). See **Figure 14** (typical). Drain any water remaining in the manifold housing and elbow.

4A. *V6*—Unclamp the upper exhaust hose. Slide hose off manifold onto exhaust tube.

4B. *V8*—Loosen the upper exhaust hose clamps. Remove the 4 fasteners holding the high-rise elbow to the exhaust manifold. Rap the elbow with a soft-faced hammer to break the gasket seal, then remove the elbow.

5. Remove the manifold attaching locknuts and washers. Discard the locknuts. Remove the manifold.

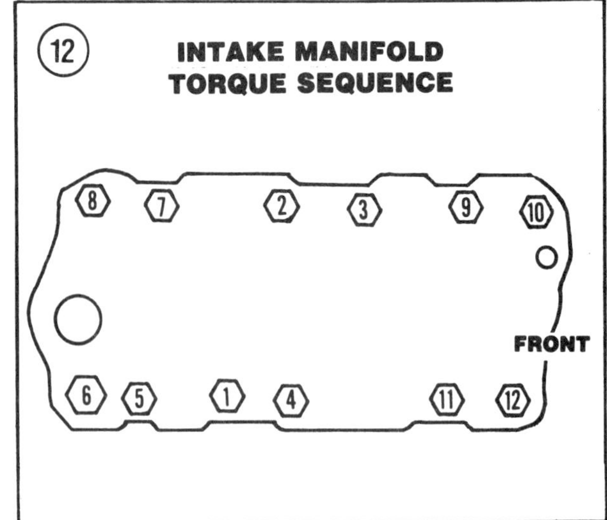

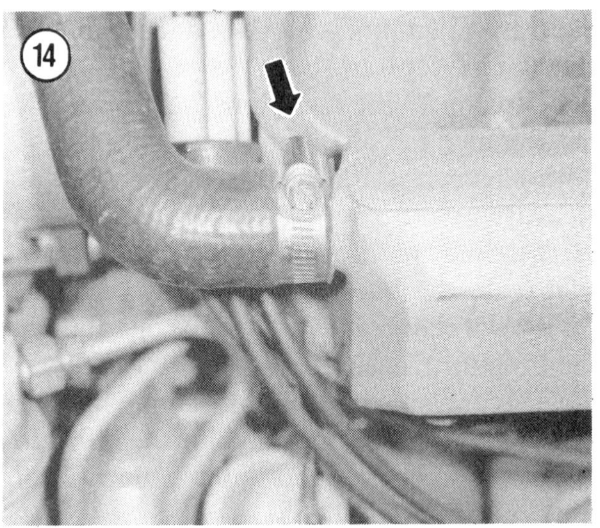

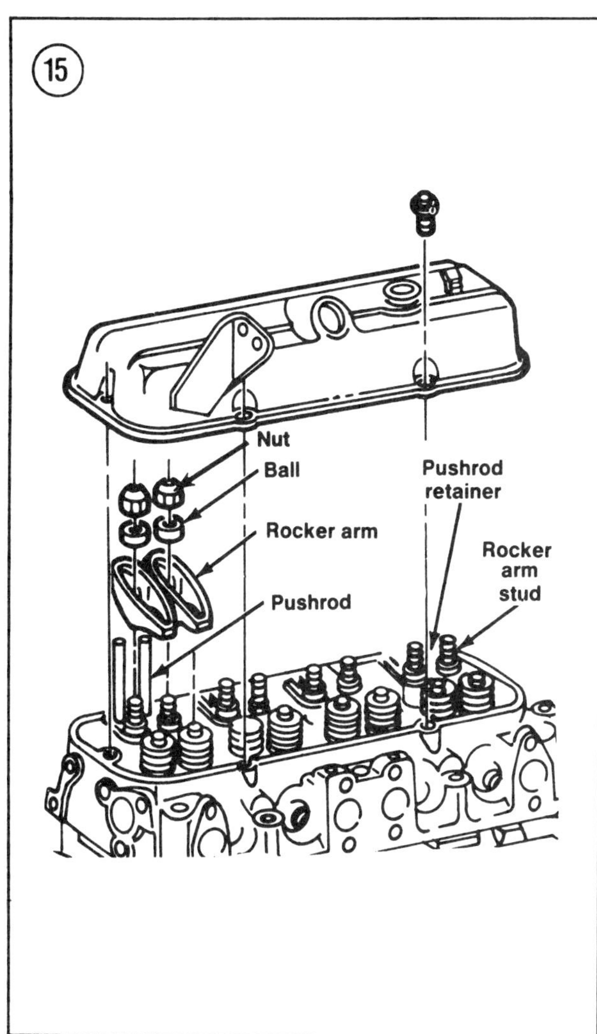

6. Clean all gasket residue from the cylinder head, manifold and high-rise elbow mating surfaces with degreaser and a putty knife.
7. Install the manifold on the cylinder head with a new gasket.
8A. *V6*—Install new washers and locknuts. Tighten the locknuts to 18-22 ft.-lb. (24-30 N•m).
8B. *V8*—Install new washers and locknuts. Tighten the locknuts to 20-26 ft.-lb. (27-35 N•m). Install high-rise elbow with a new gasket coated on both sides with OMC Gasket Sealing Compound and tighten fasteners to 10-12 ft.-lb. (14-16 N•m).
9. Reconnect the exhaust hose and reverse Steps 1-3 to complete installation.

Inspection/Cleaning

1. Inspect the engine exhaust ports for signs of rust or corrosion. Replace manifold if such signs are found.
2. Check water passage in exhaust elbow for clogging.
3. Remove pipe plugs in manifold and exhaust elbow, if so equipped. Check for sand, silt or other foreign matter.
4. Every 300 hours or 3 years, soak the manifold and elbow for 90-120 minutes in muriatic acid (available from swimming pool supply houses) to loosen deposits. Wash thoroughly with fresh water and use a stiff rod to break free any deposits inside. Repeat the washing process a second time, then wash and blow dry with compressed air.
5. Have V8 manifolds pressure-tested by a dealer. Replace manifold if it will not hold 10-15 psi.

ROCKER ARMS

Removal/Installation

Each rocker arm moves on its own pivot ball. The rocker arm and pivot ball are retained by a nut. It is not necessary to remove the rocker arm for pushrod replacement; simply loosen the nut and move the arm away from the pushrod. To remove the entire assembly, refer to **Figure 15** and proceed as follows.
1. Remove the valve cover as described in this chapter.
2. Remove the rocker arm nut and ball.
3. Remove the rocker arm.
4. Remove the valve pushrod from the cylinder block.
5. Repeat Steps 2-4 for each remaining rocker arm. Place each rocker arm and pushrod assembly in a separate container or use a rack to keep them separated for reinstallation in the same position from which they were removed.

6. Installation is the reverse of removal. If new rocker arms or balls are being installed, coat contact surfaces with engine oil or Molykote. Make sure pushrods fit into lifter sockets. Adjust the valve clearance as described in this chapter.

Inspection

1. Clean all parts with solvent and use compressed air to blow out the oil passages in the pushrods.
2. Check each rocker arm, ball, nut and pushrod for scuffing, pitting or excessive wear; replace as required. If one component is worn, replace all components servicing that valve.
3. Check pushrods for straightness by rolling them across a flat, even surface such as a pane of glass. Replace any pushrods that do not roll smoothly.
4. If a pushrod is worn from lack of lubrication, replace the corresponding lifter and rocker arm as well.

Valve Clearance Adjustment

Stem-to-rocker arm clearance must be within specifications when the hydraulic lifter is completely collapsed. If valve clearance is insufficient, the valve opens early and closes late, resulting in a rough engine idle. Excessive clearance lets the valve open too late and close too early, causing valve bounce and damage to the camshaft lobe.

Valve adjustment is required only when the cylinder head valve train has been disassembled. Adjust the valves with the lifter on the base circle of the camshaft lobe.

Engine off

1. Rotate the crankshaft until the pulley notch aligns with the zero mark on the timing tab. This positions the No. 1 cylinder at TDC. This position can be verified by placing a finger on the No. 1 rocker arms as the pulley notch nears the zero mark. If the rocker arms are moving, the engine is in the No. 4 (V6) or No. 6 (V8) firing position; rotate the crankshaft pulley one full turn to reach the No. 1 firing position.

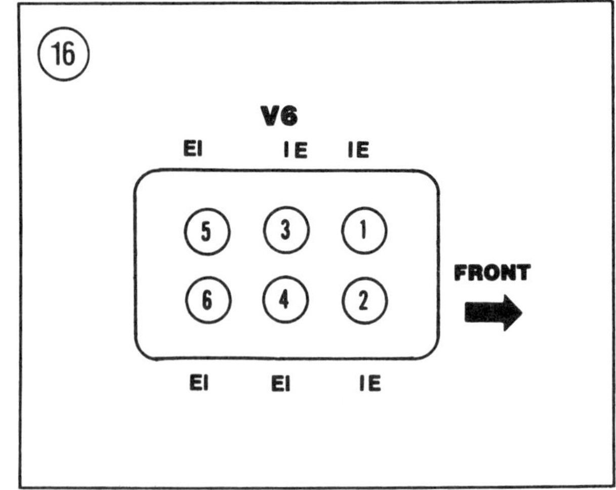

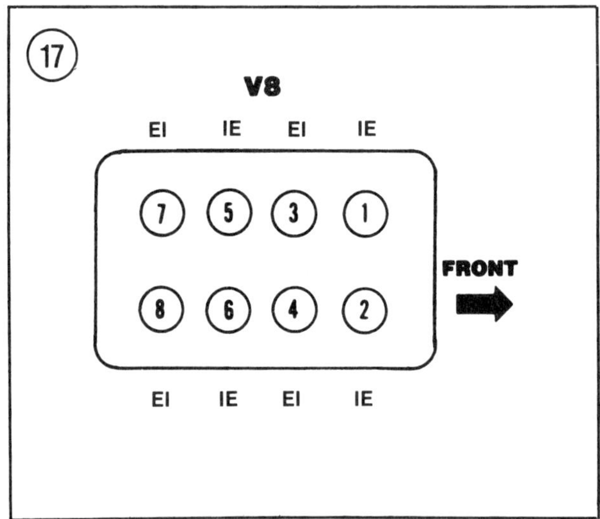

NOTE

The intake valves are those closer to the intake manifold. Exhaust valves are closer to the exhaust manifold.

2. With the engine in the No. 1 firing position, refer to **Figure 16** (V6) or **Figure 17** (V8) and adjust the following valves:
   a. Intake: 1, 2, 3 (V6) or 1, 2, 5, 7 (V8).
   b. Exhaust: 1, 5, 6 (V6) or 1, 3, 4, 8 (V8).

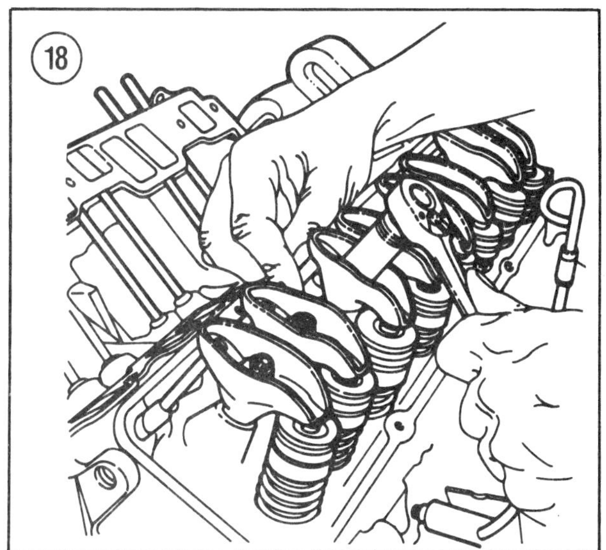

18

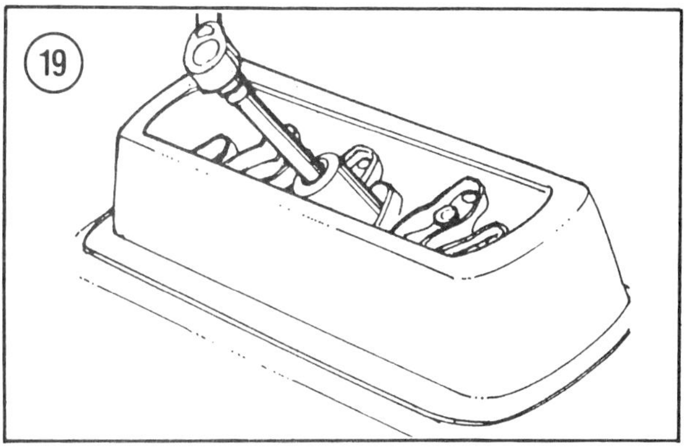

19

3. To adjust each valve, back off the adjusting nut until lash is felt at the pushrod, then turn the nut to remove all lash. When lash has been removed, the pushrod will not rotate. Turn the nut in another 3/4 turn or full turn as specified in **Table 1** to center the lifter plunger. See **Figure 18**.
4. Rotate the crankshaft one full turn to realign the pulley notch and the timing tab zero mark in the No. 4 (V6) or No. 6 (V8) firing position. Refer to **Figure 16** (V6) or **Figure 17** (V8) and adjust the following valves:
   a. Intake: 4, 5, 6 (V6) or 3, 4, 6, 8 (V8).
   b. Exhaust: 2, 3, 4 (V6) or 2, 5, 6, 7 (V8).
5. Install the valve cover as described in this chapter.

Engine running

To prevent oil from splashing out of the cylinder heads while performing this procedure, cut the top out of a used valve cover. See **Figure 19**. Tape or file the cut edges of the reworked valve cover to prevent injury to yourself while working.

1. Warm the engine to normal operating temperature with the reworked cover temporarily installed.
2. With the engine idling, back off one rocker arm nut until the rocker arm starts to clatter.
3. Tighten the rocker arm nut until the clatter stops. This will remove all lash (zero lash position).
4. Tighten the nut another 1/4 turn. Wait 10 seconds to let the engine stabilize.
5. Repeat Step 5 two more times. This will tighten the nut an additional 3/4 turn from zero lash position.
6. Repeat Steps 3-5 for each valve.
7. Stop the engine. Remove the reworked valve cover. Install the original valve cover as described in this chapter.

CRANKSHAFT PULLEY AND HARMONIC BALANCER

Removal/Installation

1. Remove the alternator drive belt. See Chapter Ten.
2. Remove the pulley attaching bolts. Remove the pulley.
3. Remove the harmonic balancer retaining bolt.
4. Install puller part No. J-23523 or equivalent to the balancer with the pulley attaching bolts and remove the harmonic balancer from the crankshaft. See **Figure 20** (typical).
5. Lubricate the front cover seal lip and the contact areas on the harmonic balancer and crankshaft with clean engine oil.

NOTE
If tool part No. J-23523 is not available for use in Step 6, pull the balancer onto the crankshaft with a thick flat washer, a full-threaded 7/16-20×4 in. bolt and a 7/16-20 nut.

6. Position the harmonic balancer over the crankshaft key and install the threaded end of tool part No. J-23523 in the crankshaft so that at least 1/2 in. of the tool threads are engaged. Install plate, thrust bearing and nut to complete tool installation.
7. Pull balancer into position as shown in **Figure 21** (typical).
8. Remove the tool, install the balancer retaining bolt and tighten to specifications (**Table 2**).
9. Install pulley and tighten attaching bolts to specifications (**Table 2**).
10. Install and adjust the alternator drive belt. See Chapter Ten.

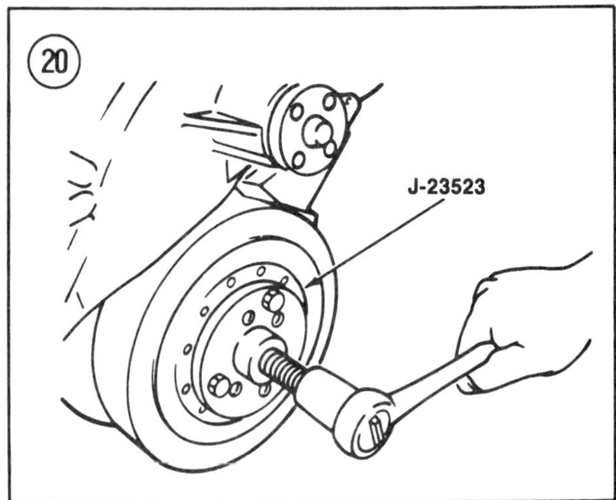

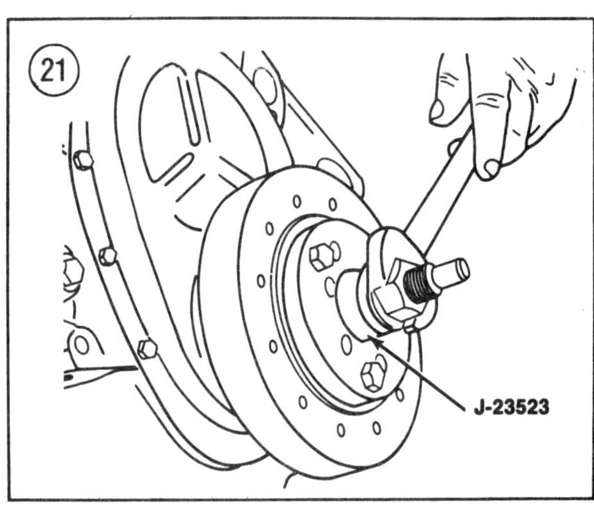

CRANKCASE FRONT COVER AND OIL SEAL

Cover Removal/Installation

1. Open the engine block drain valves and drain all the water from the block.
2. Drain the crankcase oil. See Chapter Four.
3. Remove the crankshaft pulley and harmonic balancer as described in this chapter.
4. Remove any accessory brackets attached to the engine water pump.
5. Remove the water pump pulley (**Figure 22**) and drive belt.
6. Remove the engine water pump. See Chapter Ten.
7. Remove the front cover attaching screws. Remove the front cover and gasket. Discard the gasket.
8. Cut away any excess oil pan gasket material protruding at the oil pan-to-block joint.
9. Clean the block and front cover sealing surfaces of all oil, grease and gasket residue.
10. Lubricate the timing chain and gears with engine oil.
11. Coat the gasket surfaces of the block and front cover with a water-resistant sealer and install a new gasket over the dowel pins on the engine block.
12. Apply a 1/8 in. (3 mm) bead of RTV sealant to the joint formed at the oil pan and cylinder block on each side.
13. Install the cover-to-oil pan seal. Coat the bottom of the seal with engine oil.
14. Position cover over crankshaft end and loosely install the cover-to-block upper screws.

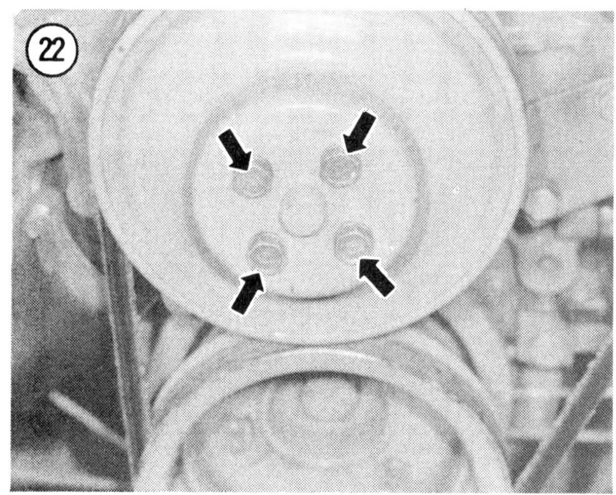

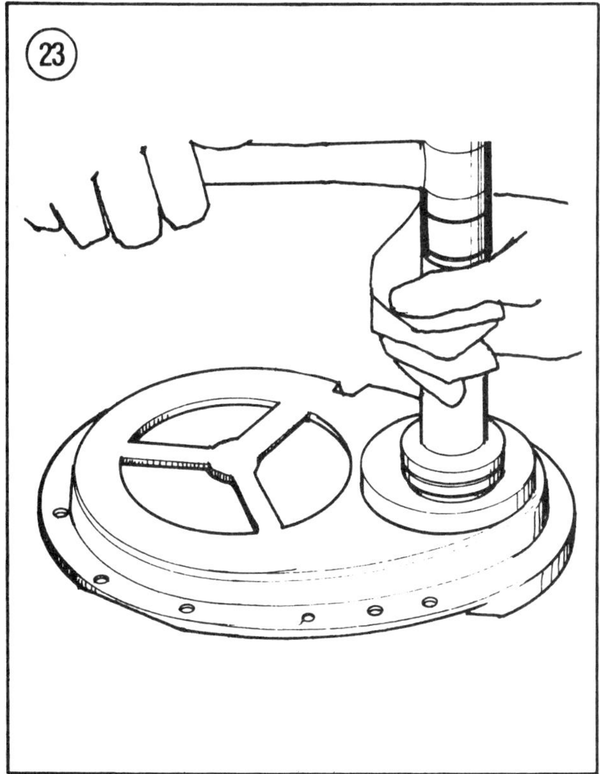

NOTE
Do not force cover on dowels in Step 15 so the cover flange or holes are distorted.

15. Press downward on the cover to align the block dowels with their corresponding cover holes, then tighten the screws in a crisscross pattern.

16. Install remaining cover screws and tighten to specifications (**Table 2**).
17. Reverse Steps 1-6 to complete installation.

Front Cover Seal Replacement

The seal can be replaced without removing the front cover. If the cover has been removed and seal replacement is necessary, support the cover on a clean workbench and perform Steps 2-4.

1. Remove the harmonic balancer as described in this chapter.
2. Pry the old seal from the cover with a large screwdriver. Work carefully to prevent damage to the cover seal surface.
3. Clean the seal recess in the cover with solvent and blow dry with compressed air.
4. Position a new seal in the cover recess with its open end facing the inside of the cover. Drive seal into place with installer part No. J-23042. See **Figure 23**.
5. Install the harmonic balancer as described in this chapter.

TIMING CHAIN AND SPROCKETS

Removal

Refer to **Figure 24** for this procedure.

1. Remove the spark plugs. See Chapter Four.
2. Remove the harmonic balancer as described in this chapter.
3. Remove the front cover as described in this chapter.
4. Temporarily reinstall the balancer bolt and washer in the end of the crankshaft. Place a wrench on the bolt and rotate the crankshaft to position the No. 1 piston at TDC with the camshaft and crankshaft sprocket marks aligned as shown in **Figure 25** (V6) or **Figure 26** (V8). Remove the balancer bolt and washer.
5. Remove the camshaft sprocket bolts. The sprocket is a light press fit and should come off easily. If not, lightly tap the lower edge of the sprocket with a plastic hammer to dislodge it from the camshaft. Remove the sprocket and timing chain as an assembly.
6. If crankshaft sprocket is to be removed, use puller part No. J-5825 or equivalent.

Installation

Refer to **Figure 24** for this procedure.

1. Install the crankshaft sprocket, if removed, with sprocket installer part No. J-5590 or equivalent.
2. Install the timing chain on the camshaft sprocket.
3. Hold the sprocket vertically with the chain hanging down. Align the camshaft and crankshaft sprocket marks as shown in **Figure 25** (V6) or **Figure 26** (V8).

NOTE

Do not drive the camshaft sprocket into place in Step 4 or you may dislodge the welch plug behind the camshaft in the rear of the block.

4. Align the camshaft dowel with the sprocket hole. Install the sprocket on the camshaft.
5. Install the camshaft sprocket mounting bolts. Tighten bolts to draw the sprocket onto the camshaft, then tighten to specifications (**Table 2**).
6. Lubricate the timing chain liberally with SAE 30 engine oil.
7. Install the front cover and harmonic balancer as described in this chapter.
8. Reinstall the spark plugs. See Chapter Four.

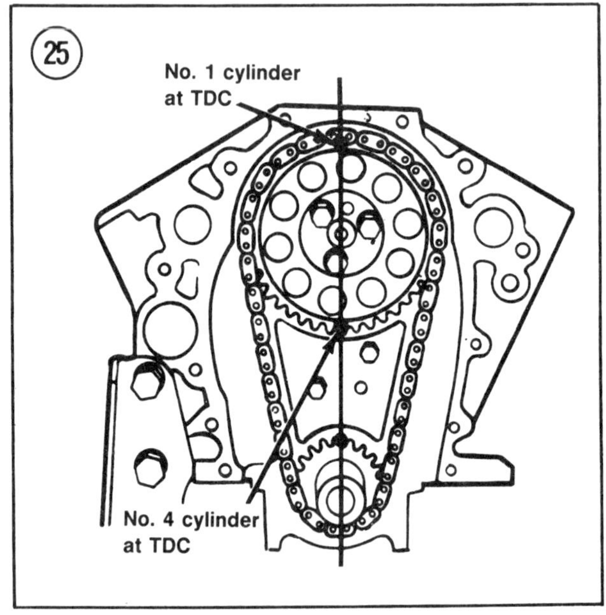

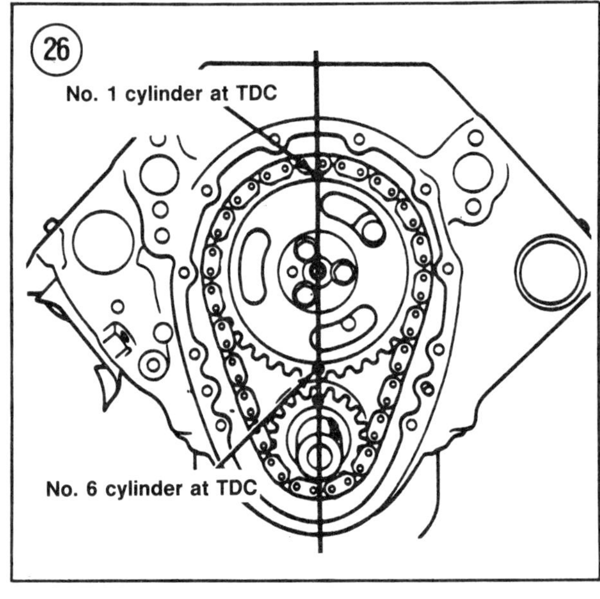

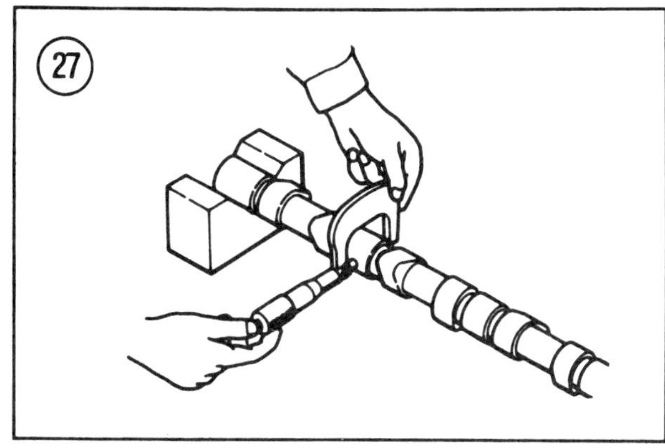

CAMSHAFT

Removal/Installation

1. Remove the valve covers as described in this chapter.
2. Remove the intake manifold as described in this chapter.
3. Loosen the rocker arm adjusting nuts, swivel the arms off the pushrods and remove the pushrods.
4. Identify each pushrod for reinstallation in its original location.
5. Remove the valve lifters with a pencil-type magnet. Place them in a rack in order of removal for reinstallation in their original locations.
6. Remove the fuel pump and pushrod. See Chapter Nine.
7. Remove the front cover, timing chain and camshaft sprocket as described in this chapter. Install two 5/16-18×4 in. bolts in the camshaft sprocket bolt holes at the end of the camshaft.

CAUTION
Do not cock the camshaft during removal. This can damage the camshaft or its bearing thrust surfaces.

8. Carefully withdraw the camshaft from the front of the engine with a rotating motion to avoid damage to the bearings.
9. Installation is the reverse of removal. Coat the camshaft lobes with GM EOS lubricant or equivalent and the journals with heavy engine oil before reinstalling in the block. Check and adjust ignition timing (Chapter Four).

Inspection

1. Check the journals and lobes for signs of wear or scoring. Lobe pitting in the toe area is not sufficient reason for replacement unless the lobe lift loss exceeds specifications.

NOTE
If you do not have precision measuring equipment, have Step 2 done by a machine shop.

2. Measure the camshaft journal diameters with a micrometer (**Figure 27**) and compare to specifications (**Table 1**). Replace the camshaft if the journals are more than 0.0009 in. (0.025 mm) out-of-round.
3. Suspend the camshaft between V-blocks and check for warpage with a dial indicator. Replace if the runout is greater than 0.015 in.

Lifter Inspection

Keep the lifters in proper sequence for installation in their original positions in the head. Clean lifters in solvent and wipe dry with a clean, lint-free cloth. Inspect and test the lifters separately to prevent intermixing of their internal parts. If any part requires replacement, replace the entire lifter.

Inspect all parts. If any lifter shows signs of pitting, scoring, galling, non-rotation or excessive wear, discard it. Check the lifter plunger. It should drop to the bottom of the body by its own weight when dry and assembled.

Lobe Lift Measurement

Camshaft lobe lift can be measured with the camshaft in the block and the cylinder head in place. The lifters must be bled down slowly in Step 6 or the readings will be incorrect.

1. Remove the valve cover as described in this chapter.
2. Remove the rocker arms and pivot assemblies as described in this chapter.
3. Remove the spark plugs. See Chapter Four.
4. Install a dial indicator on the end of a pushrod. A piece of rubber tubing will hold the dial indicator plunger in place on the center of the pushrod. See **Figure 28** (typical).
5. Rotate the crankshaft in the normal direction of rotation until the valve lifter seats on the heel or base of the cam lobe (**Figure 29**). This positions the pushrod at its lowest point.
6. Set the dial indicator at zero, then slowly rotate the crankshaft until the pushrod reaches its maximum travel. Note the indicator reading and compare to specifications (**Table 1**).
7. Repeat Steps 4-6 for each pushrod. If all lobes are within specifications in Step 6, reinstall the rocker arm assemblies and adjust the valves as described in this chapter.
8. If one or more lobes are worn beyond specifications, replace the camshaft as described in this chapter.
9. Remove the dial indicator and reverse Steps 1-3.

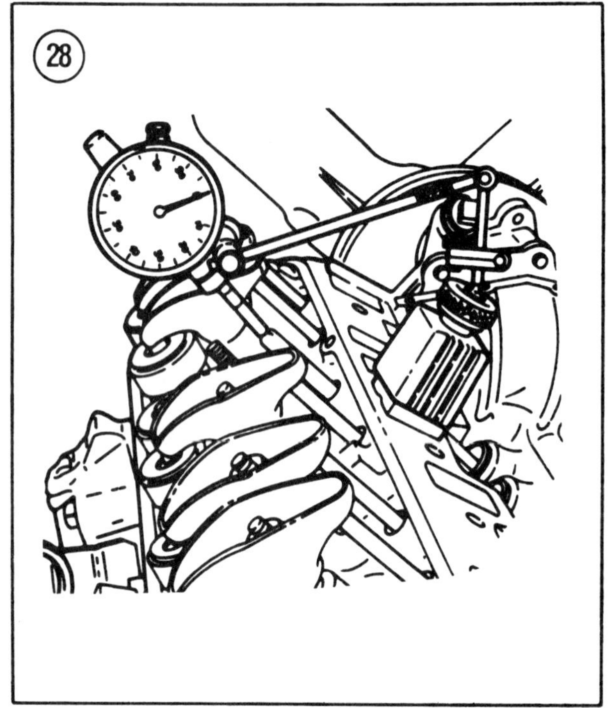

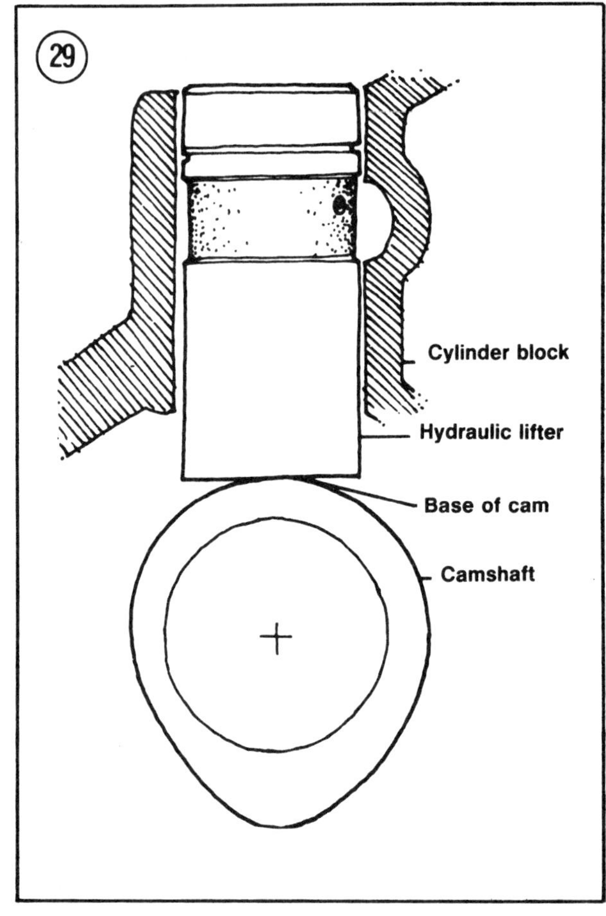

Bearing Replacement

Camshaft bearings can be replaced without complete engine disassembly. Replace bearings in complete sets. Camshaft bearing and installer tool part No. J-6098 is required for bearing replacement.

1. Remove the camshaft as described in this chapter.
2. Remove the crankshaft as described in this chapter. Leave pistons in cylinder bores.
3. Drive the camshaft welch plug from the rear of the cylinder block.

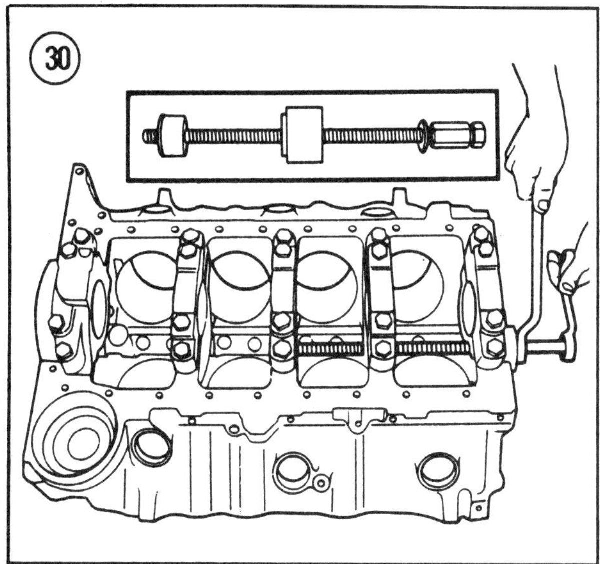

4. Secure the connecting rods to the side of the engine to keep them out of the way while replacing the cam bearings.
5. Install the nut and thrust washer to tool part No. J-6098. Index the tool pilot in the front cam bearing. Install the puller screw through the pilot.
6. Install tool part no. J-6098 with its shoulder facing the front intermediate bearing and the threads engaging the bearing.
7. Hold the puller screw with one wrench. Turn the nut with a second wrench until the bearing has been pulled from its bore. See **Figure 30**.
8. When bearing has been removed from bore, remove tool and bearing from puller screw.
9. Repeat Steps 5-8 to remove the center bearing.
10. Remove the tool and index it to the rear bearing to remove the rear intermediate bearing from the block.
11. Remove the front and rear bearings by driving them toward the center of the block.

CAUTION
Improper alignment of the rear bearing during Step 12 will restrict oil pressure reaching the valve train.

12. Installation is the reverse of removal. Use the same tool to pull the new bearings into their bores. Bearing oil holes must align with those in the block. Since the oil hole is on the top of the bearings (and cannot be seen during installation), align bearing oil hole with hole in bore and mark opposite side of bearing and block at bore to assist in positioning the oil hole during installation as follows—Position the No. 1 bearing oil holes at an equal distance from the 6 o'clock position. Align No. 5 bearing oil hole with the 12 o'clock position.
13. Wipe a new camshaft welch plug with an oil-resistant sealer and install it flush to 1/32 in. deep to maintain a level surface on the rear of the block.

7

OIL PAN

Ease of oil pan removal will depend upon the installation within a given boat. In some cases, the oil pan can be removed without removing the engine. In others, engine removal will be required to provide sufficient working space and clearance for oil pan removal.

Removal

1A. Engine in boat:
   a. Remove the oil dipstick and siphon the oil from the crankcase. See Chapter Four.
   b. Remove the oil dipstick tube.

1B. Engine out of boat:
   a. Place a suitable container under the oil pan drain plug. Remove the plug and let the crankcase drain. Reinstall the drain plug.
   b. If mounted in an engine stand, rotate the engine 180° to place the oil pan in an upright position.
   c. Remove the oil dipstick and dipstick tube.

2. Remove the oil pan attaching screws. Remove the oil pan.

3. Remove and discard the 2-piece pan gasket and the front/rear seals.

Inspection and Cleaning

1. Clean any gasket residue from the oil pan rail on the engine block and the oil pan sealing flange with degreaser and a putty knife.
2. Clean the pan thoroughly in solvent and check for dents or warped gasket surfaces. Straighten or replace the pan as required.

Installation

1. Coat the block side rails with grease and position the 2 side gaskets on the side rails.
2. Install the front pan seal on the front cover, pressing the seal into the cover holes. Tuck the side gasket front ends into the gap between the front seal groove and block.
3. Install the rear seal on the rear main bearing cap. Tuck the seal ends into the block groove openings.
4. Carefully place the oil pan in position. Make sure the gaskets and seals are not misaligned and then install a pan attaching screw finger-tight on each side of the block.
5. Install the remaining screws and tighten all to specifications (**Table 2**). Work from the center outward in each direction.
6. Install the dipstick tube and dipstick.
7. If crankcase oil was drained, refill crankcase with an oil recommended in Chapter Four.

OIL PUMP

Removal/Installation

A baffle is incorporated in the oil pickup screen assembly on some engines to eliminate pressure loss. To accommodate the baffle, the oil pump pickup tube is bent at a special angle.

1. Remove the oil pan as described in this chapter.

NOTE

The oil pump pickup tube and screen are a press fit in the pump housing and should not be removed unless replacement is required.

2. Remove the nut holding the pump to the rear main bearing cap (**Figure 31**).
3. Remove the pump, gasket (if used) and extension shaft. See **Figure 32**.
4. To install, align the slot on the extension shaft top with the drive tang on the lower end of the distributor drive shaft.

NOTE
The bottom edge of the oil pump pickup screen should be parallel to the oil pan rails when pump is installed in Step 5.

5. Install pump to rear main bearing cap with a new gasket (if used). Tighten pump nut to specifications (**Table 2**).
6. Reinstall the oil pan as described in this chapter.

Disassembly/Assembly

Refer to **Figure 33** for this procedure.

1. Remove the cover screws, cover and gasket. Discard the gasket.

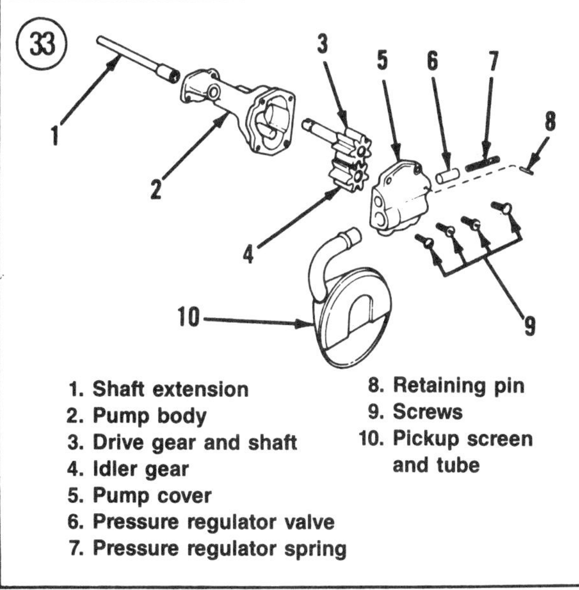

1. Shaft extension
2. Pump body
3. Drive gear and shaft
4. Idler gear
5. Pump cover
6. Pressure regulator valve
7. Pressure regulator spring
8. Retaining pin
9. Screws
10. Pickup screen and tube

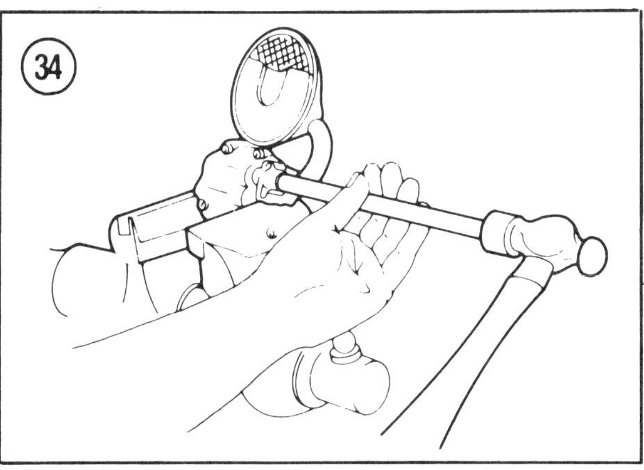

2. Mark the gear teeth for reassembly indexing and then remove the idler and drive gear with shaft from the body.
3. Remove the pressure regulator valve pin, regulator, spring and valve.
4. Remove the pickup tube/screen assembly *only* if it needs replacement. Secure the pump body in a soft-jawed vise and separate the tube from the cover.

CAUTION
Do not twist, shear or collapse the tube when installing it in Step 5.

5. If the pickup tube/screen assembly was removed, install a new one. Secure the pump body in a soft-jawed vise. Apply sealer to the new tube and gently tap in place with a soft-faced mallet. See **Figure 34**.
6. Lubricate all parts thoroughly with clean engine oil before reassembly.
7. Assembly is the reverse of disassembly. Index the gear marks, install a new cover gasket and rotate the pump drive shaft by hand to check for smooth operation. Tighten cover bolts to specifications (**Table 2**).

Inspection

NOTE
The pump assembly and gears are serviced as an assembly. If one or the other is worn or damaged, replace the entire pump. No wear specifications are provided by GM.

1. Clean all parts thoroughly in solvent. Brush the inside of the body and the pressure regulator chamber to remove all dirt and metal particles. Dry with compressed air, if available.
2. Check the pump body and cover for cracks or excessive wear.
3. Check the pump gears for damage or excessive wear.
4. Check the drive gear shaft-to-body fit for excessive looseness.

5. Check the inside of the pump cover for wear that could allow oil to leak around the ends of the gears.
6. Check the pressure regulator valve for a proper fit.

CYLINDER HEAD

Removal

Perform Steps 1-4 if engine is in boat. If engine has been removed from the boat, begin with Step 5.

1. Open the engine block drain valves and drain all water from the block.
2. Remove the intake and exhaust manifolds as described in this chapter.
3. Remove the alternator and oil filter mounting brackets.
4. Disconnect the spark plug wires and remove the wire looms from the cylinder head.
5. Remove the valve cover as described in this chapter.
6. Loosen the rocker arms and rotate them to one side. Remove the pushrods and identify each for reinstallation in their original position.
7. Loosen the cylinder head bolts, working from the center of the head to the end in each direction.
8. Remove the head bolts. Rap the end of the head with a soft-faced hammer to break the gasket seal. Remove the head from the engine.

CAUTION
Place the head on its side to prevent damage to the spark plugs or head gasket surface.

9. Remove and discard the head gasket. Clean all gasket residue from the head and block mating surfaces.

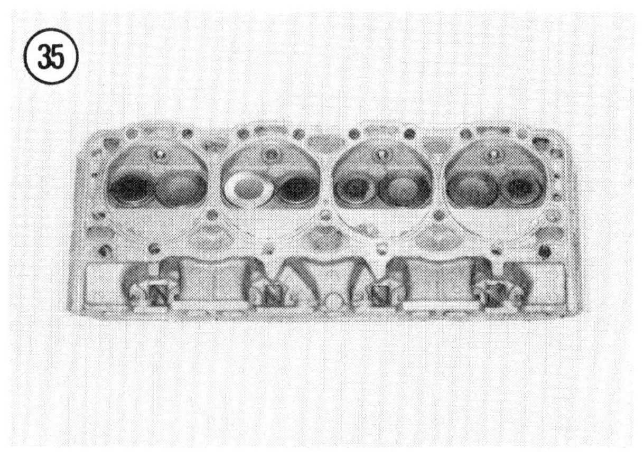

Decarbonizing

1. Without removing the valves, remove all deposits from the combustion chambers, intake ports and exhaust ports. Use a fine wire brush dipped in solvent or make a scraper from hardwood. Be careful not to scratch or gouge the combustion chambers.
2. After all carbon is removed from the combustion chambers and ports, clean the entire head in solvent.
3. Clean away all carbon on the piston tops. Do not remove the carbon ridge at the top of the cylinder bore.
4. Remove the valves as described in this chapter.
5. Clean the pushrod guides, valve guide bores and all bolt holes. Use a cleaning solvent to remove dirt and grease.
6. Clean the valves with a fine wire brush or buffing wheel.

Inspection

1. Check the cylinder head for signs of oil or water leaks before cleaning.
2. Clean the cylinder head thoroughly in solvent. While cleaning, look for cracks or other visible signs of damage. Look for corrosion or foreign material in the oil and water passages (**Figure 35**). Clean the passages with a stiff spiral brush, then blow them out with compressed air.

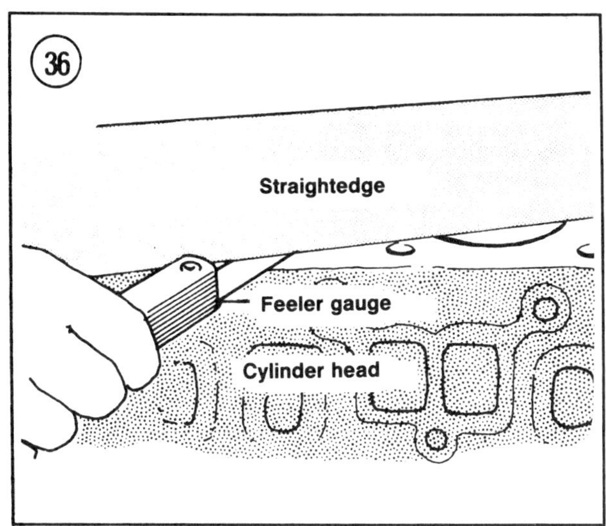

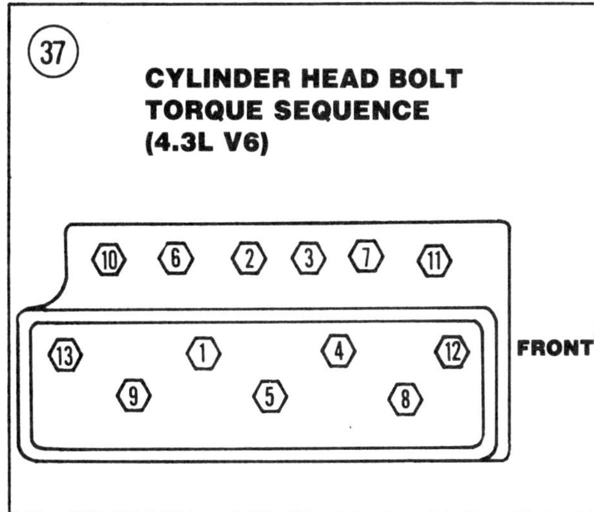

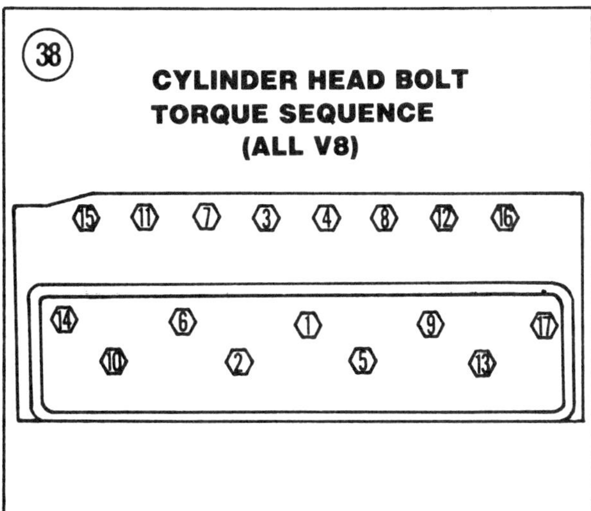

3. Check the cylinder head studs for damage and replace if necessary.
4. Check the threaded rocker arm studs or bolt holes for damaged threads; replace if necessary.
5. Check for warpage of the cylinder head-to-block surface with a straightedge and feeler gauge (**Figure 36**). Measure diagonally, as well as end to end. If the gap exceeds 0.005 in. (0.125 mm), have the head resurfaced by a machine shop. If head resurfacing is necessary, do not remove more than 0.010 in. Replace the head if a greater amount must be removed to correct warpage.

7

Installation

1. Make sure the cylinder head and block gasket surfaces and bolt holes are clean. Dirt in the block bolt holes or on the head bolt threads will affect bolt torque.
2. Recheck all visible oil and water passages for cleanliness.

CAUTION
Do not use any type of sealer with head gaskets. OMC marine head gaskets are coated with a special lacquer which provides a proper seal once the engine is warmed up.

3. Fit a new head gasket over the cylinder dowels on the block.
4. Carefully lower the head onto the cylinder block, engaging the dowel pins.
5. Wipe all head bolt threads with OMC Gasket Sealing Compound or equivalent. Install and tighten the head bolts finger-tight.
6. Tighten the head bolts 1/2 turn at a time following the sequence shown in **Figure 37** (V6) or **Figure 38** (V8) until the specified torque is reached. See **Table 2**.
7. If engine is in the boat, reverse Steps 1-6 of *Removal* in this chapter to complete installation. If engine is out of the boat, reverse Step 5 and Step 6 of *Removal* in this

chapter. Adjust the valves as described in this chapter. Check and adjust ignition timing as required. See Chapter Four.

VALVES AND VALVE SEATS

Servicing the valves, guides and valve seats must be done by a dealer or machine shop, since it requires special knowledge and expensive machine tools. A general practice among those who do their own service is to remove the cylinder heads, perform all disassembly except valve removal and take the head to a dealer or machine shop for inspection and service. Since the cost is low relative to the required effort and equipment, this is usually the best approach, even for experienced mechanics. The following procedures are given to acquaint the home mechanic with what the dealer or machine shop will do.

Valve Removal

Refer to **Figure 39** for this procedure.

1. Remove the cylinder head as described in this chapter.
2. Remove the rocker arm assemblies as described in this chapter.
3. Compress the valve spring with a compressor like the one shown in **Figure 40**. Remove the valve keys or cap locks and release the spring tension.
4. Remove the valve spring cap (or exhaust valve rotator) and valve spring.
5. Remove the valve stem seal with a pair of pliers. Discard the seal. Remove the shim and spacer, if used.

CAUTION
Remove any burrs from the valve stem lock grooves before removing the valves or the valve guides will be damaged.

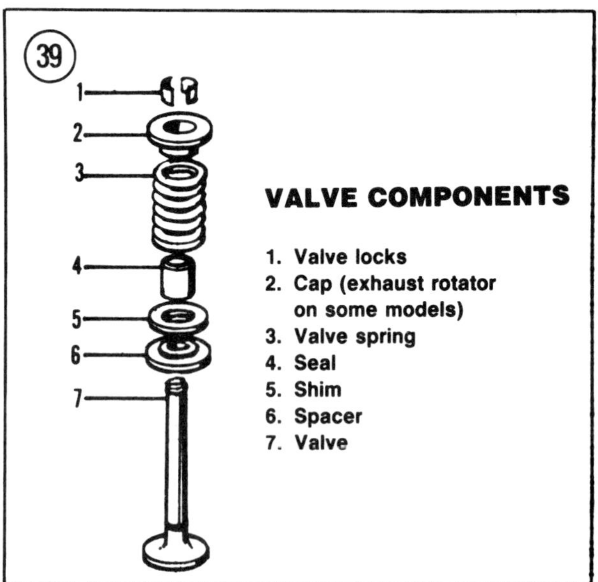

VALVE COMPONENTS

1. Valve locks
2. Cap (exhaust rotator on some models)
3. Valve spring
4. Seal
5. Shim
6. Spacer
7. Valve

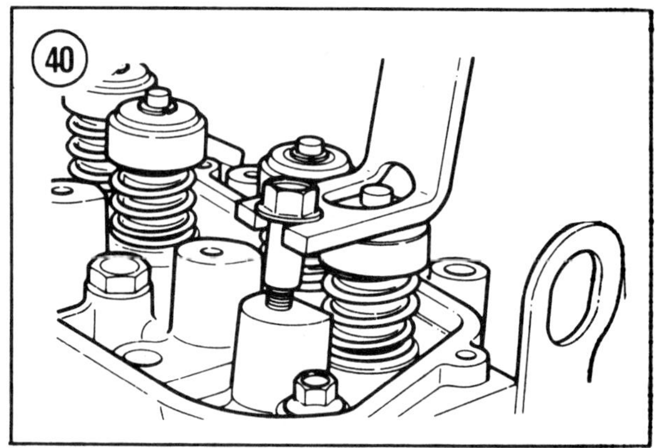

6. Remove the valve and repeat Steps 3-5 on each remaining valve.
7. Arrange the parts in order so they can be returned to their original positions when reassembled.

Inspection

1. Clean the valves with a fine wire brush or buffing wheel. Discard any cracked, warped or burned valves.
2. Measure valve stems at the top, center and bottom for wear. A machine shop can do this when the valves are ground. Also measure the length of each valve and the diameter of each valve head.

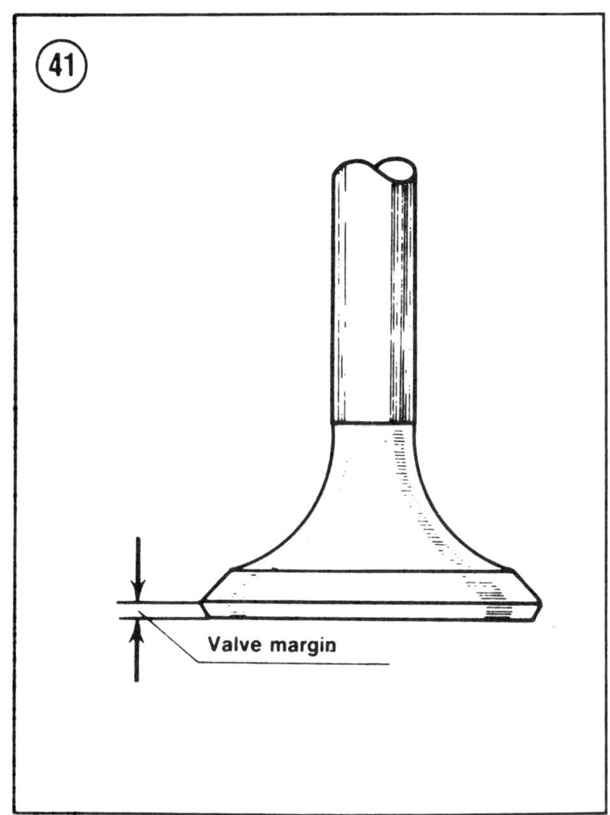

NOTE
*Check the thickness of the valve edge or margin after the valves have been ground. See **Figure 41**. Any valve with a margin of less than 1/32 in. should be discarded.*

3. Remove all carbon and varnish from the valve guides with a stiff spiral wire brush.

NOTE
The next step assumes that all valve stems have been measured and are within specifications. Replace valves with worn stems before performing this step.

4. Insert each valve into the guide from which it was removed. Holding the valve just slightly off its seat, rock it back and forth in a direction parallel with the rocker arms. This is the direction in which the greatest wear normally occurs. If the valve stem rocks more than slightly, the valve guide is probably worn.
5. If there is any doubt about valve guide condition after performing Step 4, have the valve guide measured with a valve stem clearance checking tool. Compare the results with specifications in **Table 1**. Worn guides must be reamed for the next oversize valve stem.
6. Test the valve springs under load on a spring tester (**Figure 42**). Replace any weak springs.
7. Inspect the valve seat inserts. If worn or burned, they must be reconditioned. This is a job for a dealer or machine shop, although the procedure is described in this chapter.
8. Check each spring on a flat surface with a steel square. See **Figure 43**. Slowly revolve the spring 360° and note the space between the top of the coil and the square. If it exceeds 5/16 in. at any point, replace the spring.
9. Check each valve lifter to make sure it fits freely in the block and that the end that

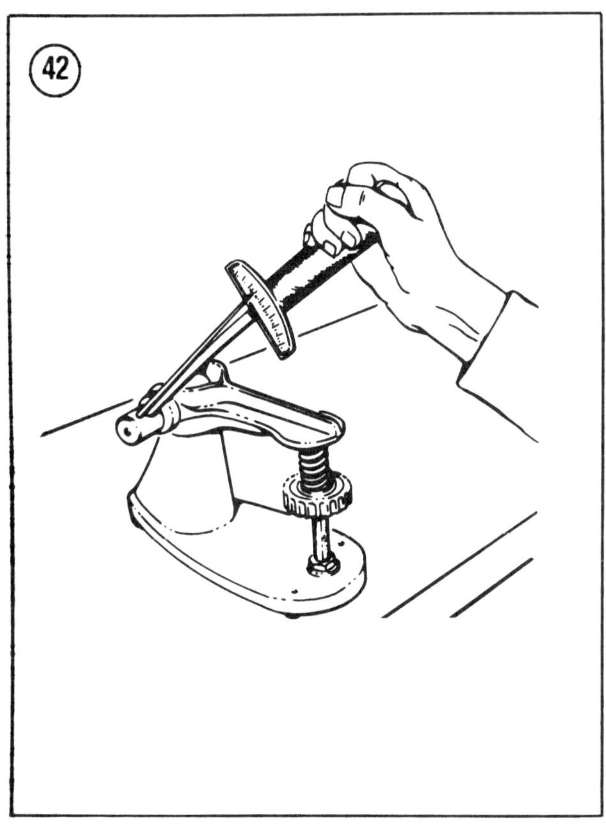

7

contacts the camshaft lobe is smooth and not worn excessively.

Valve Guide Reaming

Worn valve guides must be reamed to accept a valve with an oversize stem. These are available in 3 sizes for both intake and exhaust valves. Reaming must be done by hand (**Figure 44**) and is a job best left to an experienced machine shop. The valve seat must be refaced after the guide has been reamed.

Valve Seat Reconditioning

1. Cut the valve seats to the specified angle (**Table 1**) with a dressing stone. Remove only enough metal to obtain a good finish.
2. Use tapered stones to obtain the specified seat width when necessary.
3. Coat the corresponding valve face with Prussian blue dye.
4. Insert the valve into the valve guide.
5. Apply light pressure to the valve and rotate it approximately 1/4 turn.
6. Lift the valve out. If it seats properly, the dye will transfer evenly to the valve face.
7. If the dye transfers to the top of the valve face, lower the seat. If it transfers to the bottom of the valve face, raise the seat.

Valve Installation

NOTE
Install all parts in the same position from which they were removed.

1. Coat the valves with engine oil and install them in the cylinder head.
2. Install new oil seals on each valve. Seal should be flat and not twisted in the valve stem groove.
3. Drop the valve spring shim/spacer around the valve guide boss. Install the valve spring over the valve, the install the cap or rotator.

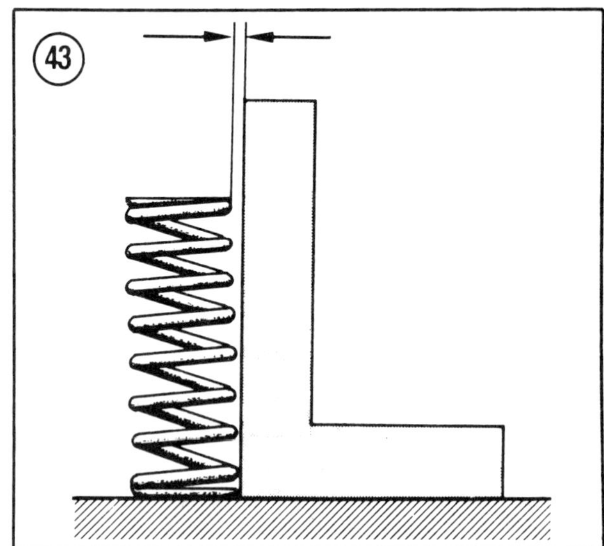

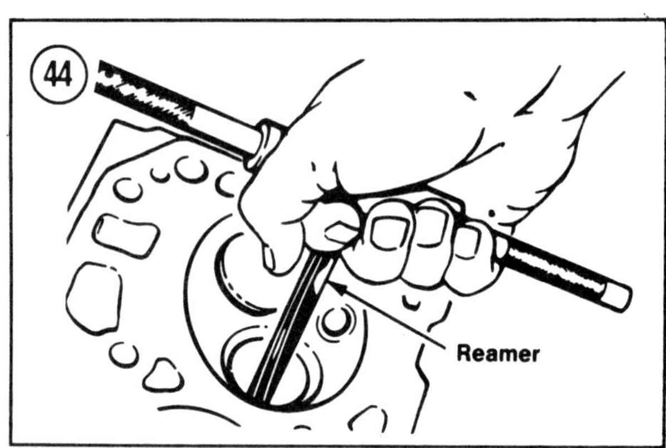

4. Compress the springs and install the keys. Make sure both keys seat properly in the upper groove of the valve stem.
5. Measure the installed spring height between the top of the valve seat and the underside of the cap or rotator, as shown in **Figure 45**. If height is greater than specifications, install an extra spring seat shim about 1/16 in. thick and remeasure the height.

VALVE LIFTERS

Removal/Installation

1. Remove the rocker arm assemblies, pushrods and intake manifold as described in this chapter.

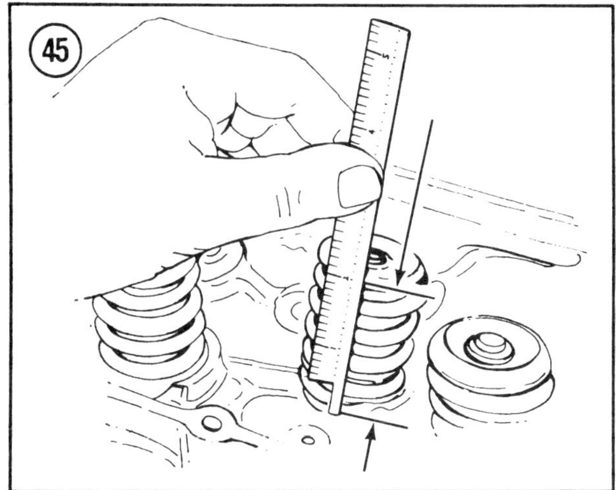

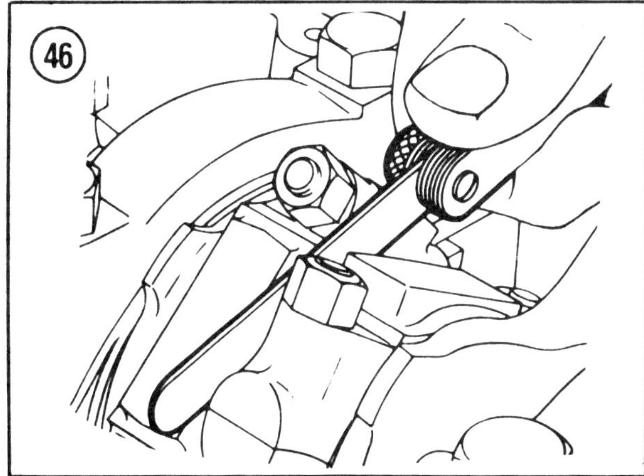

2. Remove the valve lifters. This can be done without special tools, although tool part No. J-3049 will make the job easier and faster.
3. Installation is the reverse of removal.

PISTON/CONNECTING ROD ASSEMBLY

Piston/Connecting Rod Removal

1. Remove the engine as described in this chapter.
2. Place a suitable container under the oil pan and remove the drain plug. Let the crankcase oil drain, then reinstall the drain plug.
3. Remove the intake and exhaust manifolds as described in this chapter.
4. Remove the cylinder heads as described in this chapter.
5. Remove the oil pan and oil pump as described in this chapter.
6. Rotate the crankshaft until one piston is at bottom dead center. Pack the cylinder bore with clean shop rags. Remove the carbon ridge at the top of the cylinder bores with a ridge reamer. These can be rented for use. Vacuum out the shavings, then remove the shop rags.
7. Rotate the crankshaft until the connecting rod is centered in the bore. Measure the clearance between the connecting rods with a flat feeler gauge (**Figure 46**). If the clearance exceeds specifications (**Table 1**), replace the connecting rod during reassembly.
8. Remove the nuts holding the connecting rod cap. Lift off the cap, together with the lower bearing insert.

NOTE
If the connecting rod caps are difficult to remove, tap the studs with a wooden hammer handle.

9. Use the wooden hammer handle to push the piston and connecting rod from the bore.

NOTE
Mark the cylinder number on the top of each piston with quick-drying paint. Check the cylinder numbers or identification marks on the connecting rod and cap. If they are not visible, make your own ***(Figure 47)****.*

10. Remove the piston rings with a ring remover (**Figure 48**).
11. Repeat Steps 6-10 for all remaining connecting rods.

Piston Pin Removal/Installation

The piston pins are press-fitted to the connecting rods and hand-fitted to the pistons. Removal requires the use of a press and support stand. This is a job for a dealer or machine shop equipped to fit the pistons to the pins, ream the pin bushings to the correct diameter and install the pistons and pins on the connecting rods.

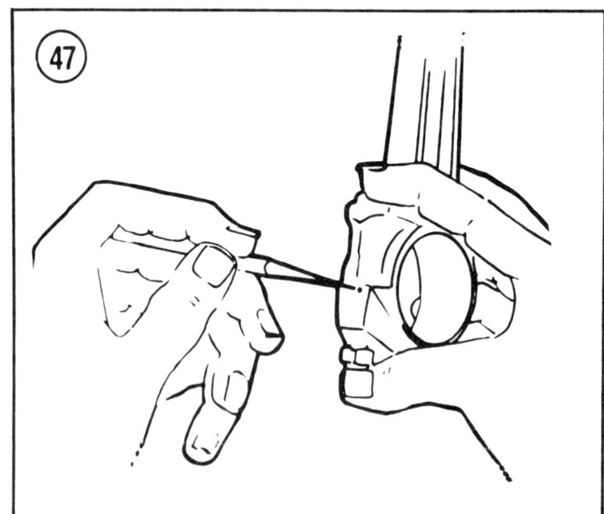

Piston Clearance Check

Unless you have precision measuring equipment and know how to use it properly, have this procedure done by a machine shop.

1. Measure the piston diameter with a micrometer (**Figure 49**) just below the rings at right angles to the piston pin bore.
2. Measure the cylinder bore diameter with a bore gauge (**Figure 50**). **Figure 51** shows the points of normal cylinder wear. If dimension A exceeds dimension B by more than 0.003 in., the cylinder must be rebored and a new piston/ring assembly installed.
3. Subtract the piston diameter from the largest cylinder bore reading. If it exceeds the specifications in **Table 1**, the cylinder must be rebored and an oversized piston installed.

NOTE
Obtain the new piston and measure it to determine the correct cylinder bore oversize dimension.

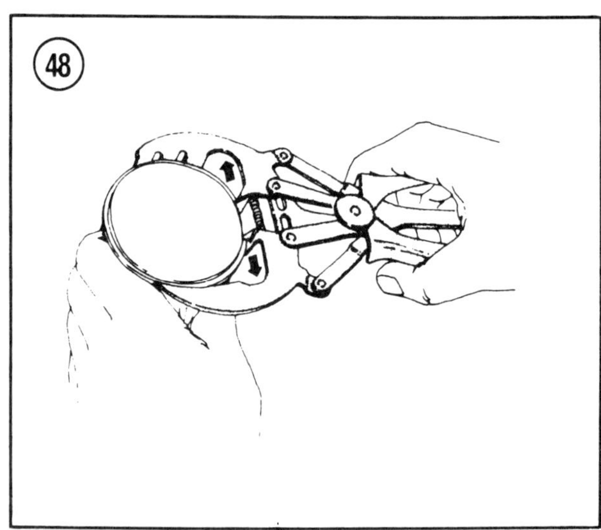

Piston Ring Fit/Installation

1. Check the ring gap of each piston ring. To do this, position the ring at the bottom of the ring travel area and square it by tapping gently with an inverted piston. See **Figure 52**.

NOTE
If the cylinders have not been rebored, check the gap at the bottom of the ring travel, where the cylinder is least worn.

2. Measure the ring gap with a feeler gauge as shown in **Figure 53**. Compare with specifications in **Table 1**. If the measurement is not within specifications, the rings must be replaced as a set. Check gap of new rings as well. If the gap is too small, file the ends of the ring to correct it (**Figure 54**).

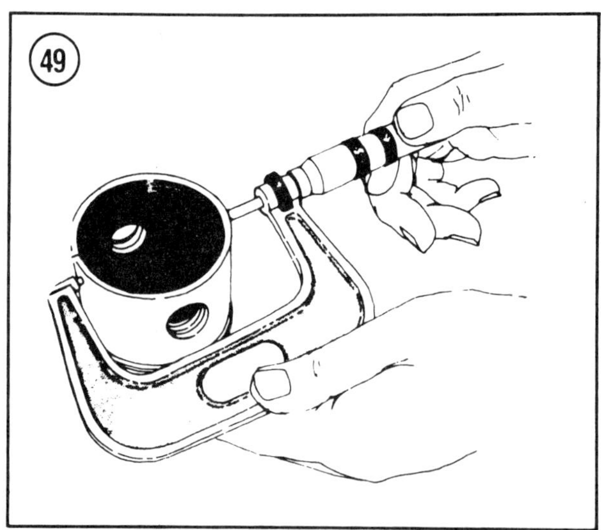

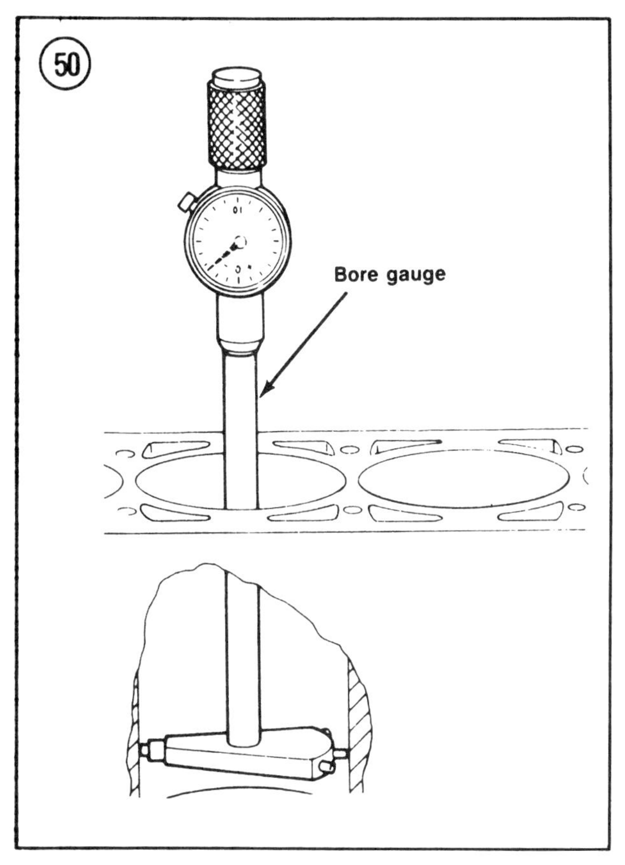
50
Bore gauge

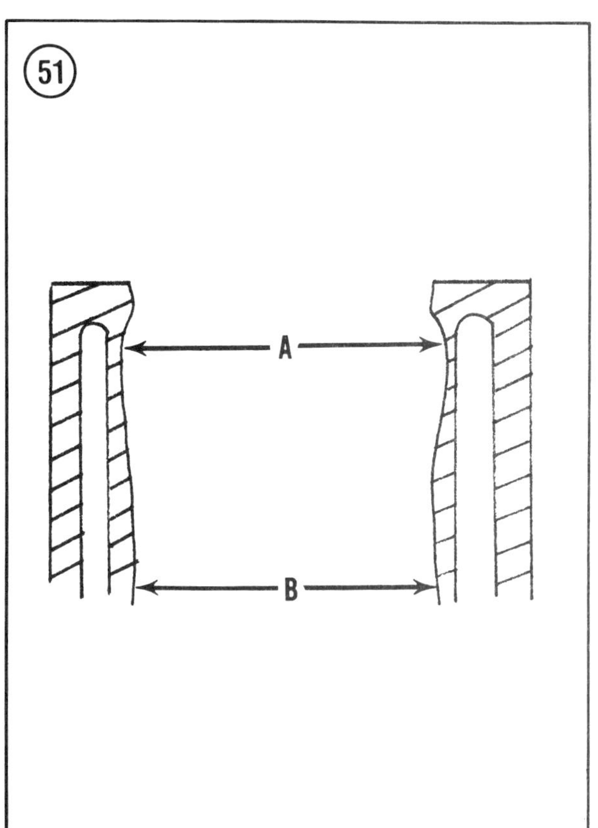
51
A
B

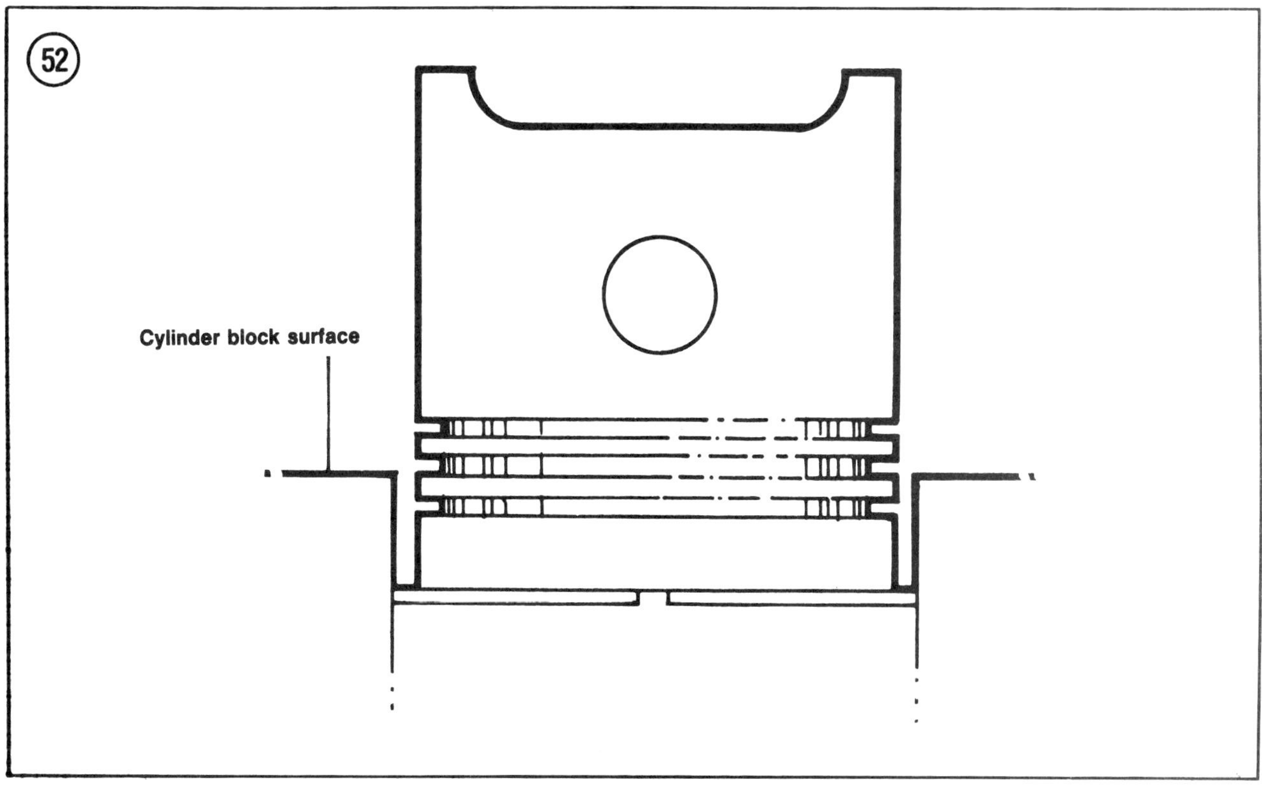
52
Cylinder block surface

3. Check the side clearance of the rings as shown in **Figure 55**. Place the feeler gauge alongside the ring all the way into the groove. If the measurement is not within specifications (**Table 1**), either the rings or the ring grooves are worn. Inspect and replace as required.
4. Using a ring expander tool (**Figure 56**), carefully install the oil control ring, then the compression rings. Oil rings consist of 3 segments. The wavy segment goes between thc flat segments to act as a spacer. Upper and lower flat segments are interchangeable. The second compression ring is tapered. The top of each compression ring is marked and must face upward.
5. Position the ring gaps as shown in **Figure 57**.

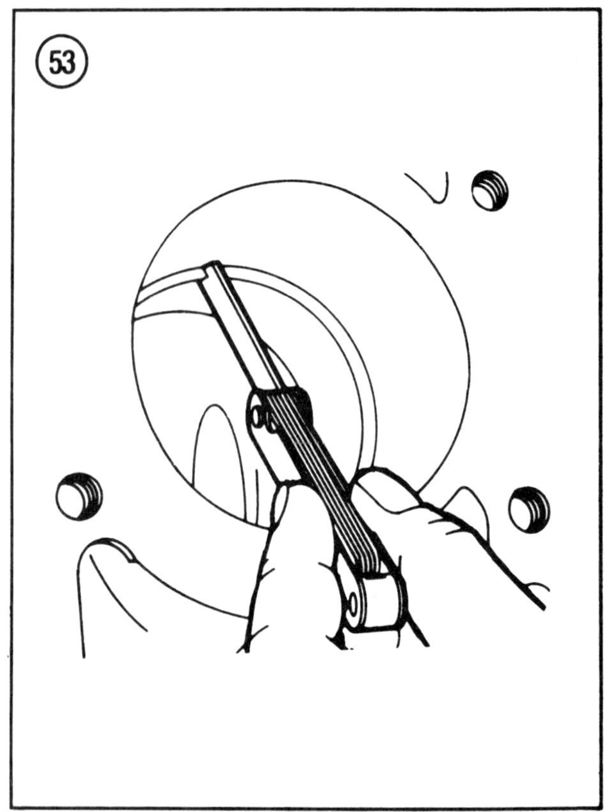

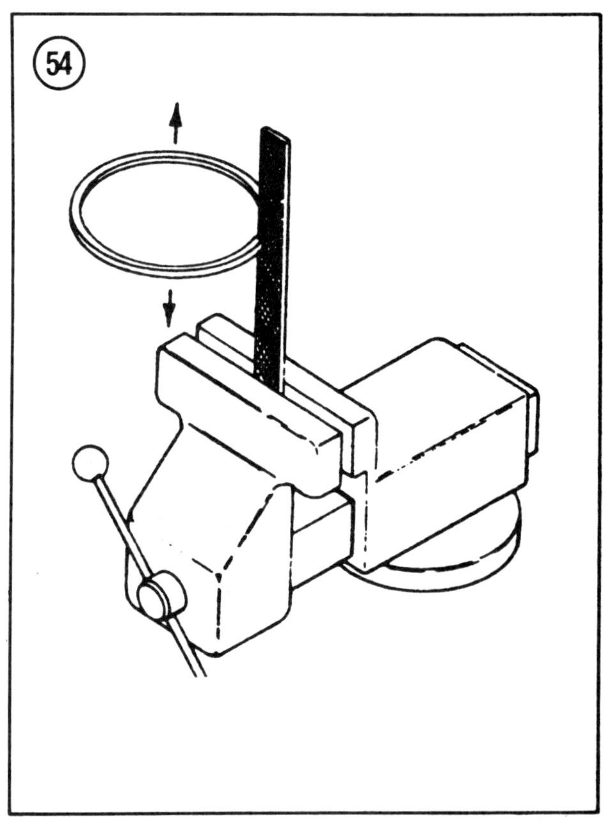

Connecting Rod Inspection

Have the connecting rods checked for straightness by a dealer or machine shop. When installing new connecting rods, have them checked for misalignment before installing the piston and piston pin. Connecting rods can spring out of alignment during shipping or handling.

Connecting Rod Bearing Clearance Measurement

1. Place the connecting rods and upper bearing halves on the proper connecting rod journals.
2. Cut a piece of Plastigage the width of the bearing. Place the Plastigage on the journal (**Figure 58**), then install the lower bearing half and cap.

NOTE
Do not place Plastigage over the journal oil hole.

3. Tighten the connecting rod cap to specifications (**Table 2**). Do not rotate the crankshaft while the Plastigage is in place.

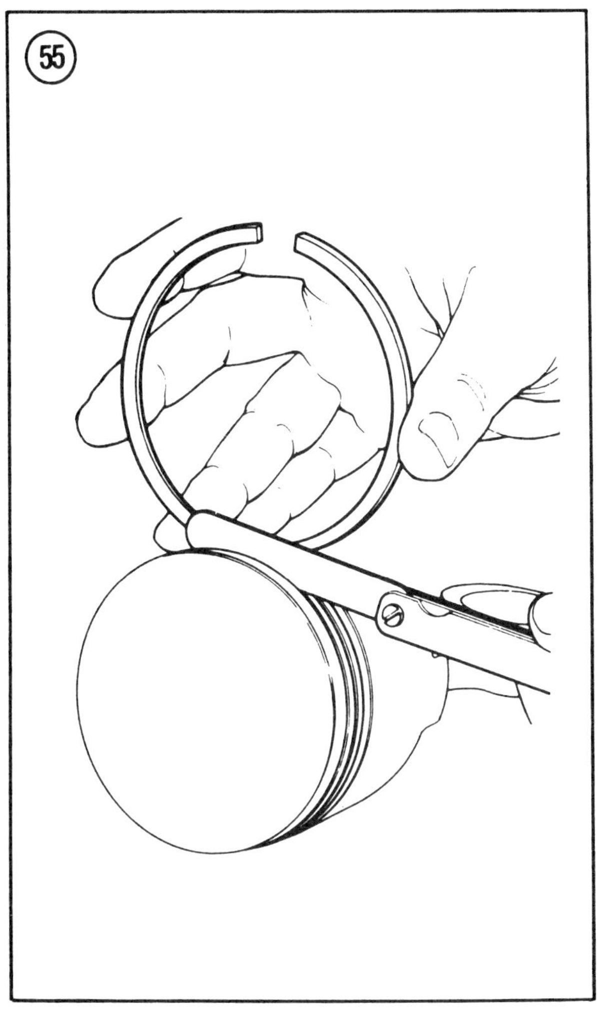
55

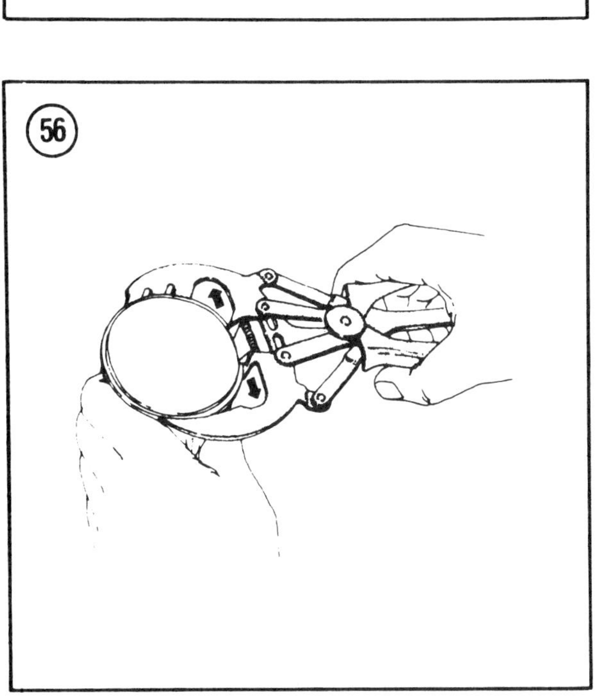
56

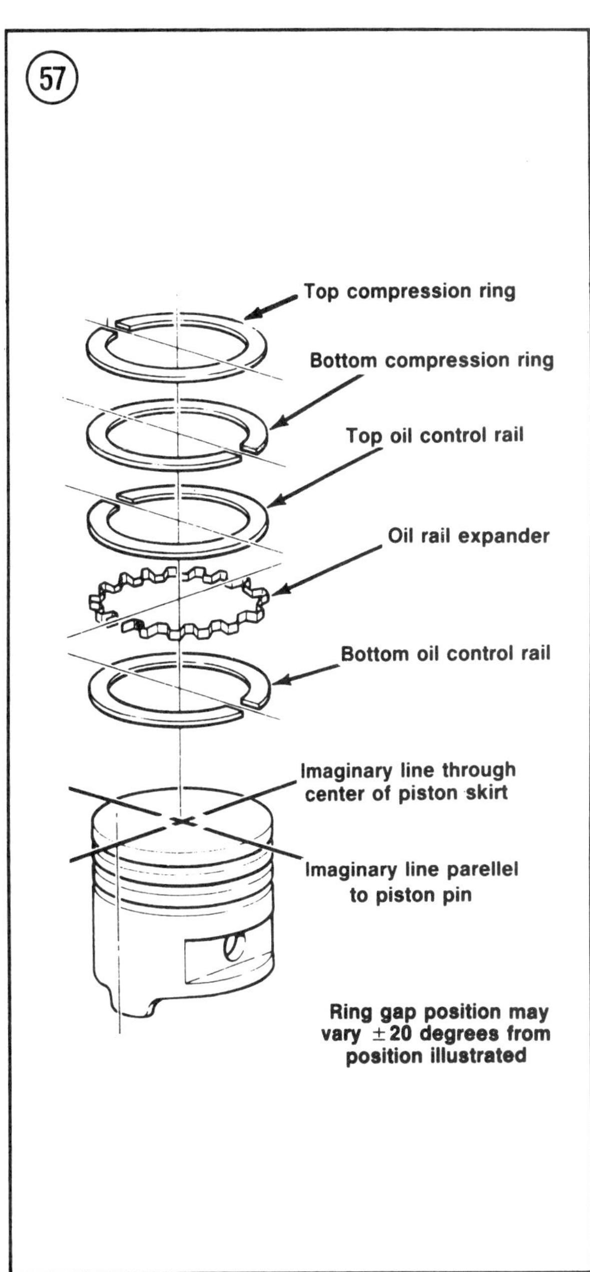
57
Top compression ring
Bottom compression ring
Top oil control rail
Oil rail expander
Bottom oil control rail
Imaginary line through center of piston skirt
Imaginary line parellel to piston pin
Ring gap position may vary ±20 degrees from position illustrated

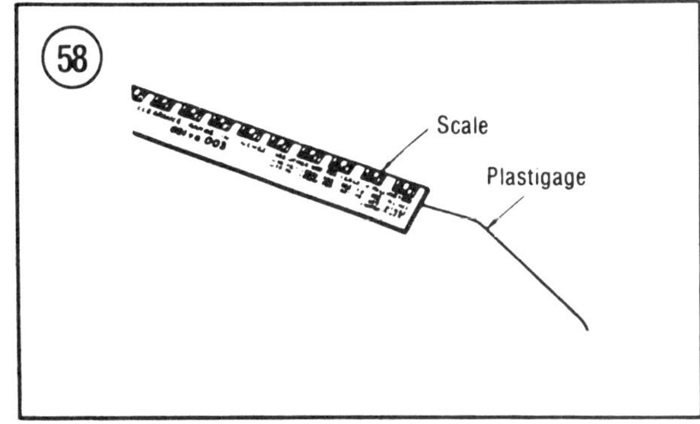
58
Scale
Plastigage

4. Remove the connecting rod caps. Bearing clearance is determined by comparing the width of the flattened Plastigage to the markings on the envelope (**Figure 59**). If the clearance is excessive, the crankshaft must be reground and undersize bearings installed.

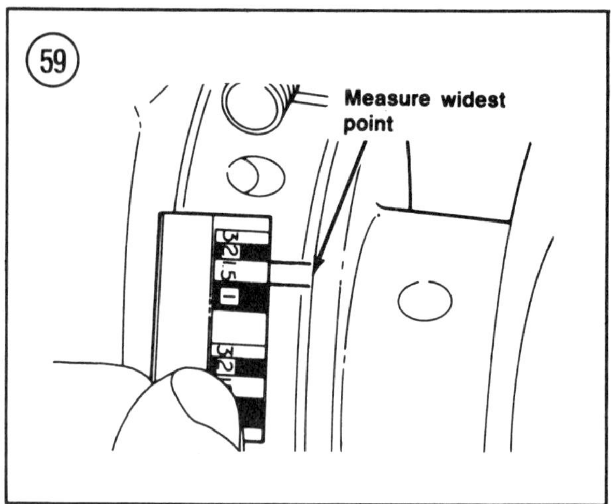

Piston/Connecting Rod Installation

1. Make sure the pistons are correctly installed on the connecting rods, if they were separated. The machined hole or cast notch on the top of the piston (**Figure 60**) and the oil hole on the side of the connecting rod must both face in the same direction.
2. Make sure the ring gaps are positioned as shown in **Figure 57**.
3. Slip short pieces of hose over the connecting rod studs to prevent them from nicking the crankshaft. Tape will work if you do not have the right diameter hose, but it is more difficult to remove.
4. Immerse the entire piston in clean engine oil. Coat the cylinder wall with oil.

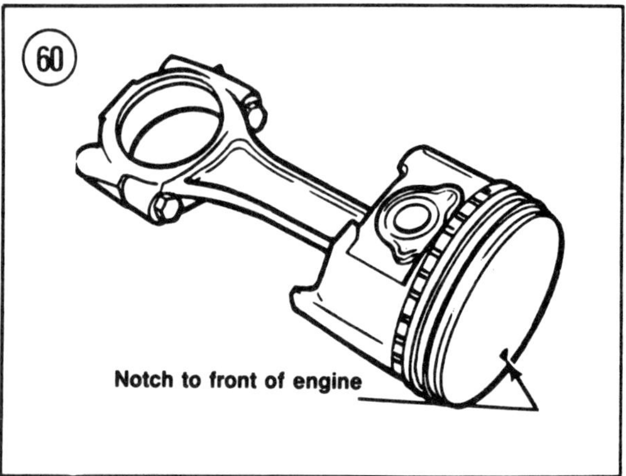

CAUTION
Use extreme care in Step 5 to prevent the connecting rod from nicking the crankshaft journal.

5. Install the piston/connecting rod assembly in its cylinder with a piston ring compressor as shown in **Figure 61**. Tap lightly with a wooden hammer handle to insert the piston. Make sure that the piston number (painted on top before removal) corresponds to the cylinder number, counting from the front of the engine.

NOTE
*The notch on the piston must face the front of the engine. See **Figure 60**.*

6. Clean the connecting rod bearings carefully, including the back sides. Coat the journals and bearings with clean engine oil. Place the bearings in the connecting rod and cap.
7. Pull the connecting rod and bearing into position against the crankpin. Remove the protective hose or tape and lightly lubricate the connecting rod bolt threads with SAE 30 engine oil.
8. Install the connecting rod cap. Make sure the rod and cap marks align. Install the cap nuts finger-tight.
9. Repeat Steps 4-8 for each remaining piston/connecting rod assembly.
10. Tighten the cap nuts to specifications (**Table 2**).
11. Check the connecting rod big-end play as described under *Piston/Connecting Rod Removal* in this chapter.

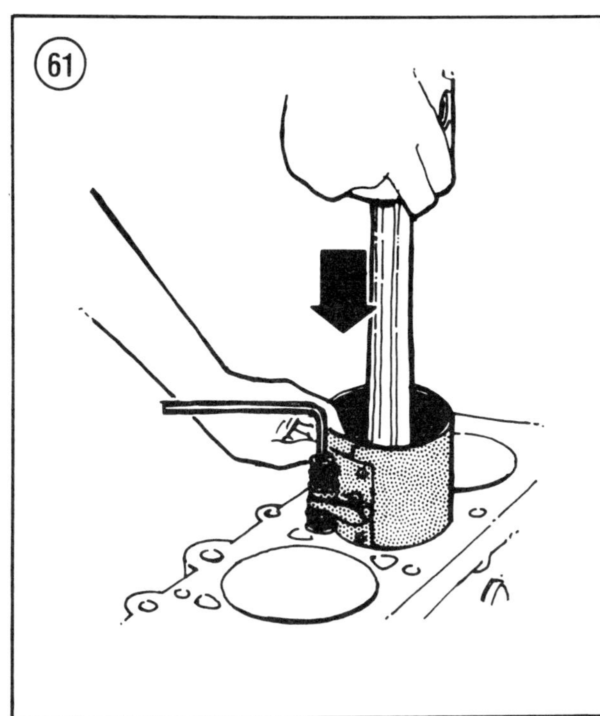

61

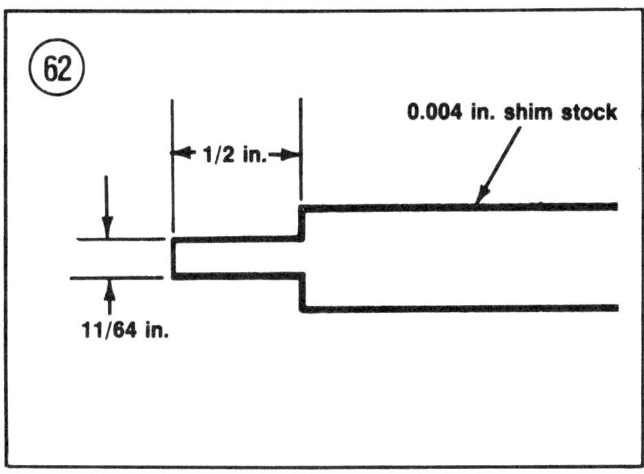

62

REAR MAIN BEARING OIL SEAL

A 2-piece neoprene seal, located under the rear main bearing cap, is used on early engines. The seal can be replaced without crankshaft removal.

A 1-piece oil seal, in a cast aluminum retainer on the rear of the block, is used with later engines. Whenever the retainer is removed, a new seal and gasket must be installed.

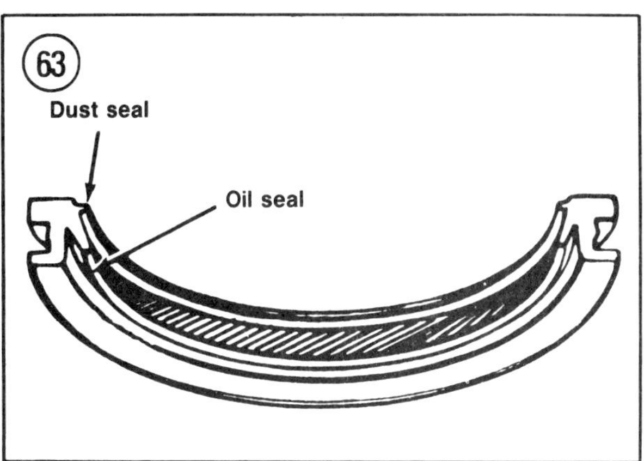

63

Replacement (2-piece Neoprene Seal)

1. Fabricate a seal installation tool as shown in **Figure 62** to protect the seal bead when positioning the new seal.
2. Remove the oil pan and oil pump as described in this chapter.
3. Remove the rear main bearing cap. Pry the oil seal from the bottom of the cap with a small screwdriver.
4. Remove the upper half of the seal with a brass pin punch. Tap the punch on one end of the seal until its other end protrudes far enough to be removed with pliers.
5. Clean all sealant from the bearing cap and crankshaft with a non-abrasive cleaner.
6. Coat the lips and bead of a new seal with light engine oil. Do not let oil touch sealing mating ends.
7. Position tip of seal installer tool (fabricated in Step 1) between crankcase and seal seat. Position seal between crankshaft and tip of tool so seal bead touches tool tip. Make sure oil seal lip faces toward front of engine. See **Figure 63**.
8. Use seal installer tool as a shoehorn and roll seal around crankshaft, protecting seal bead from sharp corners of seal seat surfaces. Keep tool in position until seal is properly seated, with both ends flush with the block.
9. Remove the tool carefully to prevent pulling seal out with it.

10. Use seal installer tool as a shoehorn again and install seal half in bearing cap. Feed seal into cap with light thumb and finger pressure.
11. Apply sealant to the areas shown in **Figure 64**. Keep sealant off the seal split line.
12. Install rear main bearing cap with seal and tighten to 10-12 ft.-lb. (14-16 N•m). Tap end of crankshaft to the rear, then to the front to align the thrust surfaces.
13. Retighten bearing cap to specifications (**Table 2**).

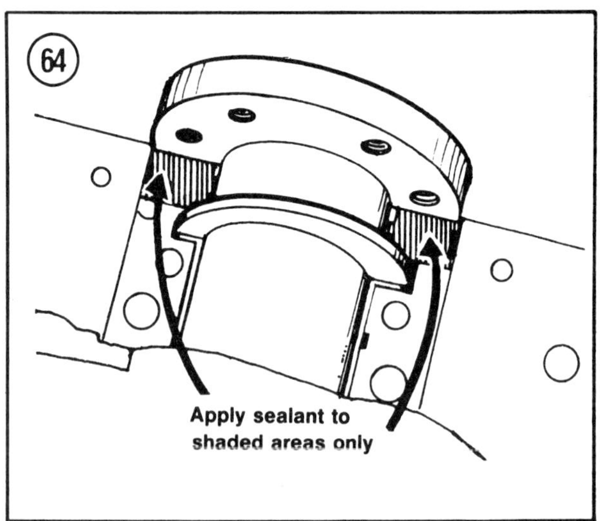

Seal Replacement (1-piece Seal)

1. Remove the engine from the boat as described in this chapter.
2. Remove the flywheel as described in this chapter.
3. Pry the old seal from the retainer with a small screwdriver or awl (**Figure 65**). Use the pry notches provided in the retainer (**Figure 66**) and work carefully to avoid scratching the outer diameter of the crankshaft with the pry tool.
4. Carefully clean and inspect the inner diameter of the seal bore and the outer diameter of the crankshaft for nicks and burrs which could affect seal performance. If any are found, the engine must be removed, disassembled and the defects corrected before a new seal is installed.
5. Lubricate the inner diameter of a new seal with clean engine oil. Install seal on mandrel of tool part No. J-35621 until it bottoms against the tool collar. See **Figure 67.**
6. Align the tool with the rear of the crankshaft and thread tool screws in place. Tighten securely with a screwdriver to make sure the seal will be installed squarely.
7. Turn the tool handle until the collar is tightly against the block and the handle has bottomed. This will push the seal into its bore and seat it properly.

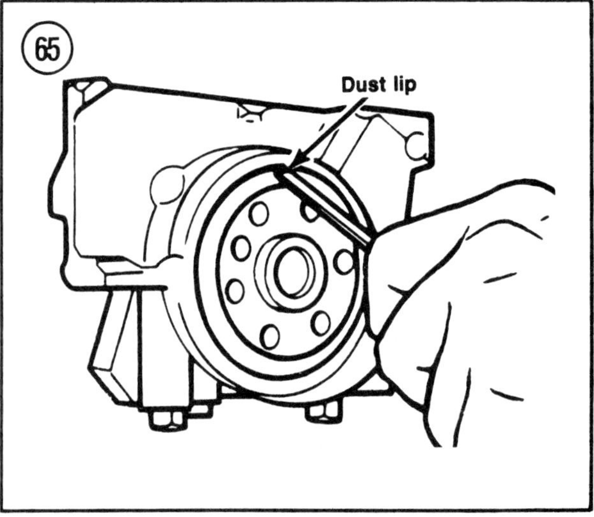

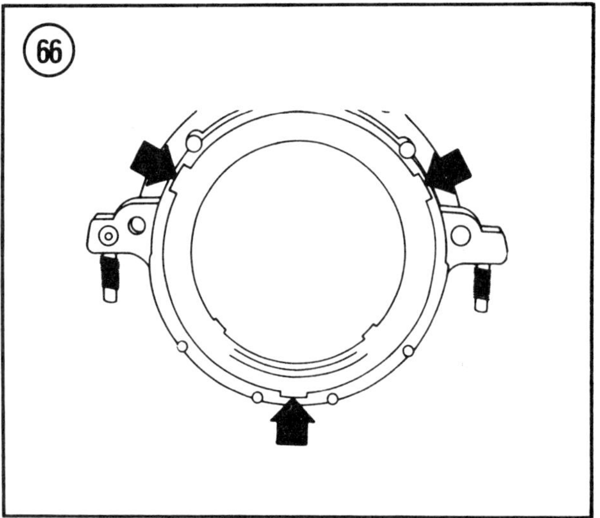

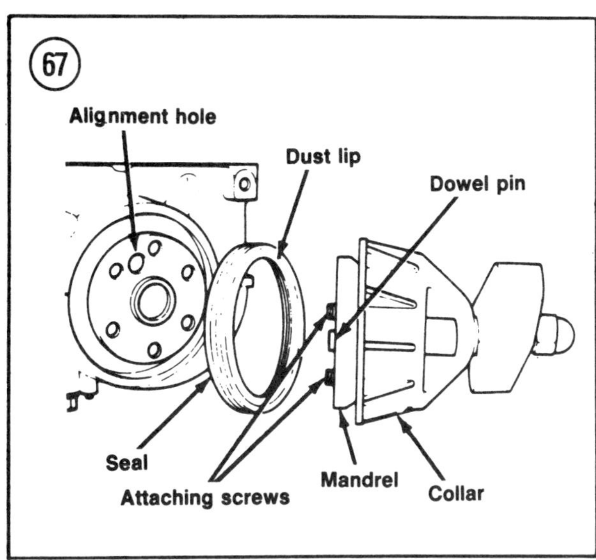

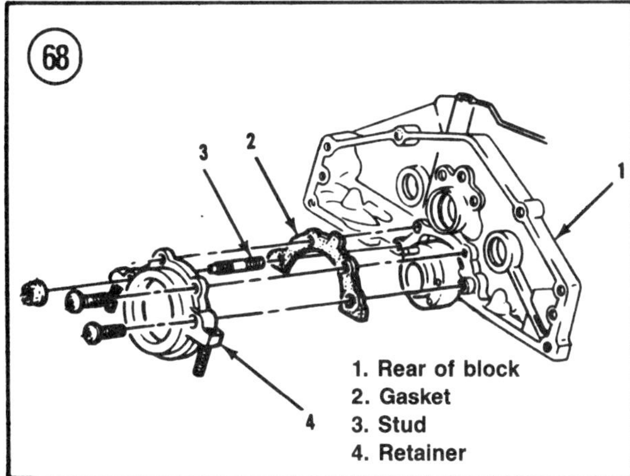

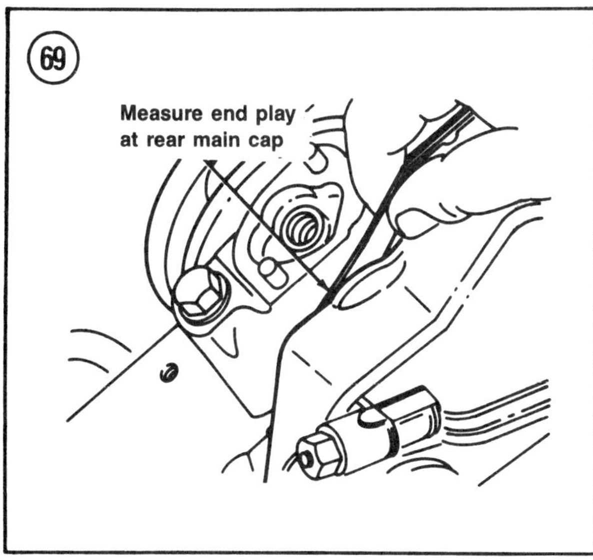

8. Back the tool handle off until it stops. Remove tool from crankshaft.
9. Check seal to make sure it is seated squarely in the bore, then reverse Step 1 and Step 2 to complete installation.

Retainer Replacement

To replace the retainer, refer to **Figure 68** and proceed as follows:

1. Remove the engine from the boat as described in this chapter.
2. Remove the flywheel and oil pan as described in this chapter.
3. Unbolt and remove the retainer/seal assembly. Remove and discard the gasket.
4. Clean all gasket residue from the retainer and block mating surfaces.
5. Fit a new gasket over the studs on the block and install the retainer. Tighten bolts to 120-150 in.-lb. (13-16 N•m).
6. Install a new seal as described in this chapter.
7. Reinstall the oil pan and flywheel as described in this chapter.
8. Reinstall the engine in the boat as described in this chapter.

CRANKSHAFT

End Play Measurement

1. Pry the crankshaft to the front of the engine with a large screwdriver.
2. Measure the crankshaft end play at the front of the rear main bearing with a flat feeler gauge. See **Figure 69**. Compare to specifications in **Table 1**.
3. If the end play is excessive, replace the rear main bearing. If less than specified, check the bearing faces for imperfections.

Removal

Refer to **Figure 70** (typical) for this procedure.

1. Remove the engine from the boat as described in this chapter.
2. Remove the flywheel as described in this chapter.
3. Mount the engine on an engine stand, if available.
4. Remove the starter motor. See Chapter Eleven.
5. Invert the engine to bring the oil pan to an upright position.
6. Remove the oil pan and oil pump as described in this chapter.
7. Remove the harmonic balancer, front cover and timing chain as described in this chapter.
8. Remove the spark plugs to permit easy rotation of the crankshaft.
9. Measure crankshaft end play as described in this chapter.
10. Rotate the crankshaft to position one connecting rod at the bottom of its stroke.
11. Remove the connecting rod bearing cap and bearing. Move the piston/rod assembly away from the crankshaft.
12. Repeat Step 10 and Step 11 for each remaining piston/rod assembly.
13. Check the caps for identification numbers or marks. If none are visible, clean the caps with a wire brush. If marks still cannot be seen, make your own with quick-drying paint.
14. Unbolt and remove the main bearing caps and bearing inserts. See **Figure 71** (typical).

NOTE
If the caps are difficult to remove, lift the bolts partway out, then lever the bolts from side to side.

15. Carefully lift the crankshaft from the engine block and place it on a clean workbench.
16. Remove the bearing inserts from the block. Place the bearing caps and inserts in order on a clean workbench.

Inspection

1. Clean the crankshaft thoroughly with solvent. Blow out the oil passages with compressed air.
2. Check the main and connecting rod journals for wear, scratches, grooves, scoring or cracks. Check oil seal surface for burrs, nicks or other sharp edges which might damage a seal during installation.

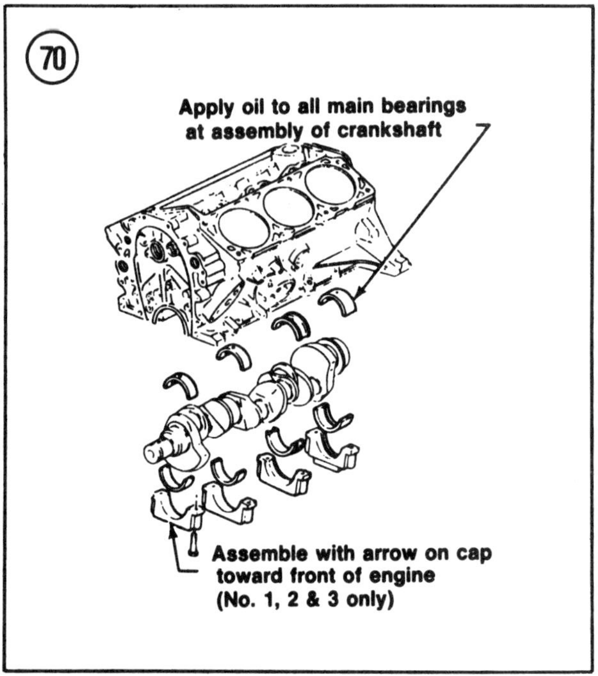
70
Apply oil to all main bearings at assembly of crankshaft
Assemble with arrow on cap toward front of engine (No. 1, 2 & 3 only)

71

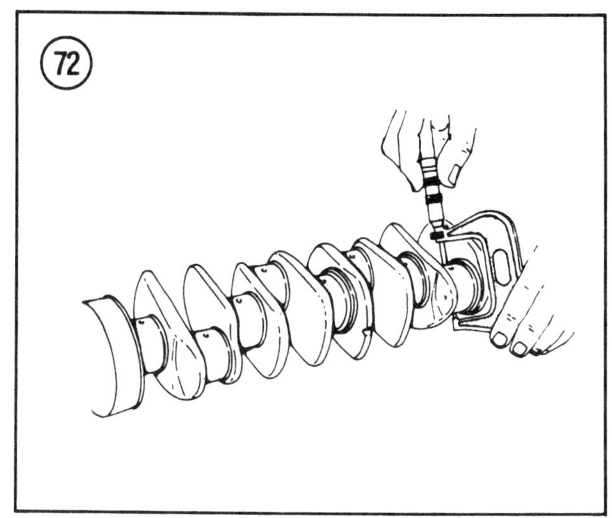

NOTE
Unless you have precision measuring equipment and know how to use it, have a machine shop perform Step 3.

3. Check all journals against specifications (**Table 1**) for out-of-roundness and taper. See **Figure 72**. Have the crankshaft reground, if necessary.

Main Bearing Clearance Measurement

Main bearing clearance is measured with Plastigage in the same manner as the connecting rod bearing clearance, described in this chapter. Excessive clearance requires that the bearings be replaced, the crankshaft be reground or both.

Sprocket Removal/Installation

1. Remove the harmonic balancer as described in this chapter.
2. Remove the front cover as described in this chapter.
3. Remove the camshaft sprocket and timing chain as described in this chapter.
4. Install tool part No. J-1619 or equivalent and remove the crankshaft sprocket.
5. Installation is the reverse of removal. Use tool part No. J-21058 or equivalent to install the sprocket to the crankshaft.

Installation

1. Install a new rear main bearing oil seal as described in this chapter.
2. Install the main bearing inserts in the cylinder block. Bearing oil holes must align with block oil holes and bearing tabs must seat in the block tab slots.

NOTE
Check cap bolts for thread damage before reuse. If damaged, replace the bolts.

3. Lubricate the bolt threads with SAE 30 engine oil.
4. Install the bearing inserts in each cap.
5. Carefully lower the crankshaft into position in the block.
6. Install the bearing caps in their marked positions with the arrows pointing toward the front of the engine and the number mark aligned with the corresponding mark on the journals.
7. Install and tighten all bolts finger-tight. Recheck end play as described in this chapter, then tighten all bolts to specifications (**Table 2**).
8. Rotate the crankshaft to make sure it turns smoothly at the flywheel rim. If not, remove the bearing caps and crankshaft and check that the bearings are clean and properly installed.
9. Reverse Steps 1-12 of *Removal* in this chapter.

FLYWHEEL

Removal/Installation

1. Remove the engine from the boat as described in this chapter.
2. Remove the flywheel housing and drive plate or coupling, if so equipped.
3. Unbolt the flywheel from the crankshaft. Remove the bolts gradually in a diagonal pattern.

4. To install, align the dowel hole in the flywheel with dowel or dowel hole in crankshaft flange and position the flywheel on studs.
5. Fit the drive plate or coupling on the studs. Install the washers and locknuts. Tighten nuts to specifications (**Table 2**).
6. Install a dial indicator on the machined surface of the flywheel and check runout. If runout exceeds 0.008 in., remove the flywheel and check for burrs. If none are found, replace the flywheel.
7. If flywheel runout is within specifications, install the flywheel housing.
8. Reinstall the engine in the boat as described in this chapter.

Inspection

1. Visually check the flywheel surface for cracks, deep scoring, excessive wear, heat discoloration and checking. If the surface is glazed or slightly scratched, have the flywheel resurfaced by a machine shop.
2. Check the surface flatness with a straightedge and feeler gauge.
3. Inspect the ring gear for cracks, broken teeth or excessive wear. If severely worn, check the starter motor drive teeth for similar wear or damage; replace as required.

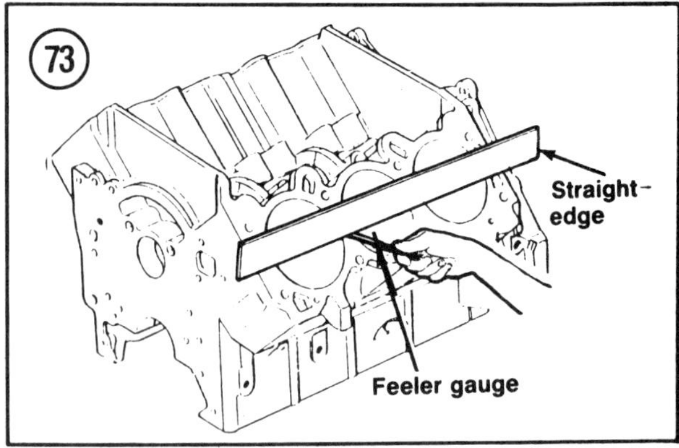

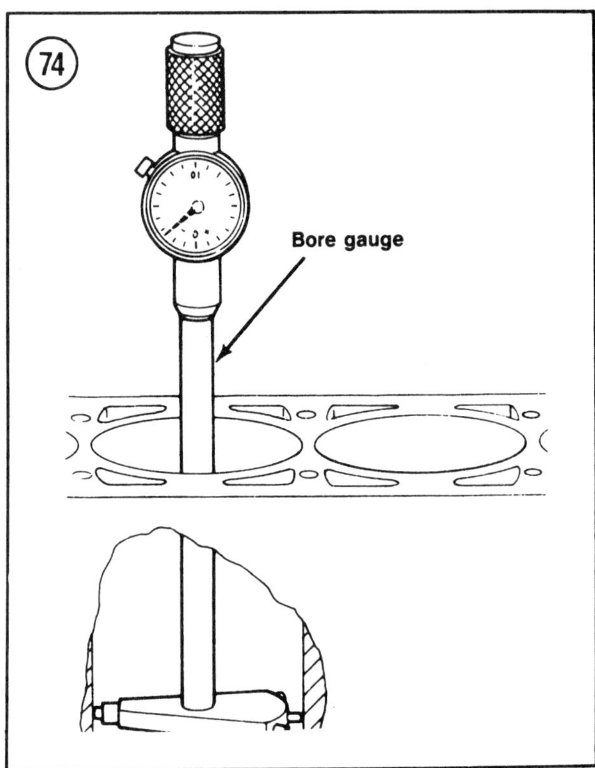

CYLINDER BLOCK

Cleaning and Inspection

1. Clean the block thoroughly with solvent. Remove any gasket or RTV sealant residue from the machined surfaces. Check all core plugs for leaks and replace any that are suspect. See *Core Plug Replacement* in this chapter. Remove any plugs that seal oil passages. Check oil and coolant passages for sludge, dirt and corrosion while cleaning. If the passages are very dirty, have the block boiled out by a machine shop. Blow out all passages with compressed air. Check the threads in the head bolt holes to be sure they are clean. If dirty, use a tap to true up the threads and remove any deposits.
2. Examine the block for cracks. To confirm suspicions about possible leak areas, use a mixture of 1 part kerosene and 2 parts engine oil. Coat the suspected area with this solution, then wipe dry and immediately apply a solution of zinc oxide dissolved in wood alcohol. If any discoloration appears in the treated area, the block is cracked and should be replaced.

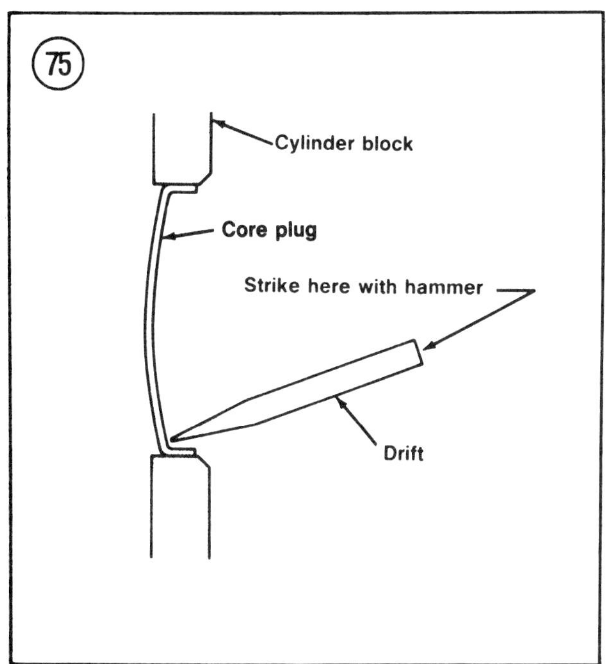

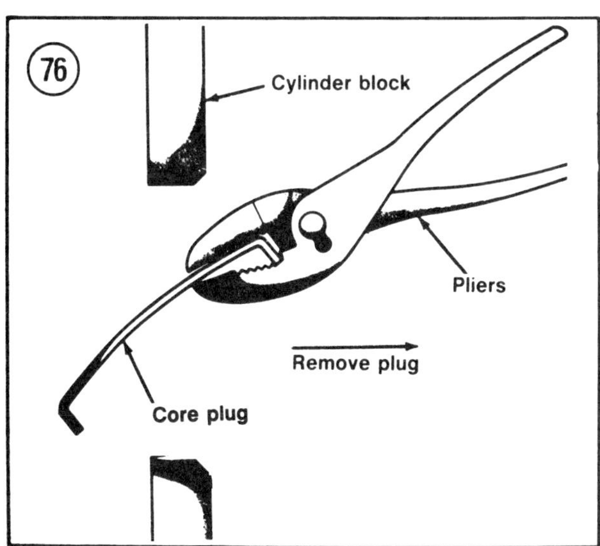

3. Check flatness of the cylinder block deck or top surface. Place an accurate straightedge on the block. If there is any gap between the block and straightedge, measure it with a flat feeler gauge (**Figure 73**). Measure from end to end and from corner to corner. Have the block resurfaced if it is warped more than 0.004 in. (0.102 mm).
4. Measure cylinder bores with a bore gauge (**Figure 74**) for out-of-roundness or excessive wear as described in *Piston Clearance Check* in this chapter. If the cylinders exceed maximum tolerances, they must be rebored. Reboring is also necessary if the cylinder walls are badly scuffed or scored.

NOTE
*Before boring, install all main bearing caps and tighten the cap bolts to specifications in **Table 2**.*

CORE PLUG REPLACEMENT

The condition of all core plugs in the block and cylinder head should be checked whenever the engine is out of the boat for service. If any signs of leakage or corrosion are found around one core plug, replace them all.

7

Removal/Installation

CAUTION
Do not drive core plugs into the engine casting. It will be impossible to retrieve them and they can restrict coolant circulation, resulting in serious engine damage.

1. Tap the bottom edge of the core plug with a hammer and drift. Use several sharp blows to push the bottom of the plug inward, tilting the top out (**Figure 75**).
2. Grip the top of the plug firmly with pliers. Pull the plug from its bore (**Figure 76**) and discard.

NOTE
Core plugs can also be removed by drilling a hole in the center of the plug and prying them out with an appropriate size drift or pin punch. On large core plugs, the use of a universal impact slide hammer is recommended.

3. Clean the plug bore thoroughly to remove all traces of the old sealer. Inspect the bore for any damage that might interfere with proper sealing of the new plug. If damage is evident,

true the surface by boring for the next oversize plug.

NOTE
Oversize plugs can be identified by an "OS" stamped in the flat on the cup side of the plug.

4. Coat the inside diameter of the plug bore and the outer diameter of the new plug with sealer. Use an oil-resistant sealer if the plug is to be installed in an oil gallery or a water-resistant sealer for plugs installed in the water jacket.
5. Install the new core plug with an appropriate size core plug replacer tool (**Figure** 77), driver or socket. The sharp edge of the plug should be at least 0.02 in. (0.5 mm) inside the lead-in chamfer.
6. Repeat Steps 1-5 to replace each remaining core plug.

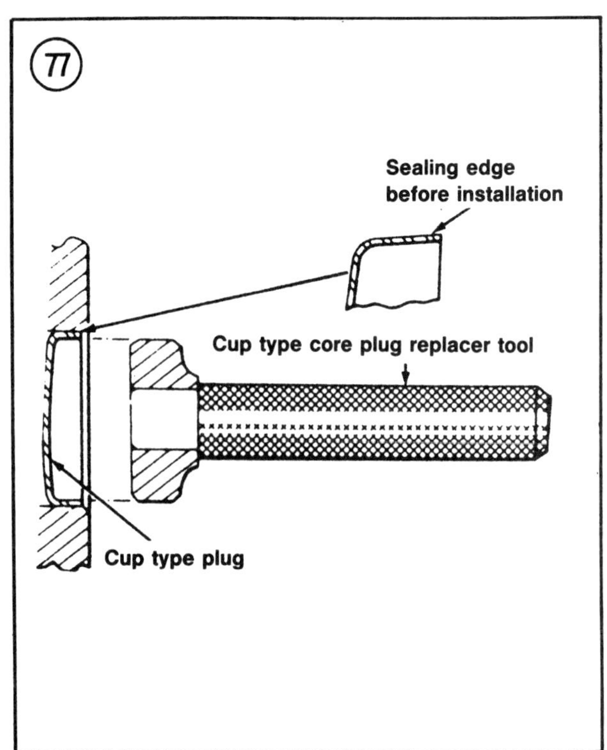

Table 1 GM V6 AND V8 ENGINE SPECIFICATIONS

Engine type	90° V6 or V8
Bore	
V6 and 5.7L V8	4.00 in.
5.0L V8	3.736 in.
Stroke	3.480 in.
Displacement	
4.3L V6	262 cid
5.0L V8	305 cid
5.7L V8	350 cid
Firing order	
V6	1-6-5-4-3-2
V8	1-8-4-3-6-5-7-2
Cylinder arrangement	
V6	
Port bank	1-3-5
Starboard bank	2-4-6
V8	
Port bank	1-3-5-7
Starboard bank	2-4-6-8

(continued)

Table 1 GM V6 AND V8 ENGINE SPECIFICATIONS (continued)

Cylinder bore	
Out-of-round	
Production	0.001 in. max.
Service	0.002 in. max.
Taper	
Production	
Thrust side	0.0005 in. max.
Relief side	0.001 in. max.
Service	0.001 in. max.
Piston clearance	
Production	0.0007-0.0017 in. max.
Service	0.0027 in. max.
Piston ring	
Ring groove clearance	
Compression	0.0012-0.0032 in.
Oil	0.002-0.007 in.
Ring gap	
Top	0.010-0.020 in.
2nd	0.010-0.025 in.
Oil	0.015-0.055 in.
Piston pin	
Diameter	0.9270-0.9273 in.
Clearance	
In piston	0.00025-0.00035 in.
Fit in rod	0.0008-0.0016 (interference)
Camshaft	
Lobe lift	
V6	
Intake	0.234 in.
Exhaust	0.257 in.
V8	
Intake	0.269 in.
Exhaust	0.276 in.
Journal diameter	1.8682-1.8692 in.
Runout	0.0015 in.
End play	0.004-0.012 in.
Crankshaft	
Main journal diameter	
No. 1	2.4484-2.4493 in.
No. 2, 3 and 4 (No. 2 and 3 V6)	2.4481-2.4490 in.
No. 5 (No. 4 V6)	2.4479-2.4488 in.
Taper	
Production	0.0002 in.
Service	0.001 in.
Out-of-round	
Production	0.0002 in.
Service	0.001 in.
Main bearing clearance	
Production	
No. 1	0.0008-0.0020 in.
No. 2, 3 and 4 (No. 2 and 3 V6)	0.0011-0.0023 in.
No. 5 (No. 4 V6)	0.0017-0.0032 in.

(continued)

7

Table 1 GM V6 AND V8 ENGINE SPECIFICATIONS (continued)

Crankshaft (cont.)	
Main bearing clearance (cont.)	
Service	
No. 1	0.001-0.0015 in.
No. 2, 3 and 4 (No. 2 and 3 V6)	0.001-0.0020 in.
No. 5 (No. 4 V6)	0.0025-0.0030 in.
End play	0.002-0.006 in.
Crankpin	
Diameter	2.0986-2.0998 in.
Taper	
Production	0.0005 in.
Service	0.001 in. max.
Out-of-round	
Production	0.0005 in.
Service	0.001 in. max.
Connecting rod	
Bearing clearance	
Production	0.0013-0.0035 in.
Service	0.0030 in. max.
Side clearance	0.008-0.014 in.
Valve train	
Lifter	Hydraulic
Rocker arm ratio	1.5:1
Valve lash	1 turn down from zero lash
Face angle	45°
Seat angle	46°
Seat width	
Intake	1/32-1/16 in.
Exhaust	1/16-3/32 in.
Stem clearance	0.0010-0.0027 in.
Valve spring	
Free length	2.03 in.
Installed height	1 23/32 in.
Damper free length	1.86 in.
Load	
Closed	76-84 lb. @ 1.70 in.
Open	194-206 lb. @ 1.25 in.

Table 2 V6 AND V8 TIGHTENING TORQUES

Fastener	ft.-lb.	N•m
Camshaft sprocket	20	27
Connecting rod caps	45	61
Cylinder head bolts	65	88
Distributor clamp	20	27
Exhaust manifold		
V6	18-22	24-30
V8		
Attaching nuts	20-26	27-35
High rise elbow	10-12	14-16

(continued)

Table 2 V6 AND V8 TIGHTENING TORQUES (continued)

Fastener	ft.-lb.	N•m
Flywheel-to-crankshaft	60	81
Front cover	7	9
Harmonic balancer	60	81
Intake manifold	30	41
Main bearing caps	70	95
Oil filter bypass valve	7	9
Oil pan		
1/4-20	7	9
5/16-18	23	30
Oil pump		
Attaching bolts	65	88
Cover screws	7	9
Temperature sending unit	20	27
Valve cover	3	5
Water pump	30	41

Table 3 STANDARD TORQUE VALUES

Fastener	ft.-lb.	N•m
Grade 5		
1/4-20	8	11
1/4-28	8	11
5/16-18	17	23
5/16-24	20	27
3/8-16	30	40
3/8-24	35	47
7/16-14	50	68
7/16-20	55	75
1/2-13	75	100
1/2-20	85	115
9/16-12	105	142
9/16-18	115	156
Grade 6		
1/4-20	10.5	14
1/4-28	12.5	17
5/16-18	22.5	31
5/16-24	25	54
3/8-16	40	34
3/8-24	45	61
7/16-14	65	88
7/16-20	70	95
1/2-13	100	136
1/2-20	110	149
9/16-12	135	183
9/16-18	150	203

Chapter Eight

Ford V8 Engines

The 302 cid (5.0L) and 351 cid (5.8L) engines are lightweight, small block V8 designs manufactured by Ford Motor Company. Both engines use a 4 inch bore; the 302 cid (5.0L) has a shorter stroke than the 351 cid (5.8L). The two engines are closely related in design, but the 351 cid (5.8L) has a taller block with longer pushrods and connecting rods. The 460 cid (7.5L) engine is a big block V8 design manufactured by Ford Motor Company.

The cylinders are numbered from front to rear: 1-2-3-4 on the starboard bank and 5-6-7-8 on the port bank. Valve arrangement from front to rear is I-E-I-E-I-E-I-E on the starboard bank and E-I-E-I-E-I-E-I on the port bank. The cylinder firing order is 1-5-4-2-6-3-7-8 on the 185 hp 302 cid (5.0L) and 460 cid (7.5L) engines and 1-3-7-2-6-5-4-8 on the 200 hp 302 cid (5.0L HO) and 351 cid (5.8L) engines. Hydraulic valve lifters and pushrods operate the rocker arms and valves. No lash adjustment is necessary in service or during assembly unless some component in the valve train has been replaced.

The crankshaft is supported by 5 main bearings, with the No. 3 bearing taking the end thrust. Crankshaft rotation is counterclockwise when seen from the drive unit end of the engine.

The chain-driven camshaft is supported by 5 bearings and is located above the crankshaft between the 2 cylinder banks.

The oil pump is located on the bottom front of the engine block and is driven by the distributor through an intermediate shaft. **Figure 1A** shows the internal components typical of the 302 cid (5.0L) and 351 cid (5.8L) engines.

Specifications (**Table 1** and **Table 2**) and tightening torques (**Table 3** and **Table 4**) are at the end of the chapter.

ENGINE SERIAL NUMBER

Engine identification is provided on a white tape label located on the front of the left valve cover. **Figure 1B** shows a typical label. This information identifies if there are unique parts or if internal changes have been made during the model year. It is important when

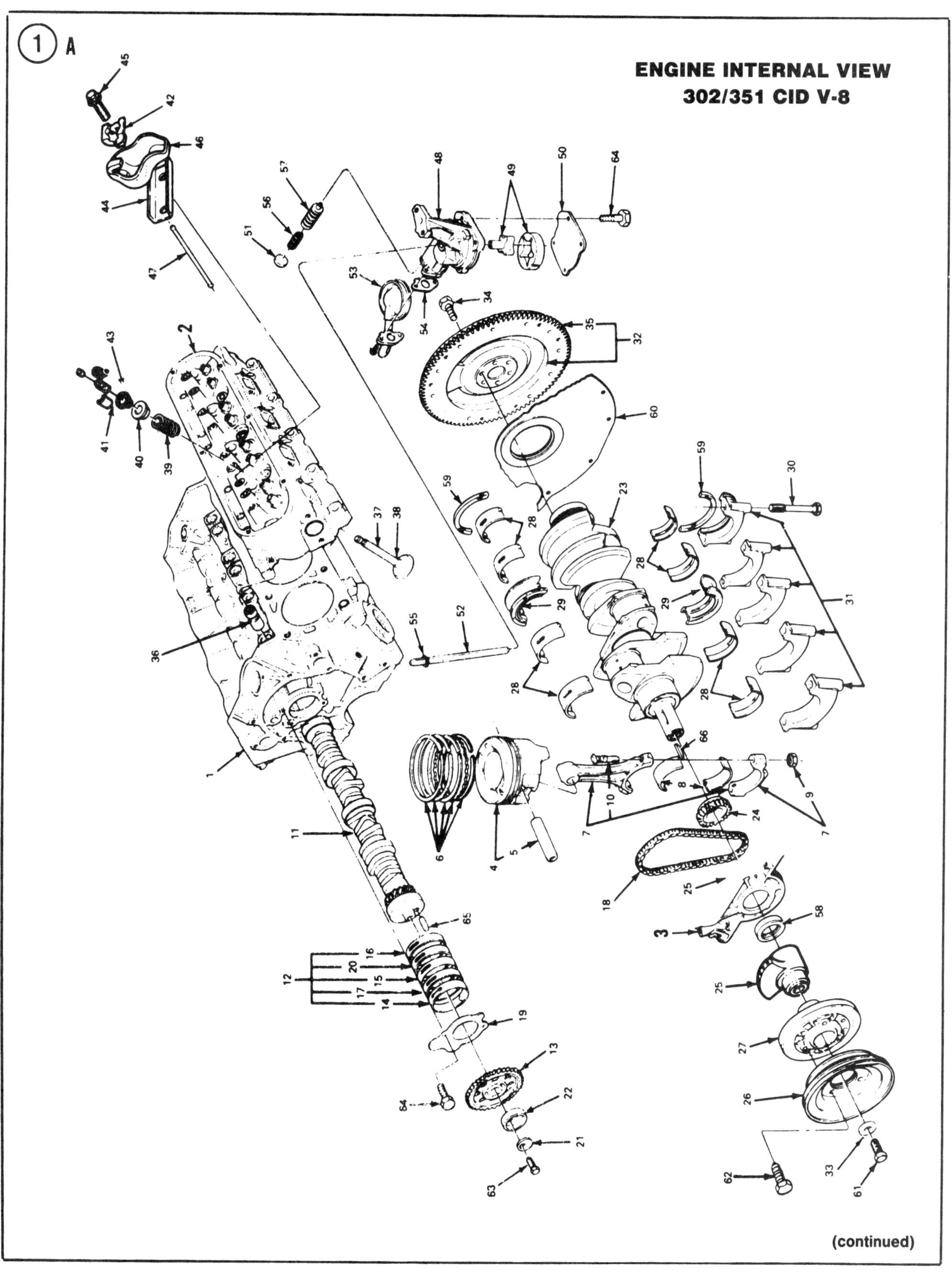
1 A
ENGINE INTERNAL VIEW
302/351 CID V-8
(continued)

1 A (continued)

1. Block assembly
2. Cylinder head
3. Cylinder front plate
4. Piston assembly
5. Piston pin
6. Piston ring set
7. Connecting rod assembly
8. Connecting rod bearing
9. Connecting rod nut
10. Connecting rod bolt
11. Camshaft
12. Camshaft bearing kit (standard)
13. Camshaft sprocket
14. Camshaft front bearing
15. Camshaft center bearing
16. Camshaft rear bearing
17. Camshaft front intermediate bearing
18. Timing chain
19. Camshaft thrust plate
20. Camshaft rear intermediate bearing
21. Camshaft sprocket washer
22. Two-piece fuel pump eccentric
23. Crankshaft assembly
24. Crankshaft sprocket
25. Crankshaft oil slinger
26. Pulley assembly
27. Crankshaft damper assembly
28. Crankshaft main bearing (except center)
29. Crankshaft bearing (center)
30. Crankshaft main bearing cap bolt
31. Main bearing cap
32. Flywheel assembly
33. Crankshaft pulley retaining washer
34. Flywheel-to-crankshaft bolt
35. Flywheel ring gear
36. Hydraulic tappet assembly
37. Exhaust valve
38. Intake valve
39. Valve spring
40. Valve spring retainer
41. Valve spring retainer key
42. Valve rocker arm fulcrum seat
43. Valve stem seal
44. Valve pushrod valley baffle
45. Valve rocker arm attaching bolt
46. Valve rocker arm
47. Valve pushrod
48. Oil pump assembly
49. Oil pump drive rotor and shaft assembly
50. Oil pump body plate
51. Oil pump relief valve plug
52. Oil pump intermediate shaft assembly
53. Oil pump screen, tube, and cover assembly
54. Oil pump inlet tube gasket
55. Oil pump intermediate shaft O-ring
56. Oil pump relief valve spring
57. Oil pump relief valve plunger
58. Cylinder front seal
59. Crankshaft rear packing
60. Engine rear plate
61. Bolt
62. Bolt
63. Bolt
64. Bolt
65. Dowel pin
66. Woodruff key

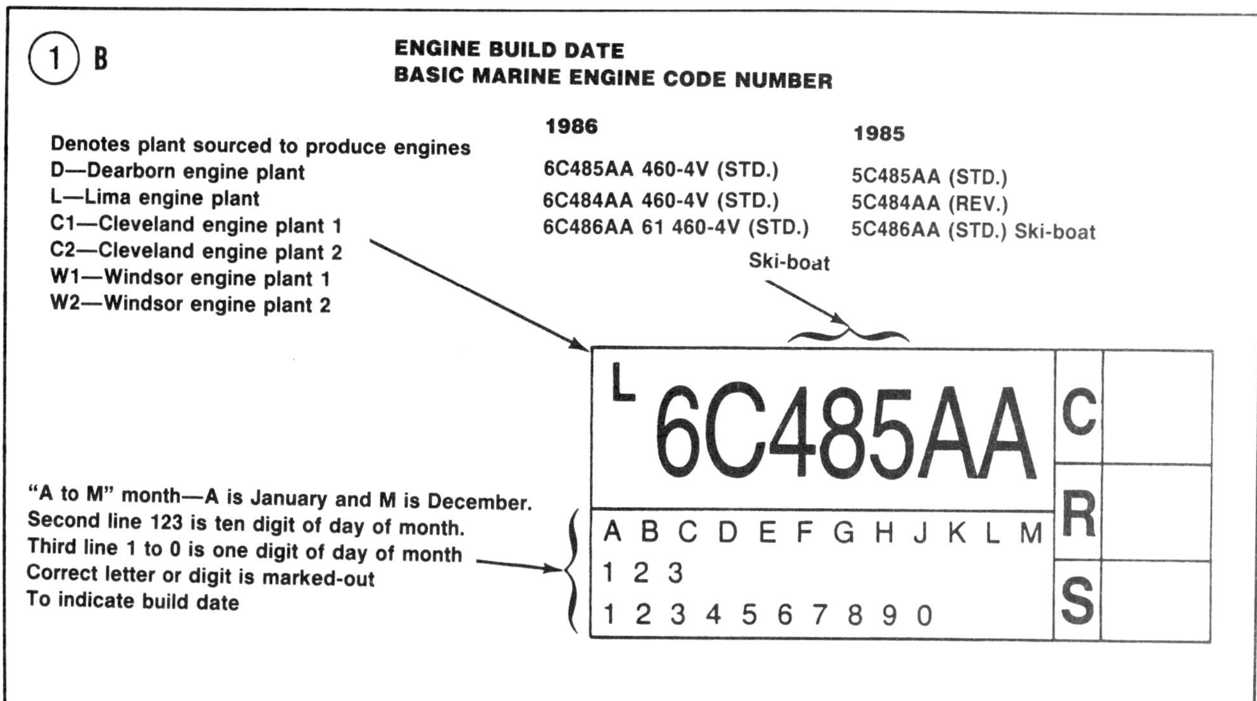

ordering replacement parts for the engine. If the label has been defaced or painted over, it will be very hard to distinguish between the various engine levels (standard output vs. low output or standard rotation vs. reverse rotation). For this reason, it is a good idea to copy the information on a 3×5 in. card and keep it in a safe place in case the information is required for engine service.

SPECIAL TOOLS

Where special tools are required or recommended for engine overhaul, the tool numbers are provided. While these tools can sometimes be rented from rental dealers, they can be purchased from Owatonna Tools Inc., 2013 4th Street N.W., Owatonna, Minnesota 55060.

GASKET SEALANT

Gasket sealant is used instead of pre-formed gaskets betwen numerous mating surfaces on the engines covered in this chapter. See *Gasket Sealant*, Chapter Six.

REPLACEMENT PARTS

Various changes are made to automotive engine blocks used for marine applications. Numerous part changes are required due to operation in fresh and salt water. For example, the cylinder head gasket must be corrosion-resistant. Marine engines use head gaskets of copper or stainless steel instead of the standard steel used in automotive applications. Brass expansion or core plugs must be used instead of the steel plugs found in automotive blocks.

Since marine engines are run at or near maximum rpm most of the time, the use of special valve lifters, springs, pistons, bearings, camshafts and other heavy-duty moving components is necessary for maximum life and performance.

For these reasons, automotive-type parts should not be substituted for marine components. In addition, OMC recommends that only OMC parts be used. Parts offered by other manufacturers may look alike, but may not be manufactured to OMC specifications.

Any damage resulting from the use of other than OMC parts is not covered by the OMC warranty.

ENGINE REMOVAL

Some service procedures can be performed with the engine in the boat; others require removal. The boat design and service procedure to be performed will determine whether the engine must be removed.

If the clearance between the front of the engine and the engine compartment bulkhead is less than 6 in., the stern drive unit must be removed in order to disengage the driveshaft from the engine coupler.

The stern drive must also be removed if engine mount height must be altered during engine removal.

WARNING
The engine is heavy, awkward to handle and has sharp edges. It may shift or drop suddenly during removal. To prevent serious injury, always observe the following precautions.
1. Never place any part of your body where a moving or falling engine may trap, cut or crush you.
2. If you must push the engine during removal, use a board or similar tool to keep your hands out of danger.
3. Be sure the hoist is designed to lift engines and has enough load capacity for your engine.
4. Be sure the hoist is securely attached to safe lifting points on the engine.
5. The engine should not be difficult to lift with a proper hoist. If it is, stop lifting, lower the engine back onto its mounts and make sure the engine has been completely separated from the vessel.

1. Remove the engine hood cover and all panels that interfere with engine removal. Place the cover and panels to one side out of the way.

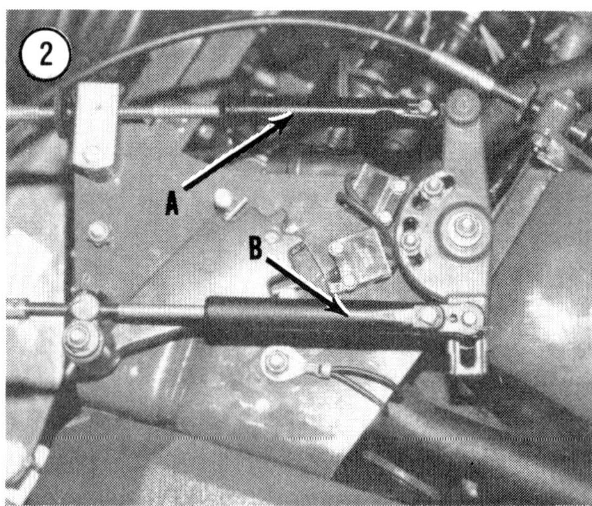

2. Disconnect the negative battery cable, then the positive battery cable. As a precaution, remove the battery from the boat.
3. Use a flare nut wrench to loosen and disconnect both power steering hydraulic lines at the actuator unit. Cap the lines and plug the actuator fittings to prevent leakage and the entry of contamination. Secure the lines at a point higher than the engine power steering pump during the remainder of this procedure to prevent damage or the loss of fluid.
4. Disconnect the fuel inlet line from the tank to the fuel filter canister at the filter canister. Cap the line and canister fitting to prevent leakage and the entry of contamination.
5. Locate and unplug all electrical harness connectors. This step will include the:
   a. Rubber 2-wire trim/tilt sender connector.
   b. Plastic 3-wire trim/tilt wire connector.
   c. Rubber 3-wire trim/tilt instrument cable connector.
   d. Rubber instrument cable connector.
   e. Battery cable lead at the starter solenoid.
   f. Black ground lead at engine stud near starter motor.
6. Loosen the 8 exhaust hose clamps. Lubricating the exhaust pipe with

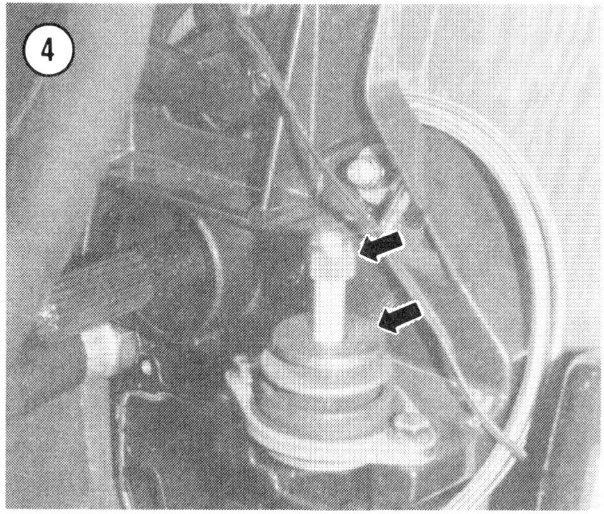

dishwashing liquid will make it easier to move the lower hose. Pry or twist the lower hose from the exhaust adapter and slide it down the exhaust pipe. Remove the adapter and upper hose from the exhaust manifold.

7. Refer to **Figure 2** and remove the remote control (A) and transom bracket (B) shift cables from the engine shift bracket. Remove the cables from each of the anchor pockets and disconnect from the shift lever. Secure the adjustable trunnion to the remote control cable with tape to prevent misadjustment when the cable is reinstalled.

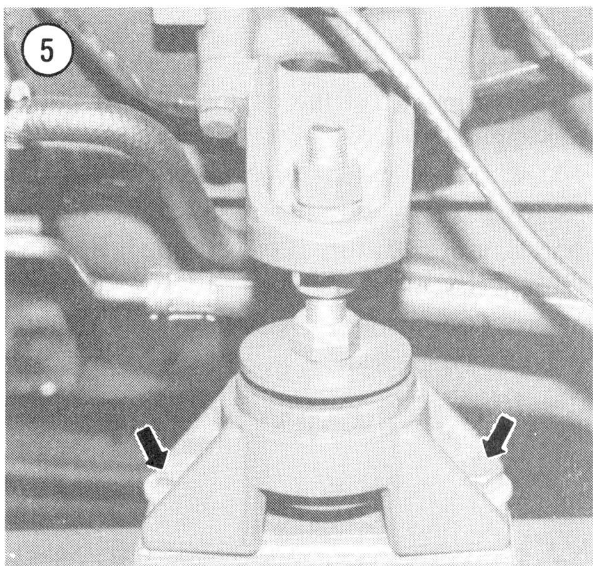

8. Disconnect the throttle cable at the carburetor and manifold anchor block. See A and B, **Figure 3**.

9. Loosen the water supply hose clamp and remove the hose from the transom bracket water tube.

10. Attach a suitable hoist to the engine lifting brackets. The hoist must have a minimum lift capacity of 1,500 lb. Raise the hoist enough to remove all slack.

NOTE
At this point, there should be no hoses, wires or linkage connecting the engine to the boat or stern drive unit. Recheck this to make sure nothing will hamper engine removal.

11. Remove and save the self-locking nut and flat washer from each rear engine mount. See **Figure 4**.

12. Remove and save the lag screws at each front engine mount. See **Figure 5**.

13A. If the stern drive was removed, lift the engine up and out of the engine compartment.

13B. If the stern drive was not removed, lift the engine enough to pull it forward and disengage the driveshaft from the engine flywheel coupler. Once the driveshaft is free of the coupler, lift the engine up and out of the engine compartment.

14. If the exhaust pipe requires service, remove the 4 retaining screws and the top port trim line clamp, if so equipped. Remove the exhaust pipe and discard the seal. Clean all residue from the transom bracket and exhaust pipe surface.

ENGINE INSTALLATION

Engine installation is the reverse of removal, plus the following:

1. If the exhaust pipe was serviced, coat a new seal with OMC Adhesive M and install in transom bracket groove. Wipe exhaust pipe screw threads with OMC Gasket Sealing Compound. Install exhaust pipe to transom bracket and tighten screws to 10-12 ft.-lb. (14-16 N•m).
2. Install any shims or adapters used with the engine mounts.
3. Install forward mount lag screws securely and tighten the rear mount self-locking nuts to 28-30 ft.-lb. (38-40 N•m).
4. If stern drive was removed, perform the *Engine Alignment* procedure as described in this chapter after securing the engine mounts.
5. Lubricate the transom bracket shift cable anchor with OMC Triple-Guard grease.
6. Fill the engine with an oil recommended in Chapter Four.
7. Fill the cooling system, if equipped with a closed system. See Chapter Five.
8. Adjust the drive belts. See Chapter Ten.
9. Adjust the timing as required. See Chapter Four.

REAR ENGINE MOUNTS

WARNING
The engine is heavy and may shift or drop suddenly. Never place your hands or any part of your body where the moving engine may trap or crush you. If you can't remove the mounts without placing your hands where the moving engine may injure them, support the engine with a jackstand as well as a hoist to be certain the engine can't fall on you.

Engine mounts are non-adjustable and rarely require service. Replace any broken or deteriorated mounts immediately to reduce strain on remaining mounts and drive line components.

Removal

1. Attach a suitable hoist to the engine lifting brackets. The hoist must have a minimum lift capacity of 1,500 lb. Raise the hoist enough to remove all slack.
2. Remove and save the self-locking nut and flat washer from each rear engine mount. See **Figure 4**.
3. Lift the engine off the rear mounts with the hoist, then remove the screws and washers holding the mount assembly. Remove the mount assembly from the transom plate.
4. To disassemble the mount, clamp it in a vise. Hold the square nut with a suitable open-end wrench and remove the bolt. Separate the mount and 2 flat washers (early models) or 1 flat and 1 conical washer (late models).
5. To reassemble the mount, place a flat washer (early model) or conical washer (late model) on the bolt (the concave side of the conical washer should face the mount). Install bolt through the flat side (bottom) of the mount. Place the other washer on the bolt and install the nut finger-tight.

NOTE
The 90 degree relationship established between the nut and mounting holes in Step 6 must be maintained or the engine mount pad slot will not engage the rear mount during installation.

6. Clamp the mount assembly in a vise. Align the mount holes 90° to any side of the square nut. Holding the mount in this position, tighten the bolt to 18-20 ft.-lb. (24-27 N•m).
7. Position the mount assembly on the transom plate. Reinstall the screws with washers and tighten to 20-25 ft.-lb. (27-34 N•m).
8. Lower the engine with the hoist until the mount pad slot engages the square nut. Reinstall the flat washer and self-locking nut. Tighten nut to 28-30 ft.-lb. (38-41 N•m).

ENGINE ALIGNMENT

To assure satisfactory engine/drivetrain life, engine alignment must be checked during reinstallation whenever stern drive unit removal is required for engine removal. Correct alignment is provided by adjusting the front mounts up or down as required. OMC alignment tool part No. 912273 with universal handle part No. 311880 is required to perform this procedure.

Slide the alignment tool through the gimbal housing from outside the boat. The tool must fit through the gimbal bearing and into the engine coupler easily. If the tool binds, adjust the front engine mounts in the proper direction to remove the binding.

Engine mount adjustment is made by loosening the nut and rearranging the shim washer on the mount screw. When alignment is correct, retighten the front mount to maintain alignment. Tighten the nut to 100-120 ft.-lb. (136-163 N•m).

DISASSEMBLY CHECKLISTS

To use the checklists, remove and inspect each part in the order mentioned. To reassemble, go through the checklists backwards, installing the parts in order. Each major part is covered in its own section in this chapter, unless otherwise noted.

Decarbonizing or Valve Service

1. Remove the valve covers.
2. Remove the intake and exhaust manifolds.
3. Remove the rocker arms.
4. Remove the cylinder heads.
5. Remove and inspect the valves. Inspect the valve guides and seats, repairing or replacing as required.
6. Assemble by reversing Steps 1-5.

Valve and Ring Service

1. Perform Steps 1-5 of *Decarbonizing or Valve Service.*
2. Remove the oil pan and oil pump.
3. Remove the pistons with connecting rods.
4. Remove the piston rings. It is not necessary to separate the pistons from the connecting rods unless a piston, connecting rod or piston pin needs repair or replacement.
5. Assemble by reversing Steps 1-4.

General Overhaul

1. Remove the engine from the boat.
2. Remove the flywheel.
3. Remove the mount brackets and oil pressure sending unit from the engine.
4. If available, mount the engine on an engine stand. These can be rented from equipment rental dealers. The stand is not absolutely necessary, but it will make the job much easier.
5. Remove the following accessories or components from the engine, if present:
   a. Alternator and mounting bracket.
   b. Power steering pump and mounting bracket.
   c. Spark plug wires and distributor cap.
   d. Carburetor and fuel lines.
   e. Oil dipstick and tube.
   f. Seawater pump, if so equipped.
6. Check the engine for signs of coolant or oil leaks.

7. Clean the outside of the engine.
8. Remove the distributor. See Chapter Eleven.
9. Remove all hoses and tubes connected to the engine.
10. Remove the fuel pump. See Chapter Nine.
11. Remove the intake and exhaust manifolds.
12. Remove the thermostat. See Chapter Ten.
13. Remove the valve covers and rocker arms.
14. Remove the crankshaft pulley, vibration damper, front cover and water pump. Remove the timing chain and sprockets.
15. Remove the camshaft.
16. Remove the cylinder heads.
17. Remove the oil pan and oil pump.
18. Remove the pistons and connecting rods.
19. Remove the crankshaft.
20. Inspect the cylinder block.
21. Assemble by reversing Steps 1-19.

VALVE COVERS

Removal/Installation

1. Disconnect the crankcase ventilation hose at the valve cover and remove the PCV valve from the cover.
2. Disconnect the spark plug cables at the plugs and remove the plug cable retainers from their brackets on the cover.
3. Remove the exhaust manifold as described in this chapter.
4. Remove the cover attaching screws.
5. Rap the valve cover with a soft-faced mallet to break the gasket seal. Remove the valve cover.
6. Clean any gasket residue from the cylinder head and valve cover with degreaser and a putty knife.
7. Coat one side of a new gasket with an oil-resistant sealer. Install the gasket sealer-side down on the cylinder head.
8. Position the valve cover on the cylinder head.
9. Install the attaching screws and tighten to specifications (**Table 3**). Wait 2 minutes, then retighten the screws to the same specification.
10. Install the spark plug cable retainers on the valve cover brackets. Connect the wires to the appropriate spark plugs. See Chapter Four.
11. Install the PCV valve in the valve cover and reconnect the crankcase ventilation hose to the PCV valve.

INTAKE MANIFOLD

Removal/Installation

Refer to **Figure 6A** (5.0L and 5.8L) or **Figure 6B** (7.5L) for this procedure.
2. Disconnect the crankcase ventilation hose from the PCV valve and carburetor.
3. Remove the flame arrestor.

6 A

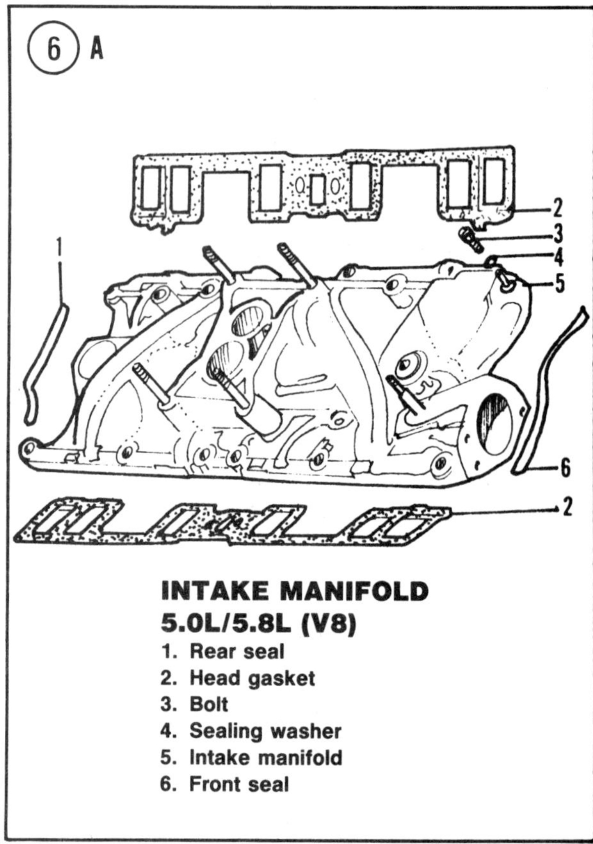

INTAKE MANIFOLD
5.0L/5.8L (V8)
1. Rear seal
2. Head gasket
3. Bolt
4. Sealing washer
5. Intake manifold
6. Front seal

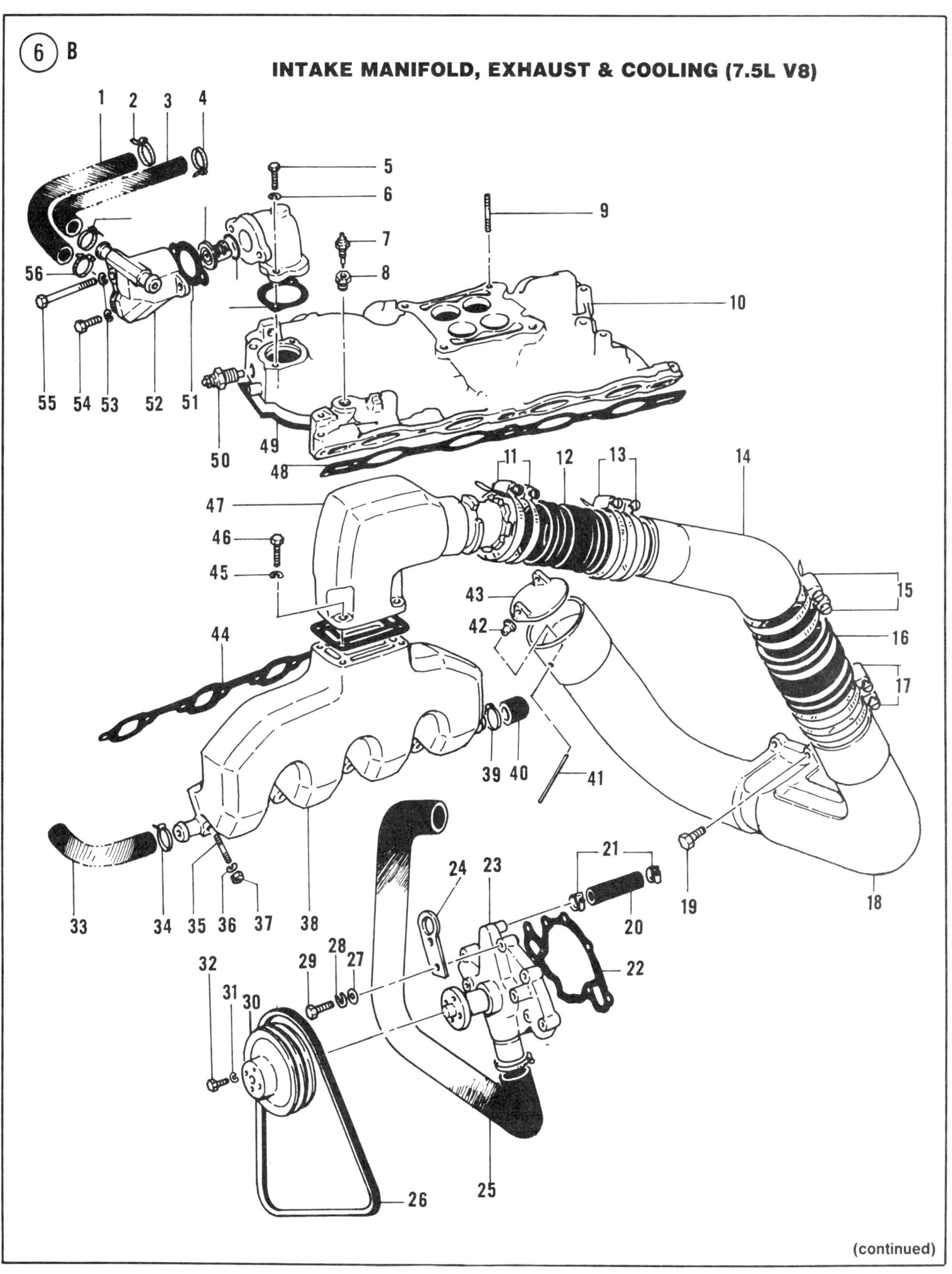
6 B
INTAKE MANIFOLD, EXHAUST & COOLING (7.5L V8)
1
2
3
4
5
6
7
8
9
10
11
12
13
14
15
16
17
18
19
20
21
22
23
24
25
26
27
28
29
30
31
32
33
34
35
36
37
38
39
40
41
42
43
44
45
46
47
48
49
50
51
52
53
54
55
56

(continued)

4. Open the cylinder block water drains and allow all water to drain. Remove the thermostat housing.
5. 7.5L—Loosen the water pump bypass hose clamp at the intake manifold.
6. Disconnect the throttle cable linkage at the carburetor and anchor block. See **Figure 7** (typical).
7. Remove the ESA module shift bracket and solenoid assembly.
8. Disconnect all electrical connectors and vacuum lines or hoses at the carburetor.
9. Disconnect the spark plug cables at the distributor cap and the coil.
10. Disconnect the fuel pump vent hose.
11. Remove the distributor cap and place it (with plug cables attached) to one side out of the way.
12. Mark the position of the distributor rotor relative to the intake manifold. Loosen the hold-down clamp and remove the distributor. See Chapter Eleven.
13. Disconnect the fuel inlet line at the carburetor. Cap the line and plug the fitting to

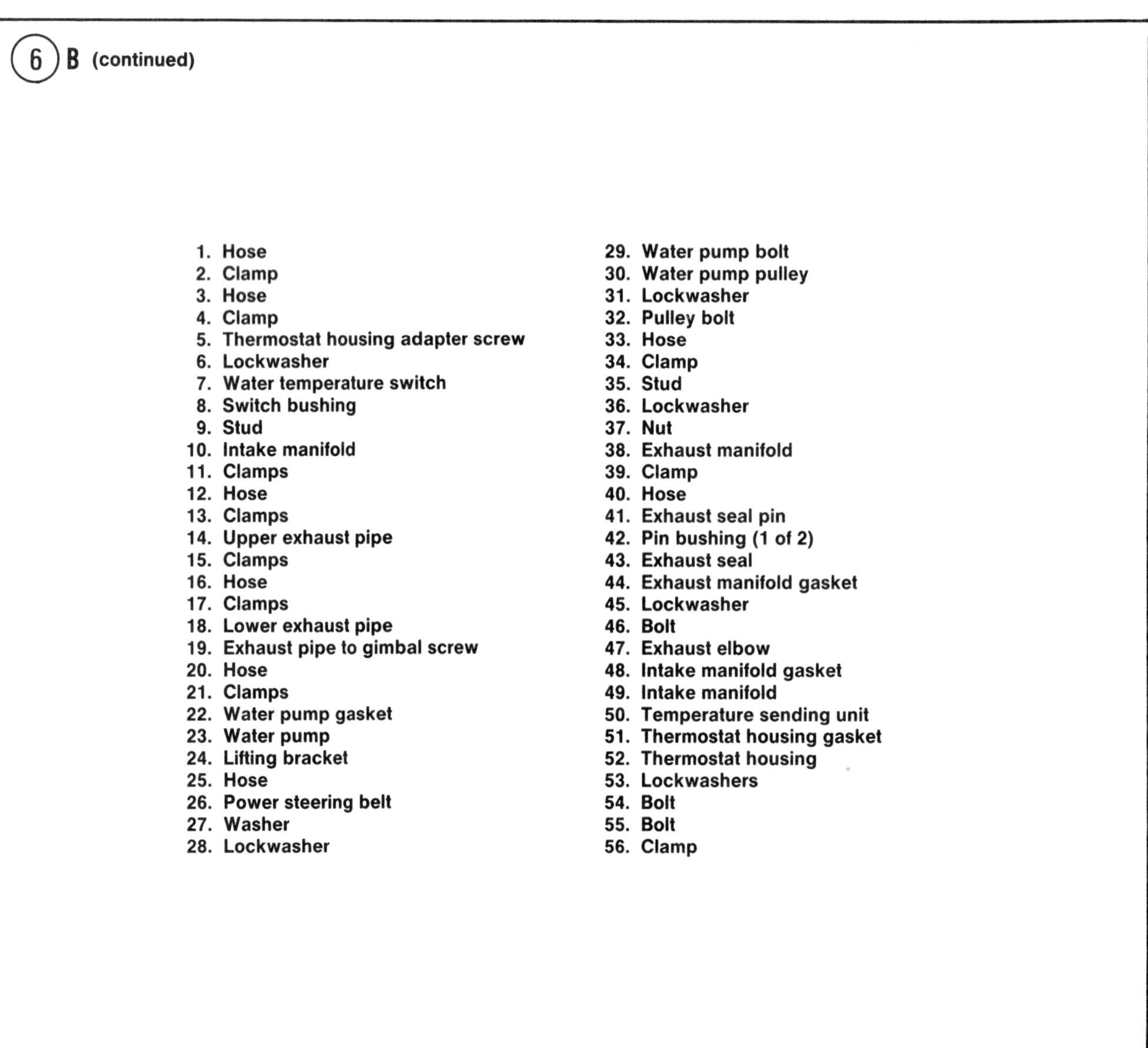

prevent leakage and the entry of contamination.

14. Remove the coil and bracket from the manifold.

15. Disconnect any remaining wire harness connections which will interfere with manifold removal.

16. Loosen and remove the intake manifold fasteners. Pry the manifold loose and remove it from the engine block with the carburetor attached.

17. Remove and discard the intake manifold gaskets and seals. Discard the attaching bolt sealing washers.

18. Clean all gasket residue from the block, cylinder heads and intake manifold with degreaser and a putty knife.

19. If the intake manifold is being replaced, transfer the carburetor, throttle cable anchor block unit, distributor clamp and temperature sending unit, if so equipped, as well as any other hardware that might be installed.

20. Run a 1/8 in. diameter bead of RTV sealant in and along the joint (full width) of the cylinder block seal mounting surface (all 4 corners). See **Figure 8**.

21. Install the new manifold-to-head gaskets and the front/rear intake manifold seals.

22. Run a 1/16 in. diameter bead of RTV sealant at the outer end of each seal (full width of seal). See **Figure 9**.

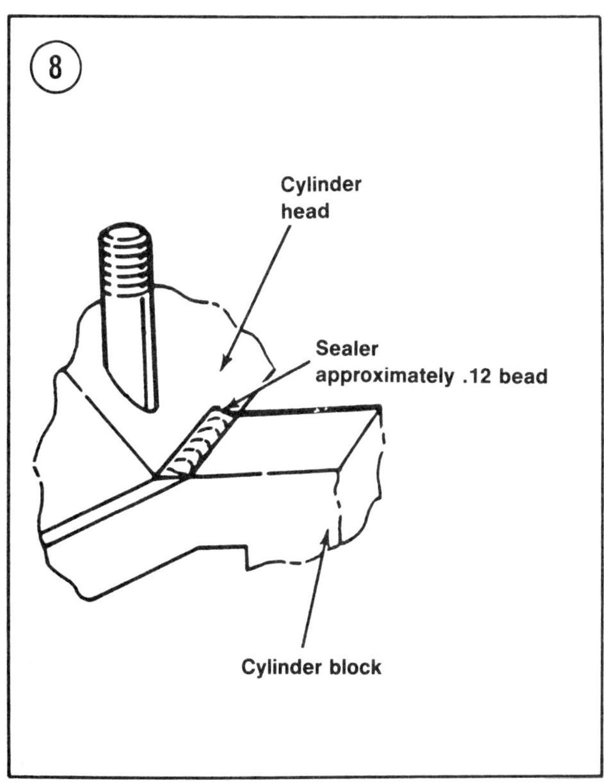

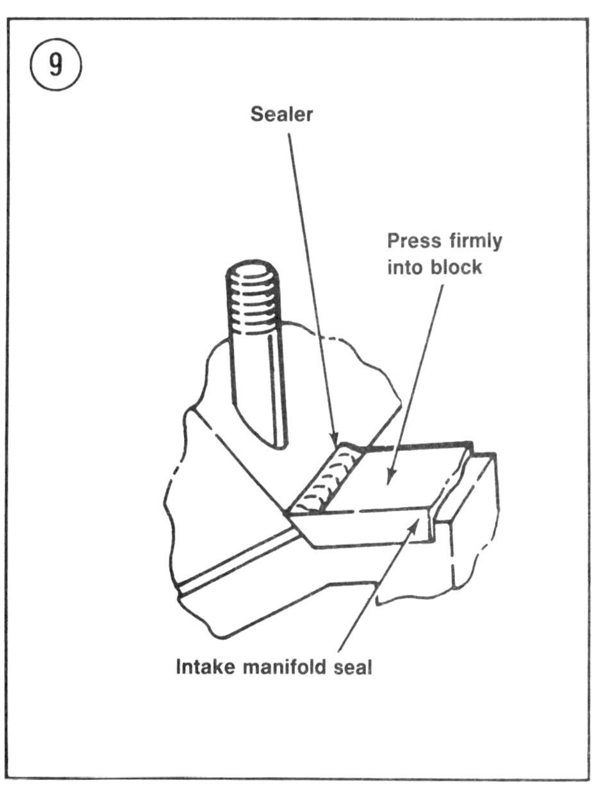

23. Lower the intake manifold into position on the cylinder block. Check the seal area to make sure the seals are in their proper position. If not, remove the manifold, correct the seal position and reinstall the manifold.
24. Install the manifold attaching fasteners. Tighten the manifold fasteners to specifications (**Table 3**) in the sequence shown in **Figure 10**.
25. Reverse Steps 1-15 to complete installation. Coat all electrical connections with OMC black neoprene dip (part No. 909570).

Inspection

1. Check the intake manifold for cracks or distortion. Replace if manifold is distorted or if cracks are found.
2. Check the mating surfaces for nicks or burrs. Small burrs may be removed with an oilstone.
3. Place a straightedge across the manifold flange/mating surfaces. If there is any gap between the straightedge and surface, measure it with a flat feeler gauge. Measure each manifold from end to end and from corner to corner. If the mating surface is not flat within 0.003 in. (0.15 mm) per 6 in. of manifold length or 0.006 in. overall, replace the manifold.

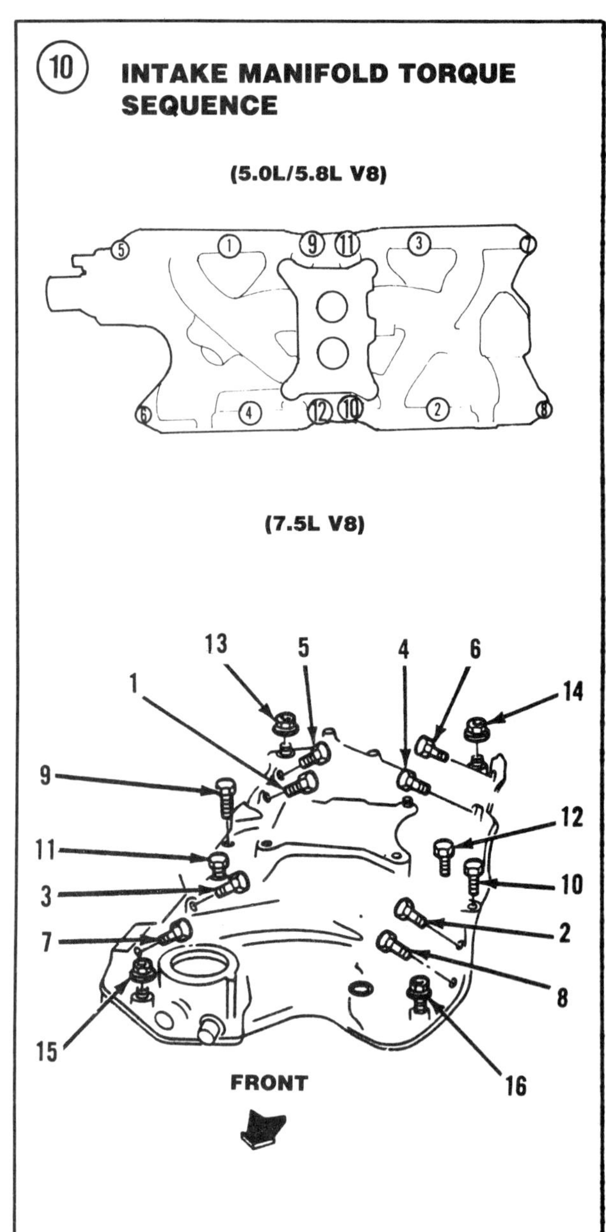

EXHAUST MANIFOLDS

Removal/Installation

Refer to **Figure 6** (typical) for this procedure.

1. Disconnect the negative battery cable.
2. Open the cylinder block water drains and remove the rubber caps **(Figure 11).** Allow all water to drain.

3A. 5.0L/5.8L—Open the cylinder block and exhaust manifold water drains.

3B. 7.5L—Disconnect the water hose(s) from the manifold(s). Drain any water remaining in the manifold housing and elbow.

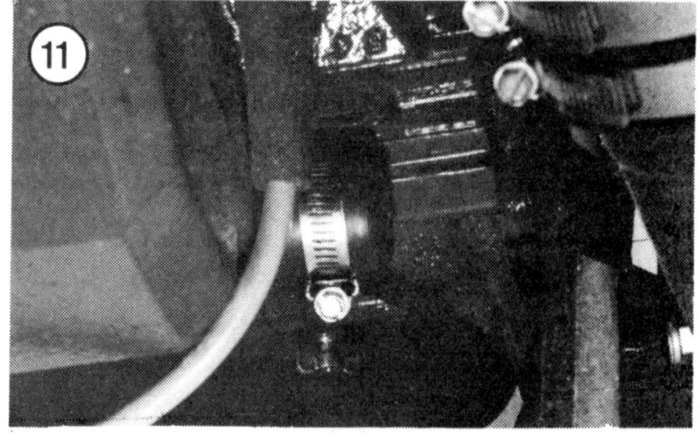

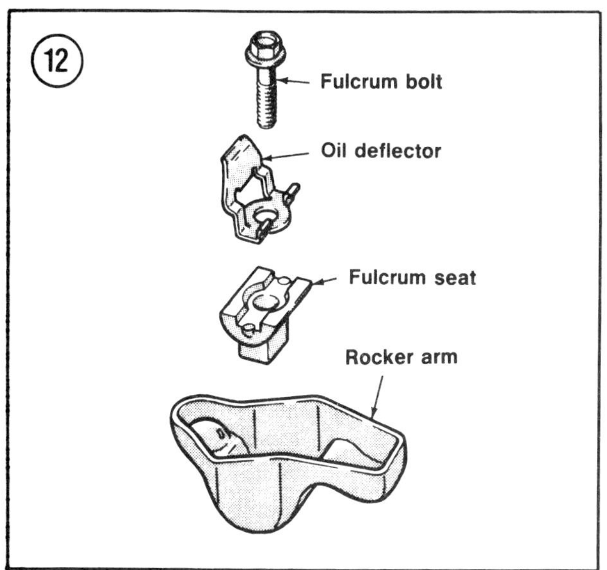

4. Unclamp the upper exhaust hose at the exhaust elbow. Lubricate the lower hose and exhaust pipe with a solution of soapy water, then slide the hose down onto the pipe.
5. Disconnect the high-rise hose from the exhaust elbow.
6. Remove the 4 fasteners holding the high-rise elbow to the exhaust manifold. Rap the elbow with a soft-faced hammer to break the gasket seal, then remove the elbow.
7. Disconnect the spark plug cables from the spark plugs.
8. Remove the manifold attaching locknuts and washers. Discard the locknuts. Remove water hose and oil dipstick tube clamps from studs if so equipped. Remove the manifold.
9. Clean all gasket residue from the cylinder head, manifold and high-rise elbow mating surfaces with degreaser and a putty knife.

NOTE

Make sure the gasket is correctly positioned in Step 10. If the connecting bar between exhaust openings is not facing down, the gasket will block off part of each exhaust port.

10. Install the manifold on the cylinder head with a new gasket.
11. Install new washers and locknuts. Tighten the locknuts to 20-26 ft.-lb. (27-35 N•m).
12. Install high-rise elbow with a new gasket coated on both sides with OMC Gasket Sealing Compound and tighten fasteners to 12-14 ft.-lb. (16-19 N•m).
13. Reconnect the spark plugs and exhaust hose, then reverse Steps 1-3 to complete installation.

Inspection/Cleaning

1. Inspect the engine exhaust ports for signs of rust or corrosion. Replace manifold if such signs are found.
2. Check water passage in exhaust elbow for clogging.
3. Remove pipe plugs in manifold and exhaust elbow, if so equipped. Check for sand, silt or other foreign matter.
4. Every 300 hours or 3 years, soak the manifold and elbow for 90-120 minutes in muriatic acid (available from swimming pool supply houses) to loosen deposits. Wash thoroughly with fresh water and use a stiff rod to break free any deposits inside. Repeat the washing process a second time, then wash and blow dry with compressed air.
5. Have manifolds pressure-tested by a dealer. Replace manifold if it will not hold 10-15 psi.

ROCKER ARMS

Removal/Installation

Each rocker arm moves on its own fulcrum seat. The rocker arm and fulcrum seat are retained by a bolt. It is not necessary to remove the rocker arm for pushrod replacement; simply loosen the bolt and move the arm away from the pushrod. To remove the entire assembly, refer to **Figure 12** and proceed as follows.

1. Remove the valve cover as described in this chapter.
2. Remove the fulcrum bolt, oil deflector (if used), fulcrum seat and rocker arm from each valve.
3. Remove the pushrod, if necessary.
4. Repeat Step 2 and Step 3 for each remaining rocker arm. Place each rocker arm and pushrod assembly in a separate container or use a rack to keep them separated for reinstallation in the same position from which they were removed.
5. Installation is the reverse of removal. Wipe the top of each valve stem, the cylinder head pushrod guide, each rocker arm fulcrum seat and seat socket with Lubriplate 777 or equivalent. Make sure that each pushrod fits into its lifter cup. Tighten each fulcrum bolt to specifications (**Table 2**). If valve train components have been replaced, check the valve clearance as described in this chapter.

Inspection

1. Clean all parts with solvent and use compressed air to blow out the oil passages in the pushrods.
2. Check each rocker arm, fulcrum, bolt and pushrod for scuffing, pitting or excessive wear. Replace as required; do not try to repair a grooved radius on the pad at the valve end of the rocker arm. If one component is worn, replace all components servicing that valve.
3. Check pushrods for straightness by rolling them across a flat, even surface such as a pane of glass. Check runout of any pushrods that do not roll smoothly with a dial indicator. If runout exceeds 0.015 in. (0.38 mm), replace the pushrod(s).
4. If a pushrod is worn from lack of lubrication, replace the corresponding lifter and rocker arm as well.

Valve Clearance Adjustment

Stem-to-rocker arm clearance must be within specifications when the hydraulic lifter is completely collapsed. If valve clearance is insufficient, the valve opens early and closes late, resulting in a rough engine idle. Excessive clearance lets the valve open too late and close too early, causing valve bounce and damage to the camshaft lobe.

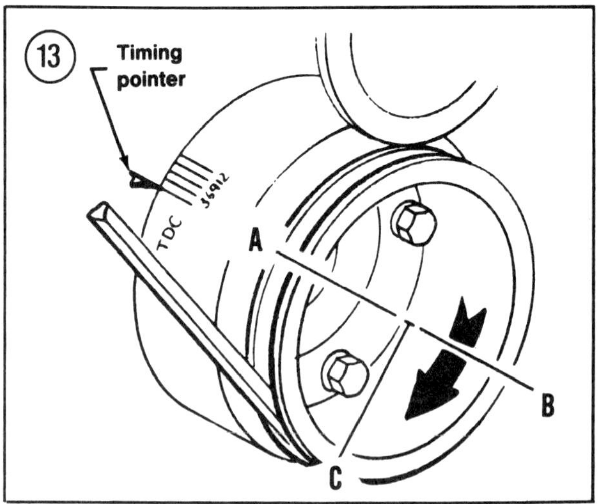

A positive stop rocker arm bolt eliminates valve clearance adjustment on these engines. However, you can compensate for wear in the valve train by installing a 0.060 in. longer or 0.060 in. shorter pushrod, as required. Whenever any component in the valve train is replaced, the following procedure should be performed to determine if pushrod replacement is necessary.

The cylinders are numbered 1-4 (starboard bank) and 5-8 (port bank) from front to rear. Valves on all engines are arranged from front to rear in the following order: I-E-I-E-I-E-I-E (starboard bank) and E-I-E-I-E-I-E-I (port bank).

Refer to **Figure 13** for this procedure.

1. Rotate the crankshaft until the pulley notch aligns with the zero mark on the timing tab. This positions the No. 1 cylinder at TDC. See A, **Figure 13.** This position can be verified by placing a finger on the No. 1 rocker arms as the pulley notch nears the zero mark. If the rocker arms are moving, the engine is

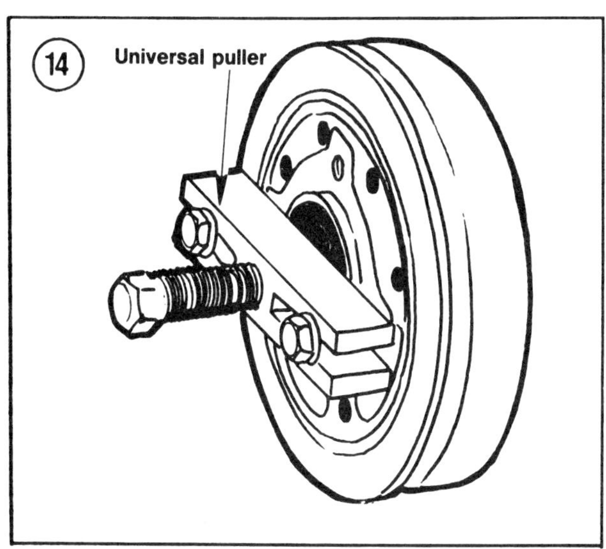

in the No. 6 firing position; rotate the crankshaft pulley one full turn to reach the No. 1 firing position.

2. Make a chalk mark at points B and C, **Figure 13**.

3. With the crankshaft in position A, **Figure 13**, install Ford tool part No. T71P-6513-A on the rocker arm of each valve listed below (in sequence). Apply pressure slowly to bleed the lifter down completely, hold the lifter down with the tool and check the clearance between the valve stem and rocker arm with a feeler gauge. Write down the clearance and repeat for each valve listed:

5.0L (Standard)/7.5L	5.0L (HO)/5.8L
a. No. 1 intake.	a. No. 1 intake.
b. No. 1 exhaust.	b. No. 1 exhaust.
c. No. 7 intake.	c. No. 4 intake.
d. No. 5 exhaust.	d. No. 3 exhaust.
e. No. 8 intake.	e. No. 8 intake.
f. No. 4 exhaust.	f. No. 7 exhaust.

4. Rotate crankshaft 180° to align position B mark with timing pointer. Repeat Step 3 to check clearance of the following valves:

5.0L (Standard)/7.5L	5.0L (HO)/5.8L
a. No. 4 intake.	a. No. 3 intake.
b. No. 2 exhaust.	b. No. 2 exhaust.
c. No. 5 intake.	c. No. 7 intake.
d. No. 6 exhaust.	d. No. 6 exhaust.

5. Rotate crankshaft another 270° to align position C mark with timing pointer. Repeat Step 3 to check clearance of the remaining valves:

5.0L (Standard)/7.5L	5.0L (HO)/5.8L
a. No. 2 intake.	a. No. 2 intake.
b. No. 3 exhaust.	b. No. 4 exhaust.
c. No. 3 intake.	c. No. 5 intake.
d. No. 7 exhaust.	d. No. 5 exhaust.
e. No. 6 intake.	e. No. 6 intake.
f. No. 8 exhaust.	f. No. 8 exhaust.

6. Allowable lifter collapsed gap (clearance) is 0.071-0.193 in. with a desired clearance of 0.096-0.165 in. for 5.0L engines, 0.098-0.198 in. with a desired clearance of 0.123-0.173 in. for 5.8L engines and 0.075-0.175 in. with a desired clearance of 0.100-0.150 in. for 7.5L engines. If clearance is less than specified, install a shorter pushrod. If greater than specified, install a longer pushrod. See dealer for pushrod selection.

8

CRANKSHAFT PULLEY AND VIBRATION DAMPER

Removal/Installation

1. Open the cylinder block water drains and allow all water to drain.

2. Remove the alternator drive belt. See Chapter Eleven.

3. Remove the pulley attaching bolts. Remove the pulley.

4. Remove the bolt and washer from the vibration damper.

5. Install a suitable puller (**Figure 14**) and remove the vibration damper from the crankshaft.

6. Remove the spacer and Woodruff key from the crankshaft.

7. To install, lubricate the vibration damper keyway and crankshaft surface with a mixture of white lead and oil.

8. Install the Woodruff key in the crankshaft slot, then install the spacer.

9. Align the vibration damper keyway with the crankshaft Woodruff key and fit the damper on the crankshaft.
10. Use a damper installer (part No. T52L-6306-AEE or equivalent) to draw the damper onto the crankshaft (**Figure 15**). Remove the installer tool.
11. Reverse Steps 1-4 to complete installation. Tighten all fasteners to specifications (**Table 3**).

CRANKCASE FRONT COVER AND OIL SEAL

Cover Removal/Installation

This procedure can generally be performed without removing the engine from the boat, providing you are careful in cutting the gasket in Step 9.

1. Open the engine block drain valves and drain all the water from the block.
2. Drain the crankcase oil. See Chapter Four.
3. Remove the crankshaft pulley and vibration damper as described in this chapter.
4. Remove the alternator. See Chapter Eleven.
5. Remove the seawater pump, if so equipped.
6. Remove any accessory brackets attached to the circulating water pump. Remove the pump pulley and drive belt. Loosen the bypass hose at the water pump.
7. Remove the fuel pump. See Chapter Nine.
8. Remove the bolts holding the front of the oil pan to the front cover.
9. Use a sharp X-acto knife to cut the oil pan gasket flush with the cylinder block face.
10. Remove the front cover bolts. Remove the cover and water pump as an assembly.
11. Remove and discard the front cover gasket.
12. Clean the block and front cover sealing surfaces of all oil, grease and gasket residue with degreaser and a putty knife.
13. Lubricate the timing chain and gears with engine oil.

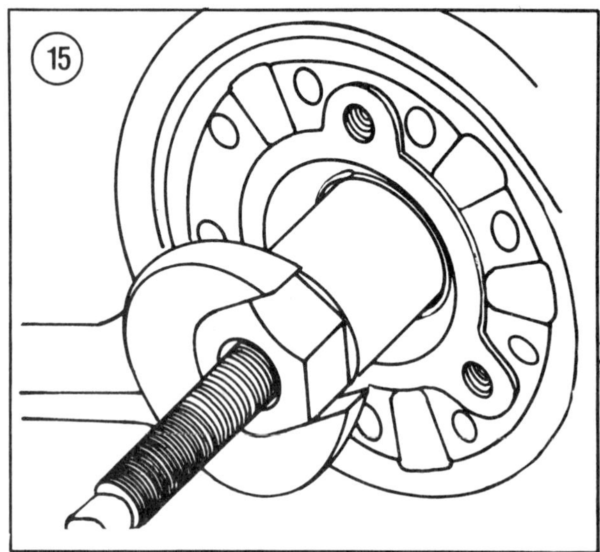

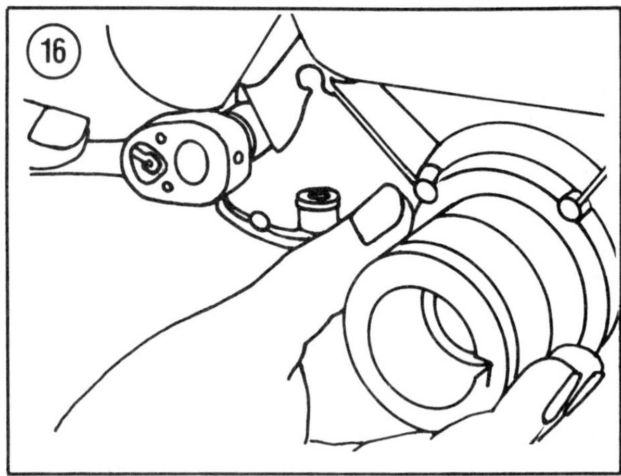

14. Coat the gasket surfaces of the block and front cover with a water-resistant sealer and install a new gasket over the dowel pins on the engine block.
15. Use the cut portion of the oil pan gasket as a template and cut a matching section from a new gasket for use in Step 16.
16. Coat the exposed surface of the oil pan flange with OMC Gasket Sealing Compound and install the gasket portion cut in Step 15. Coat the exposed gasket surface with the same sealer.
17. Position the front cover on the engine block. Work carefully to prevent damage to the oil seal or movement of the gaskets.

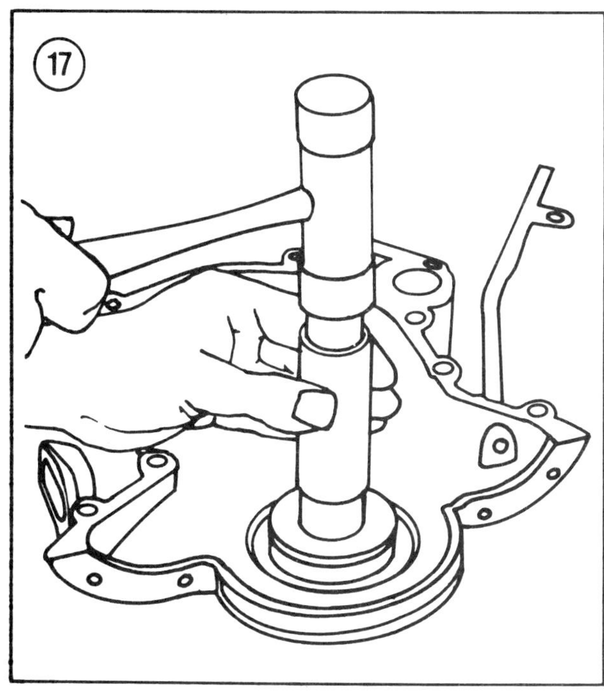

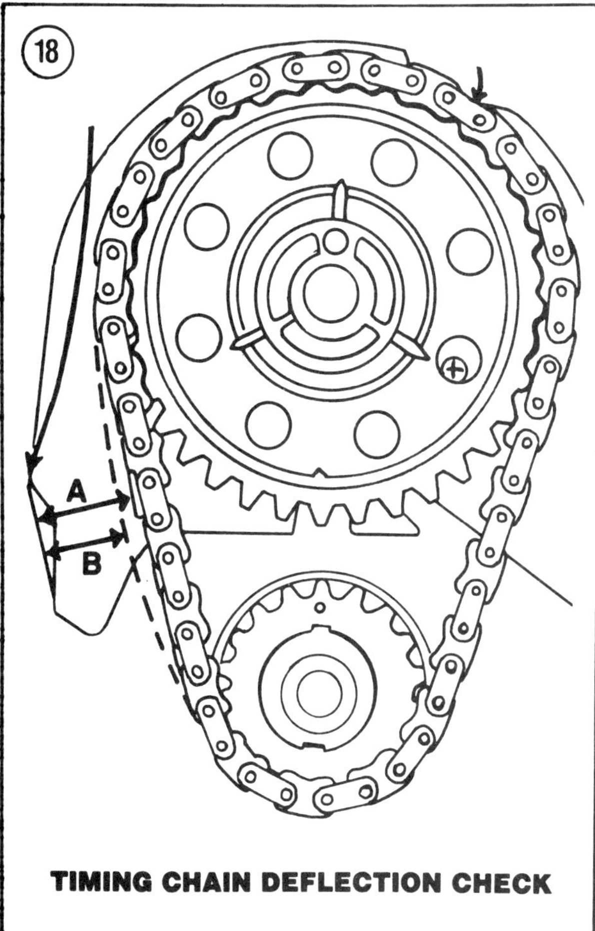

TIMING CHAIN DEFLECTION CHECK

18. Install Ford alignment tool part No. T61P-6019-B or T61P-6059-F as shown in **Figure 16**.
19. Apply downward pressure on the cover and install the oil pan attaching screws.
20. Coat the attaching bolt threads with OMC Gasket Sealing Compound. Install the bolts and tighten bolts and oil pan screws to specifications (**Table 3**).
21. Remove alignment tool and reverse Steps 1-7 to complete installation.

Front Cover Seal Replacement

1. Remove the front cover as described in this chapter.
2. Place cover on a clean flat workbench surface.
3. Use a pin punch to drive out the old seal.
4. Clean the seal recess in the cover with solvent and blow dry.
5. Wipe a new seal with Ford polyethylene grease (part No. DOAZ-19584-A) or equivalent.
6. Position new seal in cover recess and install with Ford seal installer part No. T58P-6700-B. See **Figure 17**.
7. Check seal to make sure it is fully seated and that the seal spring is properly positioned.
8. Install front cover as described in this chapter.

8

TIMING CHAIN AND SPROCKETS

Removal

1. Remove the front cover as described in this chapter.
2. Remove the crankshaft oil slinger.
3. Rotate the crankshaft clockwise to take up slack on the left side of the chain. Measure distance A, **Figure 18**, then rotate crankshaft counterclockwise to take up slack on right side of chain. Force left side of chain outward

with fingers, then measure distance B, **Figure 18**. Subtract B from A to determine timing chain deflection. If the difference or deflection exceeds 0.5 in., replace the timing chain and sprockets during reassembly.

4. Rotate crankshaft until sprocket timing marks are positioned as shown in **Figure 19.**
5. Remove camshaft sprocket capscrew, washers and fuel pump eccentric.
6. Grasp the 2 sprockets and timing chain as an assembly and slide forward to remove from the engine.

Installation

1. Assemble the timing chain to the camshaft and crankshaft sprockets with the sprocket timing marks aligned as shown in **Figure 19.**
2. Install the timing chain/sprocket assembly to the camshaft and crankshaft **(Figure 20)**. Recheck to make sure the timing marks are properly positioned.
3. Install the fuel pump eccentric, washers and camshaft sprocket capscrew. Tighten the capscrew to specifications **(Table 3)**.
4. Install the crankshaft oil slinger.
5. Install the front cover as described in this chapter.

CAMSHAFT

Removal/Installation

1. Remove the valve covers as described in this chapter.
2. Remove the intake manifold as described in this chapter.
3. Remove the front cover and timing chain as described in this chapter.
4. Loosen the rocker arm fulcrum bolts, swivel the arms off the pushrods and remove the pushrods.
5. Identify each pushrod for reinstallation in its original location.

NOTE
If the lifters are stuck in their bores, use Ford tool part No. T52T-6500-DJD or T52T-6500-D to rotate the lifter back

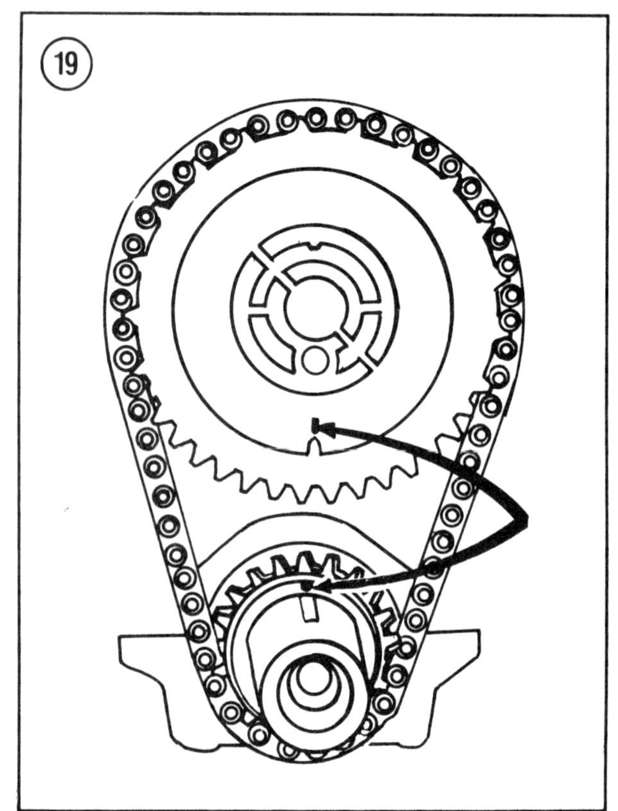

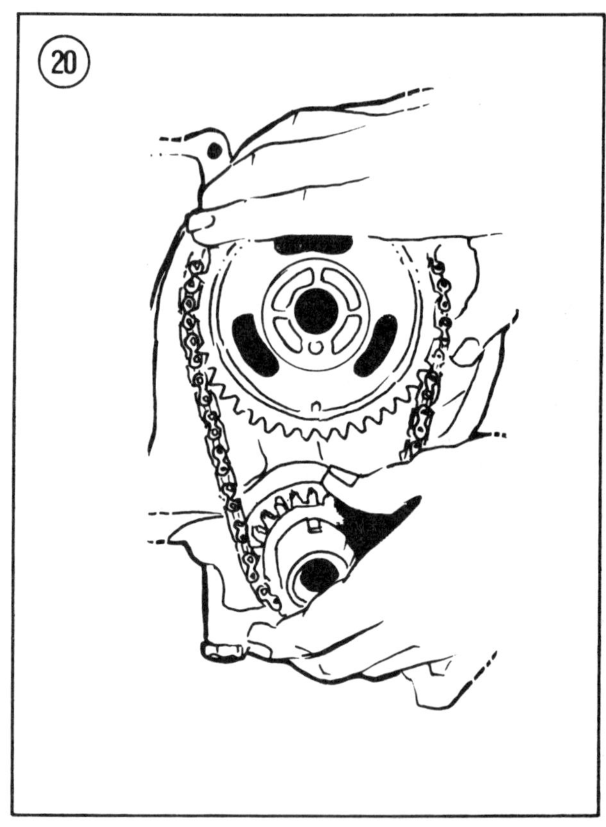

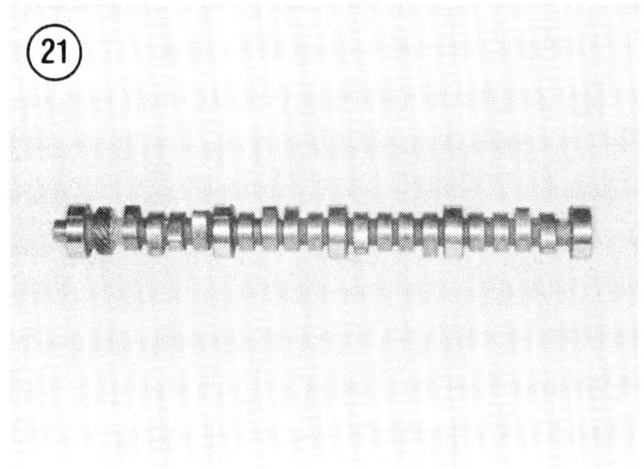

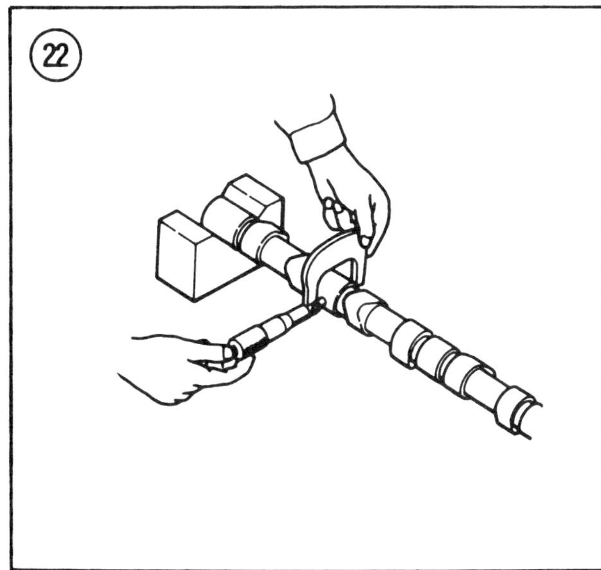

and forth. This will break the varnish or gum seal that is holding the lifter in place and allow its removal.

6. Remove the valve lifters with a pencil-type magnet. Place them in a rack in order of removal for reinstallation in their original location.
7. Remove the fuel pump and pushrod. See Chapter Nine.
8. Remove the camshaft thrust plate.

CAUTION
Do not cock the camshaft during removal. This can damage the camshaft or its bearing thrust surfaces.

9. Carefully withdraw the camshaft from the front of the engine with a rotating motion to avoid damage to the bearings.
10. Installation is the reverse of removal. Coat the camshaft lobes with Lubriplate 777 or equivalent and the journals with heavy engine oil before reinstalling in the block. Check end play as described in this chapter before tightening rocker arms in place.

Inspection

1. Check the journals and lobes for signs of wear or scoring. See **Figure 21**. Lobe pitting in the toe area is not sufficient reason for replacement unless the lobe lift loss exceeds specifications.

NOTE
If you do not have precision measuring equipment, have Step 2 and Step 3 done by a machine shop.

2. Measure the camshaft journal diameters with a micrometer (**Figure 22**) and compare to specifications (**Table 1** or **Table 2**). Replace the camshaft if one or more journals do not meet specification.
3. Suspend the camshaft between V-blocks and check for warpage with a dial indicator. See **Figure 23**. Replace if the runout is greater than specified in **Table 1** or **Table 2**.
4. Check the distributor drive gear **(Figure 24)** for excessive wear or damage. Replace camshaft if any defect is found.

Lifter Inspection

Keep the lifters in proper sequence for installation in their original position in the head. Clean lifters in solvent and wipe dry with a clean, lint-free cloth. Inspect and test the lifters separately to prevent intermixing of their internal parts. If any part requires replacement, replace the entire lifter.

Inspect all parts. If any lifter shows signs of pitting, scoring, galling, non-rotation or

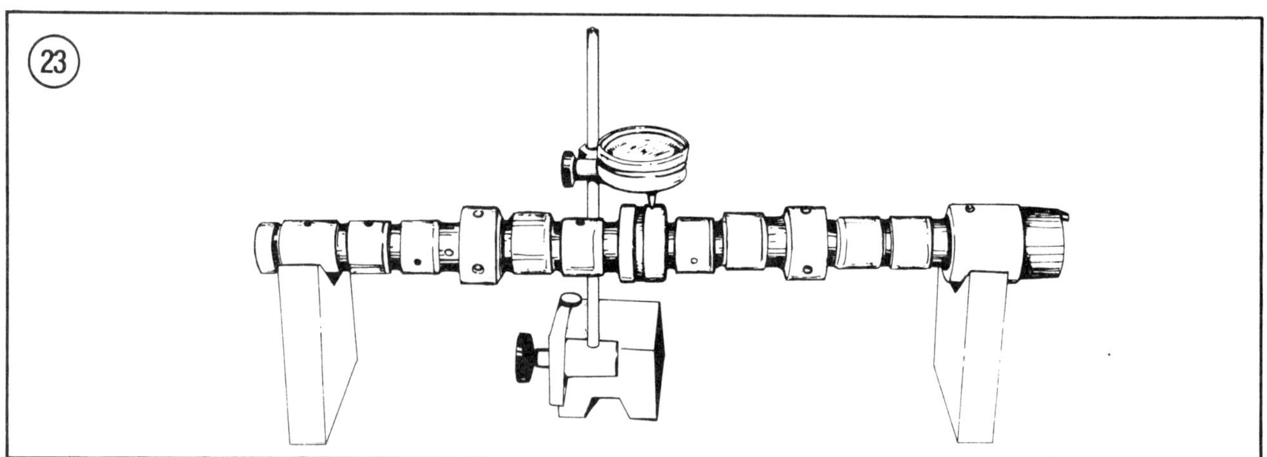

23

excessive wear, discard it. Check the lifter plunger. It should drop to the bottom of the body by its own weight when dry and assembled.

Lobe Lift Measurement

Camshaft lobe lift can be measured with the camshaft in the block and the cylinder head in place. The lifters must be bled down slowly in Step 6 or the readings will be incorrect.

1. Remove the valve cover as described in this chapter.
2. Remove the rocker arms and fulcrum assemblies as described in this chapter.
3. Remove the spark plugs. See Chapter Four.
4. Install a dial indicator on the end of a pushrod. A piece of rubber tubing will hold the dial indicator plunger in place on the center of the pushrod. See **Figure 25** (typical).
5. Rotate the crankshaft in the normal direction of rotation until the valve lifter seats on the heel or base of the cam lobe **(Figure 26).** This positions the pushrod at its lowest point.
6. Set the dial indicator at zero, then slowly rotate the crankshaft until the pushrod reaches its maximum travel. Note the indicator reading and compare to specifications (**Table 1** or **Table 2**).

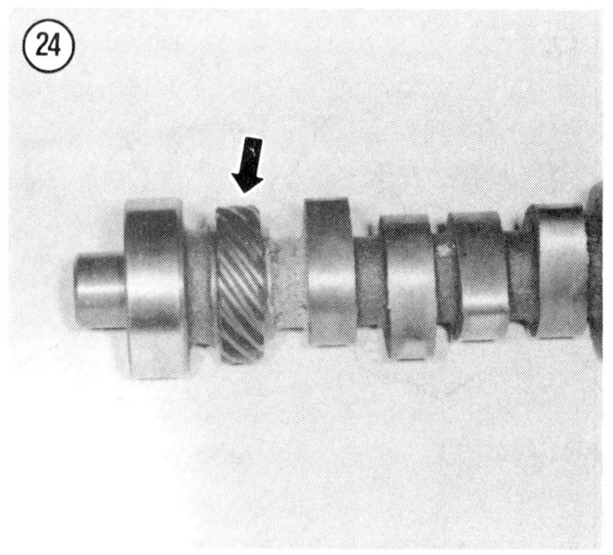

24

7. Repeat Steps 4-6 for each pushrod. If all lobes are within specifications in Step 6, reinstall the rocker arm assemblies.
8. If one or more lobes are worn beyond specifications, replace the camshaft as described in this chapter.
9. Remove the dial indicator and reverse Steps 1-3.

Bearing Replacement

Camshaft bearings are available pre-finished to the correct size and are not

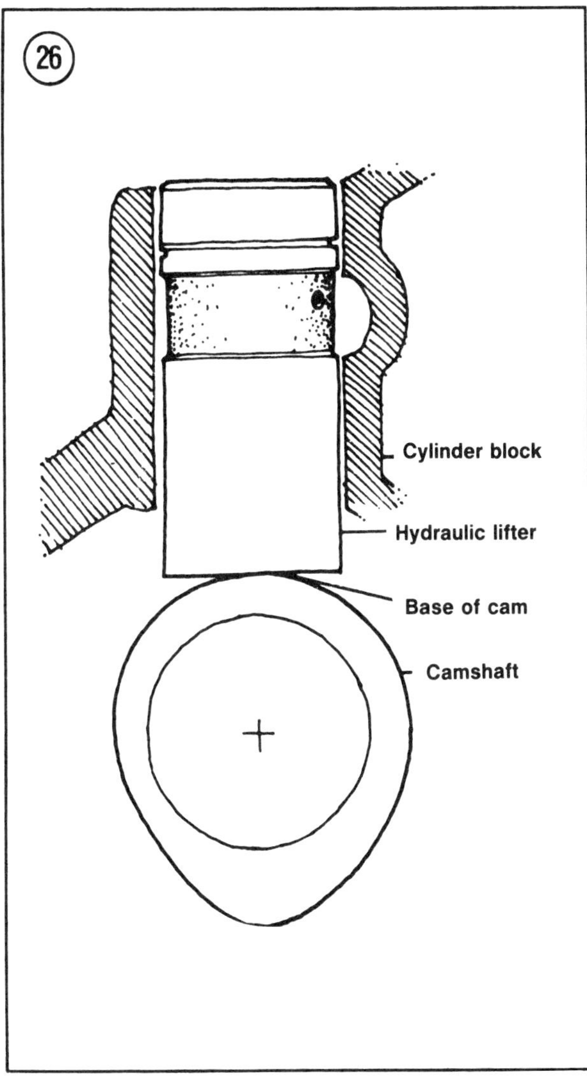

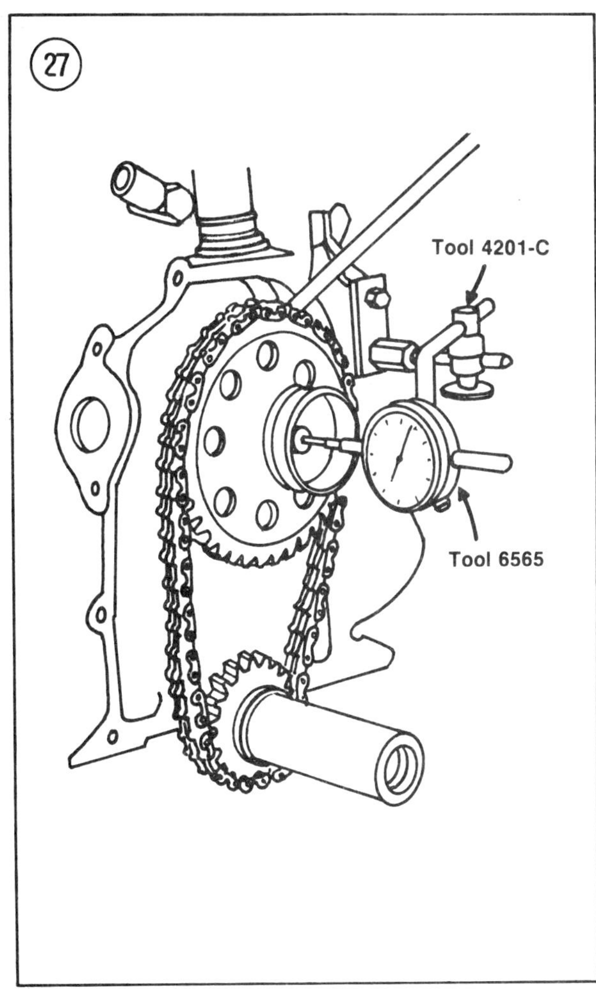

interchangeable between bores. A special puller and expanding collet are required for this procedure, which is not recommended for the amateur mechanic. Improper use of the special tools or use of the wrong expanding collet can result in severe bearing damage. If the bearings require replacement, have the job done by an OMC dealer, Ford dealer or a qualified machine shop.

End Play

Applying force against the camshaft sprocket with the valve train load on the camshaft can damage or break the sprocket. Make sure rocker arm bolts are loose before performing this procedure. Refer to **Figure 27** for this procedure.

1. Loosen the rocker arm bolts to relieve any load on the camshaft.
2. Push the camshaft to the rear of the engine as far as possible.
3. Install a dial indicator with its tip on the camshaft sprocket capscrew. Set the indicator to zero.
4. Place a large screwdriver or pry bar between the camshaft sprocket and block. Pull the camshaft forward and release it.
5. Compare the dial indicator reading with specifications (**Table 1** or **Table 2**). If end play is excessive, replace the thrust plate.
6. Tighten the rocker arm bolts.

OIL PAN

Removal

1. Remove the engine as described in this chapter.
2. Place a suitable container under the oil pan drain plug. Remove the plug and let the crankcase drain. Reinstall the drain plug.

NOTE
A modification kit is available from marine dealers to assist in draining the oil when the engine is in the boat. This kit can be installed on the engine oil pan when the engine is removed for service.

3. If mounted in an engine stand, rotate the engine 180° to place the oil pan in an upright position.
4. Remove the oil pan attaching screws. Remove the oil pan.
5. Remove and discard the 2-piece pan gasket and the front/rear seals.

Inspection and Cleaning

1. Clean any gasket residue from the oil pan rails on the engine block and the oil pan sealing flange with degreaser and a putty knife.
2. Clean the pan thoroughly in solvent and check for dents or warped gasket surfaces. Straighten or replace the pan as required.

Installation

1. Coat the block side rails with OMC Gasket Sealing Compound and position the 2 side gaskets on the side rails.
2. Install the front pan seal on the front cover with the seal tabs *over* the side gaskets.
3. Install the rear seal on the rear main bearing cap with the seal tabs *over* the side gaskets.
4. Carefully place the oil pan in position. Make sure the gaskets and seals are not misaligned and then install a pan attaching screw finger-tight on each side of the block.
5. Install the remaining screws and tighten all to specifications (**Table 3**). Work from the center outward in each direction.
6. Install the engine in the boat as described in this chapter and fill the crankcase with oil. See Chapter Four.

OIL PUMP

Removal/Installation

1. Remove the oil pan as described in this chapter.
2. Remove the oil pump attaching bolts. Remove the oil pump, gasket and intermediate drive shaft.
3. To install, fill pump with oil through either the inlet or outlet port. Rotate the pump shaft to distribute oil inside the pump body.
4. Insert the intermediate drive shaft into the oil pump and position the assembly against the crankcase. If the pump does not seat easily, rotate the drive shaft slightly so that its hex aligns with the distributor shaft.
5. Install the attaching bolts and tighten to specifications (**Table 3**).
6. Install the oil pan as described in this chapter.

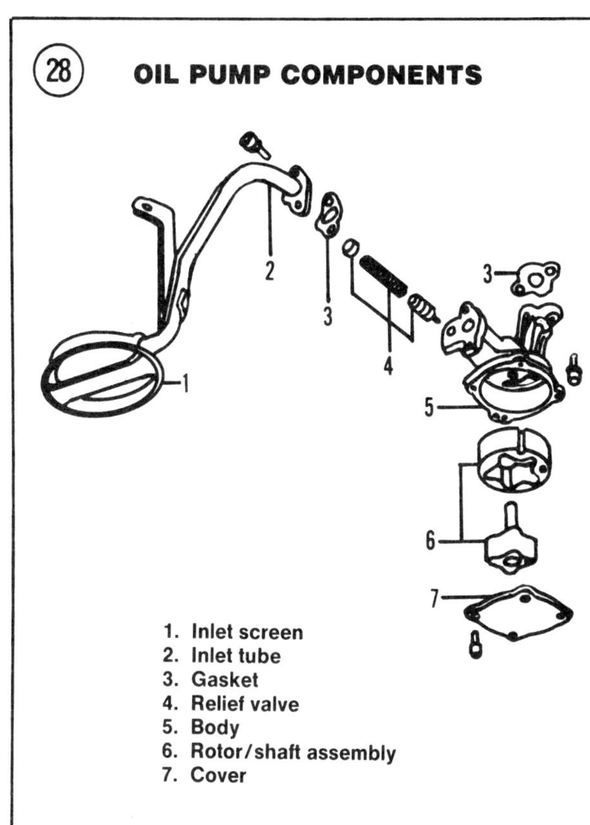

Disassembly/Assembly

Refer to **Figure 28** for this procedure.

1. Remove the oil inlet tube and gasket from the pump. Discard the gasket.
2. Remove the cover screws and cover.
3. Remove the inner rotor and shaft assembly.
4. Remove the outer race.
5. Install a self-threading sheet metal screw in the oil pressure relief valve cap. Pull cap from pump chamber.
6. Remove the pressure relief spring and plunger.
7. Oil all parts thoroughly before reassembly.
8. Install the pressure relief plunger and spring with a new cap.
9. Install the outer race, inner rotor and shaft as a unit. Make sure the identification dot on the outer race faces outward and is on the same side as the corresponding identification dot on the rotor.
10. Install cover and tighten screws to specifications (**Table 3**).
11. Install oil inlet tube with a new gasket and tighten bolts to specifications (**Table 3**).

Inspection

NOTE
The inner rotor, shaft and outer race are serviced as an assembly. If one component is defective, replace them all.

1. Clean all parts thoroughly in solvent. Brush the inside of the body and the pressure regulator chamber to remove all dirt and metal particles. Dry with compressed air, if available.
2. Check the pump body and cover for cracks or excessive wear.
3. Check the pump gears for damage or excessive wear.
4. Check the pressure relief valve spring. If worn, damaged or collapsed, replace the spring.
5. Check the relief valve plunger for scoring. Check for free operation in the pump bore.
6. Install the outer race in the pump body and check the clearance with a flat feeler gauge (**Figure 29**). If clearance exceeds specifications (**Table 1** or **Table 2**), replace the race, rotor and shaft assembly.
7. Install the rotor/shaft assembly in the pump body. Place a straightedge over the assembly and body. Measure end play between the rotor/outer race and straightedge. See **Figure 30**. If end play exceeds specifications (**Table 1** or **Table 2**), replace the race, rotor and shaft assembly.
8. Measure the drive shaft-to-housing bearing clearance. If clearance exceeds specifications (**Table 1** or **Table 2**), replace the race, rotor and shaft assembly.

CYLINDER HEAD

Removal

Perform Steps 1-4 if engine is in boat. If engine has been removed from the boat, begin with Step 5.

1. Open the engine block drain valves and drain all water from the block.
2. Remove the intake and exhaust manifolds as described in this chapter.
3. Remove the alternator and oil filter mounting brackets.
4. Disconnect the spark plug wires and remove the wire looms from the cylinder head.
5. Remove the valve cover as described in this chapter.
6. Loosen the rocker arms and rotate them to one side. Remove the pushrods and identify each for reinstallation in their original position.
7. Loosen the cylinder head bolts, working from the center of the head to the end in each direction.
8. Remove the head bolts. Rap the end of the head with a soft-faced hammer to break the gasket seal. Remove the head from the engine.

CAUTION
Place the head on its side to prevent damage to the spark plugs or head gasket surface.

9. Remove and discard the head gasket. Clean all gasket residue from the head and block mating surfaces.

Decarbonizing

1. Without removing the valves, remove all deposits from the combustion chambers, intake ports and exhaust ports. Use a fine wire brush dipped in solvent or make a scraper from hardwood. Be careful not to scratch or gouge the combustion chambers.

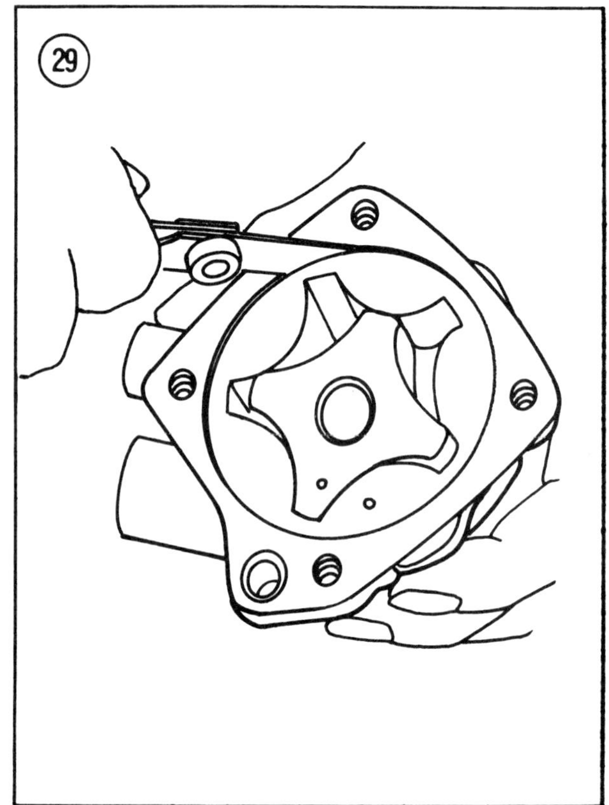

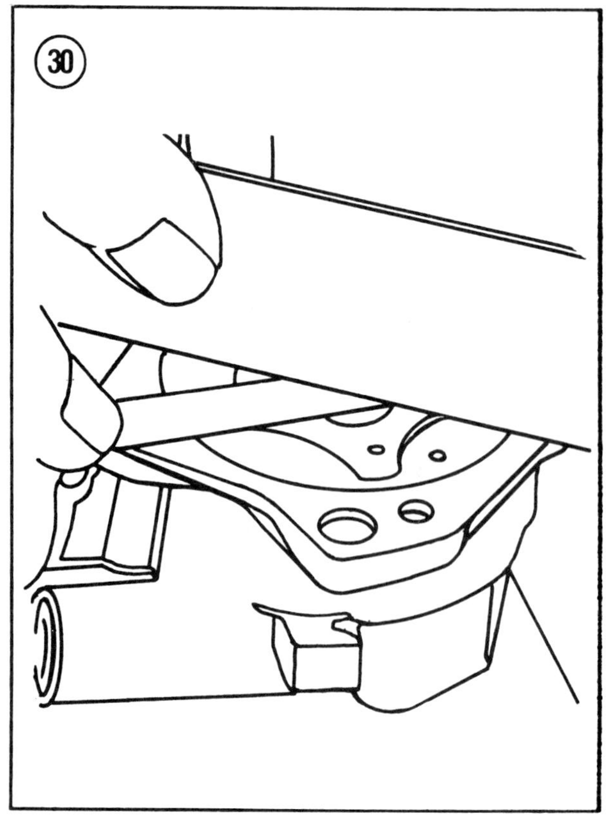

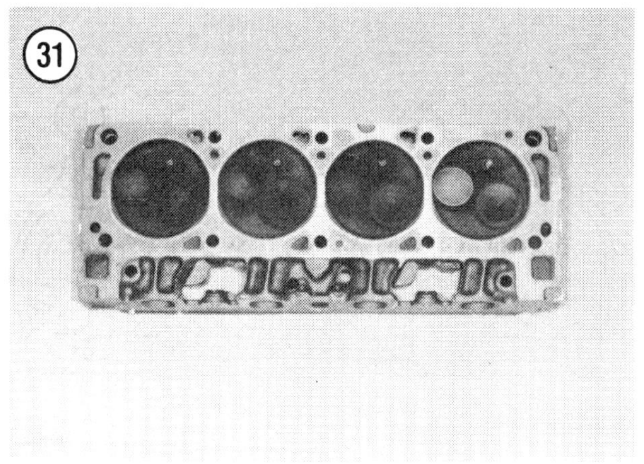

31

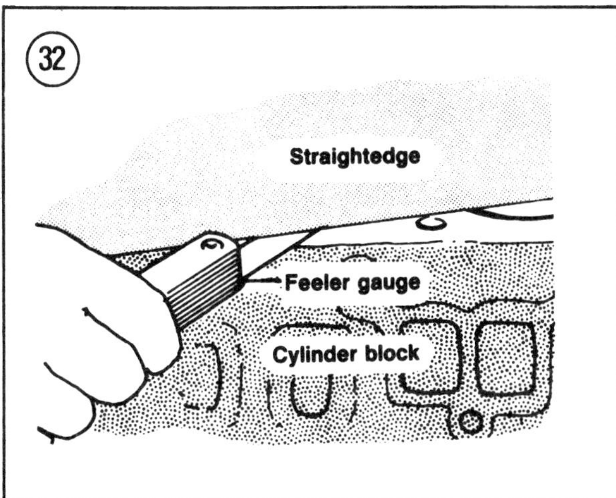

32

2. After all carbon is removed from the combustion chambers and ports, clean the entire head in solvent.
3. Clean away all carbon on the piston tops. Do not remove the carbon ridge at the top of the cylinder bore.
4. Remove the valves as described in this chapter.
5. Clean the pushrod guides, valve guide bores and all bolt holes. Use a cleaning solvent to remove dirt and grease.
6. Clean the valves with a fine wire brush or buffing wheel.

Inspection

1. Check the cylinder head for signs of oil or water leaks before cleaning.
2. Clean the cylinder head thoroughly in solvent. While cleaning, look for cracks or other visible signs of damage. Look for corrosion or foreign material in the oil and water passages (**Figure 31**). Clean the passages with a stiff spiral brush, then blow them out with compressed air.
3. Check the cylinder head studs for damage and replace if necessary.
4. Check the threaded rocker arm bolt holes for damaged threads; repair or replace if necessary.
5. Check for warpage of the cylinder head-to-block surface with a straightedge and feeler gauge (**Figure 32**). Measure diagonally, as well as end to end. If the gap exceeds specifications (**Table 1** or **Table 2**), have the head resurfaced by a machine shop. If head resurfacing is necessary, do not remove more than 0.010 in. Replace the head if a greater amount must be removed to correct warpage.

Installation

1. Make sure the cylinder head and block gasket surfaces and bolt holes are clean. Dirt in the block bolt holes or on the head bolt threads will affect bolt torque.
2. Recheck all visible oil and water passages for cleanliness.

CAUTION
Do not use any type of sealer with head gaskets.

3. Fit a new head gasket over the cylinder dowels on the block.
4. Carefully lower the head onto the cylinder block, engaging the dowel pins.
5. Install and tighten the head bolts finger-tight. Tighten the head bolts in 3 stages following the sequence shown in **Figure 33** until the specified torque is reached. See **Table 3**.
6. If engine is in the boat, reverse Steps 1-6 of *Removal* in this chapter to complete installation. If engine is out of the boat,

reverse Step 5 and Step 6 of *Removal* in this chapter. Adjust drive belt (Chapter Ten). Check and adjust carburetor and ignition timing as required. See Chapter Four.

VALVES AND VALVE SEATS

Servicing the valves, guides and valve seats must be done by a dealer or machine shop, since they require special knowledge and expensive machine tools. A general practice among those who do their own service is to remove the cylinder head, perform all disassembly except valve removal and take the head to a dealer or machine shop for inspection and service. Since the cost is low relative to the required effort and equipment, this is usually the best approach, even for experienced mechanics. The following procedures are given to acquaint the home mechanic with what the dealer or machine shop will do.

Valve Removal

Refer to **Figure 34** for this procedure.

1. Remove the cylinder head as described in this chapter.
2. Remove the rocker arm assemblies as described in this chapter.
3. Compress the valve spring with a compressor like the one shown in **Figure 35**. Remove the valve keys or cap locks and release the spring tension.
4. Remove the retainer and valve spring. On some models, there may be a sleeve on top of the retainer, a stem cap on top of the exhaust valve stem or a damper spring inside the intake valve spring.
5. Remove the valve stem seal with a pair of pliers. Discard the seal. Remove the shim and spacer, if used.

CAUTION
Remove any burrs from the valve stem lock grooves before removing the valves or the valve guides will be damaged.

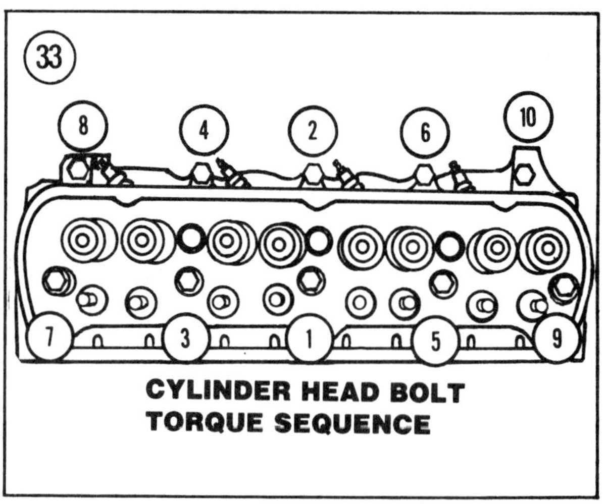

CYLINDER HEAD BOLT TORQUE SEQUENCE

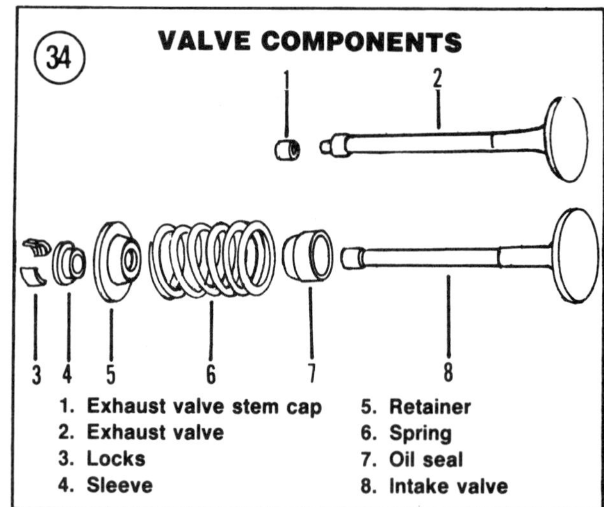

VALVE COMPONENTS

1. Exhaust valve stem cap
2. Exhaust valve
3. Locks
4. Sleeve
5. Retainer
6. Spring
7. Oil seal
8. Intake valve

6. Remove the valve and repeat Steps 3-5 on each remaining valve.
7. Arrange the parts in order so they can be returned to their original positions when reassembled.

Inspection

1. Clean the valves with a fine wire brush or buffing wheel. Discard any cracked, warped or burned valves.
2. Measure valve stems at the top, center and bottom for wear. A machine shop can do this when the valves are ground. Also measure the length of each valve and the diameter of each valve head.

35

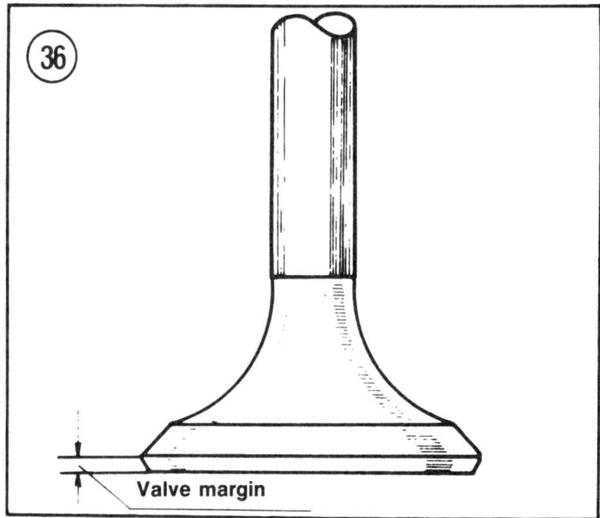

36

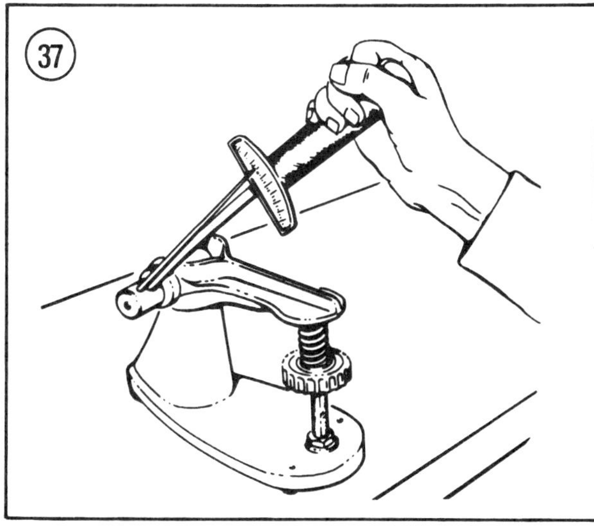

37

NOTE
*Check the thickness of the valve edge or margin after the valves have been ground. See **Figure 36**. Any valve with a margin of less than 1/32 in. should be discarded.*

3. Remove all carbon and varnish from the valve guides with a stiff spiral wire brush.

NOTE
The next step assumes that all valve stems have been measured and are within specifications. Replace valves with worn stems before performing this step.

4. Insert each valve into the guide from which it was removed. Holding the valve just slightly off its seat, rock it back and forth in a direction parallel with the rocker arms. This is the direction in which the greatest wear normally occurs. If the valve stems rocks more than slightly, the valve guide is probably worn.
5. If there is any doubt about valve guide condition after performing Step 4, have the valve guide measured with a valve stem clearance checking tool. Compare the results with specifications in **Table 1** or **Table 2**. Worn guides must be reamed for the next oversize valve stem.
6. Test the valve springs under load on a spring tester (**Figure 37**). Replace any weak springs.
7. Check each spring on a flat surface with a steel square. See **Figure 38**. Slowly revolve the spring 360° and note the space between the top of the coil and the square. If it exceeds 5/16 in. at any point, replace the spring.
8. Inspect the valve seat inserts. If worn or burned, they must be reconditioned. This is a job for a dealer or machine shop, although the procedure is described in this chapter.
9. Check each valve lifter to make sure it fits freely in the block and that the end that contacts the camshaft lobe is smooth and not worn excessively.

Valve Guide Reaming

Worn valve guides must be reamed to accept a valve with an oversize stem. These are available in 3 sizes for both intake and exhaust valves. Reaming must be done by hand (**Figure 39**) and is a job best left to an experienced machine shop. The valve seat must be refaced after the guide has been reamed.

Valve Seat Reconditioning

1. Cut the valve seats to the specified angle (**Table 1** or **Table 2**) with a dressing stone. Remove only enough metal to obtain a good finish.
2. Use tapered stones to obtain the specified seat width when necessary.
3. Coat the corresponding valve face with Prussian blue dye.
4. Insert the valve into the valve guide.
5. Apply light pressure to the valve and rotate it approximately 1/4 turn.
6. Lift the valve out. If it seats properly, the dye will transfer evenly to the valve face.
7. If the dye transfers to the top of the valve face, lower the seat. If it transfers to the bottom of the valve face, raise the seat.

Valve Installation

NOTE
Install all parts in the same position from which they were removed.

1. Coat the valves with engine oil and install them in the cylinder head.
2. Install new oil seals on each valve with a deep socket and hammer. Seal should be flat and not twisted in the valve stem groove.
3. Install the valve spring over the valve, then install the spring retainer.
4. Compress the springs and install the retainer locks. Make sure both locks seat properly in the upper groove of the valve stem.

NOTE
A 0.030 in. spacer can be installed between the spring pad and spring in Step 6 if the spring height is greater than specified, but excessive use of spacers can overstress the springs and cause spring breakage or cam lobe wear.

5. Measure the installed spring height between the spring pad surface and the underside of the spring retainer, as shown in **Figure 40**. If height is greater than specifications, replace the spring.

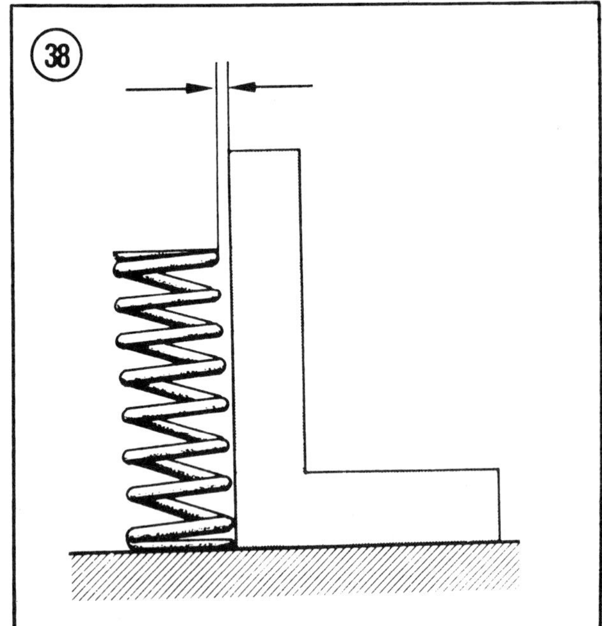

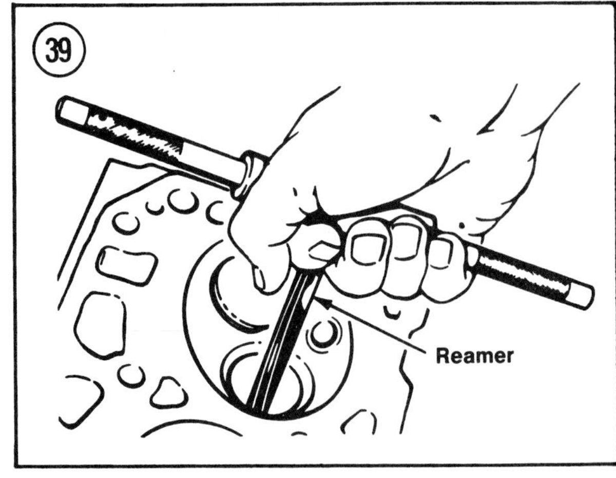

VALVE LIFTERS

Removal/Installation

1. Remove the intake manifold as described in this chapter.
2. Remove the rocker arm assemblies and pushrods as described in this chapter.
3. Remove the valve lifters. This can usually be done without special tools, although tool part No. T70L-6500-A will make the job easier and faster. If lifters are stuck, use the tool and rotate the lifter back and forth to free it from the gum or varnish deposits holding it in place.
4. Installation is the reverse of removal.

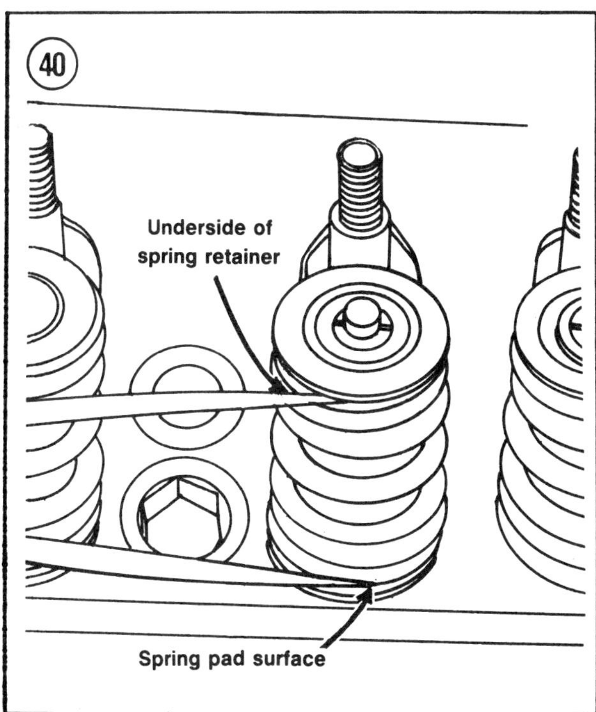

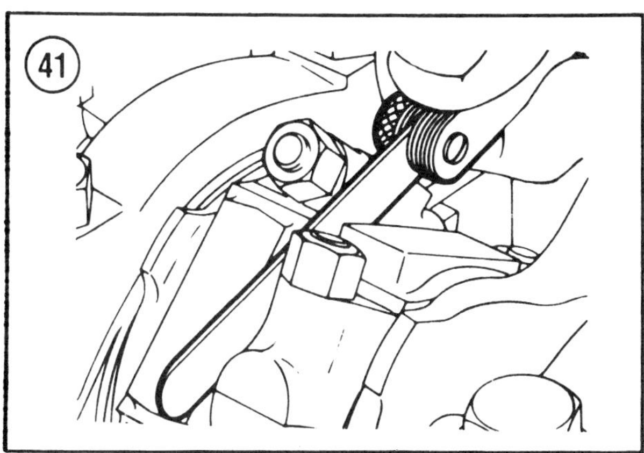

PISTON/CONNECTING ROD ASSEMBLY

Piston/Connecting Rod Removal

1. Remove the engine as described in this chapter.
2. Place a suitable container under the oil pan and remove the drain plug. Let the crankcase oil drain, then reinstall the drain plug.
3. Remove the intake and exhaust manifolds as described in this chapter.
4. Remove the cylinder heads as described in this chapter.
5. Remove the oil pan and oil pump as described in this chapter.
6. Rotate the crankshaft until one piston is at bottom dead center. Pack the cylinder bore with clean shop rags. Remove the carbon ridge at the top of the cylinder bores with a ridge reamer. These can be rented for use. Vacuum out the shavings, then remove the shop rags.
7. Rotate the crankshaft until the connecting rod is centered in the bore. Measure the clearance between the connecting rods with a flat feeler gauge (**Figure 41**). If the clearance exceeds specifications (**Table 1** or **Table 2**), replace the connecting rod during reassembly.
8. Remove the nuts holding the connecting rod cap. Lift off the cap, together with the lower bearing insert (**Figure 42**).

NOTE
*If the connecting rod caps are difficult to remove, tap the studs with a wooden hammer handle. See **Figure 43**.*

9. Use the wooden hammer handle to push the piston and connecting rod from the bore (**Figure 44**).

NOTE

Mark the cylinder number on the top of each piston with quick-drying paint. Check the cylinder numbers or identification marks on the connecting rod and cap. If they are not visible, make your own ***(Figure 45)****.*

10. Remove the piston rings with a ring remover (**Figure 46**).
11. Repeat Steps 6-10 for all remaining connecting rods.

Piston Pin Removal/Installation

The piston pins are press-fitted to the connecting rods and hand-fitted to the pistons. See **Figure 47**. Removal requires the use of a press and support stand. This is a job for a dealer or machine shop equipped to fit the pistons to the pins, ream the pin bushings to the correct diameter and install the pistons and pins on the connecting rods.

Piston Clearance Check

Unless you have precision measuring equipment and know how to use it properly, have this procedure done by a machine shop.

1. Measure the piston diameter with a micrometer (**Figure 48**) just below the rings at right angles to the piston pin bore.

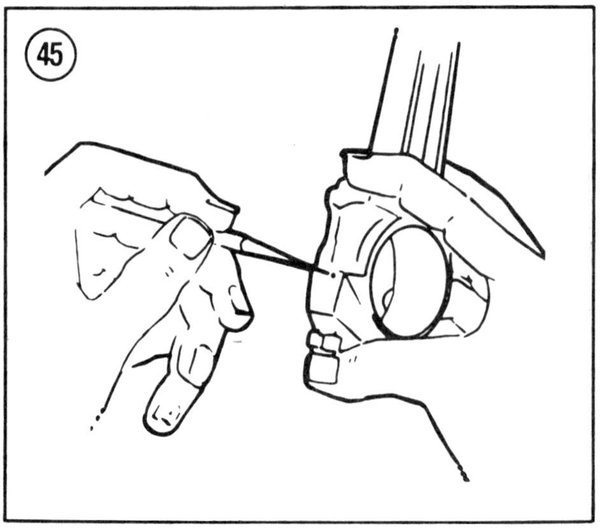

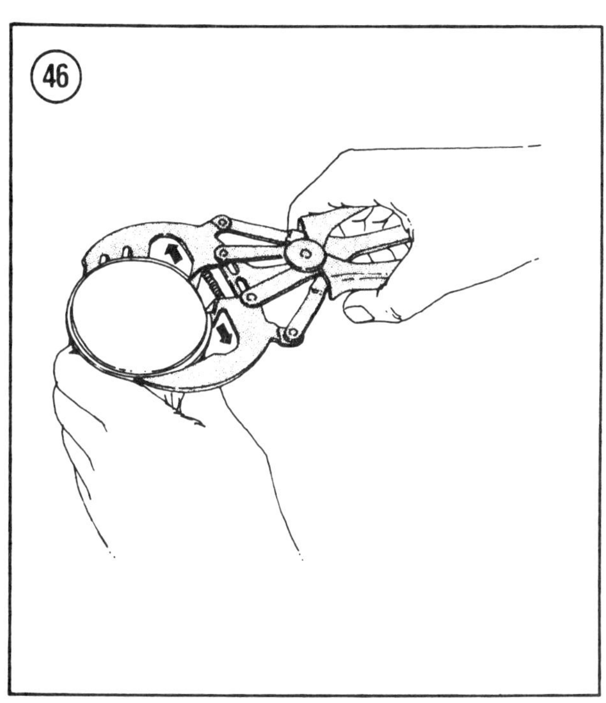

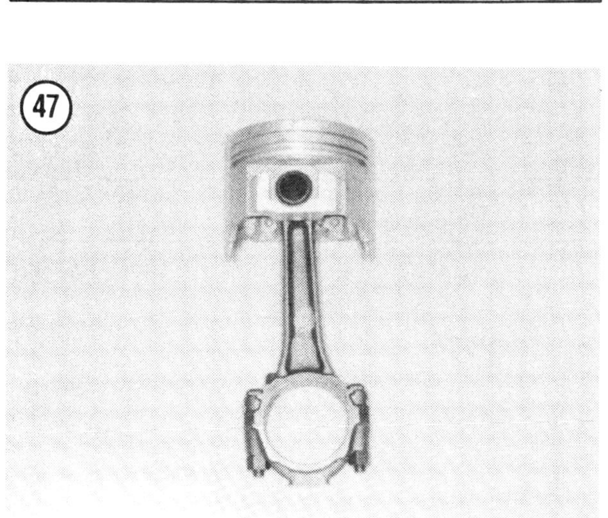

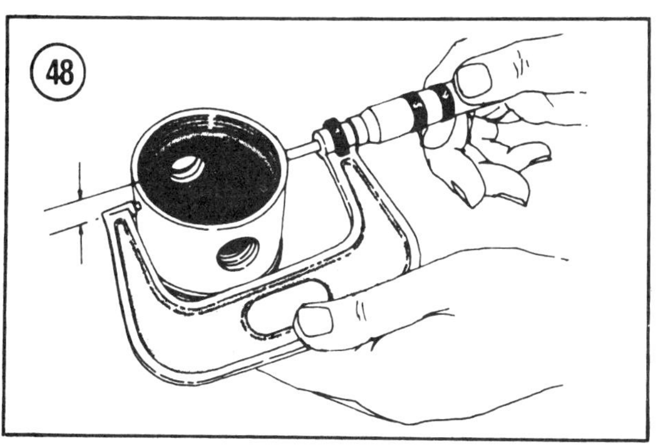

2. Measure the cylinder bore diameter with a bore gauge (**Figure 49**). **Figure 50** shows the points of normal cylinder wear. If dimension A exceeds dimension B by more than 0.003 in., the cylinder must be rebored and a new piston/ring assembly installed.

3. Subtract the piston diameter from the largest cylinder bore reading. If it exceeds the specifications in **Table 1** or **Table 2**, the cylinder must be rebored and an oversized piston installed.

NOTE
Obtain the new piston and measure it to determine the correct cylinder bore oversize dimension.

Piston Ring Fit/Installation

1. Check the ring gap of each piston ring. To do this, position the ring at the bottom of the

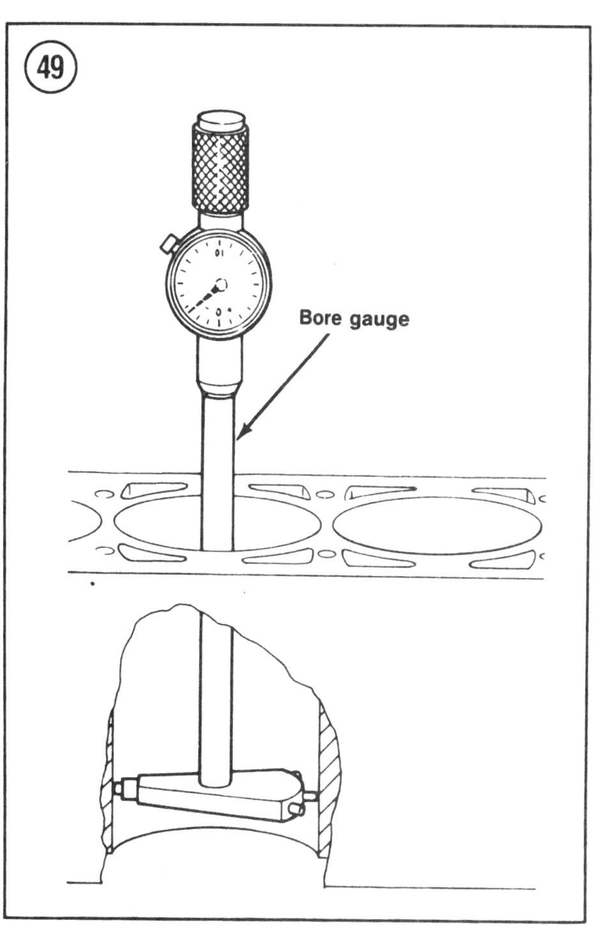

ring travel area and square it by tapping gently with an inverted piston. See **Figure 51**.

NOTE
If the cylinders have not been rebored, check the gap at the bottom of the ring travel, where the cylinder is least worn.

2. Measure the ring gap with a feeler gauge as shown in **Figure 52**. Compare with specifications in **Table 1** or **Table 2**. If the measurement is not within specifications, the rings must be replaced as a set. Check gap of new rings as well. If the gap is too small, file the ends of the ring to correct it (**Figure 53**).
3. Check the side clearance of the rings as shown in **Figure 54**. Place the feeler gauge alongside the ring all the way into the groove. If the measurement is not within specifications (**Table 1** or **Table 2**), either the rings or the ring grooves are worn. Inspect and replace as required.
4. Using a ring expander tool (**Figure 55**), carefully install the oil control ring, then the

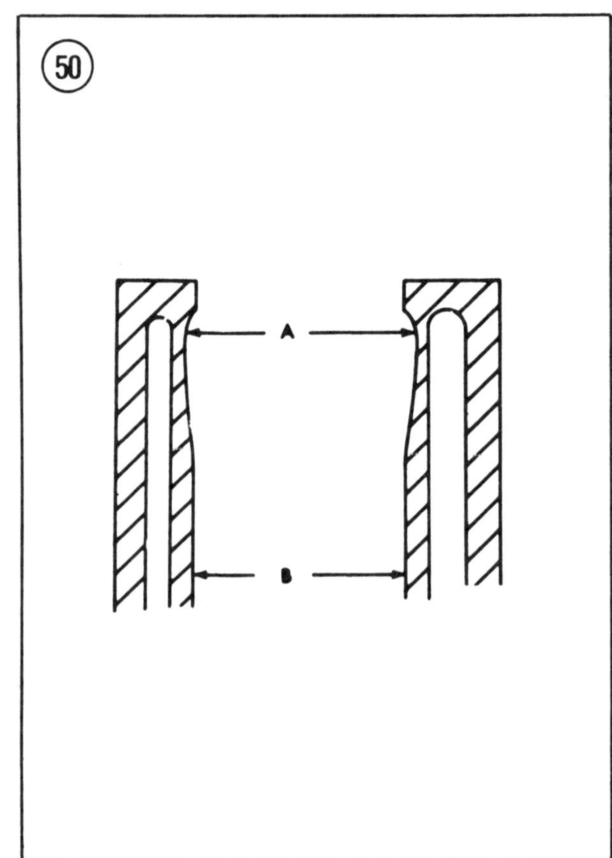

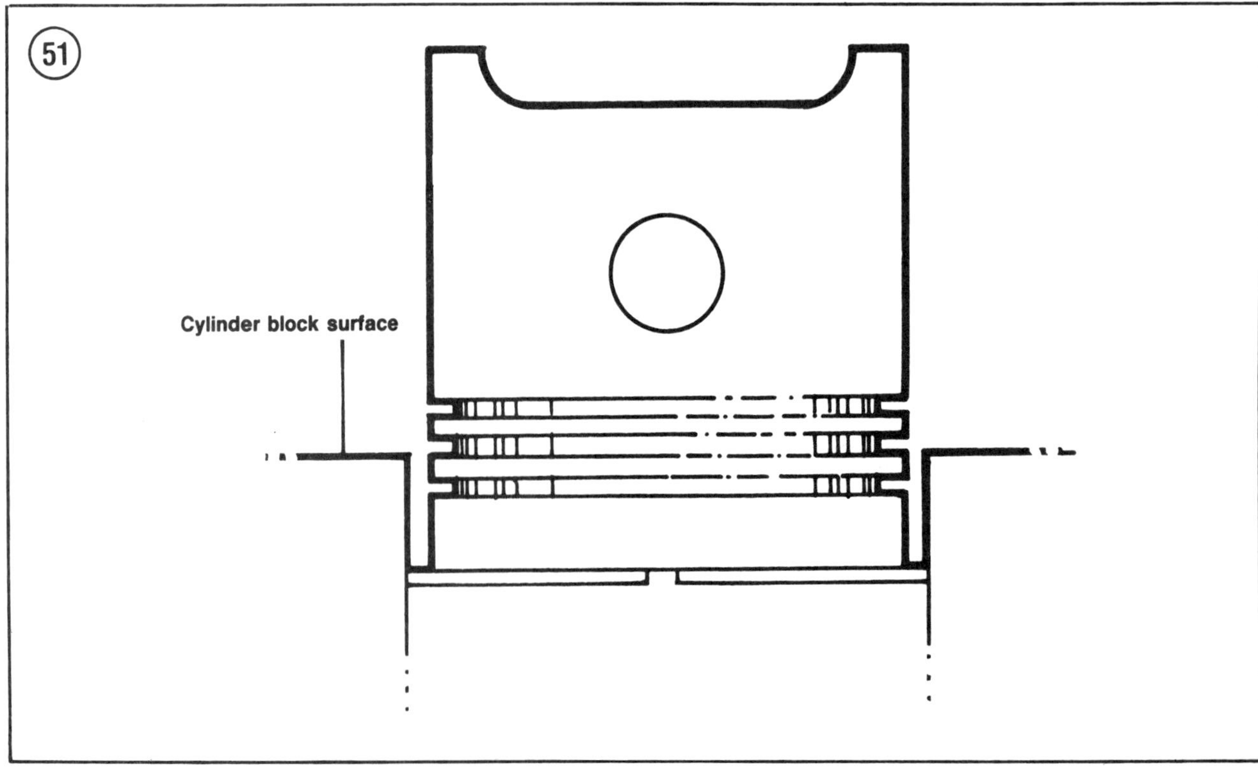

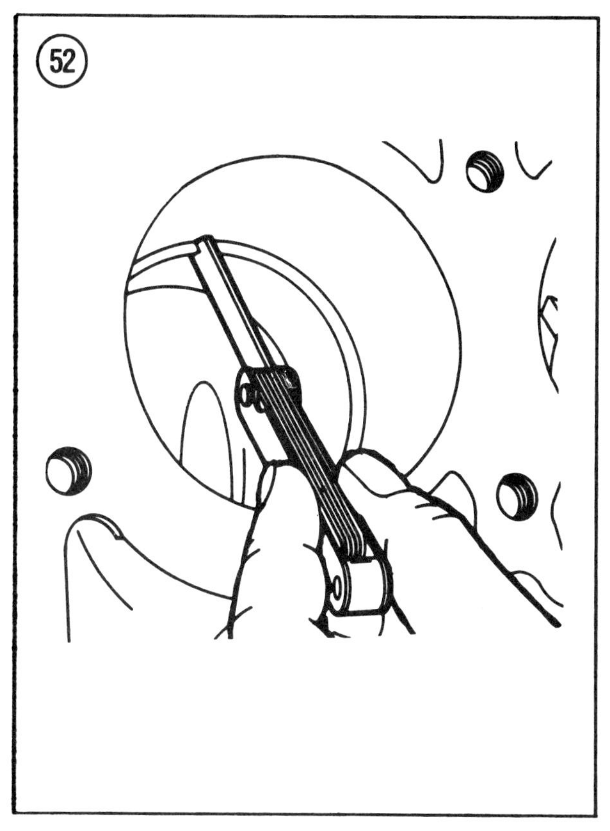
52

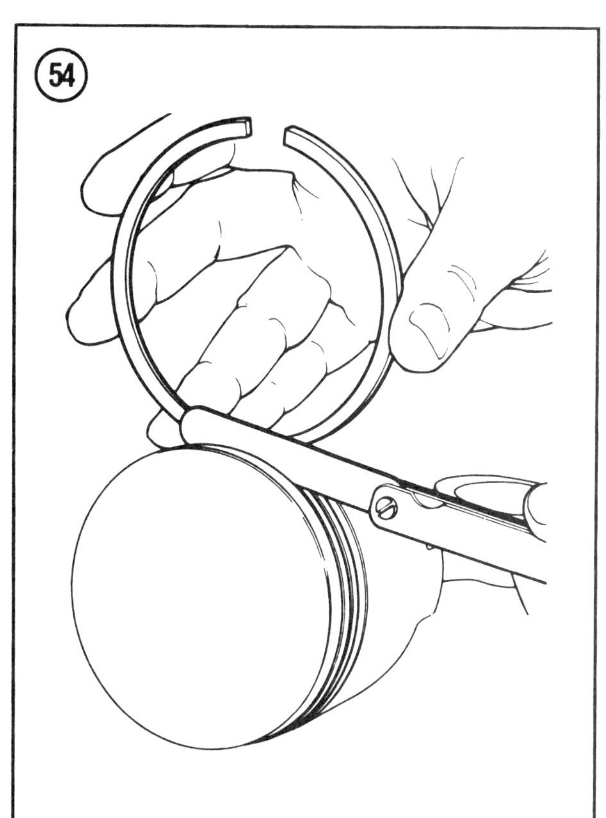
54

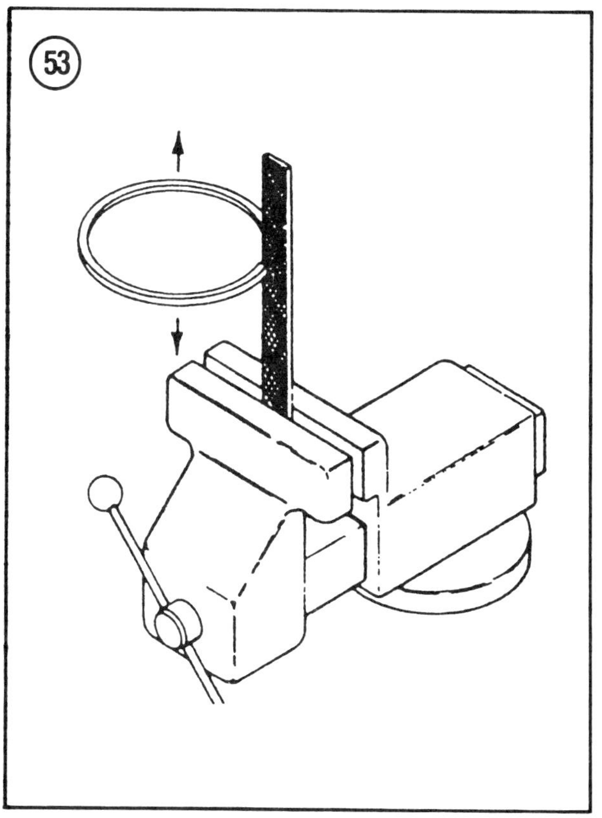
53

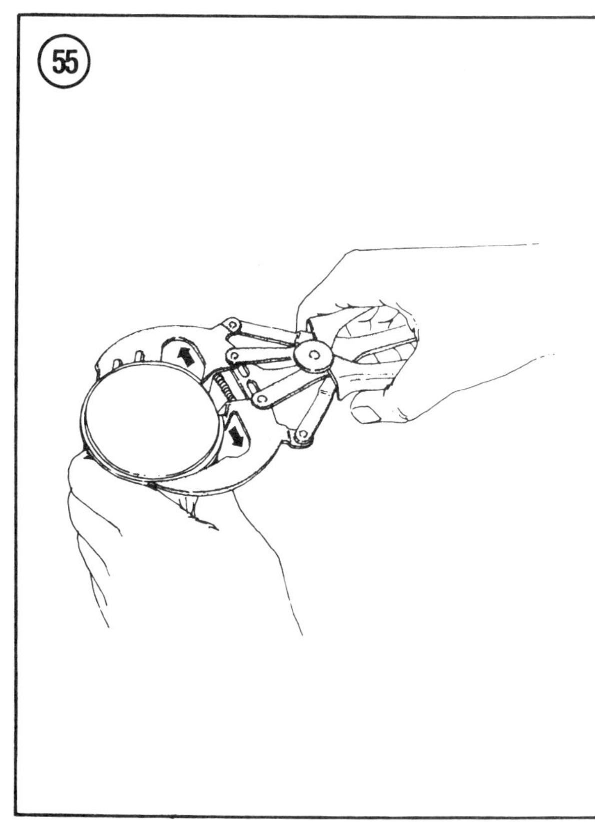
55

compression rings. Oil rings consist of 3 segments. The wavy segment goes between the flat segments to act as a spacer. Upper and lower flat segments are interchangeable.

5. Position the ring gaps as shown in **Figure 56**.

Connecting Rod Inspection

Have the connecting rods checked for straightness by a dealer or machine shop. When installing new connecting rods, have them checked for misalignment before installing the piston and piston pin. Connecting rods can spring out of alignment during shipping or handling.

Connecting Rod Bearing Clearance Measurement

1. Place the connecting rods and upper bearing halves on the proper connecting rod journals.
2. Cut a piece of Plastigage the width of the bearing. Place the Plastigage on the bearing (**Figure 57**), then install the lower bearing half and cap.

NOTE
Do not place Plastigage over the journal oil hole.

3. Tighten the connecting rod cap to specifications (**Table 3**). Do not rotate the crankshaft while the Plastigage is in place.
4. Remove the connecting rod caps. Bearing clearance is determined by comparing the width of the flattened Plastigage to the markings on the envelope (**Figure 58**). If the clearance is excessive, the crankshaft must be reground and undersize bearings installed.

Piston/Connecting Rod Installation

Connecting rods and bearing caps are numbered from 1 to 4 in the starboard bank and from 5 to 8 in the port bank. The

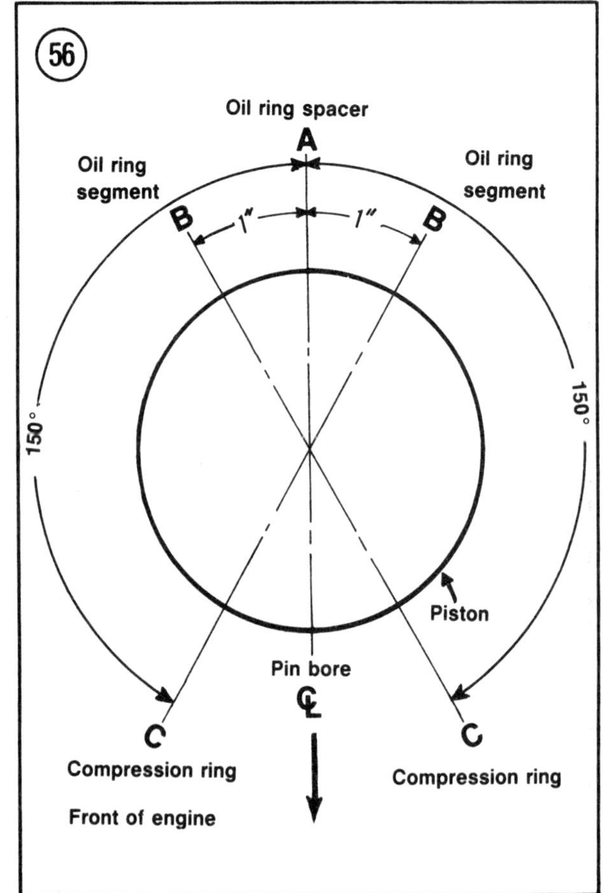

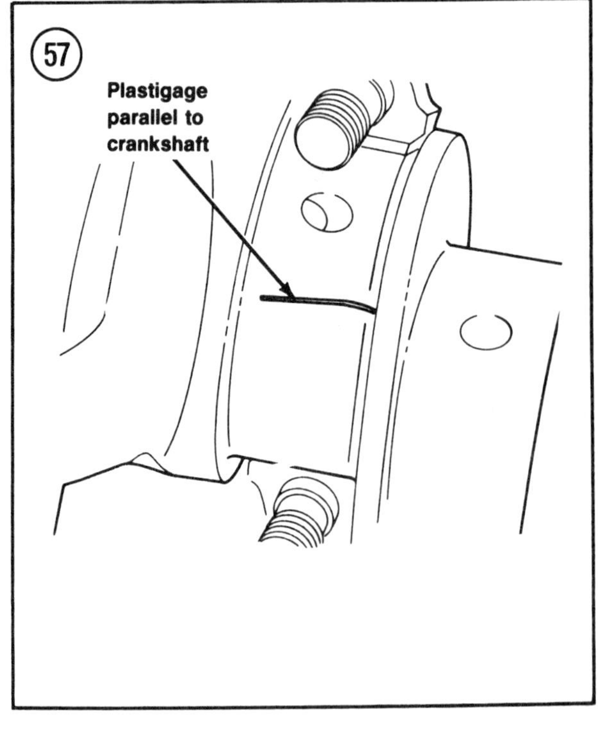

numbers on the rod and cap must be on the same side when installed in the cylinder. When switching a connecting rod from one block or cylinder to another, always fit new bearings and number the rod and cap to correspond with the new cylinder number.

1. Make sure the pistons are correctly installed on the connecting rods, if they were separated. The cylinder number side of the connecting rod and piston arrow or notch should be positioned as shown in **Figure 59**.

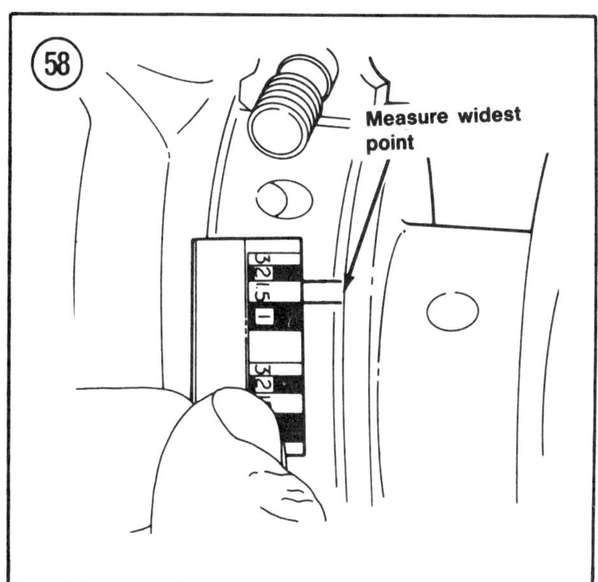

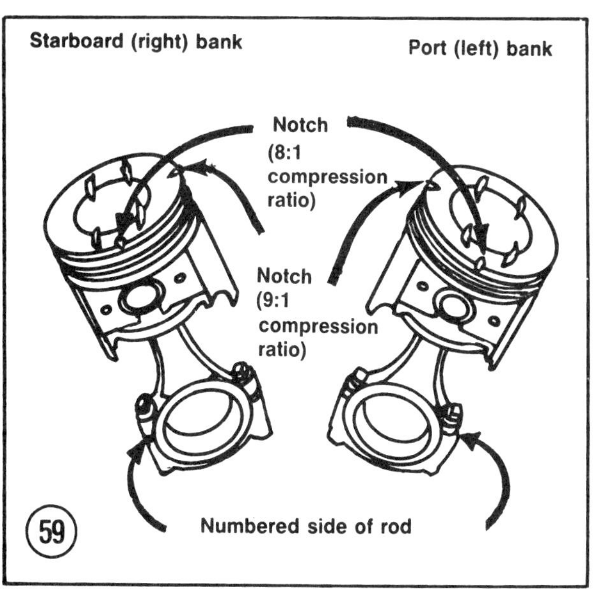

2. Make sure the ring gaps are positioned as shown in **Figure 56**.

3. Slip short pieces of hose over the connecting rod studs to prevent them from nicking the crankshaft. Tape will work if you do not have the right diameter hose, but it is more difficult to remove.

4. Immerse the entire piston in clean engine oil. Coat the cylinder wall with oil.

CAUTION
Use extreme care in Step 5 to prevent the connecting rod from nicking the crankshaft journal.

5. Install the piston/connecting rod assembly in its cylinder with a piston ring compressor as shown in **Figure 60**. Tap lightly with a wooden hammer handle to insert the piston. Make sure that the piston number (painted on top before removal) corresponds to the cylinder number, counting from the front of the engine.

NOTE
The notch on the piston must face the front of the engine.

6. Clean the connecting rod bearings carefully, including the back sides. Coat the

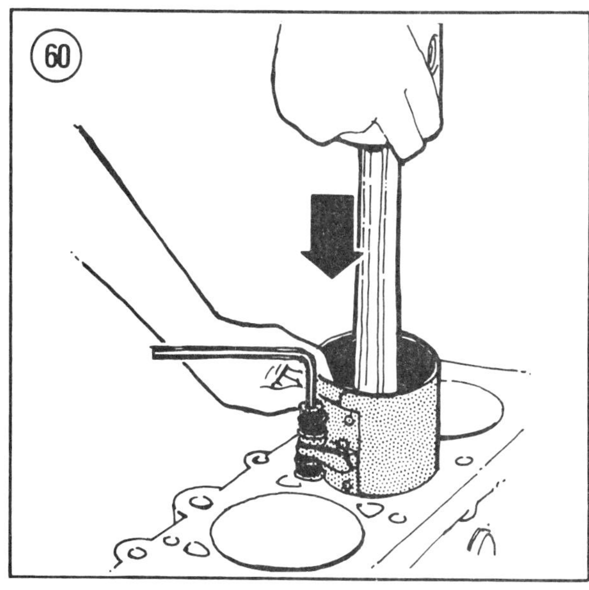

8

journals and bearings with clean engine oil. Place the bearings in the connecting rod and cap.

7. Pull the connecting rod and bearing into position against the crankpin. Remove the protective hose or tape and lightly lubricate the connecting rod bolt threads with SAE 30 engine oil.

8. Install the connecting rod cap (**Figure 42**). Make sure the rod and cap marks align. Install the cap nuts finger-tight.

9. Repeat Steps 4-8 for each remaining piston/connecting rod assembly.

10. Tighten the cap nuts to specifications (**Table 3**).

11. Check the connecting rod big-end play as described under *Piston/Connecting Rod Removal* in this chapter.

REAR MAIN OIL SEAL

Replacement seals are of the split lip variety. If the rear main cap contains a rear seal retainer pin, it must be removed to prevent damage to the new seal.

Replacement

1. Remove the engine as described in this chapter.

2. Remove the oil pan and oil pump as described in this chapter.

3. Loosen all main bearing caps enough to permit the crankshaft to be moved a maximum of 1/8 in.

4. Remove the rear main bearing cap. Remove the oil seal from the cap and cylinder block.

5. Clean the seal grooves in the cap and block with solvent and a brush.

6. Dip the 2 halves of the new seal in clean engine oil.

7. Position the cylinder block half of the seal with its undercut side facing the front of the engine. Install it by rotating it into the seal journal until about 1/8 in. remains above the parting surface. See **Figure 61**. Make sure that none of the seal rubber was shaved off by the bottom edge of the groove. If it was, discard the seal and install another.

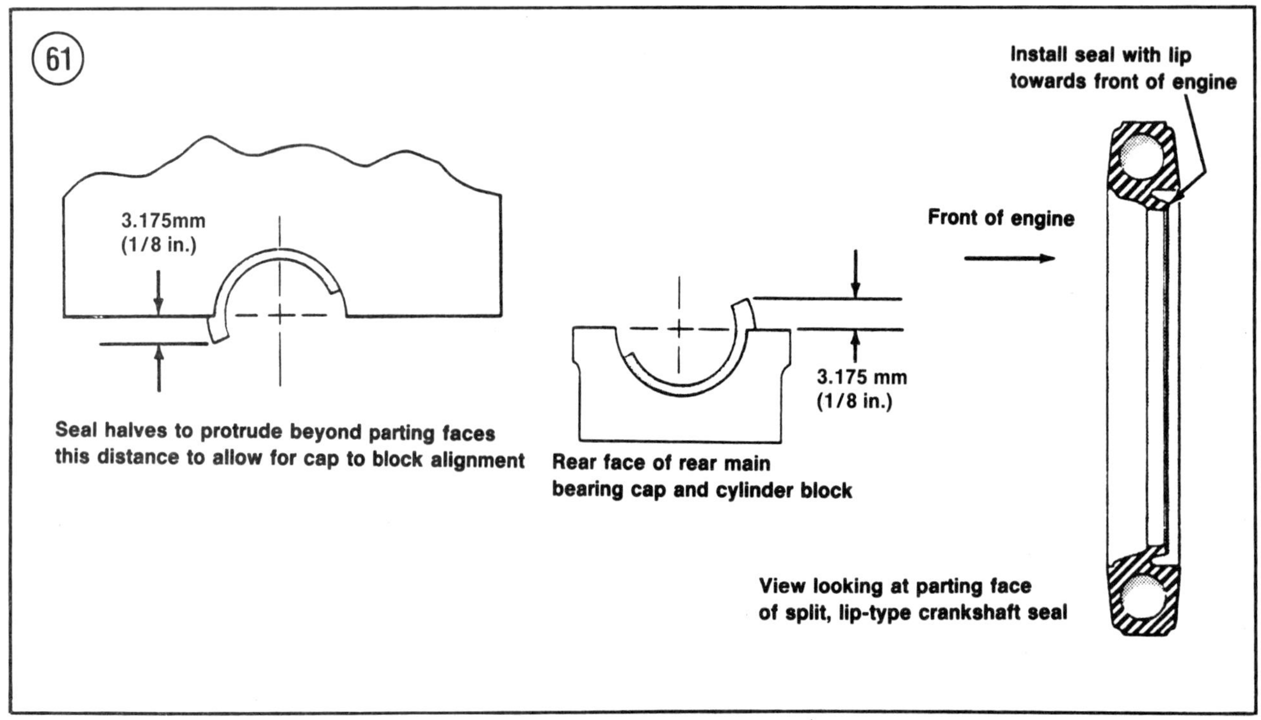

8. Tighten the loose cap bolts to specifications (**Table 3**).
9. Install the cap portion of the seal with its undercut side facing the front of the engine.

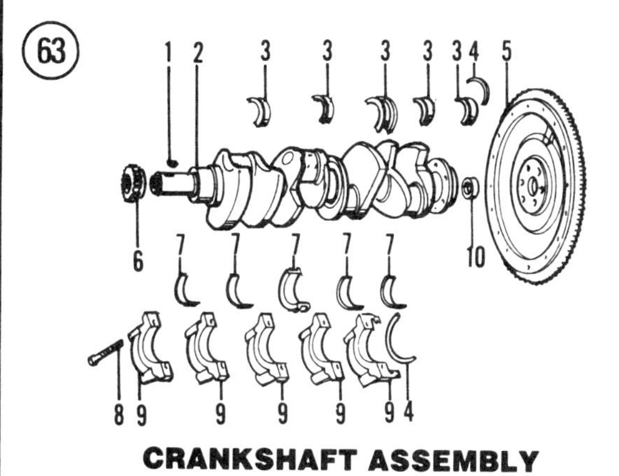

CRANKSHAFT ASSEMBLY
1. Woodruff key
2. Crankshaft
3. Upper bearing inserts
4. Rear main oil seal
5. Flywheel
6. Sprocket
7. Lower bearing inserts
8. Bolts
9. Main bearing caps
10. Pilot bearing

Again, allow about 3/8 in. of the seal end to protrude so it will mate with the other half when the cap is installed. Refer to **Figure 61**.

CAUTION
Do not apply sealant to the area forward of the side seal groove in Step 10.

10. Apply a thin coat of OMC Gasket Sealing Compound to the rear of the cap's top mating surface.
11. Install the rear main bearing cap and tighten to specifications (**Table 3**).
12. Install the oil pump and oil pan as described in this chapter.
13. Reinstall the engine in the boat as described in this chapter.

CRANKSHAFT

End Play Measurement

1. Pry the crankshaft all the way to the rear of the engine with a large screwdriver.
2. Install a dial indicator with its contact point resting against the crankshaft flange. The indicator axis should be parallel to the crankshaft axis. See **Figure 62**.
3. Set the dial indicator to zero. Force the crankshaft forward as far as it will go and compare the reading to specifications (**Table 3**).
4. Replace the thrust bearing if end play is excessive. If end play is less than specified, remove the crankshaft and recheck the thrust bearing for scratches, nicks, burrs or dirt. If none of these defects are found, improper alignment is probably the cause. Reinstall the bearing and repeat Steps 8-10 of *Installation* in this chapter.

Removal

Refer to **Figure 63** (typical) for this procedure.

1. Remove the engine from the boat as described in this chapter.

2. Remove the flywheel as described in this chapter.
3. Mount the engine on an engine stand, if available.
4. Remove the starter motor. See Chapter Eleven.
5. Invert the engine to bring the oil pan to an upright position.
6. Remove the oil pan and oil pump as described in this chapter.
7. Remove the vibration damper, front cover, timing chain and sprockets as described in this chapter.
8. Remove the spark plugs to permit easy rotation of the crankshaft.
9. Measure crankshaft end play as described in this chapter.
10. Rotate the crankshaft to position one connecting rod at the bottom of its stroke.
11. Remove the connecting rod bearing cap and bearing (**Figure 42**). Move the piston/rod assembly away from the crankshaft.
12. Repeat Step 10 and Step 11 for each remaining piston/rod assembly.
13. Check the caps for identification numbers or marks. If none are visible, clean the caps with a wire brush. If marks still cannot be seen, make your own with quick-drying paint.
14. Unbolt and remove the main bearing caps and bearing inserts. See **Figure 64** (typical).

NOTE
If the caps are difficult to remove, lift the bolts partway out, then pry them from side to side.

15. Carefully lift the crankshaft from the engine block and place it on a clean workbench.
16. Remove the bearing inserts from the block. Place the bearing caps and inserts in order on a clean workbench.

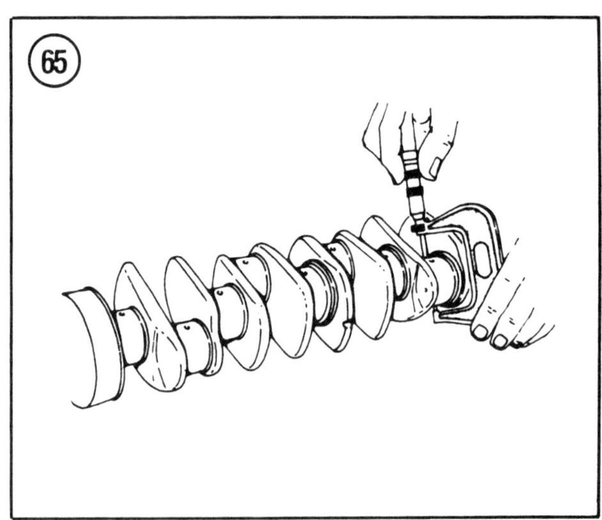

Inspection

1. Clean the crankshaft thoroughly with solvent. Blow out the oil passages with compressed air.
2. Check the main and connecting rod journals for wear, scratches, grooves, scoring or cracks. Check oil seal surface for burrs, nicks or other sharp edges which might damage a seal during installation.

NOTE
Unless you have precision measuring equipment and know how to use it, have a machine shop perform Step 3.

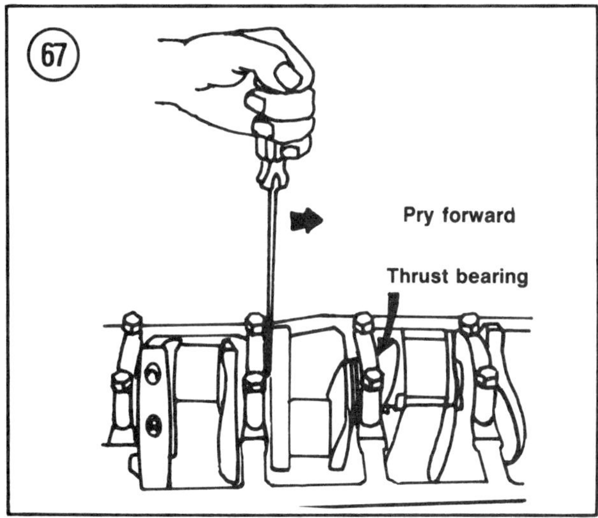

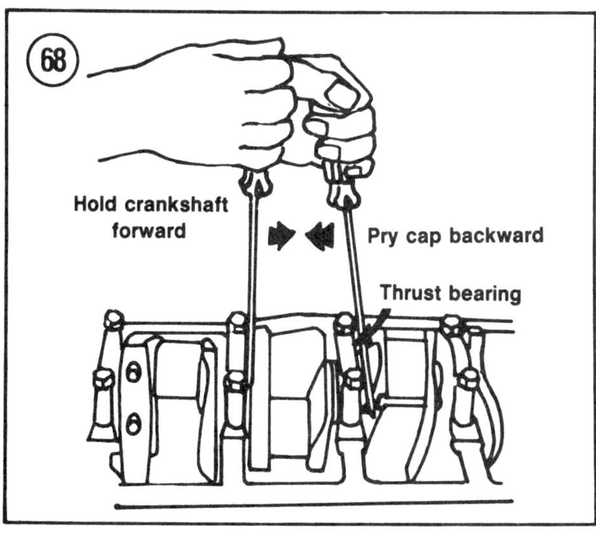

3. Check all journals against specifications (**Table 1** or **Table 2**) for out-of-roundness and taper. See **Figure 65**. Have the crankshaft reground, if necessary, and undersize bearings installed.

Main Bearing Clearance Measurement

Main bearing clearance is measured with Plastigage in the same manner as the connecting rod bearing clearance described in this chapter. Excessive clearance requires that the bearings be replaced, the crankshaft be reground or both.

Installation

Refer to **Figure 63** for this procedure.

1. Install a new rear main bearing oil seal as described in this chapter.
2. Install the main bearing inserts in the cylinder block. Bearing oil holes must align with block oil holes and bearing tabs must seat in the block tab slots.

NOTE
Check cap bolts for thread damage before reuse. If damaged, replace the bolts.

3. Lubricate the bolt threads with SAE 30 engine oil.
4. Install the bearing inserts in each cap.
5. Carefully lower the crankshaft into position in the block.
6. Install all bearing caps *except No. 3* in their marked positions with the arrows pointing toward the front of the engine (**Figure 66**) and the number mark aligned with the corresponding mark on the journals.
7. Install the No. 3 (thrust) bearing cap and tighten finger-tight.
8. Pry the crankshaft forward against the thrust surface of the upper half of the No. 3 bearing. See **Figure 67**.
9. Hold the crankshaft in this position and pry the thrust cap toward the rear of the engine (**Figure 68**) to align the thrust surfaces of both halves of the bearing.

10. Hold the crankshaft in the forward position and tighten the bearing caps to specifications (**Table 3**). See **Figure 69**.
11. Force the crankshaft to the rear of the engine and check end play as described in this chapter.
12. Reverse Steps 1-12 of *Removal* in this chapter.

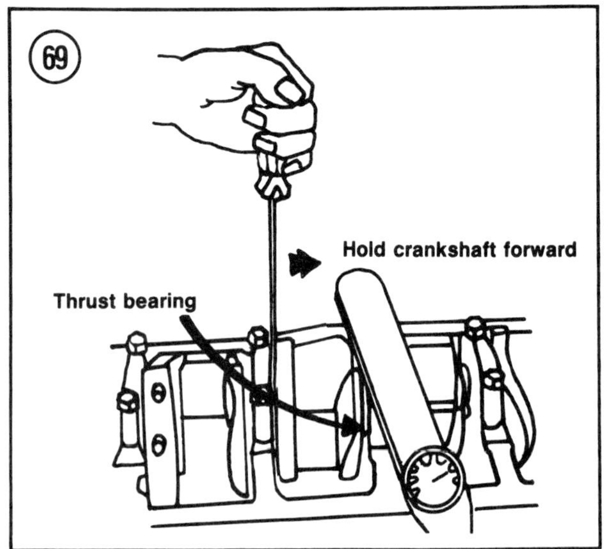

FLYWHEEL

Removal/Installation

1. Remove the engine from the boat as described in this chapter.
2. Remove the flywheel housing and drive plate or coupling, if so equipped.
3. Unbolt the flywheel from the crankshaft. Remove the bolts gradually in a diagonal pattern.
4. To install, align the dowel hole in the flywheel with dowel or dowel hole in crankshaft flange and position the flywheel on studs.
5. Fit the drive plate or coupling on the studs. Install the washers and locknuts. Tighten nuts to specifications (**Table 3**).
6. Install a dial indicator on the machined surface of the flywheel and check runout. If runout exceeds 0.008 in., remove the flywheel and check for burrs. If none are found, replace the flywheel.
7. If flywheel runout is within specifications, install the flywheel housing.
8. Reinstall the engine in the boat as described in this chapter.

Inspection

1. Visually check the flywheel surface for cracks, deep scoring, excessive wear, heat discoloration and checking. If the surface is glazed or slightly scratched, have the flywheel resurfaced by a machine shop.
2. Check the surface flatness with a straightedge and feeler gauge.

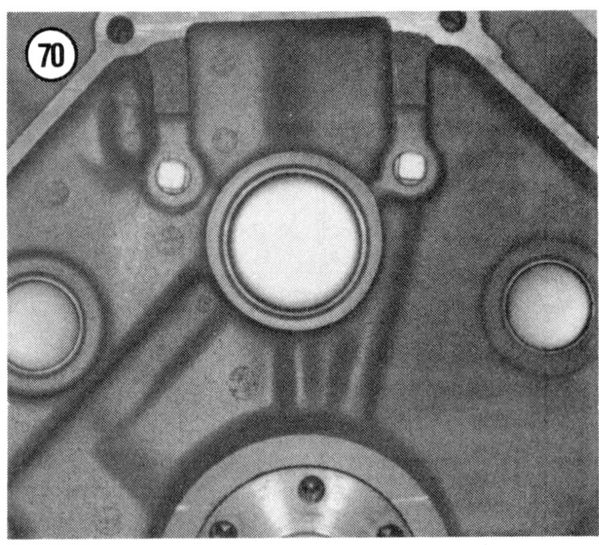

3. Inspect the ring gear for cracks, broken teeth or excessive wear. If severely worn, check the starter motor drive teeth for similar wear or damage; replace as required.

CYLINDER BLOCK

Cleaning and Inspection

1. Clean the block thoroughly with solvent. Remove any gasket or RTV sealant residue from the machined surfaces. Check all core plugs for leaks and replace any that are suspect. **Figure 70** shows typical core plug

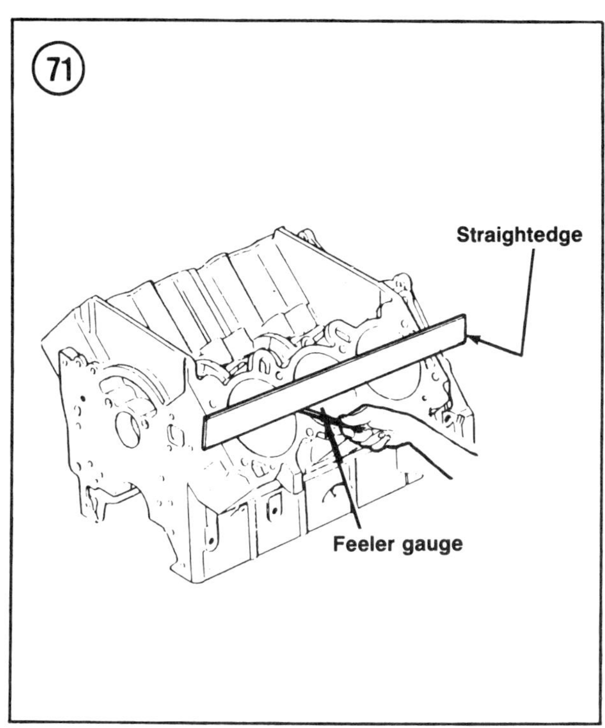

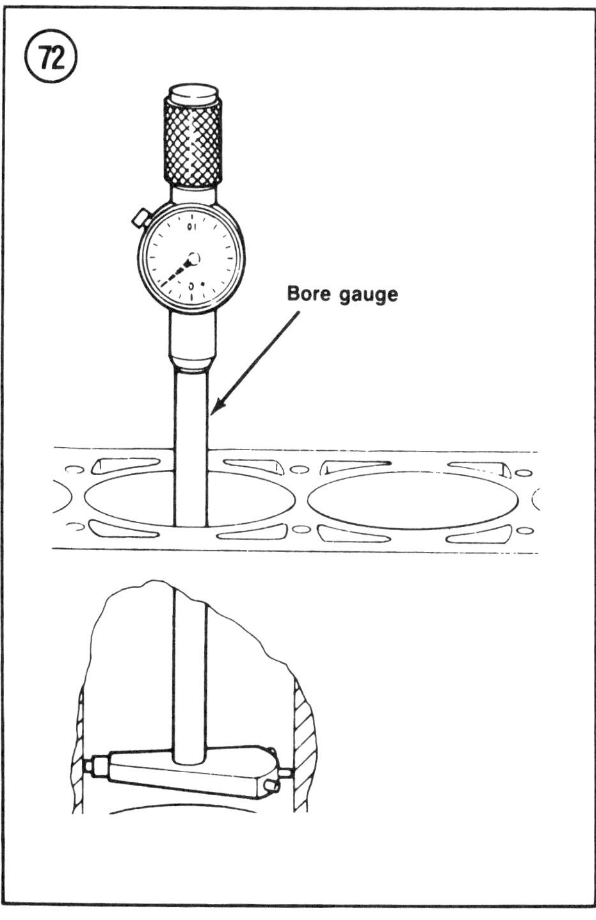

locations. See *Core Plug Replacement* in this chapter. Remove any plugs that seal oil passages. Check oil and coolant passages for sludge, dirt and corrosion while cleaning. If the passages are very dirty, have the block boiled out by a machine shop. Blow out all passages with compressed air. Check the threads in the head bolt holes to be sure they are clean. If dirty, use a tap to true up the threads and remove any deposits.

2. Examine the block for cracks. To confirm suspicions about possible leak areas, use a mixture of 1 part kerosene and 2 parts engine oil. Coat the suspected area with this solution, then wipe dry and immediately apply a solution of zinc oxide dissolved in wood alcohol. If any discoloration appears in the treated area, the block is cracked and should be replaced.

3. Check flatness of the cylinder block deck or top surface. Place an accurate straightedge on the block. If there is any gap between the block and straightedge, measure it with a flat feeler gauge (**Figure 71**). Measure from end to end and from corner to corner. Have the block resurfaced if it is warped more than 0.004 in. (0.102 mm).

4. Measure cylinder bores with a bore gauge (**Figure 72**) for out-of-roundness or excessive wear as described in *Piston Clearance Check* in this chapter. If the cylinders exceed maximumum tolerances, they must be rebored. Reboring is also necessary if the cylinder walls are badly scuffed or scored.

NOTE

*Before boring, install all main bearing caps and tighten the cap bolts to specifications in **Table 3**.*

CORE PLUG REPLACEMENT

The condition of all core plugs in the block (**Figure 70**) and cylinder head should be checked whenever the engine is out of the boat for service. If any signs of leakage or corrosion are found around one core plug, replace them all.

Removal/Installation

CAUTION
Do not drive core plugs into the engine casting. It will be impossible to retrieve them and they can restrict coolant circulation, resulting in serious engine damage.

1. Tap the bottom edge of the core plug with a hammer and drift. Use several sharp blows to push the bottom of the plug inward, tilting the top out (**Figure 73**).
2. Grip the top of the plug firmly with pliers. Pull the plug from its bore (**Figure 74**) and discard.

NOTE
Core plugs can also be removed by drilling a hole in the center of the plug and prying them out with an appropriate size drift or pin punch. On large core plugs, the use of a universal impact slide hammer is recommended.

3. Clean the plug bore thoroughly to remove all traces of the old sealer. Inspect the bore for any damage that might interfere with proper sealing of the new plug. If damage is evident, true the surface by boring for the next oversize plug.

NOTE
Oversize plugs can be identified by an "OS" stamped in the flat on the cup side of the plug.

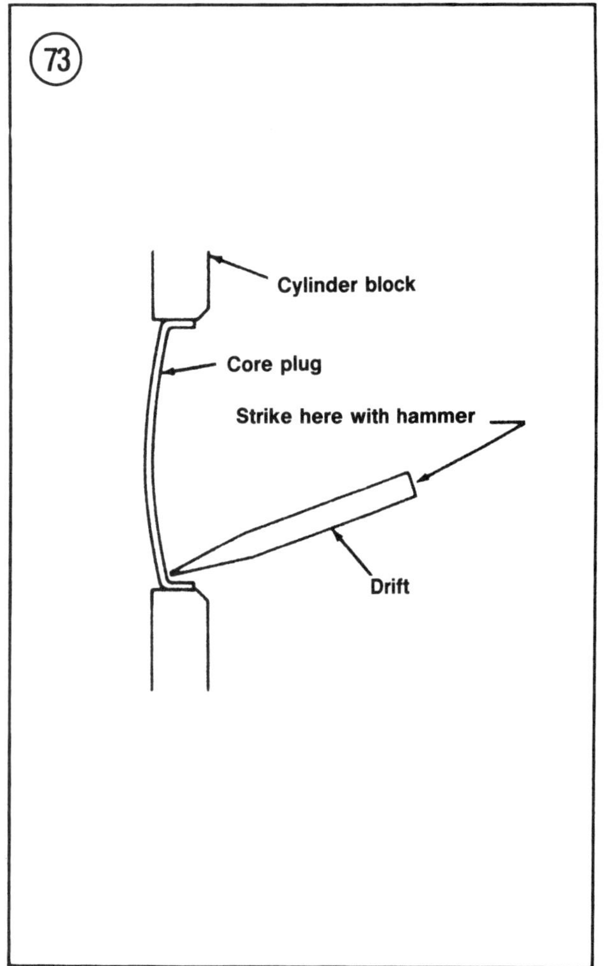

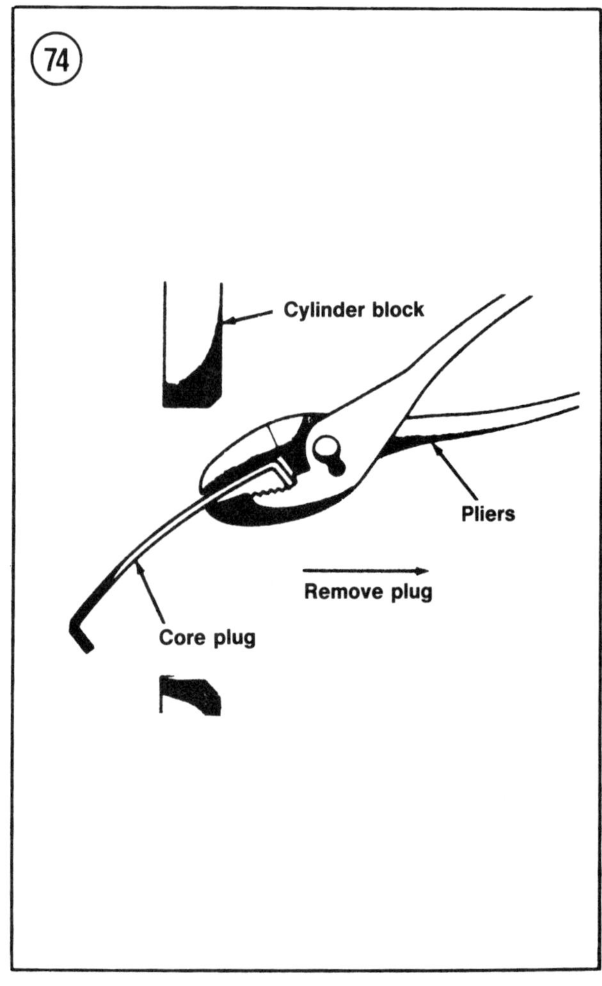

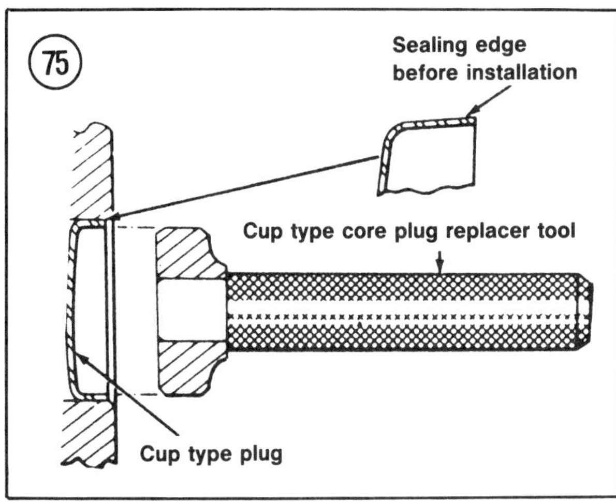

4. Coat the inside diameter of the plug bore and the outer diameter of the new plug with sealer. Use an oil-resistant sealer if the plug is to be installed in an oil gallery or a water-resistant sealer for plugs installed in the water jacket.
5. Install the new core plug with an appropriate size core plug replacer tool (**Figure 75**), driver or socket. The sharp edge of the plug should be at least 0.02 in. (0.5 mm) inside the lead-in chamfer.
6. Repeat Steps 1-5 to replace each remaining core plug.

Table 1 ENGINE SPECIFICATIONS (302 CID [5.0L] AND 351 CID [5.8L])

General specifications	
Piston displacement	
302 cid	4,949 cc (302 cu. in.)
351 cid	5,752 cc (351 cu. in.)
Bore	4.00 in.
Stroke	
302 cid	3.00 in.
351 cid	3.50 in.
Horsepower rating	
302 cid	185, 200 hp
351 cid	235 hp
Cylinder numbering (front to rear)	
Starboard bank	1-2-3-4
Port bank	5-6-7-8
Firing order	
185 hp 302 cid	1-5-4-2-6-3-7-8
All others	1-3-7-2-6-5-4-8
Cylinder bore	
Diameter	4.00 in.
Out-of-round	0.001 in. max.
Taper	
Thrust side	0.0005 in. max.
Relief side	0.001 in. max.
Piston clearance	0.0018-0.0026 in.
Piston rings	
Compression rings	
Side clearance	0.002-0.004 in.
Width	0.077-0.078 in.
Gap	0.010-0.020 in.
Oil ring	
Side clearance	Snug
Gap	0.015-0.055 in.

(continued)

Table 1 ENGINE SPECIFICATIONS (302 CID [5.0L] AND 351 CID [5.8L]) (cont.)

Piston pin	
Diameter	0.9120-0.9123 in.
Clearance	
302 cid	0.0002-0.0004 in.
351 cid	0.0003-0.0005 in.
Fit in rod	Interference
Crankshaft	
Main journal diameter	
302 cid	2.2482-2.2490 in.
351 cid	2.9994-3.0002 in.
Journal taper	0.0006 in.
Journal out-of-round	0.0006 in.
Main bearing clearance	
302 cid	
No. 1	0.0001-0.0020 in.
No. 2-5	0.0005-0.0024 in.
351 cid (all)	0.0008-0.0026 in.
End play	0.004-0.008 in.
Connecting rod journal diameter	
302 cid	2.1228-2.1236 in.
351 cid	2.3103-2.3111 in.
Journal taper	0.0006 in.
Journal out-of-round	0.0006 in.
Rod bearing clearance	0.001-0.0025 in.
Rod side clearance	0.010-0.020 in.
Camshaft	
Lobe lift (intake)	
185 hp 302 cid	0.2303 in.
200 hp 302 cid	0.260 in.
235 hp 351 cid	0.278 in.
Lobe lift (exhaust)	
185 hp 302 cid	0.238 in.
200 hp 302 cid	0.278 in.
235 hp 351 cid	0.283 in.
Journal diameter	
No. 1	2.0805-2.0815 in.
No. 2	2.0655-2.0665 in.
No. 3	2.0505-2.0515 in.
No. 4	2.0355-2.0365 in.
No. 5	2.0205-2.0215 in.
Runout	0.005 in. max.
Cylinder head	
Gasket surface flatness	0.003 in. any 6 in. or 0.007 in. overall max.
Valve system	
Lifter	Hydraulic
Rocker arm ratio	1.6:1
Face angle (intake and exhaust)	44°
Seat angle (intake and exhaust)	45°
Seat runout (all)	0.0015 in. max.
Head diameter	
Intake	1.773-1.791 in.
Exhaust	1.453-1.468 in.
Stem clearance	
Intake	0.0010-0.0027 in.
Exhaust	0.0015-0.0032 in.

(continued)

Table 1 ENGINE SPECIFICATIONS (302 CID [5.0L] AND 351 CID [5.8L]) (cont.)

Valve springs	
Free length	
Intake	
302 cid	1.94 in.
351 cid	2.06 in.
Exhaust	1.87 in.
Pressure	
302 cid	
Closed	76-84 ft.-lb @ 1.69 in.
Open	190-210 ft.-lb. @ 1.31 in.
351 cid	
Closed	71-79 ft.-lb. @ 1.79 in.
Open	190-210 ft.-lb. @ 1.31 in.
Installed height	
Intake	
302 cid	1-21/32 - 1-23/32 in.
351 cid	1-49/64 - 1-13/16 in.
Exhaust	1-19/32 - 1-5/8 in.
Oil pump	
Outer race to housing clearance	0.001-0.013 in.
Rotor end play	0.0011-0.004 in.
Drive shaft to housing bearing clearance	0.0015-0.0029 in.
Relief valve spring length	
302 cid	10.6-12.2 lbs. @ 1.704 in.
351 cid	18.2-20.2 lbs. @ 2.49 in.

8

Table 2 ENGINE SPECIFICATIONS (460 CID [7.5L])

Engine type	90° V8
Bore	4.36 in.
Stroke	3.85 in.
Displacement	460 cid (7.5 liter)
Firing order	1-5-4-2-6-3-7-8
Cylinder arrangement	
Starboard bank	1-2-3-4
Port bank	5-6-7-8
Cylinder bore	
Diameter	4.3600-4.3636 in.
Out-of-round	0.005 in. max.
Taper	0.005 in. max.
Head gasket surface flatness	0.003 in. in 6 in.
Pistons	
Diameter	
Code red	4.3585-4.3591 in.
Code blue	4.3597-4.3603 in.
0.003 oversize	4.3609-4.3615 in.
Clearance	0.0022-0.0030 in.
Ring groove width	
Compression	0.080-0.815 in.
Oil	0.188-0.189 in.
Ring width	
Compression	0.077-0.078 in.
Side clearance	
Compression	0.0025-0.0045 in.
Oil	Snug

(continued)

Table 2 ENGINE SPECIFICATIONS (460 CID [7.5L]) (cont.)

Ring gap	
Compression	0.010-0.020 in.
Oil	0.015-0.055 in.
Piston pin	
Diameter	
Standard	1.0398-1.0403 in.
0.001 oversize	1.0410-1.0413 in.
Length	3.290-3.320 in.
Clearance	Interference (press fit)
Camshaft	
Lobe lift	
Intake	0.285 in.
Exhaust	0.290 in.
Journal diameter	2.1238-2.1248 in.
Journal to bearing clearance	0.001-0.003 in.
Bearing inside diameter	2.1258-2.1273 in.
Timing chain deflection	0.5 in. max.
Runout	0.005 in.
End play	0.001-0.006 in.
Crankshaft	
Main journal diameter	2.9994-3.0002 in.
Taper	0.0005 in.
Out-of-round	0.0006 in.
Main bearing clearance	0.0008-0.0015 in.
End play	0.004-0.008 in.
Crankpin	
Diameter	2.6522-2.6530 in.
Taper	0.0004 in.
Out-of-round	0.0004 in.
Connecting rod	
Bearing clearance	0.0008-0.0015 in.
Side clearance	0.010-0.020 in.
Valve train	
Lifter	Hydraulic
Rocker arm ratio	1.73:1
Valve arrangement	
Starboard	IEIEIEIE
Port	EIEIEIEI
Face angle	44°
Seat angle	45°
Seat width	0.060-0.080 in.
Stem clearance	0.0010-0.0027 in.
Pushrod runout	0.015 in. max.
Stem diameter	
Standard	0.3416-0.3423 in.
0.003 oversize	0.3446-0.3453 in.
0.015 oversize	0.3566-0.3573 in.
0.030 oversize	0.3716-0.3723 in.
Head diameter	
Intake	2.075-2.090 in.
Exhaust	1.646-1.661 in.
Face runout	0.0020 in. max.

(continued)

Table 2 ENGINE SPECIFICATIONS (460 CID [7.5L]) (cont.)

Valve spring	
Free length	2.06 in.
Installed height	1 51/64-1 53/64 in.
Out-of-square	0.78 in. max.
Load	
Closed	87-97 lb. @ 1.82 in.
Open	300-330 lb. @ 1.32 in.
Oil pump	
Relief valve tension	20.6-22.6 lb. @ 2.490 in.
Relief valve clearance	0.0015-0.0030 in.
Drive shaft-to-housing clearance	0.0015-0.0030 in.
Rotor assembly end clearance	0.001-0.004 in.
Outer race-to-housing clearance	0.001-0.013 in.
Inner-to-outer rotor tip clearance	0.012 in.

Table 3 FORD V8 TIGHTENING TORQUES

Fastener	ft.-lb.	N•m
Alternator		
Adjusting arm		
To alternator	24-40	33-60
To water pump	35-50	48-67
Bracket-to-water pump	35-50	48-67
Pivot bolt	45-57	62-77
Camshaft sprocket	40-45	55-61
Camshaft thrust plate	9-12	13-16
Connecting rod caps		
302 cid	19-24	25-33
351 cid	40-45	54-61
460 cid	45-50	61-67
Cylinder front cover	15-21	17-24
Cylinder head bolts		
302 cid		
Step 1	50	67
Step 2	60	81
Step 3	65-70	88-95
351 cid		
Step 1	90	122
Step 2	100	136
Step 3	112	152
460 cid		
Step 1	80	108
Step 2	110	149
Step 3	130-140	177-189
Damper-to-crankshaft	70-90	95-122
Distributor clamp	17-25	24-33
Exhaust manifold		
Attaching nuts	20-26	27-35
High rise elbow	12-14	16-19
Fuel pump	19-27	26-36
Flywheel-to-crankshaft	75-85	103-115

(continued)

Table 3 FORD V8 TIGHTENING TORQUES (cont.)

Fastener	ft.-lb.	N•m
Intake manifold		
302/351 cid	23-25	31-33
460 cid	22-32	30-43
Main bearing caps		
302 cid	60-70	81-95
351/460 cid	95-105	130-143
Oil filter insert-to-adaptor	45-55	62-74
Oil filter adaptor	40-50	55-67
Oil inlet		
Tube-to-pump	12-18	17-24
To main bearing cap nut	22-32	30-43
Oil pan		
Baffle nut	22-32	30-43
Drain plug	15-25	21-33
1/4 in.	7	9
5/16 in.	9-11	13-14
Oil pump	22-32	30-43
Pulley-to-damper bolt	35-50	48-67
Valve cover	5-6	7-8
Water outlet housing	10-15	14-20
Water pump	15-21	20-28

Table 4 STANDARD TORQUE VALUES

Fastener	ft.-lb.	N•m
Grade 5		
1/4-20	8	11
1/4-28	8	11
5/16-18	17	23
5/16-24	20	27
3/8-16	30	40
3/8-24	35	47
7/16-14	50	68
7/16-20	55	75
1/2-13	75	100
1/2-20	85	115
9/16-12	105	142
9/16-18	115	156
Grade 6		
1/4-20	10.5	14
1/4-28	12.5	17
5/16-18	22.5	31
5/16-24	25	54
3/8-16	40	34
3/8-24	45	61
7/16-14	65	88
7/16-20	70	95
1/2-13	100	136
1/2-20	110	149
9/16-12	135	183
9/16-18	150	203

Chapter Nine

Fuel Delivery System

The fuel delivery system consists of the fuel tank(s), a water separating fuel filter (if so equipped), the fuel pump, carburetor, carburetor inlet filter and connecting lines. Fuel from the tank(s) is drawn through the line and water separating filter (if so equipped) by the mechanically-operated fuel pump, which then pushes it through the carburetor inlet filter into the carburetor where it is metered, mixed with air and sent to the intake manifold for delivery to the cylinders.

This chapter includes service procedures for the flame arrestor, carburetor, fuel pump and connecting lines. Regular maintenance to the fuel system is limited to replacing the fuel filter, cleaning the flame arrestor and adjusting the carburetor, as described in Chapter Four.

FLAME ARRESTOR

Removal/Installation

1. Remove the engine compartment cover or hatch and place to one side out of the way.
2. Disconnect the crankcase vent hose(s) at the flame arrestor (**Figure 1,** typical).
3. Remove the nut holding the cover **(Figure 2)** or flame arrestor **(Figure 1)** to the carburetor air horn.
4. Remove the cover, if used. Remove the flame arrestor and gasket, if used, from the carburetor air horn.
5. Installation is the reverse of removal.

Cleaning

Clean the flame arrestor in kerosene, carburetor cleaner or other commercial solvent. Do *not* use gasoline as a solvent—it is an extreme fire hazard in an open container.

1. Remove the flame arrestor as described in this chapter.
2. Submerge the flame arrestor in a container of clean solvent for several minutes to let the solution penetrate accumulated deposits of dirt, dust and other contaminants.
3. Slosh the flame arrestor in the solvent container and resubmerge for a few minutes.
4. Remove the flame arrestor from the solvent and allow it to drain, then blow dry with compressed air.
5. If the air inlet screen is deformed in any way, replace the flame arrestor.
6. Reinstall the flame arrestor as described in this chapter.

FUEL REQUIREMENTS AND QUALITY

Gasoline Requirements

OMC recommends the use of lead-free or leaded gasoline with a minimum research octane number (RON) of 93 or anti-knock index number (AKI) of 89. If the fuel used does not have a minimum 93 RON (89 AKI), you must retard the ignition timing on all engines except the 1989 2.3L, 5.0L, 5.8L and 7.5L Ford engines and 1987-1988 2.3L Ford engines to accommodate the use of lower octane fuels. Failure to retard the ignition according to the specifications provided in **Table 6**, Chapter Four may result in serious engine damage and can void your factory warranty.

Sour Fuel

The fuel used plays a large role in satisfactory engine performance. In most temperate climates, fuel will start to break down after it has been in the fuel tank about

4 months. When this happens, it forms a gum-like substance that settles at the bottom of the tank where it can clog the in-tank filter. If drawn out of the tank by the fuel pump, this substance will affect the fuel filters. It will also start to clog the jets and other small passages inside the carburetor. Such fuel gives off an odor similar to that of rotten eggs.

You should drain the fuel tank whenever the boat will not be in service for a period of time. The gasoline can be used in an automobile without harm, since it will be burned within a few days. If it is not possible or desirable to drain the tank, the use of OMC 2+4 fuel conditioner (or equivalent) is recommended to prevent the fuel from spoiling. Regular use of this additive is also recommended to prevent corrosion and gum formation in the fuel system.

Gasohol

As mentioned in Chapter Two, some gasolines sold for marine use may contain alcohol, although this fact may not be advertised. Using such fuels is not recommended, unless you can determine the nature of the blend. OMC suggests that the following precautions be observed if gasohol must be used.

1. Buy fuel only as needed and use it as soon as possible.

2. Do not spill gasohol on painted surfaces.
3. Change ignition timing according to the specifications provided in **Table 6**, Chapter Four.
4. Expect a slight decrease in power, stalling at lower speeds and somewhat greater fuel consumption.
5. Alternate the use of gasohol with regular leaded gasoline to extend valve seat life. If it is necessary to operate an engine on gasohol, do not store such fuel in the tank(s) for more than a few days, especially in climates with high humidity.

Numerous problems have been identified with the use of misblended alcohol/gasoline fuels. Some of the most important are:

a. Corrosion formation on the inside of fuel tanks and steel fuel lines.
b. Corrosion formation inside carburetors. Zinc and aluminum alloys are especially susceptible.
c. Deterioration and failure of synthetic rubber or plastic materials such as O-ring seals, diaphragms, accelerator pump cups and gaskets.
d. Premature failure of fuel line hoses.

CARBURETOR FUNDAMENTALS

A gasoline engine must receive fuel and air mixed in a precise proportion in order to operate efficiently at various speeds. Under normal conditions at sea level, the ratio is 14.7:1 at high speed and 12:1 at low speeds. Carburetors are designed to maintain these ratios while providing for sudden acceleration or increased loads.

A mixture with too much fuel is said to be "rich." One with too little fuel is said to be "lean." Incorrect mixture proportions can result from a variety of factors such as a dirty flame arrestor, defective choke, improperly adjusted idle mixture or speed screws, a leaking needle valve or a float that has absorbed fuel.

The choke valve in a carburetor provides a richer than normal mixture of fuel and air until the engine warms up. If the choke valve sticks in an open position, the engine will not start properly. A choke that sticks in a closed position will cause a flooding condition.

The throat of a carburetor is often called a "barrel." A single-barrel (1-bbl.) carburetor has only one throat. Two-barrel carburetors have 2 throats and 2 complete sets of metering devices, but only one float bowl and float. A 4-barrel carburetor has 4 throats, 4 complete sets of metering devices 1 or 2 floats depending on model.

CARBURETORS

During the years covered by this manual, the following carburetors have been used:

a. Rochester 2GC/2GV 2-bbl.
b. Rochester 4MV 4-bbl.
c. Holley 2-bbl.
d. Holley 4-bbl.

Removal, overhaul and installation procedures are provided for all models.

WARNING
Carburetors used on OMC marine engines are designed for marine use. Do not substitute an automotive carburetor or automotive carburetor parts. Fuel vapors escaping from such carburetors or as a result of incorrect parts usage can create a fire or explosion hazard.

Carburetor specifications vary with type, application and model year. The necessary specifications are provided on instruction sheets accompanying overhaul kits, along with any specific procedures required for adjustment. The specifications provided in **Table 1** should be used only if the overhaul kit instruction sheet is not available.

The carburetor model identification may be stamped on the carburetor main body or air horn casting, or on a tag attached to the carburetor by one of the air horn screws (**Figure 3**). This information is necessary to obtain the proper overhaul kit from your OMC dealer.

Carburetor Removal/Installation

1. Remove the flame arrestor as described in this chapter. If the carburetor uses a spacer on the flame arrestor mounting stud, remove and place it where it will not be lost.
2. Place a container under the fuel line connection to catch any spillage. Disconnect the fuel line at the carburetor. Use one wrench to hold the fuel inlet nut (A, **Figure 4**) while you loosen the fuel line fitting nut (B, **Figure 4**) with a second wrench. Cap the line and fitting to prevent leakage and the entry of contamination. Disconnect the fuel pump sight hose at the carburetor. See C, **Figure 4** (typical).
3. Remove and discard any tie straps holding hoses, vacuum lines or electrical wiring to the carburetor.
4. Disconnect the choke heat tube (A, **Figure 5**) or electrical connection as appropriate. If equipped with a well-type or remote choke, disconnect the choke coil rod at the carburetor (**Figure 6**).
5. Disconnect the crankcase ventilation hose at the carburetor, if so equipped.
6. Disconnect the throttle linkage.
7. Remove the carburetor flange-to-manifold fasteners and lockwashers. Remove the carburetor from the manifold.
8. Stuff a clean cloth in the intake manifold opening to prevent small parts and contaminants from falling inside.

NOTE

For ease in starting, fill the carburetor bowl with fuel before installing the carburetor. Operate the throttle lever several times and verify that fuel discharges from the pump jets before installation.

9. Installation is the reverse of removal. Clean all gasket residue from the intake manifold mating surface and install a new carburetor gasket. To prevent warpage of the carburetor base, snug the flange fasteners, then tighten the fasteners in a crisscross pattern to specifications. Tighten Rochester 2-bbl. and Holley fasteners to 12-15 ft.-lb. (16-20 N•m). Tighten Rochester 4-bbl. screws to 6-8 ft.-lb. (8-11 N•m) and nuts to 10-14 ft.-lb. (13-19 N•m).

3

4

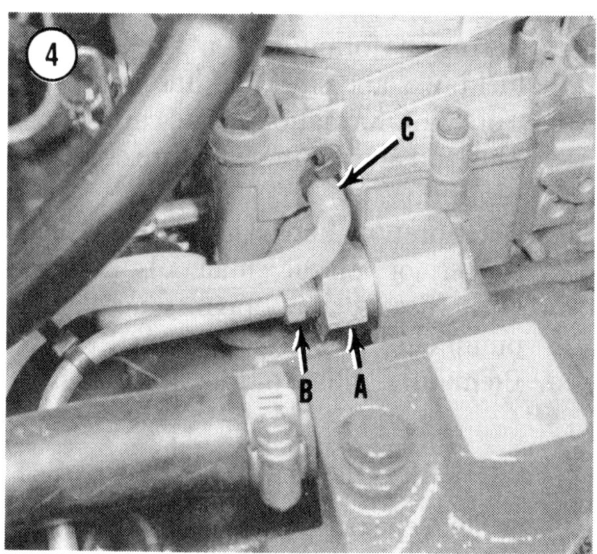

Preparation for Overhaul

Before removing and disassembling any carburetor, be sure you have the proper

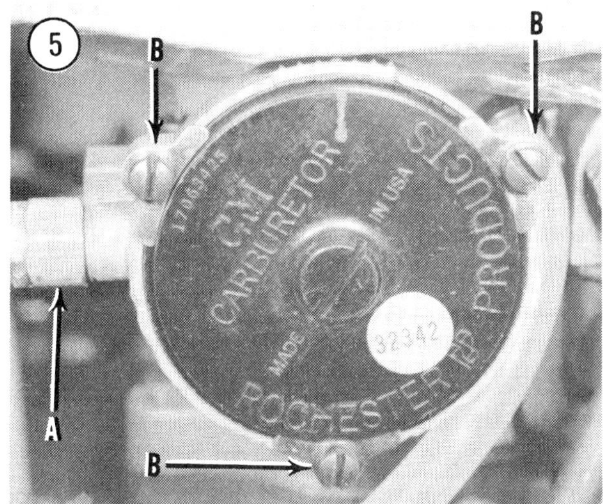

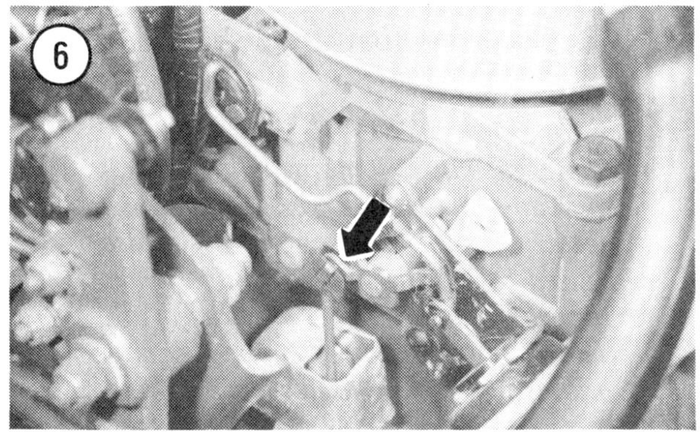

marine carburetor overhaul kit, a sufficient quantity of fresh carburetor cleaner and the proper tools. Work slowly and carefully, follow the disassembly and assembly procedures, refer to the exploded drawing of your carburetor when necessary and do not apply excessive force at any time.

It is not necessary to disassemble the carburetor linkage or remove linkage adjusting screws when overhauling a carburetor. Solenoids, dashpots and other diaphragm-operated assist devices attached to the carburetor body should be removed, as carburetor cleaner will damage them. Wipe such parts with a cloth to remove road film, grease and other contamination.

Use carburetor legs to prevent throttle plate damage while working on the carburetor. If legs are not available, thread a nut on each of four 2 1/4 in. bolts. Install each bolt in a flange hole and thread another nut on the bolt. These will hold the bolts securely to the carburetor and serve the same purpose as legs.

CAUTION
*Do **not** use the carburetor-to-manifold gasket supplied in any overhaul, gasket or repair kit unless it is specifically designed for marine application. Current OMC carburetor kits contain the correct gasket. When using kits provided by other manufacturers, it is necessary to order the correct mounting gasket from your OMC dealer.*

Some of the carburetors used on the engines covered in this manual may have riveted choke housings in accordance with Federal regulations. This adjustment is factory-set and should not be changed by the home mechanic. If the engine will not run properly after the carburetor is cleaned, reassembled and installed as described in this chapter, it is advisable to install a rebuilt carburetor.

Cleaning and Inspection

Dirt, varnish, gum, water, carbon or other contamination in or on the carburetor are often the cause of unsatisfactory performance. Gaskets and accelerating pump cups may swell or leak, resulting in carburetion problems. Efficient carburetion depends upon careful cleaning, inspection and proper installation of new parts.

The new gaskets and parts provided in a marine carburetor overhaul kit should be installed when overhauling the carburetor and the old parts discarded. Automotive carburetor overhaul kits should not be used. The gaskets included in automotive overhaul kits will allow the carburetor to vent fuel vapors directly into the engine compartment.

This venting of vapors presents a fire and explosion hazard.

Wash all parts except the choke cap, diaphragms, dashpots, solenoids and other vacuum or electrically operated assist devices in fresh commercial carburetor cleaning solvent. This can be obtained from any auto parts store. Do not leave parts in carburetor cleaner longer than necessary to loosen the gum and dirt or it will remove the sealing compound (dichromate finish) applied to the carburetor castings at the factory to prevent porosity. Cleaning with an aerosol type cleaner will do the job without damage to the sealing compound.

If a commercial cleaning solvent is used, suspend the air horn in the cleaner to prevent the solution from reaching the riveted choke cap and housing. Do not leave any parts in the cleaning solution longer than necessary to avoid removal of the sealing compound.

Rinse parts cleaned in solvent with kerosene. Blow all parts dry with compressed air. Wipe all parts which cannot be immersed in solvent with a soft cloth slightly moistened with solvent, then with a clean, dry cloth.

Force compressed air through all passages in the carburetor.

CAUTION

Do not use a wire brush to clean any part. Do not use a drill or wire to clean out any opening or passage in the carburetor. A drill or wire may enlarge the hole or passage and change the calibration.

Check the choke and throttle plate shafts for grooves, wear or excessive looseness or binding. Inspect the choke and throttle plates for nicked edges or burrs which prevent proper closure. Choke and throttle plates are positioned during production and should not be removed unless damaged.

Clean all gasket residue from the air horn, main body and throttle body sealing surfaces with a dull putty knife. Since carburetor castings are aluminum, a sharp instrument may damage them.

Inspect all components for cracks or warpage. Check floats for wear on the lip and hinge pin. Check hinge pin holes in air horn, bowl cover or float bowl for wear and elongation.

Check composition floats for fuel absorption by gently squeezing and applying fingernail pressure. If moisture appears, replace the float.

Replace the float if the arm needle contact surface is grooved. If the float or floats are serviceable, gently polish the needle contact surface of the arm with crocus cloth or steel wool. Replace the float if the shaft is worn.

NOTE

Some gasolines contain additives that will cause the viton tip on the fuel inlet needle to swell. This problem is also caused by gasoline and alcohol blends. If carburetor problems are traced to a deformed inlet needle tip, change brands of gasoline used.

Check the viton tip of the fuel inlet needle for swelling or distortion. Discard the needle if the overhaul kit contains a new needle for assembly.

Replace all screws and nuts that have stripped threads. Replace all distorted or broken springs. Inspect all gasket mating surfaces for nicks or burrs.

If a Rochester main body requires replacement, check the float bowl casting. If marked "MW," be sure to replace the main body with one marked "MW." This stands for "machined pump well" and determines the type of pump used.

Reassemble all parts carefully. It should not be necessary to apply force to any parts. If force seems to be required, you are doing something wrong. Stop and refer to the exploded drawing for your carburetor.

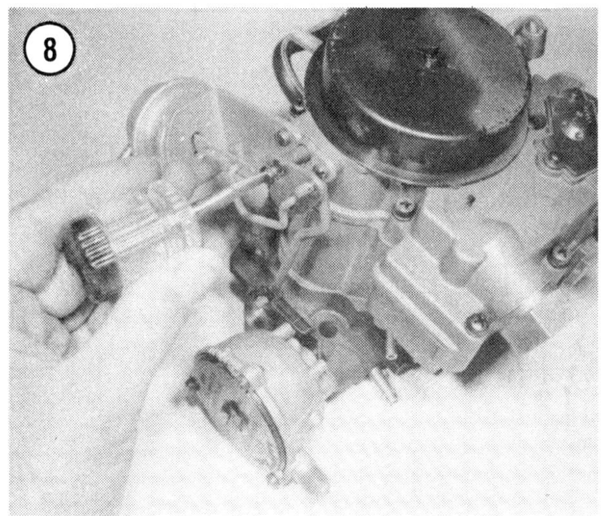

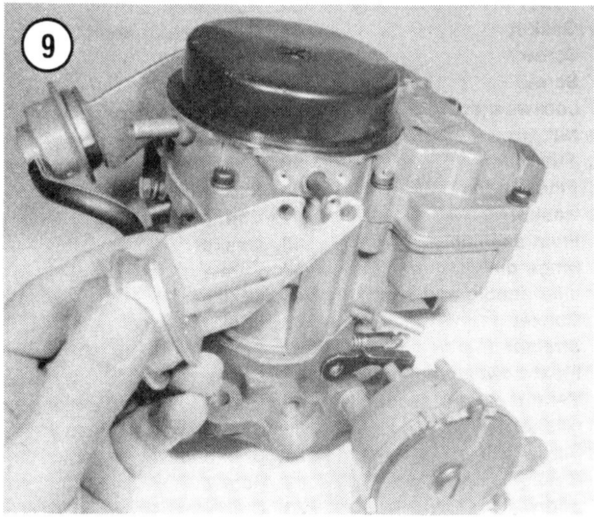

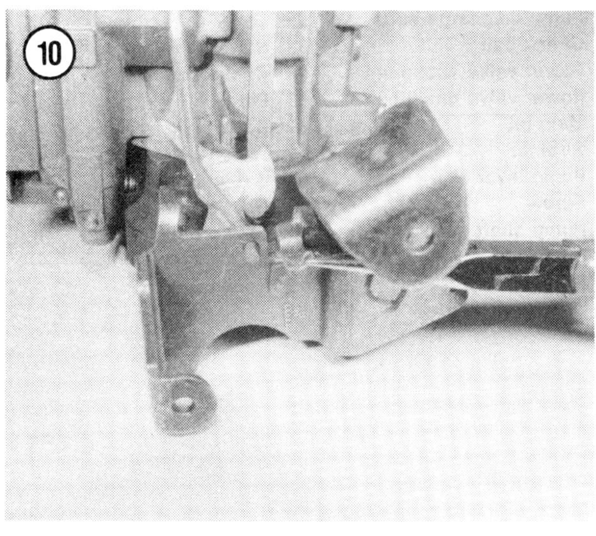

Rochester 2GC/2GV Disassembly

The Rochester 2GC uses an integral cap-type choke; the 2GV uses a remote or well-type choke. Refer to **Figure 7** as required for this procedure. Not all 2GC/2GV carburetors will use all the parts shown in **Figure 7**.

1. Use carburetor legs to prevent throttle plate damage while working on the carburetor. If legs are not available, thread a nut on each of four 2 1/4 in. bolts. Install each bolt in a flange hole and thread another nut on the bolt. These will hold the bolts securely to the carburetor and serve the same purpose as legs.
2. If choke cap is not riveted in place:
   a. Remove the cap retaining screws and retainers. See B, **Figure 5** (typical). Remove the cap cover, gasket and insulator baffle plate from the choke housing.
   b. Remove the screw holding the choke piston and lever assembly to the choke shaft. Remove the piston and lever assembly.
   c. Remove the 2 screws holding the choke housing to the bowl cover. Remove the choke housing and gasket. Discard the gasket.
3. 4.3L carburetor:
   a. Remove the screw holding the upper intermediate choke lever to the choke shaft. See **Figure 8** (typical).
   b. Disengage the lever from the choke vacuum break link.
   c. Disconnect the vacuum break hose from the throttle body, then remove the vacuum break diaphragm and bracket assembly from the bowl cover. See **Figure 9**.
   d. Disengage the intermediate choke rod from the lower choke lever.
4. Remove the hairpin retainers from each end of the pump rod with needlenose pliers. See **Figure 10** (typical). Rotate the upper rod

9

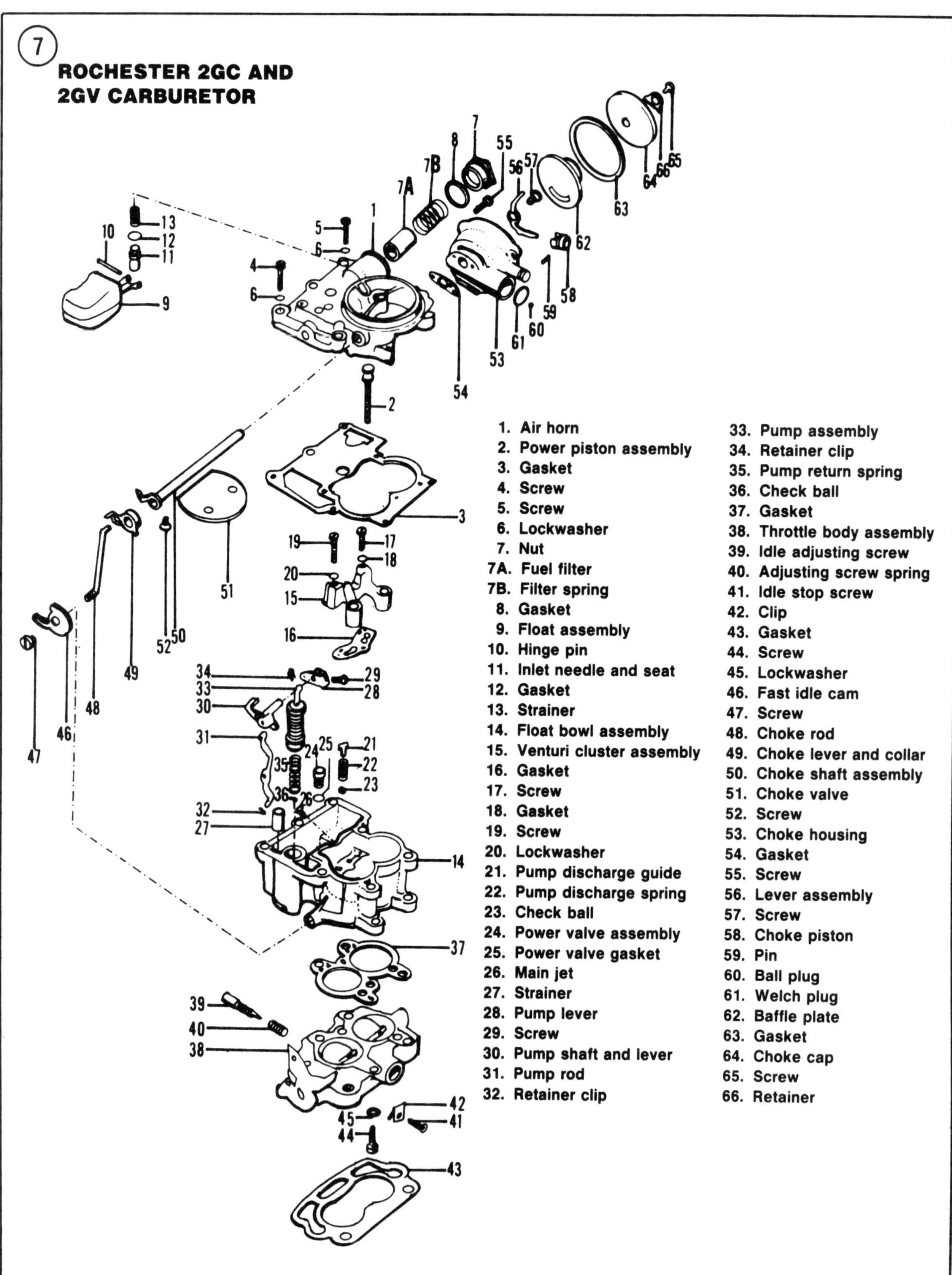
7
ROCHESTER 2GC AND
2GV CARBURETOR
1. Air horn
2. Power piston assembly
3. Gasket
4. Screw
5. Screw
6. Lockwasher
7. Nut
7A. Fuel filter
7B. Filter spring
8. Gasket
9. Float assembly
10. Hinge pin
11. Inlet needle and seat
12. Gasket
13. Strainer
14. Float bowl assembly
15. Venturi cluster assembly
16. Gasket
17. Screw
18. Gasket
19. Screw
20. Lockwasher
21. Pump discharge guide
22. Pump discharge spring
23. Check ball
24. Power valve assembly
25. Power valve gasket
26. Main jet
27. Strainer
28. Pump lever
29. Screw
30. Pump shaft and lever
31. Pump rod
32. Retainer clip
33. Pump assembly
34. Retainer clip
35. Pump return spring
36. Check ball
37. Gasket
38. Throttle body assembly
39. Idle adjusting screw
40. Adjusting screw spring
41. Idle stop screw
42. Clip
43. Gasket
44. Screw
45. Lockwasher
46. Fast idle cam
47. Screw
48. Choke rod
49. Choke lever and collar
50. Choke shaft assembly
51. Choke valve
52. Screw
53. Choke housing
54. Gasket
55. Screw
56. Lever assembly
57. Screw
58. Choke piston
59. Pin
60. Ball plug
61. Welch plug
62. Baffle plate
63. Gasket
64. Choke cap
65. Screw
66. Retainer

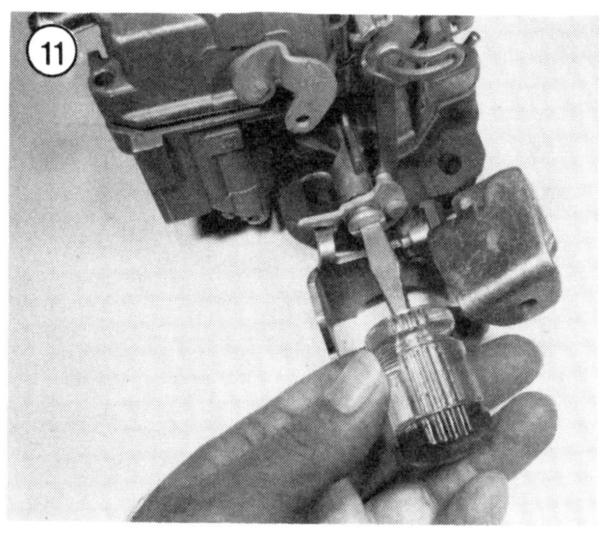

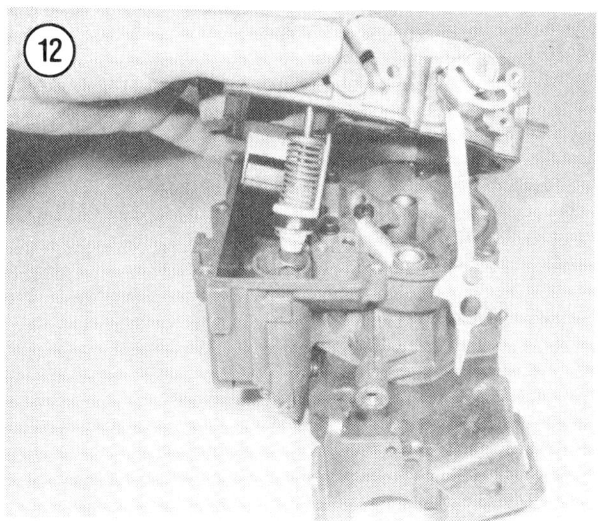

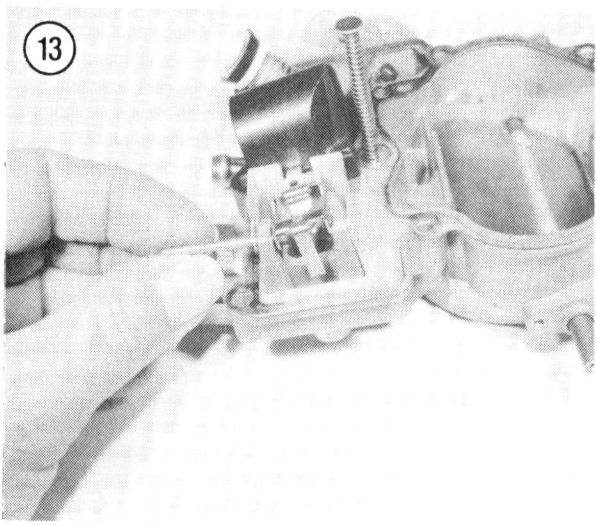

end out of the pump lever hole and remove the pump rod.

5. Remove the fast idle cam screw from the float bowl. See **Figure 11**.

6. Remove the bowl cover attaching screws and lockwashers. Rap the bowl cover, if necessary, with a soft-faced hammer to break the gasket seal (do not pry loose) and lift the assembly straight up and off the float bowl to prevent damage to the accelerator pump and power piston assembly. See **Figure 12**.

7. Invert the bowl cover and slide the float hinge pin from the retainer (**Figure 13**). Remove the float assembly from the bowl cover.

NOTE
Some models will use a pull clip on the float assembly. This will automatically remove the needle from the inlet valve. If no pull clip is used, remove the needle from its seat with needlenose pliers.

9

8. Remove and discard the bowl cover gasket. On 4.3L carburetors, remove the baffle.

9. Remove the inlet needle valve seat (**Figure 14**) with a wide-blade screwdriver. Remove and discard the gasket.

10. Unstake the power piston retaining washer. Depress and release the power piston

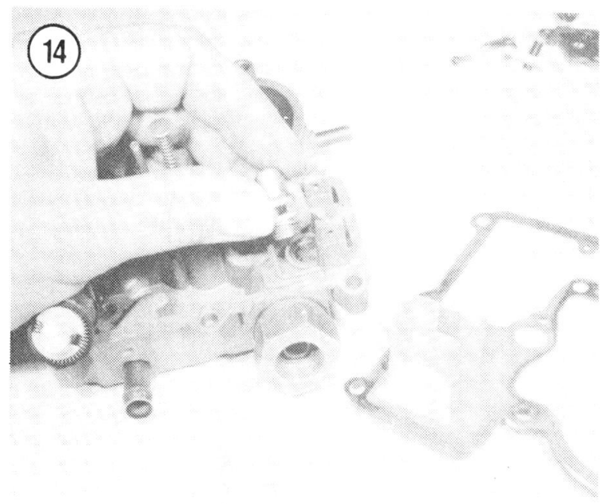

stem—it should snap free. If it does not, repeat the depress/release sequence until it does. See A, **Figure 15**.

11. Remove the accelerator pump plunger *only* if it is damaged. To do so, loosen the setscrew (B, **Figure 15**) on the plunger inner lever and break the swaged end (C, **Figure 15**). Disengage pump assembly from inner pump arm.

12. Remove the fuel inlet fitting from the bowl cover. Remove the inlet gasket, fuel filter and gasket and spring. Discard the gaskets and filter.

13. Remove the accelerator pump plunger return spring from the pump well. Invert the float bowl and catch the aluminum check ball as it falls out of the pump well (**Figure 16**).

14. Remove the pump inlet screen from the bottom of the float bowl.

15. Remove the main metering jets and power piston check valve with a wide-blade screwdriver.

16. Remove the venturi cluster attaching screws. Remove the cluster and gasket (**Figure 17**). Discard the gasket.

17. Remove the staking around the T-shaped retainer holding the discharge spring and ball in the float bowl. Remove the retainer with needlenose pliers. Invert the float bowl and remove the spring and ball.

18. Invert the float bowl and remove the throttle body attaching screws (**Figure 18**). Separate the throttle body from the float bowl and discard the gasket.

19. Turn each mixture screw clockwise until it seats *lightly*, counting the number of turns required. Write this information down for reference during reassembly. Back out and remove the idle mixture screws.

20. Clean and inspect the carburetor as described in this chapter.

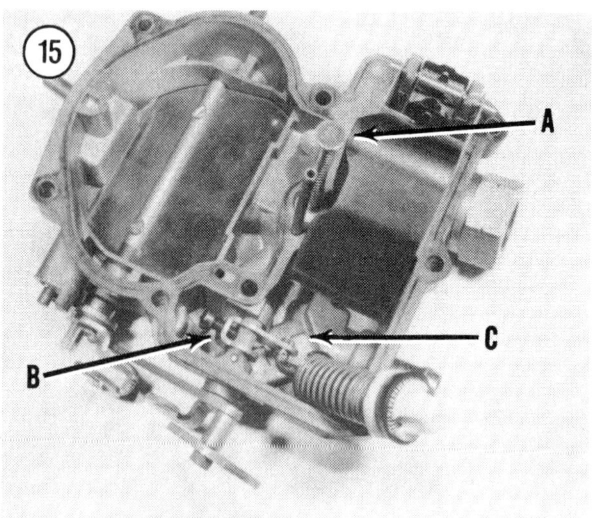

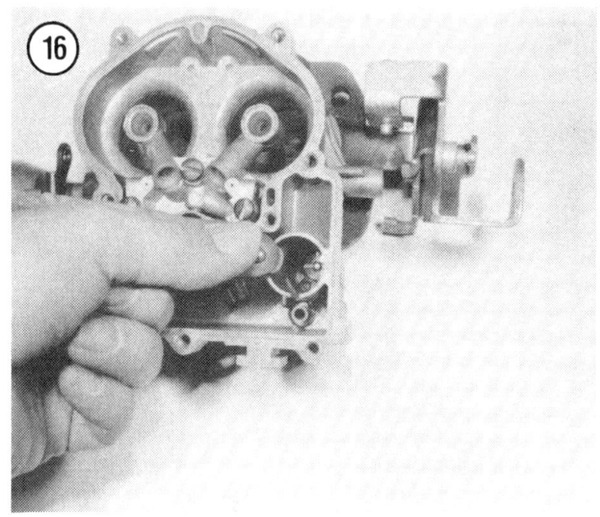

Rochester 2GC/2GV Assembly

Refer to **Figure 7** as required for this procedure. Check replacement gaskets for proper punching by comparing them with old gaskets.

1. Install each idle mixture screw and spring assembly in the throttle body. Turn the screws clockwise until they seat *lightly*, then back out the number of turns recorded during disassembly to provide a temporary idle adjustment setting.

WARNING

Make sure a non-vented gasket is used in Step 2. An automotive-type gasket will vent fuel vapors to the atmosphere during hot engine operation. This can result in an explosion or fire.

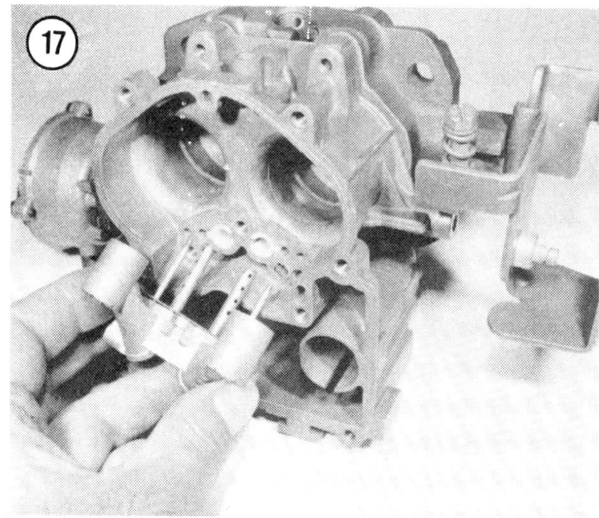

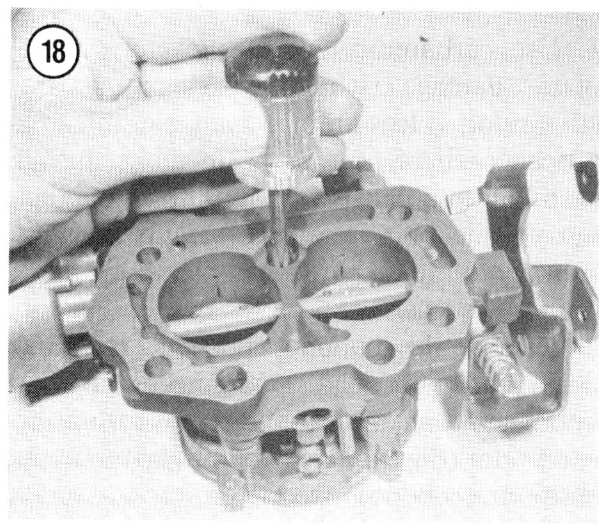

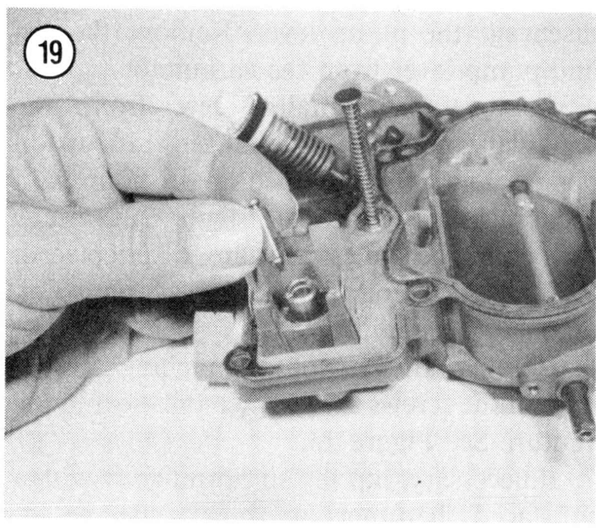

2. Invert the float bowl and install a new gasket, aligning the gasket holes with those in the casting.
3. Install the throttle body to the float bowl and tighten the attaching screws securely (**Figure 17**).
4. Drop the pump discharge check ball into the discharge well in the float bowl. Install the spring and T-shaped retainer. Stake the retainer in place flush with the top of the discharge well.
5. Fit a new gasket on the bottom of the venturi cluster and install the cluster. Tighten screws evenly and securely.
6. Reinstall the main metering jets with a wide-blade screwdriver. Fit a new gasket on the power piston check valve and install with the screwdriver.
7. Install the pump inlet check ball in the pump well (**Figure 16**). Install and center the pump return spring in the well.
8. If choke housing was removed, reinstall with a new gasket and tighten the attaching screws securely. Assemble choke piston to shaft/link assembly.
9. Install the pump inlet screen in the bottom of the float bowl.
10. If pump plunger assembly was removed, install outer pump lever and inner pump arm to bowl cover. Tighten setscrew. Connect plunger assembly to inner arm with shaft point inward and install the horseshoe retainer.
11. Install inlet needle valve seat with a new gasket (**Figure 14**). Tighten securely with a wide-blade screwdriver.
12. Install a new gasket on the bowl cover.
13. Install the power piston assembly in the bowl cover and stake housing slightly to hold piston in place.

NOTE
*On models without a float assembly pull clip, insert the inlet needle in the needle seat before installing the float in Step 14. See **Figure 19**.*

14. Connect inlet needle to float assembly and carefully reinstall in bowl cover, then insert hinge pin (**Figure 13**). Check float operation.
15. Adjust float level and drop to specifications provided with the adjustment procedure in the overhaul kit. If not available, refer to **Table 1**.
16. Install bowl cover to float bowl (**Figure 12**), making sure that the accelerator pump plunger fits into the pump well properly. Hold air horn on float bowl and check pump operation to see that the plunger operates freely.
17. Install the bowl cover screws with lockwashers, tightening evenly and securely.
18. Install the fast idle cam and tighten the screw securely (**Figure 11**).
19. Attach the accelerator pump rod and install the hairpin retainers (**Figure 10**).
20. If choke cap was removed, position the baffle plate and cover gasket on the choke housing. Install cover and rotate until index marks are aligned as specified in overhaul kit instructions (or **Table 1**). Install retainers/screws and tighten securely.
21. Install choke rod in idle cam and counterweight lever. Install idle cam to float bowl. Install choke lever to bowl cover.
22. If equipped with a vacuum break diaphragm, connect the linkage and install the diaphragm bracket screws. Reinstall the choke lever screw (**Figure 8**).

Rochester 4MV Disassembly

The Rochester 4MV is a 2-stage carburetor. Primary fuel metering is controlled by tapered metering rods operated by engine vacuum. The secondaries are larger than the primaries, with secondary metering controlled by an air valve. Refer to **Figure 20** as required for this procedure. Not all 4MV carburetors will use all the parts shown in **Figure 20**.

1. Use carburetor legs to prevent throttle plate damage while working on the carburetor. If legs are not available, thread a nut on each of four 2 1/4 in. bolts. Install each bolt in a flange hole and thread another nut on the bolt. These will hold the bolts securely to the carburetor and serve the same purpose as legs.
2. Remove the retaining clip/screw from the upper choke rod end. Disconnect rod from upper choke shaft lever and remove from the carburetor (**Figure 21**). If rod drops into main body, it can be removed later.
3. Drive the accelerator pump lever roll pin through the air horn boss just enough to disengage the pump lever. Remove the rod and pump lever from the carburetor.
4. Remove the small screw from the secondary metering rod hanger. Lift up on hanger and withdraw from air horn with metering rods attached (**Figure 22**). Leave rods on hanger unless they are to be replaced.
5. Disconnect and remove the vacuum break diaphragm assembly.
6. Remove the air horn attaching screws. Two of the screws are countersunk next to the venturi. See **Figure 23**.
7. If necessary, rap the air horn lightly with a soft-faced hammer to break the gasket

(20) **ROCHESTER 4MV CARBURETOR**

1. Air horn
2. Air valve lockout lever
3. Lockout lever roll pin
4. Secondary metering rod hanger
5. Secondary metering rod

6-8. Screw

9. Pump actuating lever
10. Pump lever roll pin
11. Pump assembly
12. Pump return spring
13. Needle and seat assembly
14. Needle and seat gasket
15. Float needle pull clip
16. Air horn gasket
17. Primary metering rod
18. Primary jet
19. Choke shaft and lever
20. Choke lever screw
21. Choke lever lockwasher
22. Choke lever nut
23. Choke valve
24. Choke valve screw
25. Float assembly
26. Hinge pin
27. Intermediate choke lever
28. Float bowl baffle
29. Choke rod
30. Choke rod clip
31. Fast idle cam
32. Vacuum diaphragm rod
33. Vacuum diaphragm rod clip
34. Vacuum diaphragm bracket
35. Bracket screw
36. Vacuum diaphragm
37. Vacuum hose
38. Power piston
39. Primary metering rod spring
40. Power piston retainer
41. Pump discharge ball retainer
42. Pump discharge ball
43. Power piston spring
44. Float bowl insert
45. Float bowl assembly
46. Idle stop screw
47. Idle stop screw spring
48. Fuel filter spring
49. Fuel filter
50. Fuel inlet nut
51. Fuel inlet gasket
52. Throttle body gasket
53. Pump rod
54. Pump rod clip
55. Throttle body
56. Idle misture needle
57. Idle needle spring
58. Throttle body screw
59. Cam lever
60. Fast idle cam
61. Lever/cam screw

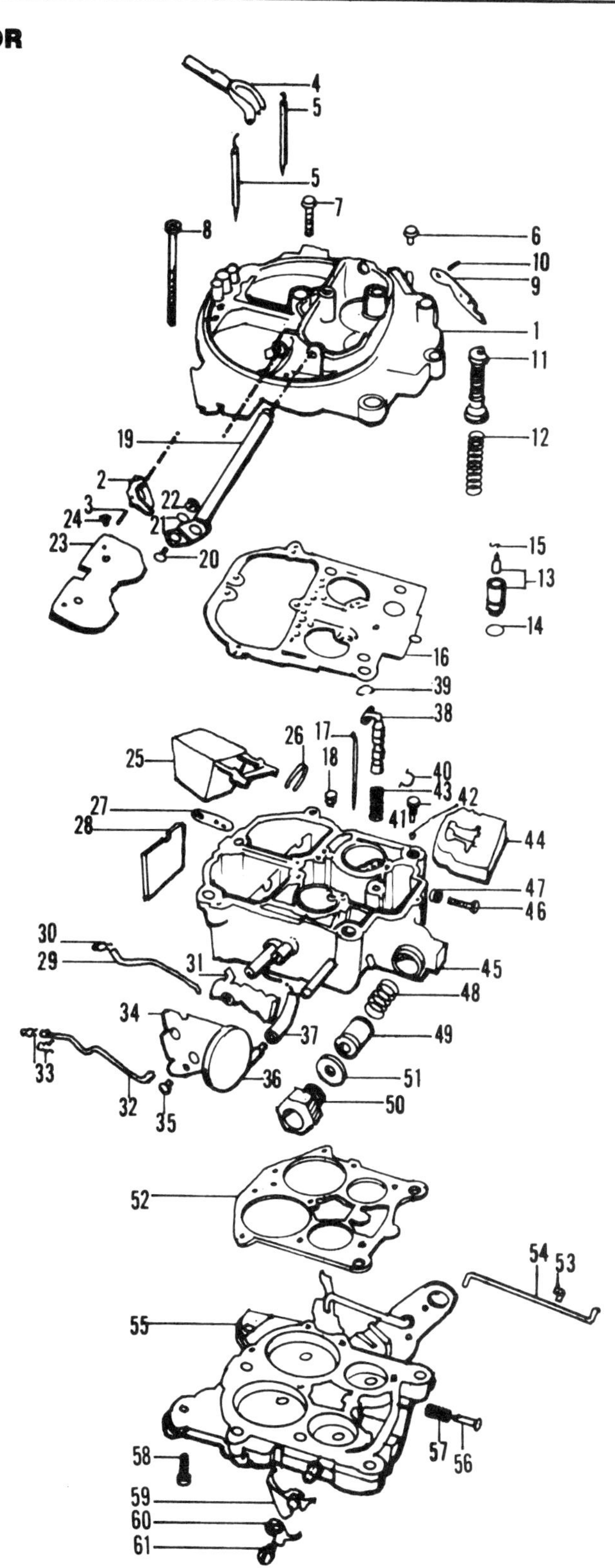

seal—do not pry free. Lift the air horn straight up and off the main body to prevent bending the main well air bleed tubes pressed into the casting. Angle the air horn slightly to disconnect the pump rod (**Figure 24**).

8. Remove the accelerating pump plunger and spring from the pump well (**Figure 25**).
9. Remove and discard the air horn-to-main body gasket.
10. Depress the rear power piston/metering rod assembly and let it snap free. On some carburetors, this may have to be done several times before the assembly will snap free. Remove the assembly with needlenose pliers (**Figure 26**), then remove the piston spring from the well.
11. Remove the plastic filler block installed over the float assembly (**Figure 27**).
12. Pull up slightly on the float retaining pin and slide it toward the pump well. Lift the float and inlet needle from the float bowl (**Figure 28**).
13. Remove the inlet needle valve seat with a wide-blade screwdriver. Remove the gasket from the seat and discard.
14. Remove the pump discharge check ball retainer with a wide-blade screwdriver. Tilt body to remove check ball.
15. Remove primary metering jets from the front of the fuel bowl with a wide-blade

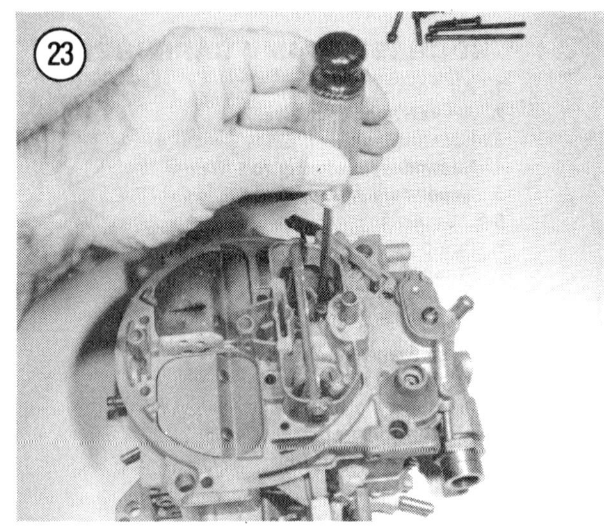

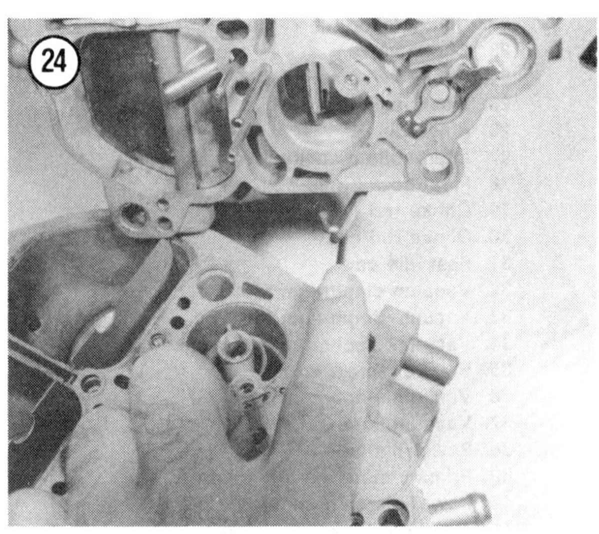

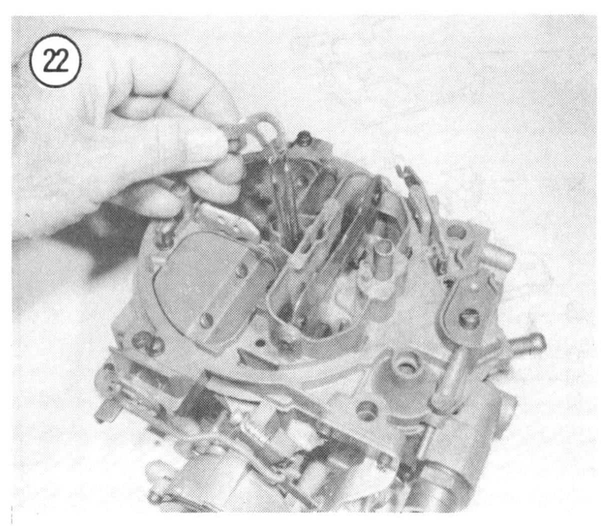

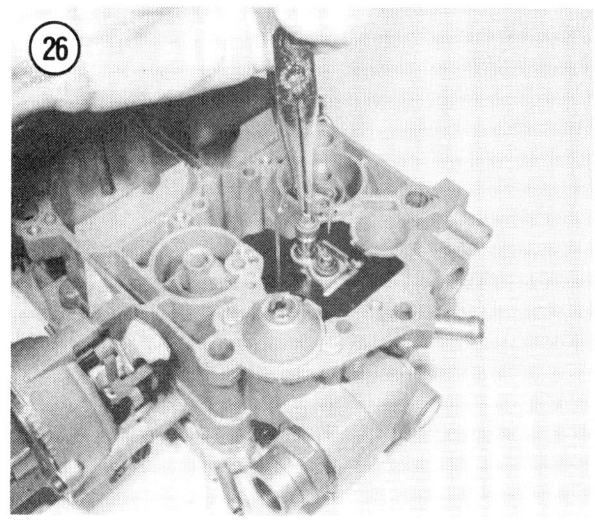

screwdriver. The secondary jets at the rear of the fuel bowl cannot be removed.

16. Remove the fuel inlet fitting from the main body. Remove the inlet gasket, fuel filter, gasket and spring. Discard the gaskets and filter.

17. Invert the main body and remove the throttle body attaching screws. Leave throttle shaft linkage attached. Separate throttle body from main body and discard the gasket.

18. Turn the mixture screws clockwise until they *lightly* seat, counting number of turns required. Write this information down for reference during reasembly. Back out and remove the screw and spring assemblies (**Figure 29**).

19. Clean and inspect the carburetor as described in this chapter.

Rochester 4MV Assembly

Refer to **Figure 20** as required for this procedure. Check replacement gaskets for proper punching by comparing them with old gaskets.

1. Install each idle mixture screw and spring assembly in the throttle body. Turn the screws clockwise until they seat *lightly*, then back out the number of turns recorded during disassembly to provide a temporary idle adjustment setting (**Figure 29**).

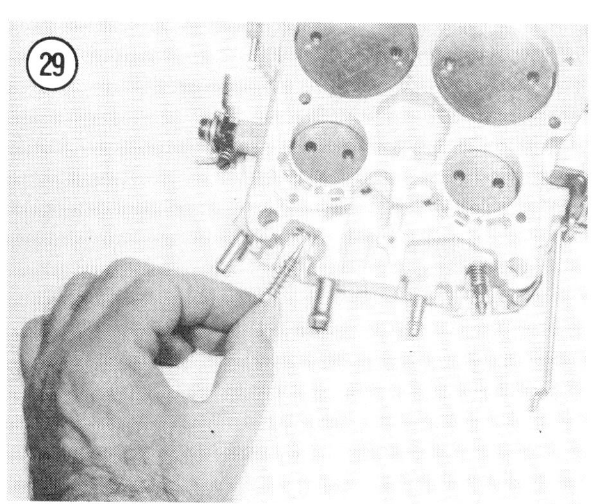

2. Position a new gasket over the throttle body dowels, then invert the carburetor body and install the throttle body. Tighten the attaching screws snugly.
3. Install fuel filter spring, a new filter and the inlet nut with new gaskets. Tighten inlet nut securely.
4. Install the lower pump rod end in the throttle lever.
5. Install the inlet needle seat with a new gasket, using a wide-blade screwdriver.
6. Drop the pump discharge check ball in the discharge well and install the pump retainer screw (**Figure 30**) with a wide-blade screwdriver.
7. Install the primary metering jets with a wide-blade screwdriver.
8. Clip fuel inlet needle over float lever arm (**Figure 31**) and lower both into the fuel bowl (**Figure 32**). Make sure the needle seats in the valve properly, then press the float retaining pin into the casting cutouts.
9. Adjust float level to specifications provided with adjustment procedure in overhaul kit. If not available, refer to **Table 1**.
10. Press the plastic filler block (**Figure 27**) over the float assembly until it is fully seated.
11. Install the rear metering rod assembly (**Figure 33**), then the power piston (**Figure**

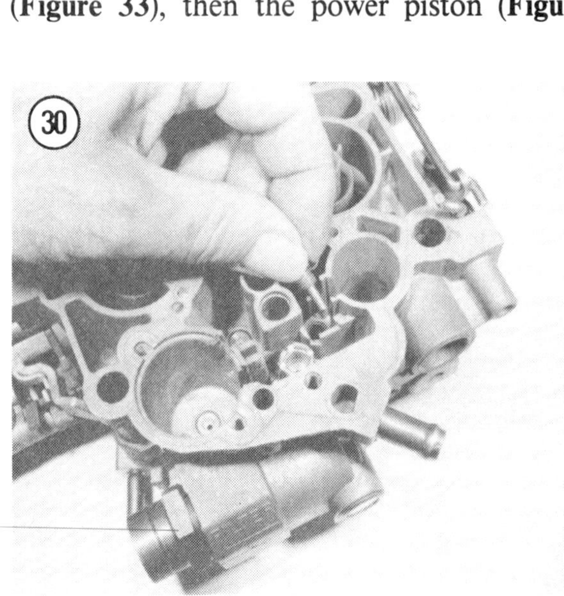
30

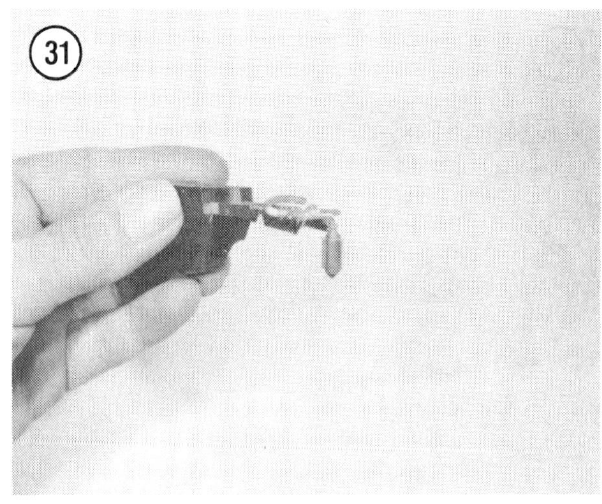
31

32

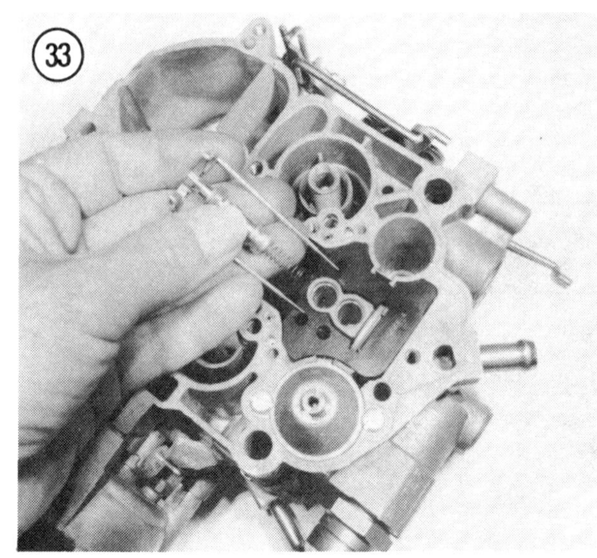
33

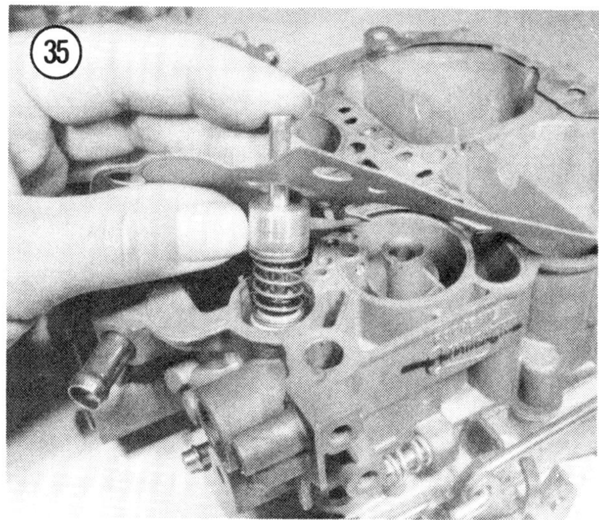

34). Make sure the metering rods enter their jets. Slide piston and spring into place.

12. Install front power piston with spring attached. Depress power piston with needlenose pliers until the raised plastic retainer on the piston rests flush with the body casting.

13. Drop the pump return spring into the pump well.

14. Install a new air horn gasket on the main body.

15. Install the accelerating pump plunger in the pump well (**Figure 35**).

16. Carefully position air horn over main body and lower into place, making sure that the vent tubes, well tubes and pump plunger fit properly through the gasket.

NOTE
Use of a magnetic screwdriver or needlenose pliers is recommended to position the screws in Step 17. If they are accidentally dropped inside the venturi, the air horn will have to be removed to retrieve them.

17. Carefully install the 2 countersunk air horn screws first (**Figure 23**).

18. Install and tighten the remaining air horn screws.

19. Install the secondary metering rods (**Figure 22**). They should drop freely into place as the hanger is lowered into the air horn. Install the hanger retaining screw snugly.

20. Install and connect the vacuum break diaphragm assembly.

21. Fit the choke rod into the bowl and connect its lower end to the lower choke lever inside. Fit the upper end in the choke shaft lever and install the retaining screw (**Figure 36**).

22. Connect the pump rod to the pump lever and pry the roll pin in place with a screwdriver blade.

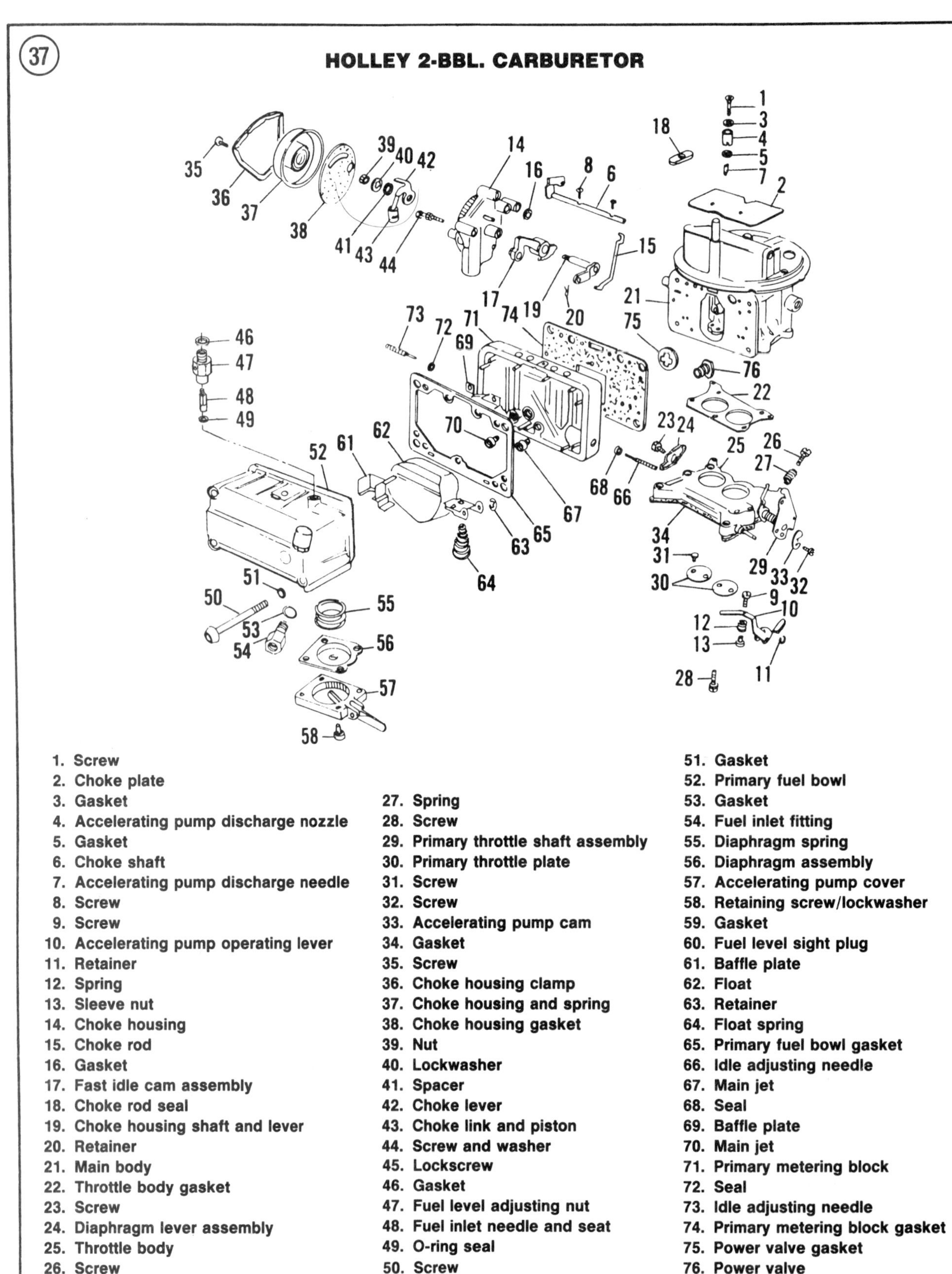

1. Screw
2. Choke plate
3. Gasket
4. Accelerating pump discharge nozzle
5. Gasket
6. Choke shaft
7. Accelerating pump discharge needle
8. Screw
9. Screw
10. Accelerating pump operating lever
11. Retainer
12. Spring
13. Sleeve nut
14. Choke housing
15. Choke rod
16. Gasket
17. Fast idle cam assembly
18. Choke rod seal
19. Choke housing shaft and lever
20. Retainer
21. Main body
22. Throttle body gasket
23. Screw
24. Diaphragm lever assembly
25. Throttle body
26. Screw
27. Spring
28. Screw
29. Primary throttle shaft assembly
30. Primary throttle plate
31. Screw
32. Screw
33. Accelerating pump cam
34. Gasket
35. Screw
36. Choke housing clamp
37. Choke housing and spring
38. Choke housing gasket
39. Nut
40. Lockwasher
41. Spacer
42. Choke lever
43. Choke link and piston
44. Screw and washer
45. Lockscrew
46. Gasket
47. Fuel level adjusting nut
48. Fuel inlet needle and seat
49. O-ring seal
50. Screw
51. Gasket
52. Primary fuel bowl
53. Gasket
54. Fuel inlet fitting
55. Diaphragm spring
56. Diaphragm assembly
57. Accelerating pump cover
58. Retaining screw/lockwasher
59. Gasket
60. Fuel level sight plug
61. Baffle plate
62. Float
63. Retainer
64. Float spring
65. Primary fuel bowl gasket
66. Idle adjusting needle
67. Main jet
68. Seal
69. Baffle plate
70. Main jet
71. Primary metering block
72. Seal
73. Idle adjusting needle
74. Primary metering block gasket
75. Power valve gasket
76. Power valve

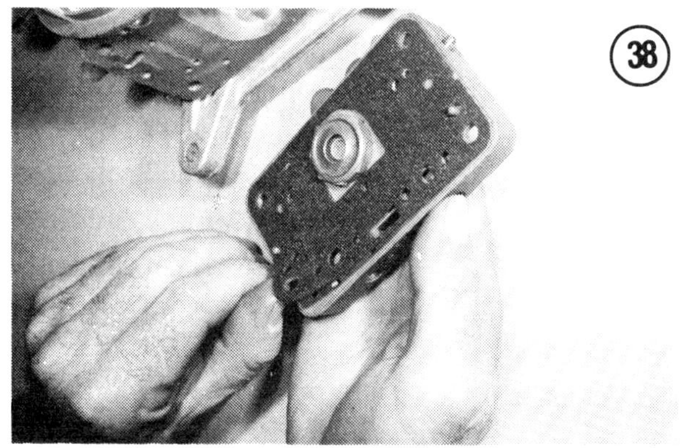
38

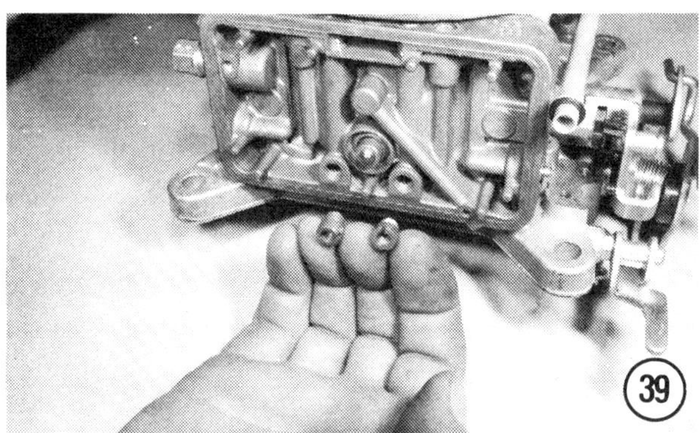
39

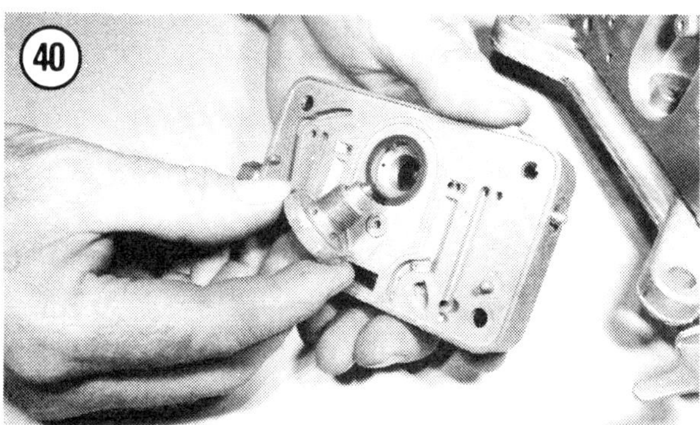
40

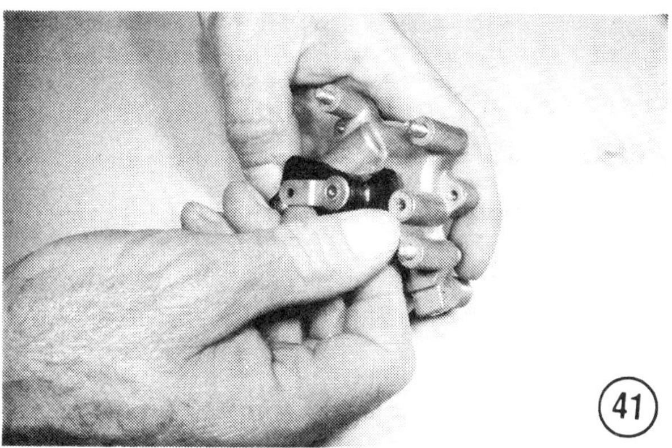
41

Holley 2-bbl. Disassembly

Refer to **Figure 37** for this procedure.

1. Use carburetor legs to prevent throttle plate damge while working on the carburetor. If legs are not available, thread a nut on each of four 2 1/4 in. bolts. Install each bolt in a flange hole and thread another nut to the bolt. This will hold the bolt securely to the carburetor and serve the same purpose as legs.
2. Remove the fuel bowl and gasket and the metering block and gasket. See **Figure 38**. Discard the gaskets.
3. Turn the idle adjusting needles clockwise until they seat *lightly*, counting the number of turns required. Write this information down for reference during reassembly. Back out and remove needles and gaskets. Discard gaskets.
4. Remove the main jets with a wide-blade screwdriver. **Figure 39** shows their location.
5. Loosen the power valve with a socket wrench. Remove the valve and discard the gasket. See **Figure 40**.
6. Remove float shaft circlip with needlenose pliers.
7. Slide float off shaft with attached spring.
8. Remove fuel inlet needle, clip and seat with gasket. The fuel inlet needle and seat are a matched assembly and is replaced as a set.
9. Remove the fuel bowl baffle plate.
10. Remove the fuel inlet fitting and gasket.
11. Invert fuel bowl. Remove accelerating pump cover, diaphragm and spring. Pump inlet check ball is *not* removable.
12. Invert carburetor. Remove throttle body attaching screws and lockwashers. Separate throttle body from main body and discard the gasket.
13. Remove choke rod retainer from choke housing shaft/lever assembly.
14. Remove thermostatic spring housing and gasket. Remove choke housing from main body. Remove and discard tiny O-ring gaskets (**Figure 41**).

15. Remove choke housing shaft nut, lockwasher and spacer. See **Figure 42**. Remove shaft and fast idle cam.
16. Remove choke piston/lever assembly. Remove choke rod and seal from main body.
17. Remove accelerating pump discharge nozzle screw. Lift pump discharge nozzle from main body with needlenose pliers (**Figure 43**). Remove and discard gaskets.
18. Invert main body and catch pump discharge needle as it falls out.
19. Remove accelerating pump operating lever from throttle body.

Holley 2-bbl. Assembly

Refer to **Figure 37** as required for this procedure. Check replacement gaskets for proper punching by comparing them with old gaskets.

1. Install accelerating pump operating lever to throttle body.
2. Drop pump discharge needle into pump well in main body. Lightly seat needle with appropriate size brass drift. Position pump nozzle and new gaskets in main body. Install retaining screw snugly. See **Figure 44**.
3. Install choke lever link/piston assembly into choke housing (**Figure 45**). Position on housing shaft and install spacer, lockwasher and nut.
4. Install new choke housing gaskets and position housing to mainbody, inserting choke rod in housing shaft lever. Projection on choke rod must be under fast idle cam to lift cam when choke is closed. Install choke rod cotter pin.
5. Fit thermostatic coil gasket to housing. Engage spring loop on spring lever, then install retainers and screws. Align index marks on housing/coil assembly to position specified in overhaul kit and tighten screws.
6. Invert main body. Install throttle body to main body with a new gasket. Fuel inlet fitting must be on same side as pump operating lever. Install and tighten attaching screws and lockwashers securely.
7. Position accelerating pump diaphragm spring and diaphragm in pump chamber with large end of lever disc against operating lever. Install cover and finger-tighten retaining screws.
8. Check to see that diaphragm is centered, then compress it with the pump operating lever and tighten the retaining screws snugly.
9. Install fuel inlet fitting with new gasket.
10. Install new fuel inlet needle, clip, gasket and seat.
11. Slide baffle plate over ridges in fuel bowl (**Figure 46**). Install spring on float and slide float over shaft with spring between ridges on boss on fuel bowl floor. Install float retainer circlip with needlenose pliers.

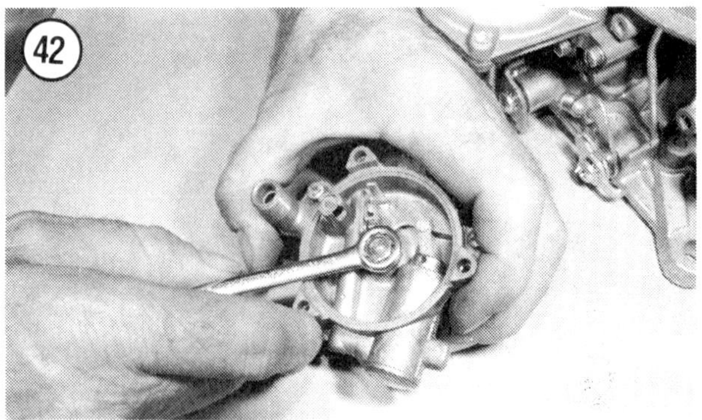

42

43

12. Adjust dry float level to specifications provided with adjustment procedure in overhaul kit.
13. Install power valve in metering block with new gasket. Tighten snugly with socket wrench.

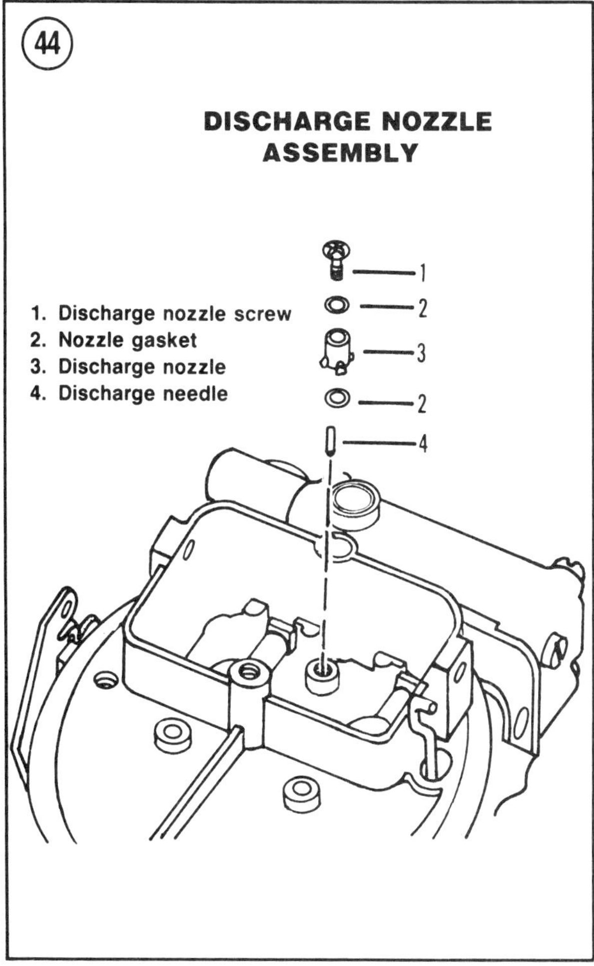

14. Install jets in metering block with wide-blade screwdriver.
15. Install idle adjusting screws in metering block with new gaskets. Turn screws clockwise until they seat *lightly*, then back them out the number of turns recorded during disassembly to provide a temporary idle adjustment setting.
16. Install a new gasket to the metering block using the dowels on the back of the block for alignment. Fit metering block and gasket to main body.
17. Position baffle plate and gasket on metering block.
18. Install retaining screws and new compression gaskets in fuel bowl.
19. Install fuel bowl to main body (**Figure 47**) and tighten retaining screws snugly.
20. Adjust accelerating pump to specifications provided with adjustment procedure in overhaul kit.

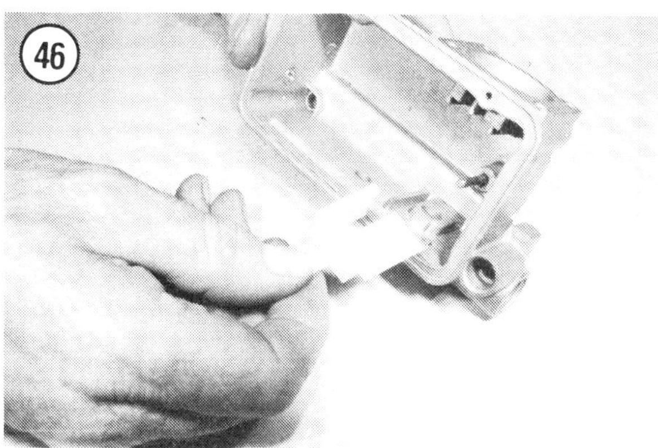

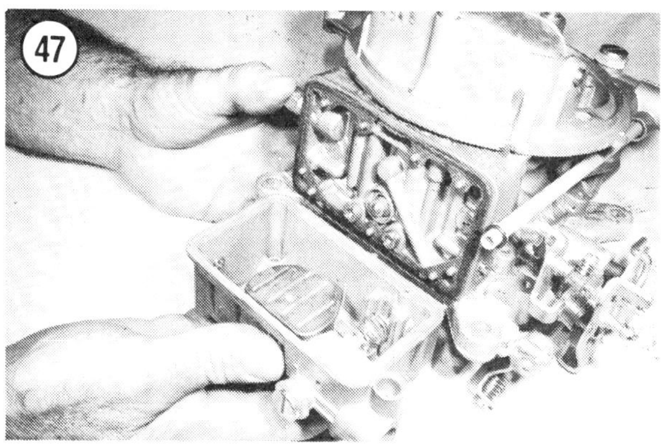

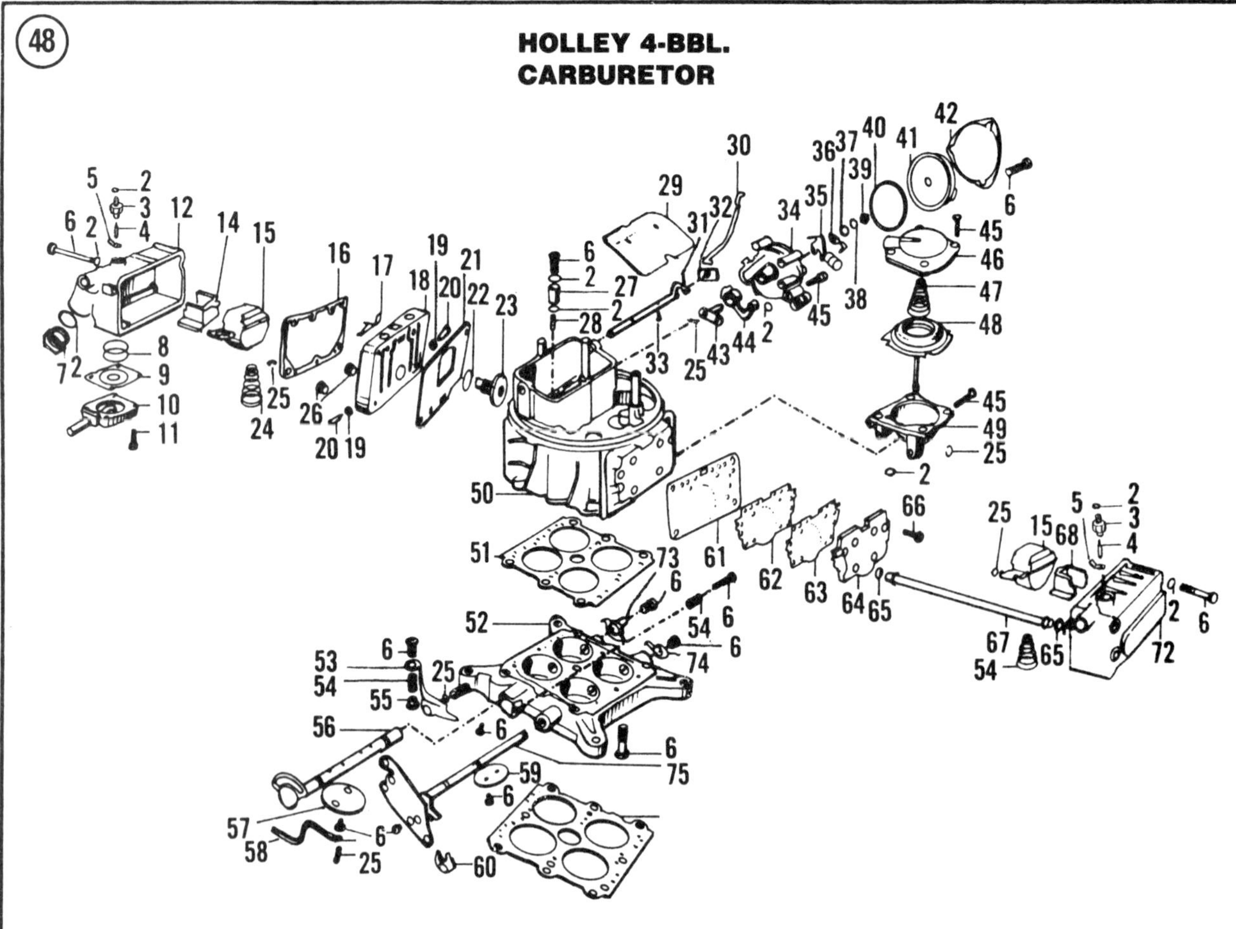

(48) **HOLLEY 4-BBL. CARBURETOR**

2. Gasket
3. Seat
4. Needle
5. Clip
6. Screw
7. Fuel inlet fitting
8. Diaphragm spring
9. Diaphragm assembly
10. Accelerating pump cover
11. Retaining screw/lockwasher
12. Primary fuel bowl
14. Baffle plate
15. Float
16. Primary fuel bowl gasket
17. Baffle plate
18. Primary metering block
19. Seal
20. Idle adjusting needle
21. Primary metering block gasket
22. Power valve gasket
23. Power valve
24. Float spring
25. Retainer
26. Main jet
27. Accelerating pump discharge nozzle
28. Accelerating pump discharge needle
29. Choke plate
30. Choke rod
31. Choke shaft
32. Choke rod seal
33. Screw
34. Choke housing
35. Choke link and piston
36. Choke lever
37. Spacer
38. Lockwasher
39. Nut
40. Choke housing gasket
41. Choke housing and spring
42. Choke housing clamp
43. Choke housing shaft/lever
44. Fast idle cam
45. Screw/washer
46. Cover
47. Diaphragm spring
48. Diaphragm assembly
49. Secondary housing
50. Main body
51. Throttle body gasket
52. Throttle body
53. Accelerating pump operating lever
54. Spring
55. Sleeve nut
56. Secondary throttle shaft
57. Secondary throttle plate
58. Throttle connecting rod
59. Primary throttle plate
60. Accelerating pump cam
61. Gasket
62. Secondary plate
63. Metering body gasket
64. Secondary metering body
65. O-ring seal
66. Clutch screw
67. Fuel distribution tube
68. Baffle plate
72. Secondary fuel bowl
73. Fast idle cam lever
74. Diaphragm lever assembly
75. Primary throttle shaft

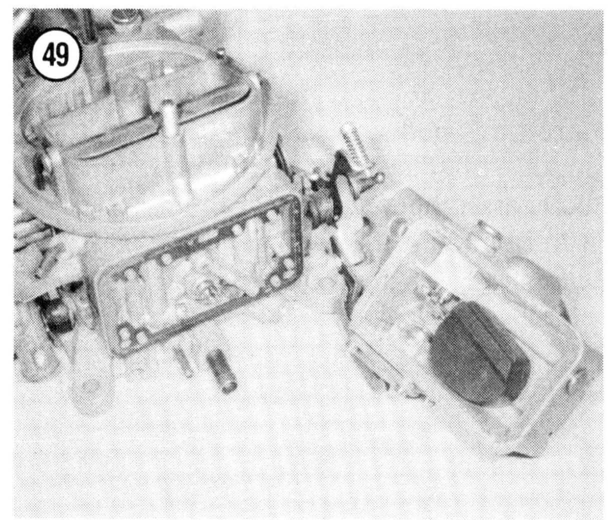
49

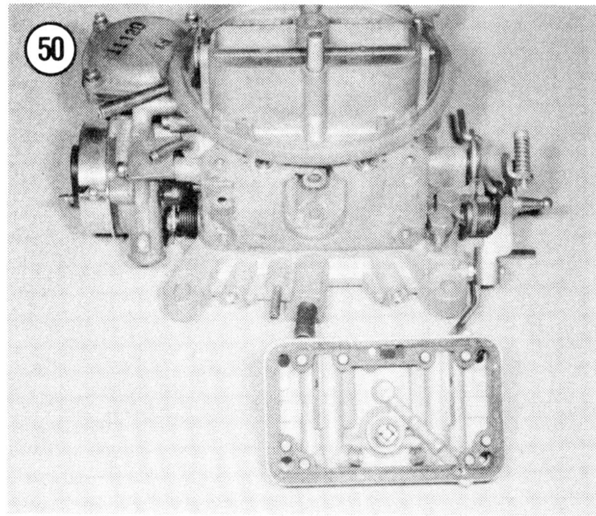
50

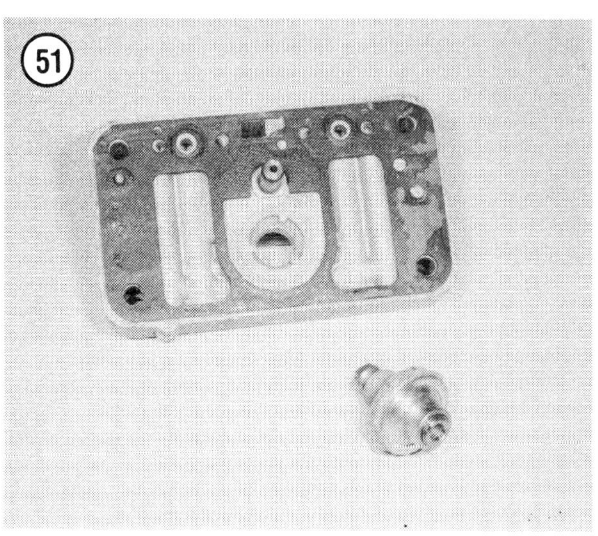
51

Holley 4-bbl. Disassembly

The primary stage of this carburetor consists of a fuel bowl, metering block and accelerating pump assembly. The secondary stage uses a fuel bowl, metering body and secondary throttle operating diaphragm. Some versions use a modulated power valve system to keep the power valve open during periods of hard acceleration when manifold vacuum might increase enough to close the valve.

CAUTION
A clutch-type screwdriver is required for removal of some fasteners on this carburetor. Substitute tools will generally only damage the screw head and should not be used.

Refer to **Figure 48** as required for this procedure. Not all carburetors will use all the parts shown in **Figure 48**.

1. Use carburetor legs to prevent throttle plate damage while working on the carburetor. If legs are not available, thread a nut on each of four 2 1/4 in. bolts. Install each bolt in a flange hole and thread another nut on the bolt. These will hold the bolts securely to the carburetor and serve the same purpose as legs.
2. Remove the primary fuel bowl and gasket (**Figure 49**).
3. Remove the metering block and gasket (**Figure 50**).
4. Remove the fuel line tube and O-ring seal. Discard the O-ring seal.
5. Turn the idle adjusting needles clockwise until they *lightly* seat, counting the number of turns required. Write this information down for reassembly reference. Back out and remove the needles and gaskets. Discard the gaskets.
6. Remove the power valve (**Figure 51**) with an appropriate socket wrench. Remove and discard the valve gasket.

7. Remove the main jets (**Figure 52**) with an appropriate jet remover. If a screwdriver is used for jet removal, work carefully to avoid casting or jet damage.

8. Remove the float shaft retainer clip with needlenose pliers. Slide float off shaft and remove the spring. See **Figure 53**.

9. Remove fuel inlet needle, clip and seat with gasket. The fuel inlet needle and seat are a matched assembly and is replaced as a set.

10. Remove the baffle plate, fuel level sight plug and gasket from the fuel bowl. Discard the gasket.

11. Remove the fuel inlet fitting, gasket and filter screen from the fuel bowl. Discard the gasket.

12. Invert the fuel bowl. Remove the accelerating pump cover, diaphragm and spring (**Figure 54**). The inlet check ball in the fuel bowl pump bore is permanently installed and no attempt should be made to remove it.

13. Remove the secondary fuel bowl and gasket. Discard the gasket.

14. Remove the metering body, plate and gaskets with a clutch-type screwdriver. See **Figure 55**. Discard the gaskets.

15. Repeat Steps 8-10 to disassemble the secondary fuel bowl components.

16. Remove the flame arrestor anchor stud.

17. Remove the C-clip at the secondary diaphragm link.

18. Invert the carburetor. Remove the throttle body retaining screws and lockwashers. Separate the throttle and main body assemblies and discard the gasket.

19. Remove the choke cover screws. Disengage the thermostat coil loop from the choke lever and remove the cover.

20. Remove the choke housing and gaskets from the main body (**Figure 56**). Discard the gaskets.

21. Remove the choke housing shaft nut, lockwasher and spacer. Lift out piston and choke link lever.

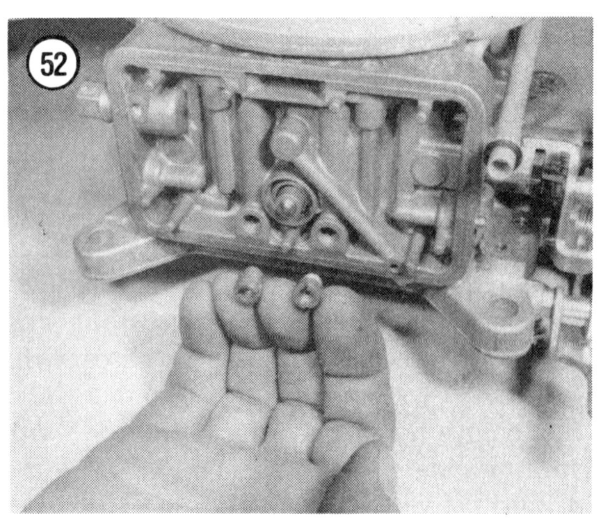

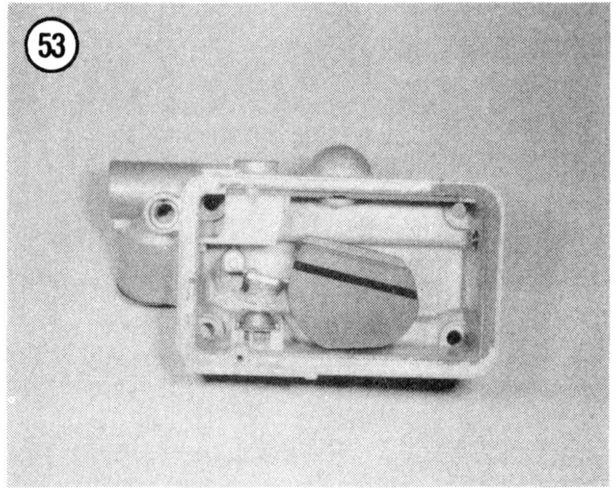

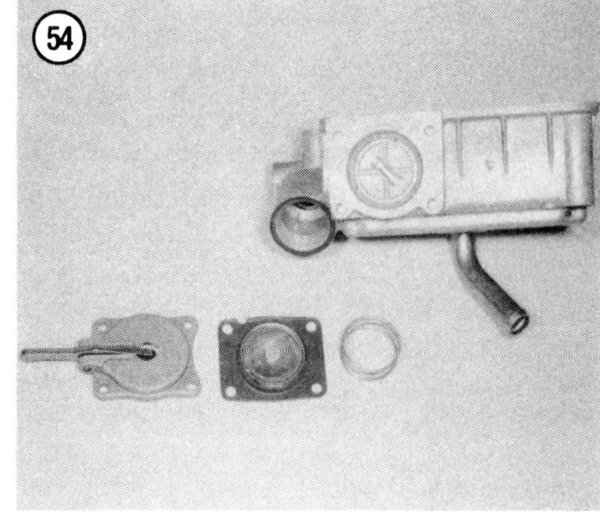

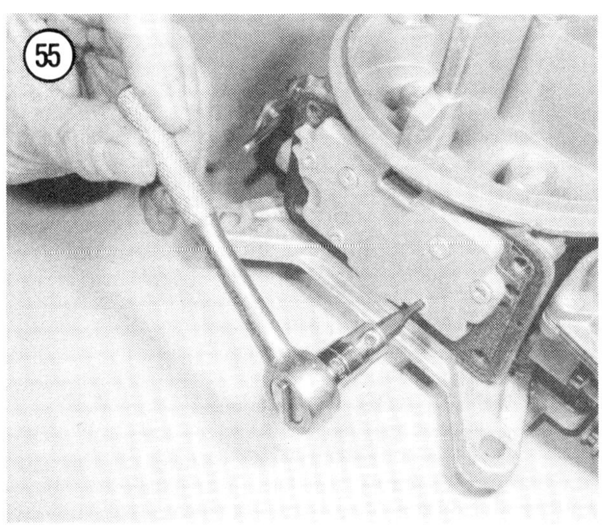

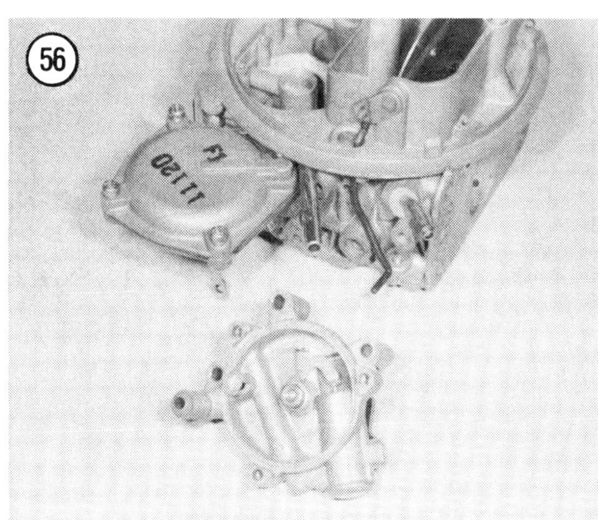

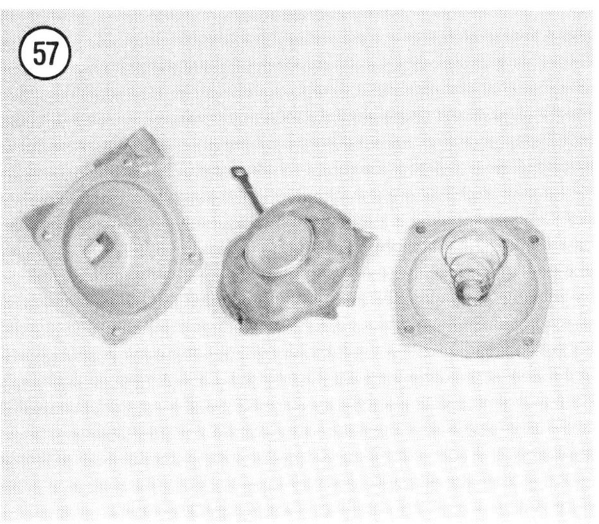

22. Remove the choke rod and seal from the main body.
23. Remove the secondary diaphragm assembly and gasket from the main body.
24. Remove the diaphragm housing cover and remove the spring and diaphragm from the housing. See **Figure 57**.
25. Remove the screw holding the accelerating pump discharge nozzle in place. Remove the nozzle and gaskets from the main body (**Figure 58**). Discard the gaskets.
26. Invert main body and catch pump discharge needle as it drops out.
27. Clean and inspect the carburetor as described in this chapter.

Holley 4-bbl. Assembly

Refer to **Figure 48** as required for this procedure. Check replacement gaskets for proper punching by comparing them with old gaskets.

1. Drop the pump discharge needle into its well. Seat needle lightly with a brass drift. Fit a new gasket on each end of the discharge nozzle and install assembly in discharge well. See **Figure 59**. Lightly stake the discharge nozzle screw in place with a flat punch. Clean any metal chips from the throttle openings before continuing this procedure.

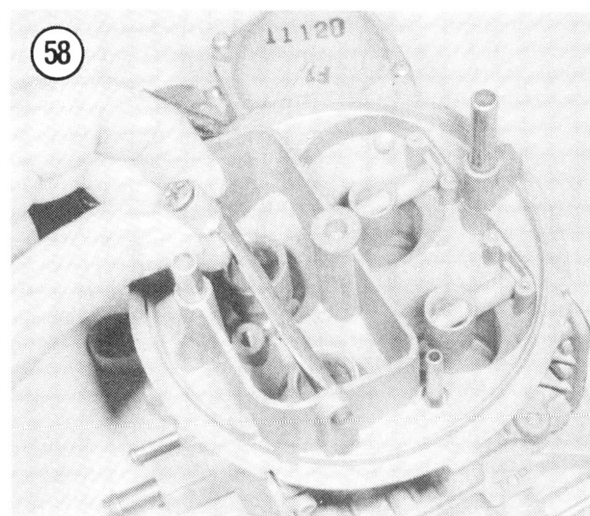

2. Position secondary diaphragm in housing and put the spring in the cover. Install cover to housing and tighten retaining screws finger-tight. Pull diaphragm rod downward as far as it will go and tighten the retaining screws snugly.
3. Fit a new gasket on the secondary vacuum passage opening in the main body. Install the diaphragm housing to the main body.
4. Fit the seal on the choke rod and install the rod with the seal fitting into the grooves underneath the flame arrestor mounting flange.
5. Refer to **Figure 60** and reassemble the choke housing as follows:

a. Install the split lever and piston in the choke housing.
b. Install the thermostatic lever and choke housing shaft assembly in the choke housing.
c. Fit the fast idle cam and choke lever on the choke housing shaft.
d. Install the spacer, star washer and nut on the choke housing shaft.
e. Install the overcenter spring between the thermostat lever and choke housing boss. See **Figure 61**.
f. Place the main body on its side and fit the choke housing gasket to the main body.
g. Guide the choke rod into the choke housing shaft lever as the housing is installed to the main body. The choke rod projection must fit under the fast idle cam.
h. Install the choke housing screws and lockwashers. Tighten screws to 5 in.-lb. (0.6 N•m) and install the choke rod cotter pin.

6. Install a new gasket on the choke housing. Connect the thermostatic coil loop to the choke lever and install the choke cover to the housing. Set cover and housing index marks

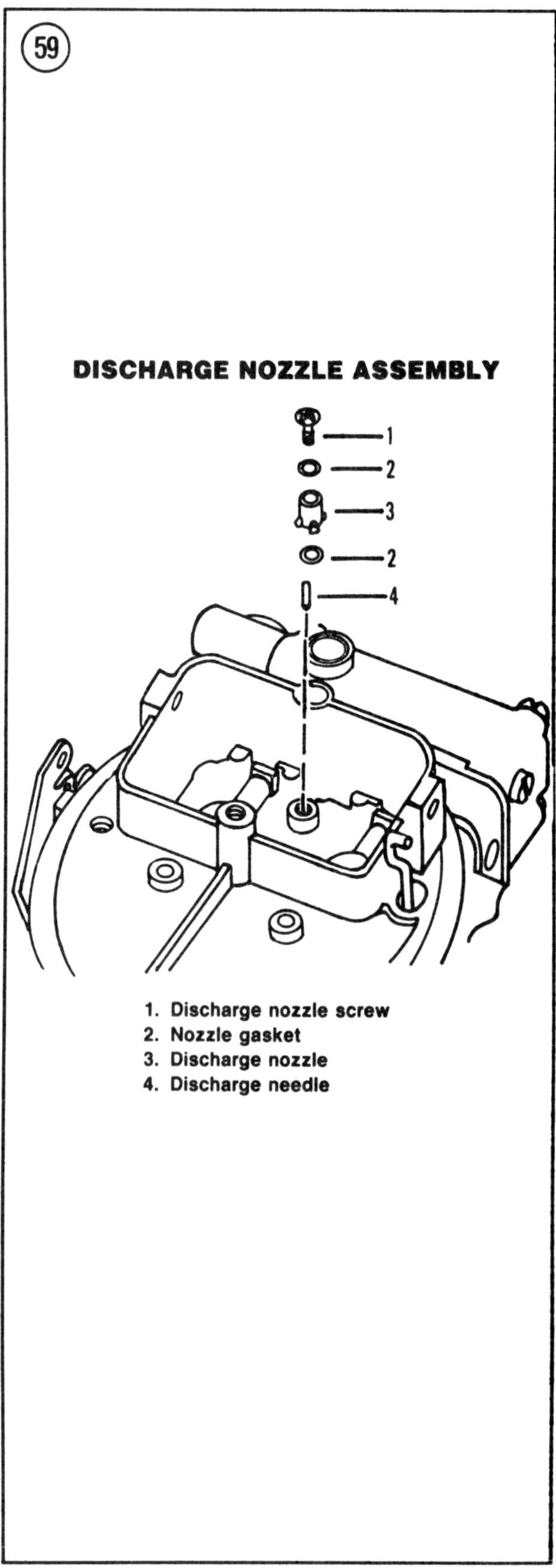

1. Discharge nozzle screw
2. Nozzle gasket
3. Discharge nozzle
4. Discharge needle

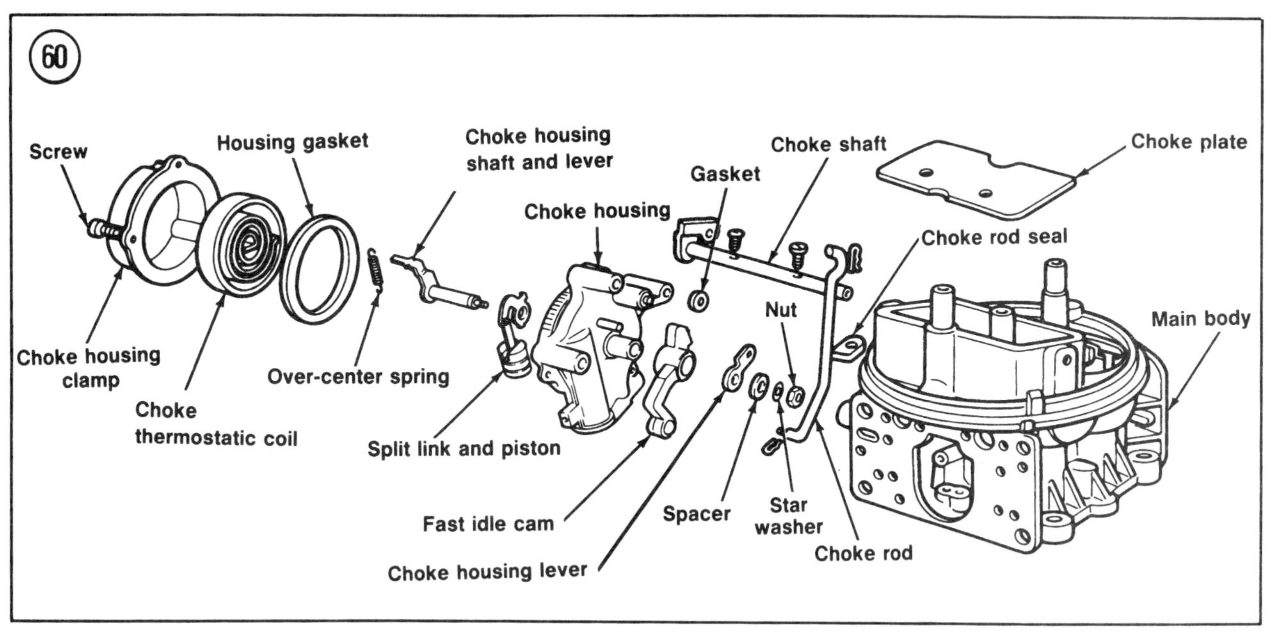

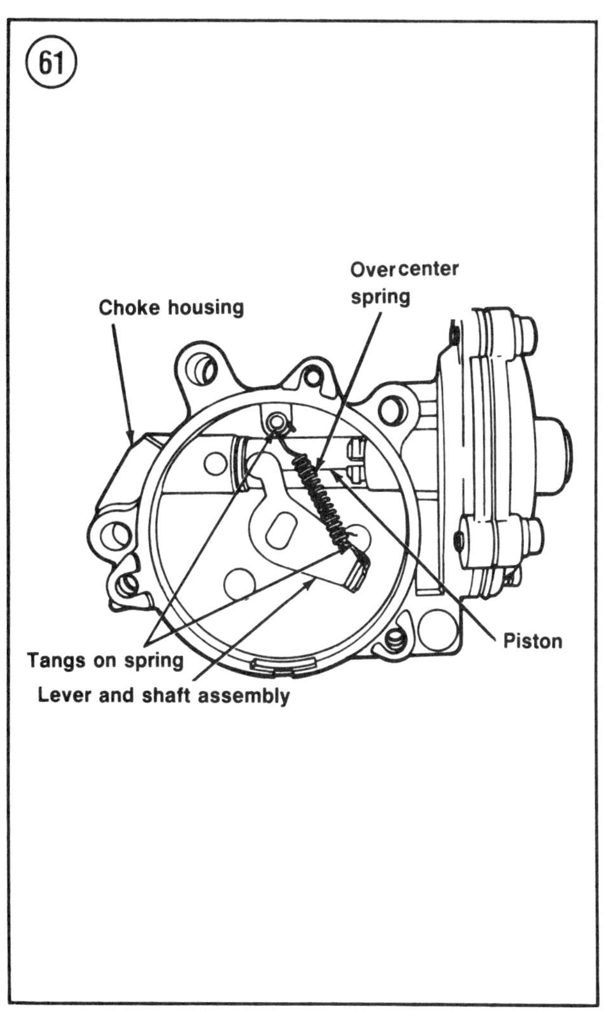

to position specified in overhaul kit instructions (or **Table 1**) and install cover screws tightly.

7. Invert the main body and position a new gasket. Fit the main body to the throttle body with the fuel inlet fitting on the same side as the accelerating pump lever, sliding the secondary diaphragm rod over the operating lever. Install the throttle body attaching screws and lockwashers and tighten to 20 in.-lb. (2.3 N•m). Install retainer on secondary diaphragm rod.

NOTE
*Refer to **Figure 62** and reassemble the primary fuel bowl first.*

8. Install new fuel inlet needle, clip, gasket and seat.

9. Slide the baffle plate over the fuel bowl ridges and install the float/spring assembly on the shaft. Float spring should fit between the ridges on the fuel bowl floor boss. Install the circlip to hold the float assembly on the shaft.

10. Adjust the dry float level to specification provided with adjustment procedure in overhaul kit instructions. If not available, refer to **Table 1**.

11. Install the power valve (**Figure 51**) in the metering block with a new gasket and tighten snugly with a socket wrench.
12. Install the main jets in the metering block with a jet installer or screwdriver blade. See **Figure 52**.
13. Install new gaskets on the idle adjusting needles. Thread needles into fuel bowl and tighten *lightly*. Back needles out same number of turns noted during disassembly.
14. Install a new gasket on the back of the metering block. Fit the metering block and gasket to the main body. Install the baffle plate and new gasket to the metering block.
15. Wipe a new fuel line tube O-ring seal with petroleum jelly and install O-ring on fuel line tube. Install this end of tube in the primary fuel bowl recess, then lubricate a second O-ring and install on the other end of the tube.
16. Install new compression gaskets on the fuel bowl screws. Insert screws through the fuel bowl, place the bowl in position on the metering block and guide the fuel line tube into the body recess. Tighten fuel bowl screws to 45 in.-lb. (5.1 N•m). These screws should be retightened to specifications once a year.
17. Reassemble the secondary fuel bowl by repeating Steps 8-10. See **Figure 63**.
18. Install a new metering body gasket to the main body. Fit the metering plate gasket, plate, gasket and metering body on the main body. Install and tighten retaining screws to 20 in.-lb. (2.3 N•m).
19. Repeat Steps 16 and 17 to install the secondary fuel bowl to the main body. Fuel bowl screws should be retightened to specifications once a year.
20. Install the accelerating pump diaphragm spring and diaphragm in pump chamber with large end of lever disc against the operating disc.
21. Install cover and finger-tighten retaining screws. Check diaphragm to make sure it is centered, then compress diaphragm with pump operating lever and tighten screws to 5 in.-lb. (0.6 N•m).
22. Adjust accelerating pump to specifications provided with adjustment procedures in overhaul kit instructions. If not available, refer to **Table 1**.

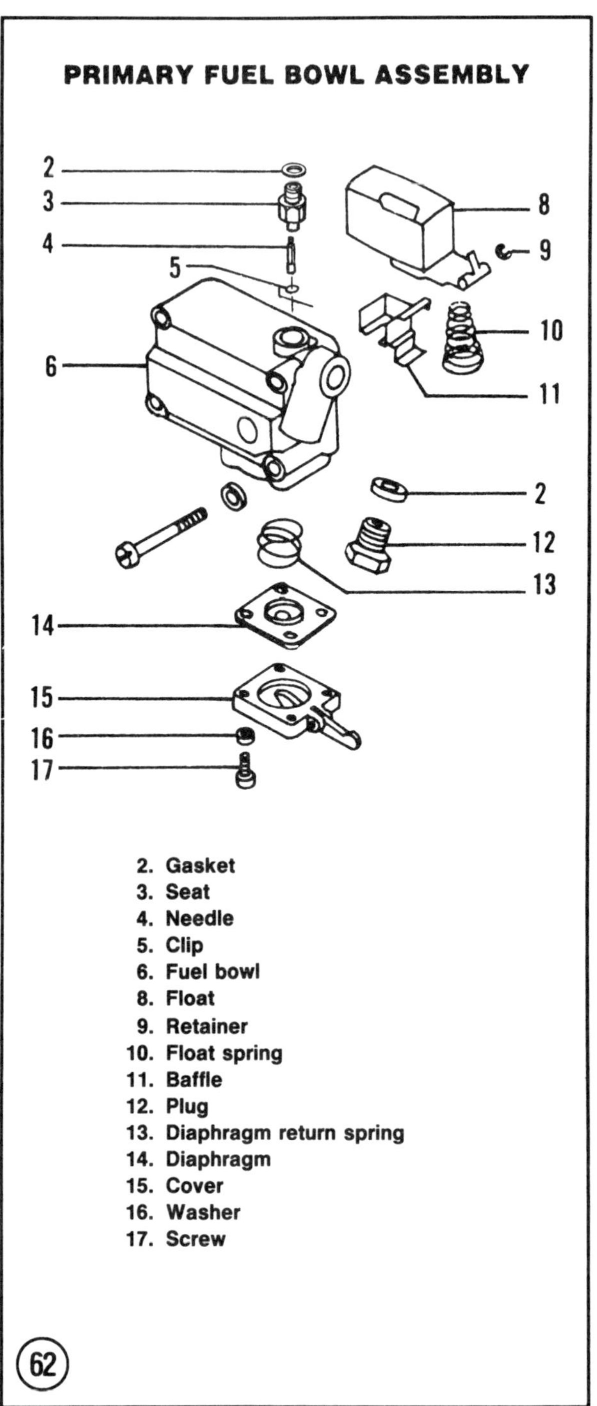

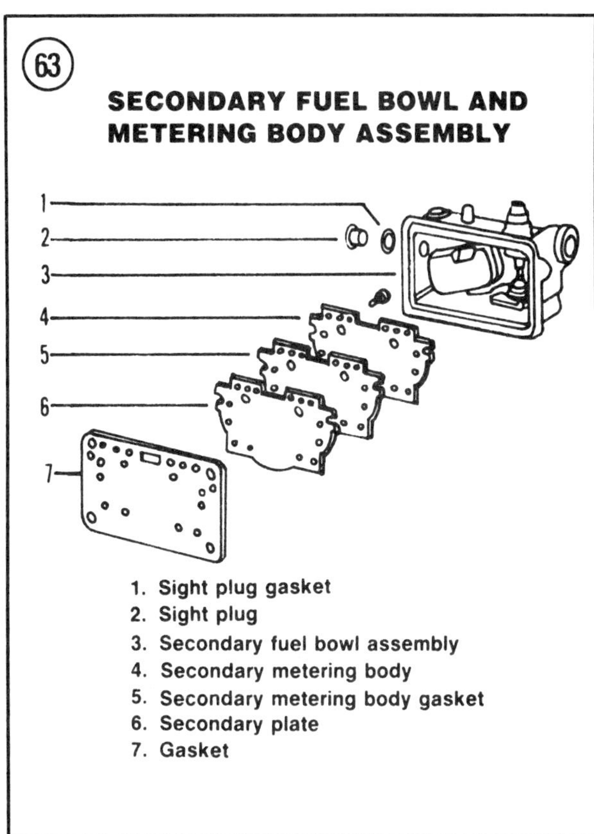

FUEL PUMP AND ANTI-SIPHON DEVICES

A non-serviceable single-action mechanical fuel pump is used with all engines. The pump rocker or lever arm is operated by and eccentric on the camshaft and provides fuel under pressure to the carburetor.

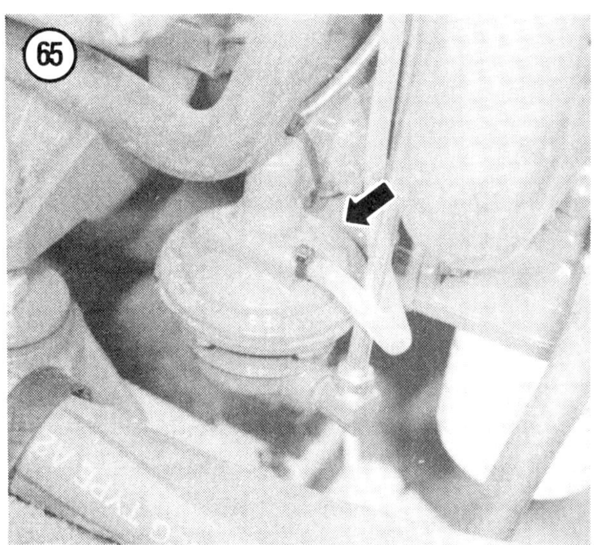

The fuel pump on the 2.5L and 3.0L engine has a metal bowl containing a filter element mounted on the pump housing and held in place by a screw-pressure swing yoke. See **Figure 64** (typical).

The fuel pump on the 7.5L engine is mounted on the engine block behind the remote oil filter and connects to a remote filter canister.

The fuel pump on all other engines is located on the engine block near the remote fuel filter canister. See **Figure 65** (typical).

Fuel pumps are fitted with a transparent overflow hose. Normally, there should be no oil or fuel in the hose. If there is, the pump diaphragm has ruptured and the pump should be replaced immediately.

In accordance with industry safety standards, all boats in which Cobra drives are used have some form of anti-siphon device installed between the fuel tank outlet and engine fuel inlet. This device is designed to shut the fuel supply off in case the boat capsizes or is involved in an accident. Quite often, the malfunction of such devices leads the owner to replace a good fuel pump in the belief that it is defective.

Anti-siphon devices can malfunction in any of the following ways:

9

a. Anti-siphon valve: orifice in valve is too small or clogs easily; valve sticks in closed or partially closed position; valve fluctuates between open and closed position; thread sealer, metal filing or debris clogs the orifice or lodges in the relief spring.
b. Solenoid-operated fuel shut-off valve: solenoid fails with valve in closed position; solenoid malfunctions, leaving valve in partially closed position.
c. Manually-operated fuel shut-off valve: valve is left in completely closed position; valve is not fully opened.

The easiest way to determine if the anti-siphon valve is defective is to bypass it by operating the engine with a remote fuel supply, such as an outboard fuel tank.

The two most common fuel pump problems are incorrect pressure and low volume. Low pressure results in a too-lean mixture and too little fuel at high speeds. High pressure will cause carburetor flooding and rsult in poor economy. Low volume also results in too little fuel at high speeds.

If a fuel system problem is suspected, check the fuel filter first. See Chapter Four. If the filter is not clogged or dirty, test the fuel pump for pressure and flow. If the pump fails either test, bypass the anti-siphon device and repeat the tests. If the pump fails a second time, replace it. If the pump passes both tests with the anti-siphon device bypassed, contact the boat manufacturer for replacement of the anti-siphon device.

Pressure Test

Refer to **Figure 66** for this procedure.

1. Connect a tachometer according to manufacturer's instructions.
2. Install a tee fitting in the fuel line between the fuel pump and carburetor. Connect a fuel pressure gauge to the fitting with a short hose.
3. Start the engine and run at idle. Record the pressure. The 2.3L, 2.5L and 3.0L fuel pump should read 3.5-6.0 psi on models prior to 1989; the 7.5L fuel pump should read 5-6 psi and all others should read 5.75-7.0 psi.

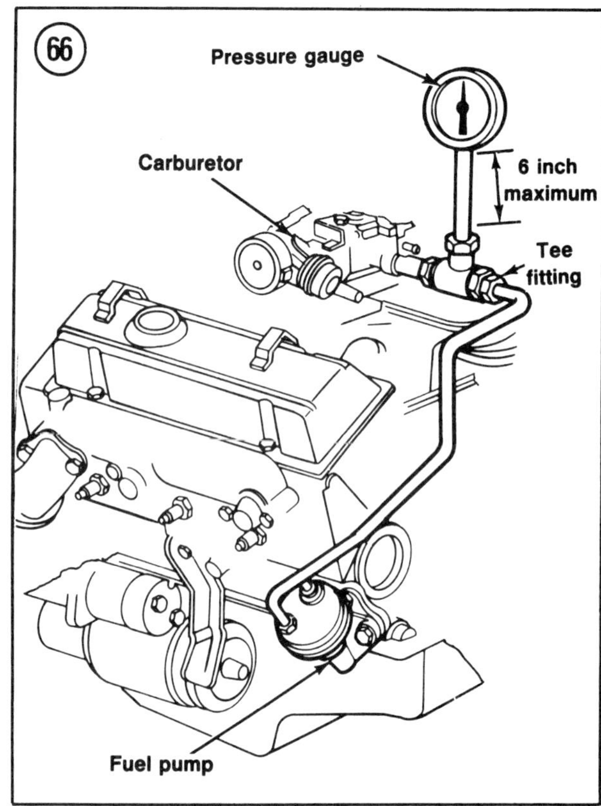

4. Gradually increase engine speed to 1,000 rpm while observing the pressure gauge. Pressure should remain constant and within specifications during the entire range between idle and 1,000 rpm.
5. If pressure is too low, check the fuel lines for kinks, leaks or restrictions; correct as required.
6. If pressure varies from specifications or changes at a higher engine speed, replace the fuel pump.
7. Shut the engine off. The pressure should drop off very slowly. If it drops off rapidly, the outlet valve in the pump is leaking and the pump should be replaced.
8. Remove the tachometer and pressure gauge. Reconnect the fuel line to the carburetor. Start the engine and check for leaks.

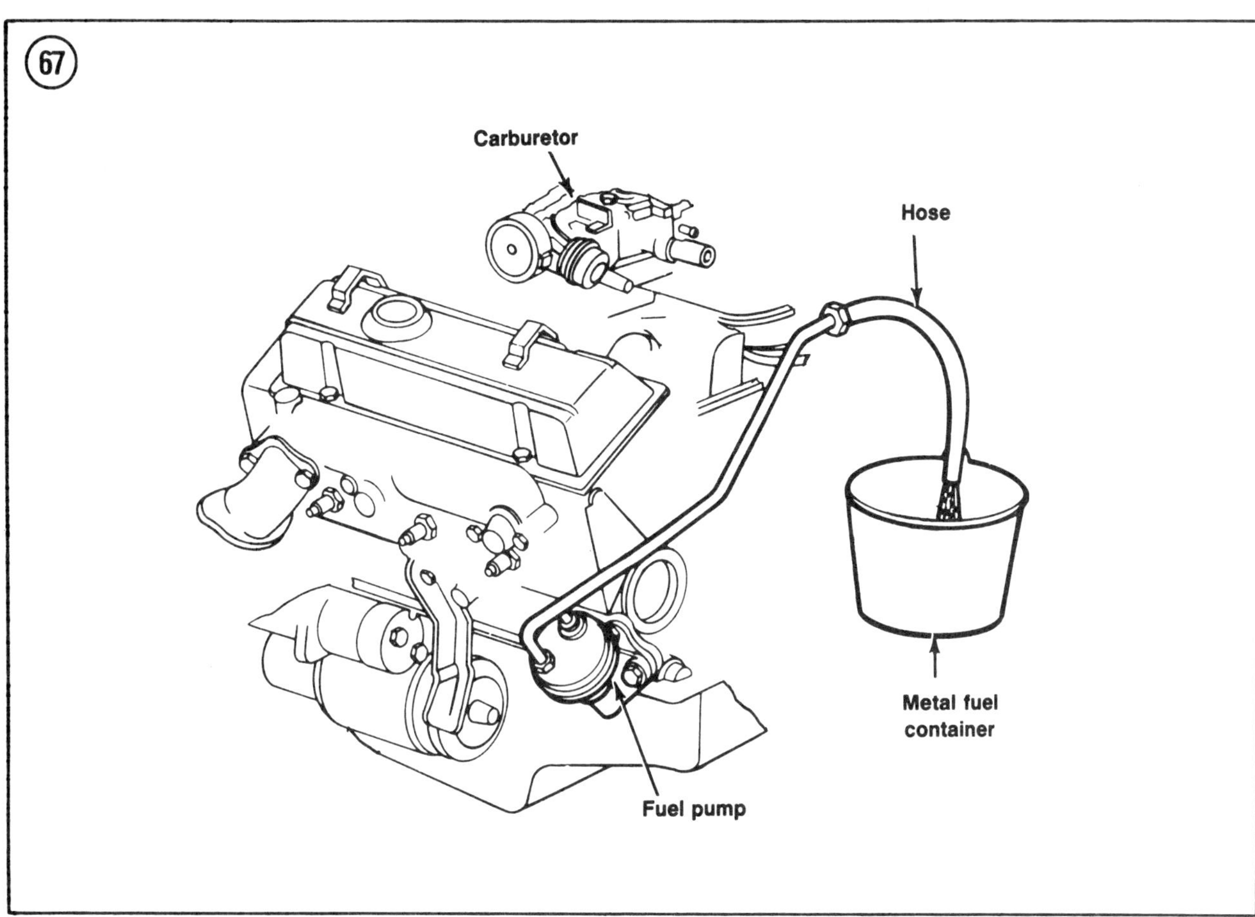

Flow Test

Refer to **Figure 67** for this procedure.

1. Disconnect the fuel inlet line at the carburetor and connect a length of flexible hose to the disconnected line.
2. Place the end of the flexible hose in a clean quart-size container.
3. Start the engine and let it run for 45 seconds (it should run this long on the fuel in the carburetor fuel bowl). Shut the engine off and check the container. It should be approximately 1/2 full within the 45 second interval. If not, check the fuel line for kinks. If none are found, disconnect the inlet line at the pump and fuel tank. Blow compressed air through the line.
4. Reconnect the inlet line and repeat the procedure. If pump volume is still too low, replace the pump.

Vacuum Test

1. Disconnect the fuel inlet line at the fuel pump. Cap the line to prevent leakage and the entry of contamination.
2. Connect OMC vacuum tester part No. 390954 or equivalent to the fuel pump inlet. Connections must be air-tight.
3. Disconnect and ground the ignition coil high tension (thick) lead.
4. Crank the engine over and note the reading on the vacuum gauge. It is is not 9-10 in. Hg at engine cranking speed, replace the fuel pump.

Removal/Installation (Except 7.5L Engine)

1. Place a container under the fuel pump to catch any spillage.

2. Disconnect the inlet and outlet lines at the pump. See **Figure 68** (typical). On V6 and V8 pumps, disconnect the fuel filter canister line at the pump. Use one wrench to hold the pump fitting and the other to loosen the line nut. Cap the lines and plug the fittings to prevent leakage and the entry of contamination.
3. Remove the overflow hose at the pump.
4. Loosen the 2 pump attaching bolts and lockwashers. See **Figure 69** (typical).
5. Connect a remote start button to the starter terminals and crank the engine over while holding the pump in place. When you feel a reduction in tension against the pump, the low point of the camshaft eccentric is resting against the pump. Remove the pump bolts and discard the gasket.
6. GM V8 engines use a pushrod between the pump rocker arm and camshaft eccentric. Remove the pushrod and check it for wear or bending.
7. Clean the pump mounting pad on the engine block to remove all gasket residue.
8. Coat both sides of a new pump gasket with OMC gasket sealing compound and install it to the pump flange.
9. If the pump uses a pushrod, apply a heavy coat of grease to one end of the pushrod and insert that end into the engine.
10. Install the pump and new gasket to the engine. Make sure the pump rocker arm rides on the camshaft eccentric or pushrod, then tighten the attaching bolts as follows:

   a. 2.5L/3.0L engines—12-14 ft.-lb. (16-19 N•m).
   b. 2.3L engines—14-21 ft.-lb. (19-28 N•m).
   c. 5.0L (302 cu. in.)/5.8L engines—19-27 ft.-lb. (26-36 N•m).
   d. All others—20-25 ft.-lb. (27-34 N•m).

11. Uncap and reconnect the fuel inlet and outlet lines and overflow hose to the pump. Reconnect the fuel filter canister line, if so equipped, and secure in place with a new tie strap.
12. Start the engine and check for leaks.

68

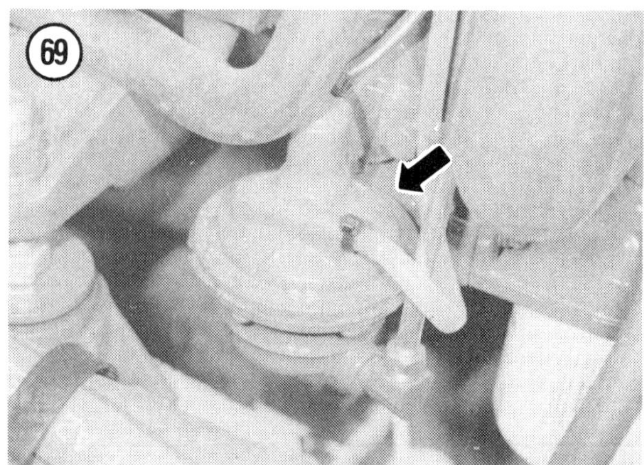
69

Removal/Installation (7.5L Engine)

1. Disconnect the fuel inlet and outlet lines at the fuel filter canister assembly.
2. Unbolt and move the remote oil filter assembly to one side out of the way.
3. Unclamp and disconnect the water hose beside the fuel filter canister assembly. Unbolt and move the filter canister assembly to one side out of the way. Discard the self-locking nuts.
4. Unbolt and remove the filter canister mounting bracket.
5. Disconnect the pump inlet and outlet lines. Cap the lines and plug the fittings to

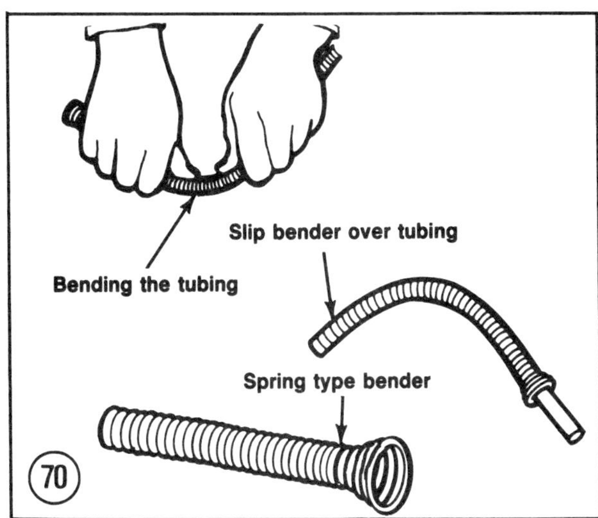

prevent leakage and the entry of contamination.

6. Cut the tie strap (if used) and disconnect the vent line at the pump housing.

7. Unbolt and remove the pump from the engine block mounting pad. Discard the gasket.

8. Installation is the reverse of removal. If a new pump is being installed, remove the elbows from the old pump. Coat their threads with OMC Pipe Sealant with Teflon and reinstall on the new pump. Use a new gasket. Tighten pump and remote oil filter assembly mounting bolts to 19-27 ft.-lb. (26-36 N•m). Start the engine and check for leaks.

FUEL LINES

Fuel lines must be Coast Guard approved (USCG Type A) with an inner diameter of at least 3/8 in. (9.5 mm). If long lines or numerous fittings are used, the inner diameter should be larger.

Fuel lines are usually a combination of rigid steel lines and flexible hoses. Flexible hose is used to connect the fuel line to the engine and absorb deflection or vibration while the engine is running. Hoses are subject to extreme temperature changes and chemical deterioration from the fuel. In areas where fuel quality is poor or gasohol is used, even the rigid steel lines will eventually deteriorate.

Damaged or leaking fuel lines and hoses must be replaced as soon as possible, and in a safe manner. While it is tempting to cut out a bad section of fuel line and insert a short length of hose as a replacement, this is not recommended except as a means of temporary repair allowing you to reach port or a marina where the line can be properly replaced. Other portions of the line may be just as weak and will fail sooner or later. Since the dangers of fire or explosion are always present when a fuel line fails, it is safer, more economical and less time-consuming to do the job right in the beginning.

Double-wrap brazed steel tubing should always be used to replace steel fuel lines. This is available from marine dealers. Do *not* use copper or aluminum tubing as neither will withstand normal engine and boat vibration. Rubber hose made specifically for fuel systems should be used. Other hose materials are not formulated to withstand chemical deterioration from gasoline.

To temporarily replace a fuel line, carry a length of fuel line hose, several worm-screw clamps and a tubing cutter with you. If it is necessary to make on-the-spot repairs, the damaged section of the line can be cut out and replaced by a length of fuel hose secured at each end with a clamp. This temporary repair should be replaced at the first available opportunity.

1. Obtain a suitable length of steel fuel line of the correct diameter.

2. Disconnect the negative battery cable.

3. Remove the damaged or deteriorated fuel line.

4. Slip a spring-type tubing bender over the tubing and carefully bend to match the old line. See **Figure 70.**

5. Remove the fittings, if any, from the old line and install on the new line.

6. Use a flaring tool to make a double lap flare on each end of the line. See **Figure 71**. This will provide a good seal and prevent the flare from cracking.

7. Install the new line and tighten the fittings securely.

8. Reconnect the negative battery cable. Start the engine and check for leaks.

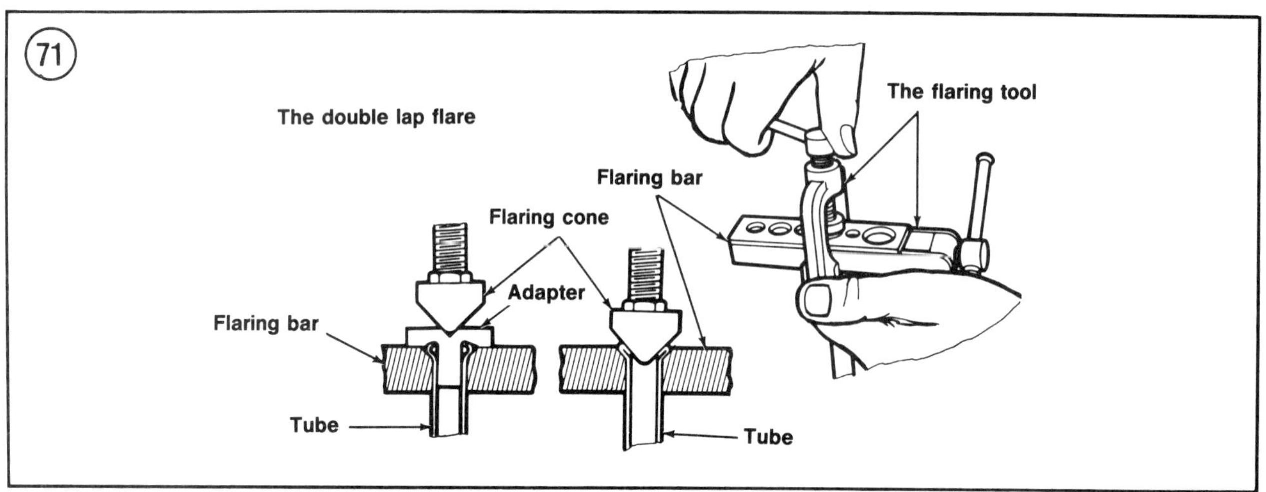

Table 1 CARBURETOR SPECIFICATIONS

Engine/bbl./ carb. No.	Float level (in.)	Float drop (in.)	Choke setting	Initial idle mixture setting
2.3L/2-bbl./ 17086107	17/32	1.75	Index	2.5 turns out
2.5L/3.0L/2-bbl./ 17086064	1/2	1.75	Index	2 turns out
4.3L/2-bbl./ 17083110 and 17085008	17/32	1.75	Index	2.5 turns out
4.3L/2-bbl./ 17082515	5/16			3.75 turns out
5.0L (305 cu. in.)/5.7L/4-bbl./ 17058286	5/16			3.75 turns out
5.7L/4-bbl./ 17059286 and 17085010	5/16			3.75 turns out
5.0L (302 cu. in.)/ 2-bbl./ E8JL-9510-AA	*		1 notch lean	1.5 turns out
5.8L/4-bbl./ E8JL-9510-CA	*		1 notch lean	1.5 turns out
7.5L/4-bbl./ L-50399	*		1 notch rich	1.5 turns out
7.5L/4-bbl./ E8JL-9510-DA	*		1 notch lean	1.5 turns out

* Parallel to fuel bowl with bowl inverted.

Chapter Ten

Cooling System

This chapter covers service procedures for the thermostat, engine and stern drive water pumps, seawater pumps, drive belts and connecting hoses in both standard and closed cooling systems.

Cooling system flushing procedures are provided in Chapter Four. Drain and refill procedures are given in Chapter Five.

Tightening torques (**Table 1**) are at the end of the chapter.

Standard Cooling System

All OMC marine engines are equipped with a standard cooling system. The water in which the boat is being operated is used as a coolant to absorb engine heat. Water from outside the boat is picked up at the water intake on each side of the stern drive lower gearcase by an impeller-type pump located in the upper portion of the upper gear housing. The pump sends the water to the engine's water pump (also called a recirculating pump) for circulation through the engine block, head(s) and manifold(s).

On some models, the water may be circulated through one or more oil coolers beore reaching the engine's water pump. The water absorbs the heat created by engine operation and then enters the exhaust elbow, where it mixes with exhaust gases before being expelled from the boat.

A thermostat controls water circulation to provide quick engine warmup and maintain a constant operating temperature.

Figure 1 shows the cooling system and circulation pattern for all Cobra drives. **Figures 2-6** show the cooling system and circulation pattern for the various OMC marine engines.

Closed Cooling System

OMC V6 and V8 marine engines may also be equipped with a closed cooling system. This cooling system is divided into two separate sub-systems; one uses seawater and the other uses a coolant mixture of distilled water and ethylene glycol antifreeze. The sub-system containing the coolant is referred to as the "fresh water" system.

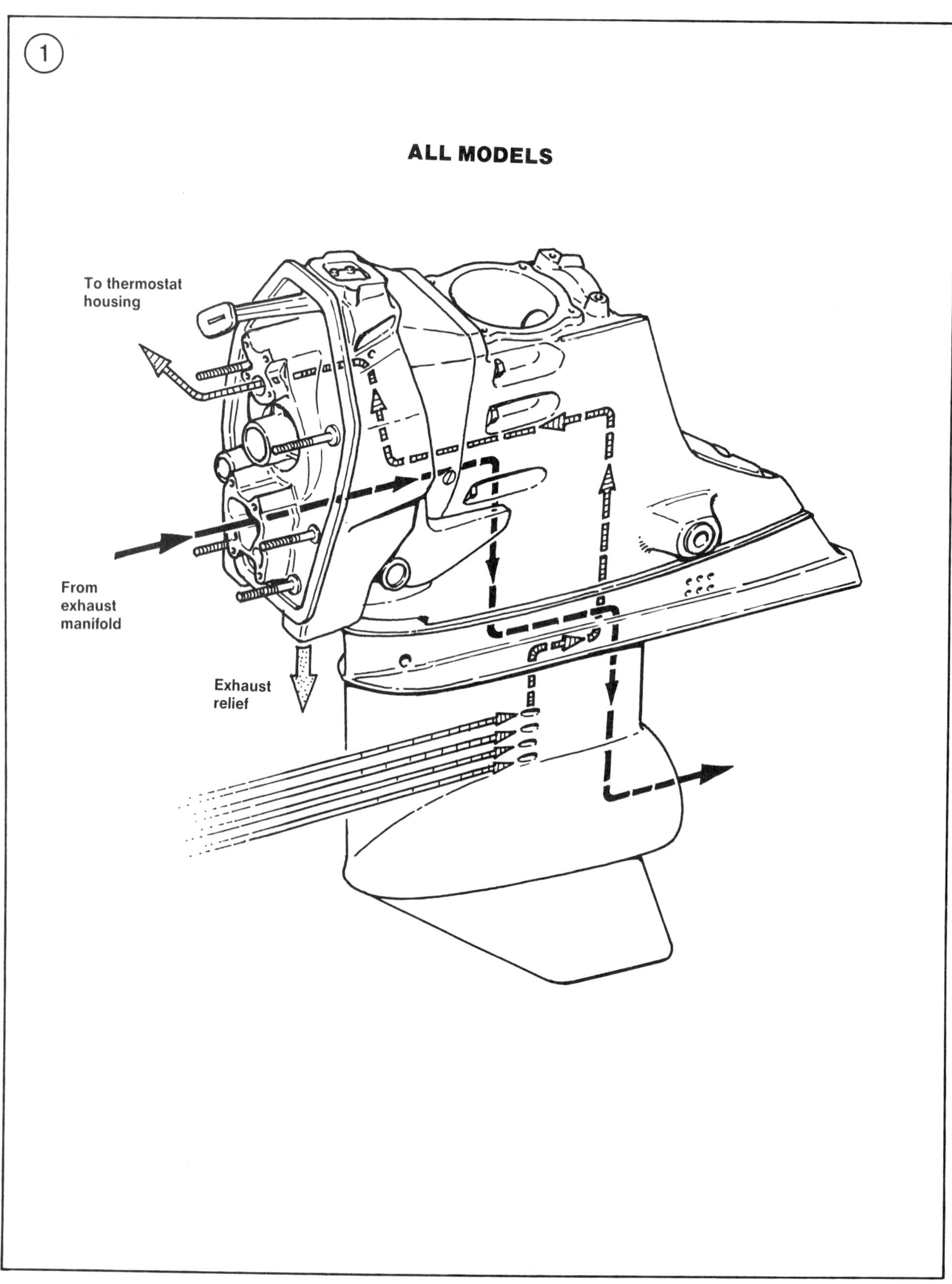
1
ALL MODELS
To thermostat housing
From exhaust manifold
Exhaust relief

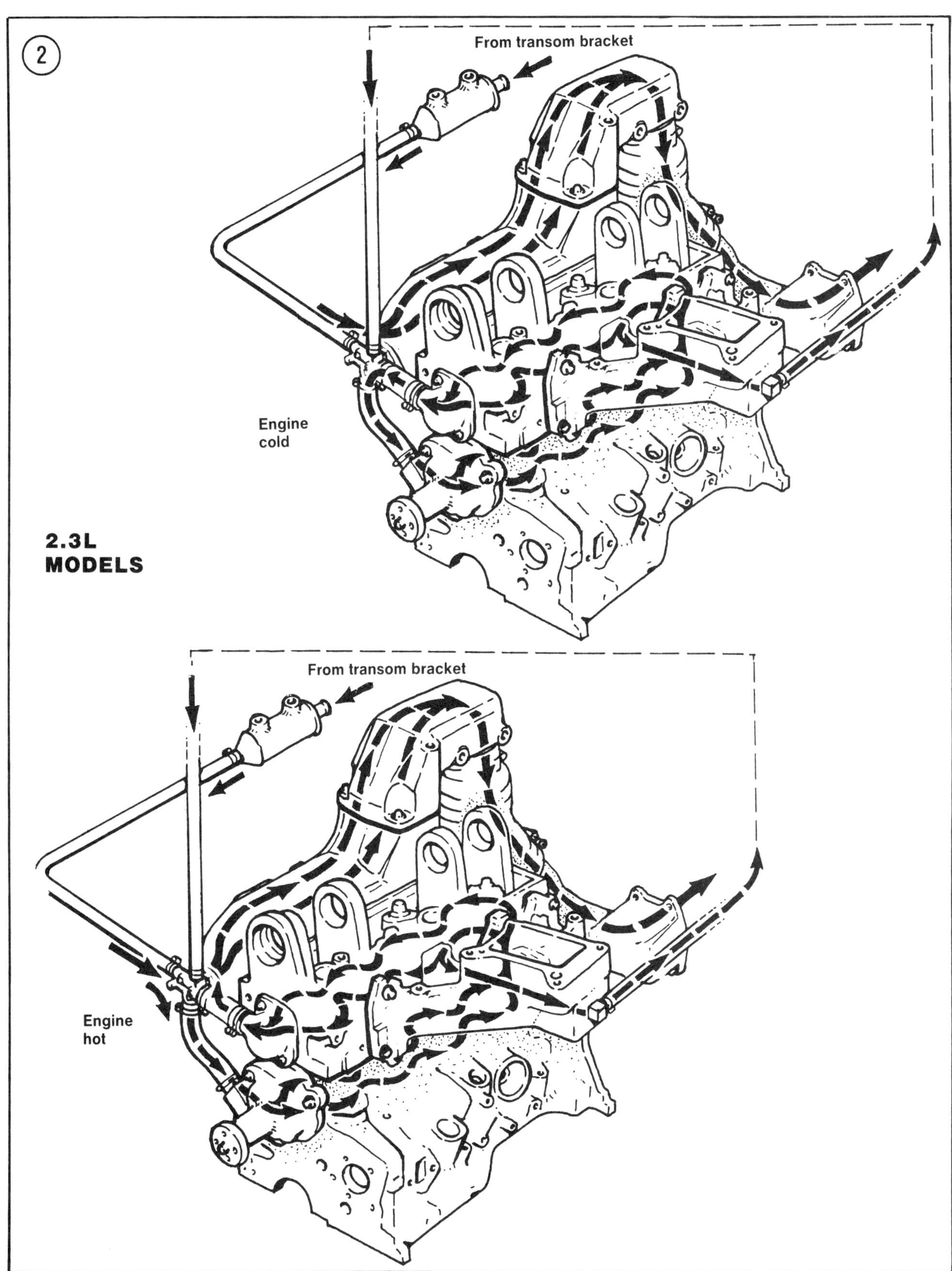
2
From transom bracket
Engine cold
2.3L MODELS
From transom bracket
Engine hot

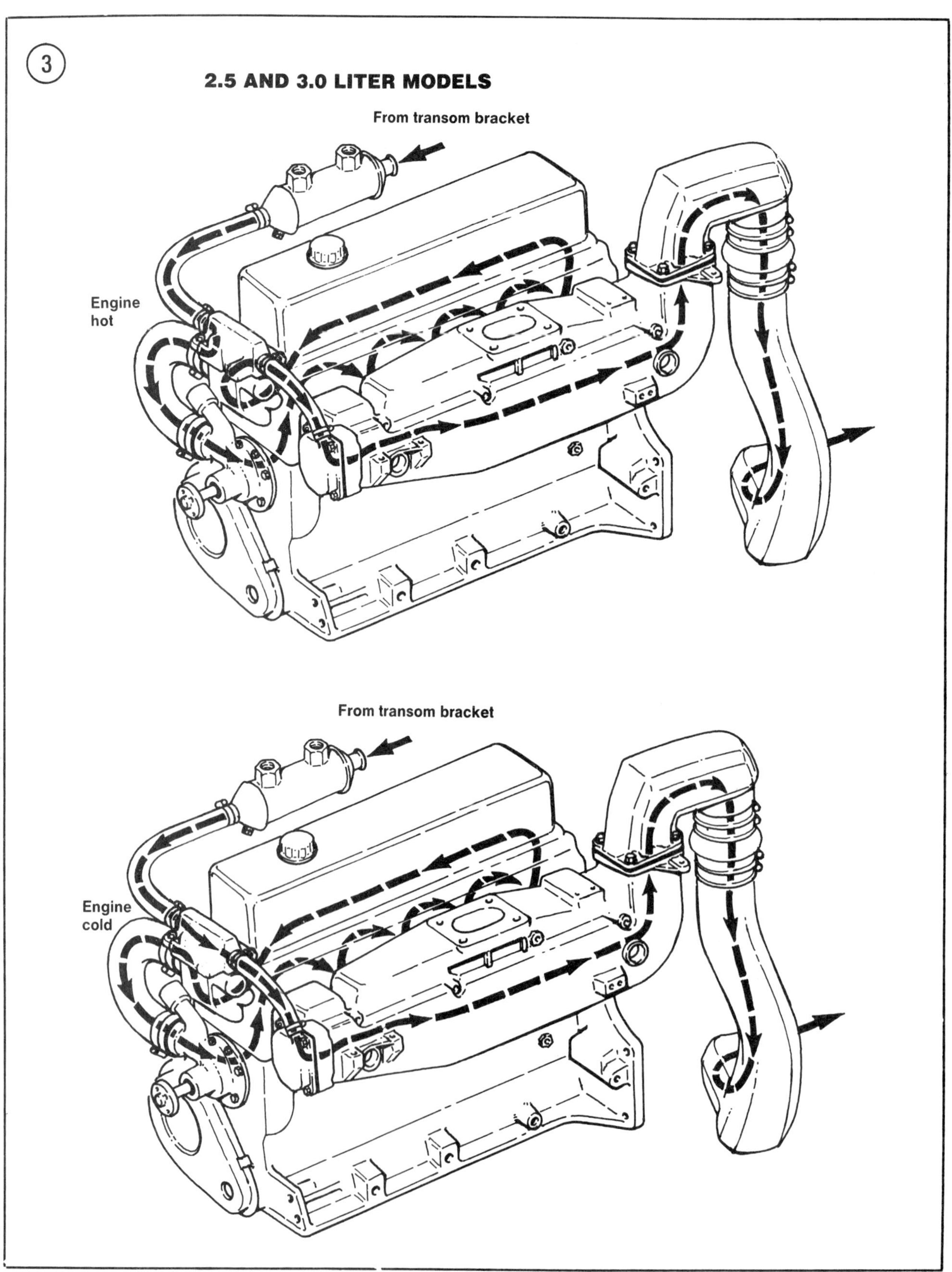
3
2.5 AND 3.0 LITER MODELS
From transom bracket
Engine hot
From transom bracket
Engine cold

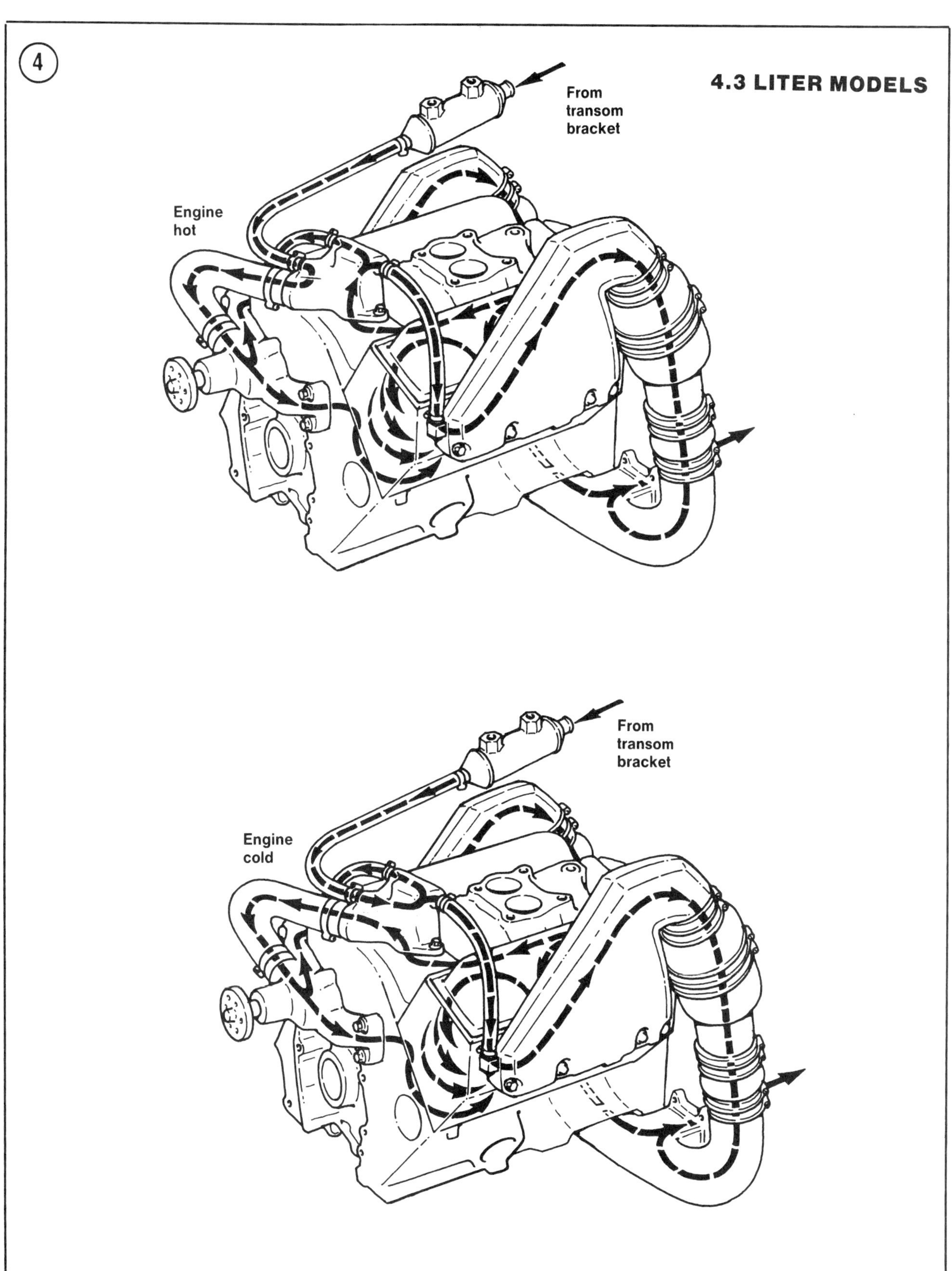
4
4.3 LITER MODELS
From
transom
bracket
Engine
hot
From
transom
bracket
Engine
cold

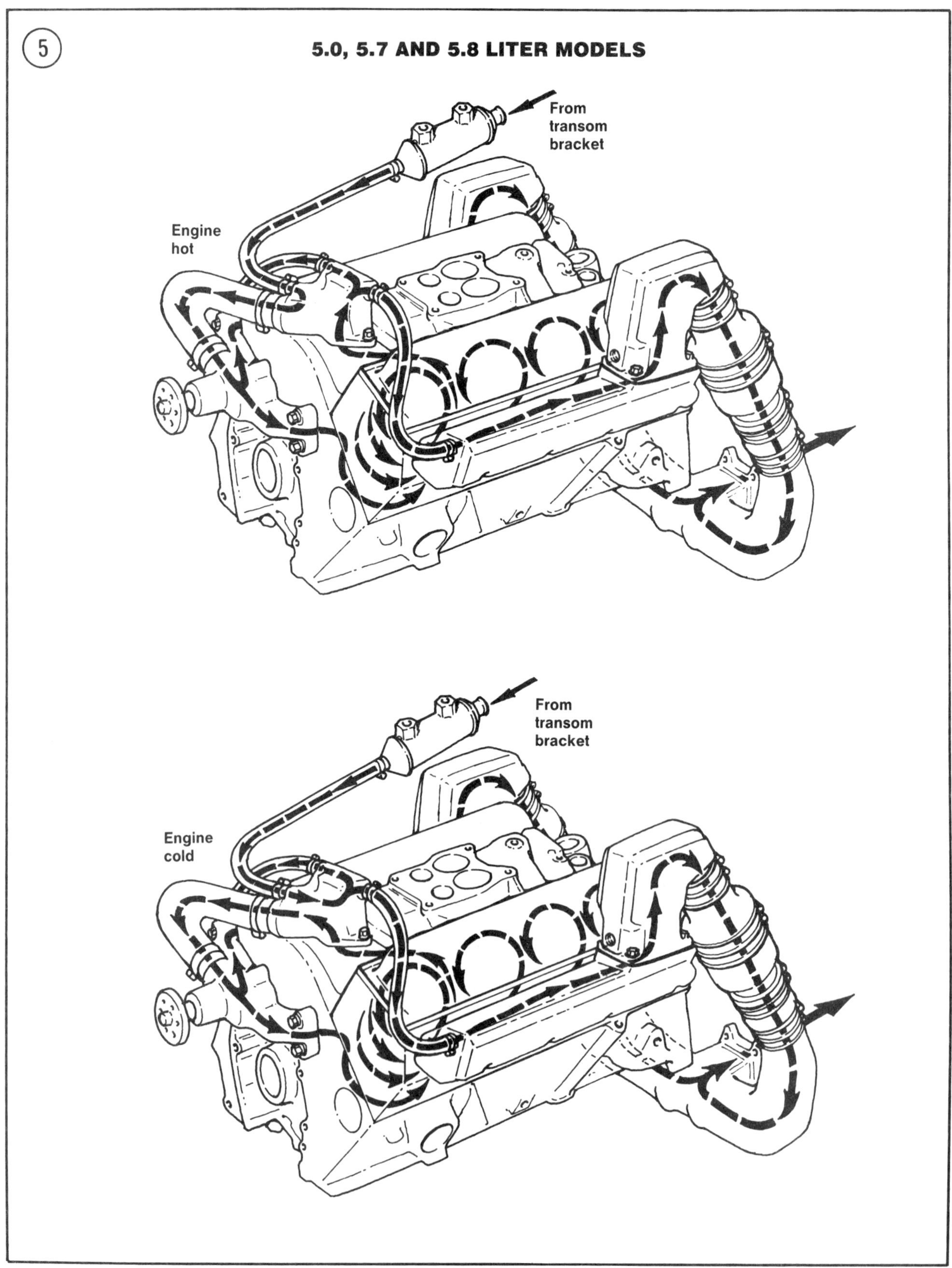
5
5.0, 5.7 AND 5.8 LITER MODELS
From transom bracket
Engine hot
From transom bracket
Engine cold

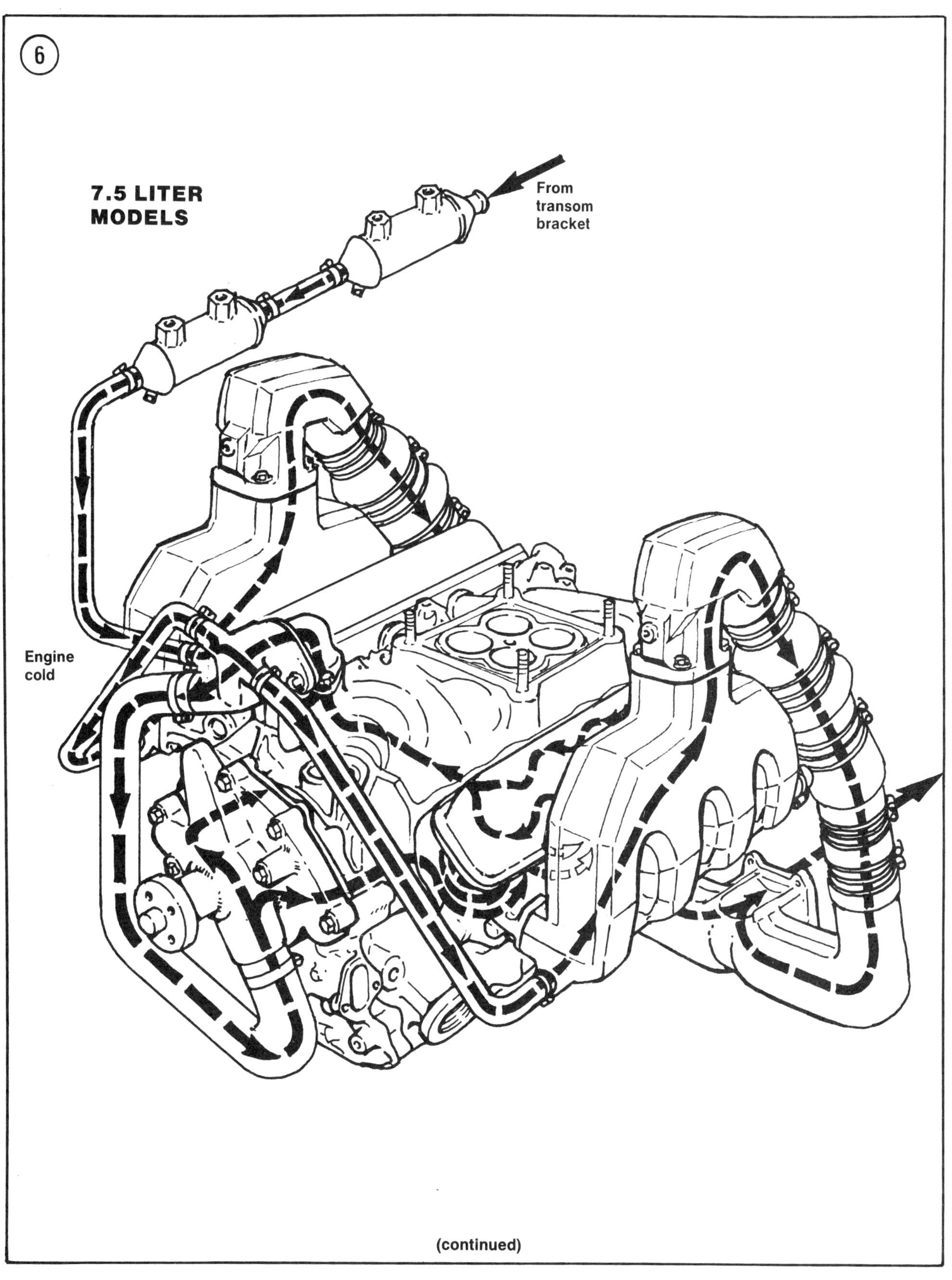

(continued)

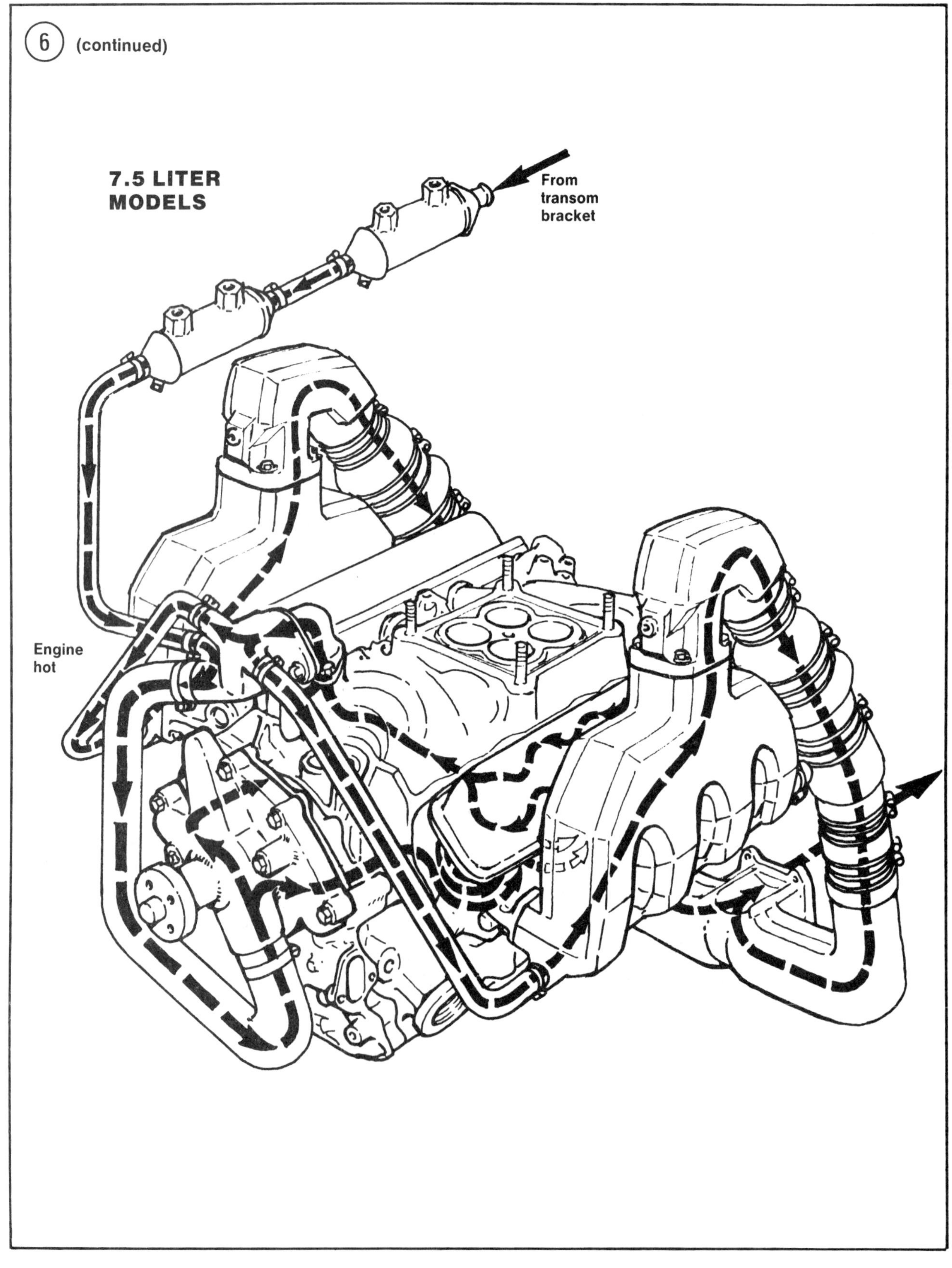
6 (continued)
7.5 LITER MODELS
From transom bracket
Engine hot

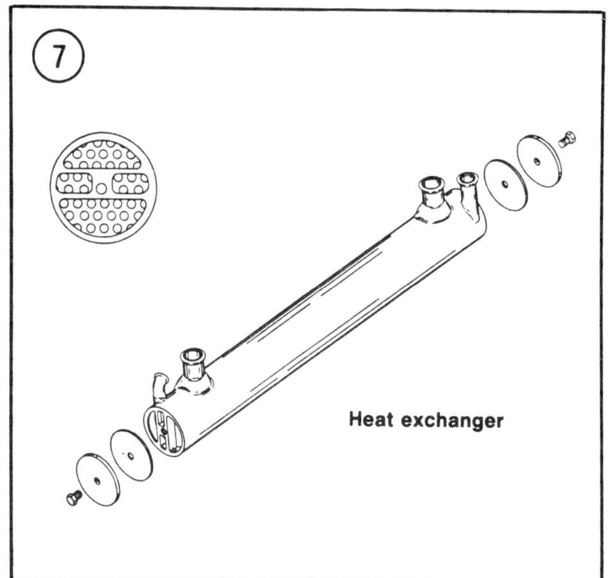

The sub-system using seawater is similar to the standard cooling system previously described. Water from outside the boat is drawn into the system by the stern drive pump. In addition, a belt-driven seawater pump is located at the front of the engine. Instead of passing directly into the engine, however, the water circulates through the power steering and oil coolers, if so equipped.

After removing heat from the cooler(s), the water travels through a series of parallel copper tubes in the heat exchanger where it absorbs engine coolant heat before returning to the exhaust elbows for discharge from the boat. **Figure 7** shows a typical heat exchanger design with a cross-section of its interior.

The "fresh water" system circulates the coolant mixture inside the engine to absorb engine heat. This coolant is then routed to the heat exchanger, where the heat absorbed from engine operation is transferred through the parallel copper tubes to the water in the seawater system.

Engine cooling is thus accomplished without seawater entering the engine. This eliminates the corrosion, deposit buildup and debris accumulation which occurs in a standard cooling system, resulting in longer engine life—especially if the boat is used in salt water.

Like an automotive cooling system, the fresh water section is pressurized at 14 psi. This raises the boiling point of the coolant to permit higher operating temperatures for increased engine efficiency.

A thermostat located in the starboard end cap of the heat exchanger controls coolant circulation. When the thermostat is closed, it prevents coolant from entering the heat exchanger, rerouting it back to the engine recirculating pump. Once the thermostat opens, it closes off the passage to the recirculating pump and sends the coolant through the heat exchanger before returning it to the engine pump. This provides quick engine warmup and maintains a constant operating temperature.

THERMOSTAT

The thermostat blocks coolant flow to the exhaust manifold (standard cooling) or heat exchanger (closed cooling) when the engine is cold. As the engine warms up, the thermostat gradually opens, allowing coolant to circulate through the system.

CAUTION

Do not operate the engine without a thermostat. This can lead to overheating and serious engine damage.

Thermostats are rated according to their opening temperature. Check the thermostat when removed to determine its opening point; the heat range should be stamped on the thermostat flange.

OMC thermostats used with standard cooling systems are rated at 160° F. They should start to open at approximately 157-163° F and should be fully open at 182° F.

OMC thermostats used with a closed cooling system differ in design and function.

10

They are not interchangeable with those used in a standard cooling system. The closed cooling system thermostat is rated at 170° F. It starts to open at approximately 168-174° F and should be fully open at about 190° F.

CAUTION

*Do **not** substitute an automotive-type thermostat. Its higher rating will cause the engine to run hotter than normal and could cause engine damage.*

Removal (Standard Cooling System)

1. Drain the engine block and exhaust manifold(s). See Chapter Five.
2. Loosen the hose clamps and disconnect the hoses from the thermostat cover.
3. Remove the thermostat cover attaching bolts and lockwashers. Remove cover with gasket. Discard the gasket. See **Figure 8** (inline) or **Figure 9** (V6 and V8), typical.
4. Remove the thermostat.

Removal (Closed Cooling System)

1. Drain the engine coolant from the block. See Chapter Five.
2. Loosen the hose clamp and disconnect the hose at the starboard end cap on the heat exchanger (**Figure 10**, typical).
3. Remove the end cap and gasket (**Figure 10**, typical). Discard the gasket.
4. Remove the thermostat.

Testing (Out of Engine)

1. Insert a 0.005 in. shim between the thermostat valve and seat. See **Figure 11**.
2. Pour some water into a container that can be heated. Submerge the thermostat in the water and suspend a thermometer as shown in **Figure 12**.

NOTE

Suspend the thermostat with wire so it does not touch the sides or bottom of the pan.

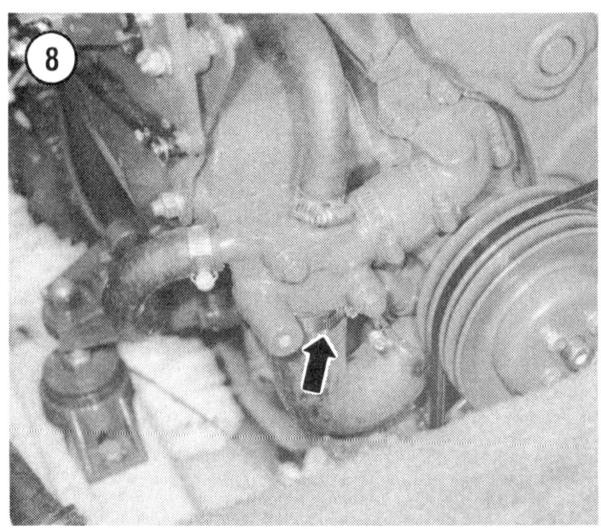

8

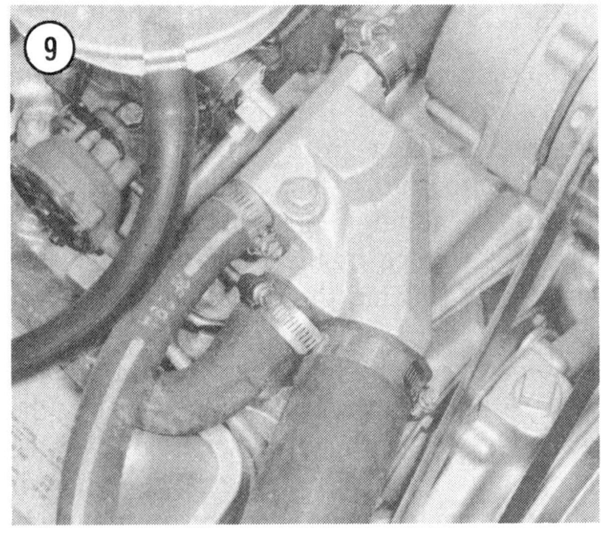

9

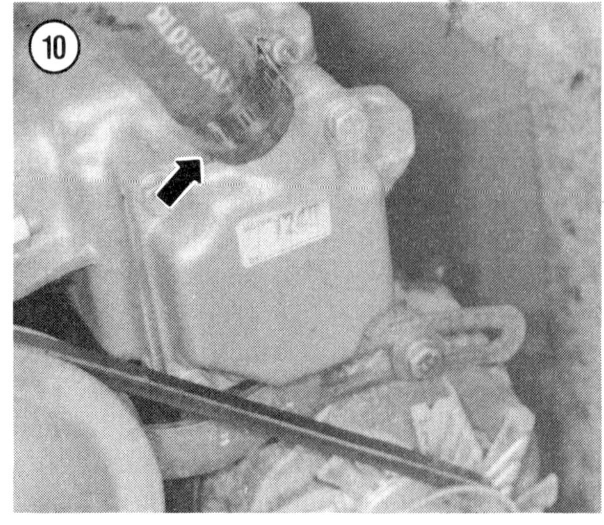

10

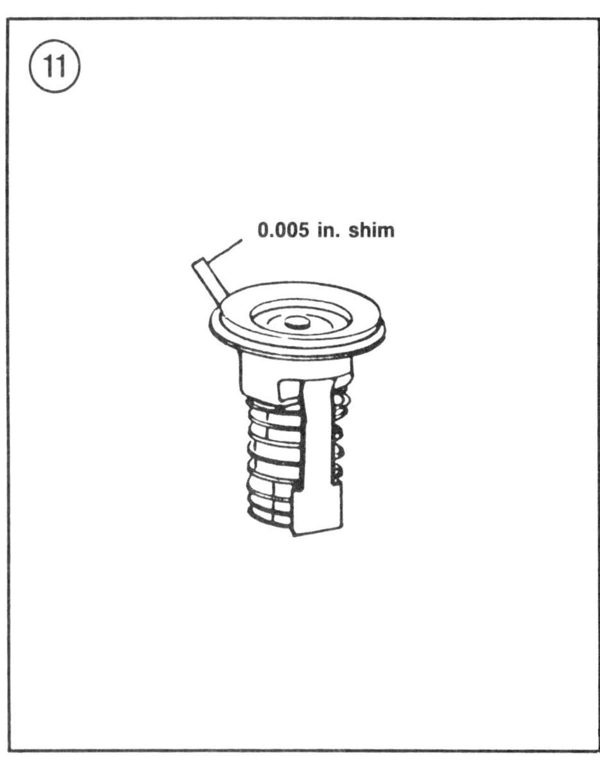

3. Heat the water until the thermostat starts to open. Check the water temperature on the thermometer. It should be approximately 160° F (standard) or 170° F (closed). The thermostat should release the shim at between 157-163° F (standard) or 168-174° F (closed). If the thermostat has not started to open at this temperature, replace it.

4. Heat the water another 25° F above the opening temperature. The thermostat should now be fully open (5/32 in.). If it is not, replace it.

5. Let the water cool to 10° *under* the thermostat's rated opening temperature. If the thermostat valve is not fully closed at this temperature, replace it.

6. Remove the thermostat from the water and let it cool to room temperature. Hold it close to a light bulb and check for leakage. If light can be seen at more than 1 or 2 tiny

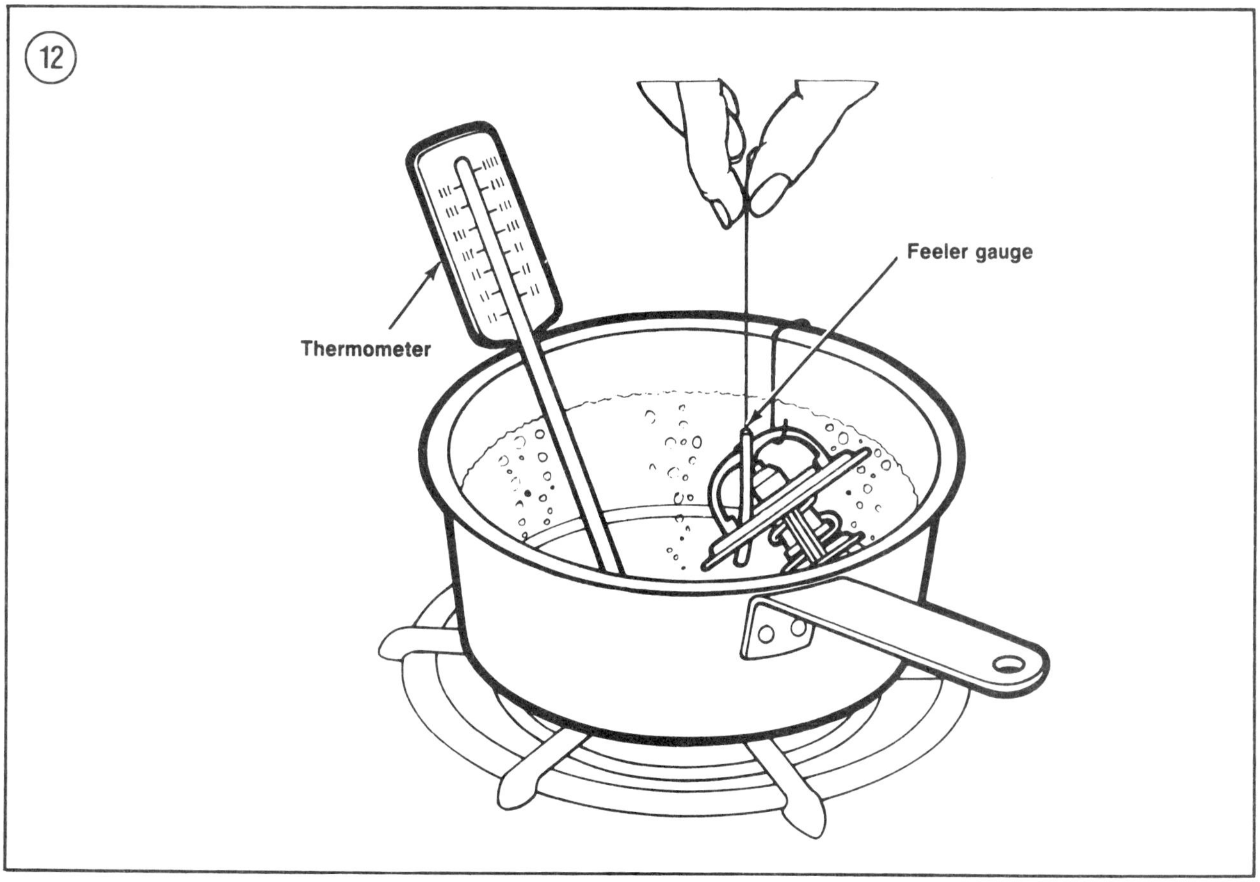

12

Feeler gauge

Thermometer

points around the edge of the valve, the thermostat is defective and should be replaced.

Testing (In Engine)

Thermostat operation can be tested without removing it from the engine or reservoir. This procedure requires the use of 2 thermomelt sticks (**Figure 13**) available from marine supply or automotive parts stores. A thermomelt stick looks like a carpenter's pencil and is made of a chemically impregnated wax material which melts at a specific temperature.

This technique can be used to check thermostat opening by marking the thermostat housing or reservoir with a 160° F or 190° F thermomelt stick, depending upon the problem. As the coolant or water reaches the first temperature, the mark made by that stick will melt. The mark made by the second stick will not melt until the coolant or water increases to that temperature.

WARNING

Do not remove the pressure fill cap from closed cooling systems when the engine is warm. Coolant may blow out of the heat exchanger and cause serious personal injury.

Overheated engine

1. Relieve the fresh water cooling system pressure on closed cooling systems by carefully removing the pressure fill cap from the heat exchanger.
2. Rub the 190° F thermomelt stick on the thermostat cover or reservoir.
3. Start the engine and run at a fast idle.
4. If no coolant or water flows through the housing-to-manifold or housing-to-exhaust elbow hoses by the time the mark starts to melt, either the thermostat is stuck closed or the water pump is failing. Remove the thermostat and test it as described in this chapter. If satisfactory, replace the water pump.

13

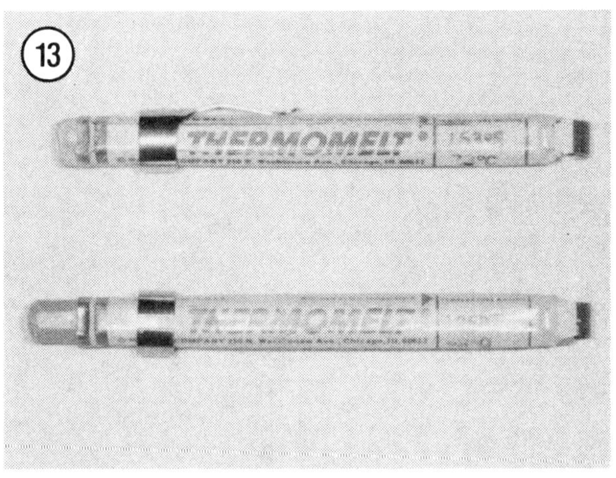

Slow engine warmup

1. Relieve the fresh water cooling system pressure on closed cooling systems by carefully removing the pressure fill cap from the heat exchanger.
2. Rub the 160° F thermomelt stick on the thermostat cover or reservoir.
3. Start the engine and run at a fast idle.
4. If no coolant or water flows through the housing-to-manifold or housing-to-exhaust elbow hoses by the time the mark starts to melt, the thermostat is stuck open and should be replaced.

Installation

1. If a new thermostat is being installed, test it as described in this chapter.
2. Clean the thermostat cover and engine or the end cap and manifold mating surfaces of all gasket residue.

3A. Standard cooling systems:
   a. Install the thermostat in the housing with its thermostatic element facing the engine. The thermostat flange must fit into the housing recess.
   b. Coat both sides of a new gasket with a water-resistant sealer and install the gasket to the thermostat cover.

c. Install the cover and tighten the bolts to specifications (**Table 1**).

3B. Closed cooling systems:

a. Install the thermostat in the heat exchanger with the thermostatic element facing outward.

b. Coat both sides of a new end cap gasket with a water-resistant sealer.

c. Position the gasket on the heat exchanger and install the end cap. Tighten the end cap bolts to specifications (**Table 1**).

4. Reverse Steps 1-2 of *Removal* to complete installation.

HOSE REPLACEMENT

Replace any hoses that are cracked, brittle, mildewed or very soft and spongy. If a hose is in doubtful condition but not definitely bad, replace it to be on the safe side. Hoses in some installations are extremely difficult to change; attention to hose condition can prevent a failure while you are off-shore.

Hose manufacturers generally rate cooling system hose life at 2 years. How long the hoses will last depends a great deal on how much you use your boat and how well you maintain the system. However, it is a good idea to change all hoses every 2 years. Always replace a cooling system hose with the same type as removed. Pleated rubber hoses do not have the same strength as reinforced molded hoses. Check the hose clamp condition and install new worm screw-type clamps with a new hose, if necessary.

Partially drain the seawater section of closed cooling systems when replacing upper hoses. Completely drain it when replacing lower hoses.

1. Loosen the clamp at each end of the hose to be removed. Grasp the hose and twist it off the fitting with a pulling motion.
2. If the hose is corroded to the fitting and will not twist free, cut it off with a sharp knife about one inch beyond the fitting. Remove the clamp and slit the remaining piece of hose lengthwise, then peel it off the fitting.
3. Clean any rust or corrosion from the fitting by wrapping a piece of medium grit sandpaper around it and rotating until the fitting surface is relatively clean and smooth.
4. Wipe the inside diameter of the hose and the outside of the fitting with dishwashing liquid. Place the new clamps on the hose and install the hose ends on the fittings with a twisting motion.
5. Position the new clamps at least 1/4 in. from the end of the hose. Make sure the clamp screw is positioned for easy access with a screwdriver or cap driver. Tighten each clamp snugly.
6. Refill the cooling system. Start the engine and check for leaks. Recheck clamps for tightness after operating the engine for a few hours.

ENGINE CIRCULATING PUMP

The circulating pump may warn of impending failure by making noise. If the seal is defective, coolant or water may leak from behind the pump pulley. The pump is serviced as an assembly and can be replaced on all models with the engine in the boat. OMC marine engine water pumps contain stainless steel components and use a special marine shaft seal assembly. Do *not* replace with an automotive-type water pump.

Removal/Installation

1. Disconnect the negative battery cable.
2. Drain the cylinder block. See Chapter Four.
3. Loosen, but do not remove, the pump pulley fasteners.
4. Loosen the alternator adjusting and pivot bolts. See **Figure 14** (typical). Swivel the alternator toward the engine and remove the drive belt. If equipped with power steering.

repeat this step to remove the power steering drive belt.

5. Remove any accessory brackets attached to the water pump or those which will interfere with its removal.
6. 2.3L—Remove the outer timing belt cover. See Chapter Six.
7. Remove the pump pulley fasteners. Remove the pulley.
8. Unclamp and disconnect the hoses from the circulating pump.
9. Remove the pump-to-cylinder block bolts. Remove the pump and gasket. Discard the gasket.
10. Clean all gasket residue from the pump and engine block mounting surfaces.
11. Installation is the reverse of removal. Tighten water pump fasteners to specifications (**Table 1**). Adjust drive belts as described in this chapter. Fill fresh water section of closed cooling systems with coolant. See Chapter Five. Start the engine and check for leaks.

STERN DRIVE PICKUP PUMP

This pump is used on all OMC Cobra drives. The water pump is located at the upper rear of the upper gear housing. **Figure 15** is an exploded view of the pump components.

CAUTION
Whenever the engine is operated, water must circulate through the stern drive or the water pump will be damaged.

Removal/Installation

The water pump assembly can be serviced without removing the stern drive unit from the boat. Refer to **Figure 15** for this procedure.

1. Remove the 3 screws holding the water pump access cover to the upper gear housing. Remove the access cover. See **Figure 16**.

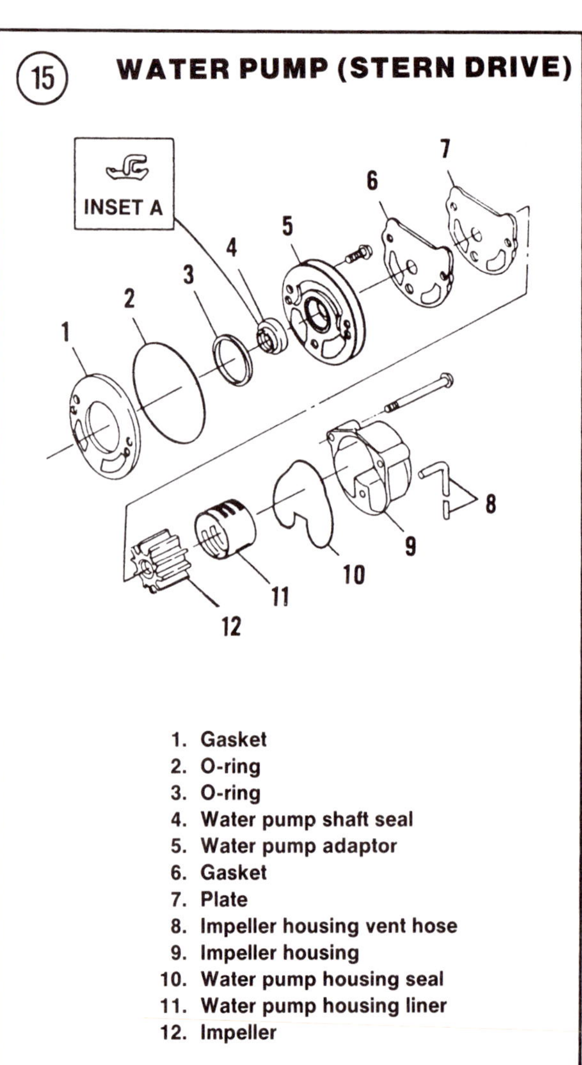

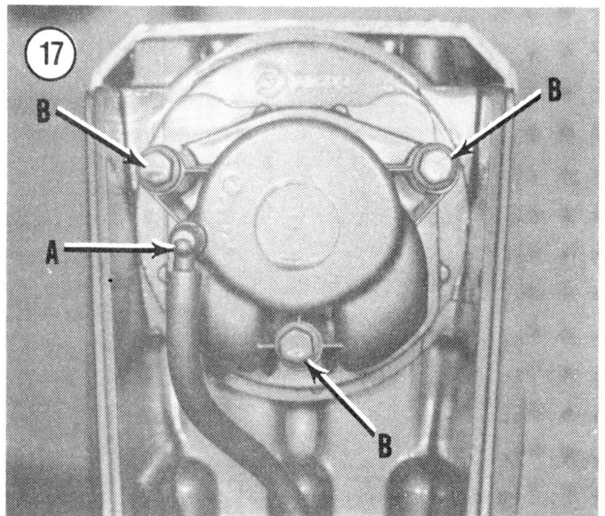

2. Disconnect the drain hose from the housing (A, **Figure 17**).

3. Remove the 3 water pump housing bolts (B, **Figure 17**). Remove the water pump housing (**Figure 18**). If the impeller does not come off with the housing, remove it from the pump shaft.

4. Pry the impeller plate from the adapter (**Figure 19**) with a gasket removal tool or putty knife. Remove and discard the gasket.

NOTE
In many cases, impeller replacement and water pump service can be carried out without further disassembly of the unit. If it is necessary to remove the entire pump assembly, or if the upper gearcase is being disassembled, continue with the procedure.

5. The water pump adapter is held in place by 2 screws, 2 O-rings and sealer. Remove the 2 screws, then carefully remove the adapter by clamping Vise Grips on the housing wall between the water passages and pulling the adapter out. See **Figure 20**. Do not damage the gasket surface around the lower screw hole. Remove and discard the adapter gasket and O-rings.

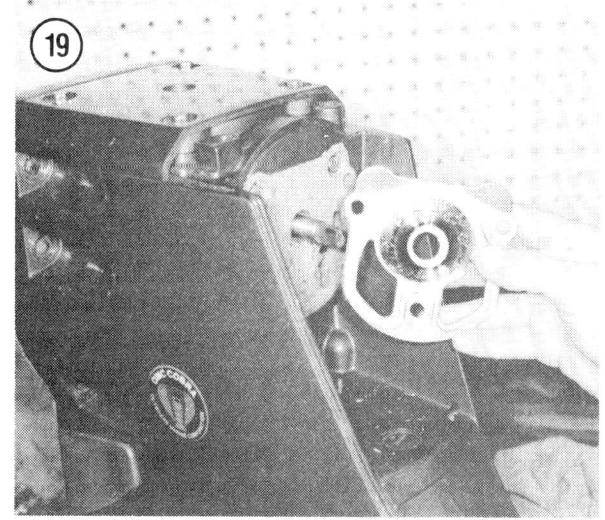

6. Disassemble, clean, inspect and reassemble the water pump as described in this chapter.
7. To reinstall the water pump assembly, coat both sides of a new adapter housing gasket with OMC Gasket Sealing Compound. Install the gasket on the rear of the adapter.
8. Wipe 2 new O-rings with OMC Gasket Sealing Compound and install them on the adapter.
9. Install the adapter housing in the gearcase (**Figure 21**), using a soft-faced hammer as required to fully seat it in place.
10. Wipe the adapter screw threads with OMC Gasket Sealing Compound. Install and tighten screws to 12-14 ft.-lb. (16-19 N•m). See **Figure 22**.
11. Lightly coat both sides of a new impeller plate gasket with OMC Gasket Sealing Compound. Install the gasket on the adapter. Make sure that the adapter plate relief slot remains open or the seal around the shaft may be pressurized and prematurely fail.
12. Install the impeller plate to the gasket surface (**Figure 23**). The side of the plate that is most worn should face the gasket.
13. Wipe a new seal ring with OMC Gasket Sealing Compound and install it in the pump cover groove.

CAUTION
The next 2 steps must be performed correctly to permit pump cover installation without disturbing the cover seal position. If the cover is not properly sealed, engine overheating will occur.

14. Position the narrow end of the impeller drive pocket directly opposite the lower screw hole in the housing cover by rotating it clockwise with a suitable screwdriver. See **Figure 24**.
15. Rotate the U-joint shaft to position the narrow end of the impeller drive shaft directly across from the lower mounting hole. See **Figure 25**.

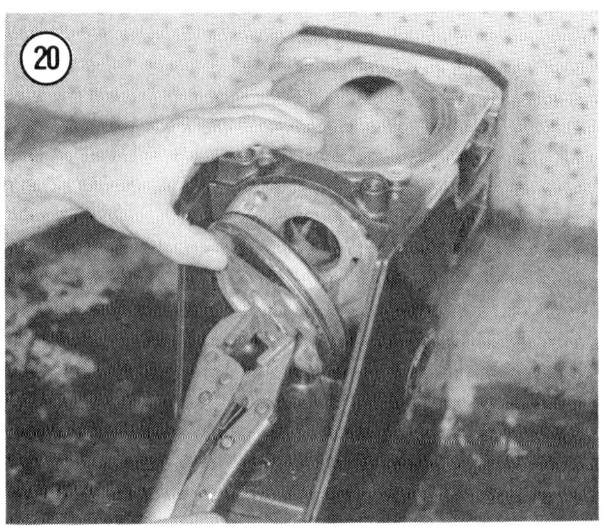

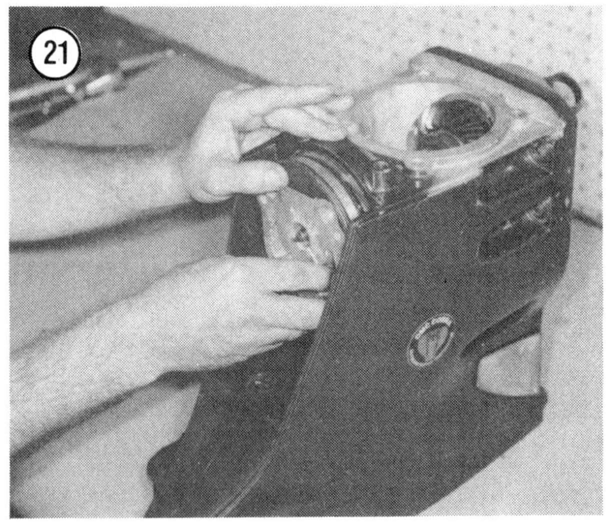

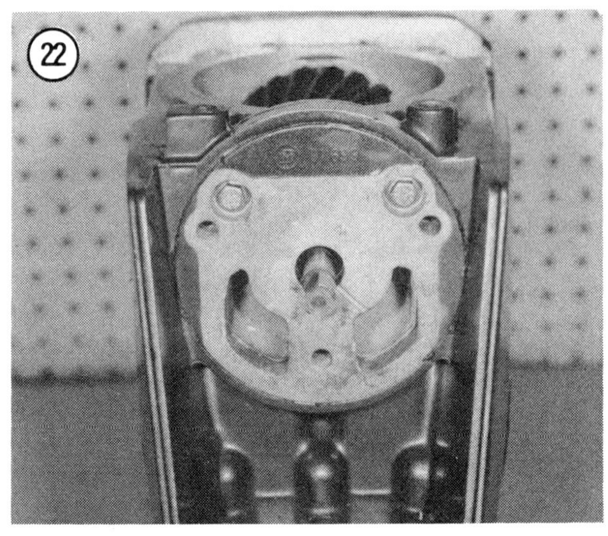

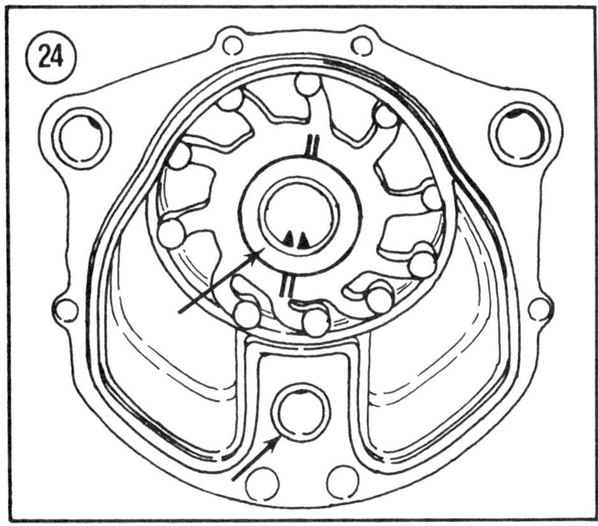

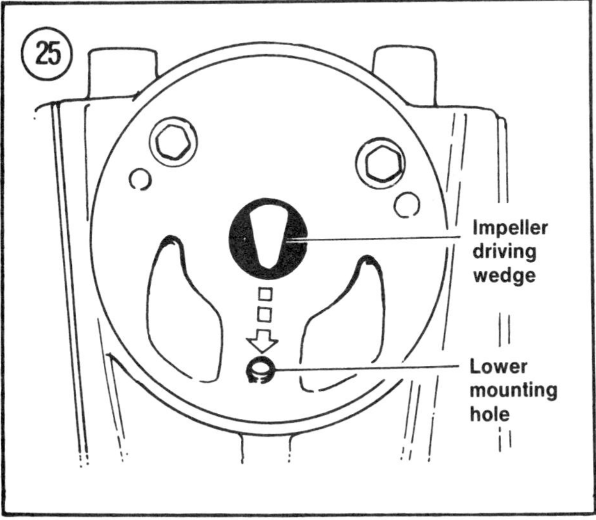

16. Install the pump cover over the shaft and push it in place against the impeller plate. If Step 14 and Step 15 have been performed correctly, the cover should fit and seat without difficulty.
17. Wipe the cover screw threads with OMC Gasket Sealing Compound. Install and tighten screws (B, **Figure 17**) to 108-132 in.-lb. (12-15 N•m).
18. Lubricate the end of the vent hose with a small quantity of dishwashing liquid and install it on the housing nipple. See A, **Figure 17**.
19. Reinstall the water pump access cover (**Figure 16**). Wipe cover screw threads with OMC Gasket Sealing Compound. Install and tighten screws to 108-132 in.-lb. (12-15 N•m).

Disassembly/Assembly

Refer to **Figure 15** for this procedure.

1. Position the adapter on a hydraulic press with its relief slot facing upward (seal cavity facing down). Press the center seal out with OMC driver part No. 912270 or equivalent, holding your hand under the press to catch the driver and seal. Discard the seal.
2. Remove and discard the O-ring seal in the impeller housing cover.
3. If the impeller remained in the housing, carefully remove it with suitable pliers. The impeller liner (**Figure 26**) should not be

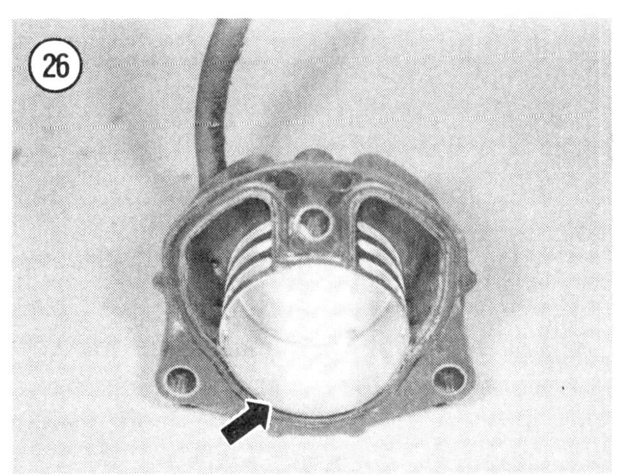

removed unless worn or scored. If removal is necessary, pull it out with pliers and discard it.

4. Clean and inspect all components as described in this chapter.

5. Position the adapter on the hydraulic press with its seal cavity facing up (relief slot facing down). Fit a new seal on OMC installer part No. 912281 or equivalent. The seal lip must face the installer tool. Wipe the metal casing on the seal with a light coat of OMC Gasket Sealing Compound.

6. Press the seal into the adapter until fully seated, then wipe the seal lips with OMC Triple-Guard grease.

7. If the liner was removed, apply a light coat of OMC Gasket Sealing Compound to the impeller housing walls which contact the liner. Push the new liner into the housing until fully seated, then wipe off any sealer that may have penetrated the liner through the water slots.

8. Lightly lubricate the impeller with OMC Hi-Vis gearcase lubricant. Holding the housing drive pocket toward you, rotate the impeller into the housing liner with a clockwise motion. See **Figure 27**.

9. Install the water pump as described in this chapter.

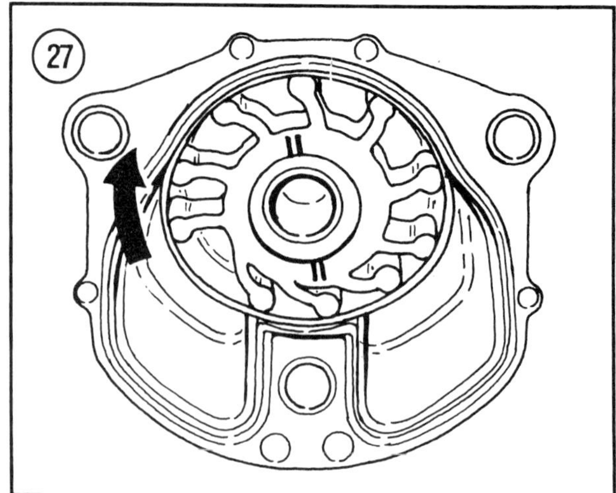

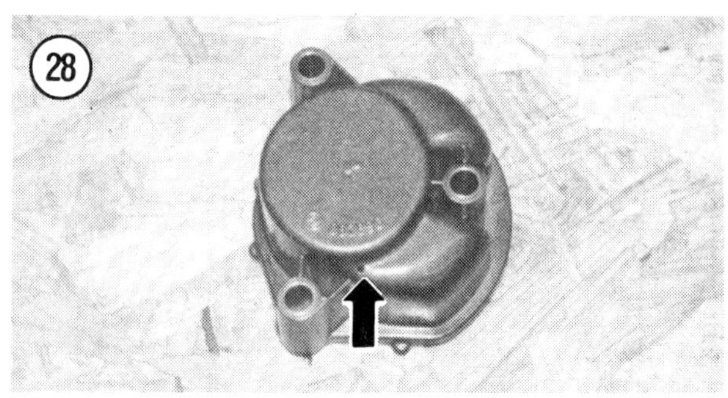

Cleaning and Inspection

1. Clean all metal parts in solvent and dry thoroughly.

2. Remove all sealer from the adapter plate surfaces. Check the O-ring grooves and gasket surfaces, removing any sharp edges that might prevent sealing.

3. Remove all sealer from the water pump housing seal groove and line cavity. Check housing for cracks and make sure the vent passage (**Figure 28**) is clear. If the passage is not clear, air pockets will form and prevent the pump from priming rapidly.

4. Check the impeller plate for wear, scoring or distortion. If only one side is worn, the plate can be turned over when reinstalled and reused. If the plate is scored or distorted, replace it.

5. Check the impeller condition. Replace the impeller if the blades have taken a set or if the edges of the blades which ride on the liner are flat instead of rounded.

Seawater (Engine) Pump Removal/Installation

A seawater pump is used with closed cooling systems. It is generally located on the starboard side at the front of the engine.

1. Loosen the hose clamps and remove the inlet and outlet hoses from the side of the pump.

2. Loosen, but do not remove the bolts holding the pump pulley to the pulley hub.

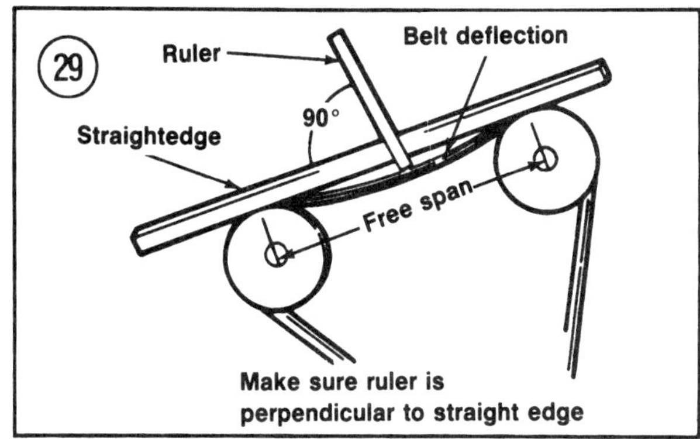

3. Loosen the pump brace bolts and mounting bracket bolt(s). Swivel pump toward the engine and remove the drive belt.
4. Remove the pump pulley fasteners. Remove the pulley.
5. Loosen the mounting bracket clamp bolt. Slide the pump from the bracket.
6. Installation is the reverse of removal. Hand-tighten all fasteners until the pump is properly positioned to align its pulley with the crankshaft pulley and its hose fittings with the hoses. Tighten the clamp bolt to 20 ft.-lb. Adjust the drive belt as described in this chapter.

DRIVE BELTS

All drive belts should be inspected at regular intervals to make sure they are in good condition and are properly tensioned. Worn, frayed, cracked or glazed belts should be replaced immediately. The components to which they direct power are essential to the safe and reliable operation of the boat. If correct adjustment is maintained on each belt, all will usually give the same service life. For this reason and because of the cost involved in replacing an inner belt (requiring the removal of the outer belt), it is a good idea to replace all belts as a set. The added expense is small compared to the cost of replacing the belts individually and eliminates the possibility of a breakdown on the water which could cost far more in time and money.

Drive belts should be properly tensioned at all times. If loose, the belt(s) will not permit the driven components to operate at maximum efficiency. The belt(s) will also wear rapidly because of the increased friction caused by slippage. Belts that are too tight will be overstressed and prone to premature failure. An excessively tight belt will also overstress the accessory unit's bearings, resulting in premature failure.

Drive belts used on OMC marine engines are heavy-duty belts and should not be replaced with drive belts designed for use with automobiles.

OMC recommends that drive belt tension be checked and adjusted using the deflection method (**Figure 29**). With the engine off, depress the belt at a point midway between the pulleys. The belt should deflect 1/4-1/2 in. if properly tensioned. **Figure 30** (2.3L), **Figure 31A** (5.0L [302 cu. in.]/5.8L), **Figure 31B** (7.5L) or **Figure 32** (all others) show typical drive belt arrangements.

Alternator Belt Adjustment (Except 4.3L Without Power Steering)

Refer to **Figure 30** (2.3L), **Figure 31A** (5.0L [302 cu. in.]/5.8L), **Figure 31B** (7.5L) or **Figure 32** (all others) for this procedure.

1. Loosen the alternator adjustment and pivot bolts.
2. Move the alternator toward or away from the engine as required to establish correct belt deflection.
3. Hold the alternator to prevent tension from changing and tighten the adjustment bolt, then the pivot bolt.
4. Recheck tension. If belt deflection is not within specifications, repeat Steps 1-3.

Alternator Belt Adjustment (4.3L Without Power Steering)

An idler pulley and bracket are used to adjust belt tension.

1. Loosen the idler pulley mounting bolt.
2. Move the idler pulley toward or away from the engine as required to establish correct belt deflection.
3. Hold the pulley to prevent tension from changing and tighten the mounting bolt.
4. Recheck tension. If belt deflection is not within specifications, repeat Steps 1-3.

Power Steering Belt Adjustment

To avoid possible pump damage, do *not* pry on the pump housing or pull on its filler neck. Refer to **Figure 31A** (5.0L [302 cu. in.]/5.8L), **Figure 31B** (7.5L) or **Figure 32** (all others except 2.3L) for this procedure. The 2.3L power steering pump is mounted on the opposite side of the engine from the alternator.

1. 7.5L engine:
   a. Loosen the 3 pump mounting bracket screws.
   b. Insert a long screwdriver blade between the water pump and the tab on the power steering pump bracket. Use these points to apply pressure and reposition the pump as required to obtain the necessary belt tension.
   c. When belt deflection is correct, maintain pressure on the bracket tab with the screwdriver and tighten the screw nearest the tab, then tighten the other 2 screws.
2. All others:
   a. Loosen the pump mounting screws.

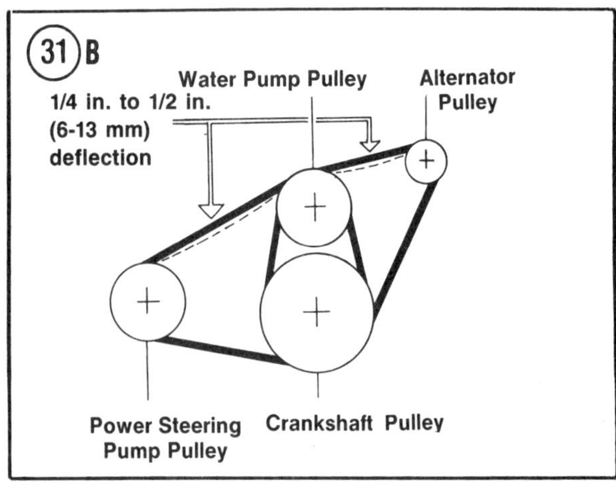

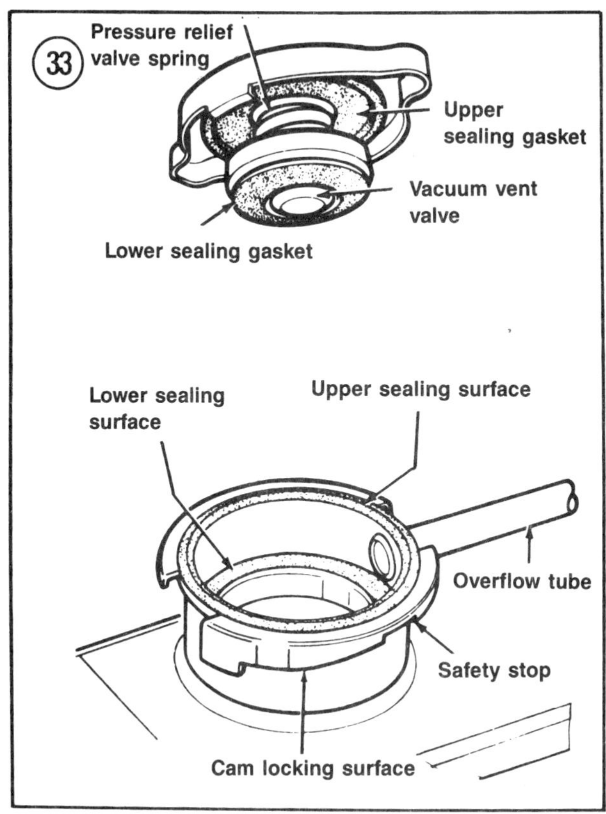

b. Insert a suitable breaker bar in the pump bracket hole and pivot the pump away from the engine.

c. When belt deflection is correct, maintain pressure on the bracket and tighten the mounting screws.

Drive Belt Replacement

Refer to **Figure 30** (2.3L), **Figure 31A** (5.0L [302 cu. in.]/5.8L), **Figure 31B** (7.5L) or **Figure 32** (all others) for this procedure.

1. Loosen the alternator, power steering pump or idler pulley bolts. The 2.3L power steering pump is mounted on the opposite side of the engine from the alternator.
2. Move the accessory unit toward the engine until there is enough slack in the belt to permit its removal from the pulleys.
3. Install a new belt over the pulleys and adjust belt tension as described in this chapter.

CLOSED COOLING SYSTEM MAINTENANCE

Pressure Testing the Fresh Water Section

When the fresh water section of a closed cooling system requires frequent topping up, it probably has a leak. Small leaks in a cooling system are not easy to locate; the hot coolant evaporates as fast as it leaks out, preventing the formation of tell-tale rusty or grayish-white stains.

A pressure test of the fresh water section will usually help to pinpoint the source of the leak. The procedure is very similar to that used in pressure testing automotive cooling systems and requires the same type of pressure tester.

1. Remove the pressure fill cap from the heat exchanger.
2. Wash the cap with clean water to remove any debris or deposits from its sealing surfaces.
3. Check the gasket (if so equipped) and rubber seal on the cap for cuts, cracks, tears or deterioration. See **Figure 33**. Replace the cap if the seal is damaged. Make sure the locking tabs on the cap are not damaged or bent.
4. Dip the cap in water and attach to a cooling system pressure tester, using the adapters supplied with the tester. See **Figure 34.**
5. Pump the pressure to 14 psi. If the cap fails to hold pressure for 30 seconds without dropping under 11 psi, replace it.
6. Inspect the filler neck seat and sealing surface **(Figure 33)** for nicks, dents, distortion or contamination. Wipe the sealing surface with a clean cloth to remove any rust or dirt. Make sure the locking cams are not bent or damaged.
7. Check coolant level; it should be within one inch of the filler neck. Top up if necessary.

8. Connect the cooling system pressure tester to the filler neck and pressurize the fresh water section to 14 psi. If pressure does not hold constant for at least 2 minutes, check all hoses, gaskets, drain plugs, drain valves, core plugs and other potential leak points for leakage. Listen for a hissing or bubbling sound while the system is under pressure.
9. If no leaks are found, disconnect the seawater outlet hose from the heat exchanger. Repressurize the system to 15 psi and note the outlet connection on the heat exchanger. If water flows from the connection, air bubbles are seen in the water or a bubbling or hissing noise is heard, there is probably a leak between the fresh and seawater sections within the heat exchanger.
10. If no signs of leakage can be found in Step 8 or Step 9, yet the coolant level continues to require frequent topping up, there is probably an internal leak. This could be caused by a blown head gasket, loose cylinder head, intake manifold, exhaust elbow, distributor block bolts or a cracked or porous head, block or manifold.

Alkalinity Test

The coolant used in the fresh water section of a closed cooling system should be replaced every 2 years. After a year's service, test the coolant for alkalinity with pink litmus paper obtained from a local drug store.
1. With the engine cold, remove the pressure fill cap from the heat exchanger.
2. Insert one end of the litmus paper into the coolant, wait a few seconds and then withdraw it.
   a. If the pink litmus paper has turned blue, the coolant alkalinity is satisfactory.
   b. If the litmus paper does not change color, the coolant has lost its alkalinity and should be replaced. Drain and refill the fresh water section of the cooling system. See Chapter Five.

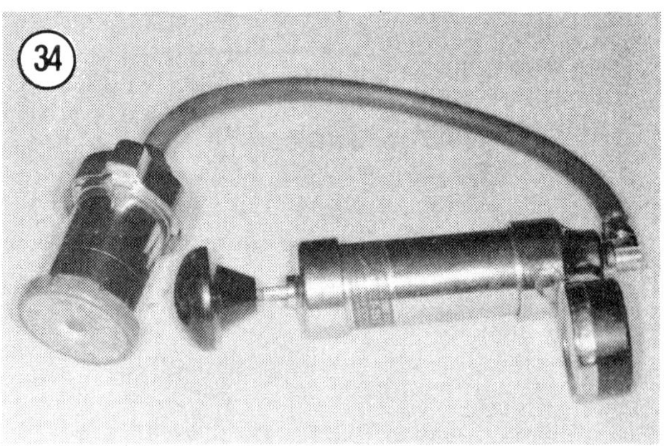

Cleaning the Fresh Water Section

The fresh water section should be flushed and cleaned every other season or 200 hours of operation. Any high quality automotive cooling system cleaning solution can be used to remove scale, rust, mineral deposits or other contamination. Use the cleaning solution according to the manufacturer's directions.

If extremely dirty or corroded, remaining deposits may be flushed out with a pressure flushing device. Follow the manufacturer's instructions regarding the connection of the pressure flushing device and procedure to be followed.

Cleaning the Seawater Section of the Heat Exchanger

Contaminants and minerals collect inside the copper tubes in the seawater section of the heat exchanger during engine operation. Such foreign material reduces the ability of the heat exchanger to operate efficiently and, if not removed periodically, will eventually lead to engine overheating. It is a good idea to remove and clean the heat exchanger whenever the coolant is changed.
1. Drain the cooling system. See Chapter Five.
2. Loosen the hose clamps and remove all hoses at the heat exchanger. Remove the attaching bolts. Remove the heat exchanger.

3. Unbolt and remove the heat exchanger end caps. Remove and discard the end cap gaskets.

NOTE
If the heat exchanger is plugged or contains heavy scale deposits, OMC suggests that you take it to an automotive radiator repair shop for proper cleaning to avoid potential damage to the unit.

4. Clean all gasket residue from the end caps and heat exchanger sealing surfaces.
5. Insert an appropriate-size wire brush into each passage in the heat exchanger. Work the brush back and forth with a vigorous motion but work carefully to avoid damage to the soldered joints.
6. Remove the brush, hold the heat exchanger vertically and blow loosened particles out with compressed air.
7. Repeat Step 5 and Step 6 as necessary to remove as much of the accumulated deposits as possible.
8. Coat both sides of new end cap gaskets with OMC Gasket Sealing Compound and reinstall the end caps. Tighten end cap bolts to specifications (**Table 1**).
9. Install the heat exchanger. Check hoses and clamps; replace any that have deteriorated. Connect hoses and tighten hose clamps securely.
10. Fill the fresh water section with coolant. See Chapter Five. Start the engine and check for leaks.

STANDARD COOLING SYSTEM MAINTENANCE

The only maintenance required for the standard cooling system is a periodic cleaning of the exhaust manifold. See the appropriate chapter for your engine.

Table 1 TIGHTENING TORQUES

Fastener	in.-lb.	ft.-lb.	N•m
Heat exchanger end cap		10-12	14-16
Power steering pump bolts		25	34
Water pump			
Engine			
2.3L		14-21	19-28
2.5L/3.0L		13-17	18-24
5.0L (302 cu. in.)/5.8L		12-18	16-24
7.5L			
Accessory bracket bolts		18-20	24-27
All others		12-15	16-20
4.3L/5.0L (305 cu. in.)/5.7L		30	41
Stern drive			
Adapter housing		12-14	16-19
Rear access cover	108-132		12-15
Water pump cover	108-132		12-15
Thermostat housing			
2.5L/3.0L		5-7	7-9
All others		20-25	27-34
Standard torque value			
1/4 in.		5-7	7-9
5/16 in.		12-14	16-19
3/8 in.		20-25	27-34
7/16 in.		32-40	43-54

Chapter Eleven

Electrical Systems

All engines covered in this manual are equipped with a 12-volt, negative-ground electrical system. Many electrical problems can be traced to a simple cause such as a blown fuse, a loose or corroded connection, a loose alternator drive belt or a frayed wire. While these are easily corrected problems which may not appear important, they can quickly lead to serious difficulty if allowed to go uncorrected.

Complete overhaul of electrical components such as the alternator, distributor or starter motor is neither practical nor economical. In many cases, the necessary bushings, bearings or other worn parts are not available for individual replacement.

If tests indicate a unit with problems other than those discussed in this chapter, replace it with a new or rebuilt marine unit. Make certain, however, that the new or rebuilt part to be installed is an exact replacement for the defective one removed. Also make sure to isolate and correct the cause of the failure before installing a replacement. For example, an uncorrected short in an alternator circuit will most likely burn out a new alternator as quickly as it damaged the old one. If in doubt, always consult an expert.

This chapter provides service procedures for the battery, charging system, starting system, ignition system and switches. Electrical specifications are provided in **Table 1** at the end of the chapter. Wiring diagrams are included at the end of the book.

BATTERY

Since batteries used in marine applications endure far more rigorous treatment than those used in an automotive charging system, they are constructed differently. Marine batteries have a thicker exterior case to cushion the plates inside during tight turning maneuvers or rough water. Thicker plates are also used, with each one individually fastened within the case to prevent failure. Spill-proof caps on the battery cells prevent electrolyte

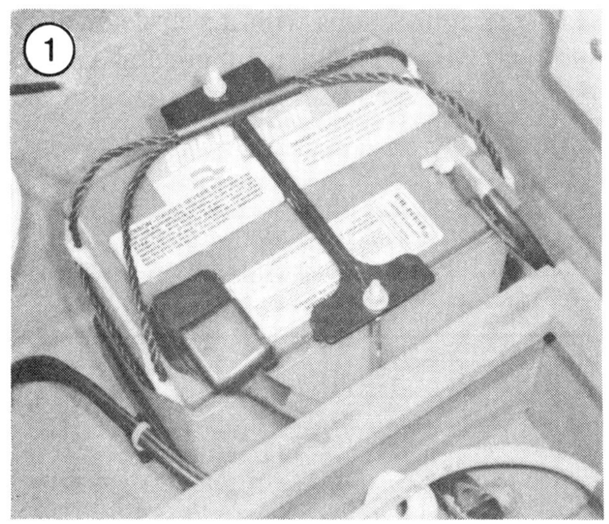

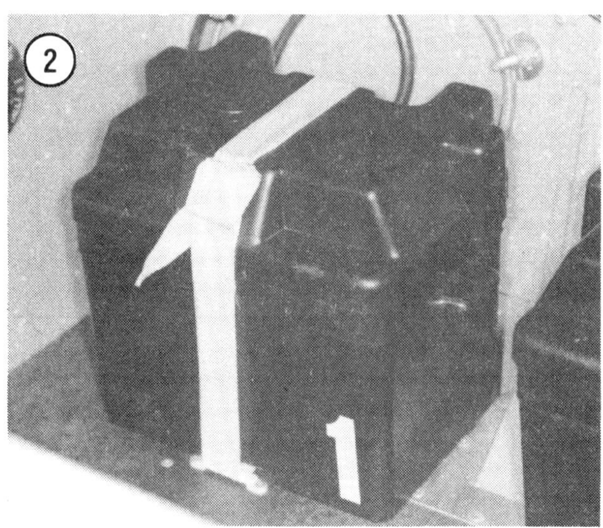

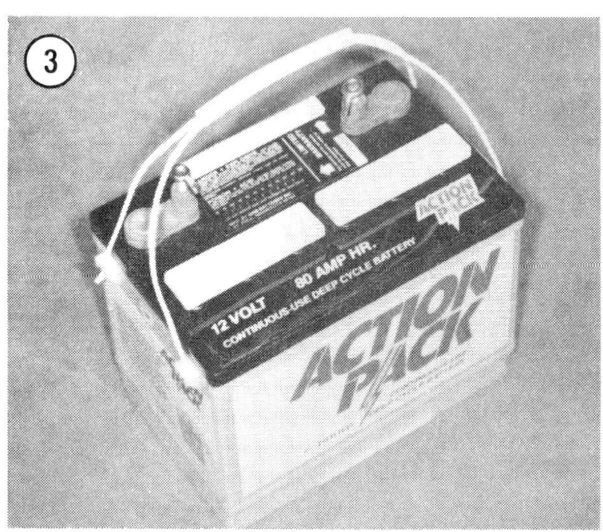

from spilling into the bilge. Automotive batteries should *only* be used in an emergency situation when a suitable marine battery is not available. If used, the automotive battery should be replaced with a suitable marine battery as soon as possible.

To assure sufficient cranking power, OMC recommends the use of a 12-volt marine battery with a minimum 360 cold cranking amperage rating and a reserve capacity rating of at least 115 minutes for all models except the 7.5L engine. With the 7.5L engine, a battery with a minimum 500 cold cranking amperage rating and a reserve capacity rating of at least 99 minutes should be used.

NOTE
A "deep cycle" battery is not suitable for use with OMC marine engines. Such batteries are designed to charge and discharge at moderate current levels. If the battery does not have a specified cold cranking amperage rating, it should not be used.

A good state of charge should be maintained in the battery. Any battery that cannot deliver at least 9.6 volts under a starting load should be recharged. If recharging does not bring it up to strength or if it does not hold the charge, replace the battery.

Care and Inspection

1. Disconnect both battery cables (negative first, then positive) and remove the battery hold-down or retainer clamp. See **Figure 1** for a typical open installation and **Figure 2** for a typical enclosed installation.

NOTE
*Some batteries have a built-in carry strap for use in Step 2. See **Figure 3**.*

2. Attach a battery carrier or carrier strap to the terminal posts and lift the battery from

the battery tray. Remove battery from the engine compartment.

3. Check the entire battery case for cracks or other damage.

4. If the battery has removable vent caps, cover the vent holes in each cap with small pieces of masking tape.

NOTE
Keep cleaning solution out of the battery cells in Step 5 or the electrolyte will be seriously weakened.

5. Scrub the top of the battery with a stiff bristle brush, using a baking soda and water solution (**Figure 4**). Rinse the battery case with clear water and wipe dry with a clean cloth or paper towels. Remove the masking tape from the filler cap vent holes, if so equipped.

6. Inspect the battery tray or container in the engine compartment for corrosion. Remove and clean if necessary with the baking soda and water solution. Rinse with clear water and wipe dry, then reinstall.

7. Clean the battery cable clamps with a stiff wire brush or one of the many tools made for this purpose (**Figure 5**). The same tool is used for cleaning the threaded battery posts (**Figure 6**).

8. Reposition the battery on the battery tray or container and remove the carrier or strap. Install and tighten the hold-down device.

9. Reconnect the positive battery cable, then the negative battery cable.

CAUTION
Be sure the battery cables are connected to their proper terminals. Connecting the battery backwards will reverse the polarity and can damage the alternator.

10. Tighten the battery cable connections to 9 ft.-lb. (12 N•m). Tightening the connections more than this can damage the battery case.

Coat the connections with a petroleum jelly such as Vaseline or a light mineral grease. Aerosol anti-corrosion sprays can also be used.

NOTE
Do not overfill the battery cells in Step 11. The electrolyte expands due to heat

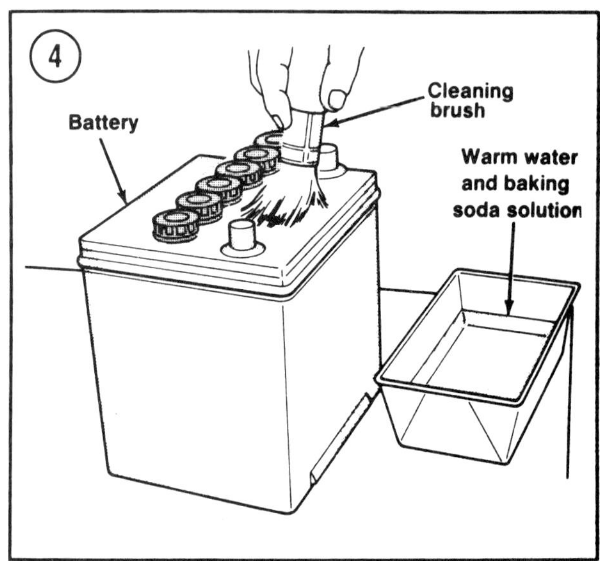

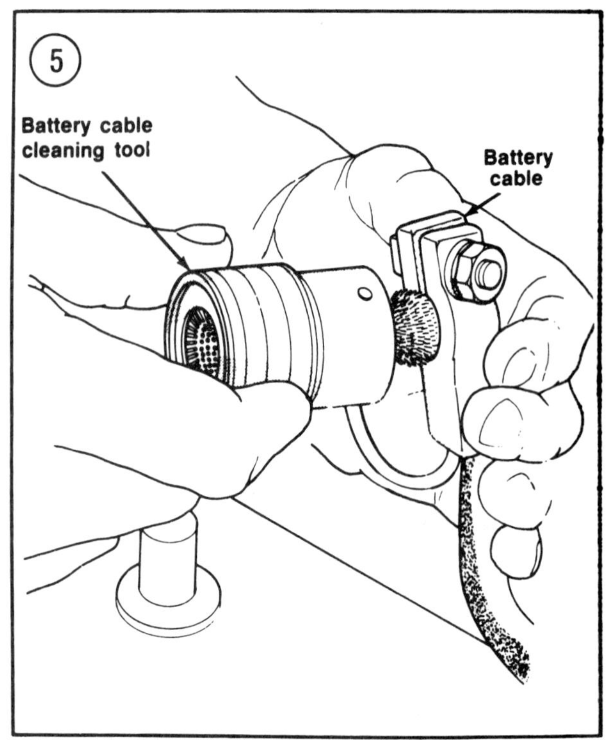

from charging and may overflow if the level is more than 1/4 in. above the battery plates.

11. Remove the filler caps and check the electrolyte level. The electrolyte should cover the battery plates by at least 1/4 in. (6 mm). See **Figure 7**. Top up with distilled water to the bottom of the fill ring in each cell, if necessary.

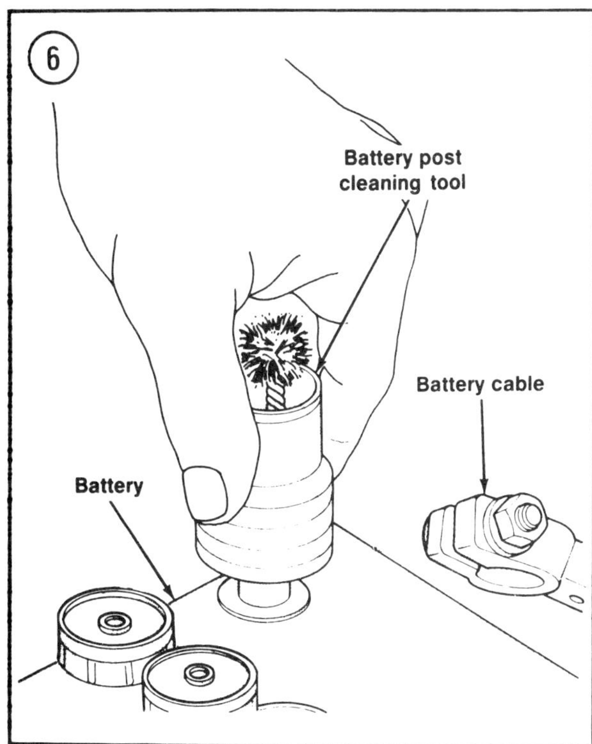

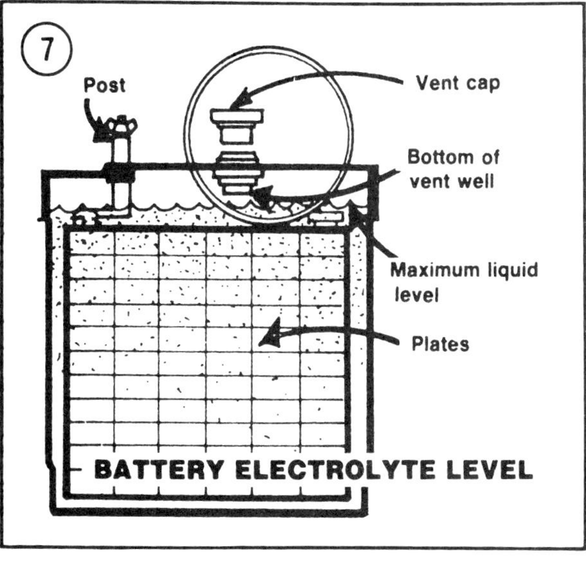

Battery Testing

Hydrometer testing is the best way to check battery condition. Use a hydrometer with numbered graduations from 1.100-1.300 rather than one with just color-coded bands. To use the hydrometer, squeeze the rubber ball, insert the tip in a cell and release the ball (**Figure 8**).

NOTE
Do not attempt to test a battery with a hydrometer immediately after adding water to the cells. Run the engine or charge the battery for 15-20 minutes to allow the water and electrolyte to mix thoroughly.

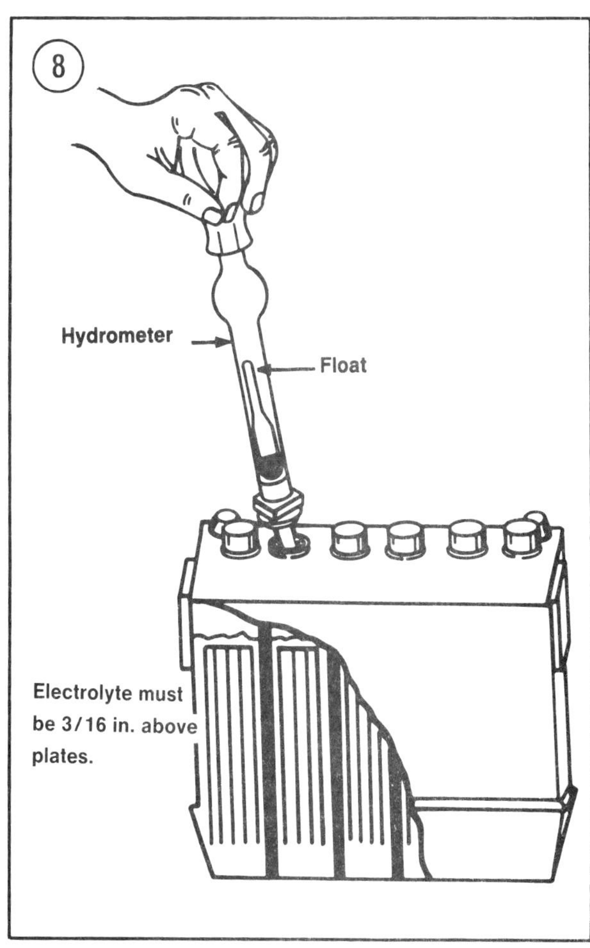

Draw enough electrolyte to float the weighted float inside the hydrometer. When using a temperature-compensated hydrometer, release the electrolyte and repeat this process several times to make sure the thermometer has adjusted to the electrolyte temperature before taking the reading.

Hold the hydrometer vertically and note the number in line with the surface of the electrolyte (**Figure 9**). This is the specific gravity for the cell. Return the electrolyte to the cell from which it came.

The specific gravity of the electrolyte in each battery cell is an excellent indicator of that cell's condition. A fully charged cell will read 1.260 or more at 80° F (27° C). If the cells test below 1.220, the battery must be recharged. Charging is also necessary if the specific gravity varies more than 0.050 from cell to cell.

NOTE

If a temperature-compensated hydrometer is not used, add 0.004 to the specific gravity reading for every 10° above 80° F (27° C). For every 10° below 80° F (27° C), subtract 0.004.

Safety Precautions

When working with batteries, use extreme care to avoid spilling or splashing the electrolyte. This solution contains sulfuric acid, which can ruin clothing and cause serious chemical burns. If any electrolyte is spilled or splashed on clothing or skin, immediately neutralize with a solution of baking soda and water, then flush with an abundance of clean water.

WARNING

Electrolyte splashed into the eyes is extremely dangerous. Safety glasses should always be worn while working with batteries. If electrolyte is splashed into the eyes, call a physician immediately, force the eyes open and flood with cool, clean water for approximately 15 minutes.

If electrolyte is spilled or splashed onto any surface, it should be immediately neutralized with a baking soda and water solution and then rinsed with clean water.

While batteries are being charged, highly explosive hydrogen gas forms in each cell. Some of this gas escapes through filler cap openings and may form an explosive atmosphere in and around the battery. This

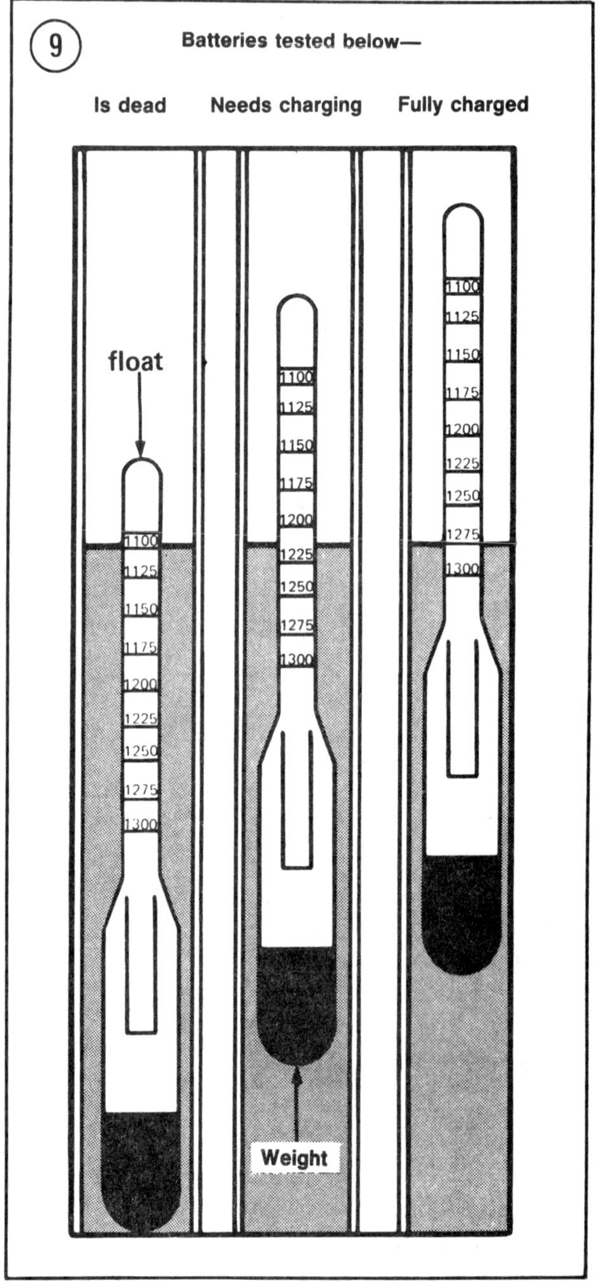

condition can persist for several hours. Sparks, an open flame or a lighted cigarette can ignite this gas, causing an internal battery explosion and possible serious personal injury.

Take the following precautions to prevent an explosion:

1. Do not smoke or permit any open flame near any battery being charged or which has been recently charged.

2. Do not disconnect live circuits at battery terminals, since a spark usually occurs when a live circuit is broken. Take care when connecting or disconnecting any battery charger. Be sure its power switch is off before making or breaking connections. Poor connections are a common cause of electrical arcs which cause explosions.

3. Take care when connecting or disconnecting any battery charger. Be sure its power switch is off before making or breaking any connection. Poor connections are a common cause of electrical arcs which cause explosions.

Charging

A good state of charge should be maintained in batteries used for starting. Check the battery with a voltmeter as shown in **Figure 10**. Any battery that cannot deliver at least 9.6 volts under a starting load should be recharged. If recharging does not bring it up to strength or if it does not hold the charge, replace the battery.

A cold battery will not accept a charge readily. If the temperature is below 40° F (5° C), the battery should be allowed to warm up to room temperature before charging.

The battery does not have to be removed from the boat for charging, but it is a recommended procedure since a charging battery gives off highly explosive hydrogen gas. In many boats, the area around the battery is not well ventilated and the gas may remain in the area for several hours after the charging procedure has been completed. Sparks or flames occuring near the battery can cause it to explode, spraying battery acid over a wide area.

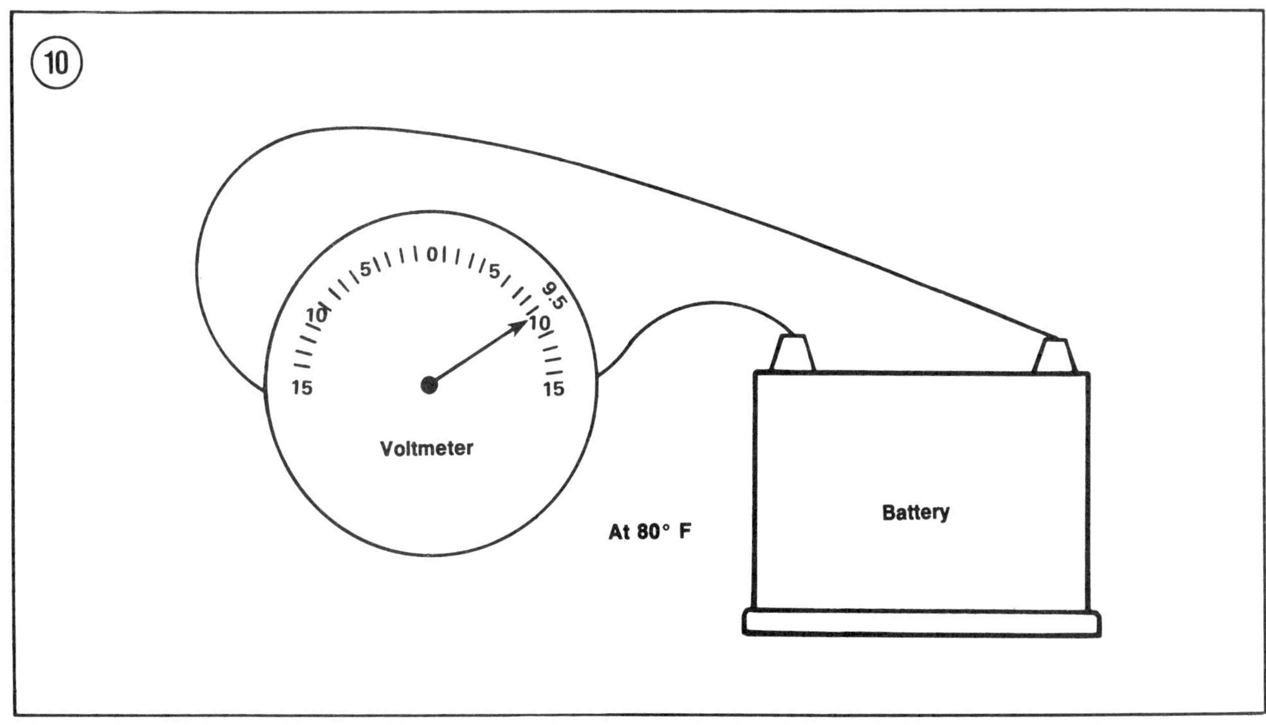

Disconnect the negative battery cable first, then the positive cable. Make sure the electrolyte is fully topped up. Remove the vent caps and place a folded paper towel over the vent openings to absorb any electrolyte that may spew as the battery charges.

Connect the charger to the battery—negative to negative, positive to positive. If the charger output is variable, select a 10-12 amp setting. Set the voltage selector to 12 volts and plug the charger in. Once the battery starts to accept a charge, the charge rate should be reduced to a level that will prevent excessive gassing and electrolyte spewing.

The length of time required to recharge a battery depends upon its size, state of charge and temperature. Generally speaking, the current input time should equal the battery amp-hour rating. For example, a 45 AH battery will require a 9-amp charging rate for 5 hours (9×5 = 45) or a 15-amp charging rate for 3 hours (15×3 = 45). Check charging progress with the hydrometer.

Jump Starting

If the battery becomes severely discharged, it is possible to start and run an engine by jump starting it from another battery. OMC does not recommend that you jump start a discharged battery due to the possible danger of explosion. Since many owners will disregard this warning, however, the following procedure is provided as the safest method to use.

Before jump starting a battery when temperatures are 32° F (0° C) or lower, check the condition of the electrolyte. If it is not visible or if it appears to be frozen, do *not* attempt to jump start the battery, as the battery may explode or rupture.

WARNING

Use extreme caution when connecting a booster battery to one that is discharged to avoid personal injury or damage to the system.

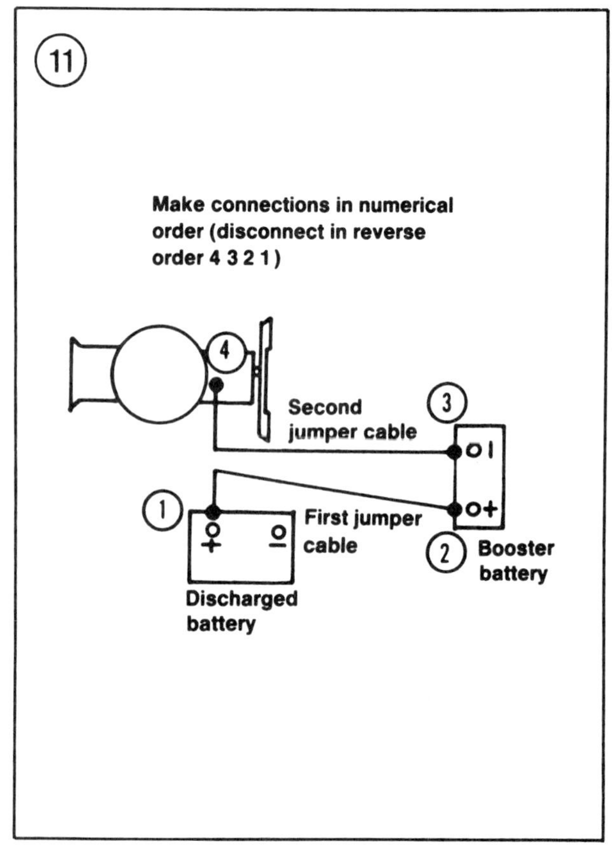

1. Connect the jumper cables in the order and sequence shown in **Figure 11**.

WARNING

An electrical arc may occur when the final connection is made. This could cause an explosion if it occurs near the battery. For this reason, the final connection should be made to the alternator mounting bracket or another good engine ground and not the battery itself.

2. Check that all jumper cables are out of the way of moving parts on both engines.
3. Start the engine with the good battery and run at a moderate speed.
4. Start the engine with the discharged battery. Once it starts, run it at a moderate speed.

CAUTION

Racing the engine may damage the electrical system.

5. Remove the jumper cables in the exact reverse order shown in **Figure 11**. Begin at point No. 4, then 3, 2 and 1.

Battery Cables

Poor terminal connections will cause excessive resistance. Defective cable insulation can cause partial short circuits. Both conditions may result in an abnormal voltage drop in the starter motor cable. When this happens, the resulting hard-start condition will place further strain on the battery. Cable condition and terminal connections should be checked periodically.

CHARGING SYSTEM

The charging system consists of the battery, alternator, voltage regulator, ignition switch, ammeter and connecting wiring. Delcotron SI-series alternators containing an integral regulator is used on some early models; all others use a Motorola alternator with a rear-mounted regulator.

Preliminary Testing

The first indication of charging system trouble is usually a slow engine cranking speed during starting or running lights that dim as engine speed decreases. This will often occur long before the ammeter indicates that there is a potential problem. When charging system trouble is first suspected, perform the following checks.

1. Check the alternator drive belt for correct tension (Chapter Ten).
2. Check the battery to make sure it is in satisfactory condition and fully charged and that all connections are clean and tight.
3. Check all connections at the alternator to make sure they are clean and tight.

If there are still indications that the charging system is not performing as it should after each of the above points has been carefully checked and any unsatisfactory conditions corrected, refer to Chapter Three and perform a charging system test.

Alternator Removal/Installation

This section provides alternator replacement procedures. Complete alternator overhaul is not practical for the amateur mechanic. Rebuilt marine-approved alternators can be purchased quite inexpensively compared to the time and effort involved in disassembly, testing, repair and reassembly. In some cases, such overhaul is not even possible since replacement components are not available.

This procedure is generalized to cover all applications. Access to the alternator is quite limited in some engine compartments and care should be taken to avoid personal injury.

1. Disconnect the negative battery cable.
2. Disconnect all wiring harnesses and leads at the rear of the alternator. See **Figure 12** (typical).
3. Loosen the alternator adjusting and pivot bolts (**Figure 13**, typical).
4. Swivel the alternator toward the engine and remove the drive belt from the alternator pulley.
5. Support the alternator with one hand and remove the adjusting and pivot bolts, noting

the position of any washers or spacers used. Remove the alternator.

6. Installation is the reverse of removal. Tighten fasteners securely (OMC provides no torque specifications). Adjust drive belt tension (Chapter Ten) before reconnecting wiring harnesses and leads to the rear of the alternator.

STARTING SYSTEM

The starting system consists of the starter motor, starter solenoid, assist solenoid, ignition switch, neutral safety or cut-out switch, battery and connecting wiring with one or more inline fuses. The neutral safety or cut-out switch is located inside the remote control box and allows starter operation only when the shift selector lever is in NEUTRAL.

OMC marine engines may be equipped with a Delco-Remy or Motorcraft positive engagement starter motor. The Delco-Remy starter solenoid is enclosed in the drive housing to protect it from exposure to dirt and adverse weather conditions.

Starter service requires experience and special tools. Troubleshooting procedures are provided in Chapter Two. The procedures described below consist of removal, installation and brush replacement. Any repairs inside the unit itself (other than brush replacement) should be done by a dealer or certified electrical shop. Installation of a professionally rebuilt marine-type unit is generally less expensive and thus more practical.

Delco-Remy Starter Solenoid Replacement

1. Remove the starter motor as described in this chapter.
2. Disconnect the field strap at the starter from the motor terminal.
3. Remove the solenoid-to-drive housing screws and the motor terminal bolt.

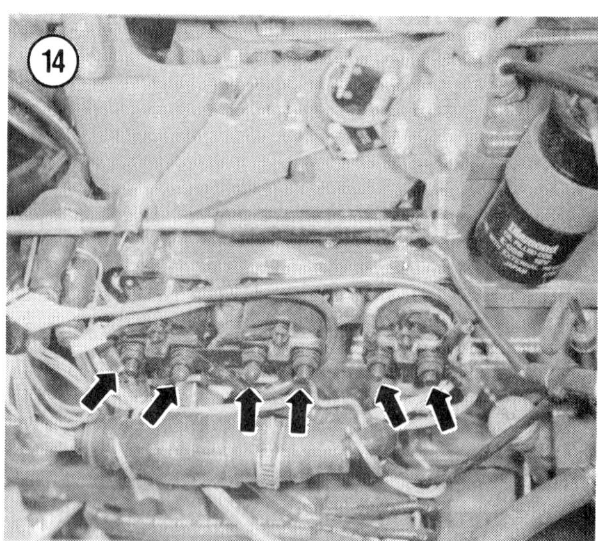

4. Rotate the solenoid 90° and remove from the drive housing with the plunger return or torsion spring.
5. Installation is the reverse of removal.

Assist Solenoid Removal/Installation

1. Disconnect the negative battery cable.
2. Disconnect the cable connector wires from the solenoid terminals. See **Figure 14**.
3. Remove the nuts holding the starter and battery cables to the solenoid. Disconnect the cables and reinstall the nuts to prevent their loss. See **Figure 14**.

4. Remove the solenoid attaching screws. Remove the solenoid.
5. Installation is the reverse of removal.

Starter Removal/Installation

1. Disconnect the negative battery cable.
2A. *Delco-Remy starter*—Disconnect the solenoid terminal wires. See **Figure 15**.
2B. *Motorcraft starter*—Disconnect the heavy starter cable at the starter terminal.
3. Remove the starter motor mounting bolts. Pull the starter motor away from the flywheel and remove it from the engine. Retrieve any mounting shims that may fall out.
4. Installation is the reverse of removal. Reinstall any shims that were removed to assure proper pinion-to-flywheel mesh. Tighten mounting bolts to 20-25 ft.-lb. (27-34 N•m). Apply OMC Black Neoprene Dip or equivalent to all terminal connections to prevent corrosion.

Starter Brush Replacement (Delco-Remy Starter)

Brush replacement requires partial diassembly of the starter. Always replace brushes in complete sets. Refer to **Figure 16** for this procedure.

1. Remove the terminal nut and disconnect the field lead from the solenoid terminal. See **Figure 17**.
2. Remove the 2 through-bolts. Separate the end frame and field frame assembly from the solenoid and drive assembly. See **Figure 18**.
3. Remove the brush lead attaching screws (**Figure 19**).
4. Remove the brush holder pivot pins.
5. Remove the 2 brush holder and spring assemblies from the field housing.
6. Check the brushes for length and condition. Replace all if any are oil-soaked or worn to 1/4 in. or less in length.
7. Make sure the brush holders are clean and that the brushes do not bind in the holders.
8. Check the brush springs. Replace if distorted or discolored.
9. Secure new brushes to the leads with the attaching screws (**Figure 20**).
10. Reverse Steps 1-3 to complete brush installation.

Starter Brush Replacement (Motorcraft Starter)

Brush replacement requires partial diassembly of the starter. Always replace brushes in complete sets. Refer to **Figure 21** for this procedure.

1. Loosen the cover band screw. Remove the cover band and drive plunger lever cover with gasket. Save gasket for reuse.
2. Note position of brushes in the brush holder. Pull back and hold the brush retaining clip with a wire hook, then remove the brush (**Figure 22**). Repeat this step to remove the remaining brushes from the holder.
3. Remove the through-bolts. Remove the brush end plate (**Figure 23**).

(16)

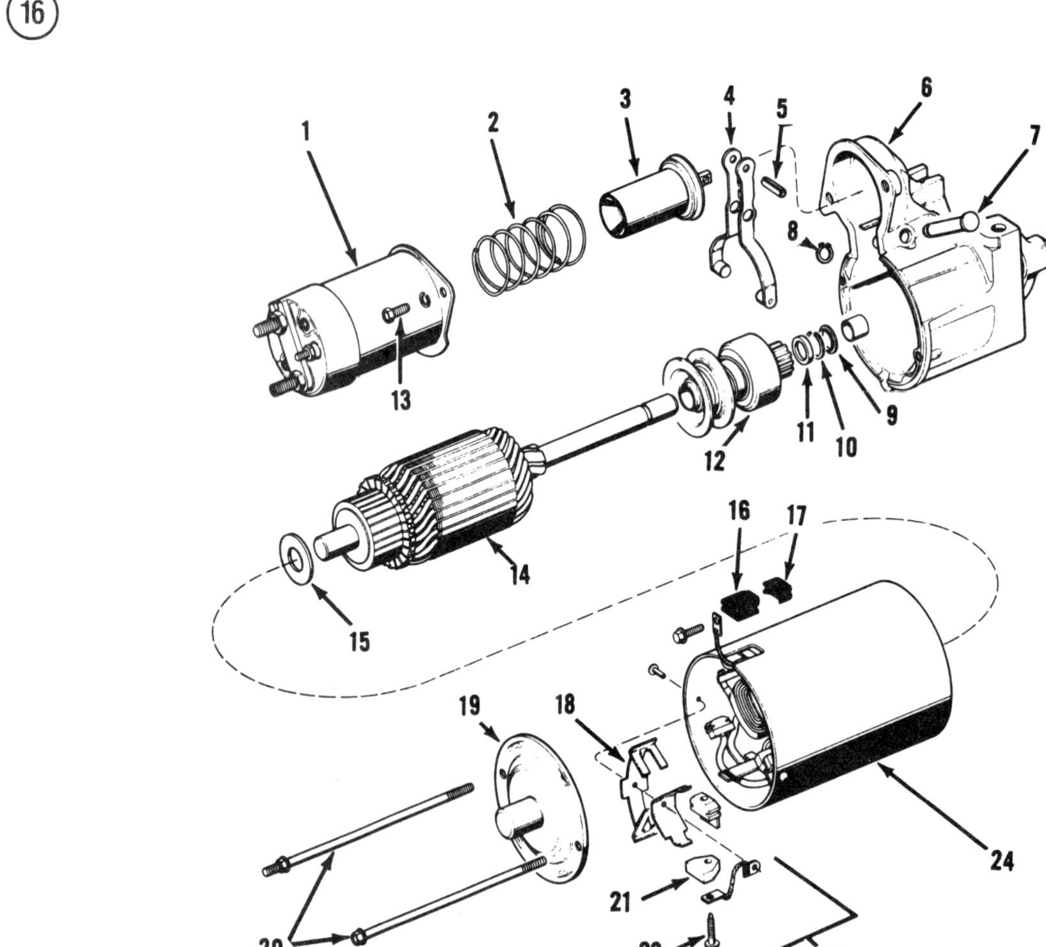

DELCO STARTER

1. Solenoid switch
2. Plunger return spring
3. Plunger
4. Shift lever
5. Plunger pin
6. Drive end housing
7. Shift lever shaft
8. Lever shaft retaining ring
9. Thrust collar
10. Pinion stop retainer ring
11. Pinion stop collar
12. Drive
13. Screw
14. Armature
15. Washer
16. Grommet
17. Grommet
18. Brush holder
19. Commutator end frame
20. Through bolt
21. Brush
22. Screw
23. Brush and holder assembly
24. Frame and field winding

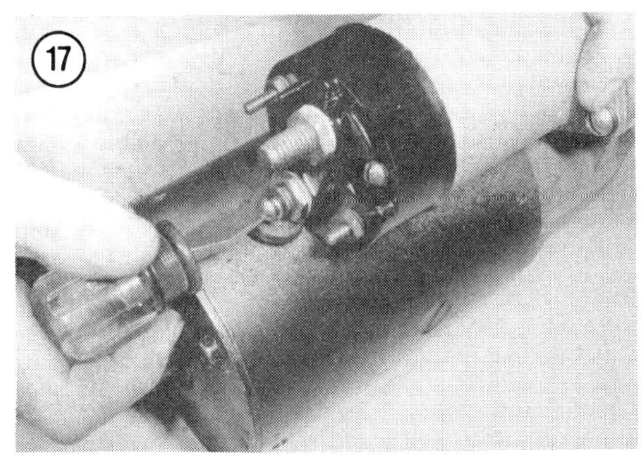

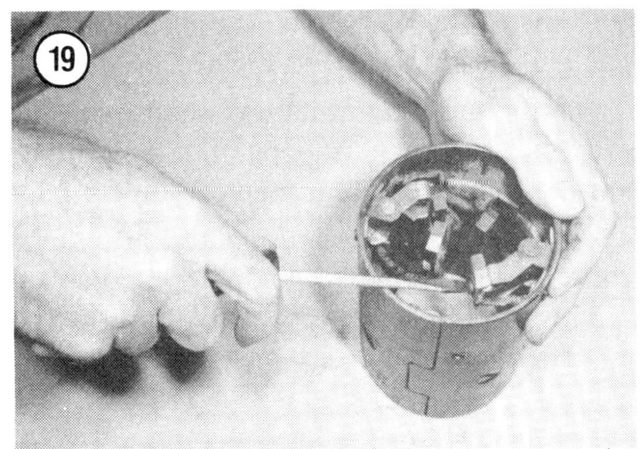

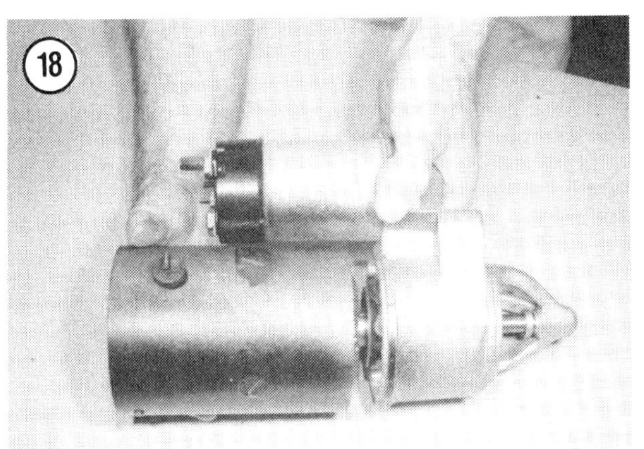

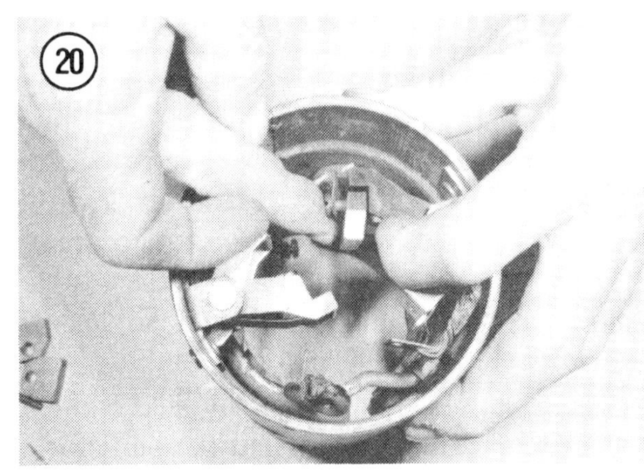

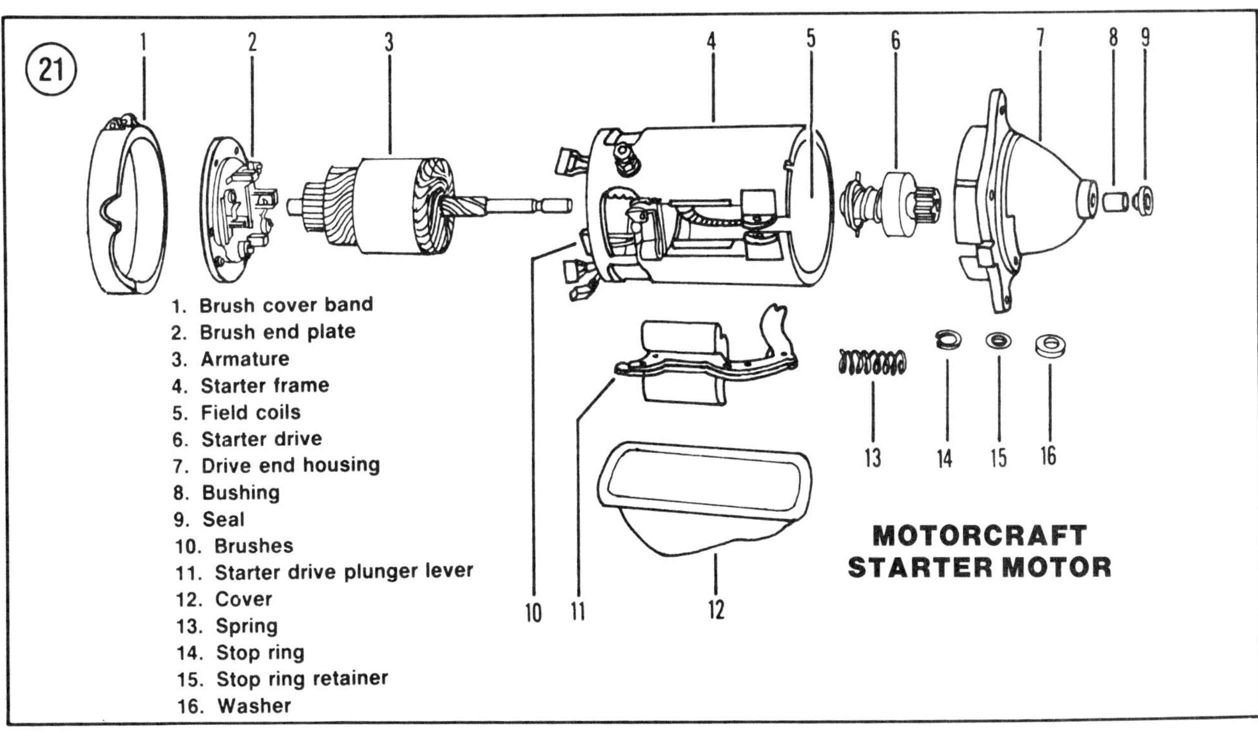
21
1
2
3
4
5
6
7
8
9
10
11
12
13
14
15
16
1. Brush cover band
2. Brush end plate
3. Armature
4. Starter frame
5. Field coils
6. Starter drive
7. Drive end housing
8. Bushing
9. Seal
10. Brushes
11. Starter drive plunger lever
12. Cover
13. Spring
14. Stop ring
15. Stop ring retainer
16. Washer
MOTORCRAFT
STARTER MOTOR

4. Remove the pivot pin holding the drive gear plunger in place. See **Figure 24**.

5. Gently tap the armature shaft with a soft-faced mallet to separate the drive housing from the field frame. See **Figure 25**.

6. Remove the drive housing and armature from the field frame.

7. Inspect the brushes. Replace all brushes if any are oil-soaked or worn to 1/4 in. or less in length.

8. To replace ground brushes, remove the brush lead attaching screws from the starter frame. Take out the brushes and install new ones.

9. To replace field coil brushes, cut the insulated brush leads as close as possible to the field coils. Attach new brush leads with the clips provided in the brush replacement kit. Solder the connections together with rosin core solder and a 300-watt soldering iron.

10. Insert the armature into the field frame, locating the drive gear so that the shift fork can engage the lip on each side of the drive gear retainer.

11. Place the armature/field frame assembly upright on the workbench. Position the small spring on the shift fork tangs and install the drive end housing. The spring should engage the hole in the housing.

12. Reinstall the pivot pin in the shift fork end, aligning the drive end housing dowel with the field frame cutout.

13. Install the brush end plate and through-bolts.

14. Pull back and hold the brush retaining clip with a wire hook, then install the brush. Repeat this step to install the remaining brushes. Make sure the brush springs rest in the small cutout on top of each brush.

15. Install the drive plunger cover and gasket, slide the cover band over the field frame and tighten the band screw.

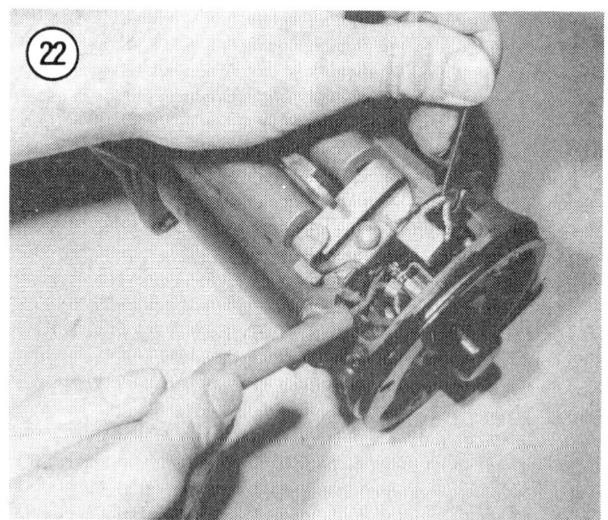
22

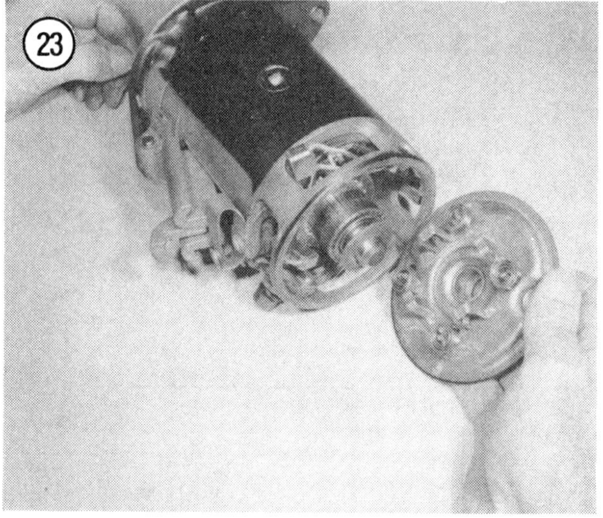
23

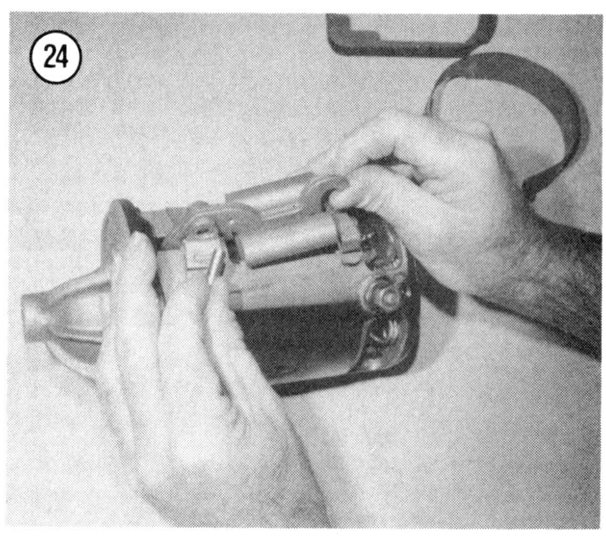
24

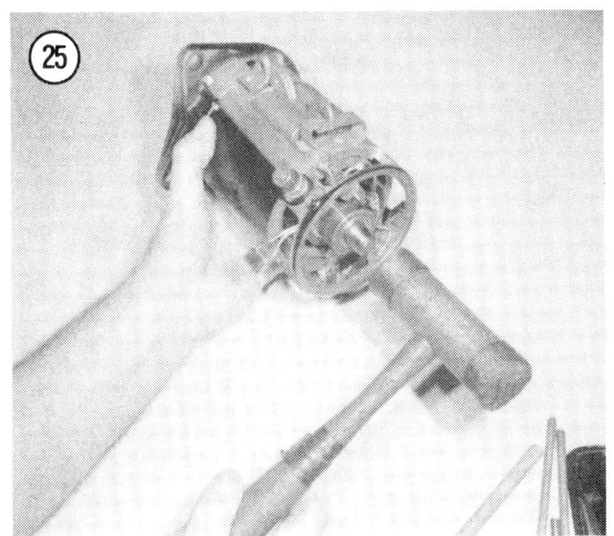

IGNITION SYSTEM

OMC marine engines are equipped with a breaker point ignition system. The breaker point system consists of a distributor (containing the breaker points and condenser), ignition coil, ignition switch, battery, spark plugs and connecting wiring. See **Figure 26** (typical).

All ignition systems contain an ignition interrupter circuit. This consists of an Electronic Shift Assist (ESA) module, converter box interrupter, overstroke switches and connecting wiring. This circuit alters engine rpm to reduce shifting effort.

26 **IGNITION SYSTEM**

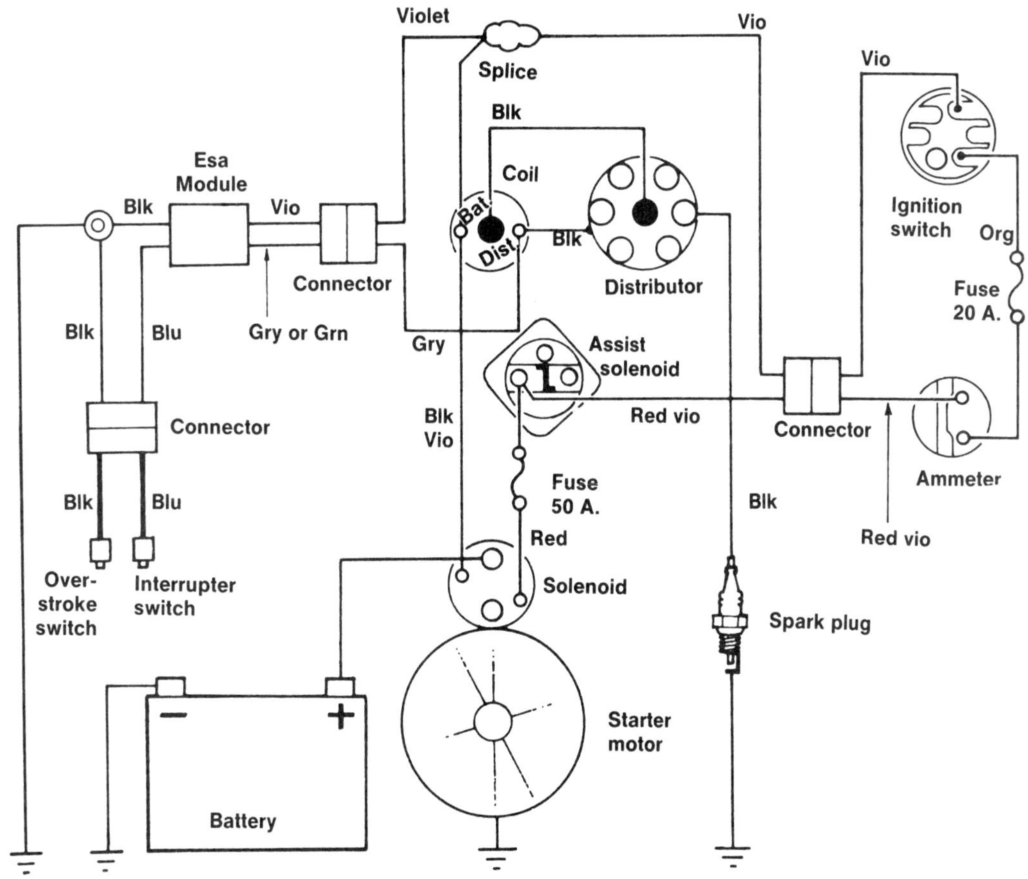

When the remote control handle is moved, the converter box shift arm senses drive train load through the shift cable. The control box switch activates the ESA module, which intermittently grounds the distributor side of the coil. Once the gear shift change has been made, the ESA shuts off and engine operation returns to normal. The second converter box switch prevents the shift mechanism from inadvertently triggering the ESA module once the engine is running in gear. **Figure 26** shows the ESA module circuitry and its relationship to the ignition system.

Distributor Servicing

OMC marine distributors are heavy-duty units manufactured with special housings, caps, advance weights and other components. They are designed to withstand climatic and environmental abuse to which the typical automotive distributor is not subjected. For this reason, automotive parts should not be substituted. Periodic care, cleaning and lubrication of the breaker point distributor is recommended for long service life.

1. Remove the distributor as described in this chapter.
2. Clean the outside of the distributor with solvent and a brush to remove all dirt, grease and other contamination.
3. Remove the distributor cap and rotor. Inspect both as described in Chapter Four. If the cap is vented, make sure the vent screen is not plugged (**Figure 27**) and that it is properly installed.
4. Have a dealer or qualified electrical shop test distributor operation on a synchroscope or distributor test machine (**Figure 28**). Have worn parts replaced as necessary.
5. Remove the breaker point and condenser assembly. See Chapter Four.
6. Remove the breaker plate attaching screws. Lift or carefully pry on breaker plate and remove from distributor bowl.
7. Remove the felt lubrication washer (if so equipped) from the center of the cam assembly. Some distributors use a tiny wire retaining clip inside the cam assembly that must be removed after removing the felt washer. See **Figure 29**.
8. Remove the cam assembly from the distributor shaft.
9. Wipe the inside of the distributor bowl with a clean dry cloth. If more than a slight film of oil or crankcase vapors is present, wash the inside of the bowl with cleaning solvent. If necessary, clean with a brush.

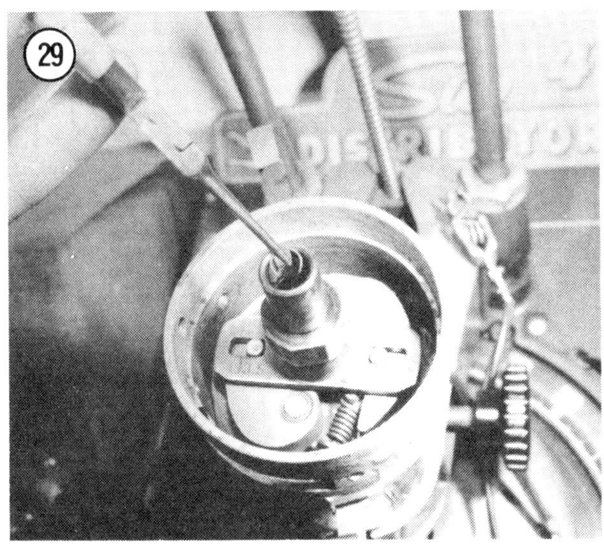

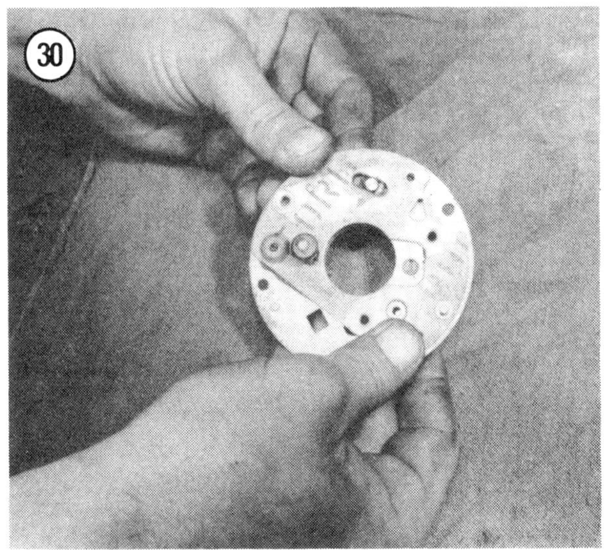

When the bowl and advance mechanism are clean, rinse in solvent and blow dry with compressed air.

10. Lightly lubricate the distributor shaft with cam grease, then install the cam assembly. Install the retaining clip, if used, and the felt washer. Place a drop or two of engine oil on the felt lubrication washer.

11. Wipe the breaker plate with a clean dry cloth. Inspect the plate for wear at its pivot points. See **Figure 30**. Lubricate the pivot points with cam grease. Reinstall the breaker plate in the distributor bowl.

NOTE
Some distributors use a felt lubricating wick mounted on the breaker plate. Other distributors may have an oil cup located on the outside of the housing bowl. Always replace the lubricating wick with a new one or put 2-3 drops of engine oil in the oil cup when replacing points or otherwise servicing the distributor.

12. Install the breaker point and condenser assembly. See Chapter Four.

13. Install the distributor in the engine as described in this chapter.

Removal

1. Unsnap the distributor retaining clips or remove retaining screws as required.
2. Remove the distributor cap with the spark plug wires attached and place to one side out of the way.
3. Disconnect the distributor primary wire at the coil.
4. Scribe a mark on the distributor housing in line with the rotor tip. Scribe a corresponding mark on the engine. See **Figure 31**.
5. Remove the distributor hold-down bolt and clamp. Remove the distributor from the engine.

Installation (Engine Not Rotated After Distributor Removal)

1. Install a new distributor mounting gasket (if used) in the engine block counterbore. Make sure the area is clean.
2. Align the rotor tip with the mark scribed on the distributor housing during removal. Turn the rotor about 1/8 turn clockwise (5.0L [302 cu. in.]/5.8L/7.5L) or 1/8 turn clockwise (all others) past the scribed mark. Position the distributor to align the housing mark with the mark scribed on the engine before removal. Slide the distributor down into the engine.

NOTE
The rotor and shaft might have to be moved slightly to engage the distributor and camshaft gears and oil pump drive tang. However, the rotor should align with the scribed mark when the distributor is in its final position.

3. Install the distributor hold-down clamp and bolt. Do not tighten at this time.
4. Install the distributor cap on the housing. Be sure the tang on the housing engages the cap slot and that the cap fits snugly on the housing.
5. Connect the distributor lead and set ignition timing. See Chapter Four. When timing is correctly adjusted, tighten the distributor hold-down bolt snugly.

Installation (Engine Rotated After Distributor Removal)

1. Remove the No. 1 spark plug. See Chapter Four. Hold a finger over the plug hole and crank the engine over or rotate the crankshaft pulley until compression pressure is felt. Continue to rotate the engine slowly until the timing mark on the crankshaft pulley aligns with the TDC (zero) mark on the timing scale.

NOTE
Always rotate the engine in the direction of normal rotation. Do not back up the engine to align the timing marks.

2. Install a new distributor mounting gasket (if used) in the engine block counterbore. Make sure the area is clean.
3. Turn the distributor shaft until the rotor tip points in the direction of the No. 1 terminal in the distributor cap. Turn the rotor 1/8 turn counterclockwise past the No. 1 terminal position. Slide the distributor into the engine.

NOTE
The rotor and shaft may have to be moved slightly to engage the distributor

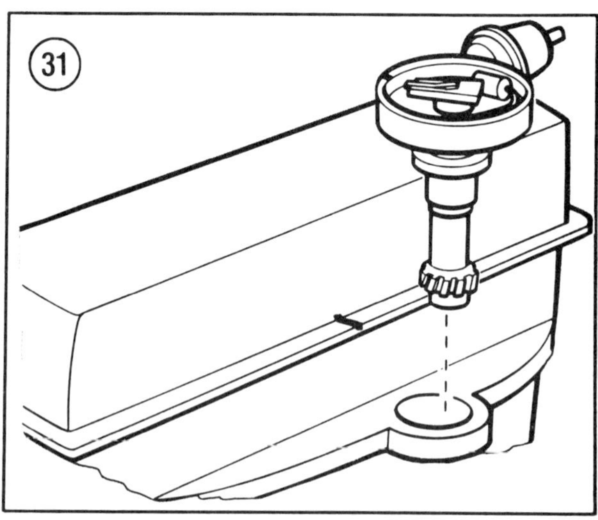

and camshaft gears and the oil pump drive tang. However, the rotor should align with the No. 1 terminal when the distributor is in place.

4. Install the distributor hold-down clamp and bolt. Do not tighten bolt at this time.
5. Install the distributor cap on the housing. Be sure the tang on the housing engages the cap slot and that the cap fits snugly on the housing.
6. Connect the distributor lead and set ignition timing. See Chapter Four. When timing is correctly adjusted, tighten the distributor hold-down bolt snugly.

IGNITION COIL

A conventional oil-filled sealed ignition coil is used. **Figure 32** shows a typical installation.

Removal/Installation

1. Disconnect the high tension (thick) lead at the coil tower.
2. Disconnect the primary and secondary electrical connections at the coil. Reinstall the nuts on the studs to prevent their loss.
3. Remove the coil clamp bracket screw. Remove the coil from the bracket.
4. Installation is the reverse of removal.

IGNITION RESISTOR WIRE

The entire engine wiring harness must be replaced if the ignition resistor wire is defective—do *not* shorten the wire as a corrective measure.

Testing

1. Disconnect the 20 gauge purple/red resistor lead at the positive terminal of the ignition coil.
2. Disconnect the purple lead at the rear of the alternator.

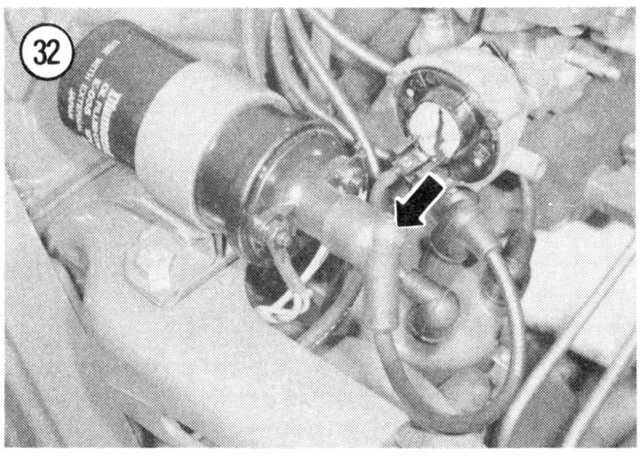

3. Connect an ohmmeter between the leads disconnected in Step 1 and Step 2.
4. If the reading is not 1.5-2.5 ohms, replace the wiring harness.

SWITCHES AND CONNECTORS

Switches can be tested with an ohmmeter or a self-powered test lamp. If a switch does not perform properly, replace it.

Many electrical problems encountered are due to poor connections in the waterproof connectors. If the pins and sockets are improperly seated in their connectors, the resulting electrical connection will be poor or non-existent.

Pins and sockets should be seated in their connectors according to the dimensions shown in **Figure 33**. When installing pins or sockets, lubricate the connector with rubbing alcohol and use insert tool (part No. 322697) to install to the proper depth.

IGNITION SWITCH

Disconnect the negative battery cable when testing the ignition switch in the boat. Refer

11

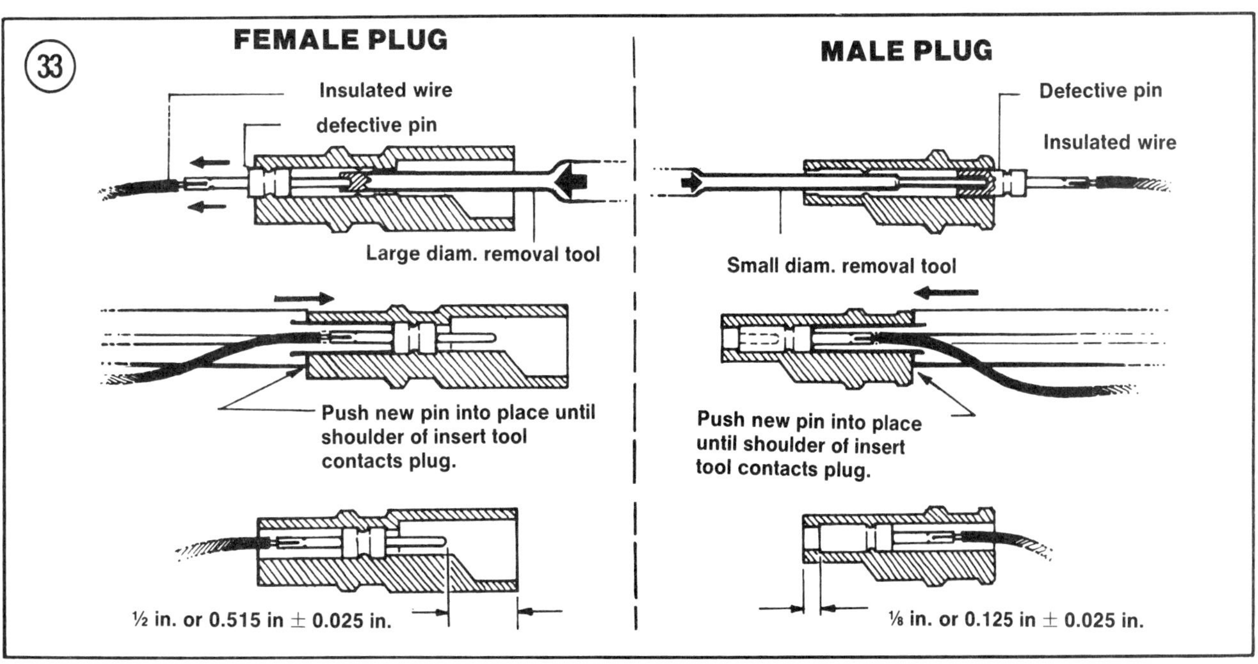

to **Figure 26** for this procedure. Terminals M and C on the switch are not used in stern drive applications.

1. Disconnect all leads at the ignition switch.
2. Connect an ohmmeter or self-powered test lamp between the B and A terminals.
3. Turn the switch ON and then to START. There should be continuity in both switch positions.
4. Move the ohmmeter lead from the A to the S terminal. Turn the key to the START position. There should be continuity.
5. If the switch fails to indicate continuity as described in any position, replace it.

NOTE
If engines equipped with a Delcotron alternator continue to run after the switch is turned off and the switch passes the continuity test, check for a shorted diode in the purple lead connected to the alternator by the rubber plug.

ESA MODULE SWITCHES

The ESA module operates an ignition interrupter switch (A, **Figure 34**) which pulses the ignition during shifting by intermittently grounding the distributor side of the coil. An overstroke switch (B, **Figure 34**) prevents the shift mechanism from inadvertently operating the module once the engine is in gear. Both switches are mounted on the shift bracket at the starboard rear of the engine.

ESA modules are stamped with an identifying mark according to engine use and must not be interchanged. When replacing a module, make sure the new one carries the same mark as the one being replaced.

A sticking interrupter switch plunger or an overstroke switch that does not engage will cause the engine to stall. A sticking interrupter switch plunger or a defective overstroke switch will cause the engine to miss continuously. A defective interrupter switch, ESA module or over-torqued overstroke switch screws will prevent the ignition from pulsing during shifting.

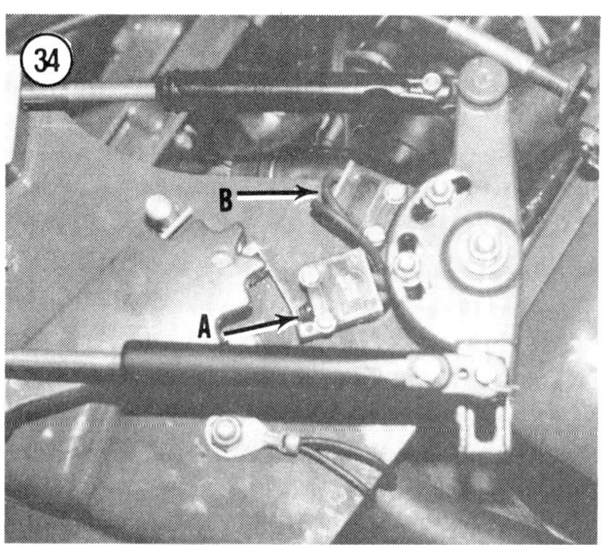

Ignition Interrupter Switch Test

1. With the boat in the water or a flushing adapter installed, start the engine and run at fast idle (800-1,000 rpm) in NEUTRAL.
2. Manually activate the interrupter switch (A, **Figure 34**). The engine should pulse and slow to 450-550 rpm until the switch is released.
3. If the engine does not react as described in Step 2, clean and tighten all connections.

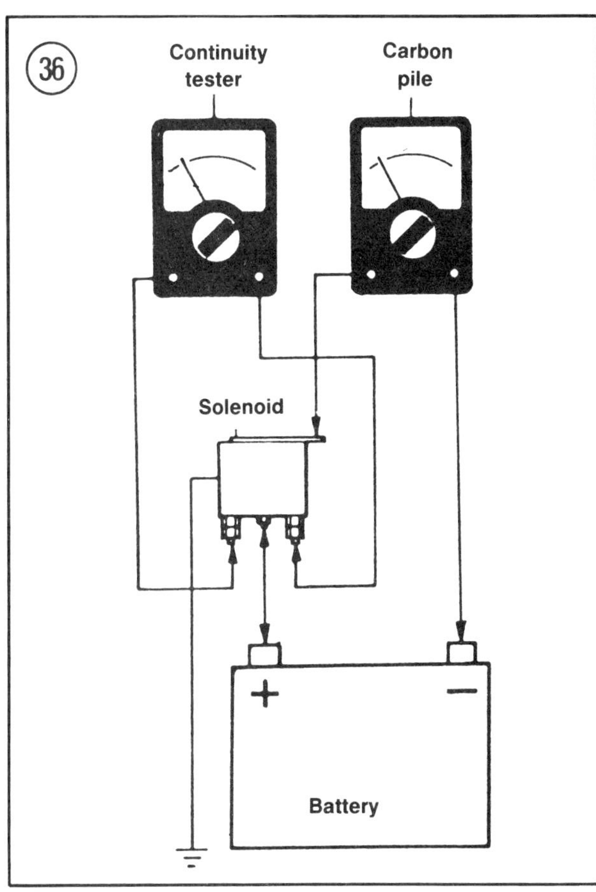

Repeat Step 2. If the engine still does not react, shut the engine off and disconnect the negative battery cable.

4. Disconnect the switch lead connector from the receptacle located behind the shift cable bracket.
5. Probe the blue wire cavities of the male connector plug (marked C and D) with an ohmmeter set on its high scale. Place the switch actuating arm lever in the V-notch of the load-sensing lever (**Figure 35**). The meter should show continuity.
6. Manually raise and lower the load-sensing lever while watching the meter scale. It should read zero when the lever is moved in either direction.
7. If it does not read zero in Step 6, check the wiring to the connector plug and repeat Step 5, then Step 6. If the meter still does not show zero in Step 6, replace the switch.

Overstroke Switch Test

1. Perform the *Ignition Interrupter Switch Test* as described in this chapter.
2. With the switch lead connector still disconnected from the receptacle located behind the shift cable bracket, probe the black wire cavities of the male connector plug (marked A and B) with an ohmmeter. The meter should show continuity.
3. Depress the switch plunger. The meter should now show no continuity.
4. If it does not show continuity in Step 3, check the wiring to the connector plug and repeat Step 2, then Step 3. If the meter still does not show continuity in Step 3, replace the switch.

SOLENOIDS

Solenoids are used with the starter and tilt motors to carry the large amount of electrical current used by the motors. The solenoid is a completely sealed and non-serviceable unit. The 2 large terminals are the battery and motor terminals. The small terminal is the switch control. Ground is internal through the solenoid bracket. If a solenoid is suspected of faulty operation, test it as follows:

11

1. Connect a volt/ohmmeter between the 2 large solenoid terminals. See **Figure 36**.
2. Connect a carbon pile as shown in **Figure 36** and reduce the voltage to under 6 volts.
3. Adjust the carbon pile until the ohmmeter or test lamp shows a complete circuit. At this point, the voltmeter should show a reading of 6-8 volts. If more than 8 volts are required to complete the circuit, replace the solenoid.

OIL PRESSURE SENDING UNIT

All engines are equipped with an oil pressure sending unit connected to the oil pressure gauge. Test the operation of the sending unit as follows:

1. Disconnect the wire at the sender terminal. See **Figure 37** (inline) or **Figure 38** (V6 and V8), typical.
2. Connect an ohmmeter between the sender termimal and a good engine ground. With the engine off, the meter should show continuity.
3. Start the engine. With the engine running, the meter should show no continuity. Replace the sender if correct test results are not noted.

WATER TEMPERATURE SENDING UNIT

All engines are equipped with a temperature sending unit connected to the temperature gauge or indicator light. Test the operation of the sending unit as follows:

1. Remove the sending unit from the engine.
2. Connect a digital ohmmeter to the sending unit.
3. Immerse the sending unit and a cooking thermometer in a container of oil.
4. Heat the container over a flameless source and note the ohmmeter reading. The ohmmeter should read as follows:
   a. 448 ohms ±10 percent at 100° F.
   b. 128 ohms ±7.5 percent at 160° F.
   c. 46.6 ohms ±5 percent at 220° F.
5. Replace the sending unit if it does not function within specified ranges at each temperature level.

FUSES

A 20 amp fuse is located between the ignition switch and ammeter to protect the electrical system. Separate inline fuses are located in fuse holders to protect the main wiring harness and the trim/tilt motor circuits. See **Figure 39** (typical). If additional electrical accessories are added to any installation, install individual fused circuits for each accessory with power takeoff at the terminal strip.

Whenever a failure occurs in any part of the electrical system, always check the fuse first to see if it is blown. Usually, the trouble is a short circuit in the wiring. This may be caused by worn-through insulation or by a wire that has worked its way loose and shorted to ground. Occasionally, the electrical overload which causes a fuse to blow may occur in a switch or motor.

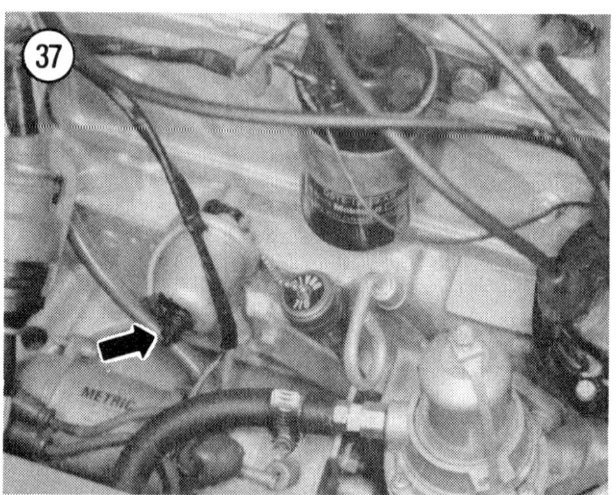

A blown fuse should be treated as more than a minor annoyance; it should serve as a warning that something is wrong in the electrical system. Before replacing a fuse, determine what caused it to blow and correct the problem. Always carry several spare fuses of the proper amperage values onboard. Never replace a fuse with one of higher amperage rating than that specified for use. Failure to follow these basic rules could result in heat or fire damage to major parts or even the loss of the entire vessel.

Table 1 ELECTRICAL COMPONENT SPECIFICATIONS

STARTER	
Delco-Remy	
No-load test	
Minimum amps	
Delco 1998318	60
Delco 1998317 and 1998570	65
Maximum amps	
Delco 1998318	85
Delco 1998317 and 1998570	95
Load test	
Volts	
Delco 1998318	4.8
Delco 1998317 and 1998570	4.3
Minimum amps	
Delco 1998318	440
Delco 1998317 and 1998570	490
Maximum amps	
Delco 1998318	430
Delco 1998317 and 1998570	560
Voltage @ rpm	
Minimum	6,800
Maximum	10,300
Solenoid current draw	
Hold-in winding	15-20 amps @ 10 volts
Both windings in parallel	47-55 amps @ 10 volts
Motorcraft	
Current draw, normal load	150 amps maximum
Cranking voltage	8 volts minimum
Stall torque @ 5 volts (min.)	
7.5L	10 ft.-lb. (14 N•m)
All others	9 ft.-lb. (12 N•m)
No-load test amperage	
7.5L	85
All others	70
Load test amperage	
7.5L	475 maximum
All others	460 maximum
IGNITION COIL	
Coil (@ 75° F)	
Resistance	
Primary	1.43-1.58 ohms
Secondary	7,500-8,700 ohms
Operating amperage	1.0 maximum

(continued)

11

Table 1 ELECTRICAL COMPONENT SPECIFICATIONS (cont.)

DISTRIBUTOR	
Breaker points	
Gap	
1986	
2.5L/3.0L/4.3L	0.019 in.
5.0L/5.7L	0.018 in.
1987	
2.3L/5.0L/5.7L	0.018 in.
3.0L/4.3L	0.019 in.
7.5L	0.017 in.
1988	
2.3L	0.018 in.
3.0L/4.3L	0.019 in.
5.0L/5.7L/5.8L/7.5L	0.018 in.
1989	
2.3L/3.0L/4.3L	0.019 in.
5.0L/5.7L/5.8L/7.5L	0.018 in.
Dwell	
1986	
2.5L/3.0L	31-34
4.3L	39 ± 2
5.0L/5.7L	30 ± 2
1987	
2.3L	36 ± 2
3.0L	31-34
4.3L	39 ± 2
5.0L/5.7L	29 ± 2
7.5L	31 ± 2
1988	
2.3L	36 ± 2
3.0L	31-34
4.3L	39 ± 2
5.0L/5.7L	30 ± 2
7.5L	31 ± 2
1989	
2.3L	36 ± 2
3.0L	31-34
4.3L	39 ± 2
5.0L/5.7L/5.8L/7.5L	29 ± 2
Condenser	
Capacity (microfarads)	
2.3L	0.25-0.31
2.5L/3.0L	0.18-0.23
All others	0.21-0.25
Centrifugal advance (° @ rpm)	
2.3L	24 @ 3,400
2.5L/3.0L	28 @ 2,100
4.3L	12 @ 3,200
5.0L (305 cu. in.)/5.7L	21 @ 3,000
5.0L (302 cu. in.)/5.8L	20 @ 5,000
7.5L	25 @ 4,600

Chapter Twelve

Stern Drive and Upper Gear Housing

Engine torque passes through a drive shaft/universal joint to a pinion and drive gear in the drive shaft (upper) housing, changing the horizontal power flow from the engine into a vertical power flow sent to the gearcase (lower) housing through a drive shaft.

Power application is controlled by shifting the lower gearcase housing. This is accomplished through a shift rod connected between the engine and drive shaft housing. A fitting in the drive shaft housing transmits horizontal motion of the engine shift rod to a vertical shift shaft which extends to the shift mechanism on the gearcase propeller shaft. The engine shift rod is connected by a shift cable to the remote control box, providing shift control at the helm.

When the unit is shifted into gear, a sliding clutch in the gearcase engages a FORWARD or REVERSE gear on the propeller shaft. This creates a direct coupling that changes the power flow back to that horizontal movement to the propeller shaft.

This chapter provides removal, installation and upper gear housing overhaul procedures for all OMC Cobra stern drive models. Repair procedures for individual subsections are given in the chapters that follow. Engine removal and installation procedures are described in the appropriate engine chapter. Refer to Chapter Six through Chapter Eight as required.

Table 1 is at the end of the chapter.

CAUTION
Elastic stop nuts should never be used more than twice. It is a good idea to replace such nuts with new ones each time they are removed. Never use worn-out stop nuts or non-locking nuts.

SERVICE PRECAUTIONS

Whenever you work on a stern drive unit, there are several precautions to keep in mind that will make your work easier, faster and more accurate.

1. Use special tools where noted. In some cases, it may be possible to perform the procedure with makeshift tools, but this procedure is not recommended. The use of makeshift tools can damage the components and may cause serious personal injury.
2. Use a vise with protective jaws to hold housings or components. If protective jaws are not available, insert blocks of soft wood on either side of the part(s) before clamping them in the vise.
3. Remove and install pressed-on parts with an appropriate mandrel, support and hydraulic press. Do not try to pry, hammer or otherwise force them on or off.
4. Refer to the appropriate table at the end of the chapter for torque values, if not given in the text. Proper torque is vital to assure long life and service from stern drive components.
5. Apply OMC Gasket Sealing Compound or Perfect Seal to the outer surfaces of all retainer and housing mating surfaces during reassembly. Do *not* allow Gasket Sealing Compound or Perfect Seal to touch O-rings or enter the bearings or gears.
6. Apply OMC Triple-Guard grease to all O-rings and seal lips.
7. Apply Loctite Type A on the outside diameter of all metal case oil seals.
8. Keep a record of all shims and where they came from. As soon as the shims are removed, inspect them for damage and write down their thickness and location. Shim material is often very thin and can be easily damaged. If the shim pack is not easily separated, do not attempt to separate it into individual shims. Wire the shims together for reassembly and place them in a safe place. Follow shimming instructions closely. If gear backlash is not properly set, the unit will be noisy and suffer premature gear failure. Incorrect bearing preload will result in premature bearing failure.
9. Work in a clean area where there is good lighting and sufficient space for components to be stored. Keep an ample number of containers available for storing small parts. Cover parts with clean shop cloths when you are not working with them.
10. Wear safety glasses when dealing with snap rings. They are often brittle and can snap during removal or installation.

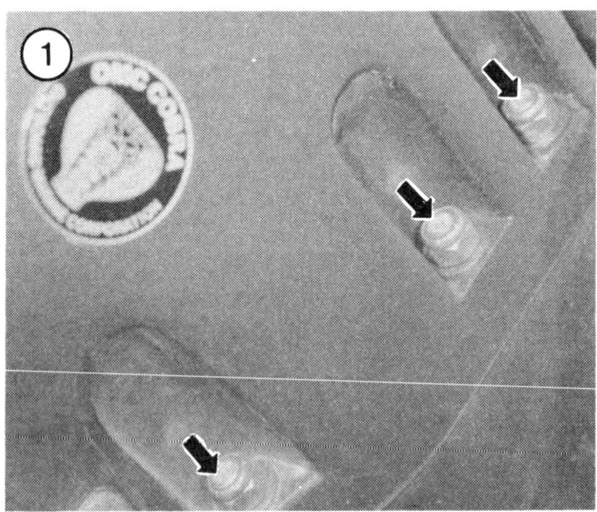

STERN DRIVE

Stern drive removal is generally a fairly simple procedure. However, if the unit has not been removed recently or if it has been subjected to considerable corrosion, it may be necessary to use force in excess of that normally required. In some cases, it may even be necessary to heat components with a welding torch to free frozen bearings or shafts.

Installation of the stern drive is more complex than removal, requiring both time and patience. Components must be properly aligned and care should be taken in mating them to prevent possible bearing, gasket or seal damage.

Removal

1. Remove the oil dipstick plug from the top of the upper gear housing. Securely install a 1/2-13 lifting eye in the plug hole.

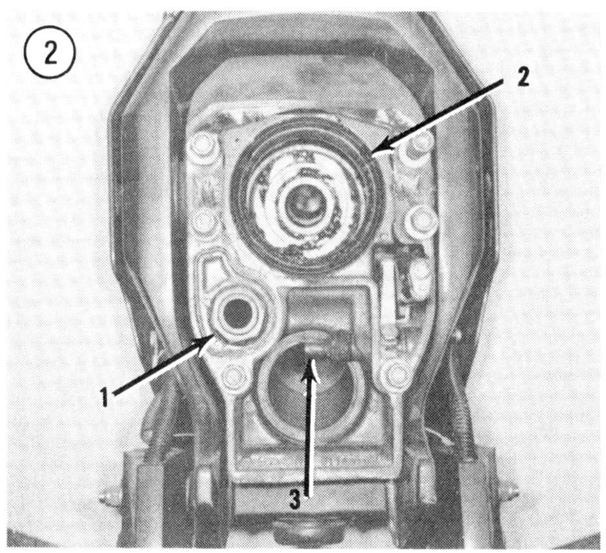

2. Disconnect the aft end of the trim/tilt cylinder on each side of the drive unit. See Chapter Sixteen.
3. Remove and discard the 6 elastic stop nuts and washers from the stern drive-to-pivot housing studs (**Figure 1**).

WARNING
Do not attempt to remove the stern drive unit from the boat in Step 4 without the aid of a hoist for support. The unit is heavy and may slip from your grasp, causing damage to the stern drive and possible personal injury.

4. Attach an overhead hoist to the lifting eye installed in the top of the upper gear housing in Step 1. Support the unit with the hoist.
5. Carefully guide the stern drive unit straight back and remove it from the boat. Support the drive shaft and U-joint coupler during removal.
6. Lower the stern drive to the ground and remove the hoist. Mount the stern drive in a suitable holding fixture, if available.
7. Remove and discard the pivot housing gasket.
8. Clean all gasket residue from the pivot housing.

Installation

1. Coat both sides of a new pivot housing gasket with OMC Gasket Sealing Compound. Install gasket on pivot housing.

2. Check condition of the small rubber seal ring (1, **Figure 2**) and the larger rubber seal inside the pivot housing (2, **Figure 2**). Replace as required. Wipe lip of large rubber seal with OMC Triple-Guard grease.

3. If engine was removed, check engine alignment as described in the appropriate chapter for your engine (Chapter Six through Chapter Eight).

4. Make sure the remote control is in its NEUTRAL position. Coat shift lever pin (3, **Figure 2**) with OMC Triple-Guard grease.

5. Lubricate drive shaft splines with OMC Triple-Guard grease. Make sure the drive shaft O-ring grooves are free of grease, then wipe both O-rings with OMC Premium 4-cycle Motor Oil (excessive grease can cause a hydraulic lock and prevent easy installation of the drive shaft in the gimbal bearing).

6. Lubricate both U-joints, the outer diameter of the U-joint coupler and the tapered end of the bearing carrier with OMC Marine Wheel Bearing Grease.

7. Place the stern drive shift rod in its NEUTRAL position (propeller should rotate freely in both directions).

8. Wipe the pivot housing mounting studs with OMC Gasket Sealing Compound.

WARNING
Do not attempt to install the stern drive unit to the boat without the aid of a hoist for support. The unit is heavy and may slip from your grasp, causing damage to the stern drive and possible personal injury.

9. Attach an overhead hoist to the lifting eye installed in the top of the upper gear housing.

NOTE
If the universal joint splines do not engage with engine coupling splines in Step 10, rotate the universal coupler with a long screwdriver or a 1/4 in. diameter bar until the splines engage the coupler.

10. Install the stern drive to the pivot housing, guiding the U-joint shaft through the gimbal housing bearing and into the engine coupling. At the same time, guide the shift shaft into the drive shaft housing opening. Do not move shift shaft assembly or coupler.
11. Install a flat washer and new elastic stop nut on each stern drive-to-pivot housing stud. Tighten nuts evenly by hand, then torque to 25 ft.-lb. (34 N•m). Torque the center nuts first, then tighten the remaining 4 nuts in a crisscross pattern. Retighten all nuts to 50 ft.-lb. (68 N•m) following the same pattern.
12. Reinstall the aft end of each trim/tilt cylinder to the stern drive housing. See Chapter Sixteen.
13. Remove the lifting eye from the upper gear housing. Reinstall the oil dipstick plug with a new seal and tighten to 48-72 in.-lb. (5-8 N•m).

UPPER GEAR HOUSING ASSEMBLY

Figure 3 is an exploded view showing the components of a typical Cobra drive upper gear housing.

Upper Gear Housing Removal

1. Place stern drive unit in a holding fixture to support the lower gearcase housing.
2. Remove the lifting eye from the upper gear housing. Leave the oil level hole open to vent the reservoir in Step 3.
3. Place a suitable container under the lower gearcase housing drain plug. Remove the drain plug and discard the nylon washer.

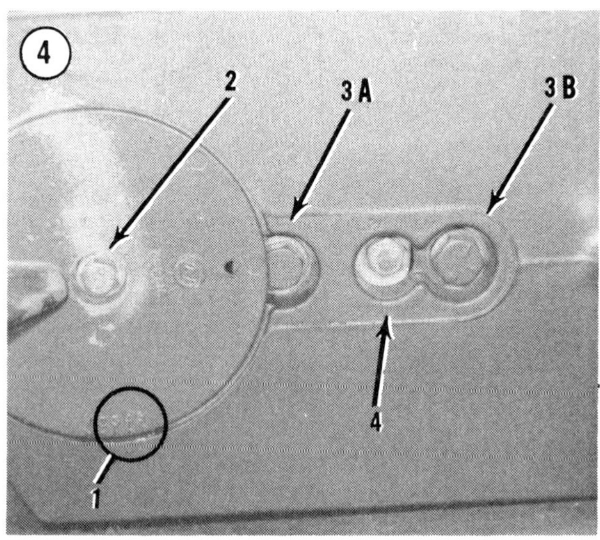

Drain the lubricant from the lower gearcase housing.

NOTE
If metallic particles are found in Step 4, remove and disassemble both the upper and lower gearcase units to inspect for damaged oil seals, oil rings and/or housing cracks. Clean all parts in solvent and blow dry with compressed air. Check magnetic drain plug tip for metallic particles and clean before reinstallation.

4. Wipe a small amount of lubricant on a finger and rub the finger and thumb together. Check for the presence of metallic particles.
5. Note color of gear lubricant. If white or cream in color, there is water in the lubricant. Inspect the drain container for signs of water separation from the lubricant.

NOTE
If there are no grid/index marks on the trim tab/gearcase housing, scribe one for reinstallation reference.

6. Note the alignment of the trim tab grid with the gearcase index mark for reinstallation reference (1, **Figure 4**). Remove the trim tab screw (2, **Figure 4**). Remove the trim tab.

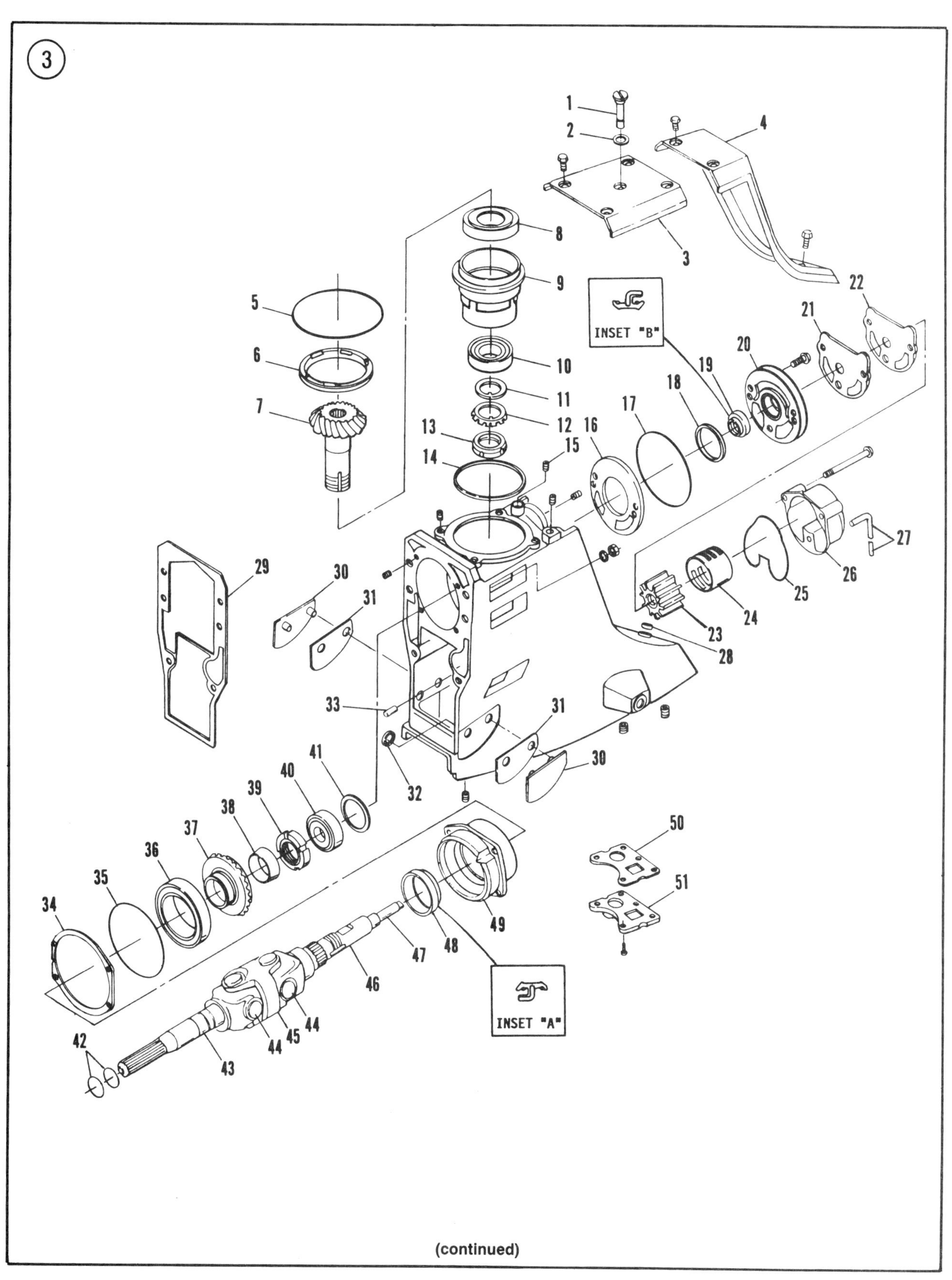
3
1
2
4
8
3
9
22
5
INSET "B"
21
6
20
10
19
18
11
7
17
13
12
16
15
14
27
29
26
30
25
31
24
23
28
33
31
41
30
40
32
39
38
50
37
36
51
35
49
34
47
48
46
INSET "A"
44
45
44
44
42
43

(continued)

(continued)

UPPER GEAR HOUSING

1. Oil dipstick
2. Dipstick gasket
3. Gear housing cover
4. Water pump access cover
5. O-ring
6. Pinion housing retainer ring
7. Pinion gear
8. Upper pinion bearing
9. Bearing carrier
10. Lower pinion bearing
11. Pinion washer
12. Nut retainer
13. Pinion nut
14. Bearing carrier shim
15. Cover insert
16. Gasket
17. O-ring
18. O-ring
19. Water pump shaft seal
20. Water pump adaptor
21. Gasket
22. Plate
23. Impeller
24. Water pump housing liner
25. Seal
26. Impeller housing
27. Impeller housing vent hose
28. Cover insert
29. Gear housing to pivot gasket
30. Thrust plate
31. Thrust plate shim
32. Thrust plate retainer ring
33. Shift rod guide
34. Bearing carrier shim
35. O-ring
36. Bearing
37. Gear
38. Centering cone
39. Gear to U-joint nut
40. U-joint shaft bearing
41. Shim
42. O-rings
43. Yoke shaft
44. U-joint
45. Center yoke
46. Stub pump shaft
47. Water pump shaft
48. Bearing carrier seal
49. Bearing carrier
50. Water passage cover
51. Cover gasket

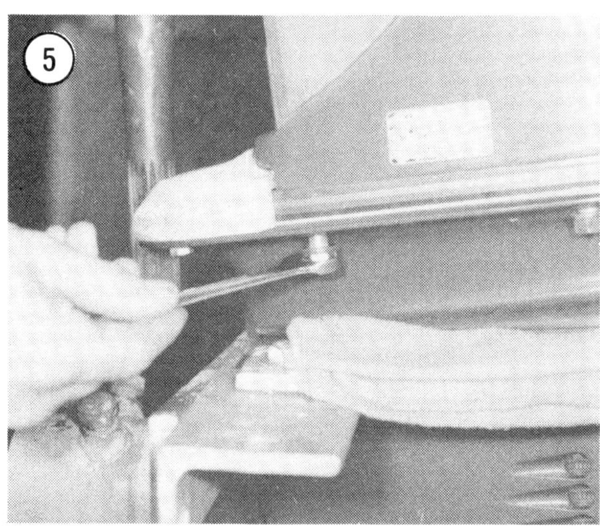

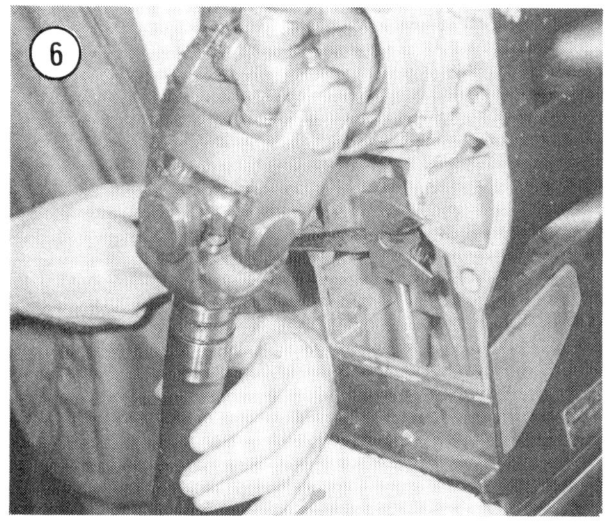

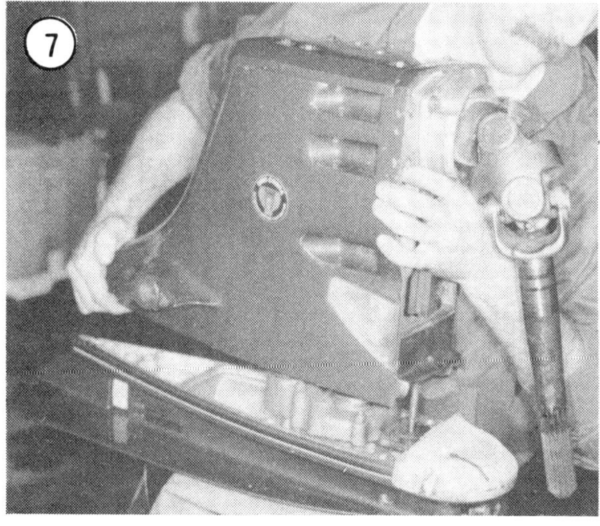

NOTE
On 2.3L, 2.5L, 3.0L and 7.5L models, one of the ventilation plate screws to be removed in Step 7 will be found inside the trim tab cavity. ***Figure 4*** *shows the 4.3L, 5.0L, 5.7L and 5.8L gearcase.*

7. Remove the 2 ventilation plate screws (3, **Figure 4**). Do *not* remove the anode screw (4, **Figure 4**).
8. Unbolt the upper gear housing from the lower gearcase housing (**Figure 5**). The two units are now held together only by O-rings. Get a firm grasp on the upper gear housing and rock from side-to-side while pulling upward to break the seal.
9. Separate gear housing enough to disengage the shift rod head from the guide pin, then turn the shift rod head 90° to port (**Figure 6**) to allow it to clear the exhaust opening.
10. Lift the upper gear housing free of the lower gearcase housing (**Figure 7**) and place unit on a clean workbench surface.

Upper Gear Housing Installation

1. Check the lower drive shaft to make sure the nylon plug is installed at the base of the splines. Wipe the splines at each end of the intermediate drive shaft with OMC Hi-Vis Gearcase Lubricant and install in the lower drive shaft.
2. Make sure the shift rod head is positioned 90° to port for installation clearance.
3. Position the upper gear housing over the lower gearcase housing. Make sure the drive shaft and water tube seat is lowered in place at the same time as the upper gear housing. When the shift rod head appears in the exhaust opening, rotate the head enough to engage the guide pin. It may be necessary to turn the U-joint shaft slightly in order to engage the drive shaft splines. The housing should seat properly with only hand pressure.
4. Clean the gear housing mounting bolts in solvent, but do not wire brush or otherwise

remove the yellow-green material on the bolt threads. This is a self-locking material to prevent the bolts from loosening. If the material is damaged or removed, install new bolts.

5. Wipe the threads of the short bolts with OMC Gasket Sealing Compound. Install and tighten evenly (**Figure 5**), then connect OMC wrench part No. 912031 to a torque wrench and tighten the bolts to 22-24 ft.-lb. (30-33 N•m).
6. Lightly wipe the ventilation plate bolt threads with OMC Gasket Sealing Compound. Install the flat washer under the large bolt (3, **Figure 4**). Tighten both bolts to 22-24 ft.-lb. (30-33 N•m).
7. Pressure and vacuum test the drive unit. See Chapter Thirteen. Pressurize to 3-6 psi and draw 3-5 in. Hg and 15 in. Hg vacuum to check the sealing of the upper gear housing and drive shaft bearing housing O-rings. The drive should not lose more than 1 psi or 1 in. Hg vacuum in 3 minutes.
8. Clean the trim tab screw threads with a wire brush and the screw hold with an appropriate thread tap. Wipe the screw threads with OMC Gasket Sealing Compound.
9. Position the trim tab with the grid/index or scribed marks aligned. If original position is unknown, set index rib with grid number 3. Install and tighten the screw to 28-32 ft.-lb. (38-43 N•m).
10. Fill the lower gearcase housing with OMC Hi-Vis Gearcase Lubricant. See Chapter Four.

Upper Gear Housing Disassembly

Refer to **Figure 3** for this procedure.

1. Install the upper gear housing in a suitable holding fixture, if available. If not, place on a clean workbench.
2. Remove the water pump access cover (**Figure 8**).

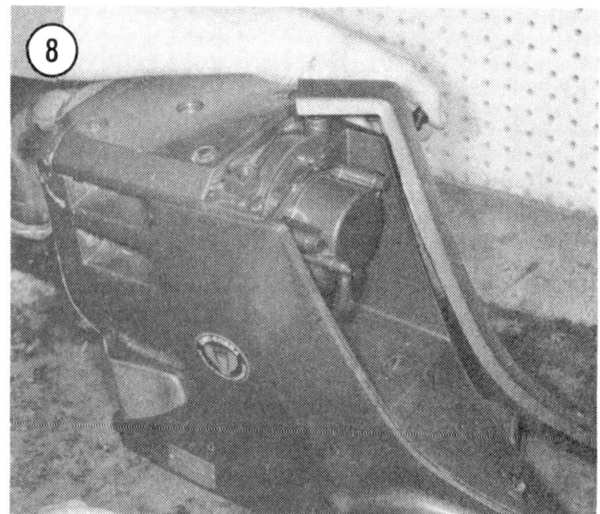

8

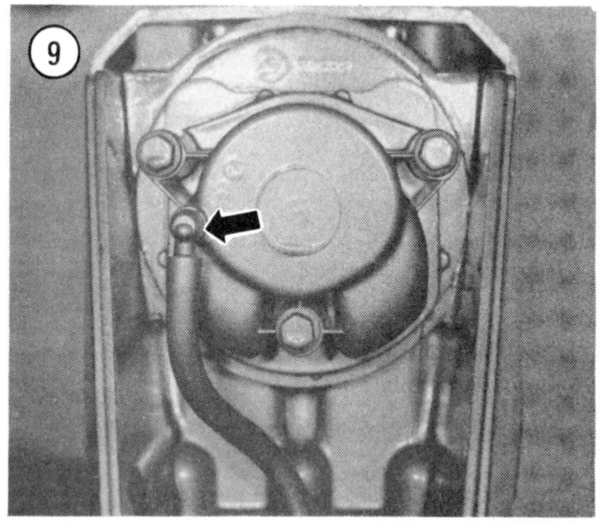

9

10

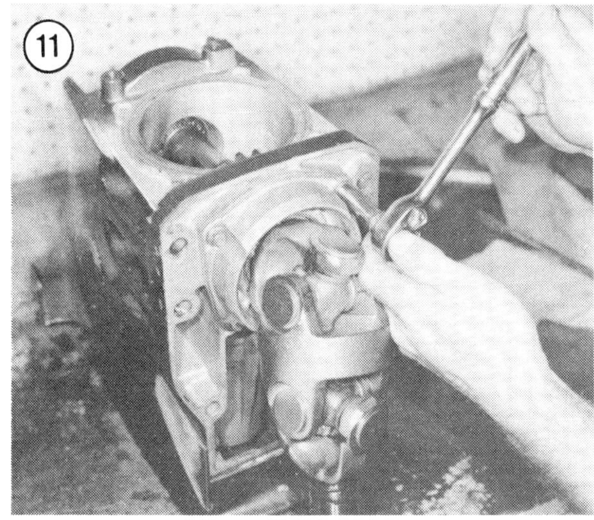

3. Disconnect the vent hose at the water pump housing (**Figure 9**). Remove the water pump assembly. See Chapter Ten.

4. Remove the screws holding the upper housing cover. Remove the cover (**Figure 10**) and discard the O-ring underneath.

5. Remove the 4 bearing carrier screws (**Figure 11**).

6. Grasp the U-joint shaft, support the shaft and pull the shaft/bearing carrier assembly from the gear housing (**Figure 12**). Remove and save the shims behind the carrier assembly.

7. Insert OMC spanner tool part No. 984330 (**Figure 13**) in the gear housing to engage the pinion bearing carrier lockring. Fasten tool to top of gear housing with 2 housing cover screws, tightening alternately and completely.

8. Connect a 1/2 in. breaker bar to the spanner tool and break the lockring free. Carefully remove the spring-loaded tool arm from the top of the housing.

9. Unscrew the lockring with the spanner tool. Remove spanner tool, then reach into the gear housing and remove the lockring (**Figure 14**).

10. Remove the pinion bearing carrier (**Figure 15**). If it does not come out easily,

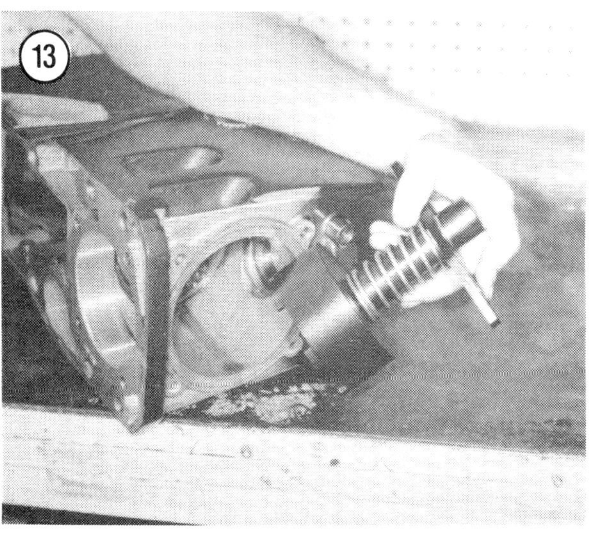

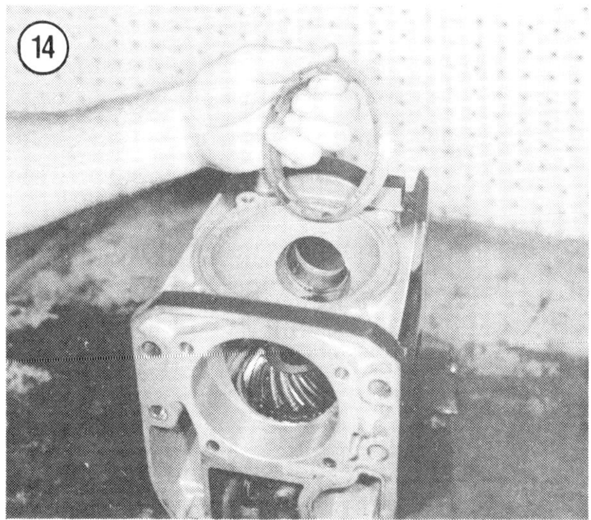

invert housing over a clean shop cloth and drive the carrier out with a 1-1 1/2 in. diameter wooden dowel and a mallet. Work carefully to avoid damage to the lockring threads in the housing.

11. Pull the water tube and seal from the water tube cover. Do not remove the water cover unless it is damaged.

12. Clean and inspect the housing as described in this chapter.

Upper Gear Housing Cleaning and Inspection

1. Clean the housing in fresh solvent. Remove all sealant from the screw holes, gasket surfaces and O-ring bores. Do not use a thread tap to clean threaded holes, as they all contain Heli-Coil inserts which will be damaged by a tap. Blow housing dry with compressed air.

2. Check the rear bearing cup for scoring, grooving, heat discoloration or other defects. If any defect is noted, remove bearing cup with remover part No. 912291 and a mallet. Retrieve the shims and discard any that are damaged.

3. Check the condition of the thrust plate on each side of the housing. If thrust plate replacement is required, carefully pry retaining rings off the studs inside the housing and remove the thrust plates.

4. Check the lockring threads for damage.

5. Remove any sharp edges in the water pump cavity, pinion carrier or U-joint carrier bore that could damage or prevent O-rings and gaskets from seating properly.

6. Inspect all cooling passages for corrosion buildup. If present, scrape passages as clean as possible with an appropriate tool.

7. If housing is to be replaced with a new unit, transfer the model plate to the new housing.

8. Check the shift rod guide pin condition. If worn excessively or broken, pull or drill out

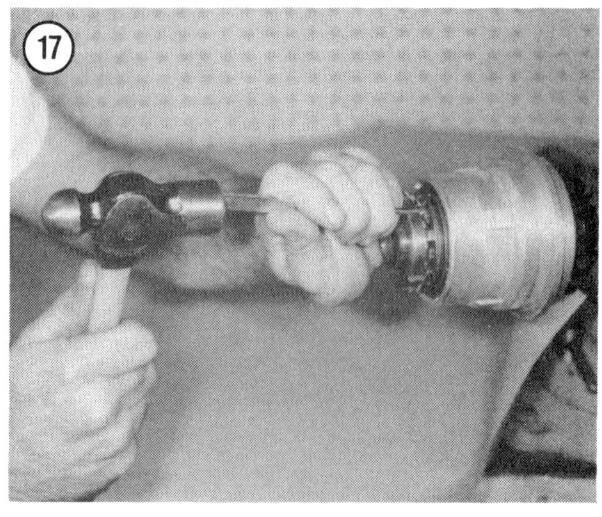

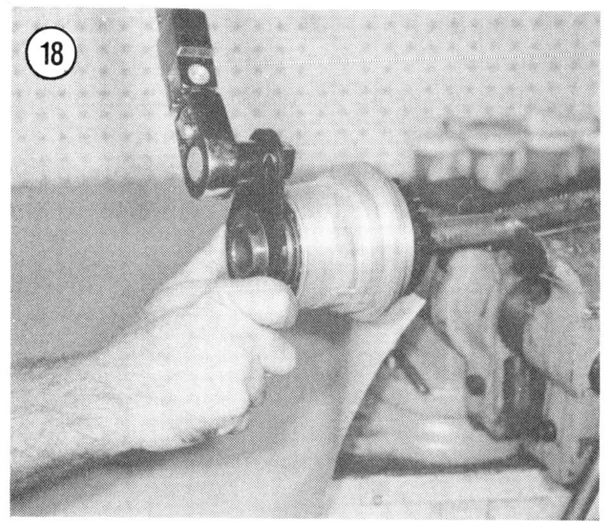

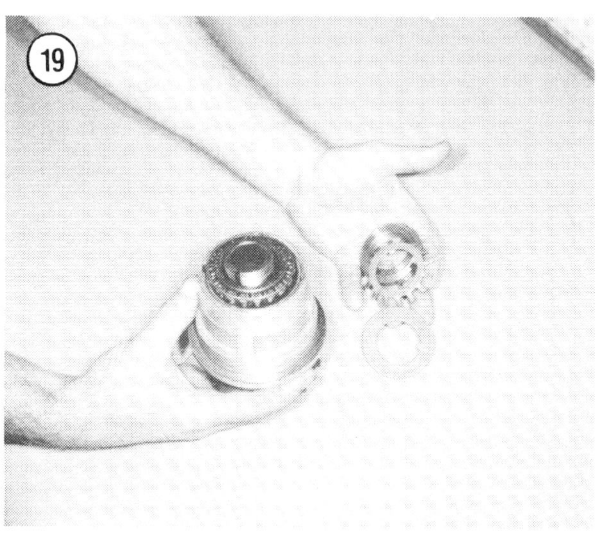

old pin and install a new one with driver part No. 912270 or equivalent. Pin height should be 0.340 in. (8.64 mm) from casting when properly installed. See **Figure 16**.

Pinion Bearing Carrier Disassembly

Refer to **Figure 3** for this procedure.

1. Clamp drive shaft spline socket (part No. 314438) horizontally in a vise and fit the bearing carrier on its end.
2. Straighten the lockwasher tab with a punch and hammer (**Figure 17**).
3. Use spanner wrench part No. 912272 and a 1/2 in. breaker bar to loosen the bearing carrier nut (**Figure 18**).
4. Remove the carrier nut, retainer and washer (**Figure 19**).
5. Press the single piece gear and shaft assembly from the lower bearing (**Figure 20**).
6. Do not remove pinion shaft bearing unless damaged. If removal is necessary, use a universal bearing separator (**Figure 21**).
7. Check the bearing cup at each end of the carrier (**Figure 22**). Do not remove cup(s) unless replacement is necessary (replace cup if bearing requires replacement). If replacement is necessary, use holding block part No. 912278, puller part No. 391259 and puller jaws part No. 391012.

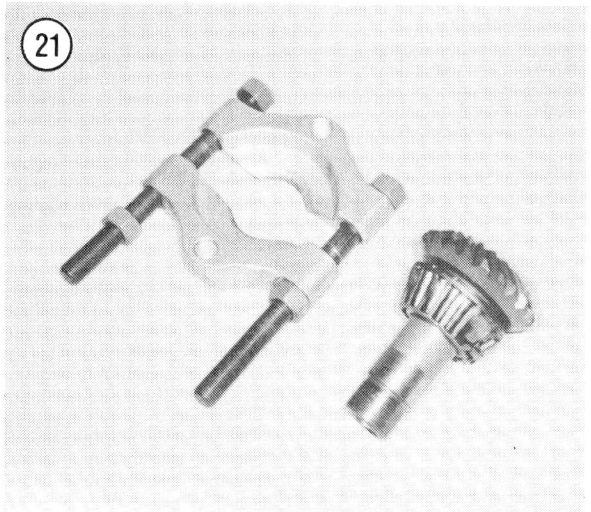

Pinion Bearing Carrier Cleaning and Inspection

1. Clean all parts in solvent and blow dry with compressed air. If bearings are washed with solvent, re-wash with soapy water to prevent scoring and pitting after unit reassembly.
2. Check carrier housing shim surface for burrs or nicks that could affect shim readings.
3. If bearing cups are removed, check the housing seats for galling.
4. Check bearings and cups for pitting, corrosion and signs of overheating (discoloration).

Pinion Bearing Carrier Assembly

Refer to **Figure 3** for this procedure.

1. If large carrier bearing cup was removed, install a new cup with combination installer part No. 912276 and a hydraulic press.
2. If small carrier bearing cup was removed, install a new cup with combination installer part No. 912276 and a hydraulic press.
3. If large pinion bearing was removed, lubricate the inside diameter of a new bearing with OMC Hi-Vis Gear Lubricant. Place bearing on combination installer part No. 912276 and press the shaft in place until the gear seats on the bearing.
4. Position carrier on pinion shaft. Lightly lubricate the inside diameter of the small bearing and place it on the shaft. Insert installer part No. 314429 inside the center of side "A" of combination installer part No. 912276. Use of part No. 314429 is required to limit bearing depth; substitute tools used in this step will not offer this safeguard and premature bearing failure is likely.
5. Install bearing on carrier assembly with a hydraulic press until the tool seats.
6. Spray OMC Locquic Primer on the shaft and spanner nut threads, then let the components dry.
7. When shaft and spanner nut threads are dry, apply OMC Ultra Lock adhesive on the nut threads. Install the washer and retainer on the shaft, then position the nut with its beveled edge facing the carrier and thread the nut onto the shaft manually as far as it will go.
8. Clamp drive shaft spline socket (part No. 314438) horizontally in a vise and fit the bearing carrier on its end. Lubricate the bearings with OMC Hi-Vis Gearcase Lubricant. Use spanner wrench part No. 912272 and a 1/2 in. breaker bar to tighten

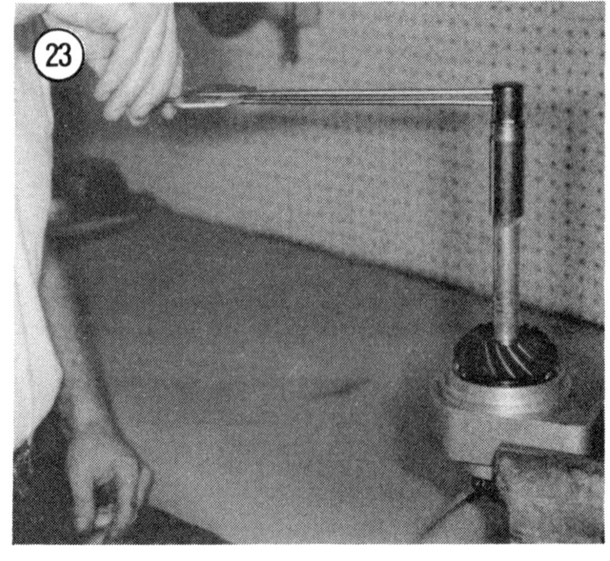

the bearing carrier nut (**Figure 18**) while rotating the carrier until all end play is removed from the shaft.

9. Remove the bearing carrier from the spline socket. Remove the spline socket from the vise. Clamp holding block part No. 912278 in the vise and insert the carrier assembly.

10. Attach drive shaft spline socket part No. 314438 to an inch-pound torque wrench. Fit the socket over the carrier nut and measure the rolling torque (torque required to turn pinion shaft). See **Figure 23**. The rolling torque should be 3-9 in.-lb., with 6 in.-lb. preferred for maximum bearing life.

11. If rolling torque is less than specified in Step 10:
   a. Tighten the carrier nut until it aligns with the next locking tab recess. Recheck torque.
   b. Continue this procedure one locking tab recess at a time until the torque reading is within specifications.

12. If rolling torque is greater than specified in Step 10:
   a. Remove the nut, retainer and washer.
   b. Remove the holding block with carrier assembly from the vise and position in a hydraulic press.
   c. Use an appropriate socket or tool to slightly press the shaft deeper in the carrier.
   d. Remove the assembly from the press, reinstall in the vise and repeat the torque measurement after reinstalling the washer, retainer and nut with OMC Ultra Lock.
   e. Repeat this step until the rolling torque is within specifications.

13. When rolling torque is correct, bend one of the retainer tabs into one of the nut's locking recesses.

14. Remove the carrier assembly from the holding block. Remove the holding block from the vise.

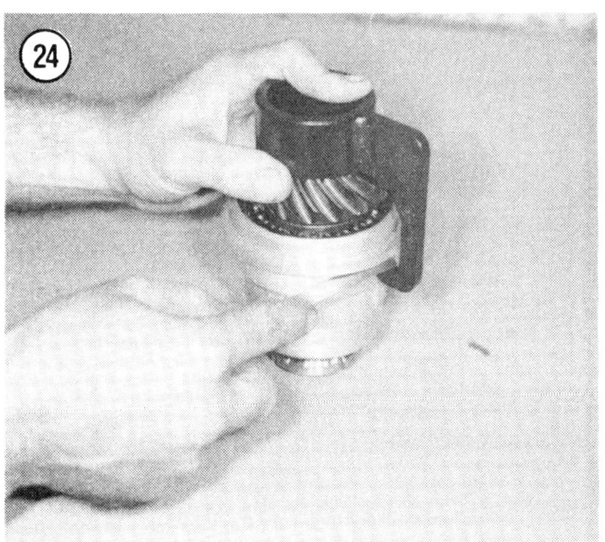
24

Pinion Bearing Carrier Shimming

The bearing carrier assembly must be properly shimmed to correctly position the pinion gear vertically relative to the horizontal drive gear. If proper shimming is not accomplished, the tooth contact pattern of the gears will be incorrect and service life of the gears will be reduced.

1. Install shim gauge part No. 912290 on the top of the gear teeth flats.

2. Measure the clearance between the underneath of the carrier rim and the tool arm with a flat feeler gauge. See **Figure 24**. 12

3. Subtract 0.020 in. from the measurement obtained in Step 2. The remainder will be the thickness of the shim(s) required to position the carrier assembly properly. As an example, suppose that the clearance measured was 0.025 in. Subtracting 0.020 in. from that measurement leaves 0.005 in. as the thickness of the shim pack to be installed on the carrier seat inside the housing.

Universal Joint Disassembly/Assembly

While complete U-joint disassembly is not required, it is always a good idea to replace the bearings and spider whenever the assembly is out of the upper gear housing for service.

Refer to **Figure 25** for this procedure.

1. Place universal joint assembly over a suitable support and remove the snap rings with a punch and hammer.
2. Install an automotive-type U-joint tool and a suitable size socket as shown in **Figure 26**. Tighten the tool to apply pressure on one bearing cap and force the other one into the socket. If the tool is not available, support the yoke between a pair of appropriate size sockets and apply pressure with a hydraulic press on one bearing cap until the opposite one is pressed into the socket, then remove the one free bearing cap.
3. Rotate the tool 180° and repeat Step 2 to press the 2nd bearing cap into the adapter, then remove the yoke.
4. Repeat Steps 1-3 to remove the remaining bearings. Remove the spider.
5. Repeat Steps 1-4 to remove the second spider/yoke assembly.
6. Position the bearing caps, yoke and cross as shown in **Figure 27**. Make sure the cross is installed with its grease fitting facing the coupling end yoke.
7. Press both bearing caps into the yoke and onto the cross, then install new C-rings (**Figure 28**).
8. Repeat Step 6 and Step 7 to install the remaining bearings.
9. Repeat Steps 6-8 to install the second spider/yoke assembly.

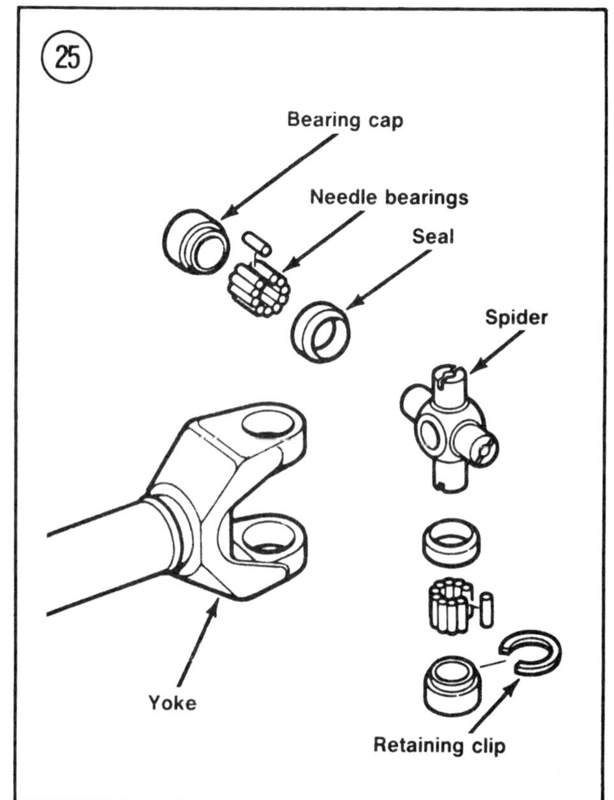

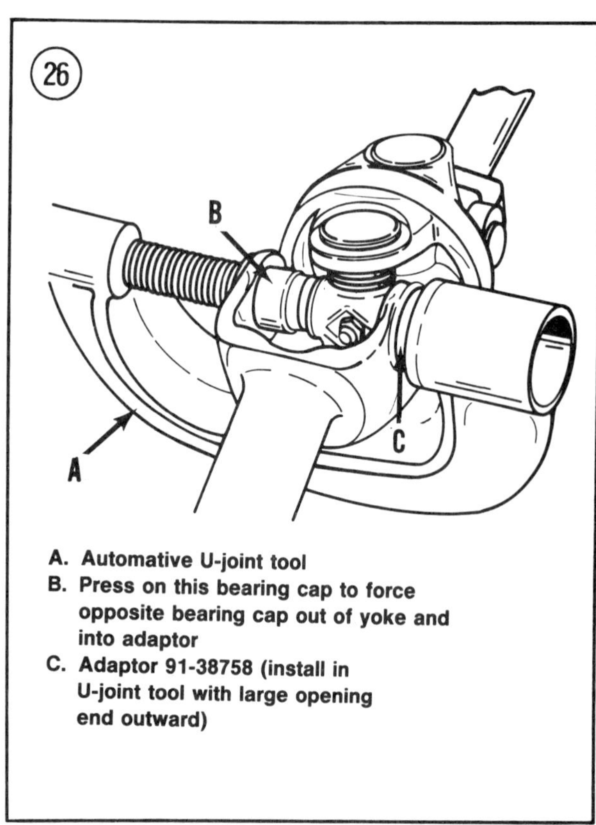

A. Automative U-joint tool
B. Press on this bearing cap to force opposite bearing cap out of yoke and into adaptor
C. Adaptor 91-38758 (install in U-joint tool with large opening end outward)

Universal Joint Shaft Disassembly

Refer to **Figure 3** for this procedure.

1. Separate the U-joint shaft from the drive shaft at the yoke nearest the bearing carrier as described in this chapter.
2. Remove the small impeller shaft bearing (**Figure 29**) using a universal bearing separator as a press plate. Install remover/installer part No. 912269 (shown in

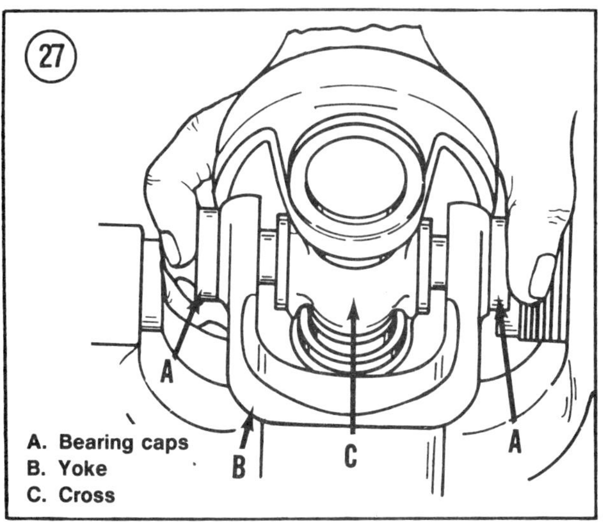

A. Bearing caps
B. Yoke
C. Cross

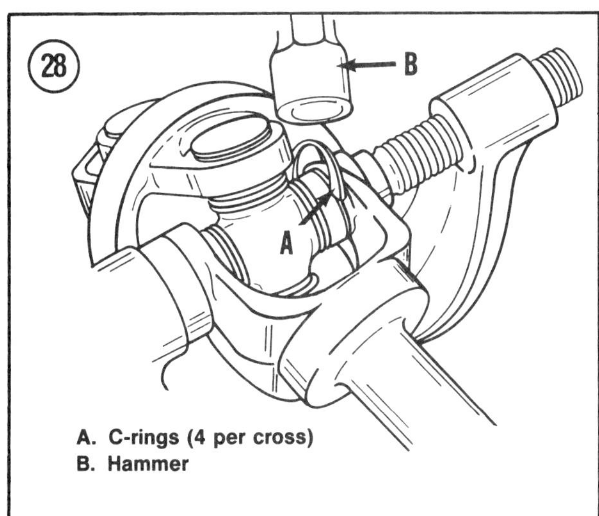

A. C-rings (4 per cross)
B. Hammer

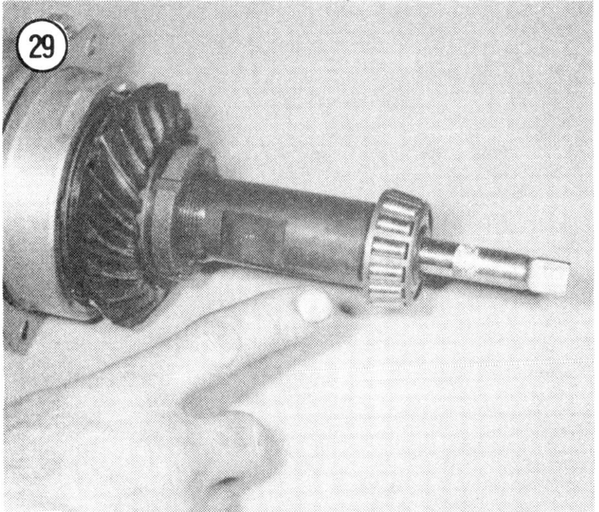

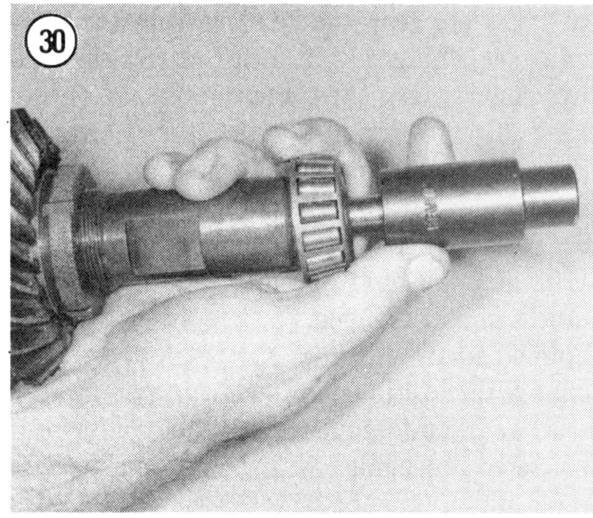

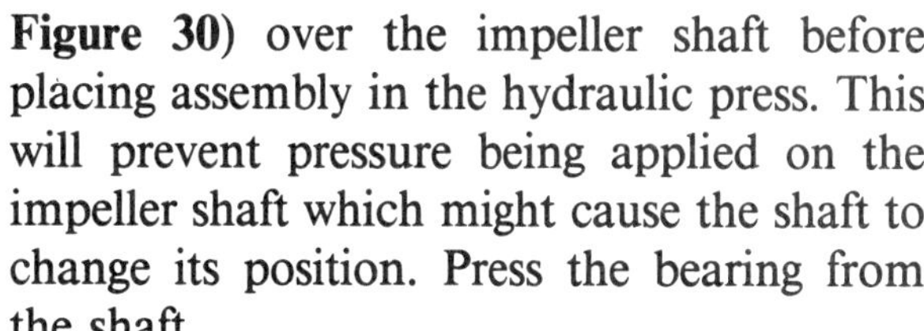
Figure 30) over the impeller shaft before placing assembly in the hydraulic press. This will prevent pressure being applied on the impeller shaft which might cause the shaft to change its position. Press the bearing from the shaft.

3. Cut a 2 7/8 in. piece of one-inch diameter pipe to make a yoke support. Install pipe in yoke ears.

CAUTION

The spanner nut to be removed in Step 4 is installed with OMC Ultra Lock and torqued to 200 ft.-lb. Use caution in removing this nut and apply heat if necessary to loosen the adhesive.

4. Insert the yoke (with yoke support installed) in a vise and clamp securely. Install spanner wrench part No. 912272 on the spanner nut and use a 3/4 in. breaker bar to break the nut loose and remove it. See **Figure 31**.

5. Install remover/installer part No. 912269 over the impeller shaft with the small diameter end of tool facing the gear. Support the bearing carrier in a hydraulic press and press the shaft from the carrier, holding one hand under the shaft to catch it as it is pressed free.

6. Press the gear and bearing from the shaft with a universal bearing separator and hydraulic press. See **Figure 32**. It is not necessary to separate the gear from the bearing unless one or the other requires replacement.
7. The impeller shaft is pressed into the U-joint shaft and should not be removed unless it is damaged. Unnecessary pressure applied to the impeller shaft will cause it to change its position. This will cause premature seal wear and may prevent the shaft from properly engaging with the impeller. If replacement is necessary:
   a. Drill a hole through the impeller shaft, attach a suitable puller and remove the impeller shaft from the U-joint shaft.
   b. Lightly lubricate a new impeller shaft with OMC Hi-Vis Gearcase Lubricant.
   c. Fit remover/installer part No. 912269 on U-joint shaft large end down.
   d. Insert new impeller shaft in remover/installer tool and press in until the shaft is flush with the end of the tool.
   e. Install the small impeller shaft bearing as described in *Universal Joint Shaft Assembly.*
8. Clean and inspect all parts as described in this chapter.

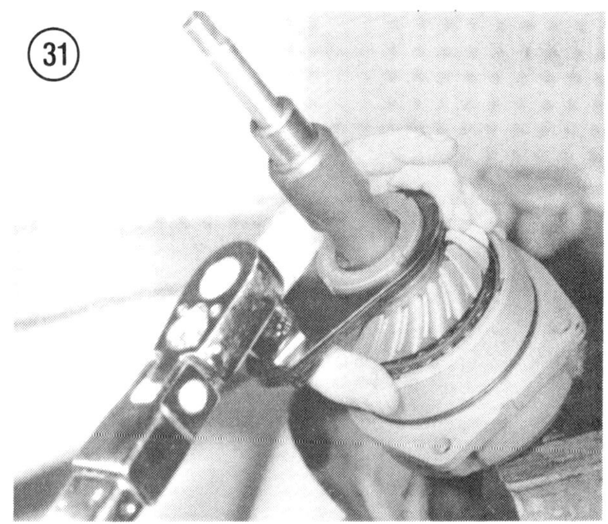

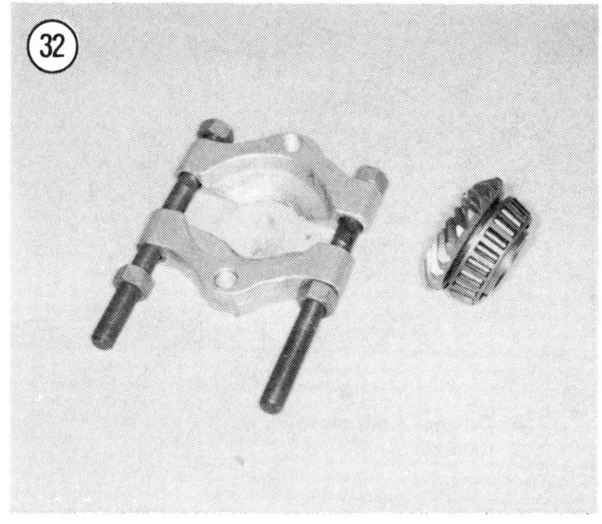

Universal Joint Shaft Assembly

Refer to **Figure 3** for this procedure.
1. Position the carrier on the drive gear bearing. After lightly lubricating the bearing rollers and U-joint shaft splines with OMC Hi-Vis Gearcase Lubricant, insert the shaft into the gear.

NOTE
The bearing will not fit tightly in the carrier when the shaft is fully seated in the gear in Step 2. Carrier movement up to 1/8 in. is to be expected.

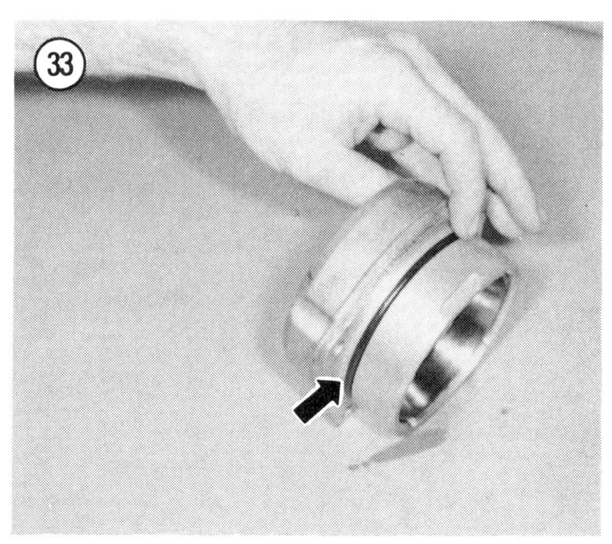

2. Support the gear and carrier assembly in a press and press the shaft into the gear until fully seated.
3. Spray OMC Locquic Primer on the shaft and spanner nut threads, then let the components dry.
4. With support tube installed in yoke, clamp the U-joint assembly in a vise.
5. Slip the centering cone onto the shaft. Seat cone tightly in the gear, using a suitable drift and mallet if necessary.
6. When shaft and spanner nut threads are dry, apply OMC Ultra Lock adhesive on the nut threads. Position the nut with its beveled edge facing the gear and thread the nut onto the shaft manually as far as it will go.
7. Attach a torque wrench to spanner wrench part No. 912272 and tighten nut to 200 ft.-lb. (271 N•m). See **Figure 31**.
8. Wipe the inner diameter of a new small bearing with OMC Hi-Vis Gearcase Lubricant.
9. Place bearing installer part No. 912269 in a press with its large end facing upward.
10. Wipe impeller shaft with OMC Extreme Pressure Grease and insert U-joint shaft into bearing and tool. Press shaft into bearing until the shaft is fully seated.

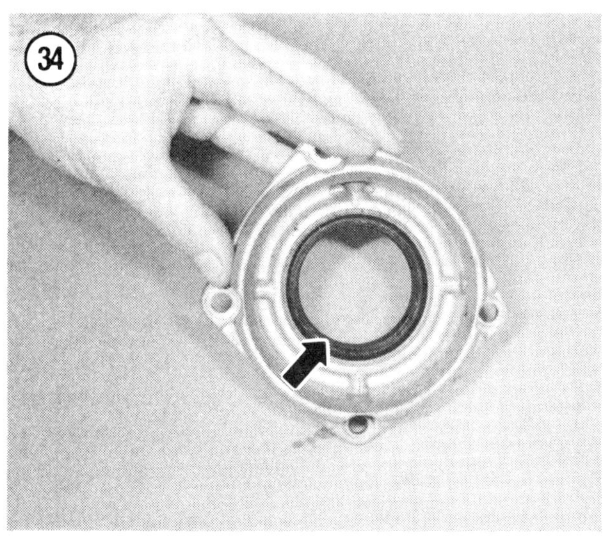

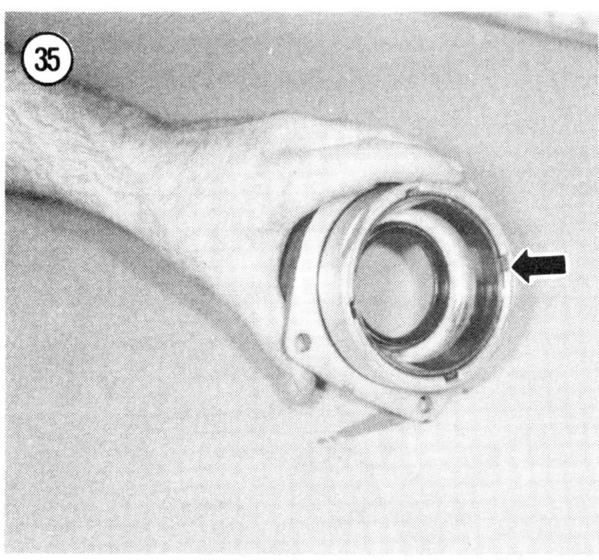

Universal Bearing Carrier Disassembly/Assembly

Refer to **Figure 3** for this procedure.
1. Remove and discard the carrier O-ring (**Figure 33**).
2. Remove the seal from the carrier (arrow, **Figure 34**) with installer part No. 912287 and a hydraulic press. Seal must be pressed out from the side shown in **Figure 34**.
3. If bearing cup (arrow, **Figure 35**) requires replacement, clamp the carrier housing in a vise with protective jaws and use a suitable 3-jaw puller to remove the cup. Make sure the jaws expand snugly behind the cup or the carrier may be damaged.
4. Clean and inspect all components as described in this chapter.
5. If the drive gear bearing was removed:
   a. Lightly lubricate the inner diameter of a new bearing.
   b. Position the gear in the press and place the bearing on top of the gear.
   c. Place the "A" side of combination installer tool part No. 912276 against the bearing.
   d. Press the bearing on the gear until it seats.

6. If the bearing cup was removed:
   a. Place the carrier in a hydraulic press.
   b. Lightly lubricate the outside of the new cup and place it on the carrier.
   c. Place the "A" side of combiantion installer tool part No. 912276 toward the cup.
   d. Press the cup into the carrier until it seats.
7. Position a new seal on installer part No. 912286 with its lip facing away from the tool. Wipe the seal case with OMC Gasket Sealing Compound.
8. Position the carrier upward in a hydraulic press. Install the seal with installer tool and coat the lips with OMC Triple-Guard grease.
9. Check the bearing carrier fit in the upper gear housing. If the carrier cannot be inserted freely in the housing, it is probably out-of-round and should be replaced.

Universal Joint Shaft and Bearing Carrier Cleaning and Inspection

1. Clean all parts in fresh solvent. Blow dry with compressed air.
2. Inspect bearing carrier for defects that would cut the O-ring and/or prevent proper sealing. Check seal bore for nicks or gouges and correct as required. If bearing cup was removed, check cup bore for the same defects as the seal bore.
3. Check the drive gear, bearings and cups for signs of corrosion, chipping, cracks, metal transfer or heat discoloration.

NOTE

If wear or corrosion is found in Step 4 or Step 5, also check engine coupling splines for the same defect.

4. Inspect coupling and gear end of U-joint for spline wear.
5. Clean all corrosion from the coupling. Replace coupling yoke if splines are partially corroded away.
6. Check the drive gear for pitting, excessive wear and chipped or broken teeth. See **Figure 36**. Replace gear if any of these defects are noted.
7. Inspect bearing cups for pitting, scoring, grooving, heat discoloration or embedded metallic particles. Replace bearing and cup if any defect is found.
8. Check condition of shim(s). Replace any that are damaged.

Universal Joint Shaft Assembly Shimming

The universal joint shaft assembly must be properly shimmed and the bearing preload

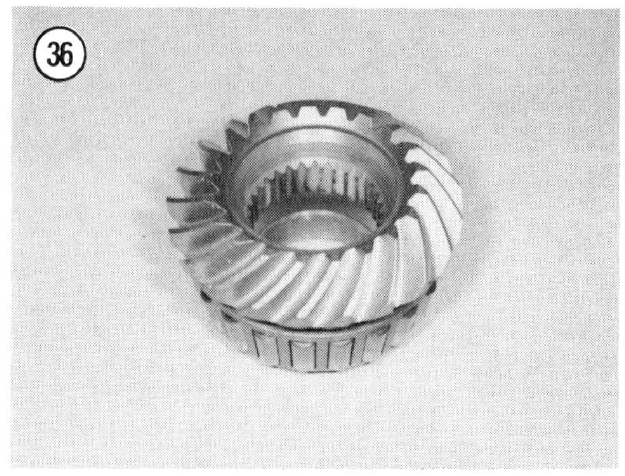

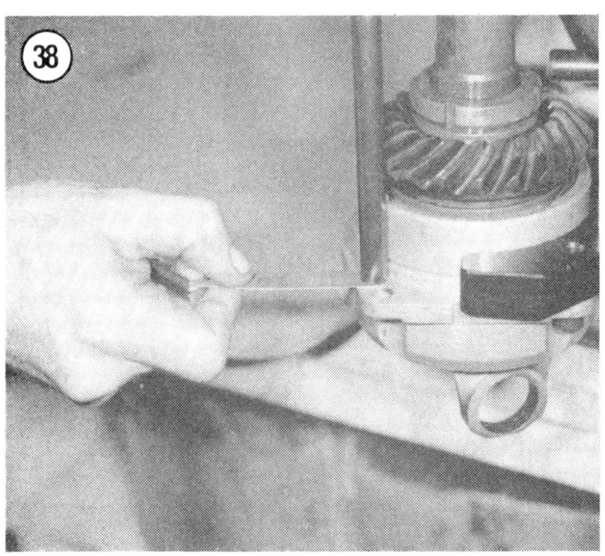

established before reinstalling the unit in the gear housing. OMC shim guage kit part No. 984329 is required for this procedure.

1. Remove the bearing carrier O-ring.
2. Place the bearing cup on the rear bearing and slide the shim fixture center adapter in place without any shimming installed.
3. Position the shaft and carrier in the fixture frame. Rotate the carrier until the 3 screw holes are aligned, then install the carrier to the frame and tighten the screws securely.
4. Tighten the preload screw until it reaches the shaft reference groove, then tighten the preload screw locknut. Rotate the shaft at least 4 full turns to seat the bearing rollers.
5. Clamp the fixture frame assembly in a vertical position with a vise. Read the gear ratio stamped on the bearing carrier and choose the correct gauge rod required for shimming the rear bearing cup to set drive gear location.
6. Install the proper rod selected in Step 5 in the inner hole of the center adapter. Tighten the screw securely and measure the clearance between the rod and one flat on the top of a gear tooth with a flat feeler gauge as shown in **Figure 37**.
7. Subtract the measurement obtained in Step 6 from 0.020 in. The remainder is the thickness of the shim pack required behind the small bearing cup. For example, if the measurement in Step 6 is 0.007 in., subtract it from 0.020 in. The remainder will be 0.013 in. or the shim pack thickness.
8. To set bearing preload, remove the rod used in Step 6 and place the long gauge rod in the outer adapter hole. Measure the clearance between the rod end and the carrier flange with a flat feeler gauge as shown in **Figure 38**.
9. The necessary shim pack thickness for correct bearing preload is determined in two steps:
   a. Add the measurement obtained in Step 8 to the thickness of the shim pack as determined in Step 7. For example, if the measurement in Step 8 is 0.021 in., you would add 0.021 in. and 0.013 in. to obtain a total of 0.034 in.
   b. Subtract 0.020 in. from the total obtained above. This would leave 0.014 in. or the correct shim pack thickness required for proper bearing preload.

Upper Gear Housing Assembly

Refer to **Figure 3** for this procedure.

12

1. If the water tube and cover was removed:
   a. Coat both sides of a new gasket with OMC Gasket Sealing Compound. Install the gasket in the housing.
   b. Wipe cover screw threads with OMC Gasket Sealing Compound. Position cover on gasket. Install and tighten screws to 12-14 ft.-lb. (16-19 N•m).
   c. Install a new seal in the cover (sealer is not required).
   d. Install water tube in cover with a twisting motion until fully seated.
2. Install the shim pack as determined in the rear bearing cup seat bore. Lubricate the outer diameter of the bearing cup and place it in its seat. Install cup with universal puller part No. 378103.

3. Install the pinion bearing carrier shim pack on the carrier seat in the housing. The locating lugs on the carrier housing must align with the locating slots in the housing (**Figure 39**). Lubricate the lugs and slots.

4. Place the housing on its side and insert the intermediate shaft in the carrier assembly. Use the intermediate shaft as a handle and insert the carrier assembly in the housing with the lugs and slots aligned. When the assembly is properly seated, the lockring threads will be fully visible and the top of the gear teeth will be 3.1 in. below the surface of the gear housing cover.

5. Wipe the lockring threads with OMC Hi-Vis Gear Lubricant and start the lockring in the housing threads (**Figure 40**). Install spanner tool part No. 984330 (**Figure 13**) on the lockring and tighten it by hand.

6. Attach the tension arm on the top of the gear housing with 2 of the cover screws and torque the lockring to 145-165 ft.-lb. (197-224 N•m). See **Figure 41**.

7. Reassemble the drive shaft to the upper bearing yoke. See *Universal Joint Diassembly/Assembly* in this chapter.

8. Fit the preload shims on the bearing carrier flange. Align the carrier and shim notches. Coat a new O-ring with OMC Gasket Sealing Compound and install it on the carrier.

9. Install the U-joint shaft assembly in the housing (**Figure 42**).

10. Wipe the carrier mounting screw threads with OMC Gasket Sealing Compound. Make sure the bearing carrier O-ring is seated, then install the mounting screws. Tighten the screws (**Figure 43**) to 12-14 ft.-lb. (16-19 N•m), then rotate the U-joint shaft at least 4 full turns to seat the bearings and permit accurate backlash checks.

11. Attach a dial indicator to the gear housing so that the indicator pin will contact the center of a gear tooth to a radius of 1.58

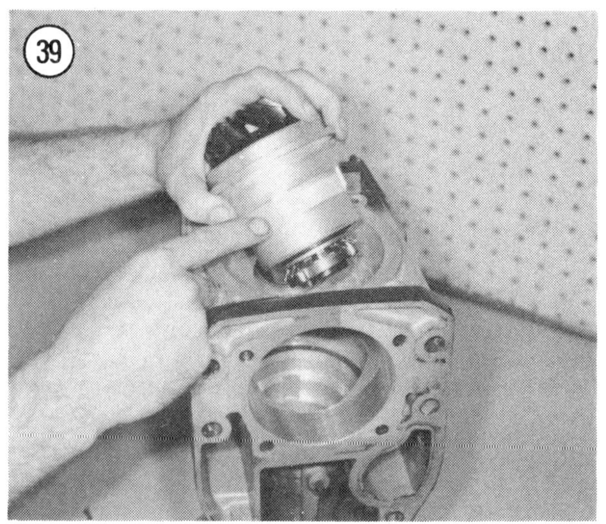

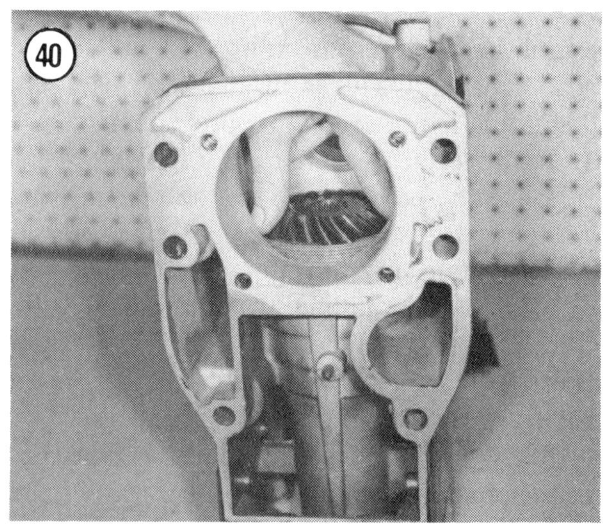

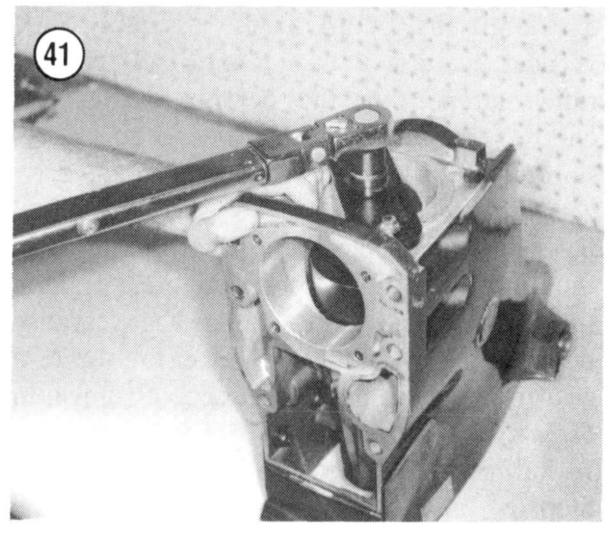

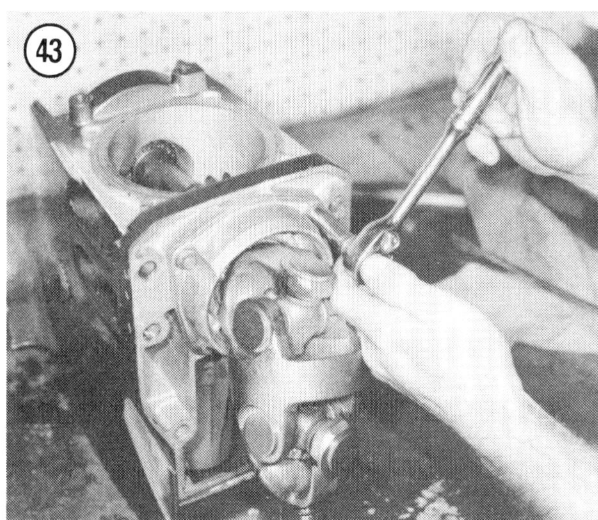

in. from the centerline of the U-joint shaft. Set the indicator to zero.

12. Rotate the shaft back and forth slowly to let the gear teeth make contact in each direction. Maximum backlash reading should be 0.009-0.015 in. (0.23-0.38 mm). If backlash is excessive, subtract 0.012 in. (mid-range or desired backlash) from the measured backlash. If backlash is insufficient, subtract the measured backlash from 0.012 in. (mid-range or desired backlash).

   a. For example, suppose the measured backlash is 0.022 in., subtracting the desired backlash of 0.012 in. would leave 0.010 in. as the amount of change required. To decrease backlash in our example, subtract 0.005 in. shims from behind the rear bearing cup and 0.005 in. shims from the U-joint bearing carrier, then add 0.005 in. shims under the pinion bearing carrier. Subtracting the shims will move the drive gear to the rear and adding the shims will move the pinion up.

   b. If the measured backlash is less than the desired mid-range, the amount of change required would be the difference between the measured backlash and the desired backlash. For example, suppose the measured backlash is 0.006 in. and the desired backlash is 0.012 in. The difference between these two is 0.006 in. To increase backlash to the desired mid-range, add 0.003 in. shims behind the rear bearing cup and and 0.003 in. shims behind the U-joint bearing carrier, then subtract 0.003 in. shims from under the pinion bearing carrier. Adding the shims will move the drive gear to the front and subtracting the shims will move the pinion down.

13. Position the gear housing in a mounting fixture to allow the U-joint shaft to hang vertically. Insert the intermediate drive shaft into the pinion carrier. Install spline socket

part No. 311875 to the intermediate drive shaft and connect a 0-50 inch-pound torque wrench.

14. Rotate the drive shaft fast enough to obtain a steady needle reading. The rolling torque should be 4-20 in.-lb. If rolling torque is not within specifications:
   a. Recheck and adjust gear backlash as required.
   b. If gear backlash is within specifications, add (to decrease) or subtract (to increase) shimming from under the U-joint carrier flange.

15. Reinstall the water pump. See Chapter Ten.

16. Wipe a new O-ring with OMC Gasket Sealing Compound and position it on the upper gear housing cover.

17. Install the cover to the upper gear housing **(Figure 44).** Wipe screw threads with OMC Gasket Sealing Compound and tighten to 12-14 in.-lb. (16-19 N•m).

18. Reinstall the rear gear housing cover. Wipe the screw threads with OMC Gasket Sealing Compound and tighten to 108-132 in.-lb. (12-15 N•m).

Table 1 TIGHTENING TORQUES

Fastener	in.-lb.	ft.-lb.	N•m
Oil level indicator		10-12	14-16
Pinion bearing carrier lockring		145-165	197-224
Pivot housing mounting nuts		50	68
Rear housing cover	108-132		12-15
Upper gear housing cover screws		12-14	16-19
U-joint carrier screws		12-14	16-19
Water pump			
Adaptor housing		12-14	16-19
Cover screws	108-132		12-15
Water tube cover		12-14	16-19

Chapter Thirteen

Gearcase Housing (Lower Unit)

Engine torque passes through a drive shaft/universal joint to a pinion and drive gear in the drive shaft (upper) housing, changing the horizontal power flow from the engine into a vertical power flow sent to the gearcase (lower) housing through a drive shaft.

Power application is controlled by shifting the gearcase housing. This is accomplished through a shift rod connected between the engine and drive shaft housing. The engine shift rod is connected by a shift cable to the remote control box, providing shift control at the helm. A fitting in the drive shaft housing transmits horizontal motion of the engine shift rod to a vertical shift shaft which extends to the shift mechanism on the gearcase propeller shaft.

When the unit is shifted into gear, a sliding clutch (clutch dog) in the gearcase engages a FORWARD or REVERSE gear on the propeller shaft, moving the selected gear into contact with the pinion gear on the vertical drive shaft. This creates a direct coupling that changes the power flow back to horizontal movement of the propeller shaft. When the shift mechanism is in NEUTRAL, the sliding clutch does not engage with either gear, so the propeller shaft does not rotate.

Since the clutch dog and drive shaft pinion gear are the central components in the shift operation, they are prone to the greatest amount of wear. The forward gear also receives more wear than the REVERSE gear.

The gearcase housing can be removed from the drive shaft housing for service without removing the entire stern drive from the boat. This chapter covers the removal, overhaul and installation of the Cobra and King Cobra gearcase housings.

Table 1 is at the end of the chapter.

FASTENER REMOVAL

Elastic stop nuts should never be used more than twice. It is a good idea to replace such nuts with new ones each time they are removed. Never use worn-out stop nuts or non-locking nuts.

SERVICE PRECAUTIONS

Whenever you work on a stern drive unit, there are several precautions to keep in mind that will make your work easier, faster and more accurate.

1. Use special tools where noted. In some cases, it may be possible to perform the procedure with makeshift tools, but this procedure is not recommended. The use of makeshift tools can damage the components and may cause serious personal injury.
2. Use a vise with protective jaws to hold housings or components. If protective jaws are not available, insert blocks of soft wood on either side of the part(s) before clamping them in the vise.
3. Remove and install pressed-on parts with an appropriate mandrel, support and hydraulic press. Do not try to pry, hammer or otherwise force them on or off.
4. Refer to the appropriate table at the end of the chapter for torque values, if not given in the text. Proper torque is vital to assure long life and service from stern drive components.
5. Apply OMC Gasket Sealing Compound or Perfect Seal to the outer surfaces of all bearing carrier, retainer and housing mating surfaces during reassembly. Do *not* allow Gasket Sealing Compound or Perfect Seal to touch O-rings or enter the bearings or gears.
6. Apply OMC Triple-Guard grease to all O-rings and seal lips.
7. Apply Loctite Type A on the outside diameter of all metal case oil seals.
8. Keep a record of all shims and where they came from. As soon as the shims are removed, inspect them for damage and write down their thickness and location. Wire the shims together for reassembly and place them in a safe place. Follow shimming instructions closely. If gear backlash is not properly set, the unit will be noisy and suffer premature gear failure. Incorrect bearing preload will result in premature bearing failure.
9. Work in a clean area where there is good lighting and sufficient space for components to be stored. Keep an ample number of containers available for storing small parts. Cover parts with clean shop cloths when you are not working with them.
10. Wear safety glasses when removing and installing snap rings. Snap rings tend to be brittle and can snap at any time, even if new.

COBRA DRIVE

The Cobra mechanical gearcase is quite similar in design to the 400/800 gearcase used with 1978-1986 OMC stern drive units. **Figure 1** is an exploded view of 2.3L, 2.5L and 3.0L gearcase housing. **Figure 2** shows the 4.3L, 5.0L, 5.7L, 5.8L and 7.5L gearcase housing components.

Early model gearcases use a horse-shoe design anode (7, **Figure 1**). Late model gearcases use a solid design anode (7, **Figure 2**). The 460 cu. in. (7.5L) King Cobra uses a two-piece water intake screen (25, **Figure 2**). The major difference in design between the 460 cu. in. (7.5L) King Cobra gearcase and the gearcase used on all other models is found in the propeller shaft bearing housing. The gearcase used on all models except 460 cu. in. (7.5L) King Cobra uses a retainer plate and 2 large snap rings not found in the 460 cu. in. (7.5L) King Cobra unit.

The Cobra and King Cobra gearcases contain the drive shaft, drive shaft bearing housing, pinion gear/bearing, shift mechanism, sliding clutch dog, FORWARD and REVERSE gears and propeller shaft/ bearing housing. See **Figure 1** and **Figure 2** for components and relationships.

Lower Gearcase Removal

The stern drive should be removed from the boat to remove the lower gearcase housing.

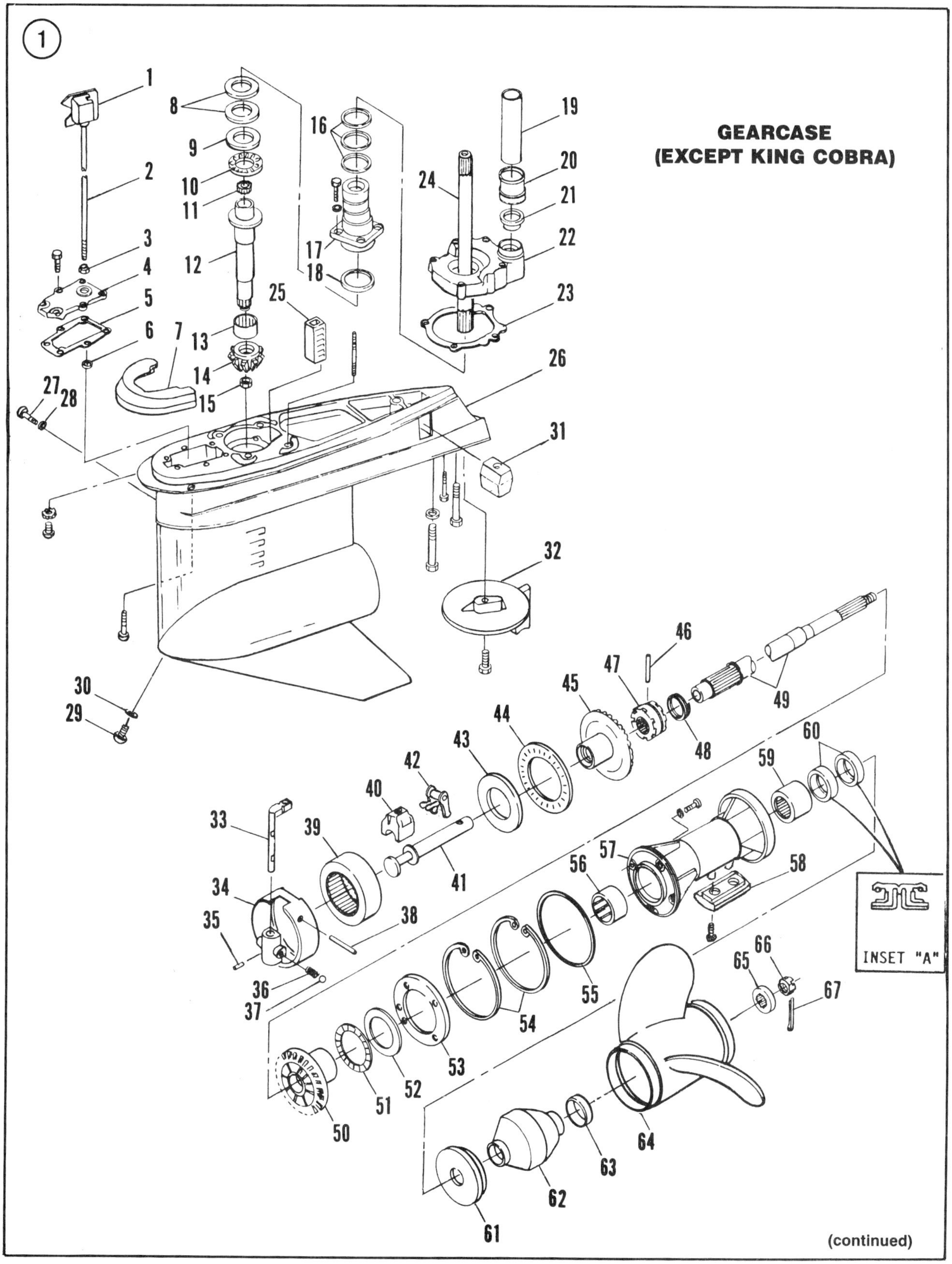

(1)

GEARCASE (EXCEPT KING COBRA)

INSET "A"

(continued)

(continued)

2.3L, 2.5L AND 3.0L GEARCASE

1. Shift rod end
2. Shift rod
3. Shift rod wiper
4. Cover and seal assembly
5. Shift rod cover gasket
6. O-ring
7. Anode
8. Shims
9. Pinion thrust washer
10. Pinion thrust bearing
11. Support shaft plug
12. Drive shaft
13. Pinion bearing
14. Pinion gear
15. Pinion gear to drive shaft nut
16. O-rings
17. Bearing housing
18. O-ring
19. Water tube
20. Water tube guide
21. Seal
22. Water passage housing
23. Water passage housing gasket
24. Drive shaft
25. Water intake screen
26. Gearcase
27. Fill plug
28. Nylon washer
29. Drain screw
30. Washer
31. Anode
32. Gearcase trim tab
33. Shifter detent
34. Housing
35. Housing pin
36. Detent spring
37. Detent ball
38. Shift lever pin
39. Needle bearing (Integral with housing [34] on 1988 and 1989 models)
40. Shifter cradle
41. Shifter shaft
42. Shift lever
43. Forward gear thrust washer
44. Forward gear thrust bearing
45. Forward gear
46. Clutch dog pin
47. Clutch dog
48. Clutch dog pin spring
49. Propeller shaft
50. Reverse gear
51. Reverse gear thrust bearing
52. Reverse gear thrust washer
53. Bearing housing retainer plate
54. Retainer rings
55. O-ring
56. Needle bearing
57. Bearing housing
58. Anode
59. Needle bearing
60. Seals
61. Thrust bushing
62. Propeller bushing
63. Bushing sleeve
64. Propeller
65. Propeller nut spacer
66. Propeller nut
67. Propeller nut cotter pin

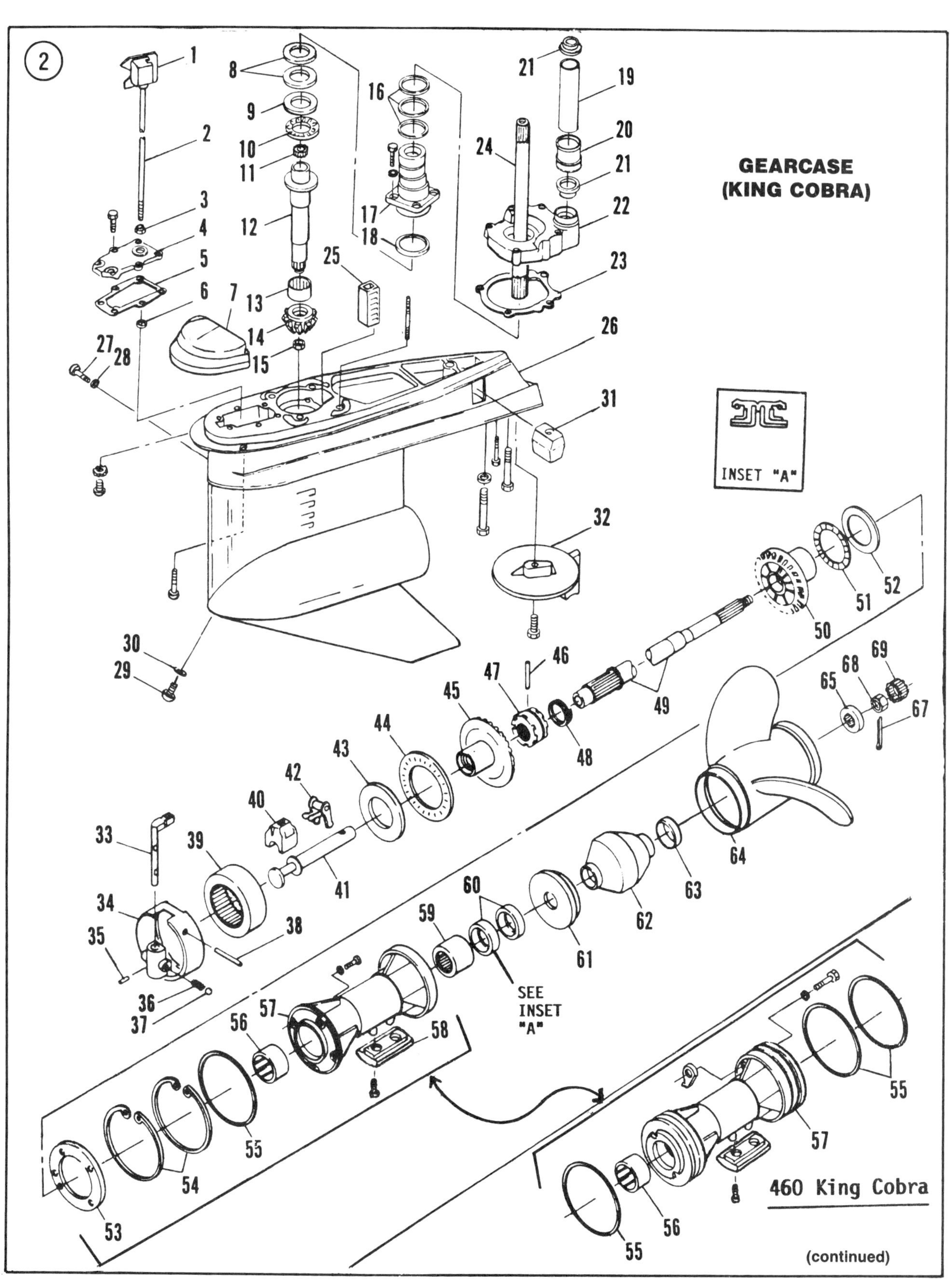
2
GEARCASE
(KING COBRA)
INSET "A"
SEE
INSET
"A"
460 King Cobra
1
2
3
4
5
6
7
8
9
10
11
12
13
14
15
16
17
18
19
20
21
22
23
24
25
26
27
28
29
30
31
32
33
34
35
36
37
38
39
40
41
42
43
44
45
46
47
48
49
50
51
52
53
54
55
56
57
58
59
60
61
62
63
64
65
67
68
69

(continued)

(2) (continued)

4.3L, 5.0L, 5.7L, 5.8L AND 7.5L GEARCASE

1. Shift rod end
2. Shift rod
3. Shift rod wiper
4. Cover and seal assembly
5. Shift rod cover gasket
6. O-ring
7. Anode
8. Shims
9. Pinion thrust washer
10. Pinion thrust bearing
11. Support shaft plug
12. Drive shaft
13. Pinion bearing
14. Pinion gear
15. Pinion gear to drive shaft nut
16. O-rings
17. Bearing housing
18. O-ring
19. Water tube
20. Water tube guide
21. Seal
22. Water passage housing
23. Water passage housing gasket
24. Drive shaft
25. Water intake screen
26. Gearcase
27. Fill plug
28. Nylon washer
29. Drain screw
30. Washer
31. Anode
32. Gearcase trim tab
33. Shifter detent
34. Housing
35. Housing pin
36. Detent spring
37. Detent ball
38. Shift lever pin
39. Needle bearing (Integral with housing [34] on 1988 and 1989 models)
40. Shifter cradle
41. Shifter shaft
42. Shift lever
43. Forward gear thrust washer
44. Forward gear thrust bearing
45. Forward gear
46. Clutch dog pin
47. Clutch dog
48. Clutch dog pin spring
49. Propeller shaft
50. Reverse gear
51. Reverse gear thrust bearing
52. Reverse gear thrust washer
53. Bearing housing retainer plate
54. Retainer rings
55. O-ring
56. Needle bearing
57. Bearing housing
58. Anode
59. Needle bearing
60. Seals
61. Thrust bushing
62. Propeller bushing
63. Bushing sleeve
64. Propeller
65. Propeller nut spacer
67. Cotter pin
68. Propeller nut
69. Propeller nut retainer

1. Place stern drive unit in a holding fixture to support the lower gearcase housing.
2. Remove the lifting eye from the upper gear housing. Leave the oil level hole open to vent the reservoir in Step 3.
3. Place a suitable container under the lower gearcase housing drain plug. Remove the drain plug and discard the nylon washer. Drain the lubricant from the lower gearcase housing.

NOTE
If metallic particles are found in Step 4, remove and disassemble both the upper and lower gearcase units to inspect for damaged oil seals, oil rings and/or housing cracks. Clean all parts in solvent and blow dry with compressed air. Check magnetic drain plug tip for metallic particles and clean before reinstallation.

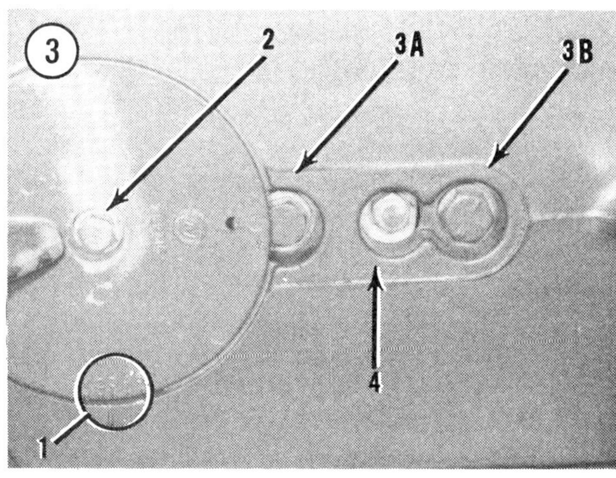

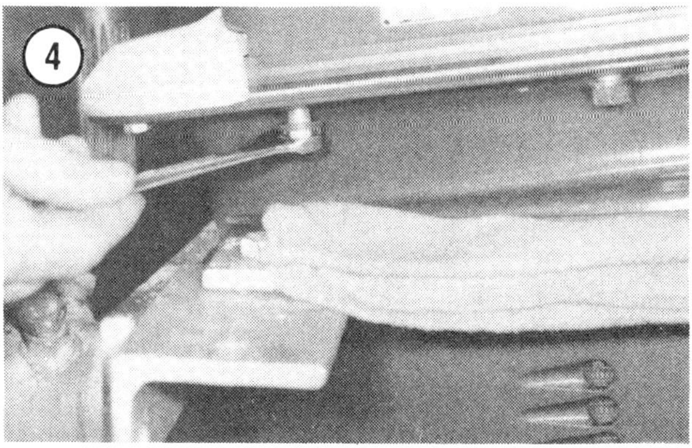

4. Wipe a small amount of lubricant on a finger and rub the finger and thumb together. Check for the presence of metallic particles.
5. Note color of gear lubricant. If white or cream in color, there is water in the lubricant. Inspect the drain container for signs of water separation from the lubricant.

NOTE
If there are no grid/index marks on the trim tab/gearcase housing, scribe one for reinstallation reference.

6. Note the alignment of the trim tab grid with the gearcase index mark for reinstallation reference (1, **Figure 3**). Remove the trim tab screw (2, **Figure 3**). Remove the trim tab.

NOTE
*On 2.3L, 2.5L, 3.0L and 7.5L models, one of the ventilation plate screws to be removed in Step 7 will be found inside the trim tab cavity. **Figure 3** shows the 4.3L, 5.0L, 5.7L and 5.8L gearcase.*

7. Remove the 2 ventilation plate screws (3, **Figure 3**). Do *not* remove the anode screw (4, **Figure 3**).
8. Unbolt the upper gear housing from the lower gearcase housing (**Figure 4**). The two units are now held together only by O-rings. Get a firm grasp on the upper gearcase and rock from side-to-side while pulling upward to break the seal.
9. Separate gear housing enough to disengage the shift rod head from the guide pin, then turn the shift rod head 90° to port (**Figure 5**) to allow it to clear the exhaust opening.
10. Lift the upper gear housing free of the lower gearcase housing (**Figure 6**) and place unit on a clean workbench surface.

13

Lower Gearcase Installation

1. Check the lower drive shaft to make sure the nylon plug is installed at the base of the

splines. Wipe the splines at each end of the intermediate drive shaft with OMC Hi-Vis Gearcase Lubricant and install in the lower drive shaft.

2. Make sure the shift rod head is positioned 90° to port for installation clearance.

3. Position the upper gear housing over the lower gearcase housing. Make sure the drive shaft and water tube seat at the same time as the upper gear housing is lowered in place. When the shift rod head appears in the exhaust opening, rotate the head enough to engage the guide pin. It may be necessary to turn the U-joint shaft slightly in order to engage the drive shaft splines. The housing should seat properly with only hand pressure.

4. Clean the gear housing mounting bolts in solvent, but do not wire brush or otherwise remove the yellow-green material on the bolt threads. This is a self-locking material to prevent the bolts from loosening. If the material is damaged or removed, install new bolts.

5. Wipe the threads of the short bolts with OMC Gasket Sealing Compound. Install and tighten evenly (**Figure 4**), then connect OMC wrench part No. 912031 to a torque wrench and tighten the bolts to 22-24 ft.-lb. (30-33 N•m).

6. Lightly wipe the ventilation plate bolt threads with OMC Gasket Sealing Compound. Install the flat washer under the large bolt (3, **Figure 3**). Tighten both bolts to 22-24 ft.-lb. (30-33 N•m).

7. Pressure and vacuum test the drive unit as described in this chapter. Pressurize to 3-6 psi and draw 3-5 in. Hg and 15 in. Hg vacuum to check the sealing of the upper gear housing and drive shaft bearing housing O-rings. The drive should not lose more than 1 psi or 1 in. Hg vacuum in 3 minutes.

8. Clean the trim tab screw threads with a wire brush and the screw hole with an appropriate thread tap. Wipe the screw threads with OMC Gasket Sealing Compound.

9. Position the trim tab with the grid/index or scribed marks aligned. If original position is unknown, set index rib with grid number 3. Install and tighten the screw to 28-32 ft.-lb. (38-43 N•m).

10. Fill the lower gearcase housing with OMC Hi-Vis Gearcase Lubricant. See Chapter Four.

Lower Gearcase Disassembly

Refer to **Figure 1** (2.3L, 2.5L and 3.0L) or **Figure 2** (4.3L, 5.0L, 5.7L, 5.8L and 7.5L) for this procedure.

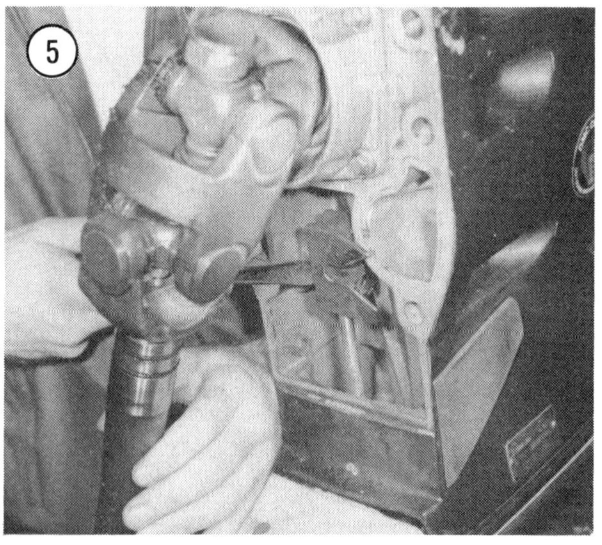
5

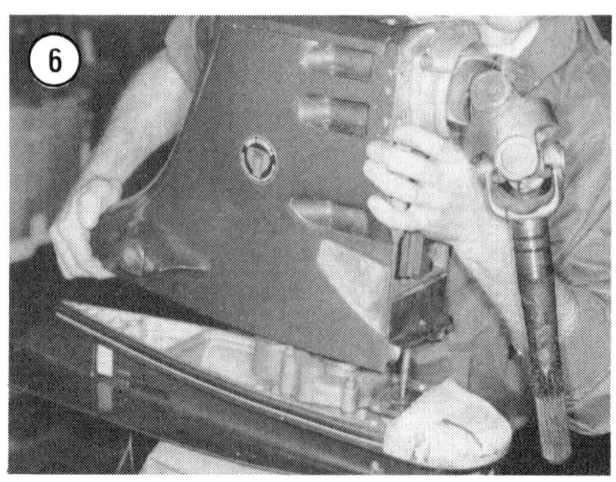
6

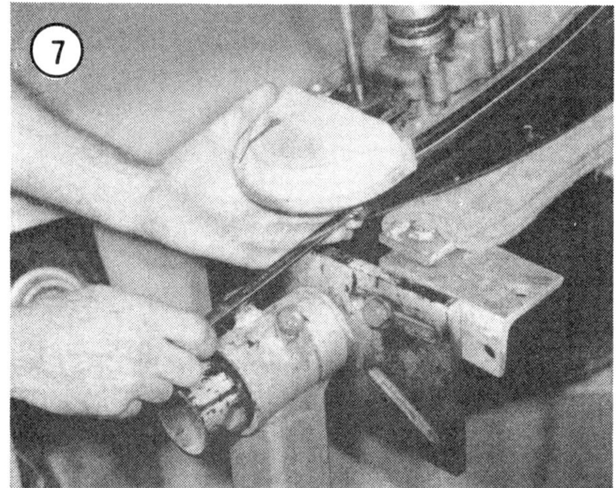

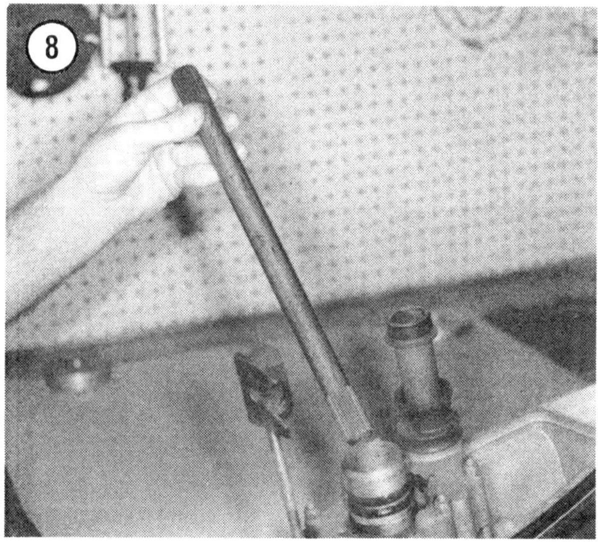

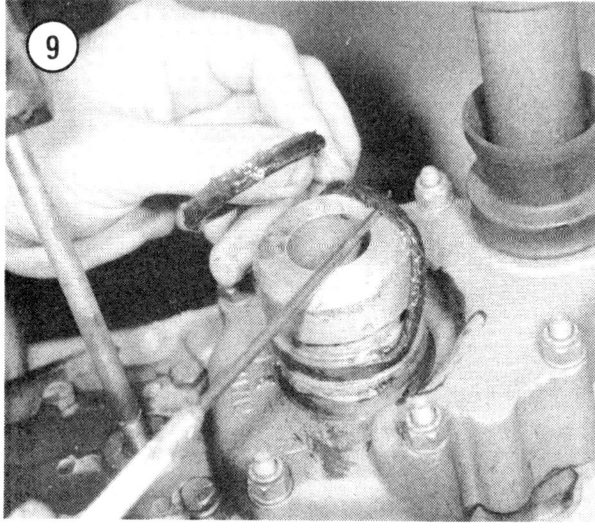

1. Remove the propeller as described in this chapter.
2. Unbolt and remove the anode (**Figure 7**). This exposes the entire shift rod cover for later removal.
3. Remove the intermediate driveshaft (**Figure 8**).
4. Remove and discard the drive shaft bearing housing O-rings (**Figure 9**).
5. Unbolt the elastic locknuts holding the water passage housing (**Figure 10**). Save the washers, but discard the locknuts.
6. Insert a screwdrive blade under the water passage housing near the 2 forward studs and carefully pry the unit free while pulling upward on the housing (**Figure 11**). Remove the housing and discard the gasket.
7. Depress the shift rod to reposition the detent lever downward. This will allow the detent lever to clear the inside of the gearcase during clutch shaft assembly removal.

NOTE
If water has entered the gearcase, the shift rod end may have corroded and may not be easily disconnected in Step 7. If this seems to be the case, move to Step 8 and remove the cover, sliding it up the shaft to provide access to the rod. Spray a quality aerosol penetrating oil on the shift rod and give it time to work, then try again to unscrew the rod. This may have to be done several times in cases of severe corrosion.

8. Unscrew the shift rod, but do not remove it from the cover unless the rod or the cover seals are to be replaced. The threads on the rod will damage the cover seals.
9. Remove the shift cover screws. Carefully pry the cover free (**Figure 12**) and remove it with the shift rod intact. Discard the gasket.
10. Remove the screws and washers holding the drive shaft bearing housing to let the drive shaft move upward while unscrewing the pinion nut. See **Figure 13**.

NOTE

The retainers on all but 460 cu. in. (7.5L) King Cobra models will be found in front of the outer rim of the bearing housing in Step 10. On 460 cu. in. (7.5L) King Cobra models, the retainers are located behind the housing outer rim.

11A. *460 cu. in. (7.5L) King Cobra*—Remove the 2 screws and retainers which hold the propeller shaft bearing carrier in the gearcase.

11B. *All others*—Remove the 4 screws which hold the propeller shaft bearing carrier in the gearcase. Remove and discard the rubber seals from the bolts.

CAUTION

The bearing carrier is an extremely tight fit in the propeller shaft bore. In some cases, it may be necessary to apply heat to the housing during the removal effort in Step 11. If heat seems to be required, apply it carefully to avoid overheating and thus damaging the housing.

12A. *2.3L and 3.0L*—Install OMC puller bolt part No. 316982 or other suitable long bolts in each of the 2 threaded holes on the carrier end. Fit OMC puller head part No. 378103 or a suitable flywheel puller on the bolts. Tighten the puller head on the bolts until the bearing carrier breaks free.

12B. *All others*—Install OMC puller head part No. 307636 and 2 puller legs (part No. 330278) or an equivalent puller with "J" bolts (**Figure 14**) to grasp the bearing carrier web and break it free of the housing.

13. Remove the bearing housing from the gearcase (**Figure 15**).

WARNING

The 2 large gearcase snap rings to be removed in Step 13 are under considerable pressure. Use the correct tool and wear safety glasses during this step to prevent accidental injury to your

10

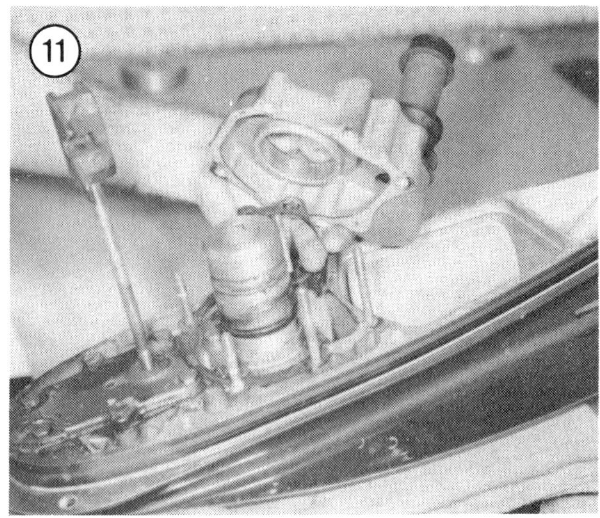

11

12

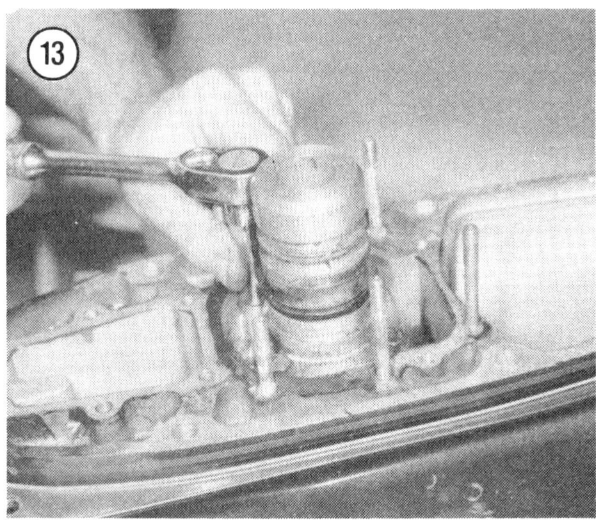

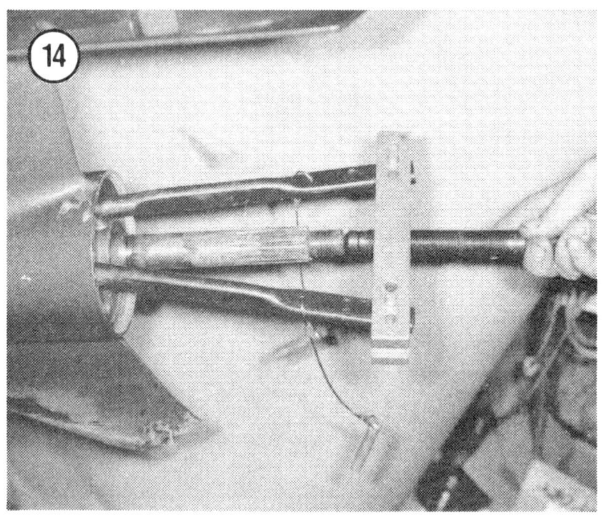

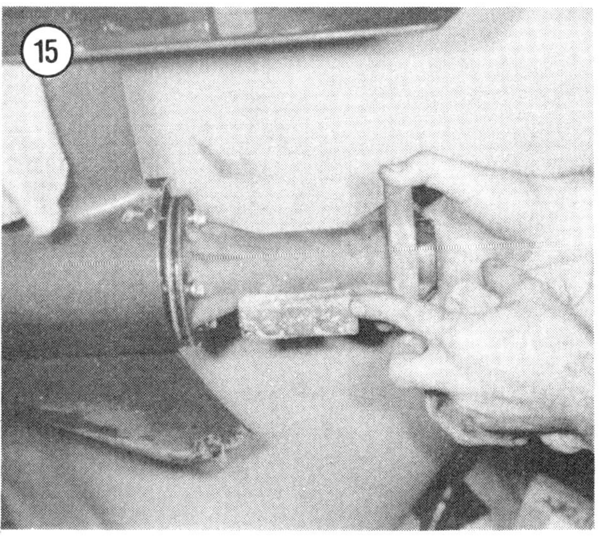

eyes if a ring breaks or unsnaps from the tool during removal.

14. All except 460 cu. in. (7.5L) King Cobra:
   a. Reach into the gearcase with OMC pliers part No. 331045 or another suitable pair of long snap ring pliers and engage the plier tips in the holes on the snap ring end.

NOTE
The procedure can be a slow, frustrating one. If the pliers contiually slip out of the snap ring ends, it may be necessary to true up the plier tips with a file, especially if they are well worn. Work slowly, carefully and with patience.

   b. Apply pressure slowly and work carefully until the snap ring is free of its groove, then ease the ring up and out of the propeller shaft bore. See **Figure 16**. With the ring on the floor, place your foot over it and release the pliers.
   c. Repeat sub-step a and sub-step b to remove the second snap ring.

15. Remove the bearing housing retaining washer (except 460 cu. in. [7.5L] King Cobra) and REVERSE gear. See **Figure 17**.

16. Remove the thrust washer and bearing (**Figure 18**).

17. To remove the pinion nut: 13
   a. Reinstall the intermediate drive shaft in the lower drive shaft, indexing the splines.
   b. Fit spline socket part No. 311875 on a breaker bar.
   c. Install socket on the intermediate drive shaft.
   d. Insert pinion nut holder part No. 334455 or a suitable open-end wrench in the propeller shaft housing and engage the pinion nut.
   e. Hold the pinion nut from moving and rotate the drive shaft counterclockwise to loosen the nut.

f. Remove the pinion nut holder/wrench and spline socket.

18. Remove the intermediate drive shaft from the lower drive shaft. Remove the bearing housing and shims (**Figure 19**).

NOTE

*The needle bearing inside the bearing housing (**Figure 20**) is not serviceable. If it is damaged, missing a roller or otherwise defective, the entire housing must be replaced as an assembly.*

19. Remove the lower drive shaft (**Figure 21**). It may be necessary to wiggle or pry the drive shaft up slightly. Remove the thrust bearing, thrust washer and shims.

20. Reach inside the propeller shaft housing and retrieve the pinion gear and nut (**Figure 22**).

21. Retrieve any loose roller bearings that fell into the gearcase when the lower drive shaft was removed. See **Figure 23**.

CAUTION

Make sure that the oil drain plug is out of the gearcase before performing Step 21. If the drain plug is installed in the case, its tip will prevent removal of the assembly and may result in damage to the plug tip or one of the components.

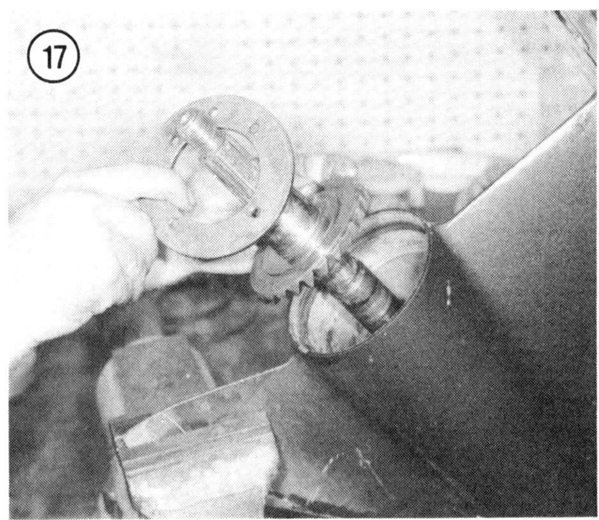

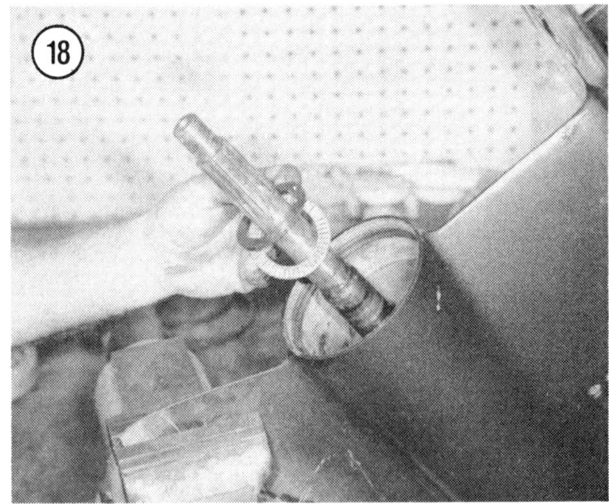

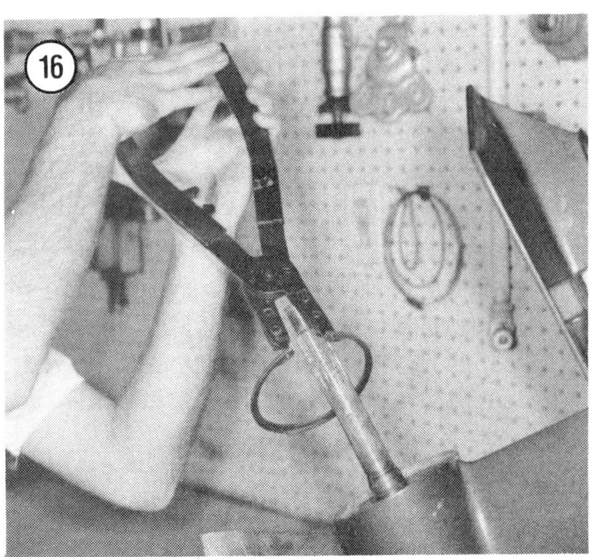

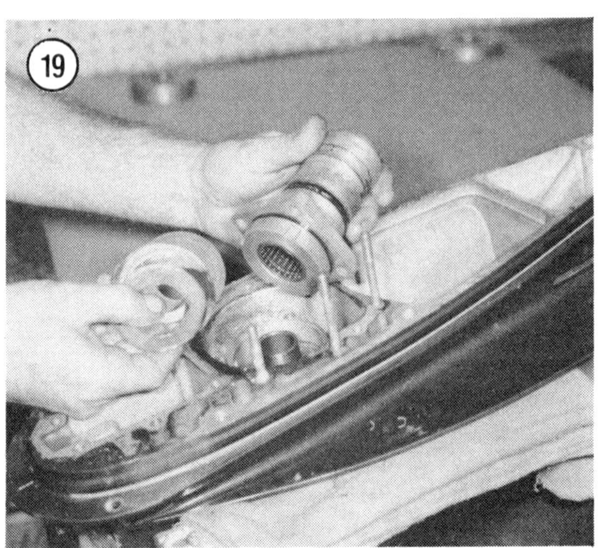

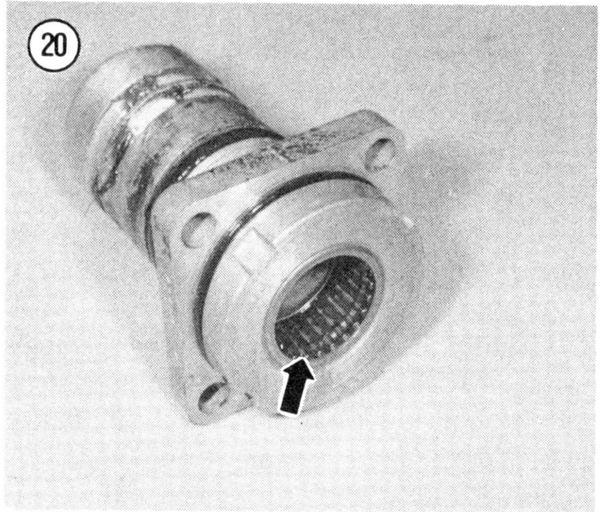

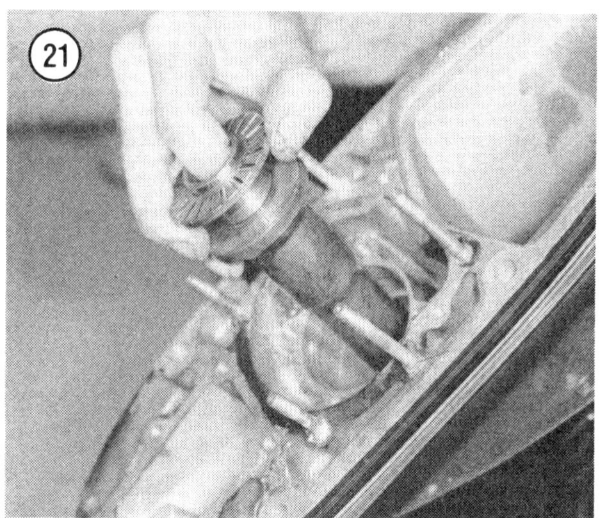

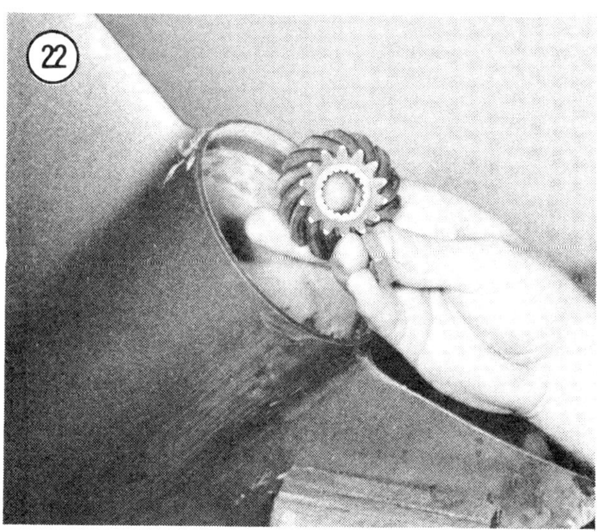

22. Reinsert the shift rod in the shift cavity and depress the shift detent. Hold the detent depressed with the shift rod and remove the propeller shaft, FORWARD gear and clutch housing assembly (**Figure 24**). This completes disassembly of the gearcase housing.
23. Clean and inspect the gearcase and components as described later in this chapter.

Propeller Shaft Bearing Housing Disassembly/Assembly

1. Check the bearing housing anode (**Figure 25**). If more than 2/3 of the anode is gone, unbolt and discard it, then install a new one.
2. Remove the back-to-back seals (**Figure 26**) with OMC bearing/seal puller part No. 391259 and OMC puller part No. 391012. Discard both seals.
3. Remove and discard the housing O-ring (A, **Figure 27**). The 460 cu. in. (7.5L) King Cobra housing uses 2 O-rings.

NOTE

*If bearings require removal in Step 4, it may be necessary to modify the jaws of puller part No. 391010 as shown in **Figure 28** in order to fit them in the puller slots behind the bearing. Grind jaws slowly and carefully. Quench frequently with water to avoid changing the temper of the metal.*

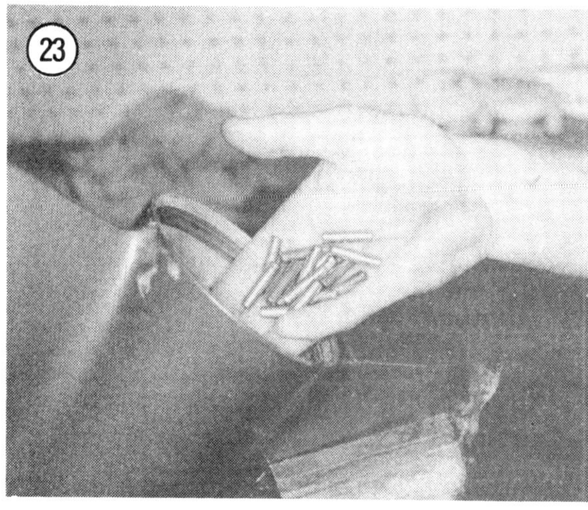

4. Check the condition of the needle bearings (B, **Figure 27**). If not damaged or otherwise defective, do not remove from housing. If the bearings require removal:
   a. Use OMC bearing/seal puller part No. 391259 and puller part No. 391010 to remove the small bearing.
   b. Use OMC bearing/seal puller part No. 391259 and puller part No. 391012 to remove the large bearing.

5. Clean the bearing housing in solvent and blow dry with compressed air, if available. Check the housing for any nicks, burrs or sharp edges in the O-ring groove that would prevent the O-ring from sealing. Correct any defects found.

6. If the needle bearings were removed:
   a. Wipe the outer edge of a new large bearing with OMC Hi-Vis Gearcase Lube. Slide the bearing on installer part No. 326562 with its lettered side facing toward the tool. Install the bearing in the housing with a suitable press.
   b. Wipe the outer edge of a new small bearing with OMC Hi-Vis Gearcase Lube. Slide the bearing on installer part No. 326562 (2.3L, 2.5L and 3.0L) or installer part No. 321517 (all others) with its lettered side facing toward the tool. Install the bearing in the housing with a suitable press.

7. Wipe the metal case of two new seals with OMC Gasket Sealing Compound. Install the seals as follows **(Figure 29)**:
   a. Place inner seal on the bearing housing with its lip facing the housing. Install the seal with the stepped side of installer part No. 326551 (2.3L, 2.5L and 3.0L) or installer part No. 326690 (all others).
   b. Place outer seal on the bearing housing with its lip facing away from the housing. Install the seal with the opposite end of installer part No. 326551 (2.3L, 2.5L and 3.0L) or installer part No. 326690 (all others).
   c. Fill the cavity between the seals with OMC Triple-Guard grease, then wipe both seal lips with the same lubricant.

8. If the anode was removed, install a new one and tighten the screws to 5-7 ft.-lb. (7-9 N•m).

9. Lightly lubricate new housing O-ring(s) with OMC Triple-Guard Grease and install on the housing. Coat housing O-ring flanges with OMC Gasket Sealing Compound. The housing is now ready for reinstallation.

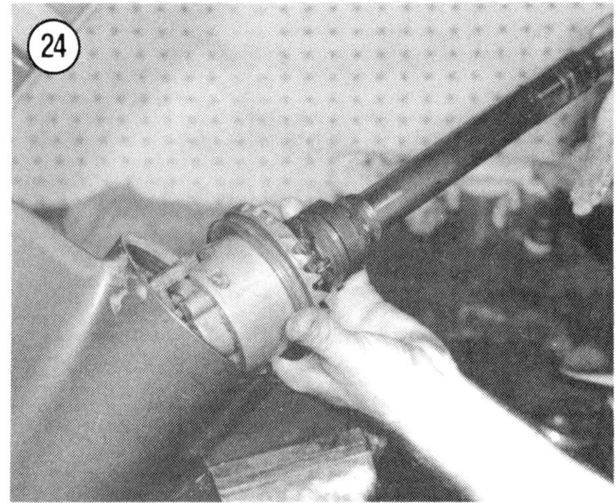

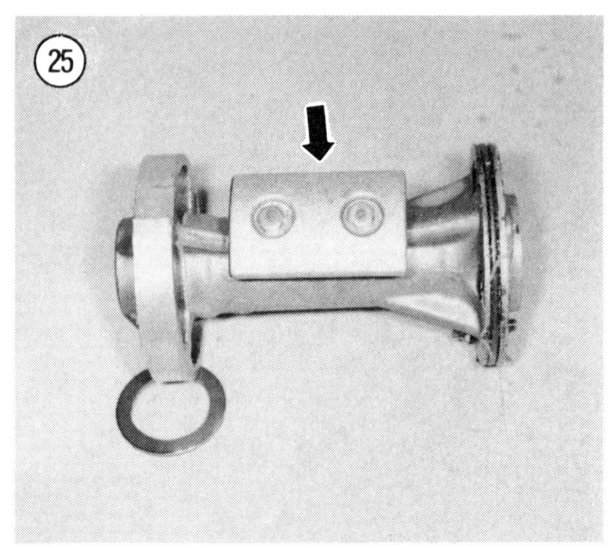

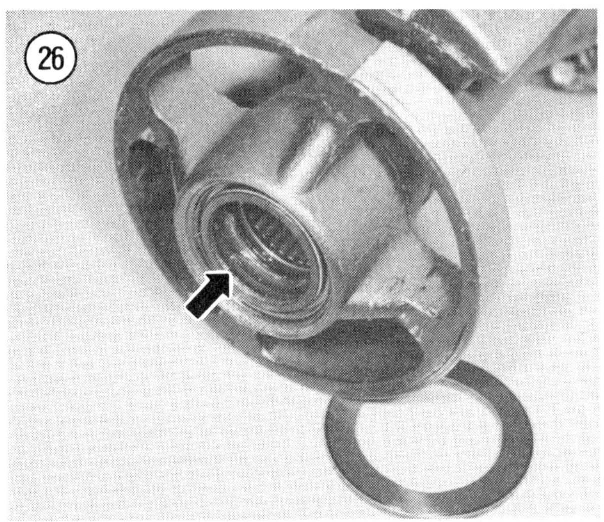

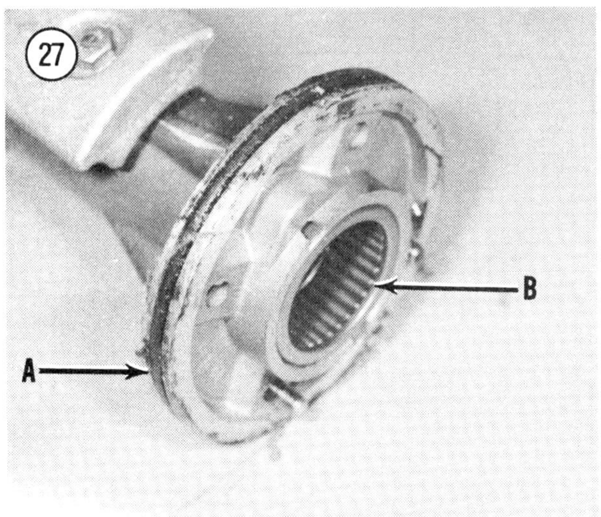

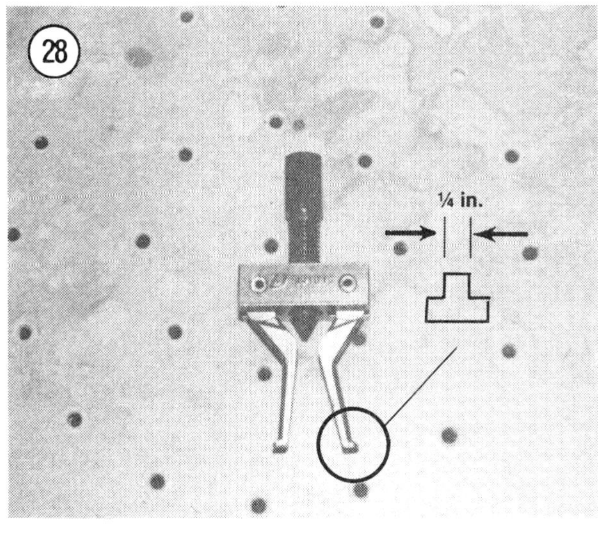

Drive Shaft Bearing Housing Disassembly

1. Remove and discard all O-rings remaining on the housing assembly. See A, **Figure 30**.

NOTE
The needle bearing inside the bearing housing (B, ***Figure 30****) is not serviceable. If it is damaged, missing a roller or otherwise defective, the entire housing must be replaced as an assembly.*

2. Check the condition of the needle bearing (B, **Figure 30**). If corroded or damaged, replace the entire housing as an assembly.
3. Wash the bearing housing in fresh solvent and blow dry with compressed air, if available. Check the housing for any nicks, burrs or sharp edges in the O-ring grooves that would prevent the O-rings from sealing. Correct any defects found.

Shift Rod Cover Disassembly/Assembly

The shift rod should not be removed from the cover unless the rod or cover sealing components must be replaced. Shift rod removal will damage the cover sealing O-ring or wiper.

1. Pull the shift rod from the cover.
2. Use an awl or sharp pick to pry the O-ring from the bottom of the bronze bushing. See **Figure 31**. Discard the O-ring.
3. Turn the cover over and repeat Step 2 to remove the wiper. Discard the wiper.
4. Clean all gasket residue from the cover surface.
5. Wash the cover in fresh solvent and blow dry with compressed air. Check the cover for signs of visible damage. If any are found, replace the cover.
6. Check the shift rod threads for wear or damage. Replace as required.

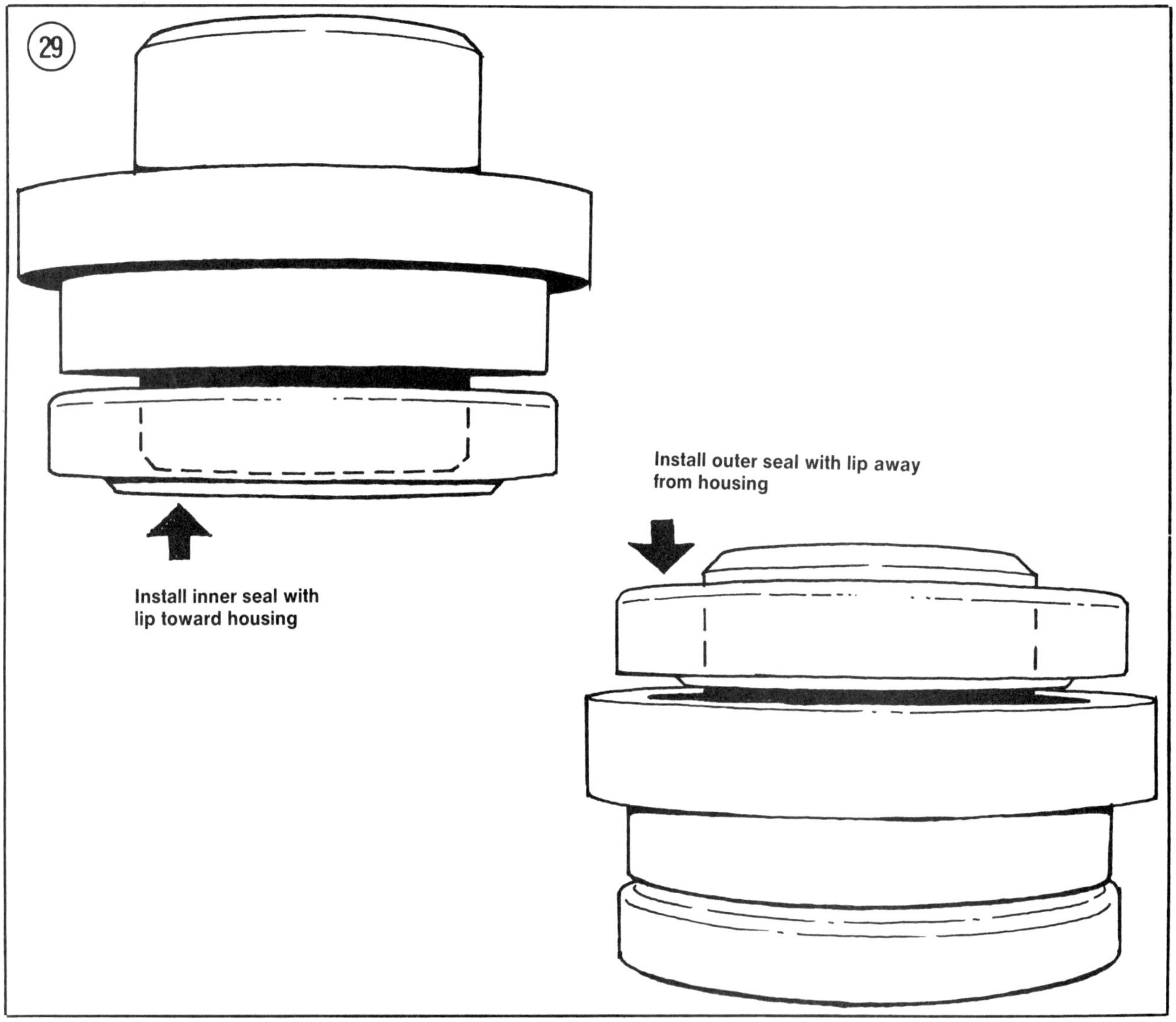

29

Install outer seal with lip away from housing

Install inner seal with lip toward housing

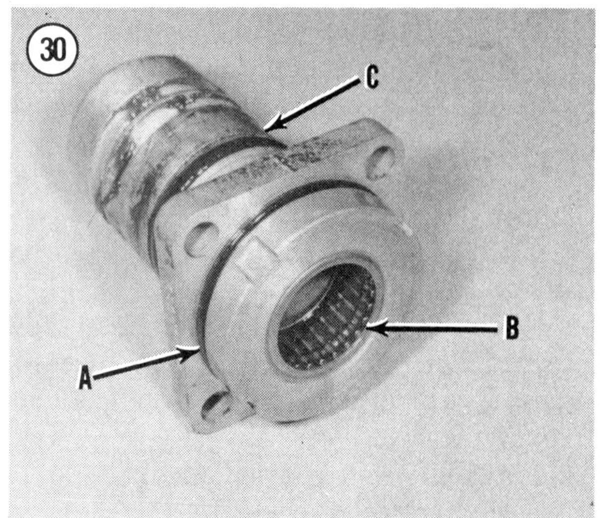

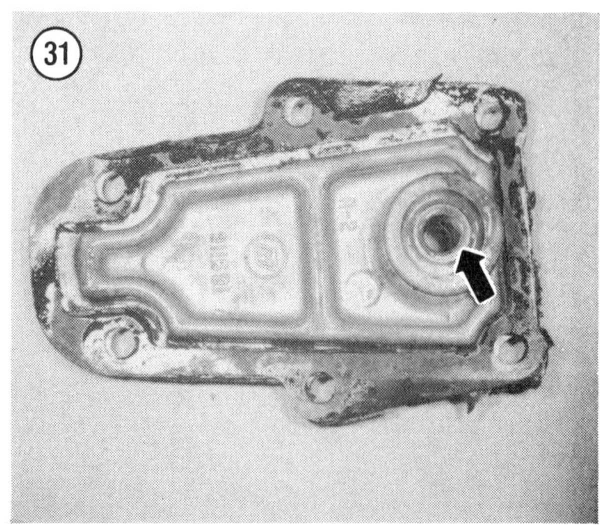

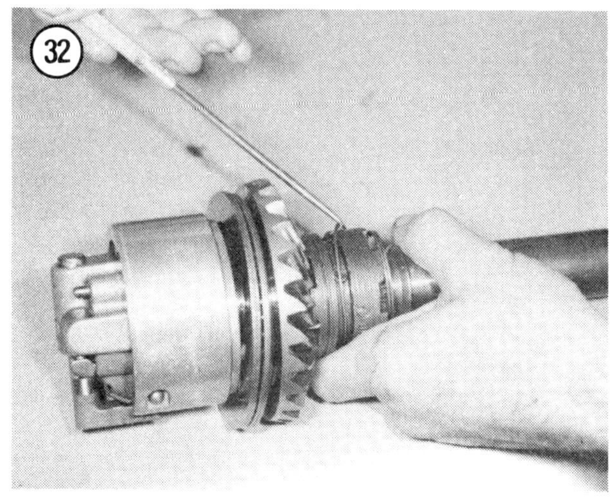

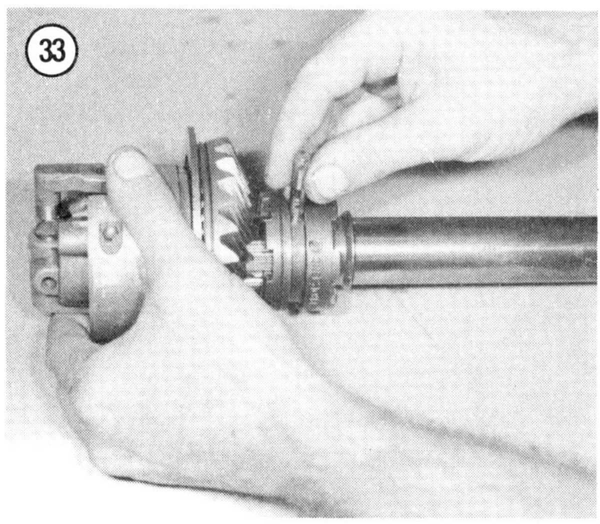

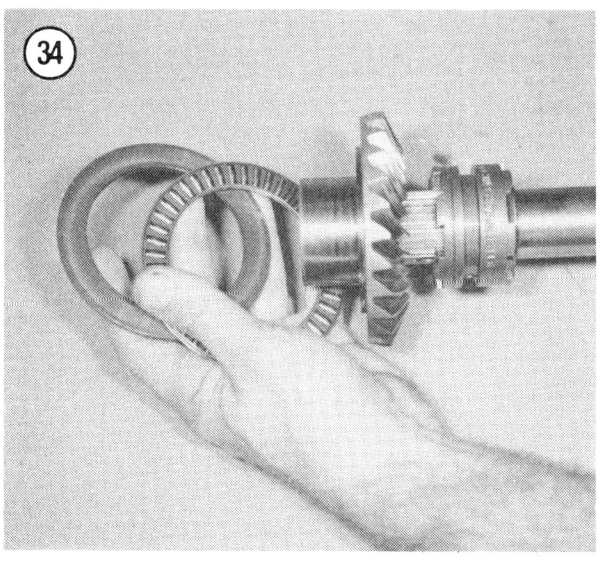

7. Wipe a new O-ring with OMC Triple-Guard Grease and install it in its seat inside the bushing.
8. Turn the cover over and repeat Step 8 to install a new wiper. Use a small screwdriver to seat the rim of the wiper in the cover.
9. Wipe the shift rod threads with OMC Triple-Guard Grease and carefully thread the shift rod through the wiper and O-ring. Once the last thread has passed through the cover sealing components, push the rod about 50 percent through the cover.

Propeller Shaft, Forward Gear and Bearing Housing Disassembly

1. Place the propeller shaft, FORWARD gear and bearing housing assembly on a clean workbench.
2. Use a small screwdriver blade, awl or pick to remove one end of the clutch dog spring from its groove (**Figure 32**), then carefully unwrap the spring from the clutch dog. Discard the spring.
3. Push the pin from the clutch dog (**Figure 33**), then separate the bearing housing assembly from the propeller shaft.
4. Remove the thrust washer, thrust bearing and FORWARD gear from the propeller shaft if they do not come off with the bearing housing. See **Figure 34**.
5. Depress the detent arm on the rear of the bearing housing and remove the shift shaft and cradle from the housing (**Figure 35**).
6. Pull up on the detent arm until it snaps into its NEUTRAL position, then remove the pivot pin from the housing (**Figure 36**).
7. Reach inside the housing and remove the shifter from its detent.
8. Wrap the housing with a shop cloth. Reach inside and turn the detent arm 90° to either side of the housing. Remove the detent arm.

9A. *2.3L, 2.5L and 3.0L models*—Remove the shifter through the opening in the top of the housing.

9B. *All other models*—Remove the shifter from the front of the bearing housing.

10. Remove the detent ball and spring (**Figure 37**).

11. This completes disassembly of the bearing housing on 2.3L, 2.5L and 3.0L models. The bearing assembly inside the bearing housing is non-serviceable and if defective, the entire unit must be replaced. On all other models, there are 25 loose roller bearings in the housing that should be removed, cleaned and inspected.

Propeller Shaft, FORWARD Gear and Bearing Housing Cleaning and Inspection

1. Clean all parts in fresh solvent. Blow dry with compressed air.
2. Check FORWARD gear (**Figure 38**) for:
   a. Broken or chipped teeth.
   b. Worn, damaged, rounded-off or discolored drive lugs.
   c. Worn or scored bronze bushing.
3. Check sliding clutch dog (**Figure 39**) for:
   a. Worn or damaged drive lugs.
   b. Worn or damaged internal splines.
   c. Elongation of the retaining pin hole.
4. Clean propeller shaft splines (**Figure 40**) with a wire brush to remove any corrosion. If

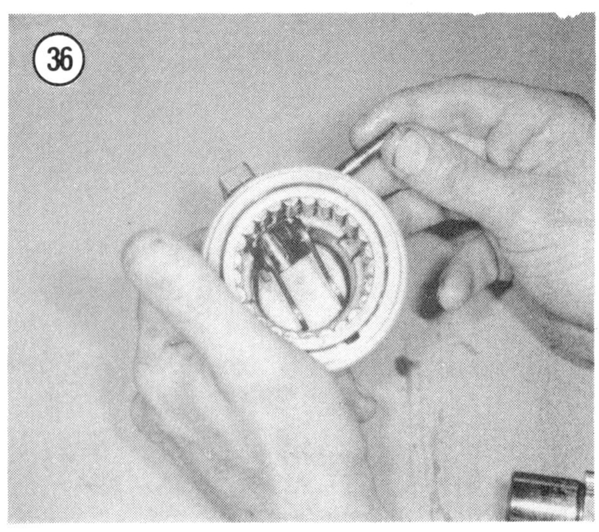

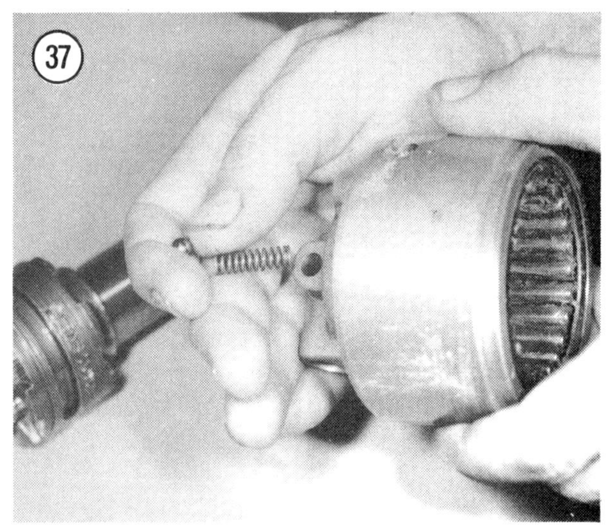

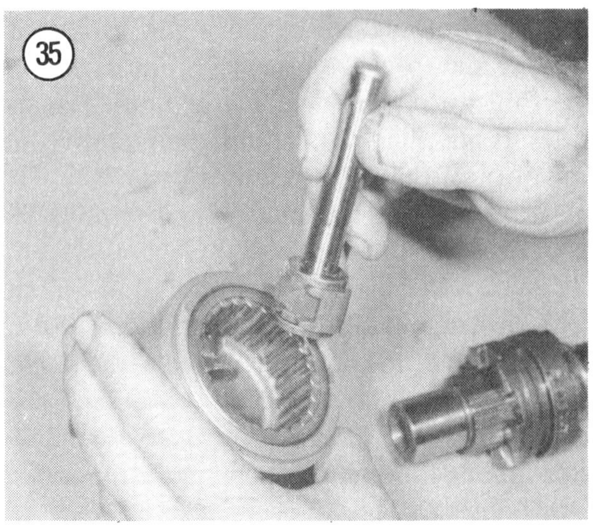

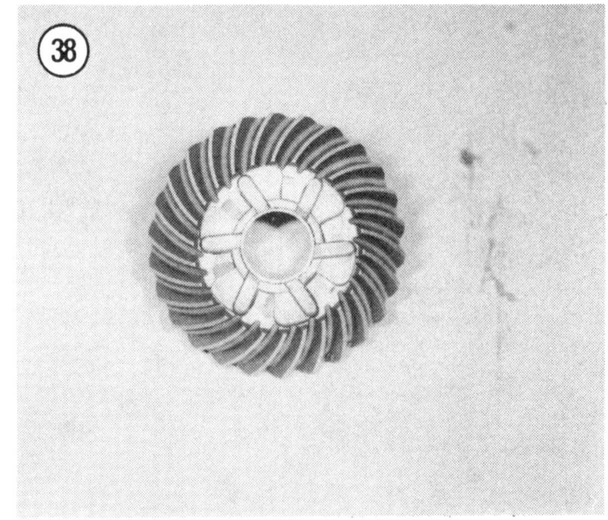

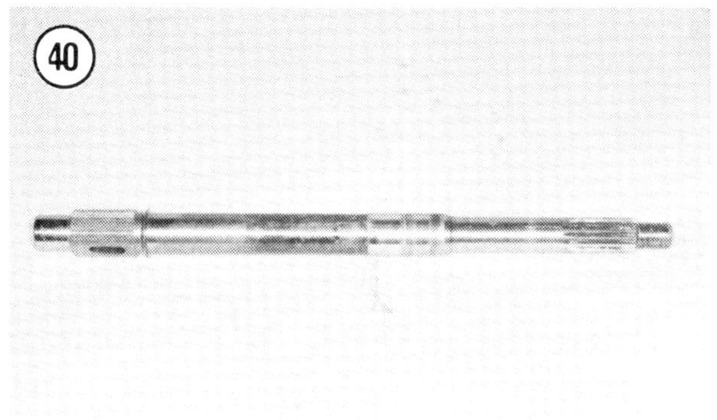

splines are partially corroded away, twisted or otherwise damaged, replace the shaft.

5. Check propeller shaft bearing and seal surfaces for signs of pitting, corrosion or heat discoloration. Replace shaft if any defects are found.

6. Check the shift detent, cradle, shifter, shaft and pin for burrs, excessive wear or damage.

7. Check the bearing housing detent lever and pivot pin holes for wear or burring that might prevent the shift mechanism from moving freely.

8. On 2.3L, 2.5L and 3.0L models, check the bearing housing bearings for pitting, corrosion, heat discoloration and free movement. If the bearings are defective, replace the entire housing assembly.

NOTE
The FORWARD gear and bearing housing are a matched assembly. If either requires replacement, replace both as a unit.

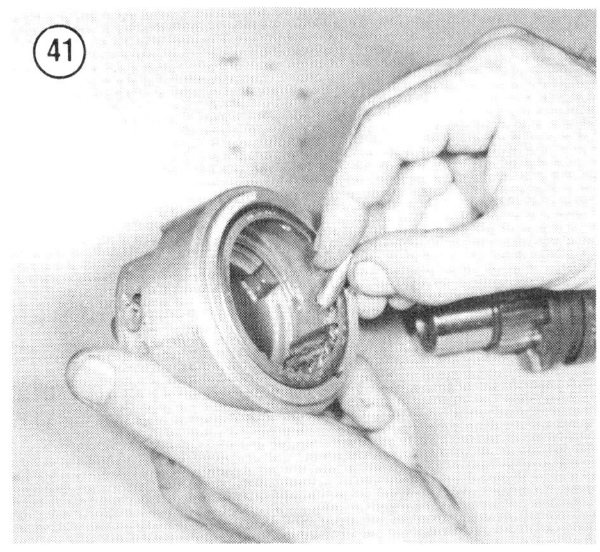

9. On all other models, inspect the loose roller bearings. If one is defective, install a new set. Do *not* use a single bearing from another assembly to replace a defective or missing bearing.

Propeller Shaft, FORWARD Gear and Bearing Housing Assembly

1. All except 2.3L, 2.5L and 3.0L—Wipe the inside of the bearing housing with OMC Needle Bearing Assembly Grease. Coat all 25 bearings with the same lubricant. Install the bearings in the housing (**Figure 41**).

2. Wipe the detent ball and spring with a light coat of OMC Needle Bearing Assembly Grease. Install the spring in the bearing housing, then the detent ball. See **Figure 37**.

3. 2.3L, 2.5L and 3.0L—Rotate the detent arm 90° to either side of the housing, then insert the shifter through the detent opening in the bearing housing.

4. Move detent arm toward one side of the bearing housing. Depress the ball and spring with a punch and push the detent into the housing. Make sure not to push detent all the way into the housing or the ball will jam the detent in the housing. When detent is beyond the ball, rotate the lever to the rear of the

housing, then move the detent to its NEUTRAL position.

5. Position the shifter with its narrow arms facing the detent. Connect the shifter to the detent neck, align its pivot holes and reinstall the retaining pin. See **Figure 36**.

6. Depress the detent as far as possible, then install the cradle and shift shaft (**Figure 35**). Connect cradle and shaft to the shifter's wide arms, then pull the detent back up to its NEUTRAL position to retain the cradle and shaft in place.

CAUTION

The clutch dog must be installed properly or it will not completely engage the REVERSE gear. This will damage both the gear and clutch dog when shifting is attempted.

7. Orient the clutch dog with the stamped words or part No. facing the rear of the propeller shaft. Align retaining pin hole in clutch dog with slot on the propeller shaft and install over the shaft splines (**Figure 42**).

8. Install the FORWARD gear, thrust washer and thrust bearing on the propeller shaft (**Figure 34**).

9. Insert the shift shaft in the propeller shaft. On models with loose roller bearings, work carefully to insert FORWARD gear in bearing housing without disturbing the bearings. Align the shaft and clutch dog holes, then install the retaining pin (**Figure 33**).

10. Slip a new retaining spring over the end of the propeller shaft. Engage one end of the spring around the clutch dog pin and then wrap the remainder of the spring in place. Work carefully to avoid stretching the spring; if stretched, discard and install another new one. Position the spring so that there are 3 coils around each end of the pin without any overlap.

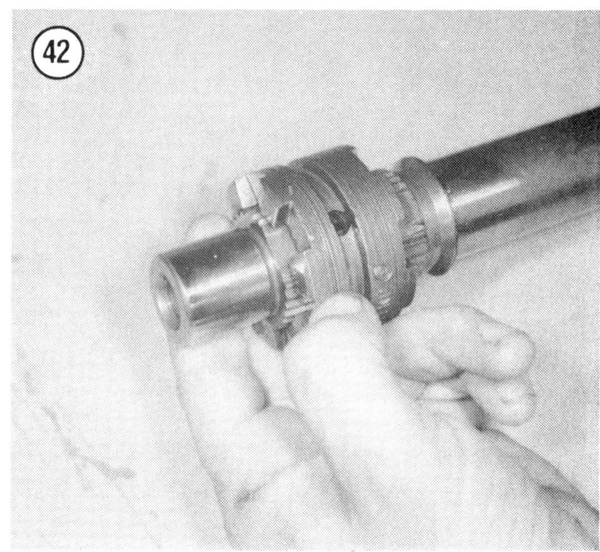

Gearcase Housing and Components Cleaning and Inspection

1. Remove all gasket and sealer residue from the shift cover and water passage cover mating surfaces.

2. Clean the gearcase housing in fresh solvent. Blow dry with compressed air, if available.

3. Clean all corrosion and sealer residue from threaded holes with an appropriate size thread tap.

4. Inspect the oil circulation hole located at the upper end of the drive shaft bore to make sure that it is not plugged. Clean or unplug as required.

5. Check all studs for looseness and damaged threads. If stud replacement is required:

   a. Install 2 suitable nuts on the stud. Unscrew the stud with a wrench on the lower nut.
   b. Clean any sealer residue from the stud hole with an appropriate size thread tap.
   c. Spray the hole threads and the threads of a new stud with Locquic Primer.
   d. Wipe the stud threads with a coat of OMC Ultra Lock.
   e. Install the stud to the depth shown in **Figure 43**.

6. Check the water intake screen. If it is plugged and cannot be satisfactorily cleaned, replace as follows:

7A. On the 460 cu. in. (7.5L) King Cobra:

a. Remove the screw located on the starboard side of the gearcase housing above the intake screen.
b. Remove the port and starboard screens.
c. Insert the port side screen first with its wide end facing down. Depress screen and push to one side until it bottoms in the cavity.
d. Insert the starboard screen and depress until it snaps into position.
e. Make sure both screens are properly positioned, then reinstall the gearcase housing screw.

7B. On all others:

a. Depress the locating tab on each side of the screen with a small screwdriver blade. Push in and up on both sides of the screen at the same time to pop it free.
b. Position new screen with its curved side facing to the front and its narrow end facing downward.
c. Depress the screen until the detents snap into place.
d. Make sure the screen covers all 4 intake openings.

8. Check the gearcase housing anodes for deterioration. If more than 2/3 of an anode is gone, install a new one.

9. Check the hydrostatic seal rings inside the bearing housing hub (7.5L) or gearcase housing (all others) for signs of damage. If rings are not in good condition, they will allow exhaust gases to enter the propeller area and result in ventilation. A gearcase with damaged seal rings should be replaced.

10. Check the lower and intermediate drive shaft threads and splines for wear, corrosion or signs of metal transfer. Make sure the oil circulation hole is open in both shafts and that the nylon shaft support plug is installed in the lower drive shaft at the base of the splines.

11. Check all thrust bearing and needle bearing surfaces for signs of heat discoloration and corrosion. Make sure the bearings rotate freely and are not pitted or worn excessively.

12. Check the REVERSE gear teeth for signs of chipping or cracking. Make sure the drive lugs are not worn or damaged. Replace gear as required.

13. Check the pinion gear teeth and internal splines for signs of chipping or cracking. Look for evidence of corrosion or metal transfer on the tapered seat of the gear. Replace gear as required.

Lower Drive Shaft Bearing Replacement

The lower drive shaft bearing should not be removed unless replacement is required. The bearing is retained by a screw on the side of the gearcase. Before removing the bearing, make sure to remove this retaining screw or the gearcase housing will be damaged when the bearing is removed.

2.3L, 2.5L and 3.0L

1. Remove pinion bearing retaining screw from the side of the gearcase housing. Discard the O-ring.

2. Assemble OMC bearing remover/installer tool part No. 391257 components as shown

in **Figure 44**. Drive the bearing down and out of the gearcase housing bore with a soft-faced hammer or mallet.

3. Assemble tool part No. 391257 components as shown in **Figure 45**. Use a 1/4-20×1/2 in. hex head screw (A), and a 1 in. O.D. flat washer (B) to attach the spacer. Use a 1/4-20×1 1/4 in. hex head screw (C) to attach the installer.
4. Wipe the outside of the bearing with OMC Needle Bearing Assembly Grease.
5. Position the lettered side of the bearing case toward the installer and slide the bearing onto the tool.
6. Insert the tool and bearing assembly into the gearcase housing bore and drive in place until the driving rod seats on the spacer.
7. Install a new O-ring on the pinion bearing retaining screw. Wipe screw threads with OMC Locquic Primer, then with OMC Nut Lock. Install and tighten screw to 48-84 in.-lb. (5-9 N•m).

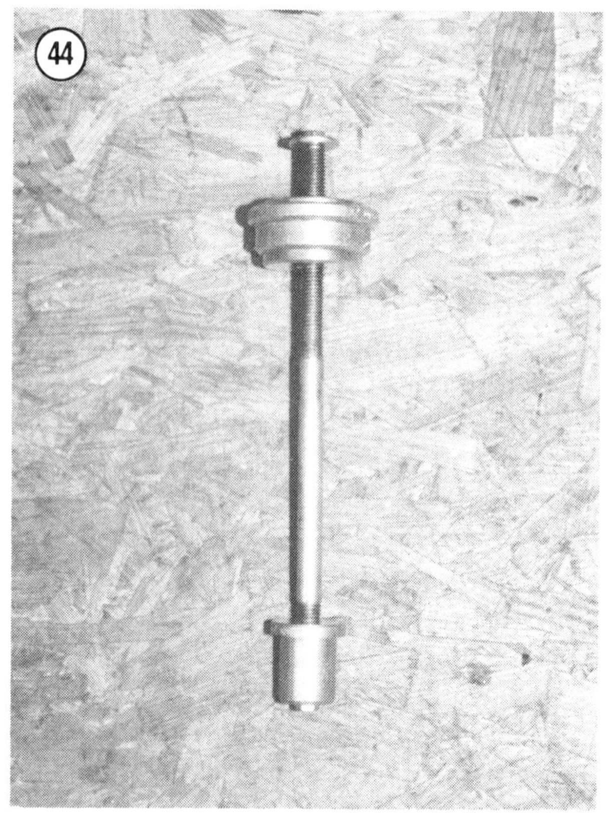

All others

1. Remove pinion bearing retaining screw from the side of the gearcase housing. Discard the O-ring.
2. Assemble OMC bearing remover/installer tool part No. 391257 components as shown in **Figure 46**. Turn the tool nut as required to pull the bearing from the gearcase housing.
3. Assemble tool part No. 391257 components as shown in **Figure 47** (except 460 cu. in. [7.5L] King Cobra) or **Figure 48** (460 cu. in. [7.5L] King Cobra). Use a 1/4-20×1/2 in. hex head screw (A), and a 1 in. O.D. flat washer (B) to attach the spacer. Use a 1/4-20×1 1/4 in. hex head screw (C) to attach the installer.
4. Wipe the outside of the bearing with OMC Needle Bearing Assembly Grease.
5. Position the lettered side of the bearing case toward the installer and slide the bearing onto the tool.

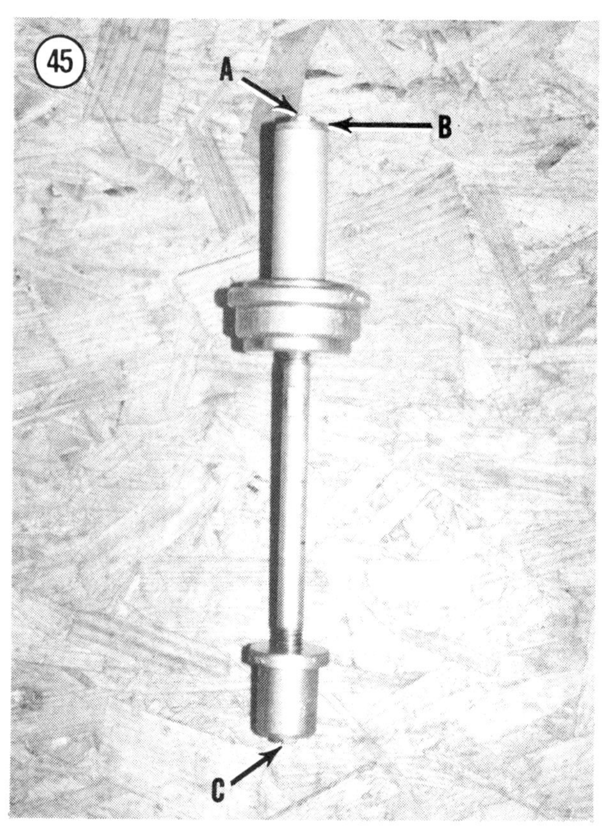

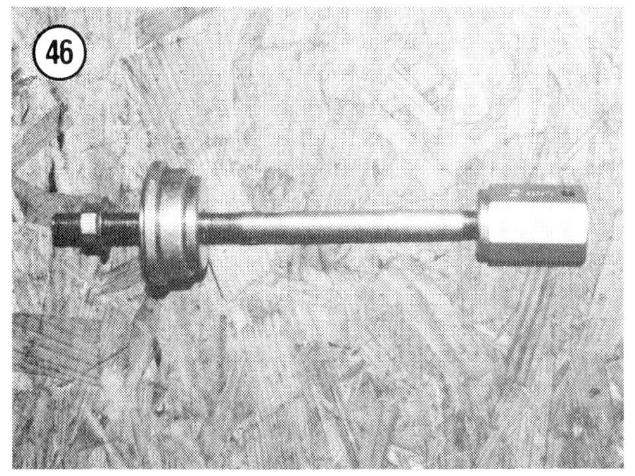

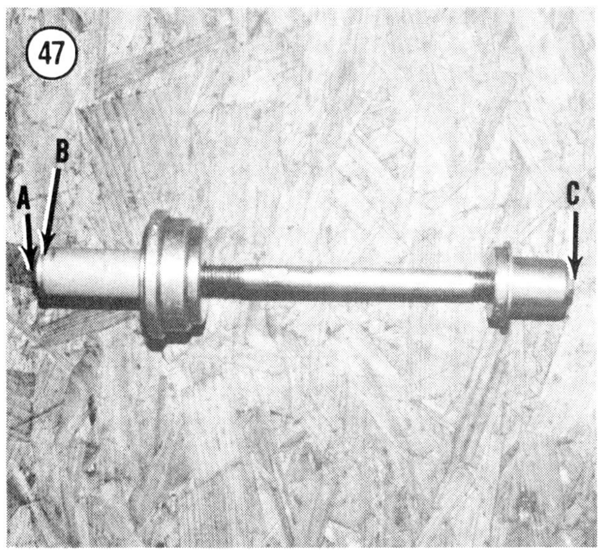

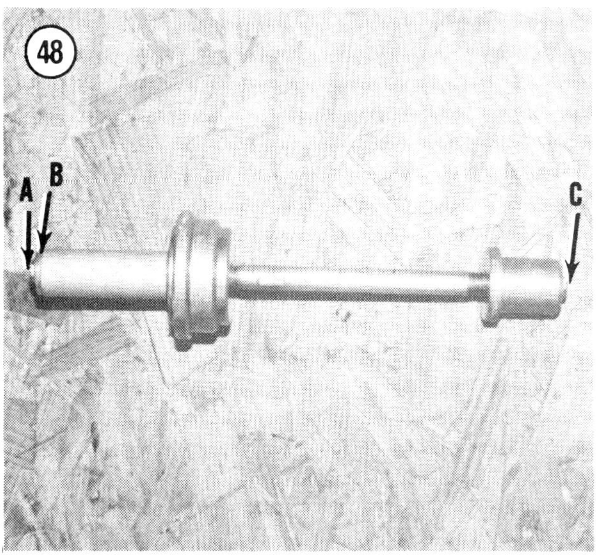

6. Insert the tool and bearing assembly into the gearcase housing bore and drive in place until the driving rod seats on the spacer.
7. Install a new O-ring on the pinion bearing retaining screw. Wipe screw threads with OMC Locquic Primer, then with OMC Nut Lock. Install and tighten screw to 48-84 in.-lb. (5-9 N•m).

Drive Shaft and Pinion Gear Shimming

If maximum service life is to be obtained from the gear train, the pinion gear must mesh precisely with the FORWARD and REVERSE gears. Shims are installed between the drive shaft bearing housing and thrust washer to ensure precise engagement of the FORWARD and REVERSE gears with the pinion gear. Whenever drive shaft or pinion components are replaced, you must determine the correct shim pack thickness to be used before reassembling the gearcase housing.
1. Secure drive shaft socket part No. 314438 in a vise. Insert the drive shaft in the socket. Install the pinion gear on the shaft and tighten the nut to 70-75 ft.-lb. (95-102 N•m). Remove the drive shaft from the socket.
2. Install the thrust bearing, thrust washer and drive shaft bearing housing (in this order) on the drive shaft without installing any of the old shims.
3. Install alignment plate (from shim gauge part No. 984329) on the drive shaft with its stepped side facing away from the bearing housing. Seat the plate against the housing, then place the drive shaft assembly and plate in shim fixture part No. 984329.
4. Tighten the fixture tension screw until the screw touches the end of the drive shaft, then continue tightening the screw until its sleeve reaches the groove on the pointed end of the screw to preload the assembly correctly. Tighten the tension screw locknut.

5. With the fixture positioned as shown in **Figure 49**, use the proper gauge bar as indicated below and measure the clearance between the gauge bar and pinion gear with a flat feeler gauge. Use gauge bar part No. 328366 (2.3L, 2.5L or 3.0L), part No. 330224 (460 cu. in. [7.5L] King Cobra) or part No. 328367 (all others). Take two or more readings (rotating the drive shaft between readings) to doublecheck your measurement.

6A. *460 cu. in. (7.5L) King Cobra*– Subtract the measurement obtained in Step 5 from 0.030 in. to determine the correct shim pack thickness. For example, if the measured clearance was 0.012 in., the correct shim pack thickness would be 0.018 in.

6B. *All others*—Subtract the measurement obtained in Step 5 from 0.020 in. to determine the correct shim pack thickness. For example, if the measured clearance was 0.012 in., the correct shim pack thickness would be 0.008 in.

7. To check your measurement, remove the drive shaft assembly from the shim fixture and install the amount of shimming determined in Step 6A or Step 6B between the thrust washer and drive shaft bearing housing. Reinstall the assembly in the fixture and measure the clearance with the feeler gauge. It should be 0.030 in. (460 cu. in. [7.5L] King Cobra) or 0.020 in. (all others).

8. Remove the drive shaft assembly from the shim fixture. Remove the bearing housing, thrust washer and thrust bearing.

9. Reinstall the drive shaft in the socket clamped in the vise. Loosen and remove the pinion nut and pinion gear from the drive shaft.

Lower Gearcase Assembly

Refer to **Figure 1** (2.3L, 2.5L and 3.0L) or **Figure 2** (4.3L, 5.0L, 5.7L, 5.8L and 7.5L) for this procedure.

1. Depress the shift detent on the FORWARD gear bearing housing as far as possible. The detent must be in its REVERSE position in order to provide sufficient clearance for propeller shaft installation.

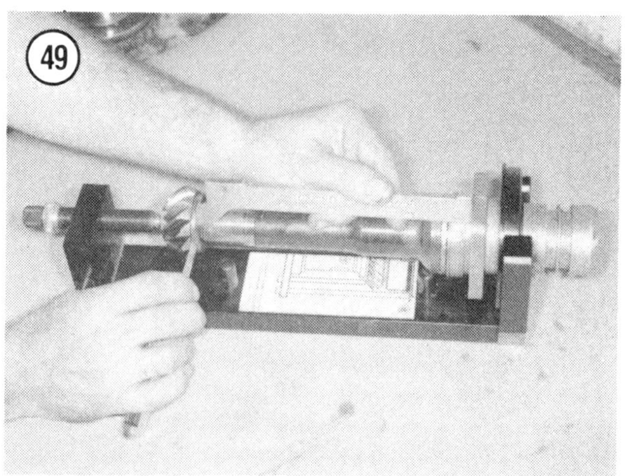
49

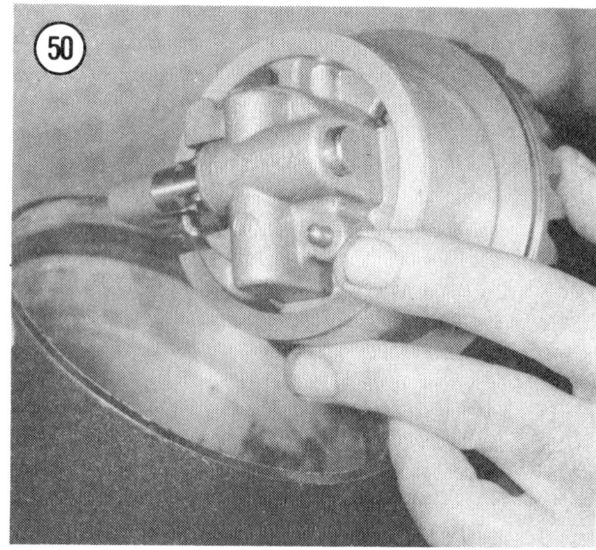
50

2. Install the gearcase housing in a suitable holding fixture with the rear of the housing elevated slightly.

3. Position the bearing housing with its detent pin aligned with the recess inside the nose of the gearcase housing. See **Figure 50**.

4. Insert the propeller shaft assembly in the gearcase housing. When the bearing housing pin engages its recess in the gearcase, the propeller shaft assembly will seat fully and the top of the detent arm can be seen centered at the bottom of the shift rod cavity.

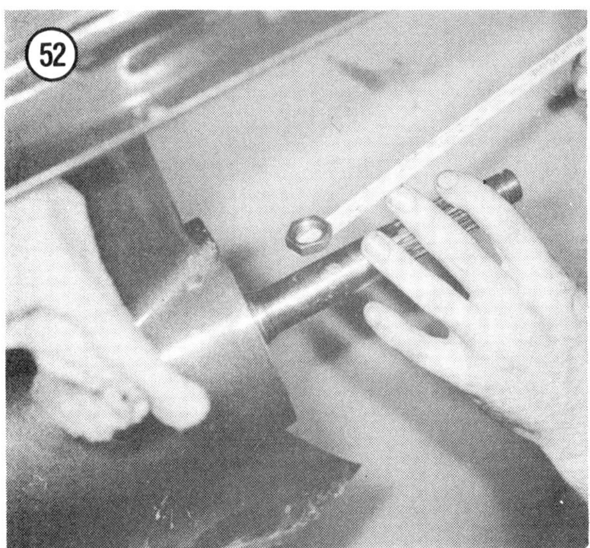

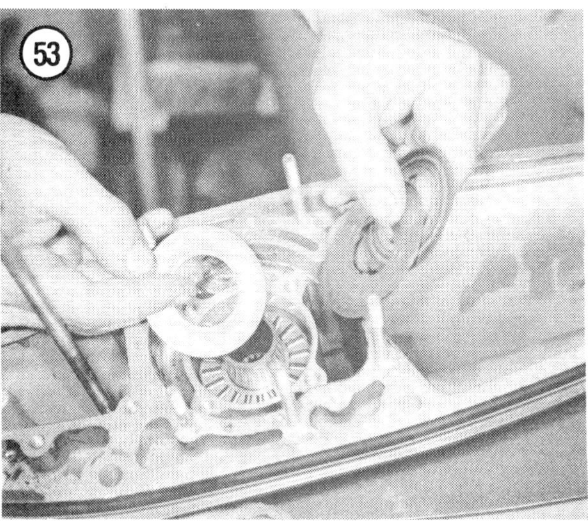

Temporarily install the shift rod and pull up on it to engage the detent in the FORWARD position. Look into the drive shaft bore and make sure the clutch dog and gear lugs are completely engaged. This will provide sufficient clearance for pinion gear and nut installation.

5. Tilt the gearcase housing up in the fixture until the drive shaft is in a vertical position, then insert the pinion gear in the housing underneath the drive shaft bearing.
6. Working slowly and carefully, insert the drive shaft into the gearcase (**Figure 51**) and through the bearing into the pinion gear.
7. Temporarily install the intermediate drive shaft in the lower drive shaft.
8. Insert the pinion nut and position it underneath the pinion gear (**Figure 52**).

CAUTION
Position the open-end wrench as close as possible to the center of the housing bore in Step 9. Do not allow wrench to press against side of housing bore as drive shaft is rotated in Step 10 or housing may be damaged.

9. Rotate the drive shaft to start the nut, then insert a thin-head 7/8 in. open-end wrench to hold the pinion gear nut from moving.
10. Install spline socket part No. 311875 on the intermediate drive shaft. Install a torque wrench in the socket and hold the pinion nut from moving with the open-end wrench while tightening the pinion nut to 100-110 ft.-lb. (136-149 N•m) on 460 cu. in. (7.5L) King Cobra and 70-75 ft.-lb. (95-102 N•m) on all other models, then remove the open-end wrench, the spline socket and intermediate drive shaft.
11. Insert the thrust bearing, thrust washer and shim pack on the drive shaft (**Figure 53**).
12. Lightly lubricate a new O-ring and install it on the drive shaft bearing housing base (**Figure 54**).
13. Install a new thick O-ring on the bottom O-ring groove of the drive shaft bearing

housing and coat the O-ring with OMC Gasket Sealing Compound.

14. Install the drive shaft bearing housing and seat with hand pressure. Fit flat washers on the retaining bolts, wipe the bolt threads with OMC Gasket Sealing Compound and tighten to 14-16 ft.-lb. (19-22 N•m). See **Figure 55**.

15. Install the REVERSE gear, thrust bearing and thrust washer (**Figure 56**) on the propeller shaft. Slide the components down into the gearcase housing.

WARNING
The 2 large gearcase snap rings installed in Step 16 are under great pressure. Use the special tool specified and wear safety glasses during this step to prevent accidental injury to your eyes if the ring breaks or unsnaps from the tool during removal.

16. All except 460 cu. in. (7.5L) King Cobra:
   a. Fit the retainer plate over the propeller shaft and slide it down into the gearcase housing.
   b. Engage the tips of retaining ring pliers part No. 331045 in the snap ring ends. Compress the ring with the pliers and position over the propeller shaft bore.

NOTE
This procedure is a slow, frustrating one. If the pliers continually slip out of the snap ring ends, it may be necessary to true up the plier tips with a file, especially if they are well worn. Work slowly, carefully and with patience.

   c. Apply pressure slowly and carefully work the snap ring into its groove in the housing, then release the pliers and remove from the propeller shaft bore.
   d. Repeat sub-steps b and c to install the second snap ring.
   e. Thread guide pins part No. 383175 into 2 of the retainer plate holes 180° from each other.
   f. Align the word UP, cast on the rear face of the propeller shaft bearing housing,

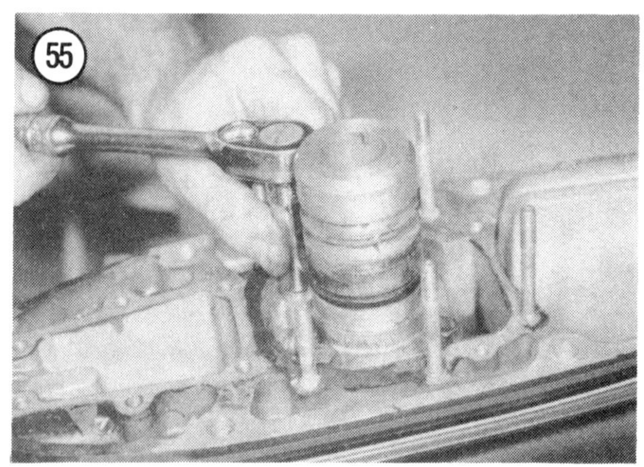

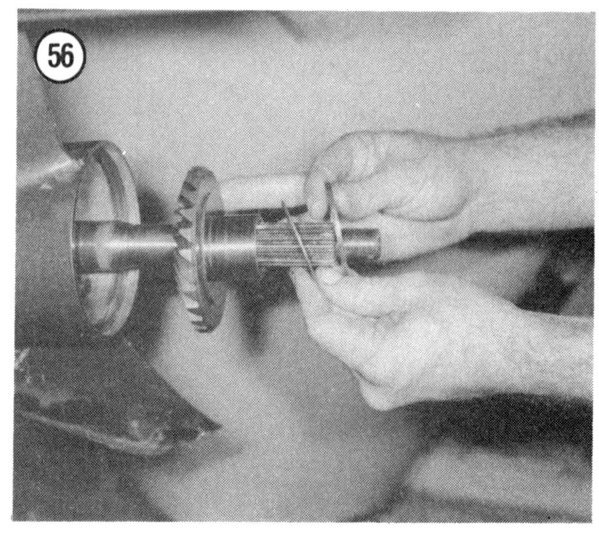

with the top of the gearcase housing. The drain slot will be positioned at the bottom.

CAUTION
Do not try to draw the bearing housing into place by tightening the screws. This can strip the retainer plate threads.

g. Slide the bearing housing over the guide pins and tap it in place below the hydrostatic rings with a soft-faced mallet.
h. Install a new seal on each of the retainer screws and coat the seal and threads with OMC Gasket Sealing Compound (**Figure 57**).

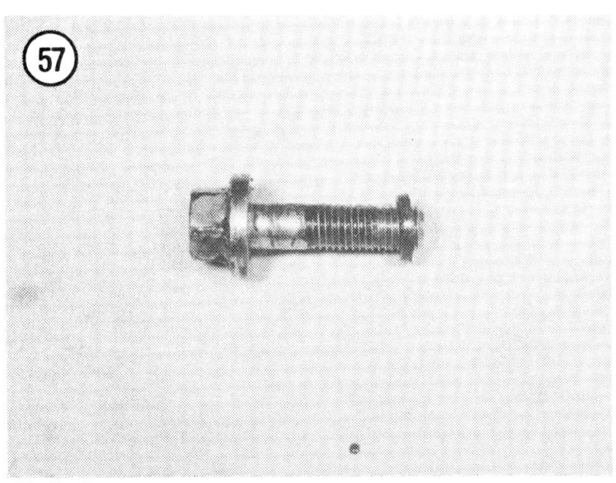

i. Install 2 screws, remove the 2 guide pins and install the remaining 2 screws. Tighten all screws to 10-12 ft.-lb. (14-16 N•m).

17. 460 cu. in. (7.5L) King Cobra:
 a. Install the propeller shaft bearing housing in the gearcase with its screw holes in a vertical position. The anode should face downward as shown in **Figure 58.**
 b. Rap the housing in place with a soft-faced mallet to seat the O-rings.
 c. Position a retainer behind one of the holes in the housing. If the retainer has a rounded edge on one side, that edge should face forward. Install a screw loosely into the retainer.
 d. Position the other retainer and install the screw.
 e. Check to make sure the retainers are properly installed. The large end should press against the gearcase housing lip with the small end between the bearing housing bosses.
 f. Tighten the screws to 18-20 ft.-lb. (24-27 N•m).

18. Coat both sides of a new water passage cover gasket with OMC Gasket Sealing Compound. Install the gasket on the gearcase and coat all water passage cover studs with the same sealer.
19. Install the water passage cover over the studs (**Figure 59**) and push into place by hand. If it will not seat completely, tap into place with a suitable hammer. Install the flat washers and new locknuts on the studs, then tighten to 9-11 ft.-lb. (12-15 N•m).
20. If water passage seal requires replacement, remove the guide and seal (**Figure 60**). Press a new seal into the cover outlet (without sealant) and reinstall the guide.
21. Wipe both sides of a new shift rod cover gasket with OMC Gasket Sealing Compound. Install the gasket and shift rod/cover

assembly (**Figure 61**). Hold the cover above the gasket and thread the shift rod into the detent 4-5 full turns, then seat the cover on the gasket.

22. Wipe the shift rod cover capscrew threads with OMC Gasket Sealing Compound. Install and tighten the capscrews to 60-84 in.-lb. (7-9 N•m).
23. Install 2 new thick O-rings on the drive shaft bearing housing. Coat the O-rings with OMC Gasket Sealing Compound (**Figure 62**), then coat the entire surface of the housing with the same sealer to prevent any buildup of corrosion between the water passage cover and bearing housing.
24. Reinstall the anode to the front of the gearcase (**Figure 63**).
25. Pressure/vacuum test the gearcase as described in this chapter.
26. Place shift rod height gauge part No. 912277 on the gearcase housing beside the shift rod. Screw the shift rod in or out as required to bring the top of the rod into contact with the bottom of the gauge reference arm. If notched side of shift rod head is not facing forward when contact is made, turn rod up to 1/2 turn in either direction to properly position the shift rod head.
27. Install the unit to the upper drive shaft housing as described in this chapter.
28. Reinstall the propeller as described in this chapter.
29. Fill the gearcase housing with the recommended type and amount of lubricant. See Chapter Four.

Lower Gearcase Pressure and Vacuum Check

Whenever the lower gearcase is overhauled, it should be pressure and vacuum tested before refilling with lubricant to make sure that the unit is correctly sealed in both directions. If leaks are not detected, water will

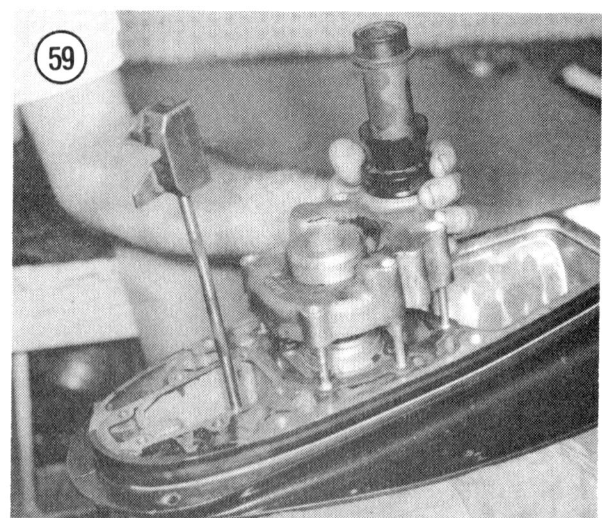
59

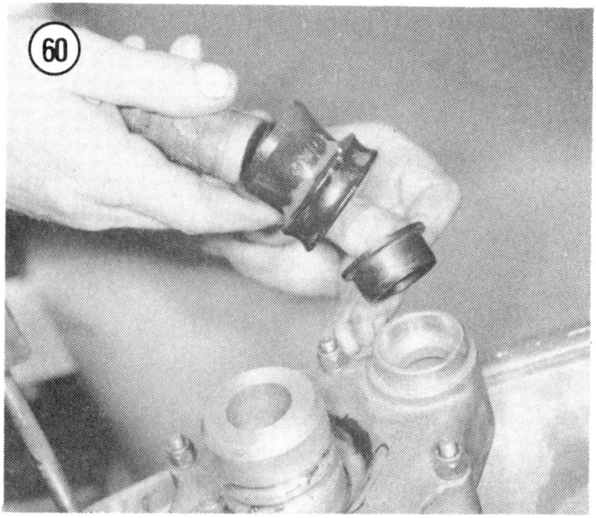
60

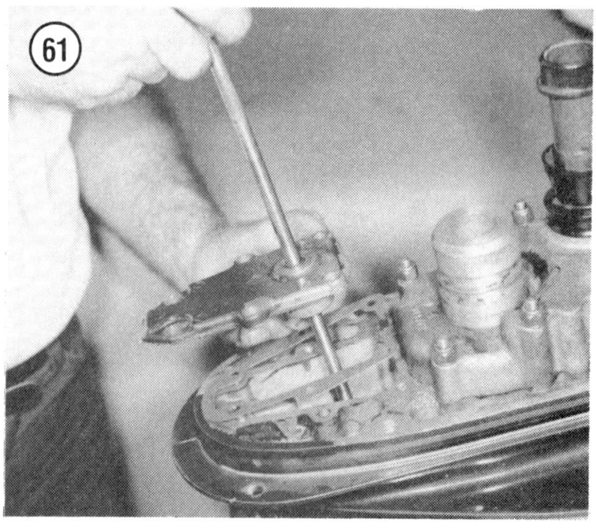
61

enter the gearcase and cause extensive damage.

OMC recommends the use of an S-34 pressure tester and a V-34 vacuum tester. If these or appropriate substitutes cannot be rented in your area, they can be purchased from the Stevens Instrument Commpany, 111 Greenwood Avenue, Waukegan, IL 60085. You will also need a one-inch expandable rubber plug for installation inside the drive shaft bearing housing.

1. Install the one-inch expandable rubber plug in the drive shaft bearing housing. Tighten the plug securely.

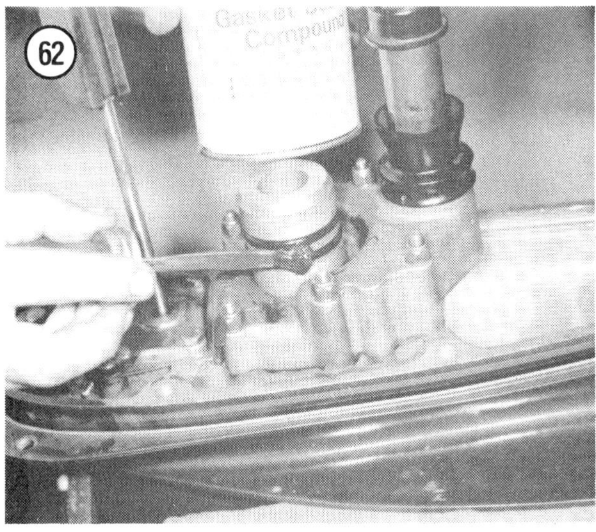

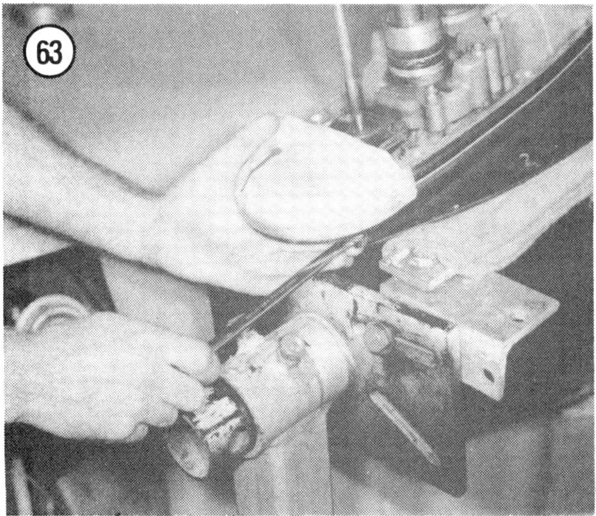

2. Install the magnetic drain plug with a new washer and tighten to 5-7 ft.-lb. (7-9 N•m).

3. Remove the oil level plug at the top of the gearcase.

4. Connect the pressure tester according to the manufacturer's instructions.

5. Pressurize the gearcase to 3-6 psi for 15 minutes and rotate the propeller shaft. If the gearcase does not maintain the pressure, submerge the unit in a tank of water to locate the air leaks.

6. Repeat Step 5 with the gearcase pressurized to 16-18 psi. The gearcase should not lose more than 1 psi in 3 minutes at this pressure.

7. Connect the vacuum tester according to manufacturer's instructions.

8. Draw 3-5 in. Hg vacuum. After 15 minutes, there should be no loss of vacuum. If the gearcase does not hold vacuum as specified, use a heavy oil on the seal and gasket surfaces to determine the source of the leak.

9. Repeat Step 8 with 15 in. Hg vacuum. The gearcase should not lose more than 1 in. Hg in 3 minutes at this vacuum.

10. If the gearcase fails to hold the pressure or vacuum as specified, disassemble and reassemble, paying special attention to sealants and gasket installation. Repeat this procedure to recheck the gearcase.

Propeller

The propeller rides on thrust bushings and is retained by a castellated nut and cotter pin. Any impact caused by hitting an underwater object is absorbed by the rubber propeller hub, which acts as a shock absorber. An underwater impact, however, may loosen the rubber hub and cause the propeller to slip.

Removal/Installation (Normal Conditions)

WARNING
Wear heavy gloves when removing or installing the propeller to protect your hands from the sharp edges of the propeller blades.

Refer to **Figure 64** (2.3L, 2.5L and 3.0L) or **Figure 65** (all others) for this procedure.

1. Make sure the remote control is in NEUTRAL and the key is removed from the ignition switch.
2. Straighten the cotter pin legs (**Figure 66**) and remove the cotter pin and keeper (if used).
3. Fit a piece of wood between the propeller and the anti-ventilation plate to prevent the propeller from turning. Loosen the propeller nut.
4. Remove the nut and spacer (**Figure 67**).
5. Remove the propeller from the prop shaft.
6. Remove the thrust bushing (**Figure 68**).
7. Wipe the propeller shaft splines with a thin coat of OMC Triple-Guard Grease.
8. Installation is the reverse of removal. Tighten the propeller nut on 2.3L, 2.5L and 3.0L to 10 ft.-lb. (14 N•m). If the cotter pin and shaft holes do not align, continue tightening until they do, then install a new cotter pin and bend the legs over. On all other models, tighten the nut to 70-80 ft.-lb. (95-108 N•m). Index the keeper on the propeller nut until it is aligned with the cotter pin hole. Install a new cotter pin and bend the legs over.

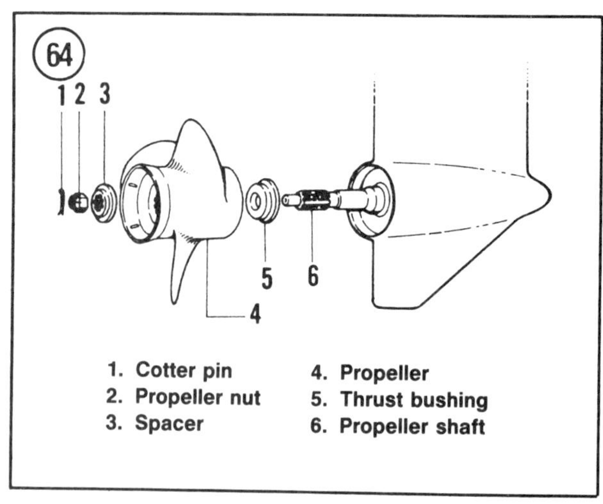

1. Cotter pin
2. Propeller nut
3. Spacer
4. Propeller
5. Thrust bushing
6. Propeller shaft

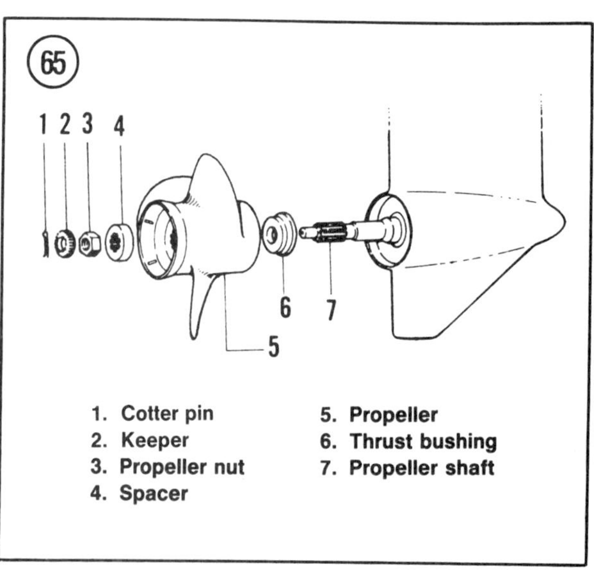

1. Cotter pin
2. Keeper
3. Propeller nut
4. Spacer
5. Propeller
6. Thrust bushing
7. Propeller shaft

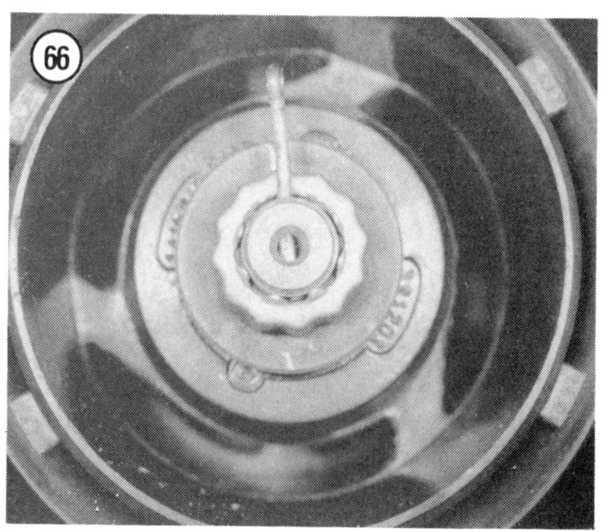

Removal/Installation (Frozen Propeller)

Under certain conditions, the propeller may not be removed easily. The rubber hub inside the propeller contains a sleeve or bushing which fits over the propeller shaft. If this sleeve becomes corroded, propeller removal can be very difficult. Striking the propeller with a soft-faced mallet is not very helpful and in many cases, may even damage the unit. The following procedure can be used in such cases.

Refer to **Figure 64** (2.3L, 2.5L and 3.0L) or **Figure 65** (all others) for this procedure.

WARNING
Wear heavy gloves when removing or installing the propeller to protect your hands from the sharp edges of the propeller blades.

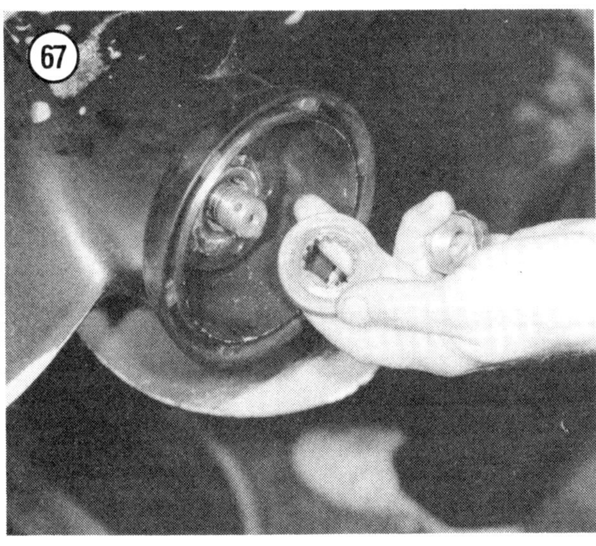

67

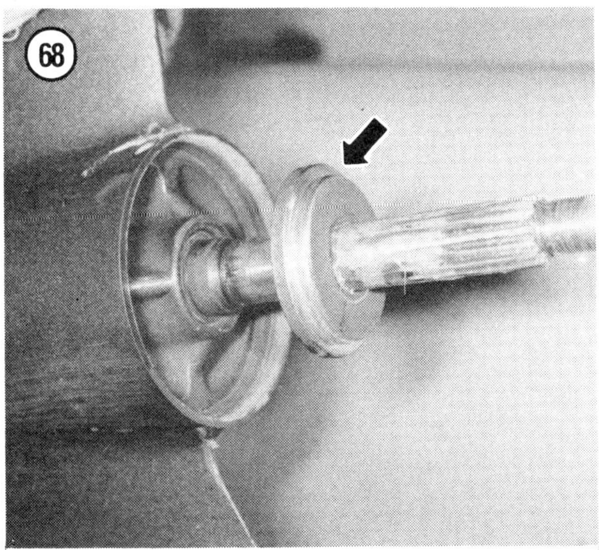

68

1. Make sure the remote control is in NEUTRAL and the key is removed from the ignition switch.
2. Straighten the cotter pin legs (**Figure 66**) and remove the cotter pin and keeper (if used).
3. Fit a piece of wood between the propeller and the anti-ventilation plate to prevent the propeller from turning. Loosen the propeller nut.
4. Remove the nut and spacer (**Figure 67**).

CAUTION
Do not apply heat to the outer surface of the propeller in Step 5. This can damage the unit beyond repair. The idea is to melt the inner rubber hub and allow the propeller to be removed leaving the inner sleeve on the propeller shaft.

5. Use an acetylene torch to apply heat to the inside diameter of the propeller. This will gradually melt the inner rubber hub. While heat is being applied, have a helper wedge a suitable wooden block between the gearcase housing and a propeller blade, using it as a pry bar to force the propeller off the inner sleeve.
6. Once the propeller has been removed, install a puller that will draw on the thrust bushing. Continue applying heat to the inner sleeve and tighten the puller. This will remove the inner sleeve and thrust bushing from the propeller shaft.
7. Once the inner sleeve has been removed, allow the propeller shaft to cool, then clean the shaft splines thoroughly and inspect for damage. If the splines are not damaged, the propeller shaft can be reused. However, if the splines are damaged, the propeller shaft should be replaced.
8. Wipe the propeller shaft splines with a thin coat of OMC Triple-Guard Grease.
9. Install the new propeller as described in this chapter.

Table 1 TIGHTENING TORQUES

Fastener	in.-lb.	ft.-lb.	N•m
Drive shaft bearing housing		14-16	19-22
Gearcase drain plug		5-7	7-9
Gearcase fill plug	60-84		7-9
Gearcase mounting bolts		22-24	30-33
Pinion bearing screw	48-84		5-9
Pinion gear nut			
460 cu. in. (7.5L) King Cobra		100-110	136-149
All others		70-75	95-102
Propeller shaft bearing housing			
460 cu. in. (7.5L) King Cobra		18-20	24-27
All others		10-12	14-16
Shift rod cover	60-84		7-9
Trim tab		28-32	38-43
Water passage cover		9-11	12-15

Chapter Fourteen

Transom Assembly

The stern drive (outside the boat) and the engine (inside the boat) must be connected by hydraulic, electrical and cooling lines. In addition, the stern drive's upper gearcase drive shaft must connect to the engine flywheel/coupler. The transom assembly serves as a waterproof passage through which these components all pass, as well as a mounting point for the stern drive unit. This chapter covers removal, overhaul and installation of the OMC Cobra transom assembly components, including the pivot housing, gimbal bearing and gimbal ring.

Transom assembly service generally involves bellows and water hose replacement, as well as gimbal bearing replacement. A defective bellows or seal will allow water to enter the boat through the transom assembly. All transom assembly service requires removal of the stern drive unit.

Figure 1 (King Cobra) and **Figure 2** (all others) show the components of the transom assembly.

Table 1 is at the end of the chapter.

PIVOT HOUSING

Removal

Refer to **Figure 1** (King Cobra) or **Figure 2** (all others) as required for this procedure.

1. Remove the stern drive. See Chapter Twelve.
2. Disconnect the shift cable at the engine. See **Figure 3** (typical).
3. Remove the retainer screw at the end of the shift lever. See A, **Figure 4** (typical). Unscrew the retainer.
4. Carefully lift the U-joint bellows from the pivot housing lip at one point. Work your finger or a flat dull tool around the inside of the bellows to disengage it from the pivot housing, then push the bellows inside the housing.

NOTE
On early models, you may find a snap ring used instead of a wire retaining ring. If so, use suitable snap ring pliers to remove it in Step 5.

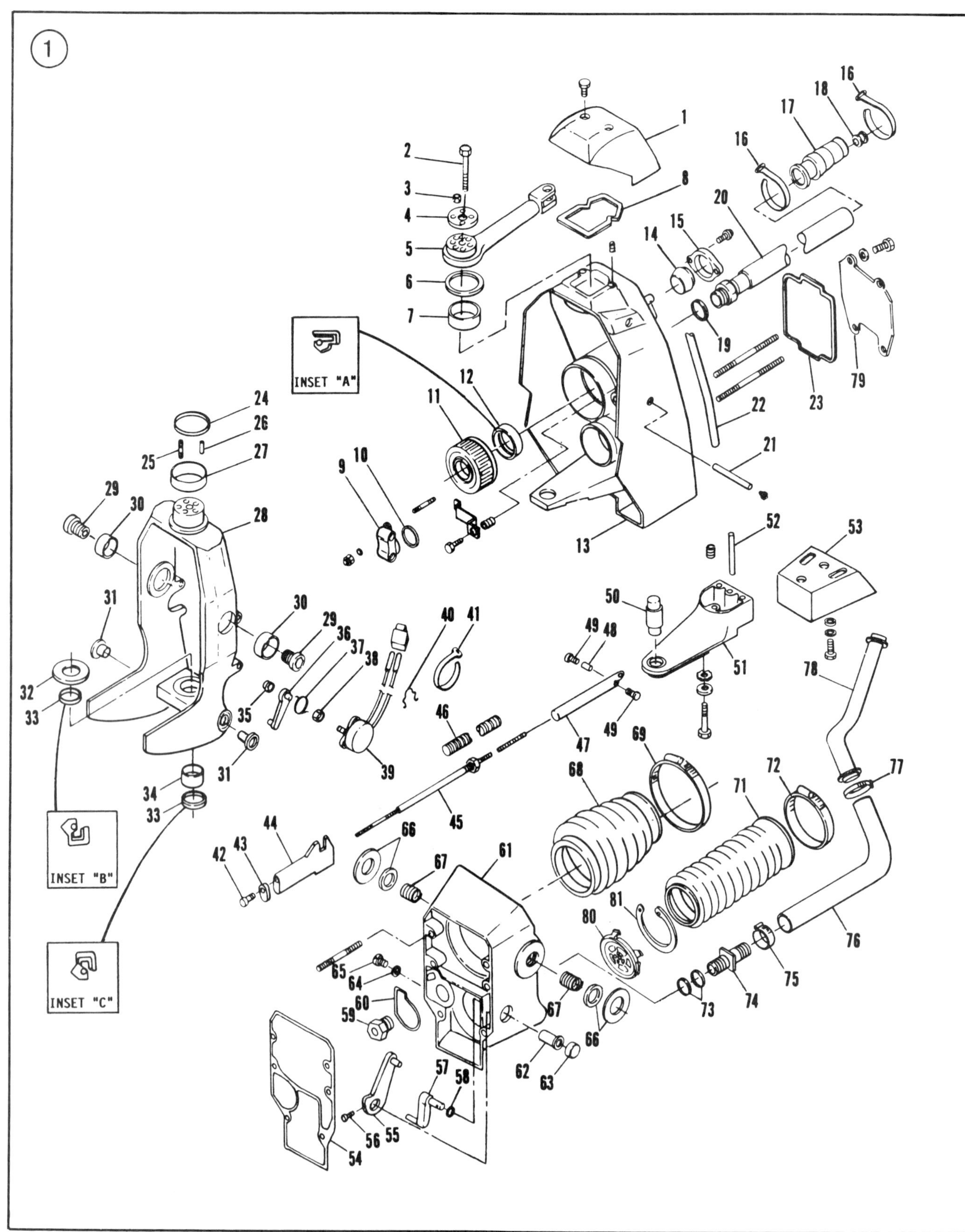
1
INSET "A"
INSET "B"
INSET "C"

TRANSOM MOUNT (KING COBRA)

1. Cover
2. Steering arm screw
3. Steering arm stud locknut
4. Steering arm plate
5. Steering arm
6. Thrust washer
7. Steering bearing
8. Gasket
9. Manifold block
10. O-ring
11. Universal joint bearing
12. Drive shaft seal
13. Gimbal housing
14. Water tube bushing
15. Water tube retainer
16. Seal-to-sleeve tie strap
17. Shift cable seal
18. Shift cable grommet
19. Sleeve and connector O-ring
20. Sleeve and connector
21. Grease tube
22. Transom seal
23. Exhaust pipe seal
24. O-ring
25. Stud
26. Steering arm dowel
27. Gimbal sleeve
28. Gimbal
29. Pivot screw
30. Steering and tilt bearing
31. Pivot pin bushings
32. Thrust washer
33. Pivot shaft seal
34. Steering and tilt bearing
35. Arm retainer
36. Arm
37. Spring
38. Nut
39. Trim sender
40. Trim sender lead retainer
41. Tie wrap (sender leads to oil line)
42. Shift cable retainer screw
43. Shift cable retainer
44. Shift cable guide
45. Shift cable core wire
46. Shift cable casing
47. Shift cable casing guide
48. Shift cable clamp
49. Setscrews
50. Steering pivot shaft
51. Steering support bracket
52. Steering support pin
53. Anode and insert assembly
54. Gear housing to pivot housing gasket
55. Shift lever and roller
56. Shift lever screw
57. Shift bellcrank
58. O-ring
59. Nipple nut
60. Water passage seal
61. Pivot housing
62. Bellcrank bushing
63. Bellcrank plug
64. O-ring
65. Plug
66. Gimbal to pivot housing washer (smaller thrust washer inboard on 1988-1989 models)
67. Pivot screw insert
68. Universal joint bellows
69. Universal joint bellows clamp
71. Exhaust bellows
72. Exhaust bellows clamp
73. O-ring(s)
74. Water inlet nipple
75. Water hose clamp
76. Water inlet hose
77. Hose clamp
78. Water tube
79. Exhaust cover plate
80. Pivot housing plug
81. Snap ring

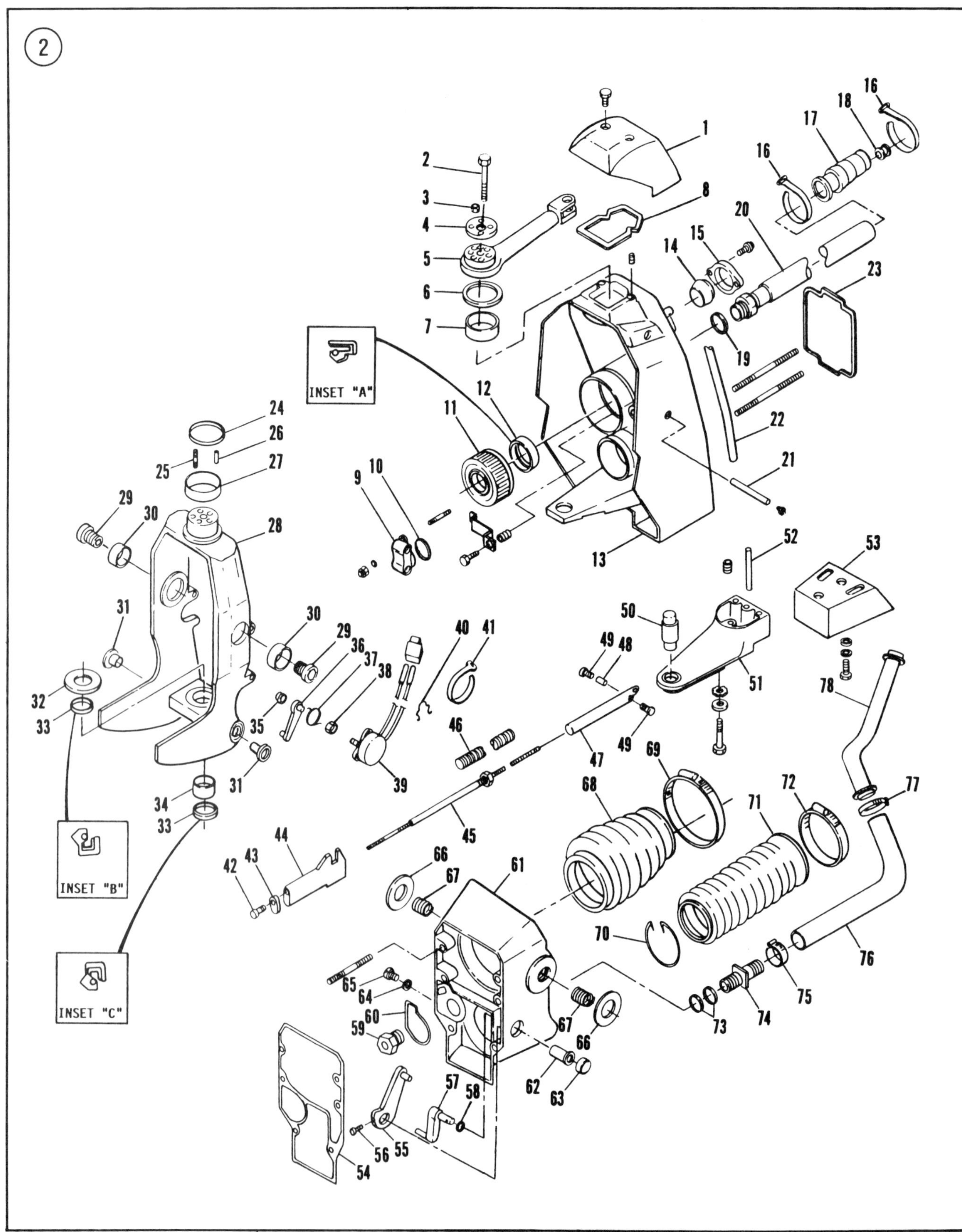
2
INSET "A"
INSET "B"
INSET "C"

TRANSOM MOUNT (EXCEPT KING COBRA)

1. Cover
2. Steering arm screw
3. Steering arm stud locknut
4. Steering arm plate
5. Steering arm
6. Thrust washer
7. Steering bearing
8. Gasket
9. Manifold block
10. O-ring
11. Universal joint bearing
12. Drive shaft seal
13. Gimbal housing
14. Water tube bushing
15. Water tube retainer
16. Seal-to-sleeve tie strap
17. Shift cable seal
18. Shift cable grommet
19. Sleeve and connector O-ring
20. Sleeve and connector
21. Grease tube
22. Transom seal
23. Exhaust pipe seal
24. O-ring
25. Stud
26. Steering arm dowel
27. Gimbal sleeve
28. Gimbal
29. Pivot screw
30. Tilt bearing
31. Pivot pin bushings
32. Thrust washer
33. Pivot shaft seal
34. Steering bearing
35. Arm retainer
36. Arm
37. Spring
38. Nut
39. Trim sender
40. Trim sender lead retainer
41. Tie wrap (sender leads to oil line)
42. Shift cable retainer screw
43. Shift cable retainer
44. Shift cable guide
45. Shift cable core wire
46. Shift cable casing
47. Shift cable casing guide
48. Shift cable clamp
49. Setscrews
50. Steering pivot shaft
51. Steering support bracket
52. Steering support pin
53. Anode and insert assembly
54. Gear housing to pivot housing gasket
55. Shift lever and roller
56. Shift lever screw
57. Shift bellcrank
58. O-ring
59. Nipple nut
60. Water passage seal
61. Pivot housing
62. Bellcrank bushing
63. Bellcrank plug
64. O-ring
65. Plug
66. Gimbal to pivot housing washer (smaller thrust washer inboard on 1988 models)
67. Pivot screw insert
68. Universal joint bellows
69. Universal joint bellows clamp
70. Exhaust bellows clip
71. Exhaust bellows
72. Exhaust bellows clamp
73. O-ring(s)
74. Water inlet nipple
75. Water hose clamp
76. Water inlet hose
77. Hose clamp
78. Water tube

5. On all except 1987 460 cu. in. (7.5L) King Cobra and 1988 350 cu. in. (5.7L) King Cobra, insert a pair of suitable pliers and grasp the ears of the wire retaining ring installed inside the exhaust bellows. Compress and remove the ring, then push the bellows inside the housing.
6. Loosen and unscrew the water hose nipple nut (B, **Figure 4**). Remove the nut and push the nipple through the housing as far as it will go.
7. Remove the pivot pin on each side of the housing (A, **Figure 5**) with a 1/2 in. hex drive socket or wrench.
8. Grasp the pivot housing securely and pull it out as far as possible. Loosen the shift cable retaining nut, then remove the housing from the cable and the transom assembly.

Disassembly

Refer to **Figure 1** (King Cobra) or **Figure 2** (all others) as required for this procedure.

1. If the bellows require removal or replacement, loosen the worm screw on each clamp. Pull the bellows from the pivot housing and discard the clamps.
2. Remove the shift cable guide from the pivot housing.
3. Remove and discard the O-ring seal installed around the cooling passage. See C, **Figure 4**.
4. Unscrew each of the 3 water drain/vent plugs. See B, **Figure 5** for typical location. Discard the plug seals.
5. Remove and discard the screw holding the shift lever in place.
6. Separate the bellcrank from the shift lever by pulling it sideways, then remove the shift lever and roller assembly. Discard the bellcrank O-ring.

NOTE
The bellcrank bushing or bearing should not be removed unless they are corroded, damaged or bind the shift lever.

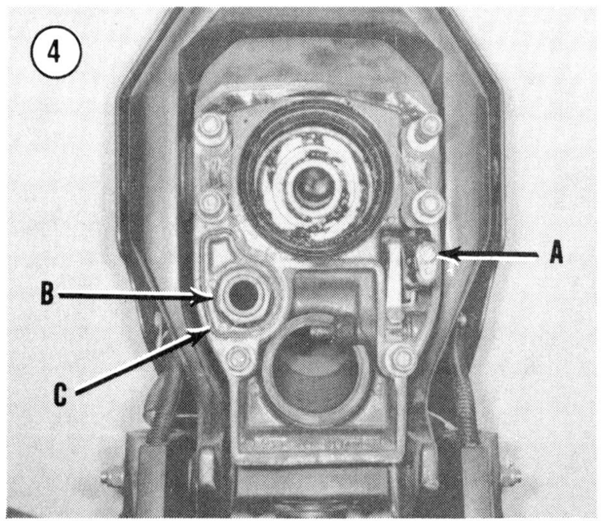

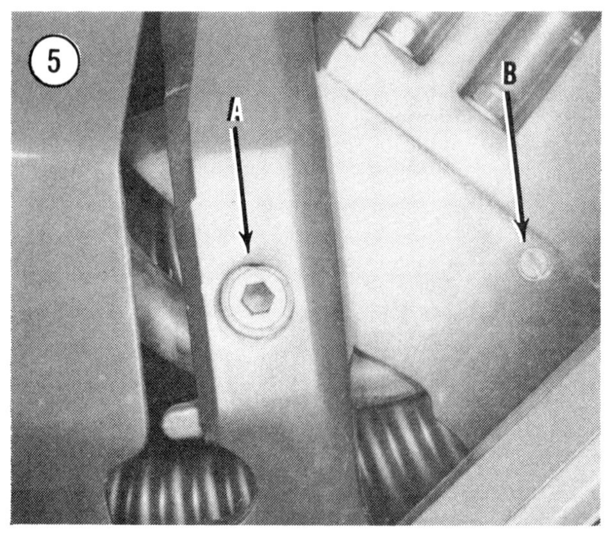

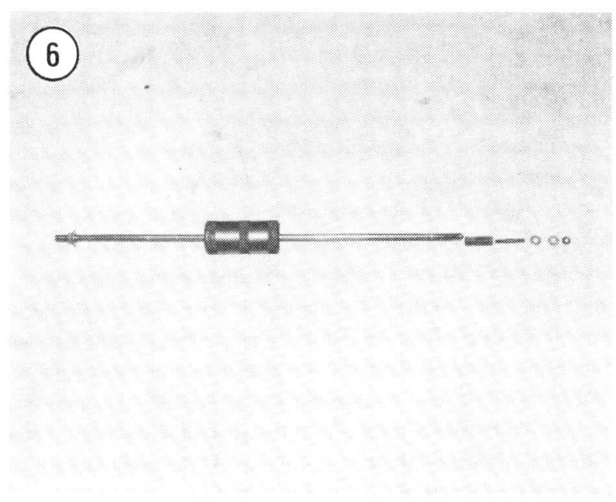

7. Check the bellcrank bushing and bearing as described in Step 5 of *Cleaning and Inspection.* If either requires replacement:
   a. Position large end of driver part No. 912270 against the bearing. Tap the driver with a hammer until the bearing is free of the pivot housing.
   b. To remove the bushing, assemble puller pin part No. 391008, adapter part No. 390898, adapter stud, 2 1/4 in. I.D.×5/8 in. O.D. flat washers and a 1/4-20 nut as shown in **Figure 6**. Insert the tool through the bushing, then install the washers and nut. Tighten the adapter and pull the bushing from the housing.
8. Check the condition of the nylon friction washers on the pivot housing bosses. If damaged or deteriorated, peel off and discard.
9. Check condition of thrust washers underneath the friction washers; replace if corroded or damaged.

Cleaning and Inspection

1. Clean the pivot housing and all metal components in fresh solvent. Blow dry with compressed air, if available.
2. Remove all sealant or adhesive residue from the pivot housing and components. Be sure to clean the shift lever bearing and bushing, pivot bosses, bellcrank, U-joint bellows opening and coolant passage opening.

CAUTION
Screw holes contain Heli-Coil inserts and should not be cleaned with a thread tap.

3. Check the bellcrank for burrs, corrosion or sharp edges on the O-ring groove. Correct or replace bellcrank as required.
4. Check the shift lever roller to make sure it rotates freely. Replace shift lever if screw hole threads are damaged.
5. Check the inside diameter of the bearing and bushing for any corrosion, burrs or distortion that can hinder or restrict free movement.
6. Inspect all mounting studs to make sure they are tightly installed and that their threads are not damaged; replace as required.
7. Make sure that the drain hole is not plugged. If it is, clean with a suitable instrument so that water can drain completely.
8. Check the coolant passage O-ring groove for nicks or burrs that will prevent proper sealing of the passage. Correct as required.

Assembly

Refer to **Figure 1** (King Cobra) or **Figure 2** (all others) as required for this procedure.

1. If the bushing was removed:
   a. Spray a new bushing with OMC Locquic Primer, then spray the bushing bore in the pivot housing with the same substance. Let both surfaces air dry.
   b. Slip a new bushing over driver part No. 912270. Lightly coat the outside of the bushing with OMC Nut Lock. Position the bushing and tool in the pivot housing bore. Tap the bushing in place with a suitable mallet.
2. If the bearing was removed:
   a. Position stop gauge part No. 984322 on the housing over the studs (this limits

bearing depth to prevent shift lever binding).

b. Spray the bearing with OMC Locquic Primer. Let it air dry, then wipe the outside of the bearing with OMC Nut Lock. Position the bearing in its bore and install with the large end of driver part No. 912270 and a suitable mallet until it contacts the stop gauge.

3. Wipe 3 new drain/vent plug O-rings with OMC Gasket Sealing Compound. Install an O-ring on each plug, then install the plugs and tighten to 50-60 in.-lb. (6-7 N•m).

4. Coat a new bellcrank O-ring with OMC Triple-Guard Grease. Install the O-ring in the bellcrank groove, then wipe the length of the shaft with the same lubricant.

5. Position the shift lever and roller assembly between the bushing and bearing. Insert the bellcrank into the shift lever so it engages the lever keyway and seats fully.

WARNING
Never reuse a shift lever screw or substitute another type of fastener. If the shift lever and bellcrank should separate, the resulting loss of control over the boat can result in a serious accident.

6. Align the screw hole in the shift lever with the recess in the bellcrank. Install a new screw and tighten to 5-7 ft.-lb. (7-9 N•m).

7. Coat the coolant passage O-ring groove with OMC Adhesive M and install a new O-ring.

8. If the pivot boss friction washers were removed, make sure that there is a good thrust washer in each pivot bore. Install new friction washers and wipe with OMC Triple-Guard Grease.

9. Position the shift lever so the cable guide will slip under the roller, then depress the shift lever to hold the guide in place.

10. If the bellows were removed, reinstall with a new worm-type clamp.

Installation

Refer to **Figure 1** (King Cobra) or **Figure 2** (all others) as required for this procedure.

1. Coat a new shift cable O-ring with OMC Gasket Sealing Compound. Slip the O-ring on the end of the cable and seat against the fitting hex. Wipe any excess sealant from the end of the cable and coat the entire length of the cable with OMC Triple-Guard Grease.

2. Fit the end of the cable through the housing and into the guide. Thread the fitting in place and tighten with a crowfoot adapter to 35-37 ft.-lb. (47-50 N•m). To assure an accurate torque reading, make sure the crowfoot adapter is installed at a 90 degree angle on the torque wrench.

3. Fit the pivot housing into the gimbal ring, guiding the water tube nipple through the housing and positioning the 2 bellows behind their respective openings.

4. Align the pivot pin holes in the gimbal housing and pivot housing on one side. Make sure that the friction washer has not slipped out of place, then install the pivot pin and screw it in until it seats.

5. Repeat Step 4 to install the other pivot pin. Pivot the housing up and down to make sure it moves freely without binding, then tighten both pivot pins to 105-120 ft.-lb. (142-163 N•m) with a 1/2 in. hex socket.

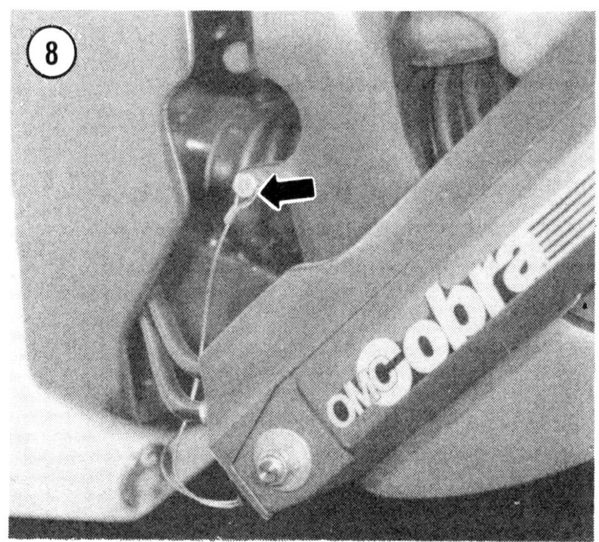

8

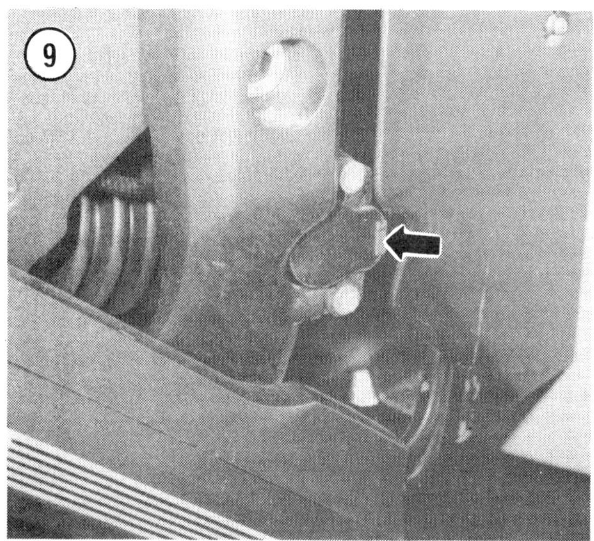

9

6. Pull the water tube through the pivot housing as far as possible, then install the nipple nut (B, **Figure 4**). Make sure the square nipple collar is located correctly behind the housing and tighten the nut to 96-120 in.-lb. (11-14 N•m). Double-check for correct collar location by trying to turn the nipple. If it can be turned, the collar is not properly seated. In this case, pull the nipple outward and turn it until the collar seats properly, then hold the pressure on the nipple and tighten the nut to the specifications above.
7. Coat the V-shaped lip inside the U-joint bellows opening with OMC Gasket Sealing Compound. Pull the bellows through the opening and seat in the groove lip. If necessary, tilt the pivot housing and reach through the exhaust opening to engage the bellows lip. Make sure that there are no flat spots on the lip (indicating the bellows has not engaged the groove), as the bellows must seal the entire circular opening.

NOTE
Do not use sealer on the exhaust bellows lip in Step 8.

8. On all except 1987 460 cu. in. (7.5L) King Cobra and 1988 350 cu. in. (5.7L) King Cobra, pull the exhaust bellows through the pivot housing and seat its channel around the pivot housing opening lip. Install the wire retaining ring or snap ring to keep it in place.

GIMBAL RING

Removal

Refer to **Figure 1** (King Cobra) or **Figure 2** (all others) as required for this procedure.

1. Remove the pivot housing as described in this chapter.
2. Remove the screw and lockwasher holding the ground wire to the port side of the gimbal ring (**Figure 8**).
3. Hold the locknut on one side of the trim/tilt cylinder shaft with one wrench and unscrew the locknut on the other side with a second wrench. Remove the locknut and washer, then withdraw the shaft completely from the gimbal ring. Carefully position the trim/tilt cylinders to prevent stressing the hydraulic lines.
4. Move the gimbal ring as far as possible to port and remove the screws holding the trim sender (**Figure 9**). Let the sender hang by its leads, which are fastened to the transom bracket.
5. Remove the 3 screws and lockwashers from the lower steering support bracket. If bracket removal is difficult after the screws

are removed, use a drift punch and mallet to drive the bracket off, rapping on alternate sides until the bracket comes free.

6. Remove the 2 screws holding the gimbal housing cover. Remove the 2 screws and steering cavity cap located under the cover. Peel the foam gasket off and discard it.

7. Remove the 4 elastic locknuts and retaining plate from the top of the steering arm. Unscrew the steering arm center bolt.

8. Position steering arm puller part No. 984146 on the 2 alignment dowels inside the steering arm and reinstall the steering arm center bolt removed in Step 7. Hold the gimbal ring with one hand and tighten the bolt to pull the steering arm off. When the steering arm comes free, remove the gimbal ring.

Disassembly

Refer to **Figure 1** (King Cobra) or **Figure 2** (all others) as required for this procedure.

1. Remove and discard the upper pivot O-ring.

2. Position the large end of remover/installer part No. 912281 so that it faces the gimbal ring (**Figure 10**). Fit the tool into one of the pivot screw tilt bearings and drive it out, then repeat the step to remove the other tilt bearing.

3. Connect puller part No. 391010 (or an equivalent 2-jaw puller) to a slide hammer and remove both nylon cylinder shaft bushings.

4. Pry the lower pivot bearing seal out with an awl or screwdriver blade (**Figure 11**), then fit the large end of remover/installer part No. 912281 in the bearing. Drive the bearing and upper seal from the gimbal ring. See **Figure 12**.

Assembly

Refer to **Figure 1** (King Cobra) or **Figure 2** (all others) as required for this procedure.

1. Lightly lubricate the outer diameter of a new lower pivot bearing and fit it on the end

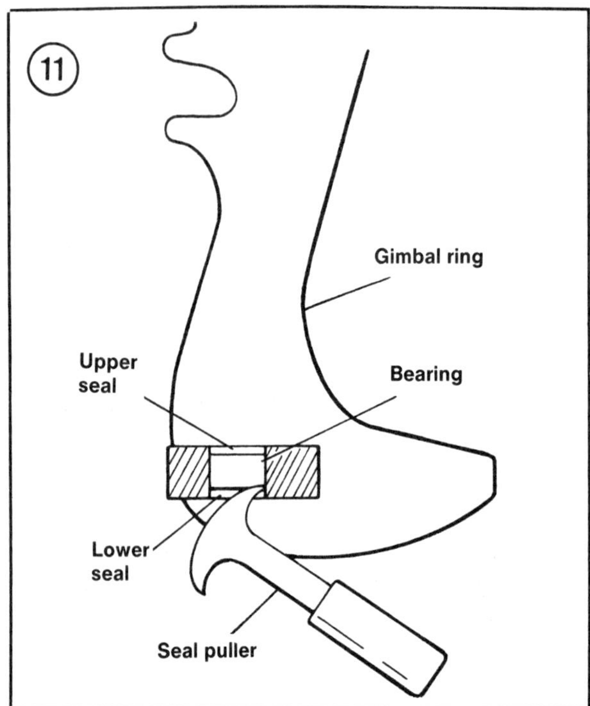

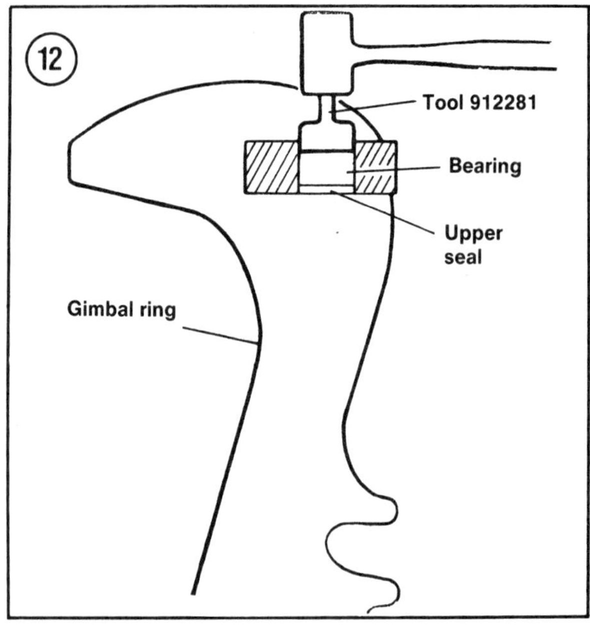

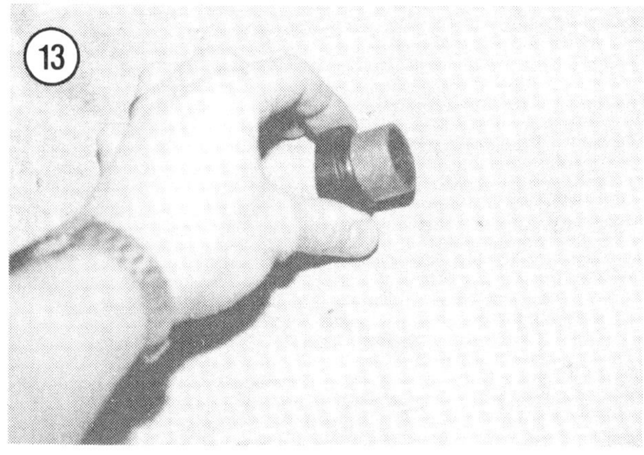

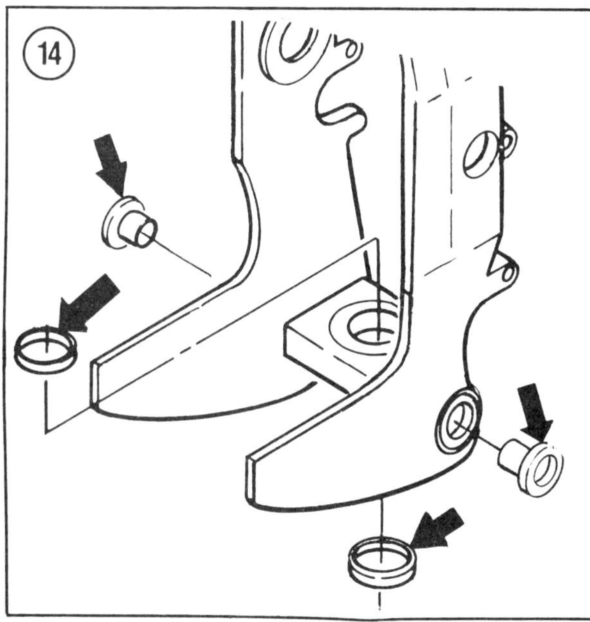

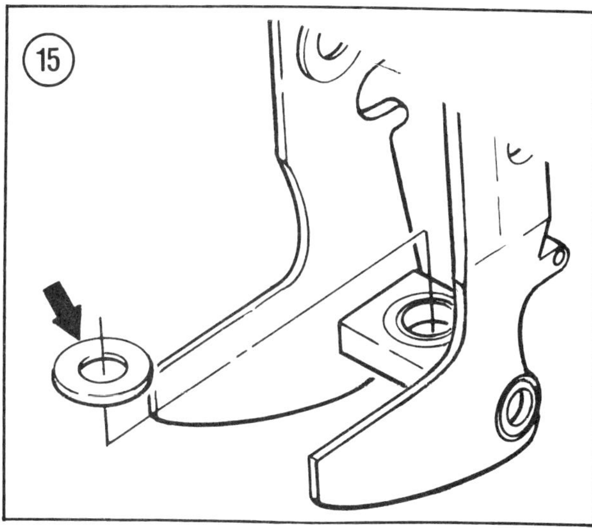

of installer part No. 912271 (**Figure 13**). Drive the bearing into the gimbal ring until it bottoms.

2. Fit a new seal on the blunt end of installer part No. 912271 with the lip facing the tool. Wipe the metal case with a light coat of OMC Gasket Sealing Compound and drive the seal in place over the bearing until it seats. Repeat this step to install the other seal.

3. Wipe the outer diameter of 2 new nylon bushings with OMC Triple-Guard Grease. Drive each bushing in place in the cylinder shaft bore with installer part No. 912281 until it seats.

4. Wipe the lips of both pivot seals and the inside of both nylon bushings with OMC Triple-Guard Grease. See **Figure 14**.

5. Fit a new tilt bearing on the blunt end of installer part No. 912281. Lightly lubricate the outside of the bearing and insert the tool and bearing into the gimbal ring from the outside. Place gimbal ring and bearing assembly into a vise and press the bearing in place by tightening the vise jaws until the bearing seats. When properly installed, the bearing should be flush to 0.010 in. below the inner surface of the gimbal ring. Repeat this step to install the other tilt bearing.

6. Wipe a new O-ring with OMC Triple-Guard Grease and install it around the upper steering post base.

Installation

Refer to **Figure 1** (King Cobra) or **Figure 2** (all others) as required for this procedure.

1. Position the thrust washer over the upper pivot bearing located inside the top of the gimbal housing.

2. Working from inside the boat, place the steering arm over the upper steering bearing inside the gimbal housing.

3. Wipe the nylon thrust washer with OMC Triple-Guard Grease and position it on top of the lower steering pivot seal (**Figure 15**).

4. If the lower pivot post fell out during disassembly, reinstall it in the lower support. Slide the gimbal ring up and over the lower steering post into the upper steering bearing and steering arm. Thread the center bolt in place finger-tight. Check to make sure the gimbal studs are flush with the top of the steering arm at this point. This indicates that the gimbal ring is correctly centered in the upper bearing. If the studs are not flush, repeat this step to correctly position it, as tightening the center bolt will damage the upper bearing. When properly centered, tighten the bolt to 65-72 ft.-lb. (88-98 N•m).
5. Fit the washer on the top of the steering arm, then install new elastic locknuts and tighten to 12-14 ft.-lb. (16-19 N•m).
6. Fit a new foam seal on the bottom of the steering cavity cap (**Figure 16**), aligning the seal notches carefully with the cap notches.
7. Install the steering cavity cap and tighten the mounting screws to 60-84 in.-lb. (7-9 N•m). Place the gimbal housing cover in position and install the mounting screws, tightening to 60-84 in.-lb. (7-9 N•m).
8. Reinstall the lower steering support bracket, seating it in place with a mallet, if necessary. Connect the ground wires to the 2 forward screws, then install the lockwashers. Install the 3 mounting screws and tighten to 18-20 ft.-lb. (24-27 N•m).
9. Rotate the gimbal ring fully to port and reinstall the trim sender unit, tightening the screws to 18-24 in.-lb. (2-3 N•m).

GIMBAL HOUSING

Disassembly/Assembly

Refer to **Figure 1** (King Cobra) or **Figure 2** (all others) as required for this procedure.

1. Remove the pivot housing as described in this chapter.

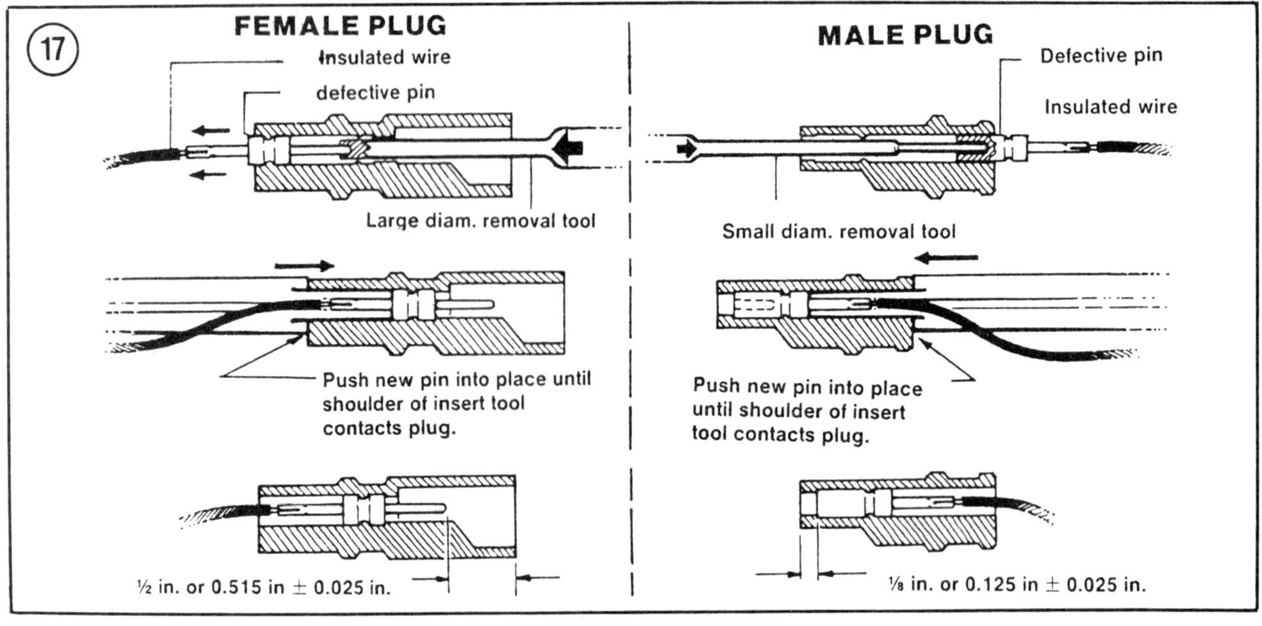

2. Remove the gimbal ring as described in this chapter.
3. Loosen the hose clamps around the exhaust and U-joint bellows and the water tube hose. Remove the bellows and hose.
4. Check the sacrificial anode. If less than 2/3 of the anode is missing, proceed to Step 5. If the anode requires replacement, remove the fasteners and ground wires holding the anode in place. Clean the anode mounting surface on the housing. Install a new anode and tighten the fasteners to 12-14 ft.-lb. (16-19 N•m).

NOTE
Whenever the trim sender is removed from the transom assembly, the component wires and its plug terminals must be removed from the connector. Connector terminals should be removed according to Step 5. Use of tools or lubricant other than specified can result in high resistance connections, short circuits between terminals or damage to the connector material.

5. Disconnect the trim sender rubber connector at the engine wiring harness.
   a. Lubricate the terminal pins with rubbing alcohol at both ends of the connector cavity.
   b. Hold the connector against the edge of a flat surface, allowing sufficient clearance for terminal removal.
   c. Insert socket removal tool part No. 322699 in the connector end of the plug and carefully push the terminals from the plug (**Figure 17**).
   d. Pull the large hairpin retaining clip from the grommet in the transom bracket, then push the grommet out of the hole with a screwdriver blade.
   e. Pull the trim sender wires through the hole and remove the trim sender and wire assembly from the gimbal housing.
6. Remove the 2 screws holding the water tube retainer. Pull the tube and grommet from the gimbal housing.
   a. If the grommet does not come out, move to the other side of the transom and push it out with a suitable punch or screwdriver blade.
   b. If the grommet is damaged or deteriorated, it must be replaced. Remove it from the water tube and discard.
7. To remove the shift cable:
   a. Slip the corrugated plastic casing off the shift cable and pull it out of the housing.
   b. Cut the tie straps holding the boot to the end of the cable sleeve inside the boat.
   c. Pull the boot from the sleeve, then pull out the cable assembly.
   d. Remove the split-ring grommet from the end of the boot and slide it off the cable.
   e. Remove the boot from the end of the cable.

NOTE
Check the condition of the gimbal bearing and upper pivot bearing in the gimbal housing. These bearings should not be removed unless they are worn or corroded and require replacement.

8. To replace the gimbal bearing:
   a. Insert a 3-jaw puller (part No. 4184 or equivalent), spreading the tool jaws behind the bearing and inner seal. Expand the jaws tightly behind the bearing and tighten the puller until the bearing comes out. Discard the bearing.
   b. Repeat sub-step a to remove the inner seal. Discard the seal.
   c. Fit a new inner seal on installer part No. 912279 with its open end facing the tool. Wipe the metal case of the seal with a light coat of OMC Gasket Sealing Compound.
   d. Thread the installer into drive handle part No. 311880. Drive the seal into the housing until fully seated, then wipe the

seal lip with OMC Triple-Guard Grease.

e. Rotate the outer band of a new gimbal bearing until it aligns with the bearing lubrication hole (**Figure 18**), then scribe a reference mark on the bearing case. This will help you to correctly position the gimbal bearing and assure that it will receive sufficient lubrication when installed.

f. Wipe the outside of the bearing case with lubricant, then insert the bearing in the housing with the scribed mark facing the extension tube opening.

g. Attach installer part No. 912279 to drive handle part No. 311880 (raised side of installer facing handle) and drive the bearing in place until it seats.

h. Lubricate the grease fitting on the starboard side of the gimbal housing with OMC Maring Wheel Bearing Grease.

9. To replace the upper pivot bearing:

a. Remove the thrust washer from the top of the bearing.

b. Insert driver part No. 912270 into installer part No. 912287. Position the assembly underneath the bearing.

c. Drive the bearing up and out of the bracket.

d. Fit installer part No. 912287 to puller rod part No. 326582. Position a new bearing on the installer and lightly lubricate the outer diameter.

e. Working from inside the boat, insert installer part No. 912286 into the steering arm cavity with its recessed side facing down.

f. Thread puller rod into the installer until it is flush with the installer. Hold the rod and tighten the nut to draw the bearing into place.

10. Reinstall the trim sender as follows:

a. Wipe the sender lead grommet with OMC Triple-Guard Grease. Route the wires through the gimbal housing rear opening and through the transom plate. Make sure they are not under any other lines (they must move freely during drive unit movement), then install and seat the grommet in the hole.

18

19

b. Reinstall the large hairpin retaining clip to the grommet inside the transom plate.

c. Lubricate the rubber connector cavity with rubbing alcohol.

d. Place socket installer part No. 322697 against the wire socket shoulder. Carefully guide the socket into the rear of the connector plug cavity and press it in place until the tool shoulder rests against the connector plug (**Figure 17**). Withdraw the installer and repeat this step to install the remaining sockets.

e. Reconnect the connector plug halves.

11. Reinstall the water tube and grommet. If the grommet was damaged or deteriorated,

slide a new grommet onto the tube. Working from inside the transom, fit the hooked end of the tube through the gimbal housing and position the retainer plate on the grommet. Hold the tube in a vertical position and install the mounting screws (**Figure 19**), then tighten them to 10-12 ft.-lb. (14-16 N•m).

12. To reinstall the shift cable:
    a. Slide the rubber boot onto the engine end of the cable. Connect the small grommet to the cable and push it into the boot.
    b. Position the cable in the sleeve, then pull the boot onto the end of the sleeve. Install new tie straps on each end of the boot to seal it to the sleeve and grommet.
    c. Wrap the plastic tubing around the cable, pushing it into the sleeve. When properly positioned, the tubing end should touch the back of the hex fitting.
13. To reinstall the water hose:
    a. Remove and discard the water hose nipple O-ring. Clean the nipple of all sealer and make sure the drain hole is clean.
    b. Wipe a new O-ring with OMC Triple-Guard Grease and install it on the nipple groove. Make sure the O-ring is not installed in the drain hole groove or freeze damage may occur during cold weather. Clean any excess grease from the drain groove and drain hole.
    c. Install a new clamp on the upper end of the hose with the screw head located so that it will be behind the port hydraulic lines.
    d. Slide the hose onto the water tube and rotate it until the nipple points directly outward. See **Figure 20**. Slip the ground strap clip under the hose clamp, then tighten the clamp screw securely. When tightened, the screw should be behind the hydraulic lines so that it will not touch the pivot housing when the stern drive is in a full tilt position.
    e. Recheck the location of the nipple drain hole. It must be facing downward. If not, loosen the nipple clamp and twist the nipple until the drain hole is properly positioned, then retighten the clamp.

14. To reinstall the exhaust and U-joint bellows:
    a. Wipe the outer diameter of the gimbal bearing bore with OMC Gasket Sealing Compound. Work carefully to avoid getting sealer on the outside of the exhaust opening.
    b. Fit a new worm-type clamp on the small end of the U-joint bellows. Push the bellows in place, making sure that the internal rib in the bellows engages the corresponding recess around the surface of the opening. On 1987 and 1988 460 cu. in. (7.5L) King Cobra installations, the exhaust relief cutout must face downward.

c. Once the U-joint bellows is properly installed, rotate the clamp until the screw head is in the one or two o'clock position (**Figure 21**), then slip the ground strap clip under the hose clamp and tighten the screw snugly. If the screw is not properly positioned, the gimbal ring will hit the clamp head during a turning maneuver and reduce the steering radius.

d. Fit a new worm-type clamp on the large end of the exhaust bellows. Push the bellows in place, making sure that the internal rib in the bellows engages the corresponding recess around the surface of the opening.

e. Once the exhaust bellows is properly installed, rotate the clamp until the screw head is in the three o'clock position (**Figure 22**), then slip the ground strap clip under the hose clamp and tighten the screw snugly.

15. Reinstall the gimbal ring and pivot housing as described in this chapter.

TRANSOM BRACKET SHIFT CABLE

Whenever the shift cable or its core wire is replaced, the cable has to be adjusted before reconnection to the engine shift bracket to provide the proper NEUTRAL position and a full range of travel.

Adjustment

1. Place the swivel retainer (A) at the end of the threads. Position the shift cable guide (B) in or out until the lower vertical edge of the guide tab and the pivot housing gasket surface (C) are flush. See **Figure 23**.
2. Move the casing guide at the engine end of the cable in or out as required until dimension "A" in **Figure 24** is 7 5/8 ±1/32 in. Measure dimension from the edge of the cable crimp (B, **Figure 24**) to the center of the shift pin hole (C, **Figure 24**).
3. Recheck to make sure that the lower vertical edge of the guide tab and the pivot housing gasket surface are still flush (readjust as required), then thread the retainer (A) on until it barely touches the guide (B) as shown

in **Figure 25**. Align the guide and retainer screw holes, then install the screw.

4. Push the cable as far as possible into the pivot housing. This will engage the shift cable guide completely and prevent any cable binding.

5. Hold the cable guide with a 9/16 in. open-end wrench to prevent it from distorting and tighten the screw installed in Step 3 to 10-12 ft.-lb. (14-16 N•m).

6. Lightly lubricate the bellcrank pin with OMC Triple-Guard Grease.

THRUST PLATES

In order to properly position the stern drive unit relative to the transom assembly and prevent binding during turns, shims are installed under a thrust plate on each side of the drive unit upper gear housing **(Figure 26.)** As the drive unit is moved in or out, the thrust plates pivot under the ears of the gimbal housing. When measured across the thrust plates, the upper gear housing width must not exceed 5.036 in.

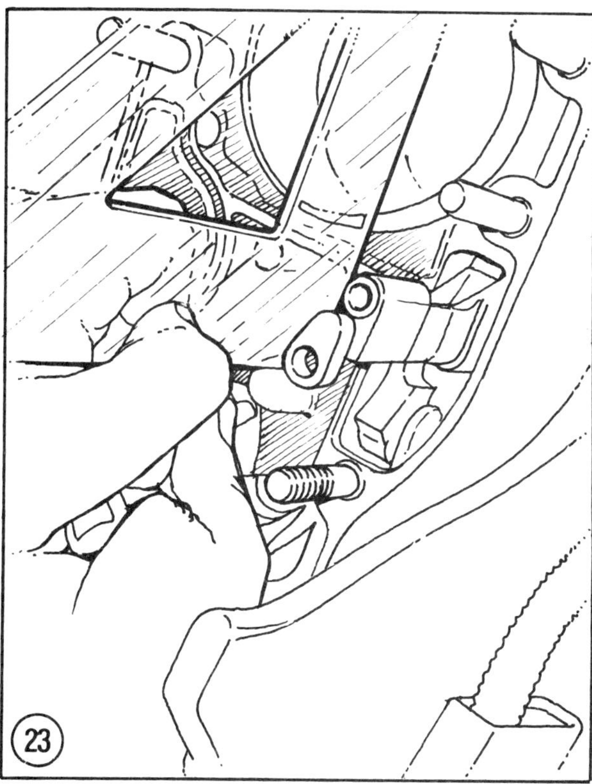

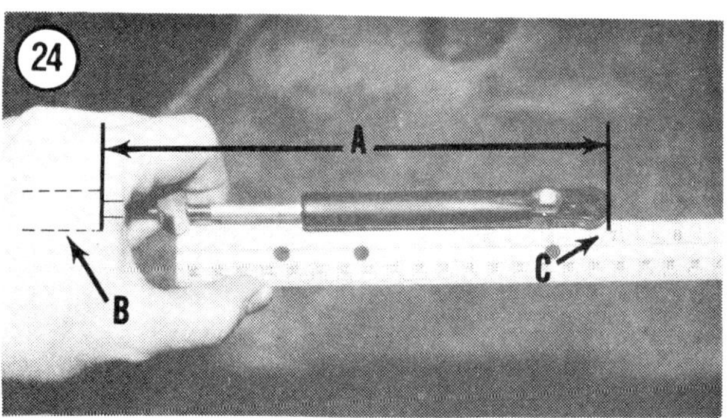

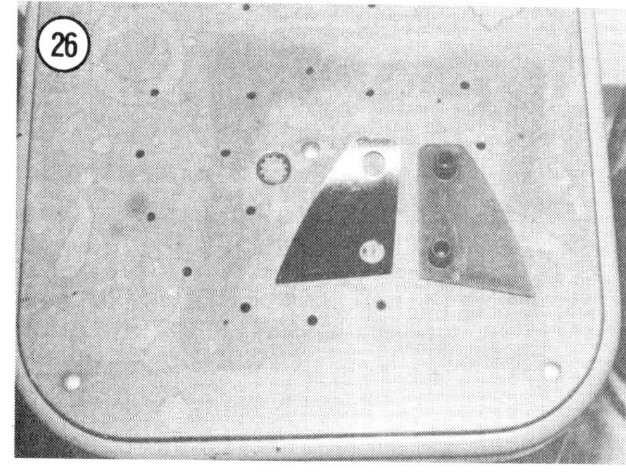

The shim material used is provided in a 0.015 in. (0.38 mm) thickness. A minimum of 1 thickness must be installed on each side, with a maximum of 4 thicknesses allowed on each side. Shims must be added in pairs. If changes are made in the shim thickness under one thrust plate, the same change must be made on the other side. That is, if one thickness is added to the port side, an equal thickness must be installed on the starboard side.

Thrust Plate Shimming

The thrust plates should not be removed unless they are damaged or the shimmed dimension exceeds specifications.

1. Measure the width across the front of the upper gear housing with a pair of 6 in. calipers at the point shown in **Figure 27**.
2. Subtract the measurement in Step 1 from 5.036 in.:
   a. In the case shown in Example 1, no additional shimming is required. 5.036 in. (required width) minus 5.021 in. (measured width) leaves a 0.015 in. difference. Since the minimum thickness of each shim is 0.015 in. and shims must be added to each side, the difference between the required and measured width must be 0.030 in. before additional shimming is added.
   b. In the case shown in Example 2, additional shimming would be needed. 5.036 in. (required width) minus 5.004 in. (measured width) leaves a 0.032 in. difference. Since the difference in this case is greater than the minimum of 0.030 in., one piece of shimming should be added under each thrust plate.
3. If additional shimming is required to reset the gear housing width correctly, carefully pry the 2 star retaining rings (**Figure 28**) from each thrust plate leg with a screwdriver blade.
4. Count the number of shims under each thrust plate. Remember that no more than 4 pieces should be on each side of the housing. If there are already 4 pieces of shimming under each plate, install new thrust plates and repeat the measuring process to determine the correct amount of shimming required.
5. Add the required shim thickness to each thrust plate. Install plate and shim pack to housing, then install a star retaining ring (concave side facing toward the inside of the housing) on each thrust plate leg.
6. Place a 1/2 in. box-end wrench over the thrust plate leg to hold the retaining ring in position and rap the thrust plate with a soft-faced mallet until the ring seats against the housing. Repeat this step to install the remaining retaining rings on the thrust plate legs.

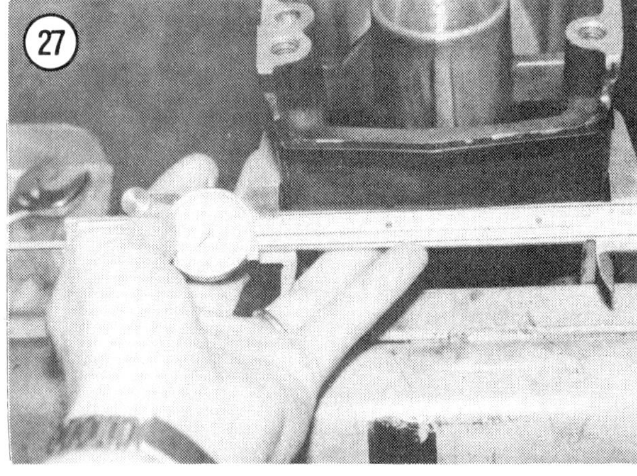

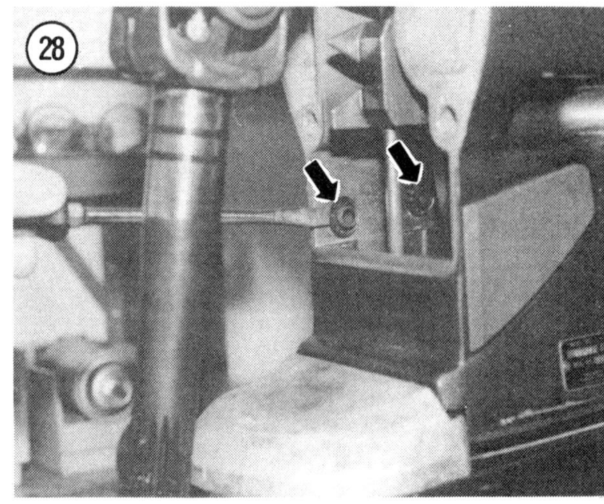

Table 1 TIGHTENING TORQUES

Fastener	in.-lb.	ft.-lb.	N•m
Drain and vent screws	50-60		6-7
Gimbal ring center bolt		65-72	88-98
Lower steering support bracket		18-20	24-27
Pivot pins		105-120	142-163
Shift cable fitting nut		35-37	47-50
Shift cable guide screw		10-12	14-16
Steering arm elastic locknuts		12-14	16-19
Steering cap screws	60-84		7-9
Trim sender screws	18-24		2-3
Water tube nut	96-120		11-14
Water tube bolts		10-12	14-16

Chapter Fifteen

Power Trim and Tilt System

Trimming describes a change in the angle of the stern drive in the water relative to the bottom of the boat. Moving the stern drive away from the transom (trimming out) raises the bow in the water; moving it toward the transom (trimming in) lowers the bow. See **Figure 1**.

Trimming may be performed with the boat at rest or at any speed in FORWARD gear. It is generally done before accelerating onto plane, after obtaining the desired engine rpm or boat speed, or when there is a change in the condition of the boat or water affecting performance. Proper trimming assures maximum performance under any given load and speed condition.

Use the bow-up position (trim out) for cruising, running *with* choppy waves or running at wide-open throttle. Too much bow-up trim causes propeller ventilation which results in propeller slippage.

Use the bow-down position (trim in) for accelerating onto plane, running at slow planing speeds or running *against* choppy waves. When bow-down trim is excessive and the boat is operated at high speeds, the bow will plow into the water and make handling difficult.

Trimming will not correct handling problems resulting from an overloaded boat or a boat whose load is improperly balanced as a result of incorrect placement.

The tilt feature is generally used to obtain sufficient clearance when mooring, launching the boat from a trailer or to provide adequate clearance during beaching. The drive may also be tilted to reduce draft for shallow water running, as long as engine speed does not exceed 1,000 rpm. You should also make sure that the lower gearcase water intakes are under water at all times when running with a tilt in shallow water. Tilting should only be performed at idle speed or at rest.

All Cobra drives are equipped with an electro-hydraulic trim/tilt system. An electric motor operates the hydraulic pump to provide pressure for raising or lowering the hydraulic actuators (trim/tilt cylinders). A malfunction of the trim/tilt system can result in the loss of reverse thrust operation and

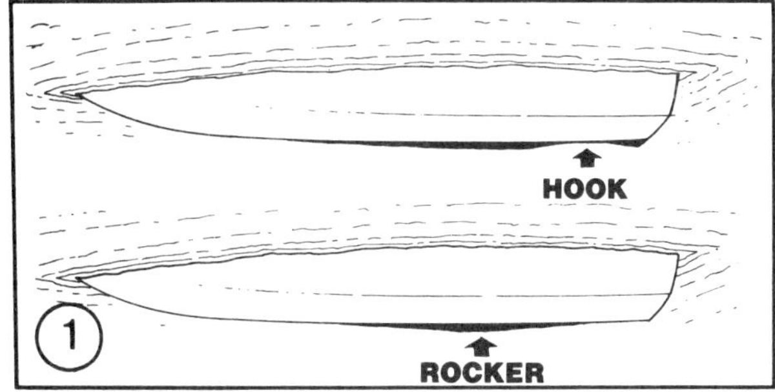

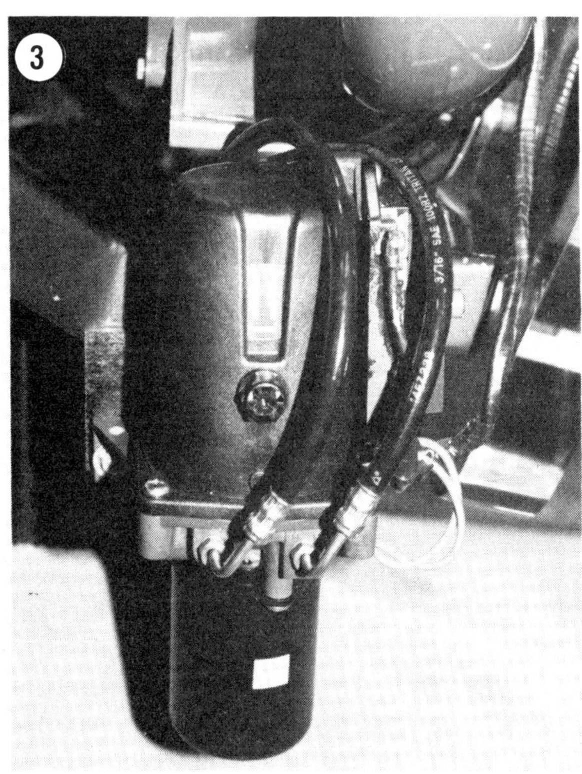

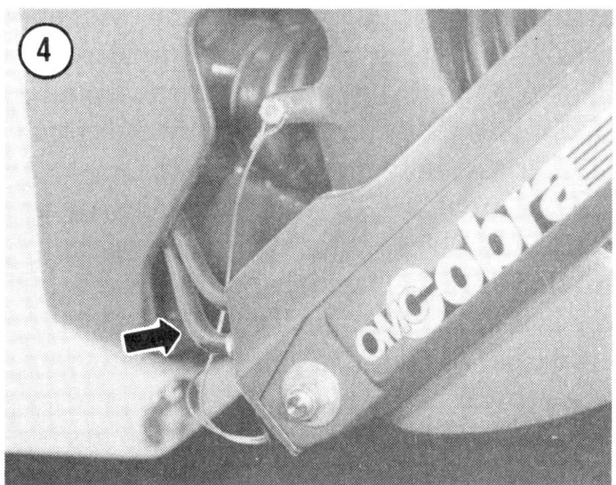

may cause of lack of shock absorbing protection in the event an underwater object is struck.

This chapter covers removal/installation and troubleshooting of the power trim/tilt system. **Table 1** and **Table 2** (*Hydraulic Pressure Specifications*) and **Table 3** and **Table 4** (*Troubleshooting Diagnostics*) are at the end of the chapter.

SYSTEM COMPONENTS

The Cobra power trim/tilt system consists of a valve body, oil pump and electric motor contained in a single pump housing (**Figure 2** 1986-1988 models or **Figure 3** 1989 models). The pump housing is connected to a hydraulic cylinder on each side of the drive unit by hydraulic lines (**Figure 4**). A sending unit is installed on the starboard side of the gimbal ring (**Figure 5**). This sending unit is electrically connected to a trim gauge on the instrument panel or dash. The trim gauge shows the bow position according to the trim angle of the drive unit. A switch installed on the remote control handle (if so equipped) or on the instrument panel/dash controls the trim/tilt operation through an UP solenoid or a DOWN solenoid mounted on the engine on 1986-1988 models and through a relay and circuit breaker assembly on 1989 models.

System is protected by two 50 amp fuses and two 20 amp fuses on 1986-1988 models and by two 50 amp fuses, a 20 amp fuse and a circuit breaker located in the relay and circuit breaker assembly on 1989 models.

A manual release valve on the pump housing can be used to lower the drive unit if an electrical malfunction occurs. When the valve is opened (turned counterclockwise), the weight of the drive unit will force it back to a vertical position.

Figure 6 shows the power trim/tilt system used with 1986-1988 GM engines; **Figure 7** shows the system used with 1989 GM engines; **Figure 8** shows the system used with 1987-1988 Ford engines; **Figure 9** shows the system used with 1989 Ford engines.

ELECTRICAL SYSTEM

Troubleshooting

If the power trim/tilt system will not operate, refer to **Figure 6** (1986-1988 GM engines), **Figure 7** (1989 GM engines), **Figure 8** (1987-1988 Ford engines) or **Figure 9** (1989 Ford engines) as appropriate and check the electrical system with the following procedure. The fuses are located at the port (2.3L) or starboard (2.5L/3.0L) side of the block or at the rear of the intake manifold (all others).

1. Make sure the battery is fully charged and that the connections are clean and tight.
2. Turn the ignition switch ON, but do not start the engine.

3A. 1986-1988—Check the condition of the 50 amp fuses between the assist solenoid, trim/tilt solenoid and the starter motor. If the fuses are good, check for battery voltage at the fuse holders with a voltmeter or 12-volt test lamp. If battery voltage is not shown, check for a problem in the wiring between the fuse holders and the battery.

3B. 1989—Check the condition of the 50 amp fuses between the assist solenoid, relay and circuit breaker assembly and the starter motor. If the fuses are good, check for battery voltage at the fuse holders with a voltmeter or 12-volt test lamp. If battery voltage is not shown, check for a problem in the wiring between the fuse holders and the battery.

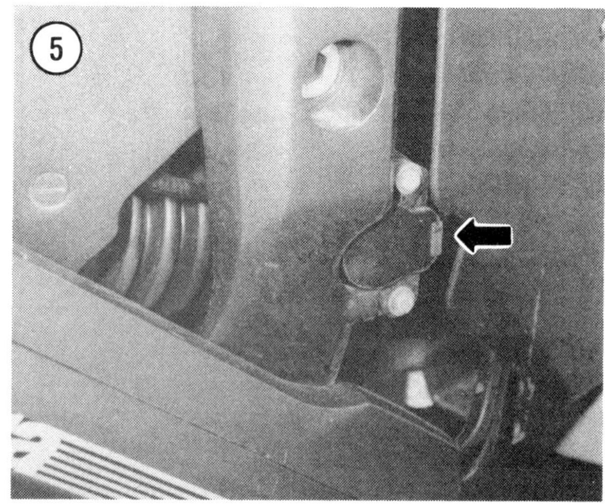

4A. 1986-1988—Check the condition of the 20 amp fuse between the trim/tilt solenoids and trim/tilt switch with a voltmeter or 12-volt test lamp. If the fuse is good, check for battery voltage at the trim/tilt switch. If battery voltage is not shown, check for a problem in the wiring between the fuse holder or trim/tilt solenoids and the trim/tilt switch. Check the solenoids as described in this chapter.

4B. 1989—Check the condition of the internal circuit breaker in the relay and circuit breaker assembly with a voltmeter or 12-volt test lamp. Battery voltage should be present at both red/purple wire terminals on the relay and circuit breaker assembly. If the circuit breaker is good, check for battery voltage at the trim/tilt switch. If battery voltage is not shown, but supply voltage is present, then replace relay and circuit breaker assembly.

5A. 1986-1988—Unplug the trim/tilt motor harness connector. Check for battery voltage at the switch side of the connector with a

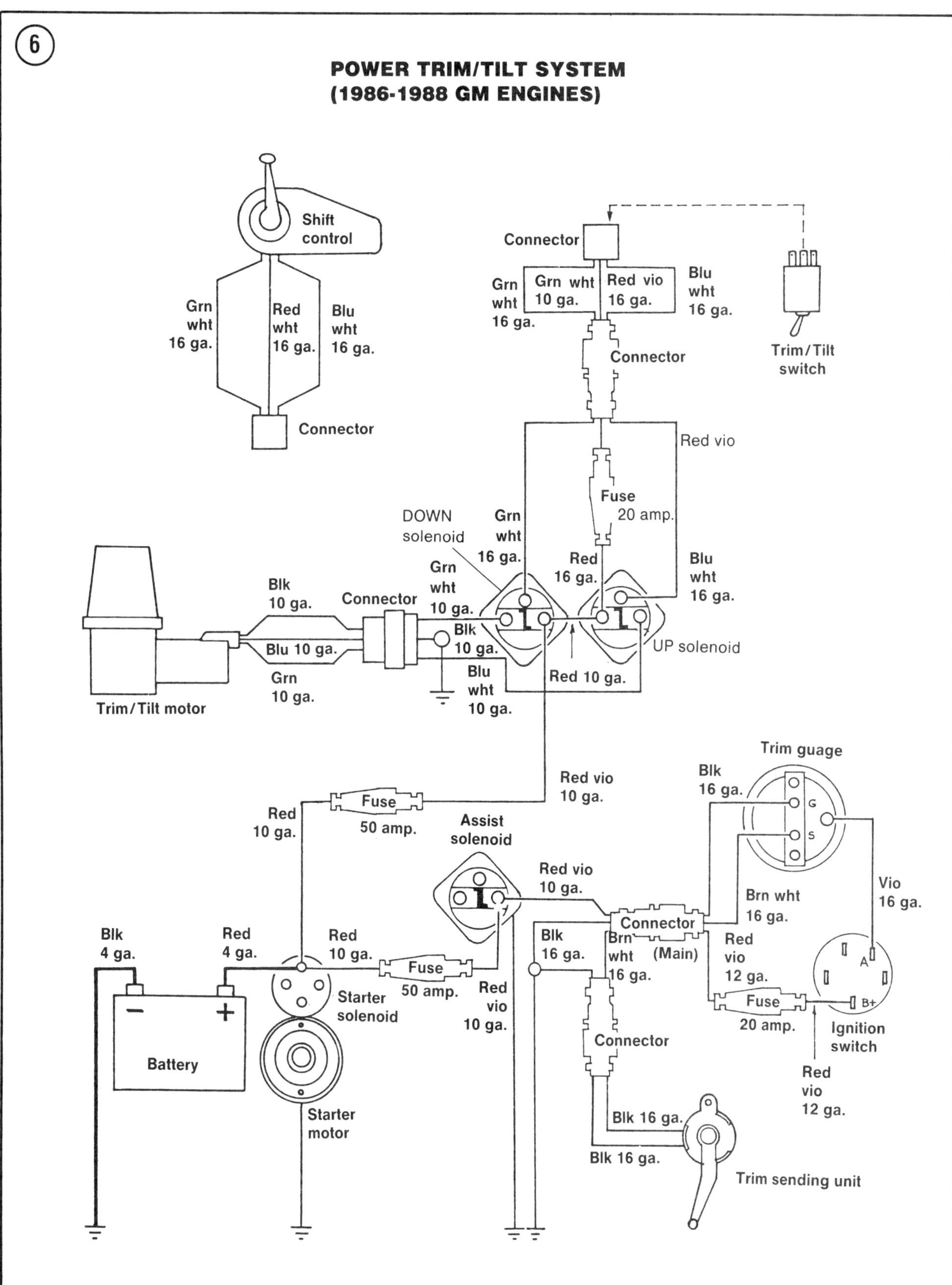
6
POWER TRIM/TILT SYSTEM
(1986-1988 GM ENGINES)
Shift control
Grn wht 16 ga.
Red wht 16 ga.
Blu wht 16 ga.
Connector
Connector
Grn wht 16 ga.
Grn wht 10 ga.
Red vio 16 ga.
Blu wht 16 ga.
Connector
Trim/Tilt switch
Red vio
Fuse 20 amp.
DOWN solenoid
Grn wht 16 ga.
Red 16 ga.
Blu wht 16 ga.
Grn wht 10 ga.
Blk 10 ga.
Connector
Blu 10 ga.
Blk 10 ga.
UP solenoid
Grn 10 ga.
Blu wht 10 ga.
Red 10 ga.
Trim/Tilt motor
Trim guage
Red vio 10 ga.
Blk 16 ga.
Red 10 ga.
Fuse 50 amp.
Assist solenoid
Red vio 10 ga.
Vio 16 ga.
Brn wht 16 ga.
Connector (Main)
Blk 4 ga.
Red 4 ga.
Red 10 ga.
Blk 16 ga.
Brn wht 16 ga.
Red vio 12 ga.
Fuse 50 amp.
Starter solenoid
Red vio 10 ga.
Fuse 20 amp.
Ignition switch
Battery
Connector
Red vio 12 ga.
Starter motor
Blk 16 ga.
Blk 16 ga.
Trim sending unit

15

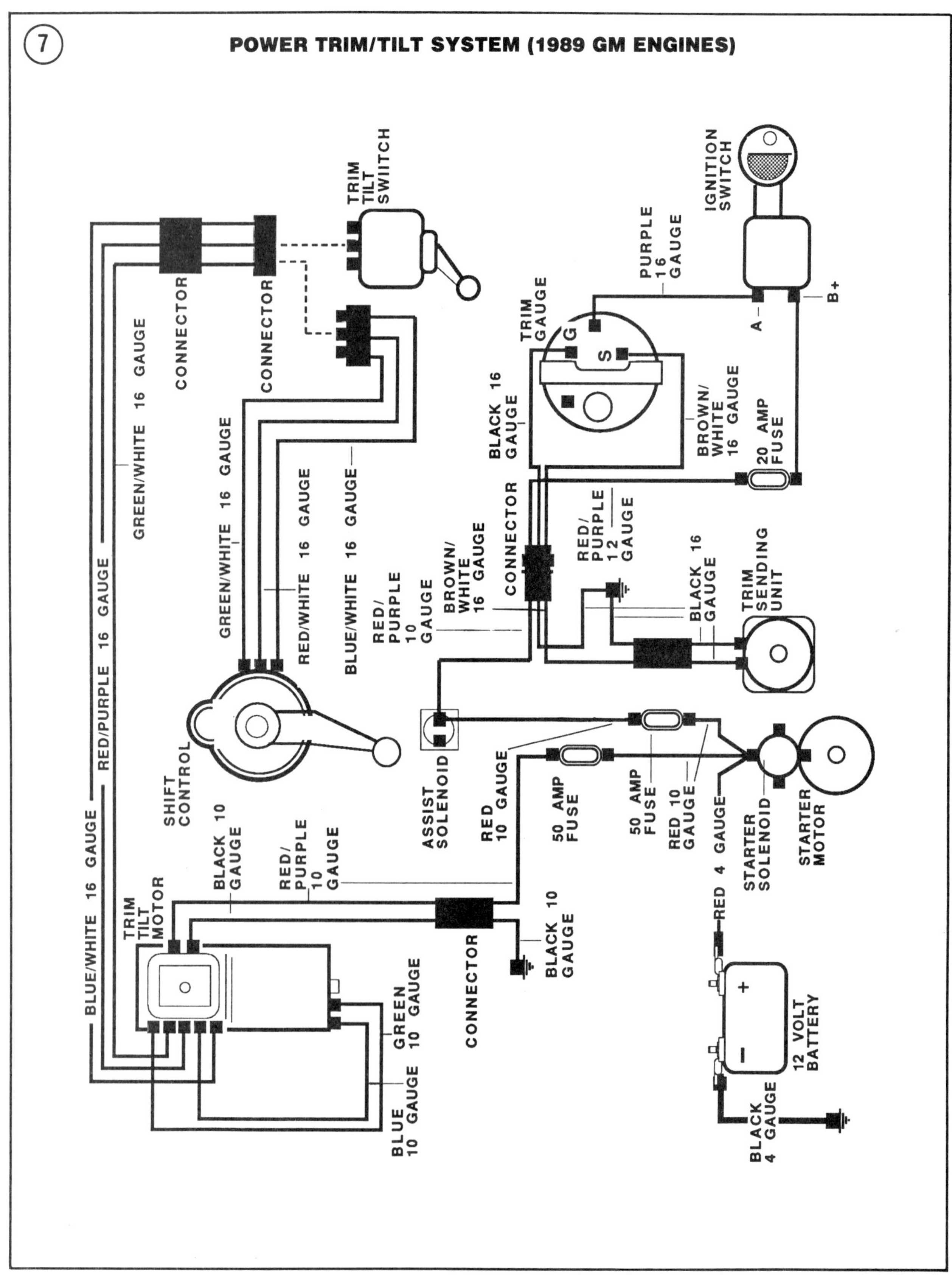

(7) **POWER TRIM/TILT SYSTEM (1989 GM ENGINES)**

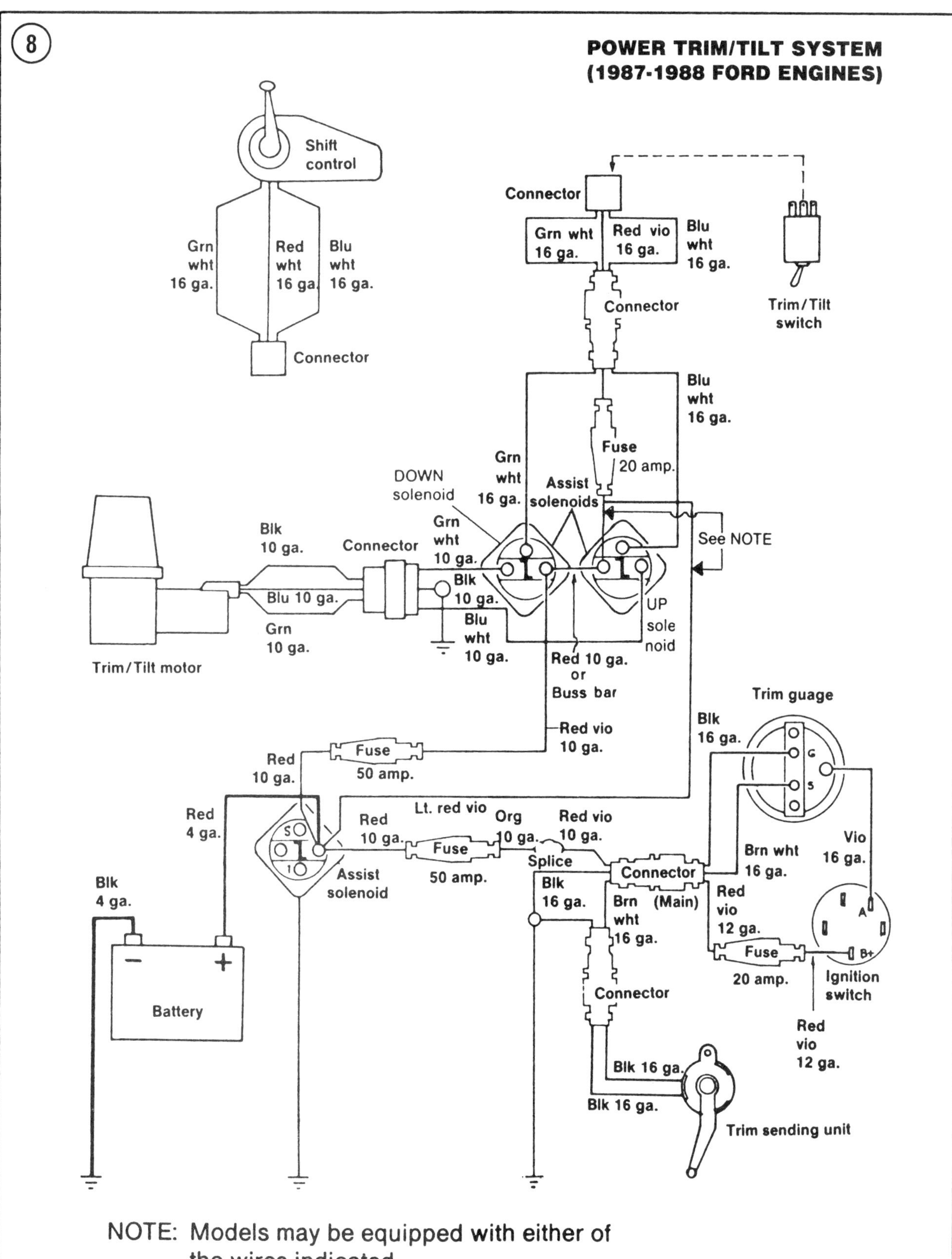
8
POWER TRIM/TILT SYSTEM
(1987-1988 FORD ENGINES)
Shift control
Grn wht 16 ga.
Red wht 16 ga.
Blu wht 16 ga.
Connector
Connector
Grn wht 16 ga.
Red vio 16 ga.
Blu wht 16 ga.
Connector
Trim/Tilt switch
Blu wht 16 ga.
Fuse
20 amp.
Grn wht 16 ga.
Assist solenoids
DOWN solenoid
Blk 10 ga.
Connector
Grn wht 10 ga.
See NOTE
Blu 10 ga.
Blk 10 ga.
Grn 10 ga.
Blu wht 10 ga.
UP solenoid
Trim/Tilt motor
Red 10 ga. or Buss bar
Trim guage
Blk 16 ga.
Red vio 10 ga.
Fuse
50 amp.
Red 10 ga.
Red 4 ga.
Red 10 ga.
Lt. red vio
Org 10 ga.
Red vio 10 ga.
Fuse
50 amp.
Splice
Assist solenoid
Blk 4 ga.
Connector
Brn wht 16 ga.
Vio 16 ga.
Blk 16 ga.
Brn (Main) wht 16 ga.
Red vio 12 ga.
Fuse
20 amp.
Ignition switch
Battery
Connector
Red vio 12 ga.
Blk 16 ga.
Blk 16 ga.
Trim sending unit
NOTE: Models may be equipped with either of the wires indicated.

15

(9)

POWER TRIM/TILT SYSTEM (1989 FORD ENGINES)

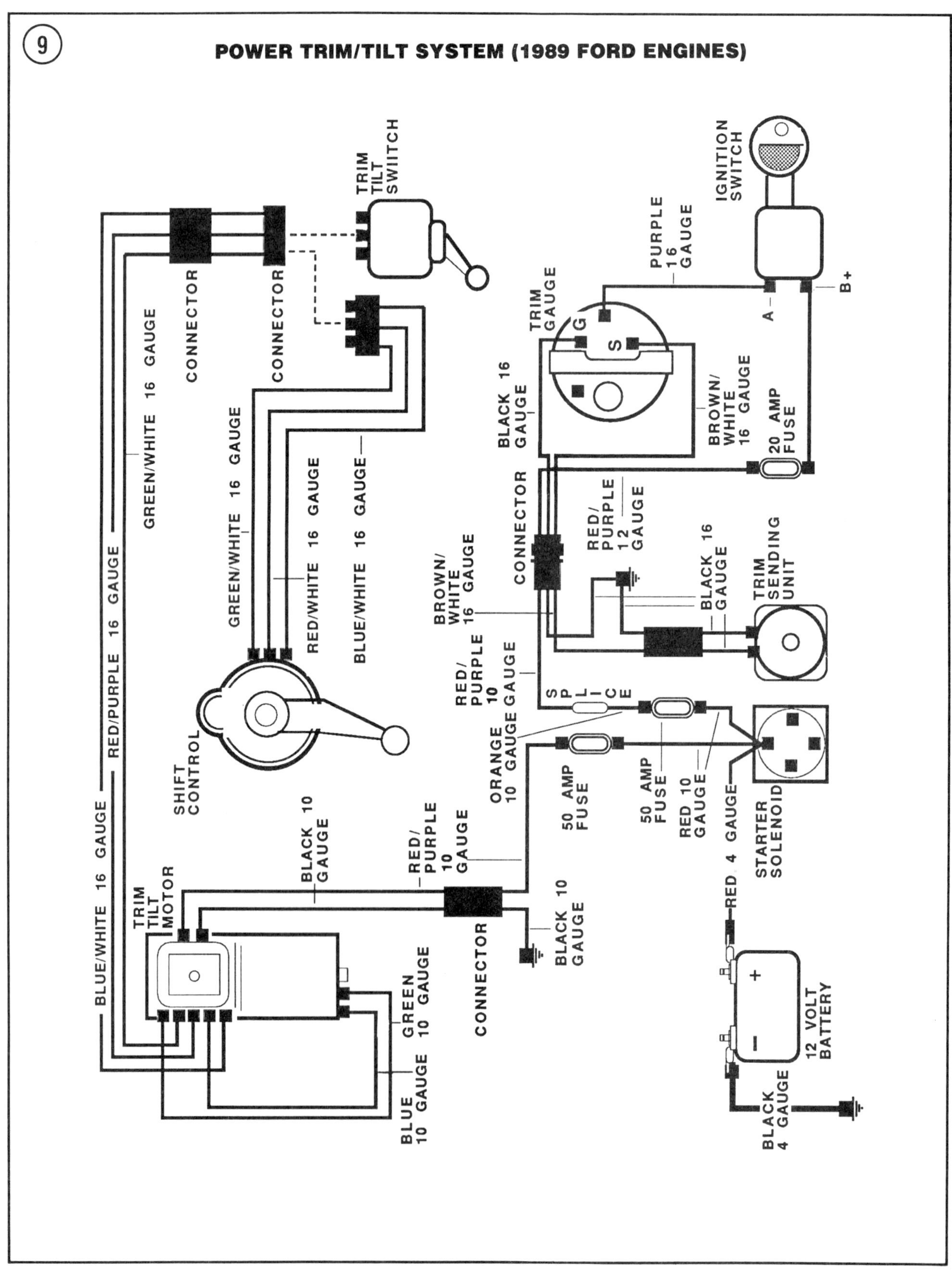

voltmeter or 12-volt test lamp with the switch in the UP position, then with the switch in the DOWN position. If battery voltage is not shown, check the trim/tilt switch as described in this chapter.

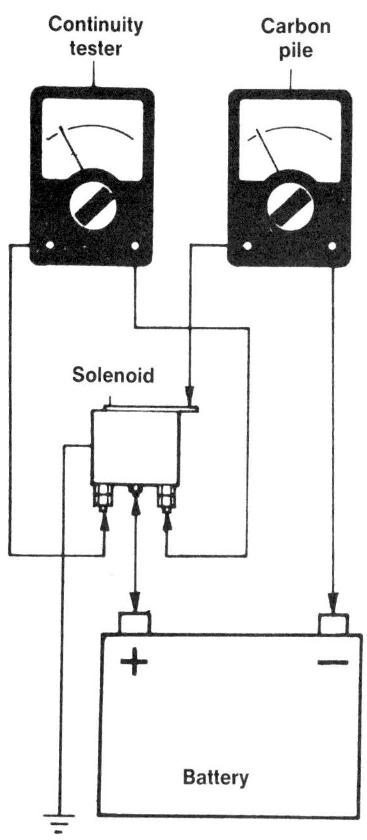

5B. 1989—Disconnect the trim/tilt motor harness connectors at the relay and circuit breaker assembly. Check for battery voltage at the terminals of the relay and circuit breaker assembly with a voltmeter or 12-volt test lamp with the switch in the UP position, then with the switch in the DOWN postion. If battery voltage is not shown, check the trim/tilt switch as described in this chapter.

6. Check the trim sending unit as described in this chapter.

Trim/Tilt Switch Test

1. Probe the red/white wire terminal at the switch for voltage with a 12-volt test lamp. If the lamp does not light, check the fuse or wiring connectors.
2. Hold the trim/tilt switch in the DOWN position and probe the green/white wire terminal for voltage with the test lamp. If the lamp does not light, replace the switch.
3. Hold the trim/tilt switch in the UP position and probe the blue/white wire terminal for voltage with the test lamp. If the lamp does not light, replace the switch.

Solenoid Test

Refer to **Figure 10** for this procedure.

1. Make sure the solenoid ground is satisfactory (ground is through the base of the unit).
2. Connect an ohmmeter between the 2 large solenoid terminals.
3. Connect a carbon pile between the solenoid and negative battery terminal. Adjust the carbon pile to reduce battery voltage to under 6 volts.
4. Connect the positive battery terminal to one of the small solenoid terminals with a jumper lead. Connect the negative battery terminal to the solenoid base with a jumper lead.
5. Adjust the carbon pile to increase battery voltage until the ohmmeter shows a completed circuit. Replace the solenoid if it requires more than 8 volts to complete the circuit.

Trim Sending Unit Test

1. Disconnect the sending unit wiring harness at the connector.
2. Connect an ohmmeter between the 2 sender leads.
3. Unbolt the sending unit and remove its cover.

4. Reach behind the bracket and manually move the sender arm through a complete up/down cycle while watching the meter scale.
5. Replace the sending unit if the meter does not show a 0-200 ±10 ohm reading for the cycle.
6. Remove the ohmmeter leads, reinstall the sending unit with cover and connect the wiring harness.

Trim Sending Unit Adjustment

If the trim/tilt gauge does not exhibit a full DOWN reading when the stern drive is in a vertical position, loosen the sending unit mounting screws, rotate the sending unit as required to provide the desired reading on the trim gauge and then tighten the mounting screws to 18-24 in. (2-3 N•m). Replace the sending unit if it cannot be rotated enough to provide a full DOWN reading on the gauge.

Trim/Tilt Motor Bench Test

If the trim/tilt motor is suspected of malfunctioning, remove it from the boat and perform a stall-torque test in each direction (UP and DOWN) to see if the motor has enough turning power to raise/lower the drive unit.

1. Remove the trim/tilt motor from the boat.
2. Clamp the motor in a vise with protective jaws. If protective jaws are not available, protect the motor housing with soft wooden blocks on either side.
3. Connect a fully charged 12-volt battery and an ammeter with a 0-200 amp scale in series with the motor. See A and B, **Figure 11**.
4. Connect the negative battery terminal to one of the tilt motor leads. Connect a voltmeter between the same tilt motor lead and the motor ground lead. See C, **Figure 11**.
5. Connect an in.-lb. torque wrench to the motor armature shaft with a suitable socket. See D, **Figure 11**.

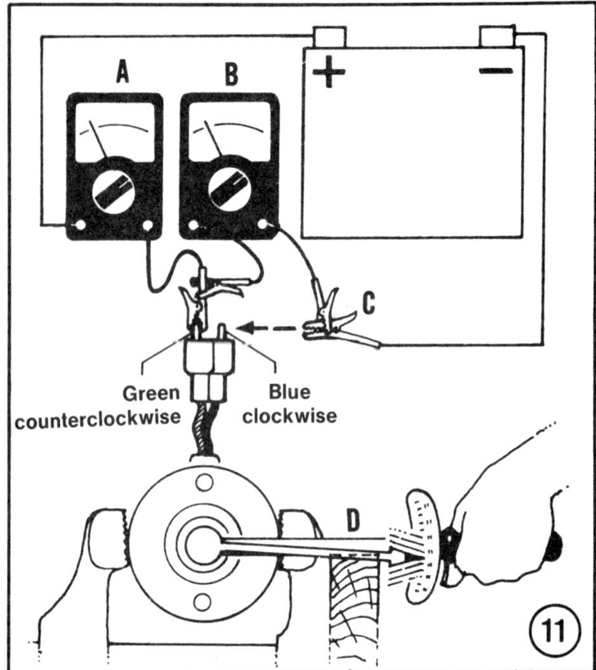

6. Holding the torque wrench, complete the electrical circuit momentarily and note the reading on the torque wrench and the ammeter.
7. Disconnect the battery lead from the tilt motor lead and connect it to the other tilt motor lead. Repeat Step 6 to check the stall-torque reading in the other direction.
8. With a voltmeter reading of at least 12 volts, the ammeter should read a maximum of 185 amps and the stall-torque reading should be at least 20.6 in.-lb.
   a. If the current and torque readings are both low, there is excessive resistance in the motor's internal connections or the brush contacts.
   b. If the current reading is high and the torque reading is low, the problem is in the field windings or armature.

1986-1988 HYDRAULIC SYSTEM

Troubleshooting

If the power trim/tilt system does not work and no problem can be located in the

electrical system, check the hydraulic system performance with the help of OMC tilt/trim pressure tester part No. 983977.

Test Connections

The tester has 2 hydraulic ports marked "A" and "B." The "A" port is always connected to the gauge and the "B" port can be closed with the use of a valve in the tester body. This allows connection of the tester to the trim/tilt valve body in 4 different ways to isolate and test the hydraulic components in the system. Perform Steps 1-3, then select the section of the system to be checked and connect the tester as described in Steps 4-7.

1. Raise the drive to its full tilt UP position and support the unit so that it will not lower by its own weight when the manual valve is opened.
2. Open the manual valve (**Figure 12**) in the pump one full turn.
3. Label the top hydraulic line for identification and place a shop cloth and drip pan under the fittings.

WARNING
Wear safety glasses and wrap a shop cloth around the hydraulic line fitting before loosening it in any of the following steps to prevent any fluid under pressure from causing personal injury.

4. Isolate the high volume side of the cylinders from the gauge and check the trim-in/tilt-down side of the valve by as follows:
   a. Disconnect the top hydraulic line at the valve body.
   b. Connect the tester hydraulic line assembly between the valve body top port and port "A" on the tester.
   c. Connect the top hydraulic line to port "B" on the tester.
5. Isolate the trim-in/tilt down side of the valve from the gauge and check the high volume side of the cylinders as follows:
   a. Disconnect the top hydraulic line at the valve body.
   b. Connect the tester hydraulic line assembly between the valve body top port and port "B" on the tester.
   c. Connect the top hydraulic line to port "A" on the tester.
6. Isolate the low volume side of the cylinders from the gauge and check the trim-out/tilt-up side of the valve as follows:
   a. Disconnect the bottom hydraulic line at the valve body.
   b. Connect the tester hydraulic line assembly between the valve body bottom port and port "A" on the tester.
   c. Connect the bottom hydraulic line to port "B" on the tester.
7. Isolate the trim-out/tilt up side of the valve from the gauge and check the low volume side of the cylinders as follows:
   a. Disconnect the bottom hydraulic line at the valve body.

b. Connect the tester hydraulic line assembly between the valve body bottom port and port "B" on the tester.
c. Connect the bottom hydraulic line to port "A" on the tester.

Test Procedure

1. Top up the trim/tilt reservoir with OMC Power Trim and Tilt fluid or DEXRON II automatic transmission fluid, if necessary.
2. Close the manual valve in the pump body (**Figure 12**).
3. Operate the trim/tilt system UP and DOWN to bleed any air that might be in the system.
4. Operate the trim/tilt system in the desired direction to the position to be tested, noting the running pressure shown by the gauge.
   a. To measure stall pressure, run the cylinders to the extreme of travel and note the gauge pressure.
   b. To check the leak-down in both cylinders and the pump valve body, run the cylinders to the extreme position and note the pressure gauge drop.
5. To isolate one portion of the trim/tilt system, run the system to its full travel position, then release the trim switch and immediately close the valve in the tester body with a screwdriver. The pressure drop on the gauge relates to that part of the system that has not been isolated.
6. Refer to **Table 1** for the normal operating pressure, maximum pressure drop and leak-down time for each mode.

1989 HYDRAULIC SYSTEM

Troubleshooting

If the power trim/tilt system does not work and no problem can be located in the electrical system, check the hydraulic system performance with the help of OMC tilt/trim pressure tester part No. 983977.

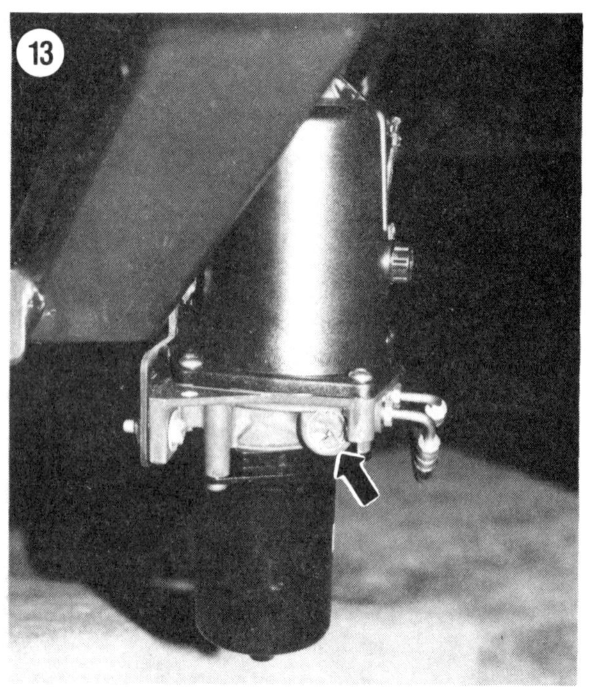

Test Connections And Test Procedures

The tester has 2 hydraulic ports marked "A" and "B". The "A" port is always connected to the gauge and the "B" port can be closed with the use of a valve in the tester body. This allows connection of the tester to the trim/tilt valve body in 4 different ways to isolate and test the hydraulic components in the system. Perform Steps 1-3, then select the section of the system to be checked and connect the tester as described in Steps 4-7.

1. Raise the drive to its full tilt UP position and support the unit so that it will not lower by its own weight when the manual valve is opened.
2. Open the manual valve (**Figure 13**) in the pump one full turn and leave open for a few seconds then close valve.
3. Label the port or starboard hydraulic line for identification and place a shop cloth and drip pan under the fittings.

WARNING
Wear safety glasses and wrap a shop cloth around the hydraulic line fitting

before loosening it in any of the following steps to prevent any fluid under pressure from causing personal injury.

4. Proceed as follows for complete circuit test showing running and stall psi during trim-out/tilt-up operation:
   a. Disconnect the port (UP) hydraulic line at the valve body.
   b. Connect the tester hydraulic line assembly between the valve body port (UP) orifice and orifice "A" on the tester.
   c. Connect the port (UP) hydraulic line to orifice "B" on tester.
   d. Completely open valve in tester body.
   e. Operate drive unit through a complete trim-out/tilt-up cycle and record running and stall psi readings. Compare readings to recommended specifications shown in **Table 2**.
5. Proceed as follows for complete circuit test showing running and stall psi during trim-in/tilt-down operation:
   a. Disconnect the starboard (DOWN) hydraulic line at the valve body.
   b. Connect the tester hydraulic line assembly between the valve body starboard (DOWN) orifice and orifice "A" on the tester.
   c. Connect the starboard (DOWN) hydraulic line to orifice "B" on tester.
   d. Completely open valve in tester body.
   e. Operate drive unit through a complete trim-in/tilt-down cycle and record running and stall psi readings. Compare readings to recommended specifications shown in **Table 2**.
6. Proceed as follows for hydraulic pump isolation test during trim-out/tilt-up operation. Test will show if malfunctioning trim/tilt operation is related to hydraulic pump or trim/tilt cylinders.
   a. Disconnect the port (UP) hydraulic line at the valve body.
   b. Connect the tester hydraulic line assembly between the valve body port (UP) orifice and orifice "A" on the tester.
   c. Connect the port (UP) hydraulic line to orifice "B" on tester.
   d. Completely open valve in tester body.
   e. Operate drive unit to complete tilt-up position, then instantaneously operate tilt/trim switch in the DOWN direction to relieve pressure on test gauge.
   f. Completely close valve in tester body.
   g. Operate drive unit in the tilt-up direction and record stall psi reading. Release tilt/trim switch, then observe pressure leakdown rate and final psi reading. Compare readings to recommended specifications shown in **Table 2**.
7. Proceed as follows for hydraulic pump isolation test during trim-in/tilt-down operation. Test will show if malfunctioning trim/tilt operation is related to hydraulic pump or trim/tilt cylinders.
   a. Disconnect the starboard (DOWN) hydraulic line at the valve body.
   b. Connect the tester hydraulic line assembly between the valve body starboard (DOWN) orifice and orifice "A" on the tester.
   c. Connect the starboard (DOWN) hydraulic line to orifice "B" on tester.
   d. Completely open valve in tester body.
   e. Operate drive unit to complete trim-in position, then instantaneously operate tilt/trim switch in the UP direction to relieve pressure on test gauge.
   f. Completely close valve in tester body.
   g. Operate drive unit in the trim-in direction and record stall psi reading. Release tilt/trim switch, then observe pressure leakdown rate and final psi reading. Compare readings to recommended specifications shown in **Table 2**.

MECHANICAL SYSTEM

Trim/Tilt Cylinder (All Models)

If a hydraulic cylinder is determined to be leaking or otherwise defective, it should be serviced (other than removal/installation) by an OMC Cobra dealer. A special tool is required to remove the end cap, and there is no guarantee that the cap can be removed (even with the special tool) without damage. Damage to the end cap renders the entire cylinder unserviceable, requiring replacement with a new unit.

Removal/Installation (All Models)

Refer to **Figure 14** for this procedure.

1. Make sure the stern drive is in its vertical (full DOWN) position. Have a suitable

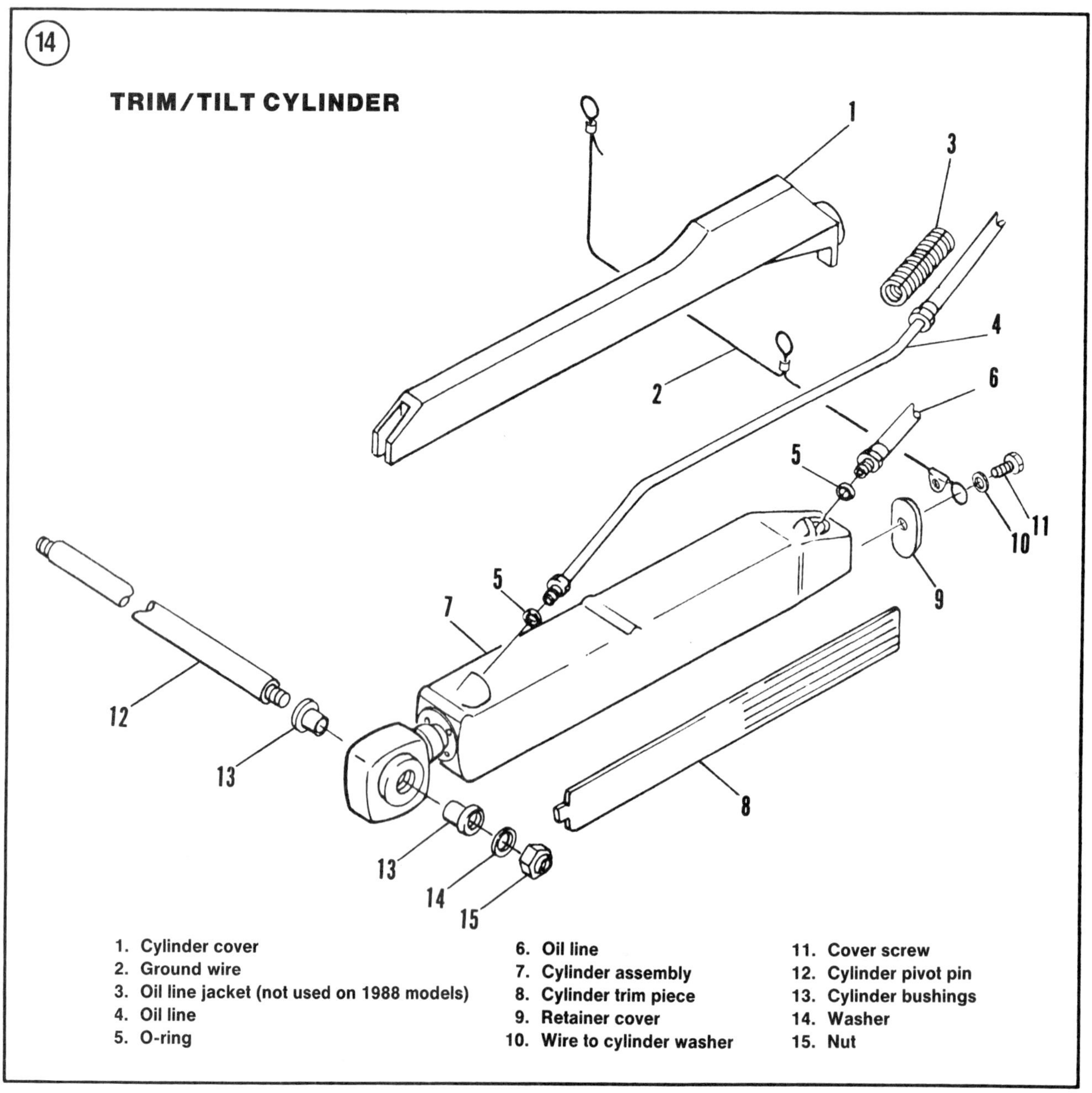

container ready to drain the fluid from the disconnected lines.

2. Loosen and remove the self-locking nut and flat washer from the trim/tilt pivot rod on each side of the drive. See **Figure 15**. Discard the locknuts.

3. Lightly tap the pivot rod out of the cylinder eye with a soft-faced hammer and remove the cylinder from the drive unit. Carefully lower the cylinder to the ground to prevent stressing the hydraulic lines. If both cylinders are to be removed, tap the pivot rod completely out of the drive unit and the other cylinder.

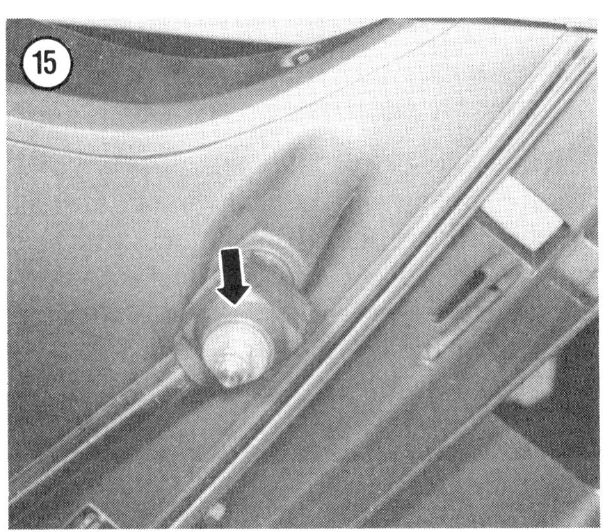

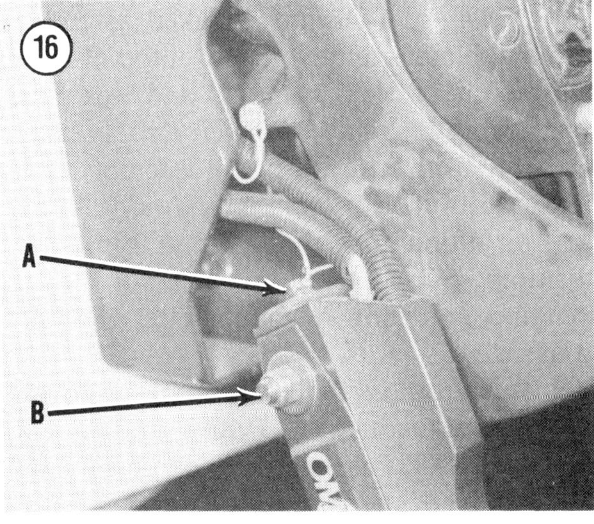

4. Remove the screw, lockwasher, ground lead and retainer from the front of the cylinder (A, **Figure 16**), then unbolt and remove the trim cylinder cover.

5. Unscrew the lower hydraulic line fitting with a flare nut wrench to avoid rounding off the corners of the fitting nut. Let the hydraulic line drain in the container. Cap the line and fitting to prevent leakage and the entry of contamination. Remove and discard the hydraulic fitting O-ring.

6. Remove the hydraulic line retainer. Loosen the remaining hydraulic line fitting with a flare nut wrench to avoid rounding the corners of the fitting nuts. Unscrew and disconnect the line from the cylinder. Cap the line and fitting to prevent leakage and the entry of contamination. Remove and discard the hydraulic fitting O-ring.

7. Hold the gimbal housing locknut on one trim/tilt cylinder (B, **Figure 16**) with a suitable wrench and loosen the locknut on the other cylinder with a second wrench. Remove the locknut and washer from one side, then slide the forward pivot shaft out of the cylinder to be removed. If both cylinders are to be removed, slide the shaft completely out of the gimbal housing and the other cylinder. Discard the locknuts.

8. Installation is the reverse of removal, plus the following:

   a. Replace any nylon bushings that are worn or damaged.
   b. Lubricate and use new O-ring seals on the hydraulic line fittings.
   c. Tighten each fitting to 14-18 ft.-lb. (19-24 N•m).
   d. Lubricate the trim/tilt pivot rod and gimbal housing pivot shaft with OMC Triple-Guard grease.
   e. Wipe the threaded end of the pivot rod and gimbal housing shaft with OMC Gasket Sealing Compound after installation. Install washer and a new self-locking nut. Hold one locknut with

a 5/8 in. box-end wrench. Tighten both locknuts on the pivot rod until the locknuts and washers bottom on the pivot rod shoulders.

f. Tighten the pivot rod and gimbal housing shaft locknuts to 32-34 ft.-lb. (43-46 N•m).

Trim/Tilt Pump (All Models)

The trim/tilt pump is installed by the boat manufacturer. For this reason, its location will vary according to manufacturer and boat design.

Removal/Installation

1986-1988

1. Place the drive unit in its full UP position. Support the drive unit with a wooden block underneath the skeg to hold it in place.
2. Place a suitable container under the pump. Turn the manual release valve one full turn counterclockwise and remove the fill plug from the reservoir. Remove the drain plug from the valve body base and drain the pump reservoir fluid. Wipe up any fluid that spills or does not enter the container.
3. Label and disconnect the hydraulic lines at the pump. Cap the lines and fittings to prevent leakage and the entry of contamination. Tie the 2 lines together and suspend them at a point higher than when connected.
4. If the O-ring seals were not removed from the pump ports with the hydraulic lines, remove and discard.
5. Unplug the electrical connector from the wiring harness.
6. Remove the 3 mounting screws and washers. Remove the trim/tilt pump from its installed position.
7. Installation is the reverse of removal. Refill the reservoir with OMC Trim and Tilt Fluid or DEXRON II automatic transmission fluid and bleed the system. See Chapter Four.

1989

1. Place the drive unit in its full UP position. Support the drive unit with a wooden block underneath the skeg to hold it in place.
2. Place a suitable container under the pump.

WARNING
It is possible that there will be residual high pressure behind the fill plug. To prevent loss, cover plug with a clean lint-free cloth during removal until any residual pressure is dissipated. To prevent potential personal injury, wear protective safety glasses.

3. Remove reservoir fill plug.
4. Label and disconnect the hydraulic lines at the pump. Place the hydraulic lines into the container to collect draining fluid. Cap the pump ports to prevent leakage and the entry of contamination.

WARNING
To prevent potential personal injury, disconnect cables from battery terminals.

5. Disconnect leads to pump electric motor from relay and circuit breaker assembly terminal block. Remove screw at top of relay and circuit breaker assembly and wire ties, then remove relay and circuit breaker assembly from trim/tilt pump assembly.
6. Remove the 2 mounting screws. Remove the trim/tilt pump assembly from its installed position. Support pump assembly over container and allow remaining reservoir fluid to drain.
7. Installation is the reverse of removal. Refill the reservoir with OMC Trim and Tilt Fluid or DEXRON II automatic transmission fluid and bleed the system. See Chapter Four.

Pump Overhaul (1986-1988)

Service to the pump should be performed by an experienced marine technician. If this is not possible, the following procedure will allow you to disassemble, inspect and reassemble the pump. However, since you are working with a hydraulic unit, cleanliness is paramount.

To prevent any possible confusion, you should also have a cupcake tin or several small containers in which you can store and properly label the numerous screws, springs, valves, circlips and other small components.

Some fasteners in the assembly have a Torx head and if removal is required, should be removed only with the proper Torx driver or the fastener head will be damaged.

Disassembly

Refer to **Figure 17** (typical) for this procedure.

1. Wipe the outside of the pump unit with a clean cloth moistened in solvent or OMC engine cleaner. Wipe the solvent or engine cleaner off with a clean lint-free cloth or paper towels.

WARNING
It is possible that there will be residual high pressure behind the check valves. To prevent their loss or potential personal injury, cover each valve with a clean lint-free cloth or paper towel during removal until any residual pressure is dissipated.

2. Remove the 3 Phillips-head screws holding the pump motor and valve body together. Separate the motor from the valve body.
3. Remove the 4 Phillips-head screws holding the pump reservoir to the valve body. Separate the reservoir from the valve body. Remove and discard the sealing O-ring from the valve body.
4. Remove the oil pump filter (1, **Figure 18**) and rotate the pump coupling (2, **Figure 18**) to check for binding.
5. Pull the pump coupling from the pump and check the condition of the rubber coupling ball (**Figure 19**). The coupling ball provides pump-to-motor cushion.
6. Remove the 3 Allen-head screws which hold the oil pump to the valve body (**Figure 20**). Remove the pump from the body. If pump requires flushing, use only clean hydraulic oil, such as OMC Trim/Tilt Fluid. If defective, the pump is replaced as an assembly.
7. The expansion valve (1, **Figure 21**) should be staked in place. Scrape away the staking with a small screwdriver blade and remove the filter valve with washer. Check the filter; it should be clean and not damaged.
8. Thread a No. 6 screw or tap into the filter valve seat and pull the seat from the valve body. Use a pencil-type magnet to remove the check ball. Remove and discard the valve core O-rings.
9. Remove and discard the 2 pump-to-valve body O-rings in the center of the assembly (2, **Figure 21**).
10. Remove the trim-in relief valve spring and valve assembly (1, **Figure 22**). Check assembly for wear or damage. The sealing tip can be replaced if necessary.
11. Remove the thermal expansion valve spring and valve core (2, **Figure 22**).
12. Bend a paper clip to form the tool shown in **Figure 23**. Repeat this step to make a second tool. Use one tool to remove the expansion valve body.
13. Expand and remove the snap ring from the manual release valve (**Figure 24**). Remove the manual release valve with a screwdriver. Remove the O-ring from the valve assembly.
14. Remove the tilt-up relief valve plug from the rear of the valve body with a screwdriver. Remove the spring and valve core. Insert the tools made in Step 12 in the plug bore and

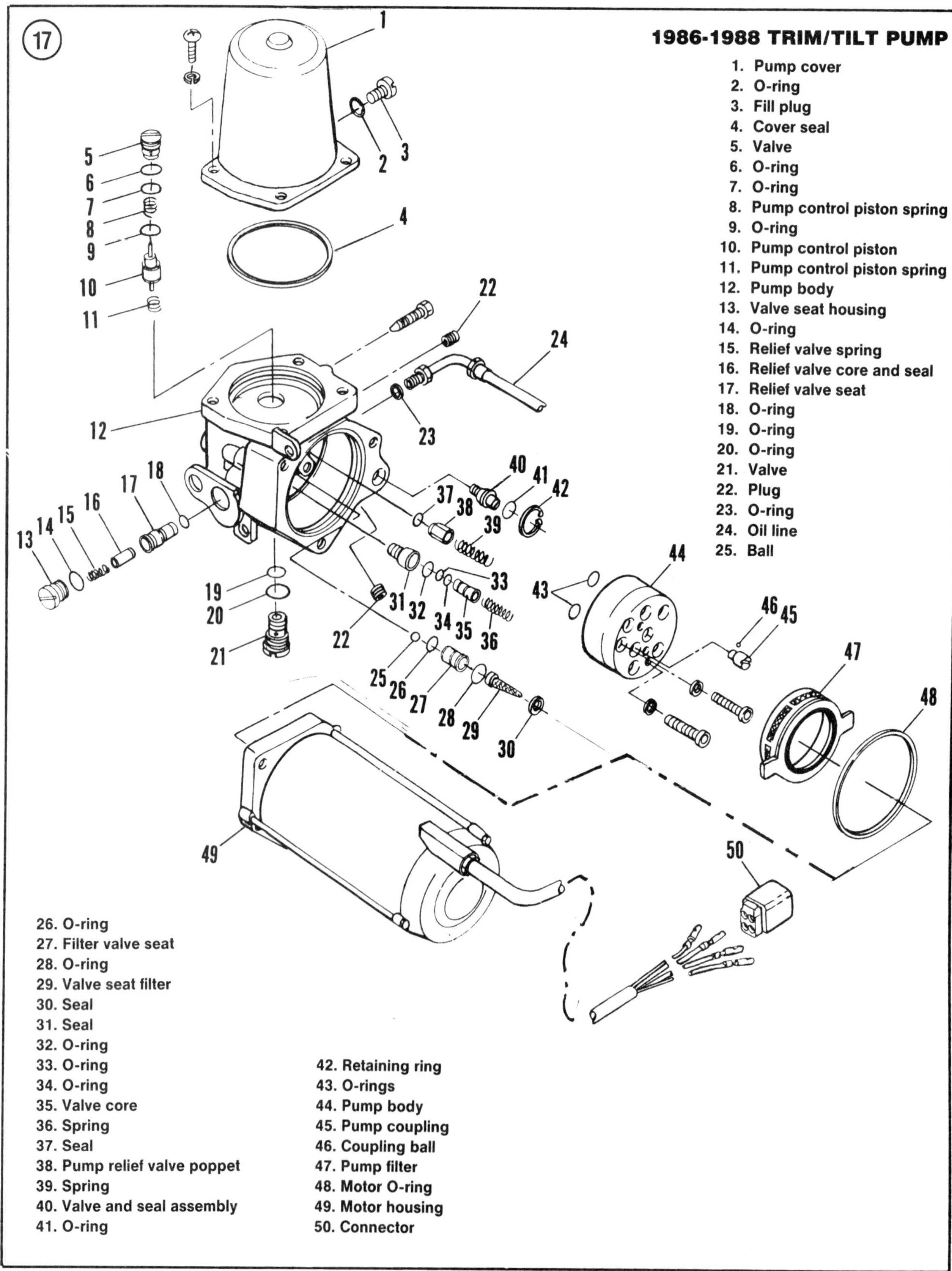
17
1986-1988 TRIM/TILT PUMP
1. Pump cover
2. O-ring
3. Fill plug
4. Cover seal
5. Valve
6. O-ring
7. O-ring
8. Pump control piston spring
9. O-ring
10. Pump control piston
11. Pump control piston spring
12. Pump body
13. Valve seat housing
14. O-ring
15. Relief valve spring
16. Relief valve core and seal
17. Relief valve seat
18. O-ring
19. O-ring
20. O-ring
21. Valve
22. Plug
23. O-ring
24. Oil line
25. Ball
26. O-ring
27. Filter valve seat
28. O-ring
29. Valve seat filter
30. Seal
31. Seal
32. O-ring
33. O-ring
34. O-ring
35. Valve core
36. Spring
37. Seal
38. Pump relief valve poppet
39. Spring
40. Valve and seal assembly
41. O-ring
42. Retaining ring
43. O-rings
44. Pump body
45. Pump coupling
46. Coupling ball
47. Pump filter
48. Motor O-ring
49. Motor housing
50. Connector

18
1
2

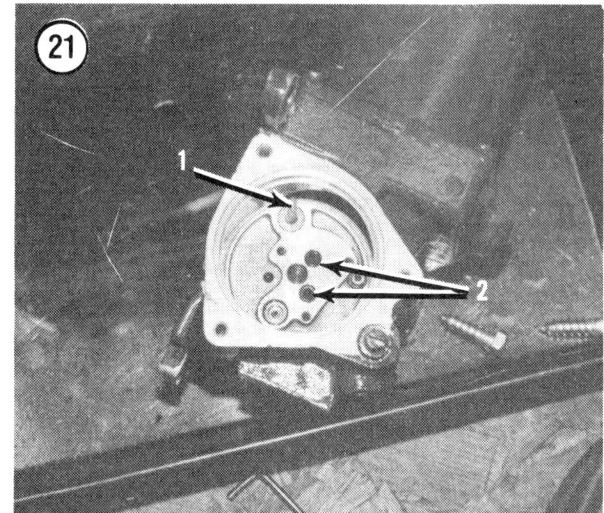
21
1
2

19

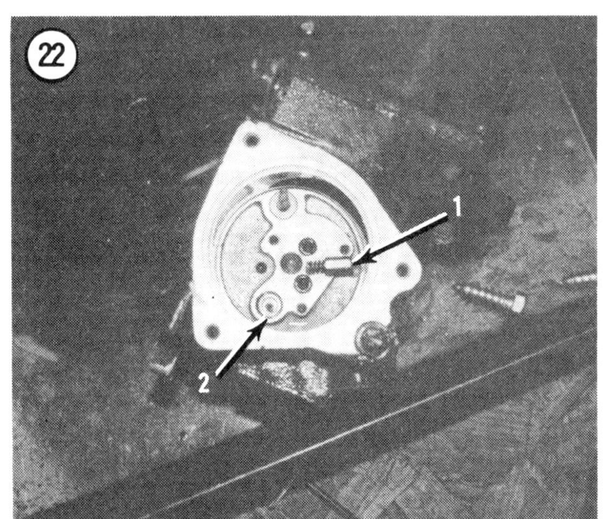
22
1
2

20

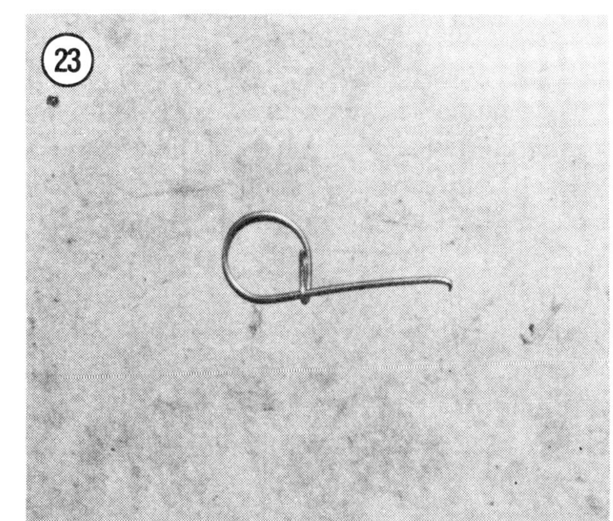
23

engage the cross holes in the valve core. Extract the valve from the bore, then use one of the tools to engage and remove the valve seat from the bore.

CAUTION
The trim-in/tilt-down and trim-out/tilt-up check valves are identical in appearance. Label or otherwise identify each properly when removed to prevent confusion during reassembly. If check valves are to be tested for leakage, do not remove the O-rings in Step 15 or Step 17.

15. Remove the trim-in/tilt-down check valve (**Figure 25**).
16. Remove the upper spring, then pull the pump control piston and lower spring (**Figure 26**) out with a pair of needlenose pliers.
17. Remove the trim-out/tilt-up check valve from the bottom of the valve body assembly.

Cleaning and Inspection

1. If all valves have been removed, clean the valve body with solvent and blow dry with low-pressure compressed air. Submerge the valve body in OMC Power Trim/Tilt fluid. This will allow the passages to fill with fluid before reassembly.
2. Check the valve seats to make sure all contamination or varnish has been removed.
3. Check all metal components for signs of excessive wear or corrosion; replace as required.
4. Check the sealing tip on all check valves. Test the check valve for free operation by inserting a length of stiff wire and gently pushing on the valve core (**Figure 27**). Remove the wire and let the valve core close by its spring action. It should close smoothly and completely.
5. Check the sealing tip on all valve cores. If damaged or otherwise defective, the tip can be replaced without replacing the entire valve core. New tips are installed with their flat side against the valve; the ribbed side will face the valve seat when installed.
6. Reinstall the oil pump coupler and submerge the pump assembly in OMC Power Trim/Tilt fluid. Rotate the coupler to check pump action. This will also fill the pump with fluid and flush the passages. Remove the coupler from the pump. If the coupler ball is damaged, defective or missing, it can be

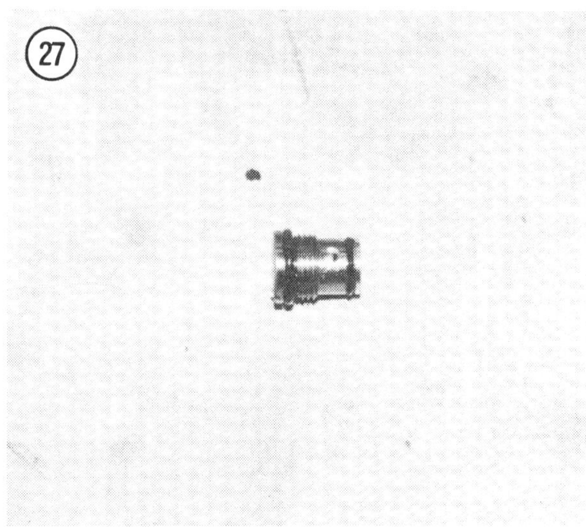

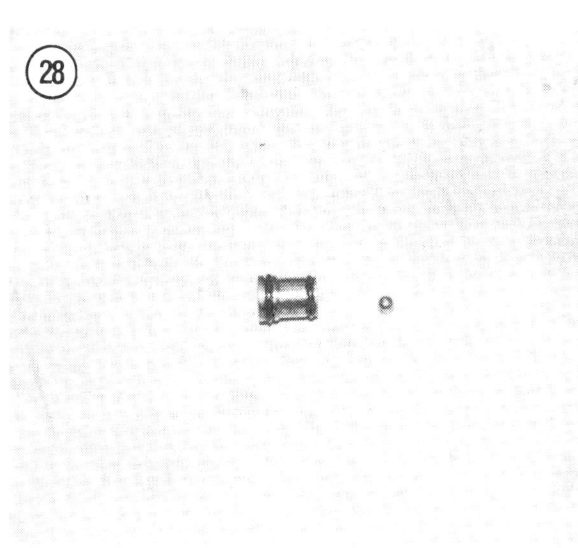

replaced without replacing the entire coupler assembly.

Assembly

Refer to **Figure 17** for this procedure.

1. If the O-rings were removed from the trim-out/tilt-up check valve, reinstall new O-rings. Wipe the O-rings with OMC Power Trim/Tilt fluid and install the valve in the bottom of the valve body. Tighten valve to 50-60 in.-lb. (5.5-7.0 N•m).
2. Install new O-rings on the tilt-up relief valve seat and cap. Wipe O-rings with OMC Power Trim/Tilt fluid and install valve seat in the bore at the rear of the valve body. Insert the spring and valve core, then install the valve cap and tighten to 50-60 in.-lb. (5.5-7.0 N•m).
3. Install the pump control piston lower spring. Install a new O-ring on the piston and lubricate with OMC Power Trim/Tilt fluid. Install piston in valve body with O-ring end first. Install upper spring in valve body.
4. If the O-rings were removed from the trim-in/tilt-down check valve, reinstall new O-rings. Wipe the O-rings with OMC Power Trim/Tilt fluid and install valve over the pump control piston assembly. Tighten valve to 50-60 in.-lb. (5.5-7.0 N•m).
5. Install new O-rings on the thermal expansion valve core. Install new pump-to-body O-rings (2, **Figure 21**). Wipe all O-rings with OMC Power Trim/Tilt fluid and install the thermal expansion valve body, core and spring in the front of the valve body (2, **Figure 22**).
6. Install trim-in relief valve and spring (1, **Figure 22**).
7. Install new O-rings on the filter valve body. Wipe O-rings with OMC Power Trim/Tilt fluid. Drop the check ball into the filter valve body (**Figure 28**) and install assembly in valve body. Install the filter and washer. Stake the washer in place with a small screwdriver or punch.

8. Insert the screws with lockwashers in the oil pump body. Since the pump can be installed only in one position, align pump body screws with valve body. Fit pump body over the valve springs and start the screws by hand. Tighten to 25-35 in.-lb. (2.8-4.0 N•m).
9. Install pump coupler. Make sure it fits into the correct hole to engage the driveshaft tang on the pump shaft. Install the oil filter assembly.
10. Install a new O-ring on the manual release valve. Install valve in housing bore. Compress and install the snap ring with snap ring pliers. See **Figure 29**.
11. Install a new O-ring on the motor mounting flange. Align the pump coupling with the mounting hole and the pump motor shaft tang with the flange mounting hole (**Figure 30**). Assemble motor to valve body and tighten the mounting screws to 60-84 in.-lb. (7-9 N•m).
12. Install a new O-ring on the reservoir mounting flange. Assemble reservoir to valve body and tighten mounting screws to 60-84 in.-lb. (7-9 N•m).
13. Install a new O-ring on the fill plug and manufacturing plug. Install the fill plug finger-tight and the manufacturing plug to 60-84 in.-lb. (7-9 N•m).

Check Valve Pressure Testing

If the trim-in/tilt-down or trim-out/tilt-up check valve is suspected of malfunctioning, it should be removed from the valve body and checked with the following procedure. The O-rings should *not* be removed before testing. This procedure requires the use of OMC Check Valve Tester (part No. 390063 and a gearcase pressure tester.

1. Connect the pressure tester to the check valve tester. Lightly lubricate the check valve O-ring and thread it into the check valve tester.
2. Pressurize the check valve to 30 psi; it should hold the pressure indefinitely.
3. Submerge the tester in a container of clear water and check for the presence of air bubbles (**Figure 31**). If bubbles appear to be coming from the outer edge (A), replace the outer O-ring. Bubbles that appear to be coming from the check valve edge (B) may be caused by a leaking inner O-ring or a defective check valve. Replace the inner O-ring and retest. If bubbles still appear, proceed with Step 4.
4. If check valve appears to be leaking, submerge assembly in clean solvent and open/close the valve several times (**Figure 27**) with a stiff wire. Dry with compressed air blown through all holes with the valve open and then closed. Repeat pressure/water test. If valve still does not function properly, replace it.

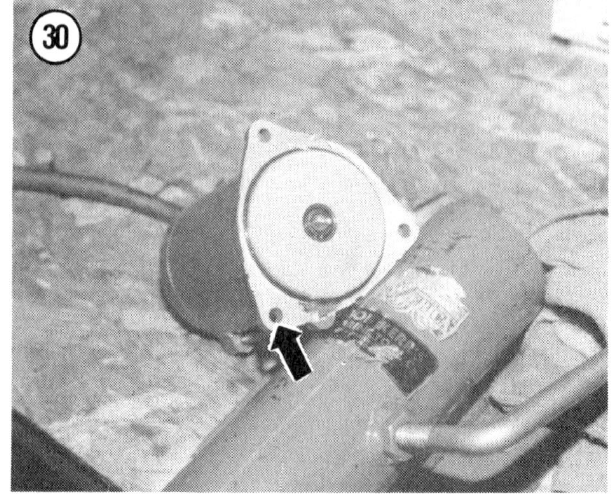

5. If the valve comes apart during testing, it can be reassembled to function properly. Insert the spring in the valve, install the valve core with the rubber seat facing out, then install the retaining disc.

Pump Overhaul (1989)

Service to the pump should be performed by an experienced marine technician. If this is not possible, the following procedure will allow you to disassemble, inspect and reassemble the pump. However, since you are working with a hydraulic unit, cleanliness is paramount.

To prevent any possible confusion, you should also have a cupcake tin or several small containers in which you can store and properly label the numerous screws, springs, valves, circlips and other small components.

Disassembly

Refer to **Figure 32** for this procedure.

1. Wipe the outside of the pump unit with a cloth moistened in solvent or OMC engine cleaner. Wipe the solvent or engine cleaner off with a clean lint-free cloth or lint-free paper towels.

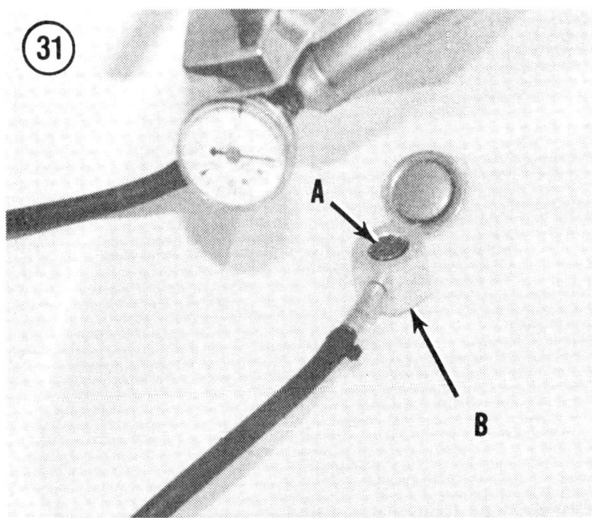

2. Remove the 3 Phillips-head screws holding the pump motor and valve body together. Separate the motor from the valve body. Remove and discard the sealing O-ring from the valve body.
3. Remove the 4 Phillips-head screws holding the pump reservoir to the valve body. Separate the reservoir from the valve body. Remove and discard the sealing O-ring from the valve body.
4. Remove the oil pump filter and rotate the pump coupling to check for binding.
5. Pull the pump coupling from the pump and check the coupling for excessive wear or any other damage.

NOTE
Use extreme care when working with gear housing or manifold. Any damage inflicted to either component can cause pump malfunction or possible personal injury.

6. Remove the 4 Allen-head screws (**Figure 33**) which hold the gear housing to the manifold in one turn increments. Note position of retainer plate (**Figure 33**), then remove the gear housing from the manifold. Make sure the 2 pump control pistons and check balls (**Figure 34**) are retained in gear housing. If gear housing requires flushing, use only clean hydraulic oil, such as OMC Power Trim and Tilt Fluid. If defective, the gear housing is replaced as an assembly with the manifold.
7. Use needle-nose pliers and extract the 2 pump control pistons (**Figure 34**) from the gear housing, then remove the check ball beneath each pump control piston (**Figure 35**).
8. Position a suitable tool through opening on top side of trim-up relief valve (large diameter valve) and push valve assembly from gear housing. Remove and discard O-ring on outside of trim-up relief valve seat (**Figure 36**).

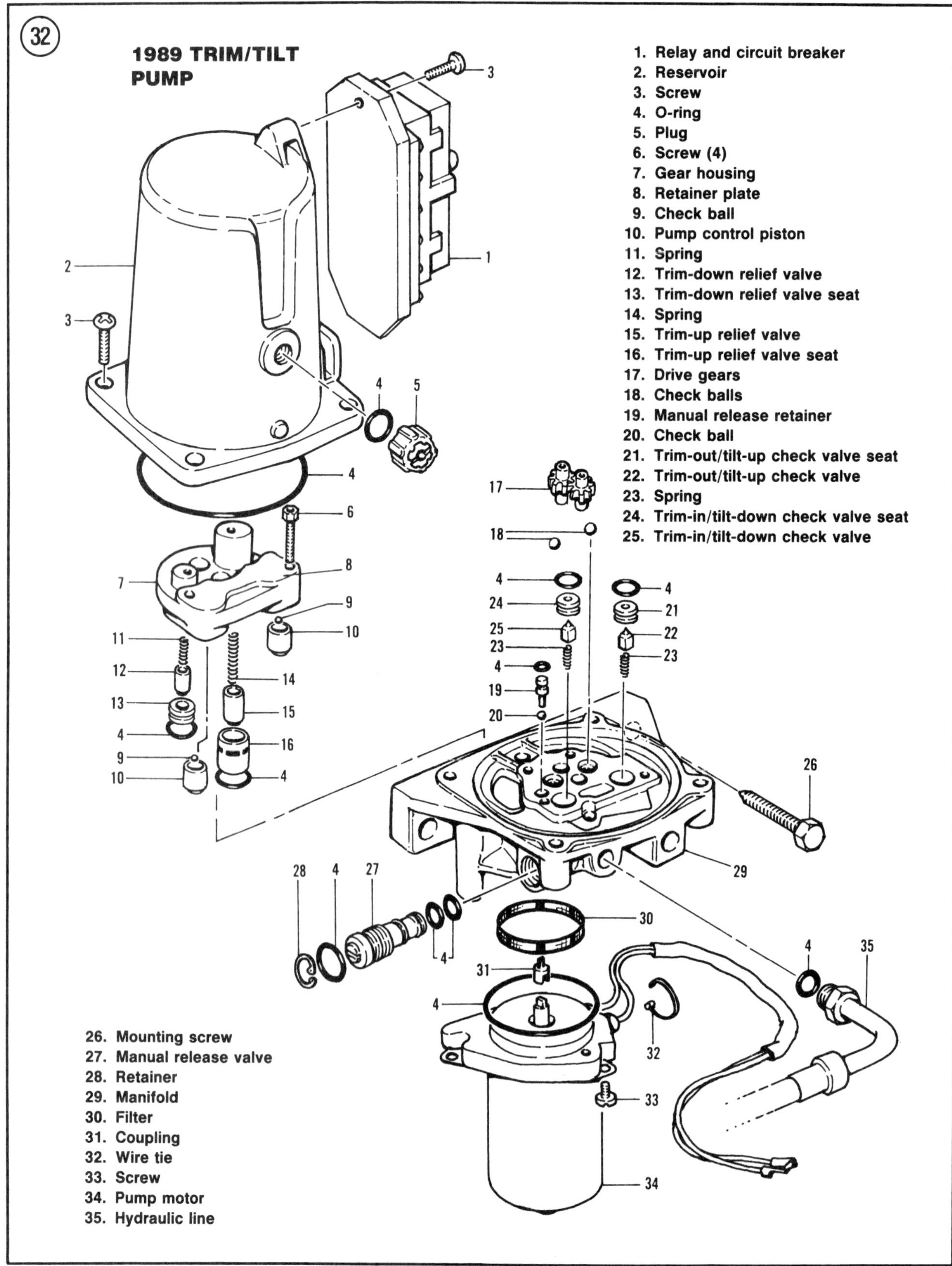

32
1989 TRIM/TILT PUMP
1. Relay and circuit breaker
2. Reservoir
3. Screw
4. O-ring
5. Plug
6. Screw (4)
7. Gear housing
8. Retainer plate
9. Check ball
10. Pump control piston
11. Spring
12. Trim-down relief valve
13. Trim-down relief valve seat
14. Spring
15. Trim-up relief valve
16. Trim-up relief valve seat
17. Drive gears
18. Check balls
19. Manual release retainer
20. Check ball
21. Trim-out/tilt-up check valve seat
22. Trim-out/tilt-up check valve
23. Spring
24. Trim-in/tilt-down check valve seat
25. Trim-in/tilt-down check valve
26. Mounting screw
27. Manual release valve
28. Retainer
29. Manifold
30. Filter
31. Coupling
32. Wire tie
33. Screw
34. Pump motor
35. Hydraulic line

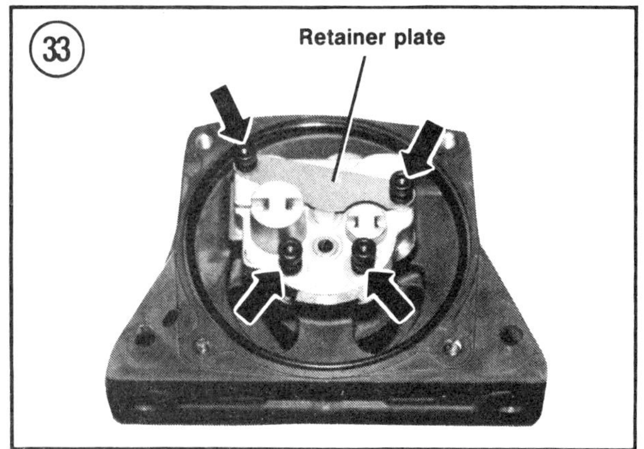

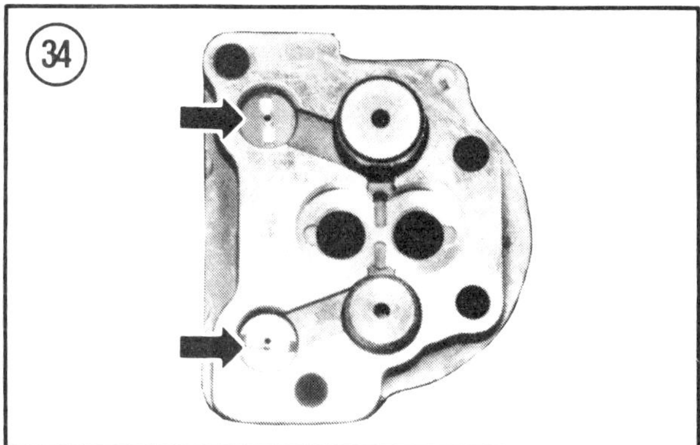

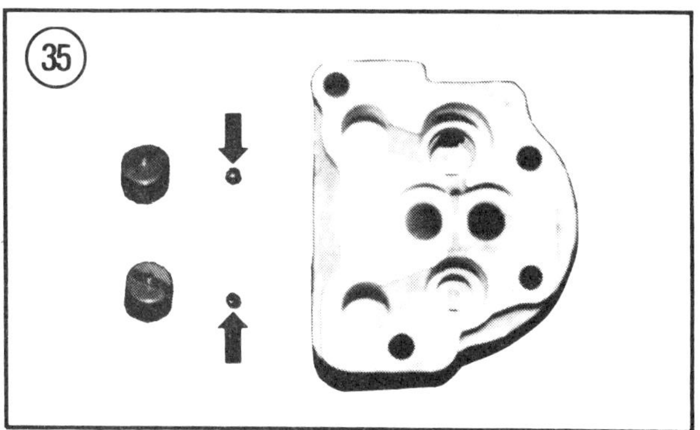

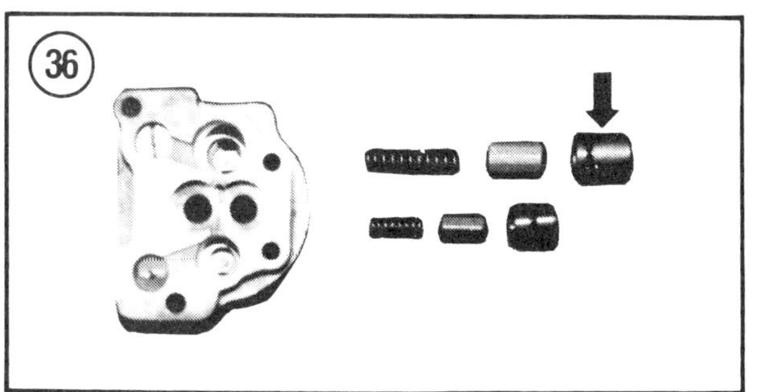

9. Position a suitable tool through opening on top side of trim-down relief valve (small diameter valve) and push valve assembly from gear housing. Remove and discard O-ring on outside of trim-down relief valve seat (**Figure 37**).

NOTE
Early model hydraulic pumps may be equipped with a short trim-down relief valve seat.

10. Remove 2 pump drive gears and 2 reservoir inlet check balls (**Figure 38**).

CAUTION
Hydraulic pressure must be used to remove the trim-out/tilt-up check valve and the trim-in/tilt-down check valve. Do not try to pry valve seats free from manifold as damage to manifold will result.

11. Fill starboard hydraulic line port in manifold with OMC Needle Bearing Grease.

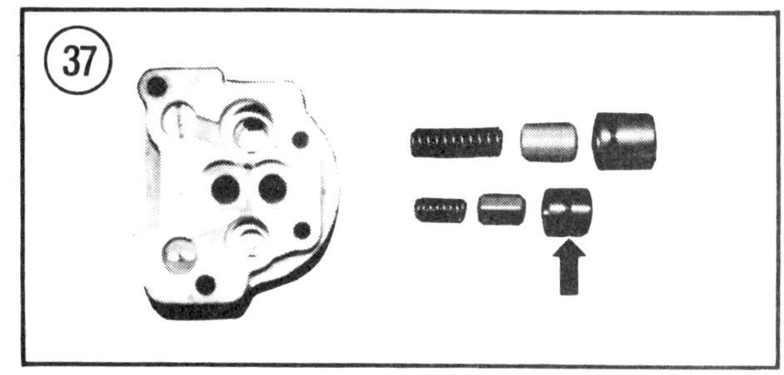

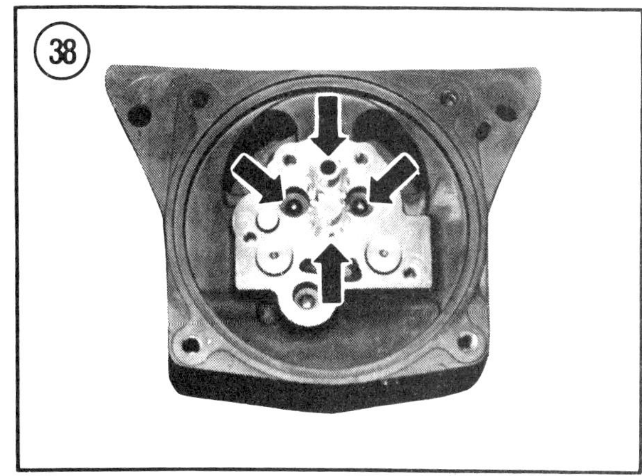

15

Cover manual release check ball hole on electric motor side of manifold, then thread a 7/16 inch fine thread bolt into the starboard manifold fitting. Withdraw bolt and add more grease as needed until the trim-in/tilt-down check valve seat becomes free. Withdraw valve and spring (**Figure 39**). Check assembly for wear or damage. Remove and discard O-ring on outside of seat.

12. Fill port hydraulic line port in manifold with OMC Needle Bearing Grease. Thread a 7/16 inch fine thread bolt into the port manifold fitting. Withdraw bolt and add more grease as needed until the trim-out/tilt-up check valve seat becomes free. Withdraw valve and spring (**Figure 40**). Check assembly for wear or damage. Remove and discard O-ring on outside of seat.

13. Position a suitable tool through opening (**Figure 41**) on electric motor side of manual release check ball, then push check ball and retainer (**Figure 42**) from manifold. Remove and discard O-ring on outside of retainer.

14. Use snap ring pliers and remove snap ring from manual release valve bore. Remove the manual release valve with a screwdriver. Remove and discard the O-rings on outside of valve (**Figure 43**).

NOTE

The thermal expansion valve is located on the inside of the manual release valve tip. If malfunction is noted in either the thermal expansion valve or the manual release valve, the complete assembly must be replaced.

Cleaning And Inspection

1. If all valves have been removed, clean the gear housing and manifold with solvent and blow dry with low-pressure compressed air. Submerge the gear housing and manifold in OMC Power Trim and Tilt fluid. This will allow the passages to fill with fluid before reassembly.

39

40

41

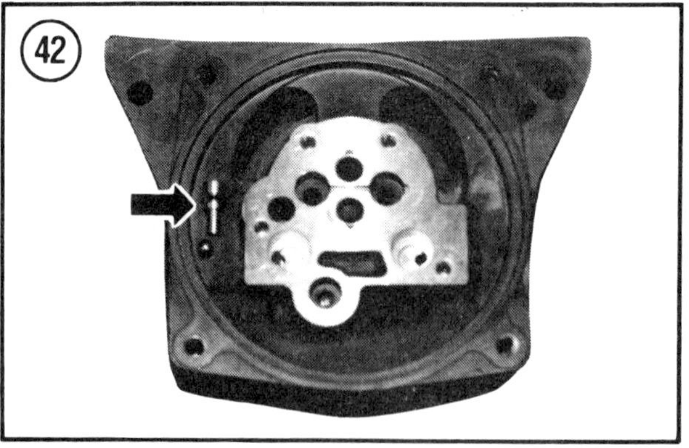

42

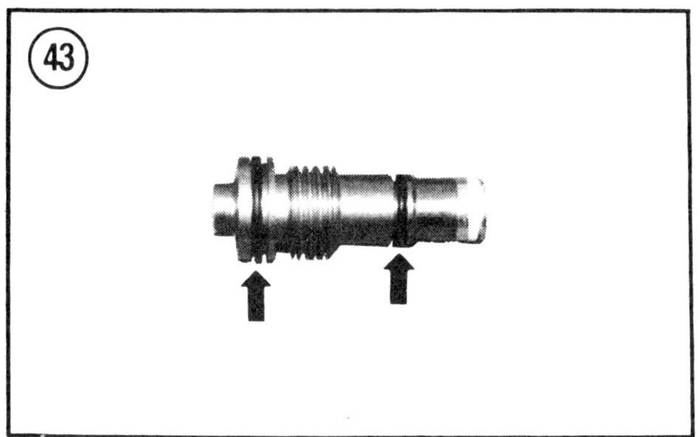

2. Check the valve seats to make sure all contamination or varnish has been removed.
3. Check all metal components for signs of excessive wear or corrosion; replace as required.
4. Check the sealing tip on all check valves; replace as required.

Assembly

Refer to **Figure 32** for this procedure.

1. Install new O-rings on manual release valve (**Figure 43**), then screw valve assembly into manifold bore until lightly seated. Use snap ring pliers and install snap ring into groove in manifold bore. Make sure snap ring properly seats in groove.
2. Install manual release check ball and retainer with a new O-ring (**Figure 42**). Press retainer into manifold until flush with manifold surface.
3. Install each spring, valve and seat, with a new O-ring, into check valve bores in manifold until properly seated (**Figure 39** and **Figure 40**).
4. Pressure test each check valve assembly as follows to ensure seat and valve properly seal.
   a. Screw a 10/32×1/2 inch screw with a 5/32 inch flat washer into the threaded hole next to the trim-out/tilt-up check valve seat (port side) to secure postion. Do not cover valve hole in center of seat with flat washer. Screw OMC Adapter (part No. 914459) onto a gearcase pressure tester. Make sure an O-ring lubricated with OMC Power Trim and Tilt Fluid is installed on the end of the OMC adapter tool. Screw adapter tool with gearcase pressure tester into port side hydraulic line orifice in manifold. Submerge manifold assembly into a container of OMC Power Trim and Tilt Fluid.

WARNING
Wear protective safety glasses to prevent any fluid or component under pressure from causing personal injury.

   b. Pump gearcase pressure tester until a reading of 30 psi is noted on pressure gauge. Then observe container of fluid for any air bubbles. If air bubbles are noted, then a determination must be made as to which component is leaking and the faulty component replaced or reseated as needed.
   c. Repeat Step 4a to test for proper sealing of trim-in/tilt-down check valve assembly (starboard side) with the exception the manual release check ball hole on the electric motor side of the manifold must be covered.
5. Install 2 reservoir inlet check balls and 2 pump drive gears (**Figure 38**).
6. Place a new O-ring on outside of trim-down relief valve seat (**Figure 37**) and lubricate with OMC Power Trim and Tilt Fluid, then install trim-down relief valve assembly into gear housing.
7. Place a new O-ring on outside of trim-up relief valve seat (**Figure 36**) and lubricate with OMC Power Trim and Tilt Fluid, then install trim-up relief valve assembly into gear housing.

8. Install the 2 pump control pistons and the check ball located beneath each piston into gear housing (**Figure 34** and **Figure 35**).
9. Position gear housing onto manifold. Install retainer plate in position noted during disassembly (**Figure 33**). Curved notch in retainer plate must position around trim-down relief valve seat. Install the 4 Allen-head screws (**Figure 33**) which hold the gear housing to the manifold and tighten in one turn increments until a final torque of 35 in.-lb. is obtained.
10. Install the pump coupling into the pump and rotate coupling to ensure no binding is noted.
11. Install oil pump filter with wide base facing toward valve body.
12. Install a new pump motor-to-valve body O-ring into valve body, then install pump motor.

NOTE
Make sure pump motor shaft properly engages pump coupling during assembly.

Tighten the 3 Phillips-head screws holding the pump motor and valve body together to 35-52 in.-lb.
13. Install a new reservoir-to-valve body O-ring into valve body, then install reservoir. Tighten the 4 Phillips-head screws holding the reservoir and valve body together to 35-52 in.-lb.

Table 1 1986-1988 HYDRAULIC PRESSURE SPECIFICATIONS

Position	Normal pressure (psi)
Trim out/tilt up	225-275
Tilt up stall	1,000-1,400
Tilt up stall/leakdown	200 maximum, 5 minutes minimum
Trim in/tilt down	400-800
Trim in/stall	400-800
Trim in stall/leakdown	200 maximum, 5 minutes minimum

Table 2 1989 HYDRAULIC PRESSURE SPECIFICATIONS

Position	Normal pressure (psi)
Tilt out/tilt up	225-275
Tilt up stall	1200-1600
Tilt up stall/leakdown	200 maximum, 5 minutes minimum
Trim in/tilt down	400-800
Trim in/stall	400-800
Trim in stall/leakdown	200 maximum, 5 minutes minimum

Table 3 1986-1988 POWER TRIM/TILT TROUBLESHOOTING DIAGNOSTICS

Condition	Probable cause
Static leakdown and/or trim-in creep when in FORWARD gear	Loose or leaking manual release valve
	Trim out/tilt up check valve sticks
	Defective thermal expansion valve
	Pump control piston sticks
	External oil leak
Trim out/tilt up creep in REVERSE gear	Trim in/tilt down check valve sticks
	Leaking check valve
	Pump control piston sticks
	External oil leak
Trim in/trim out creep	Internal leak in trim/tilt cylinder
Slow or no trim out/tilt up (motor runs)	Fill and/or bleed pump reservoir
	Loose or leaking manual release valve
	Trim out/tilt up check valve sticks
	Defective thermal expansion valve
	Pump control piston sticks
	Internal leak in trim/tilt cylinder
	Trim in/tilt down check valve sticks
	Leaking tilt-up relief valve
	Pump binds
	Defective motor

(continued)

Table 3 1986-1988 POWER TRIM/TILT TROUBLESHOOTING DIAGNOSTICS (cont.)

Condition	Probable cause
No trim out/tilt up (motor does not run)	Malfunctioning switch circuit
	Pump binds
	Defective motor
	Defective solenoid
Slow or no trim in/tilt down (motor runs)	Fill and/or bleed pump reservoir
	Trim out/tilt up check valve sticks
	Pump control piston sticks
	Trim in/tilt down check valve sticks
	Leaky check valve
	Leaking trim in relief valve
No trim in/tilt down (motor runs)	Fill and/or bleed pump reservoir
	Pump binds
	Defective motor
No trim/tilt up or down (motor runs fast)	Broken pump coupling
No trim/tilt up or down (motor does not run)	Pump binds
	Defective motor
	Defective solenoid
	Malfunctioning switch circuit
No tilt down from full tilt up position	Defective thermal expansion valve
Erratic operation or jumpy motion	Bleed pump reservoir
Continual loss of hydraulic fluid	External oil leak

Table 4 1989 POWER TRIM/TILT TROUBLESHOOTING DIAGNOSTICS

Condition	Probable cause
Static leakdown and/or creep when in FORWARD gear	Loose or leaking manual release valve
	Trim out/tilt up check valve sticks
	Defective thermal expansion valve
	Pump control piston sticks
	External oil leak
Trim out/tilt up creep in REVERSE gear	Trim in/tilt down check valve sticks
	Manual release check ball leaking
	Pump control piston sticks
	External oil leak
Trim in/trim out creep	Internal leak in trim/tilt cylinder

(continued)

Table 4 1989 POWER TRIM/TILT TROUBLESHOOTING DIAGNOSTICS (cont.)

Condition	Probable cause
Slow or no trim out/tilt up (motor runs)	Fill and/or bleed pump reservoir Loose or leaking manual release valve Trim out/tilt up check valve sticks Defective thermal expansion valve Pump control piston sticks Internal leak in trim/tilt cylinder Trim in/tilt down check valve sticks Leaking tilt-up relief valve Pump binds Defective motor
No trim out/tilt up (motor does not run)	Malfunctioning switch circuit Defective fuse or tripped circuit breaker Defective motor Defective relay and circuit breaker assembly
Slow or no trim in/tilt down (motor runs)	Fill and/or bleed pump reservoir Trim out/tilt up check valve sticks Pump control piston sticks Trim in/tilt down check valve sticks Manual release check ball leaking Leaking trim in relief valve Loose or leaking manual release valve Pump binds
No trim in/tilt down (motor runs)	Malfunctioning switch circuit Defective fuse or tripped circuit breaker Defective motor Defective relay and circuit breaker assembly
No trim/tilt up or down (motor runs fast)	Broken pump coupling
No trim/tilt up or down (motor does not run)	Defective fuse or tripped circuit breaker Defective motor Defective relay and circuit breaker assembly Malfunctioning switch circuit
No tilt down from full tilt up position	Defective thermal expansion valve
Erratic operation or jumpy motion	Bleed hydraulic system
Continual loss of hydraulic fluid	External oil leak

Chapter Sixteen

Steering Systems

OMC Cobra drives may be equipped with a manual (non-power) or power steering system. Proper operation of the stern drive steering system is essential for safe boating. The steering system should be rigged *only* by an experienced marine technician and serviced (whenever possible) by one who is equally qualified. The boater should perform routine checks and maintenance to assure that no problems develop. This chapter covers steering safety precautions, steering system troubleshooting and maintenance. **Table 1** (tightening torques) and **Table 2** (power steering troubleshooting) are at the end of the chapter.

SAFETY PRECAUTIONS

The steering system connects the stern drive unit to the steering wheel (**Figure 1**). When properly installed and maintained, the steering system gives the boater control over the vessel. A steering system that jams will prevent you from avoiding obstacles, such as other boats on the water. If the steering system is loose, the boat will weave regardless of the boater's attempt to maintain a straight course. A steering system failure will cause the boater to completely lose control, possibly resulting in a serious accident and even loss of life.

The most important safety precaution you can observe is proper lubrication and maintenance of the steering system. This is especially important whenever the stern drive unit receives a severe blow, such as hitting a piling or other object in the water, or when trailering the boat. Damaged or weak components may fail at a later time while you are on the water. Know what to look for and have any deficiencies you find corrected as soon as possible.

If you must make required adjustments yourself, make them carefully and use only the fasteners supplied with steering attachment kits or equivalent fasteners sold as replacement items by marine dealers. It is also a good idea to have your work rechecked by an experienced marine technician to make sure that no safety hazards exist.

Whenever the engine is removed or other service that affects the steering system is performed, you should make sure that:

a. Cable movement is not restricted. See **Figure 2**. Cable restrictions can result in possible jamming of the system. On power steering models, a cable restriction can cause the drive unit to go into a full turn condition without your ever turning the steering wheel.
b. The engine stringer (mount) does not interfere with the power steering pump and pulley (**Figure 3**).
c. The power steering components **(Figure 4)** and the push-pull cable function

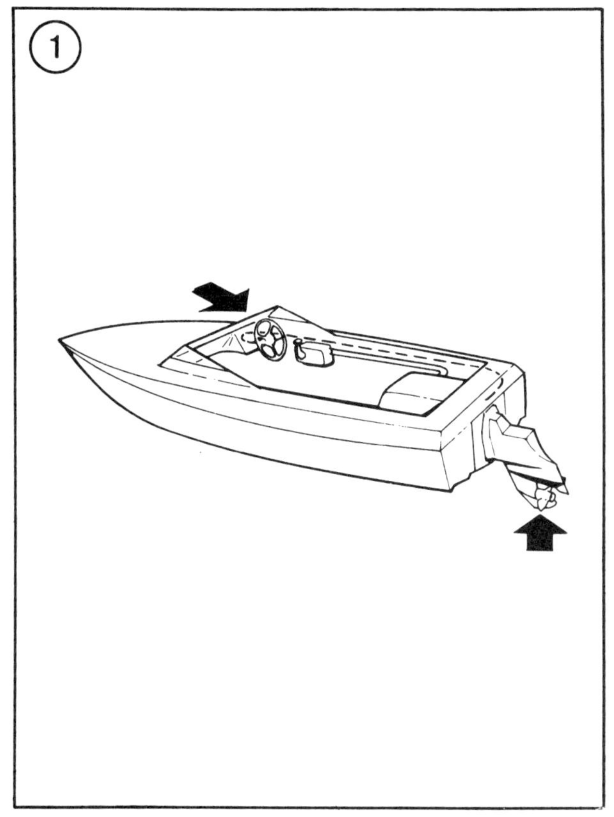

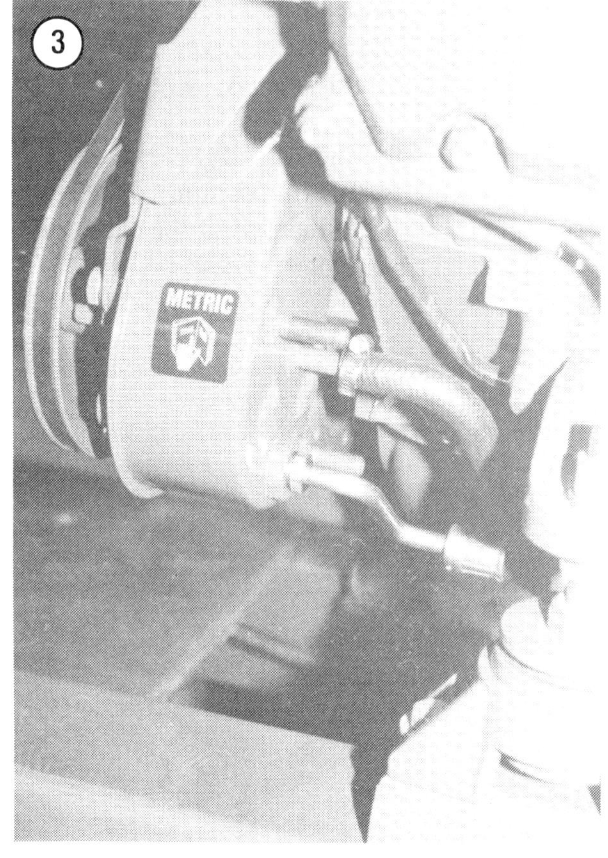

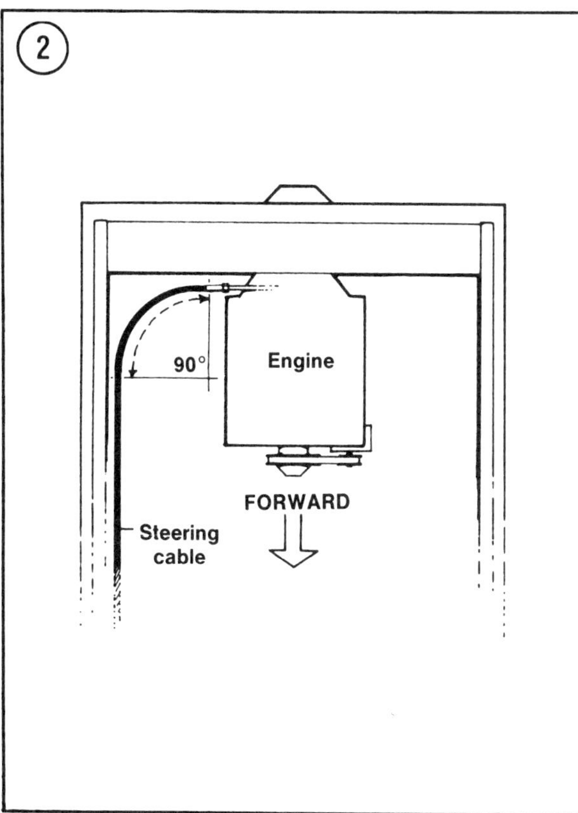

freely and will operate the power steering valve only when you turn the steering wheel.

MECHANICAL STEERING SYSTEM

A mechanical steering system **(Figure 5)** consists of the helm or steering wheel assembly, the connecting cable and hardware that attaches the steering wheel to the steering arm on the inner transom bracket.

Cable Removal/Installation

The steering cable must be serviced as an assembly.

1. Remove the cotter pin from the steering arm pin which holds the cable ram to the steering arm. See **Figure 6**. Remove the steering arm pin.
2. Turn the helm (steering wheel assembly) to the port full lock position, then loosen the

cable anchor nut (**Figure 7**) and remove the cable. **Figure 7** shows a hex-type anchor nut. A ribbed anchor nut (Inset "A," **Figure 9**) may also be used.

3. Turn the steering wheel to extend the cable ram to its full (maximum) extension, then lubricate the full length of the cable ram with OMC Triple-Guard grease.

NOTE
*The steering tube position in the anchor block is factory-set for correct centering of the steering system on 1987 and later models. Do **not** loosen the jam nut or change the steering tube position.*

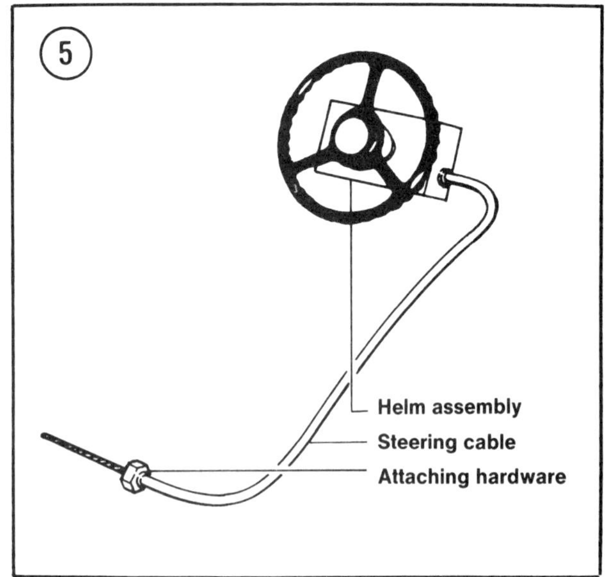

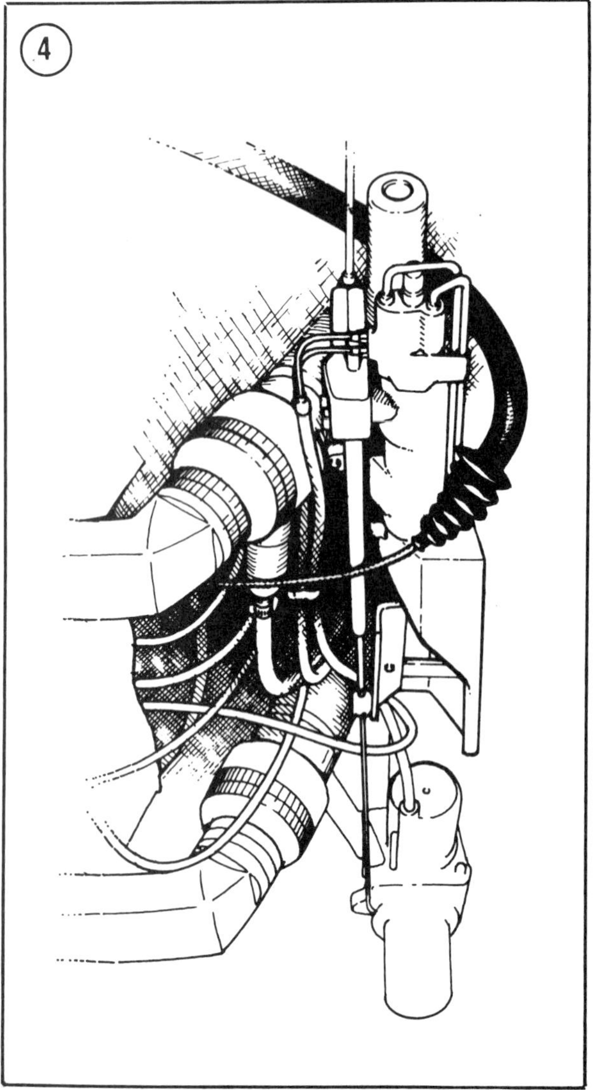

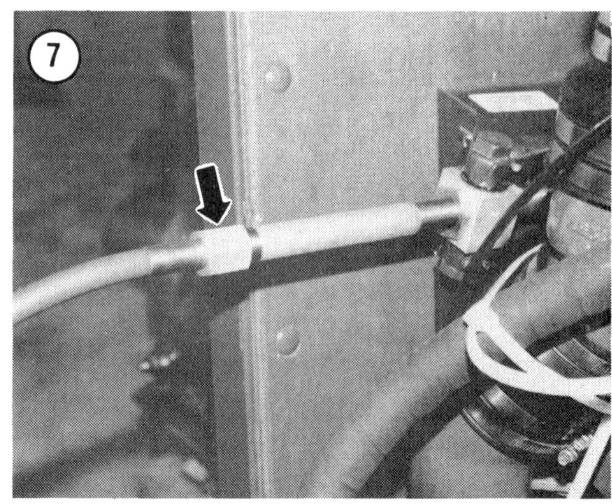

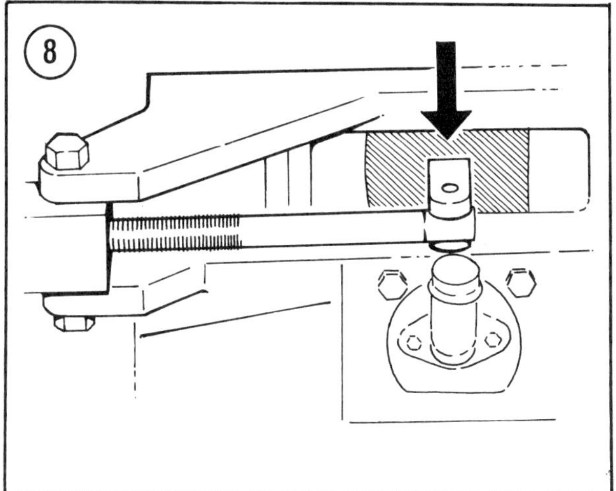

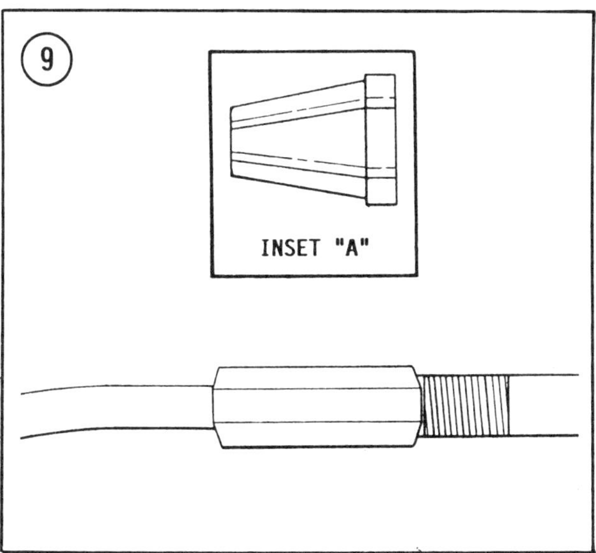

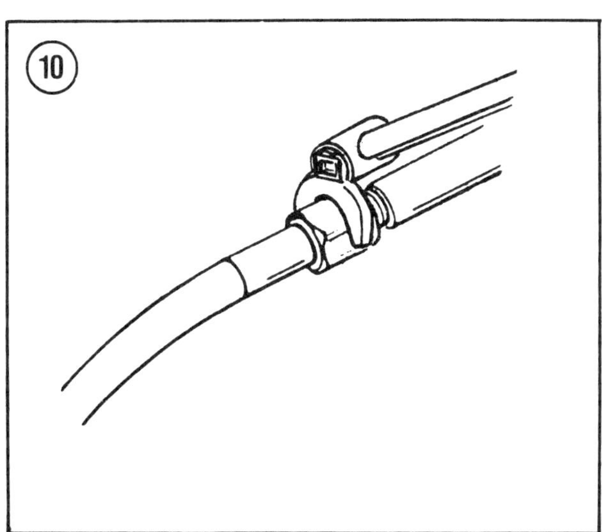

4A. On 1987 and later models, install the steering cable ram through the steering tube.

4B. On all earlier models:

a. Retract the steering cable ram completely. Count the number of steering wheel turns required to retract the ram.
b. Install the steering cable ram through the steering tube.
c. Move the stern drive steering arm to its center position (**Figure 8**).
d. Turn the steering wheel one-half of the turns counted in sub-step a to center the steering cable ram.
e. Press the cable against the steering tube (**Figure 9**). Loosen the tube locknut and rotate the tube until the hole in the cable ram aligns with the steering arm hole.
f. Position the steering tube jam nut against the tube anchor and tighten jam nut to 20-25 ft.-lb. (27-34 N•m) using OMC crowfoot adapter part No. 910103 at a 90° angle to the torque wrench.

5. Hold steering cable in tube and thread cable anchor nut onto steering tube (**Figure 9**) until it bottoms on the end of the tube.

6. Tighten the cable anchor nut to 120 in.-lb. (14 N•m) using OMC crowfoot adaptor part No. 910103 at a 90° angle to the torque wrench. See **Figure 10.**

7. Reinstall the steering arm pin (**Figure 11**). Install a new cotter pin through the hole in

the steering arm pin and spread both ends of the cotter pin to secure it in place.

8. Rotate the steering wheel to fully extend and retract the cable ram. If the installation is correct, the steering arm will move from stop to stop as the steering ram goes from a fully retracted to a fully extended position. If it does not, repeat the procedure.

Steering Tube Replacement (1987-on)

1. Loosen the jam nut, then unthread the steering tube from the anchor block. Unthread jam nut from steering tube.
2. Thread jam nut all the way onto a new steering tube.
3. Measure in 3 1/4 in. from the end of the steering tube (dimension A, **Figure 12**). Clean the next 1 1/4 in. of the tube thread with Locquic Primer and let it air dry. See dimension B, **Figure 12**.
4. Apply OMC Nut Lock to the 1 1/4 in. area of the thread that was cleaned and primed in Step 3. See dimension B, **Figure 12**.
5. Thread the anchor block onto the steering tube 3 5/32 in. from the end of the tube. See dimension A, **Figure 13**. This will position the steering tube and accurately center the steering system.
6. Hold anchor block in position and tighten jam nut against anchor block to 35-40 ft.-lb. (47-54 N•m).
7. If the anchor block was removed from the transom plate, coat both bushings with OMC Triple-Guard grease, then install the block with its original screws and tighten to 40-45 ft.-lb. (55-61 N•m) and secure with new cotter pins.

Steering System Lubrication

See Chapter Four.

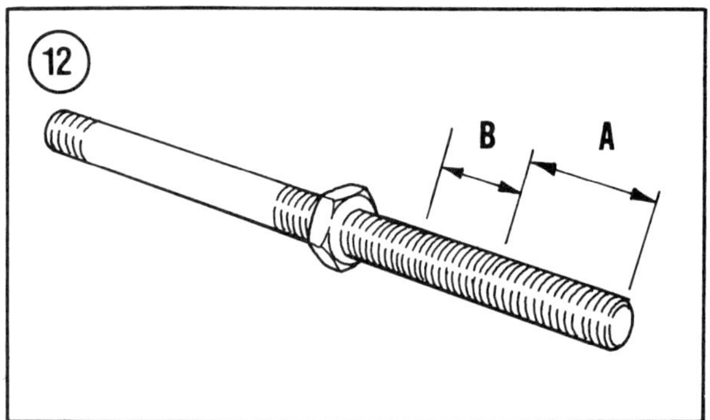

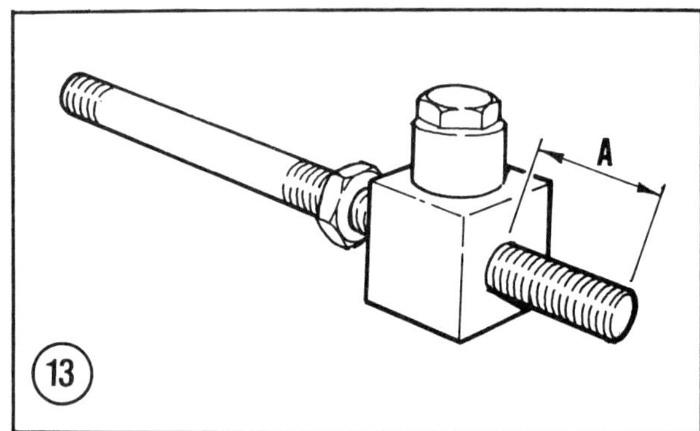

Trim Tab Adjustment

Proper adjustment of the trim tab will provide equal steering effort in both directions. If the boat seems to steer easier in one direction than the other, operate it in a straight line with a balanced load on a stretch of water where wind and current will not prove to be factors. If steering effort is not equal under these conditions, adjust the trim tab as follows:

1. Determine in which direction the steering is easier.
2. Loosen the trim tab bolt. Note that the trim tab is embossed with numbers from 0 to 6 and that one number will be aligned with an embossed mark on the anti-ventilation plate.
   a. If steering effort is easier to port, move the trim tab one number or notch to port.
   b. If steering effort is easier to starboard, move the trim tab one number or notch to starboard.

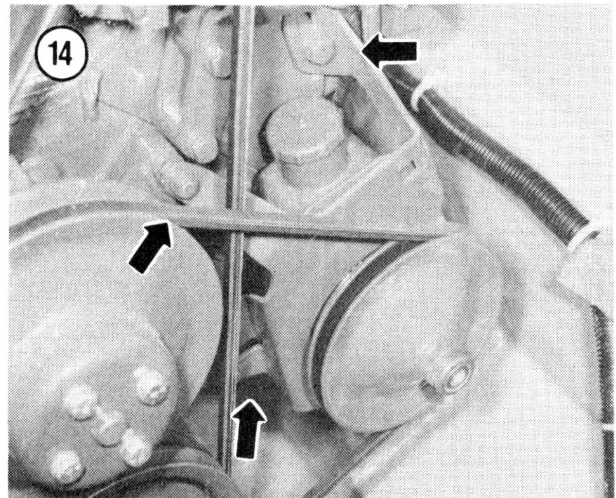

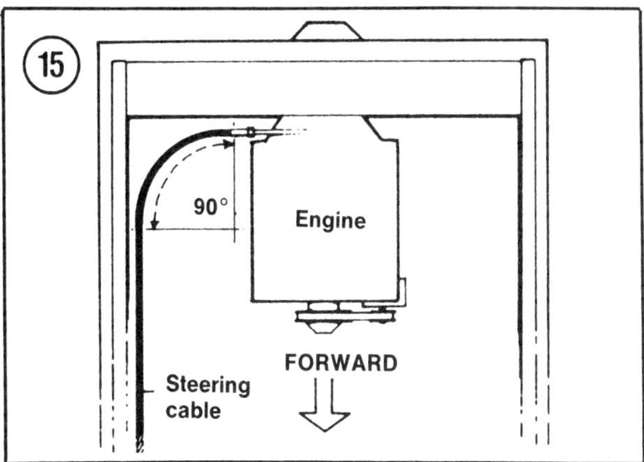

3. Tighten the trim tab bolt and recheck the steering effort by running the boat. Repeat this procedure as required to equalize the steering effort.
4. When steering effort is satisfactory in both directions, tighten the trim tab bolt to 28-32 ft.-lb. (38-43 N•m).

POWER STEERING SYSTEM

In addition to the components used in the manual steering system, the power steering system uses a power steering pump, oil cooler, steering cylinder/valve assembly and connecting hydraulic hoses. These components are all serviced as assemblies.

The power steering pump is mounted on the front of the engine and belt-driven off the crankshaft pulley (**Figure 14**, typical). The low pressure or return line connects to the upper fitting on the rear of the pump with a hose clamp; the high pressure outlet line connects to the bottom pump fitting with a molded fitting and flare nut. The control valve/piston assembly is mounted on the inner transom bracket and connects to the steering arm and steering cable ram. The valve spool in the control valve assembly moves about ⅛ in. (total) in response to movement of the steering cable casing. Although the amount of spool movement is small, it is enough to direct hydraulic pressure to the correct side of the piston. If the cable casing is restricted at the stern of the boat, it will affect the movement of the valve spool and result in hard steering in one or both directions. Make sure the area around the steering cable casing is clear and that nothing restricts cable movement near the engine. See **Figure 15** (typical). Wiring harnesses and control cables should not be tied to the steering cable.

The oil cooler is installed in the hydraulic system to prevent the fluid from overheating. This is a small heat exchanger which circulates water in one closed section to cool the hydraulic fluid passing through a second closed section. A plugged power steering oil cooler can cause an engine overheating condition.

If the power steering system loses hydraulic pressure, manual steering is still possible, although considerably more steering effort is necessary. Manual movement of the steering cable is transmitted to the actuator valve spool, which in turn transmits the same effort to the steering arm.

Fluid Level Check

Although the dipstick is marked with both HOT and COLD lines, this procedure should be performed with the engine at normal operating temperature and OFF. See **Figure 16** (typical).

1. Remove the engine compartment cover or hatch.
2. Unscrew the power steering pump reservoir cap and remove the cap/dipstick.
3. Wipe the dipstick with a clean shop cloth or paper towel. Reinstall the cap/dipstick, wait a few moments, then remove again and check the fluid level on the dipstick.
4. If fluid level is below the HOT mark on the dipstick, add sufficient GM Power Steering Fluid, DEXRON II automatic transmission fluid or OMC Power Trim and Tilt Fluid to bring the level to the specified mark on the dipstick.
5. Reinstall cap/dipstick in the power steering pump reservoir.

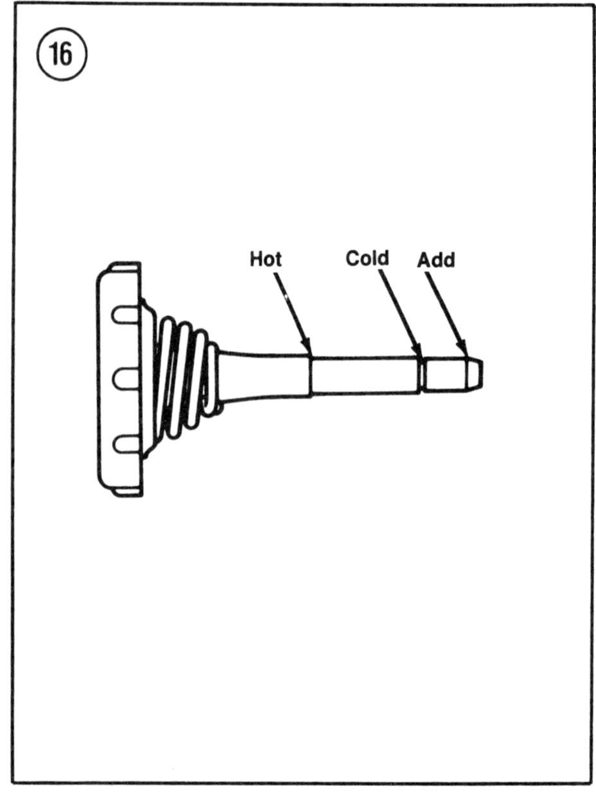

Bleeding the Hydraulic System

A low fluid level and/or air in the fluid are the most frequently encountered causes of pump noise. The power steering system must be bled to correct the problem. It must also be bled whenever a hydraulic line has been disconnected to service the system.

1. With the engine off and cold, turn the steering wheel completely to port.
2. Unscrew the power steering pump reservoir cap and remove the cap/dipstick.
3. Add sufficient GM Power Steering Fluid, DEXRON II automatic transmission fluid or OMC Power Trim and Tilt Fluid to bring the level to the COLD mark on the dipstick (**Figure 16**).
4. Reinstall the cap/dipstick in the power steering pump reservoir.
5. Start the engine, run briefly and shut it off. Repeat Steps 2-4 as required.
6. Turn the steering wheel from side-to-side without hitting the stops. Keep the fluid level in the pump reservoir just above the integral pump casting. If there is air in the fluid, it will appear light tan in color or foamy in appearance.
7. Turn the steering wheel to the center position. Start and run the engine for 2-3 minutes, then shut it off. Recheck the fluid in the reservoir. If it still contains air, repeat Step 5 and Step 6.
8. When all air has been bled from the system, run the boat on the water to make sure that the steering operates properly and is not noisy.
9. Let the system stabilize at its normal operating temperature and recheck the fluid level to make sure it is at the HOT mark on the cap/dipstick (**Figure 16**).

Power Steering Pump Removal/Installation

Metric fittings are used with all pumps. Replacement high pressure hoses must also have metric fittings and metric flare nut wrenches should be used to loosen/tighten the fitting nut to prevent rounding off the corners of the nut. Whenever the return line is removed, a new worm-type clamp should be installed.

1. Use a metric flare nut wrench to loosen the high pressure (lower) hose at the rear of the pump. Use a suitable screwdriver or cap driver to loosen the return (upper) hose clamp.
2. Place a shop cloth underneath the fittings and disconnect the lines one at a time. Cap the hose ends and pump fittings to prevent leakage and the entry of contamination. Secure both hoses in an upright position by wiring them to the alternator bracket or other convenient point to prevent fluid drainage.
3. Loosen the pump mounting fasteners (**Figure 14**, typical) and slip the drive belt off the pump pulley.
4. Unbolt the pump and remove the pump/bracket assembly from the engine.
5. If the pump is to be replaced, use pulley remover part No. 982270 or equivalent to remove the pulley from the pump. Remove the pump from the mounting bracket.
6. If the pump was removed from its mounting bracket, reposition the pump to its bracket and install the pulley with tool part No. 982271 or equivalent.
7. Position the pump assembly on the engine and install the mounting fasteners finger-tight.
8. Hand-start the high pressure hose fitting nut, then tighten the nut to 40 ft.-lb. (54 N•m). Install the return hose with a new worm-type clamp and tighten securely.
9. Fill the pump reservoir with GM Power Steering Fluid, DEXRON II automatic transmission fluid or OMC Power Trim and Tilt fluid. Rotate the pulley clockwise (as seen from the front of the pump) until no air bubbles can be seen in the fluid.

CAUTION
*Do **not** pry against the pump or pull the pump outward by its neck to adjust belt tension in Step 10. This can cause internal damage to the pump.*

10. Install the drive belt over the pump pulley and insert a 1/2 in. breaker bar in the mounting bracket slot. Pull against the mounting bracket with the breaker bar to move the pump outward and tighten one mounting bolt to hold the pump in that position.
11. Check drive belt tension. If a belt tension gauge is used, tension should be 75 lb.; if the belt deflection method is used, the belt should deflect 1/4-1/2 in. when finger pressure is applied at a point midway in the belt span.
12. When belt tension is correct, tighten all mounting bolts snugly and remove the breaker bar, then torque the mounting bolts to 25 ft.-lb. (34 N•m) and the nut to 20 ft.-lb. (27 N•m).
13. Bleed the power steering system as described in this chapter.

Power Steering Pump Disassembly/Assembly

The power steering pump can be disassembled, but internal components are not available. If the pump is defective or malfunctioning, it should be replaced. This procedure is primarily of value in cases where the engine has been submerged. In such a case, the power steering pump should be disassembled, all contamination removed and all components lightly lubricated to prevent the pump from corrosion. If properly performed, the procedure will save the pump and avoid the cost of a new one.

A new seal should be installed during reassembly. This can be obtained from any local General Motors dealer under part No. 5688044.

Refer to **Figure 17** for this procedure.

1. Remove the power steering pump as described in this chapter.
2. Drain all fluid from the pump into a suitable container.
3. Remove the fitting and control valve assemblies and the flow control spring.

17

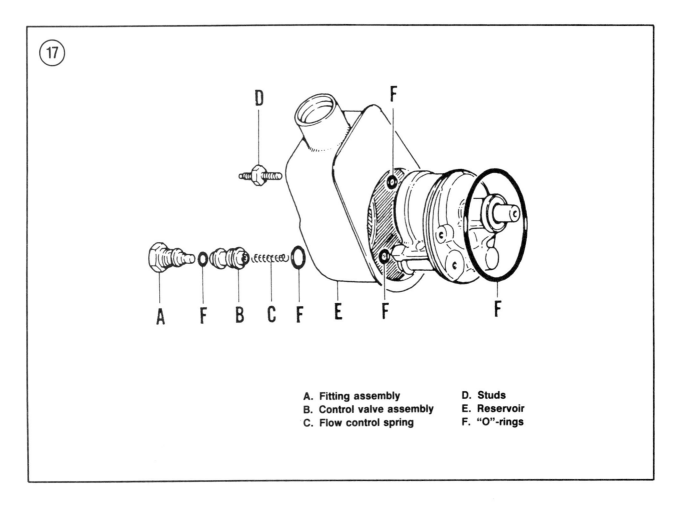

A. Fitting assembly
B. Control valve assembly
C. Flow control spring
D. Studs
E. Reservoir
F. "O"-rings

4. Remove the studs.
5. Carefully tap the reservoir from the pump housing. Remove and discard the O-rings.
6. Position the pump body retaining ring as shown in **Figure 18**. Insert an awl in the housing hole and push the ring away from its recess, then pry the ring from the pump body with a screwdriver blade.
7. Remove the pump components shown in **Figure 19**.
8. Remove and discard the 2 housing O-rings (**Figure 20**).
9. Remove the circlip holding the rotor and thrust plate on the pump shaft. Slide the rotor and thrust plate off the shaft. See **Figure 21**.
10. Remove the magnet from the pump body (**Figure 22**).
11. Clean all metal parts in fresh solvent and blow dry with compressed air.

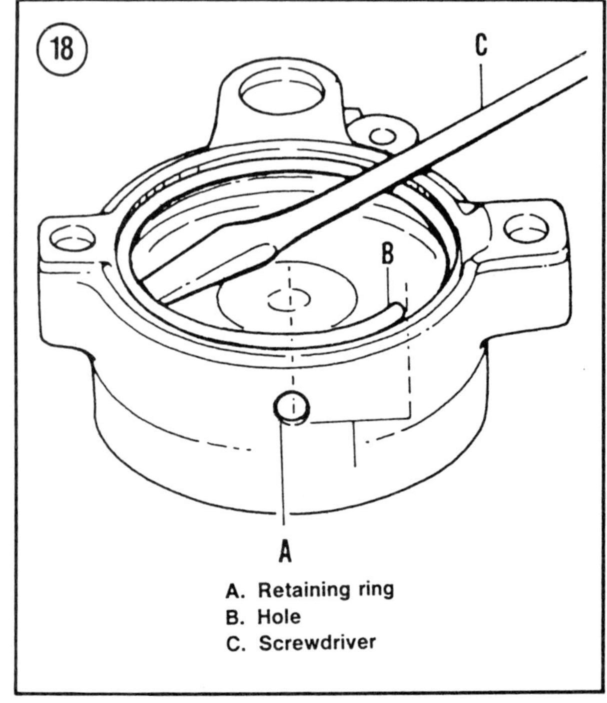

A. Retaining ring
B. Hole
C. Screwdriver

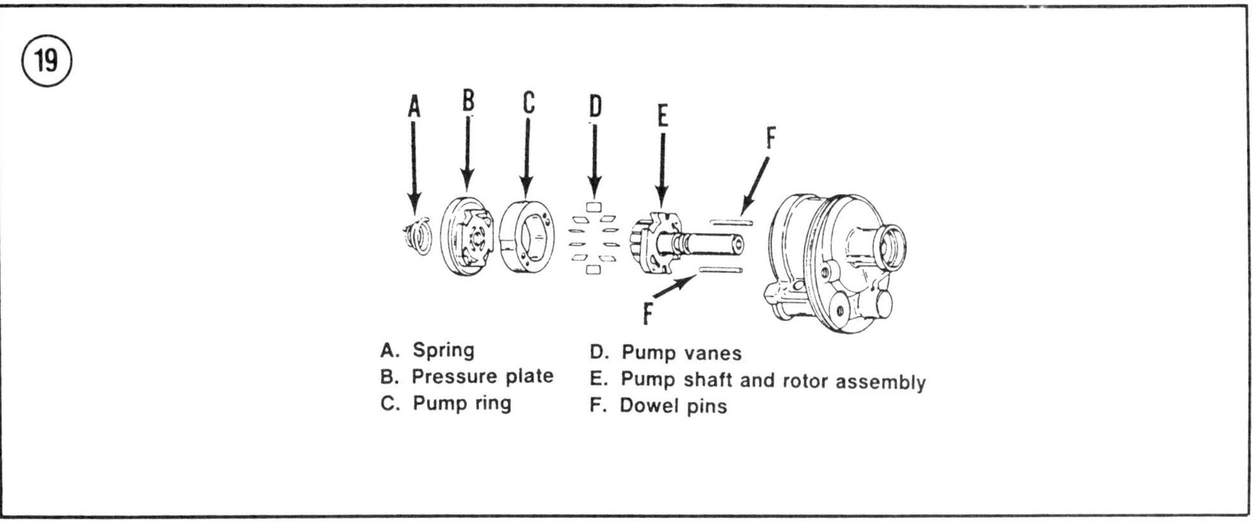

A. Spring
B. Pressure plate
C. Pump ring
D. Pump vanes
E. Pump shaft and rotor assembly
F. Dowel pins

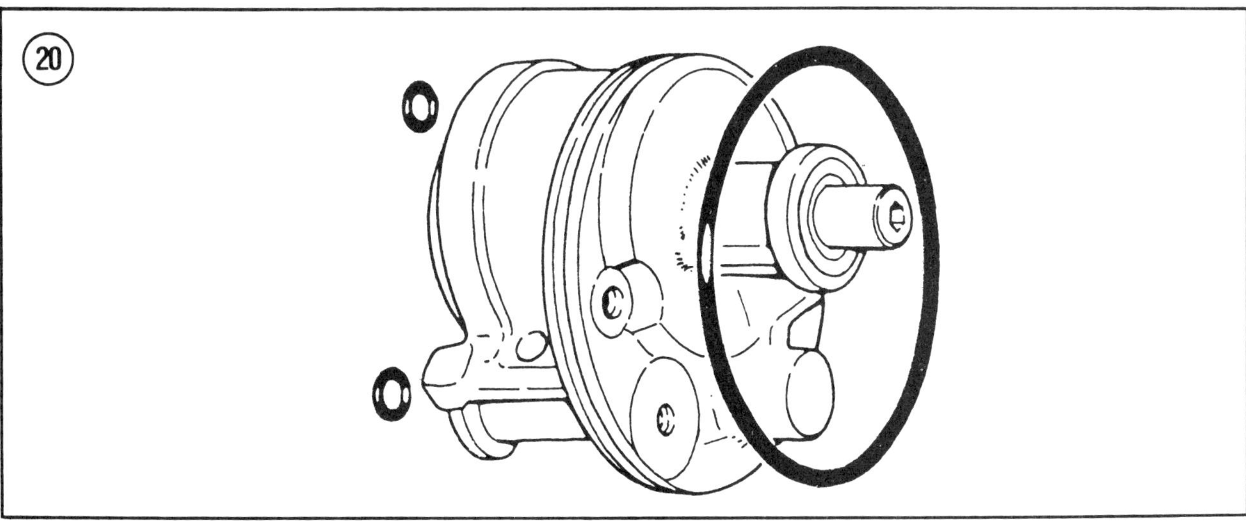

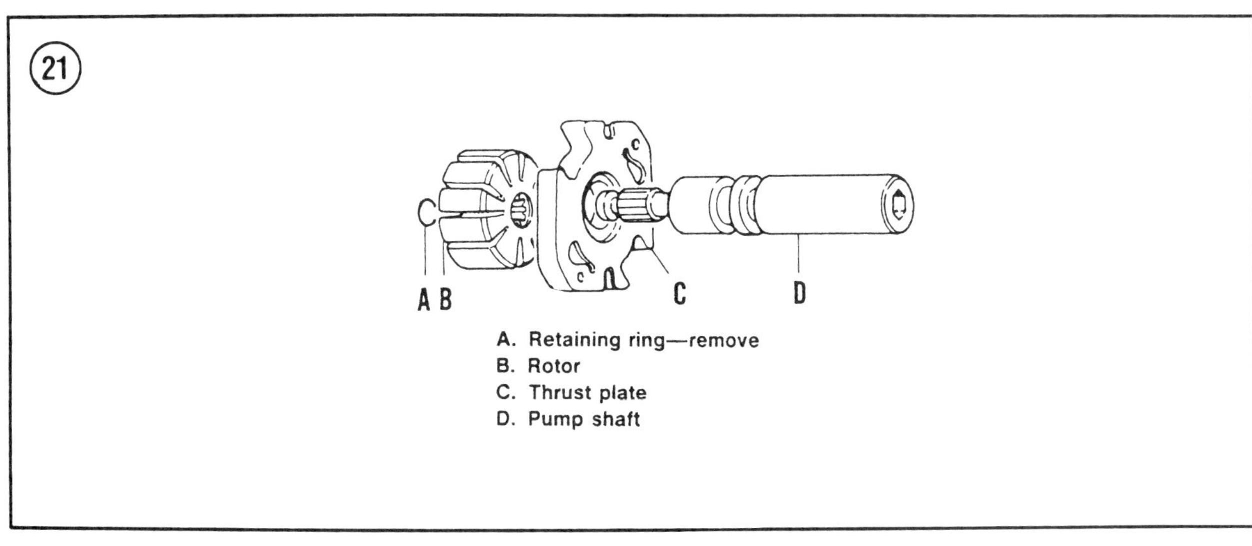

A. Retaining ring—remove
B. Rotor
C. Thrust plate
D. Pump shaft

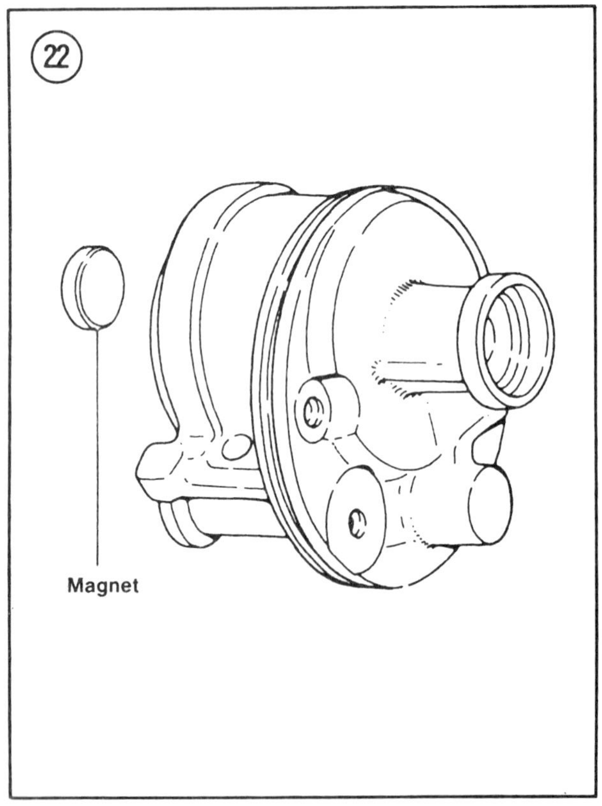

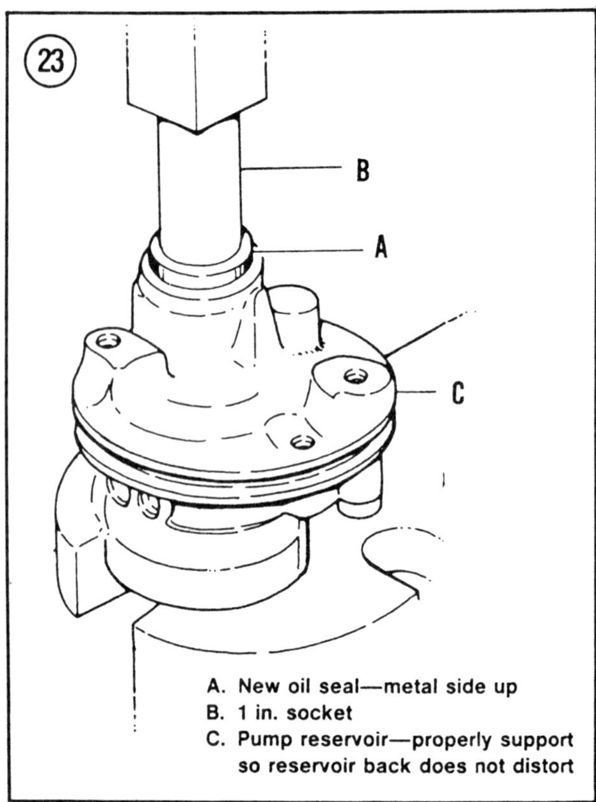

A. New oil seal—metal side up
B. 1 in. socket
C. Pump reservoir—properly support so reservoir back does not distort

12. Lubricate all metal parts with Type F or DEXRON II automatic transmission fluid.
13. Remove and discard the pump shaft seal. Place pump body on a press as shown in **Figure 23**. Position a new oil seal with its metal side facing up and use a 1 in. socket to press the seal in place. Be sure the pump body is properly supported to prevent it from distorting.
14. Install a new pressure plate O-ring in the 3rd groove in the housing, then install the dowel pins (**Figure 24**).
15. Slide the thrust plate and rotor on the pump shaft, then install the circlip (**Figure 21**).
16. Install the pump shaft and rotor assembly in the pump body (**Figure 25**).
17. Insert the pump ring, fitting the 2 smaller holes over the dowel pins. See **Figure 26**.
18. Install the vanes in the rotor slots with their rounded edges facing the pump ring (**Figure 27**). Make sure the vanes move freely.

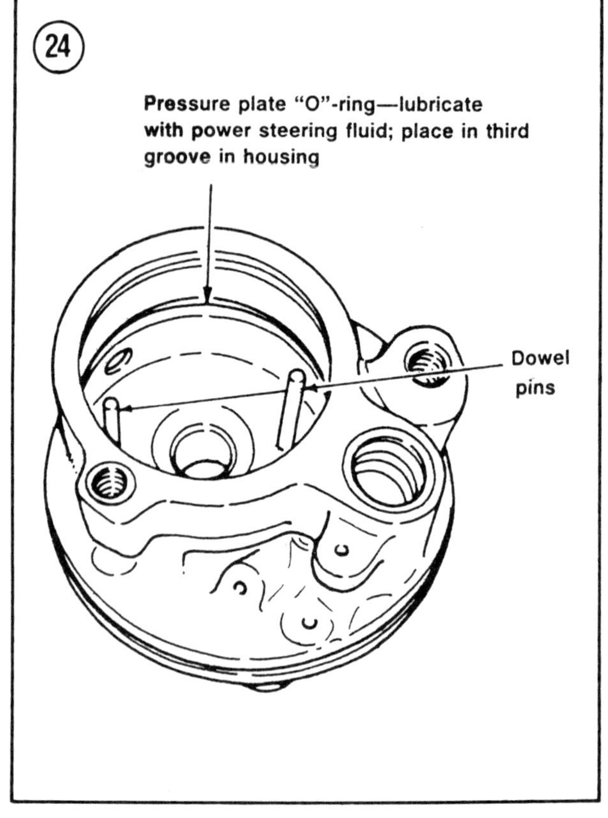

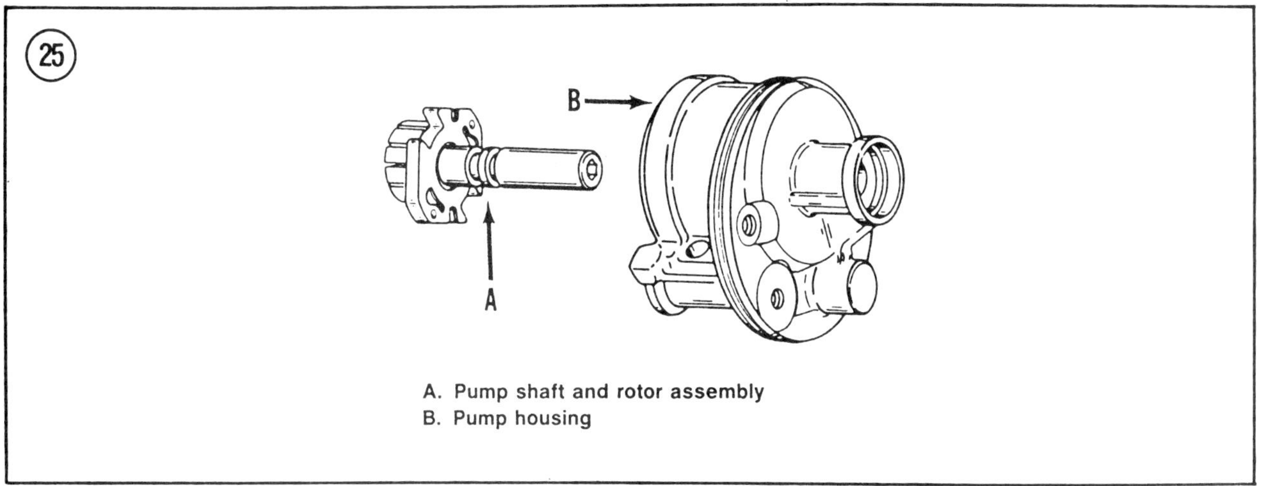

A. Pump shaft and rotor assembly
B. Pump housing

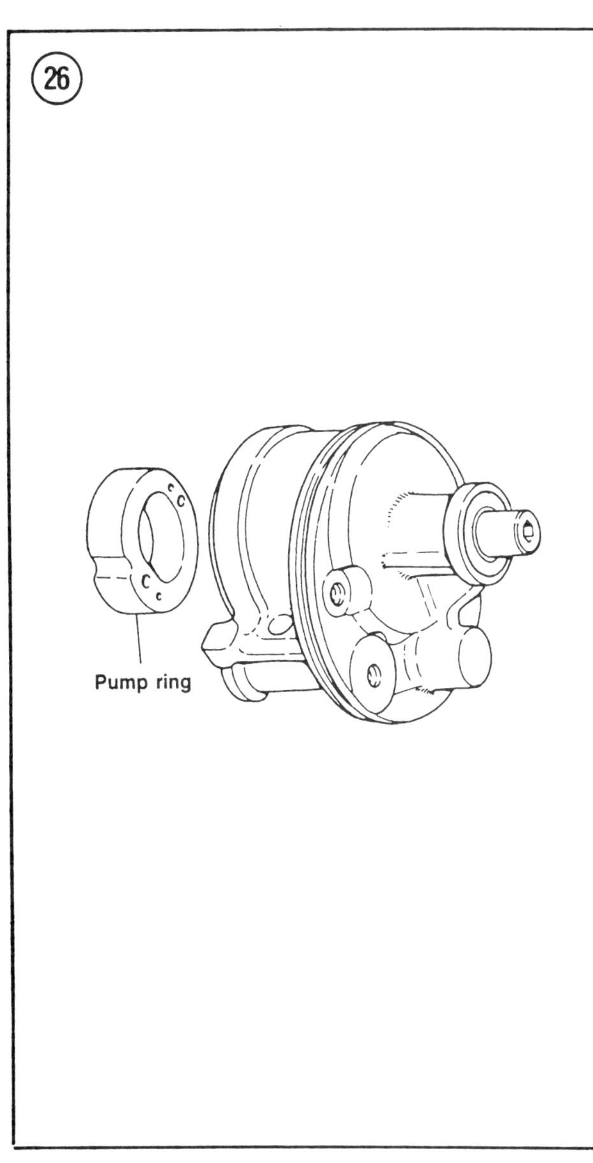

19. Install the pressure plate with its spring groove facing upward, then install a new end plate O-ring in the 2nd groove. See **Figure 28**.
20. Install the pressure plate spring and the end plate (**Figure 29**).
21. Position the housing in a press and apply pressure on the end plate to hold it down evenly. Install the retaining ring and make sure it snaps into its groove around the entire perimeter of the body.
22. Install a new large O-ring on the body and 2 new small O-rings (**Figure 30**).
23. Position the magnet on the pump body housing, then install the reservoir to the pump body and secure with the studs. Tighten studs to 35 ft.-lb. (47 N•m).
24. Install the flow control spring, control valve and fitting assemblies with new O-rings. Tighten fitting assembly to 35 ft.-lb. (47 N•m).
25. Install the pump to the bracket with installer part No. 982271, then install the pump and bracket assembly to the engine as described in this chapter.

Trim Tab Adjustment

Models equipped with power steering do not require trim tab adjustment. The trim tab is factory-set at the No. 3 position and should not be changed.

Leakage Checks

The power steering system may develop problems such as growling noises, loss of power during low-speed operation or heavy steering effort. In addition, it may require frequent addition of fluid. When any of these problems occur, the most obvious solution is to check for leaks.

Figure 31 shows the common points of pump leakage. If a leak is found at any of the points shown, the pump should be replaced as a unit. In addition to these leakage points, you should also check the following:

a. Return hose and/or clamp (replace as required).
b. Cross-threaded or loose high-pressure fitting (correct or replace as required).
c. Leakage at the power cylinder or actuator valve (replace as required).
d. Power steering fluid in the cooling system (replace the oil cooler).

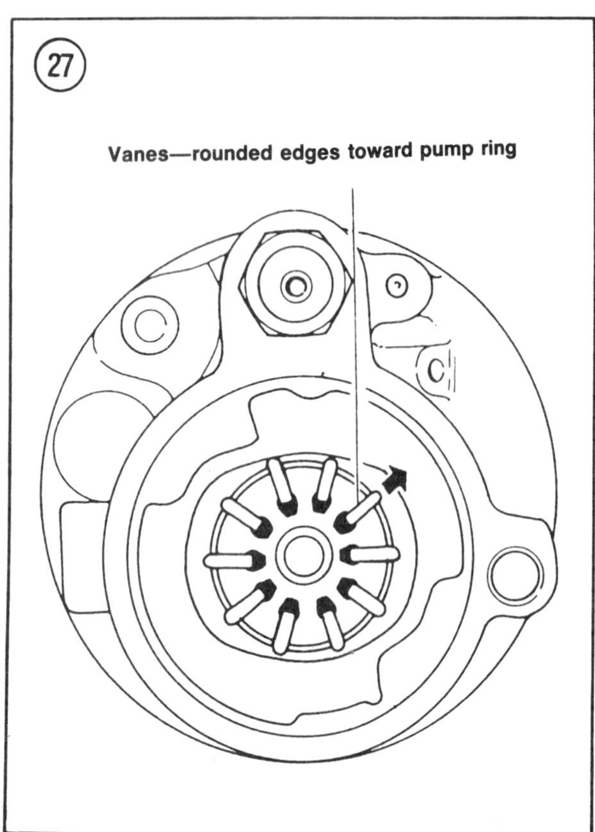

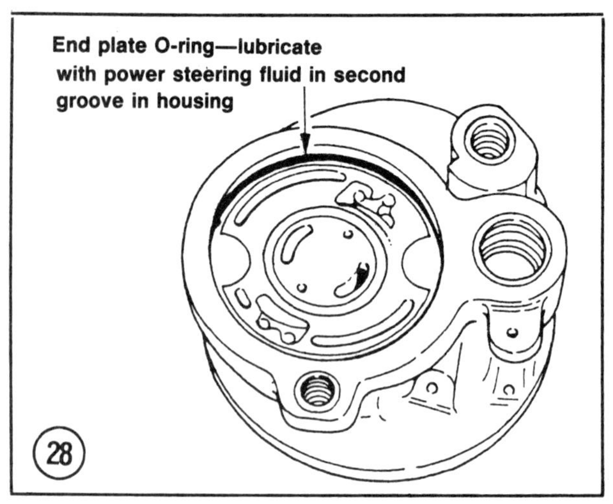

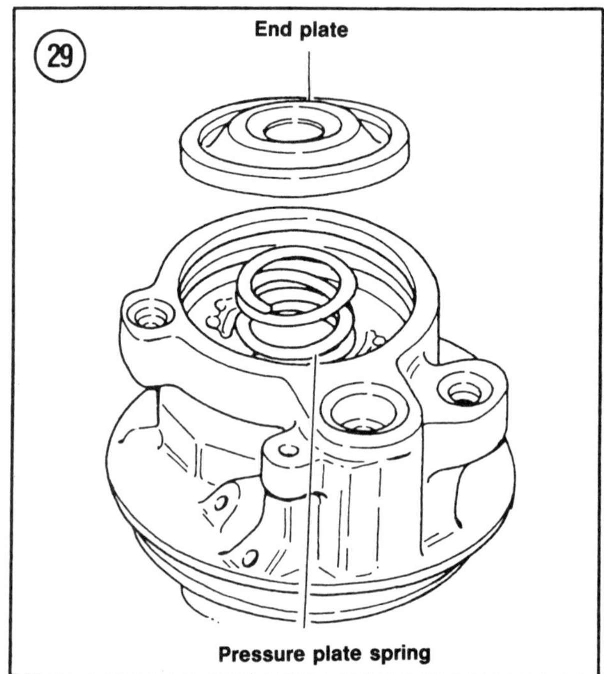

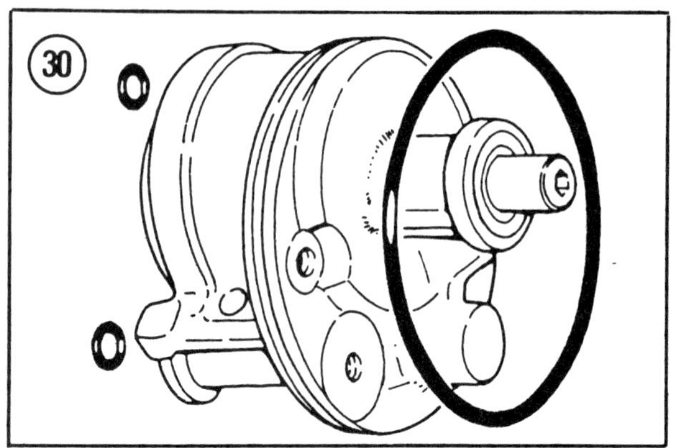

Seepage leaks are the most difficult to locate. If you keep the engine clean as suggested in Chapter Four and Chapter Five, it will be much easier to locate such leaks. To locate seepage leaks:

a. Clean the entire power steering system (pump, hoses, power cylinder/actuator valve and connecting lines).
b. Adjust the pump reservoir fluid to its correct level.
c. Start the engine and turn the steering wheel from stop-to-stop several times, then shut the engine off.
d. Recheck the areas mentioned above for dampness. Correct any deficiencies noted.

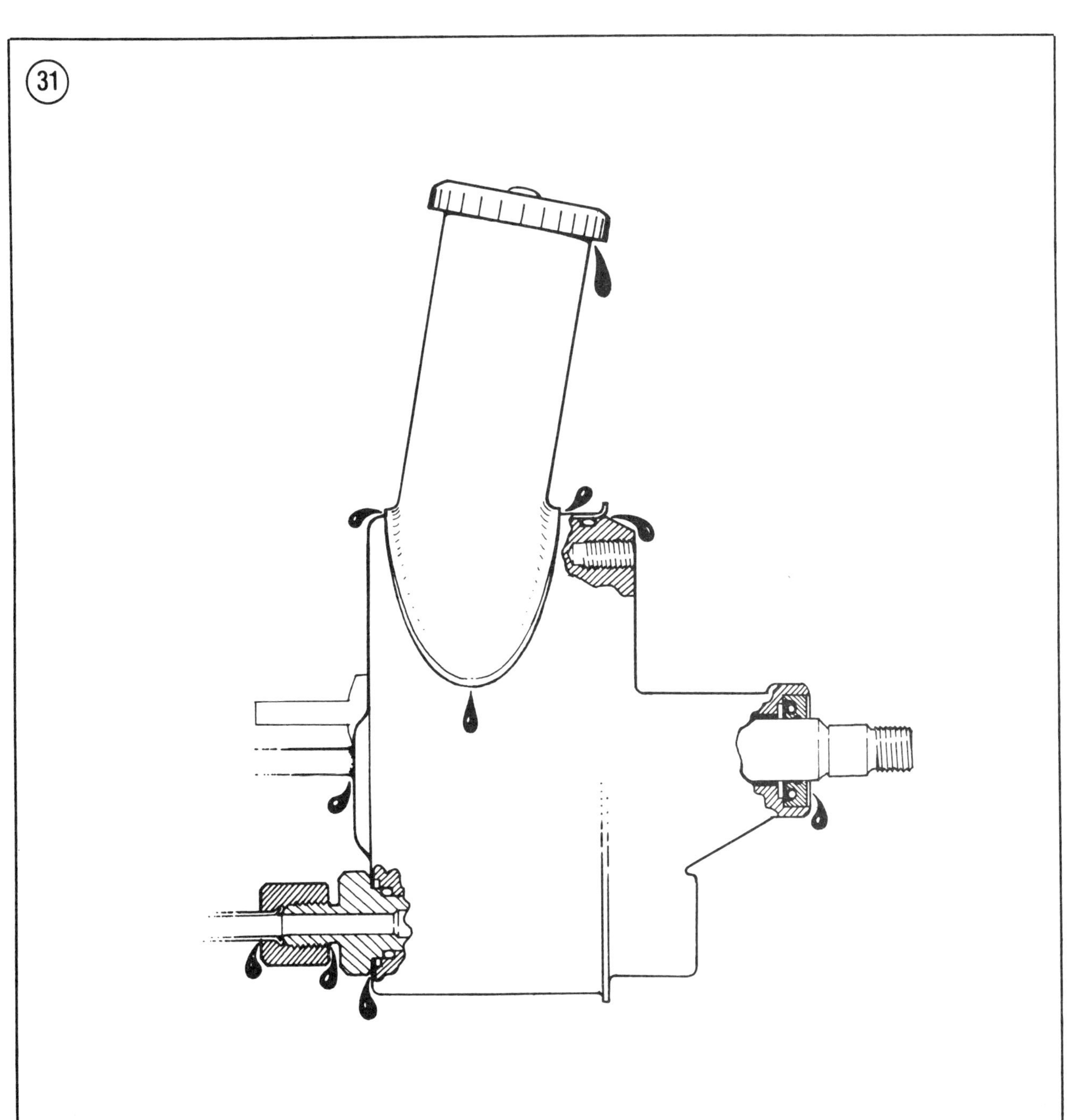

Table 1 TIGHTENING TORQUES

Fastener	in.-lb.	ft.-lb.	N•m
Actuator valve			
Adapter-to-mounting bracket		40-50	54-70
Bushing lockscrew		24-30	32-40
Control valve			
Adapter assembly-to-bracket		40-50	54-70
Hose fittings			
Inlet	103		12
Outlet		25	34
Line fittings	95-105		11-12
Jam nut			
Manual steering		20-25	27-34
Power steering		25-30	34-40
Oil cooler hose clamp	12-17		1.4-2.0
Power steering pump			
Bolts		25	34
Nut		20	27
Hose			
Fitting		40	54
Clamp	12-17		1.4-2.0
Steering assembly-to-transom plate		40-45	54-61
Steering cable anchor nut	120		14
Tube guide-to-valve stud nut		40-50	54-70

Table 2 POWER STEERING SYSTEM TROUBLESHOOTING

Symptom	Likely cause
PUMP	
Chirps or squeals	Loose drive belt
Hissing sound	Normal condition
Rattle or chuckle	Pressure hose contacting other components
	Loose steering linkage
Growl	Steering cable needs adjustment
	Hose restriction causing back pressure
Whine	Scored pump shaft bearing
Groan	Low fluid level and/or air in the system
STEERING SYSTEM	
Excessive loose steering or wheel kickback	Air in system
	Loose steering cable attachment
	Loose or worn steering ball stud
Steering wheel surge or jerk when turning	Loose drive belt
	Low fluid level
	Actuator valve sticks
	Pump pressure insufficient
	Actuator valve lacks lubrication

(continued)

Table 2 POWER STEERING SYSTEM TROUBLESHOOTING (continued)

Symptom	Likely cause
STEERING SYSTEM (cont.)	
Momentary increase in steering effort during fast turns	Slipping drive belt
	Low fluid level
	Internal pump leakage
Hard steering	
To starboard	Cable too long or restricted
To port	Cable too short or restricted
Hard steering/no assist	Internal pump or power cylinder leakage
	Cable movement restricted
	Loose drive belt
	Low fluid level
	Insufficient lubrication
	Excessive linkage friction
	Cable radius too tight @ output end
	Actuator valve sticking
	Insufficient fluid pressure
	Restricted fluid flow
Low oil pressure	Restriction in hose
	Defective power cylinder
	Loose drive belt
	Low fluid level
	Air in system
	Defective hoses
	Loose flow control valve screw
Foaming fluid	Air in system

Index

F

G

I

L

O

Wiring Diagrams

1986 OMC COBRA ENGINE CABLE

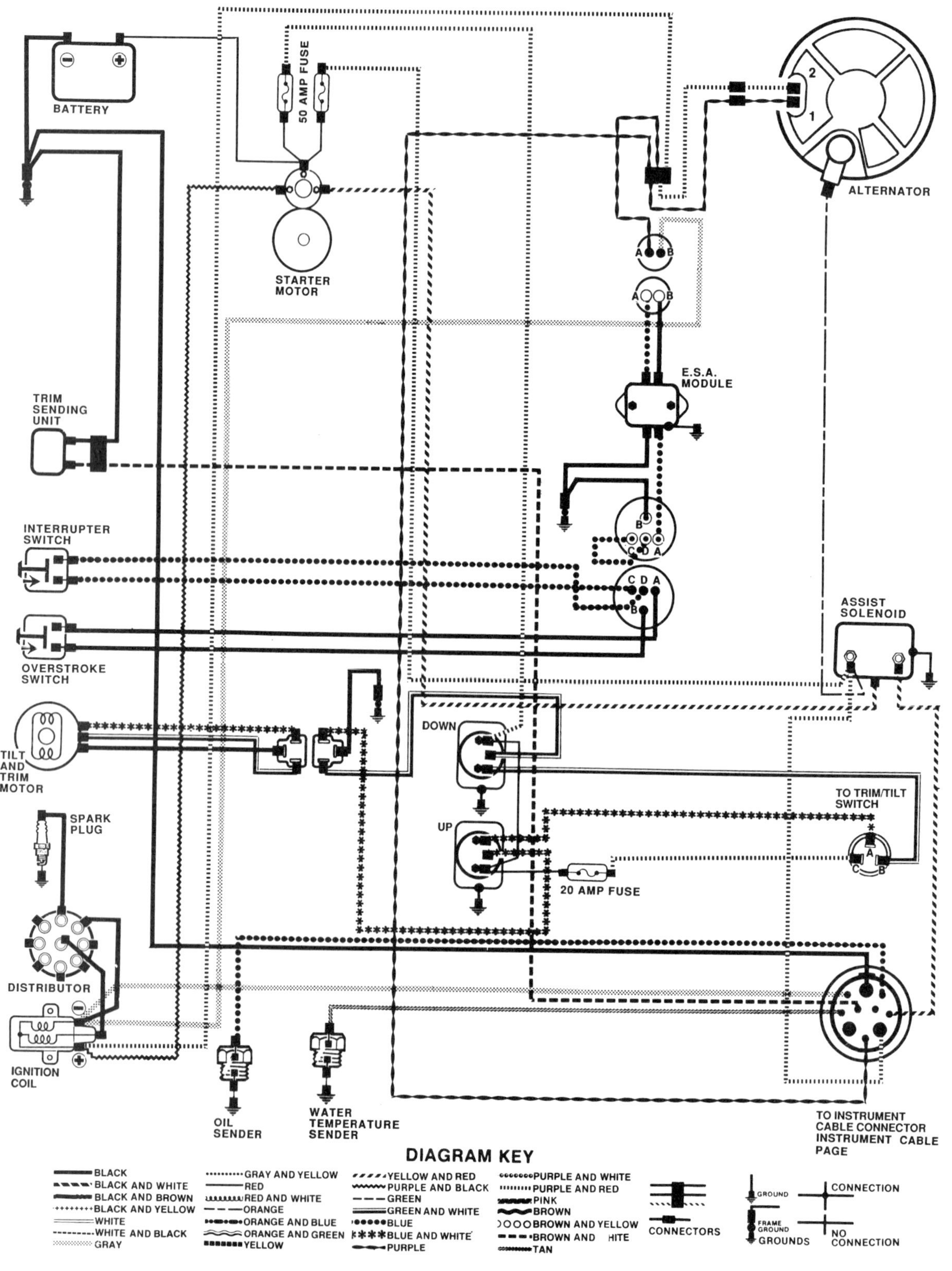

1986 OMC COBRA INSTRUMENT CABLE

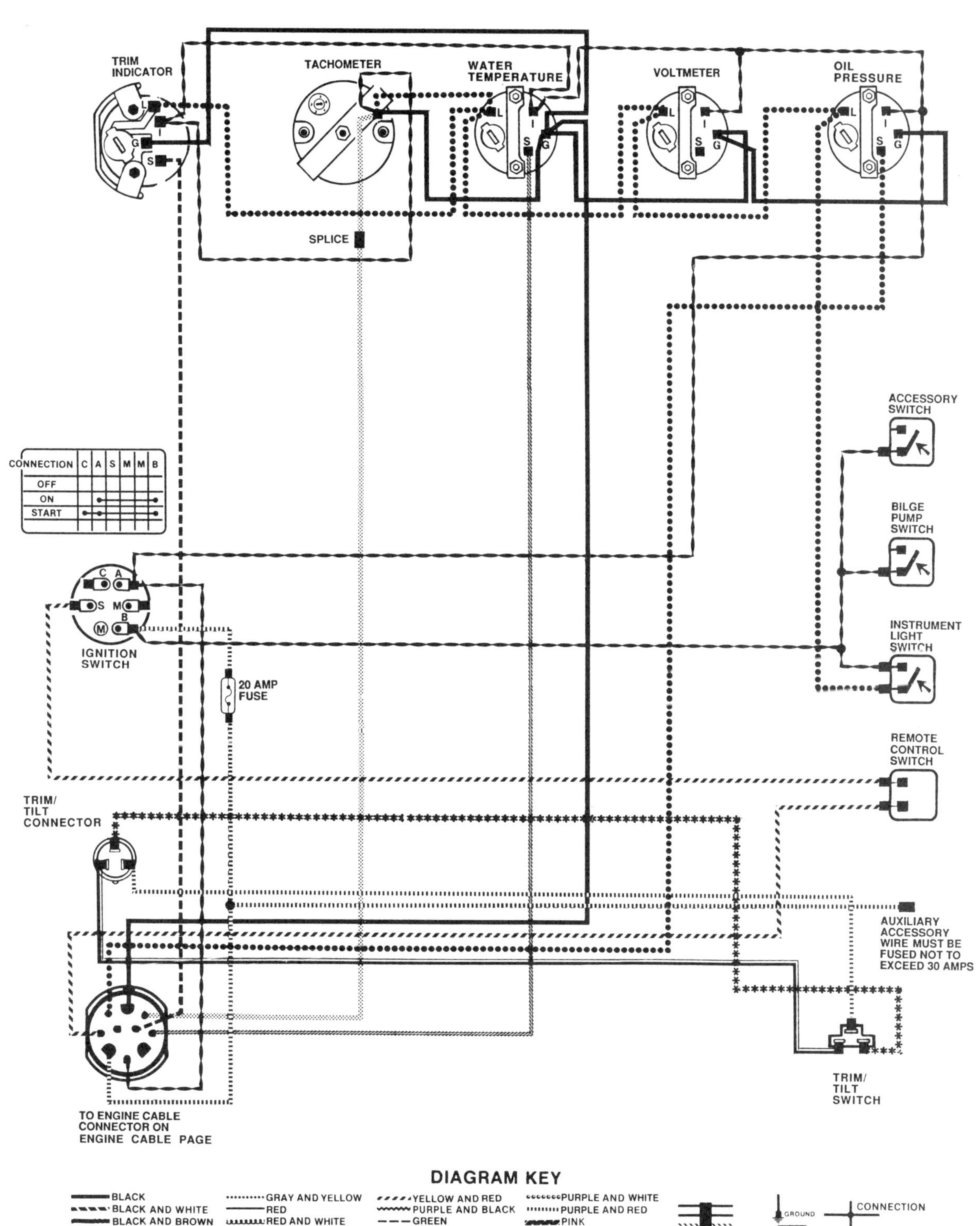

1987 OMC ENGINE CABLE 2.3 & 7.5

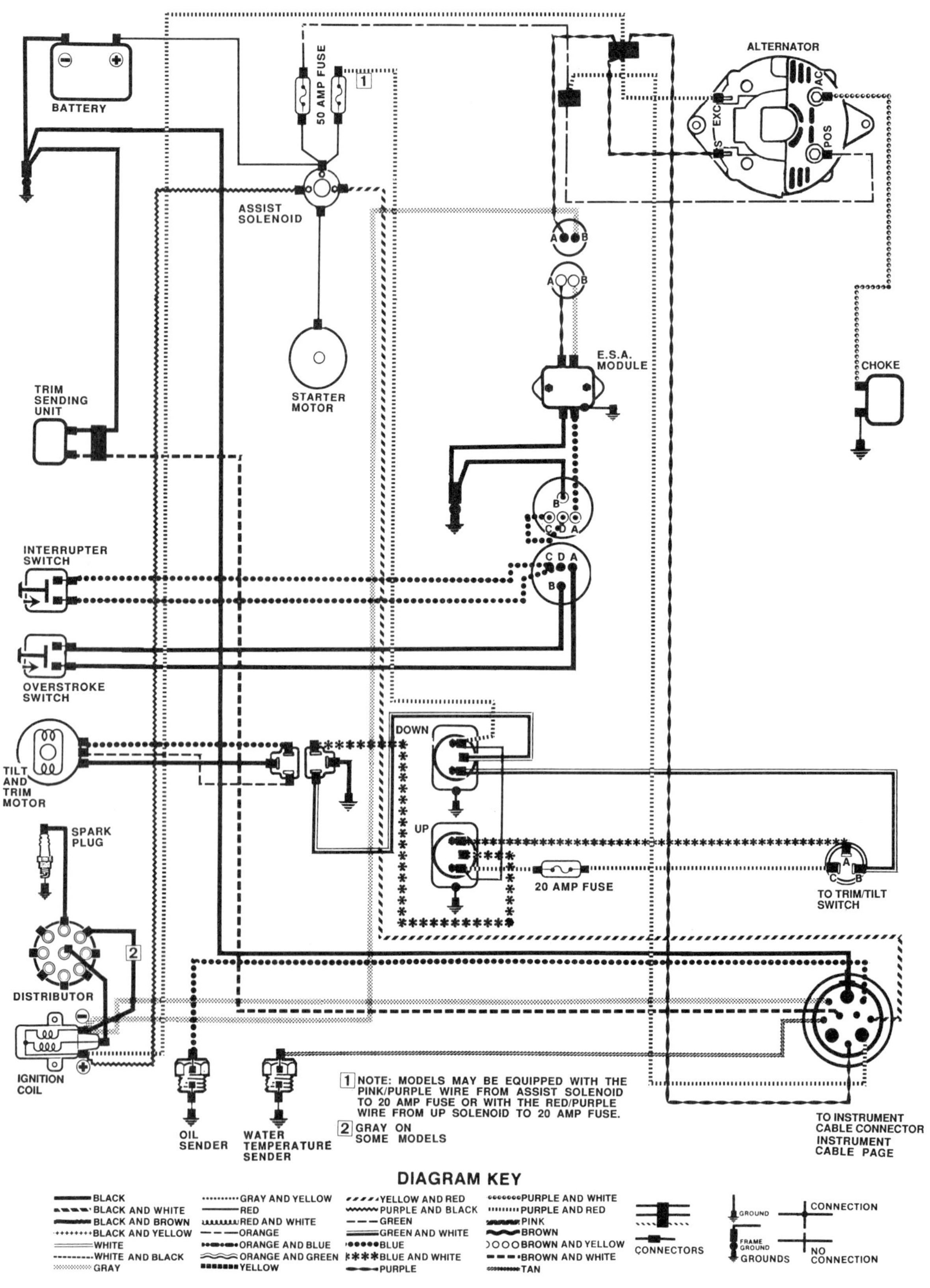

1987 OMC ENGINE CABLE 3.0, 4.3, 5.0, 5.7

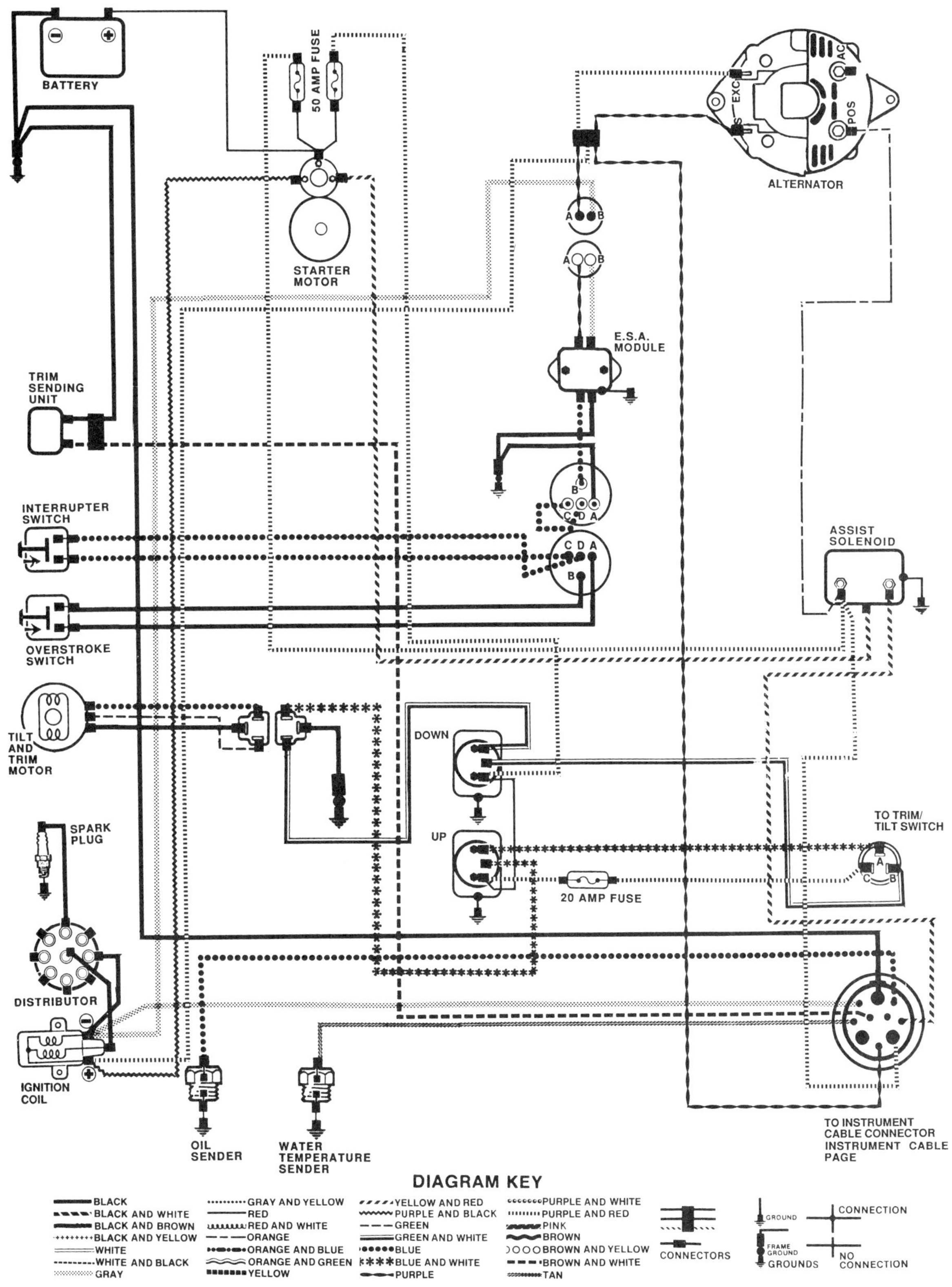

1987 OMC COBRA INSTRUMENT CABLE

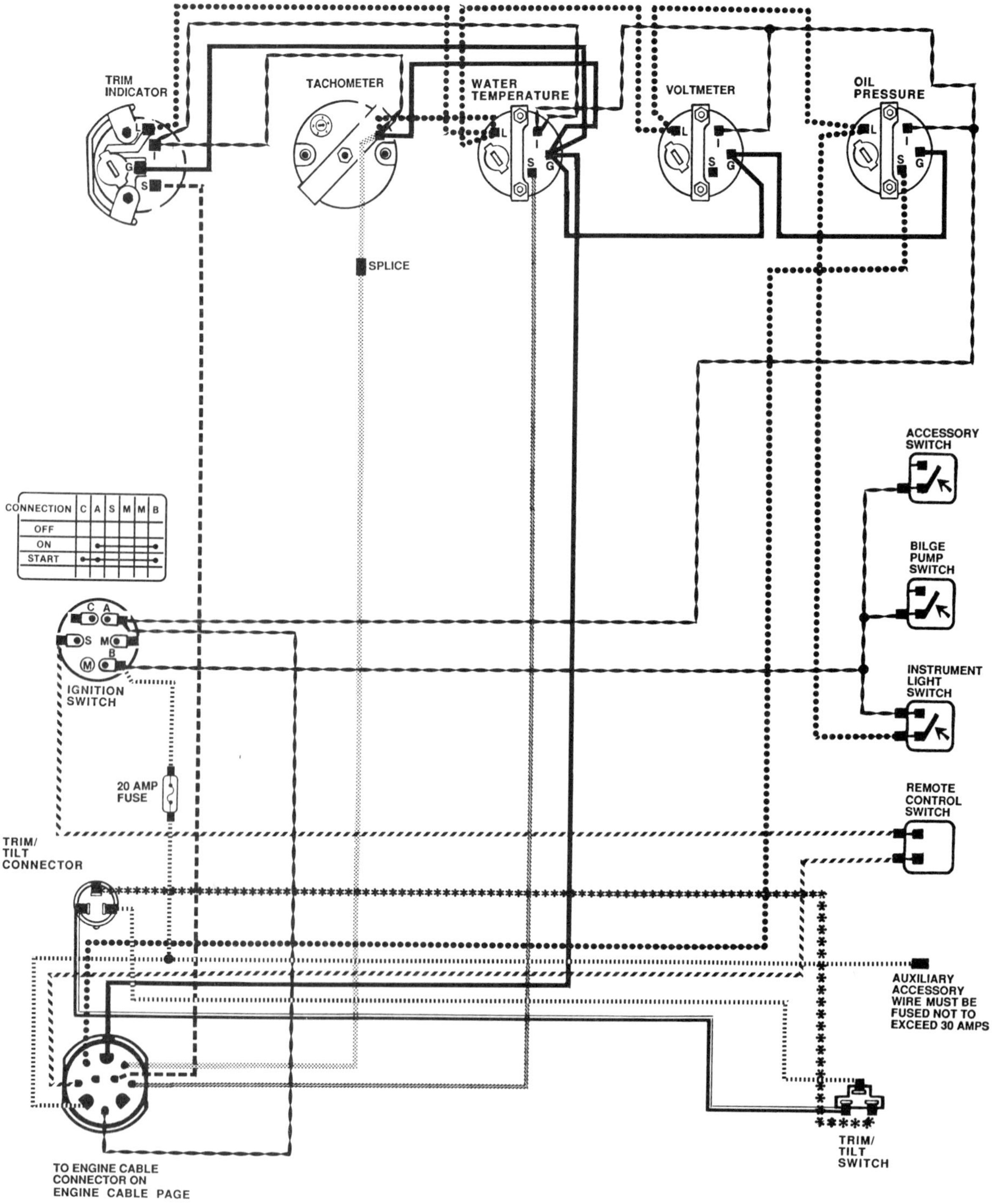

TRIM INDICATOR

TACHOMETER

WATER TEMPERATURE

VOLTMETER

OIL PRESSURE

SPLICE

ACCESSORY SWITCH

CONNECTION	C	A	S	M	M	B
OFF						
ON						
START						

BILGE PUMP SWITCH

IGNITION SWITCH

INSTRUMENT LIGHT SWITCH

20 AMP FUSE

REMOTE CONTROL SWITCH

TRIM/ TILT CONNECTOR

AUXILIARY ACCESSORY WIRE MUST BE FUSED NOT TO EXCEED 30 AMPS

TO ENGINE CABLE CONNECTOR ON ENGINE CABLE PAGE

TRIM/ TILT SWITCH

DIAGRAM KEY

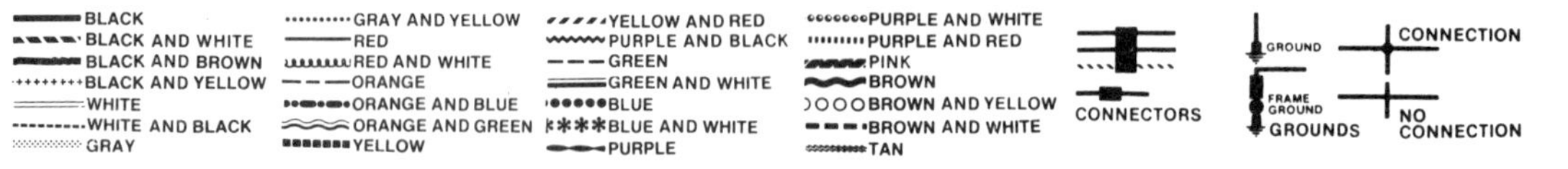

1988 OMC ENGINE CABLE 2.3 & 460 KING COBRA

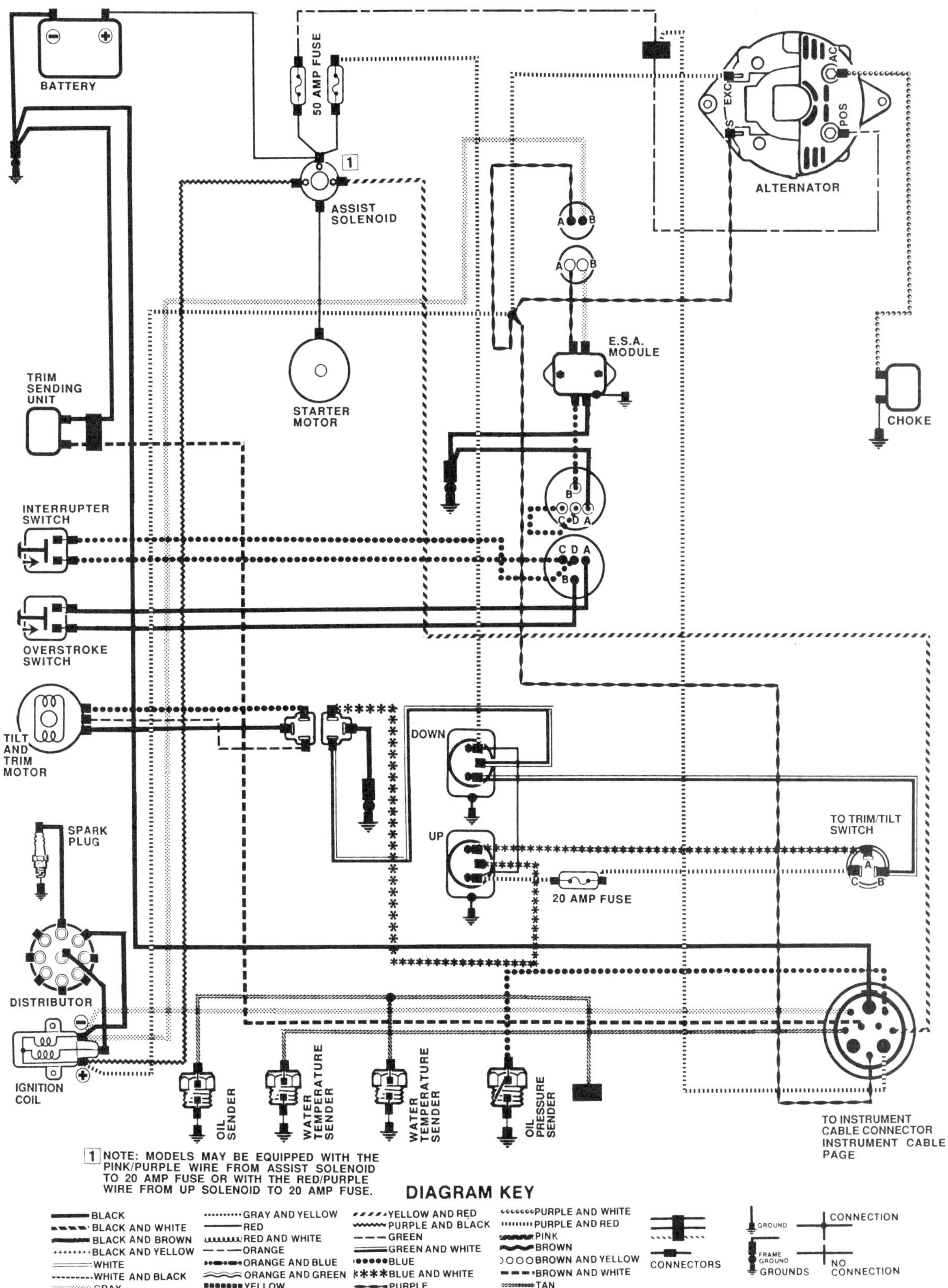

1988 OMC ENGINE CABLE 3.0, 4.3, 5.0, 5.7 & 350 COBRA

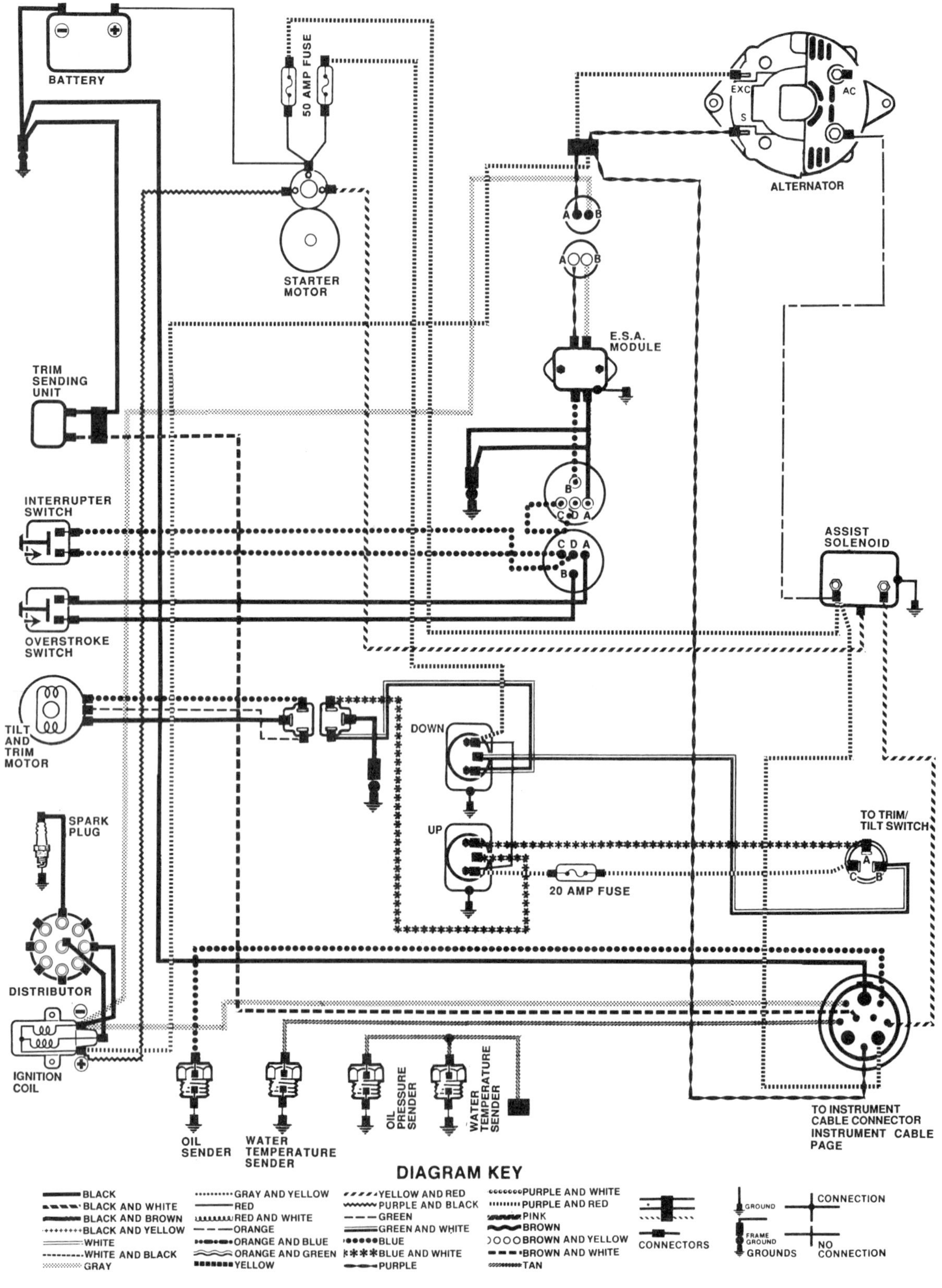

1988 OMC COBRA INSTRUMENT CABLE

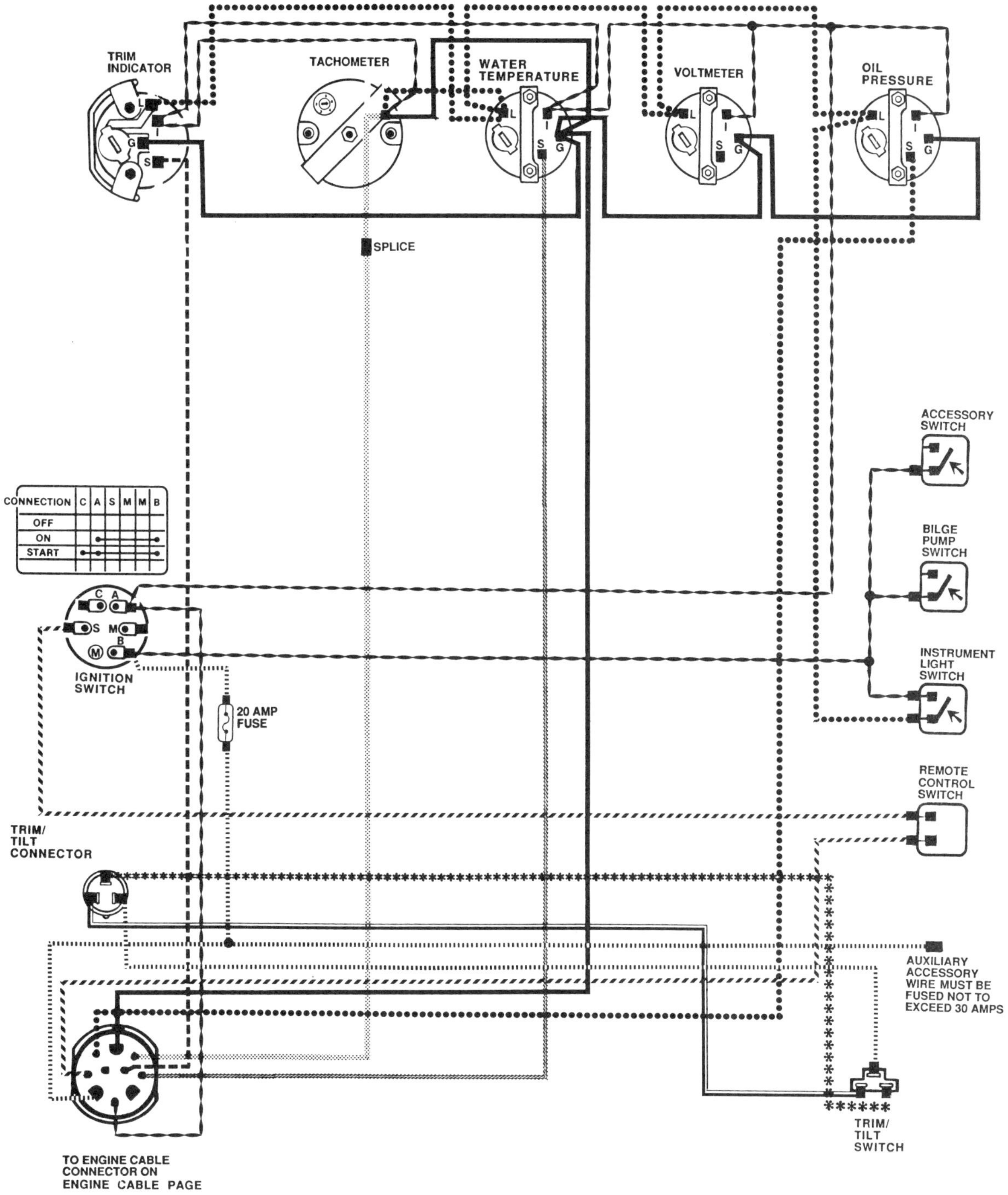

TRIM INDICATOR
TACHOMETER
WATER TEMPERATURE
VOLTMETER
OIL PRESSURE
SPLICE
ACCESSORY SWITCH
BILGE PUMP SWITCH
INSTRUMENT LIGHT SWITCH
CONNECTION C A S M M B
OFF
ON
START
IGNITION SWITCH
20 AMP FUSE
REMOTE CONTROL SWITCH
TRIM/TILT CONNECTOR
AUXILIARY ACCESSORY WIRE MUST BE FUSED NOT TO EXCEED 30 AMPS
TRIM/TILT SWITCH
TO ENGINE CABLE CONNECTOR ON ENGINE CABLE PAGE

DIAGRAM KEY

1989 OMC ENGINE CABLE 2.3, 5.0, 5.8 & 7.5

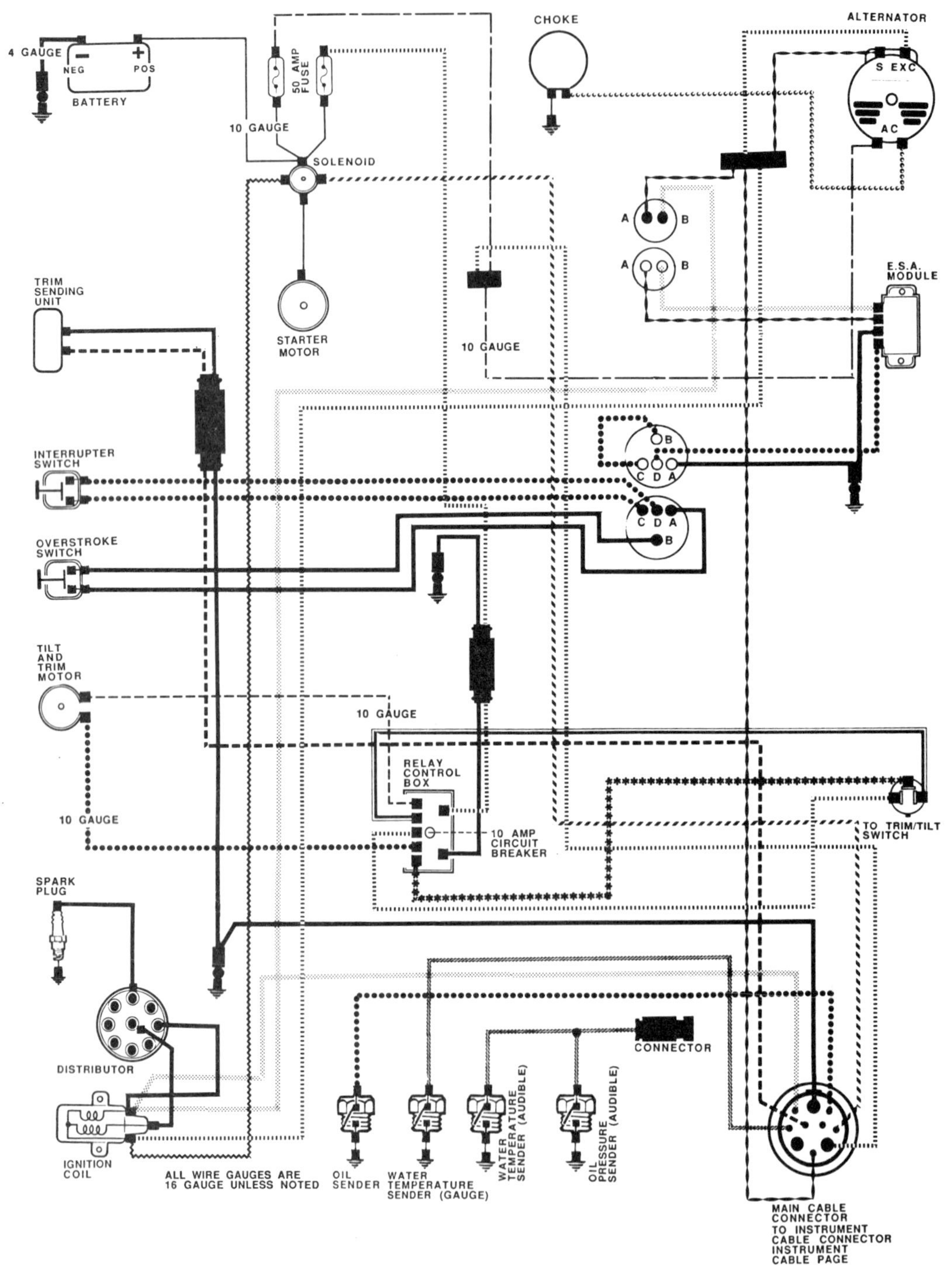

DIAGRAM KEY

BLACK
BLACK AND WHITE
BLACK AND BROWN
BLACK AND YELLOW
WHITE
WHITE AND BLACK
GRAY
GRAY AND YELLOW
RED
RED AND WHITE
ORANGE
ORANGE AND BLUE
ORANGE AND GREEN
YELLOW
YELLOW AND RED
PURPLE AND BLACK
GREEN
GREEN AND WHITE
BLUE
BLUE AND WHITE
PURPLE
PURPLE AND WHITE
PURPLE AND RED
PINK
BROWN
BROWN AND YELLOW
BROWN AND WHITE
TAN
CONNECTORS
GROUND
FRAME GROUND
GROUNDS
CONNECTION
NO CONNECTION

1989 OMC ENGINE CABLE 3.0, 4.3 & 5.7

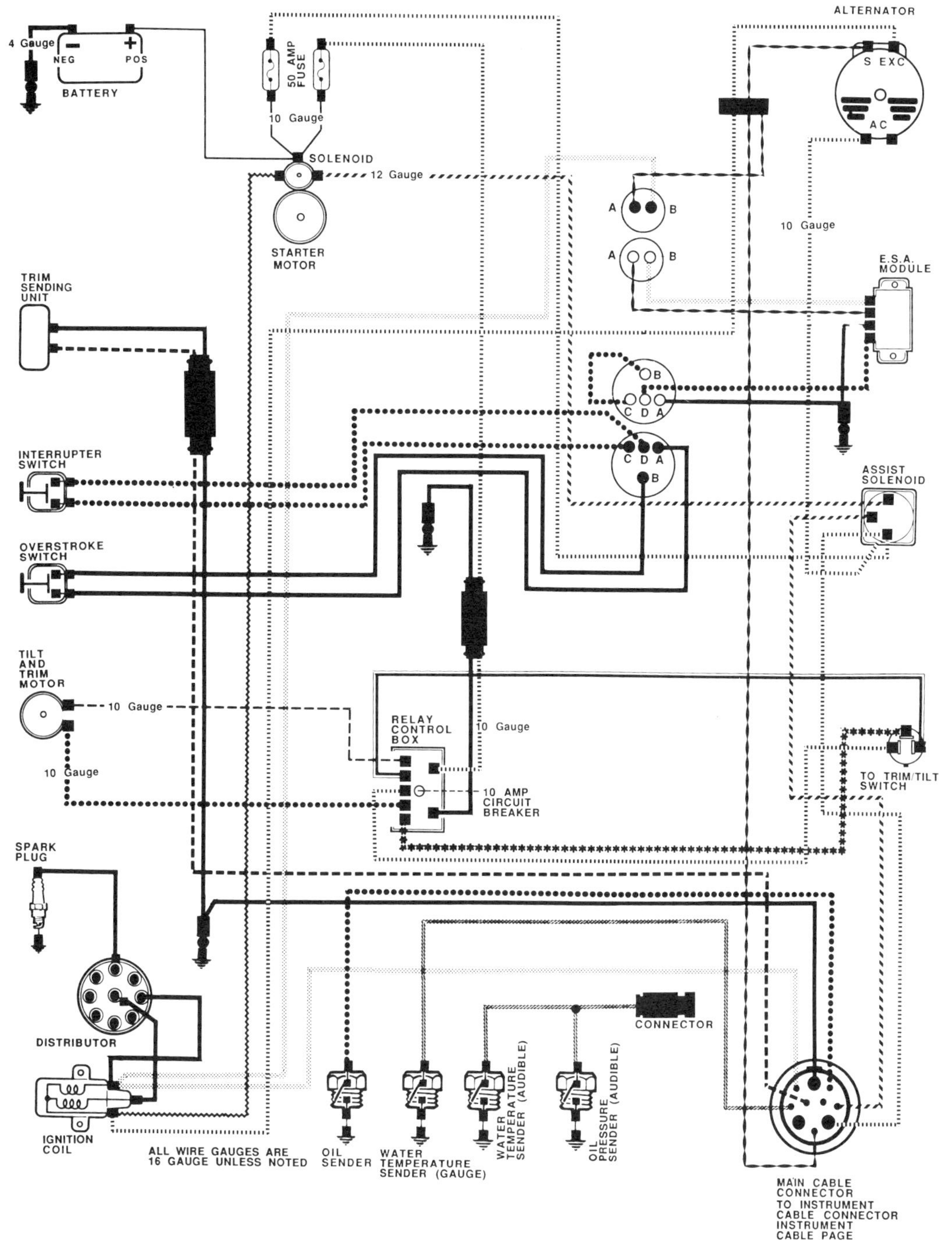

ALTERNATOR
S EXC
AC
4 Gauge
NEG
POS
BATTERY
50 AMP FUSE
10 Gauge
SOLENOID
12 Gauge
STARTER MOTOR
A B
A B
10 Gauge
E.S.A. MODULE
TRIM SENDING UNIT
B
C D A
C D A
B
INTERRUPTER SWITCH
ASSIST SOLENOID
OVERSTROKE SWITCH
TILT AND TRIM MOTOR
10 Gauge
RELAY CONTROL BOX
10 Gauge
10 Gauge
10 AMP CIRCUIT BREAKER
TO TRIM/TILT SWITCH
SPARK PLUG
DISTRIBUTOR
CONNECTOR
WATER TEMPERATURE SENDER (AUDIBLE)
OIL PRESSURE SENDER (AUDIBLE)
IGNITION COIL
ALL WIRE GAUGES ARE 16 GAUGE UNLESS NOTED
OIL SENDER
WATER TEMPERATURE SENDER (GAUGE)
MAIN CABLE CONNECTOR TO INSTRUMENT CABLE CONNECTOR INSTRUMENT CABLE PAGE

DIAGRAM KEY

1989 OMC COBRA INSTRUMENT CABLE

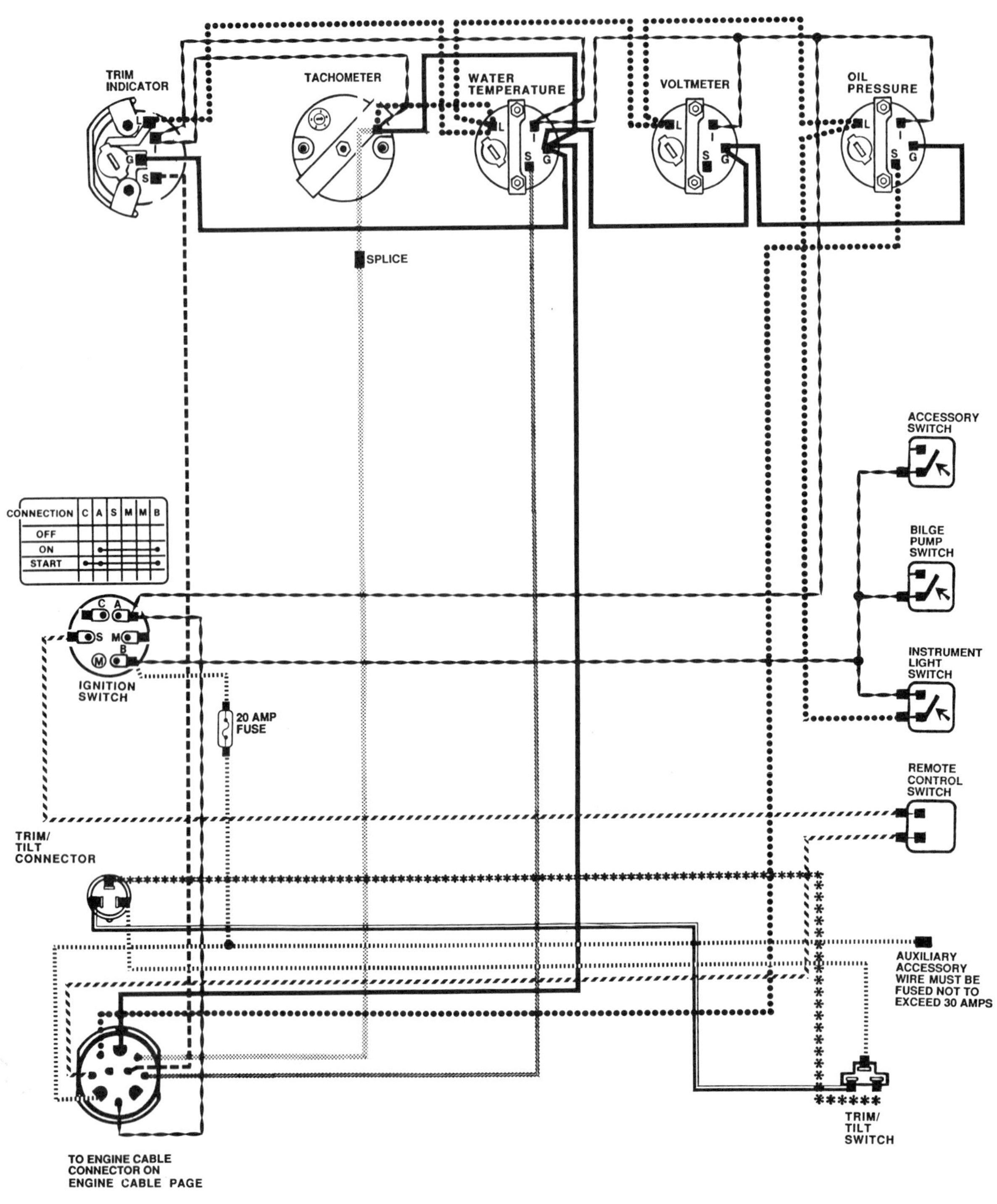

DIAGRAM KEY

BLACK
BLACK AND WHITE
BLACK AND BROWN
BLACK AND YELLOW
WHITE
WHITE AND BLACK
GRAY
GRAY AND YELLOW
RED
RED AND WHITE
ORANGE
ORANGE AND BLUE
ORANGE AND GREEN
YELLOW
YELLOW AND RED
PURPLE AND BLACK
GREEN
GREEN AND WHITE
BLUE
BLUE AND WHITE
PURPLE
PURPLE AND WHITE
PURPLE AND RED
PINK
BROWN
BROWN AND YELLOW
BROWN AND WHITE
TAN
CONNECTORS
GROUND
FRAME GROUND
GROUNDS
CONNECTION
NO CONNECTION

NOTES

NOTES

NOTES

NOTES

NOTES

NOTES